Plant Atlas 2020

Mapping Changes in the Distribution of the British and Irish Flora

Volume 2

P. A. Stroh, K. J. Walker, T. A. Humphrey,
O. L. Pescott & R. J. Burkmar

*Dedicated to field botanists throughout Britain and Ireland,
past and present, who recorded in all weathers and terrains to
provide the many millions of records that underpin this Atlas, and
especially to Gigi Crompton (1922–2020), a BSBI Vice-county
Recorder for over 40 years, whose generous legacy helped to ensure
that this book would see the light of day.*

Botanical Society of Britain and Ireland, Durham &
Princeton University Press, Princeton and Oxford

Published by

Botanical Society of Britain and Ireland,
28 Chipchase Grove, Durham, DH1 3FA
bsbi.org

Princeton University Press,
41 William Street, Princeton, New Jersey 08540
99 Banbury Road, Oxford OX2 6JX
press.princeton.edu

British Library Cataloging-in-Publication Data is available

Library of Congress Control Number 2022950179
ISBN 978-0-691-24759-5
Ebook ISBN 978-0-691-24760-1

Printed in Italy

FSC
www.fsc.org

MIX
Paper from
responsible sources
FSC® C014075

10 9 8 7 6 5 4 3 2 1

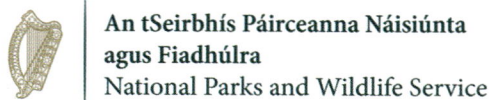

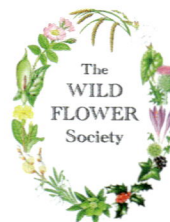

Cover artwork: CLOCKWISE FROM TOP LEFT Bean Broomrape *Orobanche crenata*, Lizard Orchid *Himantoglossum hircinum*,
Long-bracted Sedge *Carex extensa*, Annual Beard-grass *Polypogon monspeliensis*, Lousewort *Pedicularis sylvatica* ssp. *hibernica*,
Spring Gentian *Gentiana verna*, Yellow Horned-poppy *Glaucium flavum* | Chris Thorogood

(N) *Cicendia filiformis* Yellow Centaury

(L.) Delarbre

An annual herb of open, nutrient-poor heathland habitats, growing on sandy and peaty soils of relatively high base-status which are damp in winter and spring; it is also found in damp pastures, rutted tracks and woodland rides, dune-slacks and on cliffs. It can accumulate a long-lived seed bank, and requires moist, warm soils in the spring for germination. Reduced competition, caused by winter-flooding, grazing and disturbance, is essential. Lowland.

Trends *C. filiformis* underwent a substantial decline in the 19th and early 20th centuries, especially in Devon and Cornwall. Further declines, notably in Dorset, were detected in the 2002 *Atlas*, although some losses were marginally offset by new sites discovered in western Wales and southern Ireland. However, in the last two decades this dynamic species has been refound at historical

sites in areas of Pembrokeshire, southern and south-western England where it had not been seen for 50 years or more, and its 10 km square distribution would now appear to have stabilized. New locations in West Mayo and West Galway have significantly extended the known range of this species in Ireland. At sites where it has not been seen this century, dry springs are a factor in its absence, but are currently much less important than a lack of heavy grazing and disturbance (Walker *et al.*, 2017).

Biogeography Submediterranean-Subatlantic element.

Native	GB	IR
2000–19	35	34
1987–99	27	33
1970–86	30	4
pre-1970	63	21

Key refs Stewart *et al.* (1994), Walker *et al.* (2017).

P.A. STROH & R.D. PORLEY

(N) *Exaculum pusillum* Guernsey Centaury

(Lam.) Caruel

A procumbent to ascending annual herb of moist, open, short turf in coastal dune-slacks. Associates in Guernsey include *Cicendia filiformis* and *Linum radiola*. Winter-flooding and rabbit-grazing maintain the open conditions which this species requires. Lowland.

Trends Less than half a dozen populations of *E. pusillum* have been found since it was first discovered 'near Paradis' (Guernsey) in 1850. Some of these have apparently been lost to quarrying and scrub encroachment, and it only appears to survive on L'Ancresse Common (Guernsey) where its numbers vary greatly from year to year.

Biogeography Suboceanic Southern-temperate element.

	GB	IR
Long term	No trend	No trend
Short term	No trend	No trend

Native	GB	IR
2000–19	1	0
1987–99	1	0
1970–86	1	0
pre-1970	1	0

Key refs McClintock (1975).

R.D. PORLEY & P.A. STROH

N *Centaurium portense* Perennial Centaury
(Brot.) Butcher

A perennial herb of freely draining soils in open, short, grassy vegetation on coastal cliffs in Cornwall and Pembrokeshire, elsewhere an escape from cultivation in open grasslands. Lowland.

Trends *C. portense* is extant at two sites in Britain. The population at Newport Cliffs (Pembrokeshire) is stable, with sheep grazing maintaining suitable conditions. It was recently rediscovered at one of the two known Cornish sites (Porthgwarra) after an absence of perhaps 40 years (Bennallick, 2012). The second site, at Sandymouth, was destroyed following the construction of a car park. The origin of the populations on the banks and lawns of 20th century houses in West Kent and East Sussex is unknown but they are likely to have been introduced. The recent name change follows molecular studies by

Prieto *et al.* (2012) who showed that mainland European plants formerly attributed to *C. scilloides* are *C. portense* and that these are genetically distinct from *C. scilloides s.s.* from the Azores.

Biogeography Oceanic Southern-temperate element; restricted to disjunct localities along the coast of western Europe.

Native	GB	IR
2000–19	2	0
1987–99	1	0
1970–86	1	0
pre-1970	3	0

Alien	GB	IR
2000–19	4	0
1987–99	2	0
1970–86	3	0
pre-1970	1	0

	GB	IR
Long term	No trend	No trend
Short term	No trend	No trend

Key refs Bennallick (2010), Dupont (1962), Prieto *et al.* (2012), Rich (2005), Rich & McVeigh (2019), Wigginton (1999).

T.C.G. Rich

N *Centaurium erythraea* Common Centaury
Rafn

A biennial herb of short, open grassland on mildly acidic to calcareous, nutrient-poor, freely drained soils. It occurs in a range of habitats including calcareous to acid grassland, sand dunes, unshaded woodland rides and disturbed ground. Mainly below 200 m, but up to 435 m (Llyn Berwyn, Caernarvonshire).

Trends The number of 10 km square records of this ecologically wide-ranging and mobile species has increased since the 1960s, especially in northern Britain and Ireland, presumably as a result of more systematic recording. However, it is now probably much less frequent at the local level within this range due to the loss of suitable grassland niches resulting from agricultural improvement and more latterly the relaxation of grazing leading to taller, more competitive swards.

Biogeography European Southern-temperate element; widely naturalized outside its native range.

Native	GB	IR
2000–19	1745	746
1987–99	1648	600
1970–86	1113	86
pre-1970	1529	427

Alien	GB	IR
2000–19	2	2
1987–99	4	2
1970–86	1	1
pre-1970	1	1

Key refs Grime *et al.* (2007), Rich & McVeigh (2019).

T.C.G. Rich

N *Centaurium intermedium* Intermediate Centaury
(Wheldon) Druce

A biennial to perennial herb characteristic of winter-wet sides of open dune-slacks and scrapes with *Agrostis stolonifera*, *Carex arenaria*, *Centaurium* species, *Holcus lanatus* and *Salix repens*, often where disturbed by human activity. Demonstrated by Rich & McVeigh (2019) to be a fertile hexaploid species derived from hybrids between *C. erythraea* and *C. littorale*. Lowland.

Trends *C. intermedium* was first described by Wheldon in 1897 (as *Erythraea littoralis* var. *intermedia*). It is treated as a polyploid form of *C. littorale* by Stace *et al.* (2015) and Stace (2019), but as a distinct species by Rich & McVeigh (2019). The taxon is very rare in our area and currently only known from three sites covering two hectads in the Formby area (South Lancashire).

Biogeography Endemic.

		GB	IR
Long term		No trend	No trend
Short term		No trend	No trend

		GB	IR
2000–19	●	2	0
1987–99	●	0	0
1970–86	●	0	0
pre-1970	○	0	0

Key refs Rich & McVeigh (2019), Stace *et al.* (2015), Ubsdell (1976a), Ubsdell (1976b), Ubsdell (1979), Wheldon (1897).

T.C.G. RICH

N *Centaurium littorale* Seaside Centaury
(Turner ex Sm.) Gilmour

A winter-annual to short-lived perennial herb of open vegetation in dune-slacks, and occasionally the tops of saltmarshes (especially in Scotland) or rarely along paths on sea-cliffs. It favours soils that are seasonally wet, weakly saline to fresh; and is usually found in wetter conditions than *C. erythraea* when the two are growing together. Most sites are at sea level but it occurs up to *c.* 80 m in Anglesey.

Trends The overall 10 km square distribution of this species appears to have declined gradually since the 1960s with losses occurring due to succession in dune-slacks, and reclamation of saltmarshes. This decline appears to have slowed since 2000 with a number of new discoveries since then, presumably as a result of more systematic recording.

Biogeography European Temperate element.

		GB	IR
Long term			No trend
Short term			No trend

Native		GB	IR
2000–19	●	70	2
1987–99	●	70	2
1970–86	●	47	2
pre-1970	○	85	3

Alien		GB	IR
2000–19	●	0	0
1987–99	●	0	0
1970–86	●	0	0
pre-1970	○	1	0

Key refs Preston & Pearman (2000), Rich & McVeigh (2019), Stewart *et al.* (1994), Wyse Jackson *et al.* (2016).

T.C.G. RICH

N *Centaurium pulchellum* Lesser Centaury
(Sw.) Druce

A summer-annual of open niches with minimal competition on dry to damp, acidic or calcareous soils. It occurs in a range of open habitats including acid and calcareous grasslands, dry heathland, woodland rides, quarries, coastal cliffs, dune-slacks and in upper saltmarshes. Mainly lowland below 200 m, but occasionally reaching 390 m (Blaenavon, Monmouthshire).

Trends The overall 10 km square distribution of this species has remained stable, although it appears to have become more frequent in southern Britain in recent decades, perhaps benefitting from a warmer climate, though it still has a very localized distribution in northern Britain. In Ireland its distribution is almost exclusively coastal, with no no recent inland records. It is easily confused with *C. erythraea* and so some of the records on the map may be errors for that species.

Biogeography Eurosiberian Southern-temperate element.

Native	GB	IR
2000–19	364	8
1987–99	323	8
1970–86	182	8
pre-1970	353	14

	GB		IR	
Long term		◆		
Short term				

Altitude (m) / Distance north (km)

• <1%
• 1–10%
• 11–30%
• 31–40%
• 41–50%
• 51–100%

□ Apparency ■ In flower ■ In leaf

Key refs Rich & McVeigh (2019), Wyse Jackson *et al.* (2016).

T.C.G. Rich

N *Centaurium tenuiflorum* Slender Centaury
(Hoffmanns. & Link) Fritsch

A summer-annual of open seepage zones on sandy or clay soils on very unstable, slumping coastal cliffs (Dorset) and on saline ground at the top of saltmarshes (Isle of Wight). The Dorset populations are very dynamic, colonizing slumping slopes before they become vegetated. Lowland to *c.* 50 m.

Trends Though this species has a very localized distribution, populations in Dorset continue to persist. In 2006 it was recorded at the top of a saltmarsh in the Medina Estuary on the Isle of Wight (Downey *et al.*, 2021). It has not been recorded at the other historic site on the island since 1989 (King's Quay). There is a single record for Guernsey (Braye du Valle), noted by Babington in 1837. The English plants have recently been described as the endemic subsp. *anglicum*.

Biogeography Mediterranean-Atlantic element.

	GB	IR
Long term	No trend	No trend
Short term	No trend	No trend

Native	GB	IR
2000–19	3	0
1987–99	2	0
1970–86	2	0
pre-1970	5	0

Altitude (m) / Distance north (km)

• <1%
• 1–10%
• 11–30%
• 31–40%
• 41–50%
• 51–100%

□ Apparency ■ In flower ■ In leaf

Key refs Downey *et al.* (2021), Rich *et al.* (2018), Rich & McVeigh (2019), Wigginton (1999).

T.C.G. Rich

(N) *Blackstonia perfoliata* Yellow-wort
(L.) Huds.

An annual or biennial herb of open, summer-dry (but frequently winter-wet), often stony, shallow basic soils. Its main habitats are calcareous grasslands and fixed sand dunes, but it can be an abundant colonist of disturbed ground, including quarries, brownfield sites, disused airfields and railway cuttings, and on road verges, pathsides and woodland rides. Lowland.

Trends By the end of the 20th century, *B. perfoliata* had shown a slight increase in distribution and range compared with surveys undertaken for the 1962 *Atlas*. This century its reported distribution has been consolidated in southern Ireland, the English Midlands and north-western England, and with a marginal spread northwards into North Northumberland and coastal areas of eastern Scotland. Some of this increase is likely due to more systematic recording, but in part may also be related to a greater availability of suitable climate space (Berry *et al.*, 2003).

Biogeography Submediterranean-Subatlantic element.

Native	GB	IR
2000–19	740	208
1987–99	621	165
1970–86	407	27
pre-1970	638	117

Alien	GB	IR
2000–19	3	0
1987–99	4	0
1970–86	1	0
pre-1970	1	0

Key refs Berry *et al.* (2003).

R.D. PORLEY & P.A. STROH

(N) *Gentianella campestris* Field Gentian
(L.) Börner

A biennial or occasionally annual herb of open grasslands, usually on free-draining, somewhat but not always base-rich soils. In Britain its habitats include calcareous grassland, coastal slopes, sand dunes and machair, heathy but not acidic vegetation, mountain ledges and grassy slopes, tracks and forestry rides, riverbanks and shingle. In Ireland it is mainly found in coastal grasslands and dunes, and inland on limestone outcrops and eskers. Generally lowland, but reaching 915 m at Cairnwell (East Perthshire).

Trends *G. campestris* had already suffered a marked decline by 1930, and losses have continued, most notably in the lowlands of southern England, southern Wales and southern Ireland, where it is now a rare and local species due to undergrazing or neglect of pasture. It is still relatively frequent on the northern coast of Scotland, in the Scottish Highlands, and in northern and western Ireland, although overgrazing has led to losses in some areas.

Biogeography European Boreo-temperate element.

Native	GB	IR
2000–19	472	68
1987–99	418	75
1970–86	298	21
pre-1970	813	125

Key refs Rich & McVeigh (2019), Smith & Lockwood (2011), Stroh *et al.* (2019), Walker *et al.* (2017).

T.C.G. RICH & R.D. PORLEY

N *Gentianella germanica* Chiltern Gentian
(Willd.) Börner

A biennial herb of unimproved, open chalk grassland with various degrees of light scrub and occasionally in open chalk quarries, roadside banks, by railways or woodland rides. The English sites represent outliers at the north-western limit of its global distribution. Lowland.

Trends *G. germanica* has declined throughout its restricted range since the 1960s, equally across all habitats, and losses are ongoing, caused by agricultural improvement or neglect, resulting in succession to rank grassland and dense scrub and woodland. Most populations have less than 100 plants, but some have over 1,000 and a few over 5,000. In 2001 it was refound in chalk grassland in South Wiltshire (Mere Down), after an apparent absence of over 100 years. It was found at a second, completely new Wiltshire site in 2006 (Martin Down).

Biogeography European Temperate element, with a continental distribution in western Europe.

Native	GB	IR
2000–19	14	0
1987–99	21	0
1970–86	20	0
pre-1970	33	0

Alien	GB	IR
2000–19	1	0
1987–99	3	0
1970–86	2	0
pre-1970	1	0

	GB	IR
Long term		No trend
Short term		No trend

Key refs McVeigh *et al.* (2005), Rich & McVeigh (2019), Stroh *et al.* (2019).

T.C.G. RICH

N *Gentianella amarella* Autumn Gentian
(L.) Börner

A biennial herb of calcareous, freely drained, nutrient-poor soils, occurring in short, open grassland on chalk and limestone, in quarries, on coastal dunes and occasionally on roadsides, river shingle, forestry tracks and sea cliffs. Mainly lowland, ascending to 750 m (Knock Fell, Westmorland).

Trends *G. amarella* has declined since the 1960s, mainly in lowland regions on the edges of its core range due to loss of habitat through agricultural intensification and lack of management. It remains locally common in its strongholds in chalk and limestone grassland in southern and northern Britain. British populations are genetically very variable and recent taxonomic revisions now recognize four subspecies in our area. The most widespread is subsp. *amarella* which now incorporates the formerly recognized subsp. *hibernica*. The other three subspecies (subsp. *anglica*, subsp. *occidentalis*, subsp. *septentrionalis*) are mapped separately.

Biogeography Circumpolar Boreo-temperate element.

Native	GB	IR
2000–19	592	59
1987–99	610	55
1970–86	508	22
pre-1970	810	97

Alien	GB	IR
2000–19	0	0
1987–99	1	0
1970–86	0	0
pre-1970	0	0

	GB	IR
Long term		
Short term		

Key refs Pritchard (1959), Rich *et al.* (2018), Rich & McVeigh (2019).

T.C.G. RICH

Ⓝ *Gentianella amarella* subsp. *septentrionalis*
(Druce) N.M.Pritch.

A biennial herb of upland and lowland calcareous grassland or occasionally more mesotrophic grassland, in coastal pastures, dunes and road sides. It tolerates a broader range of soils on the coast than inland where it becomes confined to limestones up to 737 m (Beinn Heasgarnich, Mid Perthshire). Generally similar to subsp. *amarella*, but shorter and with creamy insides to the flowers.

Trends It is difficult to assess long-term trends for this taxon, as it is unevenly recorded, but its distribution is probably stable in northern Scotland; it is now much better recorded in northern England.

Biogeography A boreal subspecies, also occurring in Iceland and Norway.

	GB	IR
Long term	No trend	No trend
Short term	No trend	No trend

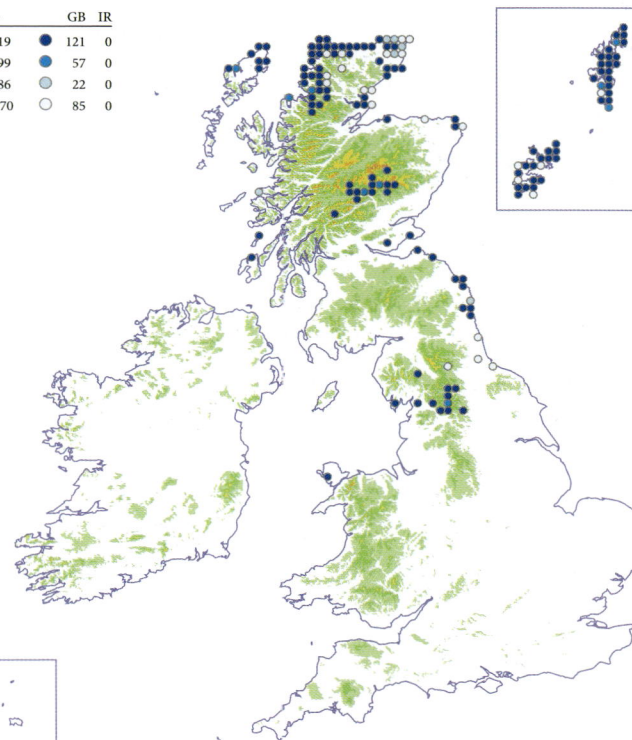

Native		GB	IR
2000–19	●	121	0
1987–99	●	57	0
1970–86	●	22	0
pre-1970	○	85	0

Key refs Pritchard (1960), Rich & McVeigh (2019).

T.C.G. Rich

Altitude (m) / Distance north (km) — dot size key: <1%, 1–10%, 11–30%, 31–40%, 41–50%, 51–100%

Apparency · In flower · In leaf — J F M A M J J A S O N D

Ⓝ *Gentianella amarella* subsp. *anglica*
(Pugsley) T.C.G.Rich & McVeigh

A biennial herb of shallow calcareous soils on chalk downland as well as old quarries, coastal slopes, sand dunes, ancient earthworks, trackways and path edges. Lowland.

Trends This taxon was formerly treated as *G. anglica* but molecular studies showed it to be very closely related to *G. amarella* subsp. *amarella* and as a consequence it is now treated at subspecific rank. It has declined markedly outside its core area on the chalk downlands of Hampshire, the Isle of Wight and Wiltshire, presumably due to spread of scrub and tall grasses where grazing levels have been reduced. Hybridization with subsp. *amarella* may be an additional threat to the survival of some but not all populations.

Biogeography Endemic.

	GB	IR
Long term	↓ ↓ · ↑ ↑	No trend
Short term	No trend	No trend

Native		GB	IR
2000–19	●	60	0
1987–99	●	81	0
1970–86	●	67	0
pre-1970	○	97	0

Alien		GB	IR
2000–19	●	1	0
1987–99	●	1	0
1970–86	●	1	0
pre-1970	○	0	0

Key refs Margetts *et al.* (1997), Rich (1997a), Rich *et al.* (2018), Rich & McVeigh (2019), Stewart *et al.* (1994), Winfield *et al.* (2003).

T.C.G. Rich

Altitude (m) / Distance north (km) — dot size key: <1%, 1–10%, 11–30%, 31–40%, 41–50%, 51–100%

Apparency · In flower · In leaf — J F M A M J J A S O N D

N ## *Gentianella amarella* subsp. *occidentalis*
T.C.G.Rich & McVeigh

A small, summer annual of species-rich dune-slacks and machair vegetation, within which it favours short, open swards on dry, nutrient-poor soils. Historically it has been referred to as *G. uliginosa* in Britain, but it was recently recognized as a morphologically distinct taxon related to the biennial *G. amarella* subsp. *amarella* (Rich *et al.*, 2018). Lowland.

Trends *G. amarella* subsp. *occidentalis* has declined, based on recent surveys in Wales and Devon which reported the loss of 15 sub-populations across three sites, with just ten sub-populations remaining across four sites (Evans & Rich, 2021). Plants discovered on Colonsay (South Ebudes) by Francis Rose in the late 1970s have been determined as a dwarfed form of *G. amarella* subsp. *amarella* by Rich & Lavery (2018). However, measurements

for the majority of Colonsay plants taken during recent fieldwork fall within the morphological range of subsp. *occidentalis* when using the characters given in Rich & McVeigh (2018). Further work is required to determine the relationship between Colonsay plants and British and European material, and in the meantime the Scottish plants are included on the mapped distribution.

Biogeography Endemic.

	GB	IR
Long term	No trend	No trend
Short term	No trend	No trend

Native		GB	IR
2000–19	●	5	0
1987–99	●	7	0
1970–86	●	7	0
pre-1970	○	6	0

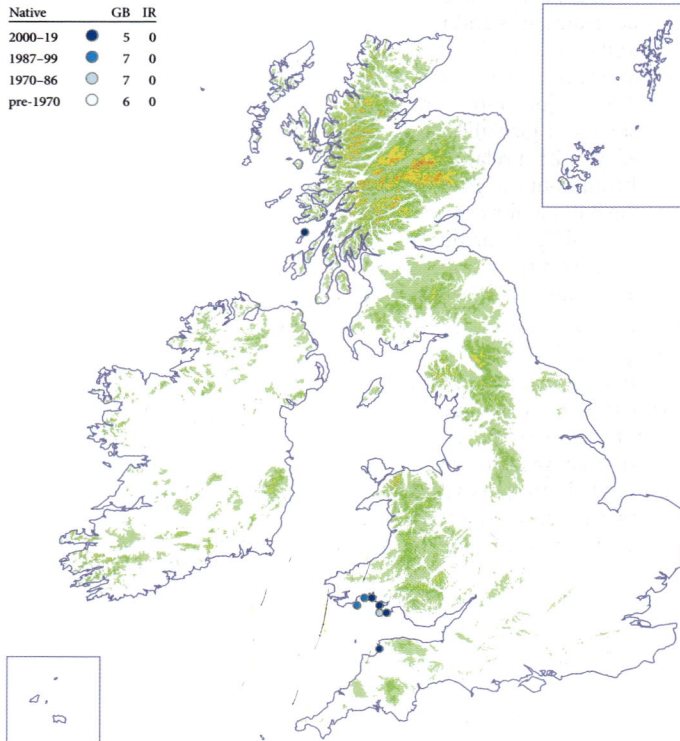

Key refs Evans & Rich (2021), Holyoak (1999), Rich (1996), Rich & Lavery (2018), Rich *et al.* (2018), Rich & McVeigh (2019), Wigginton (1999).

P.A. STROH

N? ## *Gentianopsis ciliata* Fringed Gentian
(L.) Ma

A biennial or perennial herb of short, open chalk grassland, flowering in late summer. Lowland.

Trends *G. ciliata* was first discovered in Britain at Coombe Hill (Buckinghamshire) in 1873. It was thought to have been lost from the site, and therefore from our area, after extensive searches failed to find any sign of the plant since it was last seen in 2012, but in 2021 (following the completion of *Atlas* fieldwork) two flowering plants were discovered at the same location. Plants from a second site in chalk grassland at Pitton (South Wiltshire), found in 1892, were originally recorded as *Gentiana pneumonanthe* and only correctly determined in 1995 following examination of an herbarium specimen held in the Natural History Museum (London). A specimen collected in 1910 from a site in Surrey is considered to

have been introduced. Taxonomically, it has been included in *Gentiana* and *Gentianella*, and is now in *Gentianopsis*.

Biogeography Eurosiberian Temperate element, with a continental distribution in western Europe.

	GB	IR
Long term	No trend	No trend
Short term	No trend	No trend

Native		GB	IR
2000–19	●	1	0
1987–99	●	1	0
1970–86	●	1	0
pre-1970	○	2	0

Alien		GB	IR
2000–19	●	0	0
1987–99	●	0	0
1970–86	●	0	0
pre-1970	○	1	0

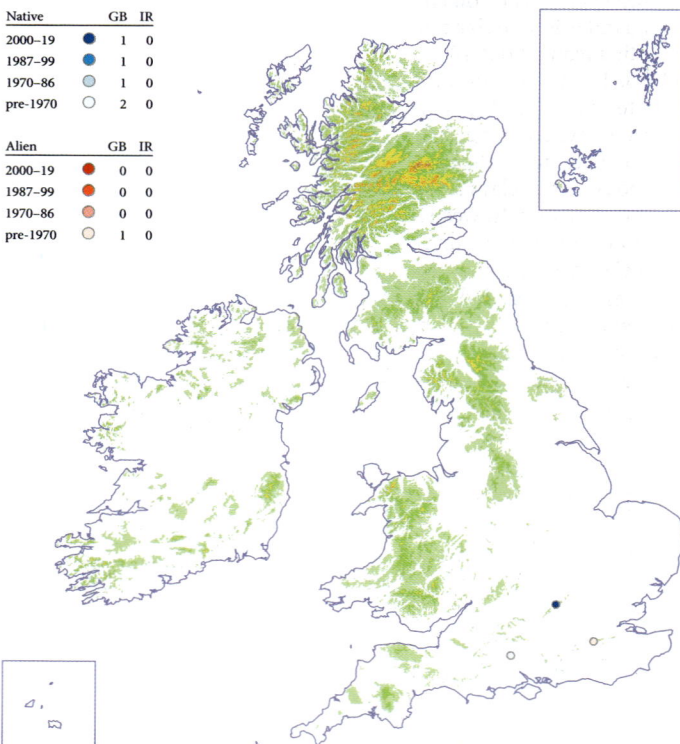

Key refs Oostermeijer *et al.* (2002), Rich & McVeigh (2019), Stroh *et al.* (2019), Wigginton (1999).

T.C.G. RICH

N *Gentiana pneumonanthe* Marsh Gentian

L.

A perennial herb of open, damp acidic heathland, grasslands and transitions between heathlands and mires, commonly associated with *Erica tetralix* and *Molinia caerulea*. The soils are mainly acidic (pH 4–6), nutrient-poor, peaty soils over glacial drift, sands and sandy clays with a relatively high water table throughout the year. The opening up of the habitat, for example by grazing or occasional light burning, favours this species by promoting flowering and the production of seed. Lowland.

Trends *G. pneumonanthe* had already undergone a dramatic decline by the 1930s due to afforestation, heathland reclamation and drainage. This decline has continued to the present day, with a lack of management now a major factor contributing to extirpation. It is now a great rarity in many counties except in South Hampshire and Dorset where the majority of British populations are now concentrated.

Biogeography Eurosiberian Temperate element.

Native	GB	IR
2000–19	35	0
1987–99	49	0
1970–86	49	0
pre-1970	127	0

Alien	GB	IR
2000–19	0	0
1987–99	1	0
1970–86	1	0
pre-1970	2	0

	GB	IR
Long term	↓ ↓	No trend
Short term	↓	No trend

Key refs Simmonds (1946), Stewart *et al.* (1994).

T.C.G. RICH

N *Gentiana verna* Spring Gentian

L.

A perennial herb of short, open, calcareous grasslands on shallow soils. In England it is an upland species, ascending from about 400 m to 730 m on Little Fell (Westmorland) and restricted to Upper Teesdale and Stainmore, where it is restricted to limestone outcrops, sugar limestone, calcareous glacial clays and in wet, calcareous flushes. In western Ireland it is a lowland plant occurring from sea level to *c.* 300 m, and occurs in dry limestone grassland, on limestone pavement and in fixed calcareous dunes. It is occasionally planted or found as a garden escape elsewhere.

Trends There has been little change in the overall 10 km square distribution of *G. verna* in Britain since the 1960s, although locally the number and size of populations has declined markedly. Similarly in Ireland, although apparently stable at the 10 km square scale, there has been a continuing loss of many small and marginal populations, mainly due to agricultural intensification or succession to scrub. It is possible that the prevalence in recent times of cold and dry winters, and dry springs, at least at its British sites, may eventually benefit *G. verna* populations, as reduced grass growth early in the year delays the return of sheep to the fells, and so allows a greater proportion of plants the time to flower and set seed.

Biogeography European Arctic-montane element; also in central Asia.

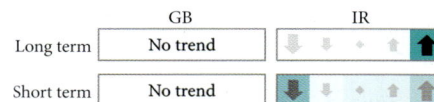

Native	GB	IR
2000–19	4	25
1987–99	4	22
1970–86	4	6
pre-1970	6	3

Alien	GB	IR
2000–19	2	0
1987–99	3	0
1970–86	1	0
pre-1970	0	0

	GB	IR
Long term	No trend	↑
Short term	No trend	↓

Key refs Elkington (1963), Elkington (1972), Halliday (1997), Rich & McVeigh (2019), Wigginton (1999).

T.C.G. RICH & R.D. PORLEY

N *Gentiana nivalis* Alpine Gentian
L.

An annual or biennial herb of open, herb-rich vegetation on mountain ledges, screes and in the associated upland grasslands on stony brown earths derived from frost-shattered, calcareous, Dalradian mica-schist. Often growing with other rare arctic-alpines at altitudes mostly within the range 850–1,095 m (Ben Lawers, Mid Perthshire).

Trends In Britain *G. nivalis* is only known from the Ben Lawers range (Mid Perthshire) and Caenlochan (Angus). The populations of this glacial relict appear to be stable at its two main sites, though numbers vary significantly from year to year and small sub-colonies may not appear every year. High levels of grazing causes high mortality, but this may mostly be offset by the corresponding control of competitors and the creation of open ground for seedlings.

Biogeography European Arctic-montane element; also in North America.

Key refs Miller (2004), Miller *et al.* (1999), Miller & Geddes (2004), Rich & McVeigh (2019), Wigginton (1999).

T.C.G. RICH & R.D. PORLEY

Ar *Vinca minor* Lesser Periwinkle
L.

An evergreen perennial herb, with procumbent vegetative stems, which root at the tips, widely grown in gardens and found naturalized in woodland, copses, plantations, scrub, hedgerows, shady roadside banks and verges, as well as on waste ground and refuse tips. Generally lowland, but reaching 380 m at Glenlivet (Banffshire).

Trends This species is similar to *V. major* but, being smaller and less invasive, is more widely cultivated for ground cover in shady areas. It was grown in gardens in Britain by medieval times (Harvey, 1981). There was an increase in records in the latter half of the 20th century that has continued this century, probably due to a genuine increase as well as more systematic recording of garden escapes.

Biogeography Apparently native to southern, western and central Europe, central and southern Russia and the Caucasus, but the limits of the native range have been obscured by its spread in cultivation.

Key refs Harvey (1981).

T.D. DINES & J.O. MOUNTFORD

768

Ne *Vinca difformis* Intermediate Periwinkle

Pourr.

A spreading evergreen perennial herb, with long trailing or arching stems that root at the tip, occasionally grown in gardens and found as a naturalized escape on grassy banks, rough ground and roadside verges. Lowland.

Trends *V. difformis* had been introduced into cultivation in Britain by 1876, and is only occasionally grown in gardens. It was first recorded in the wild in 1984 (Kent, but without locality). Since 2000 it has been recorded more frequently, especially in south-western and southern Britain, and in the extreme south of Ireland, possibly due to the more systematic recording of alien species. Both blue- and white-flowered cultivars have become naturalized.

Biogeography Native of south-western Europe, eastwards to Italy, and north-western Africa.

	GB	IR
Long term	No trend	No trend

Alien	GB	IR
2000–19	92	12
1987–99	7	1
1970–86	11	0
pre-1970	5	0

Altitude (m)

	<1%
	1–10%
	11–30%
	31–40%
	41–50%
	51–100%

Distance north (km)

J F M A M J J A S O N D

☐ Apparency ☐ In flower ☐ In leaf

T.D. DINES & J.O. MOUNTFORD

Ne *Vinca major* Greater Periwinkle

L.

A spreading evergreen perennial herb, with long trailing or arching stems that root at the tip, widely grown in gardens and found as a naturalized escape at the base of hedges, waste ground, refuse tips, disused railways, roadside verges, shaded banks and woodland. Often grown in shaded gardens, it can spread very effectively onto adjacent hedgebanks and under trees. It also occurs as a throw-out from garden waste. Lowland.

Trends *V. major* was being cultivated in Britain by 1596. It is widely grown as a ground-cover species in gardens, but its robust habit and vigorous growth means that it is frequently discarded, and often becomes well-established from garden waste in suitable habitats. It was recorded out of cultivation by 1677 (Oxfordshire). Its 10 km square distribution has increased markedly since the 1960s, possibly due in part to direct spread from gardens although, like many cultivated plants, it is also now better known due to the more systematic recording of garden escapes. It is most frequently found growing adjacent to human habitations, but some populations are nonetheless quite remote and may arise from dumping of garden waste material.

Biogeography The naturalized plant, *V. major* subsp. *major*, is a native of the European Mediterranean region; subsp. *hirsuta* is native to northern Turkey and the Caucasus.

	GB	IR
Long term		
Short term		

Alien	GB	IR
2000–19	1598	294
1987–99	1222	201
1970–86	572	9
pre-1970	815	54

Altitude (m)

	<1%
	1–10%
	11–30%
	31–40%
	41–50%
	51–100%

Distance north (km)

J F M A M J J A S O N D

☐ Apparency ☐ In flower ☐ In leaf

T.D. DINES & J.O. MOUNTFORD

Ne *Phacelia tanacetifolia* Phacelia

Benth.

An annual herb, widely cultivated in gardens, allotments and arable fields and found as a casual on refuse tips, waste ground, pavements, and as a volunteer or seed contaminant in cereal and oil-seed rape crops and in newly sown grass leys. It also occurs in birdseed and pheasant feed. Lowland.

Trends *P. tanacetifolia* has been cultivated in Britain since 1832, and was first recorded in the wild in 1881 (Mid-west Yorkshire). It remained scarce up till 1970 but has since been widely grown for green manure, game cover and as a nectar plant for bees and hoverflies that prey on aphids. Its 10 km square distribution has dramatically increased since 2000, in both density and range, and it is now widespread throughout England, southern Scotland and much of Wales, although it is almost always only of casual occurrence. It remains scarce in Ireland.

Biogeography Native of western North America (California).

Alien		GB	IR
2000–19	●	843	39
1987–99	●	188	1
1970–86	●	37	0
pre-1970	○	20	0

	GB	IR
Long term	No trend	No trend
Short term		

Key refs Briggs (1997), Crawley (2005), Leach (1997).

H.J. KILLICK

Altitude (m) / Distance north (km)
<table>
<tr><td>●</td><td><1%</td></tr>
<tr><td>●</td><td>1–10%</td></tr>
<tr><td>●</td><td>11–30%</td></tr>
<tr><td>●</td><td>31–40%</td></tr>
<tr><td>●</td><td>41–50%</td></tr>
<tr><td>●</td><td>51–100%</td></tr>
</table>

☐ Apparency ☐ In flower ☐ In leaf

N *Lithospermum officinale* Common Gromwell

L.

A shortly rhizomatous perennial herb of undisturbed places in grassland, hedgerows and wood margins, mostly on base-rich soils. Lowland.

Trends Many of the losses in Scotland and northern areas of England occurred before 1930, but it has continued to decline throughout its range due to habitat destruction. In the past *L. officinale* has been considered alien in Scotland, but its long occurrence (from 1764 in Angus) at some sites and its semi-natural, base-rich habitats (for example, rocky riversides and limestone scree) suggests that it may be native there too.

Biogeography Eurosiberian Temperate element; widely naturalized outside its native range.

Native		GB	IR
2000–19	●	435	25
1987–99	●	424	18
1970–86	●	296	11
pre-1970	○	581	51

Alien		GB	IR
2000–19	●	2	0
1987–99	●	1	0
1970–86	●	0	0
pre-1970	○	12	0

	GB	IR
Long term		
Short term		

Altitude (m) / Distance north (km)
<table>
<tr><td>●</td><td><1%</td></tr>
<tr><td>●</td><td>1–10%</td></tr>
<tr><td>●</td><td>11–30%</td></tr>
<tr><td>●</td><td>31–40%</td></tr>
<tr><td>●</td><td>41–50%</td></tr>
<tr><td>●</td><td>51–100%</td></tr>
</table>

☐ Apparency ☐ In flower ☐ In leaf

D. WELCH

(N) *Aegonychon purpureocaeruleum* Purple Gromwell
(L.) Holub

A perennial herb with creeping woody stems occurring in chalk and limestone districts in two distinct habitats. Inland, it grows in woodland edges and rides, and on lanesides and banks in partial shade. On the coast it is found amongst naturally dwarfed, open scrub on slumped cliffs, slopes and crags. It spreads by seed and from the stems rooting at nodes. It also occurs as a garden escape on roadsides and waste ground. Lowland.

Native in Britain and a neophyte in Ireland.

Trends The native distribution of this rare species seems to have remained more or less stable since 1930, though some populations have been shaded out in neglected or unmanaged woodland. It continues to increase as a naturalized alien.

Biogeography European Southern-temperate element.

Native	GB	IR
2000–19	15	0
1987–99	15	0
1970–86	14	0
pre-1970	25	0

Alien	GB	IR
2000–19	29	0
1987–99	15	1
1970–86	8	0
pre-1970	21	0

Key refs Wigginton (1999).

D. WELCH

(Ar) *Buglossoides arvensis* Field Gromwell
(L.) I.M.Johnst.

An annual herb of arable fields, occasionally found on waste ground and in other disturbed habitats, favouring light, dry, calcareous soils. The seed is short-lived and populations rely upon regular disturbance for survival. Lowland.

Trends Archaeological evidence suggests that *B. arvensis* has been an arable weed in Britain since at least the Bronze Age. It has declined substantially since the 1960s due to agricultural intensification, and in many areas it is a very rare arable weed. Seed can be transported with grain, resulting in casual populations outside its core range. In recent years it has been used as a component of seed mixtures sown along arable headlands. Due to high levels of omega-3 and omega-6 fatty acids contained in the seeds, trials are underway in some areas to grow *B. arvensis* as a crop for human consumption.

Biogeography As an archaeophyte, *B. arvensis* has a Eurosiberian Southern-temperate distribution; it is widely naturalized outside this range.

Alien	GB	IR
2000–19	126	1
1987–99	233	0
1970–86	222	1
pre-1970	592	10

Key refs Svensson & Wigren (1986).

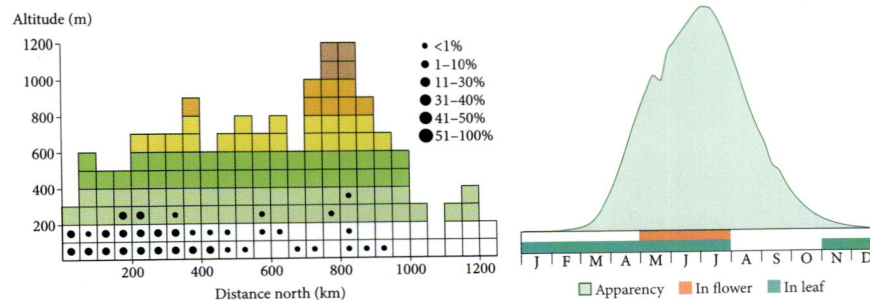

D. WELCH & P.A. STROH

(N) *Echium vulgare* Viper's-bugloss
L.

A biennial herb of grassy and disturbed habitats on well-drained soils. It is found in bare places on chalk and limestone downs, on heaths, in quarries and chalk-pits, in cultivated and waste land, along railways, tracks and roadsides, and by the coast on cliffs, sand dunes and shingle. Generally lowland, but formerly reaching 365 m as an alien at Braemar (South Aberdeenshire).

Trends The distribution of *E. vulgare* has had somewhat of a resurgence since 2000, following a decline in frequency last century due to agricultural intensification, reclamation and the development of neglected land. It is probable that it is spreading both naturally and by other means, for example as a contaminant of sand used for construction, or as an introduction in wild-flower seed

mixtures. Differentiating between native and alien occurrences has in large part become impossible, and consequently all records are mapped without status.

Biogeography Eurosiberian Temperate element; widely naturalized outside its native range.

	GB	IR
2000–19	1048	69
1987–99	809	20
1970–86	521	9
pre-1970	893	43

D. WELCH & M. SANFORD

(Ar) *Echium plantagineum* Purple Viper's-bugloss
L.

An annual or biennial herb, found in arable fields, on cliffs and in open sandy habitats by the coast. It has a long-lived seed bank, and populations vary greatly in size from year to year. It also occurs casually as a garden escape or outcast and it is occasionally found in areas that have been sown with seed mixtures to attract pollinators. Lowland.

An archaeophyte in Britain and the Channel Islands and a neophyte in Ireland.

Trends *E. plantagineum* has been known from Jersey since 1690 but was first recorded in Cornwall in 1856. It is well-established in Jersey, in West Penwith (West Cornwall) and on the Isles of Scilly, where it has been considered native by many authors. Elsewhere it is only casual.

Biogeography As an archaeophyte, *E. plantagineum* has a Mediterranean-Atlantic distribution; it is widely naturalized outside this range, and is a notorious weed in Australia.

Alien	GB	IR
2000–19	150	3
1987–99	42	0
1970–86	23	0
pre-1970	58	0

Key refs Butterfield (1999), Wigginton (1999).

D. WELCH

Ne *Echium pininana* Giant Viper's-bugloss

Webb & Berthel.

A very tall monocarpic perennial herb, occasionally grown in sheltered gardens and naturalized on rough and waste ground. Plants usually grow for several years before flowering and dying. Reproduction is by copious amounts of long-lasting seed. Lowland.

Trends 'Giant Echiums' have been grown in Britain since 1779 and it has always been assumed, but with no conclusive proof, that *E. pininana* was the species in question. It is popular in gardens in areas with very mild climates where plants can survive several winters before flowering. It was first reliably recorded from the wild in 1971 (Guernsey and Isles of Scilly). There has been a notable increase in the number of records this century, partly due to better recording of naturalized aliens, but mainly because of increased flowering due to milder winters.

Biogeography Native of the Canary Islands.

Alien	GB	IR
2000–19	127	37
1987–99	25	1
1970–86	13	0
pre-1970	8	0

	GB	IR
Long term	No trend	No trend
Short term		

D.A. Pearman & T.D. Dines

• <1%
• 1–10%
• 11–30%
• 31–40%
• 41–50%
• 51–100%

Apparency In flower In leaf

Ne *Cerinthe major* Greater Honeywort

L.

An annual herb, widely grown in gardens, self-seeding freely, and occasionally occurring as a casual on pavements, dumped soil and in waste places close to human habitations. Lowland.

Trends A popular species in cultivation, frequently spreading by seed to waste places and disturbed soils. A casual usually killed by frost over winter so rarely becoming established.

Biogeography Native of southern Europe and the Mediterranean region.

Alien	GB	IR
2000–19	150	2
1987–99	2	0
1970–86	1	0
pre-1970	1	0

	GB	IR
Long term	No trend	No trend
Short term		No trend

• <1%
• 1–10%
• 11–30%
• 31–40%
• 41–50%
• 51–100%

Apparency In flower In leaf

M.N. Sanford

Ne *Pulmonaria officinalis* Lungwort

L.

A perennial herb, naturalized in woodlands and scrub, on banks and rough ground, and also occurring on refuse tips and waste ground. Generally lowland, but reaching 424 m (Ashgill, Cumberland).

Trends This species was cultivated in Britain by 1596, and is now commonly grown in gardens. Though some occurrences were in the past treated as possibly native, it is now regarded as an introduction; it was first recorded from the wild by 1793 (West Kent). The number of records has increased in all areas since the 1960s, reflecting both increased abundance and more systematic recording of garden escapes.

Biogeography A European Temperate species, absent as a native from much of western Europe.

Alien	GB	IR
2000–19	1050	19
1987–99	487	5
1970–86	248	4
pre-1970	315	1

Key refs Meeus *et al.* (2013).

D. WELCH & J.O. MOUNTFORD

N *Pulmonaria obscura* Suffolk Lungwort

Dumort.

A perennial herb of poorly drained chalky boulder clay, occurring in three ancient woodlands dominated by *Acer campestre*, *Corylus avellana* and *Fraxinus excelsior* and with a long history of coppice management, especially by rides and clearings. It will tolerate deep shade but flowers best in more open areas. It reproduces by seed and by rhizomatous spread, occasionally forming patches. Lowland.

Trends *P. obscura* is considered native in Britain because its habitat and associated species are similar to native sites in Europe, and because it is rarely cultivated here. First recorded in 1842, it is currently known from three privately owned woods, all within about a kilometre of each other in Suffolk. Populations experienced some decline in numbers in the 20th century due to the cessation of coppicing, but the reinstatement of woodland management in recent decades has resulted in healthy populations in two of the woods, and its continued presence in the third.

Biogeography European Temperate element, with a continental distribution in western Europe.

	GB	IR
Long term	No trend	No trend
Short term	No trend	No trend

Native	GB	IR
2000–19	1	0
1987–99	1	0
1970–86	0	0
pre-1970	0	0

Key refs Birkinshaw & Sanford (1996), Sanford & Fisk (2010), Stroh *et al.* (2014), Wigginton (1999).

D. WELCH & J.O. MOUNTFORD

Pulmonaria rubra Red Lungwort
Schott

Ne

A perennial herb found as a naturalized garden escape in woodland, scrub, hedges and rough grassland. Lowland.

Trends *P. rubra* was being cultivated in Britain by 1903 and is popular in gardens. It was first recorded from the wild in 1969 (Frilford, Berkshire) and has been recorded much more frequently this century than in the past.

Biogeography Native to mountain forests in the Carpathians and the Balkan Peninsula.

	GB	IR
Long term	No trend	No trend
Short term		No trend

Alien		GB	IR
2000–19	●	55	0
1987–99	●	14	0
1970–86	●	4	0
pre-1970	○	1	0

	<1%
	1–10%
	11–30%
	31–40%
	41–50%
	51–100%

Altitude (m)

Distance north (km)

Apparency   In flower   In leaf

T.D. Dines & J.O. Mountford

Pulmonaria longifolia Narrow-leaved Lungwort
(Bastard) Boreau

N

A perennial herb of lightly shaded habitats, mostly on base-rich clay soils, in coppiced woodland, wood-pasture and amongst *Pteridium aquilinum* on heathland; it also grows in hedgebanks and marl-pits. Though it seeds freely and reproduces vegetatively, even vigorous colonies seldom spread into apparently suitable contiguous ground. Non-native populations often occur in amenity woodland. Lowland.

Trends Although the number of 10 km squares in which *P. longifolia* is mapped as a native has remained stable since the 1960s, this is mainly due to more intensive recording, and some colonies have been lost, particularly in central parts of its range, whilst at some extant sites there has been a crash in numbers. The main factors for deterioration of suitable habitat or loss of a population include shading, inappropriate ride, hedgebank or railway bank management, and grazing. It is sometimes grown in gardens, and escapes have been noted thinly scattered through Britain.

Biogeography Oceanic Temperate element.

	GB	IR
Long term		No trend
Short term		No trend

Native		GB	IR
2000–19	●	16	0
1987–99	●	18	0
1970–86	●	18	0
pre-1970	○	20	0

Alien		GB	IR
2000–19	●	4	0
1987–99	●	5	0
1970–86	●	3	0
pre-1970	○	17	0

	<1%
	1–10%
	11–30%
	31–40%
	41–50%
	51–100%

Altitude (m)

Distance north (km)

Apparency   In flower   In leaf

Key refs Rand & Mundell (2011), Stewart *et al.* (1994).

D. Welch & J.O. Mountford

Symphytum officinale Common Comfrey
L.

A tall perennial herb of riverbanks, streamsides and associated ditches, fens and marshes. It is also an occasional escape from cultivation on waste ground and roadsides. The identification of *S. officinale* requires not only the long wings on the stem, but also very narrow upper stem leaves with a broad (1–2 cm) leaf decurrence at the stem junction and an absence of blue or violet coloration in the flowers. Lowland.

Trends *S. officinale* is thought to be native in lowland England and the Welsh borders. Elsewhere, records are often misidentifications of *S. ×uplandicum* in the uplands of these countries. The diploid subsp. *bohemicum* with cream flowers (2n=24) seems to be confined to the Fenlands of East Anglia, and the rivers draining into them; the taller tetraploid subsp. *officinale* (2n=48), with either cream or carmine (purplish-red) flowers, is more widespread. Records of cream-flowered plants from riverine habitats can be relied upon and indicate a sparse but widespread native distribution along the river systems of the Wessex Basin, the Severn and the Wye, and the upper and middle Thames; also in East Anglia, from Essex to West Norfolk and Lincolnshire. However, the great majority of 10 km square records shown for *S. officinale* on both riverine and non-riverine sites elsewhere are likely to be purple-flowered *S. ×uplandicum*. As it has become impossible to determine the native range with any certainty, all records are mapped without status.

Biogeography European Temperate element; also in central Asia and widely naturalized outside its native range.

Key refs Leaney (2015), O'Reilly (2006).

R.M. Leaney & D. Welch

Symphytum asperum × officinale = S. ×uplandicum Russian Comfrey
Nyman

A very tall and robust perennial herb of moist, fertile soils, long established on woodland margins, hedgebanks, road verges, tracks, waste ground, railway embankments, stream- and ditch-banks; also a relic of cultivation on allotments and in old gardens. It forms clonal patches competing with tall grass and herbage, seldom with associated seedling plants. It continues to extend its range away from roads along footpaths, tracks and riverside paths. Mainly spread vegetatively by cutting machinery. Generally lowland, but up to 470 m south of Glenmore Lodge (Easterness).

A cultivated hybrid (alien × alien).

Trends Introduced in the 1790s from the palace gardens of St Petersburg as an ornamental, then promoted as a forage plant in the mid-19th century. First recorded in the wild in 1861 (Marlborough, North Wiltshire), and now by far the commonest comfrey throughout our area; its distribution is independent from that of the parents, and seems to be increasing. The usual pink-, purple- or violet-flowered forms can have very long stem-winging and continue to be regularly misidentified as the carmine-flowered form of *S. officinale*.

Biogeography This hybrid is known from the Caucasus; it has been spread in cultivation and is naturalized in temperate Europe.

Key refs Hills (1976), Leaney (2016), Stace *et al.* (2015).

R.M. Leaney & D. Welch

Ne *Symphytum asperum* Rough Comfrey

Lepech.

A very tall comfrey, morphologically similar to *S. ×uplandicum* and, like that species, able to compete with tussocky grasses and rank vegetation, but occurring only very occasionally on road verges, tracksides and in churchyards. It produces abundant seedling plants around clonal patches, but, unlike *S. ×uplandicum*, is probably not resistant to frequent mowing. Lowland.

Trends *S. asperum* was introduced to our area as an ornamental by Conrad Loddiges in 1799 and was subsequently imported in the mid-19th century as a fodder plant. It appears to have always been extremely scarce in the wild, indeed Wade (1958) was only able to confirm around 20 records over a period of 120 years. This suggests that many of the new hectad records are likley to be errors for the blue-flowered form of *S. ×uplandicum*. In Norfolk,

there have been no new records this century, yet a population of many hundreds of plants has persisted for over 40 years in an area left unmown in a churchyard, but has not spread into the surrounding mown turf.

Biogeography Native of north-eastern Turkey, the Caucasus and northern Iran. Formerly cultivated and now naturalized in western and central Europe.

	GB	IR
Long term	No trend	No trend
Short term	⬇⬇◆⬆⬆	No trend

Alien	GB	IR
2000–19	69	2
1987–99	34	0
1970–86	27	4
pre-1970	33	2

Key refs Hills (1976), Wade (1958).

D. Welch & R.M. Leaney

Ne *Symphytum tuberosum* Tuberous Comfrey

L.

A perennial herb, spreading vegetatively by partially tuberous rhizomes to form extensive colonies. It is found naturalized along stream, river and ditch banks, in woodland and on road verges and waste ground. It is reported to spread by seed. Generally lowland, but reaching 365 m near Greenhow (Mid-west Yorkshire).

Trends Formerly treated as a native in Scotland and northern England (Preston *et al.*, 2002a) but now classed as an introduction throughout its British and Irish range (Pearman, 2007). This conclusion is based on its late discovery in the wild (1765 along the Water of Leith, Midlothian), continued spread (indicative of a fairly recent arrival), and northerly distribution being at odds with a southerly European range. It is now thought to have originated as a medicinal herb in Scotland (as a

substitute for *S. officinale*) (Braithwaite, 2021), and its 10 km square distribution has increased markedly since the 1960s, largely as a result of garden escapes.

Biogeography Native of western, central and southern Europe extending to north-western Anatolia.

	GB	IR
Long term	⬇⬇◆⬆⬆	⬇⬇◆⬆⬆
Short term	⬇⬇◆⬆⬆	⬇⬇◆⬆⬆

Alien	GB	IR
2000–19	659	60
1987–99	482	22
1970–86	286	6
pre-1970	445	11

Key refs Braithwaite (2014), Braithwaite (2021), Pearman (2007).

D. Welch, R.M. Leaney & K.J. Walker

(Ne) *Symphytum grandiflorum* Creeping Comfrey
DC.

A perennial herb, spreading vegetatively by rhizomes which produce long, leafy stolons and potentially forming very large clonal colonies. Widely planted as ground cover in gardens and parks and found on roadsides, in hedgerows, woods, and plantations and on streamsides, often where dumped in garden waste although some populations have clearly originated from material washed down streams. Often confused with *S. ×hidcotense* but less frequent in semi-natural habitats and less likely to spread by seed. Usually lowland, but reaching 400 m in the Clun Forest (Shropshire).

Trends Introduced to cultivation not long before 1900 but already recorded from the wild by 1898, in contrast with *S. ×hidcotense* which was not recorded in the wild until 1979. Its 10 km square distribution has increased dramatically since the 1960s and especially in the last 20 years due to the more systematic recording of garden escapes. However, the earlier recognition as a wild plant may have resulted in its being over-recorded for *S. ×hidcotense* during most of the 20th century and even today.

Biogeography Native of the Caucasus.

Alien		GB	IR
2000–19	●	696	6
1987–99	●	235	0
1970–86	●	76	0
pre-1970	○	37	1

	GB	IR
Long term	No trend	No trend
Short term	↓ ↓ · ↑ **⬆**	No trend

Key refs Perring (1994).

D. WELCH & R.M. LEANEY

Altitude (m) — Distance north (km)

● <1%
● 1–10%
● 11–30%
● 31–40%
● 41–50%
● 51–100%

☐ Apparency ☐ In flower ☐ In leaf

J F M A M J J A S O N D

(Ne) *Symphytum orientale* White Comfrey
L.

A clump-forming perennial herb, sometimes grown in gardens (where it can become a weed) and found on roadsides, waste ground, and in churchyards and cemeteries. It forms small clonal patches which compete poorly with taller vegetation, but regenerate vegetatively after cutting and produce abundant seedlings. Lowland.

Trends *S. orientale* was introduced from Russia as an ornamental by 1752 and first recorded in the wild in 1849 (Cambridgeshire). It has long been out of favour with gardeners due to it tendency to become a weed, but is nevertheless still extending its range and has spread noticeably this century into rural villages and nearby road verges and hedgebanks. Since the 1960s it has spread out from its former strongholds in East Anglia and the East Midlands, across much of southern Britain, with more scattered records in northern England, Scotland and eastern Ireland. There have been many more records this century which have maintained the same pattern of distribution, mostly filling in the southern range.

Biogeography Native of southern Russia, north-western Turkey and the Caucasus.

Alien		GB	IR
2000–19	●	681	4
1987–99	●	385	1
1970–86	●	213	0
pre-1970	○	193	1

	GB	IR
Long term	↓ ↓ · **↑** ↑	No trend
Short term	↓ ↓ · ↑ **⬆**	No trend

Key refs Perring (1994), Sanford & Fisk (2010).

D. WELCH & R.M. LEANEY

Altitude (m) — Distance north (km)

● <1%
● 1–10%
● 11–30%
● 31–40%
● 41–50%
● 51–100%

☐ Apparency ☐ In flower ☐ In leaf

J F M A M J J A S O N D

Ne *Symphytum caucasicum* Caucasian Comfrey
M.Bieb.

A perennial herb, spreading to form large, vigorous colonies, widely grown in gardens and found as an occasional garden throw-out on road verges or waste ground, or as a garden or allotment relic. Lowland.

Trends *S. caucasicum* was being grown as early as 1820, and has been present in the wild since 1879 (Milverton, Warwickshire). It is widely grown in gardens and the recent increase in records probably reflects both increased awareness of the taxon and more systematic recording of garden escapes. Some plants sold as this species show evidence of hybridization with other taxa in the *S. ×uplandicum* complex.

Biogeography Native of the Caucasus.

	GB	IR
Long term	No trend	No trend
Short term		No trend

Alien	GB	IR
2000–19	98	0
1987–99	10	0
1970–86	9	0
pre-1970	11	0

Key refs Leaney (2014), Perring (1994).

R.M. LEANEY & T.D. DINES

Ne *Brunnera macrophylla* Great Forget-me-not
(Adams) I.M.Johnst.

A shortly rhizomatous clump-forming perennial herb, found as a persistent garden escape or throw-out. It occurs in rough grassland, woodland and on refuse tips. Lowland.

Trends This species has been cultivated in British gardens since 1825 and remains very popular. It was recorded in the wild by 1926 (Moretonhampstead, South Devon). It may previously have been under-recorded, the name having sometimes been mistakenly applied to *Omphalodes verna*, but even so it is evidently increasing.

Biogeography Native of the Caucasus and northern Asia.

	GB	IR
Long term	No trend	No trend
Short term		No trend

Alien	GB	IR
2000–19	196	0
1987–99	87	1
1970–86	26	0
pre-1970	17	0

D. WELCH

Ne *Anchusa officinalis* Alkanet
L.

A tall perennial herb of rough and
waste ground, hedgerows, railway
banks and refuse tips, originating from
gardens or from birdseed. Populations
are generally impermanent, but
are occasionally naturalized, as, for
example, on sand dunes at Phillack
Towans (West Cornwall). Lowland.

Trends *A. officinalis* has been grown
in British gardens since 1752, and
was formerly also cultivated for
fodder. It was first formally recorded
in the wild in 1799 at Hartley
Links, South Northumberland.

Biogeography A European Temperate
species.

	GB	IR
Long term	No trend	No trend
Short term		No trend

Alien	GB	IR
2000–19	91	4
1987–99	46	1
1970–86	26	1
pre-1970	88	1

Altitude (m)

	<1%
	1–10%
	11–30%
	31–40%
	41–50%
	51–100%

Distance north (km)

☐ Apparency ☐ In flower ☐ In leaf

D. WELCH

Ne *Anchusa azurea* Garden Anchusa
Mill.

A tall perennial herb of rough and
waste ground, and refuse tips. It
occurs as a garden escape, but also
arises from grain and birdseed. It
is rarely naturalized. Lowland.

Trends *A. azurea* was once grown as a
fodder plant and was also introduced
as an impurity in grain seed. It was
introduced into cultivation by 1759 and
is now widely grown in gardens, much
more so than *A. officinalis*. It was first
recorded in the wild in 1866 (Surrey),
and has been naturalized at Phillack
Towans (West Cornwall) since 1914.

Biogeography Native of southern
Europe, the Mediterranean region and
western Asia.

	GB	IR
Long term	No trend	No trend
Short term		No trend

Alien	GB	IR
2000–19	25	0
1987–99	19	0
1970–86	15	0
pre-1970	35	0

Altitude (m)

	<1%
	1–10%
	11–30%
	31–40%
	41–50%
	51–100%

Distance north (km)

☐ Apparency ☐ In flower ☐ In leaf

D. WELCH

Ar *Lycopsis arvensis* Bugloss
L.

An annual weed of well-drained, usually sandy, soils in arable fields, but also occurring near the sea on sandy heaths, in disturbed dunes and on waste ground. Lowland, but with a casual record at 420 m near Ballater (South Aberdeenshire).

Trends *L. arvensis* declined in the latter half of the 20th century as a result of agricultural intensification, including the increased use of herbicides. Since 2000 the distribution appears to have stabilized, and has increased locally in some areas.

Biogeography As an archaeophyte, *L. arvensis* has a Eurosiberian Temperate distribution; it is widely naturalized outside this range.

Alien	GB	IR
2000–19	1133	43
1987–99	1054	38
1970–86	691	28
pre-1970	1206	51

D. Welch & P.A. Stroh

Altitude (m)

- <1%
- 1–10%
- 11–30%
- 31–40%
- 41–50%
- 51–100%

Apparency In flower In leaf

Ne *Nonea lutea* Yellow Nonea
(Desr.) DC.

An annual herb, occasionally grown in gardens and found as a casual or persistent garden weed, and locally established in stony gateways, roadsides and waste ground. Lowland.

Trends This species was being cultivated in Britain by 1805 but was not recorded as a naturalized plant until 1956 when it was found as a lawn weed in a Cambridge garden (Leslie, 2019). It remained very rare but since 2000 it has become much more frequent and may be spreading, especially in southern and eastern England, although some of the increase is undoubtedly due to the more systematic recording of aliens over the last 20 years.

Biogeography Native of Russia, Ukraine and south-western Asia but spreading farther west in Europe.

	GB	IR
Long term	No trend	No trend
Short term		No trend

Alien	GB	IR
2000–19	69	0
1987–99	6	0
1970–86	4	0
pre-1970	0	0

Key refs Leslie (2019).

Altitude (m)

- <1%
- 1–10%
- 11–30%
- 31–40%
- 41–50%
- 51–100%

Apparency In flower In leaf

J.O. Mountford

Ne *Pentaglottis sempervirens* Green Alkanet

(L.) Tausch ex L.H.Bailey

An erect perennial herb, found naturalized close to human habitations in lightly shaded habitats, including waste ground, pavements, tracksides, roadsides, hedgerows, scrub, woodland and by rivers and streams. It reproduces prolifically from seed, has a deep tap root, and can be very invasive in woodlands (Millar, 2012). Generally lowland, but reaching 420 m Clun Forest, (Shropshire).

Trends *P. sempervirens* was introduced to British gardens by 1596 where it frequently becomes a weed and is consequently discarded in garden waste. It was known from the wild by 1724 (Rochester, West Kent) and was already widespread by the 1960s. Its 10 km square distribution has continued to increase since then and it is now commonly found throughout much of Britain, and appears to be spreading in Ireland. This spread appears to have been mostly by seed but possibly also from root fragments as the deep roots are very brittle and, as any gardener knows, "any piece left in the soil will sprout freely" (Brickell, 2016).

Biogeography Native of south-western Europe, but naturalized in western Europe north of its native range.

Alien	GB	IR
2000–19	1905	154
1987–99	1588	59
1970–86	916	22
pre-1970	1059	31

Key refs Ballantyne (2013), Brickell (2016), James (2013), Millar (2012), Smith (2013b).

D. WELCH & K.J. WALKER

Ne *Borago officinalis* Borage

L.

An annual herb, found as a casual garden escape on roadsides and waste ground. It also arises from birdseed and as a relic of cultivation as a minor crop. It is rarely naturalized. Lowland, with an exceptional record at 425 m (Alston, Cumberland).

Trends *B. officinalis* has been grown in gardens since at least medieval times (Harvey, 1981). It was first recorded from the wild in 1724, and Dunn (1905) described it as a frequent escape from gardens. It is increasingly planted as a nectar-source for bees and occasionally cultivated as a crop. It is treated as a cultivated archaeophyte by Stace & Crawley (2015).

Biogeography Native of the Mediterranean area; the limits of its native range have been obscured by its spread in cultivation.

Alien	GB	IR
2000–19	1061	89
1987–99	675	14
1970–86	298	7
pre-1970	446	12

Key refs Dunn (1905), Harvey (1981), Stace & Crawley (2015).

D. WELCH

Ne *Trachystemon orientalis* Abraham-Isaac-Jacob
(L.) G.Don

A rhizomatous perennial herb, widely grown in gardens and occasionally naturalized in damp woods, streamsides, laneside banks and other shaded places. Lowland.

Trends Cultivated in Britain by 1752, this species was recorded from the wild by 1844 (Keswick, Cumberland). It is long-lived once established and appears to be gradually increasing.

Biogeography Native of eastern Bulgaria, northern Turkey and the western Caucasus.

	GB	IR
Long term	No trend	No trend

Alien	GB	IR
2000–19	219	10
1987–99	108	4
1970–86	51	0
pre-1970	39	0

Altitude (m)

- <1%
- 1–10%
- 11–30%
- 31–40%
- 41–50%
- 51–100%

Distance north (km)

J F M A M J J A S O N D

Apparency   In flower   In leaf

D. Welch

Ne *Amsinckia lycopsoides* Scarce Fiddleneck
Lehm.

An annual herb, found on arable land and waste ground on light, sandy soils. It arises as a contaminant of grain and, formerly, from wool shoddy. Lowland.

Trends *A. lycopsoides* has been naturalized on the Farne Islands since 1922, but confusion with *A. micrantha* means that scattering of records elsewhere probably exaggerates the true distribution of this species.

Biogeography Native of western North America.

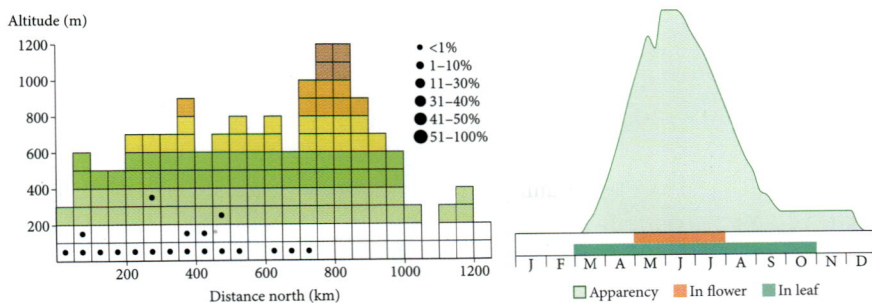

	GB	IR
Long term	No trend	No trend
Short term	No trend	No trend

Alien	GB	IR
2000–19	7	0
1987–99	16	0
1970–86	8	0
pre-1970	52	0

Altitude (m)

- <1%
- 1–10%
- 11–30%
- 31–40%
- 41–50%
- 51–100%

Distance north (km)

J F M A M J J A S O N D

Apparency   In flower   In leaf

M.N. Sanford

Ne *Amsinckia micrantha* Common Fiddleneck
Suksd.

An annual herb of arable land and waste ground. It is sometimes an abundant or even pernicious weed on light, sandy soils. It arises as a contaminant of grain, soil and, formerly, from wool shoddy. Predominantly lowland, but reaching 329 m at Lainchoil (Moray).

Trends *A. micrantha* was first recorded from the wild in 1888 (Penzance, West Cornwall), when it was introduced as a seed impurity. It has increased steadily since the 1960s, and is clearly much more frequent now than formerly, often being introduced as a casual with imported soil and spreading to become naturalized on light soils. Now a persistent weed in eastern England (especially in parts of East Anglia) and eastern Scotland. It has been much confused with *A. lycopsoides*.

Biogeography Native of western North America; widely naturalized in other parts of the world.

	GB	IR
Long term	No trend	No trend
Short term		No trend

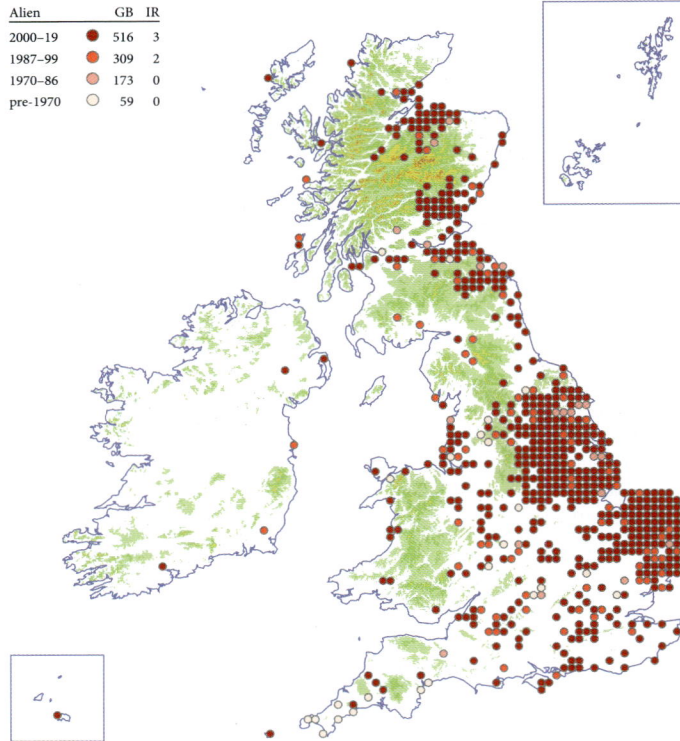

Alien	GB	IR
2000–19	516	3
1987–99	309	2
1970–86	173	0
pre-1970	59	0

Key refs Beckett & Bull (1999), Clement (1999), Simpson (1982).

D. Welch

N *Mertensia maritima* Oysterplant
(L.) Gray

A perennial herb of gravelly beaches and shingle, occasionally on sand. It can also colonize earth and rocks tipped at the coast (Randall, 1988). Seeds can survive prolonged immersion in sea water, and dispersal by sea currents enables colonization of new, but sometimes transient, sites. Lowland.

Trends *M. maritima* is a highly mobile species and consequently its 10 km square distribution has varied markedly since 1800. In Britain, continued expansion in northern Scotland has been balanced by contraction in the south, to the extent that it no longer occurs in England and Wales. Such 'range shift' may represent a response to climate change, with declines linked to increased storm damage and higher winter temperatures possibly inhibiting seed production, alongside other pressures such as shingle removal and

grazing. In Ireland its distribution is generally stable, following losses in the 19th and early 20th centuries.

Biogeography European Boreo-arctic Montane element; a coastal species also found in eastern Asia and North America.

	GB	IR
Long term		
Short term		

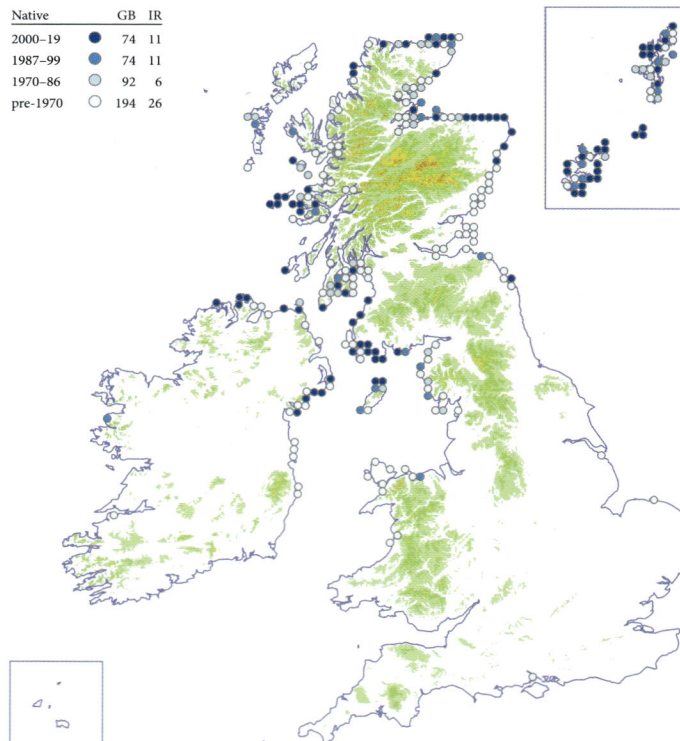

Native	GB	IR
2000–19	74	11
1987–99	74	11
1970–86	92	6
pre-1970	194	26

Key refs Randall (1988), Scott (1963a), Stewart *et al.* (1994), Welch & Innes (1999).

D. Welch & P.A. Stroh

N *Myosotis scorpioides* Water Forget-me-not
L.

A stoloniferous or rhizomatous perennial herb of damp or wet habitats, usually in fertile, calcareous to mildly acidic soils. It is usually terrestrial, occurring by lakes, ponds, rivers and streams, in marshes and in fens, but may sometimes be aquatic, forming submerged patches or floating rafts. 0–600 m (Moor House, Westmorland).

Trends The distribution of *M. scorpioides* has been generally stable over many decades. It has sometimes been confused with *M. secunda*, and some of these errors may be included on the map. However, the surprising lack of records this century in parts of Wales, and areas of western and northern Scotland, may reflect better differentiation of these two taxa in the field, rather than actual loss, but also under-recording in the more remote areas.

Biogeography Eurosiberian Temperate element; widely naturalized outside its native range.

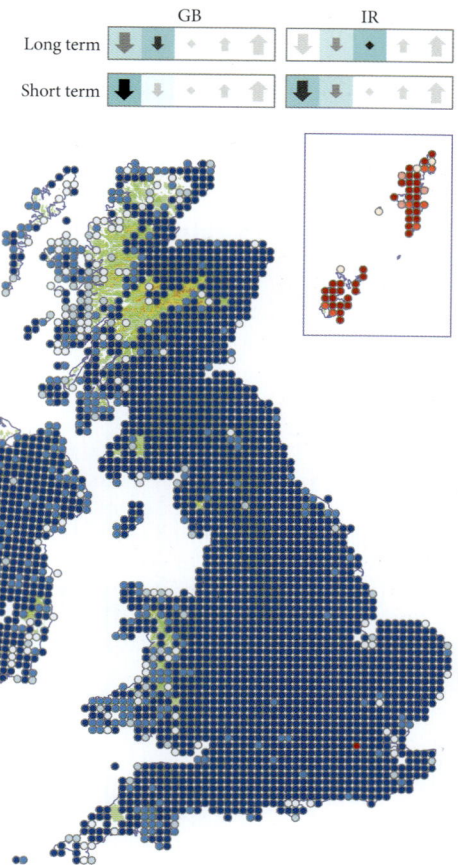

Native		GB	IR
2000–19	●	2040	578
1987–99	●	2033	542
1970–86	●	1546	111
pre-1970	○	2038	426

Alien		GB	IR
2000–19	●	38	0
1987–99	●	40	0
1970–86	●	21	0
pre-1970	○	41	0

Altitude (m) chart

- ● <1%
- ● 1–10%
- ● 11–30%
- ● 31–40%
- ● 41–50%
- ● 51–100%

Distance north (km)

☐ Apparency ■ In flower ■ In leaf

J F M A M J J A S O N D

Key refs Grime *et al.* (2007), Preston & Croft (1997), Welch (1967).

D. WELCH & P.A. STROH

N *Myosotis secunda* Creeping Forget-me-not
Al.Murray

A stoloniferous annual to perennial herb of the margins of acidic rills, streams and pools, in marshy pastures, moorland flushes and springs. It prefers acid peaty soils, and usually avoids richer calcareous situations. 0–805 m (Carnedd Llewelyn, Caernarvonshire).

Trends This species has sometimes been confused in the past with *M. scorpioides* and *M. laxa*, and the map in the 1962 *Atlas* certainly contained some errors. It is now more comprehensively recorded, and there appears to have been little change in its 10 km square distribution, other than some decline at the margins of its range. It was mapped as 'all records' in the 1962 *Atlas*.

Biogeography Oceanic Temperate element.

Native		GB	IR
2000–19	●	1554	479
1987–99	●	1427	398
1970–86	○	828	60
pre-1970	○	1200	229

Alien		GB	IR
2000–19	●	0	0
1987–99	●	1	0
1970–86	●	0	0
pre-1970	○	0	0

Altitude (m) chart

- ● <1%
- ● 1–10%
- ● 11–30%
- ● 31–40%
- ● 41–50%
- ● 51–100%

Distance north (km)

☐ Apparency ■ In flower ■ In leaf

J F M A M J J A S O N D

Key refs Welch (1967).

D. WELCH

N *Myosotis stolonifera* Pale Forget-me-not
(DC.) J.Gay ex Leresche & Levier

A perennial herb growing in rills, soakways, ditches and the backwaters of streams, and along base-rich spring-lines and flushes. Mainly upland, reaching 820 m on Cross Fell (Cumberland), and down to 130 m in the Lune valley (Cumberland).

Trends This species was first collected in the North Pennines in 1919, and was initially described as an endemic, *M. brevifolia* (Salmon, 1926). It was inadequately recorded for the 1962 *Atlas*, the plant not being sought in areas distant from the original sites. However, following a study of its characteristic features, *M. stolonifera* became better known and it has been found more widely, notably in southern Scotland. The absence of recent records for some historical sites is likely to reflect a lack of recording of fairly remote and uninviting habitats, rather than actual loss. In some upland areas it appears to be threatened by hybridization with *M. secunda* (*M. ×bollandica*) (Jepson *et al.*, 2012). The remarkable discovery of *M. stolonifera* on Exmoor (Somerset) in 2016 (Wilcox, 2016) is now thought to be an error.

Biogeography Oceanic Boreal-montane element; confined to Portugal, Spain and Britain.

Native	GB	IR
2000–19	97	0
1987–99	96	0
1970–86	84	0
pre-1970	63	0

Key refs Jepson *et al.* (2012), Salmon (1926), Stewart *et al.* (1994), Welch (1967), Wilcox (2016).

D. WELCH & P.A. STROH

N *Myosotis laxa* Tufted Forget-me-not
Lehm.

An annual or biennial herb of wet ground, often growing in open places trampled by livestock or where there has been other disturbance. It occurs in marshes, fen-meadows, rush-pastures, and by lakes, ponds, canals, rivers and streams. Lowland to 650 m in flushes on the east side of Ben Buck (West Perthshire).

Trends *M. laxa* appears stable throughout much of its range, and its distribution in Ireland is now much better known due to more systematic recording. However, local losses in south-eastern England, reported in the 2002 *Atlas*, appear to have continued this century to the extent that decline is more visible at the 10 km square scale. Much of this decline is most likely attributable to undergrazing, drainage and habitat degradation. It was mapped as 'all records' in the 1962 *Atlas*.

Biogeography Circumpolar Boreo-temperate element, with a disjunct distribution.

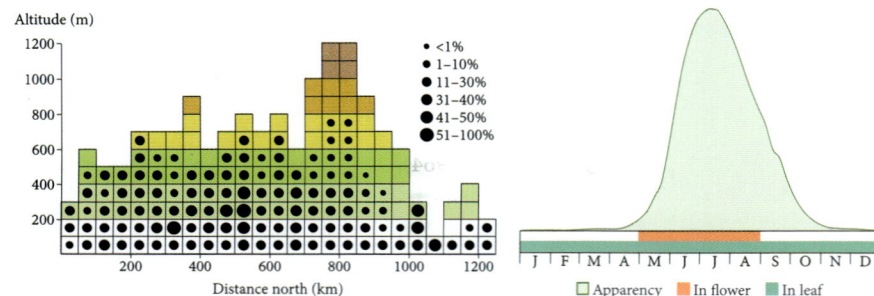

Native	GB	IR
2000–19	2176	701
1987–99	2096	643
1970–86	1333	111
pre-1970	1812	449

Alien	GB	IR
2000–19	1	0
1987–99	1	0
1970–86	1	0
pre-1970	1	0

D. WELCH & P.A. STROH

N *Myosotis sicula* Jersey Forget-me-not
Guss.

	GB	IR
Long term	No trend	No trend
Short term	No trend	No trend

An annual herb recorded from two sites on Jersey; in damp places on Ouaisné Common and by a small pool near the coast at Noirmont. Lowland.

Trends *M. sicula* was discovered at both its Jersey localities by A.J. Wilmott in 1922. It was last seen at Ouaisné Common in 1957. The Noirmont population disappeared in the 1980s when the pool became shaded by willows but these were cleared in 1983 and it was rediscovered at the site in 1992. The very small population there maintains a precarious existence and has been recorded several times since 2000.

Biogeography Mediterranean-Atlantic element.

Native	GB	IR
2000–19	1	0
1987–99	1	0
1970–86	0	0
pre-1970	1	0

Key refs Le Sueur (1984).

D. WELCH

N *Myosotis alpestris* Alpine Forget-me-not
F.W.Schmidt

	GB	IR
Long term	No trend	No trend
Short term	No trend	No trend

A perennial herb of two contrasting upland habitats in Britain. In the North Pennines it grows in short limestone grassland where the turf is kept open by preferential grazing by sheep and rabbits in areas otherwise dominated by acid grassland and blanket bog. In Scotland it is found on mica-schist rock ledges and amongst small herbs in the grassy slopes below. Reproduction is by seed, and flowering occurs mainly in June and July. From 685 m in Upper Teesdale (North-west Yorkshire and Westmorland) to 1,180 m on Ben Lawers (Mid Perthshire).

Trends The 10 km square distribution of *M. alpestris* is unchanged since the 1960s. In England, flowering stems are usually heavily grazed and this has led to the development of a dwarf ecotype which is morphologically distinct from ungrazed (rock ledge) Scottish populations. The overall number of plants on Ben Lawers appears to have declined by a third between 1994 and 2015, although monitoring plants growing on inaccessible cliff ledges can be challenging. In the North Pennines populations at three locations range from a few hundred (Green Castle, Mickle Fell) to possibly in excess of 50,000 individuals (Little Fell). Flowering is also adversely affected by prolonged periods of dry weather.

Biogeography Circumpolar Arctic-montane element, with a disjunct distribution.

Native	GB	IR
2000–19	5	0
1987–99	5	0
1970–86	5	0
pre-1970	7	0

Alien	GB	IR
2000–19	0	0
1987–99	0	0
1970–86	0	0
pre-1970	1	0

Key refs Elkington (1964), Walker (2015c), Wigginton (1999).

S.H. WATTS & D. WELCH

Myosotis sylvatica Wood Forget-me-not
Ehrh. ex Hoffm.

An erect biennial or perennial herb growing as a native, at least in England, on damp, fertile soils in woodland and rocky grassland. It is much more widespread in a wider range of habitats as a garden escape. 0–485 m (East Stone Gill, North-west Yorkshire).

Trends The native range of *M. sylvatica* has been completely obscured by garden escapes, and all records are mapped here without status. Alien plants were once similar to the natives but are now often recognizable by their more varied, brighter flower colours. An attempt was made to exclude such escapes from the map in the 1962 *Atlas*. Large-flowered variants of *M. arvensis* may have been reported as this species.

Biogeography Eurasian Temperate element; widely naturalized outside its native range.

		GB	IR
2000–19	●	1895	116
1987–99	●	1500	22
1970–86	●	874	1
pre-1970	○	874	2

Altitude (m)

●	<1%
●	1–10%
●	11–30%
●	31–40%
●	41–50%
●	51–100%

Distance north (km)

Apparency   In flower   In leaf

Key refs Rich & Jermy (1998).

D. Welch & P.A. Stroh

Myosotis arvensis Field Forget-me-not
(L.) Hill

An annual or biennial herb of open or disturbed ground, especially cultivated fields but also woodland edges, open grassland, hedges, scrub, roadsides, walls and quarries. 0–610 m (Nenthead, Cumberland), and exceptionally at 845 m on Great Dun Fell (Westmorland).

Trends Despite changes in agricultural practice, the distribution of *M. arvensis* has remained stable since the 1960s, due in part to its flexible life history and long-lived seed. The larger-flowered var. *sylvestris* is often mistaken for *M. sylvatica*, but such errors are unlikely to have affected the distribution shown on the map.

Biogeography As an archaeophyte, *M. arvensis* has a Eurosiberian Boreo-temperate distribution; it is widely naturalized outside this range.

Alien		GB	IR
2000–19	●	2505	748
1987–99	●	2409	593
1970–86	●	1496	81
pre-1970	○	2348	519

Altitude (m)

●	<1%
●	1–10%
●	11–30%
●	31–40%
●	41–50%
●	51–100%

Distance north (km)

Apparency   In flower   In leaf

Key refs Grime *et al.* (2007), Rich & Jermy (1998).

D. Welch

Ⓝ *Myosotis ramosissima* Early Forget-me-not
Rochel

An annual herb of open habitats or bare ground on dry, relatively infertile soils. It is found in chalk and limestone grassland, on sandy heaths and banks, stabilized sand dunes, the borders of sandy cultivated fields, railway tracks, rocks, walls, gravel-pits, quarry spoil and waste ground. 0–430 m (above Swindale, Brough, Westmorland).

Trends There have been some local losses of *M. ramosissima* since the 1960s, with much of this loss linked to the absence of formerly close-grazed semi-natural communities in inland areas. However, as a diminutive, early flowering species, it may have been overlooked in some areas previously, and intensive recording this century has revealed many new locations inland, and also by the coast, most notably in the Outer Hebrides and West Sutherland, extending the northern and north-western range limits. It was mapped as 'all records' in the 1962 *Atlas*.

Biogeography European Southern-temperate element.

Native	GB	IR
2000–19	986	42
1987–99	911	33
1970–86	566	17
pre-1970	856	28

Key refs Grime *et al.* (2007).

D. WELCH & P.A. STROH

Ⓝ *Myosotis discolor* Changing Forget-me-not
Pers.

An annual herb of open grassland and disturbed ground occurring in a wide range of habitats, including fen- and hay-meadows, pastures, moorland edges, marshes, dune-slacks, arable field margins, road verges, railway tracks, chalk- and gravel-pits, rocks, pavements and walls. Generally lowland, but reaching 610 m on Little Fell (Westmorland) and 845 m on Great Dun Fell (Westmorland).

Trends *M. discolor* has suffered a widespread decline in southern and eastern England since the 1960s, with much of this loss taking place in the latter half of the 20th century. It is, however, now much more comprehensively recorded in southern, western and central England, and in Ireland. Two subspecies occur in our area; subsp. *discolor* occurs on dry, sandy or peaty ground and on ultrabasic rocks, whereas subsp. *dubia* prefers damp, base-poor pastures, moorland edges and muddy tracks. Further investigation is required to delineate the range of the two subspecies.

Biogeography European Temperate element.

Native	GB	IR
2000–19	2131	509
1987–99	1849	419
1970–86	1090	58
pre-1970	1714	229

Alien	GB	IR
2000–19	2	0
1987–99	0	0
1970–86	2	0
pre-1970	1	0

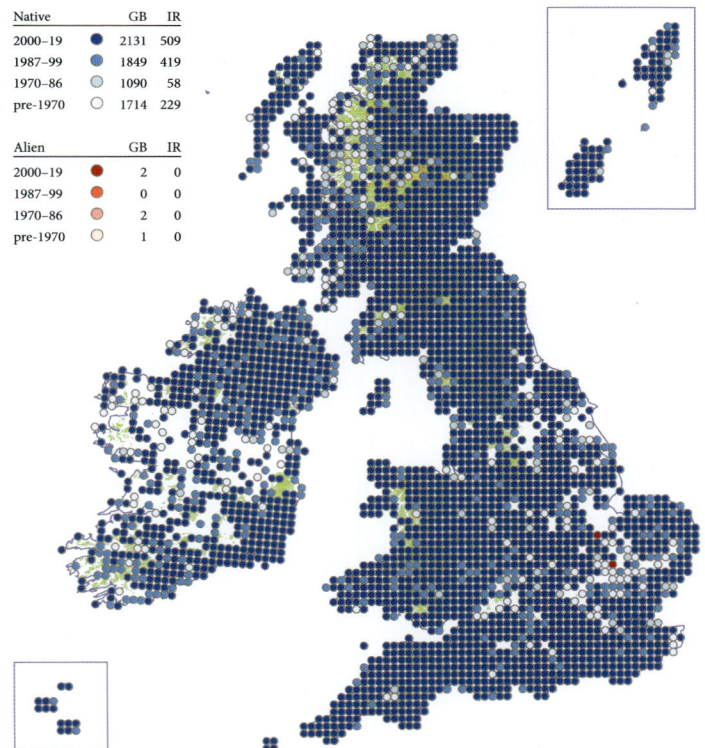

Key refs Chater (2010b), Jones (2018), Sell & Murrell (2009).

D. WELCH & P.A. STROH

N *Myosotis stricta* Upright Forget-me-not
Link ex Roem. & Schult.

An erect, patent-hairy annual herb of droughted, nutrient- and calcium-poor sand dune slopes dominated by *Syntrichia ruraliformis* (Sand-hill Screw-moss), *Vulpia fasciculata* and *Phleum arenarium*. Also recorded from a wall top and perhaps formerly on gravelly banks and open ground on limestone headlands. It would appear to occupy a narrow ecological niche, is rather thermophilous and scarce where it occurs. Lowland.

Trends First recorded at Petit Tor on the Torquay limestones (South Devon) in 1859 and subsequently from Helensburgh (Dunbarton) in 1967, but generally dismissed as a casual, or an error. Specimens in the Natural History Museum herbarium collected in Wensleydale (North-west Yorkshire) in 1902 and at Sandscale (Westmorland) in 1914 were identified as this by Jones & Rumsey (2019), and it was refound at the latter site in 2020. Plants collected as *M. collina* var. *mittenii* in the 1880s at Mickleham Downs (Surrey) and on Dawlish Warren (South Devon) are also believed to represent this species, which may be overlooked elsewhere.

Biogeography Widely distributed throughout Eurasia, introduced in North America.

Native	GB	IR
2000–19	1	0
1987–99	0	0
1970–86	0	0
pre-1970	0	0

	GB	IR
Long term	No trend	No trend
Short term	No trend	No trend

Key refs Jones & Rumsey (2019).

F.J. RUMSEY & R.A. JONES

Ne *Lappula squarrosa* Bur Forget-me-not
(Retz.) Dumort.

An annual herb, found as a casual on waste ground and refuse tips where it is introduced in birdseed, grass-seed, grain and, formerly, wool shoddy. Lowland.

Trends This species was first recorded from the wild in 1839 (Southwold, East Suffolk). It had undergone a widespread decline by 1930, possibly due to a decline in grain imports from Europe. Since then it has remained a very rare casual.

Biogeography *L. squarrosa* has a Eurosiberian Temperate distribution, but it is rare in western Europe; it is widely naturalized in North America and elsewhere.

Alien	GB	IR
2000–19	13	0
1987–99	11	3
1970–86	9	1
pre-1970	86	1

	GB	IR
Long term	No trend	No trend
Short term	No trend	No trend

D. WELCH

Ne *Omphalodes verna* Blue-eyed-Mary

Moench

A creeping perennial herb, found as a garden escape or outcast naturalized in woodland and along lanes. Lowland.

Trends *O. verna* was cultivated in Britain by 1633, but appears to be less frequent in gardens than formerly. It was known from the wild by 1794 (Moray), and Dunn (1905) described it as 'occasionally recorded in England as naturalized near gardens'. It can be very persistent. Perhaps still over-recorded for *Brunnera macrophylla*.

Biogeography Native of the mountains of southern-central and south-eastern Europe.

	GB	IR
Long term	No trend	No trend
Short term		No trend

Alien	GB	IR
2000–19	58	1
1987–99	36	1
1970–86	17	0
pre-1970	56	0

Altitude (m) histogram; symbol key: <1%, 1–10%, 11–30%, 31–40%, 41–50%, 51–100%. Distance north (km).

Apparency, In flower, In leaf (J F M A M J J A S O N D)

Key refs Dunn (1905).

D. WELCH

N *Cynoglossum officinale* Hound's-tongue

L.

A biennial herb of disturbed ground, growing mostly on dry, often base-rich soils. Its habitats include coastal sand dunes and shingle, open grassland, woodland margins and clearings, field edges, cleared land and gravelly waste. It is unpalatable to grazing animals and is often frequent on disturbed ground by rabbit warrens and badger setts. Generally lowland, but reaching 400 m on Eglwyseg Rocks, Llangollen (Denbighshire).

Trends *C. officinale* declined sharply in the latter decades of the 20th century, loss of habitat and herbicide spraying doubtless being major factors. Although declines have continued, it remains frequent on parts of the East Anglian coast, the Brecklands of Norfolk and Suffolk and the South Downs. A few old records in northern Scotland and Ireland are considered to be relics of cultivation by herbalists.

Biogeography Eurosiberian Temperate element; widely naturalized outside its native range.

	GB	IR
Long term		
Short term		

Native	GB	IR
2000–19	435	10
1987–99	425	11
1970–86	308	9
pre-1970	621	43

Alien	GB	IR
2000–19	8	0
1987–99	6	0
1970–86	3	0
pre-1970	10	4

Altitude (m) histogram; symbol key: <1%, 1–10%, 11–30%, 31–40%, 41–50%, 51–100%. Distance north (km).

Apparency, In flower, In leaf (J F M A M J J A S O N D)

Key refs de Jong *et al.* (1990), Upadhyaya *et al.* (1988).

D. WELCH

N *Cynoglossum germanicum* Green Hound's-tongue
Jacq.

A biennial or short-lived perennial herb occurring in glades or the margins of deciduous lowland woodland, usually *Fagus sylvatica*, *Quercus* spp. or *Fraxinus excelsior*; occasionally in hedgebanks. It is found mainly on calcareous, freely draining, loamy soils. It relies on animal or human vectors for the dispersal of its barbed fruits, which are long-lived in the soil, and requires disturbance in order to germinate, hence it is often associated with areas of badger or rabbit activity, public footpaths or areas of woodland cleared following storms. Lowland.

Trends The reasons for a marked decline before 1930 are unclear, but may be more apparent than real as many old records appear to have been of transient populations. Whilst sites continued to be lost throughout much of the 20th century, the great storm of 1987 opened up its woodland habitats, resulting in the appearance

of huge populations in Surrey, where it still has healthy numbers. With the number of sites in Oxfordshire doubling since 2000, there are now upwards of 30 established sites across south-eastern and central England.

Biogeography European Temperate element, with a continental distribution in western Europe.

Native	GB	IR
2000–19	13	0
1987–99	5	0
1970–86	4	0
pre-1970	50	0

Alien	GB	IR
2000–19	5	0
1987–99	2	0
1970–86	0	0
pre-1970	7	0

Key refs Wigginton (1999).

D. Welch & T. Smith

N *Convolvulus arvensis* Field Bindweed
L.

A trailing or climbing perennial herb, found on waste or cultivated ground, waysides, railway banks, open scrub and rough or short grassland, including disturbed chalk downland. Lowland.

Trends There is no evidence for a marked change in the distribution of *C. arvensis* within southern and eastern Britain since the 1960s although it has declined in northern and western Britain, and in Ireland, presumably due to the decline in small-scale arable cultivation over recent decades. It remains one of the most persistent garden and arable weeds in many regions and once established is almost impossible to eradicate.

Biogeography Eurosiberian Southern-temperate element, but widely naturalized so that distribution is now Circumpolar Southern-temperate.

Native	GB	IR
2000–19	1598	319
1987–99	1628	322
1970–86	1192	54
pre-1970	1646	243

Alien	GB	IR
2000–19	1	0
1987–99	5	0
1970–86	1	0
pre-1970	2	0

Key refs Grime *et al.* (2007), Weaver & Riley (1982).

G.M. Kay & K.J. Walker

Calystegia soldanella Sea Bindweed
(L.) R.Br.

A trailing perennial herb found on sand dunes, and above the strand-line on sand and shingle beaches, often growing with *Eryngium maritimum*. Lowland.

Trends The loss of sand dunes and increased recreational disturbance on those that remain have resulted in many losses of this species during the 20th century, particularly in southern and eastern England, although it seems to be relatively resistant to trampling. Its distribution since the 1990s appears to be stable, save for coastal areas in eastern Scotland, where there are very few recent records.

Biogeography Mediterranean-Atlantic element; also in western North America and widely naturalized outside its native range.

Native	GB	IR
2000–19	223	67
1987–99	200	53
1970–86	141	14
pre-1970	245	36

Alien	GB	IR
2000–19	0	0
1987–99	0	0
1970–86	0	0
pre-1970	1	0

Key refs Stroh *et al.* (2014).

G.M. Kay & J.O. Mountford

Calystegia sepium Hedge Bindweed
(L.) R.Br.

A perennial climber of moist, fertile habitats, occurring in hedges, scrub, woodland edges, banks of watercourses, tall-herb fens, in open willow- and alder-carr, and on railway banks and waste ground. More rarely, it is present on coastal sands and dunes. It also occurs in artificial habitats in built-up areas near human habitations. 0–370 m (Beaufort, Breconshire).

Trends There has been no appreciable change in the range of this species since the 1960s, other than possibly a slight spread in western Ireland and inland in northern Scotland. Two subspecies occur in our area: subsp. *sepium* is found throughout the range of the species and subsp. *roseata* is mapped separately. A third, subsp. *spectabilis*, was formerly recorded as a garden relic in Merionethshire.

Biogeography Circumpolar Temperate element.

Native	GB	IR
2000–19	2207	904
1987–99	2051	797
1970–86	1342	111
pre-1970	1765	631

Alien	GB	IR
2000–19	25	1
1987–99	16	1
1970–86	7	0
pre-1970	12	1

Key refs Grime *et al.* (2007).

G.M. Kay & J.O. Mountford

N *Calystegia sepium* subsp. *roseata*
Brummitt

A perennial climber that typically occurs in brackish habitats at the upper edges of saltmarshes, in reedbeds and in grassy waste places in coastal regions. It is also found inland on riversides, on ditch-banks and in fens, as well as on rough ground. Lowland.

Trends *C. sepium* subsp. *roseata* was first described in 1967 and mapped by Perring & Sell (1968). It is now far better recorded and has been shown to be frequent in both Broadland and Fenland, where it may have been the typical taxon of undrained fens. The pink form of the nominate subspecies, *C. sepium* subsp. *sepium* f. *colorata*, also occurs in fen sites and there is some possibility of confusion (Leslie, 2019). Other than recent discovery of these eastern English sites, and a substantial number of new records for Ireland, the distribution appears to be largely stable.

Biogeography Oceanic Temperate element; also known from temperate South America, Easter Island and Australasia.

Native	GB	IR
2000–19	148	143
1987–99	72	76
1970–86	20	3
pre-1970	48	12

Alien	GB	IR
2000–19	3	0
1987–99	6	0
1970–86	1	0
pre-1970	0	0

	GB	IR
Long term	No trend	No trend
Short term	No trend	No trend

Key refs Brummitt & Chater (2000), Leslie (2019), Sell (1967).

G.M. Kay & J.O. Mountford

Hy *Calystegia sepium* × *silvatica* = *C.* ×*lucana*
(Ten.) G.Don

This hybrid occupies similar habitats to the parents, including scrub, hedges, ditches, marshes, reedbeds, road banks, the tops of saltmarshes and shingle beaches, fence-lines and waste ground. It is perhaps commonest in urban areas. Clones vary in fertility, from highly fertile to nearly sterile. Lowland.

A spontaneous hybrid (native × alien).

Trends Trends in the distribution of this hybrid are difficult to ascertain, and though the map shows that it is widespread, concentrations in those few areas where recorders have been competent to record it suggest that its distribution in our area is still imperfectly known.

Biogeography Widespread in southern Europe and northern Africa.

	GB	IR
2000–19	257	43
1987–99	97	2
1970–86	29	0
pre-1970	48	1

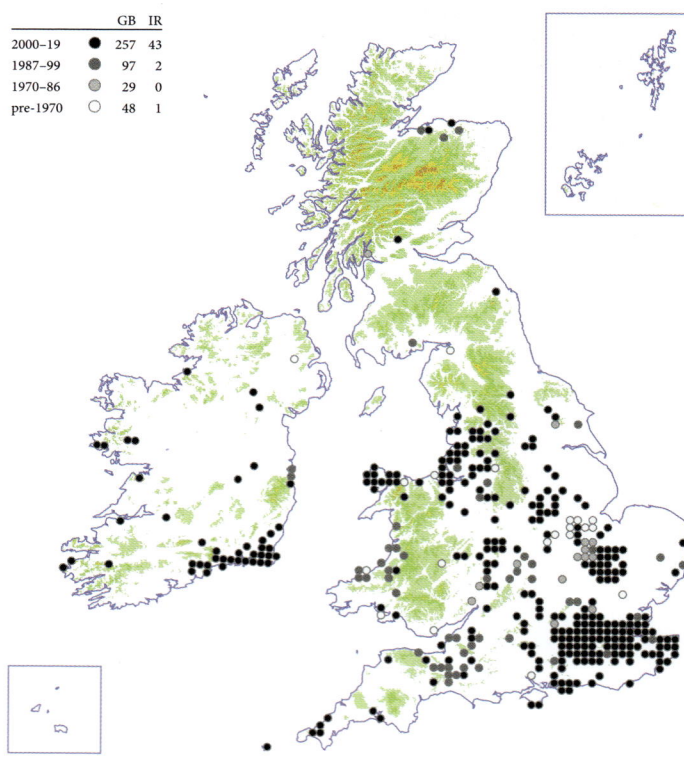

	GB	IR
Long term	No trend	No trend
Short term	No trend	No trend

Key refs Stace *et al.* (2015).

C.A. Stace, C.D. Preston & D.A. Pearman

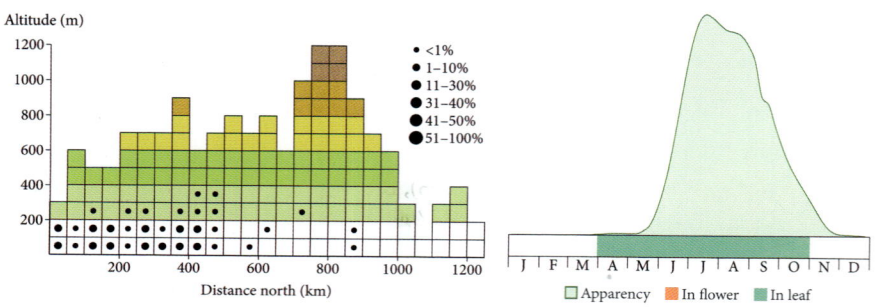

Ne *Calystegia pulchra* Hairy Bindweed
Brummitt & Heywood

A climbing perennial herb, found naturalized in hedges and on waste ground, usually close to human habitations. Reproduction is mainly vegetative and seed rarely ripens in our area, though when established populations may persist for many decades. Lowland to 399 m on rock outcrops at Cwm Clydach (Carmarthenshire).

Trends *C. pulchra* has been cultivated in Britain since 1823. The earliest specimens from our area were collected in 1867 (Twickenham, Middlesex) and 1884 (Edinburgh, Midlothian), and retrospectively identified from herbarium material following its recognition as a distinct species by Brummitt & Heywood (1960). The evidence of better recording (and thus wider distribution) that was noted in the 2002 *Atlas* has continued.

Biogeography Origin unknown, either originating in cultivation or a native of north-eastern Asia; widely naturalized in northern and central Europe.

Alien	GB	IR
2000–19	546	136
1987–99	470	88
1970–86	368	31
pre-1970	267	14

Key refs Brummitt & Heywood (1960), Brummitt & Chater (2000).

G.M. Kay & J.O. Mountford

Ne *Calystegia silvatica* Large Bindweed
(Kit.) Griseb.

A climbing or scrambling perennial herb of hedges, fences, gardens and waste ground. It also spreads into semi-natural habitats away from human habitations, possibly as a result of dispersal by agricultural machinery (Sell & Murrell, 2009). Seed-set is often very poor. 0–382 m at Robbery Gate (South Somserset).

Trends *C. silvatica* has been cultivated in Britain since 1815. It was collected from the wild in 1863 but not generally recognized as distinct from *C. sepium* until 1948 (Hough End Clough, South Lancashire), by which time it was widespread. The distribution is now generally stable although there is evidence of local spread into more rural sites, especially in Ireland. Two subspecies occur in Britain; subsp. *disjuncta* is common over much of Britain, whereas subsp. *silvatica* may be more frequent in western Britain and Ireland.

Biogeography Native of the Mediterranean region and south-western Asia.

Alien	GB	IR
2000–19	1742	439
1987–99	1570	274
1970–86	882	59
pre-1970	1297	100

Key refs Brummitt (1996), Brummitt & Chater (2000), Lousley (1948a), Sell & Murrell (2009).

G.M. Kay & J.O. Mountford

Ne *Cuscuta campestris* Yellow Dodder
Yunck.

A rootless, annual parasitic herb, introduced on a range of ornamental plants and agricultural and horticultural seed and birdseed. It usually occurs on garden plants, on crops (especially of carrot, beetroot and lucerne) and on tomato plants at sewage works. It rarely sets seed in Britain. Lowland.

Trends *C. campestris* was first recorded in the wild in 1927 (Bristol, West Gloucestershire). Its overall frequency of introduction appears to be stable.

Biogeography Native of North America; widely naturalized in other continents.

Alien	GB	IR
2000–19	43	0
1987–99	10	0
1970–86	20	0
pre-1970	17	0

T.D. Dines

N *Cuscuta europaea* Greater Dodder
L.

An annual, rarely perennial, rootless twining holoparasite of damp nitrophilous places, especially the banks of rivers, but also hedges and ditchbanks. Its primary host is usually *Urtica dioica*, rarely *Humulus lupulus* or other species, whence it can spread to a wide spectrum of secondary hosts. It often grows close to flowing water, which may disperse the seeds. Lowland.

Trends While *C. europaea* continues to be found in new sites, presumably due to better recording, its distribution suggests many losses away from particular hot-spot areas usually closely associated with a river system or watercourse. In these its populations are dynamic, fluctuating in number and location, but appearing fairly stable at a broader scale over the longer term.

Biogeography Eurosiberian Temperate element; widely naturalized outside its native range.

Native	GB	IR
2000–19	45	0
1987–99	52	0
1970–86	42	0
pre-1970	104	0

Alien	GB	IR
2000–19	2	0
1987–99	1	0
1970–86	1	0
pre-1970	17	0

Key refs Stewart *et al.* (1994), Verdcourt (1948).

F.J. Rumsey

Ⓝ *Cuscuta epithymum* Dodder
(L.) L.

An annual, rarely perennial, rootless twining herb, parasitic on the stems of a wide variety of small shrubs and herbs, most frequently *Calluna vulgaris*, *Thymus drucei*, *Ulex gallii* and *U. minor*, on lowland and coastal heathlands, chalk downland and fixed dune grasslands. It was also previously casual on field crops and in arable field-borders at the northern and western extent of its range. Almost exclusively lowland, but to 485 m at Hameldown Beacon (South Devon).

Trends Historically, this species underwent a dramatic decline in its natural habitats during the 19th and 20th centuries due to the loss of lowland heath, ploughing of chalk downland and an increase in scrub. Improved seed cleaning also drastically reduced its casual occurrence as a weed of fodder and other crops, which resulted in a marked contraction of its range southwards in Britain. Whilst it still

may be locally abundant, there are considerable annual fluctuations in population size related to management and climate. The results of a stratified random survey conducted between 2008 and 2013 focusing on post-1970 locations reported high survivorship and some stablisation of distribution (Walker *et al.*, 2017), though across its range it continues to be lost from sites, and it remains vulnerable to changes in habitat management.

Biogeography Eurosiberian Southern-temperate element; widely naturalized outside its native range.

Native		GB	IR
2000–19	●	223	17
1987–99	●	214	17
1970–86	○	190	8
pre-1970	○	483	23

Alien		GB	IR
2000–19	●	1	0
1987–99	●	0	0
1970–86	●	0	0
pre-1970	○	20	0

Key refs Walker *et al.* (2017).

F.J. Rumsey

Ⓝ𝐞 *Lycium* Teaplant
L.

The two species of *Lycium* in our area (*L. barbarum* and *L. chinense*) are deciduous shrubs, spreading vegetatively by tip-rooting of the arching stems or by suckering. They are found most often planted in hedges bounding gardens from where they often escape if left untended, also occasionally bird-sown or established from dumped material on waste land, refuse tips, shingle, riverbanks, hedgebanks and walls. 0–350 m (near Brassington, Derbyshire).

Trends Botanists and gardeners have long attempted to distinguish these two species but they are probably best treated as one very variable species, and this is the approach adopted here. They were introduced before 1696 and were first recorded from the wild in 1848 (as *L. barbarum*). There has been no appreciable change in their distribution since the 1960s and any local increases

are undoubtedly due to the better recording of aliens in recent decades.

Biogeography Both *L. barbarum* and *L. chinense* are natives of China.

Alien		GB	IR
2000–19	●	858	63
1987–99	●	855	54
1970–86	●	501	20
pre-1970	○	803	25

Key refs Bean (1973), Coats (1963).

T.D. Dines & K.J. Walker

(N) *Atropa belladonna* Deadly Nightshade
L.

A robust rhizomatous perennial herb of dry disturbed ground, field margins, grassland, hedgerows and open woodland. It is native only on calcareous soils, particularly those overlying chalk and limestone, but it occurs on a wider range of soils as an alien, where it is often a relic of cultivation as a medicinal herb. Dispersal is mainly by bird-distributed seed. Lowland.

Native in Britain and a neophyte in Ireland and the Channel Islands.

Trends Although highly persistent, *A. belladonna* has declined due to agricultural improvement and, in some cases, targeted eradication. Some populations may well be ancient introductions and it is difficult to determine the status of many populations, even within its core area.

Biogeography European Temperate element.

Native	GB	IR
2000–19	240	0
1987–99	276	0
1970–86	192	0
pre-1970	332	0

Alien	GB	IR
2000–19	61	2
1987–99	39	9
1970–86	34	6
pre-1970	90	8

Key refs Butcher (1947).

T.D. DINES

(Ar) *Hyoscyamus niger* Henbane
L.

An annual to biennial herb, found in a wide variety of disturbed habitats including arable field margins, tracks and roadsides, sand dunes, open areas in calcareous grassland, refuse tips, old sand- and gravel-pits and waste ground. It prefers disturbed ground, including rabbit warrens, badger setts and building sites, mostly on calcareous or other free-draining soils, particularly those overlying chalk. Although usually casual, it is often sporadic in occurrence, sometimes emerging in large numbers, suggesting that it forms a long-term persistent seed bank. It is occasionally introduced in seed mixtures amongst legume crops and on newly sown verges (Leslie, 2019). Generally lowland, but to 371 m in Soutra Aisle (East Lothian).

Trends There is a continuous archaeological record of *H. niger* in Britain from the Bronze Age onwards. It was formerly cultivated for medicinal use. Declines before 1930, particularly in Ireland, were evident by the 1950s and have continued, with an almost halving of hectad occurrences since 2000. The reasons for decline are not clear but are likely to include increased use of herbicides and other control measures on farmland (due to its toxicity to livestock), gentrification of waste and derelict land and a long-term decline in cultivation.

Biogeography As an archaeophyte, *H. niger* has a Eurosiberian Southern-temperate distribution, but it is widely naturalized so that it is now Circumpolar Southern-temperate.

Alien	GB	IR
2000–19	236	7
1987–99	304	16
1970–86	341	13
pre-1970	677	79

Key refs Leslie (2019), Stewart *et al.* (1994).

T.D. DINES, S.M. SMART & K.J. WALKER

Ne *Nicandra physalodes* Apple-of-Peru

(L.) Gaertn.

A large annual herb, occasionally grown as an ornamental in gardens but also arising from birdseed. Usually occurring as a casual in gardens and allotments, on refuse tips, on disturbed ground and on soil and manure heaps. It seeds can overwinter, resulting in established populations in milder areas, some apparently self-sowing (especially in allotments and gardens). Lowland.

Trends *N. physalodes* was grown in Britain by 1759 and it was first recorded in the wild in 1850 (Isle of Wight). Its size and appearance mean that it is unlikely to be overlooked and its distribution has increased dramatically since the 1960s.

Biogeography Native of South America (Peru).

Alien		GB	IR
2000–19	●	429	10
1987–99	●	153	2
1970–86	●	107	0
pre-1970	○	66	1

T.D. Dines

Ne *Datura stramonium* Thorn-apple

L.

An annual herb of waste ground, refuse tips, cultivated and disturbed ground. Most populations are casual, but the species can become naturalized, or reappear after long periods from dormant seeds. It most frequently arises from birdseed, but also from oil-seed and grain. Lowland.

Trends *D. stramonium* was cultivated in Britain by 1596 and was grown commercially for alkaloids used to treat asthma. It was first recorded in the wild in 1690. As a casual at many locations, changes within its range are difficult to assess, with much turnover apparent. However, new records this century have extended the species' range into Ireland and into northern Scotland, with a first record for Orkney in 2006.

Biogeography Native range unknown, possibly the Americas or the Black Sea region; now widespread in temperate and sub-tropical regions.

Alien		GB	IR
2000–19	●	657	21
1987–99	●	417	1
1970–86	●	343	8
pre-1970	○	597	7

Key refs Mabey (1996), Weaver & Warwick (1984).

T.D. Dines & S.M. Smart

Ne *Datura ferox* Longspine Thorn-apple

L.

An annual herb, found as a casual on arable fields and refuse tips originating as a grain impurity, and formerly from wool shoddy. It is also occasionally grown in gardens, from which most recent records probably originate. Lowland.

Trends *D. ferox* was first cultivated in Britain in 1731. It was recorded from the wild in 1895 (Halfway, Berkshire). It remains infrequent but has been recorded in a small number of new locations in northern and western England and in mid-eastern Scotland since 2000.

Biogeography Native of China; widely naturalized elsewhere.

	GB	IR
Long term	No trend	No trend
Short term	↓ ↓ · ↑ **↑**	No trend

Alien		GB	IR
2000–19	●	31	0
1987–99	●	7	1
1970–86	●	9	0
pre-1970	○	14	0

Altitude (m)

- <1%
- 1–10%
- 11–30%
- 31–40%
- 41–50%
- 51–100%

Distance north (km)

☐ Apparency   ☐ In flower   ☐ In leaf

T.D. DINES & S.M. SMART

Ne *Physalis peruviana* Cape-gooseberry

L.

A rhizomatous perennial herb which occurs on refuse tips and waste ground. It is usually casual but a few populations in southern England are naturalized. It arises from birdseed, oil-seed and from food refuse, and formerly from wool shoddy. Lowland.

Trends *P. peruviana* was first cultivated in Britain in 1772, but it is assumed that all early records are of plants arising from imported fruit or seed impurities. It was first recorded from the wild in 1918 (Bradford, South-west Yorkshire) and appears to be increasing, possibly through the increased popularity of its sweet, edible fruit. It is now cultivated here on a small scale.

Biogeography Native of South America; widely naturalized elsewhere.

	GB	IR
Long term	No trend	No trend
Short term	↓ ↓ · ↑ **↑**	No trend

Alien		GB	IR
2000–19	●	92	1
1987–99	●	33	1
1970–86	●	13	0
pre-1970	○	13	0

Altitude (m)

- <1%
- 1–10%
- 11–30%
- 31–40%
- 41–50%
- 51–100%

Distance north (km)

☐ Apparency   ☐ In flower   ☐ In leaf

Key refs Vaughan & Geissler (2009).

T.D. DINES & D.A. PEARMAN

Ne *Alkekengi officinarum* Chinese-lantern

Moench

A perennial herb, grown in gardens and allotments for its bright orange calyces, but with long rhizomes that can lead to it being thrown-out. It has been found on waste ground and refuse tips, on roadside verges, railway banks and other waste places. Most records are of established colonies; dispersal by seed is limited and the majority of populations are probably derived from garden throw-outs. It is very persistent when established. Lowland.

Trends *A. officinarum* was introduced from southern Europe by 1548, and is often cultivated for its ornamental fruits. It was known from the wild by 1597. It has been gradually increasing in range since the 1960s.

Biogeography Native of central and southern Europe and south-western and central Asia.

		GB	IR
Long term		No trend	No trend
Short term	↓ ↓ · ↑ **↑**		No trend

Alien		GB	IR
2000–19	●	126	0
1987–99	●	43	0
1970–86	●	35	0
pre-1970	○	33	0

Altitude (m) chart — Distance north (km)

<1%, 1–10%, 11–30%, 31–40%, 41–50%, 51–100%

Apparency · In flower · In leaf

T.D. DINES & K.J. WALKER

N? *Solanum nigrum* Black Nightshade

L.

An annual herb of cultivated and waste ground, especially where the soil is nutrient-rich. On Colonsay (South Ebudes) subsp. *schultesii* occurs along strandlines at the top of beaches. Usually lowland, but reaching 480 m at Eisteddfa Gurig (Cardiganshire).

Native or alien in Britain and the Channel Islands and a neophyte in Ireland.

Trends *S. nigrum* may be native in south-eastern England and parts of Wales, but it is certainly introduced and usually casual in northern England, Scotland and Ireland. It was recorded in the wild by 1597. Its range has extended westwards and northwards since the 1960s but it is not clear to what extent these comprise alien occurrences; some records may refer to subsp. *schultesii*, an alien from southern Europe.

Biogeography Eurasian Southern-temperate element; widely naturalized outside its native range.

		GB	IR
Long term	↓ ↓ · **↑** ↑		↓ ↓ · · **↑**
Short term	↓ ↓ · **↑** **↑**		↓ ↓ · · **↑**

Native		GB	IR
2000–19	●	1352	0
1987–99	●	1171	0
1970–86	●	721	0
pre-1970	○	954	0

Alien		GB	IR
2000–19	●	80	177
1987–99	●	31	41
1970–86	●	27	8
pre-1970	○	61	23

Altitude (m) chart — Distance north (km)

<1%, 1–10%, 11–30%, 31–40%, 41–50%, 51–100%

Apparency · In flower · In leaf

Key refs Bassett & Munro (1985).

T.D. DINES & K.J. WALKER

Ne *Solanum nigrum* subsp. *schultesii*
(Opiz) Wessely

An annual which occurs on cultivated land, around docks, on beaches, and refuse tips and other waste ground. Populations may be casual, but are often naturalized. Lowland.

Trends *S. nigrum* subsp. *schultesii* was not recognized in Britain until 1980, but the first herbarium record dates back to 1946 (Rainham, South Essex). It is still almost certainly under-recorded and thus trends in its distribution are difficult to assess.

Biogeography Subsp. *schultesii* has a more southerly distribution than subsp. *nigrum* in Europe and is widespread in warm-temperate regions elsewhere.

	GB	IR
Long term	No trend	No trend
Short term	No trend	No trend

Alien		GB	IR
2000–19	●	59	1
1987–99	●	23	0
1970–86	●	15	0
pre-1970	○	2	0

Altitude (m)

- ● <1%
- ● 1–10%
- ● 11–30%
- ● 31–40%
- ● 41–50%
- ● 51–100%

Distance north (km)

☐ Apparency ■ In flower ■ In leaf

T.D. DINES

Ne *Solanum nitidibaccatum* Green Nightshade
Bitter

An annual herb, found as an arable weed, as well as in abandoned fields, on waste land and refuse tips. The majority of populations are casual, but the species can occasionally become established. Lowland.

Trends *S. nitidibaccatum* was first recorded in the wild in 1893 (Milverton, Warwickshire). It has increased in recent decades, especially as a seed contaminant, and is sometimes found in abundance, particularly in crops of sugar-beet. It is still increasing but may be under-recorded in some areas.

Biogeography Native of South America, and western North America, now frequently naturalized in Europe and elsewhere.

	GB	IR
Long term	No trend	No trend
Short term	⬇ ⬇ ◆ ⬆ ⬆	No trend

Alien		GB	IR
2000–19	●	246	1
1987–99	●	172	2
1970–86	●	99	0
pre-1970	○	20	0

Altitude (m)

- ● <1%
- ● 1–10%
- ● 11–30%
- ● 31–40%
- ● 41–50%
- ● 51–100%

Distance north (km)

☐ Apparency ■ In flower ■ In leaf

T.D. DINES & D.A. PEARMAN

Ne *Solanum sarrachoides* Leafy-fruited Nightshade
Sendtn.

An erect or decumbent annual herb, found as a casual on cultivated ground, refuse tips and waste ground. Rarely, it becomes naturalized. Lowland.

Trends *S. sarrachoides* was recorded in the wild in 1922 (Avonmouth, West Gloucestershire). In common with several other casual American aliens, it is often associated with carrot seed, and was imported by this means during the Second World War. It appears to be increasing in Britain, but some records may result from confusion with the more widespread *S. nitidibacccatum*.

Biogeography Native of South America.

Alien	GB	IR
2000–19	19	0
1987–99	35	0
1970–86	57	0
pre-1970	38	0

Key refs Heslop Harrison (1953).

T.D. DINES

N *Solanum dulcamara* Bittersweet
L.

A scrambling, woody perennial of woodland, thickets, hedgerows, ditches and, as var. *marinum*, on shingle beaches. It often grows in moist habitats and is common in swamps and tall-herb fens and beside rivers and lakes, where it can even grow in shallow water. Generally lowland, but up to 444 m at Bad an Teachdaire (South Aberdeenshire).

Trends *S. dulcamara* is now better recorded in Scotland and Ireland but there has been no appreciable change in its overall 10 km square distribution since the 1960s.

Biogeography Eurasian Southern-temperate element, but naturalized in North America so distribution is now Circumpolar Southern-temperate.

Native	GB	IR
2000–19	1928	622
1987–99	1843	493
1970–86	1419	81
pre-1970	1706	204

Alien	GB	IR
2000–19	28	1
1987–99	9	1
1970–86	3	0
pre-1970	9	0

Key refs Grime *et al.* (2007).

T.D. DINES & K.J. WALKER

803

Ne *Solanum tuberosum* Potato
L.

A rhizomatous perennial herb, widely cultivated for its edible tubers, found on dumped soil, refuse tips, waste land, and on coastal sand and shingle where domestic waste has been dumped. In disturbed habitats it is usually casual, but the production of tubers allows some populations in more stable sites to become established. Lowland.

Trends Potatoes have been cultivated in the Andes for at least 7,000 years. *S. tuberosum* was introduced to England in about 1590, becoming a staple food of the poor, especially in Scotland and Ireland, by 1800. It was known from the wild by 1835 (Galloway), and its distribution is likely to be stable, but like many crop casuals, the species is ignored and under-recorded by many botanists.

Biogeography Native of South America.

	GB	IR
Long term	No trend	No trend

Short term

Alien		GB	IR
2000–19	●	1030	155
1987–99	●	598	63
1970–86	●	210	2
pre-1970	○	109	3

● <1%
● 1–10%
● 11–30%
● 31–40%
● 41–50%
● 51–100%

Key refs Hawkes (1990), Jackson (1986), Phillips & Rix (1993).

T.D. DINES

☐ Apparency ☐ In flower ☐ In leaf

Ne *Solanum lycopersicum* Tomato
L.

A herb that is widely cultivated in gardens and allotments and found as a frequent casual on waste ground, refuse tips, railway lines, pavements and sewage works. The species behaves as a perennial in its native range, but both the plant and, to a lesser extent, its seeds are frost-sensitive. Most populations in our area are therefore killed each year, with new plants arising from seeds discarded as fresh fruit or from human sewage. Generally lowland, but reaching 480 m in Nant Nod lead mine (Cardiganshire).

Trends *S. lycopersicum* was being cultivated by Gerard in 1596, and is now very widely grown. It was first recorded from the wild in 1798, on ballast hills at Sunderland, County Durham. Casual plants have not been recorded systematically until relatively recently and are still ignored by many recorders.

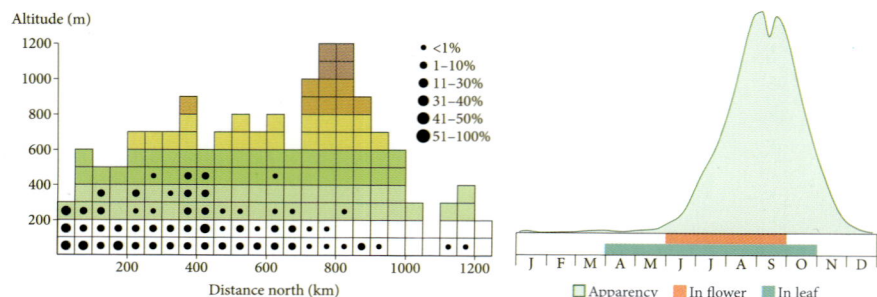

Biogeography Native of Central and South America; a frequent casual in Europe but not truly naturalized here.

	GB	IR
Long term	No trend	No trend

Short term

Alien		GB	IR
2000–19	●	861	95
1987–99	●	467	39
1970–86	●	200	4
pre-1970	○	127	1

● <1%
● 1–10%
● 11–30%
● 31–40%
● 41–50%
● 51–100%

Key refs Smart & Simmonds (1995), Vaughan & Geissler (2009).

T.D. DINES & D.A. PEARMAN

☐ Apparency ☐ In flower ☐ In leaf

Ne *Solanum laciniatum* Kangaroo-apple
Aiton

An evergreen frost-tender shrub that is normally grown as a conservatory plant or as an annual in our area. It occurs on rough and waste ground, and on coastal sand. Most populations are casual, but it is naturalized in the Channel Islands and on the Isles of Scilly, where it often perennates. Lowland.

Trends *S. laciniatum* was introduced into cultivation in Britain in 1772, and is increasingly popular for its large leaves and deep purplish-blue flowers. It has been naturalized in our area since 1920 (Isles of Scilly, West Cornwall).

Biogeography Native of south-eastern Australia, Tasmania and New Zealand.

Alien	GB	IR
2000–19	42	7
1987–99	20	2
1970–86	8	0
pre-1970	9	0

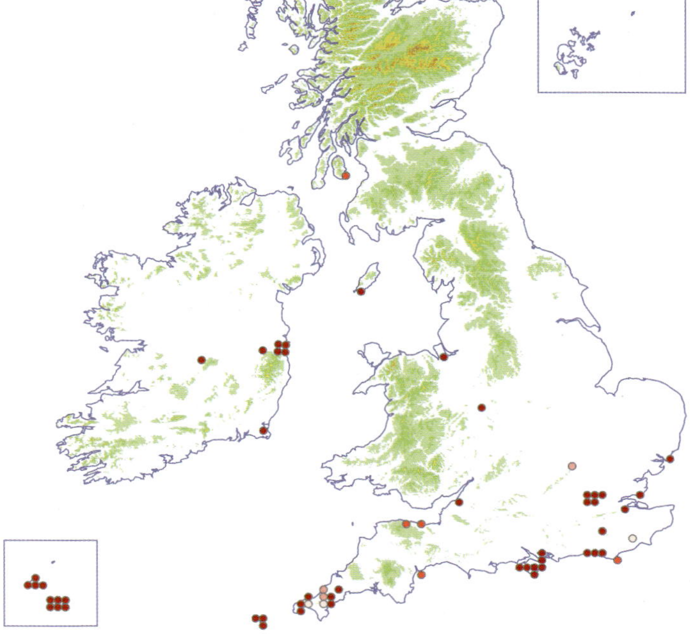

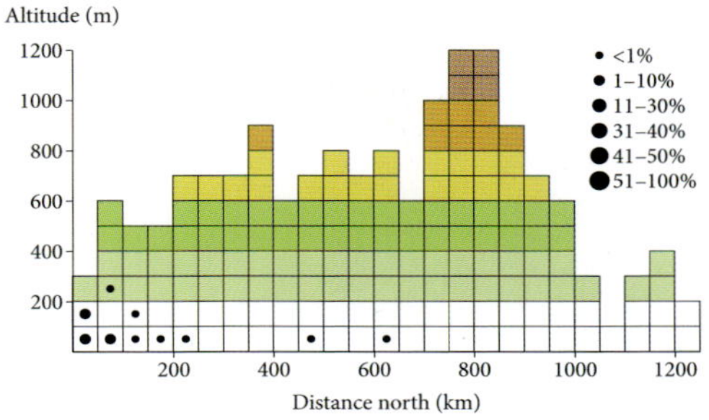

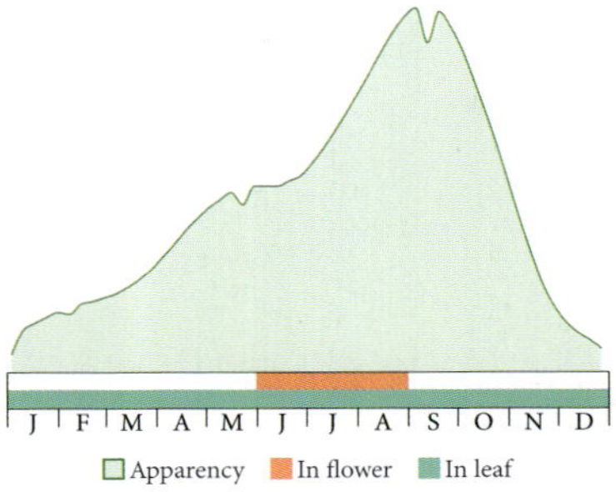

	GB	IR
Long term	No trend	No trend
Short term		

Altitude (m)
- <1%
- 1–10%
- 11–30%
- 31–40%
- 41–50%
- 51–100%

Apparency In flower In leaf

T.D. DINES & D.A. PEARMAN

Ne *Solanum rostratum* Buffalo-bur
Dunal

An erect annual herb, found as a casual of arable fields, refuse tips, waste places and roadsides where it is introduced with grain, birdseed, and formerly with wool shoddy. Lowland.

Trends *S. rostratum* was first recorded in the wild in 1882 (Kingswood, Bristol, West Gloucestershire), and appears to be in decline, perhaps reflecting cessation in the use of wool shoddy as a fertilizer.

Biogeography Native of south-eastern North America and Mexico.

Alien	GB	IR
2000–19	50	0
1987–99	53	0
1970–86	40	1
pre-1970	28	0

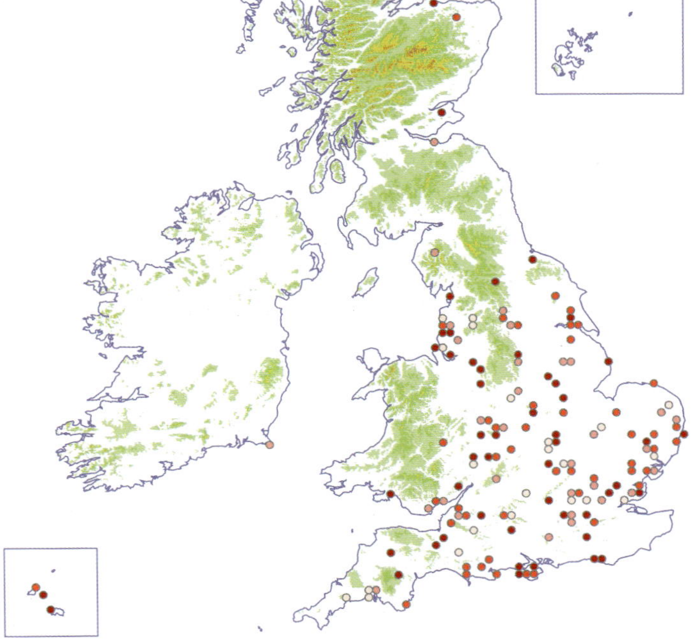

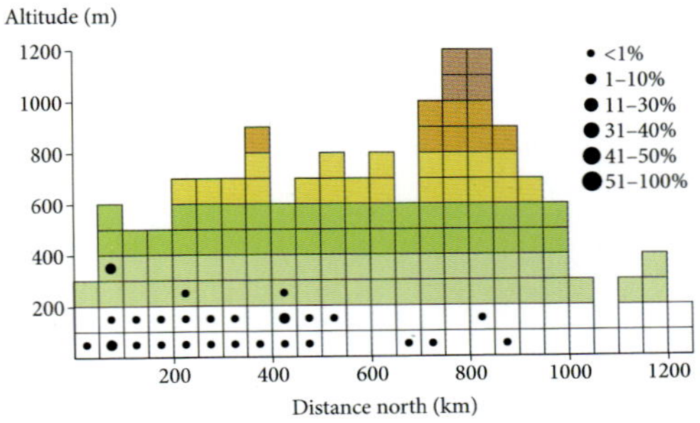

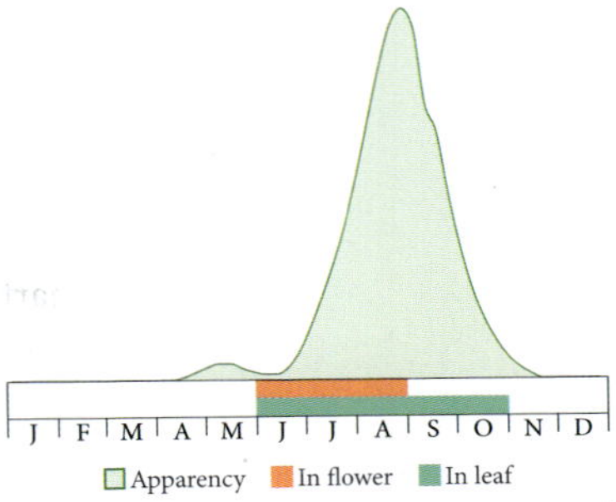

	GB	IR
Long term	No trend	No trend
Short term		No trend

Altitude (m)
- <1%
- 1–10%
- 11–30%
- 31–40%
- 41–50%
- 51–100%

Apparency In flower In leaf

T.D. DINES & D.A. PEARMAN

Ne ***Nicotiana alata*** Sweet Tobacco
Link & Otto

A potentially large, erect annual, occurring as a casual on refuse tips and waste and cultivated ground, sometimes persisting for a few years. Reproduction is by seed. Lowland.

Trends *N. alata* was first cultivated in Britain in 1829, and was recorded in the wild in 1912 (Hayes, West Kent). It is frequently cultivated for its scented flowers, and is surprisingly uncommon in the wild given its popularity with gardeners. This is the species from which most of the ornamental cultivars are derived, and hybrids with *N. forgetiana* (*N. ×sanderae*) are common in gardens and may have been overlooked for this species.

Biogeography Native of southern South America.

GB		IR
Long term	No trend	No trend
Short term	↓	No trend

Alien	GB	IR
2000–19	71	1
1987–99	51	1
1970–86	21	0
pre-1970	20	0

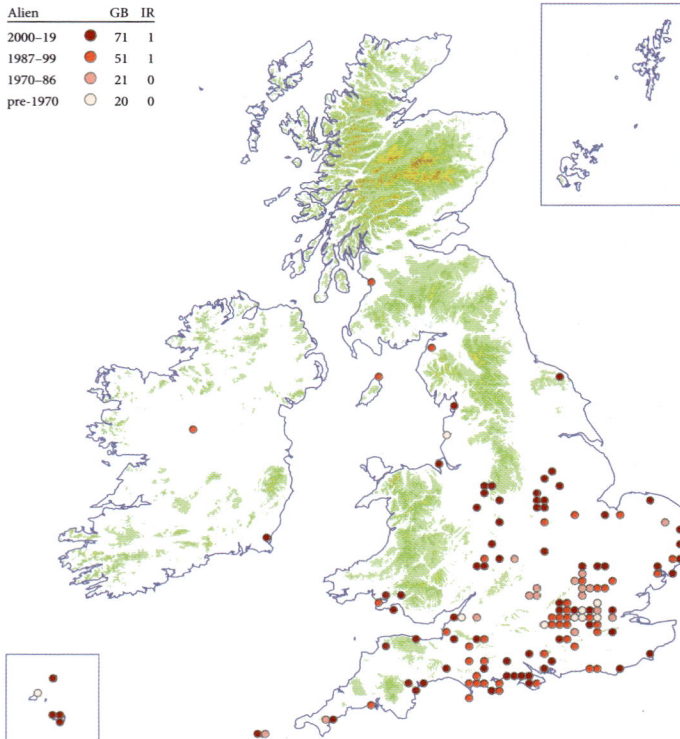

T.D. DINES & D.A. PEARMAN

Hy ***Nicotiana alata × forgetiana = N. ×sanderae***
W. Watson

A partially hardy annual hybrid occurring as a garden escape on refuse tips, roadsides, landfill sites, old allotments and gardens, and waste ground. Lowland.

A cultivated hybrid (alien × alien).

Trends *N. ×sanderae* was raised in England by Messrs Sander & Sons of St Albans in 1903, and named by Watson (1904) from their material. It is often grown in gardens as a bedding plant, and was first recorded in the wild in 1965 (North Oxford tip, Oxfordshire). Though there has been an increase in records since 2000, it is probably still under-recorded, and overlooked for its parents, particularly *N. alata*.

Biogeography A hybrid of garden origin.

GB		IR
Long term	No trend	No trend
Short term	No trend	No trend

	GB	IR
2000–19	101	1
1987–99	45	1
1970–86	6	0
pre-1970	2	0

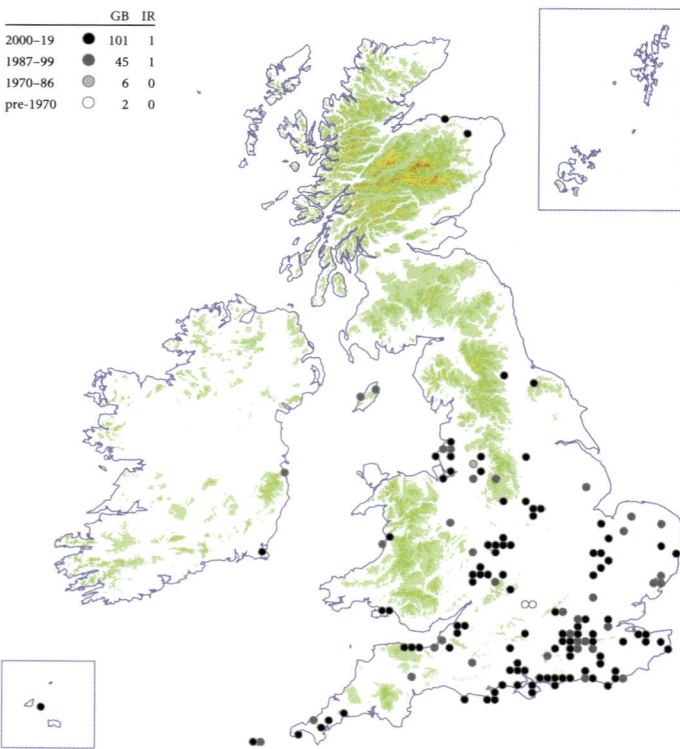

Key refs Stace *et al.* (2015), Watson (1904).

C.A. STACE, C.D. PRESTON & D.A. PEARMAN

Hy *Petunia axillaris × integrifolia = P. ×hybrida* Petunia
(Hook.) Vilm.

A procumbent to erect annual hybrid, found as single plants, in small numbers, or occasionally in larger quantities on urban streetsides (where they often seed themselves from hanging baskets or window-boxes) and on dumped soil, disturbed roadsides, waste ground and refuse tips. It is usually casual, but sometimes persists for a few years. It is fertile, and sets abundant, but frost-sensitive, seed. Lowland.

A cultivated hybrid (alien × alien).

Trends *P. ×hybrida* was raised by 1837 and is extremely popular in cultivation. There were relatively few records pre-2000, and the considerable increase this century is most likely due to the fuller recording of aliens, coupled with a greater interest in recording urban flora. It was first recorded as a casual from Hanwell (Middlesex) in 1948.

Biogeography A hybrid of garden origin.

	GB	IR
2000–19	257	12
1987–99	63	1
1970–86	17	0
pre-1970	14	0

	GB	IR
Long term	No trend	No trend
Short term	↑	↑

Key refs Stace *et al.* (2015).

C.A. STACE, C.D. PRESTON & D.A. PEARMAN

Hy *Forsythia suspensa × viridissima = F. ×intermedia* Forsythia
Zabel

A deciduous shrub found frequently as a relic of cultivation in hedges and by roads, rivers and canals; it may also survive from discarded material on commons, refuse tips and waste ground. The hybrid sometimes spreads by suckering. All plants in the wild seem to be derived from vegetative fragments and it does not appear to set viable seed. Lowland.

A cultivated hybrid (alien × alien).

Trends *F. ×intermedia* was found as a chance seedling in Germany in 1878, close to its supposed parents, and was first grown in Britain ten years later. It has been known from the wild since at least 1970, when it was found on waste ground at Heamoor (West Cornwall), although a record of *F. europaea* from Bury St Edmunds (West Suffolk) from 1952 was probably this hybrid. It is a very common and

vigorous garden plant, which appears to be increasing in the wild with continued dumping of garden waste, though the spread of this species in recent decades must also be a reflection of the fuller recording of aliens, and particularly of planted shrubs.

Biogeography A hybrid of garden origin.

	GB	IR
2000–19	195	0
1987–99	174	3
1970–86	41	0
pre-1970	12	0

	GB	IR
Long term	No trend	No trend
Short term	↓	No trend

Key refs Bean (1973), Coats (1963), Stace *et al.* (2015).

C.A. STACE, C.D. PRESTON & D.A. PEARMAN

807

Ne *Jasminum officinale* Summer Jasmine
L.

A scrambling, twining, deciduous shrub which is naturalized on walls, pavements, roadsides, banks and waste ground, seldom far from human habitations. It also occurs as a throw-out on roadsides and refuse tips, and as a relic of cultivation. Reproduction by seed has been reported, although vegetative spread is the more common mechanism; the trailing stems root freely. Lowland.

Trends *J. officinale* was being grown in British gardens by 1548, and probably long before. It was first recorded from the wild in 1967 (East Suffolk). Although it can be found throughout our area, it appears to be most frequent in the London area, though some of these records may be of planted individuals in gardens.

Biogeography Native of China and the Himalayas.

GB	IR
Long term	No trend	No trend
Short term		

Alien	GB	IR
2000–19	84	8
1987–99	14	1
1970–86	9	0
pre-1970	5	0

Altitude (m) legend:
- <1%
- 1–10%
- 11–30%
- 31–40%
- 41–50%
- 51–100%

Distance north (km)

J F M A M J J A S O N D

☐ Apparency ☐ In flower ☐ In leaf

Key refs Bean (1973).

J. PARMENTER & T.D. DINES

Ne *Jasminum nudiflorum* Winter Jasmine
Lindl.

A deciduous, scrambling or trailing winter-flowering shrub, found as a garden escape in woods, scrub and hedgerows, and on walls, roadsides and waste ground, but seldom far from human habitations. It also occurs as a throw-out on roadsides and refuse tips, and as a relic of cultivation. Although deciduous, the stems are winter-green and bear flowers in winter and early spring. Reproduction by seed can occur, although vegetative spread is the more common mechanism; the trailing stems root freely. Lowland.

Trends *J. nudiflorum* was introduced into cultivation in Britain in 1844 and is extremely common in gardens, where it is grown for its yellow winter flowers. It was first recorded from the wild in 1940 (Cambridgeshire) and appears to be increasing its range. Although it can be found throughout Britain and Ireland, it appears to be most common in and around London, though some of these records may be from gardens.

Biogeography Native of China.

GB	IR
Long term	No trend	No trend
Short term		

Alien	GB	IR
2000–19	137	8
1987–99	15	0
1970–86	7	0
pre-1970	7	0

Altitude (m) legend:
- <1%
- 1–10%
- 11–30%
- 31–40%
- 41–50%
- 51–100%

Distance north (km)

J F M A M J J A S O N D

☐ Apparency ☐ In flower ☐ In leaf

Key refs Bean (1973).

J. PARMENTER & T.D. DINES

Fraxinus excelsior Ash
L.

A deciduous tree of woodland, scrub and hedgerows, especially on moist, basic soils, but also frequent on rock scars and cliffs, stabilized scree, and the grikes of limestone pavement. It can tolerate periodically waterlogged soils, being found around springs and in alder- and willow-carr, but it is susceptible to drought. In managed woodland it may be grown as a timber tree or coppice. It is a rapid colonizer of abandoned arable land, waste ground, disused quarries, and railway banks. Seed production can be prolific, with periodic mast years, although seedling mortality is usually very high. Mitchell *et al.* (2014) provide a review of the biodiversity of other taxonomic groups associated with this species, whilst Thomas (2016) has comprehensively updated its Biological Flora. 0–840 m (Cairn Mairg, Glen Lyon, Mid Perthshire).

Trends *F. excelsior* is near-ubiquitous at the 10 km square scale and its range appears to be stable. In northern Scotland it is native on limestone and widely planted elsewhere; differentiating native from alien populations can therefore be difficult. Whilst ash dieback fungus *Hymenoscyphus fraxineus* is no doubt affecting ash mortality at small scales, whether it will affect the large-scale distribution remains to be seen. For example, in continental Europe, some reports of mortality at the site level are under 50% (*e.g.* Lõhmus & Runnel, 2014), meaning that extirpation from entire hectads would seem unlikely in the short term.

Biogeography European Temperate element.

Native	GB	IR
2000–19	2447	938
1987–99	2386	909
1970–86	1761	180
pre-1970	2367	856

Alien	GB	IR
2000–19	105	4
1987–99	67	3
1970–86	34	1
pre-1970	65	5

• <1%
• 1–10%
• 11–30%
• 31–40%
• 41–50%
• 51–100%

Key refs Grime *et al.* (2007), Lõhmus & Runnel (2014), Mitchell *et al.* (2014), Rackham (1980), Rackham (2014), Thomas (2016), Wardle (1961).

O.L. PESCOTT & T.D. DINES

Fraxinus angustifolia Narrow-leaved Ash
Vahl

A tall deciduous tree, up to 25 m tall, grown predominately in gardens, parks and as a street tree. Lowland.

Trends *F. angustifolia* was apparently introduced in 1815, and there is little evidence of regeneration from seed, though seedlings have been reported from Cambridgeshire (Leslie, 2019). It is certainly confused with *F. excelsior* by some recorders. There are two subspecies present in our area, subsp. *angustifolia* and subsp. *oxycarpa*, and probably the latter is the more widely grown.

Biogeography Native to the Mediterranean region, east-central Europe and south-western Asia.

Alien	GB	IR
2000–19	169	2
1987–99	5	0
1970–86	1	0
pre-1970	0	0

• <1%
• 1–10%
• 11–30%
• 31–40%
• 41–50%
• 51–100%

Key refs Bean (1973), Leslie (2019).

D.A. PEARMAN

Ne *Fraxinus ornus* Manna Ash
L.

A very leafy deciduous tree, up to 20 m tall. Widely planted as a garden and street tree, in other amenity plantings and occasionally in more open countryside. Lowland.

Trends *F. ornus* was grown here by 1710. Self-sown plants are frequently encountered in Cambridgeshire, and have also been recorded in London near to planted trees, and it is probable that seedlings are often present where *F. ornus* is planted.

Biogeography Native of the Mediterranean region, south-central Europe, and south-western Asia.

Long term	GB	IR
	No trend	No trend
Short term		No trend

Alien	GB	IR
2000–19	138	1
1987–99	43	0
1970–86	12	0
pre-1970	11	0

Key refs Bean (1973).

D.A. Pearman

Ne *Syringa vulgaris* Lilac
L.

A deciduous shrub, widely planted in gardens, parkland, churchyards, plantations and hedges and along roadsides and railways. It is also found as a relic of cultivation in sites of former human habitation and occasionally establishes where garden waste has been dumped. Reproduction is mostly via suckering and establishment from seed is rare, usually on walls, wall-tops and pollarded willows in urban areas (Leslie, 2019). Generally lowland, but reaching 410 m on a trackside south of Bulhope Law (East Lothian).

Trends *S. vulgaris* was in cultivation in Britain by 1596, becoming extremely popular in parks and gardens in the 19th century, with a multitude of cultivars. It was known from the wild by at least 1879 (Oxfordshire). The astonishing increase in records since the 1960s is probably due to both a better recording of aliens and a genuine increase in planting and garden escapes.

Biogeography Native of south-eastern Europe, but modified by selection and cultivation.

	GB		IR	
Long term				
Short term				

Alien	GB	IR
2000–19	1561	238
1987–99	1224	127
1970–86	647	5
pre-1970	310	49

Key refs Bean (1980), Fiala (1988), Leslie (2019).

T.D. Dines & D.A. Pearman

N *Ligustrum vulgare* Wild Privet
L.

A deciduous to semi-evergreen shrub found as a native in hedgerows, woodland and scrub, preferring well-drained, calcareous or base-rich soils. It is also very widely planted, particularly in hedges and woodland, and occurs as a garden escape and a relic of cultivation. 0–490 m (Craig y Cilau, Breconshire).

Trends There has been no appreciable change in the native range of *L. vulgare* since the 1960s, although it can be difficult to know whether some populations are alien or native. Most records in mountainous areas, in Scotland and also in intensive arable areas such as Fenland, are probably alien in origin. In Ireland it is mapped as alien but may be native at some coastal sites. Some records may be errors for the common garden plant *L. ovalifolium*.

Biogeography European Temperate element; widely naturalized outside its native range.

Native	GB	IR
2000–19	1473	0
1987–99	1438	0
1970–86	1033	0
pre-1970	1359	0

Alien	GB	IR
2000–19	339	723
1987–99	297	656
1970–86	134	58
pre-1970	389	624

T.D. Dines & J.O. Mountford

Ne *Ligustrum ovalifolium* Garden Privet
Hassk.

A semi-evergreen or evergreen shrub, abundantly planted for hedging and commonly found as a persistent relic in old gardens, or a garden throw-out in hedges, refuse tips, waste land and on railway banks. Plants very occasionally arise from bird-sown seed although it seldom flowers freely in gardens due to the constant trimming of boundary hedges. Lowland.

Trends *L. ovalifolium* has been cultivated in Britain since 1842, and was first recorded from the wild in 1939 (Hampstead, Surrey). Trends in its distribution are difficult to assess due to past recorders frequently ignoring planted hedges. However, in recent years more attention has been paid to such occurrences and a combination of more comprehensive recording and a real increase in sites is reflected in the latest map, where it is only absent from upland areas and parts of Ireland.

Biogeography Native of Japan.

Alien	GB	IR
2000–19	1720	460
1987–99	1273	225
1970–86	474	7
pre-1970	155	10

Key refs Bean (1973).

T.D. Dines & J.O. Mountford

N *Digitalis purpurea* Foxglove
L.

A biennial or short-lived perennial herb, frequent on acidic soils in hedgebanks, open woods and woodland clearings, on heathland and moorland margins, riverbanks, montane rocky slopes, sea-cliffs, walls and waste land. A major factor in its success is its prolific seed production and persistent seed bank; as a consequence, it is often found in great abundance in disturbed or burnt areas, such as recently felled forestry plantations. 0–880 m (Mt Brandon, South Kerry).

Trends The distribution of *D. purpurea* is near-ubiquitous at the 10 km square resolution and appears to be stable, although the number of recorded squares has increased in Ireland due to more systematic recording. It is a common garden plant and can occur as an escape outside its native range and also on calcareous soils, and these probably account for the majority of the recent increases in England. It is questionable whether its native and introduced ranges can now be differentiated with any certainty, although an attempt to demarcate them is presented on the map.

Biogeography Suboceanic Southern-temperate element; widely naturalized outside its native range.

Native	GB	IR
2000–19	2565	816
1987–99	2493	747
1970–86	1653	116
pre-1970	2295	639

Alien	GB	IR
2000–19	78	7
1987–99	35	4
1970–86	20	0
pre-1970	20	1

Key refs Grime *et al.* (2007).

A. HORSFALL

Altitude (m)

• <1%
• 1–10%
• 11–30%
• 31–40%
• 41–50%
• 51–100%

Distance north (km)

Apparency In flower In leaf

Ne *Digitalis lutea* Straw Foxglove
L.

A winter-green biennial to perennial herb, sometimes grown in gardens, and naturalized on roadside verges and banks, quarries, walls and waste ground. Reproduction is by seed and it is often self-sown. Lowland.

Trends *D. lutea* was grown in Britain by 1629. It was recorded from the wild in 1919 (Looe, East Cornwall) and seems to be increasing.

Biogeography Native of western and western-central Europe, from Belgium and Spain east to Austria and southern Italy.

	GB	IR
Long term	No trend	No trend
Short term		No trend

Alien	GB	IR
2000–19	38	0
1987–99	14	0
1970–86	9	0
pre-1970	6	0

Altitude (m)

• <1%
• 1–10%
• 11–30%
• 31–40%
• 41–50%
• 51–100%

Distance north (km)

Apparency In flower In leaf

T.D. DINES & D.A. PEARMAN

Erinus alpinus Fairy Foxglove

L.

This short-lived, evergreen perennial herb occurs in the crevices of old walls and on rock outcrops, often on limestone (including railway cuttings) or bricks with lime mortar but also on more acidic substrates. It seeds freely and thrives in full sun, often forming large colonies, often in places remote from human habitations. Generally lowland, but reaching 410 m at Inchrory (Banffshire).

Trends *E. alpinus* is a popular garden plant, cultivated by 1759. It was known from the wild by 1867 (Tanfield, North-west Yorkshire). There seems to have been a considerable spread since the 1960s, continuing in the 21st century, perhaps in part a result of the greater propensity of botanists to record plants on garden walls.

Biogeography Native of the mountains of south-western and south-central Europe.

Alien	GB	IR
2000–19	357	100
1987–99	249	50
1970–86	149	12
pre-1970	149	6

A. HORSFALL & J.O. MOUNTFORD

Veronica officinalis Heath Speedwell

L.

A perennial herb of open woods and woodland rides, on banks, infertile acid or calcareous grassland and on heathland. It grows in well-drained, often moderately acidic or leached soils on calcareous substrates, and in some grasslands is confined to raised ground or anthills. 0–880 m (Cadair Idris, Merionethshire).

Trends The overall 10 km square distribution of *V. officinalis* is little changed since the 1960s, though there were local declines in the 20th century where its habitats were lost, particularly in the English Midlands. The mapped distribution for Ireland reflects better recording this century. It was mapped as 'all records' in the 1962 *Atlas*.

Biogeography European Boreo-temperate element; widely naturalized outside its native range.

Native	GB	IR
2000–19	2313	742
1987–99	2253	623
1970–86	1392	99
pre-1970	2305	520

Alien	GB	IR
2000–19	0	1
1987–99	0	0
1970–86	0	1
pre-1970	0	0

P.A. STROH & A. HORSFALL

Veronica alpina Alpine Speedwell

L.

A small montane perennial herb of areas of late snow-lie in open, often rocky places on well-drained but slightly moist ground. It grows on both acidic and calcareous substrates, but most of its sites are subject to some base-enrichment from flushing. From 760 m above Loch Callater (South Aberdeenshire) to 1,190 m on Aonach Beag (Westerness).

Trends There seems to have been no appreciable change in the 10 km distribution of *V. alpina* since the 1960s. It was found at a new site in Easterness (Creag Meagaidh) in 2015, and at three 10 km squares this century where there had been no records since the 1970s. Although it is probably extant in most of the 10 km squares for which there are only pre-2000 records, changes in the duration of snow cover as a result of climate warming are likely to alter future competitive plant-plant interactions, to the detriment of poor competitors such as *V. alpina* (Rixon *et al.*, 2014).

Biogeography Eurosiberian Arctic-montane element; also in central Asia and North America.

Native	GB	IR
2000–19	19	0
1987–99	20	0
1970–86	28	0
pre-1970	29	0

Key refs Rixen *et al.* (2014), Stewart *et al.* (1994).

P.A. STROH & M.J. WIGGINTON

Veronica montana Wood Speedwell

L.

A perennial herb of damp basic to mildly acidic soils in long-established, mixed deciduous woodland, scrub and shaded hedgebanks. It is found on loamy and sandy soils and on heavy clay. Generally lowland, but reaching 451 m at Dinorwic Slate Quarry (Caernarvonshire).

Trends The 10 km square distribution of *V. montana* has increased since the 1960s, especially in Ireland, Scotland and eastern areas of England. In many regions it is a very localized species that is easily overlooked, and much confused with *V. chamaedrys*, and so recent increases are likely due to more intensive recording.

Biogeography European Temperate element.

Native	GB	IR
2000–19	1775	698
1987–99	1644	473
1970–86	1146	94
pre-1970	1389	125

Alien	GB	IR
2000–19	2	0
1987–99	1	0
1970–86	1	0
pre-1970	0	0

Key refs Grime *et al.* (2007).

P.A. STROH & A. HORSFALL

Veronica scutellata Marsh Speedwell
L.

A perennial herb of wetland habitats, including pond and lake margins, marshes, fens and fen-meadows, wet grassland, hillside flushes, bogs and wet heath, often on acidic soils. It occurs in both open habitats and amongst tall vegetation. 0–780 m on Cross Fell (Cumberland).

Trends A widespread decline of *V. scutellata* was reported in the 2002 *Atlas*, with losses most concentrated in central and southern England and central Ireland due to the drainage of its wetland habitats. Losses have continued, with undergrazing and neglect likely to be contributory factors alongside degraded hydrology, to the extent that it has become an uncommon species throughout much of lowland Britain. It was mapped as 'all records' for the 1962 *Atlas*.

Biogeography Eurosiberian Boreo-temperate element; also in North America and widely naturalized outside its native range.

Native	GB	IR
2000–19	1411	495
1987–99	1326	455
1970–86	919	102
pre-1970	1389	276

Alien	GB	IR
2000–19	1	0
1987–99	0	0
1970–86	0	0
pre-1970	0	0

P.A. Stroh & A. Horsfall

Veronica beccabunga Brooklime
L.

A robust perennial herb of all but the most infertile substrates in a wide range of wetland habitats including shallow water by rivers, streams and ponds, ditches, marshy hollows in pastures, flushes, wet woodland rides and rutted tracks. It thrives in fairly open habitats, competing poorly in dense stands of taller plants. Propagation is by seed and vegetatively from rooted stems. 0–845 m (Great Dun Fell, Westmorland).

Trends The 10 km square distribution of *V. beccabunga* has remained stable since the 1960s, but has been better recorded in northern Scotland this century.

Biogeography Eurosiberian Temperate element; widely naturalized outside its native range.

Native	GB	IR
2000–19	2274	886
1987–99	2213	838
1970–86	1627	125
pre-1970	2128	725

Key refs Grime *et al.* (2007), Preston & Croft (1997).

P.A. Stroh & A. Horsfall

N *Veronica anagallis-aquatica* Blue Water-speedwell
L.

An annual to perennial herb of fertile substrates by rivers, streams and ponds, in ditches and in flooded clay- and gravel-pits. It grows as a vegetative plant submerged in shallow water, as a flowering emergent, or as a terrestrial plant in marshy habitats and disturbed ground at the water's edge. Although the habitat preferences of the two water-speedwells overlap considerably, *V. anagallis-aquatica* is probably commonest by flowing water whereas *V. catenata* is generally most abundant in still water, such as drainage channels. Reproduction is by seed and by rooted stem fragments. 0–380 m (Malham Tarn, Mid-west Yorkshire).

Trends *V. anagallis-aquatica* was mapped as 'all records' in the 1962 *Atlas* but early trends may be confounded by confusion with *V. catenata* which was not distinguished until 1921. The decline since the 1960s might therefore partly reflect improved recognition of the two species, although some losses have certainly taken place as a result of the drainage and eutrophication of wetlands, or severe watercourse management. The species may be over-recorded for its hybrid with *V. catenata* in some areas.

Biogeography Eurasian Southern-temperate element; widely naturalized outside its native range.

Native	GB	IR
2000–19	914	450
1987–99	900	393
1970–86	685	65
pre-1970	939	198

Alien	GB	IR
2000–19	1	0
1987–99	3	0
1970–86	1	0
pre-1970	2	0

Key refs Burnett (1997), Pennell (1921), Preston & Croft (1997).

A. Horsfall & J.O. Mountford

Altitude (m) / Distance north (km)
- <1%
- 1–10%
- 11–30%
- 31–40%
- 41–50%
- 51–100%

Apparency | In flower | In leaf

Hy *Veronica anagallis-aquatica × catenata = V. ×lackschewitzii*
J.B.Keller

This annual or sometimes perennial hybrid is found in similar habitats to its parents, including the shallow edges of ponds, lakes, ditches, streams and rivers. It is also recorded from sand- and gravel-pits. It can often be found with both parents, but may occur in the absence of one or both, and in Hampshire replaces the parents over a large area (Brewis *et al.*, 1996). The F$_1$ hybrid is usually highly sterile, but F$_2$ and later generations can be more fertile.

A spontaneous hybrid (native × native).

Trends Records of this hybrid have gradually accumulated since it was first described in 1929 but it is almost certainly under-recorded, especially in Ireland.

Biogeography Widespread in temperate Europe, and also recorded from North America where *V. anagallis-aquatica* is an introduction.

	GB	IR
2000–19	114	9
1987–99	71	22
1970–86	62	0
pre-1970	81	6

	GB	IR
Long term	No trend	No trend
Short term	No trend	No trend

Key refs Brewis *et al.* (1996), Stace *et al.* (2015).

Altitude (m) / Distance north (km)
- <1%
- 1–10%
- 11–30%
- 31–40%
- 41–50%
- 51–100%

Apparency | In flower | In leaf

A. Horsfall

N *Veronica catenata* Pink Water-speedwell
Pennell

A usually annual herb of shallow water and the muddy edges of rivers, streams, ponds and lakes, in dune-slacks, and in clay-, gravel- and chalk-pits. Although often found with *V. anagallis-aquatica*, its habitats are more restricted, being more frequent on the muddy edges of standing waters, especially drainage channels on coastal and floodplain levels. 0–344 m (Cusop, Herefordshire).

Trends The 10 km square distribution of *V. catenata* has changed little since the 1960s, but it is now much better recorded, and particularly in Ireland since the turn of the century due to more systematic recording.

Biogeography Circumpolar Temperate element, with a disjunct distribution.

Native	GB	IR
2000–19	815	212
1987–99	761	196
1970–86	583	49
pre-1970	657	67

Alien	GB	IR
2000–19	1	0
1987–99	0	0
1970–86	0	0
pre-1970	0	0

Altitude (m)

Apparency   In flower   In leaf

Key refs Burnett (1997), Pennell (1921), Preston & Croft (1997).

A. HORSFALL & J.O. MOUNTFORD

Ne *Veronica peregrina* American Speedwell
L.

An annual herb, found as a weed in parks, gardens, pavements, nurseries, allotments and other cultivated ground, and by streams and in damp waste places. It rarely seems to persist for long. Lowland.

Trends *V. peregrina* was introduced by 1680, apparently from mainland Europe. It was first recorded in the wild in 1836 (Strabane, Tyrone). It has spread in our area since then, markedly so since 1970 in Northern Ireland and South Lancashire. It is very inconspicuous and may have been overlooked elsewhere.

Biogeography Native of North and South America.

Alien	GB	IR
2000–19	161	86
1987–99	72	29
1970–86	58	6
pre-1970	80	19

Long term   No trend   No trend

Short term

Altitude (m)

Apparency   In flower   In leaf

Key refs Bangerter (1964), Bangerter (1966).

A. HORSFALL & P.A. STROH

Veronica serpyllifolia Thyme-leaved Speedwell
L.

A low perennial herb with creeping and rooting stems, widespread in both natural and artificial habitats, including woodland rides, grassland, heathland, flushes, damp rock ledges, cultivated land, gardens, damp tracks and paths, and waste ground. It seems indifferent to soil pH and fertility, and often occurs in areas disturbed by humans. 0–1,160 m (Braeriach, South Aberdeenshire).

Trends The 10 km square distribution of *V. serpyllifolia* appears to be stable. Subsp. *serpyllifolia* occurs throughout the range of the species up to altitudes of 825 m (Cross Fell, Cumberland); subsp. *humifusa* is mapped separately.

Biogeography Circumpolar Boreo-temperate element; widely naturalized outside its native range.

Native	GB	IR
2000–19	2671	939
1987–99	2543	810
1970–86	1507	108
pre-1970	2352	615

Alien	GB	IR
2000–19	0	1
1987–99	0	1
1970–86	0	0
pre-1970	0	0

P.A. STROH & A. HORSFALL

Veronica serpyllifolia subsp. *humifusa*
(Dickson) Syme

A creeping, perennial herb of damp rock ledges, flushes and wet gravels in upland regions, ascending from 120 m (north of Daviot, Easterness) to 1,160 m on Braeriach (South Aberdeenshire).

Trends *V. serpyllifolia* subsp. *humifusa* has been erratically recorded since it was first mapped by Perring & Sell (1968) and this may account for the losses shown on the map. Since 2000 it has been found at a number of new localities within its known range in Scotland and Wales, though there are also many areas where the taxon probably still persists but has not been recorded this century. Historical records for north-western England may be errors for subsp. *serpyllifolia*.

Biogeography Circumpolar Arctic-montane element, with a disjunct distribution.

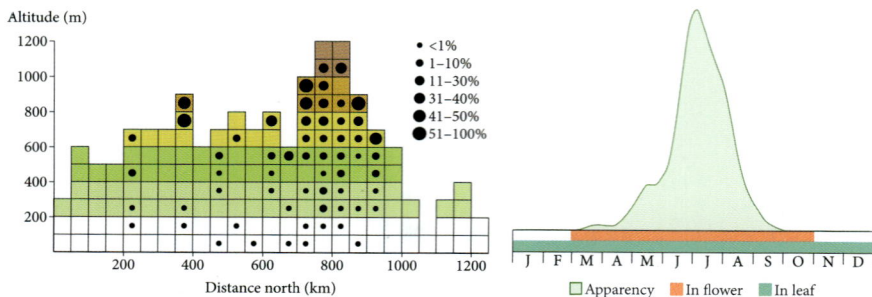

	GB	IR
Long term	No trend	No trend
Short term	No trend	No trend

Native	GB	IR
2000–19	65	0
1987–99	69	0
1970–86	40	0
pre-1970	104	0

P.A. STROH & A. HORSFALL

Ne # *Veronica longifolia* Garden Speedwell
L.

A woody-based perennial herb, widely grown in gardens and found as a naturalized escape or casual in rough grassland and hedgerows and on roadsides, waste ground, old chalk-pits, railway sidings and refuse tips. Lowland.

Trends *V. longifolia* was cultivated in Britain by 1731, and is popular in gardens. It was first recorded in the wild in 1910 (Leith, Midlothian). It appears to be increasing, but could often have been misrecorded for garden forms of *V. spicata* and, especially, the fertile hybrid *V. longifolia × V. spicata*.

Biogeography A Eurasian Boreo-temperate species, which is absent as a native from western Europe.

	GB	IR
Long term	No trend	No trend
Short term	↓ ↓ · ↑ ↑	No trend

Alien		GB	IR
2000–19	●	93	0
1987–99	●	72	0
1970–86	●	46	0
pre-1970	○	43	0

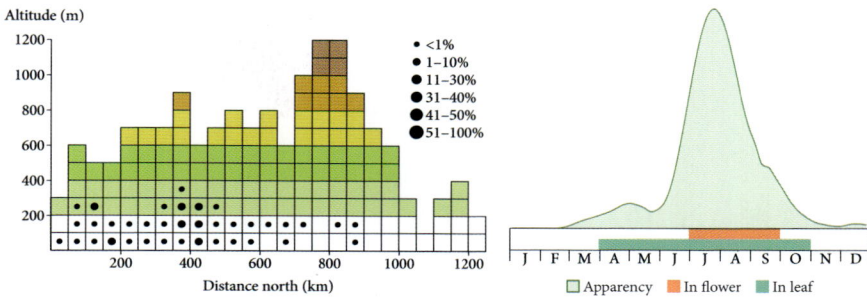

T.D. Dines & P.A. Stroh

Altitude (m) / Distance north (km) histogram; phenology chart (Apparency, In flower, In leaf)

Hy # *Veronica longifolia × spicata*

A perennial herb with a woody base, found as a naturalized garden escape on sand dunes, in grassland and by grassy tracks. It is intermediate between the parents and fertile. Lowland.

A cultivated hybrid (native × alien).

Trends Various forms of this hybrid are widely cultivated in gardens. It has only recently been recorded from the wild, in 1991 (Sheffield, South-west Yorkshire), but it may have been misidentified previously as *V. longifolia*.

Biogeography A hybrid of garden origin.

	GB	IR
Long term	No trend	No trend
Short term	No trend	No trend

		GB	IR
2000–19	●	13	0
1987–99	●	2	0
1970–86	●	0	0
pre-1970	○	0	0

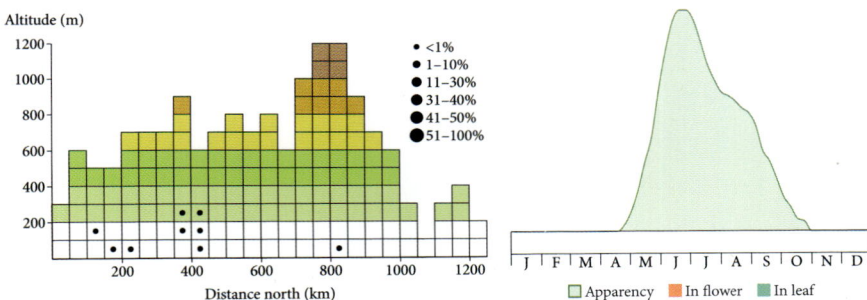

Key refs Stace *et al.* (2015).

C.A. Stace, C.D. Preston & D.A. Pearman

Altitude (m) / Distance north (km) histogram; phenology chart (Apparency, In flower, In leaf)

N *Veronica spicata* Spiked Speedwell
L.

A perennial herb of well-drained, infertile soils. In eastern England, subsp. *spicata* grows in open, short grassland on at least mildly base-rich soils derived from glacial drift and interglacial sands. In north-western and south-western England and in Wales, it is a plant of thin soils in short calcareous grassland on rock ledges and rocky slopes, mainly of limestone, and more rarely in maritime heath. Generally lowland, but reaching 400 m in Ribblesdale (Mid-west Yorkshire).

Trends British populations of *V. spicata* have been separated into two subspecies; subsp. *spicata* in eastern England and subsp. *hybrida* in western England and Wales. However, morphological distinguishing features are neither clear-cut, nor constant. There are nevertheless ecological differences (see above), and differing trends, between the eastern and western populations. Whilst its western

10 km square distribution has changed little since the 1960s, in eastern England the species has declined substantially, with more than 80% of populations lost by the 1990s. There are now only three extant sites, excluding introductions; Newmarket Heath (Cambridgeshire), Wiltonhill Wood (West Suffolk), and Weeting Heath (West Norfolk).

Biogeography Eurosiberian Temperate element, with a continental distribution in western Europe.

Native	GB	IR
2000–19	19	0
1987–99	21	0
1970–86	22	0
pre-1970	25	0

Alien	GB	IR
2000–19	18	1
1987–99	12	0
1970–86	13	0
pre-1970	11	0

	GB	IR
Long term		No trend
Short term		No trend

Altitude (m) distribution chart; Distance north (km)

Phenology: Apparency, In flower, In leaf — J F M A M J J A S O N D

Dot size key: <1%, 1–10%, 11–30%, 31–40%, 41–50%, 51–100%

Key refs Houston *et al.* (2000), Kay & John (1995), Leslie (2019), Porter & Halliday (2014), Sanford & Fisk (2010), Stewart *et al.* (1994), Stroh *et al.* (2019), Wigginton (1999).

P.A. STROH & A. HORSFALL

Ar *Veronica hederifolia* Ivy-leaved Speedwell
L.

An annual herb, frequently found as a weed of cultivated land, as well as waste ground, woodland rides, hedgebanks, walls, track and road verges, gardens and allotments, pavements, and active and disused railways, found on sandy, loam or clay soils. It seeds freely, with germination in spring or autumn. 0–380 m (Malham Moor, Mid-west Yorkshire).

Trends The overall 10 km square distribution of *V. hederifolia* remains stable although it is now better recorded in upland regions of Britain and in Ireland than in the 1960s. Two cytologically distinct subspecies are widely recorded in our area (subsp. *hederifolia*, subsp. *lucorum*) and, although often difficult to separate in the field, they are mapped separately here. They appear to be equally widespread, although the records suggest that subsp. *hederifolia* is more common on arable

land, while subsp. *lucorum* favours shady, woodland habitats, but they are often found growing together.

Biogeography As an archaeophyte, *V. hederifolia* has a European Southern-temperate distribution; it is widely naturalized outside this range.

Alien	GB	IR
2000–19	1946	427
1987–99	1794	286
1970–86	1185	32
pre-1970	1509	88

	GB	IR
Long term		
Short term		

Altitude (m) distribution chart; Distance north (km)

Phenology: Apparency, In flower, In leaf — J F M A M J J A S O N D

Dot size key: <1%, 1–10%, 11–30%, 31–40%, 41–50%, 51–100%

Key refs Salisbury (1964).

A. HORSFALL & P.A. STROH

Veronica triphyllos Fingered Speedwell

Ar

L.

An annual herb of sandy calcareous or slightly acidic soils found on the margins of arable fields and on sandy banks. It was formerly also known from tracks, fallow fields, gravel-pits and waste ground. Regular disturbance is needed to exclude competition and maintain sufficient open ground for germination. Lowland.

Trends *V. triphyllos* was first recorded in Britain in 1670, and it has been long-established in the Breckland region of East Anglia. It disappeared from many sites before 1930, and since the 1970s it has been confined to very few localities, with the main reasons for loss including the widespread application of fertilizers and herbicides, irrigation, development, afforestation, and atmospheric nitrogen deposition (Pankhurst *et al.*, 2021). Conservation management is ensuring its survival at five extant sites, four of which support deliberate introductions. At one of these (Weeting Heath), over one million plants were recorded in 2019.

Biogeography As an archaeophyte, *V. triphyllos* has a European Temperate distribution, with a continental distribution in western Europe.

Alien	GB	IR
2000–19	4	0
1987–99	3	0
1970–86	11	0
pre-1970	30	0

	GB	IR
Long term	No trend	No trend
Short term	No trend	No trend

Key refs Pankhurst *et al.* (2021), Wigginton (1999).

A. HORSFALL & P.A. STROH

Veronica fruticans Rock Speedwell

N

Jacq.

A small, rather woody perennial herb with numerous ascending, often branching shoots. It is restricted and localized in the southern and central Scottish Highlands to upland calcareous substrates where it colonizes exposed soils with minimal competition on dry, open montane slopes and rock ledges that are usually south-facing and inaccessible to grazing animals. The optimum flowering period is the end of June to end of July, and the deep azure-blue corollas fall off after only a few days. Montane, from 540 m (Meall an Fhiodhain, Mid Perthshire) to 1,100 m (Ben Lawers, Mid Perthshire).

Trends The 10 km square range of *V. fruticans* appears to have contracted this century. Some populations are known to have been lost, and the numbers of plants at extant sites are generally small. The largest population occurs within Ben Lawers National Nature Reserve, where total numbers were stable during monitoring from 1993 to 2016. Elsewhere, localized declines have been caused by landslips, rockfalls, sheep activity or competition from taller, more vigorous species.

Biogeography European Arctic-montane element; also in Greenland.

Native	GB	IR
2000–19	13	0
1987–99	17	0
1970–86	15	0
pre-1970	18	0

Alien	GB	IR
2000–19	0	0
1987–99	0	0
1970–86	0	0
pre-1970	1	0

	GB	IR
Long term		No trend
Short term		No trend

Key refs Watts (2016), Wigginton (1999).

S.H. WATTS

Ne *Veronica filiformis* Slender Speedwell
Sm.

A perennial herb of mown areas of amenity grassland including garden lawns, large parks and churchyards, as well as on grass by roadsides and paths and on grassy banks and streamsides. It is self-incompatible, rarely setting seed in our area, and spreading vegetatively by slender, procumbent stems and from fragments dispersed by mowing machinery. Generally lowland, but reaching 450 m at Nenthead (Cumberland).

Trends This species was cultivated in Britain by 1805 but was not widely grown until the 20th century. It was first recorded out of cultivation in 1927 by the River Ayr (Ayrshire). Thereafter it spread rapidly, and was widespread by the time of the 1962 *Atlas*. Since then it has further increased and greatly consolidated its range, especially in northern England, Scotland and Ireland.

Biogeography Native of northern Turkey and the Caucasus.

Alien		GB	IR
2000–19	●	1920	398
1987–99	●	1868	358
1970–86	●	1122	59
pre-1970	○	1048	116

Key refs Bangerter & Kent (1957), Bangerter & Kent (1962), Bangerter & Kent (1965), Harris & Lovell (1980).

A. HORSFALL & P.A. STROH

Ar *Veronica agrestis* Green Field-speedwell
L.

A spring-germinating annual herb, typically a colonist of cultivated land, waysides, gardens and allotments. It prefers soils which are well-drained and mildly acidic or neutral, occurring on calcareous substrates only when there is surface leaching. 0–410 m on Malham Moor (Mid-west Yorkshire) and 455 m in East Perthshire.

Trends The 10 km square distribution of *V. agrestis* had declined by the 1960s (Salisbury, 1961) and continued to do so for the remainder of the 20th century due to agricultural intensification. It is no longer a familiar cornfield weed. Since 2000 this decline has continued in many areas, though the rate of decline has slowed, and in a few counties in central and south-eastern England it appears to have made somewhat of a recovery, perhaps due to more systematic recording of arable habitats. It is sometimes confused with *V. polita*.

Biogeography As an archaeophyte, *V. agrestis* has a European Temperate distribution; it is widely naturalized outside this range.

Alien		GB	IR
2000–19	●	1352	128
1987–99	●	1134	60
1970–86	●	750	31
pre-1970	○	1215	120

Key refs Salisbury (1961).

A. HORSFALL & P.A. STROH

Ne *Veronica polita* Grey Field-speedwell
Fr.

An annual herb, found most frequently as a weed of cultivated fields, but also in gardens and allotments, tracks and pavements, railways, old pits and other disturbed ground, typically growing on light, well-drained, sandy, often calcareous soils. Generally lowland, but reaching 409 m in the Clun Forest (Shropshire).

Trends *V. polita* was first recorded from the wild in Britain in 1747. Its general distribution appears stable, with a slight increase this century in southern and eastern England and Wales. More systematic recording has led to many more records in Ireland since 2000. It is sometimes confused with *V. agrestis*, though capsule hair characters readily separate the two species.

Biogeography A Eurosiberian Southern-temperate species.

Alien		GB	IR
2000–19	●	1076	107
1987–99	●	837	42
1970–86	●	576	10
pre-1970	○	851	78

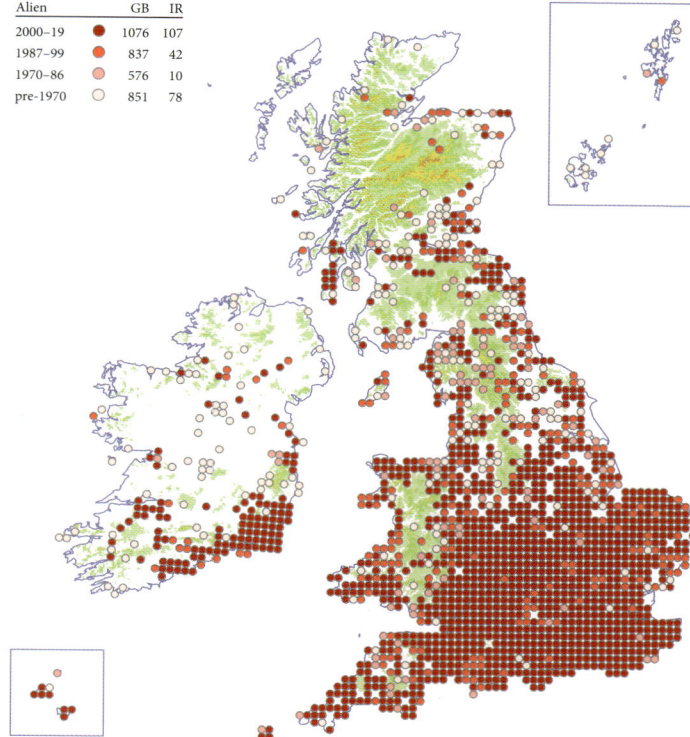

A. HORSFALL & P.A. STROH

Ne *Veronica persica* Common Field-speedwell
Poir.

An annual herb, found mainly as a naturalized weed of arable fields, as well as gardens, allotments, pavements, railways, tracks and roadsides, waste ground, and other disturbed ground, found on a wide range of fertile soils. It is self-fertile and seeds prolifically, forming a persistent seed bank and germinating throughout the year. It also spreads vegetatively from stem fragments. 0–413 m (Dalehead, Derbyshire).

Trends This species was first recorded in Britain in 1825 (Brimpton, Berkshire) and rapidly extended its range during the 19th century; by the 1960s it was ubiquitous throughout the lowlands of Britain and Ireland. It has continued to consolidate its range since then, particularly in upland regions. It remains frequent on arable land, including intensively managed fields, where it is associated with a wide range of crops.

Biogeography Probably native to mountains of the Caucasus and northern Iran, where it may have originated by the hybridization of *V. ceratocarpa* and *V. polita*. Widespread as a weed in Europe, northern Africa, North America, Japan and New Zealand.

Alien		GB	IR
2000–19	●	2088	801
1987–99	●	1998	616
1970–86	●	1213	59
pre-1970	○	1943	425

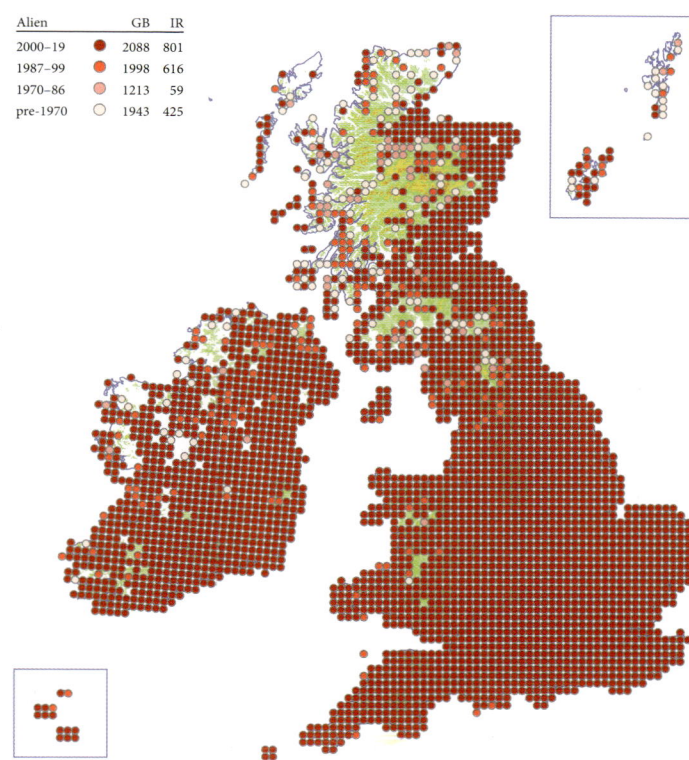

Key refs Fischer (1987), Grime *et al.* (2007).

A. HORSFALL & P.A. STROH

Ne *Veronica teucrium* Large Speedwell
L.

A perennial herb, grown in gardens and found as a naturalized escape on open and rough ground, especially sand dunes. Lowland.

Trends *V. teucrium* was in cultivation in Britain by 1597; it is very widely grown in gardens and several cultivars are available. It was first recorded from the wild in 1917 (Surrey). The recent increase in records presumably reflects the more systematic recording of garden escapes since 2000.

Biogeography A variable species with a European Temperate distribution.

	GB	IR
Long term	No trend	No trend
Short term	↓ ↓ · ↑ **↑**	No trend

Alien	GB	IR
2000–19	29	0
1987–99	12	0
1970–86	6	0
pre-1970	10	2

Altitude (m) / Distance north (km) chart with dot size key: <1%, 1–10%, 11–30%, 31–40%, 41–50%, 51–100%

Apparency / In flower / In leaf phenology chart

T.D. DINES & P.A. STROH

N *Veronica chamaedrys* Germander Speedwell
L.

A stoloniferous perennial herb of woods, hedgebanks, grassland, rock outcrops, upland screes, road verges, railway banks and waste ground, found on most soil types except the most impoverished. It also occurs on anthills on chalk downland. It spreads vegetatively by prostrate stems which root at the nodes; reproduction from seed appears to be comparatively rare. 0–750 m (Meal na Teanga, Loch Lochy, Westerness), with an unlocalized record of 820 m elsewhere in the Scottish Highlands.

Trends There has been no appreciable change in the 10 km square distribution of *V. chamaedrys* since the 1960s, though like many species, its local distribution is now much better known due to more systematic recording this century.

Biogeography Eurosiberian Boreo-temperate element; widely naturalized outside its native range.

	GB	IR
Long term	↓ · · ↑	↓ · · ↑
Short term	↓ ↓ · ↑ ↑	↓ ↓ · ↑ ↑

Native	GB	IR
2000–19	2618	961
1987–99	2557	927
1970–86	1736	187
pre-1970	2513	872

Alien	GB	IR
2000–19	11	0
1987–99	16	0
1970–86	3	0
pre-1970	15	0

Altitude (m) / Distance north (km) chart with dot size key: <1%, 1–10%, 11–30%, 31–40%, 41–50%, 51–100%

Apparency / In flower / In leaf phenology chart

Key refs Grime *et al.* (2007).

P.A. STROH & A. HORSFALL

Veronica arvensis Wall Speedwell
L.

An annual herb of cultivated land, open grassland, heaths, sand dunes, gravelled paths and tracks, waste ground, banks, walls and pavements, usually on dry soils. In closed grassland it may be restricted to anthills. Seed remains viable in the soil for several years. Generally lowland, but reaching at least 820 m in the Breadalbanes (Mid Perthshire) and exceptionally at 845 m on Great Dun Fell (Westmorland).

Trends There is no evidence of any significant change in the 10 km square distribution of *V. arvensis*, other than it is now better recorded in Ireland and upland regions of Britain due to more systematic surveying.

Biogeography European Southern-temperate element, but widely naturalized so that distribution is now Circumpolar Southern-temperate.

		GB	IR
Native			
2000–19	●	2573	811
1987–99	●	2418	673
1970–86	○	1438	69
pre-1970	○	2234	455

Key refs Grime *et al.* (2007).

P.A. STROH & A. HORSFALL

Veronica verna Spring Speedwell
L.

An annual herb of infertile, skeletal, sandy soils, occurring in short grassland and uncultivated, sometimes flinty, sparsely vegetated places including the edges of rabbit warrens and tracksides. Historically, it was also known from Rye fields. In recent decades *V. verna* has been introduced to cultivated arable margins, but native populations depend on intensive grazing by rabbits or sheep with additional disturbance to keep its habitat open. Lowland.

Trends Unlike the other 'Breckland speedwells' (*V. praecox*, *V. triphyllos*), *V. verna* is primarily a plant of semi-natural habitats and is therefore considered to be a native species. It is currently found at nine localities within two 10 km squares, centered around Icklingham, Eriswell and Lakenheath (all West Suffolk). However, re-establishing and then maintaining suitable disturbance and grazing regimes may lead to its appearance at some sites where it has not been seen since the turn of the century. It was introduced to an arable plant reserve at Weeting (West Norfolk) in 1970, where it still persists, sometimes in large numbers, along disturbed margins and within the crop.

Biogeography Eurosiberian Temperate element, with a continental distribution in western Europe.

		GB	IR
Native			
2000–19	●	2	0
1987–99	●	2	0
1970–86	○	4	0
pre-1970	○	8	0
Alien			
2000–19	●	0	0
1987–99	●	0	0
1970–86	●	0	0
pre-1970	○	2	0

	GB	IR
Long term	No trend	No trend
Short term	No trend	No trend

Key refs Stroh *et al.* (2019), Wigginton (1999).

P.A. STROH & A. HORSFALL

Ne ## *Veronica salicifolia* Narrow-leaved Hebe
G.Forst.

An evergreen shrub found planted or
as a garden escape on roadsides and
in hedgerows, quarries and pavement
cracks, as well as on sea-cliffs and on
walls. It reproduces freely by seed,
and can become well-established,
especially in coastal areas. Lowland.

Trends This species was first recorded
in the wild in 1913 (Lostwithial, East
Cornwall), but trends in distribution
are difficult to assess. *V. salicifolia* is the
parent of many cultivated hybrids, and
some records may be in error for these.

Biogeography Native of South America
(Chile) and New Zealand.

	GB	IR
Long term	No trend	No trend

Alien	GB	IR
2000–19	146	34
1987–99	71	16
1970–86	15	4
pre-1970	9	2

Key refs Bean (1973).

T.D. DINES & P.A. STROH

Altitude (m)

	<1%
	1–10%
	11–30%
	31–40%
	41–50%
	51–100%

J F M A M J J A S O N D
☐ Apparency ▮ In flower ▮ In leaf

Hy ## *Veronica salicifolia × elliptica = V. ×lewisii* Lewis's Hebe
J.B.Armstr.

An evergreen shrub found as a
naturalized garden escape on walls
and rocky and waste ground near the
sea, and in coastal scrub. Lowland.

A cultivated hybrid (alien × alien).

Trends *V. ×lewisii* was first recorded
from the wild in 1972 at Bawdsey
Cliffs (East Suffolk). It has been over-
recorded in the past for *V. ×franciscana*.

Biogeography A hybrid of garden
origin. It parents are natives of New
Zealand.

	GB	IR
Long term	No trend	No trend

	GB	IR
2000–19	15	4
1987–99	17	4
1970–86	5	0
pre-1970	2	1

Key refs Chalk (1986), Clement (1985a), Green (1973), Stace
(1975), Stace *et al.* (2015).

C.A. STACE, C.D. PRESTON & D.A. PEARMAN

Altitude (m)

	<1%
	1–10%
	11–30%
	31–40%
	41–50%
	51–100%

J F M A M J J A S O N D
☐ Apparency ▮ In flower ▮ In leaf

Hy *Veronica elliptica × speciosa = V. ×franciscana*
Eastw.

An evergreen shrub found naturalized on sea-cliffs, where colonies have originated as self-sown plants derived from nearby hedges or ornamental plantings. It also occurs as self-sown individuals in other habitats, especially old walls but also cliff-top scrub, sand dunes, disused quarries, gravel-pits, rocky road cuttings, roadsides, waste ground, refuse tips, and as a street weed at the base of walls or in pavement cracks. The hybrid is fully fertile and reproduces abundantly by seed. Lowland.

A cultivated hybrid (alien × alien).

Trends This hybrid was first raised in 1859, with the most frequent cultivar, 'Blue Gem', being raised in 1868. It is extremely popular in gardens, especially in coastal areas. It was first recorded in the wild at Killiney Bay (County Dublin) in 1904. There are very many more records this century compared with the map in the 2002 *Atlas*; this is most likely due to a combination of factors, including a real increase in naturalized occurrences, and fuller recording of hybrids this century. It is probable that the map also includes some records of planted material. In a few cases there may have been some confusion with *V. ×lewisii*, though this is much the rarer of the two hybrids.

Biogeography A hybrid of garden origin; both parents are native of New Zealand, though the hybrid is not known there despite the two species growing together.

	GB	IR
Long term	No trend	No trend
Short term	No trend	No trend

	GB	IR
2000–19 ●	245	129
1987–99 ●	109	36
1970–86 ●	26	1
pre-1970 ○	21	8

Key refs Stace *et al.* (2015).

C.A. STACE, C.D. PRESTON & D.A. PEARMAN

N *Sibthorpia europaea* Cornish Moneywort
L.

A procumbent perennial herb of thin acidic soils in humid, sheltered areas that have surface or ground water seepage and periodic disturbance. It is found in woodland on steep-sided gorges, banks by small streams and ditches (often creeping over a carpet of mosses and liverworts), on wet grassy heaths, cattle-poached wet meadows and marshes, shaded paths and lawns, damp shaded roadside verges, and on thin soil over granite walls or other masonry. 0–515 m (Connor Hill, South Kerry).

Trends Improved recording of this inconspicuous species over the past 40 years has resulted in a much better understanding of its ecological niche, range and frequency. Whilst the 10 km square distribution of *S. europaea* appears stable, records at a finer resolution show that it is a highly localized plant throughout its British range. Away from its core south-western stronghold it is present in the Sussex Weald, where it contributes to a western Atlantic flora which has persisted in suitable microhabitats. In Ireland, it is only present on the Dingle Peninsula, where it appears to co-exist with the non-native *Epilobium brunnescens*, which has a preference for similar habitat.

Biogeography Oceanic Temperate element.

	GB	IR
Long term		
Short term		

Native	GB	IR
2000–19 ●	92	8
1987–99 ●	90	7
1970–86 ●	81	5
pre-1970 ○	100	9

Alien	GB	IR
2000–19 ●	5	0
1987–99 ●	3	1
1970–86 ●	1	1
pre-1970 ○	6	3

Key refs French (2020), Pryce & Chater (2000), Stewart *et al.* (1994), Stroh (2015c).

P.A. STROH & A. HORSFALL

Ne *Antirrhinum majus* Snapdragon
L.

An annual or short-lived perennial herb, widely naturalized on old walls, waysides, pavement cracks and gutters, road verges, quarries and gravel-pits, waste ground, derelict housing sites, rock faces and railway land, but seldom far from human habitations. Populations can be long-lived, and the species reproduces readily from seed. It is recommended for planting as a pollinator nectar source by several authorities following study of its structural genetics in relation to pollinator attraction. Lowland.

Trends *A. majus* has been cultivated here since Elizabethan times and is very popular in gardens. It was first recorded in the wild in 1698 (Margam Abbey, Glamorganshire). Its distribution has increased substantially since the 1950s and it is now one of the most frequent self-sown garden escapes in towns and villages. This is probably due to a genuine spread as well as the better recording of aliens.

Biogeography Native of south-western Europe and the western Mediterranean region.

Alien		GB	IR
2000–19	●	1178	177
1987–99	●	903	78
1970–86	●	420	2
pre-1970	○	447	11

Key refs Dyer *et al.* (2007).

A. Horsfall & N. Aspey

Ar *Chaenorhinum minus* Small Toadflax
(L.) Lange

A spring-germinating annual herb of open habitats on well-drained, often calcareous soils, including cultivated fields, disturbed track edges, on rough waste ground, old walls, quarries, coastal shingle, pavements and especially along railways where it is typical of open cinders and ballast that are somehow protected from herbicide management. 0–525 m (Garn Goch, Glamorganshire).

Trends This species appears to have expanded its range along the railway network in the 19th century (Sargent, 1985) but from the 1960s onwards, it declined in many areas, due to the abandonment of many rural railway lines. It was once a familiar weed of cultivated farmland, but agricultural intensification has now rendered it much rarer in this habitat. In the second half of the 20th century, it was much more likely to be found along railways and in railway yards but, more recently, there is some evidence of decline there also.

Biogeography As an archaeophyte, *C. minus* has a European Temperate distribution; it is widely naturalized outside this range.

Alien		GB	IR
2000–19	●	970	131
1987–99	●	1013	85
1970–86	●	806	13
pre-1970	○	1119	105

Key refs Grime *et al.* (2007), Sargent (1985).

A. Horsfall & J.O. Mountford

Ar *Misopates orontium* Weasel's-snout
(L.) Raf.

An annual of light soils, found in arable and other cultivated ground including among horticultural crops, and in gardens, allotments and waste places. It reproduces by seed, but cold, wet summers inhibit its germination and growth. Lowland.

Trends *M. orontium* declined because of agricultural intensification and the more widespread sowing of crops in the autumn months. Salisbury (1961) noted that it appeared to be less frequent than formerly, and since then it has declined sharply, disappearing from almost half of its 10 km squares in south-eastern England by the end of the 20th century (Preston *et al.*, 2002a). Losses have continued, although its distribution appears to have stabilized in some areas, even showing local signs of recovery in south-western England and south-western Wales. Its range extends as far north as the Firth of Tay, but it is only

ever frequent in the warmer climate of southern Britain.

Biogeography As an archaeophyte, *M. orontium* has a Eurosiberian Southern-temperate distribution; it is widely naturalized outside this range.

Alien		GB	IR
2000–19	●	260	10
1987–99	●	255	4
1970–86	●	190	6
pre-1970	○	419	24

Key refs Salisbury (1961), Wilson (1991).

A. HORSFALL & P.A. STROH

Ne *Asarina procumbens* Trailing Snapdragon
Mill.

A stoloniferous perennial herb which is naturalized on dry banks, walls and cliffs. Reproduction is by seed. Lowland.

Trends *A. procumbens* was in cultivation in Britain by 1699 and is popular in gardens. It was recorded from the wild in 1938 (Oxford, Oxfordshire) and appears to be increasing, with a slight expansion farther north in Scotland and west into Wales.

Biogeography Native of southern France and north-eastern Spain.

Alien		GB	IR
2000–19	●	66	0
1987–99	●	31	0
1970–86	●	18	0
pre-1970	○	4	0

T.D. DINES & N. ASPEY

Ne *Cymbalaria muralis* Ivy-leaved Toadflax

G.Gaertn., B.Mey. & Scherb.

A winter-green, trailing perennial herb, still sold as a rockery plant, but now well-established both within and outside gardens, mostly on old walls and bridges, but also on pavements and in other well-drained rocky and stony places, usually near to human habitations. It is also found as large, prostrate patches on railways and shingle beaches. It can root from fragments or from nodes, and its seeds germinate readily on brick and stone mortar. 0–570 m (Hartside Quarry, Cumberland).

Trends *C. muralis* was grown in gardens by 1617, and records from the wild date from 1640 (Hatfield, Hertfordshire). Two subspecies are recorded: subsp. *muralis* and subsp. *visianii*. The latter was first recorded in 1970 at Wisley, Surrey.

Biogeography Native of the mountains of southern-central and south-eastern Europe; widely naturalized through much of temperate and southern Europe.

Alien	GB	IR
2000–19	2042	629
1987–99	1895	531
1970–86	1077	49
pre-1970	1767	344

Key refs Salisbury (1964), Wilcox & Ruhsam (2020).

D.A. Pearman & A. Horsfall

Ne *Cymbalaria pallida* Italian Toadflax

(Ten.) Wettst.

A perennial herb found as a garden escape on walls, pavements, shingle, rocky banks and waste ground. Populations are often naturalized, spreading readily by seed. Generally lowland, but reaching 407 m at Allenheads (South Northumberland).

Trends This species was introduced into cultivation in Britain before 1879 and was first recorded from the wild in 1924 at Bardsea, Westmorland, where it was naturalized on a shingle beach until 1977. It is difficult to assess any changes in its distribution, especially as some populations may have been overlooked, but others may have been recorded in error for pale-flowered variants of *C. muralis*.

Biogeography Native of the mountains of central Italy.

Alien	GB	IR
2000–19	180	4
1987–99	58	1
1970–86	24	0
pre-1970	26	0

Key refs Wilcox & Ruhsam (2020).

D.A. Pearman & T.D. Dines

Ar *Kickxia elatine* Sharp-leaved Fluellen

(L.) Dumort.

An annual herb of disturbed, light soils overlying chalk and calcareous boulder-clay, found on the headlands and margins of arable fields (particularly those cultivated for cereals), and less commonly on tracks, waste ground and in gardens. It is also found on sandy soils, and has been recorded on open peaty ground (County Cork). It has a similar ecology to *K. spuria* and is often found growing with it. Lowland.

Trends Although this species is often only present in small and scattered populations, its overall distribution appears to have remained relatively stable since the 1960s. Its ability to germinate in the late summer has possibly limited declines as a result of herbicide applications (Simpson, 1982) and in recent decades it has also benefitted from conservation management of arable field margins as part of agri-environment schemes (Walker *et al.*, 2007).

Biogeography As an archaeophyte, *K. elatine* has a European Southern-temperate distribution; it is widely naturalized outside this range.

Alien	GB	IR
2000–19	796	42
1987–99	690	20
1970–86	465	11
pre-1970	748	30

Key refs Simpson (1982), Walker *et al.* (2007).

A. HORSFALL

Ar *Kickxia spuria* Round-leaved Fluellen

(L.) Dumort.

An annual herb of arable land and open waste ground, usually on calcareous soils. Found in similar places to *K. elatine* but often more frequent and in a wider range of habitats including woodland rides and cleared areas in boulder clay woods. Lowland.

Trends Like *K. elatine*, the overall distribution of *K. spuria* appears to have remained relatively stable since the 1960s, possibly due to its ability to germinate in the late summer and thereby avoid herbicide applications (Simpson, 1982). In recent decades it has also benefitted from conservation management of arable field margins as part of agri-environment schemes (Walker *et al.*, 2007).

Biogeography As an archaeophyte, *K. spuria* has a European Southern-temperate distribution.

Alien	GB	IR
2000–19	523	0
1987–99	456	0
1970–86	334	0
pre-1970	517	0

Key refs Simpson (1982), Walker *et al.* (2007).

A. HORSFALL

N *Linaria vulgaris* Common Toadflax
Mill.

A perennial herb of open grassland, on stony and waste ground, hedgebanks, road verges, railway embankments and cultivated land, especially on calcareous soils. It reproduces by seed and also spreads by creeping rhizomes. 0–404 m on the south-west side of the A9, Slochd Mor (Easterness).

Trends The overall 10 km square range of *L. vulgaris* would appear to be relatively stable in southern areas, although there have been substantial losses in the north of its British range and in some areas of Ireland. It was mapped as 'all records' in the 1962 *Atlas*.

Biogeography Eurasian Boreo-temperate element, but naturalized in North America so distribution is now Circumpolar Boreo-temperate.

Native	GB	IR
2000–19	1677	71
1987–99	1713	36
1970–86	1200	19
pre-1970	1736	57

Alien	GB	IR
2000–19	7	1
1987–99	5	2
1970–86	4	0
pre-1970	12	1

Key refs Grime *et al.* (2007), Saber *et al.* (1995).

A. HORSFALL

Hy *Linaria repens × vulgaris = L. ×sepium*
G.J.Allman

A perennial hybrid that typically occurs on railway clinker, a favoured habitat for both parents, but also on rocky hedgebanks, disused chalk-pits and chalk rubble, roadside verges, field edges, by footpaths and on arable land and waste ground. It often occurs in the absence of one or both parents; it is fertile and back-crosses readily to form swarms of intermediates. Lowland.

A spontaneous hybrid (native × alien).

Trends The lack of correspondence between the sites mapped by Perring & Sell (1968) and the more recent records is striking, and suggests that at many stations populations of the hybrid are relatively short-lived and are lost as sites become overgrown or modified by development.

Biogeography Widespread in western and central Europe.

	GB	IR
Long term	No trend	No trend
Short term	No trend	No trend

	GB	IR
2000–19	58	0
1987–99	71	0
1970–86	51	0
pre-1970	82	2

Key refs Stace *et al.* (2015).

C.A. STACE, C.D. PRESTON & D.A. PEARMAN

Ne *Linaria purpurea* Purple Toadflax
(L.) Mill.

A perennial herb, very widely grown in gardens from where it frequently escapes or occurs as an outcast on pavements, walls, waste ground, roadsides, banks, refuse tips and in quarries. Mainly lowland but up to 410 m at Lady Canning's Plantation (Derbyshire).

Trends *L. purpurea* was introduced into cultivation by 1599 and is a popular garden plant with several named cultivars. It was known from the wild by 1834 (Hampstead, Middlesex), and its distribution has greatly increased since the 1960s, especially in northern Britain, Wales and Ireland, probably due to both better recording and a genuine spread.

Biogeography Native of central and southern Italy and Sicily.

Alien	GB	IR
2000–19	1729	153
1987–99	1350	67
1970–86	702	11
pre-1970	501	7

A. HORSFALL

Hy *Linaria purpurea* × *repens* = *L.* ×*dominii*
Druce

L. ×*dominii* is often found on dismantled railway lines or in adjacent railway yards; its other habitats include roadside banks, chalk-pits, disused quarries, walls, refuse tips and waste ground. It is sometimes recorded in the absence of *L. purpurea* or of both parents. Lowland.

A spontaneous hybrid (alien × alien).

Trends Druce (1913) first named this plant from hybrids which arose spontaneously in his Oxford garden. It was first recorded in the wild in *c.* 1950 in a chalk-pit at Dunstable Downs (Bedfordshire), and in recent decades it has been found at an increasing number of sites, coinciding with the spread of the neophyte *L. purpurea* into the range of the archaeophyte *L. repens*.

Biogeography *L. purpurea* has a restricted native range (Italy, Sicily) which does not overlap with the Suboceanic Temperate native range of *L. repens*.

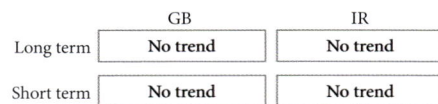

	GB	IR
	Long term	No trend	No trend
	Short term	No trend	No trend

	GB	IR
2000–19	66	0
1987–99	41	0
1970–86	20	0
pre-1970	6	0

Key refs Druce (1913), Stace *et al.* (2015).

C.A. STACE, C.D. PRESTON & D.A. PEARMAN

Ar *Linaria repens* Pale Toadflax
(L.) Mill.

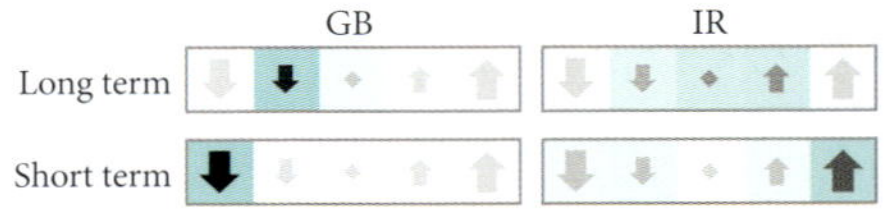

A perennial herb, spreading by slender rhizomes, found on rough and waste ground, stony and cultivated land, grassy banks and along railway tracks, usually on dry, calcareous or base-rich soils. 0–415 m (Angler's Retreat, Cardiganshire).

Trends Many new sites for *L. repens* have been found this century, but such gains mask a high turnover in 10 km squares since the 1960s, perhaps reflecting the tendency for it to behave as a transient colonist of open habitats.

Biogeography As an archaeophyte, *L. repens* has a Suboceanic Temperate distribution; it is widely naturalized outside this range.

Alien	GB	IR
2000–19	457	15
1987–99	485	8
1970–86	376	10
pre-1970	478	18

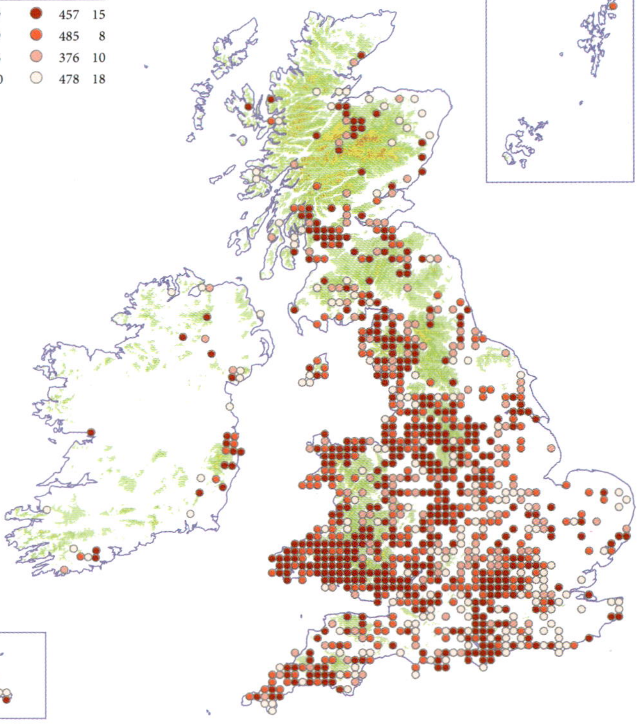

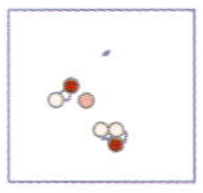

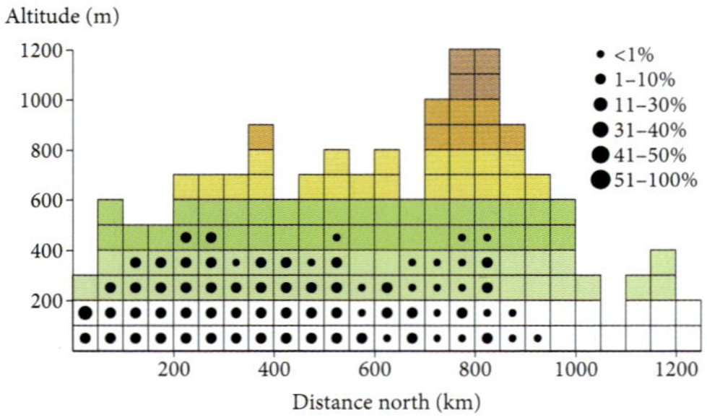

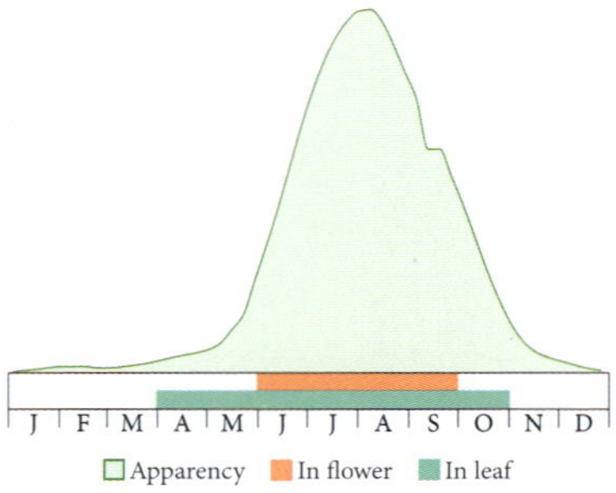

A. HORSFALL

Ne *Linaria supina* Prostrate Toadflax
(L.) Chaz.

An annual herb found on sandy sea-shores, waste places and walls near the sea, and on roadside embankments and beside railways. It is naturalized in some parts of south-western Britain, but occurs only as a rare casual elsewhere. Lowland.

Trends *L. supina* was being grown in Britain in 1728, but there is no evidence that it was ever a garden plant. It was first recorded in the wild in 1839 at Par (East Cornwall), where it was formerly considered to be native. It was last seen at Par in 2003, but is still persistent at Falmouth Docks Station (West Cornwall), where it has been known since 1972, despite annual street cleansing with herbicides.

Biogeography Native of south-western Europe, extending east to Croatia. It is also found in North Africa.

	GB	IR
Long term	No trend	No trend
Short term	No trend	No trend

Alien	GB	IR
2000–19	8	0
1987–99	14	0
1970–86	14	0
pre-1970	26	0

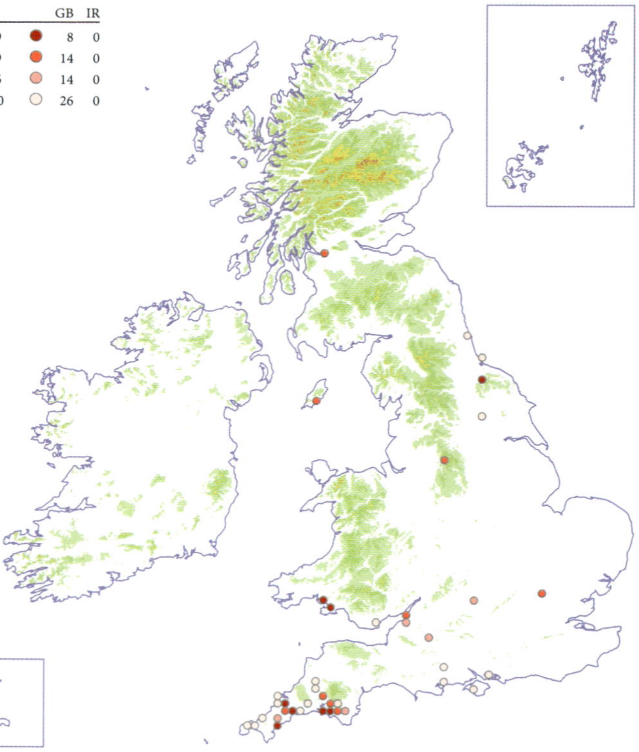

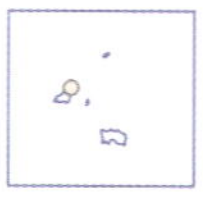

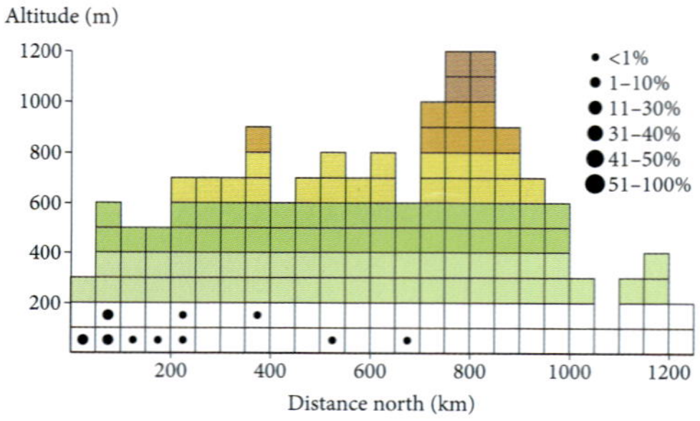

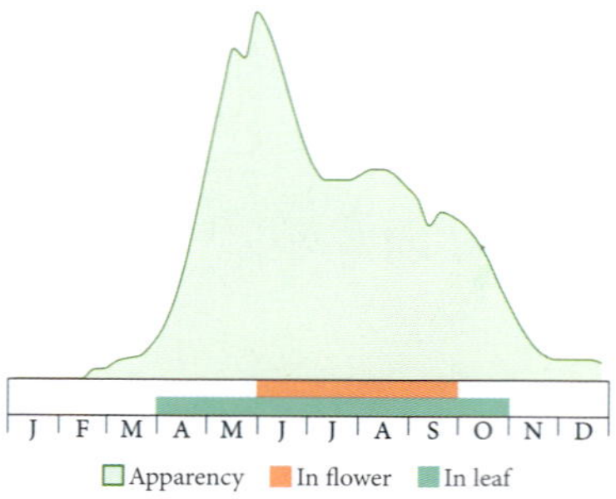

Key refs FitzGerald (1990), French (2020).

D.A. PEARMAN & T.D. DINES

Ne *Linaria pelisseriana* Jersey Toadflax
(L.) Mill.

An annual herb, found as a casual
of hedgebanks, rough ground
and rocky places. Lowland.

Trends *L. pelisseriana* was first recorded
from the wild in St Ouen's Bay, Jersey in
1837, where it was seen sporadically at
scattered localities until 1955. It is often
regarded as a native to the island, but its
history suggests that it is more likely to
be an alien. It is only casual elsewhere.

Biogeography A Mediterranean-
Atlantic species.

	GB	IR
Long term	No trend	No trend
Short term	No trend	No trend

Alien	GB	IR
2000–19	3	0
1987–99	0	0
1970–86	1	0
pre-1970	17	0

•	<1%	
•	1–10%	
●	11–30%	
●	31–40%	
●	41–50%	
●	51–100%	

Altitude (m)

Distance north (km)

J F M A M J J A S O N D

☐ Apparency ☐ In flower ☐ In leaf

A. HORSFALL

Ne *Linaria maroccana* Annual Toadflax
Hook.f.

An annual herb, found as a casual
on refuse tips, waysides and in
waste places, usually near human
habitations, originating from garden
waste and birdseed. It has also been
recorded on sea-cliffs. The seeds
germinate readily. Lowland.

Trends *L. maroccana* was introduced
into cultivation in Britain in 1871
and was first recorded from the
wild in 1927 at Thorner, near York
(Mid-west Yorkshire). Its overall
distribution appears to have increased
substantially this century.

Biogeography Native of northern Africa
(Morocco).

	GB	IR
Long term	No trend	No trend
Short term		No trend

Alien	GB	IR
2000–19	118	1
1987–99	39	0
1970–86	26	0
pre-1970	30	0

•	<1%	
•	1–10%	
●	11–30%	
●	31–40%	
●	41–50%	
●	51–100%	

Altitude (m)

Distance north (km)

J F M A M J J A S O N D

☐ Apparency ☐ In flower ☐ In leaf

A. HORSFALL

N *Plantago coronopus* Buck's-horn Plantain
L.

A perennial herb of dry, open, often heavily trampled habitats on acidic to basic stony or sandy soils, and in rock crevices. It occurs in open grassland, on heathlands, sand dunes and shingle, sea-cliffs and sea-walls, waste ground, amenity grassland and by paths. Although it has always been known from inland habitats in southern and eastern England, it is increasingly being recorded from beside salt-treated roads. 0–455 m (Titterstone Clee, Shropshire).

Trends Although some sites were lost as heathland was destroyed in the last century, the distribution of *P. coronopus* has increased substantially in southern and central England this century along roadsides, in urban areas as a pavement weed and in mown grassland. Its coastal distribution is stable.

Biogeography Eurosiberian Southern-temperate element; widely naturalized outside its native range.

Native	GB	IR
2000–19	1728	322
1987–99	1312	280
1970–86	709	92
pre-1970	1152	228

Alien	GB	IR
2000–19	16	0
1987–99	16	0
1970–86	5	0
pre-1970	9	0

Key refs Dodds (1953).

Altitude (m) / Distance north (km)

• <1%
• 1–10%
• 11–30%
• 31–40%
• 41–50%
• 51–100%

Apparency   In flower   In leaf

G.M. KAY & P.A. STROH

N *Plantago maritima* Sea Plantain
L.

A perennial herb of the middle and upper zones of saltmarshes, coastal turf, rocks and cliffs, on coastal heaths and occasionally on shingle beaches and inland saltmarshes. In the uplands it is found in species-rich pastures, on stream banks, rock ledges and scree, and in stony flushes. It is also found along inland road verges. 0–790 m (Caernarvonshire, Mid Perthshire and County Mayo).

Trends The 10 km square distribution of *P. maritima* in coastal and montane habitats shows little change since the 1960s. It continues to spread on the verges of salt-treated roads in Scotland, but is rare as an inland halophyte elsewhere.

Biogeography Eurosiberian Wide-boreal element; also in North America.

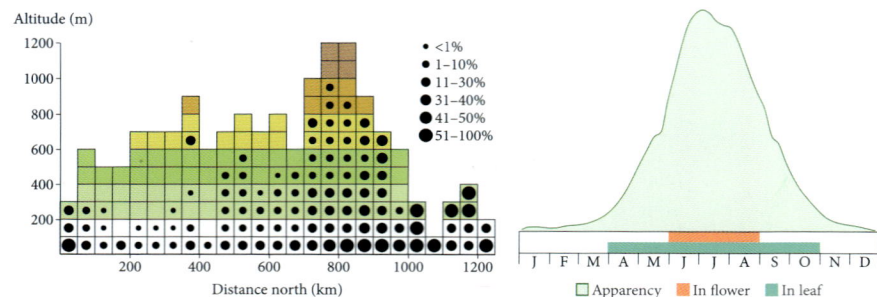

Native	GB	IR
2000–19	1277	395
1987–99	1159	350
1970–86	710	131
pre-1970	1095	311

Alien	GB	IR
2000–19	9	0
1987–99	4	0
1970–86	4	0
pre-1970	4	0

Altitude (m) / Distance north (km)

• <1%
• 1–10%
• 11–30%
• 31–40%
• 41–50%
• 51–100%

Apparency   In flower   In leaf

G.M. KAY & P.A. STROH

N *Plantago major* Greater Plantain

L.

A perennial herb of open habitats; it is most frequent on trampled paths and tracks, disturbed field edges and roadsides, and in gardens, but it also occurs in some closed grasslands. It grows in a wide range of soils, avoiding only very acidic sites, and can produce a large and persistent seed bank. 0–700 m (Raehowe End, Cumberland), with an exceptional record at 845 m on Great Dun Fell (Westmorland).

Trends The distribution of this ubiquitous species appears to be stable at the 10 km square level. Subsp. *major* occurs throughout the range of the species; subsp. *intermedia* is mapped separately.

Biogeography Eurasian Wide-temperate element, but naturalized in North America so distribution is now Circumpolar Wide-temperate.

Native		GB	IR
2000–19	●	2783	997
1987–99	●	2717	954
1970–86	◐	1766	155
pre-1970	○	2637	896

Key refs Grime *et al.* (2007), Hawthorn (1974), Sagar & Harper (1964).

G.M. KAY

N *Plantago major* subsp. *intermedia*

(Gilib.) Lange

An annual or perennial herb of damp, open habitats, including somewhat saline soils by coastal creeks and the upper end of saltmarshes, the edge of rivers and streams, damp mud exposed in summer by ponds and reservoirs, and winter-flooded hollows in arable fields. It has also been recorded beside salt-treated roads and as a garden weed. Lowland.

Trends This subspecies was first recognized in Britain by Lousley (1958), but not described in standard Floras until Clapham *et al.* (1987). Wolff & Morgan-Richards (1999) have suggested that it is specifically distinct from subsp. *major*, but the morphological separation in our area is not clear-cut. It is better recorded in recent decades, but the patchy distribution of records demonstrates that it is still under-recorded.

Biogeography Subsp. *intermedia* is widespread in Europe; its wider distribution is uncertain.

	GB	IR
Long term	No trend	No trend
Short term	No trend	No trend

Native		GB	IR
2000–19	●	413	255
1987–99	●	154	28
1970–86	◐	34	5
pre-1970	○	25	7

Key refs Doogue & Akeroyd (1988), Lousley (1958), Preston & Whitehouse (1986), Wolff & Morgan-Richards (1999).

G.M. KAY

N *Plantago media* Hoary Plantain
L.

A perennial herb of chalk and limestone soils as well as heavy clays. Its main habitats are chalk and limestone downland, track edges, calcareous pasture and mown grassland (such as churchyards); it is less frequent in hay meadows and on fixed sand dunes, and is sometimes found in flood-meadows which receive calcareous water (Grose, 1957). Seed appears to be short-lived. 0–540 m (east of Hartside summit, Cumberland).

Native in Britain and a neophyte in Ireland and the Channel Islands.

Trends *P. media* has declined around the limits of its core area since the 1960s, mainly due to the ploughing-up or improvement of permanent pasture. In recent decades it has been included in wild-flower seed mixtures, and locally some new records may represent intentional sowing of this species.

Biogeography Eurasian Temperate element; widely naturalized outside its native range.

Key refs Grose (1957), Sagar & Harper (1964).

G.M. Kay & P.A. Stroh

N *Plantago lanceolata* Ribwort Plantain
L.

A perennial herb, found in most grassland habitats over all but the most acidic soils. It occurs in meadows and pastures, in upland grasslands, on rock ledges and crevices, sand dunes and sea cliffs (including sites subject to sea-spray), on roadsides and riverbanks, in cultivated and waste ground, in lawns and on walls. Seed is moderately long-lived. 0–790 m in Atholl (East Perthshire), and 845 m on Great Dun Fell (Westmorland).

Trends *P. lanceolata* is ubiquitous at the 10 km square level and its distribution has not changed appreciably since the 1960s. It is genetically and phenotypically highly variable.

Biogeography Eurosiberian Southern-temperate element, but widely naturalized so that distribution is now Circumpolar Southern-temperate.

Key refs Cavers *et al.* (1980), Grime *et al.* (2007), Sagar & Harper (1964).

G.M. Kay

Ne *Plantago arenaria* Branched Plantain

Waldst. & Kit.

An annual herb, found in open sandy places, including waste ground, and in docklands, usually casual but sometimes naturalized. Lowland.

Trends *P. arenaria* arrived as a grain impurity and was first recorded in the wild in 1820; it is now of only rare occurrence. There has been much nomenclatural confusion between this species and the allied *P. afra*; some historical records may be errors for the latter.

Biogeography *P. arenaria* has a Eurosiberian Southern-temperate distribution; its native range has been obscured by its spread as a weed and it is widely naturalized on other continents.

	GB	IR
Long term	No trend	No trend
Short term	No trend	No trend

Alien	GB	IR
2000–19	6	0
1987–99	8	0
1970–86	8	0
pre-1970	55	1

G.M. Kay

N *Littorella uniflora* Shoreweed

(L.) Asch.

A perennial herb of oligotrophic or mesotrophic waters, found in lakes, reservoirs, rivers, streams, ponds and winter-flooded dune-slacks, growing on stones, gravel, sand, peat, marl or soft mud. It grows to a depth of about 4 metres and can form a dense band in the draw-down zone around lakes and reservoirs. It reproduces by seed and vegetatively by rooting stolons. Seeds remain viable for decades. 0–840 m (Lochanager, South Aberdeenshire).

Trends *L. uniflora* can be difficult to monitor due to highly variable population levels at many sites and the inaccessibility of populations growing in deep water. However, drainage had resulted in the loss of many lowland sites for this species before 1930, especially in southern England, and further losses have occurred since then, even with better recording effort. Since 2000 the low-level decrease across its general range has continued, mainly associated with eutrophication leading to increased shading, reduced carbon dioxide supply and heightened nitrate levels.

Biogeography Suboceanic Temperate element.

Native	GB	IR
2000–19	960	344
1987–99	1000	337
1970–86	650	91
pre-1970	922	246

Alien	GB	IR
2000–19	0	0
1987–99	1	0
1970–86	0	0
pre-1970	1	0

Key refs Preston & Croft (1997), Robe & Griffiths (1992), Robe & Griffiths (1994).

M.J. Wigginton & N. Aspey

Hippuris vulgaris Mare's-tail
L.

A herbaceous perennial that occurs in two growth forms. Plants with long, flaccid stems grow as submerged aquatics, and are sometimes abundant in clear calcareous water. More rigid, stiffly erect shoots grow as emergents at the edge of lakes and ponds, in swamps or in upland flushes. These may be very robust when growing on deep, eutrophic mud. 0–900 m (Moine Mhor, Easterness), but rare above 400 m.

Trends The map suggests the possibility of a gradual reduction in the frequency of *H. vulgaris* in many areas. It seems improbable that this is attributable solely to the uneven recording of aquatic species, and it requires further study. In Broadland *H. vulgaris* proved relatively tolerant of turbid water (George, 1992) but it has declined in calcareous streams in south-west Germany (Schütz, 1995) and colonies in shallow water on lake margins are vulnerable to overgrowth by taller emergents following eutrophication (Sand-Jensen *et al.*, 2008). *H. vulgaris* persists in some sites to which it has been introduced.

Biogeography Circumpolar Boreo-temperate element.

Native	GB	IR
2000–19	800	290
1987–99	809	315
1970–86	570	94
pre-1970	844	244

Alien	GB	IR
2000–19	34	0
1987–99	22	0
1970–86	8	0
pre-1970	3	0

Key refs George (1992), Preston & Croft (1997), Sand-Jensen *et al.* (2008), Schütz (1995).

C.D. Preston

Callitriche hermaphroditica Autumnal Water-starwort
L.

A herb of mesotrophic lakes, gravel-pits and occasionally in canals. It is usually annual, although some populations may perennate. 0–568 m Gameshope loch (Peeblesshire).

Trends *C. hermaphroditica* is widespread and locally abundant. There have been recent losses from some sites which may be due to deteriorating water quality, but at the same time there have been new records from gravel-pits in Lincolnshire and canals in the English Midlands. It is likely that these changes involve different subspecies, with subsp. *hermaphroditica* increasing and subsp. *macrocarpa* declining.

Biogeography Circumpolar Boreal-montane element.

Native	GB	IR
2000–19	189	49
1987–99	217	72
1970–86	228	29
pre-1970	233	59

Alien	GB	IR
2000–19	1	0
1987–99	1	0
1970–86	0	0
pre-1970	0	0

Key refs Lansdown (2008), Martinsson (1991b), Preston & Croft (1997), Stewart *et al.* (1994).

R.V. Lansdown

N *Callitriche truncata* Short-leaved Water-starwort

Guss.

An annual or occasionally perennial herb, growing in rivers, canals, ditches, lakes and gravel-pits, typically in base-rich mesotrophic or eutrophic waters, and rarely as a terrestrial plant on wet mud. Lowland.

Trends *C. truncata* appears to be increasing and spreading northwards in Britain. It has been discovered since the 1960s in Essex, Lincolnshire and Anglesey, and its range now overlaps with that of *C. hermaphroditica*. It appears to have been lost from the Gloucester & Sharpness Canal and the Bridgewater Canal, but it is not clear why.

Biogeography Mediterranean-Atlantic element. *C. truncata* is also spreading northwards in mainland Europe. British and Irish plants are referable to subsp. *occidentalis*.

	GB	IR
Long term		No trend
Short term		No trend

Native	GB	IR
2000–19	46	2
1987–99	33	2
1970–86	23	1
pre-1970	31	1

Altitude (m) chart, Distance north (km)

- <1%
- 1–10%
- 11–30%
- 31–40%
- 41–50%
- 51–100%

☐ Apparency ■ In flower ■ In leaf

Key refs Lansdown (2008), Preston & Croft (1997), Stewart *et al.* (1994).

R.V. Lansdown

N *Callitriche stagnalis s.l.* Common Water-starwort

An annual or perennial herb found on rutted tracks, in ephemeral pools and at the margins of ditches and rivers, as well as in seepages and flushes, particularly in the uplands, as well as rarely in deep water in chalk streams. 0–610 m on Great Dun Fell (Westmorland), and possibly to 890 m on Foel Grach (Caernarvonshire).

Trends As in previous atlases, records of *C. platycarpa* are included here with *C. stagnalis s.s.* The name *Callitriche stagnalis* is still (mis)applied by recorders to any water-starwort species with floating leaves and as a consequence it is not possible to produce a reliable map of this segregate. *C. stagnalis s.s.* is probably widespread and abundant throughout much of the region, particularly in the north and west of Britain. It is more difficult to assess the accuracy of its distribution in the

south and east due to limited critical distinction from *C. platycarpa*.

Biogeography European Temperate element; it also occurs as an alien (naturalized) in Australia, Chile, the Falkland Islands, New Caledonia, New Zealand and North America.

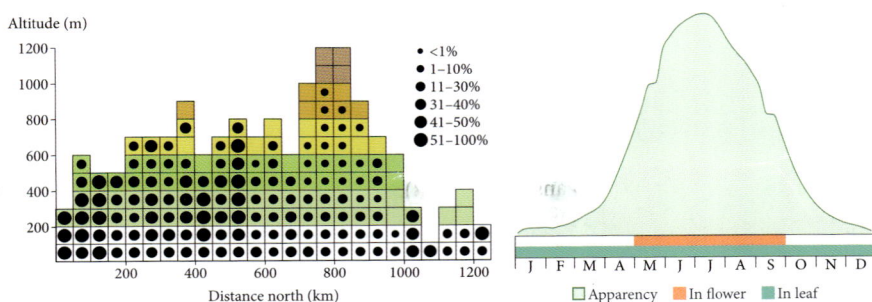

	GB	IR
Long term		
Short term		

Native	GB	IR
2000–19	2436	599
1987–99	2400	627
1970–86	1595	107
pre-1970	1996	550

Altitude (m) chart, Distance north (km)

- <1%
- 1–10%
- 11–30%
- 31–40%
- 41–50%
- 51–100%

☐ Apparency ■ In flower ■ In leaf

Key refs Lansdown (2008), Preston & Croft (1997).

R.V. Lansdown

843

N *Callitriche platycarpa* Various-leaved Water-starwort

Kütz.

A perennial herb, occurring in most types of water body and as a terrestrial form on damp mud, most frequent in eutrophic waters, particularly ditches and canals. Generally lowland, but reaching 520 m at Llynnoedd Ieuan (Cardiganshire).

Trends *C. platycarpa* is widespread and abundant in the lowlands of southern Britain, becoming less frequent in the north and west. It appears to be spreading northwards, but this apparent trend may be a result of limited critical recording in the past. Historical records for Orkney and Shetland are now considered doubtful. It is relatively widespread in Ireland but the patchiness of the map shows it is under-recorded. It was mapped with *C. stagnalis* in the 1962 *Atlas*.

Biogeography European Temperate element.

	GB	IR
Long term	No trend	No trend
Short term	↓	↓

Native	GB	IR
2000–19	562	117
1987–99	635	129
1970–86	552	25
pre-1970	450	56

Key refs Lansdown (2008), Martinsson (1991a), Preston & Croft (1997).

R.V. LANSDOWN

N *Callitriche palustris* Narrow-fruited Water-starwort

L.

An annual or possibly perennial herb occurring in a range of water body types, but generally found where water levels drop to expose sandy or silty substrates on which *C. palustris* develops terrestrial forms, including the drawdown zones of lakes and reservoirs, as well as river bars and backwaters. Generally lowland in the region, it extends to high altitudes elsewhere.

Trends *C. palustris* was found in a turlough in western Ireland (Gort, County Mayo) in 1999, then new to Scotland (Endrick, Stirlingshire) in 2000 and more recently in England (Haweswater, Westmorland) in 2017. It is possible that it has been overlooked due to limited critical recording of *Callitriche*. However, the possibility that it is a relatively recent introduction cannot be dismissed.

Biogeography Circumpolar Boreal-temperate element.

	GB	IR
Long term	No trend	No trend
Short term	No trend	No trend

Native	GB	IR
2000–19	6	2
1987–99	0	1
1970–86	0	0
pre-1970	0	0

Key refs Lansdown (2008).

R.V. LANSDOWN

Callitriche obtusangula Blunt-fruited Water-starwort
Le Gall

A perennial herb typical of permanent, still or slow-flowing mesotrophic to eutrophic waters, particularly chalk streams, ditches and field ponds, extending into brackish water in coastal grazing marshes. It also grows in a terrestrial form on wet mud as water levels drop. Generally lowland, but reaching 424 m at Byrgwm Pool (Radnorshire).

Trends *C. obtusangula* is widespread in lowland Britain. It is better recorded in the Fenland basin and in Northern Ireland than before 2000, due to more systematic recording, but has not been found from many hectads since the 1960s, suggesting a genuine decline.

Biogeography Suboceanic Southern-temperate element.

Native		GB	IR
2000–19	●	440	121
1987–99	●	491	137
1970–86	○	373	14
pre-1970	○	423	45

	GB	IR
Long term		
Short term		

Altitude (m) / Distance north (km)

● <1%
● 1–10%
● 11–30%
● 31–40%
● 41–50%
● 51–100%

J F M A M J J A S O N D
☐ Apparency ☐ In flower ☐ In leaf

Key refs Lansdown (2008), Preston & Croft (1997), Schotsman (1967).

R.V. LANSDOWN

Callitriche brutia Pedunculate Water-starwort
Petagna

An annual or perennial herb growing in poached muddy ground, and in permanent and seasonal water bodies, from lakes and pools to rivers, streams and ditches, but almost always in oligotrophic conditions. 0–950 m (Ben Lawers, Mid Perthshire).

Trends This appears to be the most abundant *Callitriche* species in upland regions of Britain and Ireland, as well as in areas such as the New Forest (South Hampshire) and the Lizard Peninsula (West Cornwall). There is no evidence of a change in 10 km square distribution and the map probably provides a good indication of its distribution, but only limited comparison of trends is possible as the two subspecies (subsp. *brutia*, subsp. *hamulata*) were mapped as one species, *C. intermedia*, in the 1962 *Atlas* and few populations are confirmed critically. There is, however, some evidence for loss in south-eastern England which might be real given its requirement for oligotrophic conditions, but this requires confirmation.

Biogeography European Southern-temperate element; it also occurs in Greenland and as an alien in Australia and the west coast of North America.

Native		GB	IR
2000–19	●	1157	158
1987–99	●	1215	205
1970–86	○	839	51
pre-1970	○	1024	120

	GB	IR
Long term		
Short term		

Altitude (m) / Distance north (km)

● <1%
● 1–10%
● 11–30%
● 31–40%
● 41–50%
● 51–100%

J F M A M J J A S O N D
☐ Apparency ☐ In flower ☐ In leaf

Key refs Lansdown (2008), Preston & Croft (1997).

R.V. LANSDOWN

Ne *Verbascum blattaria* Moth Mullein
L.

A usually biennial, winter-green herb, sometimes grown in gardens and found as an escape on waste ground, rough grassland, field-borders, roadsides, active and disused railways, old quarries and gravel-pits, refuse tips and gardens. Occurrences are generally casual, but some populations can be persistent and large. Lowland.

Trends *V. blattaria* was known from the wild by 1629 (Dartford, West Kent). Dunn (1905) described it as scattered irregularly over the central and southern counties of England and its distribution remains much the same, although it appears to have increased over the last 20 years for reasons that are not clear.

Biogeography *V. blattaria* has a Eurosiberian Southern-temperate distribution. It is naturalized in Europe north of its native range.

Alien		GB	IR
2000–19	●	259	4
1987–99	●	124	0
1970–86	●	40	0
pre-1970	○	269	1

	GB	IR
Long term	No trend	No trend
Short term		No trend

Key refs Dunn (1905), Gross & Werner (1978).

A. HORSFALL

Ne *Verbascum virgatum* Twiggy Mullein
Stokes

A usually biennial, winter-green herb, naturalized on dry banks, walls, field margins, rough grassland, pastures and sheltered sea-cliffs in south-western England; elsewhere found as a casual or sometimes persisting on waste ground, refuse tips, re-seeded road verges, sand-pits, tracks, active and disused railways and disturbed coastal dunes. It reproduces by seed, easily colonizing open habitats, but does not tolerate much competition. Lowland.

Trends *V. virgatum* was first recorded in the wild in Britain in 1787 (Worcestershire). Its 10 km square distribution appears stable in Devon and Cornwall, where it has often been considered to be possibly native, but has gradually increased elsewhere, especially in eastern England, where it is much more common now than 30 years ago (Leslie, 2019).

Biogeography A Suboceanic Southern-temperate species.

Alien		GB	IR
2000–19	●	190	33
1987–99	●	170	8
1970–86	●	126	1
pre-1970	○	226	7

	GB	IR
Long term		
Short term		

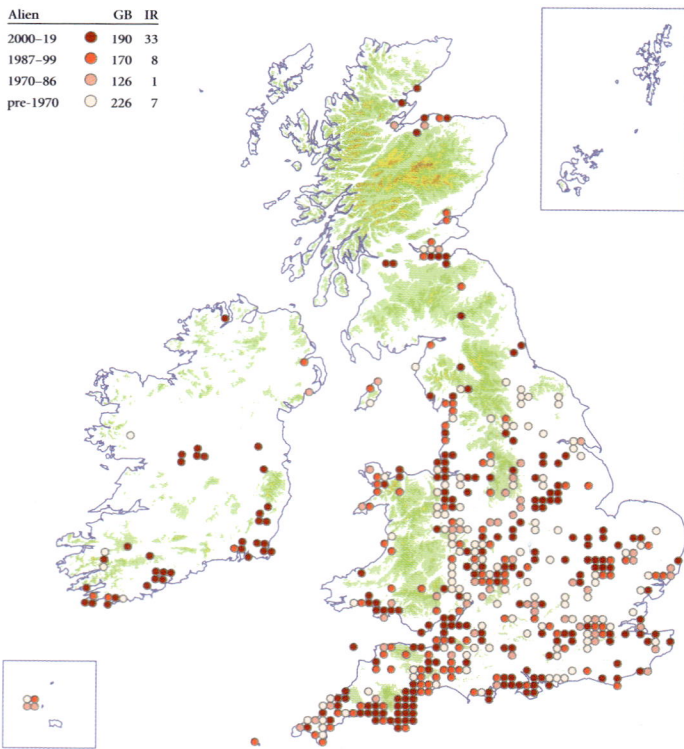

Key refs Leslie (2019), Stewart *et al.* (1994).

A. HORSFALL

Ne *Verbascum phoeniceum* Purple Mullein

L.

A perennial herb, grown in gardens and found as an escape or birdseed alien on refuse tips and waste ground. Lowland.

Trends *V. phoeniceum* had been introduced into cultivation in Britain by 1596, and is not infrequently grown in gardens. It was first recorded from the wild in 1803 (Beaumaris, Anglesey). Its distribution shows a very gradual expansion of both range and density of records over time.

Biogeography Native of Europe and south-western Asia, from Germany and Italy east to Iran, and the Altai mountains.

GB	IR
Long term	No trend	No trend
Short term	⬇ ⬇ ◆ ⬆ ⬆	No trend

Alien	GB	IR
2000–19	26	0
1987–99	13	0
1970–86	7	0
pre-1970	8	0

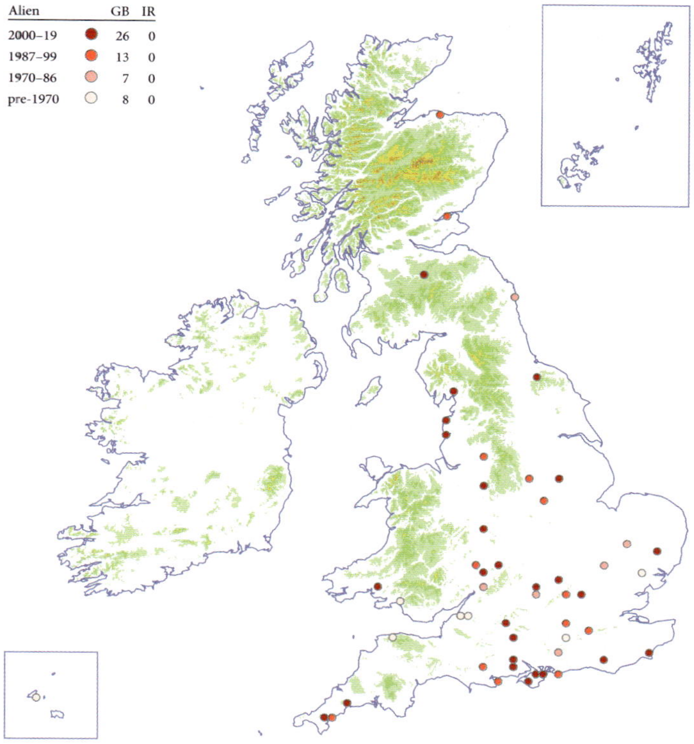

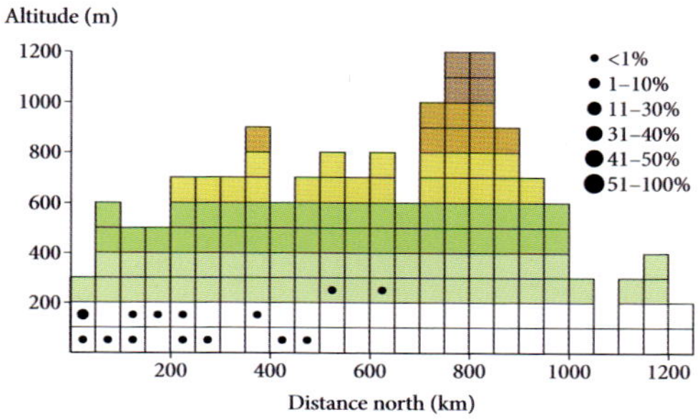

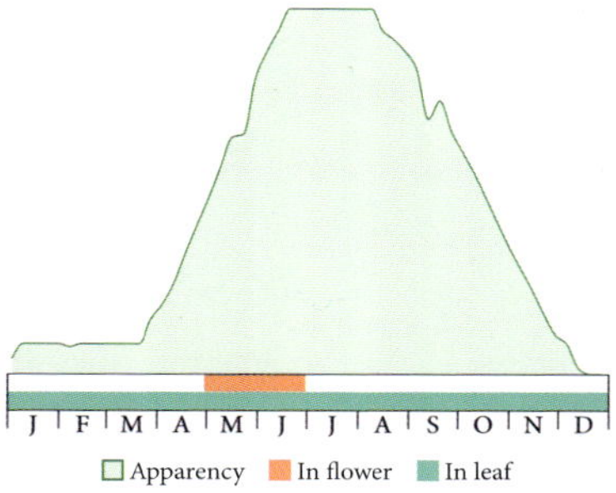

J. PARMENTER & T.D. DINES

Ne *Verbascum phlomoides* Orange Mullein

L.

A winter-green biennial herb, occasionally grown in gardens and found as an escape on roadsides, hedgebanks, open rough ground, refuse tips, old pits, active and disused railways and along field margins, generally on sandy or stony soils. It is sometimes naturalized in central and southern Britain, but occurrences are usually short-lived despite seed being freely produced. Lowland.

Trends *V. phlomoides* was introduced into cultivation in Britain by 1739 and was known from the wild by 1836 (Offington, East Sussex). Although now rarely cultivated, its 10 km square distribution appears to have increased steadily over the last 30 years.

Biogeography *V. phlomoides* has a European Temperate distribution.

GB	IR
Long term	No trend	No trend
Short term	⬇ ⬇ ◆ ⬆ ⬆	⬇ ⬇ ◆ ⬆ ⬆

Alien	GB	IR
2000–19	179	10
1987–99	156	0
1970–86	98	0
pre-1970	122	0

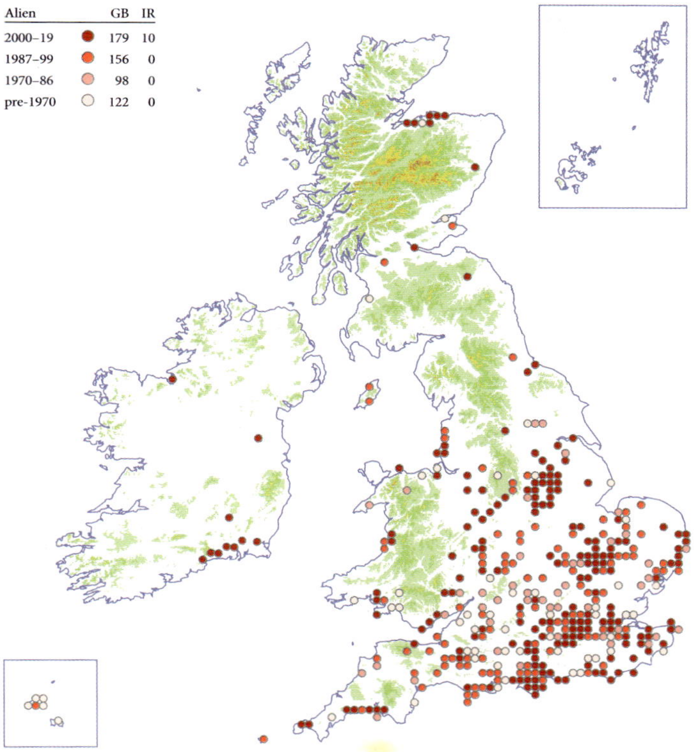

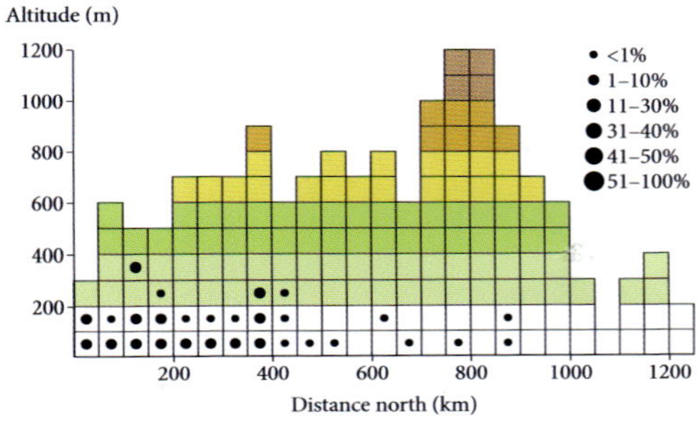

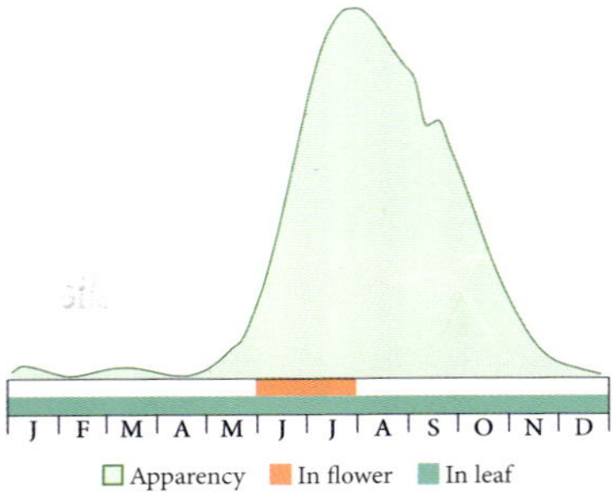

A. HORSFALL

Ne *Verbascum densiflorum* Dense-flowered Mullein
Bertol.

A large, winter-green biennial herb, occasionally grown in gardens and found as an escape on waste ground, roadsides and refuse tips. Populations are usually casual, but occasionally may persist for a few years. Lowland.

Trends This species has been grown in gardens since 1817. The earliest report out of cultivation is from St Anne's (West Lancashire) in 1907, though according to Dunn (1905) it was occasionally recorded as a garden escape in England. It may be over-recorded for *V. thapsus*, and for *V. phlomoides* and its hybrids, but appears to have been recorded more frequently in south-eastern England in the last 20 years.

Biogeography A European Temperate species, but rare or absent as a native from westernmost Europe.

		GB	IR
Long term	No trend		No trend
Short term			

Alien		GB	IR
2000–19	●	110	4
1987–99	●	77	3
1970–86	●	13	0
pre-1970	○	22	0

Key refs Dunn (1905).

Altitude (m) — Distance north (km)

● <1%
● 1–10%
● 11–30%
● 31–40%
● 41–50%
● 51–100%

Apparency | In flower | In leaf

S. Lambert & T.D. Dines

N *Verbascum thapsus* Great Mullein
L.

A biennial herb of open scrub and hedgebanks, waysides, railway banks and sidings, rough grassy places, waste ground and quarries. It prefers well-drained soils, especially those over a sand, gravel or chalk substrate. It produces copious quantities of long-lived seed and may become an abundant colonist. It is cultivated in gardens and frequently escapes, becoming established on refuse tips or where thrown out. 0–570 m (Hartside Quarry, Cumberland).

Trends There has been little change in the overall 10 km square distribution of *V. thapsus* since the 1960s. The map probably overestimates its occurrence as a native and underestimates the extent to which it occurs as an alien.

Biogeography Eurosiberian Temperate element; widely naturalized outside its native range.

		GB	IR
Long term			
Short term			

Native		GB	IR
2000–19	●	1843	406
1987–99	●	1689	305
1970–86	●	1126	46
pre-1970	○	1498	137

Alien		GB	IR
2000–19	●	49	4
1987–99	●	40	7
1970–86	●	21	0
pre-1970	○	26	3

Key refs Gross & Werner (1978).

Altitude (m) — Distance north (km)

● <1%
● 1–10%
● 11–30%
● 31–40%
● 41–50%
● 51–100%

Apparency | In flower | In leaf

A. Horsfall

Hy *Verbascum nigrum × thapsus = V. ×semialbum*
Chaub.

This sterile, often short-lived perennial is not infrequent where the parents grow together (Easy, 2006), and has been recorded in the apparent absence of *V. nigrum*. It is perhaps most frequent on disturbed chalky soil but is also known from sand-pits, coastal shingle beaches, disused railway lines and sidings, waste ground and refuse tips. Lowland.

A spontaneous hybrid (native × native).

Trends *V. ×semialbum* was first known to British botanists as a spontaneous hybrid which appeared in the garden of E. Robson in 1790, and only subsequently discovered in the wild, at Barton near Swaffham (West Norfolk), by Dawson Turner. It is probably under-recorded.

Biogeography Widespread in Europe.

	GB	IR
Long term	No trend	No trend
Short term	No trend	No trend

	GB	IR
2000–19	32	0
1987–99	27	0
1970–86	17	0
pre-1970	28	0

Key refs Easy (2006), Stace *et al.* (2015).

C.A. STACE, C.D. PRESTON & D.A. PEARMAN

Altitude (m)

<1%
1–10%
11–30%
31–40%
41–50%
51–100%

Distance north (km)

Apparency In flower In leaf

J F M A M J J A S O N D

Ne *Verbascum chaixii* Nettle-leaved Mullein
Vill.

A biennial or perennial herb with a well-branched inflorescence and usually yellow flowers. It arises as a grain contaminant or, increasingly, as a garden escape and occurs on waste and rough ground. It is naturalized at several sites, but is usually casual. Lowland.

Trends *V. chaixii* was introduced into cultivation in Britain in 1818, and is a popular garden plant. It was known from the wild by 1892 (Abbotsbury, Dorset). Early records may have been confused with *V. pyramidatum*. It may also be overlooked for *V. nigrum*. Records are scattered throughout England and extend into Scotland.

Biogeography *V. chaixii* has a Eurosiberian distribution; native of southern and central Europe, and western Asia.

	GB	IR
Long term	No trend	No trend
Short term		No trend

Alien	GB	IR
2000–19	35	0
1987–99	10	0
1970–86	2	0
pre-1970	9	0

Altitude (m)

<1%
1–10%
11–30%
31–40%
41–50%
51–100%

Distance north (km)

Apparency In flower In leaf

J F M A M J J A S O N D

J. PARMENTER & T.D. DINES

N *Verbascum nigrum* Dark Mullein
L.

A biennial or short-lived perennial herb of road verges and embankments, in hedgebanks and other grassy places, on walls and in cultivated ground, including arable field margins. It prefers well-drained calcareous soils. 0–354 m (Garchory, South Aberdeenshire).

Native in Britain and the Channel Islands and a neophyte in Ireland.

Trends *V. nigrum* is a mobile species with a dynamic life-history; changes in the management of hedgebanks and roadsides may be responsible for local losses, but can also be of benefit in assisting the dispersal of seed to new areas. This species is often grown in gardens, and the distinction between native and alien populations has become more blurred as garden escapes become more frequent.

Biogeography Eurosiberian Temperate element.

Native		GB	IR
2000–19	●	397	0
1987–99	●	351	0
1970–86	○	232	0
pre-1970	○	385	0

Alien		GB	IR
2000–19	●	177	6
1987–99	●	107	3
1970–86	●	86	0
pre-1970	○	132	1

Altitude (m) chart — key:
● <1%
● 1–10%
● 11–30%
● 31–40%
● 41–50%
● 51–100%

Distance north (km)

J F M A M J J A S O N D
☐ Apparency ☐ In flower ☐ In leaf

A. HORSFALL

Ne *Verbascum speciosum* Hungarian Mullein
Schrad.

A winter-green biennial herb, grown in gardens and found as an escape on roadsides and tracksides, waste ground, spoil heaps, railway sidings and other disturbed habitats. Populations are usually short-lived, although it persists at a few sites. Lowland.

Trends *V. speciosum* was introduced into cultivation in Britain in 1818 and is quite widely grown in gardens. It was first recorded from the wild in 1909 (West Gloucestershire); its distribution is much better known this century.

Biogeography Native of south-eastern Europe and south-western Asia.

	GB	IR
Long term	No trend	No trend
Short term		No trend

Alien		GB	IR
2000–19	●	81	0
1987–99	●	17	0
1970–86	●	11	0
pre-1970	○	12	0

Altitude (m) chart — key:
● <1%
● 1–10%
● 11–30%
● 31–40%
● 41–50%
● 51–100%

Distance north (km)

J F M A M J J A S O N D
☐ Apparency ☐ In flower ☐ In leaf

J. PARMENTER & T.D. DINES

N? *Verbascum pulverulentum* Hoary Mullein
Vill.

A monocarpic perennial herb of roadside verges and railway banks, in old quarries and gravel-pits, in hedgebanks, rough ground, and locally on coastal shingle and dry grassland over river terrace deposits (its only 'natural' habitats). Outside its core area it is usually a casual of waste ground. Seed remains viable for many years and new populations can appear after soil disturbance. Lowland.

Native or alien in Britain and a neophyte in the Channel Islands.

Trends *V. pulverulentum* was first recorded in Britain in 1670. Since the 1960s its 10 km square distribution has become much better known as a result of more systematic recording, and it appears to spreading away from its two main centres of distribution; the first on shingle and dry grasslands between Snettisham and Heacham (West Norfolk), and the second on river terrace deposits near Norwich (East Norfolk). In recent years the latter population has expanded out onto road verges, arable field margins and other dry, disturbed habitats in the surrounding area.

Biogeography Submediterranean-Subatlantic element.

Native	GB	IR
2000–19	42	0
1987–99	41	0
1970–86	35	0
pre-1970	38	0

Alien	GB	IR
2000–19	42	0
1987–99	23	0
1970–86	16	0
pre-1970	22	0

Key refs Beckett & Bull (1999), Stewart *et al.* (1994).

A. HORSFALL, M. SANFORD & J. PARMENTER

N *Verbascum lychnitis* White Mullein
L.

A biennial, or occasionally short-lived perennial, herb of dry, usually calcareous soil, occurring in rough pastures, recently cleared woodland, on railway embankments, tracksides and road verges and in quarries and waste places. It produces large amounts of seed that remains viable for many years. It freely hybridizes with other *Verbascum* species. Lowland.

Native in Britain and a neophyte in Ireland.

Trends There has been little change in the overall 10 km square distribution of *V. lychnitis* since the 1960s, but because it depends on periodic disturbance its abundance locally can vary markedly from year to year. Large populations can arise where woodland is cleared in forestry operations or as a result of storm damage.

Biogeography European Temperate element.

Native	GB	IR
2000–19	22	0
1987–99	24	0
1970–86	24	0
pre-1970	35	0

Alien	GB	IR
2000–19	56	2
1987–99	49	0
1970–86	31	0
pre-1970	100	0

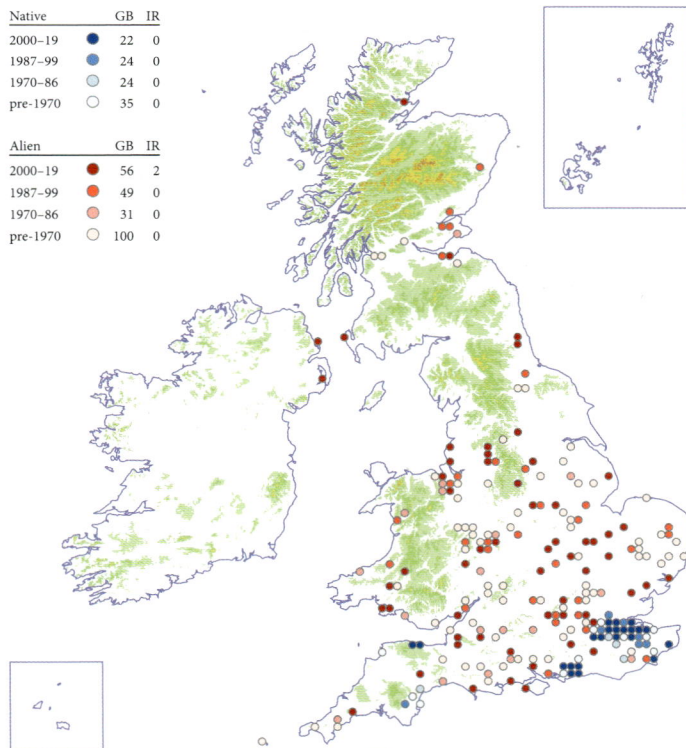

Key refs Stewart *et al.* (1994).

A. HORSFALL & M. SANFORD

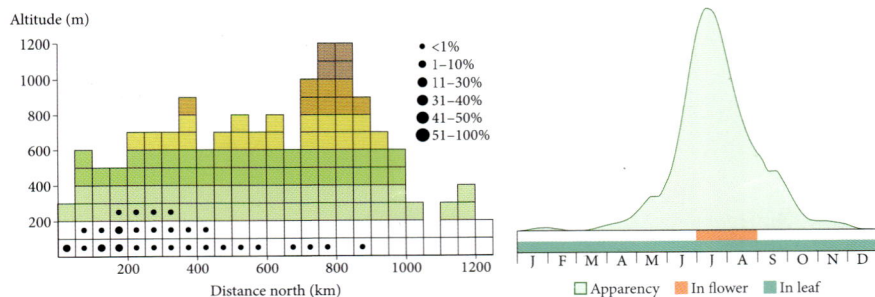

Scrophularia nodosa Common Figwort
L.

A perennial herb of open or shaded habitats, preferring fertile soils and found in damp woodland, woodland rides, hedgebanks, ditches and riversides, and sometimes in drier sites on waste ground. Generally lowland, but reaching 504 m near Great Punchard Gill (North-west Yorkshire).

Trends *S. nodosa* is now much better recorded in Scotland and Ireland than in the 1960s and its overall 10 km square distribution appears to be stable.

Biogeography Eurosiberian Temperate element.

Native		GB	IR
2000–19	●	2292	879
1987–99	●	2174	789
1970–86	○	1374	110
pre-1970	○	2102	625

Altitude (m)

- <1%
- 1–10%
- 11–30%
- 31–40%
- 41–50%
- 51–100%

Distance north (km)

Apparency   In flower   In leaf

A. HORSFALL & K.J. WALKER

Scrophularia auriculata Water Figwort
L.

A partially winter-green perennial herb that grows on the margins of ponds, pits, lakes, rivers, streams and canals, and in ditches, fen drains, marshes, wet meadows, fens and wet woodlands. It is occasionally found also growing on disused railways, waste ground and walls. *S. auriculata* is much more strongly associated with water than *S. nodosa*, with which it is sometimes confused. Usually lowland, but reaching 410 m at Trefil (Breconshire) and 442 m at Gwaun Helen (Glamorganshire).

Trends The 10 km square distribution of *S. auriculata* is broadly similar to that in the 1960s although the expansion in range noted the 2002 *Atlas* appears to have continued and it is now much more widespread in northern England, Scotland, Wales and Ireland. Although this undoubtedly reflects more thorough recording it may represent a genuine increase in some areas. Its status in Scotland is uncertain and a number of records from northern Scotland have been discounted as errors for *S. nodosa*.

Biogeography Suboceanic Southern-temperate element.

Native		GB	IR
2000–19	●	1573	640
1987–99	●	1392	409
1970–86	○	1046	35
pre-1970	○	1275	251

Alien		GB	IR
2000–19	●	60	0
1987–99	●	13	0
1970–86	○	3	0
pre-1970	○	5	0

Altitude (m)

- <1%
- 1–10%
- 11–30%
- 31–40%
- 41–50%
- 51–100%

Distance north (km)

Apparency   In flower   In leaf

A. HORSFALL & K.J. WALKER

Scrophularia umbrosa Green Figwort

N

Dumort.

A rhizomatous perennial herb of fertile soils by streams, rivers, canals, along floodplain ditches and in damp woodlands, scrub and carr, in both open and shaded places. Also an occasional garden weed. Generally lowland.

Trends Although *S. umbrosa* is treated as native it may be a relatively recent colonist. It was first recorded in Britain in 1840 (Shropshire) and in Ireland in 1895 (County Dublin). Its patchy distribution is puzzling, though it continues to be found in new sites, perhaps in part due to better recording. Since 2000 the known northern limits of *S. umbrosa* have been extended to South Aberdeenshire, although populations here are thought to be of garden origin.

Biogeography Eurosiberian Temperate element, with a continental distribution in western Europe.

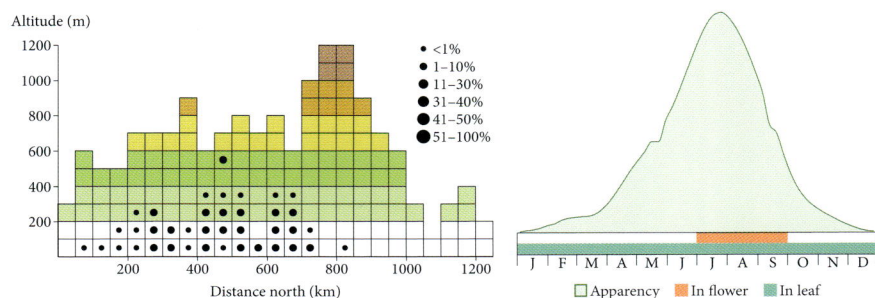

Native	GB	IR
2000–19	125	6
1987–99	128	9
1970–86	120	4
pre-1970	128	9

Alien	GB	IR
2000–19	4	0
1987–99	1	0
1970–86	0	0
pre-1970	2	0

Key refs Stewart *et al.* (1994).

A. HORSFALL & N. ASPEY

Scrophularia scorodonia Balm-leaved Figwort

Ne

L.

A long-lived perennial herb of hedgebanks, scrubby field-borders, rough ground on cliff-tops, waste places, disused quarries and old walls. Lowland.

Trends *S. scorodonia* was known in Jersey from 1690 and in Cornwall since 1700. It is often claimed as a probable native, but it is more likely to have been accidentally introduced, as for nearly 300 years mainland sites were in ruderal habitats near to ports (Pearman, 2007). In the last two decades there has been a very marked expansion in Cornwall and Devon and a number of new records farther afield, most notably in southern Wales and Scotland.

Biogeography Oceanic Southern-temperate element; as a native confined to western Europe and north-western Morocco.

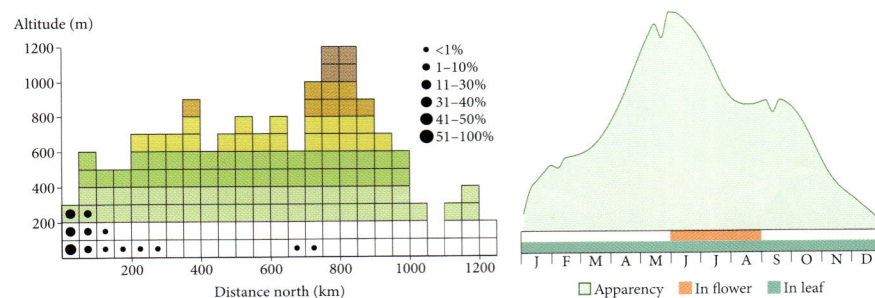

Alien	GB	IR
2000–19	83	0
1987–99	63	0
1970–86	35	0
pre-1970	48	0

Key refs Dupont (1962), Pearman (2007), Wigginton (1999).

D.A. PEARMAN

Ne *Scrophularia vernalis* Yellow Figwort
L.

A winter-green biennial to perennial herb, occasionally grown in gardens and found naturalized on pavements, road verges and waste ground and in woodland clearings, plantations, hedgebanks and rough waste ground, usually in shade. Lowland.

Trends *S. vernalis* was grown in gardens by 1617, but has always been an uncommon garden plant. It was first recorded in the wild in 1762 (Mitcham, Surrey) though Parkinson noted it as a weed in his garden before 1640. By the 18th century it was known from several localities in, for example, Surrey, Sussex and north Wales, and it had become naturalized throughout Britain by 1930. The number of records has substantially increased since the 1960s, particularly in eastern and north-eastern Scotland.

Biogeography Native of the mountains of central and southern Europe and the Caucasus.

Alien		GB	IR
2000–19	●	90	0
1987–99	●	115	0
1970–86	●	81	0
pre-1970	○	124	0

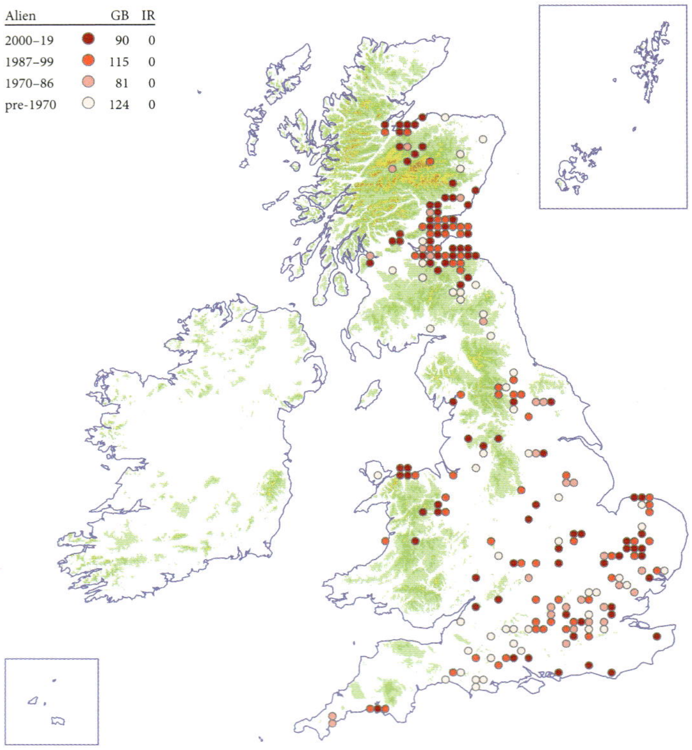

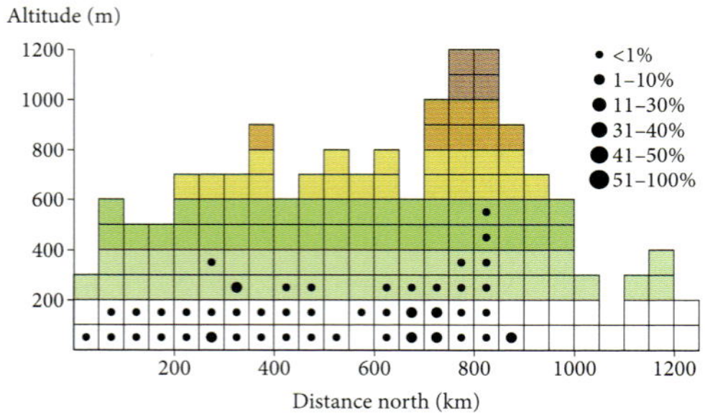

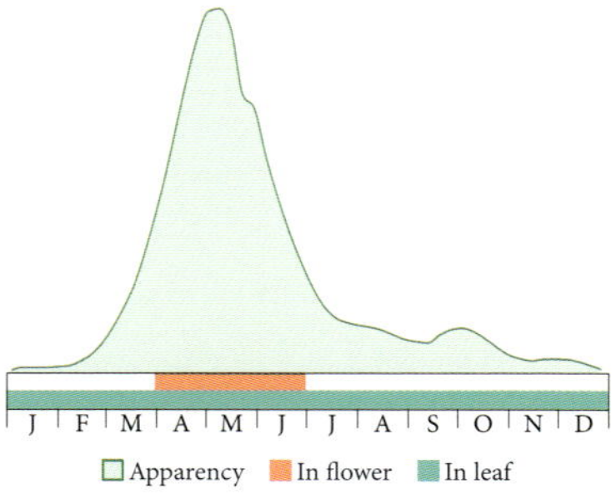

Key refs Salisbury (1964).

D.A. Pearman

Ne *Phygelius capensis* Cape Figwort
E.Mey. ex Benth.

An evergreen shrub which was naturalized on a river bank at Little Bray (County Dublin) and also occurs on rough ground near gardens, and as a relic of cultivation. Reproduction is mainly vegetative, by suckers, but also by seed. Usually lowland, but to 347 m north-east of Glenmazeran Lodge (Easterness).

Trends *P. capensis* was introduced into cultivation in Britain in 1855. It was recorded from the wild in 1960 (near Newton Stewart, Wigtownshire). However, many of the plants recorded or sold as this might well be the hybrid with *P. aequalis* (*P.* ×*rectus*) which is now much more widely grown.

Biogeography Native of South Africa.

Alien		GB	IR
2000–19	●	59	18
1987–99	●	13	0
1970–86	●	3	1
pre-1970	○	1	0

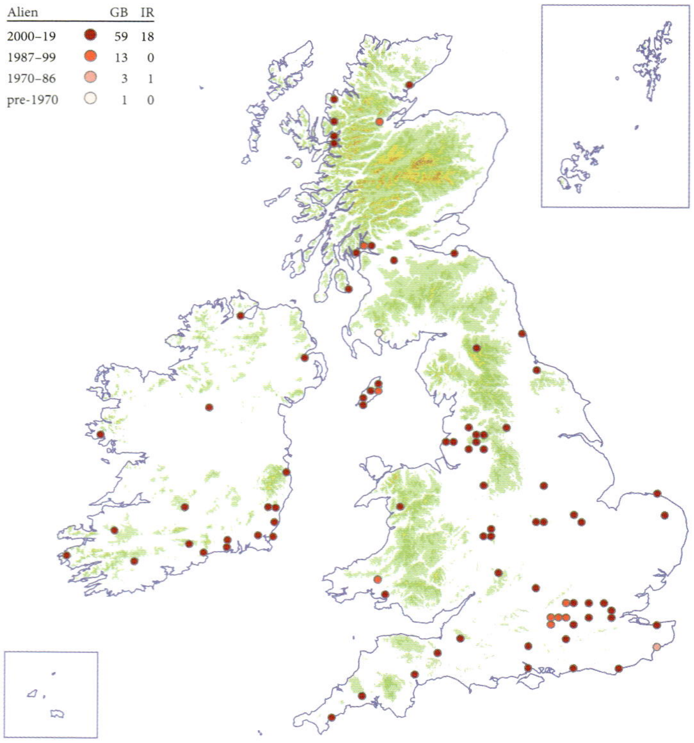

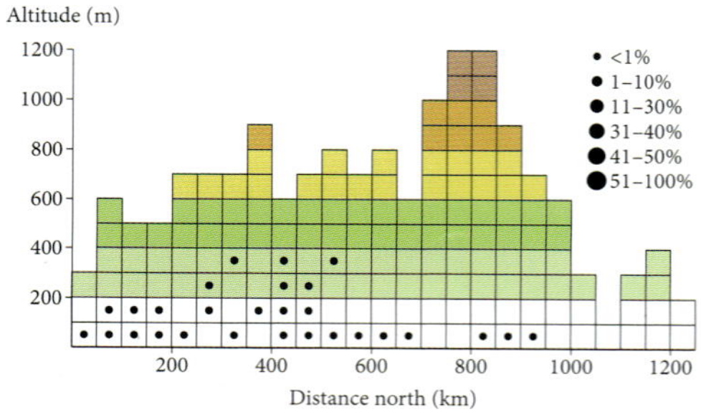

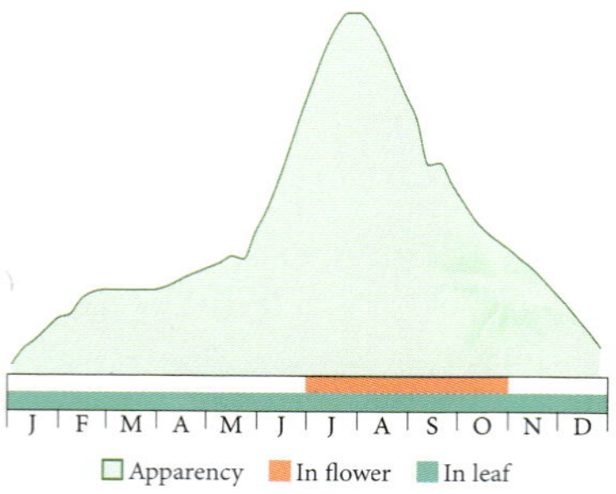

Key refs Bean (1976).

T.D. Dines & D.A. Pearman

Ne *Chaenostoma cordatum* Bacopa
Benth.

A perennial herb, woody at the base, but here grown mainly as an annual, particularly for hanging baskets, pots and window boxes. It readily self-sows onto pavements where it can persist for a year or two. Lowland.

Trends *C. cordatum* was introduced here possibly by 1816, but certainly by 1845. However, it was not until the latter half of the 20th century that it became a popular plant in hanging baskets. It was first recorded in the wild in 1997 (Birmingham, Warwickshire), and the many records since then reflect its increasing recent popularity.

Biogeography Native of South Africa.

	GB	IR
Long term	No trend	No trend
Short term	↑	No trend

Alien	GB	IR
2000–19	107	5
1987–99	3	0
1970–86	0	0
pre-1970	0	0

D.A. Pearman

Altitude (m) — Distance north (km)

● <1%
● 1–10%
● 11–30%
● 31–40%
● 41–50%
● 51–100%

☐ Apparency ☐ In flower ☐ In leaf

J F M A M J J A S O N D

Ne *Nemesia strumosa* Cape-jewels
Benth.

An annual herb, widely grown in gardens and in hanging baskets and window boxes, and available in a wide range of colours. It is found occasionally as a garden outcast such as on refuse tips, or self-sown on pavements. Lowland.

Trends *N. strumosa* was introduced by Suttons Seeds in 1892, and apparently first recorded in 1912 (Pitstone Hill, Buckinghamshire) (Druce, 1926). An increase in records this century is probably related to a greater interest in the recording of street weeds

Biogeography A native of the coast in Western Cape, South Africa.

	GB	IR
Long term	No trend	No trend
Short term	↑	No trend

Alien	GB	IR
2000–19	46	0
1987–99	4	0
1970–86	0	0
pre-1970	2	0

Key refs Druce (1926).

Altitude (m) — Distance north (km)

● <1%
● 1–10%
● 11–30%
● 31–40%
● 41–50%
● 51–100%

☐ Apparency ☐ In flower ☐ In leaf

J F M A M J J A S O N D

D.A. Pearman

Limosella aquatica Mudwort

L.

An annual herb of the muddy edges of rivers, lakes, reservoirs, pools, ditches, rutted tracks, roadsides and other ephemeral wet habitats. In the Burren (County Clare) it also occurs in limestone solution hollows. It may prefer mildly acidic, nutrient-enriched soils. Plants reproduce by seed and also spread by stolons. 0–455 m (Malham Moor, Mid-west Yorkshire).

Trends This species is erratic in appearance, with natural and substantial seasonal fluctuations in populations. Although many losses occurred before 1930, the species continued to decline into the latter half of the 20th century, mainly due to drainage of wetlands, the infilling of ponds and lack of grazing. However, there has been a notable increase in records, most apparent in Scotland and to a lesser extent in Ireland and northern England,

largely as a result of the creation of new wetland habitats and its dispersal by wildfowl, in particular resident populations of Greylag *Anser anser* and Canada Geese *Branta canadensis*.

Biogeography Circumpolar Boreo-temperate element.

Native	GB	IR
2000–19	113	12
1987–99	77	7
1970–86	47	8
pre-1970	164	6

Alien	GB	IR
2000–19	0	0
1987–99	0	0
1970–86	0	0
pre-1970	1	0

Key refs Stewart *et al.* (1994).

Altitude (m) / *Distance north (km)*

Apparency *In flower* *In leaf*

A. HORSFALL & N. ASPEY

Limosella australis Welsh Mudwort

R.Br.

An annual to short-lived perennial herb of intertidal mudflats and saltmarsh pools, occurring as scattered plants or in dense swards. Reproduction by seed occurs, but plants spread mostly by stolons. Lowland.

Trends This species was first recorded in Glamorganshire in 1897, but colonies in south Wales had probably died out by the 1940s. It was not found in north Wales until 1921. It can be locally abundant, but numbers fluctuate markedly from year to year. It has been suggested that it might be a recent arrival, or even a ballast-alien (Jones, 1991), but the evidence for this remains inconclusive (Jones, 2020b).

Biogeography Oceanic Boreo-temperate element; in Europe restricted to Wales, but widespread in coastal regions of eastern North America.

	GB	IR
Long term	No trend	No trend
Short term	No trend	No trend

Native	GB	IR
2000–19	5	0
1987–99	4	0
1970–86	3	0
pre-1970	4	0

Key refs Jones (1991), Jones (2020b), Kay & John (1995), Wigginton (1999).

Altitude (m) / *Distance north (km)*

Apparency *In flower* *In leaf*

A. HORSFALL & S. LAMBERT

Ne *Buddleja davidii* Butterfly-bush

Franch.

A large deciduous or semi-evergreen shrub, now very commonly encountered on waste ground, by railways and canals, in abandoned quarries, on roadsides and in a wide variety of micro-habitats in urban areas including pavements, walls and derelict buildings. It prefers dry, disturbed ground where large populations can develop from its wind-dispersed seed. It can form dense thickets reducing ground flora and invertebrate diversity locally, especially in chalk grassland, such as at Folkestone Warren (East Kent). Usually lowland, but reaching 404 m at Lady Canning's Plantation (Derbyshire).

Trends *B. davidii* was introduced into cultivation in 1896, and quickly became very popular in gardens. It was known to be naturalized in the wild by 1922 (Harlech, Merionethshire). Its range increased greatly on bomb-damaged sites in urban areas after 1945 and it was well-established in southern England by the 1960s. Its distribution continues to increase, with many more records in the 21st century from northern Britain and Ireland.

Biogeography Native of China.

Alien	GB	IR
2000–19	2000	601
1987–99	1435	262
1970–86	665	21
pre-1970	481	23

Key refs Clay & Drinkall (2001).

T.D. DINES & N. ASPEY

Hy *Buddleja davidii × globosa = B. ×weyeriana* Weyer's Butterfly-bush

Weyer

A deciduous or semi-evergreen shrub which occurs as a naturalized garden escape, and as a planted shrub, in hedgerows and on roadsides and rough ground. Lowland.

A cultivated hybrid (alien × alien).

Trends This hybrid was first exhibited in 1920, and was first recorded from the wild in 1976 (Truro, West Cornwall). Some of the records on the map are likely to be of planted origin.

Biogeography A hybrid of garden origin.

	GB	IR
2000–19	60	3
1987–99	20	0
1970–86	4	0
pre-1970	1	0

Key refs Stace *et al.* (2015).

C.A. STACE, C.D. PRESTON & D.A. PEARMAN

Ne *Buddleja globosa* Orange-ball-tree
Hope

A large deciduous or semi-evergreen shrub, found as a garden escape or throw-out, and as a planted shrub, on buildings, roadsides, railway-banks, in hedges, woodland edge, waste ground, by streams, ponds and as a relic of cultivation. Reproduction is by seed. Lowland.

Trends Introduced into cultivation in 1774, *B. globosa* has become a popular garden plant. It was rarely recorded in the wild in the 20th century, but since 2000 there are many more records. This might in part be due to better recording of aliens, but there is almost certainly also an element of genuine spread and naturalization.

Biogeography Native of South America (Chile, Peru).

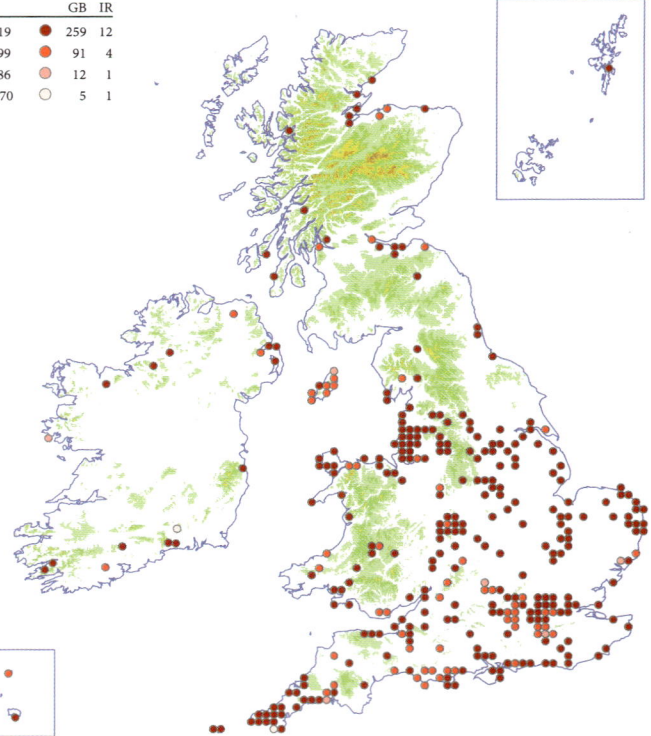

Alien		GB	IR
2000–19	●	259	12
1987–99	●	91	4
1970–86	●	12	1
pre-1970	○	5	1

	GB	IR
Long term	No trend	No trend
Short term	↓ ↓ · ↑ **↑**	↓ ↓ · ↑ **↑**

Key refs Bean (1970), Coats (1963).

Altitude (m)

• <1%
● 1–10%
● 11–30%
● 31–40%
● 41–50%
● 51–100%

Distance north (km)

J F M A M J J A S O N D
☐ Apparency ■ In flower ■ In leaf

T.D. DINES & N. ASPEY

Ne *Acanthus mollis* Bear's-breech
L.

A robust, clump-forming perennial herb, persisting where it is dumped from gardens in sites such as roadsides, railway banks, waste places and in woodlands. Flowering is irregular, particularly in shaded sites. Although seed is produced, spread is almost exclusively through dispersal of root fragments. Lowland.

Trends This plant is popular in gardens for its attractive foliage, and has been cultivated in our area since at least 1548. It was first recorded in the wild in 1820 (Penzance, West Cornwall), and is increasingly found naturalized near gardens, around urban fringes and where garden refuse is tipped. In the extreme south-west of Britain it is more likely to be found in semi-natural vegetation. While undoubtedly better recorded, there has

been a continuing genuine increase in the wild since the 2002 *Atlas*.

Biogeography Native of the Mediterranean region.

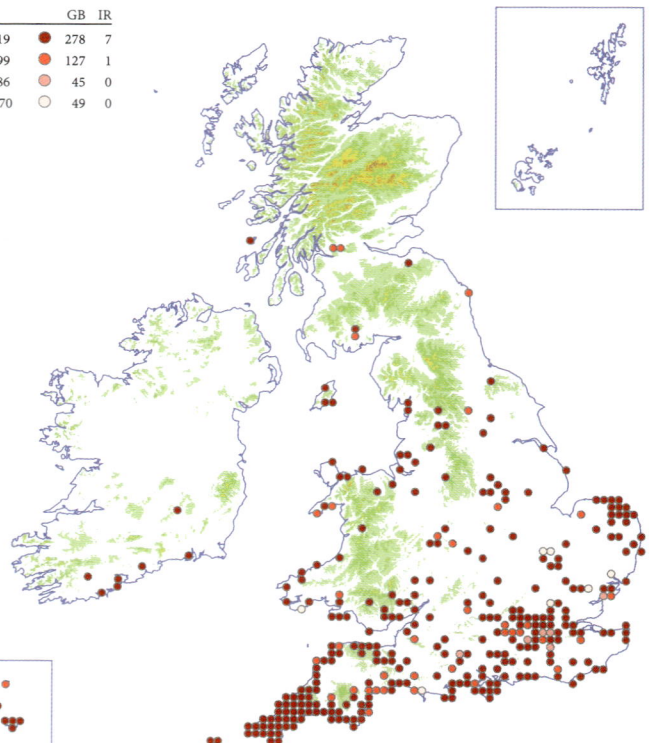

Alien		GB	IR
2000–19	●	278	7
1987–99	●	127	1
1970–86	●	45	0
pre-1970	○	49	0

	GB	IR
Long term	No trend	No trend
Short term	↓ ↓ · ↑ **↑**	↓ ↓ · ↑ **↑**

Altitude (m)

• <1%
● 1–10%
● 11–30%
● 31–40%
● 41–50%
● 51–100%

Distance north (km)

J F M A M J J A S O N D
☐ Apparency ■ In flower ■ In leaf

F.J. RUMSEY, T.D. DINES & N. ASPEY

Ne *Acanthus spinosus* Spiny Bear's-breech
L.

A large perennial herb found as a naturalized garden escape on roadsides, railway banks, by canals, in scrub and on waste ground. Lowland.

Trends *A. spinosus* had been introduced into cultivation in Britain by 1629, and possibly as early as during Roman times. It is popular in gardens for its decorative foliage and flowers. It was known from the wild by 1942 (Bristol, West Gloucestershire), and may be increasing its naturalized range due to climate warming.

Biogeography Native of the Mediterranean region, from Italy eastwards.

	GB	IR
Long term	No trend	No trend
Short term		No trend

Alien	GB	IR
2000–19	50	0
1987–99	22	0
1970–86	10	0
pre-1970	11	0

Altitude (m) — Distance north (km)

- <1%
- 1–10%
- 11–30%
- 31–40%
- 41–50%
- 51–100%

Apparency — In flower — In leaf

T.D. DINES & N. ASPEY

N *Pinguicula lusitanica* Pale Butterwort
L.

An insectivorous perennial herb which retains its insect-trapping leaves through the winter. It grows on damp bare peat and at the bases of grass, rush or sedge tussocks beside moorland rills, drainage ditches on former bogs, acidic flushes and wet heaths, often in places trampled by livestock or deer. 0–490 m (Dartmoor, South Devon, and the Mourne Mountains, County Down).

Trends *P. lusitanica* is an easily overlooked species which has declined in some lowland areas since the 1960s, largely through loss of habitat, changes in management and scrub encroachment, though overall its distribution appears to have stabilized this century, and with many new locations discovered, most notably in Ireland, due to fuller recording.

Biogeography Oceanic Temperate element.

	GB	IR
Long term		
Short term		

Native	GB	IR
2000–19	404	256
1987–99	342	215
1970–86	188	40
pre-1970	446	190

Altitude (m) — Distance north (km)

- <1%
- 1–10%
- 11–30%
- 31–40%
- 41–50%
- 51–100%

Apparency — In flower — In leaf

Key refs Dupont (1962), Heslop-Harrison (2004).

F.J. RUMSEY

Pinguicula alpina Alpine Butterwort

L.

A small, rosette-forming, insectivorous perennial herb formerly known from one site, described as a bog or moor. In mainland Europe, it grows in base-rich flushes, stony mires and the drier parts of open boggy heathland, often at high altitude. Lowland.

Trends *P. alpina* was known from a single site near Avoch (Easter Ross), where it was first reported in 1831 and last recorded before 1919. It gradually declined as its site was encroached upon by cultivation and colonized by seedling conifers; it was also heavily collected. Its restriction to this single, otherwise unremarkable, lowland mire has led to suspicions that it may have been planted.

Biogeography Eurosiberian Arctic-montane element.

	GB	IR
Long term	No trend	No trend
Short term	No trend	No trend

Native	GB	IR
2000–19	0	0
1987–99	0	0
1970–86	0	0
pre-1970	1	0

Key refs Heslop-Harrison (2004), Lusby (1998), Marren (1999).

F.J. RUMSEY

Pinguicula vulgaris Common Butterwort

L.

A rosette-forming, insectivorous perennial herb of damp, nutrient-poor, acidic or base-rich habitats, overwintering as a rootless bud. It is found in blanket bogs, in crevices of irrigated rocks and rock ledges, in base-poor as well as base-rich open flushes, and in open bryophyte-dominated communities in fens. 0–1,020 m (Meall Garbh, Mid Perthshire).

Trends Many lowland sites of *P. vulgaris* were lost before the end of the 19th century due to drainage and agricultural intensification. This loss has continued, with over half the 10 km squares which remained in central and southern areas of lowland England after 1930 now lost, including many in Norfolk. Its distribution elsewhere appears to be stable. Small, isolated populations in the lowlands appear to have lower seed-set due to infection by the anther smut *Microbryum pinguiculae* (Smith *et al.*, 2021b).

Biogeography Circumpolar Boreal-montane element, with a disjunct distribution.

Native	GB	IR
2000–19	1204	376
1987–99	1229	371
1970–86	816	77
pre-1970	1378	339

Alien	GB	IR
2000–19	1	0
1987–99	0	0
1970–86	1	0
pre-1970	2	0

Key refs Heslop-Harrison (2004), Smith *et al.* (2021b).

F.J. RUMSEY

N *Pinguicula grandiflora* Large-flowered Butterwort
Lam.

A rosette-forming, insectivorous perennial herb, overwintering as a rootless bud which also functions as a vegetative propagule. It is found on wet rocks, flushed moorland and acidic bogs. 0–950 m (Howling Ridge, Carrauntoohil, South Kerry).

Native in Ireland and a neophyte in Britain.

Trends There has been little change in the native Irish range of *P. grandiflora*, where this species may be locally abundant. It has been planted in damp places and is occasionally naturalized in Britain, although perhaps unsurprisingly there have been a greater proportion of losses in these introduced sites.

Biogeography Oceanic Temperate element.

		GB	IR
Long term	No trend		
Short term	No trend		

Native		GB	IR
2000–19	●	0	69
1987–99	●	0	65
1970–86	●	0	10
pre-1970	○	0	25

Alien		GB	IR
2000–19	●	5	2
1987–99	●	8	2
1970–86	●	7	2
pre-1970	○	8	3

Key refs Scully (1916).

F.J. RUMSEY

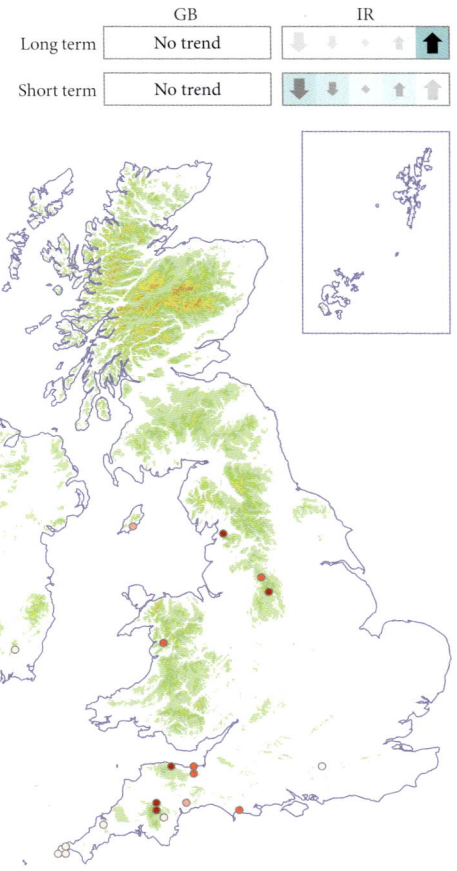

N *Utricularia vulgaris* agg.

Free-floating, insectivorous perennial herbs of still or sluggish, acidic to basic, nutrient-poor waters over inorganic or peaty substrates. Flowering is irregular, and reproduction is usually by turions. Generally lowland, but reaching 640 m in Atholl (East Perthshire).

Trends This aggregate, which comprises *U. australis* and *U. vulgaris*, is much better recorded in Scotland and Northern Ireland than it was in the 1962 *Atlas*. It has declined in many areas, mainly due to drainage, peatland destruction and eutrophication. The two species can only be distinguished from one another with certainty when flowering, and the incidence of this decreases northwards.

Biogeography The distribution of the two species is given in their respective accounts.

	GB	IR
Long term	No trend	No trend
Short term	No trend	No trend

Native		GB	IR
2000–19	●	300	148
1987–99	●	392	167
1970–86	●	189	61
pre-1970	○	522	177

Alien		GB	IR
2000–19	●	6	0
1987–99	●	9	0
1970–86	●	0	0
pre-1970	○	4	0

Key refs Taylor (1989).

F.J. RUMSEY

Utricularia vulgaris Greater Bladderwort

L.

A free-floating, insectivorous perennial herb of oligotrophic and mesotrophic, base-rich waters. Habitats include sheltered bays in limestone lakes, ponds, ditches and pools in calcareous fens and grazing marshes, and flooded clay-, marl-, and gravel-pits. Flowering is temperature dependent, variable annually, and less frequent in the north of its range. Generally lowland, but the precise upper altitudinal limit is unknown.

Trends The map is based largely on flowering plants together with records of vegetative plants identified by Taylor (1989), and the range of the species is probably to an extent underestimated. Distributional changes are difficult to determine, but the species does appear to have declined in lowland England due to acidification and eutrophication of its wetland habitats.

Biogeography Eurosiberian Temperate element.

Native	GB	IR
2000–19	67	26
1987–99	85	42
1970–86	59	27
pre-1970	135	24

Alien	GB	IR
2000–19	2	0
1987–99	3	0
1970–86	0	0
pre-1970	1	0

Key refs Preston & Croft (1997), Taylor (1989).

F.J. Rumsey

Altitude (m)

• <1%
• 1–10%
• 11–30%
• 31–40%
• 41–50%
• 51–100%

Distance north (km)

☐ Apparency   ■ In flower   ■ In leaf

Utricularia australis Bladderwort

R.Br.

A free-floating, insectivorous perennial herb of acidic water, found in lakes, ponds, reservoirs, slow-flowing streams, ditches, canals, and swampy ground over mineral or peaty soil. It can also occur, however, in moderately calcareous sites. It spreads primarily through fragmentation and dispersal of the overwintering turions. Generally lowland, but reaching 335 m on Lambrigg Fell (Westmorland), and probably at 500 m in Llyn Anafon (Caernarvonshire).

Trends *U. australis* can only be satisfactorily distinguished from *U. vulgaris*, from which it may have been derived through hybridization, when flowering. The vast majority of records accepted for mapping are of flowering material only, though a minority are of vegetative plants keyed using the leaf-teeth bristle character in

Poland & Clement (2009), which may not be reliable. Most flowering within the genus is in the south, and therefore records are likely to have a southern bias and greatly underestimate the true range. Distributional change is difficult to assess, though it has decreased in lowland England and elsewhere through eutrophication of water bodies.

Biogeography Eurasian Boreo-temperate element.

Native	GB	IR
2000–19	79	25
1987–99	79	17
1970–86	56	11
pre-1970	90	23

Alien	GB	IR
2000–19	4	0
1987–99	5	0
1970–86	0	0
pre-1970	1	0

Key refs Poland & Clement (2009), Preston & Croft (1997), Thor (1979).

F.J. Rumsey

Altitude (m)

• <1%
• 1–10%
• 11–30%
• 31–40%
• 41–50%
• 51–100%

Distance north (km)

☐ Apparency   ■ In flower   ■ In leaf

Utricularia intermedia agg. Bladderworts

Perennial, insectivorous herbs, strongly dimorphic with photosynthetic non-trapping leaves flattened to often submerged surfaces, with colourless trap-bearing shoots descending into sloppy humic substrates. It is most frequent in shallow, oligotrophic water in acidic and peaty sites, though also occurring in calcareous sites in species-rich fen. Plants rarely flower, and reproduction is mainly by turions. From sea level to at least 825 m (Meall Garbh, Mid Perthshire), occurring in sloping micaceous runnels with *Carex microglochin*, and possibly higher elsewhere on the Ben Lawers range.

Trends A poorly known complex of three species, *U. intermedia s.s.*, *U. ochroleuca* and *U. stygia*, for which there are rather few reliable records. The last two are almost certainly derived from the first through hybridization

with *U. minor*. The aggregate has declined, especially in the southern part of its range, due to habitat destruction and eutrophication. It is, however, much better recorded in Scotland and Ireland than in the 1962 *Atlas*. In spite of clearer guidance the segregates are still poorly recorded and much confused, with misinterpretation of the sometimes difficult-to-see quadrifid trap hair characters perhaps responsible.

Biogeography Circumpolar Boreal-montane element.

Native	GB	IR
2000–19	242	69
1987–99	277	86
1970–86	125	29
pre-1970	266	103

Key refs Preston & Croft (1997), Taylor (1989), Thor (1979), Thor (1987), Thor (1988).

F.J. RUMSEY

Utricularia stygia Nordic Bladderwort

G. Thor

A perennial insectivorous plant with strongly dimorphic foliage, found in shallow strongly acidic to weakly calcareous waters, from bog-pools to montane micaceous runnels. Flowering is very rare and seed is not set, with reproduction by the overwintering turions. From sea level to c. 825 m (Ben Lawers Range, Mid Perthshire).

Trends *U. stygia* was only described as a separate species in 1987 and is now known to be derived through hybridization between *U. intermedia* and *U. minor*, as is the similar and regularly confused *U. ochroleuca*. *U. stygia* more closely approaches its *U. intermedia* parent in morphology and arguably in ecology. Discrimination largely relies on accurate interpretation of the form of the quadrifid trap hairs, a microscopic character only really visible in fresh material and sometimes difficult to

interpret. Probably still under-recorded and much confused with other members of the *U. intermedia* aggregate. Many of the hectad losses shown on the map are records made in the 1990s during the Scottish Loch Survey which have not been relocated this century.

Biogeography Boreal-montane element; its wider extra-European distribution is still unclear.

Native	GB	IR
2000–19	144	13
1987–99	131	3
1970–86	1	0
pre-1970	1	0

Key refs Taylor (1989).

F.J. RUMSEY

Utricularia ochroleuca Pale Bladderwort
R.W.Hartm.

A perennial insectivorous herb with rather dimorphic foliage, the traps borne predominantly on colourless shoots descending into rather sloppy humic substrates, the photosynthetic leaves often rather flattened on submerged substrates in shallow acidic to weakly calcareous waters, from bog-pools to upland lochans. It rarely flowers and does not set seed, reproduction being exclusively by overwintering turions. 0–500 m near to Loch nan Eun (Wester Ross).

Trends *U. ochroleuca* is now known to be derived through hybridization between *U. intermedia* and *U. minor*, as is the similar and regularly confused *U. stygia*. *U. ochroleuca* more closely approaches its *U. minor* parent in morphology and arguably in ecology. Discrimination largely relies on accurate interpretation of the form of the quadrifid trap hairs, a microscopic character only really visible in fresh material and sometimes difficult to interpret. The predominance of records made between 1987 and 1999 reflects the critical recording during the Scottish Loch Survey in the 1990s, which has not been repeated. There is no indication of a genuine decline and it is certainly still under-recorded and much confused with other members of the *U. intermedia* aggregate, particularly *U. stygia*.

Biogeography Circumpolar Boreal-montane element.

		GB	IR
Long term	No trend		No trend
Short term	No trend		No trend

Native		GB	IR
2000–19	●	5	0
1987–99	●	37	1
1970–86	○	1	0
pre-1970	○	0	0

Key refs Taylor (1989).

F.J. RUMSEY

Utricularia minor Lesser Bladderwort
L.

A perennial insectivorous free-floating submerged herb of nutrient-poor, acidic, or sometimes base-rich, shallow water in bog pools and abandoned peat cuttings, at the edges of lakes amongst emergent vegetation, in ditches and small ponds, and in fens. 0–600 m (Haystacks Tarn, Cumberland), and possibly to 685 m in Scotland.

Trends *U. minor* is free-flowering, and can be reliably identified on both flowering and vegetative characters. A decline was apparent by the 1960s, and this has continued in southern and eastern England, and perhaps also in south-eastern Ireland, due to habitat destruction and eutrophication. It may still be under-recorded in the northern and western parts of its range.

Biogeography Circumpolar Boreo-temperate element.

	GB	IR
Long term		
Short term		

Native		GB	IR
2000–19	●	346	182
1987–99	●	360	209
1970–86	○	181	56
pre-1970	○	448	254

Key refs Preston & Croft (1997).

F.J. RUMSEY

N ## *Utricularia bremii* New Forest Bladderwort
Heer ex Koell.

A perennial insectivorous herb of nutrient-poor acidic, shallow water in bog pools, or deeper water (to *c.* 2 m) in ditches and abandoned peat cuttings. Free-floating or affixed in open sloppy humic substrates. Lowland.

Trends *U. bremii* is only known with certainty from a single site in the New Forest (South Hampshire), where it was first recorded in 2008, but it is potentially overlooked elsewhere as it is only able to be discriminated from *U. minor* when flowering. Non-flowering herbarium specimens from Moray were identified as this early in the 20th century but have never been confirmed. Similar plants occurred at Spur Bog (Dorset) where other non-native insectivorous plants have been introduced, raising questions over its status in Britain.

Biogeography Native of central Europe and perhaps more widely but not always separable from *U. minor* and hence overlooked.

	GB	IR
Long term	No trend	No trend
Short term	No trend	No trend

Native	GB	IR
2000–19	1	0
1987–99	0	0
1970–86	0	0
pre-1970	0	0

Key refs Bailey & McPherson (2016), Taylor (1991).

F.J. Rumsey

Ar ## *Verbena officinalis* Vervain
L.

A perennial herb of open habitats or bare ground on freely draining, often calcareous soils. It is most frequently found in rough grassland and scrub, on roadsides, along active and disused railway lines and on sheltered coastal cliffs and rock outcrops; less often in quarries and gravel-pits, streamsides, wood-borders and walls. Lowland.

Trends *V. officinalis* has been growing around human settlements since the Neolithic, and it was widely cultivated in medieval gardens. The overall 10 km square distribution appears to have changed little since the 1960s in the core of its range in southern Britain, whereas there has been a high degree of turnover in other parts of its range where it is less common, particularly in central and northern Britain and in Ireland.

Biogeography As an archaeophyte, *V. officinalis* has a Eurasian Southern-temperate distribution; it is widely naturalized outside this range.

Alien	GB	IR
2000–19	756	55
1987–99	590	41
1970–86	351	12
pre-1970	727	71

Key refs Woodward (1997).

S. Lambert & R.M. Burton

Ne *Verbena bonariensis* Argentinian Vervain

L.

An annual to perennial herb, recently widely planted in gardens and municipal areas where it self-sows prolifically. It is found as an escape on pavements, at the base of walls and fences, as well as on refuse tips and waste ground. Generally lowland, but reaching 480 m near Pym Chair car park in Cheshire.

Trends *V. bonariensis* had been introduced into British gardens by 1732 and was first recorded out of cultivation in Bristol in 1949. It has become a very popular ornamental in recent years and this has led to a remarkable increase in its 10 km square distribution since 2000 in southern Britain, mostly near to human habitations or in urban areas. Some early records of plants arising from wool shoddy may have been misidentifications of *V. litoralis*.

Biogeography Native of eastern South America.

Alien		GB	IR
2000–19	●	618	43
1987–99	●	12	0
1970–86	●	4	0
pre-1970	○	17	0

	GB	IR
Long term	No trend	No trend
Short term	⬆	⬆

S. Lambert & T.D. Dines

Ne *Stachys byzantina* Lamb's-ear

K.Koch

A winter-green perennial herb that spreads by stolons to form dense mats. It is now very popular in gardens but spreads vigorously and so is frequently discarded in garden waste. It is found on roadsides, refuse tips, waste ground, pathsides, on dumped soil or rubble, and in quarries. It self-sows quite readily, often from planted sources, but the offspring are likely to be casual. It is often persistent where dumped or sometimes survives as a relic of cultivation. Lowland.

Trends This species, introduced into cultivation in 1782, was first recorded in the wild in 1854 (Thirsk, North-east Yorkshire). Its distribution has increased dramatically since the 1960s, especially since 2000 in southern and central England, although many of the records in the London area are likely to be from gardens.

Biogeography Native of south-western Asia.

Alien		GB	IR
2000–19	●	528	18
1987–99	●	147	3
1970–86	●	29	0
pre-1970	○	13	0

	GB	IR
Long term	No trend	No trend
Short term	⬆	⬆

K.J. Walker

N *Stachys germanica* Downy Woundwort

L.

A biennial or short-lived perennial herb of woodland margins, grassy banks, ancient hedgerows and green lanes overlying oolitic limestone; occasionally recorded from stony fields and quarries. The reappearance of plants following disturbance and scrub clearance suggests that seeds remain viable over long periods. Lowland.

Trends *S. germanica* may have been more widespread than the current map suggests, but it declined markedly in the 19th century. As a native it became confined to the present small area of Oxfordshire before 1930. Here it has been recorded in 11 sites since the 1950s, but has only been reliably recorded in five of these sites since 2000. Its disappearance is often associated with a lack of disturbance and succession to coarse vegetation and scrub, and annual conservation work is needed to maintain suitable conditions.

Biogeography European Temperate element.

GB		IR
Long term	No trend	No trend
Short term	No trend	No trend

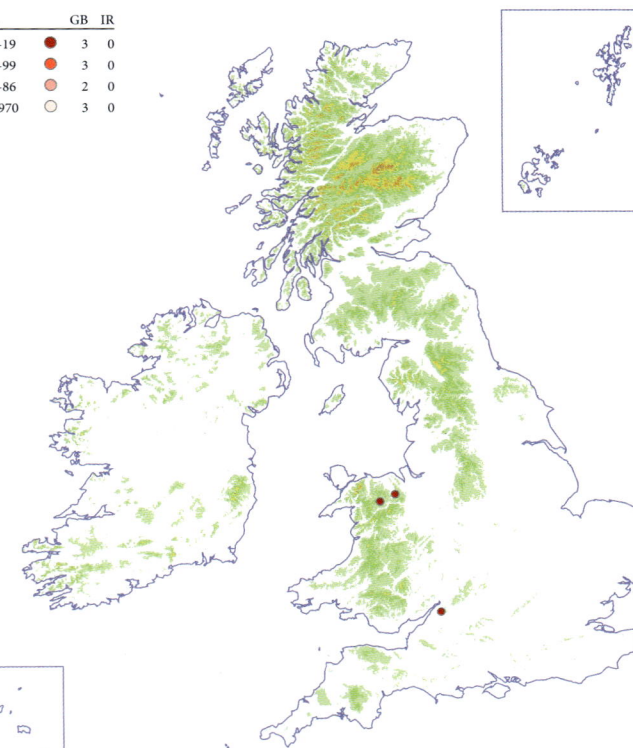

Native		GB	IR
2000–19	●	3	0
1987–99	●	3	0
1970–86	●	5	0
pre-1970	○	10	0

Alien		GB	IR
2000–19	●	2	0
1987–99	●	1	0
1970–86	●	1	0
pre-1970	○	15	0

Altitude (m)

- <1%
- 1–10%
- 11–30%
- 31–40%
- 41–50%
- 51–100%

Distance north (km)

☐ Apparency ■ In flower ■ In leaf

J F M A M J J A S O N D

Key refs Dunn (1997), Marren (1988), Wigginton (1999).

K.J. WALKER

N? *Stachys alpina* Limestone Woundwort

L.

A short-lived perennial herb, now only occurring in a few sites in open woodlands, wood-borders, hedgebanks and trackways on thin soils overlying calcareous rock. Lowland.

Trends *S. alpina* was cultivated in Britain by 1597 and was first discovered in the wild in 1897 (Wotton-under-Edge, Gloucestershire). Initially considered to be native, its genetics, dynamics and late discovery subsequently supported the view that it was an introduction (Kay & John, 1995; Pearman, 2007). Recently, however, Jones (2011) and Rich (2022) have offered an alternative view, presenting a case for it being more likely native than introduced. The Gloucestershire population may have spread shortly after its discovery, but is now maintained artificially by sowing seed. It was found in Denbighshire in 1908 (Jones, 2011), and though the five or so sub-populations that survive appear to be slowly declining, trends are obscured due to repeated conservation plantings. It can reappear after disturbance and buried seed may exist at some of its former sites.

Biogeography Native of western, central and southern Europe.

GB		IR
Long term	No trend	No trend
Short term	No trend	No trend

Alien		GB	IR
2000–19	●	3	0
1987–99	●	3	0
1970–86	●	2	0
pre-1970	○	3	0

Altitude (m)

- <1%
- 1–10%
- 11–30%
- 31–40%
- 41–50%
- 51–100%

Distance north (km)

☐ Apparency ■ In flower ■ In leaf

J F M A M J J A S O N D

Key refs Jones (2011), Kay & John (1995), Pearman (2007), Rich (2022), Wigginton (1999).

K.J. WALKER

N *Stachys sylvatica* Hedge Woundwort
L.

A perennial herb, with long creeping rhizomes, found in woods, hedgerows, the banks of rivers and streams, rough grassland and waste places, and, locally, as a persistent garden weed. It characteristically grows in moist, fertile, mildly acidic to basic soils in disturbed or lightly to moderately shaded sites. It spreads by vigorous rhizomatous extension and by seed. 0–500 m (above Malham, Mid-west Yorkshire), with an exceptional record at 845 m on Great Dun Fell (Westmorland).

Trends There is no evidence for a change in the overall 10 km square distribution of *S. sylvatica* since the 1960s although it is now much better recorded in Scotland and Ireland.

Biogeography Eurosiberian Temperate element.

Native	GB	IR
2000–19	2447	836
1987–99	2380	722
1970–86	1597	105
pre-1970	2314	577

Key refs Grime *et al.* (2007), Taylor & Rowland (2010).

K.J. WALKER

Hy *Stachys palustris × sylvatica = S. ×ambigua* Hybrid Woundwort
Sm.

A sterile rhizomatous perennial herb occurring in the habitats of either parent, but frequently in the absence of both. It grows as well-established, vegetatively reproducing colonies by lakes, reservoirs, ponds, streams, rivers and canals, in ditches, at the edges of woods and scrub and on wet woodland rides, in rough grassland, on roadsides, and as a weed of cultivated and disturbed ground. It reproduces by rhizome fragments. 0–435 m (Block Wood, Montgomeryshire).

A spontaneous hybrid (native × native).

Trends Although localized declines have been reported (*e.g.* Mountford, 1994), there is no evidence for an appreciable change in the 10 km square distribution of *S. ×ambigua*; indeed, it may be more frequent than the current map suggests.

Biogeography Widespread in Europe.

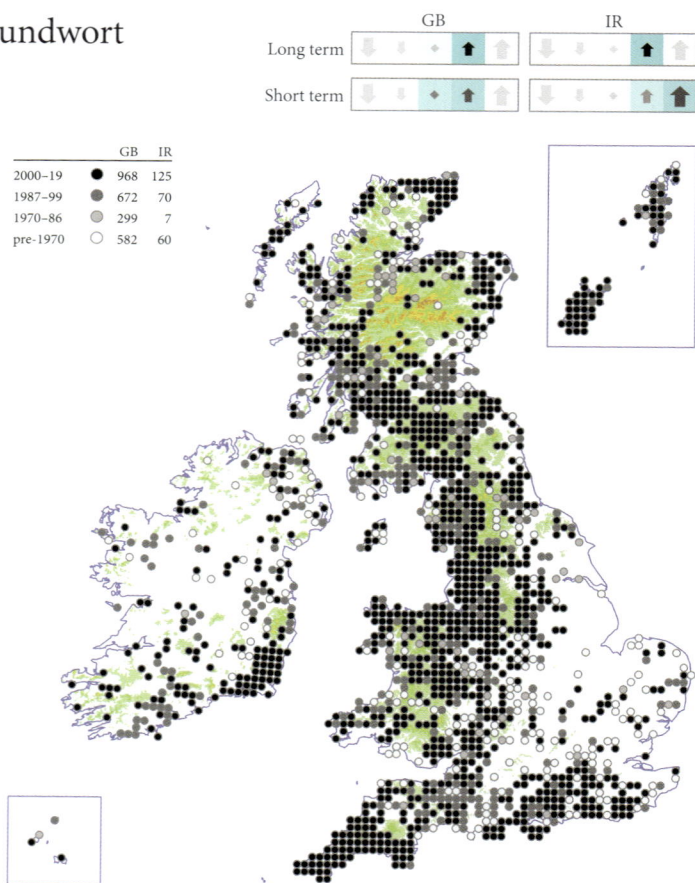

	GB	IR
2000–19	968	125
1987–99	672	70
1970–86	299	7
pre-1970	582	60

Key refs Mountford (1994), Stace *et al.* (2015)

C.A. STACE, C.D. PRESTON & D.A. PEARMAN

N *Stachys palustris* Marsh Woundwort
L.

A perennial herb with long rhizomes that produce small tubers at the apex in the autumn. It is found most frequently on the banks and margins of streams, rivers, ditches and ponds, in fens, marshes and swamps, and occasionally in damp woodland and hedgerows and on damp shingle on beaches, woodland rides, waste ground and cultivated fields. It is typically found on intermittently flooded and poorly drained soils. 0–540 m (Moor House, Teesdale, Westmorland).

Trends There has been an small increase in the overall 10 km square distribution of *S. palustris* since the 1960s, presumably due to better recording of wetland habitats but also due to the widespread creation of wetlands, either intentionally or accidentally through the abandonment of former mining, industrial and quarrying sites. It is also occasionally planted with other waterside plants in new wetlands or occurs as an obvious escape near to human habitations. Broad-leaved forms of *S. ×ambigua* have formerly been mistaken for *S. palustris* by visitors to Scotland, and some such errors may still be mapped.

Biogeography Circumpolar Boreo-temperate element.

Native	GB	IR
2000–19	2242	937
1987–99	2055	859
1970–86	1300	111
pre-1970	1938	675

Alien	GB	IR
2000–19	1	0
1987–99	2	0
1970–86	1	0
pre-1970	1	0

Key refs Jones & Wilcock (1974), Morton (1973), Taylor & Rowland (2011).

K.J. WALKER

Ar *Stachys arvensis* Field Woundwort
(L.) L.

An annual herb, found most frequently as a weed on arable margins, also along tracks and paths, in allotments and gardens, on waste ground and on road verges, usually on non-calcareous soils, though it occurs on limestone outcrops in western Ireland. Generally lowland, but reaching 412 m at Wellshead Allotment (South Somerset).

Trends *S. arvensis* was formerly a frequent weed of arable land that has declined substantially since the 1960s, especially in southern, central, eastern and northern England and Scotland where it is now a rare plant and largely absent from this habitat. It remains locally abundant in parts of western Britain, especially coastal regions, as well as parts of East Anglia and southern Ireland, but only on light, infertile soils that have been less amenable to agricultural improvement and where conservation measures to reduce agricultural inputs have been widely implemented (Walker *et al.*, 2007).

Biogeography As an archaeophyte, *S. arvensis* has a Suboceanic Southern-temperate distribution; it is widely naturalized outside this range.

Alien	GB	IR
2000–19	857	145
1987–99	830	134
1970–86	696	12
pre-1970	1139	119

Key refs Walker *et al.* (2007).

K.J. WALKER

Ne *Stachys annua* Annual Yellow-woundwort

(L.) L.

An annual found in arable fields, on waste ground and occasionally in gardens. It is usually casual but sometimes persists for several years, and originates as a contaminant of grain and oil-seed. Lowland.

Trends This species was cultivated in Britain by 1713. It was recorded in the wild by 1830 (Kent) and was at one time so abundant in parts of south-eastern England that it was considered to be native. It has declined appreciably, presumably due to improvements in seed cleaning techniques. It is now a very rare casual.

Biogeography A variable species with a European Temperate distribution; absent as a native from western Europe.

	GB	IR
Long term	No trend	No trend
Short term	No trend	No trend

Alien		GB	IR
2000–19	●	7	0
1987–99	●	4	0
1970–86	●	9	0
pre-1970	○	64	0

Key refs Styles (1976).

Altitude (m) chart. Distance north (km).

● <1%
● 1–10%
● 11–30%
● 31–40%
● 41–50%
● 51–100%

☐ Apparency ☐ In flower ☐ In leaf

K.J. WALKER

N *Betonica officinalis* Betony

L.

A perennial herb of grassland, hedgebanks, heathland, open woods and woodland rides and margins. It is occasionally found in cliff-top grassland, sometimes as the genetically dwarf var. *nana*. It favours mildly acidic soils, but is also found on those that are neutral or strongly calcareous. 0–480 m (Afon Myherin, Cardiganshire) and possibly higher at Gau Craig (Merionethshire).

Trends *B. officinalis* is a good indicator of ancient habitats and though its 10 km square distribution seems relatively stable this century, many populations have been lost since the 1960s following the destruction of its grassland habitats. It is now widely planted both within and beyond its native range and this has to some extent obscured its native distribution, especially in southern and eastern areas of Scotland.

Biogeography European Temperate element; also in central Asia.

	GB	IR
Long term		
Short term		

Native		GB	IR
2000–19	●	1379	13
1987–99	●	1399	16
1970–86	●	1009	4
pre-1970	○	1417	33

Alien		GB	IR
2000–19	●	34	0
1987–99	●	9	0
1970–86	●	2	1
pre-1970	○	5	2

Key refs Grime *et al.* (2007), Rackham (1980).

Altitude (m) chart. Distance north (km).

● <1%
● 1–10%
● 11–30%
● 31–40%
● 41–50%
● 51–100%

☐ Apparency ☐ In flower ☐ In leaf

K.J. WALKER

Ar *Ballota nigra* Black Horehound
L.

A foetid, winter-green perennial herb of hedgerows, field-borders, walls, waysides and waste ground, often on disturbed nutrient-rich soils near habitations. Lowland, though it has been recorded as a casual at 480 m on Helvellyn (Cumberland).

Trends Archaeological evidence suggests that *B. nigra* is an ancient introduction, having been associated with human settlements since the Iron Age. Its overall distribution is stable. Our plants are all believed to be subsp. *meridionalis*; subsp. *nigra* may be overlooked as a casual.

Biogeography As an archaeophyte, *B. nigra* has a European Southern-temperate distribution.

Alien	GB	IR
2000–19	1231	17
1987–99	1249	19
1970–86	789	12
pre-1970	1199	52

Key refs Halliday (1997).

K.J. WALKER

N *Marrubium vulgare* White Horehound
L.

A perennial herb, probably native only near the sea on open, exposed cliff-top grasslands and slopes overlying limestone and chalk, and on sandy banks and verges in Breckland. It is cultivated for tea for its medicinal properties, and is naturalized in rough ground and waste places; it also formerly occurred as a wool shoddy alien. Usually lowland, but at 371 m above Dinbren Uchaf (Denbighshire), on the underhang of a south-facing cliff.

Native in Britain and a neophyte in Ireland and the Channel Islands.

Trends The distinction between native and alien populations, particularly in coastal areas, can be difficult to ascertain. Its native distribution appears to be stable although localized declines have occurred due to lack of grazing. Its decline as an alien, already apparent in the 1960s, has continued, especially on arable land inland.

Biogeography Eurosiberian Southern-temperate element; widely naturalized outside its native range.

Native	GB	IR
2000–19	30	0
1987–99	33	0
1970–86	27	0
pre-1970	43	0

Alien	GB	IR
2000–19	55	1
1987–99	91	1
1970–86	98	0
pre-1970	430	25

Key refs Mabey (1996), Stewart *et al.* (1994).

K.J. WALKER

Ne *Leonurus cardiaca* Motherwort

L.

A winter-green perennial herb, formerly grown as a medicinal plant but now only as an ornamental. Widely naturalized on banks by roads and tracks and on waste ground, often near human habitations, and often persisting for long periods. Lowland.

Trends *L. cardiaca* was first introduced from continental Europe in the Middle Ages as a medicinal herb and later as an impurity of imported grain. It was recorded in the wild by 1548. The marked contraction in range that was evident by the 1960s has continued as a result of the gradual extinction of established populations and a decreasing rate of introduction, the latter due in part to more effective seed cleaning.

Biogeography *L. cardiaca* is a Eurosiberian Temperate species, but the limits of its native range have been obscured by its spread in cultivation.

GB	IR
Long term	No trend	No trend
Short term		No trend

Alien	GB	IR
2000–19	56	0
1987–99	29	0
1970–86	24	0
pre-1970	230	4

Key refs Mabey (1996).

K.J. Walker

N *Lamiastrum galeobdolon* subsp. *galeobdolon*

(L.) Ehrend. & Polatschek

A stoloniferous perennial herb of mixed ancient deciduous woodlands, woodland edges and hedgerows. Usually growing on moist, mildly acidic to neutral soils. Lowland.

Trends *L. galeobdolon* subsp. *galeobdolon* is a diploid and was first recorded in Britain by Wegmüller (1971). It has been confirmed cytologically only from three privately owned woods in the North Lincolnshire Wolds, and Kirkcudbrightshire, although at the latter site it was probably introduced. It is possible that it may still be overlooked elsewhere because of its similarity to the widespread subsp. *montanum*. Perhaps the most reliable character to separate the two taxa are the hairs on the lower half of the stem: these are almost entirely confined to the angles in subsp. *galeobdolon*, whereas subsp. *montanum*

has a more or less equal distribution of hairs on the faces and the angles.

Biogeography European Temperate element; this subspecies extends farther north and east than subsp. *montanum*.

GB	IR
Long term	No trend	No trend
Short term	No trend	No trend

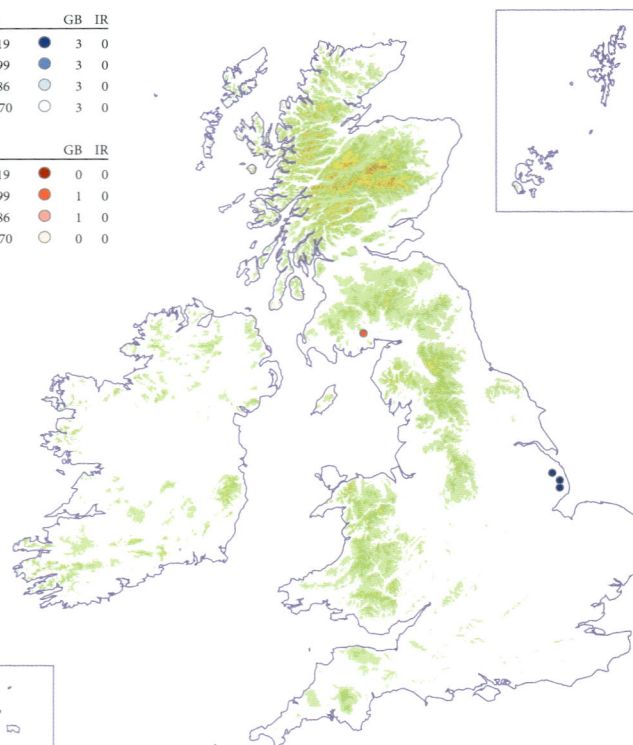

Native	GB	IR
2000–19	3	0
1987–99	3	0
1970–86	3	0
pre-1970	3	0

Alien	GB	IR
2000–19	0	0
1987–99	1	0
1970–86	1	0
pre-1970	0	0

Key refs Wegmüller (1971).

K.J. Walker & J.O. Mountford

N *Lamiastrum galeobdolon* subsp. *montanum*

(Pers.) Ehrend. & Polatschek

A winter-green stoloniferous perennial herb of moist woodland, hedges, roadsides and the grikes of limestone pavement, usually on heavy soils. It is often associated with ancient woods and wood-relic hedges (Rackham, 1980), particularly in eastern England. 0–425 m (Ystradfellte, Breconshire).

Trends Although the overall 10 km square distribution of subsp. *montanum* is stable, it appears to be declining at a more local scale due to the cessation of management in many woods and grazing by deer in eastern England. In some ancient woods variegated garden plants (subsp. *argentatum*) can be abundant but this subspecies does not appear to be replacing subsp. *montanum*.

Biogeography European Temperate element; subsp. *montanum* occurs in the southern and western part of the species' range.

Native		GB	IR
2000–19	●	853	8
1987–99	●	830	6
1970–86	●	305	8
pre-1970	○	319	12

Alien		GB	IR
2000–19	●	22	0
1987–99	●	15	0
1970–86	●	13	0
pre-1970	○	10	0

Key refs Grime *et al.* (2007), Packham (1983), Rackham (1980), Rich & Jermy (1998).

K.J. WALKER

Ne *Lamiastrum galeobdolon* subsp. *argentatum*

(Smejkal) Stace

A winter-green perennial herb, with long, vigorous stolons, widely grown in gardens as an ornamental ground cover, growing on a variety of soils, and naturalized in scrub, copses, secondary woodland and plantations, hedgebanks, riverbanks, on roadside verges and on tracksides. Usually in shaded places near to human habitations where garden rubbish has been dumped. Usually lowland, but reaching 400 m in the Clun Forest (Shropshire).

Trends The history of this plant in our area is obscure. It was not recognized taxonomically until Smejkal described it as a new taxon in 1975 and Rutherford & Stirling (1987) brought it to the attention of British and Irish botanists. It was probably introduced in the late 1960s, possibly from Germany; the first record in the wild was in 1974 (Chippinghurst,

Oxfordshire). Since then it has increased rapidly in most lowland regions. The spread in Ireland is even more recent, commencing in the late 1980s. Certainly in western England it is found far from human habitations, forming dense smothering patches. These are most unlikely to have originated from garden waste and it therefore must be spreading by other means.

Biogeography Origin uncertain; perhaps a cultivated variant of subsp. *montanum*.

Alien		GB	IR
2000–19	●	1883	325
1987–99	●	1082	75
1970–86	●	183	0
pre-1970	○	48	0

Key refs Clement & Foster (1994), Rich & Jermy (1998), Rutherford & Stirling (1987).

K.J. WALKER & D.A. PEARMAN

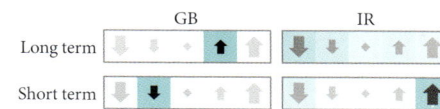

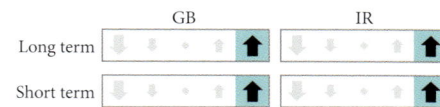

Ar *Lamium album* White Dead-nettle
L.

A winter-green rhizomatous or sometimes stoloniferous perennial, seeding everywhere. It is most often found on waste ground and on the verges and banks of paths, tracks and roads, also on the margins of arable fields, as a weed of streets, walls and gardens, railways, disturbed areas in woodland and on riverbanks, often growing on fertile soils close to human habitations and tolerant of shade and full sun. 0–465 m (Flash, Staffordshire).

Trends There has been no appreciable change in the overall distribution of *L. album* since the 1960s, although it appears to have declined towards the margins of its range in Scotland, Wales and Ireland, possibly due to a decline in small-scale cultivation in upland and coastal regions.

Biogeography As an archaeophyte, *L. album* has a Eurasian Boreo-temperate distribution; it is widely naturalized outside this range.

Alien	GB	IR
2000–19	1764	121
1987–99	1717	134
1970–86	1225	20
pre-1970	1734	108

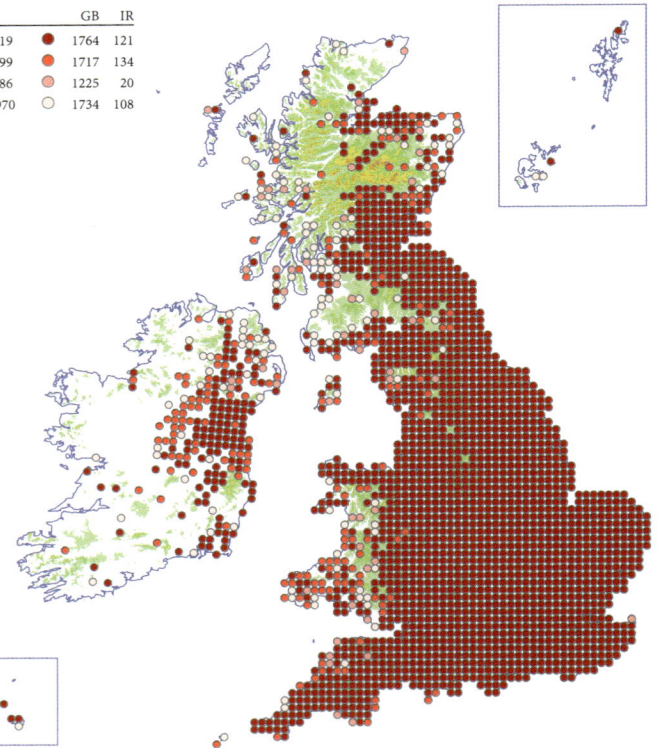

Key refs Grime *et al.* (2007).

K.J. WALKER

Altitude (m)

● <1%
● 1–10%
● 11–30%
● 31–40%
● 41–50%
● 51–100%

Distance north (km)

☐ Apparency ■ In flower ■ In leaf

J F M A M J J A S O N D

Ne *Lamium maculatum* Spotted Dead-nettle
(L.) L.

A winter-green rhizomatous or stoloniferous perennial herb, much grown in gardens for its silver-striped leaves and readily established where garden waste has been dumped or by self-sowing. Widely naturalized on the banks and verges of tracks and roads, pavements, rough ground, refuse tips and waste places, usually close to human habitations. Generally lowland, but recorded at 490 m above Garrigill (Cumberland).

Trends This species was introduced into cultivation from Italy in 1683, and recorded in the wild in 1747 (Oxford). It is still widely grown in gardens and its range has increased since the 1960s.

Biogeography A European Temperate species, absent as a native from much of western Europe.

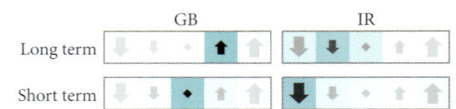

Alien	GB	IR
2000–19	976	6
1987–99	731	9
1970–86	337	0
pre-1970	412	7

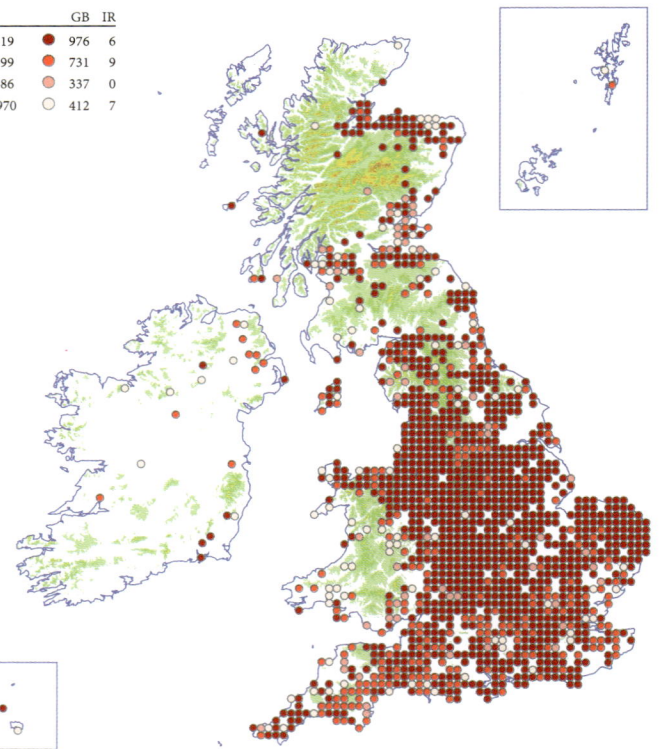

Altitude (m)

● <1%
● 1–10%
● 11–30%
● 31–40%
● 41–50%
● 51–100%

Distance north (km)

☐ Apparency ■ In flower ■ In leaf

J F M A M J J A S O N D

K.J. WALKER

Ar *Lamium purpureum* Red Dead-nettle
L.

An annual herb of fertile and disturbed soils, including cultivated and waste ground, gardens, hedgerows, on roadside verges, along railways, around rock outcrops and in rough grassland. 0–610 m (Grasshill, County Durham).

Trends As in the 1962 *Atlas*, *L. purpureum* is present in nearly all lowland areas but the current map suggests a decline in Scotland in recent decades, possibly due to the abandonment of marginal arable land.

Biogeography As an archaeophyte, *L. purpureum* has a European Temperate distribution; it is widely naturalized outside this range.

Alien		GB	IR
2000–19	●	2186	701
1987–99	●	2177	628
1970–86	●	1352	66
pre-1970	○	2250	452

Altitude (m)

● <1%
● 1–10%
● 11–30%
● 31–40%
● 41–50%
● 51–100%

Distance north (km)

☐ Apparency   ☐ In flower   ☐ In leaf

Key refs Grime *et al.* (2007).

K.J. WALKER

Ar *Lamium hybridum* Cut-leaved Dead-nettle
Vill.

An annual herb, most often found as an arable weed, often of broad-leaved crops, but also in a range of other disturbed habitats including waste ground, dumped soils and gravels, refuse tips, gardens, allotments, roadside verges, disused railway lines and old gravel-pits. Mainly on dry soils. 0–320 m (Derbyshire).

Trends There has been a considerable increase in the distribution of *L. hybridum* since the 1960s, presumably because it is adapted to highly fertile soils. However, it is often confused with *L. purpureum*, so may previously have been under-recorded. It is possibly still overlooked in some areas, and may be even more common than the current map suggests.

Biogeography As an archaeophyte, *L. hybridum* has a European Temperate distribution.

Alien		GB	IR
2000–19	●	1074	265
1987–99	●	920	176
1970–86	●	542	33
pre-1970	○	613	65

Altitude (m)

● <1%
● 1–10%
● 11–30%
● 31–40%
● 41–50%
● 51–100%

Distance north (km)

☐ Apparency   ☐ In flower   ☐ In leaf

K.J. WALKER

Ar *Lamium confertum* Northern Dead-nettle

Fr.

An annual of cultivated and waste ground. Generally lowland, but formerly recorded as a casual at 320 m in Derbyshire.

Trends *L. confertum* is often confused with other dead-nettles and as such it is difficult to make an assessment of change. It appears to have declined in Scotland since the 1960s, presumably due to the increased use of herbicides as well as a decline in the area of land under cultivation. Naturalized populations no longer exist in England, where it is now present only as a casual. In Ireland the number of recent records from County Wexford and County Down suggest that is under-recorded.

Biogeography As an archaeophyte, *L. confertum* has a European Boreal-montane distribution; it also occurs in Greenland.

Alien		GB	IR
2000–19	●	208	31
1987–99	●	212	18
1970–86	●	113	3
pre-1970	○	269	42

Altitude (m)

- <1%
- 1–10%
- 11–30%
- 31–40%
- 41–50%
- 51–100%

Distance north (km)

Apparency   In flower   In leaf

K.J. Walker

Ar *Lamium amplexicaule* Henbit Dead-nettle

L.

An annual herb, most often found as a weed of cultivated ground on light, dry soils. It also occurs as a weed in gardens and allotments, on pavements and at the base of walls, on waste ground and dumped soil, by railways, in old pits and on sand dunes. 0–455 m (Atholl, East Perthshire).

Trends Although now much better recorded than it was in the 1962 *Atlas*, the map suggests a slight decline in this species, especially in southern England and north-eastern Scotland. Locally, it has appreciably declined as a weed of cultivated land because of the increased use of herbicides (Brewis *et al.*, 1996), and possibly also due to the decline in cultivation in regions that are agriculturally marginal. However, it appears to be increasing as a ruderal, and many modern records are now from urban habitats.

Biogeography As an archaeophyte, *L. amplexicaule* has a Eurosiberian Southern-temperate distribution, but it is widely naturalized so that distribution is now Circumpolar Southern-temperate.

Alien		GB	IR
2000–19	●	1075	58
1987–99	●	1052	29
1970–86	●	736	6
pre-1970	○	1127	55

Key refs Brewis *et al.* (1996).

Altitude (m)

- <1%
- 1–10%
- 11–30%
- 31–40%
- 41–50%
- 51–100%

Distance north (km)

Apparency   In flower   In leaf

K.J. Walker & P.A. Stroh

Ar

Galeopsis segetum Downy Hemp-nettle

Neck.

An annual herb of arable and waste ground, most frequently found as a casual in root crops. Lowland.

Trends This species was formerly established at one site near Bangor (Caernarvonshire), where it has often been regarded as a native, and though it used to appear annually following its discovery there in 1802, it has not been seen since 1975, and is now presumed to be extinct. Elsewhere it is a rare and declining casual. The sole 21st century record is of a self-sown plant in disturbed ground at the National Botanic Garden of Wales (Carmarthenshire), where it is grown as part of their rare Welsh plant collection.

Biogeography As an archaeophyte, *G. segetum* has a Suboceanic Temperate distribution.

	GB	IR
Long term	No trend	No trend
Short term	No trend	No trend

Alien	GB	IR
2000–19	1	0
1987–99	2	0
1970–86	2	0
pre-1970	40	1

K.J. WALKER & P.A. STROH

Ar

Galeopsis angustifolia Red Hemp-nettle

Ehrh. ex Hoffm.

An annual herb of arable land, waste places and open ground on calcareous substrates, including disturbed track edges, chalk heaps and pits, quarries, limestone pavements and scree; also found on eskers and on coastal sand and shingle. This late-flowering species often fails to set seed within winter-sown crops, and numbers fluctuate widely from year to year. 0–357 m (Earl Sterndale, Derbyshire).

Trends *G. angustifolia* was formerly a common cornfield weed in some areas (Druce, 1927), but there was a sharp contraction in range by 1950, a decline which accelerated following a shift from spring- to winter-sown crops and cleaner crop husbandry. It is now a rare species in our area and is largely restricted as an ancient archaeophyte to limestone scree, disturbed track edges in chalk grassland, pits and quarries, conservation headlands and coastal shingle in southern England and Ireland. In recent decades it has been introduced into some areas under the auspices of cornfield weed restoration initiatives.

Biogeography European Temperate element.

Alien	GB	IR
2000–19	80	8
1987–99	97	11
1970–86	174	4
pre-1970	598	32

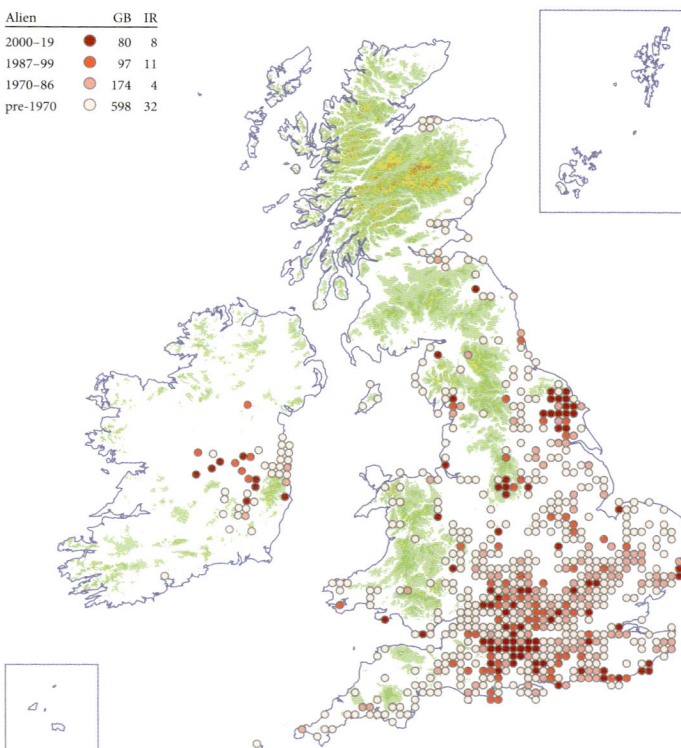

Key refs Druce (1927), Stewart *et al.* (1994), Townsend (1962).

K.J. WALKER & P.A. STROH

877

Ar *Galeopsis speciosa* Large-flowered Hemp-nettle
Mill.

An annual herb of cultivated, marginal and waste ground, often within root crops, especially potatoes and sugar beet on peaty soils. 0–445 m (Clun Forest, Shropshire).

Trends Formerly a locally common weed of peaty fields but now much more local and rarely found in any quantity. This species declined markedly in the latter half of the 20th century, especially in southern Britain, and this trend has continued since 2000, most clearly in areas of central and northern England, and Wales. It is often associated with traditional arable farming and has suffered where modern methods of cultivation and weed control have been introduced.

Biogeography As an archaeophyte, *G. speciosa* has a Eurosiberian Boreo-temperate distribution; it is widely naturalized outside this range.

Alien		GB	IR
2000–19	●	381	25
1987–99	●	435	37
1970–86	●	403	12
pre-1970	○	824	64

K.J. WALKER & P.A. STROH

N *Galeopsis tetrahit* agg. Common Hemp-nettles

Annual herbs of moist, moderately shaded semi-natural habitats such as woodland clearings, ditches, fens, riverbanks, roadside verges and wet heaths, but perhaps more frequently encountered in disturbed arable, waste and cultivated ground. 0–610 m (Corrie Fee, Angus).

Trends Records of *G. bifida* and *G. tetrahit* are included on this map, which is equivalent to the map of *G. tetrahit* agg. in the 1962 *Atlas*. The two segregates are mapped separately.

Biogeography The world distribution of the two segregates is given in the relevant accounts.

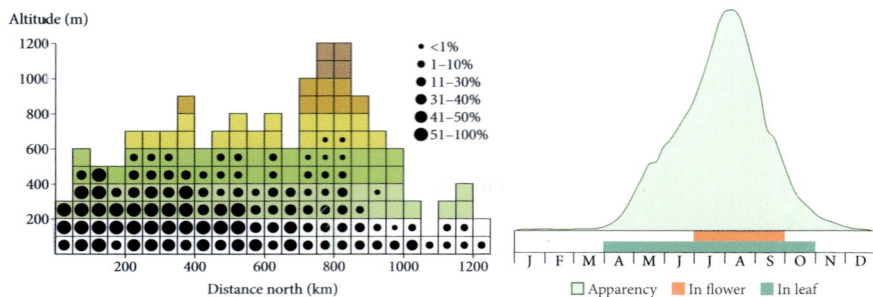

Native		GB	IR
2000–19	●	2269	342
1987–99	●	2194	381
1970–86	○	1471	62
pre-1970	○	2245	463

Alien		GB	IR
2000–19	●	0	3
1987–99	●	1	9
1970–86	●	0	0
pre-1970	○	0	7

K.J. WALKER

Galeopsis tetrahit Common Hemp-nettle
L.

An annual herb of woodland clearings, ditches, fens, riverbanks, roadside verges and wet heaths, but perhaps more frequent in disturbed arable, waste and cultivated ground. 0–610 m (Corrie Fee, Angus).

Trends The known distribution of this species has increased markedly in Britain, especially since 2000, due to greater efforts in separating it from *G. bifida*, rather than as a result of a genuine spread.

Biogeography European Boreo-temperate element.

Native	GB	IR
2000–19	2022	247
1987–99	1720	205
1970–86	670	38
pre-1970	663	276

Alien	GB	IR
2000–19	0	1
1987–99	1	5
1970–86	0	0
pre-1970	0	3

Key refs Grime *et al.* (2007), O'Donovan & Sharma (1987).

P.A. STROH & K.J. WALKER

Galeopsis bifida Bifid Hemp-nettle
Boenn.

An annual herb of arable, waste and cultivated ground, and less often woodland clearings and ditch-sides. It is found in similar places to *G. tetrahit*, and often grows with it, although it is more frequent on arable land. Generally lowland, but reaching 460 m at Brown Clee (Shropshire).

Trends *G. bifida* was mapped within *G. tetrahit* agg. in the 1962 *Atlas*. As a consequence, it is difficult to assess long-term changes in distribution, although it was mapped in the 2002 *Atlas*. The substantial number of new 10 km square records since 2000 is likely to reflect better recognition and recording of this taxon, rather than genuine spread.

Biogeography Eurasian Boreo-temperate element, but naturalized in North America so distribution is now Circumpolar Boreo-temperate.

Native	GB	IR
2000–19	1311	104
1987–99	950	96
1970–86	371	8
pre-1970	316	46

Alien	GB	IR
2000–19	0	0
1987–99	0	0
1970–86	3	0
pre-1970	0	0

Key refs Grime *et al.* (2007), O'Donovan & Sharma (1987).

P.A. STROH & K.J. WALKER

Hy *Galeopsis bifida* × *tetrahit* = *G.* ×*ludwigii*
Hausskn.

A largely sterile hybrid rarely recorded with its parents at the edge of woods, in hedgerows, on grassy roadside banks, lakesides, old railway sidings and at the edges of arable fields. Lowland.

A spontaneous hybrid (native × native).

Trends Many field botanists struggle to separate the parents of this hybrid consistently, so it is not surprising that there have been only a few scattered records of *G.* ×*ludwigii* in our area since it was first discovered by J.L. Gilbert at Old Weston (Huntingdonshire) in 1955 (Gilbert, 1956).

Biogeography Known from Sweden, the Netherlands, and central Europe.

	GB	IR
Long term	No trend	No trend
Short term	No trend	No trend

		GB	IR
2000–19	●	1	0
1987–99	●	7	0
1970–86	●	4	0
pre-1970	○	4	0

Key refs Gilbert (1956), Stace *et al.* (2015).

C.A. STACE, C.D. PRESTON & D.A. PEARMAN

Ne *Phlomis fruticosa* Jerusalem Sage
L.

An evergreen shrub, much grown in gardens and amenity plantings, which occurs as a naturalized garden escape on sand dunes, coastal cliffs, banks, walls, field edges and rough ground. Most plants appear to be self-sown but it also occurs as a casual throw-out on roadsides and refuse tips. Lowland.

Trends *P. fruticosa* was already grown in British gardens by 1562, and is now a very popular ornamental plant. It was known at Ball Hill, Polden Hills (North Somerset) from 1896 and persisted there until 1957. It appears to be increasing in some areas.

Biogeography Native of the Mediterranean region from Sardinia eastwards to western and south-western Turkey and Cyprus.

	GB	IR
Long term	No trend	No trend
Short term		

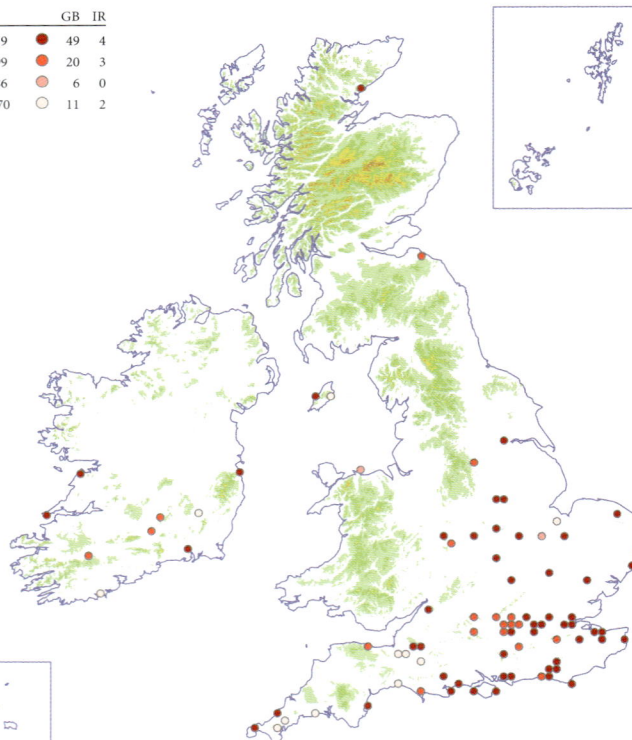

Alien		GB	IR
2000–19	●	49	4
1987–99	●	20	3
1970–86	●	6	0
pre-1970	○	11	2

Key refs Bean (1976).

T.D. DINES & D.A. PEARMAN

Melittis melissophyllum Bastard Balm
L.

An attractive, strong-smelling perennial herb of woodland, wood-borders and clearings, scrub, hedgebanks and river valleys on damp base-rich soils. In the New Forest (South Hampshire), it is a plant of ancient woodland. It favours light shade and can be abundant in cleared or coppiced woodland. It is intolerant of grazing. Lowland.

Trends A survey of historic localities of *M. melissophyllum* has shown localized declines due to a lack of grazing or coppicing in its main strongholds in Devon and Cornwall (Walker *et al.*, 2017). It has also declined in the New Forest and Dorset as a result of overshading and pony and deer grazing, although at some sites it has reappeared after scrub clearance and coppicing. In comparison, the Welsh population is very small but appears to be stable.

Biogeography European Temperate element.

Native		GB	IR
2000–19	●	69	0
1987–99	●	69	0
1970–86	●	69	0
pre-1970	○	105	0

Alien		GB	IR
2000–19	●	3	0
1987–99	●	0	0
1970–86	●	2	0
pre-1970	○	7	0

Key refs Brewis *et al.* (1996), Kay & John (1995), Stewart *et al.* (1994), Walker *et al.* (2017).

K.J. Walker

Scutellaria galericulata Skullcap
L.

A perennial herb of a variety of wetland habitats including ponds, rivers, canals, marshes, fens, fen-meadows, wet woodland and dune-slacks. It also grows on coastal boulder beaches in Scotland. Generally lowland, but reaching 365 m at High Cup Gill (Westmorland).

Trends *S. galericulata* was mapped as 'all records' in the 1962 *Atlas*. Though still frequent across Britain, it appears to have declined in many areas since 2000. There are many new 10 km square records in Ireland due to intensive recording this century.

Biogeography Eurosiberian Boreo-temperate element; also in North America.

Native		GB	IR
2000–19	●	1427	184
1987–99	●	1397	147
1970–86	●	954	50
pre-1970	○	1381	124

Alien		GB	IR
2000–19	●	1	0
1987–99	●	0	0
1970–86	●	1	0
pre-1970	○	0	0

K.J. Walker & S.M. Smart

N *Scutellaria minor* Lesser Skullcap

Huds.

A perennial herb of wet heaths, bogs, marshes and moist, heathy woodlands on acidic, oligotrophic or slightly mesotrophic soils. 0–545 m (Yes Tor, South Devon).

Trends Many populations of *S. minor* were lost before 1930. The species' range has continued to contract in core areas as a result of drainage and habitat loss, with declines most evident in south-western Ireland and the English Midlands.

Biogeography Suboceanic Southern-temperate element.

Native		GB	IR
2000–19	●	601	108
1987–99	●	586	82
1970–86	●	377	9
pre-1970	○	598	102

Key refs Dupont (1962).

S.M. SMART & K.J. WALKER

N *Teucrium scorodonia* Wood Sage

L.

A rhizomatous perennial herb of well-drained, acidic to mildly calcareous mineral soils, occurring in a wide range of habitats including woodland, hedgerows, scrub, heaths, limestone grassland and pavement, mountain ledges, dunes and shingle, and amongst bracken in pastures. It is an occasional weed by railways and on disturbed ground. It is sensitive to grazing and trampling. 0–550 m (Pistyll Rhaeadr, Montgomeryshire) and possibly higher on Craig y Dulyn, above Dulyn Reservoir (Caernarvonshire).

Trends There is no evidence for an appreciable change in the 10 km square range of *T. scorodonia* since the 1960s, though it may be better recorded in Ireland and has spread into some disturbed sites in central and eastern England.

Biogeography Suboceanic Southern-temperate element.

Native		GB	IR
2000–19	●	2192	554
1987–99	●	2139	517
1970–86	●	1342	97
pre-1970	○	2139	430

Alien		GB	IR
2000–19	●	5	0
1987–99	●	2	0
1970–86	●	3	0
pre-1970	○	1	0

Key refs Grime *et al.* (2007), Hutchinson (1968).

K.J. WALKER & J.O. MOUNTFORD

Teucrium chamaedrys Wall Germander

N?

L.

A perennial herb thought to be native only in cliff-top chalk grassland at Cuckmere Haven (East Sussex) where a small, almost prostrate variety has been known since 1945 (Rose, 1988a; Rumsey, 2018). Elsewhere it occurs as a naturalized introduction on walls, rocks and dry banks. Lowland.

Native or alien in Britain and a neophyte in Ireland and the Channel Islands.

Trends *T. chamaedrys* was first recorded in the wild in 1710 and has experienced an overall decline as a garden escape, and although it is reasonably stable in its putative native station at Cuckmere Haven, the number of plants has decreased slightly since the early 1980s. The identity of extant populations often needs to be checked as the normal garden plant is probably the hybrid between *T. chamaedrys* and *T. lucidum*.

Some populations are very long-lived; one has been known on a wall at Curry Mallet (South Somerset) from 1922 until at least 2008, whilst a population on a railway bank survived for over a century.

Biogeography European Southern-temperate element, with a continental distribution in western Europe.

Native	GB	IR
2000–19	1	0
1987–99	1	0
1970–86	1	0
pre-1970	2	0

Alien	GB	IR
2000–19	32	1
1987–99	21	1
1970–86	21	0
pre-1970	59	3

Key refs Clement & Foster (1994), Rose (1988a), Rumsey (2018), Sussex Botanical Recording Society (2018), Wigginton (1999).

K.J. WALKER & J.O. MOUNTFORD

Teucrium scordium Water Germander

N

L.

A stoloniferous winter-green perennial herb of wetland habitats with fluctuating water levels, including the margins of dune-slack pools, reed-fen, clay-pits and the banks of rivers, ponds and ditches. In Ireland it is often recorded from turloughs. Flowering and seed production can be poor. Lowland.

Trends The long-term decline of *T. scordium* in England was apparent by the 1960s and continued as a result of drainage, reclamation and eutrophication of its wetland habitats. By the 1990s it was confined to three sites in England: two former quarries in Cambridgeshire (Bassenhally Pits and Upware North Pit) and an area of dune-slacks at Braunton Burrows (North Devon). Although the Devon population is relatively stable, the Cambridgeshire sites are threatened by

lack of management, scrub encroachment and shading. Due to this vulnerability a small number of plants were introduced into an ex-arable wetland restoration scheme adjacent to one of the native sites (Upware North Pit), where it has since established and spread via stolon fragments on lake-shores that resemble its Irish sites. The introduced population has recently been estimated at hundreds of thousands of plants, whereas the native site supports fewer than 20 individuals. In Ireland, populations appear stable in the Shannon Basin and margins of the Burren.

Biogeography Eurosiberian Southern-temperate element.

Native	GB	IR
2000–19	3	9
1987–99	3	10
1970–86	5	7
pre-1970	25	11

Alien	GB	IR
2000–19	2	0
1987–99	0	0
1970–86	0	0
pre-1970	1	0

Key refs Beecroft *et al.* (2007), Smith *et al.* (2016), Wigginton (1999).

K.J. WALKER & J.O. MOUNTFORD

Ne ***Teucrium botrys*** Cut-leaved Germander
L.

A biennial herb of bare ground within open grassland, arable field margins, and open fallow overlying chalk and limestone; occasionally recorded on spoil-tips and in disused quarries. Lowland.

Trends *T. botrys* was cultivated in Britain by 1599, first recorded in the wild at Box Hill (Surrey) in 1844, and has sometimes been considered to be native. It has declined since 1930 due to agricultural intensification, scrub encroachment and lack of grazing. However, it benefits from disturbance and at some sites thousands of plants have been recorded since 2000, following cultivation or conservation management such as harrowing and turf cutting.

Biogeography European Temperate element, but absent as a native from much of western Europe.

	GB	IR
Long term	No trend	No trend
Short term	No trend	No trend

Alien	GB	IR
2000–19	7	1
1987–99	7	0
1970–86	8	0
pre-1970	12	0

Key refs Rich (1997b), Wigginton (1999).

K.J. Walker & J.O. Mountford

N ***Ajuga reptans*** Bugle
L.

A winter-green perennial herb with a short rhizome and long leafy stolons of damp deciduous woods and woodland rides, shaded places and unimproved grassland on neutral or acidic soils, sometimes occurring in flushed ground. 0–894 m (Beinn nan Eachan, Mid Perthshire).

Trends The distribution of *A. reptans* has not changed appreciably since the 1960s, and its true distribution in Ireland is now much better understood due to more intensive recording since 2000.

Biogeography European Temperate element.

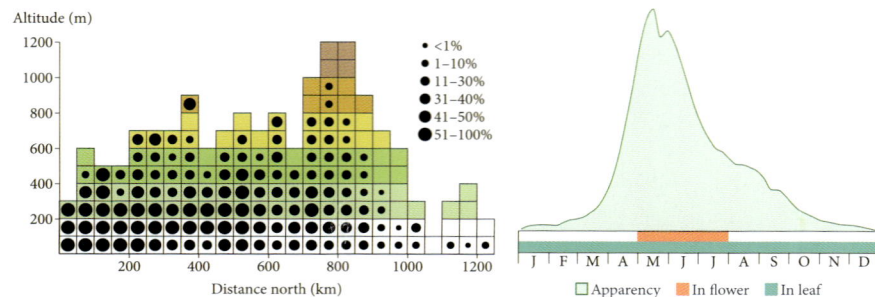

	GB	IR
Long term		
Short term		

Native	GB	IR
2000–19	2362	731
1987–99	2297	620
1970–86	1559	118
pre-1970	2252	452

Alien	GB	IR
2000–19	23	1
1987–99	4	0
1970–86	3	0
pre-1970	3	0

P.A. Stroh & K.J. Walker

N *Ajuga pyramidalis* Pyramidal Bugle
L.

A rhizomatous perennial herb of free-draining rocky slopes, rock crevices and shallow peat in open heathland and grassland overlying infertile, moderately acidic to basic soils. The majority of British and Irish populations are coastal, small in size and are largely made up of non-flowering rosettes. Reproduction is mainly from seed, which is long-lived and often germinates after disturbance. 0–680 m on Ill Bell (Westmorland).

Trends *A. pyramidalis* remains a very scarce plant in Britain and Ireland but has been found in many new sites since the 1960s, particularly in the remoter parts of northern and western Ireland and north-western Scotland, often as a result of targeted surveys of suitable habitats (e.g. Rich *et al.*, 1999b; Pearman *et al.*, 2008). The number of new populations discovered since 2000 suggest that it is still overlooked in some areas, especially when not in flower, and further populations almost certainly await discovery. The only English colony, discovered in 1869, occurs on a precipitous crag in the Lake District where around a dozen plants survive. Some coastal populations in north-western Scotland may have been lost through more intensive grazing by sheep and deer, but the difficulties in finding this species makes any assessment of change problematic.

Biogeography European Boreal-montane element.

Native	GB	IR
2000–19	61	7
1987–99	51	6
1970–86	41	6
pre-1970	73	4

Key refs Gulliver (1997), Pearman *et al.* (2008), Rich *et al.* (1999b), Stewart *et al.* (1994), Stroh *et al.* (2019).

K.J. WALKER

N? *Ajuga chamaepitys* Ground-pine
(L.) Schreb.

An annual or biennial herb of arable field margins and bare tracks and rabbit scrapes on chalk downland. Its seeds are long-lived and this has led to its reappearance following disturbance at some sites. Lowland.

Native or alien in Britain and a neophyte in the Channel Islands.

Trends Known as a British plant since 1551, *A. chamaepitys* declined considerably between 1950 and 1990 due to herbicide spraying, abandonment of fallow land and succession to coarse grassland, scrub and woodland on chalk slopes. Over the past 30 years its distribution has remained relatively stable, with an improvement of its fortunes on some arable sites due to increased protection and more sympathetic management, often as part of conservation initiatives and agri-environment schemes (e.g. uncropped margins with reduced herbicide and fertilizer applications).

Biogeography European Southern-temperate element.

Native	GB	IR
2000–19	17	0
1987–99	15	0
1970–86	20	0
pre-1970	49	0

Alien	GB	IR
2000–19	0	0
1987–99	5	0
1970–86	3	0
pre-1970	7	0

Key refs Stewart *et al.* (1994), Wigginton (1999).

K.J. WALKER

Ar *Nepeta cataria* Cat-mint
L.

A winter-green perennial herb, found along the margins of arable fields, as well as the verges of tracks and roads on chalky soils. It also occurs on hedgebanks, rough fields, waste ground, refuse tips, pits and ancient chalk banks. It occasionally escapes from gardens or is deliberately planted in areas sown with wild-flower seed mixtures. The seed is long-lived. Lowland.

Trends *N. cataria* has declined since the 1960s largely as a result of the intensification of arable cropping and possibly more locally due to the growth of scrub, following the loss of grazing. Some populations have also been lost due to the removal of hedgerows (Gent *et al.*, 1995).

Biogeography As an archaeophyte, *N. cataria* has a Eurosiberian Temperate distribution; it is widely naturalized outside this range.

Alien	GB	IR
2000–19	178	2
1987–99	181	0
1970–86	133	0
pre-1970	432	9

	GB	IR
Long term	↓ ↓	No trend
Short term	↓	No trend

Key refs Gent & Wilson (1995).

K.J. Walker

Hy *Nepeta nepetella × racemosa = N. ×faassenii* Garden Cat-mint
Bergmans ex Stearn

A rhizomatous perennial herb found as a garden throw-out on roadsides, stone walls, coastal dunes, refuse tips and waste ground; some of the plants are said to be self-sown. Most populations are small and probably casual, but it can persist and spread by means of its extensive rhizomes. The hybrid is sterile; fertile plants have been recorded but these may be referable to *N. racemosa*. Lowland.

A cultivated hybrid (alien × alien).

Trends This hybrid was in cultivation by 1876 and is extremely popular in gardens. It was first recorded in the wild from waste ground at Kingsknowe Station (Midlothian) in 1902, and may be increasing in the wild, though much of this spread must be due to better recording of both aliens and hybrids in recent decades.

Biogeography A hybrid of garden origin.

	GB	IR
2000–19	182	7
1987–99	86	0
1970–86	33	0
pre-1970	30	0

	GB	IR
Long term	No trend	No trend
Short term	↑ ↑	↑

Key refs Stace *et al.* (2015).

C.A. Stace, C.D. Preston & D.A. Pearman

N *Glechoma hederacea* Ground-ivy
L.

A carpet-forming stoloniferous perennial herb of woods, grassland, hedgerows and waste places, usually on fertile soils. It usually spreads vegetatively by rapid growth of its creeping stems, and seed-set is often very low. 0–570 m (Hartside Quarry, Cumberland).

Trends Although there has been no appreciable change in the 10 km square distribution of *G. hederacea* since the 1960s, in recent decades it has apparently increased within lowland woods, particularly in south-eastern England, where excessive deer grazing has led to a decline in more palatable woodland ground-flora species (Cooke, 1994). The increases in remoter parts of Scotland and in Ireland are likely to reflect more systematic recording since 2000.

Biogeography Eurasian Boreo-temperate element, but naturalized in North America so distribution is now Circumpolar Boreo-temperate.

Native	GB	IR
2000–19	2185	691
1987–99	2145	644
1970–86	1489	109
pre-1970	2090	493

Alien	GB	IR
2000–19	4	0
1987–99	7	0
1970–86	4	0
pre-1970	19	0

Key refs Grime *et al.* (2007), Hutchings & Price (1999).

K.J. WALKER

N *Prunella vulgaris* Selfheal
L.

A patch-forming winter-green perennial herb that is almost ubiquitous in fertile and infertile grasslands on both acid and calcareous soils, growing in meadows, pastures, lawns, woodland clearings and rides, tracks, paths, roadsides and waste ground, possibly achieving its greatest abundance on moist, heavier soils. It forms clonal patches in short-grazed turf and spreads by seed and the detachment of daughter ramets. 0–755 m (Knock Fell, Westmorland), and 845 m on Great Dun Fell (Westmorland).

Trends *P. vulgaris* is very frequent throughout our area, and there is no evidence for a change in its overall distribution since the 1960s. It is now a frequent constituent of wild-flower seed mixtures and is likely to be increasing as an introduction in areas that are often sown, such as road verges and newly landscaped areas.

Biogeography Circumpolar Wide-temperate element; widely naturalized outside its native range.

Native	GB	IR
2000–19	2806	998
1987–99	2755	942
1970–86	1900	205
pre-1970	2663	895

Alien	GB	IR
2000–19	1	0
1987–99	1	0
1970–86	0	0
pre-1970	1	0

Key refs Grime *et al.* (2007).

K.J. WALKER

Ne *Prunella laciniata* Cut-leaved Selfheal

(L.) L.

A perennial herb, with a short rhizome and an erect to decumbent stem rooting at the nodes. Found naturalized in dry, calcareous grassland, on roadsides, on waste ground and along woodland rides. Lowland.

Trends *P. laciniata* was formerly regarded as a possible native but is now considered to be a neophyte due to the late year of its discovery in the wild (1886), its association with sown clover leys and its lack of persistence at many sites (Pearman, 2007). It suffered widespread losses before 1930, possibly due to a decline in the sowing of clover leys, and these losses have continued since then. It is now rare, though new sites are occasionally found.

Biogeography *P. laciniata* has a European Temperate distribution.

	GB	IR
Long term	No trend	No trend
Short term	No trend	No trend

Alien		GB	IR
2000–19	●	13	2
1987–99	●	14	1
1970–86	●	10	0
pre-1970	○	57	0

Key refs Clement (1985b), Morton (1973), Pearman (2007).

K.J. WALKER

Ne *Melissa officinalis* Balm

L.

A winter-green perennial herb with a shortly spreading rhizome, widely grown in gardens for its lemon-scented foliage and seeding prolifically. Usually found established where discarded in garden waste but also clearly self-sown or spreading in soil and gravel. Often found on banks and road verges close to human habitations, and on refuse tips and waste ground. Lowland.

Trends *M. officinalis* was being cultivated in British gardens by 995 (Harvey, 1981) and was recorded in the wild by 1763. It is a popular culinary herb and has spread rapidly northwards in our area since the 1960s.

Biogeography A native of southern Europe, the Mediterranean region and south-western Asia, but its native range is obscured by naturalized populations farther north.

	GB	IR
Long term		
Short term		

Alien		GB	IR
2000–19	●	1061	61
1987–99	●	543	18
1970–86	●	206	2
pre-1970	○	355	22

Key refs Harvey (1981), Mabey (1996).

K.J. WALKER

Clinopodium menthifolium Wood Calamint

(Host) Stace

A rhizomatous perennial herb of lightly shaded woodland edges and scrub overlying chalk. Lowland.

Trends This species has been known since 1843 from a single dry chalk valley on the Isle of Wight. Although once abundant, the cessation of coppicing led to a marked decline and by the late 1950s it was almost extinct. Since then, annual conservation work to remove invasive ground-cover and to reinstate coppicing has led to a considerable increase to around 2,000 plants along a laneside bordering the wood (Marston, 2007). Since 2007 a handful of colonies have also been successfully established from seed and plug-plants in woodland nearby. It recently escaped from cultivation in Breconshire and is now established under a hedge along an old bridleway.

Biogeography European Temperate element.

Native		GB	IR
2000–19	●	1	0
1987–99	●	1	0
1970–86	○	1	0
pre-1970	○	1	0

Alien		GB	IR
2000–19	●	1	0
1987–99	●	0	0
1970–86	●	0	0
pre-1970	○	0	0

	GB	IR
Long term	No trend	No trend
Short term	No trend	No trend

Key refs Marston (2007), Wigginton (1999).

K.J. WALKER

Clinopodium ascendens Common Calamint

(Jord.) Samp.

A rhizomatous winter-green perennial herb of dry, sunny banks and verges next to hedgerows, tracks, fields and roads, usually on calcareous soils. It also occurs in old sand-, gravel- and chalk-pits, railway sidings, rough scrubby grassland, rocky outcrops, churchyards, walls and woodland margins. It occasionally occurs near to human habitations as a relic of cultivation. Generally lowland, but reaching 380 m at Conistone (Mid-west Yorkshire).

Trends *C. ascendens* has declined since the 1960s due to habitat loss, succession as a result of a lack of grazing in its grassland habitats, and changes to road verge management which have favoured more competitive species. However, in some areas it seems to be spreading in anthropogenic habitats such as railway sidings, disused railways and disused quarries. It is a late-flowering and often very local plant and this may have resulted in it being overlooked in some areas in the past.

Biogeography European Temperate element.

Native		GB	IR
2000–19	●	518	52
1987–99	●	462	41
1970–86	○	338	5
pre-1970	○	495	36

Alien		GB	IR
2000–19	●	38	1
1987–99	●	17	1
1970–86	●	3	0
pre-1970	○	18	1

K.J. WALKER

N *Clinopodium nepeta* Lesser Calamint

(L.) Kuntze

A short-lived winter-green perennial herb of dry, south-facing banks and rough grassland on calcareous, sandy or gravelly soils. Formerly a pasture plant, it is now largely confined to roadsides, hedgebanks, railway banks, old pits, scrubby grassland, churchyards and waste ground. Lowland.

Trends The native range of *C. nepeta* is uncertain because of former confusion with *C. ascendens* and the occurrence of garden escapes. Despite these uncertainties it is clear that its range contracted in the latter half of the 20th century, with many colonies lost following habitat destruction or changes to cutting regimes in its grassland habitats. However, its distribution appears to have stabilized over the past 20 years, and with small increases in some areas on road verges and on old railway lines. It is

grown in gardens and has escaped and become naturalized in a few places.

Biogeography Submediterranean-Subatlantic element.

Native	GB	IR
2000–19	68	0
1987–99	67	0
1970–86	62	0
pre-1970	113	0

Alien	GB	IR
2000–19	9	0
1987–99	2	0
1970–86	1	0
pre-1970	5	0

	GB	IR
Long term		No trend
Short term		No trend

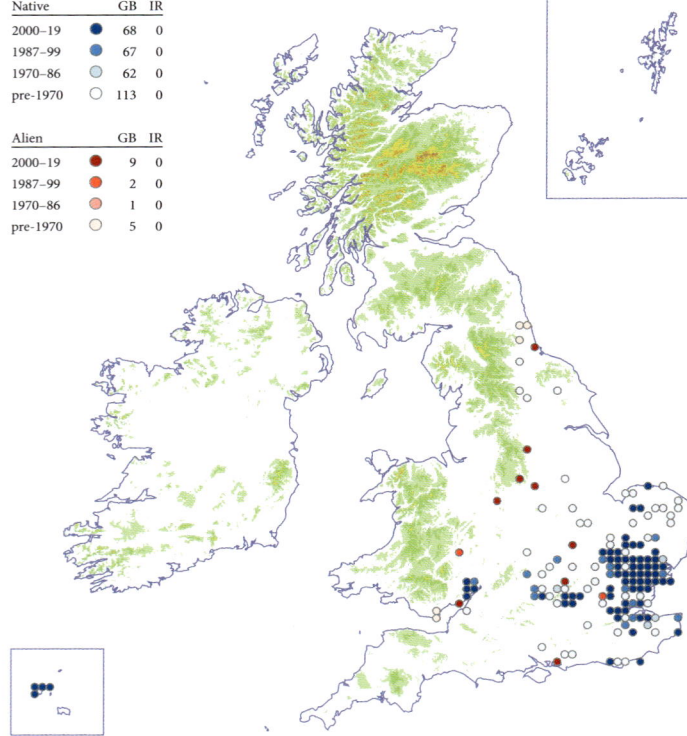

Key refs Stewart *et al.* (1994), Stroh *et al.* (2019).

K.J. Walker

N *Clinopodium vulgare* Wild Basil

L.

A rhizomatous winter-green perennial herb of hedgebanks, woodland margins, coarse scrubby grassland, coastal cliffs and sand dunes, typically on dry calcareous soils. It is also found on arable land, waste ground, old quarries, and track- and railway-sides. 0–490 m (Cwar yr Hendre, Breconshire).

Native in Britain and the Channel Islands and a neophyte in Ireland.

Trends *C. vulgare* appears to have become much less common in some regions, most clearly north of the Humber, presumably due to the loss of species-rich calcareous grasslands. It may be increasing as a garden escape in some areas.

Biogeography Circumpolar Temperate element, with a disjunct distribution.

Native	GB	IR
2000–19	1054	0
1987–99	1000	0
1970–86	777	0
pre-1970	1124	0

Alien	GB	IR
2000–19	15	8
1987–99	4	1
1970–86	0	0
pre-1970	2	7

	GB	IR
Long term		
Short term		

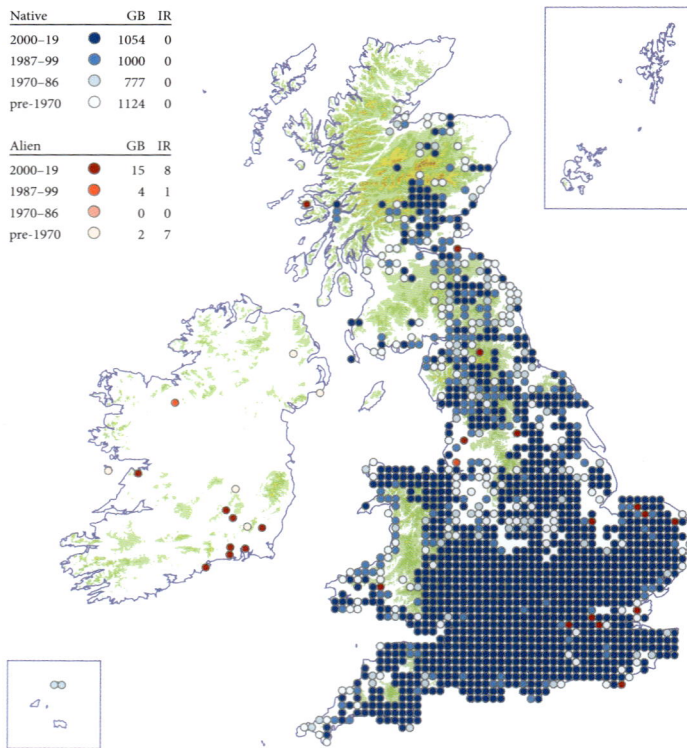

Key refs Grime *et al.* (2007).

K.J. Walker

Clinopodium acinos Basil Thyme

(L.) Kuntze

An annual or short-lived perennial herb of disturbed soils in dry grassland, rocky ground and arable fields. In Britain it mainly grows on calcareous soils, and more rarely on sands and gravels; in Ireland it is a plant of sandy and gravelly sites, including eskers. It is also a rare casual of waste ground, quarries, pits and banks by roads and railways. 0–394 m (Creigiau Eglwyseg, Denbighshire).

Trends *C. acinos* has declined substantially since the 1960s as a result of more efficient methods of weed control on arable land and, in Ireland, gravel extraction. In many areas it is no longer found in arable fields, surviving only in less intensively managed habitats on chalk and limestone where periodic disturbance reduces competition and creates the gaps it needs for regeneration. The only recent record for Scotland is from a golf course near to Elgin (Moray) in 2009 in an area where it has been known since 1862. It is considered to be alien in Ireland (Scannell & Synnott, 1987).

Biogeography European Temperate element; also in central Asia.

Native	GB	IR
2000–19	220	0
1987–99	259	0
1970–86	261	0
pre-1970	506	0

Alien	GB	IR
2000–19	5	16
1987–99	4	20
1970–86	1	7
pre-1970	13	26

Key refs Scannell & Synnott (1987), Stroh *et al.* (2019).

K.J. Walker

Origanum vulgare Wild Marjoram

L.

A perennial herb of dry, infertile, calcareous soils, occurring in grassland, hedgebanks and scrub, and a colonist of bare or sparsely vegetated ground, including quarries, pavements and road verges. It is occasionally naturalized from gardens. It is intolerant of heavy grazing. 0–510 m (Pennant Dyfi, Craig Ty Nant, Merionethshire).

Native in Britain and Ireland and a neophyte in the Channel Islands.

Trends *O. vulgare* declined slightly in the latter half of the last century in areas outside of its chalk and limestone strongholds. Since 2000, however, it appears to have had something of a revival. This is most likely due to a combination of factors, including more systematic recording and natural spread onto verges, railway banks and cuttings (*e.g.* Leslie, 2019), but also as a result of its use as a component in wild-flower seed mixtures, and an increase in records as a naturalized garden escape.

Biogeography Eurasian Southern-temperate element; widely naturalized outside its native range.

Native	GB	IR
2000–19	1104	165
1987–99	886	134
1970–86	604	9
pre-1970	889	109

Alien	GB	IR
2000–19	340	38
1987–99	83	18
1970–86	24	6
pre-1970	47	27

Key refs Grime *et al.* (2007), Leslie (2019).

P.A. Stroh & K.J. Walker

891

(Ne) *Thymus vulgaris* Garden Thyme
L.

An evergreen dwarf shrub, widely cultivated in gardens and found naturalized on old walls, stony banks, in rough grassland and on waste ground, where it can be self-sown. Usually lowland, but at 450 m on limestone spoil at Mynydd Ddu (Carmarthenshire).

Trends *T. vulgaris* was cultivated in Britain by medieval times (Harvey, 1981). It is very popular in gardens where it is grown for its aromatic leaves and occurs in scores of forms and cultivars. It was first recorded in the wild, as completely naturalized on a garden wall, in 1839 (Hythe, East Kent). Though it appears to be increasing, it could simply be more frequently recorded.

Biogeography Native of the western Mediterranean region, east to south-eastern Italy.

Alien	GB	IR
2000–19	75	3
1987–99	36	2
1970–86	22	0
pre-1970	10	0

	<1%
	1–10%
	11–30%
	31–40%
	41–50%
	51–100%

Key refs Bean (1980), Harvey (1981).

T.D. DINES & D.A. PEARMAN

(N) *Thymus pulegioides* Large Thyme
L.

A prostrate evergreen perennial dwarf shrub of bare ground, short turf or coarse grassland on chalk and limestone, more rarely on sands and gravels on heaths and fixed sand dunes. It is more tolerant of competition than *T. drucei* but more restricted to calcareous substrates. Generally lowland, but reaching 410 m at Vagar Hill (Herefordshire).

Trends This species was formerly confused with *T. drucei* but is now rather better recorded. It is usually very localized and is still overlooked in many areas. It has clearly declined since the 1960s, especially at the edges of its range, often due to a loss of short turf where rabbit and sheep grazing has declined.

Biogeography European Temperate element.

Native	GB	IR
2000–19	254	0
1987–99	300	0
1970–86	188	0
pre-1970	385	3

Alien	GB	IR
2000–19	12	0
1987–99	3	0
1970–86	4	0
pre-1970	7	0

	<1%
	1–10%
	11–30%
	31–40%
	41–50%
	51–100%

Key refs Pigott (1955).

K.J. WALKER

Thymus drucei Wild Thyme

Ronniger

An evergreen dwarf perennial shrub of free-draining, calcareous or base-rich substrates, including chalk, limestone, sands and gravels, often on anthills. It occurs in short grassland on heaths, downland, sea-cliffs and sand dunes, and around rock outcrops and hummocks in calcareous mires. It is also frequent in upland grassland and on montane cliffs, rocks and ledges. 0–1,125 m (Ben Lawers, Mid Perthshire).

Trends *T. drucei* is still very abundant in suitable habitats. There is evidence for some losses in the southern part of its range since the 1960s, especially away from its strongholds on chalk and limestone, due to habitat destruction and succession to coarse grass and scrub following the relaxation or absence of grazing.

Biogeography European Boreo-temperate element.

Native	GB	IR
2000–19	1974	429
1987–99	1994	411
1970–86	1296	103
pre-1970	2037	358

Alien	GB	IR
2000–19	17	1
1987–99	5	0
1970–86	3	0
pre-1970	0	0

Key refs Grime *et al.* (2007), Pigott (1955).

K.J. WALKER

Thymus serpyllum Breckland Thyme

L.

A small prostrate evergreen dwarf shrub confined to dry sandy heaths and grasslands overlying chalk drift, and on inland dunes, especially in areas disturbed by rabbits or sheep. Lowland.

Trends *T. serpyllum* was first recorded in 1773, but since then many sites have been lost to forestry and cultivation. However, the recovery of rabbit populations and increase in sheep grazing has ensured the maintenance of suitable conditions at many of its remaining sites in Breckland, and its overall distribution appears to be stable.

Biogeography European Boreo-temperate element, with a continental distribution in western Europe; widely naturalized outside its native range.

	GB	IR
Long term	No trend	No trend
Short term	No trend	No trend

Native	GB	IR
2000–19	6	0
1987–99	6	0
1970–86	7	0
pre-1970	8	0

Key refs Pigott (1955), Trist (1979), Wigginton (1999).

K.J. WALKER

N *Lycopus europaeus* Gypsywort
L.

A rhizomatous perennial herb of wet habitats on organic and mineral soils, including the banks of rivers, streams, lakes and ditches, the margins of ponds and gravel-pits, fens, swamps, wet woodland, the tops of beaches and dune-slacks. It is tolerant of temporary flooding, and is often an early colonist of exposed mud and shallow standing water in newly created wetlands. 0–485 m (Lochan Learg nan Lunn, Mid Perthshire).

Trends The distribution of *L. europaeus* appears to have been generally stable since the 1960s, and is now better known in Ireland due to more systematic recording. Localized losses as a result of drainage and clearance of watercourses are likely to have been more than compensated for by colonization of new sites.

Biogeography Eurosiberian Temperate element; widely naturalized outside its native range.

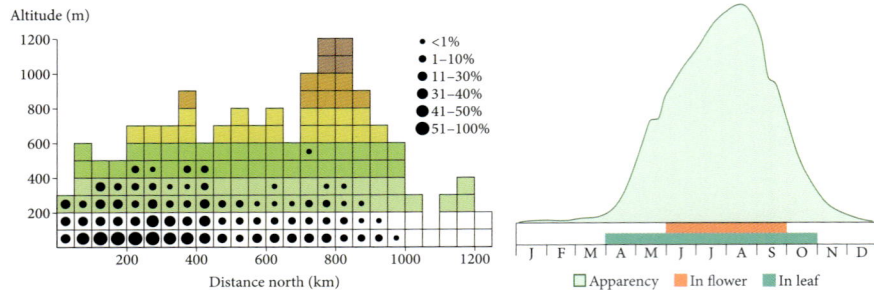

Native	GB	IR
2000–19	1598	339
1987–99	1515	289
1970–86	1071	67
pre-1970	1389	160

Alien	GB	IR
2000–19	1	0
1987–99	0	0
1970–86	0	0
pre-1970	0	0

P.A. STROH & K.J. WALKER

N *Mentha arvensis* Corn Mint
L.

A rhizomatous perennial, rarely annual, herb of arable fields, woodland rides and clearings, marshy pastures, ditches, pond and lake margins, tracksides and waste places; overlapping in habitat with *M. aquatica* but typically replacing it in drier habitats or where water levels fluctuate markedly, such as dried-up margins of ponds and lakes. 0–435 m (Llyn Hir, Cardiganshire).

Trends There has been a decline in the distribution of *M. arvensis* since the 1960s, as the damp, unintensively farmed ploughland which it favours has been improved or changed to pasture. However, its distribution is now better understood and many new discoveries have been made in areas where it is very local and was previously under-recorded. Some early records may refer to *M. ×verticillata*.

Biogeography Circumpolar Boreo-temperate element; widely naturalized outside its native range.

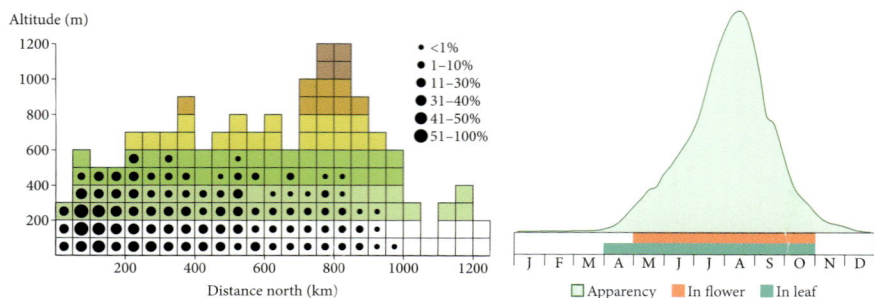

Native	GB	IR
2000–19	1371	213
1987–99	1383	222
1970–86	1063	41
pre-1970	1644	325

Alien	GB	IR
2000–19	4	0
1987–99	2	0
1970–86	1	0
pre-1970	1	0

Key refs Graham (1950), Stace (1975).

K.J. WALKER

Hy *Mentha aquatica* × *arvensis* = *M.* ×*verticillata* Whorled Mint

L.

A perennial herb that spreads by rhizomes and/or stolons and which may be frequent in places where the water levels fluctuate greatly, such as the edges of rivers, streams, lakes, reservoirs and ponds; it also grows in wet woodland, on woodland rides, in fens and swamps, on canal banks, in ditches, damp pastures, dune-slacks, old quarries, arable fields, and by damp tracks and roadsides. It often grows in slightly drier habitats than *M. aquatica*. It is usually sterile; highly fertile plants are sometimes found and may be back-crosses. Generally lowland, but reaching 447 m at Craig Bron-banog (Denbighshire).

A spontaneous hybrid (native × native).

Trends Though it has been found in many new 10 km squares this century, this naturally occurring hybrid has certainly been lost from some wetland sites in the past 50 years (Mountford, 1994) and, presumably, from some arable sites as well.

Biogeography Frequent in mainland Europe, although rare in the Mediterranean region.

	GB	IR
Long term	No trend	No trend
Short term	No trend	No trend

	GB	IR
2000–19	878	212
1987–99	827	153
1970–86	483	31
pre-1970	882	85

Key refs Mountford (1994), Stace *et al.* (2015).

C.A. Stace, C.D. Preston & D.A. Pearman

Hy *Mentha aquatica* × *arvensis* × *spicata* = *M.* ×*smithiana* Tall Mint

R.A.Graham

A rhizomatous or stoloniferous perennial herb, occasionally arising spontaneously where *M. spicata* and *M.* ×*verticillata* occur together, but more typically occurring as a garden throw-out. It is recorded from a wide range of damp semi-natural habitats, including sand dunes, fens, wet meadows and pastures, streamsides and riverbanks, as well as by houses, canals and village ponds, and on rubbish tips and waste ground. It is usually sterile. Lowland.

A cultivated hybrid (native × native × alien).

Trends This hybrid was first recorded in the wild in 1724. Many of the records mapped were compiled by Perring & Sell (1968). Declines have been reported but it is unclear whether these are due to genuine losses, to to under-recording, or through the loss of casual or naturalized populations.

Biogeography This hybrid occurs widely in central Europe.

	GB	IR
Long term	No trend	No trend
Short term	No trend	No trend

	GB	IR
2000–19	108	4
1987–99	112	10
1970–86	73	0
pre-1970	355	2

Key refs Stace *et al.* (2015).

K.J. Walker

Hy *Mentha arvensis × spicata = M. ×gracilis* Bushy Mint
Sole

A rhizomatous perennial herb of the banks of lakes, reservoirs, ponds, rivers, streams and ditches, and in damp meadows and marshy pastures. It also grows on roadside verges, dismantled railways, by village ponds, in farmyards, derelict allotments, and on waste ground and refuse tips, often in the absence of either parent. 0–385 m (Brown Clee Hill, Shropshire).

A cultivated hybrid (native × alien).

Trends Plants arising spontaneously are pubescent, but glabrous clones are more commonly established as garden escapes or throw-outs. The mapped distribution is similar to that in Perring & Sell (1968) and the 2002 *Atlas*, in the north and west of our area, but there are few eastern records this century, perhaps reflecting the loss of casual or naturalized populations. It has been

misidentified as *M. ×verticillata* and as the non-British *M. ×dalmatica*.

Biogeography This hybrid is frequently cultivated and occurs widely in Europe.

	GB	IR
Long term	No trend	No trend
Short term	No trend	No trend

		GB	IR
2000–19	●	198	34
1987–99	●	201	18
1970–86	●	173	11
pre-1970	○	403	13

Key refs Stace *et al.* (2015).

K.J. Walker

Altitude (m) — distribution chart
- ● <1%
- ● 1–10%
- ● 11–30%
- ● 31–40%
- ● 41–50%
- ● 51–100%

Distance north (km)

Apparency | In flower | In leaf

N *Mentha aquatica* Water Mint
L.

A rhizomatous perennial herb of permanently wet habitats adjacent to open water, often partially or wholly submerged. It grows by ditches, ponds, rivers, and streams and in marshes, wet pastures, dune-slacks, fens, and wet woodlands. It spreads clonally by extensive rhizomes, and by detached rhizome fragments, which are often dispersed by water. 0–490 m (Cwar yr Hendre, Breconshire).

Trends With the exception of the Scottish Highlands, *M. aquatica* has a near-ubiquitous distribution at the 10 km square scale which has changed very little since the 1960s, except in Ireland and northern Scotland where it is now known to be more widespread as a result of more systematic recording in recent decades.

Biogeography European Temperate element; widely naturalized outside its native range.

		GB	IR
Native			
2000–19	●	2439	927
1987–99	●	2350	887
1970–86	○	1807	198
pre-1970	○	2231	790

	GB	IR
Long term		
Short term		

Key refs Grime *et al.* (2007).

K.J. Walker

Altitude (m) — distribution chart
- ● <1%
- ● 1–10%
- ● 11–30%
- ● 31–40%
- ● 41–50%
- ● 51–100%

Distance north (km)

Apparency | In flower | In leaf

Hy *Mentha aquatica × spicata = M. ×piperita* Peppermint
L.

A rhizomatous or stoloniferous perennial herb of damp ground on edges of lakes, reservoirs, ponds, rivers and streams, and in flushes, marshes, wet pastures and wet woodland, and also on waste ground and refuse tips. Glabrous plants are thought to be garden escapes or throw-outs, while pubescent forms are likely to have arisen spontaneously. 0–450 m (Grwyne Fawr, Monmouthshire).

A cultivated hybrid (native × alien).

Trends The distribution of this hybrid has not changed appreciably since it was mapped by Perring & Sell (1968), who included pubescent plants formerly misdetermined as *M. ×dumetorum* (*M. aquatica × M. longifolia*), though it appears to have declined in eastern England, perhaps reflecting the loss of casual or naturalized populations that once arose from cultivated stock. The extent of spontaneous hybridization is unclear because glabrous and hairy forms are rarely recorded separately.

Biogeography Widespread in Europe, both as a spontaneous hybrid and as a garden escape.

	GB	IR
Long term	No trend	No trend
Short term	No trend	No trend

		GB	IR
2000–19	●	564	96
1987–99	●	542	51
1970–86	●	355	16
pre-1970	○	691	60

Key refs Stace *et al.* (2015).

C.A. STACE, C.D. PRESTON & D.A. PEARMAN

Ar *Mentha spicata* Spear Mint
L.

A rhizomatous perennial herb, widely grown in gardens and found naturalized in a variety of damp or wet habitats, and on rough and waste ground, usually close to human habitations. Generally lowland, but reaching 403 m at Mynydd Llanybydder (Carmarthenshire).

Trends *M. spicata* was probably under-recorded in the 1962 *Atlas* because of confusion with *M. longifolia*, *M. suaveolens* and their hybrids. It is very commonly cultivated and spreads vigorously, so it is often discarded with garden rubbish, and in some areas it is now the most common naturalized garden mint.

Biogeography Derived from *M. longifolia* and *M. suaveolens* by hybridization and chromosome doubling. It probably arose in cultivation.

Alien		GB	IR
2000–19	●	1382	68
1987–99	●	1188	41
1970–86	●	744	16
pre-1970	○	864	32

Key refs Graham (1958).

K.J. WALKER

Hy *Mentha longifolia × spicata = M. ×villosonervata* Sharp-toothed Mint
Opiz

A perennial herb that occurs as a garden escape and throw-out, and as a relic of cultivation. Although the hybrid is sometimes recorded on streamsides, ditchsides, wet marshy ground and damp roadsides, many records are from drier habitats, such as hedgebanks, road cuttings and lanesides, derelict allotments and gardens, waste ground and refuse tips. Lowland.

A cultivated hybrid (alien × alien).

Trends This hybrid is commonly cultivated in gardens and was known from the wild by 1906 (Colinton, Midlothian). The apparent increase shown on the map may be due to former taxonomic difficulties, particularly confusion with *M. spicata* and *M. ×villosa*, taxa from which it is not readily separable. It is still probably under-recorded.

Biogeography Probably widespread in Europe, but the distribution is uncertain due to confusion with *M. ×villosa*.

	GB	IR
Long term	No trend	No trend
Short term	No trend	No trend

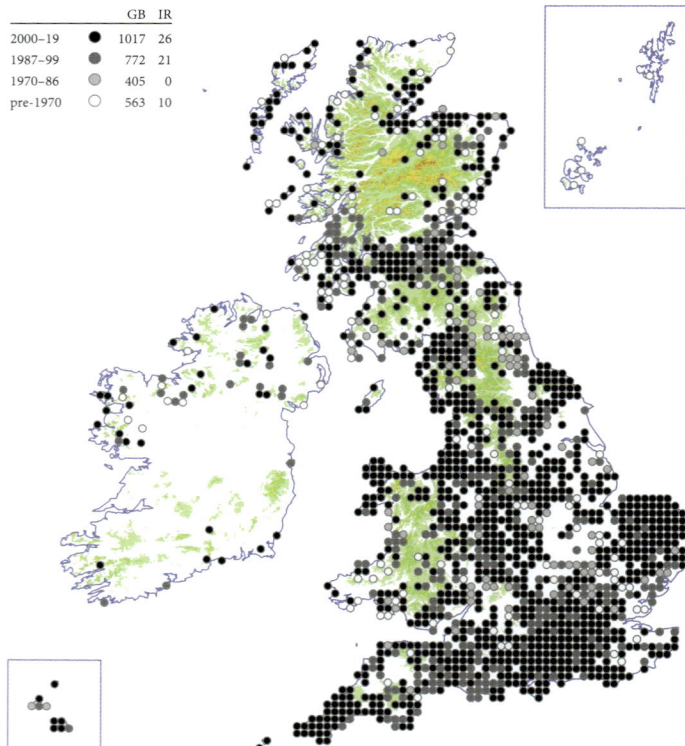

		GB	IR
2000–19	●	83	0
1987–99	●	80	1
1970–86	●	55	0
pre-1970	○	61	1

Key refs Stace *et al.* (2015).

C.A. STACE, C.D. PRESTON & D.A. PEARMAN

Hy *Mentha spicata × suaveolens = M. ×villosa* Apple-mint
Huds.

A rhizomatous perennial herb, widespread and naturalized in damp, rough and waste ground, and on roadsides. It sometimes spreads to form large patches. There are many cultivated variants; probably the most widespread is var. *alopecuroides*, a uniform hybrid possibly represented in our area by a single clone, to which the name Apple-mint probably applies. 0–382 m (Totley Moss, Derbyshire).

A cultivated hybrid (native × alien).

Trends *M. ×villosa* was known from the wild by at least 1882 and is an increasing garden escape. It was mapped as *M. ×niliaca* by Perring & Sell (1968), but at that stage it was thought to be under-recorded. It may still be more frequent than the current map suggests. *M. scotica*, formerly considered as a separate species or a variant of *M. ×villosa*, has now been

placed within *M. spicata* pending further study. *Mentha* species and hybrids are taxonomically difficult and rather unfashionable with recorders; there is no illustrated handbook so recording effort has been decidedly uneven.

Biogeography Widespread in Europe.

	GB	IR
Long term	No trend	No trend
Short term	No trend	No trend

		GB	IR
2000–19	●	1017	26
1987–99	●	772	21
1970–86	●	405	0
pre-1970	○	563	10

Key refs Stace *et al.* (2015).

C.A. STACE, C.D. PRESTON & D.A. PEARMAN

Hy *Mentha longifolia* × *suaveolens* = *M.* ×*rotundifolia* False Apple-mint

(L.) Huds.

	GB	IR
Long term	No trend	No trend
Short term	No trend	No trend

A perennial herb intermediate between its parents and found as a garden escape or throw-out on refuse tips, waste ground and roadsides. Lowland.

A cultivated hybrid (native × alien).

Trends As with all hybrid mints, uncertainties in identification and nomenclatural confusion mean that this hybrid is under-recorded, so it is difficult to assess changes in distribution. It was first recorded in the wild from Ben Lester Burn, Arran (Clyde Isles) in 1929. It is often confused with its parents and with *M.* ×*villosa*.

Biogeography Frequent with the parents in Europe and south-western Asia.

	GB	IR
2000–19	34	1
1987–99	32	5
1970–86	33	0
pre-1970	29	1

Key refs Stace (1975), Stace *et al.* (2015).

K.J. WALKER

N *Mentha suaveolens* Round-leaved Mint

Ehrh.

A rhizomatous perennial herb of damp places, probably native only in coastal parts of south-western England and Wales; elsewhere it is increasing as a garden escape, often forming extensive colonies on roadsides and waste ground. Lowland.

Native in Britain and a neophyte in Ireland and the Channel Islands.

Trends The native distribution of *M. suaveolens* is difficult to define with certainty due to garden escapes and former confusion with *M.* ×*villosa* (*cf.* Brewis *et al.*, 1996; Halliday, 1997). However, its overall native range appears to be stable whereas it has increased dramatically elsewhere, especially in Ireland, Wales and northern England, partly due to more systematic recording but mainly due its increased prevalence as a garden escape.

Biogeography Submediterranean-Subatlantic element.

Native	GB	IR
2000–19	66	0
1987–99	65	0
1970–86	37	0
pre-1970	89	0

Alien	GB	IR
2000–19	213	84
1987–99	175	39
1970–86	136	12
pre-1970	256	73

Key refs Brewis *et al.* (1996), Halliday (1997).

K.J. WALKER

(N) *Mentha pulegium* Pennyroyal
L.

A short-lived perennial herb of seasonally inundated grassland overlying silt and clay. The majority of native populations are now confined to pools, runnels, ruts and poached areas on heavily grazed village greens, but habitats also include damp heathy pastures, lake shores and coastal grassland. Lowland.

Trends *M. pulegium* was lost from many sites before 1930, and declined further during the 20th century due to the drainage of wetlands, filling-in of ponds and the loss of traditional grazing on commons and village greens. Since the 1980s an erect variety originating from North America has been introduced in seed mixtures used for amenity and landscaping and, as a consequence, it is now more common as a naturalized alien, especially in southern and central England, where it occurs in habitats such as newly sown road verges, the margins of reservoirs, restored riverside pastures and former gravel-pits. This variety often occurs in areas where native populations of *M. pulegium* were known, leading to suspicions to those not familiar with the alien variety that it may have been overlooked as a native or reappeared from long-buried seed banks.

Biogeography European Southern-temperate element.

Native	GB	IR
2000–19	27	8
1987–99	22	5
1970–86	18	4
pre-1970	238	41

Alien	GB	IR
2000–19	123	3
1987–99	53	0
1970–86	19	0
pre-1970	78	1

Key refs Kay & John (1995), Stewart *et al.* (1994), Stroh *et al.* (2019), Wigginton (1999).

K.J. WALKER

(Ne) *Mentha requienii* Corsican Mint
Benth.

A perennial herb which occurs as a weed in cultivated ground and occasionally as well-established populations in damp grassy and rocky places, in woodlands, along tracks, paths and pavements and on refuse tips. It also occurs where planted. Generally lowland, but reaching 305 m on Slieve Gullion (County Armagh).

Trends This species was apparently introduced in 1829 and is frequent in cultivation. It was first recorded in the wild in 1872 (Castletownshend, West Cork) and was mapped by Perring & Sell (1968). It is a slightly tender plant; there are more records in the last 50 years, probably largely due to improved recording, though milder winters might also be a factor in recent increases.

Biogeography Native of Corsica, Sardinia and the nearby Italian island of Montecristo; possibly naturalized in Portugal, but rare in mainland Europe.

Alien	GB	IR
2000–19	51	14
1987–99	27	3
1970–86	13	1
pre-1970	17	6

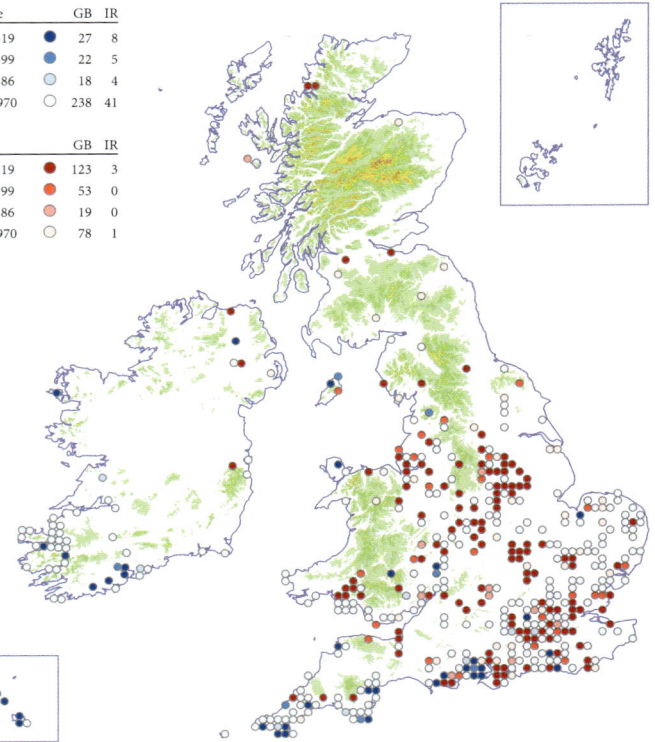

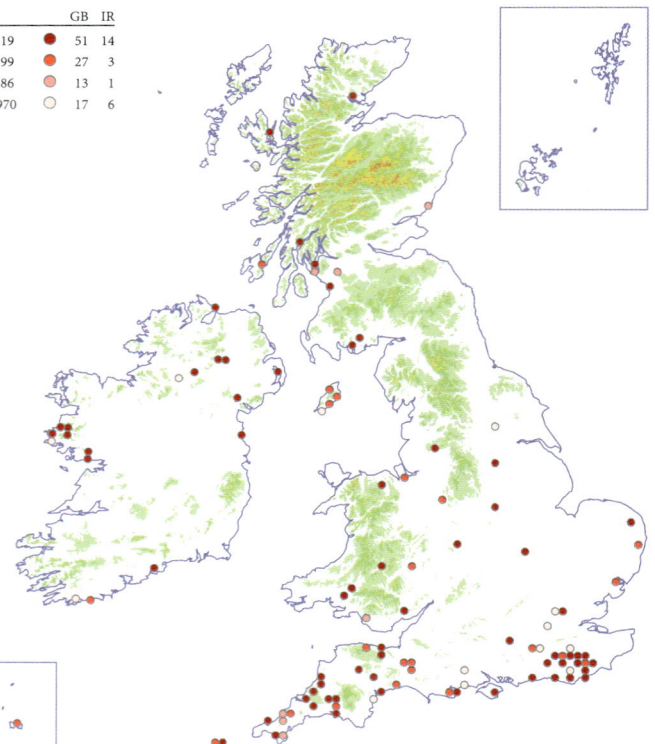

K.J. WALKER

Ne *Lavandula angustifolia* Garden Lavender

Mill.

An evergreen shrub, very widely grown in gardens, with a multiplicity of cultivars, and spreading from plantings and occasionally by seed. It is also increasingly planted as a field crop, albeit still on a small scale. Lowland.

Trends *L. angustifolia* has been cultivated in our area since at least the 13th century (Harvey, 1981), and probably earlier. The first record from the wild that we have traced is 1982 (Chelsea, Middlesex) but this late record is probably more a reflection of its absence from earlier Floras and a general increase in the recording of garden escapes since the 1980s. The majority, perhaps all self-sown plants are of this species, and not of the hybrid *L. ×intermedia*, which is mainly sterile (Stace *et al.*, 2015).

Biogeography A native of the western Mediterranean region; it is widely cultivated elsewhere.

Alien	GB	IR
2000–19	356	11
1987–99	48	0
1970–86	5	0
pre-1970	1	0

Key refs Harvey (1981), Stace *et al.* (2015), Upson & Andrews (2004).

D.A. PEARMAN & K.J. WALKER

Ne *Rosmarinus officinalis* Rosemary

L.

An evergreen shrub, widely grown in gardens for its flowers and its use as a herb. It is usually found as a throw-out or relic of cultivation, almost always close to human habitations but self- and bird-sown plants have been recorded from walls, pavement cracks and waste ground. Lowland.

Trends *R. officinalis* has been cultivated as a herb in Britain since at least 1548 and is now extremely popular in gardens. Rather surprisingly it was not recorded from the wild until 1969. Since then its distribution has increased substantially, although many of the records in and around London may be from gardens. A large number of cultivars are available, and have been recorded from the wild, including the white-flowered 'Albiflora'.

Biogeography Native of the south-western Europe, the Mediterranean region and the Caucasus.

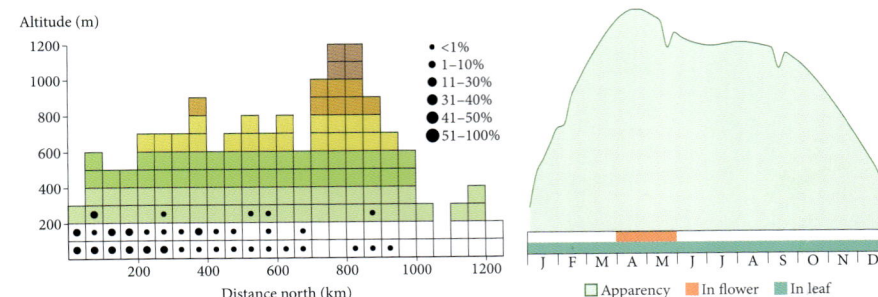

Alien	GB	IR
2000–19	297	14
1987–99	80	0
1970–86	12	0
pre-1970	2	0

Key refs Bean (1980).

K.J. WALKER

(N?) *Salvia pratensis* Meadow Clary
L.

A long-lived perennial herb of unimproved grassland, lanesides, road verges and disturbed ground on well-drained soils overlying chalk and limestone. It is occasionally established from gardens or as a casual in waste places. Lowland.

Trends *S. pratensis* is considered a probable British native, although the relatively late year of discovery (1696) and association with ancient roads and trackways could suggest an ancient introduction. Most of the losses of native sites seem to have taken place before 1950, and there is little evidence for a significant decline in recent years, although numbers have reduced on some sites either due to lack of management or the regular mowing of road verges with the trimmings left *in situ* (Stroh *et al.*, 2019). The bulk of the 26 extant populations are in the Cotswolds, with about half in Oxfordshire. It became extinct in its sole native Welsh site in 2008, but has been recently reintroduced there. In the late 18th and early 19th centuries *S. pratensis* was widely introduced via the import of foreign grain, but more recent introductions are mainly of garden escapes (Rich *et al.*, 1999c; Moughan *et al.*, 2021).

Biogeography European Temperate element.

Native	GB	IR
2000–19	17	0
1987–99	20	0
1970–86	21	0
pre-1970	34	0

Alien	GB	IR
2000–19	47	0
1987–99	27	0
1970–86	16	0
pre-1970	112	0

Key refs Kay & John (1995), Moughan *et al.* (2021), Rich *et al.* (1999c), Stroh *et al.* (2019), Wigginton (1999).

K.J. WALKER

(N) *Salvia verbenaca* Wild Clary
L.

A long-lived, winter-green, clump-forming perennial herb of dry, open grassland on sunny banks, tracksides, roadsides, disused railway lines, and coastal shingle and sand dunes; usually on infertile, well-drained, acidic or base-rich soils. It also occurs as an introduction on waste ground or in newly sown grassland on road verges and areas that have been landscaped. In Ireland, it is almost exclusively coastal. Lowland.

Trends The native 10 km square range of *S. verbenaca* has declined since the 1960s due to the loss of unimproved grassland. However, it has increased substantially as an alien, especially in central and northern England. As a consequence, it has become increasingly difficult to differentiate its native range with certainty.

Biogeography Mediterranean-Atlantic element.

Native	GB	IR
2000–19	313	9
1987–99	309	11
1970–86	205	9
pre-1970	432	19

Alien	GB	IR
2000–19	99	0
1987–99	12	1
1970–86	3	0
pre-1970	21	1

Key refs Mabey (1996).

K.J. WALKER

Ne ## *Salvia officinalis* Sage

L.

A small semi-evergreen shrub, long grown as a herb and for ornament, and found on pavements and walls and in waste places. Usually a garden outcast but also self-seeding. Lowland.

Trends *S. officinalis* has been grown in Britain from at least the 12th century (Harvey, 1981), and is frequently found in the wild as a short-lived plant. It was first recorded at Old Storridge, Worcestershire, in 1867.

Biogeography A native of southern Europe, widely planted elsewhere.

	GB	IR
Long term	No trend	No trend
Short term	↓↓ • ↑ **↑**	No trend

Alien	GB	IR
2000–19	66	2
1987–99	23	0
1970–86	1	0
pre-1970	7	0

Key refs Bean (1980), Harvey (1981), Vaughan & Geissler (2009).

D.A. PEARMAN

Altitude (m)

Distance north (km)

• <1%
• 1–10%
● 11–30%
● 31–40%
● 41–50%
● 51–100%

J F M A M J J A S O N D

□ Apparency ■ In flower ■ In leaf

Ne ## *Salvia reflexa* Mintweed

Hornem.

An annual herb which occurs in fields and on refuse tips and waste ground. It arises from birdseed, grain, grass-seed and, formerly, from wool shoddy. Lowland.

Trends *S. reflexa* was first recorded in the wild in Britain in 1928 (Fritton, East Norfolk), but is now much less commonly recorded with the reduction in the number of refuse tips and access to them, changes to the contents of birdseed, and a decline in the use of wool shoddy.

Biogeography Native of North America; naturalized in Australia, where its high nitrate content renders it toxic to livestock.

	GB	IR
Long term	No trend	No trend
Short term	No trend	No trend

Alien	GB	IR
2000–19	10	0
1987–99	15	0
1970–86	22	0
pre-1970	26	0

Key refs Spooner (1982).

T.D. DINES & D.A. PEARMAN

Altitude (m)

Distance north (km)

• <1%
• 1–10%
● 11–30%
● 31–40%
● 41–50%
● 51–100%

J F M A M J J A S O N D

□ Apparency ■ In flower ■ In leaf

Ne *Salvia viridis* Annual Clary
L.

An annual herb, occasionally grown in gardens and occurring as a garden escape or birdseed alien on roadsides, refuse tips and waste ground. It is usually casual, but some populations persist for a few years. Lowland.

Trends This species was introduced to cultivation in Britain by 1596 and was recorded from the wild by 1858. In the 1970s it was a frequent casual on refuse tips but has declined in frequency as these tips have been closed and access to the few that remain has become more difficult (Leslie, 2019).

Biogeography Native of the Mediterranean region and south-western Asia.

	GB	IR
Long term	No trend	No trend
Short term		No trend

Alien	GB	IR
2000–19	19	0
1987–99	14	0
1970–86	22	0
pre-1970	73	0

Key refs Leslie (2019).

K.J. WALKER

Ne *Salvia verticillata* Whorled Clary
L.

A foetid perennial herb, commonly grown in gardens, usually occurring as a casual, but sometimes naturalized, on road verges, waste ground and by railways. Most plants appear to be self-sown from gardens or more rarely as a grain contaminant. Lowland.

Trends *S. verticillata* was introduced into cultivation in Britain by 1658, and was recorded from the wild by 1857. Most populations are short-lived and there are few recent records, although it persisted at Phillack Towans (West Cornwall) from 1918 to 1970 together with several other garden plants.

Biogeography A European Southern-temperate species, absent as a native from north-western Europe.

	GB	IR
Long term	No trend	No trend
Short term		No trend

Alien	GB	IR
2000–19	19	0
1987–99	19	0
1970–86	18	0
pre-1970	130	0

K.J. WALKER

Ne ***Erythranthe*** Monkeyflowers
Spach

A genus of vigorous, yellow-flowered, stoloniferous perennials which have become widely naturalized in damp places, including pond and lake margins, stream and river shingles, wet woodland, springs and flushes, and damp pastures. 0–750 m (Allt a' Choire Chais in the Cairngorms, Easterness).

Trends *Erythranthe* taxa were cultivated as waterside garden plants by 1759. They have been known to be established in the wild since at least 1830 and some have hybridized both in cultivation and in the wild to form a critical complex of closely related taxa. Because of identification difficulties, the individual taxa are probably under-recorded. Many cultivars of *Erythranthe* are now commercially available and further garden escapes can be expected.

Biogeography An aggregate comprising non-native species from North and South America, and their hybrids.

Native	GB	IR
2000–19	3	0
1987–99	3	0
1970–86	0	0
pre-1970	3	0

Alien	GB	IR
2000–19	1505	196
1987–99	1373	188
1970–86	1043	61
pre-1970	1362	129

	GB	IR
Long term	No trend	No trend
Short term	No trend	No trend

Key refs Puzey & Vallejo-Marín (2014), Rich & Jermy (1998), Silverside (1994), Vallejo-Marín (2012), Vallejo-Marín & Lye (2013).

A. HORSFALL & M. VALLEJO-MARÍN

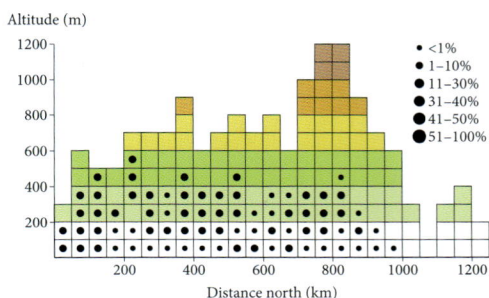

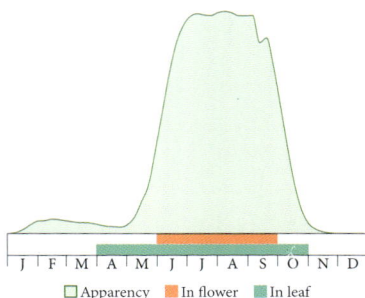

Ne ***Erythranthe moschata*** Musk
(Douglas ex Lindl.) G.L.Nesom

A decumbent perennial herb, found in damp, often shaded places, including the muddy edges of ditches, wooded swamps, damp woodland rides, by ponds and in damp pasture, usually naturalized but occasionally occurring as a casual. Its seeds are very long-lived in the soil. 0–476 m (Knotbury, Staffordshire).

Trends *E. moschata* was introduced to gardens in 1826, spreading from there into semi-natural habitats; it was first recorded from the wild by 1866. It is a very distinct species which has not hybridized with the other monkeyflowers. Consequently, there has been little confusion with other species and it is well recorded. Its 10 km square distribution appears to be stable.

Biogeography Native of western North America.

Alien	GB	IR
2000–19	171	7
1987–99	187	5
1970–86	174	3
pre-1970	212	8

Key refs Rich & Jermy (1998).

A. HORSFALL & M. VALLEJO-MARÍN

Ne *Erythranthe guttata* Monkeyflower

(DC.) G.L.Nesom

A vigorous perennial herb, established in wet places by streams, rivers and ponds, in damp meadows, marshy ground and open woodland. It produces abundant fertile pollen and seeds and spreads both by seed and vegetatively, rooting from the nodes in wet mud or gravel. Generally lowland, but ascending to 650 m at Glenshee Ski Centre (South Aberdeenshire).

Trends *E. guttata* is thought to have been introduced to cultivation in 1812. It soon became established in semi-natural habitats, being known in the wild by 1824. Previously a popular garden plant, it is now rarely cultivated. Its distribution is probably stable although local populations are very dynamic and vary in size from year to year. It is often confused with *E. lutea* and *E. ×robertsii*.

Biogeography Native of western North America, from Mexico to Alaska. Non-native populations are found in continental Europe, the Faroe Islands, New Zealand, and eastern North America.

Alien	GB	IR
2000–19	1085	131
1987–99	882	88
1970–86	529	15
pre-1970	446	20

Key refs Puzey & Vallejo-Marín (2014), Rich & Jermy (1998), Silverside (1994), Vallejo-Marín & Lye (2013).

A. HORSFALL & M. VALLEJO-MARÍN

Hy *Erythranthe guttata × lutea × cuprea*

A stoloniferous perennial herb naturalized in similar places to *E. ×robertsii*, growing on river gravels or in marginal vegetation or shallow water by lakes, streams and rivers, and more rarely, in lowland ditches. It arises as a garden escape and is sterile. Generally lowland but reaching 496 m at Bellanby Burn (Banffshire).

A cultivated hybird (alien × alien × alien).

Trends A colony at Grasmere (Westmorland) was first noted by L. Holmes in 1974 and was still present in 1982. Webster (1978) published a record of material she had collected in 1975 by a small burn running into Loch Ness at Brachla (Easterness). There are few records for the hybrid this century, and it is likely to be under-recorded.

Biogeography A hybrid of garden origin.

	GB	IR
Long term	No trend	No trend
Short term	No trend	No trend

	GB	IR
2000–19	4	0
1987–99	15	0
1970–86	15	0
pre-1970	0	0

Key refs Rich & Jermy (1998), Silverside (1994), Stace (1975), Stace *et al.* (2015), Webster (1978).

C.A. STACE, C.D. PRESTON & D.A. PEARMAN

Hy *Erythranthe guttata × lutea = E. ×robertsii* Hybrid Monkeyflower

(Silverside) G.L.Nesom

A perennial hybrid of damp and wet places, well-established in marshes and by lakes, ponds, streams and rivers, often growing as large colonies on riverside shingle or in marginal vegetation, and sometimes choking shallow streams and ditches. It is partially fertile, and can spread vegetatively from stem fragments. Although concentrated in the uplands, ascending to over 440 m above Garrigill (Cumberland), it extends down to rivers and ditches into the lowlands of the north and west. The amphidiploid *E. peregrina* derives from *E. ×robertsii* and resembles the F₁ hybrid closely, but differs mainly in its fertility (Vallejo-Marin, 2012).

A cultivated hybrid (alien × alien).

Trends *E. ×robertsii* was first recognized in Britain by Roberts (1964), by which time it appears to have been widely naturalized, but it was not named as such until 1990. Herbarium records show that it was present in Scotland by 1848 (Pentland Hills, Midlothian) and in Ireland by 1865 (Fassaroe, County Wicklow). It is the commonest taxon of high ground, and many records of *Erythranthe* agg., *E. lutea* and even *E. guttata* are probably referable to this hybrid, which is therefore likely to be under-recorded.

Biogeography A hybrid of garden origin.

	GB	IR
Long term	No trend	No trend
Short term	No trend	No trend

		GB	IR
2000–19	●	459	63
1987–99	●	378	109
1970–86	●	228	46
pre-1970	○	103	23

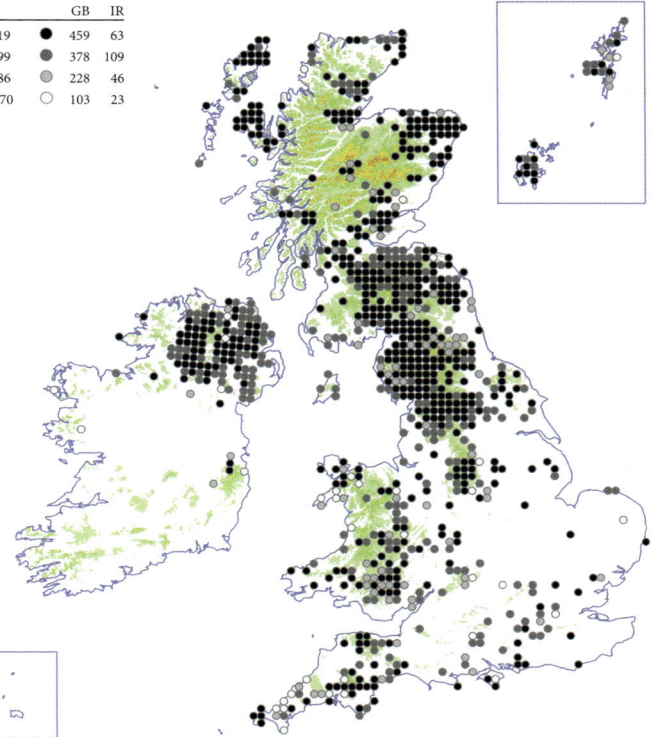

Key refs Roberts (1964), Stace *et al.* (2015), Vallejo-Marín (2012).

C.A. STACE, C.D. PRESTON & D.A. PEARMAN

N *Erythranthe peregrina* New Monkeyflower

(Vall.-Marín) G.L.Nesom

A vigorous perennial herb of stream sides. This species, discovered in 2011, is an allopolyploid derived from the hybrid between *E. guttata* and *E. lutea* (*E. ×robertsii*). It is capable of reproducing both via seeds and through clonal propagation via lateral stems that root at the nodes. It shares the morphological characteristics of *E. ×robertsii* but possesses twice the genome size and number of chromosomes (2n = 6× = 92), and is characterized by high (>90%) pollen fertility (Vallejo-Marín, 2012). 300–360 m.

Trends *E. peregrina* is a newly described taxon discovered in South Lanarkshire in 2011. It was discovered in Orkney in 2014, where it appears to be more abundant, but population sizes seem to fluctuate from year to year.

Biogeography Scottish endemic.

	GB	IR
Long term	No trend	No trend
Short term	No trend	No trend

Native		GB	IR
2000–19	●	3	0
1987–99	●	0	0
1970–86	●	0	0
pre-1970	○	0	0

Key refs Vallejo-Marín (2012), Vallejo-Marín *et al.* (2015).

M. VALLEJO-MARÍN

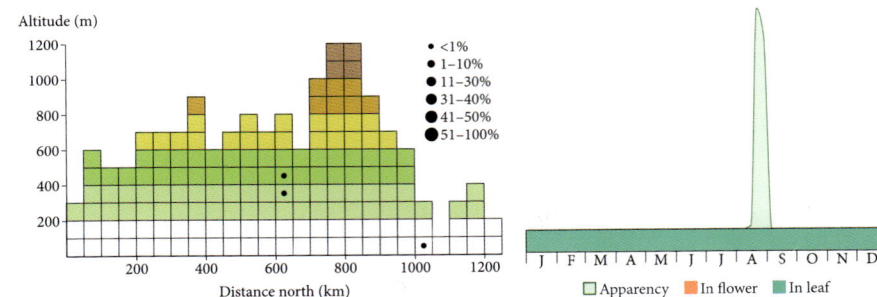

Hy *Erythranthe cuprea × guttata = E. ×burnetii* Coppery Monkeyflower
(S.Arn.) Silverside

Like *E. guttata* and *E. lutea* this hybrid occurs in marshy ground by watercourses, in flushes and on river shingle, though it may be more restricted to the upper reaches of rivers than other members of the genus. It is also known as a rare casual of pavement cracks and waste ground in southern England (Green *et al.*, 1997; Maycock & Woods, 2005). It is usually sterile, but on rare occasions sets a few viable seeds. Generally lowland, but reaching 415 m above Garrigill (Cumberland).

A cultivated hybrid (alien × alien).

Trends Initially identified as *E. cuprea*, which is not naturalized in Britain, it was only recognized as a hybrid after Roberts (1964, 1968) published his detailed studies of the genus, establishing the hybrid nature of the British populations. Plants were raised by Dr Burnet of

Aberdeen in 1901, and were first collected from the wild by Thirlmere (Cumberland) in 1931; they were apparently well-established by 1957.

Biogeography A hybrid of garden origin; the parents *E. cuprea* (South America) and *E. guttata* (North America) are allopatric.

	GB	IR
Long term	No trend	No trend
Short term	No trend	No trend

		GB	IR
2000–19	●	35	0
1987–99	●	54	0
1970–86	●	48	0
pre-1970	○	16	0

Key refs Green *et al.* (1997), Maycock & Woods (2005), Roberts (1964), Roberts (1968), Stace *et al.* (2015).

C.A. STACE, C.D. PRESTON & D.A. PEARMAN

Ne *Erythranthe lutea* Blood-drop-emlets
(L.) G.L.Nesom

A creeping perennial herb naturalized in damp or wet places including marshes and flushes, and on riversides and river shingle. Reproduction is by seed and, to some extent, vegetatively through lateral stems that root at the nodes. Generally lowland.

Trends *E. lutea* was introduced into cultivation by 1826. It is very local and has been much over-recorded for its hybrid with *E. guttata* (*E. ×robertsii*). and so the map is likely to include errors for the hybrid. It is currently rare, with few confirmed populations.

Biogeography Native of South America (Andes).

	GB		IR	
Long term	↓		↓	
Short term	↓		No trend	

Alien		GB	IR
2000–19	●	52	2
1987–99	●	53	4
1970–86	●	90	0
pre-1970	○	165	3

Key refs Rich & Jermy (1998), Silverside (1994), Vallejo-Marín & Lye (2013), Vallejo-Marín *et al.* (2016).

A. HORSFALL & M. VALLEJO-MARÍN

Hy *Erythranthe cuprea × lutea = E. ×maculosa* Scottish Monkeyflower
(W.Bull ex T.Moore) Mabb.

A stoloniferous perennial herb naturalized in wet places, including marshy ground by streams and rivers, in flushes, and on river shingle, where it arises as a garden escape. This hybrid is partially fertile and may set viable seed. Lowland.

A cultivated hybrid (alien × alien).

Trends Introduced into cultivation in Britain by 1863, the earliest specimen of a naturalized plant was collected in 1963 from the River Tweed near Peebles (Peeblesshire), and the first published record was also from shingle by the Tweed, at Neidpath in the same county. It may be under-recorded.

Biogeography A hybrid of garden origin.

	GB	IR
Long term	No trend	No trend
Short term	No trend	No trend

	GB	IR
2000–19	14	0
1987–99	14	0
1970–86	14	0
pre-1970	1	0

Altitude (m)
<1%
1–10%
11–30%
31–40%
41–50%
51–100%

Distance north (km)

Apparency   In flower   In leaf

Key refs Stace *et al.* (2015).

C.A. STACE, C.D. PRESTON & D.A. PEARMAN

N *Melampyrum cristatum* Crested Cow-wheat
L.

An annual hemiparasite of various woody and herbaceous species; mostly found on the margins of ancient *Quercus robur* woodlands, their clearings and rides and in associated field hedgebanks and adjacent protected road verges on chalky boulder-clay soils. It is very rarely found in open meadow grassland. Lowland.

Trends Much of the loss of *M. cristatum* had taken place before 1930, but the range has further contracted since then, most notably in woodlands due to the cessation of traditional coppice management and a lack of ride cutting. Although targeted surveys this century have refound this species at a number of historical road verge sites where it was previously thought to be lost, many populations were not present, with the reasons for loss thought to be a result of neglect, 'cut and drop'

regimes that lead to an accumulation of thatch, cutting before seed-set, and herbicide drift from adjacent arable farmland. It has apparently gone from its sole meadow site, in South Essex, through trampling by horses and inappropriate management.

Biogeography Eurosiberian Temperate element, with a continental distribution in western Europe.

	GB	IR
Long term		No trend
Short term		No trend

Native	GB	IR
2000–19	21	0
1987–99	15	0
1970–86	23	0
pre-1970	62	0

Alien	GB	IR
2000–19	0	0
1987–99	0	0
1970–86	0	0
pre-1970	2	0

Altitude (m)
<1%
1–10%
11–30%
31–40%
41–50%
51–100%

Distance north (km)

Apparency   In flower   In leaf

Key refs Horrill (1972), Stewart *et al.* (1994), Walker *et al.* (2017).

F.J. RUMSEY

Ne *Melampyrum arvense* Field Cow-wheat
L.

An annual hemiparasite, mainly on the roots of grasses. Formerly an arable weed, it now occurs in open grassland beside hedges and ditch-banks, field-borders, in a disused brick-pit and on slumping chalk cliff-faces. The largest remaining populations are a natural occurrence in a garden on old arable land and in several conservation sites where it has been deliberately sown. Lowland.

Trends Although an archaeophyte in parts of northern Europe, this conspicuous species was not recorded in Britain until 1716 (West Suffolk). Originally introduced with crop-seed, it has declined due to improved seed cleaning, agricultural intensification and a lack of disturbance at some sites. It was rare by 1930, and has continued to decline since then, persisting only through management at four sites

since 2000 (Species Recovery Trust, 2016). It has been deliberately planted at some of these sites, which now hold the majority of the British population.

Biogeography *M. arvense* has a European Temperate distribution, although it is absent from much of western Europe.

Alien	GB	IR
2000–19	5	0
1987–99	8	0
1970–86	8	0
pre-1970	52	0

	GB	IR
Long term		No trend
Short term	No trend	No trend

Key refs Species Recovery Trust (2016), Wigginton (1999).

F.J. RUMSEY

N *Melampyrum pratense* Common Cow-wheat
L.

An annual hemiparasite with two subspecies with contrasting habitat associations present in our area: *M. pratense* subsp. *pratense* occurs in open woods, scrub, dry heathlands and upland moorlands on well-drained, nutrient-poor acidic soils; *M. pratense* subsp. *commutatum*, which is mapped separately, occurs more rarely in scrub, in hedgerows and deciduous woodland on chalk and limestone. A variable species, its host range is not well known but will include various trees and ericaceous sub-shrubs. The large seeds have an elaiosome and are distributed by ants. Lowland to 960 m (Macgillycuddy's Reeks, South Kerry).

Trends *M. pratense* was mapped as 'all records' in the 1962 *Atlas*. Many of the losses apparent on the map occurred before 1930, but the decline has accelerated since then in lowland

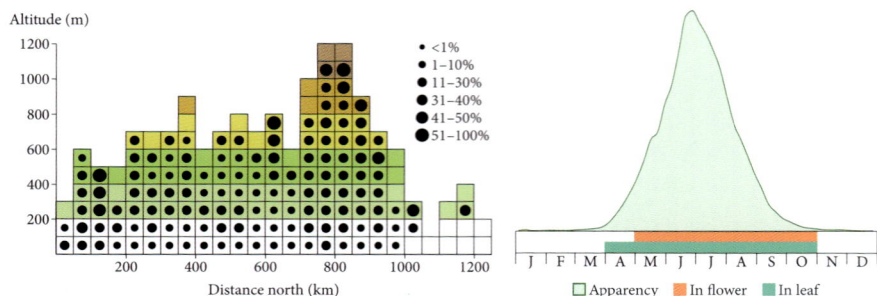

England. This is due to habitat loss and particularly the cessation of traditional woodland management.

Biogeography Eurosiberian Boreo-temperate element.

Native	GB	IR
2000–19	1126	248
1987–99	1202	204
1970–86	927	77
pre-1970	1477	200

Alien	GB	IR
2000–19	0	0
1987–99	0	0
1970–86	0	0
pre-1970	1	0

	GB	IR
Long term		
Short term		

Key refs Smith (1963b).

F.J. RUMSEY

Melampyrum pratense subsp. *commutatum*

(Tausch ex A.Kern.) C.E.Britton

An annual hemiparasite of scrub, hedgerows and open deciduous woodland on calcareous soils derived from chalk, limestones and the Headon beds in the New Forest, but largely replaced on the chalky boulder clays of East Anglia by *M. cristatum*. Its host range is not well known but will include various trees. The large seeds are distributed by ants. Lowland.

Trends Although this broad-leaved calcicolous form of *M. pratense* has been known since the work of Smith (1963b) it has not been well recorded and is almost certainly under-represented on the map. It is likely that as with the nominate subspecies it has declined markedly as a consequence of the cessation of traditional woodland management and the increase in ranker woodland understoreys.

Biogeography Eurosiberian Boreo-temperate element. The precise distribution of this poorly recorded taxon is not well established.

Native		GB	IR
2000–19	●	10	0
1987–99	●	7	1
1970–86	●	5	0
pre-1970	○	32	0

	GB	IR
Long term	No trend	No trend
Short term	No trend	No trend

Key refs Smith (1963b).

F.J. Rumsey

Melampyrum sylvaticum Small Cow-wheat

L.

An annual hemiparasite of humid, lightly shaded situations on damp, usually somewhat enriched, acidic soils; in wooded ravines, in grassy hollows and on banks in woodlands and on upland cliff ledges. A long lost north Wales site near Llanrwst (Denbighshire) was probably associated with lead-rich soils. Near sea level to 760 m on Aonach air Chrith (West Ross).

Trends This species has previously been confused with some forms of *M. pratense* which makes assessing trends difficult. It has definitely been lost in the southern and lowland parts of its range, and also in Northern Ireland, with many losses occurring before 1930. It is extinct in England, being last seen near to Winch Bridge (North-west Yorkshire) in 1976, and from north Wales where it was lost over a century earlier. Since the

2002 *Atlas* more concerted efforts have been made to record this species, and the decline shown this century is likely to be real and not as a consequence of under-recording. The causes are not fully known but will include afforestation, nutrient enrichment, grazing and trampling by livestock.

Biogeography European Boreal-montane element.

Native		GB	IR
2000–19	●	21	1
1987–99	●	22	3
1970–86	●	19	3
pre-1970	○	68	17

Alien		GB	IR
2000–19	●	1	0
1987–99	●	0	0
1970–86	●	0	0
pre-1970	○	0	0

	GB	IR
Long term		No trend
Short term		No trend

Key refs Dalrymple (2007), Rich *et al.* (1998b), Stewart *et al.* (1994).

F.J. Rumsey

N *Euphrasia* Eyebrights
L.

A critical aggregate of small, annual herbs hemiparasitic on the roots of a diverse range of herbs and small shrubs, mainly found in permanent or semi-permanent grasslands. 0–1,210 m (Ben Lawers, Mid Perthshire).

Trends This map includes all the *Euphrasia* taxa in our area. Hybridization, sometimes involving back-crossing and the formation of locally distinct populations, and morphological plasticity mean that identification can be very challenging, and comments on distributional trends for many taxa are tentative. The aggregate has declined due to habitat loss and agricultural improvement. Most taxa are under-recorded.

Biogeography For the distribution of the component taxa, see the relevant accounts.

	GB	IR
Long term	No trend	No trend
Short term	No trend	No trend

Native	GB	IR
2000–19	2065	671
1987–99	2238	738
1970–86	1630	169
pre-1970	2468	753

Key refs Grime *et al.* (2007), Silverside (1998), Stace (1975), Yeo (1978).

F.J. Rumsey

N *Euphrasia officinalis* subsp. *pratensis* Rostkov's Eyebright
Schübl. & G.Martens

A hemiparasitic annual herb of rather damp, herb-rich hay meadows, riverside grasslands, lightly grazed pastures and grassy roadsides. It is replaced in shorter turf and more acidic sites by *E. officinalis* subsp. *anglica*, with which it completely intergrades. Generally lowland, but reaching 430 m at Llanddewi Brefi (Cardiganshire).

Trends This diploid taxon has undoubtedly declined through agricultural improvement and loss of habitat, although as with other critical taxa in the genus it has not been well-recorded, especially in Ireland. It is regarded as a species, *E. rostkoviana*, by Metherell & Rumsey (2018), as it was in the 2002 *Atlas*. The presence of several distinct local taxa with longish glandular hairs in northern and central Scotland suggests a wider past distribution of diploid taxa in the north.

Biogeography European Boreo-temperate element.

	GB	IR
Long term		
Short term		

Native	GB	IR
2000–19	81	10
1987–99	98	20
1970–86	74	5
pre-1970	112	78

Key refs Metherell & Rumsey (2018), Stewart *et al.* (1994).

F.J. Rumsey

Euphrasia officinalis subsp. *monticola* Montane Eyebright
Silverside

A hemiparasitic annual herb of upland hay meadows, primarily of relatively dry soils but also in wet meadows and upland fens, rarely if ever colonizing agriculturally improved grasslands. Most sites are at 200 m to 455 m (Smallburn, North Northumberland), but it has been recorded at 100 m.

Trends This diploid taxon is difficult to separate from subsp. *pratensis* (*E. rostkoviana*) with which it may hybridize. Its distribution is uncertain through difficulties of identification, but it is undoubtedly declining as hay meadows are lost or agriculturally improved. It is regarded as a species, *E. montana*, by Metherell & Rumsey (2018).

Biogeography European Boreo-temperate element.

Key refs Metherell & Rumsey (2018), Stewart *et al.* (1994).

F.J. RUMSEY

Euphrasia officinalis subsp. *anglica* English Eyebright
(Pugsley) Silverside

A diploid hemiparasitic annual herb of grazed habitats on damp acidic substrates. It grows in old pastures, heathlands, moorlands, and disused quarries. It is particularly frequent on the acid leached areas overlying limestones in and around Cheddar Gorge (North Somerset). Generally lowland, but reaching 450 m at Llanddewi Brefi (Cardiganshire).

Trends This is perhaps the most distinctive of the subspecies recognized by Stace (2019) within *E. officinalis* and it is treated as a species, *E. anglica*, by Metherell & Rumsey (2018), as it was in the 2002 *Atlas*. It is most distinct in south-western England; elsewhere material can be difficult to name (Silverside, 1991). It frequently occurs in mixed populations showing introgression with a range of tetraploid species, and some of these local forms

have become stabilized and show distinct ecological preferences. Because of these difficulties, the distribution, as with most of our *Euphrasia* species, is imperfectly known, but the species has undoubtedly declined through habitat loss and degradation, often associated with undergrazing.

Biogeography Endemic; the identification of similar plants in northern France requires confirmation (Yeo, 1978).

Key refs Metherell & Rumsey (2018), Silverside (1991), Yeo (1978).

F.J. RUMSEY

913

Hy *Euphrasia officinalis* subsp. *anglica* × *tetraquetra*

	GB	IR
Long term	No trend	No trend
Short term	No trend	No trend

Plants thought to be hybrids between these two taxa show the compact 'cruciform' habit of *E. tetraquetra* together with many of the long, flexuous glandular hairs of the other parent. Metherell & Rumsey (2018) treat subsp. *anglica* as a species, *E. anglica*. Lowland.

A spontaneous hybrid (native × native).

Trends Specimens identified as this hybrid by L.J. Margetts were first collected by R.E.N. Smith in 2009 on heathland in Hembury Woods, Dartmoor (South Devon), and similar plants were found in 2011 at two other Dartmoor localities; Ideford Common and north-west of Throwleigh. Both parents occur on Dartmoor, though neither was seen in the first site and only subsp. *anglica* was found in the second two. C. Metherell, however, determined the plants collected as an unusual form of subsp. *anglica*, rather than the hybrid (Smith *et al.*, 2016).

Biogeography Wider distribution uncertain.

	GB	IR
2000–19	3	0
1987–99	0	0
1970–86	0	0
pre-1970	0	0

Key refs Metherell & Rumsey (2018), Smith *et al.* (2016), Stace *et al.* (2015).

A.J. SILVERSIDE

N *Euphrasia rivularis* Cumbrian Eyebright
Pugsley

	GB	IR
Long term		No trend
Short term		No trend

A hemiparasitic annual herb of upland rocky flushes, seepage areas and wet rock ledges on montane cliffs. It grows from 250 m at Llanddeusant (Carmarthenshire) to *c.* 750 m on Snowdon (Caernarvonshire), although a specimen identified as this from Rossal Farm (Mid Ebudes) grew at 5 m altitude.

Trends *E. rivularis* is diploid and is closely allied to *E. officinalis* subsp. *pratensis*, from which it has probably arisen through hybridization with *E. micrantha*. Its distribution appears to be stable in the Lake District. In Wales, many new sites have been discovered in Carmarthenshire, although recent searches have failed to re-find it in some sites in southern Snowdonia. It is, however, easily overlooked and probably under-recorded. If correct, the sole Scottish record, made in 2014, represents a significant extension of geographic and altitudinal range.

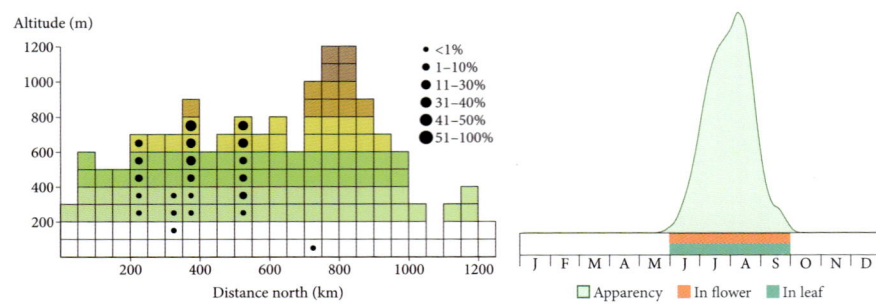

Biogeography Endemic.

Native	GB	IR
2000–19	13	0
1987–99	10	0
1970–86	7	0
pre-1970	12	0

Key refs Metherell & Rumsey (2018), Wigginton (1999).

F.J. RUMSEY

N *Euphrasia vigursii* Cornish Eyebright

Davey

A hemiparasitic annual herb that is characteristic of *Agrostis curtisii–Ulex gallii* heaths. In coastal areas it occurs mainly on cliff-tops in patches of short, species-rich turf around rock outcrops, and by tracks and paths, where scrub is suppressed but the vegetation is not too open. Inland it occurs on lightly grazed damp heaths and open moorland. Generally lowland, but reaching 330 m on Kit Hill (East Cornwall).

Trends This diploid species has declined markedly since the 1960s at its inland sites through habitat dereliction and destruction, including the decline of grazing. *E. vigursii* is believed to have arisen as a stabilized segregate following introgression between *E. officinalis* subsp. *anglica* and *E. micrantha*. Hybridization poses an ongoing threat, with hybrids replacing pure populations of *E. vigursii* at a significant number of sites.

Biogeography Endemic.

Native	GB	IR
2000–19	11	0
1987–99	8	0
1970–86	25	0
pre-1970	31	0

	GB	IR
Long term	No trend	No trend
Short term	No trend	No trend

Key refs French *et al.* (1999), Wigginton (1999).

F.J. RUMSEY

N *Euphrasia arctica* Arctic Eyebright

Lange ex Rostrup

A hemiparasitic annual herb of meadows, unimproved pastures, machair grasslands and roadsides, often replacing *E. nemorosa* over much of northern and western Britain and regularly hybridizing with it and other sympatric *Euphrasia* taxa. Mainly below 500 m, but reaching 1,049 m on Coire nam Beitheach (Main Argyll).

Trends This species is probably under-recorded in southern England, although frequently now present here only in a hybridized state. The species has undoubtedly declined through the improvement of its grassland communities, drainage, changes to management and grazing practices, most notably undergrazing and neglect. Previously it was treated as two distinct subspecies, with the glandular subsp. *borealis* being the more widespread and common plant. The larger and earlier flowering, more decumbent and eglandular subsp. *arctica* is the more frequent subspecies in the Orkneys and Shetland, but the distinguishing characters are now believed to show so much overlap that Metherell & Rumsey (2018) treat them as an aggregate, which is how they are mapped here.

Biogeography Native of north-western Europe, largely restricted to southern Scandinavia, the Faeroes and Britain and Ireland, but closely allied plants are found south to the Carpathians and eastwards to central Russia.

Native	GB	IR
2000–19	782	342
1987–99	424	268
1970–86	349	51
pre-1970	910	373

Alien	GB	IR
2000–19	0	0
1987–99	1	0
1970–86	0	0
pre-1970	1	0

Key refs Metherell & Rumsey (2018).

F.J. RUMSEY

Hy *Euphrasia arctica × nemorosa*

A highly fertile hybrid, often occurring in the absence of both parents and likely to be found on a wide variety of soils, from damp grazed pasture and grassy heathland to hay meadows, machair, limestone and granite quarries, the margins of scrub, woodland rides, downland and roadsides. In southern Scotland it seems to be especially common along old railways. Generally lowland but ascending to 754 m in Keppel Cove, Hellvellyn (Westmorland).

A spontaneous hybrid (native × native).

Trends This hybrid was not mapped in previous atlases. The two species from which the hybrid derives are themselves very variable and probably closely genetically linked (French, 2008), with some suggesting that they might be better treated as a single rather variable species; identification of the hybrid is, therefore, fraught with difficulty, and consequently it is almost certainly under-recorded.

Biogeography Wider distribution uncertain.

		GB	IR
	Long term	No trend	No trend
	Short term	No trend	No trend

		GB	IR
2000–19	●	106	26
1987–99	●	29	5
1970–86	●	20	0
pre-1970	○	15	2

Key refs French *et al.* (2008), Stace *et al.* (2015).

A.J. Silverside, C. Metherell & F.J. Rumsey

Altitude (m) / Distance north (km) chart with legend: <1%, 1–10%, 11–30%, 31–40%, 41–50%, 51–100%

Phenology chart: J F M A M J J A S O N D — Apparency, In flower, In leaf

Hy *Euphrasia arctica × confusa*

A highly fertile hybrid of a wide range of habitats including stony, heathy slopes, grassy heathland and moorland, sheep-grazed acidic pastures, moist neutral pastures, hay meadows, limestone grassland, sea-cliffs and sand dunes, riverside rocks, roadsides, railway cuttings and embankments, quarries, lead-mine spoil and disused ash tips. Generally lowland, but the precise upper altitudinal limit is unknown.

A spontaneous hybrid (native × native).

Trends This hybrid may occur in uniform colonies which replace its parents, but also forms hybrid swarms where its parents meet. It is not always separable from depauperate forms of *E. arctica* and is certainly under-recorded.

Biogeography Wider distribution uncertain.

		GB	IR
	Long term	No trend	No trend
	Short term	No trend	No trend

		GB	IR
2000–19	●	94	6
1987–99	●	22	3
1970–86	●	32	0
pre-1970	○	69	2

Key refs Rich & Jermy (1998), Stace (1975), Stace *et al.* (2015).

F.J. Rumsey & A.J. Silverside

Altitude (m) / Distance north (km) chart with legend: <1%, 1–10%, 11–30%, 31–40%, 41–50%, 51–100%

Phenology chart: J F M A M J J A S O N D — Apparency, In flower, In leaf

Hy *Euphrasia arctica × micrantha = E. ×difformis*
F.Towns.

	GB	IR
Long term	No trend	No trend
Short term	No trend	No trend

A highly fertile hybrid frequent in places where the grassland species *E. arctica* meets the heathland and moorland specialist *E. micrantha*. Typical habitats include heath-grassland mosaics, the grassy sides of roads and streams passing through moorland, and coastal turf on cliffs and dunes. More rarely, it occurs in hay meadows and on railway embankments. Generally lowland but ascending to 529 m near to Lochan na Lairige (Mid Perthshire).

A spontaneous hybrid (native × native).

Trends The binomial is based on material collected by Townsend with the parents on moorland and rocky ground by the River Sheil at Sheil Bridge (Westerness) in 1896. It is probably under-recorded, either for one of the parent species, or confused with the not dissimilar hybrid between *E. arctica* and *E. scottica*.

Biogeography Wider distribution uncertain.

	GB	IR
2000–19	41	4
1987–99	11	0
1970–86	12	0
pre-1970	37	3

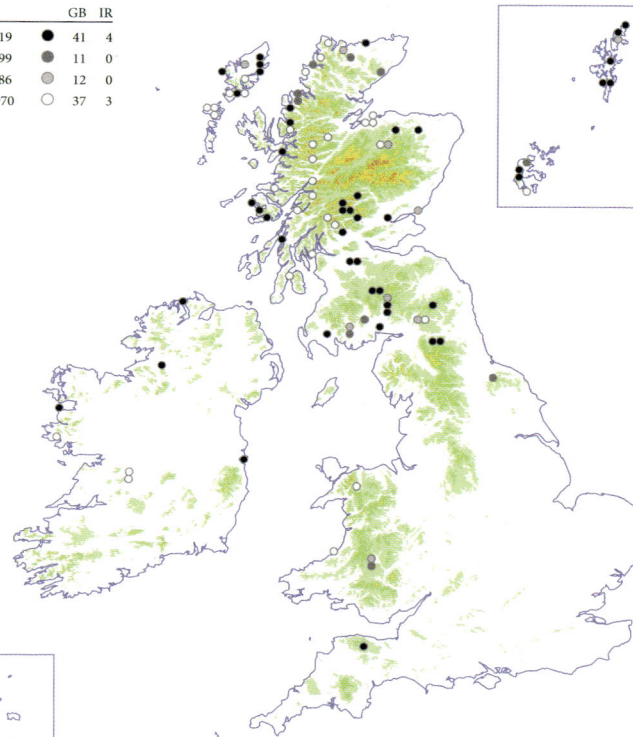

Key refs Stace *et al.* (2015).

A.J. SILVERSIDE

N *Euphrasia tetraquetra* Western Eyebright
(Bréb.) Arrond.

	GB	IR
Long term		
Short term		

A hemiparasitic annual herb of short turf on exposed coastal cliffs and sand dunes, but also very locally inland on chalk and limestone pastures in south-western England, where it is more vulnerable to hybridization and is progressively replaced by its fertile persistent hybrids. 0–364 m (Sourton Tor, North Devon).

Trends The distribution of this species has not changed markedly since it was mapped by Perring & Sell (1968), although it is now better recorded in some areas. Whilst usually distinct, this tetraploid species is often confused with other *Euphrasia* taxa, particularly in northern Scotland where dwarf forms of *E. nemorosa* and *E. foulaensis* can be very similar, the latter effectively replacing it in its coastal niche. Recent records from the far north of Scotland have accordingly been omitted in the absence of determined specimens.

Biogeography Oceanic Temperate element.

Native	GB	IR
2000–19	220	134
1987–99	174	84
1970–86	95	20
pre-1970	265	68

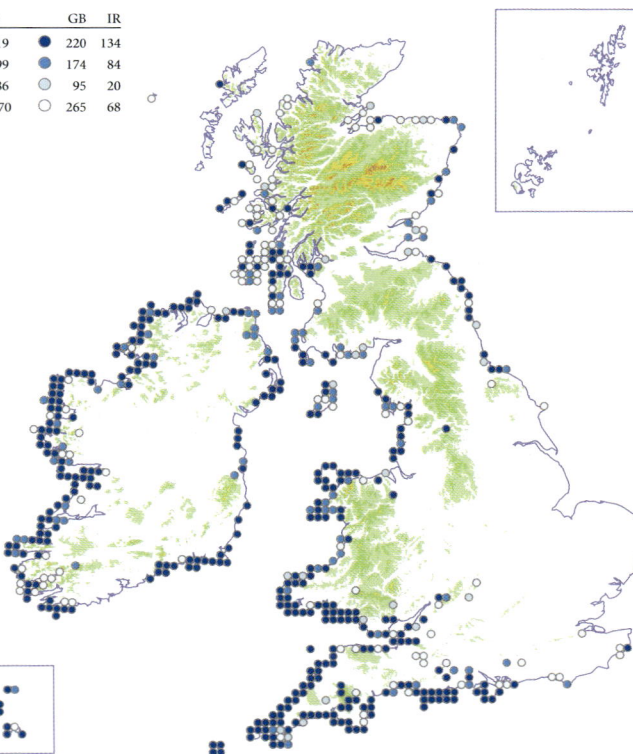

Key refs Yeo (1978).

F.J. RUMSEY

N *Euphrasia nemorosa* Common Eyebright
(Pers.) Wallr.

A hemiparasitic annual herb of short grassland, heathlands, chalk and limestone downland, sand dunes, open scrub, woodland rides and upland moorlands. It is absent from agriculturally improved land. 0–825 m (Cross Fell, Cumberland).

Trends This tetraploid species has not shown any marked change in its range aside from Scotland, where there would appear to have been a marked decline. This is, however, more likely a function of previous misidentifications, although losses to hybridization have occurred. It is the most widespread and ecologically tolerant of our *Euphrasia* species, becoming more restricted to coastal habitats and calcareous soils at lower altitudes in northern Britain. However, it forms hybrids with many other *Euphrasia* species, and introgressed

populations can be locally abundant, making identification difficult.

Biogeography European Temperate element.

Native	GB	IR
2000–19	1021	159
1987–99	905	119
1970–86	675	39
pre-1970	1136	109

Alien	GB	IR
2000–19	1	0
1987–99	1	0
1970–86	1	0
pre-1970	1	0

Key refs Metherell & Rumsey (2018).

F.J. RUMSEY

Hy *Euphrasia nemorosa × confusa*

A widespread fertile hybrid recorded from a wide range of dry and moist grasslands and heathy grasslands, extending from sand dunes and cliffs on the coast to sheep-grazed pastures in the uplands; it also colonizes waste from coal and lead mines. Generally lowland, but reaching 570 m at Llyn Llygad Rheidol (Cardiganshire).

A spontaneous hybrid (native × native).

Trends This hybrid may occur in large uniform colonies in the absence of one or both parents, and may entirely replace them in some districts. It tends to become restricted to coastal areas in the northern part of its range, as does *E. nemorosa*. Hybrid plants are variable and form a complete continuum between the parental taxa; they are certainly under-recorded.

Biogeography Wider distribution uncertain.

	GB	IR
2000–19	156	9
1987–99	99	3
1970–86	29	0
pre-1970	60	1

	GB	IR
Long term	No trend	No trend
Short term	No trend	No trend

Key refs Stace *et al.* (2015).

F.J. RUMSEY & A.J. SILVERSIDE

Hy *Euphrasia nemorosa × micrantha* = E. ×areschougii
Wettst.

A highly fertile hybrid, frequently encountered where the parents grow together in heathy grassland. It is also recorded from short montane turf, lead mine spoil, and the serpentine communities of Unst (Shetland). Lowland but reaching 495 m on Widdybank Pasture (Durham).

A spontaneous hybrid (native × native).

Trends This hybrid was not mapped in previous atlases. Thought to be one of the more common *Euphrasia* hybrids in our area (Metherell & Rumsey, 2018), it is certainly under-recorded.

Biogeography Wider distribution uncertain, although it is known from continental Europe.

		GB	IR
Long term		No trend	No trend
Short term		No trend	No trend

		GB	IR
2000–19	●	22	4
1987–99	●	10	0
1970–86	●	17	0
pre-1970	○	24	0

Key refs Metherell & Rumsey (2018), Stace *et al.* (2015).

A.J. SILVERSIDE

- • <1%
- • 1–10%
- ● 11–30%
- ● 31–40%
- ● 41–50%
- ● 51–100%

Altitude (m) / Distance north (km)

☐ Apparency ☐ In flower ☐ In leaf

N *Euphrasia pseudokerneri* Chalk Eyebright
Pugsley

A late-summer flowering hemiparasitic annual of herb-rich calcareous grassland on chalk and soft limestones, occasionally found on harder limestones in Ireland or as f. *elongata* in damp fens, and also known from calcareous flushes, a lead mine and coastal grassland in Cardiganshire. Lowland.

Trends *E. pseudokerneri*, a tetraploid, is decreasing through the ploughing up of its habitat and agricultural improvement of downland pastures. Changes in land management have favoured other *Euphrasia* species, particularly *E. nemorosa*, which may, in turn, have increased the incidence of hybridization.

Biogeography Endemic; it is replaced by *E. stricta* in Europe.

	GB	IR
Long term		No trend
Short term		No trend

Native		GB	IR
2000–19	●	86	1
1987–99	●	81	1
1970–86	●	69	0
pre-1970	○	153	4

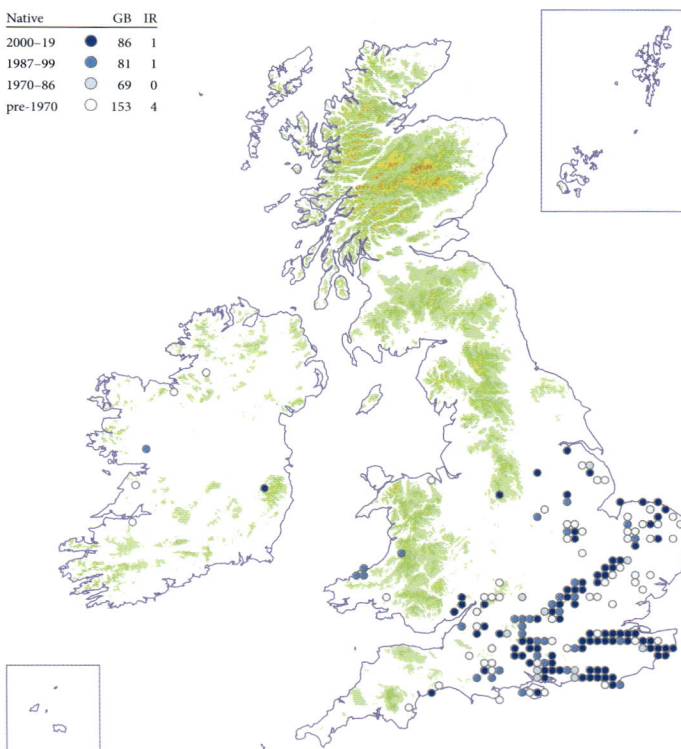

Key refs Stewart *et al.* (1994), Stroh *et al.* (2019).

F.J. RUMSEY

- • <1%
- • 1–10%
- ● 11–30%
- ● 31–40%
- ● 41–50%
- ● 51–100%

Altitude (m) / Distance north (km)

☐ Apparency ☐ In flower ☐ In leaf

N *Euphrasia confusa* Confused Eyebright
Pugsley

A hemiparasitic annual herb of grazed pasture and grassy heathland on free-drained, acidic or calcareous soils. It is especially characteristic of upland pastures in northern and western Britain, but is occasionally found in open vegetation on sandy soils elsewhere. It is rare and mainly coastal in Ireland. It can withstand intense grazing pressure. 0–740 m (Craig Cwm Sere, Breconshire).

Trends *E. confusa* is a widespread and frequent tetraploid species but one which hybridizes readily. As with other *Euphrasia* taxa, the extensive hybridization makes identification difficult. Although now better recorded than when mapped by Perring & Sell (1968), it is difficult to know whether there has been as appreciable a decline as mapping suggests, as it is likely to still be under-recorded.

Biogeography Oceanic Boreo-temperate element.

Native	GB	IR
2000–19	645	34
1987–99	400	25
1970–86	408	7
pre-1970	722	19

Key refs Metherell & Rumsey (2018), Rich & Jermy (1998), Stace (1975).

F.J. RUMSEY

Hy *Euphrasia confusa × micrantha*

A highly fertile hybrid found in grassland or in communities variously intermediate between grassland and heathland in open country and on roadsides, railway embankments, forest tracks, streamsides and in coastal turf. They may form hybrid swarms or show incipient speciation, and sometimes persist as uniform and attractive populations in areas from which *E. micrantha* appears to have gone. Generally lowland but ascending to 614 m on Black Hill (Herefordshire) and possibly higher in Scotland.

A spontaneous hybrid (native × native).

Trends In common with all *Euphrasia* hybrids, it is likely to be under-recorded, and may often be confused with either parent, or with the similar hybrids *E. ×areschougii* and *E. ×difformis* (Metherell & Rumsey, 2018).

Biogeography Wider distribution uncertain.

	GB	IR
2000–19	45	0
1987–99	21	0
1970–86	9	0
pre-1970	40	0

	GB	IR
Long term	No trend	No trend
Short term	No trend	No trend

Key refs Metherell & Rumsey (2018), Stace *et al.* (2015).

A.J. SILVERSIDE

OROBANCHACEAE | *Euphrasia*

Hy *Euphrasia confusa × scottica*

A fertile hybrid of flushes and damp stream banks in upland areas, with populations occasionally extending into short, dry turf, heathy grassland and heathy communities on steep rocky slopes. The hybrid is found throughout much of the range of *E. scottica* and absent only where *E. confusa* is rare. It is, however, often found in the absence of one or other parent. Generally lowland but ascending to over 700 m in Cwm Idwal (Caernarvonshire).

A spontaneous hybrid (native × native).

Trends This hybrid is certainly under-recorded. Populations of the hybrid are frequent in upland areas and locally may be more common than *E. scottica*.

Biogeography Wider distribution uncertain.

	GB	IR
2000–19	25	0
1987–99	22	0
1970–86	48	0
pre-1970	39	0

Long term: GB No trend, IR No trend
Short term: GB No trend, IR No trend

Key refs Stace *et al.* (2015).

F.J. Rumsey & A.J. Silverside

N *Euphrasia frigida* Upland Eyebright
Pugsley

A hemiparasitic annual herb of damp or wet, usually rather basic, cliff ledges. It occurs at 200 m on Foula (Shetland), but is usually found above 400 m, reaching 1,190 m on Aonach Beag (Westerness).

Trends This species, although better recorded than when mapped by Perring & Sell (1968), is almost certainly still under-recorded. As a consequence, the mapped losses in remote upland areas of northern Scotland and in the southern extremes of its Irish range may be more apparent than real.

Biogeography Eurosiberian Arctic-montane element; also in North America.

Native	GB	IR
2000–19	69	2
1987–99	41	2
1970–86	41	4
pre-1970	93	7

Key refs Stewart *et al.* (1994).

F.J. Rumsey

921

N *Euphrasia foulaensis* Foula Eyebright
F. Towns. ex Wettst.

A low-growing compact hemiparasitic annual herb of damp, open turf on coastal cliff-tops, and at the upper fringe of saltmarshes. Its cliff-top sites are subject to sea spray, but it avoids the most exposed sites. *E. foulaensis* seems unable to survive in rank turf, and grazing by sheep or rabbits is essential for its survival. It largely replaces *E. tetraquetra*, with which it has been confused, in Scotland. Lowland.

Trends This small-flowered inbreeding tetraploid species can be locally abundant. Some sites have been lost through agricultural improvement or the cessation of grazing. It was discovered in Ireland in 2017, where further sites are to be expected. Any apparent decline may rather reflect under-recording. However, it is much better recorded now than when mapped by Stewart *et al.* (1994).

Biogeography Oceanic Boreal-montane element.

Native		GB	IR
2000–19	●	104	1
1987–99	●	54	0
1970–86	○	48	0
pre-1970	○	120	0

	GB	IR
Long term		No trend
Short term		No trend

Key refs Metherell & Rumsey (2018), Stewart *et al.* (1994).

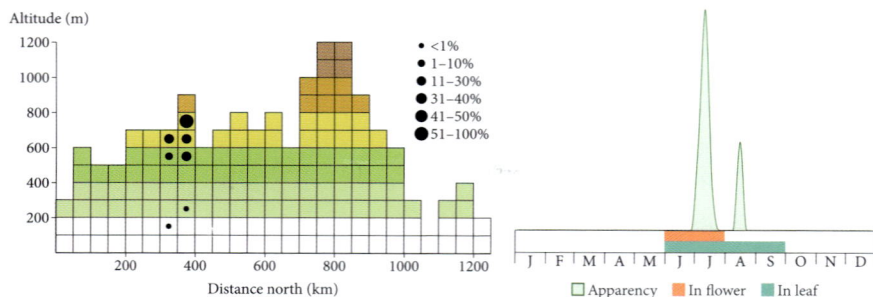

F.J. RUMSEY

N *Euphrasia cambrica* Welsh Eyebright
Pugsley

A dwarf hemiparasitic annual herb of well-drained, basic, sheep-grazed grassland on mountain slopes. More rarely it grows in wetter, base-enriched flushes where it can occur with *E. rivularis* and *E. scottica*, hybridizing with the latter. An upland species, reaching 880 m on Cadair Idris (Merionethshire).

Trends *E. cambrica*, a tetraploid species, is easily overlooked because of its small size and inconspicuous flowers. It has been confused in the past with *E. ostenfeldii*, from which it may be derived and with which it forms hybrids, as at Cwm Idwal (Caernarvonshire). Recently it has only been recorded from sites on Snowdon and the Glyders, the apparent losses possibly resulting from under-recording rather than representing a true decline, as its habitat remains largely unchanged.

Biogeography Endemic.

Native		GB	IR
2000–19	●	1	0
1987–99	●	3	0
1970–86	○	2	0
pre-1970	○	4	0

	GB	IR
Long term	No trend	No trend
Short term	No trend	No trend

Key refs Metherell & Rumsey (2018), Wigginton (1999).

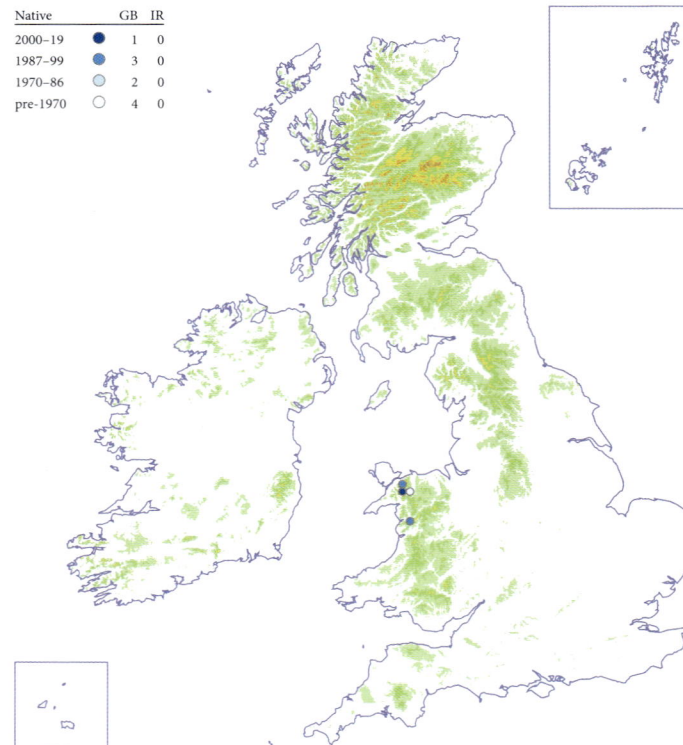

F.J. RUMSEY

Euphrasia ostenfeldii Ostenfeld's Eyebright

(Pugsley) Yeo

A hemiparasitic annual herb of sparsely vegetated areas in very well-drained, exposed and often base-rich habitats, including dry limestone rock ledges (where it may parasitize *Dryas octopetala*), eroding sea-cliffs, fine-gravel screes, bare serpentine debris and sandy coastal turf. 0–810 m (Rum, North Ebudes).

Trends An apparently variable and still poorly understood species complex, into which eglandular hairy examples of the genus have been 'shoe-horned'. Many plants now recognized as this tetraploid species were previously referred to *E. curta*. The current taxonomic treatment dates from 1971 but *E. ostenfeldii* is still both under-recorded and regularly misidentified, perhaps reflecting the rather unsatisfactory treatment. Further research is clearly needed. It has been confused with

eglandular hairy forms of *E. nemorosa* (which probably deserve taxonomic recognition), *E. marshallii* and *E. rotundifolia*, and hybrids are known with eight other *Euphrasia* species to add further confusion. Plants occur in good quality habitat and the apparent decline may be real, but the quality of recording precludes any confident assessment of trends in its distribution over either the short or long term.

Biogeography Oceanic Boreo-arctic Montane element.

Native	GB	IR
2000–19	40	1
1987–99	16	0
1970–86	20	0
pre-1970	40	0

Key refs Metherell & Rumsey (2018), Stewart *et al.* (1994).

F.J. RUMSEY

Euphrasia marshallii Marshall's Eyebright

Pugsley

A hemiparasitic annual herb of coastal rocks and eroding sea-cliff edges below maritime heath dominated by *Calluna vulgaris* and *Empetrum nigrum*. It is usually closely associated with *Plantago* species, particularly *P. maritima*, and these may act as hosts. Lowland.

Trends This tetraploid species was first described in 1929, and despite its relative distinctiveness, past confusion with other species and current under-recording of *Euphrasia* taxa make it difficult to assess changes in distribution. There have undoubtedly been losses through cultivation of cliff-tops and through the threat of extensive hybridization with *E. foulaensis*, *E. arctica* and *E. nemorosa*. In more basic situations, *E. marshallii* is often replaced by its hybrid with *E. nemorosa*.

There are many more recent records than when mapped by Wigginton (1999).

Biogeography Endemic.

Native	GB	IR
2000–19	21	0
1987–99	10	0
1970–86	16	0
pre-1970	31	0

Key refs Metherell & Rumsey (2018), Stewart *et al.* (1994), Wigginton (1999).

F.J. RUMSEY

N *Euphrasia rotundifolia* Pugsley's Eyebright
Pugsley

	GB	IR
Long term	No trend	No trend
Short term	No trend	No trend

A hemiparasitic annual herb of flushed basic turf on sea-cliffs. At its currently known sites, *Primula scotica* is a constant associate, although *Plantago maritima* is probably its usual host. Lowland.

Trends Though a reinterpretation of herbarium material (Metherell & Rumsey, 2018) has resulted in a more restrictive view of this tetraploid taxon than that adopted in Perring & Sell (1968), its taxonomic status remains uncertain and it is still often over-recorded through confusion with *E. marshallii* and its hybrids. It is itself apparently derived through hybridization between *E. foulaensis* and *E. marshallii* and is sometimes hardly distinguishable from the last, with which it regularly grows, when both are dwarfed. Apparently restricted to a single small site on the Caithness coast until rediscovered on the Shetland Islands in 2016 (Heylor, Ronas Voe).

Biogeography Endemic.

Native	GB	IR
2000–19	3	0
1987–99	2	0
1970–86	1	0
pre-1970	5	0

Key refs Metherell & Rumsey (2018), Wigginton (1999).

F.J. RUMSEY

N *Euphrasia campbelliae* Campbell's Eyebright
Pugsley

	GB	IR
Long term	No trend	No trend
Short term	No trend	No trend

A hemiparasitic annual herb of damp, mossy, grazed heathy turf near the sea, in sedge-rich communities or in grassy dwarf-shrub heath, especially where *Calluna vulgaris* and *Erica tetralix* are kept short by grazing. Lowland.

Trends This tetraploid taxon was first described in 1940, and is probably of complex hybrid origin. Hybrids are formed with all sympatric *Euphrasia* species, the most frequent being that with *E. micrantha*, almost certainly a parent to *E. campbelliae*. Fieldwork carried out in 2013 suggests hybridization must pose a threat to the integrity of the few known populations of this species (Metherell & Rumsey, 2018). Although there are more records now than when mapped by Wigginton (1999), with new finds in south-east Lewis, it has apparently been lost from several 10 km squares within its very restricted endemic range.

Biogeography Endemic.

Native	GB	IR
2000–19	10	0
1987–99	6	0
1970–86	3	0
pre-1970	10	0

Key refs Metherell & Rumsey (2018), Wigginton (1999).

F.J. RUMSEY

N *Euphrasia micrantha* Slender Eyebright
Rchb.

A hemiparasitic annual herb of dry or damp places on acid heathlands. It also grows on open clay and sandy substrates in disturbed habitats, such as disused gravel-pits and old airfields. Typically associated with *Calluna vulgaris* which is presumed to be its primary host. 0–731 m (Firthhope Rig, Dumfriesshire) and possibly higher in the Cairngorms.

Trends This slender tetraploid species has continued to decline markedly due to habitat loss and degradation through lack of management, but also as a consequence of increased hybridization. As with all *Euphrasia* species, some apparent losses are perhaps due to under-recording, or former confusion with other taxa, although it is one of the most distinctive species. Many populations show signs of hybridization with *E. nemorosa*. In north-western

Scotland it is apparently largely replaced by its hybrid with *E. scottica*, although this taxon is still under-recorded.

Biogeography European Temperate element.

Native	GB	IR
2000–19	589	123
1987–99	392	88
1970–86	354	21
pre-1970	770	139

Key refs Rich & Jermy (1998), Yeo (1978).

F.J. RUMSEY

N *Euphrasia scottica* Scottish Eyebright
Wettst.

A hemiparasitic annual herb typically associated with flush communities and wet moorland in upland areas. It is similar to *E. micrantha* and perhaps not specifically distinct from it. 0–915 m (Sgurr na Lappaich, Glen Strathfarrar, Easterness).

Trends The distribution of this tetraploid species is somewhat uncertain because of confusion with other taxa and hybridization, although it is among the more distinctive of British and Irish *Euphrasia* species. Even so it is certainly still under-recorded. In north-western Scotland it is largely replaced by its hybrid with *E. micrantha*, although the very few records of this hybrid fail to capture this. As the *Euphrasia* species most strongly restricted to very damp habitats, it is likely to be most

susceptible to drainage and increasing aridification through climatic change.

Biogeography European Boreal-montane element.

Native	GB	IR
2000–19	472	60
1987–99	321	38
1970–86	265	12
pre-1970	342	43

Key refs Metherell & Rumsey (2018).

F.J. RUMSEY

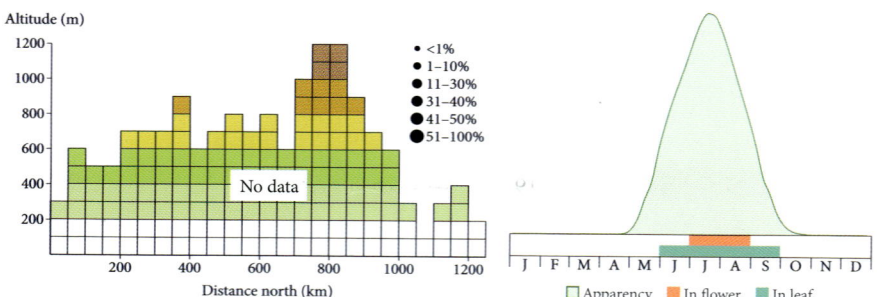

Euphrasia heslop-harrisonii Heslop-Harrison's Eyebright
Pugsley

A hemiparasitic annual herb largely restricted to short turf in saltmarshes immediately above the high water mark, where it is associated with *Plantago* species. More rarely it occurs on grassy banks in the spray zone and on coastal cliff tops. Lowland, but to *c.* 300 m on Rum, South Ebudes.

Trends Though first described in 1945, this tetraploid species of probable hybrid origin [although clarified by both Yeo (1978) and Silverside (1983)] has remained poorly understood, largely because its diagnostic features are subtle and not always well demonstrated. Since it was mapped by Perring & Sell (1968) it has been recorded at more sites, but is almost certainly still under-recorded. It was discovered in Ireland for the first time in 2019. The survival of *E. heslop-harrisonii*

is dependent on the continuation of grazing of its saltmarsh habitat.

Biogeography Endemic to Britain and Ireland.

Native		GB	IR
2000–19	●	31	1
1987–99	●	15	0
1970–86	◐	8	0
pre-1970	○	11	0

	GB	IR
Long term		No trend
Short term		No trend

● <1%
● 1–10%
● 11–30%
● 31–40%
● 41–50%
● 51–100%

□ Apparency ■ In flower ■ In leaf

Key refs Silverside (1983), Wigginton (1999), Yeo (1978).

F.J. RUMSEY

Euphrasia salisburgensis Irish Eyebright
Funck

A hemiparasitic annual herb of calcareous grasslands on limestone, maritime sand dunes and montane limestone cliffs. 0–550 m (Ben Bulben, County Sligo).

Trends The distribution of this distinctive and variable tetraploid species appears to be stable. Plants from cliffs on Ben Bulben approach the boreal species *E. lapponica* in appearance, but may alternatively be derived through introgression with *E. frigida*. Hybrids between *E. salisburgensis* and other *Euphrasia* species are rare, and are largely but not completely sterile. A specimen from Yorkshire collected in 1885 or 1886 is now considered to have resulted from confusion, or mislabelling, in the herbarium.

Biogeography European Boreo-arctic Montane element; Irish material is referable to the endemic var. *hibernica*, treated as an endemic species by P.D. Sell (Sell & Murrell, 2009).

Native		GB	IR
2000–19	●	0	47
1987–99	●	0	31
1970–86	◐	0	20
pre-1970	○	0	36

	GB	IR
Long term	No trend	
Short term	No trend	

● <1%
● 1–10%
● 11–30%
● 31–40%
● 41–50%
● 51–100%

No data

□ Apparency ■ In flower ■ In leaf

Key refs Sell & Murrell (2009), Sledge (1975), Yeo (1975), Yeo (1978).

F.J. RUMSEY

Odontites vernus Red Bartsia

(Bellardi) Dumort.

An annual hemiparasitic herb of short, often trampled grasslands, tracks, waste places, the edges of arable fields, gravelly and rocky seashores and saltmarshes. 0–595 m (Ben Lawers, Mid Perthshire).

Trends The distribution of this species has not altered significantly since the 1960s. Three subspecies are represented in our area: the aestival subsp. *vernus* is widespread, the autumnal subsp. *serotinus* is concentrated in southern Britain and Ireland, and the maritime subsp. *litoralis* (which is mapped separately).

Biogeography Eurasian Temperate element; widely naturalized outside its native range.

Native		GB	IR
2000–19	●	2216	851
1987–99	●	2009	758
1970–86	○	1295	92
pre-1970	○	1992	614

Alien		GB	IR
2000–19	●	3	0
1987–99	●	1	0
1970–86	●	2	0
pre-1970	○	1	0

F.J. Rumsey

Odontites vernus subsp. *litoralis*

(Fr.) Nyman

An annual hemiparasitic herb of coastal grasslands on stabilized sand dunes, gravelly and rocky seashores, the upper margins of saltmarshes, and on waste ground near the sea. Lowland.

Trends This coastal subspecies has been confused with depauperate specimens of the two weedy widespread subspecies, which may also occur in its coastal habitats. It was mapped by Perring & Sell (1968), but is still under-recorded, which may account for many of the apparent losses on remote sections of the Scottish coasts.

Biogeography European Boreo-temperate element. *O. vernus* subsp. *litoralis* was described from the Baltic; plants from southern Sweden southwards may be a distinct taxon, subsp. *pumilus*.

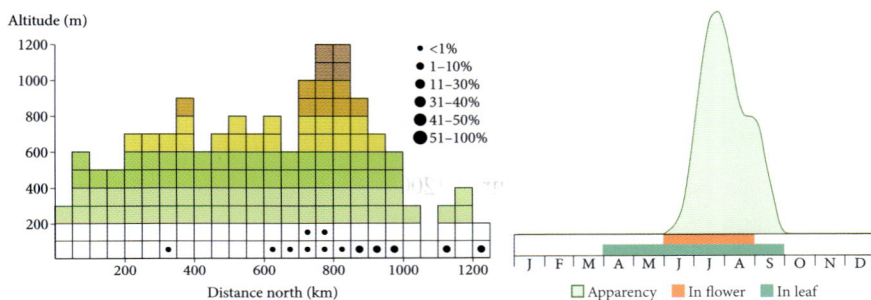

	GB	IR
Long term	No trend	No trend
Short term	No trend	No trend

Native		GB	IR
2000–19	●	20	0
1987–99	●	24	0
1970–86	●	2	0
pre-1970	○	33	0

Key refs Sell (1967), Snogerup (1982).

F.J. Rumsey

N *Bartsia alpina* Alpine Bartsia

L.

A shortly rhizomatous perennial herb of base-rich soils. In England it is restricted to drier hummocks in base-rich flushes and mires and runnels in damp upland pastures, and of steep, flushed, species-rich banks next to rivers. In the Breadalbanes (Mid Perthshire) it grows on the periodically inundated ledges of mica-schist crags. Seed-set is poor. From 245 m at Orton (Westmorland) to 950 m on Beinn Heasgarnich (Mid Perthshire).

Trends *B. alpina* has been lost from a number of pastures through overgrazing, trampling by cattle and drainage and this threat continues, with most English populations now comprising very few plants, and with declining numbers and little apparent recruitment. Scottish ledge communities, which were previously considered largely unaffected (Preston *et al.*, 2002a), appear to have shown losses,

particularly from the eastern end of its range, for reasons which are unclear.

Biogeography European Arctic-montane element; also in North America.

Native	GB	IR
2000–19	13	0
1987–99	13	0
1970–86	17	0
pre-1970	19	0

Key refs Taylor & Rumsey (2003), Wigginton (1999).

F.J. RUMSEY

N *Parentucellia viscosa* Yellow Bartsia

(L.) Caruel

A hemiparasitic annual herb of damp, open grassy places on sandy soils, often by tracks. It normally occurs in drier dune-slacks and in reclaimed heath-pasture, but is also found on pathsides, rough and scrubby grassland and field-borders, and increasingly in re-seeded amenity grasslands and waste places. It thrives on disturbance. Lowland.

Trends This species has continued to expand its range northwards and eastwards in Britain, largely through introductions from seed mixtures. In many sites the species has only appeared as a casual, although it has persisted in some areas. The re-seeding of old pasture has led to some decline at inland sites in south-western England. In Ireland, it appears to be relatively stable in the north, but it has apparently declined and contracted in range in the south-west.

Biogeography Mediterranean-Atlantic element; widely naturalized outside its native range.

Native	GB	IR
2000–19	136	62
1987–99	125	50
1970–86	106	17
pre-1970	145	63

Alien	GB	IR
2000–19	120	0
1987–99	76	0
1970–86	31	0
pre-1970	38	0

Key refs Stewart *et al.* (1994).

F.J. RUMSEY

Ne *Rhinanthus angustifolius* Greater Yellow-rattle
C.C.Gmel.

An annual hemiparasite, formerly a widespread weed of arable land but now virtually confined to grassland and open scrub on chalk (North Downs), on peat in an area of cleared bracken and on railway ballast (Lincolnshire) and sandy coastal grassland (Angus). Lowland.

Trends This species was first recorded in the wild in 1722 (North Northumberland). Nearly all its arable sites were lost before 1930. It was not discovered on the North Downs until 1966 (Lousley, 1976) and this is now the species' main British centre, with an increasing number of new sites in reserves and conservation areas. It was first found in West Kent in 2011. Hay cutting after flowering at some of its North Downs sites and unwitting dispersal through other conservation activities may have assisted

its spread. Some old records may be errors for the variable *R. minor*.

Biogeography Eurosiberian Boreo-temperate element.

Alien	GB	IR
2000–19	14	0
1987–99	11	0
1970–86	11	0
pre-1970	83	0

Key refs Lousley (1976), Wigginton (1999).

F.J. RUMSEY

N *Rhinanthus minor* Yellow-rattle
L.

An annual hemiparasitic herb of nutrient-poor grasslands, including permanent pastures, hay meadows, the drier parts of fens, flushes in lowland and upland grasslands, and on montane ledges; also on roadsides and waste ground. It is also now widely sown to help diversify species-poor grasslands. 0–1,065 m (Ben Lawers, Mid Perthshire).

Trends *R. minor* declined throughout the 20th century in semi-natural grasslands. It is now included in many wild-flower seed mixtures, often being used as a 'conservation tool' to help suppress grasses and thereby diversify species-poor swards (Pywell *et al.*, 2004). It is very variable and six intergrading and apparently inter-fertile subspecies have been recognized in our area, and are mapped separately. However, whilst they show broad geographic and ecological

distinctions, some populations cannot be clearly assigned to any of them.

Biogeography European Boreo-temperate element; widely naturalized outside its native range.

Native	GB	IR
2000–19	2541	735
1987–99	2363	702
1970–86	1564	122
pre-1970	2344	670

Alien	GB	IR
2000–19	11	0
1987–99	4	0
1970–86	2	0
pre-1970	3	0

Key refs Grime *et al.* (2007), Pywell *et al.* (2004), Westbury (2004).

F.J. RUMSEY

Ⓝ *Rhinanthus minor* subsp. *minor*
L.

A little-branched, early summer-flowering ecotype found in a range of lowland grassy, well-drained, nutrient-poor, basic habitats, including unimproved pasture, hay meadows, road verges and rough grassland. 0–570 m (Moor House, Westmorland).

Trends The poor coverage of this subspecies in many areas reflects the fact that most recorders have not distinguished the type subspecies from the others and simply recorded the aggregate. The remarks on the trends in the distribution of *R. minor* also apply to this subspecies.

Biogeography European Boreo-temperate element; occurring almost throughout the range of the species but rarer in the boreal zone than subsp. *stenophyllus*.

		GB	IR
Long term		No trend	No trend
Short term		No trend	No trend

Native		GB	IR
2000–19	●	275	5
1987–99	●	285	4
1970–86	●	176	20
pre-1970	○	571	222

Alien		GB	IR
2000–19	●	3	0
1987–99	●	5	0
1970–86	●	1	0
pre-1970	○	4	0

Altitude (m) histogram, with dot size key: <1%, 1–10%, 11–30%, 31–40%, 41–50%, 51–100%.

Apparency / In flower / In leaf phenology chart (J F M A M J J A S O N D).

Key refs Westbury (2004).

F.J. Rumsey

Ⓝ *Rhinanthus minor* subsp. *stenophyllus*
O.Schwarz

A much-branched, floriferous, late-flowering ecotype which occurs in fens and damp grasslands in southern England, but largely replaces subsp. *minor* in a wide variety of habitats over much of northern England and Scotland. 0–500 m (Loch Callater, South Aberdeenshire).

Trends A widespread but critical taxon, not always easy to distinguish from other subspecies, which is certainly under-recorded in northern and western Britain and in Ireland. The losses in south-eastern England are probably real, as much of its habitat there has been agriculturally improved.

Biogeography European Boreo-montane element.

		GB	IR
Long term		No trend	No trend
Short term		No trend	No trend

Native		GB	IR
2000–19	●	297	74
1987–99	●	175	35
1970–86	●	170	3
pre-1970	○	528	62

Alien		GB	IR
2000–19	●	1	0
1987–99	●	2	0
1970–86	●	1	0
pre-1970	○	0	0

Altitude (m) histogram, with dot size key: <1%, 1–10%, 11–30%, 31–40%, 41–50%, 51–100%.

Apparency / In flower / In leaf phenology chart (J F M A M J J A S O N D).

Key refs Westbury (2004).

F.J. Rumsey

(N) *Rhinanthus minor* **subsp.** *monticola*
(Sterneck) O.Schwarz

A squat, branched, but few-flowered autumnal-flowering ecotype of base-rich grassland, serpentine heath and basic rock ledges. It grows at sea level in northern and western Scotland and western Ireland, is perhaps most frequent above 200 m and ascends to at least 855 m on Helvellyn (Cumberland).

Trends This often heavily pigmented, dull-flowered plant is not unduly difficult to identify but it is probably greatly under-recorded, as it suffers from the same neglect as the other segregates of this difficult complex. The level of recording makes assessment of change difficult but there is an indication of a decline in the Scottish uplands. Further research is needed on this and other montane ecotypes of this species.

Biogeography European Boreo-montane element.

	GB	IR
Long term	No trend	No trend
Short term	No trend	No trend

Native		GB	IR
2000–19	●	85	0
1987–99	●	28	2
1970–86	○	52	1
pre-1970	○	90	1

Key refs Westbury (2004).

F.J. RUMSEY

(N) *Rhinanthus minor* **subsp.** *calcareus*
(Wilmott) E.F.Warb.

A much-branched, many-noded, late-flowering ecotype of dry, basic downland turf. Lowland.

Trends A critical taxon which is not always easy to distinguish. Almost all of the records mapped are those collected from herbaria by Perring & Sell (1968). This taxon is possibly declining with the loss of semi-natural grassland, but it is much too poorly recorded to be sure. Plants from the Burren resemble this subspecies but British experts do not regard them as sufficiently similar to be included within it (Webb & Scannell, 1983).

Biogeography A little-known taxon, not recorded outside our area.

	GB	IR
Long term	No trend	No trend
Short term	No trend	No trend

Native		GB	IR
2000–19	●	14	0
1987–99	●	8	0
1970–86	○	12	0
pre-1970	○	44	0

Key refs Webb & Scannell (1983).

F.J. RUMSEY

Ⓝ *Rhinanthus minor* subsp. *lintonii*
(Wilmott) P.D.Sell

A late-flowering ecotype of montane grassland, flushes and damp rock ledges. It has been recorded from 550 m (Coire Chailein, Main Argyll) to 915 m or more (Ben Avon, Banffshire).

Trends This subspecies is probably derived from hybridization between subsp. *borealis*, subsp. *monticola* and subsp. *stenophyllus*. It was mapped for the first time in the 2002 *Atlas* and is almost certainly still under-recorded, as are all of the subspecies of *R. minor*. The level of recording makes assessment of change difficult but it is likely to have shown declines, in common with other species of its montane habitats.

Biogeography Not recorded outside Britain.

	GB	IR
Long term	No trend	No trend
Short term	No trend	No trend

Native		GB	IR
2000–19	●	11	0
1987–99	●	12	0
1970–86	○	4	0
pre-1970	○	11	0

Key refs Sell (1967).

F.J. Rumsey

Ⓝ *Rhinanthus minor* subsp. *borealis*
(Sterneck) P.D.Sell

A small, unbranched, late-flowering ecotype of grassy places, cliffs and flushes on mountains. It is also recorded from sea-cliffs in Shetland. An upland plant ascending to 1,065 m on Ben Lawers (Mid Perthshire).

Trends Like the other subspecies of *R. minor*, this taxon is certainly under-recorded. However, some records may be misidentifications of the less well-known subsp. *lintonii*. While the under-recording greatly complicates assessment of change it is likely that the taxon has declined markedly.

Biogeography European Boreo-arctic Montane element; Hultén & Fries (1986) treat this taxon as conspecific with the North American *R. groenlandicus*.

	GB	IR
Long term	No trend	No trend
Short term	No trend	No trend

Native		GB	IR
2000–19	●	18	0
1987–99	●	20	0
1970–86	○	45	0
pre-1970	○	89	0

Key refs Westbury (2004).

F.J. Rumsey

Pedicularis palustris Marsh Lousewort
L.

An annual to biennial hemiparasitic herb of a wide range of base-rich to acidic, moist habitats, including wet heaths, valley bogs, wet meadows, ditches, fens and hillside flushes. Its sites are usually more enriched than those preferred by *P. sylvatica*. 0–670 m (Knock Ore Gill, Westmorland).

Trends The decline of *P. palustris* in central and southern England and many parts of Ireland was already apparent by the 1960s and the species has suffered a further substantial decline in these areas since then, mostly through habitat loss due to drainage and agricultural improvement. It appears to be more stable in its core upland strongholds in northern England and Scotland with only local losses and many recent gains as a result of more systematic recording.

Biogeography European Boreo-temperate element.

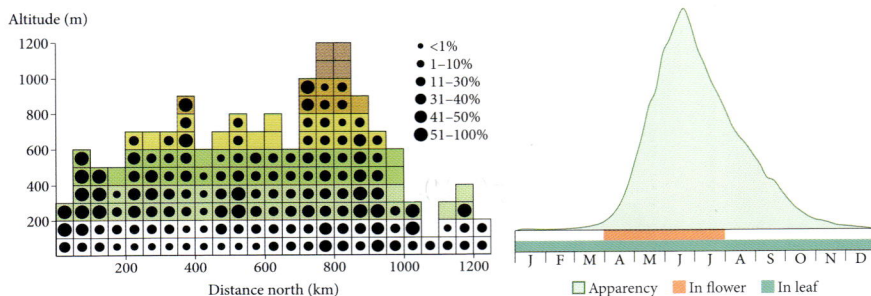

Native	GB	IR
2000–19	1123	373
1987–99	1180	428
1970–86	860	113
pre-1970	1447	398

F.J. RUMSEY

Pedicularis sylvatica Lousewort
L.

A perennial, rarely biennial, hemiparasitic herb of acidic soils, found on damp grassy heaths, moorlands, upland flushed grasslands and the drier parts of bogs and marshes. 0–915 m (Macgillycuddy's Reeks, South Kerry).

Trends *P. sylvatica* was mapped as 'all records' in the 1962 *Atlas*. There has been a widespread decline in southern and eastern England since the 1960s, which can be attributed to the loss of heathlands and unimproved grasslands. Two subspecies occur in our area: subsp. *sylvatica* occurs throughout the range of the species; subsp. *hibernica* is mapped separately.

Biogeography European Temperate element.

Native	GB	IR
2000–19	1709	708
1987–99	1731	611
1970–86	1078	112
pre-1970	1940	527

Alien	GB	IR
2000–19	1	0
1987–99	1	0
1970–86	1	0
pre-1970	0	0

F.J. RUMSEY

Ⓝ *Pedicularis sylvatica* subsp. *hibernica*

D.A.Webb

This subspecies, which differs in its hairy calyx, largely replaces subsp. *sylvatica* in western Ireland, where it occurs on damp moorlands and blanket bogs. 0–330 m (east of Tregaron, Cardiganshire).

Trends This taxon was first described and mapped by Webb (1956) from Ireland and the Outer Hebrides. It has only comparatively recently been recorded in England and Wales and may yet prove be more widespread in western and north-western Britain than the map suggests. Intermediates with subsp. *sylvatica* occur, especially in the eastern portion of its Irish range.

Biogeography Oceanic Boreal-montane element; its relationship to the pubescent *P. sylvatica* subsp. *lusitanica* of the Iberian Peninsula requires clarification.

	GB	IR
Long term	No trend	No trend
Short term	No trend	No trend

Native	GB	IR
2000–19	81	203
1987–99	59	115
1970–86	23	0
pre-1970	25	66

Key refs Rich (1994c), Webb (1956).

F.J. RUMSEY

Ⓝ *Lathraea squamaria* Toothwort

L.

A perennial herb that is parasitic on the roots of a range of woody plants, especially *Corylus avellana*, *Fraxinus excelsior* and *Ulmus glabra*. It is primarily a plant of deciduous woodland, but it also occurs under hedges and on river and stream banks. Generally lowland, but reaching 350 m at Alston (Cumberland).

Trends The 10 km square distribution of *L. squamaria* has changed very little since the 1960s, although it is now much better recorded locally, especially in Ireland, with many recent discoveries made there. Losses have, however, occurred throughout its range for reasons that are not clear, and these have continued since 2000. Sites in hedgerows and narrow woodland strips in farming land appear particularly susceptible, along with coniferized ancient woodlands.

Biogeography European Temperate element; also in central Asia.

	GB	IR
Long term		
Short term		

Native	GB	IR
2000–19	483	131
1987–99	429	86
1970–86	398	43
pre-1970	494	65

Alien	GB	IR
2000–19	0	1
1987–99	2	1
1970–86	0	0
pre-1970	3	0

M.J.Y. FOLEY & M.W. RAND

Ne *Lathraea clandestina* Purple Toothwort

L.

A parasitic perennial herb, mainly found on alders, willows and poplars, but occasionally also on bamboos, as at Newby Hall (Mid-west Yorkshire). It usually occurs in damp, shaded places in open woodland, coppices and along hedgerows, and especially near streams and rivers where it is likely to be dispersed in floodwaters. Such sites often resemble its habitat in its native range in continental Europe. Lowland.

Trends *L. clandestina* was introduced to cultivation in Britain in 1888. It is grown in gardens as an attractive curiosity, from where many populations are likely to have originated. It was first reported from the wild in 1908 at Coe Fen in Cambridge (Cambridgeshire), where it was probably deliberately planted and where it still survives. It appears to be increasing, with localized losses heavily outweighed by its discovery at scores of new sites in the last two decades.

Biogeography A Suboceanic Temperate species, native to Belgium, France, Spain and Italy.

Alien	GB	IR
2000–19	103	1
1987–99	85	3
1970–86	38	0
pre-1970	35	1

Key refs Atkinson (1996), Atkinson & Atkinson (2020).

M.J.Y. FOLEY & M.W. RAND

N *Orobanche rapum-genistae* Greater Broomrape

Thuill.

A perennial parasite of leguminous shrubs, especially *Ulex europaeus* and *Cytisus scoparius*, but also known to occur occasionally on *Genista tinctoria* and *G. anglica*. Its habitat, governed by that of its hosts, is mainly scrub on acid soils, but hedgebanks and tracksides are also favoured. On sea-cliffs in south-western England and on the Channel Islands a form occurs which is parasitic on *C. scoparius* subsp. *maritimus*. Lowland.

Trends This species suffered a dramatic decline in the 19th and early 20th century. This is largely unexplained, although changes in land-use were probably at least partly responsible. The decline continued throughout the 20th century, although there have been resurgences, as following the great storms of 1987 when windthrow briefly opened habitats, stimulating growth of its main hosts. New populations have been found, although on sites where the species probably previously occurred, indicating a long-persistent seed bank. Colonization of genuinely novel sites where the hosts abound, as created on motorway banksides, has not occurred, suggesting poor dispersal capability.

Biogeography Suboceanic Southern-temperate element.

Native	GB	IR
2000–19	83	10
1987–99	91	5
1970–86	90	7
pre-1970	399	27

Key refs Rumsey & Jury (1991), Rumsey & Headley (1998), Stewart *et al.* (1994).

M.J.Y. FOLEY & F.J. RUMSEY

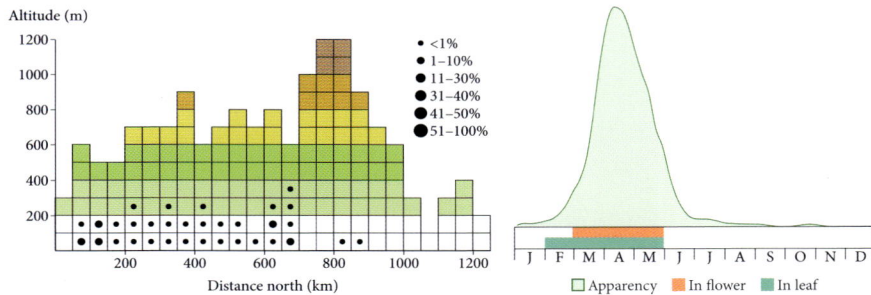

Orobanche caryophyllacea Bedstraw Broomrape
Sm.

A parasite mainly of *Galium album* and *G. verum*, probably perennial and sometimes long-lived. It occurs in stabilized sand dune grassland, and in scrub and hedgebanks on chalk downs and undercliffs. Most populations are small, but some of those on sand dunes are of a considerable size. Lowland.

Trends Populations of this species on the North Downs (East Kent) are small to absent in many years and declining because of habitat change, but those on sand dunes seem reasonably secure, although vulnerable to increasing visitor pressure. Native records from other parts of Britain, including Scotland, are now considered to be errors. It persisted for over 50 years in the natural order beds at Royal Botanic Gardens Kew (Surrey), where it was introduced from France.

Biogeography European Temperate element, with a continental distribution in western Europe.

	GB	IR
Long term	No trend	No trend
Short term	No trend	No trend

Native		GB	IR
2000–19	●	2	0
1987–99	●	4	0
1970–86	○	5	0
pre-1970	○	5	0

Alien		GB	IR
2000–19	●	0	0
1987–99	●	1	0
1970–86	●	0	0
pre-1970	○	1	0

Key refs Rumsey & Jury (1991), Thorogood & Rumsey (2021), Wigginton (1999).

M.J.Y. FOLEY & F.J. RUMSEY

Orobanche elatior Knapweed Broomrape
Sutton

Apparently perennial, this species is almost exclusively parasitic upon *Centaurea scabiosa*, and is mainly found in lightly grazed or ungrazed chalk and limestone grassland. It may also form substantial populations in man-made habitats such as road verges, railway banks and quarries. Lowland.

Trends There appears to have been a gradual contraction in the range of *O. elatior*, especially in areas outside its core range where populations tend to be small. Most losses are probably due to habitat destruction, or long-term neglect. The distribution is apparently stable in its core areas.

Biogeography Eurosiberian Temperate element, with a continental distribution in western Europe.

	GB	IR
Long term	↓	No trend
Short term	↓	No trend

Native		GB	IR
2000–19	●	170	0
1987–99	●	173	0
1970–86	○	147	0
pre-1970	○	231	0

Key refs Rumsey & Jury (1991).

M.J.Y. FOLEY

Ⓝ *Orobanche alba* Thyme Broomrape

Stephan ex Willd.

An annual, or possibly perennial, parasite of *Thymus drucei*. Its principal habitat is base-rich rocky coastal slopes, but it also occurs inland on vegetated scree below limestone outcrops in northern England. Generally lowland, but reaching *c.* 490 m at Nappa Scar, Wensleydale (North-west Yorkshire).

Trends A variable species elsewhere represented at this western extreme of range by intensely coloured plants described originally as *O. rubra*. Populations can vary greatly in size from year to year, but the overall range of the species appears to be stable. It is probably still present in many of the remote Scottish 10 km squares where it has not been recorded since 1987. Numbers in northern England have consistently been critically low in recent years. It has been

occasionally over-recorded for other *Orobanche* species in the lowlands.

Biogeography European Temperate element; also in central Asia.

Native	GB	IR
2000–19	49	26
1987–99	45	24
1970–86	30	12
pre-1970	76	33

Alien	GB	IR
2000–19	0	0
1987–99	1	0
1970–86	2	0
pre-1970	1	0

Key refs Ballantyne (1992), Rumsey & Jury (1991), Stewart *et al.* (1994).

M.J.Y. FOLEY & F.J. RUMSEY

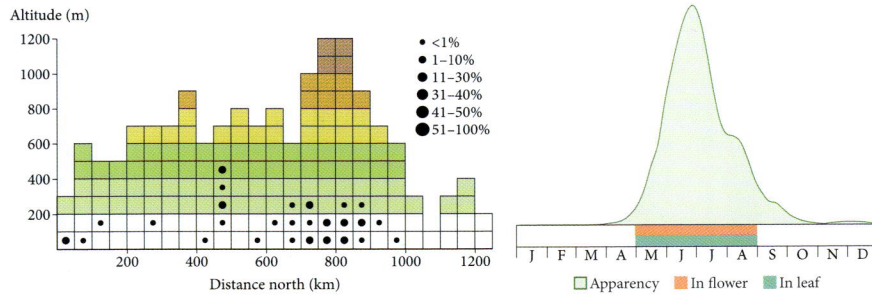

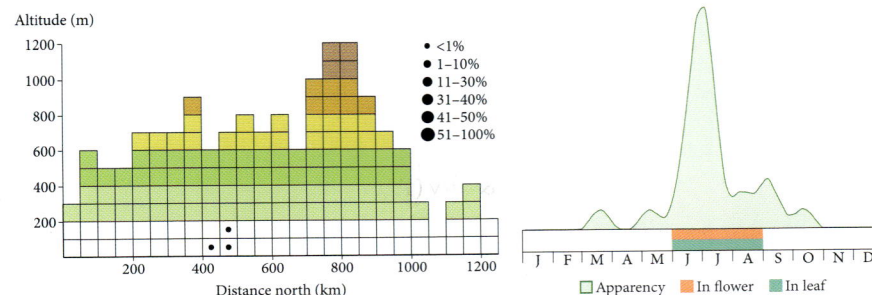

Ⓝ *Orobanche reticulata* Thistle Broomrape

Wallr.

An annual to weakly perennial root parasite of *Cirsium arvense* and occasionally *C. eriophorum*, typically occurring in rough grassland on riverbanks or adjacent floodplains, where it is sometimes transient, but also on road verges, in coppiced woodland, ungrazed limestone grassland, the edge of a flooded gravel-pit and in old quarries. Along the River Ure (North-west Yorkshire, Mid-west Yorkshire) its occurrence suggests that seed is readily dispersed by water. It is almost restricted to Magnesian limestone districts. Lowland.

Trends Although the overall 10 km square distribution of *O. reticulata* appears to be stable, there has been much turnover at the site level. A number of core and outlying populations, such as the sole North-east Yorkshire site by Linton-on-Ouse, may have been lost, but a few new

populations have also been found in recent years. Numbers fluctuate markedly from year to year, making assessment of trends over time difficult, but many extant sites are in poor condition and lack effective management. It is only thriving consistently on nature reserves such as at Quarry Moor, Ripon (Mid-west Yorkshire) and Wharram Quarry (South-east Yorkshire); at both sites it may have been introduced. The seed bank is extremely persistent which gives hope for recovery at past locations with no recent records.

Biogeography European Temperate element, with a continental distribution in western Europe; also in central Asia. Our plant is subsp. *pallidiflora*, which has a lowland distribution in Europe and is quite distinct from the montane *O. reticulata* subsp. *reticulata*.

Native	GB	IR
2000–19	7	0
1987–99	6	0
1970–86	6	0
pre-1970	5	0

Key refs Foley (1993), Foley (2000a), Newlands & Smith (1998), Rumsey & Jury (1991), Stroh *et al.* (2019), Wigginton (1999).

M.J.Y. FOLEY & F.J. RUMSEY

Ne *Orobanche crenata* Bean Broomrape

Forssk.

		GB	IR
Long term		No trend	No trend
Short term		No trend	No trend

A parasitic annual herb, which is a pernicious weed in the Mediterranean region. Formerly a very rare casual, occasionally occurring in gardens often on *Pelargonium* species, but now a more frequent parasite of crops of peas and beans and then persisting on a range of native legumes in adjacent field margins. Flowering can occur late in summer and seed set is relatively poor, although seed may lie dormant for decades. Lowland.

Trends *O. crenata* was first recorded in Britain in 1845 from a locality in Charlton (West Gloucestershire) which supported a range of Mediterranean weed species, including *Phelipanche ramosa*. Its most persistent British metapopulation has been in the Cranham area (South Essex) where it was originally discovered in a garden in 1950. It was found in a nearby crop-field in the 1970s, when there were tens of thousands of plants, and subsequently in adjacent rough grassland, where it was last recorded in 2013, but may still recur. There have been major outbreaks following introduction with imported seed in recent years in Kent and Hertfordshire, with small numbers appearing in surrounding areas in the following years in the former. It has been recorded on a newly seeded roundabout elsewhere in Kent and is likely to become a more regular and potentially economically damaging, if attractive, component of our flora.

Biogeography Native of the Mediterranean region and south-western Asia, eastwards to Iran.

Alien		GB	IR
2000–19	●	4	0
1987–99	●	3	0
1970–86	●	1	0
pre-1970	○	5	0

Key refs Rumsey & Jury (1991).

F.J. RUMSEY

N *Orobanche hederae* Ivy Broomrape

Duby

		GB				IR		
Long term			↑				↑	↑
Short term				↑				↑

An annual or perennial parasite which grows on the roots of *Hedera* species, especially *Hedera hibernica* and, rarely, on other cultivated Araliaceae and members of the Apiaceae. It is a plant of coastal cliffs, open rocky woodland, quarries, hedgebanks and other similar habitats. Increasingly found in urban areas, in churchyards, car parks and gardens. Lowland.

Trends Populations of *O. hederae* in coastal habitats appear to be stable. Elsewhere it has been recorded with increasing frequency in gardens and urban areas. There has been an assumption in the past that inland populations in 'artificial' habitats, especially in eastern England, established accidentally as a contaminant of topsoil, though its light seeds are just as likely to have arrived naturally to many localities via long-distance dispersal on the wind.

Biogeography Submediterranean-Subatlantic element.

Native		GB	IR
2000–19	●	239	137
1987–99	●	148	94
1970–86	●	118	16
pre-1970	○	142	63

Key refs Jones (1987), Rumsey & Jury (1991), Stewart *et al.* (1994).

M.J.Y. FOLEY & F.J. RUMSEY

Orobanche picridis Oxtongue Broomrape

F.W.Schultz

An annual or rarely perennating parasite occurring mainly on the edges and ledges of coastal chalk cliffs and their undercliffs where it parasitizes *Picris hieracioides* and, rarely, *Pilosella* species and *Inula conyzae*. Previously known from chalky arable and a nearby chalk pit in Cambridgeshire where it occurred over a *c.*70-year period, and from a small number of other sites including Giltar Point, Pembrokeshire, where it only appeared transiently. Numbers fluctuate markedly from year to year, presumably as a consequence of climatic variables yet to be fully elucidated. Lowland.

Trends Although increasing rates of coastal erosion and the development of scrub on some undercliff areas have caused losses and pose threats, this species is probably maintaining its numbers. Losses on cliffs have been offset by increases on adjacent downlands and disturbed grasslands in both Kent and the Isle of Wight. The largest Kent population, on Kingsdown Ranges, is however potentially threatened by development. A major new population was found on the south Wales coast in 2021, following the end of fieldwork for this *Atlas*, although a specimen in the British Herbarium in the Natural History Museum (BM) suggests it has been overlooked in the area for over a century. It is easily mistaken for *O. minor* and this has been responsible for both over- and potentially also under-recording.

Biogeography European Southern-temperate element.

	GB	IR
Long term	No trend	No trend
Short term	No trend	No trend

Native		GB	IR
2000–19	●	3	0
1987–99	●	2	0
1970–86	●	2	0
pre-1970	○	9	0

Key refs Rumsey & Jury (1991), Thorogood & Rumsey (2021), Wigginton (1999).

F.J. RUMSEY

Altitude (m) chart; < 1%, 1–10%, 11–30%, 31–40%, 41–50%, 51–100%. Distance north (km).

Apparency · In flower · In leaf

Orobanche minor Common Broomrape

Sm.

This usually annual root parasite occurs on a wide range of hosts, but mainly on species of Fabaceae and Asteraceae. Speciation is apparently underway, driven through host specificity with genetically distinct but poorly morphologically defined lineages now recognized as infra-specific taxa (Thorogood & Rumsey, 2021). This process may be recent, with *O. minor* var. *heliophila* primarily parasitizing *Brachyglottis* ×*jubar*, a host only introduced to Britain in the 20th century. The most frequent of these taxa, var. *minor*, is probably alien and is usually found on cultivated land (often introduced with grass or fodder crop seed) and other disturbed ground. However other taxa are native, with subsp. *maritima* found on cliffs and dunes on the south coast, with *Daucus carota* subsp. *gummifer* as its main host. Lowland.

Native in Britain and the Channel Islands and a neophyte in Ireland.

Trends The frequent introductions of this species give it a dynamic distribution, so that long-term trends in frequency are difficult to assess. The native subspecies and variants appear to be stable, although scrub encroachment on coastal slopes and damage to beach and dune systems may be having some negative impact. Var. *heliophila* has increased markedly in urban and amenity areas where its host is widely planted.

Biogeography European Southern-temperate element; widely naturalized outside its native range.

	GB	IR
Long term		
Short term		

Native		GB	IR
2000–19	●	634	0
1987–99	●	616	0
1970–86	●	429	0
pre-1970	○	656	0

Alien		GB	IR
2000–19	●	5	101
1987–99	●	8	71
1970–86	●	8	25
pre-1970	○	7	85

Key refs Rumsey & Jury (1991), Thorogood *et al.* (2009), Thorogood & Rumsey (2020), Thorogood & Rumsey (2021).

F.J. RUMSEY & M.J.Y. FOLEY

Altitude (m) chart; < 1%, 1–10%, 11–30%, 31–40%, 41–50%, 51–100%. Distance north (km).

Apparency · In flower · In leaf

N *Phelipanche purpurea* Yarrow Broomrape
(Jacq.) Soják

An annual or possibly perennial herb, *P. purpurea* is parasitic on *Achillea millefolium*. It typically occurs on dry, somewhat basic soils in cliff-top grassland and on roadsides and grassy banks, usually near the sea. Inland it has occurred in pasture, by allotments and in churchyard lawns as well as on roadsides. Flowers can reappear after decades of absence, suggesting that the seeds are long-lived or that plants can persist without flowering for many years. Lowland.

Trends Increased rates of coastal erosion, and the loss of some habitats to housing development, may pose future threats for the species. In recent years the loss or decline of some populations has to some extent been balanced by the appearance, or reappearance, of others. The population at Maryport Docks (Cumberland) has increased rapidly since its discovery in 1983 and a new population was discovered on a roadside in North Hampshire in 2019, not far from the location of a long-disputed record by Goodyer from the 17th century.

Biogeography European Temperate element.

Key refs Rumsey & Jury (1991), Stroh *et al.* (2019), Wigginton (1999).

M.J.Y. FOLEY & F.J. RUMSEY

N *Ilex aquifolium* Holly
L.

An evergreen shrub or tree of deciduous woodlands and wood-pasture, especially those on acidic soils in which *Fagus sylvatica* and *Quercus* predominate; often a frequent or locally dominant undershrub but rarely dominating the canopy. Its susceptibility to heavy browsing can limit regeneration. It is also found in scrub and hedgerows, and on ledges of acidic cliffs, and is often planted in amenity areas and parkland. 0–600 m (Eel Crags, Cumberland).

Trends Widespread planting has completely obscured the native distribution of this species and all records are mapped without status. There is little discernible change in its overall 10 km square distribution, save for the remoter parts of Scotland and Ireland where more systematic recording has led to new discoveries in recent decades. At a finer scale, however, Rackham (2003) reports a general increase in *I. aquifolium* in eastern England in the last 150 years, and as a species known to be sensitive to winter cold, it is possible that its local abundance in other areas farther north may also have increased, as it has done at the eastern limit of its European range in mainland Europe.

Biogeography Suboceanic Southern-temperate element.

Key refs Peterken (1975), Peterken & Lloyd (1967), Rackham (2003).

G.T.D. WILMORE & K.J. WALKER

Hy *Ilex aquifolium × perado = I. ×altaclerensis* Highclere Holly

(hort. ex Loudon) Dallim.

A large evergreen shrub or small tree widely planted and sometimes self-sown shrub in woods, especially on large estate, hedges, parks, churchyards and cemeteries, gardens and quarries, and on banks of rivers and streams, roadsides and waste ground; it also occurs as a relic of cultivation. The hybrid is fully fertile. Lowland.

A cultivated hybrid (native × alien).

Trends *I. ×altaclerensis* arose in cultivation in 1838, with the first wild record of self-sown plants in Lesness Abbey Woods (West Kent). Like *I. aquifolium*, it is available as numerous cultivars which are extremely popular in gardens. Separating the two taxa can be very difficult, and the hybrid is almost certainly under-recorded. The current map suggests that it is frequently found in those areas where recorders have learnt to recognize it.

Biogeography A hybrid of garden origin.

	GB	IR
2000–19 ●	450	5
1987–99 ●	166	2
1970–86 ●	25	0
pre-1970 ○	5	0

Key refs Stace *et al.* (2015).

C.A. STACE, C.D. PRESTON & D.A. PEARMAN

N *Campanula patula* Spreading Bellflower

L.

A biennial herb of dry, well-drained, sunny sites on fairly infertile sandy or gravelly soils subject to periodic disturbance. It is found mainly in marginal habitats such as woodland borders and clearings, footpaths, hedgebanks, riverbanks, railway embankments, road sides and field edges. It can form a persistent seed bank, allowing plants to reappear following disturbance after long absences above-ground. Lowland.

Trends The decline of *C. patula* was already apparent in the 1960s and it has since been lost from many more sites through the cessation of coppicing and other disturbance in woodland, and the increased use of herbicides on roadsides and railway banks. Surveys this century have shown that the total population is now critically small (Walker *et al.*, 2017) and, as a consequence, seed return and

genetic effects mean that the chances of regeneration from the seed bank are now very low (De Vere *et al.*, 2012).

Biogeography European Temperate element, with a continental distribution in western Europe; widely naturalized outside its native range.

Native	GB	IR
2000–19 ●	31	0
1987–99 ●	37	0
1970–86 ●	43	0
pre-1970 ○	122	0

Alien	GB	IR
2000–19 ●	14	0
1987–99 ●	6	0
1970–86 ●	4	0
pre-1970 ○	34	0

Key refs de Vere *et al.* (2012), Stewart *et al.* (1994), Walker *et al.* (2017).

T.D. DINES & K.J. WALKER

Ar *Campanula rapunculus* Rampion Bellflower
L.

	GB	IR
Long term	↓	No trend
Short term	↓ ↑	No trend

A perennial herb found naturalized in rough grassland and on roadsides, railway banks and in quarries. It also occurs as a relic of cultivation. Reproduction is from seed and rhizome fragments. Lowland.

Trends *C. rapunculus* was once frequently grown in gardens in our area for ornament and its edible roots. It was recorded from the wild as early as 1597, but fell out of favour as a vegetable around 1700 and as a consequence it is now rarely encountered, either in cultivation or in the wild.

Biogeography *C. rapunculus* is a variable species with a European Southern-temperate distribution; it is naturalized in Europe north of its native range.

Alien	GB	IR
2000–19	15	1
1987–99	10	0
1970–86	16	0
pre-1970	117	0

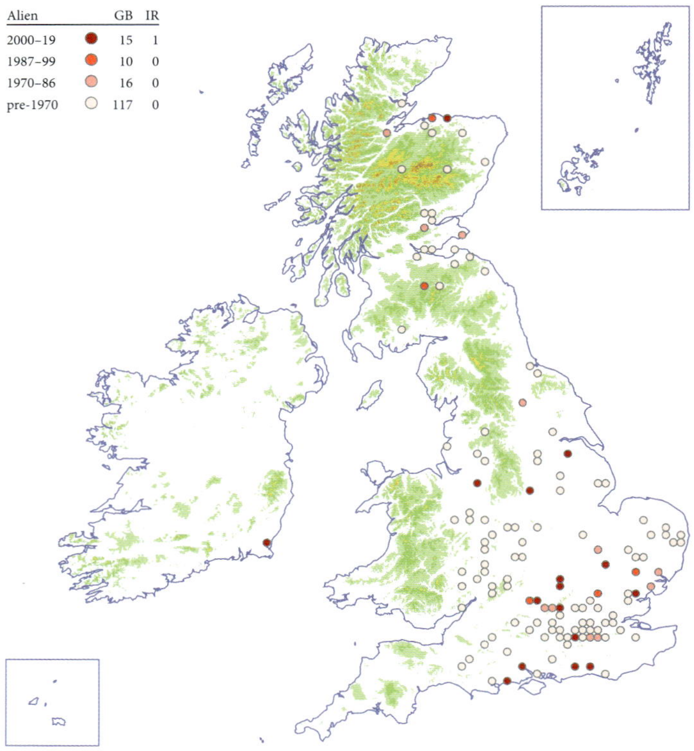

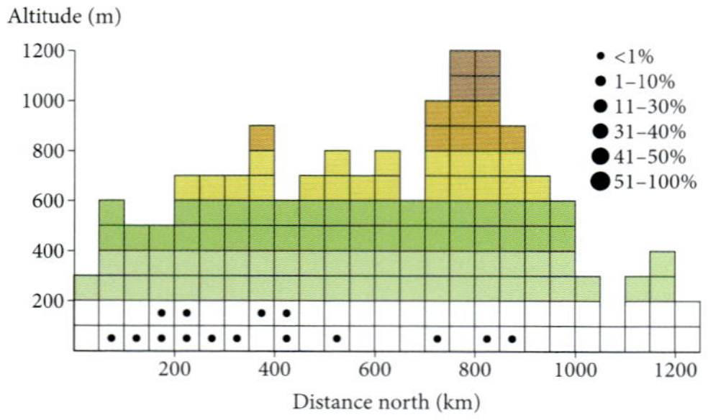

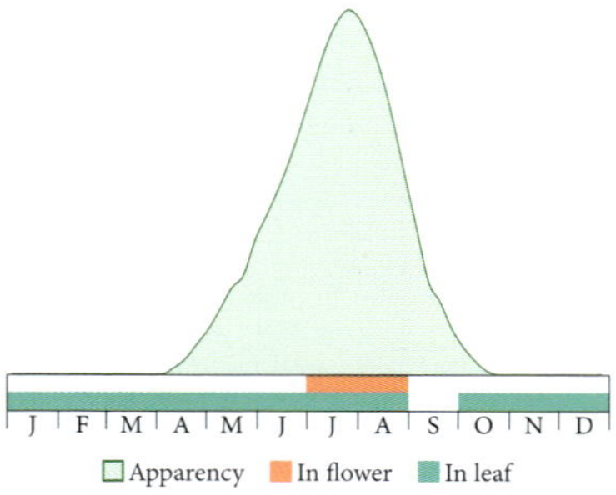

Altitude (m)
1200
1000
800
600
400
200
<1%
1–10%
11–30%
31–40%
41–50%
51–100%
200
400
600
800
1000
1200
Distance north (km)

J F M A M J J A S O N D
Apparency
In flower
In leaf

T.D. Dines & K.J. Walker

Ne *Campanula lactiflora* Milky Bellflower
M.Bieb.

	GB	IR
Long term	No trend	No trend
Short term	↑	No trend

An upright, clump-forming perennial herb, grown in gardens and naturalized beside streams, on roadsides and paths, and on rough and waste ground, particularly on damp soil. It is occasionally found as a relic of cultivation. Reproduction is by seed. Lowland.

Trends *C. lactiflora* was introduced into cultivation in Britain in 1814, and is widely grown in gardens, with many cultivars. It is increasingly recorded from the wild, where it was first recorded in 1954 (Scarborough, North-east Yorkshire, and at Dess and at Ballater, South Aberdeenshire).

Biogeography Native of north-eastern Turkey, the Caucasus and north-western Iran.

Alien	GB	IR
2000–19	61	0
1987–99	19	0
1970–86	21	0
pre-1970	15	0

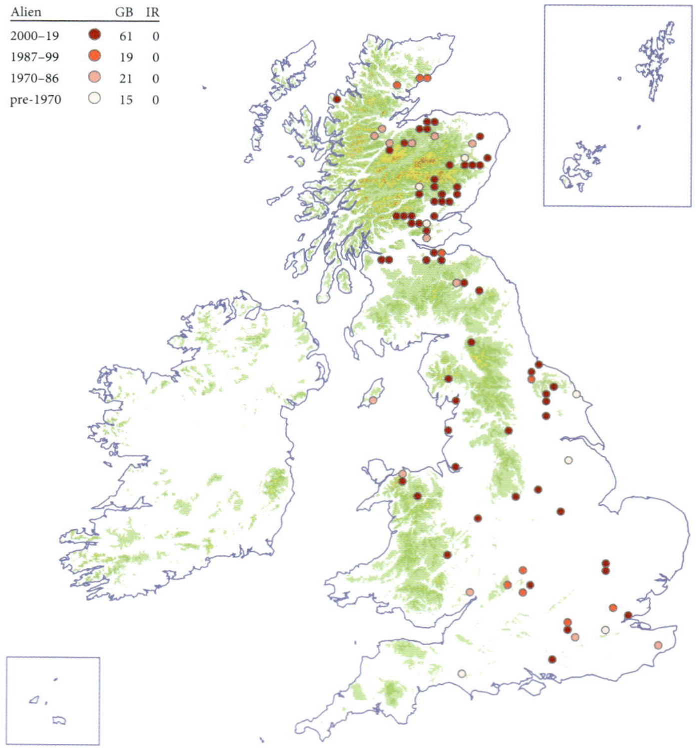

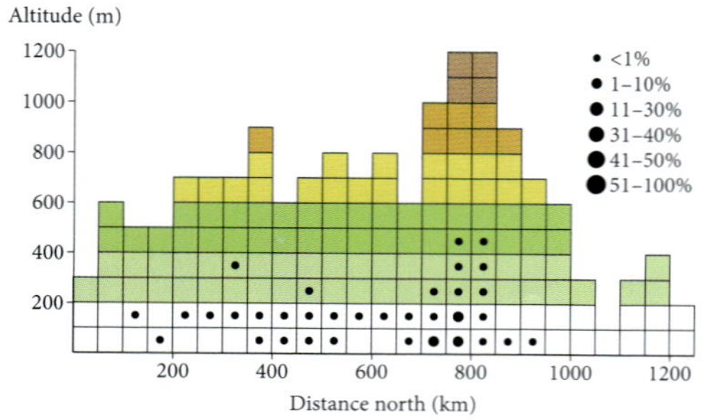

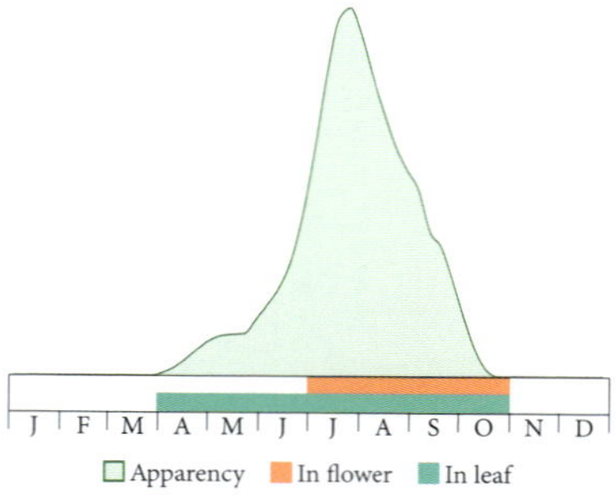

Altitude (m)
1200
1000
800
600
400
200
<1%
1–10%
11–30%
31–40%
41–50%
51–100%
200
400
600
800
1000
1200
Distance north (km)

J F M A M J J A S O N D
Apparency
In flower
In leaf

T.D. Dines & D.A. Pearman

Ne *Campanula persicifolia* Peach-leaved Bellflower
L.

A winter-green perennial herb with shortly creeping rhizomes, much grown in gardens and found on pavements, along boundaries and waysides, on waste ground, on the banks and verges of roadsides, in hedgerows and woods. It is frequently found self-sown, and often naturalized, forming persistent populations. Lowland.

Trends *C. persicifolia*, introduced into cultivation before 1596, was claimed as native by Druce (1903), but the evidence for this is very unconvincing and has never been accepted. The first record in the wild dates from 1802 (Woods of Cullen, Banffshire). The large and continuing increase in records since the 1960s is probably due to continued escapes from cultivation, as well as to better recording of aliens.

Biogeography A European Temperate species, absent as a native from much of western Europe.

Alien	GB	IR
2000–19	628	4
1987–99	307	1
1970–86	127	0
pre-1970	90	0

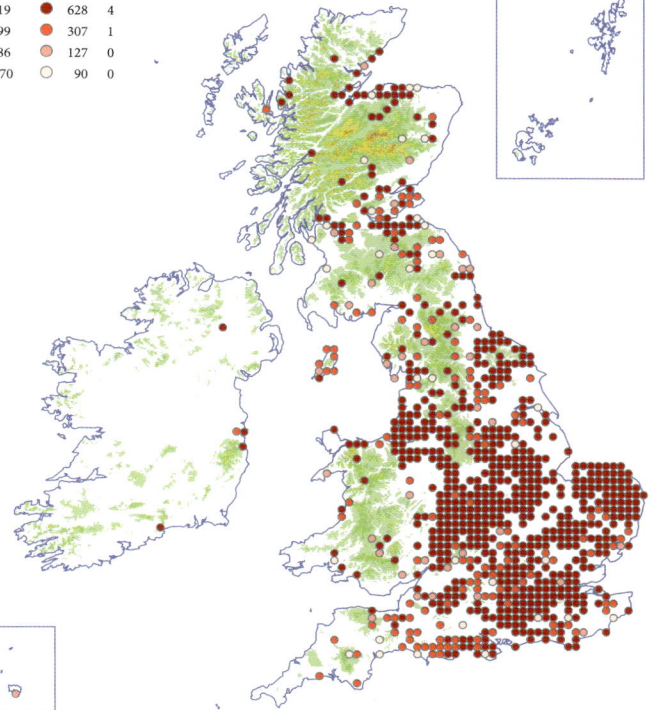

	GB	IR
Long term	↑	No trend
Short term	↑	No trend

Key refs Druce (1903).

T.D. Dines & D.A. Pearman

Ne *Campanula medium* Canterbury-bells
L.

A winter-green biennial herb, commonly grown in gardens, and found on disturbed waste ground, refuse tips, dumped soil, disused railway lines, road verges and banks. It is usually casual but can become established, particularly on railway embankments and on chalk soils. Lowland.

Trends *C. medium* was introduced to Britain from Europe by 1597 and is now common in cultivation. It was first recorded in the wild in 1870. It was not mapped in the 1962 *Atlas*, so changes in its distribution are difficult to assess but it is probably increasing in some areas as a garden outcast.

Biogeography Native of south-eastern France and northern and central Italy.

Alien	GB	IR
2000–19	65	2
1987–99	73	0
1970–86	46	0
pre-1970	47	0

	GB	IR
Long term	No trend	No trend
Short term	↓	No trend

T.D. Dines & K.J. Walker

(N) *Campanula glomerata* Clustered Bellflower
L.

A perennial herb of short calcareous grassland, scrub, open woodland, cliffs and sand dunes. It is most frequent on chalk and oolite, and curiously absent from apparently suitable habitat on other limestones and base-rich substrates. It also occurs as a garden escape on roadsides and waste ground. 0–355 m (Oddendale, Westmorland) and up to 470 m as an alien in Quarnford Churchyard (Staffordshire).

Trends This species has seen a gradual decline both within and outside its core areas, due to habitat loss and a decline in grazing leading to increased competition from tall grasses. Many populations are small, often consisting of only a few plants (Green *et al.*, 1997). *C. glomerata* is widely grown in gardens and seems to be increasing as a naturalized escape.

Biogeography Eurasian Temperate element, with a continental distribution in western Europe.

Native	GB	IR
2000–19	259	0
1987–99	288	0
1970–86	244	0
pre-1970	379	0

Alien	GB	IR
2000–19	45	0
1987–99	39	0
1970–86	21	0
pre-1970	32	0

Key refs Green *et al.* (1997).

T.D. DINES

(Ne) *Campanula portenschlagiana* Adria Bellflower
Schult.

A partially winter-green perennial herb, with subterranean runners, much grown on walls and rockeries in gardens and frequently establishing on the tops and exterior faces of garden walls, as well as in pavement cracks, on rocky banks, and on waste ground. Populations arise from seed and stem fragments, which root readily. It appears less able than *C. poscharskyana* to self-sow away from human habitations. Lowland.

Trends *C. portenschlagiana* was introduced into cultivation in 1835, and is now very popular in gardens where it can become a troublesome weed. It was first recorded in the wild in 1922 (Cardiff, Glamorganshire), and Clement (1978a) described it as "often seen questionably wild about gardens", giving only one locality. It was brought to the wider attention of botanists in our area by Grenfell (1982) and Stace (1991);

it is still unevenly recorded, although the western range shown by the map is probably genuine. It is increasing rapidly in some areas, although it is often confused with the more common *C. poscharskyana* which also grows on walls. Some of the records might be of *C. garganica* or other similar species.

Biogeography Native of the eastern Adriatic region.

Alien	GB	IR
2000–19	787	73
1987–99	352	13
1970–86	34	1
pre-1970	7	1

Key refs Clement (1978a), Grenfell (1982).

T.D. DINES, D.A. PEARMAN & K.J. WALKER

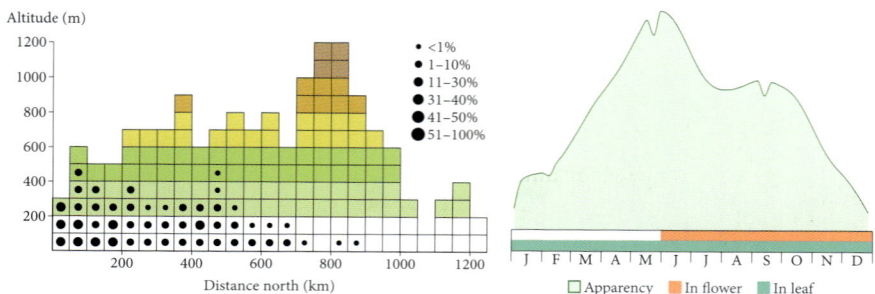

Ne *Campanula poscharskyana* Trailing Bellflower
Degen

A partially winter-green perennial herb, widely grown on walls and rockeries in gardens, frequently established on the tops and exterior faces of garden walls, in pavement cracks, on rocky banks and in waste ground. Populations arise from seed and stem fragments, which root readily, and more occasionally from garden throw-outs. It appears to have a greater ability than *C. portenschlagiana* to self-sow farther away from human habitations. Lowland.

Trends *C. poscharskyana* was introduced into cultivation in 1931 and is frequently grown on walls and rockeries in gardens. It was first recorded in the wild in 1957 (Worgret, Dorset), and possibly before that from a quarry in the Malvern Hills (Herefordshire or Worcestershire). Like *C. portenschlagiana* most botanists were not aware of it until it was described and illustrated by Grenfell (1982) and

included in Stace (1991). Its range appears to be increasing very rapidly in some areas although it is still unevenly recorded and possibly confused with the more localized *C. portenschlagiana* by some recorders. It was first recorded in Ireland in 1995, but it must have been overlooked before that.

Biogeography Native of the eastern Adriatic region.

Alien		GB	IR
2000–19	●	1101	53
1987–99	●	467	8
1970–86	●	71	0
pre-1970	○	15	0

Key refs Grenfell (1982).

T.D. DINES, D.A. PEARMAN & K.J. WALKER

N *Campanula latifolia* Giant Bellflower
L.

A large perennial herb of damp shaded habitats such as woodland, riversides and hedgerows, usually on fertile, neutral or calcareous soils. It is also grown in gardens, occurring as an established alien on waste ground, roadsides and hedgebanks. Generally lowland, but reaching 390 m at Ingleborough (Mid-west Yorkshire).

Trends Within its native range, this species has shown little change in overall distribution since the 1960s. It is, however, becoming more frequent as an alien. It is regarded as an alien in Ireland (Scannell & Synnott, 1987).

Biogeography European Temperate element; also in central Asia.

Native		GB	IR
2000–19	●	628	0
1987–99	●	691	0
1970–86	●	600	0
pre-1970	○	726	0

Alien		GB	IR
2000–19	●	54	21
1987–99	●	43	24
1970–86	●	47	13
pre-1970	○	74	11

Key refs Scannell & Synnott (1987).

T.D. DINES

945

N *Campanula trachelium* Nettle-leaved Bellflower

L.

A large perennial herb, found as a native on base-rich, usually calcareous soils in woodland, scrubby grassland and hedgebanks; in Ireland it is also reported from riverbanks and swamp woodland. It is also grown in gardens, and occurs as a naturalized alien on a wider range of soils and habitats. Generally lowland, but reaching 320 m in Monk's Dale (Derbyshire).

Trends This species has declined in many regions through habitat loss arising from the cessation of coppicing and the removal of hedgerows. It may be increasing as an escape from gardens and as a consequence its native range is difficult to determine with certainty, especially in northern England where many populations occur in the same habitats as in regions where it is definitely native. It is often confused with *C. latifolia* and some of these errors may have been included on the map.

Biogeography European Temperate element; also in central Asia.

Native	GB	IR
2000–19	432	15
1987–99	456	10
1970–86	338	4
pre-1970	430	14

Alien	GB	IR
2000–19	150	7
1987–99	67	3
1970–86	40	6
pre-1970	59	8

Key refs Goodwillie (1999a).

T.D. DINES & K.J. WALKER

Ne *Campanula rapunculoides* Creeping Bellflower

L.

A perennial herb, spreading by long slender rhizomes, grown in gardens but soon becoming a weed. It most often found on the banks and verges of roads and tracks where it can survive being mown, as well as railway banks, old pits and occasionally woodland and arable field-borders. Generally lowland, but reaching 365 m near Felindre (Radnorshire).

Trends This species was cultivated in Britain by 1683 and was first recorded from the wild by 1708 (Hoxton, Oxfordshire). It was frequently grown in gardens where it spreads vigorously by rhizomes and seed and is therefore often discarded. Although it can be persistent, most populations in the wild are often short-lived and this may help to explain its decline, which was already evident in the 1960s and has continued and even accelerated since then.

Biogeography A European Temperate species, apparently native north to the Netherlands, but naturalized to southern Fennoscandia.

Alien	GB	IR
2000–19	138	3
1987–99	250	2
1970–86	211	2
pre-1970	463	14

T.D. DINES & D.A. PEARMAN

N *Campanula rotundifolia* Harebell

L.

A rhizomatous perennial herb found in a wide range of dry, open, infertile grasslands, as well as fixed dunes, rock ledges, roadsides and railway banks. It tolerates a wide range of soil pH, being found on both mildly acidic and calcareous substrates, and heavy-metal tolerant races are known. 0–1,210 m (Ben Lawers, Mid Perthshire).

Trends Although *C. rotundifolia* remains very widespread it is certainly less common in the lowlands where it has declined, along with many other grassland species, as a result of habitat loss, agricultural improvement and reductions in levels of grazing (Stroh *et al.*, 2014). In calcareous grassland and heathland this decline has also been attributed to increasing deposition of pollutants such as nitrogen which has favoured more competitive grasses and herbs (Maskell *et al.*, 2010; Van Den

Berg *et al.*, 2010). Its absence from some apparently suitable areas, especially in south-western England, is puzzling.

Biogeography Circumpolar Boreo-temperate element.

Native	GB	IR
2000–19	2007	228
1987–99	2068	219
1970–86	1362	71
pre-1970	2132	189

Alien	GB	IR
2000–19	6	0
1987–99	4	0
1970–86	3	0
pre-1970	5	0

Key refs Grime *et al.* (2007), Maskell *et al.* (2010), Stevens *et al.* (2012), Stroh *et al.* (2014), van den Berg *et al.* (2010).

T.D. DINES & K.J. WALKER

Ar *Legousia hybrida* Venus's-looking-glass

(L.) Delarbre

An annual herb, found in or on the margins of land cultivated for a wide range of crops, mainly on calcareous soils, especially on chalk. It also occurs as a casual in disturbed sites such as track or road verges, waste ground, chalk-pits, and disused railway lines. Lowland.

Trends *L. hybrida* has significantly declined since the 1940s because of the use of herbicides and changing methods of arable cultivation, but remains locally abundant on chalk escarpments in southern England, especially on arable fields managed as part of agri-environment schemes (Walker *et al.*, 2007). The seed is long-lived and populations can reappear after long periods of absence.

Biogeography As an archaeophyte, *L. hybrida* has a European Southern-temperate distribution.

Alien	GB	IR
2000–19	238	0
1987–99	318	0
1970–86	297	0
pre-1970	471	1

Key refs Walker *et al.* (2007).

T.D. DINES & K.J. WALKER

Ne *Legousia speculum-veneris* Large Venus's-looking-glass
(L.) Chaix

An annual herb, naturalized on the margins of a few arable fields in North Hampshire. It also arises as a casual garden escape and grain impurity, and more recently, as a grass-seed contaminant. Lowland.

Trends *L. speculum-veneris* was being grown in Britain long before 1680, but has always been rare in the wild, where it was first recorded 1727 (Bingley, South-west Yorkshire). It has been known from a small area around Upper Wootton, North Hampshire, since 1916, where conservation management is currently in place to preserve it along with a number of other rare arable weeds (Walker *et al.*, 2007).

Biogeography *L. speculum-veneris* has a Submediterranean-subatlantic distribution.

	GB	IR
Long term	No trend	No trend
Short term	No trend	No trend

Alien	GB	IR
2000–19	2	0
1987–99	1	0
1970–86	5	0
pre-1970	10	0

Key refs Walker *et al.* (2007).

T.D. Dines & D.A. Pearman

Altitude (m)

- <1%
- 1–10%
- 11–30%
- 31–40%
- 41–50%
- 51–100%

Distance north (km)

☐ Apparency ☐ In flower ☐ In leaf

N *Wahlenbergia hederacea* Ivy-leaved Bellflower
(L.) Rchb.

A small, low-growing perennial herb of damp, wet or boggy places on acidic soils, occurring on heathlands, heathy pastures and moorlands, in open woodland and willow-carr, and by streams and in flushes. In Ireland, it is most frequent beside streams and is absent from pastures. It prefers areas with moving, rather than standing, water. 0–485 m (Killakee, County Dublin), and up to 700 m on the Cambrian Way, near Craig Cwmoergwm (Breconshire).

Trends *W. hederacea* appears to have declined from the edges of its range by the 1960s, but its distribution is now much better understood due to more intensive recording, especially in Wales and Ireland, and new populations continue to be found, though this is balanced by localized losses throughout its range due to habitat destruction, improvement of pastures, increased grazing pressure and peat extraction.

Biogeography Oceanic Southern-temperate element.

Native	GB	IR
2000–19	204	15
1987–99	206	13
1970–86	158	7
pre-1970	262	35

Alien	GB	IR
2000–19	6	0
1987–99	3	0
1970–86	0	0
pre-1970	6	3

Key refs Stroh *et al.* (2019).

T.D. Dines & K.J. Walker

Altitude (m)

- <1%
- 1–10%
- 11–30%
- 31–40%
- 41–50%
- 51–100%

Distance north (km)

☐ Apparency ☐ In flower ☐ In leaf

Phyteuma spicatum Spiked Rampion
L.

(N?)

A long-lived perennial herb of damp, fertile, acid soils on road verges, streamsides and in coppiced woodland. Reproduction is by seed, which is long-lived, but recruitment at some sites is negligible. Lowland.

Trends *P. spicatum* has been grown for centuries as a medicinal plant, and was first recorded in the wild in 1640. Plants in Sussex were first recorded in 1824, suggesting that although traditionally regarded as native, it might be an introduction there. It was formerly more widespread and more abundant within this stronghold. It cannot tolerate shade and has been lost from a number of sites through a lack of coppicing and the growth of tall vegetation along rides. Over the last decade around 350 plants have been recorded annually across nine sites. It has also been reintroduced to a few sites within this narrow native range.

Biogeography European Temperate element.

	GB	IR
Long term	No trend	No trend
Short term	No trend	No trend

Native	GB	IR
2000–19	4	0
1987–99	4	0
1970–86	3	0
pre-1970	8	0

Alien	GB	IR
2000–19	1	0
1987–99	0	0
1970–86	1	0
pre-1970	12	0

Key refs Wheeler & Hutchings (1999), Wheeler & Hutchings (2002), Wigginton (1999).

T.D. DINES & K.J. WALKER

Phyteuma orbiculare Round-headed Rampion
L.

(N)

A perennial herb of species-rich chalk grassland, open scrub, earthworks and road verges. It is tolerant of grazing, and seems to prefer short turf, but it also grows in neighbouring ungrazed grassland. Propagation is mostly by seed but it also spreads by stoloniferous growth. Lowland.

Trends Most losses of *P. orbiculare* took place before 1930 due to ploughing of chalk grassland. Its 10 km square distribution has not changed appreciably since the 1960s, although like many short plants it is a poor competitor and has declined locally due to the relaxation of grazing and succession to coarse grass or scrub on some sites.

Biogeography European Boreo-temperate element; at low altitudes in western Europe and in mountains of central Europe.

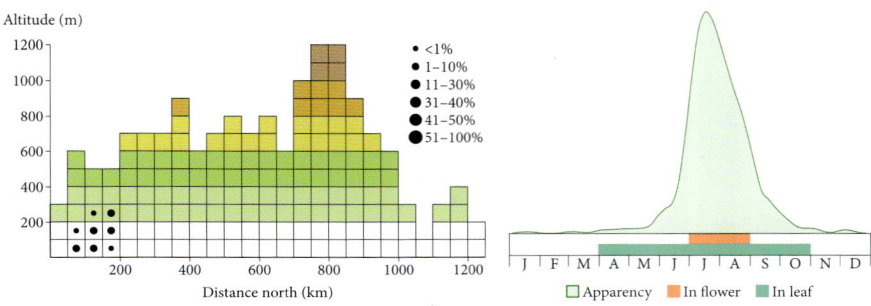

	GB	IR
Long term	↓ ↓ ◆ ↑ ↑	No trend
Short term	↓ ↓ ◆ ↑ ↑	No trend

Native	GB	IR
2000–19	40	0
1987–99	39	0
1970–86	33	0
pre-1970	48	0

Alien	GB	IR
2000–19	0	0
1987–99	0	0
1970–86	0	0
pre-1970	2	0

Key refs Stewart *et al.* (1994).

T.D. DINES & K.J. WALKER

(N) *Jasione montana* Sheep's-bit
L.

A partially winter-green biennial herb of acidic, shallow, well-drained soils. It occurs on sea-cliffs, in maritime grasslands and heathlands and on stabilized sand dunes, and inland on dry heathland, stone walls, hedgebanks and railway cuttings. Propagation is by seed, and disturbed open sites and recently burnt ground are frequently colonized. 0–955 m (Mt Brandon, South Kerry).

Trends *J. montana* was lost from many sites in central, southern and eastern England before 1930, and it has further declined throughout its British range since then, but especially away from its coastal strongholds in the west. Reasons for losses include the destruction of lowland heaths and the growth of coarser vegetation following a decline in rabbit and livestock grazing, and possibly also eutrophication caused by atmospheric deposition of nitrogen. Its distribution is considered to be more stable in Ireland.

Biogeography European Temperate element.

Native		GB	IR
2000–19	●	623	379
1987–99	●	702	354
1970–86	●	526	58
pre-1970	○	986	301

Alien		GB	IR
2000–19	●	0	0
1987–99	●	5	0
1970–86	●	4	0
pre-1970	○	4	0

Key refs Parnell (1985).

T.D. DINES & K.J. WALKER

(N) *Lobelia urens* Heath Lobelia
L.

A rhizomatous perennial herb of rough pastures and grassy heaths dominated by *Molinia caerulea*. It is confined to infertile moderately acidic soils that are often seasonally waterlogged. Reproduction is by seed, which may be long-lived, and germination seems to be stimulated by disturbance. Most populations fluctuate erratically in size. Lowland.

Trends *L. urens* has decreased gradually and it is now known from only six native localities. A few recent records from Devon may be transient and are likely to be due to movement of people or ponies. Populations have been lost to afforestation and agricultural improvement, with continued threats from lack of appropriate habitat management. Many of the extant populations are very small and rely on periodic disturbance in order to halt woodland succession and to stimulate germination from the seed bank (Dinsdale *et al.*, 2003).

Biogeography Oceanic Southern-temperate element.

Native		GB	IR
2000–19	●	7	0
1987–99	●	6	0
1970–86	●	9	0
pre-1970	○	12	0

Alien		GB	IR
2000–19	●	3	0
1987–99	●	2	0
1970–86	●	0	0
pre-1970	○	3	0

Key refs Brightmore (1968), Dinsdale *et al.* (2000), Stroh *et al.* (2019), Wigginton (1999).

T.D. DINES & K.J. WALKER

Ne *Lobelia erinus* Garden Lobelia
L.

A winter-green perennial herb that is widely grown as an annual in hanging baskets and window boxes in our area. It is most frequently found along the base of walls as well as on pavements, waste ground, and refuse tips. It is usually a casual, often arising from seed, but some populations persist in sheltered urban sites. Lowland.

Trends *L. erinus* was cultivated in Britain by 1752 and is widely grown as an ornamental, but was not recorded from the wild until 1905 (Southport, South Lancashire). It is still unevenly recorded and changes in distribution are difficult to assess given the more comprehensive recording of garden escapes in recent decades.

Biogeography Native of South Africa.

Alien	GB	IR
2000–19	743	67
1987–99	346	11
1970–86	66	0
pre-1970	22	0

	GB	IR
Long term	No trend	No trend

T.D. Dines, D.A. Pearman & K.J. Walker

N *Lobelia dortmanna* Water Lobelia
L.

A small, rosette-forming perennial herb of oligotrophic lakes and long-established reservoirs, growing on gravelly, stony or silty acidic substrates. It is slow-growing, with little ability to withstand shade or competition and is therefore confined to shallow water less than 2 m deep. Reproduction and dispersal is by seed, which can remain viable for at least 30 years. 0–745 m (Llyn Bach, Caernarvonshire).

Trends *L. dortmanna* is still frequent in the north and west of our area, and its distribution has been largely stable since 2000. Declines from the east of its range in both Britain and Ireland had mostly taken place by the early 20th century, due to eutrophication. Apparent losses in south-western Scotland this century are more likely to be a result of under-recording rather than of genuine loss.

Biogeography European Boreal-montane element; also in North America.

Native	GB	IR
2000–19	416	125
1987–99	465	126
1970–86	277	39
pre-1970	449	134

	GB	IR
Long term		
Short term		

Key refs Farmer (1989), Preston & Croft (1997), Woodhead (1951b).

P.A. Stroh & T.D. Dines

Ne ## *Pratia angulata* Lawn Lobelia
(G.Forst.) Hook.f.

A small, patch-forming procumbent herb with stems that root at the nodes, found naturalized on damp lawns, mainly in parks and botanic gardens. Lowland.

Trends *P. angulata* was introduced into cultivation in Britain in 1828, and is increasingly popular in rock gardens, and with many more records this century than in the past. It has been known in the lawns of the Royal Botanic Garden, Edinburgh (Midlothian) since the 1930s. Some of the records mapped may refer to *P. pedunculata* which was first identified in 2000 but now appears to be more frequent than *P. angulata* in somewhat drier places in southern Britain (Stace, 2019).

Biogeography Native of New Zealand (*P. pedunculata* is native to Australia).

Alien	GB	IR
2000–19	36	2
1987–99	12	0
1970–86	8	0
pre-1970	4	0

	GB	IR
Long term	No trend	No trend
Short term		No trend

T.D. Dines & J.O. Mountford

N ## *Menyanthes trifoliata* Bogbean
L.

A rhizomatous perennial herb which grows as an emergent at the shallow edge of lakes, pools or slow-flowing rivers, or in swamps, flushes or dune-slacks. It tolerates a wide range of water chemistry, but is intolerant of shade. The species is distylous and pin or thrum colonies become established by clonal growth. 0–1,030 m (Beinn Heasgarnich, Mid Perthshire).

Trends Although this species remains frequent over much of our area, it has decreased in south-eastern England because of the drainage of wetlands in both historic and recent times. In some of these areas it is now more frequent as a planted ornamental than as a native.

Biogeography Circumpolar Boreo-temperate element.

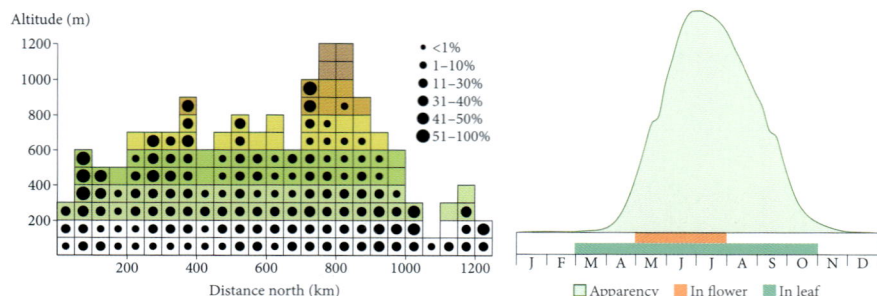

Native	GB	IR
2000–19	1557	695
1987–99	1512	685
1970–86	1048	160
pre-1970	1512	509

Alien	GB	IR
2000–19	216	2
1987–99	97	0
1970–86	25	0
pre-1970	49	0

Key refs Hewett (1964), Preston & Croft (1997), van Rossum *et al.* (2015).

C.D. Preston

N *Nymphoides peltata* Fringed Water-lily
Kuntze

A rhizomatous perennial which grows in water 0·5–2 m deep in lakes, ponds, slowly flowing rivers, canals and large fenland ditches. As a native it is a plant of calcareous and eutrophic water. The species is distylous and large pin or thrum colonies become established by clonal growth. Generally lowland, but reaching 410 m at Llanelly Hill in Breconshire.

Native in Britain and a neophyte in Ireland and the Channel Islands.

Trends *N. peltata* had declined as a native in the Thames valley by 1960, but remains frequent in the fenlands of East Anglia (where all apparently native plants are the pin morph). It is popularly grown as an ornamental, and has become widely naturalized from material deliberately planted in the wild or discarded as surplus stock.

Biogeography Eurasian Temperate element; widely naturalized outside its native range.

Native	GB	IR
2000–19	37	0
1987–99	35	0
1970–86	20	0
pre-1970	42	0

Alien	GB	IR
2000–19	538	16
1987–99	463	11
1970–86	161	2
pre-1970	151	5

Key refs Preston & Croft (1997), Stewart *et al.* (1994).

C.D. PRESTON

Ne *Echinops sphaerocephalus* Glandular Globe-thistle
L.

A clump-forming perennial herb, occasionally grown in gardens and found as an escape on roadsides, walls, railway embankments, arable margins, waste ground and in disused quarries. It is usually casual but sometimes persists for many years. Lowland.

Trends *E. sphaerocephalus* was grown in Britain by John Gerard in 1596, but was not recorded from the wild until 1903 (Jersey, Channel Islands). It is less common in gardens than *E. bannaticus* or *E. exaltatus* and possibly over-recorded because of confusion with these more widely grown species.

Biogeography *E. sphaerocephalus* has a Eurosiberian Southern-temperate distribution, extending north into western Europe to central France.

Alien	GB	IR
2000–19	37	0
1987–99	71	0
1970–86	49	0
pre-1970	37	1

	GB	IR
Long term	No trend	No trend
Short term		No trend

Key refs Kent (1968).

F.H. PERRING & D.A. PEARMAN

Ne *Echinops exaltatus* Globe-thistle
Schrad.

A clump-forming perennial herb, widely grown in gardens and found on roadsides and waste ground. It is occasionally naturalized, but is more often only casual. Lowland.

Trends *E. exaltatus* was first cultivated in Britain in 1822, but is less frequent in gardens than *E. bannaticus* and is much rarer in the wild. It was first recorded in 1907 (Minto Crag, Roxburghshire), but it no longer appears to be available commercially and so may be over-recorded for *E. bannaticus*.

Biogeography Native of east-central and southern Europe.

	GB	IR
Long term	No trend	No trend
Short term		No trend

Alien		GB	IR
2000–19	●	84	0
1987–99	●	45	0
1970–86	●	21	0
pre-1970	○	16	0

Key refs Kent (1968).

Altitude (m) chart, distance north (km)

● <1%
● 1–10%
● 11–30%
● 31–40%
● 41–50%
● 51–100%

☐ Apparency ▮ In flower ▮ In leaf

F.H. PERRING & D.A. PEARMAN

Ne *Echinops bannaticus* Blue Globe-thistle
Rochel ex Schrad.

A clump-forming perennial herb, commonly grown in gardens and found naturalized on roadsides, railway embankments and waste ground as well as refuse tips and other areas where garden waste has been dumped. Lowland.

Trends *E. bannaticus* was first brought into cultivation around 1832 and is now widely available to gardeners, especially as the variety 'Taplow Blue'. It is now the most frequent *Echinops* species found in the wild, from where it was first recorded in 1938 (Dorset), and it appears to be increasing. It is thought that most, if not all, records of *E. ritro* refer to this species (Clement & Foster, 1994; Stace, 2019).

Biogeography Native of south-eastern Europe, east to the Crimea.

	GB	IR
Long term	No trend	No trend
Short term		No trend

Alien		GB	IR
2000–19	●	218	1
1987–99	●	114	1
1970–86	●	27	0
pre-1970	○	25	0

Key refs Clement & Foster (1994), Kent (1968).

Altitude (m) chart, distance north (km)

● <1%
● 1–10%
● 11–30%
● 31–40%
● 41–50%
● 51–100%

☐ Apparency ▮ In flower ▮ In leaf

F.H. PERRING & D.A. PEARMAN

N *Carlina vulgaris* Carline Thistle
L.

A usually biennial or short-lived perennial monocarpic herb, typically occurring in well-grazed grassland on dry, infertile calcareous or base-rich soils, but also in more open habitats, including rock exposures, screes, quarry floors, pits, tracksides, coastal cliffs and sand dunes. 0–490 m (Cwar yr Hendre, Breconshire).

Trends *C. vulgaris* declined in the second half of the 20th century largely due to habitat destruction and succession due to a lack of grazing. Since 2000 its known range has stabilized and records have even increased in some areas due to more systematic recording, especially in north-western Scotland and Ireland. It has occasionally been recorded as an accidental introduction on waste ground or old mine workings inland (Chater, 2010b).

Biogeography Eurosiberian Temperate element.

Native	GB	IR
2000–19	836	176
1987–99	821	178
1970–86	622	32
pre-1970	989	153

Alien	GB	IR
2000–19	1	0
1987–99	1	0
1970–86	1	0
pre-1970	2	0

Key refs Chater (2010b), Greig-Smith & Sagar (1981), Grime *et al.* (2007), Hackney (1992).

F.H. PERRING & K.J. WALKER

Ar *Arctium lappa* Greater Burdock
L.

A monocarpic perennial herb of streamsides and riverbanks, roadside verges, tracks and waysides, field-borders, waste land and other disturbed places. Lowland.

Trends *A. lappa* was probably over-recorded in the 1962 *Atlas* because '*Arctium lappa*' was used as the name of the *Arctium* aggregate at that time. This problem continues, with Stace (2019) and Sell & Murrell (2006) having different interpretations of the taxon. The distribution seems stable. It may only be a recent colonist outside its core area in England, and appears to be increasing in northern England and Wales.

Biogeography As an archaeophyte, *A. lappa* has a Eurosiberian Temperate distribution, but it is widely naturalized so that its distribution is now Circumpolar Temperate.

Alien	GB	IR
2000–19	953	2
1987–99	822	3
1970–86	521	0
pre-1970	721	2

Key refs Gross *et al.* (1980), Perring (1960), Sell & Murrell (2006), Werner & Hawthorn (1980).

F.H. PERRING & J.O. MOUNTFORD

(N) *Arctium minus s.l.* Lesser & Wood Burdocks

Monocarpic perennial herbs that occur on waysides, field-borders, banks of watercourses, waste ground and in woodlands and on wood borders. Usually lowland, but up to 540 m at Brown Clee (Shropshire).

Trends The recording of *A. minus s.l.* has been confused by varying understanding of the taxon, with Stace (2019) separating *A. nemorosum* from the two subspecies of *A. minus* (subsp. *minus*, subsp. *pubens*) whilst Sell and Murrell (2006) treat all three taxa as subspecies of *A. lappa*. The distribution of *A. nemorosum*, *A. minus* subsp. *minus*, and *A. minus* subsp. *pubens* are mapped at the aggregate level here. Their overall distribution at the 10 km square level appears to be stable, with some localized increases along coarse roadside

verges and in disturbed woodlands.

Biogeography Throughout most of Europe and western Asia; introduced in North and South America as well as New Zealand.

Native	GB	IR
2000–19	2392	730
1987–99	2336	769
1970–86	1443	83
pre-1970	1878	375

Alien	GB	IR
2000–19	1	0
1987–99	0	0
1970–86	0	0
pre-1970	0	0

Key refs Grime *et al.* (2007), Sell & Murrell (2006), Werner & Hawthorn (1980).

J.O. MOUNTFORD

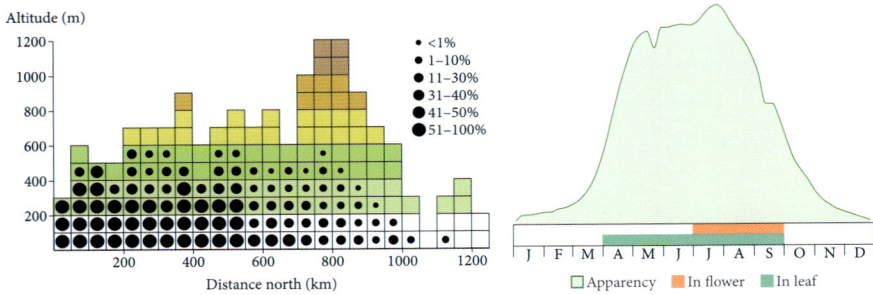

(N) *Saussurea alpina* Alpine Saw-wort

(L.) DC.

A perennial herb of damp, base-rich cliffs, rock ledges, screes and other open ground, occasionally found in flushed areas and sometimes washed down mountain streams to become established on rocky stream banks and riverside shingle. It reproduces by seed, and spreads vegetatively by new rosettes arising from stolons. From near sea level in Caithness and Westerness, to 1,207 m on Ben Lawers (Mid Perthshire).

Trends *S. alpina* shows no appreciable change in its 10 km square distribution since the 1960s. There is evidence of local declines in the Lake District (Porter & Halliday, 2014) and on Irish mountains (Curtis & McGough, 1988), possibly due to overgrazing by sheep, although there have been recent discoveries in West Mayo (Corranabinna), West Galway (Maumturk Mountains) and South

Kerry (Mount Brandon). Several new populations have also been found this century in Scotland, and an absence of recent records from some areas where it was found in the late 20th century (Preston *et al.*, 2002a) probably reflects difficulties of recording in remote locations, and also the inaccessibility of some sites, rather than genuine loss. For example, at its most southerly site in England (Ingleborough), it is confined to a single precipitous rock ledge that can only safely be approached using ropes.

Biogeography Eurasian Arctic-montane element.

Native	GB	IR
2000–19	173	12
1987–99	164	10
1970–86	116	8
pre-1970	177	20

Key refs Godwin (1975), Porter & Halliday (2014).

P.A. STROH & F.H. PERRING

N *Carduus tenuiflorus* Slender Thistle
Curtis

An annual or biennial herb of dry, coastal grasslands, seabird colonies, sea-walls, the upper edges of beaches, sandy waste ground and roadsides. Inland, it occurs on well-drained soils, often, but not always, as an alien. Lowland.

Trends The coastal distribution of *C. tenuiflorus* is similar to that of the 1960s but in England it has spread inland over recent decades, especially in eastern counties such as Cambridgeshire (Leslie, 2019). In the past it was mainly recorded as a wool alien inland but most recent records are from salt-treated roadsides, cultivated fields and railway sidings. Some of these probably result from natural spread but given the difficulties in establishing their origin most have been mapped as alien. It is at its northern limit in East Sutherland and Caithness, but in continental Europe it reaches only the southern tip of the Netherlands.

Biogeography Suboceanic Southern-temperate element.

Native		GB	IR
2000–19	●	314	69
1987–99	●	328	68
1970–86	●	196	15
pre-1970	○	360	92

Alien		GB	IR
2000–19	●	119	0
1987–99	●	57	0
1970–86	●	38	0
pre-1970	○	88	0

Key refs Leslie (2019).

F.H. Perring & K.J. Walker

N *Carduus crispus* Welted Thistle
L.

A biennial, winter-green herb of the margins and rides of woods, banks and the verges of tracks and roads, ditch-banks, damp hedge bottoms, streamsides, pastures and meadows, railway banks, old pits, arable margins and waste places, especially on chalk and clay soils with a high nutrient status. In Ireland, it is confined as a native to dry banks and waste places. Populations expand considerably following disturbance or scrub clearance. Generally lowland, but reaching 365 m above Castleton (Derbyshire).

Trends The core distribution of *C. crispus* is stable. It was formerly considered to be a casual on the periphery of its range in Scotland but its habitats and persistence there suggests that it is more likely to to be a natural colonist, and so all records are mapped as native.

Biogeography Eurosiberian Temperate element, but widely naturalized so that distribution is now Circumpolar Temperate.

Native		GB	IR
2000–19	●	1250	26
1987–99	●	1255	28
1970–86	●	846	3
pre-1970	○	1209	41

Alien		GB	IR
2000–19	●	2	0
1987–99	●	2	0
1970–86	●	1	0
pre-1970	○	1	1

Key refs Bain *et al.* (1988).

F.H. Perring & K.J. Walker

Hy *Carduus crispus × nutans = C. ×stangii*

H.Buek ex Nyman

This hybrid is often found where the parents grow close to one another, in a range of grassland types (including calcareous grassland), disused chalk- and sand-pits, roadside verges, tracksides, cultivated land and waste ground. Most records are of single plants or small numbers in mixed populations of the parents, but rarely there are records of the hybrid in the presence of only one parent, as in Aberystwyth (Cardiganshire), where it grew with *C. nutans* (Chater, 2010b). Lowland.

A spontaneous hybrid (native × native).

Trends Trends in distribution are difficult to discern due to the general inconsistencies associated with recording hybrids. It is probably under-recorded.

Biogeography Widespread in Europe.

	GB	IR
2000–19	62	0
1987–99	27	0
1970–86	21	0
pre-1970	54	0

	GB	IR
Long term	No trend	No trend
Short term	No trend	No trend

Key refs Chater (2010b), Stace *et al.* (2015).

C.A. STACE, C.D. PRESTON & D.A. PEARMAN

Ne *Carduus acanthoides* Broad-winged Thistle

L.

An annual to biennial herb, a casual of rough ground and waste places, possibly originating as a contaminant from imported grain and birdseed mixtures. Lowland.

Trends The origin, distribution, abundance and persistence of *C. acanthoides* is unclear due to taxonomic and nomenclatural confusion with *C. crispus*. The earliest record so far traced is from 1895 (Reigate, Surrey), but the map should be treated as provisional as the majority of records mapped are not backed by herbarium specimens.

Biogeography Europe (rare in the west) and south-west Asia.

Alien	GB	IR
2000–19	13	0
1987–99	5	0
1970–86	4	0
pre-1970	0	0

	GB	IR
Long term	No trend	No trend
Short term	No trend	No trend

D.A. PEARMAN & K.J. WALKER

N ***Carduus nutans*** Musk Thistle

L.

A biennial, or sometimes perennial, herb, typically found on chalk, limestone or lime-enriched soils, but also occurring on sandy or shingly ground. It is found in rough, often overgrazed or recently established pastures, on roadsides and in disturbed places. Generally lowland, but reaching *c.* 530 m at High Cup Nick (Westmorland).

Native in Britain and the Channel Islands and a neophyte in Ireland.

Trends The overall distribution of *C. nutans* has not changed markedly since the 1960s, but it is now better recorded in many areas. It has always been rare in Ireland, where it is generally considered to have been introduced as a seed contaminant.

Biogeography Eurosiberian Temperate element; widely naturalized outside its native range.

Native		GB	IR
2000–19	●	1034	0
1987–99	●	1081	0
1970–86	●	733	0
pre-1970	○	1032	0

Alien		GB	IR
2000–19	●	31	10
1987–99	●	23	17
1970–86	●	21	10
pre-1970	○	34	23

Key refs Bain *et al.* (1988).

F.H. PERRING

N ***Cirsium eriophorum*** Woolly Thistle

(L.) Scop.

A robust monocarpic perennial herb occurring in dry, often ungrazed grasslands, open scrub and woods on limestone, chalk and lime-rich clay. It also grows in disturbed habitats created by quarrying. 0–310 m (Hassop Mines, Derbyshire).

Trends Although the overall distribution of *C. eriophorum* has not changed markedly since the 1960s, it has declined along its eastern, northern and western margins for reasons that are not clear. Today, it is a very uncommon plant away from its strongholds on the chalk and limestone.

Biogeography European Temperate element.

Native		GB	IR
2000–19	●	317	0
1987–99	●	318	0
1970–86	●	243	0
pre-1970	○	362	0

Alien		GB	IR
2000–19	●	3	0
1987–99	●	2	0
1970–86	●	1	0
pre-1970	○	9	0

Key refs Braithwaite *et al.* (2006), Tofts (1999).

F.H. PERRING & S.M. SMART

N *Cirsium vulgare* Spear Thistle
(Savi) Ten.

A monocarpic perennial occurring in a wide array of habitats, including overgrazed pastures and rough grassland, sea-cliffs, dunes, drift lines and well-drained, fertile, disturbed habitats including arable fields, spoil heaps, waste ground and burnt areas in woodland. 0–685 (Breadalbanes, Mid Perthshire), and exceptionally at 845 m on Great Dun Fell (Westmorland).

Trends *C. vulgare* is a near-ubiquitous weed at the 10 km scale throughout our area. It was listed as an 'injurious weed' in the UK in 1959 under the Weeds Act, but despite signficant attempts by land managers to control it on agricultural land since then, using both chemical and biological controls, its distribution has remained unchanged at the 10 km square level and it remains a very common and persistent species within human-modified landscapes.

Recent evidence suggests it may have increased in frequency and become more abundant in arable land and upland grassland, but declined in linear features such as roadsides and hedges (Maskell *et al.*, 2020).

Biogeography Eurosiberian Temperate element; widely naturalized outside its native range.

Native	GB	IR
2000–19	2771	974
1987–99	2757	946
1970–86	1865	156
pre-1970	2650	891

Key refs Grime *et al.* (2007), Klinkhamer & de Jong (1993), Maskell *et al.* (2020).

F.H. Perring & S.M. Smart

N *Cirsium dissectum* Meadow Thistle
(L.) Hill

A shortly stoloniferous perennial herb of fens, fen-meadows, flood-pastures, bog margins and poorly drained meadows on acid to neutral, usually peaty, soils. It often grows in sites subject to marked vertical or lateral movement of base-rich water. 0–595 m (Annacouna in the Ben Bulbin range, County Sligo).

Trends *C. dissectum* underwent a dramatic decline in lowland Britain in the 19th and 20th centuries due to the drainage of wetlands and habitat degradation caused by agricultural improvement. These losses have continued to the present day and it is now a very uncommon plant in much of southern, central and eastern Britain. The species is now better recorded in Ireland where it remains locally common. In Scotland it is restricted to Islay, Jura, the adjacent mainland and Colonsay (South Ebudes), where

it was discovered at its most northerly global location in 2018. The contrast between the distribution of *C. dissectum* and *C. heterophyllum* remains one of the unresolved biogeographical problems in the British and Irish flora.

Biogeography Oceanic Temperate element.

Native	GB	IR
2000–19	290	515
1987–99	372	422
1970–86	293	82
pre-1970	433	407

Alien	GB	IR
2000–19	1	0
1987–99	3	0
1970–86	0	0
pre-1970	0	0

Key refs de Vere (2007), Kay & John (1994), Stroh *et al.* (2019).

F.H. Perring & S.M. Smart

Hy *Cirsium dissectum × palustre = C. ×forsteri*
(Sm.) Loudon

	GB	IR
Long term	No trend	No trend
Short term	No trend	No trend

This hybrid usually occurs with both parents, sometimes abundantly, on peaty soil on the margins of bogs, and in dune-slacks, swamps, wet meadows and calcareous fens. Generally lowland, but reaching over 300 m at Kings Nympton (North Devon).

A spontaneous hybrid (native × native).

Trends *C. ×forsteri* was first found in a wood near Frant (East Sussex) by T.F. Forster in 1817 (Forster & Forster, 1842), and was first mapped in the 2002 *Atlas*. In southern England it is likely to have suffered the same fate as many populations of *C. dissectum*, succumbing to drainage and habitat destruction. Though the hybrid has been found at many new sites in south-western England this century, it probably remains under-recorded in our area. Chater (2010b) reported that

isozyme analysis of leaf samples taken from a population in Cardiganshire which, on morphological grounds, appeared to be pure *C. dissectum*, contained multiple examples of the hybrid, suggesting that the genetic composition of our *C. dissectum* populations requires further study.

Biogeography *C. ×forsteri* is recorded from the mainland of western Europe (France and the Netherlands).

	GB	IR
2000–19	36	5
1987–99	23	6
1970–86	10	5
pre-1970	31	19

Altitude (m)

- <1%
- 1–10%
- 11–30%
- 31–40%
- 41–50%
- 51–100%

Distance north (km)

J F M A M J J A S O N D

☐ Apparency ☐ In flower ☐ In leaf

Key refs Chater (2010b), Forster & Forster (1842), Stace *et al.* (2015).

F.H. PERRING & K.J. WALKER

N *Cirsium tuberosum* Tuberous Thistle
(L.) All.

	GB	IR
Long term		No trend
Short term		No trend

A perennial herb of old chalk and limestone grassland and maritime cliff top vegetation, often on slopes with a northerly or north-westerly aspect, and usually occurring in tall vegetation that is not or only lightly grazed. It spreads by producing axillary basal rosettes to form clonal patches, and also reproduces by seed. Where heavy grazing reduces swards heights to less than 15 cm tall, it frequently hybridizes with *C. acaule*. Many of these populations contain puzzling intermediates which may represent a complex history of introgression between the hybrids and parents. Lowland.

Trends The overall 10 km square distribution of *C. tuberosum* has not changed appreciably since the 1960s, although locally there have been losses due to habitat destruction, overgrazing, coastal erosion and hybridization with *C. acaule*. It became extinct at its sole Cambridgeshire locality when the site

was ploughed in 1973, but has recently been reintroduced to a site nearby (Wimpole Hall) using plants retained in cultivation at Cambridge University Botanic Garden, following an earlier failed attempt in 1987 (Pigott, 1988). It has not been seen at its sole Dorset site for many years and many populations in North Wiltshire have declined in numbers due to overgrazing and introgression with *C. acaule*. Its stronghold is Salisbury Plain in Wiltshire, where many populations have been protected from overgrazing and agriculture due to military occupancy, although forestry planting and tank manoeuvres continue to cause localized declines. The Glamorganshire populations are largely free from hybridization and introgression with *C. acaule*, though some are threatened from agricultural improvement and coastal erosion.

Biogeography Suboceanic Southern-temperate element.

Native	GB	IR
2000–19	17	0
1987–99	18	0
1970–86	14	0
pre-1970	11	0

Alien	GB	IR
2000–19	2	0
1987–99	1	0
1970–86	1	0
pre-1970	2	0

Altitude (m)

- <1%
- 1–10%
- 11–30%
- 31–40%
- 41–50%
- 51–100%

Distance north (km)

J F M A M J J A S O N D

☐ Apparency ☐ In flower ☐ In leaf

Key refs Kay & John (1994), Pigott (1988), Stroh *et al.* (2019), Wigginton (1999).

F.H. PERRING, S.M. SMART & K.J. WALKER

N *Cirsium heterophyllum* Melancholy Thistle
(L.) Hill

A tall perennial herb of upland hay meadows, damp roadside verges and streamsides, the grykes of limestone pavement, montane ledges and steep banksides, and moist woodland margins, usually on base-rich soils. Mostly upland, reaching 760 m in the Breadalbanes (Mid Perthshire) and possibly to 975 m elsewhere in Scotland.

Trends *C. heterophyllum* has retracted from the lowland margins of its range since the 1960s, where it was always likely to have been rare, and therefore more vulnerable to land use change. Here, as elsewhere, it has declined due to a shift from low intensity (traditional) hay meadow management to intensive silage making, and changes to the management of road verges that provided a refuge for this species in many areas (Bradshaw, 2009). These losses have been partially offset by a

number of new records throughout its British range since 2000 due to more systematic recording. In Ireland it is now confined to a single locality (as a native) in County Fermanagh where two groups of 16 individuals were recorded in 2005 (Forbes & Northridge, 2012).

Biogeography Eurosiberian Boreal-montane element.

Native	GB	IR
2000–19	577	1
1987–99	536	1
1970–86	396	1
pre-1970	618	1

Alien	GB	IR
2000–19	14	0
1987–99	16	2
1970–86	5	0
pre-1970	15	0

	GB	IR
Long term		No trend
Short term		No trend

Key refs Bradshaw (2009), Forbes & Northridge (2012), Stroh *et al.* (2019).

F.H. Perring, S.M. Smart & K.J. Walker

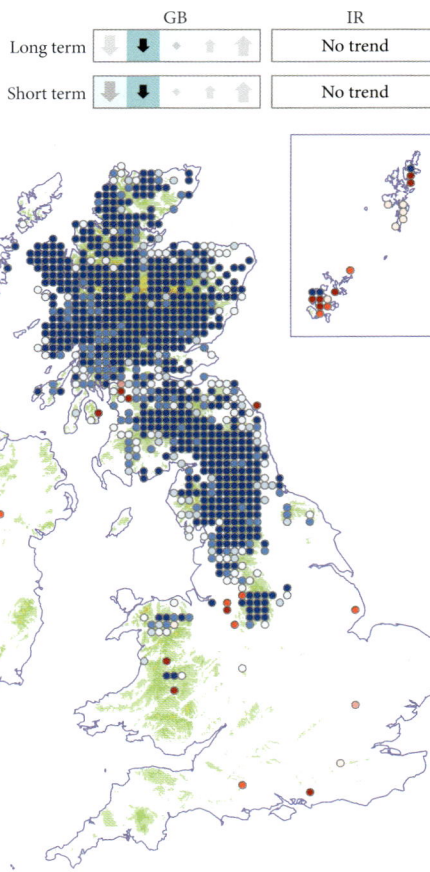

N *Cirsium acaule* Dwarf Thistle
(L.) Scop.

A rosette-forming perennial herb of short, heavily grazed chalk or limestone grassland and more rarely in mesotrophic grasslands on deeper soils. Its northerly and westerly British limits are determined by summer warmth, and towards the margins of its range (*e.g.* Yorkshire Wolds, Derbyshire, Flintshire) it is almost wholly confined to south-west-facing slopes. It benefits from grazing reducing sward heights to less than 10–15 cm, or frequent mowing, but is destroyed by heavy trampling. Long-stemmed forms occur in ranker grasslands (*C. acaule* var. *caulescens*) allowing it to persist under little or no grazing. Generally lowland, but reaching 460 m at Blaen Onneu (Breconshire).

Trends The distribution of this species has declined since the 1960s due to the ploughing-up or improvement of calcareous grassland, and more recently

the relaxation of grazing on many sites and spread of tall grasses and scrub. Despite new records in Carmarthenshire and Glamorganshire, the map indicates a contraction in its distribution, a pattern consistent with change in tetrad frequency (Braithwaite *et al.*, 2006).

Biogeography European Temperate element.

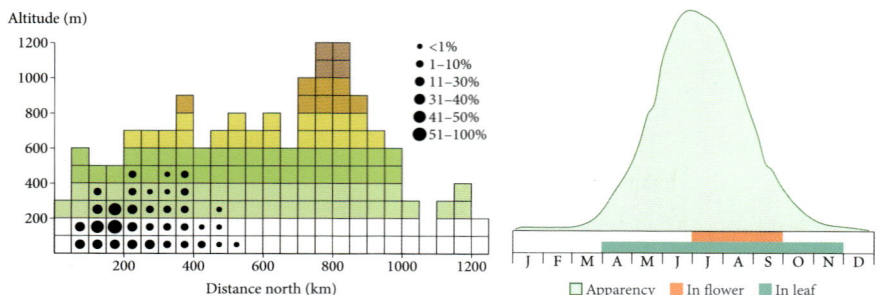

Native	GB	IR
2000–19	546	0
1987–99	591	0
1970–86	431	0
pre-1970	644	0

Alien	GB	IR
2000–19	1	0
1987–99	2	0
1970–86	1	0
pre-1970	2	0

	GB	IR
Long term		No trend
Short term		No trend

Key refs Braithwaite *et al.* (2006), Pigott (1968).

F.H. Perring & S.M. Smart

(N) *Cirsium palustre* Marsh Thistle
(L.) Scop.

A monocarpic perennial herb of mires, fens, marshes, damp grassland, rush-pastures, wet woodland, montane springs and flushes, and tall-herb vegetation on mountain ledges. It reproduces by seed, which may persist for many years, as, for example, during the dark phase of a coppice cycle. 0–845 m (Great Dun Fell, Westmorland), and 910 m on An Stuc (Mid Perthshire).

Trends *C. palustre* is a near-ubiquitous species at the 10 km square resolution and there has been no overall change in its distribution since the 1960s, though its local distribution is now much better known.

Biogeography Eurosiberian Boreo-temperate element; widely naturalized outside its native range.

Native	GB	IR
2000–19	2706	974
1987–99	2635	929
1970–86	1841	167
pre-1970	2555	838

Key refs Baude *et al.* (2016), Grime *et al.* (2007).

F.H. Perring & S.M. Smart

(Hy) *Cirsium arvense* × *palustre* = *C.* ×*celakovskianum*
Knaf

A tall, rhizomatous hybrid that usually grows with both parents in woods, fens, riverside meadows and a wide variety of damp, disturbed habitats including roadside verges, track edges, gravel-pits, quarries, cornfields and waste ground. Lowland.

A spontaneous hybrid (native × native).

Trends *C.* ×*celakovskianum* is the most frequently encountered thistle hybrid in Britain and Ireland. The first confirmed record was from a wood near Holme Lacy (Herefordshire) in 1888; earlier records lack supporting specimens and may be errors. Despite many recent records it is almost certainly under-recorded, especially in Ireland, and it should be searched for wherever the two parents flower together in damp, disturbed habitats.

Biogeography Also recorded in central Europe.

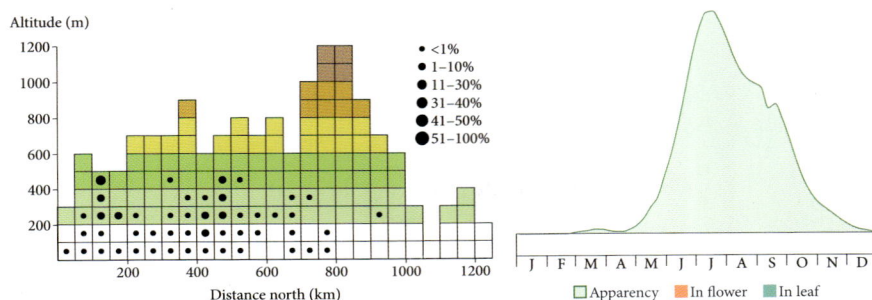

		GB	IR
2000–19	●	96	15
1987–99	●	15	0
1970–86	●	11	1
pre-1970	○	20	0

	GB	IR
Long term	No trend	No trend
Short term	No trend	No trend

Key refs Stace *et al.* (2015).

K.J. Walker

N *Cirsium arvense* Creeping Thistle
(L.) Scop.

A perennial herb of heavily grazed and fertilized pastures, nutrient-rich grasslands, roadsides, arable fields and other cultivated land, waste ground and in disturbed upland habitats. Plants regenerate freely from rhizome fragments which are broken up by ploughing or other disturbance and are probably widely dispersed in top-soil. It is also reproduces prolifically by seed. 0–700 m (Breadalbanes, Mid Perthshire), and at 845 m on Great Dun Fell (Westmorland).

Trends *C. arvense* is a near-ubiquitous weed of human-modified habitats at the 10 km and even 2 km and 1 km square scales throughout Britain and Ireland. It was listed as an 'injurious weed' in the UK in 1959 under the Weeds Act, but despite significant attempts by land managers to control it on agricultural land since then, using both chemical and biological controls, its distribution has remained unchanged at the 10 km square level and it remains one of the most successful and persistent plant species within human-modified landscapes.

Biogeography Eurasian Temperate element, but naturalized in North America so distribution is now Circumpolar Temperate.

Native	GB	IR
2000–19	2755	996
1987–99	2698	938
1970–86	1855	174
pre-1970	2581	883

Key refs Grime *et al.* (2007), Kay (1985), Maskell *et al.* (2020), Moore (1975), Tiley (2010).

F.H. PERRING & S.M. SMART

Ar *Onopordum acanthium* Cotton Thistle
L.

A winter-green biennial herb, often found on the margins of fields, on the verges of tracks and roads, on refuse tips and in other waste places. It is frequently associated with market gardens and farm buildings, and perhaps dispersed to new sites with manure or contaminated straw. 0–330 m (near Alston, Cumberland).

An archaeophyte in Britain and the Channel Islands and a neophyte in Ireland.

Trends There is archaeological evidence for the presence of *O. acanthium* in Britain from the Iron Age onwards. Tall plants appear to be of garden origin and are usually casual. Smaller plants that form persistent populations on arable edges and adjacent roadsides in Breckland may represent a native variant (Leslie, 2019). It has increased in frequency since the 1960s, possibly as an escape from gardens where it is frequently grown for ornament.

Biogeography As an archaeophyte, *O. acanthium* has a Eurosiberian Temperate distribution; it is widely naturalized outside this range.

Alien	GB	IR
2000–19	624	1
1987–99	533	2
1970–86	337	0
pre-1970	487	4

Key refs Leslie (2019).

F.H. PERRING & K.J. WALKER

Ne *Cynara cardunculus* Globe Artichoke

L.

A large perennial herb which is sometimes present as long-established populations in rough and waste ground. It arises as a garden escape or relic of cultivation. Lowland.

Trends *C. cardunculus* was in cultivation in Britain by 1530, and is very widely grown as a vegetable and for ornament. It was recorded from the wild in 1904 (Slateford and Leith, Midlothian). There are two varieties grown here, the edible Globe Artichoke (var. *scolymus*) and the Cardoon (var. *cardunculus*), a magnificent stately giant reaching two metres or more in height. The early records given above are of the former variety, but the identity of the variety is not known for the vast majority of recent records, nor why there has been such a large increase, although it is possible that records of sown vegetables within allotments have made a contribution.

Biogeography Native of the western Mediterranean region, but also an invasive weed in Mediterranean climates around the world.

Alien	GB	IR
2000–19	94	7
1987–99	23	0
1970–86	10	0
pre-1970	8	0

	GB	IR
Long term	No trend	No trend
Short term		

Key refs Vaughan & Geissler (2009).

D.A. PEARMAN & T.D. DINES

Ar *Silybum marianum* Milk Thistle

(L.) Gaertn.

An annual or winter-green biennial herb, grown in gardens for its impressive rosettes, found in rough pasture, on grassy banks of roads and tracks, in hedgerows, on waste ground, on refuse tips and dumped soil, along active and disused railway lines and on arable field margins. It is locally well-established and persistent, especially in coastal habitats in southern England, but is also a widespread casual, mainly from bird seed. Lowland.

Trends *S. marianum* occurs as an introduction with birdseed, grass-seed and oil-seed, and as a garden escape. Its overall distribution appears to be stable; the high turnover of records shown on the map simply reflects the casual nature of many records, with large losses having been compensated by more recent gains.

Biogeography Native of the Mediterranean region; naturalized or casual throughout much of Europe and in North America and Australia.

Alien	GB	IR
2000–19	376	9
1987–99	252	14
1970–86	195	15
pre-1970	398	52

	GB	IR
Long term		
Short term		

Key refs Doogue, D.; Nash, D.; Parnell, J.; Reynolds, S.; Wyse Jakson, P (1998).

F.H. PERRING & K.J. WALKER

N *Serratula tinctoria* Saw-wort
L.

A clump-forming perennial herb of calcareous and acid grassland, damp meadows, fen-meadows, wet heaths and heathy mires, open scrub and woodland, rocky lake shores and maritime cliff-tops; occasionally also found on roadside verges, railway banks and in gravel-pits. It is found on soils with a pH range of 4·8–7·5. British populations may comprise two distinct ecotypes with widely differing habitat requirements (Jefferson & Walker, 2017). 0–560 m (Fur Tor, Dartmoor, South Devon), and reportedly up to 630 m on Snowdon (Caernarvonshire).

Trends *S. tinctoria* has been declining in Britain since the 1900s, especially in eastern, central and northern England, due to drainage, the improvement of pastures and the loss of grasslands in woods and on wood-margins. It is now a very localized species, even in its core areas in south-west England, and almost exclusively confined to ancient, undisturbed habitats. As a consequence, it has been categorized as an axiophyte in 16 of the 18 counties (89%) in which it occurs (out of 24 counties with axiophyte lists). It was first recorded in Ireland as a casual in 1893 and has not been recorded there since 1950.

Biogeography European Temperate element.

Native		GB	IR
2000–19	●	601	0
1987–99	●	679	0
1970–86	●	516	0
pre-1970	○	755	0

Alien		GB	IR
2000–19	●	2	0
1987–99	●	1	0
1970–86	●	0	0
pre-1970	○	5	2

Key refs Jefferson & Walker (2017), Rackham (1980).

F.H. PERRING & K.J. WALKER

N *Centaurea scabiosa* Greater Knapweed
L.

A tufted, winter-green, perennial herb of dry, usually calcareous soils, and found in chalk and limestone grassland, scrub, woodland margins, and on cliffs, roadsides, railway banks, arable field margins, and waste ground. It is also widely introduced in wild-flower seed mixtures. 0–320 m (Matlock, Derbyshire).

Trends The distribution of *C. scabiosa* declined during the 20th century due to the ploughing-up or improvement of infertile, species-rich grasslands. This downward trend appears to have continued, with abandonment, the relaxation of grazing and the unsympathetic management of roadsides and other grasslands now greater threats than outright habitat destruction. However, local increases are occurring due to the colonization of disturbed habitats, such as quarries and railway sidings, as well as widespread sowing in seed mixtures. Coastal plants with entire or subentire basal leaves and capitula with long peduncles have been named var. *succisifolia* (Sell & Murrell, 2006), though their taxonomic status has been questioned in the past (*e.g.* Valentine, 1980); var. *scabiosa* is uncontroversially the common plant found in our area.

Biogeography Eurosiberian Temperate element; widely naturalized outside its native range.

Native		GB	IR
2000–19	●	975	72
1987–99	●	1004	73
1970–86	●	774	10
pre-1970	○	1047	90

Alien		GB	IR
2000–19	●	58	1
1987–99	●	26	2
1970–86	●	11	0
pre-1970	○	35	3

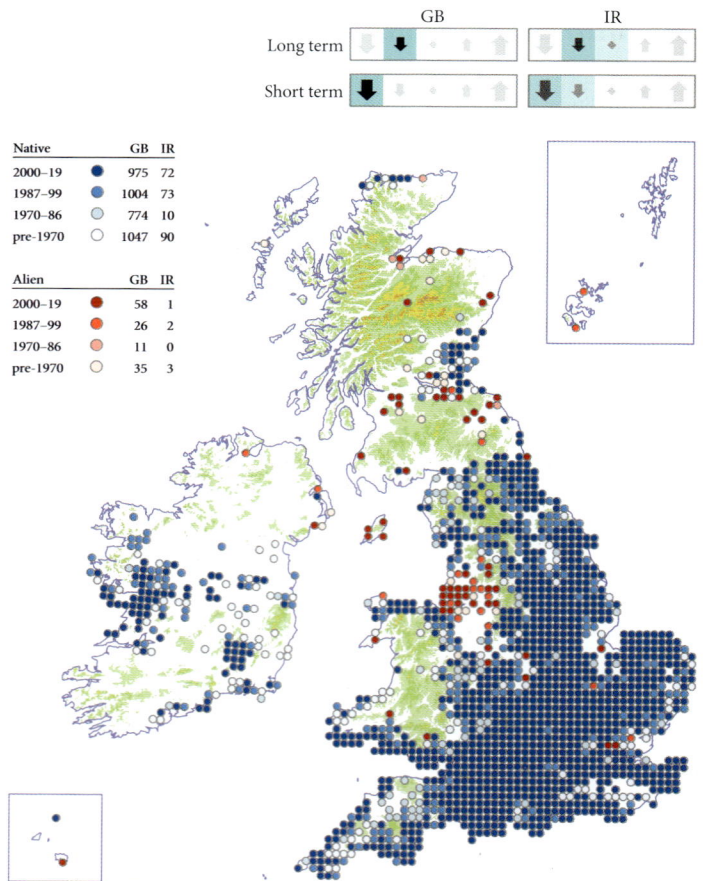

Key refs Grime *et al.* (2007), Grose (1957), Sell & Murrell (2006), Valentine (1980).

P.A. STROH & F.H. PERRING

Ne *Centaurea montana* Perennial Cornflower

L.

A vigorous perennial herb, spreading by rhizomes and increasingly naturalized on road verges, waste ground, railway banksides, grass verges and churchyards, and in a range of other urban habitats. Mainly lowland, reaching 465 m at Flash (Staffordshire).

Trends *C. montana* was introduced to cultivation in Britain by 1596; it is widely grown in gardens and was known from the wild by 1844 (Gradbitch, Warwickshire). It was not included in the 1962 *Atlas*, but its spread was clearly evident in the 2002 *Atlas*. Its range has continued to expand this century and it is now commonly encountered on roadsides in towns and villages throughout Britain, although it is still curiously uncommon in much of Ireland. It is very persistent, and many populations are very long-established.

Biogeography Native of the mountains of central and southern Europe.

Long term	GB	IR
	No trend	No trend

Short term

Alien	GB	IR
2000–19	1197	16
1987–99	747	5
1970–86	265	0
pre-1970	94	0

Altitude (m)

- <1%
- 1–10%
- 11–30%
- 31–40%
- 41–50%
- 51–100%

Distance north (km)

☐ Apparency ☐ In flower ☐ In leaf

P.A. Stroh & F.H. Perring

Ar *Centaurea cyanus* Cornflower

L.

An annual herb, formerly a 'pestilential weed' of cereal crops, now almost exclusively found as a casual of pavements, allotments, waste places, roadsides and refuse tips arising from gardens and, most especially in recent decades, in areas sown with wild-flower seed mixtures. Such populations are usually casual, although plants may appear in subsequent years from a disturbed seed bank. 0–350 m (Blackwell, Derbyshire).

Trends *C. cyanus* is known to have been present in Britain from the Iron Age onwards. It was a serious weed of cereal crops until seed cleaning caused a rapid decline, which was accelerated by the large-scale use of inorganic herbicides from the 1950s onwards. Its distribution began to recover in the 1980s as a result of its inclusion in wild-flower seed mixtures, and it is now an almost ubiquitous component in readily available seed packets, leading to a substantial increase this century. Godwin (1975) believed that its natural habitat in our area was on scree slopes and alluvial deposits in late glacial tundra.

Biogeography As an archaeophyte, *C. cyanus* has a distribution centred on the European Temperate region; it has been widely naturalized outside this range.

	GB	IR
Long term		
Short term		

Alien	GB	IR
2000–19	869	65
1987–99	472	18
1970–86	289	1
pre-1970	683	46

Altitude (m)

- <1%
- 1–10%
- 11–30%
- 31–40%
- 41–50%
- 51–100%

Distance north (km)

☐ Apparency ☐ In flower ☐ In leaf

Key refs Godwin (1975), Stewart *et al.* (1994), Wigginton (1999).

F.H. Perring & P.A. Stroh

Ar ## *Centaurea calcitrapa* Red Star-thistle
L.

A biennial herb of waste ground, field edges, horse paddocks, refuse tips, gravel-pits and tracksides in dry grassland, and on banks on well-drained sandy, gravelly or light chalky soils. In Sussex it can be locally abundant, forming extensive dense patches (Sussex Botanical Recording Society, 2018). Lowland.

Trends There is a single archaeological record of this species from a Roman site, and it was recorded in the historic period by 1597. It is sometimes regarded as native in Sussex on dry chalky banks, where it grows in habitats similar to those near the Somme Estuary in northern France (Wigginton, 1999). It is also established in East Kent, where it has been known since 1839 at Chatham. Elsewhere it is a declining casual from wool, birdseed, lucerne and esparto.

Biogeography Native of the Mediterranean region; widespread as an introduction farther north but now declining outside its native range.

Alien	GB	IR
2000–19	13	0
1987–99	11	0
1970–86	21	0
pre-1970	157	1

	GB	IR
Long term		No trend
Short term		No trend

Key refs Sussex Botanical Recording Society (2018), Wigginton (1999).

F.H. PERRING & P.A. STROH

Ne ## *Centaurea solstitialis* Yellow Star-thistle
L.

An annual or, rarely, biennial herb introduced with grain, birdseed, lucerne or sainfoin seed, and found most frequently in cornfields and on waste ground. Lowland.

Trends *C. solstitialis* was known from the wild by at least 1617, and formerly persisted in lucerne and sainfoin fields. Dunn (1905) described it as "of frequent occurrence in Southern England", but it is much less common than it was before 1930, and now known only as a rare casual.

Biogeography Native of southern Europe and south-western Asia; widely naturalized elsewhere.

Alien	GB	IR
2000–19	7	0
1987–99	7	0
1970–86	32	0
pre-1970	257	1

	GB	IR
Long term	No trend	No trend
Short term	No trend	No trend

Key refs Dunn (1905).

F.H. PERRING & P.A. STROH

Ne *Centaurea diluta* Lesser Star-thistle
Aiton

A perennial herb, often behaving as an annual in our area, found as a casual of waste places and refuse tips, mainly from birdseed but also from wool and grain and is now possibly derived from sown in wild-flower seed mixtures. Lowland.

Trends *C. diluta* was introduced into cultivation in 1781. It was first recorded in the wild in 1904, and the species is now a very rare casual, with only two records in our area this century, both in areas that had been sown with wild-flower seed.

Biogeography A native of south-western Spain, north-western Africa and the Atlantic Islands.

Alien	GB	IR
2000–19	2	0
1987–99	13	0
1970–86	48	0
pre-1970	73	0

	GB	IR
Long term	No trend	No trend
Short term	No trend	No trend

F.H. PERRING & P.A. STROH

Ne *Centaurea jacea* Brown Knapweed
L.

An erect perennial herb with light-brown involucral scales, found in grassland sown with wild-flower seed mixtures, but possibly also as a natural colonist in Essex (Adams, 2020). Lowland.

Trends *C. jacea* was first recorded from the wild in 1775 from Hardwick, West Suffolk. It appears to have been formerly more common in south-eastern England, though it may be overlooked in some areas, and some records may be in error for the hybrid with *C. debeauxii* (*C. ×moncktonii*).

Biogeography Native in Europe, to western Siberia and the Caucasus.

Alien	GB	IR
2000–19	14	1
1987–99	12	0
1970–86	2	0
pre-1970	43	1

	GB	IR
Long term	No trend	No trend
Short term	No trend	No trend

Key refs Adams (2020).

P.A. STROH

N *Centaurea nigra s.l.* Common Knapweed

A perennial herb of a wide range of grasslands including hay meadows, pastures, chalk and limestone downland, fen-meadows, cliff-top grassland, roadsides, cemeteries, railway banks, scrub, woodland edges, field borders and waste ground. It occurs on a wide variety of soils ranging from mildly acidic to calcareous and from waterlogged to free-draining. It is now a near-universal constituent of wild-flower seed mixtures used for conservation, amenity and landscaping purposes. 0–580 m (Cadair Idris, Merionethshire) and exceptionally at 845 m on Great Dun Fell (Westmorland).

Trends *C. nigra s.l.* includes both *C. nigra s.s.* (*C. nigra* subsp. *nigra*) and *C. debeauxii* which was formerly treated as *C. nigra* subsp. *nemoralis*. These taxa have had a complicated taxonomic history and have been very unevenly recorded by British and Irish botanists, with most recorders not distinguishing between the two. To complicate matters further,

intermediates occur where both species grow together, and also in the absence of *C. debeauxii*. It is, therefore, not possible to map their separate distributions and range with any confidence. *C. nigra s.l.* has a near-ubiquitous distribution which appears to be stable. *C. nigra s.s.* occurs throughout the range of the species whereas *C. debeauxii* appears to be more restricted to light, often calcareous soils in southern Britain (south of a line from Carmarthenshire to North Lincolnshire, but with a scattering of records north to the Scottish lowlands). As noted above, *C. nigra* has been sown in wild-flower seed mixtures throughout the range of the species since the 1980s. Only a small proportion of this seed is likely to be of native provenance with the majority imported from Europe or possibly elsewhere.

Biogeography Suboceanic Temperate element; widely naturalized outside its native range.

Native	GB	IR
2000–19	2642	988
1987–99	2591	949
1970–86	1743	184
pre-1970	2522	900

Alien	GB	IR
2000–19	7	0
1987–99	3	0
1970–86	6	0
pre-1970	6	0

Key refs Adams (2020), Sell & Murrell (2006).

P.A. STROH & K.J. WALKER

Ne *Carthamus tinctorius* Safflower
L.

An annual to biennial herb appearing as a casual on waste ground, refuse tips, where farmyard manure has been dumped, in gardens and on arable land, probably always originating from birdseed. Lowland.

Trends This species has been in cultivation in Britain since at least 1551, when it was grown for the oil extracted from its achenes and the red and saffron dyes from its flowers. It was not formally recorded from the wild, however, until 1899 (Dorset). It appears to be increasing as a birdseed alien.

Biogeography *C. tinctorius* is not known as a wild plant, but it has long been cultivated in southern Europe, south-western and south-central Asia and elsewhere.

Alien	GB	IR
2000–19	61	2
1987–99	46	1
1970–86	46	0
pre-1970	42	1

Key refs De Rougemont (1989), Zohary & Hopf (2000).

F.H. PERRING & K.J. WALKER

Ar *Cichorium intybus* Chicory
L.

A winter-green perennial herb, typically found on the grassy banks and verges of paths, tracks and roads, but also on arable field margins, in rough grassland, on waste ground and riverbanks. Lowland.

Trends Though *C. intybus* was formerly regarded as a native, at least in England and Wales, doubt is now cast on that status in most counties, and it is almost always treated as a relic of cultivation. Historically, it was cultivated for its seed (subsp. *intybus*) and more recently for its roots, which were used to flavour coffee. Today it is widely sown in mixed forage crops and in wild-flower seed mixtures and these introductions have reversed the decline in its distribution identified in the 2002 *Atlas*.

Biogeography As an archaeophyte, *C. intybus* has a Eurosiberian Southern-temperate distribution, but it is widely naturalized so that its distribution is now Circumpolar Southern-temperate.

Alien	GB	IR
2000–19	1102	82
1987–99	742	18
1970–86	509	7
pre-1970	1109	50

F.H. PERRING & K.J. WALKER

Ar *Arnoseris minima* Lamb's Succory
(L.) Schweigg. & Körte

An annual weed of cornfields or fallow ground on the most infertile, acidic, sandy soils. It was particularly associated with soils over Lower Greensand. Lowland.

Trends Although widely scattered in the 18th and 19th centuries, *A. minima* was probably persistent only in eastern and south-eastern England. It declined from the start of the 20th century and by 1953 was limited to about 12 localities. Except for deliberate introductions in the 1980s in East Suffolk and on an experimental arable weed plot in Buckinghamshire, in both cases where it failed to persist, it has not been seen since it was last recorded near to Stokenchurch (Oxfordshire) in 1971. Its decline was due to the increased use of fertilizers and herbicides, and improved seed screening methods.

Biogeography As an archaeophyte, *A. minima* has a European Temperate distribution.

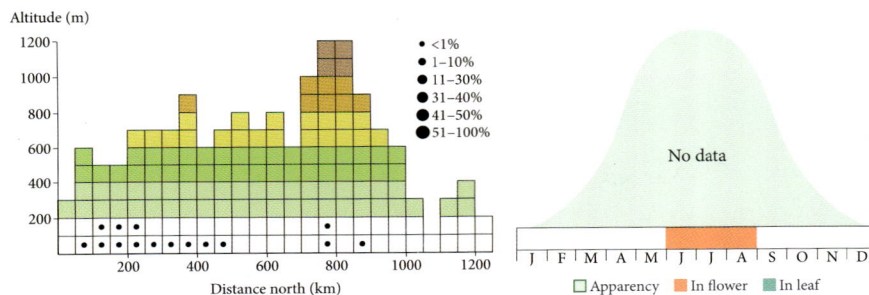

Alien	GB	IR
2000–19	0	0
1987–99	2	0
1970–86	3	0
pre-1970	87	0

Key refs Silverside (1990a).

F.H. PERRING

N? *Lapsana communis* Nipplewort
L.

An annual to perennial herb of disturbed and shaded places, and thriving over a wide range of soil acidity and moisture. Its habitats include open woodland, scrub, hedgerows, waste and cultivated ground, railway banks, roadsides and old walls. 0–481 m (Dolfawr, Shropshire), and reportedly higher in West Perthshire.

Trends There has been no discernible change in the 10 km square range of *L. communis* since the 1960s. Almost all our plants are subsp. *communis*, but the normally perennial subsp. *intermedia*, a well-established introduction, has been recorded from a few sites in lowland England.

Biogeography European Temperate element; also in central Asia and widely naturalized outside its native range.

Native	GB	IR
2000–19	2397	908
1987–99	2326	828
1970–86	1509	111
pre-1970	2259	696

Alien	GB	IR
2000–19	4	0
1987–99	3	0
1970–86	5	0
pre-1970	6	0

Key refs Sell (1981).

F.H. PERRING & K.J. WALKER

N *Hypochaeris radicata* Cat's-ear
L.

A perennial herb of meadows, pastures, lawns, heathlands, cliff-tops, sand dunes, roadsides, railway banks and waste ground, on slightly acidic, usually free-draining soils. It is very tolerant of drought, and is absent from sites subject to prolonged waterlogging. 0–610 m (Macgillycuddy's Reeks, South Kerry), and to 845 m at Great Dun Fell (Cumberland).

Trends There has been no discernible change in the range of *H. radicata* although it has undoubtedly increased at a local scale in recent decades, partly as a result of widespread planting in wild-flower seed mixtures on roadsides, arable margins and in amenity areas.

Biogeography European Southern-temperate element; widely naturalized outside its native range.

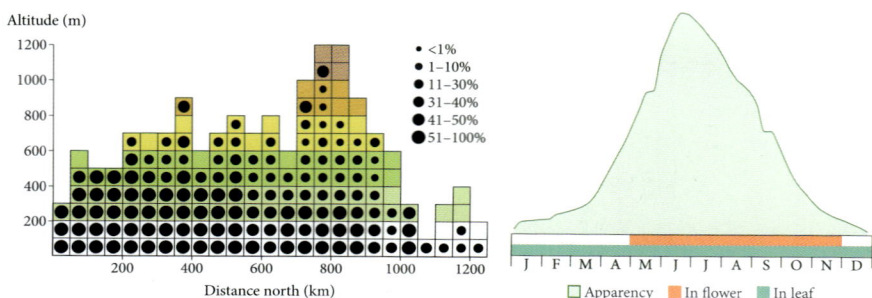

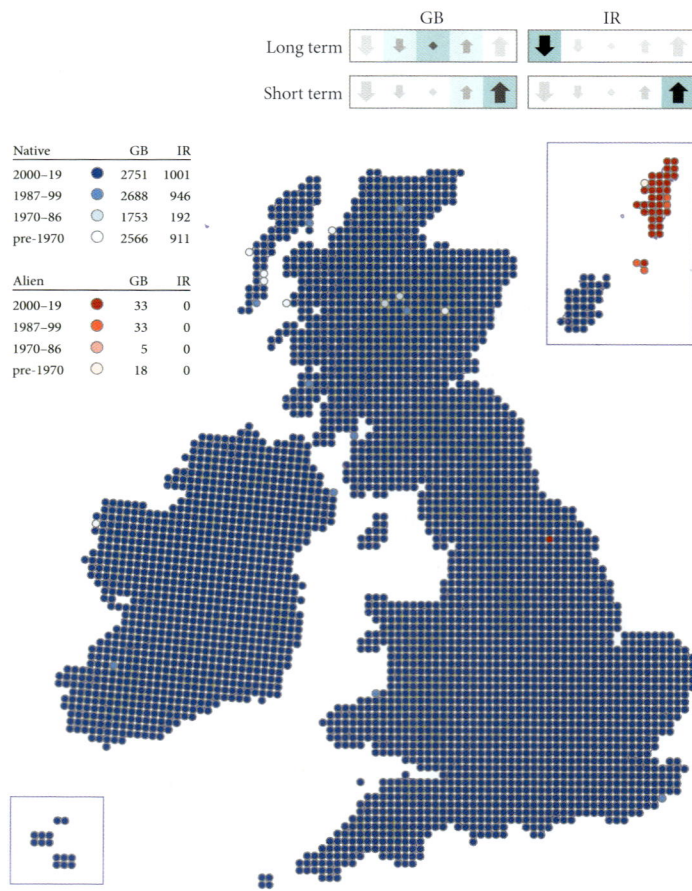

Native	GB	IR
2000–19	2751	1001
1987–99	2688	946
1970–86	1753	192
pre-1970	2566	911

Alien	GB	IR
2000–19	33	0
1987–99	33	0
1970–86	5	0
pre-1970	18	0

Key refs Aarssen (1981), Grime *et al.* (2007), Scott & Palmer (1987), Turkington & Aarssen (1983).

F.H. PERRING & K.J. WALKER

N *Hypochaeris glabra* Smooth Cat's-ear

L.

An annual herb of open summer-parched grasslands, heathy pastures, and arable margins on usually acidic, nutrient-poor, sandy or gravelly soils; also occurring in dune grassland and on sandy shingle. It was formerly widespread as a wool shoddy alien. Lowland.

Trends *H. glabra* declined historically as a result of agricultural improvement and an absence of grazing, but these losses have been compensated to some extent by recent discoveries (*e.g.* in Cambridgeshire) where it appears to be spreading and is possibly benefitting from warmer winters. It can be easily overlooked, particularly as the flowers close in the afternoon.

Biogeography European Southern-temperate element; widely naturalized outside its native range.

Native		GB	IR
2000–19	●	195	2
1987–99	●	137	3
1970–86	○	138	1
pre-1970	○	244	4

Alien		GB	IR
2000–19	●	1	0
1987–99	●	2	0
1970–86	●	3	0
pre-1970	○	8	0

Key refs Fone (1989), Stroh *et al.* (2019).

F.H. PERRING & K.J. WALKER

N *Hypochaeris maculata* Spotted Cat's-ear

L.

A perennial herb of free-draining, usually base-rich substrates, including superficial deposits of sands and gravels (or wind-blown loess soils). It occurs on chalk and limestone downland, on coastal cliffs over limestone and serpentine, and on wind-blown calcareous sand on the north Cornwall coast. In Jersey, it grows on exposed granite cliffs. Some of the few remaining populations are confined to ancient man-made features, such as tumuli and earthworks, that escaped conversion to arable. Lowland.

Trends *H. maculata* is now known from only half the sites it was recorded from in the 19th century. These losses, all inland, have been due to habitat destruction by ploughing, or lack of grazing followed by invasion of coarse grasses and scrub. Of the eight surviving populations only one has more than 1,000 plants (Knocking Hoe, Bedfordshire); two have critically low numbers, with fewer than ten individuals recorded in recent years (Risby, Suffolk; Devil's Dyke, Cambridgeshire).

Biogeography Eurosiberian Temperate element, with a continental distribution in western Europe.

Native		GB	IR
2000–19	●	8	0
1987–99	●	10	0
1970–86	○	9	0
pre-1970	○	19	0

Alien		GB	IR
2000–19	●	0	0
1987–99	●	1	0
1970–86	●	0	0
pre-1970	○	2	0

Key refs Stroh *et al.* (2019), Wells (1976), Wigginton (1999).

F.H. PERRING & K.J. WALKER

(N) *Scorzoneroides autumnalis* Autumn Hawkbit
(L.) Moench

A clump-forming, winter-green perennial herb, found mostly on grassy banks and in meadows, pastures, lawns, cemeteries and churchyards, as well as wet grassland, fen, open scrub, heathland, saltmarsh, fixed dunes and roadsides in the lowlands, and also screes, flushes and lake margins in the uplands. It is a common weed of pavements, arable land and waste ground. 0–1,140 m (Ben Nevis, Westerness).

Trends *S. autumnalis* is a ubiquitous species that appears to tolerate high levels of competition, disturbance and eutrophication. Its overall 10 km square range is stable and it may be increasing locally within anthropogenic habitats. It is very variable, with several ecotypes ranging from tall, hairy plants on montane cliff ledges to small, virtually glabrous plants in saltmarshes.

Biogeography European Boreo-temperate element; widely naturalized outside its native range.

Native	GB	IR
2000–19	2801	970
1987–99	2733	888
1970–86	1708	180
pre-1970	2569	792

Key refs Allen (1957), Grime *et al.* (2007).

F.H. PERRING & K.J. WALKER

(N) *Leontodon hispidus* Rough Hawkbit
L.

A perennial herb of dry, neutral or calcareous soils, occurring in hay meadows, pastures, chalk and limestone downland and other dry grasslands, on roadside verges, railway banks, rock ledges and in quarries. It readily spreads by wind-dispersed seeds into open habitats. 0–575 m (Harwood Dale, North Northumberland) and exceptionally at 845 m on Great Dun Fell (Westmorland).

Trends There has been no discernible change in the 10 km square distribution of *L. hispidus* since the 1960s although it has probably increased locally as an introduction on roadsides where it is frequently sown with wild-flower seed mixtures. It is possibly over-recorded in some areas in error for *L. saxatilis*. Almost all Scottish Highland records have been treated as dubious or as introductions if found in locations where wild-flower seed is likely

to have been sown (*e.g.* roadsides, industrial estates). Almost or wholly glabrous plants occasionally occur and have been named var. *glabratus*.

Biogeography European Temperate element.

Native	GB	IR
2000–19	1617	217
1987–99	1543	194
1970–86	1122	26
pre-1970	1508	157

Alien	GB	IR
2000–19	14	0
1987–99	8	0
1970–86	0	0
pre-1970	5	0

Key refs Grime *et al.* (2007).

F.H. PERRING & K.J. WALKER

Leontodon saxatilis Lesser Hawkbit
Lam.

A winter-green usually perennial herb of heavily grazed calcareous grassland, dry heathland, stony banks, limestone and other basic rock outcrops, fixed sand dunes, tracks, and sand- and gravel-pits. It prefers well-drained, calcareous to mildly acidic soils, but also occurs in periodically wet habitats such as dune-slacks, rutted tracks and pond margins on sandy soils. It is often less common than *L. hispidus*, with which it is frequently confused, and more restricted to shorter, less dense turf on chalk and sands. 0–500 m (Brown Clee Hill, Shropshire).

Trends Although the overall 10 km square distribution of *L. saxatilis* is stable it appears to have declined in northern and western Britain and in Ireland. It is frequently confused with *L. hispidus* and so some of these losses may reflect misidentifications.

However, it seems to replace *L. hispidus* over much of western and northern Scotland where it appears to be native.

Biogeography Suboceanic Southern-temperate element; widely naturalized outside its native range.

Native	GB	IR
2000–19	1386	518
1987–99	1314	485
1970–86	915	71
pre-1970	1139	405

Alien	GB	IR
2000–19	14	0
1987–99	4	0
1970–86	5	0
pre-1970	2	0

F.H. PERRING & K.J. WALKER

Picris hieracioides Hawkweed Oxtongue
L.

A native, winter-green, biennial or perennial herb, mainly of calcareous soils, occurring in the less heavily grazed swards in chalk and limestone grassland, on roadsides and railway banks, and in quarries and lime-pits. It is intolerant of heavy grazing and is a poor competitor in dense vegetation. Lowland.

Native in Britain and the Channel Islands and a neophyte in Ireland.

Trends *P. hieracioides* has shown little change in distribution since the 1960s, although there have been some losses in the northern and eastern parts of its range, presumably due to habitat loss and changes in grassland management. Over much of its range loss has to some extent been compensated by new discoveries, which are likely to represent other subspecies (subsp. *grandiflora*, subsp. *villarsii*), introduced

from elsewhere in Europe, perhaps in wild-flower seed mixtures. However, it has not been possible to differentiate between native and non-native occurrences within its accepted native range due to difficulties in separating the subspecies. It has been introduced to Ireland, where it has spread towards the south and west along railways.

Biogeography Eurasian Temperate element.

Native	GB	IR
2000–19	684	0
1987–99	666	0
1970–86	444	0
pre-1970	687	0

Alien	GB	IR
2000–19	21	22
1987–99	7	12
1970–86	7	2
pre-1970	13	4

F.H. PERRING & K.J. WALKER

Ar *Helminthotheca echioides* Bristly Oxtongue
(L.) Holub

An annual to winter-green biennial herb, most frequently found on recently disturbed banks and verges of paths, tracks and roads as well as open grassland, margins of arable fields, cliffs and scree slopes, riverbanks, sea-walls, gardens and allotments and waste places, especially on lime-rich clay soils. Mainly a lowland plant, but reaching to 370 m in Rassau (Breconshire).

Trends *H. echioides* was mapped with a somewhat patchy distribution in the 1962 *Atlas*, being found mainly south of a line from the Severn to the Humber. Since then it has consolidated within that range and spread northwards and westwards, especially in coastal areas over the last 20 years. The majority of populations in Ireland, north-eastern England and Scotland appear to be only casual.

Biogeography As an archaeophyte, *H. echioides* has a European Southern-temperate distribution; it is widely naturalized outside this range.

Alien	GB	IR
2000–19	1358	84
1987–99	1105	18
1970–86	653	8
pre-1970	859	15

F.H. PERRING & P.A. STROH

N? *Scorzonera humilis* Viper's-grass
L.

A perennial herb of damp, unimproved grasslands and fen-meadows on relatively infertile, neutral or mildly acidic soils. Lowland.

Trends This species was first recorded in Britain in Dorset (Wareham Meadows) in 1914. It is currently known from four locations; two in Dorset, and two in Glamorganshire. It was found new to Guernsey (L'Ancresse Common) in 2016. Wareham Meadows supports much the largest English population, with an estimated 23,000 plants recorded in 2007. In Wales, where the species was first discovered in 1996, several thousand plants occur in five fields at Cefn Cribwr. In Warwickshire, a small population discovered in 1954 had gone by 1967. The native status of this species is sometimes questioned, but as its habitats are similar to those in continental Europe, most authorities accept it as a native in Britain.

Biogeography European Temperate element.

Native	GB	IR
2000–19	4	0
1987–99	3	0
1970–86	1	0
pre-1970	3	0

Alien	GB	IR
2000–19	0	0
1987–99	0	0
1970–86	0	0
pre-1970	1	0

Key refs Stroh *et al.* (2019), Wigginton (1999).

P.A. STROH & F.H. PERRING

Tragopogon pratensis Goat's-beard
L.

(N)

An annual to perennial herb of tall, unmown grassland on banks, verges, hedgerows and field margins, as well as in meadows and pastures, calcareous grassland, old pits, sand dunes, roadsides, railway banks and waste ground. 0–470 m (Flash, Staffordshire).

Trends The 10 km square distribution of *T. pratensis* has changed little since the 1960s, although it is now better recorded in Ireland and Scotland where it may be spreading. It tolerates occasional mowing, but with the decline of traditional hay meadows has become increasingly restricted to more disturbed habitats. The native subsp. *minor* occurs throughout the range of the species, the alien subsp. *pratensis* is mapped separately.

Biogeography Eurosiberian Temperate element; widely naturalized outside its native range.

Native	GB	IR
2000–19	1598	141
1987–99	1564	90
1970–86	992	24
pre-1970	1477	54

Alien	GB	IR
2000–19	44	6
1987–99	38	6
1970–86	29	5
pre-1970	44	5

Key refs Barling (1955), Rich & Jermy (1998).

F.H. PERRING & K.J. WALKER

Tragopogon pratensis subsp. *pratensis*
L.

(Ne)

An annual to perennial herb, found most often in dry grassland, and on roadsides, refuse tips and waste ground. It is usually casual in the north and west of its range. Lowland.

Trends This subspecies was first recorded in Britain in 1836 (Middlesex). It may be slightly over-recorded; only records based on freshly opened flowers are reliable because the characters separating the subspecies become obscure very soon after fertilization (Rich & Jermy, 1998). Its origin is unclear but a frequent association with road verges suggests that it might have been introduced in wild-flower seed mixtures imported from western and central Europe where it is native. It appears to be increasing.

Biogeography Subsp. *pratensis* occurs throughout much of the European range of the species.

	GB	IR
Long term	No trend	No trend
Short term	No trend	No trend

Alien	GB	IR
2000–19	110	1
1987–99	52	0
1970–86	28	3
pre-1970	53	0

Key refs Barling (1955), Rich & Jermy (1998).

F.H. PERRING & K.J. WALKER

Ne *Tragopogon porrifolius* Salsify
L.

	GB	IR
Long term	No trend	No trend
Short term		

A biennial herb, grown as a root vegetable and probably also introduced in wild-flower seed mixtures. It is found most often as an escape from cultivation on the banks and verges of tracks and roads, sea-walls, cliffs, rough grassland, arable land, and waste ground, especially in south-eastern England. It also occurs as a weed of urban flower-beds, gardens and allotments. Many records are either casual or persist only for a few years. Lowland.

Trends This species was first recorded in the wild in Britain in 1596 (Whalley, South Lancashire). Its range has increased dramatically since the 1960s, partly as a result of more systematic recording of aliens but probably also due to increased cultivation and introduction via seed. Most records appear to be of the common cultivated plant (subsp. *porrifolius*) with flowers equalling the involucral bracts.

Biogeography Native of the Mediterranean region; the native range of the cultivated subsp. *porrifolius* is uncertain but it is widely naturalized in temperate Europe.

Alien	GB	IR
2000–19	368	6
1987–99	273	3
1970–86	106	1
pre-1970	221	12

Altitude (m)

• <1%
• 1–10%
• 11–30%
• 31–40%
• 41–50%
• 51–100%

Distance north (km)

☐ Apparency ☐ In flower ☐ In leaf

F.H. Perring & K.J. Walker

N *Sonchus palustris* Marsh Sow-thistle
L.

	GB	IR
Long term		No trend
Short term		No trend

A perennial herb of tall vegetation beside rivers on damp peaty or silty soils rich in nitrogen. It is also moderately tolerant of saline conditions, and can grow near tidal river mouths. Lowland.

Trends Whilst urban developments caused a decline in *S. palustris* in the Thames Valley and in Kent by the end of the 20th century, there is some evidence of recovery in recent years, and also an increase in Broadland and East Suffolk. It became extinct in Cambridgeshire through drainage long before 1930, but has spread from a colony introduced to Woodwalton Fen (Huntingdonshire) and is now scattered through the Middle Level by drains and the River Nene. The Hampshire populations, though first found in 1959, appear to be native. The Yorkshire plants are thought to have been introduced with willows from East Anglia. A small colony in Bedfordshire, found on edge of a shallow ditch by a roadside verge, is of unknown provenance, but has persisted for over 50 years.

Biogeography Eurosiberian Temperate element.

Native	GB	IR
2000–19	28	0
1987–99	26	0
1970–86	21	0
pre-1970	45	0

Alien	GB	IR
2000–19	23	0
1987–99	11	0
1970–86	11	0
pre-1970	7	0

Altitude (m)

• <1%
• 1–10%
• 11–30%
• 31–40%
• 41–50%
• 51–100%

Distance north (km)

☐ Apparency ☐ In flower ☐ In leaf

Key refs Boon & Outen (2011), Stewart *et al.* (1994).

F.H. Perring & J.O. Mountford

N *Sonchus arvensis* Perennial Sow-thistle

L.

A creeping perennial herb of roadside verges, ditches and riverbanks, sea-walls and the upper parts of beaches and saltmarshes, particularly along strand lines; it is also frequent in arable fields, where it can be a troublesome weed, spreading by root fragments, and on waste ground. It prefers disturbed, nutrient-enriched soils and often grows with halophytes on salted inland road verges. 0–490 m (Hartside, Cumberland).

Trends There has been no appreciable change in the overall 10 km square distribution of *S. arvensis* since the 1960s, although it is now better recorded in Ireland and it appears to have increased in our area as a weed of arable crops and also on salted roadside verges inland. A glabrous form, subsp. *uliginosus*, has been recorded throughout Britain, usually from wetter habitats. Its taxonomic status and ecology require further study.

Biogeography Eurosiberian Temperate element, but widely naturalized so that its distribution is now Circumpolar Temperate.

Native	GB	IR
2000–19	2211	772
1987–99	2126	704
1970–86	1353	79
pre-1970	2005	532

Key refs Lemna & Messersmith (1990), Lousley (1968).

F.H. PERRING & K.J. WALKER

N *Sonchus oleraceus* Smooth Sow-thistle

L.

An overwintering annual herb of disturbed or trampled grasslands, coastal cliff-slopes, roadside verges, arable fields, manure heaps, walls, pavement cracks, gardens and waste places. It is intolerant of grazing but is an invasive weed of bare ground. It is more frequent in coastal habitats than *S. asper* but less frequent in the uplands. 0–570 m (Hartside Quarry, Cumberland).

Trends There has been no discernible change in the 10 km square distribution of *S. oleraceus* since the 1960s although it is now better recorded in Scotland and Ireland. It is a highly variable taxon but only two varieties appear to be distinct ecotypes (var. *litoralis*, var. *oleraceus*).

Biogeography European Southern-temperate element, but widely naturalized so that distribution is now Circumpolar Southern-temperate.

Native	GB	IR
2000–19	2360	956
1987–99	2176	857
1970–86	1341	119
pre-1970	2116	710

Alien	GB	IR
2000–19	14	1
1987–99	7	1
1970–86	3	0
pre-1970	9	1

Key refs Grime *et al.* (2007), Hutchinson *et al.* (1984), Lewin (1948).

F.H. PERRING & K.J. WALKER

(N) ***Sonchus asper*** Prickly Sow-thistle

(L.) Hill

An overwintering annual herb of rough grassland, scrub, roadside verges, quarries, rock outcrops, railway lines, arable fields, manure heaps, gardens and waste places. It prefers dry, disturbed, sandy soils and is intolerant of grazing, but can be an invasive weed of bare ground. *S. asper* tolerates rather wetter conditions than *S. oleraceus* and is more frequent in the uplands. Plants that are highly variable in leaf shape, and often approaching *S. oleraceus* in colour and the lack of prickles, can only be separated with certainty by the rugosity of the achenes. 0–628 m (Killhope Cross, County Durham).

Trends The known 10 km square distribution of *S. asper* has increased in our area since the 1960s, and since the start of the 21st century

the species has been better recorded throughout Scotland and Ireland relative to past atlas surveys.

Biogeography European Southern-temperate element, but widely naturalized so that distribution is now Circumpolar Southern-temperate.

Native	GB	IR
2000–19	2681	985
1987–99	2481	917
1970–86	1476	125
pre-1970	2230	802

Alien	GB	IR
2000–19	0	1
1987–99	0	1
1970–86	0	0
pre-1970	0	1

Key refs Grime *et al.* (2007), Hutchinson *et al.* (1984), Lewin (1948).

F.H. Perring & K.J. Walker

(Ar) ***Lactuca serriola*** Prickly Lettuce

L.

An annual or biennial herb of roadsides, field margins, waste ground, gravel-pits and sea-walls, often rapidly colonizing newly turned soil. Also occasionally in semi-natural habitats, such as shingle banks and sand dunes. Lowland.

An archaeophyte in Britain and the Channel Islands and a neophyte in Ireland.

Trends *L. serriola*, first recorded in Britain in 1632, spread rapidly during the 20th century, often as a consequence of road and motorway developments. Since the 1960s, it has continued its advance westwards and northwards, colonizing much of the English Midlands and Lancashire by the 1990s, extending to much of Teesside and Tyneside this century. It was first recorded in Ireland in 1996 and is now widespread in the east. Two forms are

present in our area (f. *integrifolia* and f. *serriola*), of which the first appears much the commonest though seemingly without any ecological distinction.

Biogeography As an archaeophyte, *L. serriola* has a Eurosiberian Southern-temperate distribution; it is widely naturalized outside this range.

Alien	GB	IR
2000–19	1222	51
1987–99	988	3
1970–86	458	0
pre-1970	433	0

Key refs Bowra (1992), Carter & Prince (1985), Reynolds (1999).

F.H. Perring & J.O. Mountford

Ne *Lactuca sativa* Garden Lettuce
L.

An annual or biennial herb, long cultivated as a salad plant, and occasionally escaping onto waste ground or persisting on abandoned arable land; also a birdseed alien occurring casually on refuse tips. Lowland.

Trends *L. sativa* has been cultivated in Britain since at least 1200 (Harvey, 1981), or possibly the Roman era, and is treated by Stace & Crawley (2015) as a cultivated archaeophyte. However, it was not recorded in the wild until 1859 (Blackrock, Dublin). There are many cultivated varieties, including *L. sativa* var. *sativa* (cabbage lettuce) and *L. sativa* var. *crispa* (cos lettuce). Although often thought to be under-recorded, more rigorous recent recording of casuals and agricultural species suggests it is genuinely quite uncommon.

Biogeography *L. sativa* was derived in cultivation from wild relatives, the closest of which is *L. serriola*. The first evidence for its cultivation comes from Ancient Egypt.

	GB	IR
Long term	No trend	No trend
Short term	↓ ↓ · ↑ **↑**	No trend

Alien	GB	IR
2000–19	46	4
1987–99	18	0
1970–86	21	0
pre-1970	20	0

Key refs Harvey (1981), Stace & Crawley (2015), Zohary & Hopf (2000).

F.H. Perring & J.O. Mountford

Altitude (m)

< 1%
1–10%
11–30%
31–40%
41–50%
51–100%

Distance north (km)

Apparency In flower In leaf

N *Lactuca virosa* Great Lettuce
L.

An annual or biennial herb occurring as a native on coastal cliffs, inland rock outcrops and perhaps sand dunes, but much more widespread as a plant of rank calcareous grassland, woodland margins, road banks, quarries, tracks and rough ground. It is sensitive to grazing. Lowland.

Trends *L. virosa* was first recorded in Britain in 1570 but it was often recorded in error for *L. serriola* f. *integrifolia* before 1930, so it may have been rarer then than historical records suggest. Road and urban developments have greatly assisted its spread since the 1970s, and the dramatic increase shown in the 2002 *Atlas* has continued in the 21st century both in terms of overall spread and consolidation within its core distribution in eastern England. It is close to impossible now to distinguish its original native distribution, and consequently all records are mapped as if they are native.

Biogeography Suboceanic Southern-temperate element.

	GB	IR
Long term	↓ ↓ · **↑** ↑	No trend
Short term	↓ ↓ · **↑** ↑	No trend

Native	GB	IR
2000–19	788	1
1987–99	539	0
1970–86	255	0
pre-1970	386	3

Key refs Boorman & Fuller (1984), Oswald (2000), Salisbury (1953).

F.H. Perring & J.O. Mountford

Altitude (m)

< 1%
1–10%
11–30%
31–40%
41–50%
51–100%

Distance north (km)

Apparency In flower In leaf

N *Lactuca saligna* Least Lettuce
L.

An autumn- or spring-germinating annual herb of disturbed, sandy shingle and old south-facing sea-walls and embankments, growing on sparsely vegetated ground; also formerly on the banks of rivers and ditches in East Anglia, and, rarely, on paths and cliffs in Essex. Lowland.

Trends *L. saligna* suffered a severe decline owing to sea-wall refurbishment and river engineering. It was extirpated from about half its known sites by 1930, and survived in East Anglia only until 1953 (Leslie, 2019). Inundation by sea water caused a dramatic decline in the Sussex population in the 1990s from which it has recovered, and the Essex population continues to thrive, benefitting from cattle grazing. It was refound in West Kent in 1999, on the Isle of Grain, and at Sheppey in 2000 after an absence of about 20

years. Here it grows with *Bupleurum tenuissimum* and *Hordeum marinum*. Although its extant sites seem relatively secure, it is vulnerable to a lack of grazing, which would appear to preclude its establishment elsewhere.

Biogeography European Southern-temperate element.

| Long term | GB No trend | IR No trend |
| Short term | No trend | No trend |

Native	GB	IR
2000–19	5	0
1987–99	3	0
1970–86	5	0
pre-1970	36	0

Alien	GB	IR
2000–19	0	0
1987–99	0	0
1970–86	1	0
pre-1970	7	0

Key refs Kitchener (2022), Leslie (2019), Wigginton (1999).

F.H. Perring & J.O. Mountford

N *Cicerbita alpina* Alpine Blue-sow-thistle
(L.) Wallr.

A tall perennial herb of ledges inaccessible to most grazing animals on moist, predominantly north-facing acidic rocks, often where there is late snow-lie. In countries where grazing pressure is lower, such as Norway, it is found in birch and conifer woodlands from sea level to above the treeline. From 700 m in Glen Doll (Angus) to 1,090 m on Lochnagar (South Aberdeenshire), but formerly at 530 m in Glen Canness (Angus).

Trends *C. alpina* is one of Britain's rarest mountain plants with only four populations currently known. The main threat is from trampling or grazing by Red Deer *Cervus elaphus* and sheep. It is an outbreeding though self-compatible species with most colonies comprising fewer than 20 clones. Seed production is poor and germination has never been observed

in natural populations. Since 2017 it has been planted at several new sites as part of a conservation programme to conserve the species in our area.

Biogeography European Boreal-montane element; a woodland and sub-montane meadow species across much of its European range.

| Long term | GB No trend | IR No trend |
| Short term | No trend | No trend |

Native	GB	IR
2000–19	3	0
1987–99	4	0
1970–86	4	0
pre-1970	4	0

Alien	GB	IR
2000–19	2	0
1987–99	0	0
1970–86	1	0
pre-1970	0	0

Key refs Marren *et al.* (1986), Michl *et al.* (2010), Wigginton (1999).

A. Finger & F.H. Perring

Ne *Cicerbita macrophylla* Common Blue-sow-thistle
(Willd.) Wallr.

A tall perennial herb, strongly rhizomatous with the potential to become a serious weed in gardens and therefore often discarded. It is also occasionally self-sown. Widely naturalized on roadsides, pond margins and riverbanks where, with its long rhizomes, it forms large clonal patches. Generally lowland, but reaching 320 m at Tomintoul (Banffshire), and 460 m at Flash (Staffordshire).

Trends This species had been introduced into British gardens by 1823, and was first recorded as naturalized by a roadside at Glenridding, Ullswater (Cumberland) in 1915. There was a dramatic expansion in range during the 20th century although this increase has now slowed, possibly because it is less often grown in gardens.

Biogeography Our plant is subsp. *uralensis* from the Urals; subsp. *macrophylla* is found in the Caucasus.

Alien		GB	IR
2000–19	●	622	31
1987–99	●	552	23
1970–86	●	410	21
pre-1970	○	285	13

		<1%
	●	1–10%
	●	11–30%
	●	31–40%
	●	41–50%
	●	51–100%

Key refs Sell (1986).

P.A. STROH & F.H. PERRING

N *Mycelis muralis* Wall Lettuce
(L.) Dumort.

A winter-green perennial herb of rock outcrops, limestone pavement and hedgebanks, and in woodland, wood margins and scrub, especially on chalk and limestone but also on acidic rocks in some areas. It is also an increasing weed of shaded walls, pavements and waste ground in urban areas. 0–500 m (Alston Moor, Cumberland), and 570 m at Hartside Quarry (Cumberland).

Native in Britain and a neophyte in Ireland.

Trends The overall distribution of *M. muralis* has remained largely unchanged since the 1960s, though there are now many more records from eastern England, Scotland and Ireland. It is almost certainly an introduction in Ireland, where it continues to spread in both semi-natural and anthropogenic habitats. Likewise, its status is uncertain in Scotland and parts of England where its native habitats are scarce and it is largely confined to urban habitats such as walls, pavements, gardens, railway lines and roadsides.

Biogeography European Temperate element.

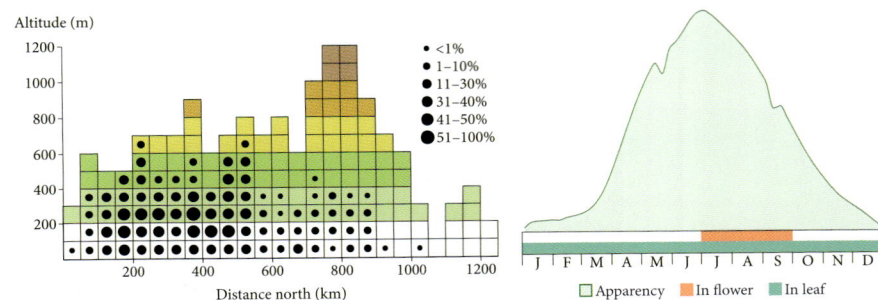

Native		GB	IR
2000–19	●	1276	0
1987–99	●	1142	0
1970–86	●	769	0
pre-1970	○	1048	0

Alien		GB	IR
2000–19	●	3	166
1987–99	●	4	77
1970–86	●	2	13
pre-1970	○	8	42

		<1%
	●	1–10%
	●	11–30%
	●	31–40%
	●	41–50%
	●	51–100%

Key refs Clabby & Osborne (1999), Grime *et al.* (2007), Webb & Scannell (1983).

F.H. PERRING & K.J. WALKER

(N) *Taraxacum* Dandelions
F.H.Wigg.

These winter-green, tap-rooted perennial herbs are ubiquitous in a wide variety of habitats. They are most abundant in disturbed, grassy habitats such as pastures, roadside verges, lawns, tracks, paths, gardens and waste ground, but some microspecies are confined to natural or semi-natural habitats, including sand dunes, calcareous grassland, hay meadows, fens, mires, flushes and cliffs. 0–1,220 m (Aberdeenshire).

Trends The 10 km square distribution of the *Taraxacum* aggregate is stable. Dandelions comprise a large and complex group of predominantly apomictic taxa which currently comprises 239 microspecies in our area, of which 58 are endemic and 45 are introduced (Richards, 2021). The alien taxa are rarely recorded as such, and all records are mapped here without status.

Biogeography Circumpolar Wide-temperate element.

	GB	IR
2000–19	2800	998
1987–99	2767	951
1970–86	2346	300
pre-1970	2670	868

Key refs Dudman & Richards (1997), Grime *et al.* (2007), Richards (2021).

T.D. DINES & K.J. WALKER

(N) *Crepis paludosa* Marsh Hawk's-beard
(L.) Moench

In the uplands, this perennial herb is found on rocky, wooded streamsides, where it often grows on water-splashed rocks, and also in sheltered gullies and on flushed banks. At lower altitudes it occurs in fens, damp hay meadows, wet woodland, ditches and on roadside verges. Lowland to 1,000 m (Easterness).

Trends Although there were losses of *C. paludosa* at the southern edges of its range last century following habitat destruction and the drainage of lowland marshes, overall its distribution has remained fairly stable since the 1960s, and in recent years there have been many new sites found in Ireland, southern Wales, and areas of northern Scotland due to more systematic recording.

Biogeography European Boreo-temperate element.

Native	GB	IR
2000–19	1037	343
1987–99	989	262
1970–86	672	88
pre-1970	951	203

P.A. STROH & F.H. PERRING

Crepis mollis Northern Hawk's-beard

(Jacq.) Asch.

A winter-green perennial of tall herb-rich grassland on shallow, slightly flushed base-rich sandstone and limestone substrates, often on north-facing slopes. Typically found in upland pastures and hay meadows, but also in wood pasture and on stream banks, roadsides and limestone pavement. From 90 m beside the Swarland Burn (North Northumberland) to 670 m in Caenlochan (Angus).

Native in Britain and a neophyte in Ireland.

Trends *C. mollis* had gone from many of its localities by the late 19th century, and declines continued into the 20th century, with significant losses reported from 1970 onwards. However, surveys since 2000 suggest that at least some of this apparent decline may have been due to under-recording; the plant can be difficult to relocate due to the remoteness of many sites, the small size of populations, confusion with other yellow-flowered composites and a lack of flowering. Its overall 10 km square distribution would now appear stable, albeit there have been localized losses, and many populations are small and vulnerable.

Biogeography European Temperate element, with a continental distribution in western Europe.

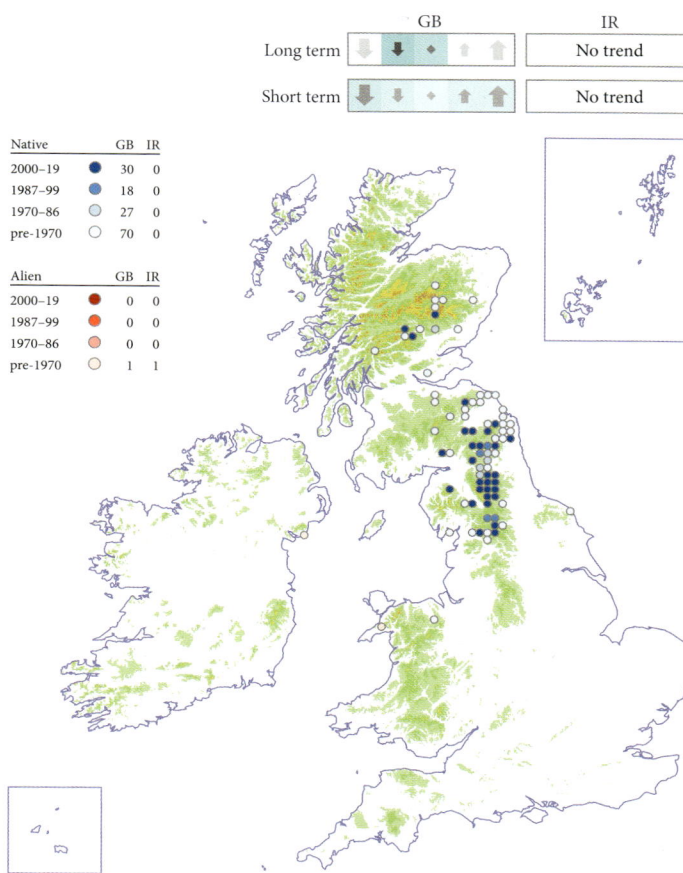

Native	GB	IR
2000–19	30	0
1987–99	18	0
1970–86	27	0
pre-1970	70	0

Alien	GB	IR
2000–19	0	0
1987–99	0	0
1970–86	0	0
pre-1970	1	1

Key refs Stewart *et al.* (1994), Stroh *et al.* (2019).

P.A. STROH & F.H. PERRING

Crepis biennis Rough Hawk's-beard

L.

A stout, biennial herb that is probably native only in rough grassland and woodland margins on chalk soils in south-eastern England. Elsewhere it seems likely to have been introduced, often with grass seed, persisting locally in pastures, in arable fields and on field margins, roadsides, dry banks and waste ground. Lowland.

Native in Britain and a neophyte in Ireland.

Trends The expansion in the range of *C. biennis* observed in the 20th century has continued this century, particularly in central and northern England and in Ireland, where it is classed as an alien. This spread may in part be due to its introduction as a contaminant of seed mixtures sown on road verges and on field headlands, or in transported soil. As a consequence, the limits of its native range are almost impossible to determine with any certainty although in northern and western Britain it often behaves like a casual. There have, however, been losses from apparently native sites in southern England since the 1960s, the reasons for which are unclear.

Biogeography European Temperate element.

Native	GB	IR
2000–19	233	0
1987–99	173	0
1970–86	141	0
pre-1970	222	0

Alien	GB	IR
2000–19	265	163
1987–99	173	109
1970–86	121	21
pre-1970	168	48

F.H. PERRING & K.J. WALKER

N *Crepis capillaris* Smooth Hawk's-beard
(L.) Wallr.

This morphologically variable winter-green annual to biennial occurs in a wide variety of grassy habitats including banks and verges beside paths, tracks and roads, rough fields, meadows and pastures, lawns and rocky banks. It is also an early colonist of open habitats such as chalk- and gravel-pits, railways, waste ground, streets and gardens, set-aside and arable margins. It is a poor competitor in closed vegetation but often survives and flowers in mown turf. 0–585 m (Hopetoun Craig, Dumfriesshire).

Trends The known distribution of *C. capillaris* has expanded since the 1960s, presumably as a result of more systematic recording, especially in Ireland and Scotland, but also because of localized increases in man-made habitats.

Biogeography European Temperate element; widely naturalized outside its native range.

Native	GB	IR
2000–19	2403	905
1987–99	2338	815
1970–86	1461	106
pre-1970	2218	747

Alien	GB	IR
2000–19	4	0
1987–99	3	0
1970–86	5	0
pre-1970	3	0

Key refs Grime *et al.* (2007).

F.H. Perring & K.J. Walker

Ne *Crepis vesicaria* Beaked Hawk's-beard
L.

A usually biennial winter-green herb, sometimes annual or perennial, found on the verges of paths, tracks and roads, rough grassland and meadows, old pits, lawns, railway banks, arable margins, set-aside, pavements, gardens, allotments and in waste places. 0–482 m (Hilltop, Staffordshire).

Trends In Britain, this species was first recorded in 1713 in Kent. It spread rapidly, reaching the western coast of Ireland in 1896. It is now the commonest spring-flowering yellow composite along roadsides in the southern halves of Britain and Ireland. It has spread northwards since 1960s, especially in the east, and it is now well-established in north-eastern England. There are also many more records in western England, Wales and Ireland than in the two previous atlases. Most of our plants are regarded as subsp. *taraxacifolia*, which has all the achenes with long beaks, but other subspecies are likely to be present.

Biogeography Native of the Mediterranean region and south-western Asia.

Alien	GB	IR
2000–19	1262	277
1987–99	1166	252
1970–86	707	16
pre-1970	905	106

F.H. Perring & K.J. Walker

Ne ## *Crepis setosa* Bristly Hawk's-beard
Haller f.

An annual to biennial herb which is most frequent in recently sown grassland, but is also found in arable fields, on waste ground and in areas sown with wild-flower seed mixtures; it sometimes persists but is usually casual. Lowland.

Trends This species was first recorded from North Essex in 1843, and from North Yorkshire in 1857. It appears to be less frequent now than formerly.

Biogeography *C. setosa* has a European Southern-temperate distribution.

	GB	IR
Long term	No trend	No trend
Short term	↓	No trend

Alien	GB	IR
2000–19	19	1
1987–99	69	3
1970–86	51	0
pre-1970	60	0

F.H. Perring & K.J. Walker

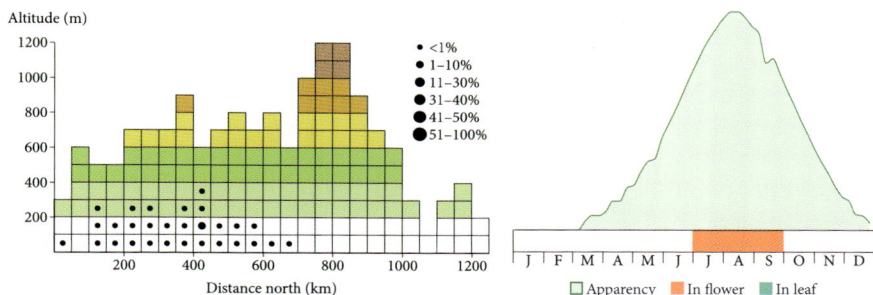

Ar ## *Crepis foetida* Stinking Hawk's-beard
L.

An annual or biennial herb now found only on disturbed coastal shingle in Sussex and Kent, but formerly also in open sandy or chalky habitats inland. Lowland.

Trends *C. foetida* is now only known from one natural site and two established populations nearby. At Dungeness, where it was believed to have been extirpated by 1980, new populations were established in a shingle-heath community, including in several nearby gardens, following reintroduction in 1992, although the majority of these subsequently died out. However, in 2010 an overlooked population was discovered close to an historic site in Lydd where it had not been introduced and is unlikely to have colonized from reintroductions. This large population therefore represents the only surviving natural population in Britain. In 2000 the species was reintroduced to a second shingle location at Rye Harbour (East Sussex), was almost lost due to grazing by rabbits, but recovered after the area was enclosed in a rabbit-proof fence in 2005. Numbers then increased rapidly and now exceed 3,000 in some years. Attempts to introduce it to three chalk pits in North Kent all failed. The main reasons for its long-term decline are unclear but grazing may be a key factor, as reintroduced populations have only survived where rabbits have been excluded. A genetic study has shown that the species has not suffered from a genetic bottleneck (Squirrell *et al.*, 2006). The Dungeness plant is subsp. *foetida*; the rare casual records may be referable to the central and south-eastern European subsp. *commutata*, or to subsp. *rhoeadifolia*.

Biogeography As an archaeophyte, *C. foetida* has a Eurosiberian Southern-temperate distribution.

	GB	IR
Long term	No trend	No trend
Short term	No trend	No trend

Alien	GB	IR
2000–19	2	0
1987–99	2	0
1970–86	1	0
pre-1970	35	0

Key refs Ferry *et al.* (2010), Kitchener (2022), Squirrell *et al.* (2006), Wigginton (1999).

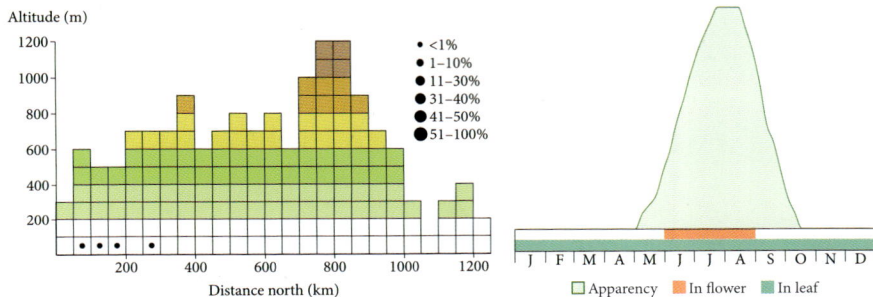

P.A. Stroh, K.J. Walker & F.H. Perring

Ⓝ *Crepis praemorsa* Leafless Hawk's-beard
(L.) F.Walther

A perennial herb, confined to low banks of limestone drift within 10 m of a stream at the edges of a hay meadow and grazed pasture, at an altitude of 250–275 m (Orton Pasture, Westmorland).

Trends This species was discovered as new to Britain and western Europe in Westmorland in 1988. In 2009, the population comprised about 30 distinct colonies along half a kilometre of streamside, with around 2,000 shoots but only three flowering stems (Roberts, 2009b). This is a much larger total than when the population was first discovered, although the reasons for this increase are unknown. Doubt has been expressed about its status, and it is regarded as an archaeophyte in some European countries. However, the similarity of its British and Scandinavian habitats, together with the undisturbed nature of the site, suggest that it may be native in our area.

Biogeography Eurosiberian Temperate element, with a continental distribution in western Europe.

Native	GB	IR
2000–19	1	0
1987–99	1	0
1970–86	0	0
pre-1970	0	0

	GB	IR
Long term	No trend	No trend
Short term	No trend	No trend

Key refs Halliday (1997), Roberts (2009b), Stroh *et al.* (2019), Wigginton (1999).

F.H. PERRING & K.J. WALKER

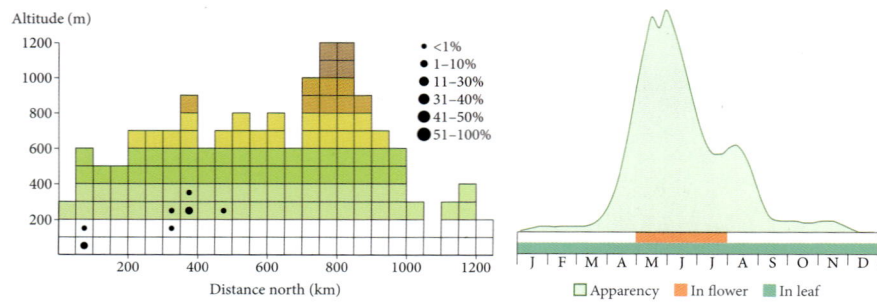

Ⓝ *Pilosella peleteriana* Shaggy Mouse-ear-hawkweed
(Mérat) F.W.Schultz & Sch.Bip.

A perennial herb, spreading by short, thick stolons, occurring on steep, well-drained slopes in chalk and limestone grassland (especially on the edges of paths, on small terraces and at the edge of sea-cliffs), on dry dolerite rock shelves and quarry waste, on shallow soils overlying granite, and on dunes. Lowland.

Trends *P. peleteriana* was first mapped by Perring & Sell (1968) and now includes three subspecies, although Stace (2010) suggests that they are better treated as varieties. The current map shows some losses before 1970, but the species is now better recorded in Dorset and Staffordshire and the overall distribution is stable. It was recently rediscovered in Derbyshire and at a second site on the Isle of Wight.

It occurs throughout the Channel Islands where it largely replaces *P. officinarum*. There is no specimen supporting the Merionethshire record mapped in Perring & Sell (1968) and the plant has not been refound.

Biogeography Suboceanic Boreo-temperate element.

Native	GB	IR
2000–19	21	0
1987–99	18	0
1970–86	11	0
pre-1970	19	0

	GB	IR
Long term	No trend	No trend
Short term	No trend	No trend

Key refs Stroh *et al.* (2019), Wigginton (1999).

F.H. PERRING & K.J. WALKER

N *Pilosella officinarum* Mouse-ear-hawkweed

F.W.Schultz & Sch.Bip.

A perennial, stoloniferous herb of dry habitats, including short grassland, heathlands, sand dunes, screes, rock outcrops, quarries and cliffs. It grows on both base-rich and acidic substrates. 0–915 m (Ben Macdui, South Aberdeenshire).

Trends There has been no discernible change in the distribution of *P. officinarum* since the 1960s. It is variable, and seven subspecies have been recognized. However, all are more or less connected by intermediates, and are not or only partially discrete geographically and ecologically; Stace (2010) considers they are no more than varieties. They have not been recorded consistently by British or Irish botanists and so there has been no attempt to map them here.

Biogeography European Temperate element; widely naturalized outside its native range.

Native	GB	IR
2000–19	2598	873
1987–99	2481	803
1970–86	1709	139
pre-1970	2452	737

Alien	GB	IR
2000–19	1	1
1987–99	1	1
1970–86	0	0
pre-1970	1	0

Key refs Bishop & Davy (1994), Grime *et al.* (2007), Rich & Jermy (1998).

F.H. PERRING & K.J. WALKER

Ne *Pilosella flagellaris* subsp. *flagellaris* Spreading Mouse-ear-hawkweed

(Willd.) P.D.Sell & C.West

A perennial, stoloniferous herb, sometimes grown in gardens and found naturalized on roadsides, railway banks, disused railways, disused colliery sites and lawns, as well as in churchyards and sand pits. Reproduction is by seed and vegetative spread. Lowland.

Trends This subspecies has been cultivated in Britain since 1816. It was first recorded in the wild in 1869 on railway banks at Granton, Edinburgh (Midlothian), where it may have escaped from the Botanic Garden. It has increased since the 1960s especially in the central belt of Scotland and in Nottinghamshire, where it has been spreading since 1976, mainly on disused railways, roadsides and on disused colliery sites.

Biogeography *P. flagellaris* subsp. *flagellaris* has a European Boreo-temperate range, with a continental distribution in western Europe.

Alien	GB	IR
2000–19	57	0
1987–99	47	0
1970–86	32	0
pre-1970	20	0

Key refs Shaw (2020).

F.H. PERRING & K.J. WALKER

N *Pilosella flagellaris* subsp. *bicapitata* Shetland Mouse-ear-hawkweed
P.D.Sell & C.West

An endemic perennial herb of grassy limestone rocky outcrops, heathy granulitic gneiss and feldspathic rocky sea-banks in three localities in Shetland, where it was first described in 1962. Lowland.

Trends There has been no change in the distribution of this subspecies at the 10 km scale. However, two of its three localities are accessible to sheep, and increased grazing pressure in recent years has suppressed flowering and might have reduced the size of populations, which probably only numbers several hundred plants in total (Scott *et al.*, 2002). The occurrence of this endemic subspecies in Shetland at such a distance from native populations of subsp. *flagellaris* in central and southern Europe presents a fascinating biogeographic puzzle.

Biogeography Endemic.

	GB	IR
Long term	No trend	No trend
Short term	No trend	No trend

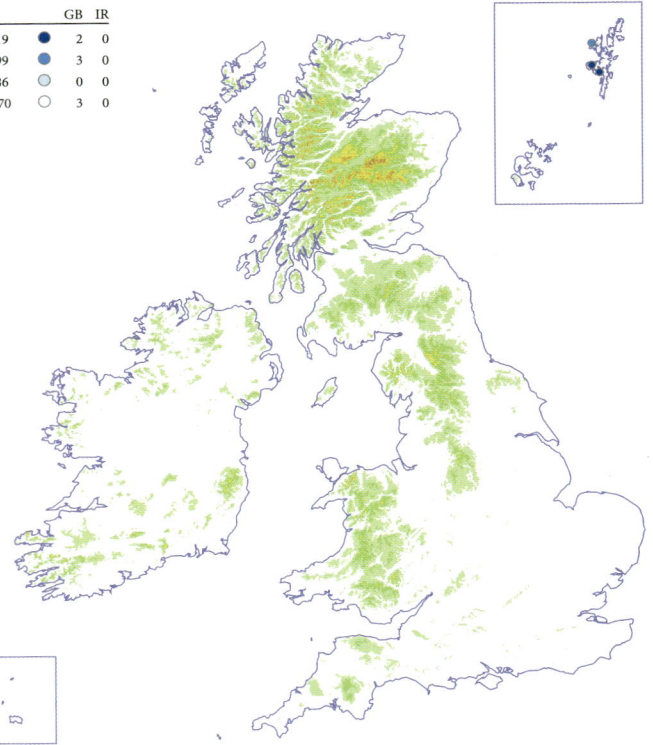

Native	GB	IR
2000–19	2	0
1987–99	3	0
1970–86	0	0
pre-1970	3	0

Key refs Scott (1968), Scott *et al.* (2002), Wigginton (1999).

F.H. Perring & K.J. Walker

Ne *Pilosella praealta* Tall Mouse-ear-hawkweed
(Vill. ex Gochnat) F.W.Schultz & Sch.Bip.

A perennial herb, with or without stolons, which is naturalized on roadside verges, walls, railway banks and rough ground. It arises as a garden escape. Lowland.

Trends *P. praealta* is grown only rarely in gardens. It was recorded from the wild in 1851 (Culross, Fife), and is now better recorded than when mapped by Perring & Sell (1968).

Biogeography Widespread as a native in temperate Europe.

	GB	IR
Long term	No trend	No trend
Short term	No trend	No trend

Alien	GB	IR
2000–19	33	0
1987–99	18	0
1970–86	8	0
pre-1970	24	0

T.D. Dines

Ne *Pilosella caespitosa* Yellow Fox-and-cubs
(Dumort.) P.D.Sell & C.West

A perennial herb, spreading by stolons and rhizomes, which is naturalized on grassy banks, riverbanks, sand dunes, roadsides, pavements, walls, railway banks and rough ground. It arises as a garden escape. Lowland.

Trends *P. caespitosa* was introduced into British gardens before 1819. It was recorded in the wild in 1868 (River Ettrick, Selkirkshire). It has always been a rare alien, continues to occur sporadically, and was last recorded in Ireland in 1977.

Biogeography *P. caespitosa* is widespread in temperate Europe and is naturalized in North America.

	GB	IR
Long term	No trend	No trend
Short term	No trend	No trend

Alien		GB	IR
2000–19	●	24	0
1987–99	●	10	0
1970–86	●	11	1
pre-1970	○	26	1

Altitude (m) / Distance north (km)

●	<1%
●	1–10%
●	11–30%
●	31–40%
●	41–50%
●	51–100%

Apparency   In flower   In leaf

T.D. DINES & K.J. WALKER

Hy *Pilosella caespitosa × lactucella = P. ×floribunda* Irish Fox-and-cubs
(Wimm. & Grab.) Arv.-Touv.

A perennial herb, spreading by stolons and rhizomes, naturalized in grassy heath on a roadside verge in South Hampshire, on an old colliery waste tip near Cannock Wood (Staffordshire), on a disused railway line near Lymm (Cheshire), and formerly also in a limestone quarry at Cave Hill (County Antrim). Lowland.

A cultivated hybrid (alien × alien).

Trends This hybrid was recorded at Cave Hill (County Antrim) in 1897 and was last seen there in 1910. It was discovered on a roadside verge in the New Forest (South Hampshire) in 1991, and in 2008 a population of the hybrid was found on an old colliery waste tip at Cannock Wood (Staffordshire). A fourth population discovered in 2015 on a disused railway line in Lymm (Cheshire) was confirmed by flow cytometry.

Biogeography Native of northern and central Europe, east to the Carpathians.

	GB	IR
Long term	No trend	No trend
Short term	No trend	No trend

		GB	IR
2000–19	●	2	0
1987–99	●	1	0
1970–86	●	0	0
pre-1970	○	0	2

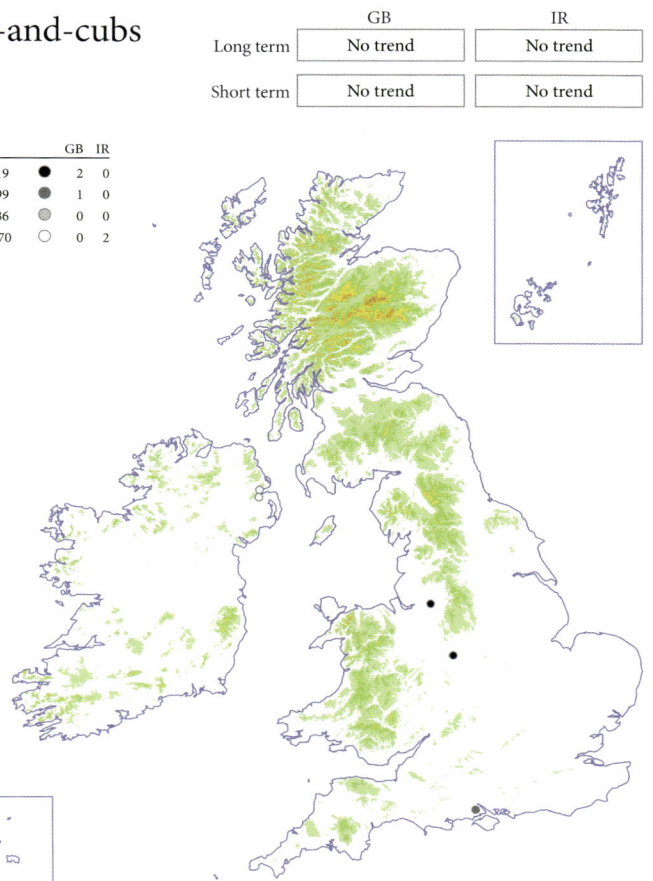

Altitude (m) / Distance north (km)

●	<1%
●	1–10%
●	11–30%
●	31–40%
●	41–50%
●	51–100%

Apparency   In flower   In leaf

Key refs Stace *et al.* (2015).

C.A. STACE, C.D. PRESTON & D.A. PEARMAN

Ne *Pilosella aurantiaca* Fox-and-cubs
(L.) F.W.Schultz & Sch.Bip.

A winter-green perennial herb, spreading via its vigorous stolons or by seed. It is widely grown in gardens for its attractive reddish orange flowers from where it often escapes to form naturalized populations in mown grassland on roadsides and in churchyards. It is also recorded from railway banks, waste ground, walls, pavements, and other waste places, usually close to human habitations. 0–490 m (Ben Lawers, Mid Perthshire).

Trends *P. aurantiaca* was grown in gardens by 1629 and recorded from the wild by 1793. It has increased considerably in range since the 1960s and it is now one of the commonest aliens encountered in regularly mown grasslands in man-made habitats. Two subspecies are recognized in our area, subsp. *aurantiaca* and the more widespread subsp. *carpathicola* that

occurs throughout the range of the species. Although expertly determined records of these were mapped by Perring & Sell (1968), they have not been comprehensively recorded since then and are not mapped separately here.

Biogeography *P. aurantiaca* has a European Boreal-montane distribution; it is naturalized outside this range in Europe, North America and elsewhere.

Alien	GB	IR
2000–19	1951	197
1987–99	1205	60
1970–86	604	18
pre-1970	484	13

Key refs Shaw (2020).

F.H. PERRING & K.J. WALKER

N *Hieracium* Hawkweeds
L.

This aggregate includes about 420 microspecies of *Hieracium* recorded in our area, ranging from the variable diploid *H. umbellatum* to the numerous endemic apomictic polyploids such as *H. attenboroughianum* (McCosh & Rich, 2018). Collectively they occur on acid to calcareous, free-draining, often nutrient-poor soils from sea level to the highest summits of Scottish mountains in ungrazed open, usually rocky habitats. 0–1,220 m (Cairngorms, South Aberdeenshire).

Trends The aggregate map shows little change since the 1960s at the 10 km square scale, but this masks the marked declines or extirpation of some native taxa, the spread of a small number of non-natives, and also the fuller recording of the distribution of many *Hieracium*

following the publication of regional and national identification guides.

Biogeography Circumpolar Wide-boreal element.

	GB	IR
2000–19	2399	253
1987–99	2231	239
1970–86	1687	63
pre-1970	1947	202

Key refs McCosh & Rich (2018).

T.C.G. RICH

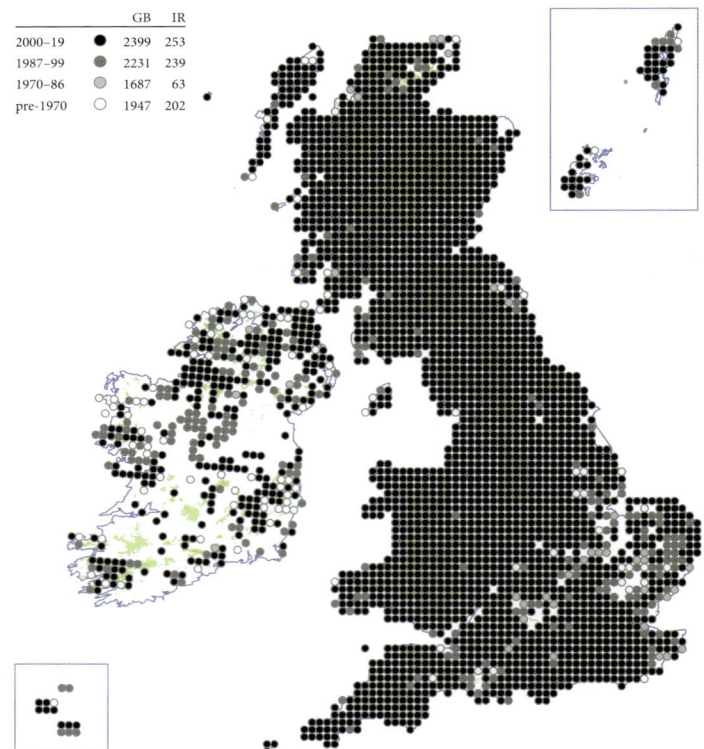

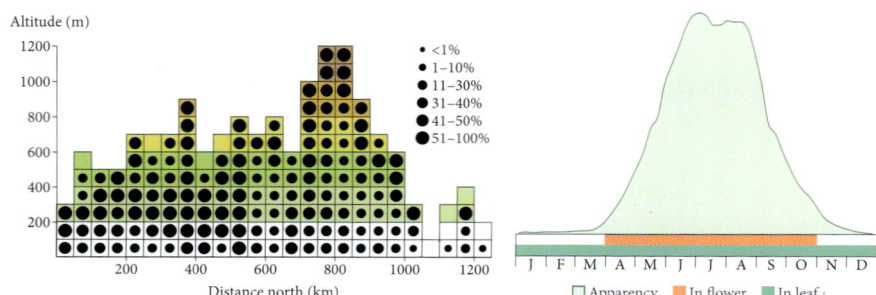

N *Filago germanica* Common Cudweed

L., non Huds.

An autumn- or spring-germinating annual herb of dry, open, acidic to neutral and occasionally calcareous habitats including arable fields, track sides, open grassland, quarries and rocky ledges, sand-pits, sand dunes, sandy heaths, tracks and waste ground. Lowland to 390 m (Llanelly, Breconshire).

Trends *F. germanica* suffered a decline in range in Britain during the second half of the 20th century due to changing agricultural practices, cultivation of marginal land, and abandonment, re-routing or improvement of tracksides or paths, leading to a lack of gaps for regeneration. It remains locally abundant on dry, sandy soils in eastern Britain and, since 2000, there have been many new records in southern, central and northern England, suggesting an expansion in range for reasons that are unclear. In Ireland declines in the north were apparent by the mid-20th century, and although it remains a rare species, its distribution is now much better known, at least in the south-east.

Biogeography European Southern-temperate element; also recorded in central Asia. It reaches its northern limit in Scotland and Jutland.

Native	GB	IR
2000–19	854	39
1987–99	548	14
1970–86	394	2
pre-1970	847	67

Alien	GB	IR
2000–19	2	0
1987–99	2	0
1970–86	1	0
pre-1970	3	0

Key refs Stroh *et al.* (2019).

T.C.G. Rich, G. Halliday & K.J. Walker

N? *Filago lutescens* Red-tipped Cudweed

Jord.

A winter- or spring-germinating annual herb of arable field margins, tracks and paths, open sandy ground, sand-pits and commons or heathland, usually in very open, therophyte communities with other cudweeds. Lowland.

Trends This species declined before the 1960s due to changes in agricultural practices in arable sites and lack of disturbance on tracks and heathland. Since then its range has remained largely stable with an increase in sites since 2000, partly due to increased awareness and more systematic recording of arable weeds, and possibly also a warming climate.

Biogeography European Temperate; it reaches its northern limit in England.

Native	GB	IR
2000–19	20	0
1987–99	20	0
1970–86	16	0
pre-1970	81	0

Alien	GB	IR
2000–19	0	0
1987–99	3	0
1970–86	1	0
pre-1970	2	0

Key refs Rich (1999b), Wigginton (1999).

T.C.G. Rich

Ar *Filago pyramidata* Broad-leaved Cudweed
L.

An annual herb of arable fields, disturbed road and track sides, heathlands, commons and quarries and pits, where it grows in open, drought-prone grassland vegetation or in arable weed communities, often with other cudweed species. It was once most frequent as an arable weed on calcareous or acidic sandy soils, but is now mostly confined to chalk quarries or on chalk spoil. Lowland.

Trends *F. pyramidata* declined gradually up to the 1970s due to changes in agricultural practices in arable fields and from tracks and roadsides due to reduced disturbance. Since 2000, 13 populations have been recorded, mainly from chalk quarries and pits, often adjacent to arable fields, with only two populations on arable margins including one that is now managed exclusively for rare arable weeds (Ranscombe Farm, North Kent) (Shellswell *et al.*, 2021). In 2013 an extensive population was discovered on disturbed track edges of a tank driver training area on Salisbury Plain (Wiltshire) where it had clearly been overlooked by many previous botanists who had visited the area.

Biogeography As an archaeophyte, *F. pyramidata* has a Submediterranean-Subatlantic distribution. It reaches its northern limit in England, and is declining in the eastern part of its European range.

Alien	GB	IR
2000–19	17	0
1987–99	15	0
1970–86	14	0
pre-1970	138	0

Key refs Rich (1999a), Shellswell *et al.* (2021), Wigginton (1999).

T.C.G. RICH & K.J. WALKER

N *Logfia minima* Small Cudweed
(Sm.) Dumort.

An annual herb of dry, open, infertile, acidic to neutral soils in arable fields, open grassland, quarries and mine spoil, woodland tracks, sandy heaths, sand-pits and dunes. Lowland to 430 m (Mynydd Llangatwg, Breconshire).

Trends The 10 km square distribution of *L. minima* declined in the latter half of the 20th century, especially in south-eastern and eastern England and eastern Scotland, due to the intensification of arable cultivation and the widespread loss of infertile sandy and heathy grasslands. Its distribution this century is much more stable, and it may even be increasing in some regions (*e.g.* English Midlands, eastern Scotland) for reasons that are unclear.

Biogeography European Temperate element; it reaches its northern limit in Scotland.

Native	GB	IR
2000–19	582	69
1987–99	438	49
1970–86	290	15
pre-1970	669	72

Alien	GB	IR
2000–19	2	0
1987–99	2	0
1970–86	0	0
pre-1970	1	0

T.C.G. RICH & G. HALLIDAY

Logfia gallica Narrow-leaved Cudweed

(L.) Coss. & Germ.

An annual herb of open sandy or gravelly soils in drought-prone vegetation on arable field margins, open acid grasslands, gravel-pits, quarries, tracks and roadsides, usually growing with other cudweeds. Lowland.

Trends Once known from at least 30 sites in south-eastern England but extinct there by 1955 due to more intensive agricultural management. It was reintroduced at its last known site in Essex (Berechurch Common) in 1994 using local seed but it has not persisted, with a last record from 2004. Introductions in Suffolk have also failed. It survives on Sark (Channel Islands).

Biogeography Native of the Mediterranean region; it is probably introduced in the northern part of its Submediterranean-Subatlantic range.

	GB	IR
Long term	No trend	No trend
Short term	No trend	No trend

Alien	GB	IR
2000–19	3	0
1987–99	6	0
1970–86	3	0
pre-1970	24	0

Altitude (m)

Distance north (km)

- <1%
- 1–10%
- 11–30%
- 31–40%
- 41–50%
- 51–100%

Apparency ■ In flower ■ In leaf

Key refs Rich *et al.* (1999a), Wigginton (1999).

T.C.G. RICH

Antennaria dioica Mountain Everlasting

(L.) Gaertn.

A winter-green, dioecious perennial herb, spreading by short stolons and restricted to very infertile, free-draining basic to mildly acidic soils. In the lowlands, it is confined to very short vegetation with low competition including chalk and limestone grassland, maritime and dry heathland, coastal cliff-tops, sand dunes and machair. In upland regions its habitats include rock ledges, streamsides, scree, fell field, well-drained acidic and calcareous grasslands, heathy pastures and dwarf-shrub heaths. 0–983 m (Aonach Beag, Westerness).

Trends *A. dioica* has declined markedly throughout lowland regions of Britain and Ireland since the mid-19th century, most notably in lowland England where it now survives in just five widely distributed sites in Cornwall, Somerset, Wiltshire, Gloucestershire and Northamptonshire. All these populations are small, single-sex and comprise only one or a few genets. Although most losses took place before 1950, the decline continued for much of the remainder of the 20th century due to the ploughing of its habitats and the intensification of grassland management. Its 10 km square distribution appears to be more stable in upland regions, but there have been notable declines locally, even in areas where the habitats appear largely unchanged. Increased atmospheric deposition of sulphate and inorganic nitrogen, resulting in acidification and eutrophication of soils and increased competition, is likely to have accounted for these localized losses or reductions in size of populations at some sites.

Biogeography Eurasian Boreo-temperate element.

	GB	IR
Long term		
Short term		

Native	GB	IR
2000–19	627	192
1987–99	620	212
1970–86	405	59
pre-1970	829	260

Alien	GB	IR
2000–19	1	0
1987–99	0	0
1970–86	0	0
pre-1970	0	0

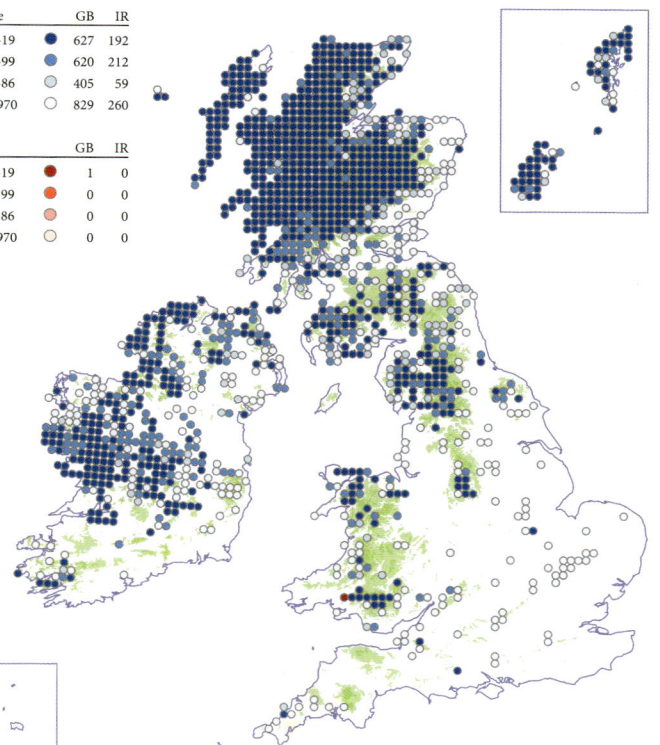

Altitude (m)

Distance north (km)

- <1%
- 1–10%
- 11–30%
- 31–40%
- 41–50%
- 51–100%

Apparency ■ In flower ■ In leaf

Key refs Stroh *et al.* (2019).

P.A. STROH, G. HALLIDAY & K.J. WALKER

Ne *Anaphalis margaritacea* Pearly Everlasting

(L.) Benth.

A rhizomatous perennial herb, grown in gardens and established on waste ground and in short grassland, especially on roadside verges, lane- and railwaysides, coal mine slag-heaps and in open areas in woodland. Generally lowland, but reaching 521 m at Mynydd Ty-isaf (Glamorganshire).

Trends *A. margaritacea* was being grown in British gardens by 1588. It was reported in the wild by 1700 when it was already well-naturalized along the Rhymney River, Glamorgan. It has increased in overall distribution since the 1960s, with many more recent scattered records, especially in southeastern England and eastern Scotland.

Biogeography Native of North America and north-eastern Asia; widely naturalized in northern and central Europe.

	GB	IR
Long term	No trend
Short term	No trend

Alien		GB	IR
2000–19	●	134	4
1987–99	●	120	1
1970–86	●	92	1
pre-1970	○	163	11

Key refs Wade *et al.* (1994).

G. HALLIDAY

Altitude (m)

● <1%
● 1–10%
● 11–30%
● 31–40%
● 41–50%
● 51–100%

Distance north (km)

☐ Apparency ☐ In flower ☐ In leaf

N *Omalotheca norvegica* Highland Cudweed

(Gunnerus) Sch.Bip. & F.W.Schultz

A perennial herb of ungrazed rock ledges, crags, gorges, screes and steep gullies, preferring a southerly or easterly aspect and an acidic, well-drained mineral soil. From 600 m (Aonach air Chrith, West Ross) to 980 m (Sgurr na Lapaich, Easterness).

Trends A targeted survey of *O. norvegica* in the 1990s led to the discovery of many new locations, and at least some sites have not been visited this century, leading to difficulties in interpreting trends. However, it would appear to have suffered a sharp decline, with some populations having been searched for without success in recent years; for example, it has almost certainly been lost from Caenlochan (Angus) due to overgrazing and excessive trampling by sheep and Red Deer *Cervus elaphus* (Geddes & Payne, 2006). Many surviving populations are small and vulnerable

to rock falls and avalanches, though new habitat is also created in this way.

Biogeography European Arctic-montane element; also in central Asia and North America.

	GB	IR
Long term	No trend
Short term	No trend

Native		GB	IR
2000–19	●	6	0
1987–99	●	16	0
1970–86	●	8	0
pre-1970	○	14	0

Key refs Geddes & Payne (2006), Wigginton (1999).

P.A. STROH & G. HALLIDAY

Altitude (m)

● <1%
● 1–10%
● 11–30%
● 31–40%
● 41–50%
● 51–100%

Distance north (km)

☐ Apparency ☐ In flower ☐ In leaf

Omalotheca sylvatica Heath Cudweed
(L.) Sch.Bip. & F.W.Schultz

A short-lived perennial herb of open communities on infertile, damp or dry, often sandy or gravelly acidic soils. Habitats include heaths and heathy pastures, sand-pits, sand dunes, the edges of farm tracks and, especially, canopy gaps in woodland and along the edges of forestry rides and tracks in areas of former heathland. 0–850 m (Breadalbanes, Mid Perthshire).

Trends *O. sylvatica* was once widespread throughout much of our area but appears to have declined substantially since the 1960s, despite extensive afforestation programmes occurring throughout the same time period that should, theoretically, have been beneficial. As a dynamic species with a persistent seed bank, it is possible that declines are slightly exaggerated; certainly a number of sites where it was not found in the 1990s, but where it was present in the 1960s, have been located since. However, countering this are a number of factors, including habitat loss, depletion of the seed bank by widespread application and drift of herbicides and agrochemicals, the fragmentation and isolation of sites, a prolonged cessation of ride management (or conversely, perhaps, too-frequent deep churning of the soils by heavy vehicles), and increased soil nutrient enrichment resulting in the spread of competitive species such as *Pteridium aquilinum* (Walker *et al.*, 2017; Stroh *et al.*, 2019).

Biogeography Eurosiberian Boreo-temperate element; also in North America.

Key refs Stewart *et al.* (1994), Stroh *et al.* (2019), Walker *et al.* (2017).

P.A. STROH & G. HALLIDAY

Omalotheca supina Dwarf Cudweed
(L.) DC.

A dwarf, perennial herb of mountain-top fell-field communities, wet grassy slopes, cliffs, moraines and late snow-patches, where it grows in sites that are relatively well-drained and stony and which dry out in summer. Usually from 455 to 1,305 m (Ben Macdui, South Aberdeenshire), but descending to 300 m on river gravels at Killin (Mid Perthshire).

Trends The 10 km square distribution of *O. supina* is probably stable. A slight retraction in range this century most likely reflects the difficulties in surveying remote and difficult terrain, rather than actual loss. Petraglia *et al.* (2014) suggest that a combination of a warming climate leading to increased nutrient availability as a result of mineralization, and atmospheric deposition, may benefit the growth and reproduction of this species, but it is likely that such advantages will be offset by increased competition from the surrounding vegetation.

Biogeography European Arctic-montane element; also in central Asia and North America.

Key refs Petraglia *et al.* (2014).

P.A. STROH & G. HALLIDAY

N *Gnaphalium uliginosum* Marsh Cudweed
L.

An annual herb of open, muddy ground, usually subject to waterlogging during the winter. It is characteristic of trampled field entrances, compacted arable and cultivated land, the margins of reservoirs and the edges of summer-dry ponds trampled by cattle. It is also found on rutted tracks on heaths and wet rides in woodland. It prefers mildly to quite strongly acidic soils. 0–590 m (north of Cwmystwyth, Cardiganshire) and exceptionally to 919 m at Stob Coire Sgriodan (Westerness).

Trends The distribution of *G. uliginosum* has increased this century, especially in Ireland and northern Scotland, probably due to a combination of more systematic recording, and a preference for disturbed habitats.

Biogeography Eurasian Boreo-temperate element, but naturalized in North America so distribution is now Circumpolar Boreo-temperate.

Native	GB	IR
2000–19	2377	734
1987–99	2138	623
1970–86	1285	57
pre-1970	1844	350

P.A. STROH & G. HALLIDAY

Ne *Laphangium luteoalbum* Jersey Cudweed
(L.) Tzvelev

An annual to winter-green biennial herb of sandy fields, dune-slacks and waste ground. The vast majority of recent records are mainly of casual plants in waste places, including pavements, gravel drives, railway sidings, china clay waste, tracks and refuse tips. It is thought to have a long-lived, persistent seed bank. Lowland.

Trends *L. luteoalbum* was first recorded in 1689 (Jersey, Channel Islands), with the first mainland record from Little Shelford (Cambridgeshire) in 1802. Over the next two centuries it was found in the Breckland, Norfolk, Kent and Dorset, with many authors claiming it as a native. Far more likely is that it arrived and was subsequently spread by humans (although it is also reportedly spread by birds), and so it is mapped as a neophyte here following the assessment of its status by Pearman (2007). Since

2000 there has been a fifty-fold increase in the number of hectad records for reasons that are unclear but might include a warming climate, spreading of aggregates for hardcore, repeated import via horticulture, as well as more intensive recording. The records from the Channel Islands too seem far more indicative of casual alien occurrences. In some places it might been over-recorded for *Pseudognaphalium undulatum* or even the newly reported *P. stramineum*.

Biogeography Eurosiberian Southern-temperate element, reaching its northern limit in southern Sweden. But it is widely naturalized outside its native range, and indeed is regarded as a world-wide weed.

Alien	GB	IR
2000–19	107	18
1987–99	18	0
1970–86	7	0
pre-1970	25	0

Key refs Clement (2004), Pearman (2007), Wigginton (1999).

D.A, PEARMAN, G. HALLIDAY AND K.J. WALKER

Ar *Inula helenium* Elecampane
L.

A rather robust, conspicuous and persistent perennial herb, widely if sparsely established from garden outcasts on roadsides and lanes and by woodland margins, but seldom far from human habitations. In Scotland it can occur in very remote locations that mark the sites of long abandoned crofts. Lowland.

Trends *I. helenium* has been grown in gardens for its medicinal, culinary and ornamental value since at least 995 (Harvey, 1981). It is less frequently planted now and although very persistent it appears to be in gradual decline in many regions.

Biogeography Native of western and central Asia; widely naturalized in temperate Europe and elsewhere.

Alien	GB	IR
2000–19	359	67
1987–99	275	45
1970–86	188	11
pre-1970	476	64

Key refs Harvey (1981).

G. HALLIDAY & K.J. WALKER

N *Inula salicina* Irish Fleabane
L.

A perennial herb confined to the northern half of Lough Derg (North Tipperary), where it has been recorded along the limestone shoreline and on the islands, occupying an intermediate, stony habitat between the flood level and the surrounding scrub. Lowland.

Trends Populations of *I. salicina* have progressively declined. It was last recorded from the south-eastern Galway side of Lough Derg in 1970 and is now restricted to North Tipperary where a single naturally occurring population comprising a small patch of the species is known. Its decline has been attributed to a combination of factors: changes in the lake water-levels associated with the hydroelectric scheme at the southern end of the lake, increased eutrophication of the lake and lake-shore, and scrub development associated with reduced levels of lakeshore grazing. Between 1996 and 2006 it was transplanted to six sites on the North Tipperary shoreline and has persisted at one of these (*c.* 500 m from a former location). Material from two populations (one extant, one extinct) are maintained in *ex situ* cultivation.

Biogeography Eurasian Temperate element, with a continental distribution in western Europe.

Native	GB	IR
2000–19	0	1
1987–99	0	1
1970–86	0	1
pre-1970	0	3

Alien	GB	IR
2000–19	0	0
1987–99	0	1
1970–86	0	0
pre-1970	0	1

	GB	IR
Long term	No trend	No trend
Short term	No trend	No trend

G. HALLIDAY & M. WYSE JACKSON

Inula conyzae Ploughman's-spikenard
(Griess.) Meikle

A winter-green biennial to perennial herb found most often on dry banks, mainly on chalk or limestone, less frequently on sands and gravels, typically in places where the vegetation cover is broken or in areas of open soil or stony ground. It occurs in dry grassland, on banks, woodland margins, rides and scrub, in quarries and pits, screes (but rarely on cliffs), on the more vegetated parts of sand dunes, on roadsides and rough ground. Most sites have a southerly aspect and are unshaded. 0–360 m (Darren Ddu, Breconshire).

Native in Britain and the Channel Islands and a neophyte in Ireland.

Trends There has been a noticeable increase in the distribution of *I. conyzae* in eastern England where it appears to have spread along road and rail networks since the 1960s.

New populations in ruderal habitats appear to be more short-lived.

Biogeography European Temperate element; it reaches its northern limit in Jutland.

Key refs Grime *et al.* (2007).

G. HALLIDAY & K.J. WALKER

Limbarda crithmoides Golden-samphire
(L.) Dumort.

A perennial herb of sea-cliffs where it grows on ledges, in crevices and in open turf on calcareous or base-rich rocks, where it is often rooted in soil enriched with calcareous shell sand. In south-eastern England it also occurs in saltmarshes, growing in low-marsh sites on coarse sand and above this on moderately organic soils, frequently where drift-litter accumulates. Lowland.

Trends *L. crithmoides* is much better recorded now than before 1960. Its known distribution is stable or possibly increasing due to more systematic recording, with most losses from outlying squares having occurred in the 19th century.

Biogeography Mediterranean-Atlantic element; it reaches its northern limit in Scotland.

Key refs Malloch & Okusanya (1979), Okusanya (1979a), Okusanya (1979b), Okusanya (1979c), Stewart *et al.* (1994).

G. HALLIDAY & K.J. WALKER

Dittrichia graveolens Stinking Fleabane

(L.) Greuter

Ne

A strongly smelling annual which formerly occurred in arable fields, arising from wool shoddy. However, all recent records are from motorways and other major roads, where it must be spread by passing vehicles, presumably, initially at least, by those coming from mainland Europe.

Trends *D. graveolens* first arose in the wild from wool shoddy in 1913 (Galashiels, Selkirkshire). There were only one or two records in the period 1970 to 2005, but since then it has spread along the motorway network in southern England (M3, M27, A34, M20), mirroring a similar spread along the motorways of central Europe.

Biogeography Native of the Mediterranean region and south-western Asia, now extending north into central and western Europe; naturalized in Australia and elsewhere.

Alien	GB	IR
2000–19	58	0
1987–99	0	0
1970–86	4	0
pre-1970	12	0

	GB	IR
Long term	No trend	No trend
Short term	⬆	No trend

Altitude (m)

- <1%
- 1–10%
- 11–30%
- 31–40%
- 41–50%
- 51–100%

Distance north (km)

☐ Apparency ☐ In flower ☐ In leaf

Key refs Rand & Leach (2007).

D.A. Pearman

Pulicaria dysenterica Common Fleabane

(L.) Bernh.

N

A perennial, stoloniferous herb of damp or wet, open habitats including damp meadows and pastures, marshes, water- and fen-meadows, tall-herb fens, by rivers, streams, canals and ditches, in dune-slacks, wet hollows and seepages on sea-cliffs, damp woodland rides, roadside verges, arable margins, setaside and waste ground. It is found on a wide range of acidic and base-rich soil types but seems to favour areas subject to disturbance that are also nutrient-rich. 0–420 m (Rassau, Breconshire).

Trends The distribution of *P. dysenterica* has increased since the 1960s, especially in northern Britain and in Ireland, possibly due to an increase in the availability of disturbed, nutrient-rich ground associated with human activities.

Biogeography Eurosiberian Southern-temperate element; it reaches its northern limit in eastern Denmark.

Native	GB	IR
2000–19	1466	397
1987–99	1407	292
1970–86	1011	69
pre-1970	1310	262

Alien	GB	IR
2000–19	13	0
1987–99	5	0
1970–86	3	0
pre-1970	3	0

	GB					IR				
Long term	⬇	⬇	◆	⬆	⬆	⬇	◆			
Short term	⬇	⬇	◆	⬆	⬆	⬇	◆	⬆	⬆	

Altitude (m)

- <1%
- 1–10%
- 11–30%
- 31–40%
- 41–50%
- 51–100%

Distance north (km)

☐ Apparency ☐ In flower ☐ In leaf

G. Halliday & K.J. Walker

N *Pulicaria vulgaris* Small Fleabane

Gaertn.

An annual herb of damp, winter-flooded hollows in unimproved grassland on New Forest 'lawns', on commons and village greens, on rutted tracks and in floodplains. Extant sites are mostly grazed or trodden by livestock, this disturbance creating the open conditions needed for seedling survival. Extreme disturbance can create population explosions occasionally running into hundreds of thousands of plants, while fluctuations may reduce populations to a handful. Lowland.

Trends Most sites for this species, which was once widespread in southern England, were lost before 1930. More recently, outside the New Forest (South Hampshire), it was lost from Wiltshire in the 1970s, was last seen in Surrey in 1996, and its last North Hampshire record was in 2003. Losses are largely due to lack of grazing on commons, the infilling of ponds and drainage, and lack of appropriate management. In the New Forest it continues to hold its own and occasionally new sites in the Avon catchment are discovered, but it is threatened on some holdings by discontinuation of commoning practices.

Biogeography Eurosiberian Temperate element; it is declining throughout Europe and now reaches its extant northern native limit in South Hampshire.

Native	GB	IR
2000–19	7	0
1987–99	9	0
1970–86	8	0
pre-1970	127	0

Alien	GB	IR
2000–19	0	0
1987–99	2	0
1970–86	0	0
pre-1970	1	0

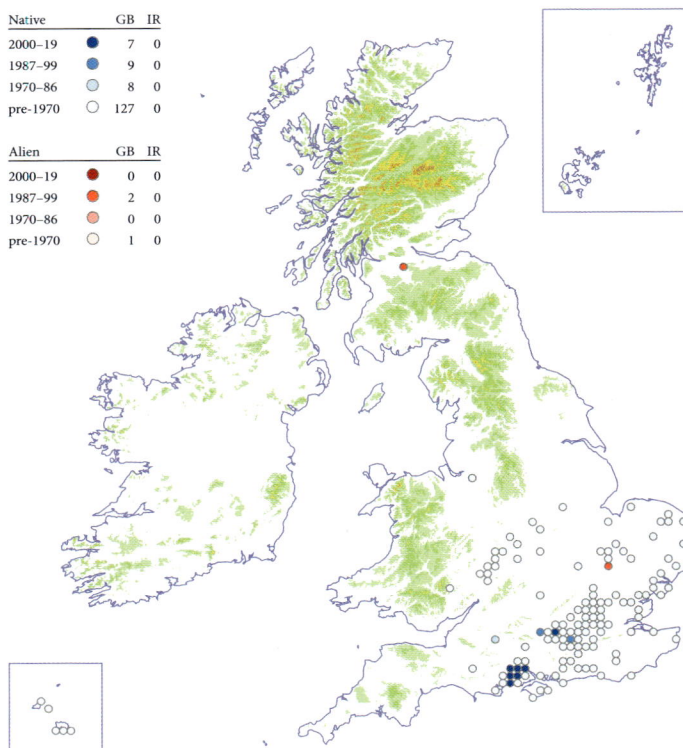

Key refs Chatters (1991), Chatters (2021), Prince & Hare (1981), Rand & Chatters (2010), Wigginton (1999).

G. HALLIDAY & M.W. RAND

Ne *Buphthalmum speciosum* Yellow Oxeye

Schreb.

A robust perennial herb, quickly spreading by rhizomes and occurring as a garden escape or occasionally as a deliberate introduction in rough grassland, and by ditchbanks, lakes and rivers. It seems to prefer damp soils and is sometimes well-naturalized. Generally lowland, but reaching 480 m at Axe Edge Moor (Derbyshire).

Trends *B. speciosum* has been cultivated since 1739 and is fairly frequently grown in gardens. It was first recorded in the wild near Croxdale (County Durham) in 1905. It might well be mistaken for some of the large species of *Inula*. It was planted at Woodwalton Fen (Huntingdonshire) in the 1930s as a nectar source for butterflies (Wells, 2003) and is now well-naturalized.

Biogeography Native of the mountains of eastern-central Europe, the Balkan Peninsula, northern Turkey and the Caucasus; widely naturalized in central Europe.

Alien	GB	IR
2000–19	76	2
1987–99	43	1
1970–86	17	0
pre-1970	21	0

Key refs Sutton (2001), Wells (2003).

G. HALLIDAY & D.A. PEARMAN

(N) *Solidago virgaurea* Goldenrod
L.

A perennial herb of free-draining, usually acidic (occasionally basic) substrates in a wide range of habitats. In the lowlands these include woods, hedgebanks, heaths, banks and coastal cliff-tops; in the uplands, cliff ledges, rocks by waterfalls, rocky streamsides, tall-herb communities in gullies, limestone pavements, montane grass-heath and fell-field. 0–1,140 m (Cairntoul, South Aberdeenshire).

Trends Many populations of *S. virgaurea* in lowland Britain have disappeared since the 1960s due to habitat loss and it is now a very localized species in areas dominated by intensive agriculture. Upland populations appear to have fared much better although it is likely to have suffered localized declines due to overgrazing and moorland burning. It is a very variable species, with many different ecotypes, although only two have so far been recognized in Britain (subsp. *virgaurea*; subsp. *minuta*).

Biogeography Eurasian Boreo-temperate element.

Native	GB	IR
2000–19	1604	449
1987–99	1659	394
1970–86	1101	61
pre-1970	1785	344

Alien	GB	IR
2000–19	6	0
1987–99	4	0
1970–86	3	0
pre-1970	2	0

Key refs Grime *et al.* (2007), Halliday (1997).

G. HALLIDAY & K.J. WALKER

(Ne) *Solidago canadensis* Canadian Goldenrod
L.

A tall, rhizomatous perennial herb, grown in gardens and naturalized on roadsides, by railways and on river banks, waste ground, refuse tips and spoil heaps, uncultivated arable margins on a wide range of soil types but most frequent on light, sandy or chalky soils. Garden throw-outs can be very persistent; the plants are fertile and spread by seed. Generally lowland, but reaching 329 m at Warslow (Staffordshire).

Trends *S. canadensis* was introduced into cultivation in Britain in 1648, and it was very popular in gardens, although now possibly eclipsed by cultivated hybrids. It was recorded in the wild in 1849 in Bristol, but did not become widespread until 1930. Although formerly confused with *S. gigantea*, the maps are probably reliable in indicating that *S. canadensis* is the more common of the two species in southern Britain. It increased dramatically in the second half of the 20th century, but much less so since.

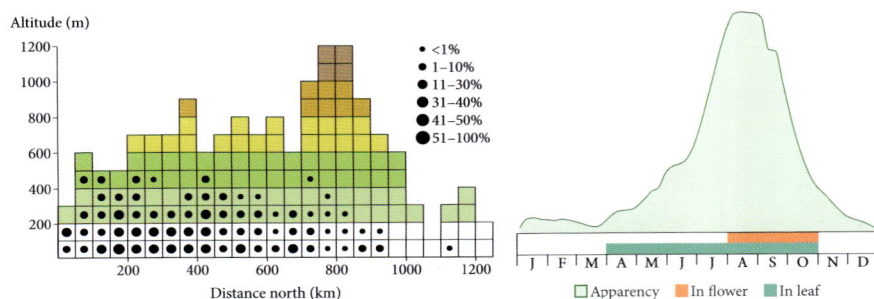

Biogeography Native of North America; widely naturalized in Europe.

Alien	GB	IR
2000–19	1038	15
1987–99	873	21
1970–86	505	4
pre-1970	342	0

Key refs Werner *et al.* (1980).

G. HALLIDAY & K.J. WALKER

Ne *Solidago gigantea* Early Goldenrod
Aiton

A tall, rhizomatous perennial herb, grown in gardens and naturalized in waste places, by active and disused railways, on roadside verges, riverbanks, refuse tips, old pits and in new woodlands and plantations on a wide range of soil types. Most plants in the wild originate from the dumping of garden rubbish and probably spread further by seed. Generally lowland, but reaching 328 m north of Moffat (Dumfriesshire).

Trends *S. gigantea* was cultivated in Britain by 1758, and it is now commonly grown in gardens. It was known from the wild by 1909 but, like *S. canadensis*, it did not become widespread until after 1930. It has increased dramatically since the 1960s but possibly less so since 2000. It often occurs with *S. canadensis*, especially on refuse tips, but is much less common.

Biogeography Native of North America; widely naturalized in Europe.

Alien	GB	IR
2000–19	797	15
1987–99	566	2
1970–86	287	0
pre-1970	128	1

G. Halliday & K.J. Walker

Ne *Symphyotrichum* Michaelmas-daisies
Nees

These perennial herbs are often naturalized on hedgebanks, roadsides, railways, rubbish tips, waste ground and also riverbanks, lakesides, saltmarshes and in fens. Most colonies arise from discarded garden material, followed by rhizomatous spread or regeneration by seed. 0–345 m (Garrigill, Cumberland).

Trends This map includes the species of *Symphyotrichum* of North American origin, and their hybrids. These have been grown in Britain since 1710 and are very difficult to separate. Plants are often recorded as *Symphyotrichum* agg., and these and more precisely determined records are mapped here. *S. schreberi* was known from one site in Renfrewshire and *S. laeve* is a rare escape; the other three species and two hybrids are mapped separately. The maps must be regarded as provisional.

Biogeography Natives of North America.

Alien	GB	IR
2000–19	1133	51
1987–99	1068	37
1970–86	546	14
pre-1970	456	12

Key refs Oliver (1998).

T.D. Dines

Ne *Symphyotrichum novae-angliae* Hairy Michaelmas-daisy
(L.) G.L.Nesom

A roughly hairy, clump-forming perennial herb naturalized on waste ground, by railways and on roadside verges. Lowland.

Trends Introduced into cultivation in 1710, *S. novae-angliae* is commonly grown in gardens, but being vigorous and long-lived, any excess garden material tends to be dumped surreptitiously and it readily becomes established. It is likely that further spread by seed from these initial colonies takes place. It was first recorded from the wild in 1823. Its overall distribution appears stable although it may be increasing in and around London as a garden escape.

Biogeography Native of eastern North America; widely naturalized in central Europe.

Alien	GB	IR
2000–19	46	0
1987–99	48	1
1970–86	24	0
pre-1970	39	0

G. HALLIDAY & K.J. WALKER

Hy *Symphyotrichum laeve × novi-belgii = S. ×versicolor*
(Willd.) G.L.Nesom

Late Michaelmas-daisy

A perennial herb, rather variable but always intermediate between the parents and usually with bluish-purple ligules. Naturalized colonies of the hybrid are recorded from wet and dry, inland and coastal habitats, including sand dunes, the upper edges of saltmarshes, coastal scrub, reed-swamps, lake, river, stream and canalsides, hedgebanks and roadside verges, railways, waste ground and refuse tips. 0–345 m (Garrigill, Cumberland).

A cultivated hybrid (alien × alien).

Trends This vigorous hybrid originated in cultivation in Britain in 1790, and was first recorded from the wild in 1817 at Park Place Wood (Berkshire). As with most alien *Symphyotrichum* taxa, opinions differ markedly on its frequency, reflecting the taxonomic problems posed by these plants; hybrids appear to form a complete spectrum between the parents, presumably as a result of back-crossing. However, actual proof of this, and of the fertility of the primary hybrids, is lacking.

Biogeography A hybrid of garden origin; it is not known in North America but is widely naturalized in central Europe.

	GB	IR
2000–19	149	0
1987–99	258	1
1970–86	43	2
pre-1970	32	0

Key refs Stace *et al.* (2015).

C.A. STACE, C.D. PRESTON & D.A. PEARMAN

Ne *Symphyotrichum novi-belgii* Confused Michaelmas-daisy
(L.) G.L.Nesom

A rhizomatous, partially winter-green, perennial herb, grown in gardens for its autumnal display and widely naturalized on hedgebanks, railway sidings, roadsides, refuse tips and waste ground. In addition, it sometimes occurs on riverbanks, lakesides and in fen vegetation. Lowland.

Trends *S. novi-belgii* was introduced as a garden plant in 1710. It was recorded in the wild by 1860 and the extant population at Wicken Fen (Cambridgeshire) was found in 1864. It is a very variable plant, with many cultivars, and is much hybridized with other species. As a consequence, it has been much over-recorded for S. ×*salignum* and, no doubt, also for S. ×*versicolor*.

Biogeography Native of eastern North America; widely naturalized in north-western and central Europe.

Alien	GB	IR
2000–19	450	12
1987–99	472	5
1970–86	276	7
pre-1970	233	5

Key refs Briggs *et al.* (1989).

G. HALLIDAY & K.J. WALKER

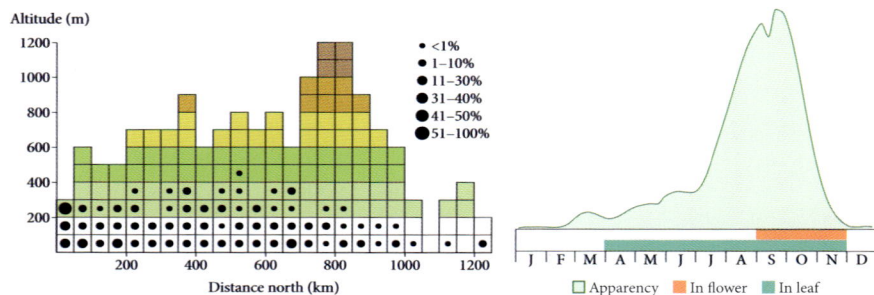

Hy *Symphyotrichum novi-belgii* × *lanceolatum* = S. ×*salignum*
(Willd.) G.L.Nesom

Common Michaelmas-daisy

A vigorous hybrid which has become widely naturalized, often as extensive colonies, in a similar range of habitats to those of S. ×*versicolor*, including river and lakeside habitats, but also in drier sites on sand dunes, in grassland and scrub, in commons and heathland. 0–305 m (Hardendale, Westmorland).

A cultivated hybrid (alien × alien).

Trends This hybrid is thought to have been introduced into cultivation in Britain in 1815, and was first recorded in the wild in 1861 at Redgrave Fen (East Suffolk). It is much confused with both its parents; for example, a famous clone which had been recorded at Wicken Fen (Cambridgeshire) since 1864 as S. ×*salignum* was shown to be S. *novi-belgii* by Briggs *et al.* (1989).

Some of the taxonomic problems might arise from back-crossing, as the hybrid is reportedly somewhat fertile. It is probably under-recorded.

Biogeography A hybrid of garden origin; widely naturalized in northern and central Europe.

	GB	IR
2000–19	282	11
1987–99	360	6
1970–86	93	2
pre-1970	50	3

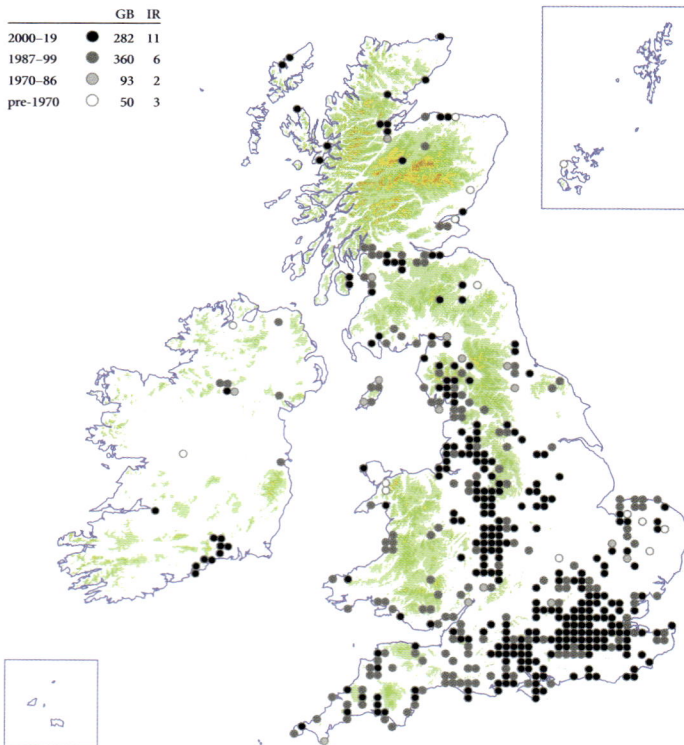

Key refs Briggs *et al.* (1989), Stace *et al.* (2015).

C.A. STACE, C.D. PRESTON & D.A. PEARMAN

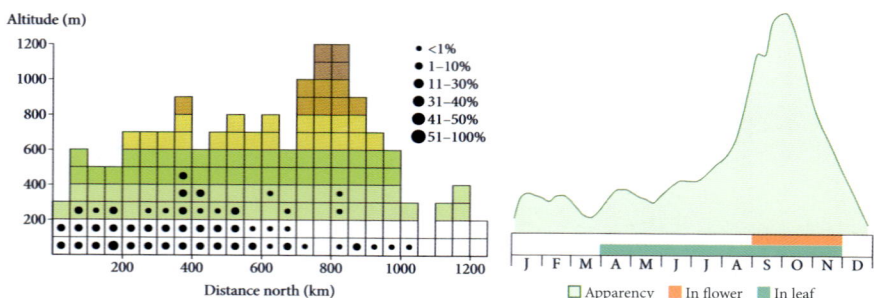

Ne *Symphyotrichum lanceolatum* Narrow-leaved Michaelmas-daisy
(Willd.) G.L.Nesom

A rhizomatous, partially winter-green perennial herb, established along railways and riverbanks, on roadsides and by car parks and on waste ground and refuse tips. Lowland.

Trends *S. lanceolatum* has been cultivated since 1811 and was recorded from the wild by 1860. According to Stace (2019) it is second only to *S. ×salignum* in frequency in Britain, yet several county Floras record it as rare. This may indicate regional variation, but is more likely to reflect under-recording. Its known distribution has certainly increased since 2000 due to better recording of michaelmas-daisies in general. Most occurrences have arisen from garden outcasts, but it may have been accidentally introduced by North American servicemen in Wiltshire (Oliver, 1998).

Biogeography Native of eastern North America; widely naturalized in western and central Europe.

Alien		GB	IR
2000–19	●	266	14
1987–99	●	185	3
1970–86	●	51	2
pre-1970	○	49	1

Key refs Oliver (1998).

	<1%
●	1–10%
●	11–30%
●	31–40%
●	41–50%
●	51–100%

Altitude (m) / Distance north (km)

Apparency   In flower   In leaf

G. HALLIDAY & K.J. WALKER

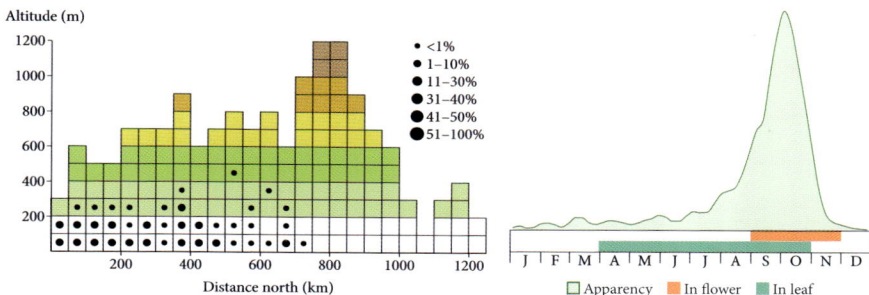

N *Galatella linosyris* Goldilocks Aster
(L.) Rchb.f.

A perennial herb of shallow soil in open, grassy habitats on limestone sea-cliffs and rocky slopes, cliff-top grassland and wind-pruned heath overlying limestone. It is a poor competitor, and is usually intolerant of heavy grazing, although in Pembrokeshire it is found in low-growing, sheep-grazed, cliff-top grassland and heath. It seems to be self-incompatible and some small populations appear to represent single, self-sterile clones. Plants grown in cultivation can spread vigorously when free of competition. Lowland.

Trends The distribution of *G. linosyris* is stable at the hectad scale, but this masks localized declines. Of the dozen sites known it has not been seen on Humphrey Head (Westmorland) since 2007 and on the Great Orme (Caernarvonshire) all its populations are declining as a result

of scrub encroachment (McCarthy & Bratton, 2010). Less is known about populations elsewhere but all are critically small and susceptible to scrub encroachment where not grazed.

Biogeography European Temperate element, with a continental distribution in western Europe; it reaches its northern limit on Öland and Gotland.

	GB	IR
Long term	No trend	No trend
Short term	No trend	No trend

Native		GB	IR
2000–19	●	7	0
1987–99	●	7	0
1970–86	●	7	0
pre-1970	○	8	0

Alien		GB	IR
2000–19	●	0	0
1987–99	●	1	0
1970–86	●	1	0
pre-1970	○	6	0

Key refs McCarthy & Bratton (2010), Wigginton (1999).

	<1%
●	1–10%
●	11–30%
●	31–40%
●	41–50%
●	51–100%

Altitude (m) / Distance north (km)

Apparency   In flower   In leaf

G. HALLIDAY, M.J. WIGGINTON & K.J. WALKER

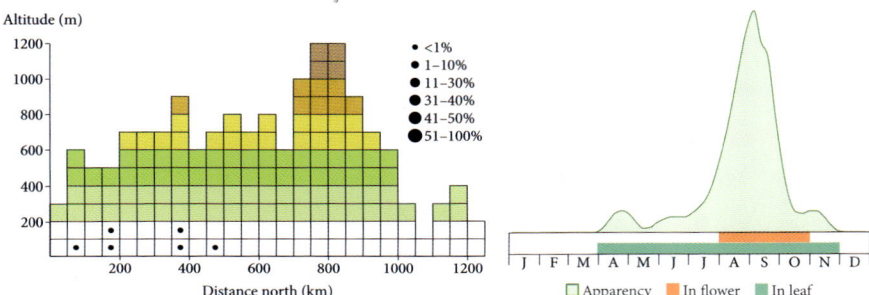

(N) *Tripolium pannonicum* Sea Aster
(Jacq.) Dobrocz.

An annual, biennial to short-lived perennial herb occurring at low elevations in ungrazed or lightly grazed saltmarshes, especially along creek-sides, and also on muddy sea-banks, tidal riverbanks (in some cases a long way inland) and in brackish ditches. In western Britain and Ireland it also grows amongst rocks and on exposed sea-cliffs. It also occurs very locally in inland saltmarshes and beside salt-treated roads. Lowland.

Trends The distribution of *T. pannonicum* has not changed appreciably since the 1960s and it has not spread inland in the same way as many other halophytes have since the 1970s. The rayless form, var. *flosculosum*, was mapped by Perring & Sell (1968).

Biogeography Eurasian Temperate element.

Native	GB	IR
2000–19	626	262
1987–99	577	229
1970–86	381	96
pre-1970	601	183

Alien	GB	IR
2000–19	4	0
1987–99	2	0
1970–86	3	0
pre-1970	6	0

Key refs Clapham *et al.* (1942), Lee (1977).

G. HALLIDAY

(Ne) *Erigeron speciosus* Garden Fleabane
(Lindl.) DC.

A perennial herb, very popular in gardens from where it escapes and sometimes establishes on walls, rough and disturbed ground and dunes, particularly in coastal areas. Lowland.

Trends *E. speciosus* was first noted in the wild in 1921 (Bexhill, East Sussex), and on coastal dunes in South Lancashire in 1951 where it still persists. It has a wide distribution in England but is not so far recorded in the other countries, except for a single site in north Wales. It is likely to be very unevenly recorded.

Biogeography Native of western North America.

Alien	GB	IR
2000–19	50	0
1987–99	8	0
1970–86	2	0
pre-1970	2	0

M.W. RAND

Ne *Erigeron glaucus* Seaside Daisy

Ker Gawl.

A decumbent perennial herb found as a garden escape in pavement cracks and on walls, banks, sea-cliffs and shingle. Lowland.

Trends This species has been cultivated in Britain since 1812 and is now commonly grown in gardens, particularly near the coast. It was first recorded from the wild in 1942 on sea-cliffs at Bournemouth (South Hampshire). In the last two decades it has extended its range into northern Scotland and Ireland; there are now more inland sites and they are no longer concentrated in a few metropolitan areas. It is invasive on shingle and soft cliffs on the south coast of England.

Biogeography Native of North America.

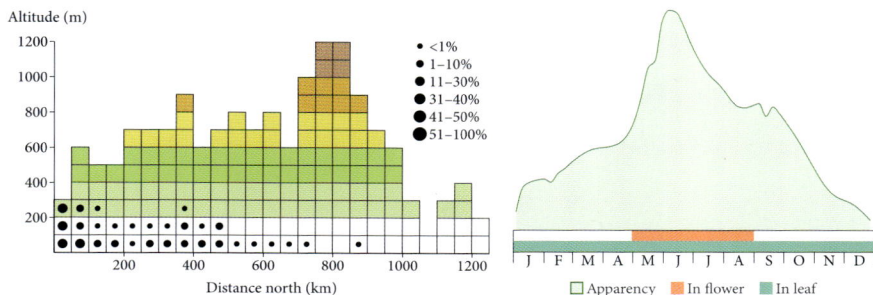

	GB	IR
Long term	No trend	No trend
Short term	↑	↑

Alien	GB	IR
2000–19	345	22
1987–99	173	1
1970–86	36	0
pre-1970	38	0

Altitude (m)

- • <1%
- • 1–10%
- ● 11–30%
- ● 31–40%
- ● 41–50%
- ● 51–100%

J F M A M J J A S O N D

☐ Apparency ▬ In flower ▬ In leaf

G. Halliday & M.W. Rand

N *Erigeron borealis* Alpine Fleabane

(Vierh.) Simmons

A perennial rhizomatous herb of basic montane cliff ledges which are adjacent to grazed, herb-rich grassland. It only occurs in Caenlochan (Angus) and on mica-schists in the Breadalbane Hills (Mid Perthshire), typically in south-facing locations where most direct sunlight is received during the morning. These surviving sites are inaccessible to sheep and deer; plants which establish below crags do not survive long under intensive grazing. From 640 m on Craig Maud (Angus) to 1,100 m on Creag an Fhitich (Mid Perthshire).

Trends Although *E. borealis* was lost from a number of sites in the eastern Highlands of Scotland before 1930, its current 10 km square distribution appears to be stable. The size of some populations fluctuates widely from year to year, and long-term trends are difficult to determine due to the

challenges involved with monitoring plants located in remote areas and on high cliff ledges. Declines have been reported at Caenlochan since 1986, but the Ben Lawers population has been relatively stable since 1981.

Biogeography Eurosiberian Arctic-montane element; it reaches its southern limit in Scotland, being replaced by the very similar *E. neglectus* in the Alps.

	GB	IR
Long term	No trend	No trend
Short term	No trend	No trend

Native	GB	IR
2000–19	5	0
1987–99	6	0
1970–86	5	0
pre-1970	10	0

Altitude (m)

- • <1%
- • 1–10%
- ● 11–30%
- ● 31–40%
- ● 41–50%
- ● 51–100%

J F M A M J J A S O N D

☐ Apparency ▬ In flower ▬ In leaf

Key refs Cole (2012), Wigginton (1999).

S.H. Watts, G. Halliday & M.J. Wigginton

Ne *Erigeron karvinskianus* Mexican Fleabane
DC.

A perennial herb, well-established on walls, rock outcrops and cliffs, in cracks in pavements and on stony banks, to which it has usually spread by seed from nearby gardens. Lowland.

Trends *E. karvinskianus* has been cultivated in Britain since 1856 and is widely grown in frost-free areas, particularly in the Channel Islands, in coastal areas of south-western England and south Wales and in sheltered urban sites. It was first recorded as naturalized in 1891, at St Peter Port, Guernsey, where it was locally abundant by the end of the 19th century. The marked increase noted in the 2002 *Atlas* has continued, and has resulted in a scattering of new sites in coastal Scotland; elsewhere it has consolidated its position, particularly in inland areas. On species-rich anthropogenic sites such as old walls it can be invasive, eliminating almost all other taxa.

Biogeography Native of Central America (Mexico); naturalized in western and southern Europe.

Alien	GB	IR
2000–19	926	98
1987–99	290	32
1970–86	79	8
pre-1970	85	8

Key refs McClintock (1975).

G. HALLIDAY & M.W. RAND

N *Erigeron acris* Blue Fleabane
L.

An annual or perennial herb of open, well-drained, skeletal neutral or calcareous soils, often on warm, south-facing slopes. Habitats include sand dunes, sand- and gravel-pits, spoil and waste heaps from quarries, railway ballast, industrial waste and cinders. It also grows on rock outcrops, especially of chalk and limestone and on mortared walls. 0–430 m (Banffshire).

Trends The overall 10 km square range of *E. acris* has increased markedly since the 1960s, especially in the English Midlands, northern England, Scotland and Ireland, where it largely occurs in disturbed, anthropogenic habitats. It was formerly treated as alien in Scotland, but is found in the same habitats as farther south, and so has been mapped as a native here.

Biogeography Circumpolar Boreo-temperate element.

Native	GB	IR
2000–19	946	79
1987–99	795	43
1970–86	505	10
pre-1970	742	58

Alien	GB	IR
2000–19	0	0
1987–99	0	0
1970–86	0	0
pre-1970	1	0

Key refs Grime *et al.* (2007).

G. HALLIDAY & K.J. WALKER

Ne *Erigeron canadensis* Canadian Fleabane
L.

An erect annual herb of well-drained, open habitats in urban areas such as pavements, waste places, walls and railway ballast. It also occurs as a weed on cultivated land, and on coastal sand dunes and sandy ground inland. 0–369 m (Dylife, Montgomeryshire).

Trends This species has been known in the London area since 1690. Its range has expanded markedly in Britain since the 1960s, and it was first recorded in Ireland in 1983. That expansion has continued in the last two decades and, although still very much a plant of the lowlands, it occurs much more frequently now in northern Britain and in Ireland. Where it occurs with *E. floribundus* and *E. sumatrensis*, there are often marked fluctuations in the relative sizes of populations and in some years it is almost totally replaced by them.

Biogeography Native of North America; naturalized throughout Europe and in similar climatic regions almost worldwide.

Alien	GB	IR
2000–19	1262	61
1987–99	983	11
1970–86	494	2
pre-1970	686	0

G. HALLIDAY & M.W. RAND

Ne *Erigeron floribundus* Bilbao Fleabane
(Kunth) Sch.Bip.

An erect annual herb of open habitats in urban areas such as pavements, waste places, walls and disturbed roadsides, but spreading more widely in rural areas than either *E. canadensis* or *E. sumatrensis*. It is also a frequent weed of cultivated land. Lowland.

Trends The first records for *E. floribundus* in our area were made in Rosbercon, Ireland in 1992 (Reynolds, 1997) and in and around Southampton in Britain in 1994 (Stanley, 1996). For the next few years most British records were centered around southern Hampshire and London, but by 2010 it had spread to much of southern England and southern Wales, the Midlands and south-eastern Ireland, and it continues to advance northwards and westwards. It is a highly variable plant and may comprise more than one taxon.

Biogeography Native of South America.

Alien	GB	IR
2000–19	576	177
1987–99	21	3
1970–86	0	0
pre-1970	1	0

Key refs Reynolds (1997), Stanley (1996).

M.W. RAND

Ne *Erigeron sumatrensis* Guernsey Fleabane
Retz.

A tall and very conspicuous annual herb of well-drained, open and disturbed ground, such as pavements, waste ground, the disturbed edges of paths, tracks and roads, active and disused railways, docks, chiefly in urban areas but also on coastal sand and shingle and in set-aside and fallow fields on light soils in warmer rural regions. It also formerly occurred as a wool casual. Lowland.

Trends The first record for *E. sumatrensis* in our area was from Guernsey in 1961. It was found naturalized in South Essex in 1974 and was well established in the London area by 1984. It spread rapidly in parts of southern England in the 1990s, and was first recorded in Ireland in 1990. This rapid spread has continued northwards and westwards over the last two decades, although it is still rare over much of northern Britain, Wales and Ireland. Plants with smaller capitula are rare but may represent a different taxon.

Biogeography Native of South America; widely naturalized in Europe.

Alien	GB	IR
2000–19	759	24
1987–99	175	1
1970–86	9	0
pre-1970	4	0

	GB	IR
Long term	No trend	No trend
Short term		

Key refs Wurzell (1988).

G. Halliday & M.W. Rand

Altitude (m)

- <1%
- 1–10%
- 11–30%
- 31–40%
- 41–50%
- 51–100%

Distance north (km)

☐ Apparency ☐ In flower ☐ In leaf

Ne *Erigeron bonariensis* Argentine Fleabane
L.

An annual herb of cultivated land, waste ground, railway sidings and docks. It arose formerly mostly from wool shoddy and populations were usually casual, but its routes of introduction are now more diverse and it is more frequently naturalized (*e.g.* in Middlesex). Lowland.

Trends Although *E. bonariensis* was being cultivated in Britain by 1732, it most likely originated in the wild from wool shoddy. The first record in 1843 (Kew Bridge, Surrey) appears to have been of a casual occurrence and naturalized plants were not reported until 1993 (Middlesex). The species is sometimes confused with *E. sumatrensis*. Its distribution is increasing.

Biogeography Native of tropical America; widely naturalized elsewhere.

Alien	GB	IR
2000–19	90	2
1987–99	11	0
1970–86	7	0
pre-1970	16	0

	GB	IR
Long term	No trend	No trend
Short term		No trend

Altitude (m)

- <1%
- 1–10%
- 11–30%
- 31–40%
- 41–50%
- 51–100%

Distance north (km)

☐ Apparency ☐ In flower ☐ In leaf

T.D. Dines & M.W. Rand

Ne *Callistephus chinensis* China Aster
(L.) Nees

An annual herb, commonly grown
in gardens, found as a garden
escape or throw-out on refuse tips
and waste ground. Lowland.

Trends *C. chinensis* was grown in
Britain by 1732 and is a popular annual
bedding plant in gardens. It had
been recorded from the wild by 1903
(Leith, Midlothian). It was formerly
a fairly uncommon escape, but due
to much work by plant breeders, it is
now much more commonly grown.

Biogeography Native of China.

	GB	IR
Long term	No trend	No trend
Short term	⬆	No trend

Alien		GB	IR
2000–19	●	28	0
1987–99	●	4	1
1970–86	●	10	0
pre-1970	○	21	0

Altitude (m) / Distance north (km)

● <1%
● 1–10%
● 11–30%
● 31–40%
● 41–50%
● 51–100%

☐ Apparency ☐ In flower ☐ In leaf

Key refs Sutton (2001).

T.D. DINES & D. PEARMAN

Hy *Olearia avicenniifolia × moschata = O. ×haastii* Daisy-bush
Hook.f.

An evergreen shrub recorded from
scattered localities, especially in
coastal regions. It is known as a garden
outcast, relic of amenity planting and
occasionally as a self-sown plant in
woodland, scrub, rough grassland
and waste ground. Reproduction by
seed is occasional, and seedlings have
been recorded on walls. Lowland.

A cultivated hybrid (alien × alien).

Trends This hardy hybrid has been
cultivated in British gardens since 1858,
and continues to be extremely popular.
It was not recorded from the wild until
1978, when it was found at Knock Bay
(Wigtownshire); self-sown seedlings
were first recorded on the harbour wall
in Weymouth (Dorset) in 1979. There
are many more records than when
mapped in the 2002 *Atlas*, although in
a number of cases it is not clear if they

are of naturalized plants and, more
likely, the map instead reflects a greater
interest in recording planted specimens.

Biogeography Native of New Zealand,
where occasional individual hybrid
plants are found.

	GB	IR
Long term	No trend	No trend
Short term	⬆	No trend

		GB	IR
2000–19	●	58	1
1987–99	●	16	1
1970–86	●	10	0
pre-1970	○	3	0

Altitude (m) / Distance north (km)

● <1%
● 1–10%
● 11–30%
● 31–40%
● 41–50%
● 51–100%

☐ Apparency ☐ In flower ☐ In leaf

Key refs Stace *et al.* (2015).

C.A. STACE, C.D. PRESTON & D.A. PEARMAN

Ne *Olearia macrodonta* New Zealand Holly
Baker

An evergreen shrub, found in hedges and scrub, and on roadsides, banks, sea-cliffs, sand dunes and waste ground. It is usually found as a garden escape or throw-out, and can become well-established in suitable habitats. Reproduction is by seed. Lowland.

Trends This species was first introduced to British gardens in 1884; it is now extremely popular, especially in coastal areas, and increasingly, in urban areas. By 1936 it had been recorded from the wild at Tintagel, East Cornwall, though it is always difficult to separate planted from wild plants.

Biogeography Native of New Zealand.

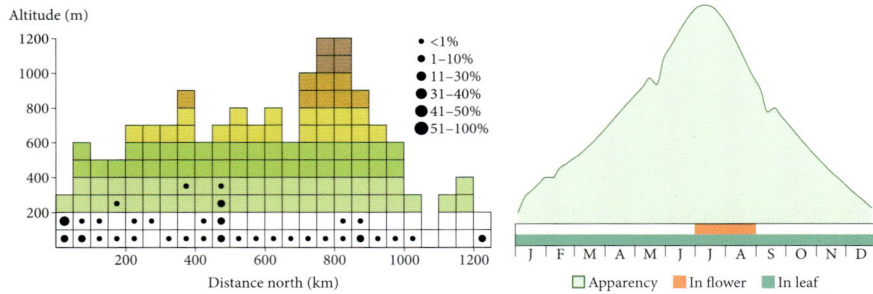

	GB	IR
Long term	No trend	No trend

Alien	GB	IR
2000–19	115	46
1987–99	45	27
1970–86	13	1
pre-1970	6	0

Key refs Sutton (2001).

G. Halliday & D.A. Pearman

- • <1%
- • 1–10%
- ● 11–30%
- ● 31–40%
- ● 41–50%
- ● 51–100%

Altitude (m) / Distance north (km)

□ Apparency ■ In flower ■ In leaf

Ne *Olearia traversii* Ake-ake
(F.Muell.) Hook.f.

An evergreen shrub or small tree which is sometimes grown as hedging in areas with a mild climate and which occurs as a garden escape in rough grassland. It can become naturalized, reproducing by seed, although it can be shy to flower. Lowland.

Trends *O. traversii* was introduced into cultivation in Britain in 1887. It is recorded in the wild with increasing frequency, with the first record in 1966 (west of Dingle, South Kerry)

Biogeography Native of the Chatham Islands.

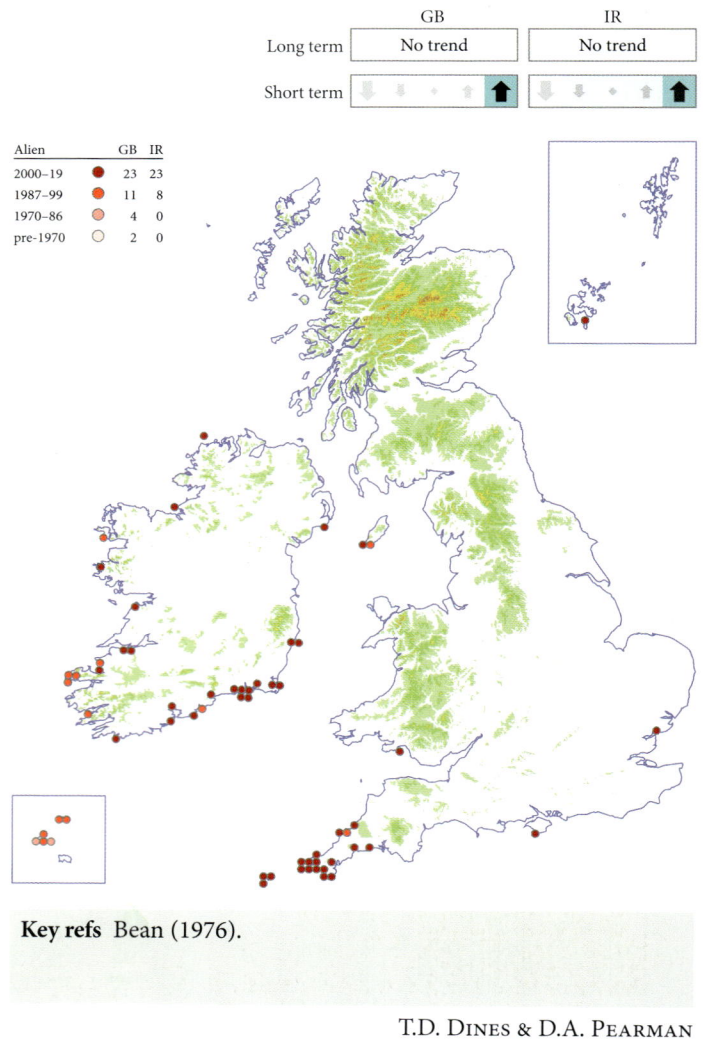

	GB	IR
Long term	No trend	No trend

Alien	GB	IR
2000–19	23	23
1987–99	11	8
1970–86	4	0
pre-1970	2	0

Key refs Bean (1976).

- • <1%
- • 1–10%
- ● 11–30%
- ● 31–40%
- ● 41–50%
- ● 51–100%

Altitude (m) / Distance north (km)

□ Apparency ■ In flower ■ In leaf

T.D. Dines & D.A. Pearman

Bellis perennis Daisy
L.

A rosette-forming, winter-green, shortly stoloniferous perennial which grows in mown or heavily grazed or trampled grassland. It occurs in practically all types of neutral and calcareous grassland but it does best in those that are relatively wet for at least part of the year. It is most familiar as a weed of lawns and recreational areas, roadside verges and pastures, but more natural habitats include stream banks, lake margins, dune-slacks and the margins of upland flushes. 0–915 m (Caenlochan, Angus).

Trends *B. perennis* is almost ubiquitous at the 10 km square resolution in Britain and Ireland and as such shows virtually no change in its overall distribution since the 1960s except for small increases in montane and coastal regions due to more systematic recording.

Biogeography European Temperate element; widely naturalized outside its native range.

Native	GB	IR
2000–19	2821	1003
1987–99	2783	967
1970–86	1893	180
pre-1970	2690	900

Key refs Grime *et al.* (2007).

G. HALLIDAY

Tanacetum parthenium Feverfew
(L.) Sch.Bip.

An aromatic winter-green perennial herb, formerly grown as a medicinal herb and still widely cultivated as an ornamental in gardens and found naturalized on pavements, at the base of walls, on tracksides, refuse tips, waste ground and as a weed of gardens and allotments. It seeds freely, but has a poorly formed pappus, and disperses for only short distances; it is therefore most frequent near human habitations. It can appear in pavements after glyphosate treatment. Several cultivars occur including forms with double flowers and golden foliage. 0–570 m (Hartside Quarry, Cumberland).

Trends *T. parthenium* was being grown in gardens for medicinal use by medieval times. Its distribution and altitudinal range may not have not changed significantly since the 1960s but recent recording of aliens has been more systematic, leading to a consolidation of its known range in some areas. It has benefitted from the increased urbanization in many lowland regions.

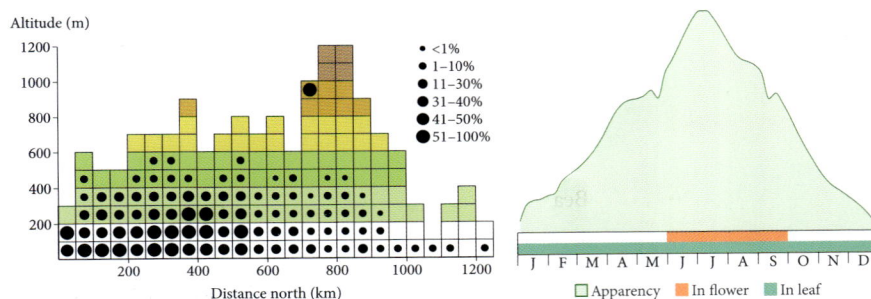

Biogeography Apparently native to the Balkan Peninsula; now widespread in temperate regions throughout the world.

Alien	GB	IR
2000–19	2001	373
1987–99	1864	338
1970–86	1046	45
pre-1970	1683	138

H.J. KILLICK

(N) *Tanacetum vulgare* Tansy
L.

An aromatic, rhizomatous perennial herb of nutrient-rich grassy places by rivers, roads and railways, and on waste ground. 0–380 m (Glenlivet, Banffshire).

Native in Britain and the Channel Islands and a neophyte in Ireland.

Trends *T. vulgare* was grown in medieval gardens as a medicinal or culinary herb, and escapes from cultivation are widely naturalized. For this reason it is often impossible to differentiate native plants from those of garden origin, and all those in Britain are mapped without status; it is considered to be alien in Ireland. There has been no significant change in its distribution.

Biogeography Eurasian Boreo-temperate element, but naturalized in North America so distribution is now Circumpolar Boreo-temperate.

	GB	IR
2000–19 ●	1767	141
1987–99 ●	1659	116
1970–86 ●	1009	26
pre-1970 ○	1624	179

Altitude (m)
Distance north (km)

● <1%
● 1–10%
● 11–30%
● 31–40%
● 41–50%
● 51–100%

□ Apparency   ■ In flower   ■ In leaf

Key refs Mabey (1996).

H.J. KILLICK

(Ar) *Artemisia vulgaris* Mugwort
L.

A tall aromatic perennial herb of waste places, refuse tips, rough ground, farmyards, roadside verges and waysides, usually on relatively alkaline, fertile soils. The seeds, lacking a pappus, are often spread by human activities, especially in urban areas and along road and rail systems. Generally lowland, but reaching 350 m north of Shap summit (Westmorland), 410 m in Llyn y Gwaith (Cardiganshire) and 465 m in Flash (Staffordshire).

Trends The spread of *A. vulgaris* reflects its preference for anthropogenic habitats and its drought tolerance. However, the species remains rare in some Scottish counties.

Biogeography As an archaeophyte, *A. vulgaris* has a Eurosiberian Temperate distribution; it is widely naturalized outside this range.

Alien	GB	IR
2000–19 ●	1927	225
1987–99 ●	1906	280
1970–86 ●	1234	44
pre-1970 ○	1807	361

Altitude (m)
Distance north (km)

● <1%
● 1–10%
● 11–30%
● 31–40%
● 41–50%
● 51–100%

□ Apparency   ■ In flower   ■ In leaf

Key refs Braithwaite *et al.* (2006), Grime *et al.* (2007).

H.J. KILLICK & P.A. STROH

Ne *Artemisia verlotiorum* Chinese Mugwort
Lamotte

A tall rhizomatous perennial herb, naturalized and locally abundant on waysides, and in waste places and rough ground. It rarely sets seed, and its spread is often by detached pieces of rhizome. Lowland.

Trends *A. verlotiorum* was first collected from the wild in Britain in 1908 (Hounslow, Middlesex) but not recognized as a distinct species until 1938–39. By 1950 it was well-established in Surrey and Middlesex and it is now most abundant there and near Tyneside. By 1987 it had hybridized with *A. vulgaris*. Elsewhere it has continued to appear scattered in many places but with substantial turnover, with many mid- to late 20th century records not refound this century.

Biogeography Native of south-western China; widely naturalized in western and central Europe and other continents.

	GB	IR
Long term	No trend	No trend
Short term	⬇ ⬇ ◆ ⬆ ⬆	No trend

Alien		GB	IR
2000–19	●	97	0
1987–99	●	61	0
1970–86	●	53	0
pre-1970	○	64	0

Altitude (m) — Distance north (km)
●<1% ●1–10% ●11–30% ●31–40% ●41–50% ●51–100%

☐ Apparency ☐ In flower ☐ In leaf

Key refs Brenan (1950), Burton (1983), James *et al.* (2000).

H.J. KILLICK

Ar *Artemisia absinthium* Wormwood
L.

A tall, grey, aromatic, wind-pollinated perennial herb grown in some gardens and allotments, found as a relic or self-sown in open industrial areas, base- and nutrient-rich skeletal soils, waste and rough ground, waysides, dry banks, railway sidings, farmyards, refuse tips, gravel-pits and quarries. It is often persistent, especially in urban and maritime locations where it is less at risk from frost damage. Cattle and horses avoid it. 0–375 m (Hengwym Annedd, Cardiganshire).

Trends *A. absinthium*, which was being grown in British gardens by medieval times (Harvey, 1981), has been cultivated for medicine, absinthe and flavouring; it was also a folk cure for insomnia. It is surviving well in its English Midlands heartland, but declines have been reported outside of this core area since fieldwork for the 2002 *Atlas* commenced. It has become a scarce and threatened species in Ireland.

Biogeography As an archaeophyte, *A. absinthium* has a Eurosiberian Temperate distribution; it is widely naturalized outside this range.

	GB	IR
Long term	⬇ ⬇ ◆ ⬆ ⬆	⬇ ◆ ◆ ⬆
Short term	⬇ ◆ ◆ ⬆ ⬆	⬇ ◆ ◆ ⬆ ⬆

Alien		GB	IR
2000–19	●	466	5
1987–99	●	603	6
1970–86	●	443	5
pre-1970	○	796	44

Altitude (m) — Distance north (km)
●<1% ●1–10% ●11–30% ●31–40% ●41–50% ●51–100%

☐ Apparency ☐ In flower ☐ In leaf

Key refs Braithwaite *et al.* (2006), Chater (2010b), Erskine *et al.* (2018), Grime *et al.* (2007), Harvey (1981), Smith *et al.* (2016), Thomas *et al.* (1985), Trueman *et al.* (2013).

H.J. KILLICK & P.A. STROH

N *Artemisia norvegica* Norwegian Mugwort
Fr.

A small rhizomatous perennial herb of mountain tops, usually occurring in exposed situations on or near summit ridges and plateaus on bare stony ground, *Racomitrium* heath, bouldery crests of solifluction terraces, and sometimes hollows between rocks. The relative importance of sexual and vegetative reproduction in British populations is uncertain. From 700 m at Culmoor (West Ross) to 907 m at Seana Bhraigh (East Ross).

Trends This species was discovered on Cul Mor in West Ross in 1950, and subsequently on two additional summits in the same vice-county. Its populations fluctuate in size, but appear to be stable. It is one of a handful of British arctic-montane species that may go extinct as the climate warms over coming decades (Walmsley *et al.*, 2007).

Biogeography European Arctic-montane element; rare in the Arctic zonobiome and absent from mountains of central Europe.

	GB	IR
Long term	No trend	No trend
Short term	No trend	No trend

Native	GB	IR
2000–19	3	0
1987–99	3	0
1970–86	3	0
pre-1970	3	0

Key refs Wigginton (1999).

M.J. WIGGINTON & K.J. WALKER

Ne *Artemisia biennis* Slender Mugwort
Willd.

A large annual to biennial herb, found on waste ground, roadsides, muddy reservoir banks, and in pavement cracks. It arises from oil-seed, birdseed and as a grain impurity, and is sometimes naturalized, although most populations are casual. It must also be spread by bird or by human agency, and was formerly introduced with wool shoddy. Lowland.

Trends *A. biennis* was first found in the wild in 1903 (West Kent). It remains rare, but can form dense swards in suitable habitats, such as around Chew Lake reservoir in North Somerset, where it has been known since 1961.

Biogeography Native of western North America; naturalized in eastern North America and Europe.

	GB	IR
Long term	No trend	No trend
Short term	No trend	No trend

Alien	GB	IR
2000–19	9	1
1987–99	13	1
1970–86	10	0
pre-1970	31	1

Key refs Hultén (1968).

T.D. DINES & D.A. PEARMAN

N *Artemisia campestris* Field Wormwood

L.

A wind-pollinated perennial herb of infertile, sandy grassland, coastal and inland sand dunes, forest rides and tracks, and roadsides; it does not persist in tall, closed turf but sometimes reappears following disturbance. Lowland.

Native in Britain and a neophyte in Ireland.

Trends Two subspecies of *A. campestris* occur in Britain and Ireland. *A. campestris* subsp. *campestris* occurs as a native in the Breckland region of East Anglia where many populations have been lost to agriculture, forestry, building development, and succession. Only three of the original sites survive, though several new populations have been established using native seed. It requires periodic soil disturbance to persist, and numbers have recovered recently at one of its native sites (Brandon, West Suffolk) following turf-stripping. Plants identified as subsp. *maritima* found on sand dunes in Glamorganshire (Crymlyn Burrows) and in South Lancashire (Crosby-Sefton dunes) are almost certainly introductions, probably arriving as seed contaminants (Jones & Rumsey, in press).

Biogeography Eurosiberian Temperate element, with a continental distribution in western Europe.

Native	GB	IR
2000–19	2	0
1987–99	2	0
1970–86	2	0
pre-1970	11	0

Alien	GB	IR
2000–19	4	0
1987–99	4	0
1970–86	3	0
pre-1970	17	1

Key refs Clement (2006), Smith & Wilcox (2006), Wigginton (1999).

H.J. KILLICK

N *Artemisia maritima* Sea Wormwood

L.

An aromatic perennial herb typically found in the upper, drier parts of saltmarshes, as well as on shingle, sea-cliffs, waste ground and walls close to the sea, by brackish dykes of drained estuarine marshes, on the banks of tidal rivers, and rarely as an halophyte along inland roadsides. It is wind-pollinated, and rarely produces seed. Lowland.

Trends *A. maritima* was lost from many sites during the 20th century due to, for example, land reclamation and the erosion of saltmarshes ('coastal squeeze'). Its distribution now appears to be stable and it remains locally abundant in some areas. It is now better recorded, or perhaps increasing, in Ireland and in East Anglia it is spreading inland along salted road verges.

Biogeography Suboceanic Temperate element.

Native	GB	IR
2000–19	169	20
1987–99	159	9
1970–86	135	7
pre-1970	204	18

Alien	GB	IR
2000–19	0	0
1987–99	1	0
1970–86	2	0
pre-1970	1	1

Key refs Evans (2007), Leach (1984), Ryves (1984).

H.J. KILLICK

1019

Ne *Santolina chamaecyparissus* Lavender-cotton
L.

A small pale-leaved evergreen scented shrub, with yellow button-like flowers, widely cultivated as a hedging plant and for ground cover. Found as a garden outcast or self-sown in pavement cracks, brick paths and walls; it can persist on refuse tips, rough ground, and as a relic of cultivation, and has become established on some sandy shores. Lowland.

Trends This species was introduced to cultivation in Britain by 1573, and is now very widely grown in gardens. It was recorded as a garden escape by 1902 (Weir Head, East Cornwall), and on Oxford refuse tip in 1954. There were few other records before 1970 but since then its 10 km square distribution has increased. In the London area, where it has been systematically recorded, it is now very widespread; it has also spread elsewhere

in England and the Isle of Man, and to a lesser extent in Scotland and Wales. Two subspecies occur in our area (subsp. *chamaecyparissus* and subsp. *tomentosus*) but these have rarely been distinguished by recorders.

Biogeography Native of the Mediterranean region.

Alien	GB	IR
2000–19	76	1
1987–99	34	0
1970–86	14	1
pre-1970	17	1

	GB	IR
Long term	No trend	No trend
Short term	↑	No trend

Key refs Dunn (1905).

H.J. KILLICK

N *Achillea ptarmica* Sneezewort
L.

A perennial herb of damp or wet, infertile, acidic habitats on a wide range of soils, including fen- and water-meadows, rush-pasture, marshes, streamsides, wet heath, springs and flushes on hill slopes and occasionally in blanket bog and wet woodland. It is also occasionally found as a garden escape or planting (sometimes as a double-flowered form) in churchyards, and on roadsides and waste ground. 0–770 m (Cross Fell, Cumberland).

Native in Britain and Ireland and a neophyte in the Channel Islands.

Trends *A. ptarmica* has declined since the 1960s, especially in southern England, mainly due to drainage and habitat destruction as a result of changes in agricultural management. It is now a notable species in many lowland vice-counties and often listed as a

county rarity or axiophyte. Elsewhere its distribution appears to be stable or even increasing at the 10 km square resolution, for example in the Highlands of Scotland and Ireland, although this is likely due to more systematic recording rather than a genuine increase.

Biogeography Eurasian Boreo-temperate element; widely naturalized outside its native range.

Native	GB	IR
2000–19	2136	422
1987–99	2066	374
1970–86	1406	89
pre-1970	2113	372

Alien	GB	IR
2000–19	23	3
1987–99	14	1
1970–86	12	0
pre-1970	15	0

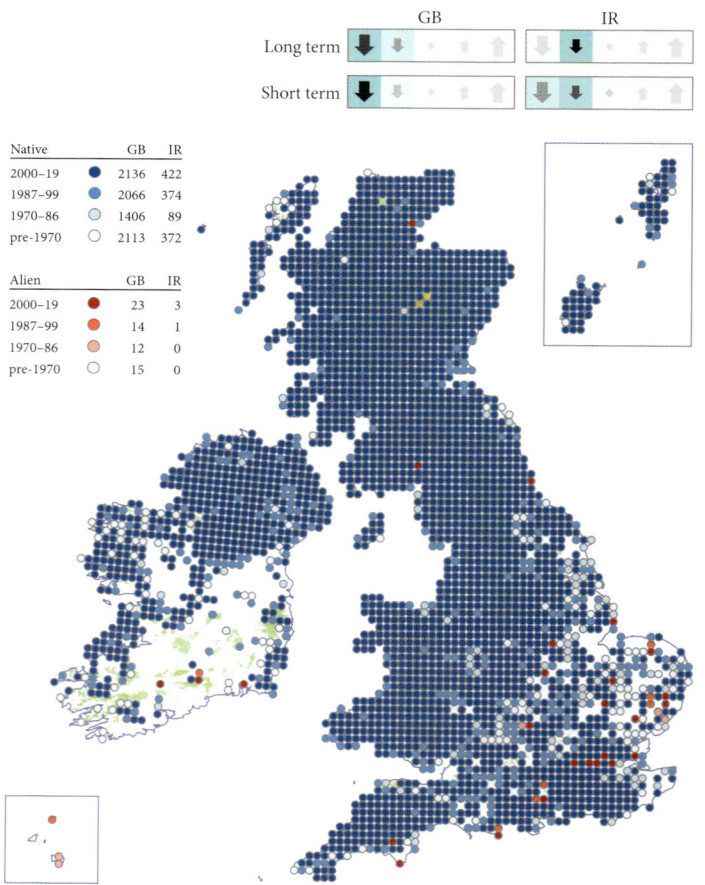

	GB	IR
Long term	↓	↓
Short term	↓	↓

Key refs Chater (2010b).

H.J. KILLICK & K.J. WALKER

N *Achillea millefolium* Yarrow
L.

A strongly scented perennial herb that grows in all kinds of grassland habitats, ranging from lawns to pastures and montane communities irrigated by melting snow-beds; also found on coastal sand dunes and stabilized shingle, waysides and waste ground. It tolerates drought, and grows in most soils except the most nutrient-poor, permanently waterlogged or strongly acidic; var. *compacta* grows on sandy shores and cliffs. 0–1,210 m (Ben Lawers, Mid Perthshire).

Trends *A. millefolium* is ubiquitous at the 10 km square resolution and there has been no significant change in its distribution since the 1960s. It is now very widely grown in gardens and sown in wild-flower seed mixtures in wild locations, even in upland regions (*e.g.* Cardiganshire). These sown plants vary widely in terms of provenance, colour, morphology and flowering time, including a form with ray florets only.

Biogeography Eurasian Boreo-temperate element, but naturalized in North America so distribution is now Circumpolar Boreo-temperate.

Native		GB	IR
2000–19	●	2793	978
1987–99	●	2751	927
1970–86	●	1920	167
pre-1970	○	2672	886

Key refs Black & Warwick (1982), Chater (2010b), Grime *et al.* (2007).

H.J. KILLICK

Ne *Achillea filipendulina* Fern-leaf Yarrow
Lam.

A perennial herb with a woody stock and long, thin, rhizomes, now very popular in gardens, especially the cultivars 'Gold Plate' and 'Cloth of Gold'. It is frequently discarded in garden waste and establishes along roadsides, hedgerows and railways. Also naturalized on garden walls, old buildings and in churchyards where it is clearly self-sown. Lowland.

Trends *A. filipendulina* was introduced from the Caucasus in 1803, and first found in the wild in 1909 (Ware, Hertfordshire).

Biogeography Native of the Caucasus, Iran, Afghanistan and central Asia.

Alien		GB	IR
2000–19	●	52	0
1987–99	●	18	0
1970–86	●	7	0
pre-1970	○	2	0

Key refs Sutton (2001).

D.A. PEARMAN

(N) *Achillea maritima* Cottonweed
(L.) Ehrend. & Y.P.Guo

A small shrubby perennial herb with silvery leaves and small tubular yellow flower-heads, found in sand dunes and on stabilized shingle. Lowland.

Trends *A. maritima* was first recorded in our area in the early 17th century, but has declined sharply and inexplicably since 1850. It is no longer found in Britain, with last records from Cornwall in 1933 and the Isles of Scilly in 1936. In the Channel Islands the species has not been seen since 1879 (Jersey). It is extant at just two sites in Ireland, both in County Wexford, although one site is a reintroduction following an absence of the species for over 30 years; just one plant was found here in 2014. At the second site it has declined catastrophically in recent years due to competition with *Ammophila arenaria*, with just 12 plants recorded in 2018 (Wyse Jackson *et al.*, 2016).

Biogeography Mediterranean-Atlantic element; more frequent on stable Mediterranean beaches than on the stormy Atlantic coast.

	GB	IR
Long term	No trend	No trend
Short term	No trend	No trend

Native	GB	IR
2000–19	0	1
1987–99	0	2
1970–86	0	1
pre-1970	29	6

Alien	GB	IR
2000–19	0	0
1987–99	0	1
1970–86	0	0
pre-1970	0	0

Key refs Hurst (1901), Le Sueur (1984), Lousley (1971), Marren (1999), Wyse Jackson *et al.* (2016).

H.J. KILLICK & K.J. WALKER

(N) *Chamaemelum nobile* Chamomile
(L.) All.

C. nobile is a small aromatic perennial mat-forming herb with daisy-like heads and dissected leaves. It is found in moderately acidic, unfertilized, seasonally wet grassland on dry, sandy or gleyed soils, especially on commons and pastures where mowing, trampling or grazing discourage competitors; also on lawns, and in coastal grassland and on cliffs, where exposure and trampling maintain a short sward. 0–465 m (near Priestleap, South Kerry).

Trends *C. nobile* had decreased considerably by 1930, presumably due to the enclosure of common lands during the 18th and 19th centuries; this decline continued throughout much of the 20th century due to drainage, habitat fragmentation and the cessation of grazing. For example, over 90% of the sites recorded in Dorset in the 1930s were lost by 1993 (Byfield & Pearman,

1996). Its distribution now appears to be fairly stable within core native areas. All populations in northern England (north of Derbyshire) and Scotland are considered to be naturalized or planted, some for the creation of chamomile lawns, although some populations in Scotland (for example, on Colonsay, South Ebudes) are in habitats identical to those in areas of southern England where it is assumed to be native.

Biogeography Suboceanic Southern-temperate element.

	GB	IR
Long term		
Short term		

Native	GB	IR
2000–19	158	65
1987–99	150	60
1970–86	120	5
pre-1970	309	95

Alien	GB	IR
2000–19	31	0
1987–99	21	0
1970–86	14	0
pre-1970	71	3

Key refs Byfield *et al.* (1996), Kay & John (1994), Stewart *et al.* (1994), Stroh *et al.* (2019), Westerhoff & Clark (1992).

H.J. KILLICK

Ne *Anthemis punctata* Sicilian Chamomile

Vahl

A perennial herb grown in gardens and found naturalized, especially on walls, but also on roadsides, railway banks, pathsides, cliffs and waste ground. It also arises as a grain impurity, and some populations are only casual. Lowland.

Trends *A. punctata* was first cultivated in Britain in 1818 and is popular in gardens, especially in areas with a mild climate as an early flowering, persistent, wall-plant. It has been naturalized on cliffs near Fishguard (Pembrokeshire) since 1923. It appears to be increasing, or possibly better-recorded.

Biogeography Native of Sicily (subsp. *cupaniana*) and north-western Africa (*A. punctata* subsp. *punctata*). Our plant is the former subspecies.

	GB	IR
Long term	No trend	No trend
Short term		No trend

Alien	GB	IR
2000–19	72	2
1987–99	39	2
1970–86	14	0
pre-1970	7	0

Key refs Sutton (2001).

T.D. DINES & D.A. PEARMAN

Ar *Anthemis arvensis* Corn Chamomile

L.

An aromatic annual herb with daisy-like flowers and dissected leaves, formerly most frequent as a weed of arable crops, especially cereals, on light calcareous or sandy soils. It is now mostly found in open grassland, leys, field-borders and waste places, and on roadsides and disturbed ground near the sea. Lowland.

An archaeophyte in Britain and the Channel Islands and a neophyte in Ireland.

Trends *A. arvensis* declined substantially in the 20th century, especially in the latter half, and this trend has continued since 2000. It was fairly resistant to the first phenoxy herbicides but less so to later compounds, and has now largely disappeared from arable land. It is, however, still widespread in East Anglia and Lancashire. Many northern occurrences are casual. It has been introduced as a contaminant of grass-seed and has been advertized as a component of cornfield seed mixtures, but in many cases the species may have been misidentified for *Cota austriaca*.

Biogeography As an archaeophyte, *A. arvensis* has a European Southern-temperate distribution; it is widely naturalized outside this range.

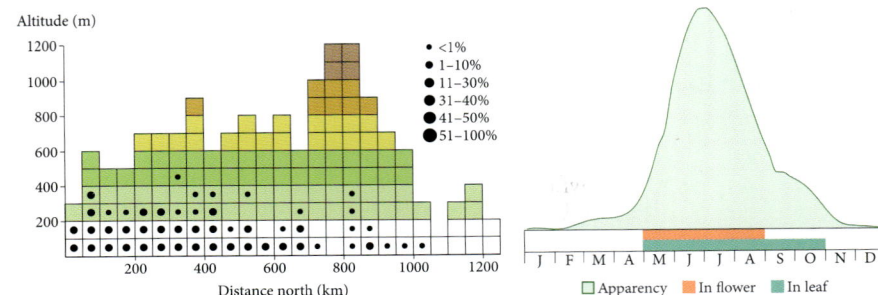

	GB	IR
Long term		
Short term		

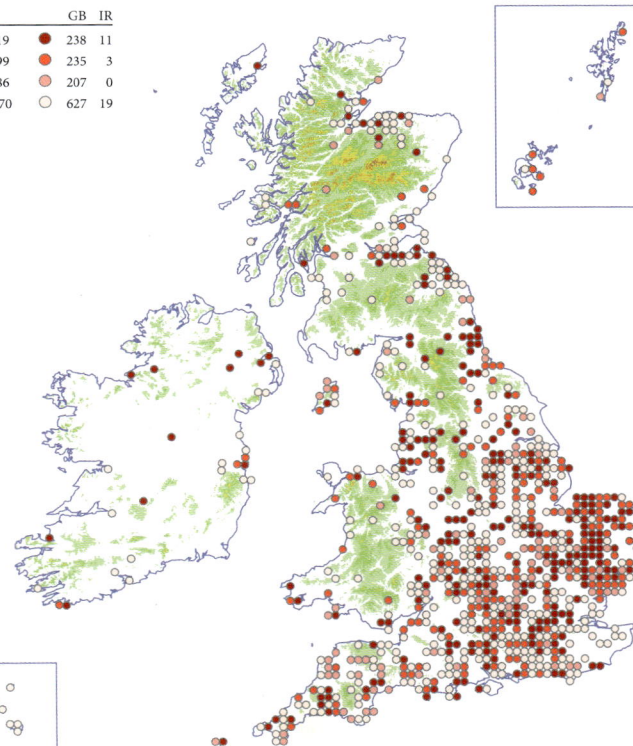

Alien	GB	IR
2000–19	238	11
1987–99	235	3
1970–86	207	0
pre-1970	627	19

Key refs Braithwaite *et al.* (2006), Erskine *et al.* (2018), Kay (1971b), Willmot & Moyes (2015).

H.J. KILLICK

Ar *Anthemis cotula* Stinking Chamomile

L.

A foetid annual herb of cereals and other arable crops, favouring heavy soils, including clay, clay-loam and marl, but it can also grow on light soils, including those over chalk. It is toxic to dogs, cats and horses, and unpleasant to handle. It is a grain-seed casual in Ireland. Lowland.

Trends *A. cotula* has been a serious and therefore unpopular weed of cereals and other arable crops, probably since the Iron Age. Although fairly resistant to the first phenoxy herbicides, it was much reduced by later ones and is now mostly relegated to waste places. It had declined in many areas (especially in northern England) by 1970, and very many of the records reported in the latter decades of the 20th century have not been repeated.

Biogeography As an archaeophyte, *A. cotula* has a European Southern-temperate distribution; it is widely naturalized outside this range.

Alien		GB	IR
2000–19	●	472	8
1987–99	●	571	9
1970–86	●	426	4
pre-1970	○	970	56

Key refs Braithwaite *et al.* (2006), Kay (1971a).

H.J. KILLICK

Ne *Cota tinctoria* Yellow Chamomile

(L.) J.Gay

An aromatic biennial or perennial herb with large yellow flower-heads; it yields a yellow dye and is grown in gardens from where it may escape onto waste, rough and marginal land, usually on dry soils. Populations are usually small, and do not persist; they attract many insects. There are a number of subspecies and cultivars, which have hybridized after escaping. Lowland.

Trends *C. tinctoria*, introduced by 1561, was first noted in the wild in 1690 (Durham). It is a casual or an established escape, and perhaps also a birdseed alien.

Biogeography A Eurosiberian Temperate species, which has spread northwards in Europe as an escape from cultivation.

Alien		GB	IR
2000–19	●	120	6
1987–99	●	84	4
1970–86	●	74	0
pre-1970	○	123	0

Key refs Trueman *et al.* (2013).

H.J. KILLICK

Ne *Cota austriaca* Austrian Chamomile

(Jacq.) Sch.Bip.

An annual to biennial herb of dumped soil, waste ground and areas sown with grass seed, often as a constituent of wild-flower seed mixtures. Possibly also in birdseed, and formerly in wool shoddy. Lowland.

Trends Although *C. austriaca* was known from the wild by 1878 it was scarcely recorded during the 20th century. However, its distribution has increased dramatically since 2000 due to its inclusion in 'cornfield' and 'wild-flower' seed mixtures which have been widely sown on road verges and in amenity areas in cities, towns and villages. It closely resembles *Anthemis arvensis*, and is often sown as, and then misrecorded for, that species.

Biogeography Native of east-central and south-eastern Europe, Turkey and the Causasus; introduced farther north.

Alien	GB	IR
2000–19	182	16
1987–99	5	1
1970–86	1	0
pre-1970	3	0

K.J. WALKER

Ar *Glebionis segetum* Corn Marigold

(L.) Fourr.

An annual herb of arable fields on light, sandy or loamy soils that are deficient in calcium, as well as on disturbed soils on roadsides, waste ground and refuse tips; it is also increasingly sown in wild-flower seed mixtures in urban areas. The seeds are long-lived in the soil leading to unexpected mass emergence following disturbance. It germinates mainly in spring. 0–410 m (Eisteddfa Gurig, Cardiganshire).

Trends There is a continuous archaeological record of *G. segetum* in Britain from the Iron Age onwards. It has been so abundant in the past that Henry II ordered its eradication. A once colourful but serious weed of oats and potatoes in Victorian times, it is now much reduced due to improved seed cleaning, liming, herbicides and the shift to autumn-sown crops, but it remains locally abundant where the intensity of management has

remained low (*e.g.* on light soils in coastal areas). Many recent records are from sown wild-flower mixtures.

Biogeography As an archaeophyte, *G. segetum* has a European Southern-temperate distribution; it is widely naturalized outside this range.

Alien	GB	IR
2000–19	1064	192
1987–99	946	241
1970–86	707	58
pre-1970	1390	364

Key refs Braithwaite *et al.* (2006), Howarth & Williams (1972), Walker *et al.* (2017), Wilson (1991).

H.J. KILLICK & P.A. STROH

Ne ***Glebionis coronaria*** Crown Daisy
(L.) Cass. ex Spach

An annual herb, sometimes grown
for ornament. Found in arable
fields, waste places, rubbish tips,
roadsides and pathsides. It arises as
a contaminant of birdseed and grain
and as a garden escape. Lowland.

Trends *G. coronaria* was cultivated
in Britain by 1629 and is fairly
common in gardens. It was
recorded in the wild before 1900
(Oulton Broad, East Suffolk).

Biogeography Native of the
Mediterranean region and south-western
Asia. Naturalized elsewhere in Asia and
in California.

	GB	IR
Long term	No trend	No trend
Short term		No trend

Alien	GB	IR
2000–19	19	1
1987–99	16	0
1970–86	7	0
pre-1970	20	0

- <1%
- 1–10%
- 11–30%
- 31–40%
- 41–50%
- 51–100%

Apparency | In flower | In leaf

T.D. Dines

Ne ***Leucanthemella serotina*** Autumn Oxeye
(L.) Tzvelev

A large, rhizomatous perennial herb
which is naturalized in damp areas
on heathland, commons and sand
dunes, by ditches and ponds and on
waste ground. It arises as a garden
escape or throw-out. Lowland.

Trends *L. serotina* was introduced
into cultivation in Britain in 1825
and is widely grown in gardens. It
was recorded from the wild in 1909
(Oxford, Oxfordshire), and is now
much more frequently recorded.

Biogeography Native of south-eastern
Europe.

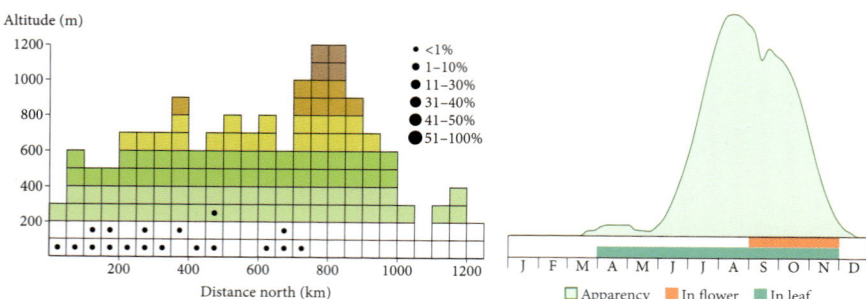

	GB	IR
Long term	No trend	No trend
Short term		No trend

Alien	GB	IR
2000–19	48	1
1987–99	33	0
1970–86	13	0
pre-1970	14	0

- <1%
- 1–10%
- 11–30%
- 31–40%
- 41–50%
- 51–100%

Apparency | In flower | In leaf

Key refs Sutton (2001).

T.D. Dines

N *Leucanthemum vulgare* Oxeye Daisy
Lam.

A perennial herb of a wide range of grassland habitats, especially meadows, pastures and downland which are cut or moderately grazed, preferring well-drained, neutral to base-rich soils; also on coastal cliffs, stabilized sand dunes, waste ground, by railways and in newly sown roadsides. 0–845 m (Great Dun Fell, Westmorland).

Trends *L. vulgare* has been spread by human activities throughout much of its range. In recent decades it has become an almost ubiquitous component of wild-flower seed mixtures, and robust forms can soon dominate created grasslands, producing spectacular displays for a limited time. The 2002 *Atlas* suggested a surprising decline in Highland Scotland, presumably in semi-natural habitats, but more systematic recording this century has resulted in many of the gaps being filled. It has, however, become increasingly

difficult to distinguish native from alien populations, and many 10 km squares will have a mixture of native and sown alien varieties and subspecies.

Biogeography Eurosiberian Boreo-temperate element, but widely naturalized so that distribution is now Circumpolar Boreo-temperate.

Native	GB	IR
2000–19	2442	909
1987–99	2308	846
1970–86	1549	95
pre-1970	2379	828

Alien	GB	IR
2000–19	11	5
1987–99	6	5
1970–86	2	0
pre-1970	3	1

Key refs Grime *et al.* (2007), Howarth & Williams (1968).

P.A. STROH & H.J. KILLICK

Hy *Leucanthemum lacustre* × *maximum* = *L.* ×*superbum* Shasta Daisy
(Bergmans ex J.W.Ingram) D.H.Kent

A perennial herb which is well-established as a throw-out from gardens and from sowing wild-flower seed mixtures. Habitats include meadows, roadsides and tracksides, railway banks, churchyards, disused quarries, sea-cliffs, river banks, waste ground and on mounds of tipped soil. Although a hybrid, it is fully fertile. Lowland.

A cultivated hybrid (alien × alien).

Trends *L.* ×*superbum*, first introduced to cultivation in Britain in 1901, is now commonly sown in amenity and conservation schemes, sometimes to the exclusion of *L. vulgare*. It was first recorded from the wild at Watergate, Newquay (West Cornwall) in 1913. Though much better recorded this century, it is possible that the hybrid name has on occasion been used to cover other introduced members of the extremely variable *L. vulgare* complex.

Biogeography A hybrid of garden origin.

	GB	IR
2000–19	987	43
1987–99	761	9
1970–86	218	0
pre-1970	151	0

Key refs Stace *et al.* (2015).

C.A. STACE, C.D. PRESTON & D.A. PEARMAN

Ar *Matricaria chamomilla* Scented Mayweed
L.

A small aromatic annual herb, typically found on arable land, especially in cereal crops, as well as on disturbed and other waste ground, such as gateways, tracks, disused railways and old pits. It does best in fairly open, neutral to alkaline ground fairly rich in nitrate and occurs usually on light soils, but sometimes on loams and heavy clays. 0–470 m (Clun Forest, Shropshire).

An archaeophyte in Britain and the Channel Islands and a neophyte in Ireland.

Trends At the beginning of the 20th century *M. chamomilla* was a very widespread weed of arable crops, mainly of cereals, on sandy and loam soils in England and Wales. It declined as an arable weed from the mid-20th century onwards due to the widespread use of herbicides, but often survived in field edges, corners and gateways and other

areas of waste ground on farms as well as in urban areas. It is still locally abundant across much of Britain and can appear in large numbers, from buried seed, during new developments such as road schemes, or on set-aside land.

Biogeography As an archaeophyte, *M. chamomilla* has a European Southern-temperate distribution, but it is widely naturalized so that its distribution is now Circumpolar Southern-temperate.

Alien	GB	IR
2000–19	1562	65
1987–99	1396	33
1970–86	900	6
pre-1970	1084	18

Key refs Braithwaite *et al.* (2006), Trueman *et al.* (2013).

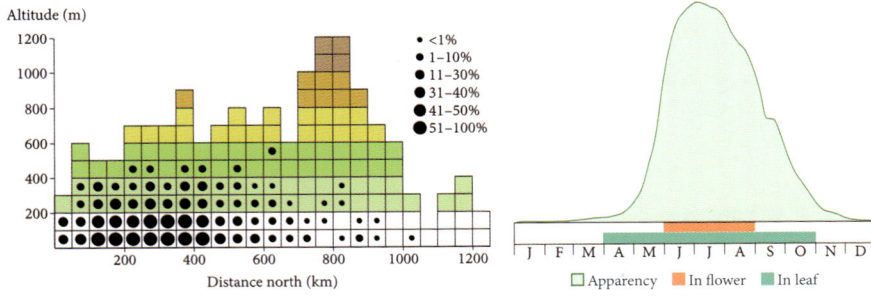

Altitude (m)

- <1%
- 1–10%
- 11–30%
- 31–40%
- 41–50%
- 51–100%

☐ Apparency   ☐ In flower   ☐ In leaf

H.J. KILLICK

Ne *Matricaria discoidea* Pineappleweed
DC.

An annual herb of disturbed, open, usually fertile, near-neutral to base-rich ground including pavements, roadsides, waste ground, improved pastures, tracks, field gateways and arable margins. Generally lowland, but reaching 845 m on Great Dun Fell (Westmorland).

Trends *M. discoidea* was first recorded in the wild in Britain as an escape from Kew Gardens (Surrey) in 1869 and in Ireland in 1894. It became one of the fastest spreading plants in the 20th century, aided by the transport of seeds on tyres and footwear. By 2000 it was a near-ubiquitous weed at the 10 km square level, except for the Scottish Highlands, and its distribution has continued to expand, both locally, and into previously unoccupied 10 km squares.

Biogeography Probably native of northern and southern Asia and perhaps

adjacent parts of North America; in the 19th and 20th centuries it spread to boreal and temperate zones throughout the Northern Hemisphere.

Alien	GB	IR
2000–19	2672	965
1987–99	2580	895
1970–86	1555	120
pre-1970	2517	821

Key refs Grime *et al.* (2007), Salisbury (1964).

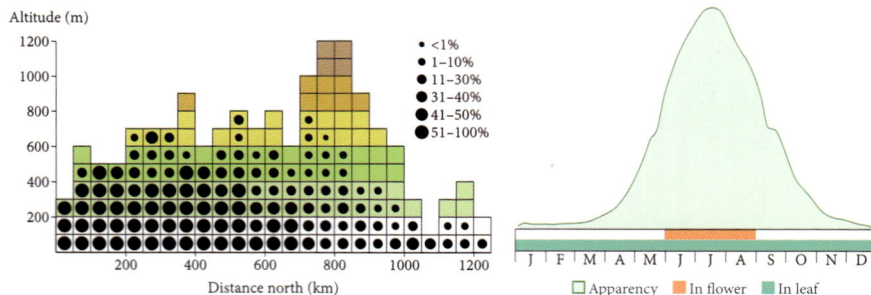

Altitude (m)

- <1%
- 1–10%
- 11–30%
- 31–40%
- 41–50%
- 51–100%

☐ Apparency   ☐ In flower   ☐ In leaf

H.J. KILLICK

N *Tripleurospermum maritimum* Sea Mayweed

(L.) W.D.J.Koch

A perennial, sometimes biennial, herb with fleshy dissected leaves and white ray florets. It occurs in a wide range of coastal habits usually influenced by salt spray including open sand, shingle, screes, sea cliffs, walls and waste and disturbed ground; especially in seabird colonies; also rarely inland on road verges. Sell and Murrell (2006) have recognized three subspecies; subsp. *maritimum* occurs throughout the range of the species, the red-tinged subsp. *vinicaule* is confined to southern England and subsp. *nigriceps* is only found in northern Scotland. Lowland.

Trends Records for *T. maritimum s.s.* and *T. inodorum* were mapped together in the 1962 *Atlas*. Many older records are, therefore, only referable to the aggregate. Since then, *T. maritimum s.s.* has been increasingly well recorded around nearly all the coasts of Britain and Ireland and its distribution appears stable.

Biogeography Circumpolar Wide-boreal element.

Native	GB	IR
2000–19	922	331
1987–99	789	272
1970–86	238	67
pre-1970	263	37

Alien	GB	IR
2000–19	1	0
1987–99	3	0
1970–86	0	0
pre-1970	0	0

Key refs Chater (2010b), Kay (1972), Sell & Murrell (2006).

H.J. KILLICK

Ar *Tripleurospermum inodorum* Scentless Mayweed

(L.) Sch.Bip.

An annual herb, found in a wide range of habitats on disturbed, fertile soils including arable fields (but much sparser here than formerly), farm tracks, gateways, roadsides, railway ballast, quarries, spoil heaps, pavements, and waste ground. It rapidly colonizes newly disturbed soil on construction sites. It is occasionally abundant in stubble fields. Generally lowland, but reaching 590 m in Atholl (East Perthshire).

Trends There is a continuous archaeological record of *T. inodorum* from British sites from the Bronze Age onwards. It was not recognized as a full species distinct from *T. maritimum* until 1969 and while recorders are increasingly separating the two taxa, this will not have happened everywhere. Its 10 km square distribution appears to be stable although it has declined in abundance on arable land.

Biogeography As an archaeophyte, *T. inodorum* has a Eurosiberian Temperate distribution, but it is widely naturalized so that its distribution is now Circumpolar Temperate.

Alien	GB	IR
2000–19	2184	487
1987–99	2028	413
1970–86	1047	40
pre-1970	898	45

Key refs Grime *et al.* (2007), Kay (1969), Kay (1994).

H.J. KILLICK

Ne *Cotula coronopifolia* Buttonweed
L.

An annual to perennial herb, widely grown in gardens and also found as a wool alien. It has become naturalized in wet and marshy places, in greatest abundance on intertidal mud, but also at inland sites, often in areas of mining subsidence that are flooded in winter. Lowland.

Trends This species, which was cultivated in Britain by 1683, has been known in the wild since 1869 (Highbury, Middlesex). It was known from north-western England by 1985, and other southern locations and the Channel Islands by 1999. It has spread recently, and extended its range into non-saline areas and Ireland (Dublin and Cork), but has also been lost from many previous locations.

Biogeography Native of South Africa, naturalized (especially in coastal regions) in western Europe, western North America, South America, Australasia and elsewhere.

Alien	GB	IR
2000–19	75	4
1987–99	38	0
1970–86	11	1
pre-1970	12	1

	GB	IR
Long term	No trend	No trend
Short term	↓ ↓ · ↑ **↑**	No trend

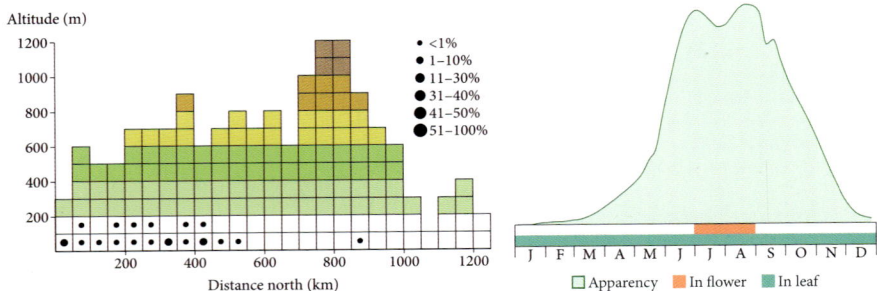

Key refs Clement (1993), Martin (1993).

H.J. KILLICK

Ne *Cotula alpina* Alpine Cotula
(Hook.f.) Hook.f.

A low-growing perennial herb with stems rooting at the nodes. Occasionally grown in garden lawns and rockeries and naturalized on tracks and roadside verges, and occasionally areas of burnt heather and peaty ditches, mainly on moorlands managed for Red Grouse *Lagopus lagopus scotica*. It flowers profusely and spreads by seed dispersed on vehicles and livestock. It has also been recorded as a casual on an urban roadside and is naturalized in gardens and parkland. The origin of British populations is unknown. 0–430 m (Ouster Bank, Upper Nidderdale, Mid-west Yorkshire).

Trends *C. alpina* has long been cultivated in gardens but was not reported from the wild until 2009. However, following this discovery, earlier records extending back to 1975 subsequently came to light from Upper Nidderdale (Mid-west Yorkshire),

where it is abundant along *c.* 35 km of moorland tracks and roadsides. It occurs in very similar habitats on the North York Moors (North-east Yorkshire) and on the Coigach Peninsula (Wester Ross); it is spreading rapidly within all three areas.

Biogeography Native of south-eastern Australia (New South Wales, Victoria) and Tasmania.

Alien	GB	IR
2000–19	13	0
1987–99	1	0
1970–86	1	0
pre-1970	0	0

	GB	IR
Long term	No trend	No trend
Short term	No trend	No trend

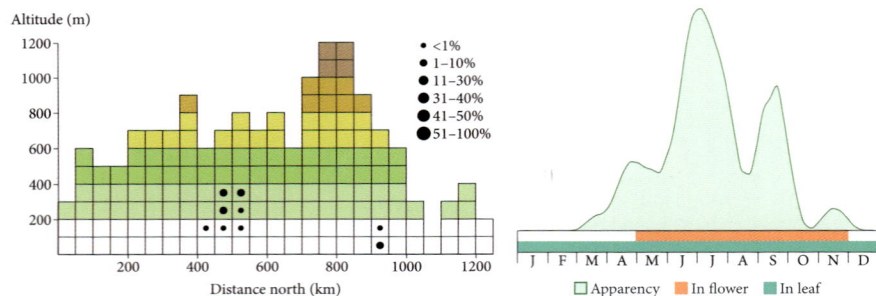

Key refs Robinson (2009), Walker *et al.* (2020).

K.J. WALKER

Ne *Senecio inaequidens* Narrow-leaved Ragwort
DC.

A clump-forming, winter-green perennial herb with a woody base, now thoroughly naturalized in a range of ruderal habitats including paths, tracks, roadsides, pavements, bridges, railways, spoil and dung heaps, derelict buildings and waste ground. Also occurring on river shingle and sandy beaches and as a casual on arable land. Lowland.

Trends *S. inaequidens* was first recorded in the wild in 1836 (St Davids, Fife). The majority of 19th and 20th century records originate from wool shoddy, but it may have arrived in East Kent by 1978 as a natural extension of its naturalized alien range in France. Its 10 km square distribution started to increase in 1999 and since then it has spread rapidly throughout Britain and Ireland, mainly along major transport networks, and it is now locally abundant in many urban areas, often forming huge colonies on railway sidings and on derelict land. In Ireland, it has spread throughout the island since 1999 and is now locally abundant around Dublin.

Biogeography Native of South Africa; widely naturalized in Europe, especially by major roads and railways.

Alien		GB	IR
2000–19	●	527	46
1987–99	●	23	2
1970–86	●	4	0
pre-1970	○	13	0

	GB	IR
Long term	No trend	No trend
Short term		

Key refs Burton (1979).

T.D. DINES & J.O. MOUNTFORD

Altitude (m) — <1%, 1–10%, 11–30%, 31–40%, 41–50%, 51–100%
Distance north (km)

Apparency · In flower · In leaf

Ne *Senecio sarracenicus* Broad-leaved Ragwort
L.

A tall perennial clump-forming herb, grown in gardens and occurring as a relic of cultivation and as a naturalized escape by streams and rivers, and in fens, fen-woodland, swamps and marshy grassland. Predominantly lowland, but to 403 m near Malham Tarn (Mid-west Yorkshire).

Trends This species was introduced by 1620 and was originally grown for medicinal use (as Saracens' Consound). It was first recorded in the wild in 1632 (Gwarthlow, Shropshire). It is locally abundant in some areas, for example along the River Eden in Cumberland and in the Somerset Levels, and this suggests independent spread from several different foci. It is now widely grown in gardens, so many recent records are probably garden escapes.

Biogeography *S. sarracenicus* has a Eurosiberian Temperate distribution; it is naturalized in north-western Europe beyond its native range.

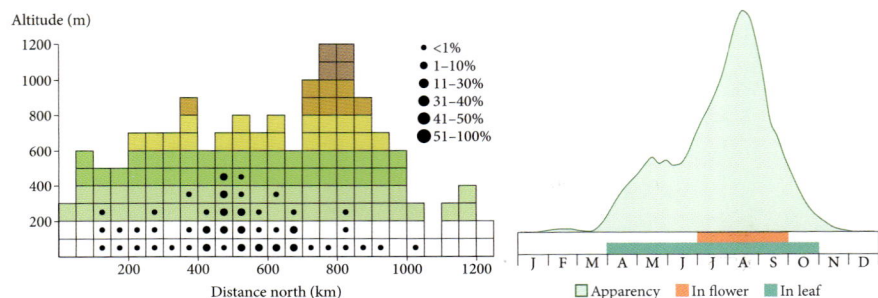

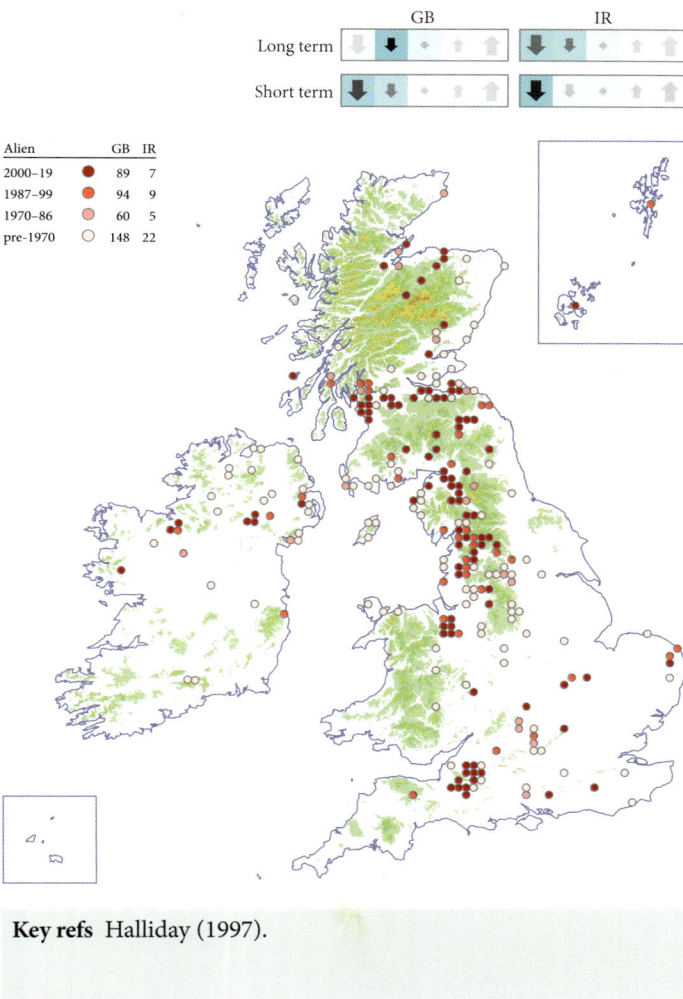

Alien		GB	IR
2000–19	●	89	7
1987–99	●	94	9
1970–86	●	60	5
pre-1970	○	148	22

	GB	IR
Long term		
Short term		

Key refs Halliday (1997).

H.J. KILLICK

Altitude (m) — <1%, 1–10%, 11–30%, 31–40%, 41–50%, 51–100%
Distance north (km)

Apparency · In flower · In leaf

Ne *Senecio smithii* Magellan Ragwort
DC.

A tall rhizomatous perennial herb, found as a naturalized garden escape or relic of cultivation in open, fertile grassy meadows and pastures, on cliffs and roadsides, by lakes and streams and in ditches. Mostly lowland (to 350 m).

Trends *S. smithii* was introduced to Britain in 1801, with a first record in the wild by 1918 (near Corgarff, South Aberdeenshire). Legend has it that it was introduced by whalers who brought it back from Patagonia and Chile, and it is known locally in Scotland as 'Falkland Islands Daisy'. Scott & Palmer (1987) conclude that most Shetland populations originate as escapes from gardens. Its overall 10 km square distribution has changed very little since the 1960s.

Biogeography Native of temperate South America.

	GB	IR
Long term	No trend	No trend
Short term	⬇ ⬇ ◆ ⬆ ⬆	No trend

Alien	GB	IR
2000–19	32	0
1987–99	33	0
1970–86	22	0
pre-1970	23	0

Key refs Druce (1928), Scott & Palmer (1987).

H.J. KILLICK

Ne *Senecio squalidus* Oxford Ragwort
L.

A winter-green annual to short-lived perennial herb, found most often as a street weed, where it is found at the base of walls, as well as on other disturbed or waste ground on well-drained soils including railways, cinders, roadsides and gardens. Lowland.

Trends *S. squalidus* was first recorded in the wild in 1794 as an escape from Oxford Botanic Garden, and at Bideford, North Devon, sometime before 1830. It spread rapidly after reaching the railway in Oxford in *c.*1879 and by the 1960s it was present over much of southern Britain and was starting to colonize other habitats. This increase continued until the 1980s but since then its distribution has declined, especially since 2000, possibly due to street cleansing and redevelopment of derelict urban sites, though this temporal and spatial pattern of distribution does shows signs of the 'boom-bust' cycle (Strayer *et al.*, 2017) observed for other initially invasive alien species. In Ireland it was naturalized in Cork city by 1845 but it then spread relatively slowly.

Biogeography *S. squalidus* appears to have arisen in cultivation in the Oxford Botanic Garden (Abbott *et al.*, 2000).

	GB	IR
Long term	⬇ ◆ ◆ ⬆ ⬆	◆ ◆ ◆ ⬆ ⬆
Short term	⬇ ◆ ◆ ⬆ ⬆	⬇ ◆ ◆ ⬆ ⬆

Alien	GB	IR
2000–19	1117	44
1987–99	1285	62
1970–86	932	15
pre-1970	1006	21

Key refs Abbott *et al.* (2000), Abbott & Lowe (2004), Allan & Pannell (2009), Braithwaite *et al.* (2006), Grime *et al.* (2007), Harris (2002), Sell & Murrell (2006), Strayer *et al.* (2017).

H.J. KILLICK & P.A. STROH

Hy *Senecio squalidus* × *vulgaris* = *S.* ×*baxteri*
Druce

An annual or biennial herb arising spontaneously in gardens where the parents grow as weeds, as well as on disused railway lines, refuse tips and waste ground. It is a sterile triploid which is unable to reproduce vegetatively or by seed. This triploid F_1 hybrid has given rise by chromosome number doubling to the amphidiploid hexaploid species *S. cambrensis*. Lowland.

A spontaneous hybrid (native × alien).

Trends This hybrid has been known since 1892 (Oxfordshire) and 1906 (Glamorganshire), and appears sporadically.

Biogeography Wider distribution uncertain.

	GB	IR
Long term	No trend	No trend
Short term	No trend	No trend

	GB	IR
2000–19	14	1
1987–99	25	3
1970–86	28	0
pre-1970	32	5

Altitude (m) / Distance north (km)

- <1%
- 1–10%
- 11–30%
- 31–40%
- 41–50%
- 51–100%

Apparency   In flower   In leaf

Key refs Stace *et al.* (2015).

C.A. STACE, C.D. PRESTON & D.A. PEARMAN

Hy *Senecio squalidus* × *viscosus* = *S.* ×*londinensis*
Lousley

An annual or biennial herb found in mixed populations of its parents, often as just one or a few plants but sometimes in greater abundance. Many records are from railway land but it is also recorded from old quarries, sand- and gravel-pits, roadsides, refuse tips and coastal shingle. It is completely sterile, with infertile pollen and no ripe fruits, and there is no evidence of introgression. Lowland.

A spontaneous hybrid (alien × alien).

Trends This hybrid was discovered in the London area in 1944, when it was particularly frequent on bombed sites. It is now much less often recorded.

Biogeography This hybrid was originally described from Romania, but its distribution in mainland Europe is not well-documented.

	GB	IR
Long term	No trend	No trend
Short term	No trend	No trend

	GB	IR
2000–19	31	0
1987–99	58	1
1970–86	64	1
pre-1970	41	0

Altitude (m) / Distance north (km)

- <1%
- 1–10%
- 11–30%
- 31–40%
- 41–50%
- 51–100%

Apparency   In flower   In leaf

Key refs Stace *et al.* (2015).

C.A. STACE, C.D. PRESTON & D.A. PEARMAN

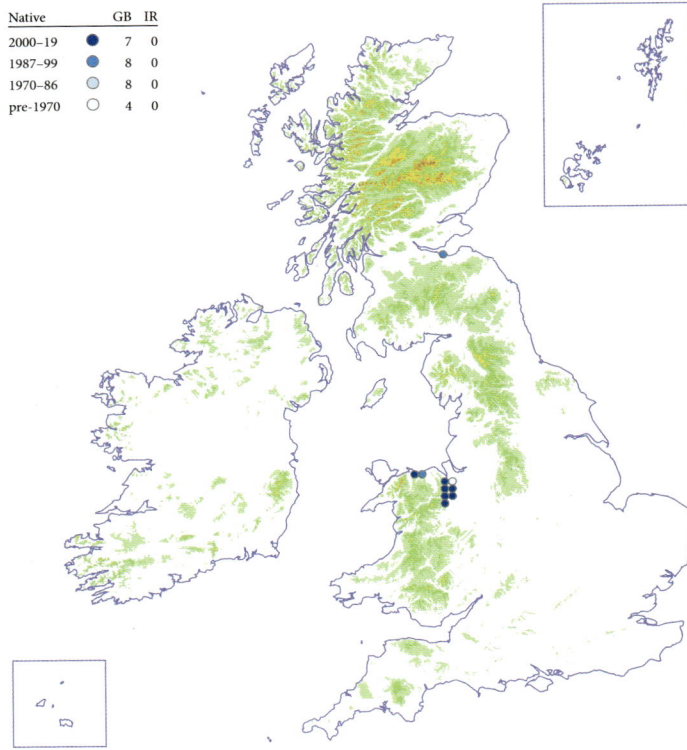

N *Senecio cambrensis* Welsh Groundsel
Rosser

A small annual, or sometimes short-lived perennial of open or disturbed sites, including waste and rough ground, on roadsides and footpaths, mine spoil and dumped rubble, and in cracks in walls. Lowland.

Trends The earliest collection of *S. cambrensis* was from Brynteg (Denbighshire) in 1925, but it was only in 1948, following the discovery of a site at Cefn-y-bedd (Flintshire), that the species was recognized as distinct; a formal description followed in 1955. It arose from the hybrid between *S. vulgaris* and *S. squalidus* by chromosome doubling. A survey in 2010 found only twelve localities, compared with 35 known in the early 1980s, triggering conservation efforts to propagate plants *ex situ* (*e.g.* at Cambridge Botanic Garden, where it is occasionally found as a weed). It appears to have been lost

from two 10 km squares in north Wales this century, and also from its sole Scottish locality at Leith (Midlothian), where it was last seen in 1993.

Biogeography Endemic.

Native	GB	IR
2000–19	7	0
1987–99	8	0
1970–86	8	0
pre-1970	4	0

	GB	IR
Long term	No trend	No trend
Short term	No trend	No trend

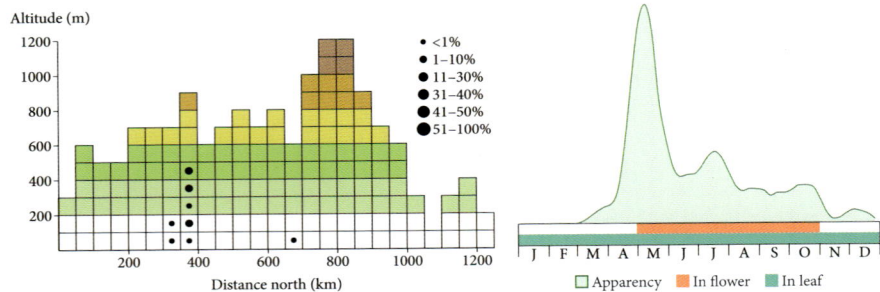

Key refs Abbott & Lowe (2004), Abbott *et al.* (2009), Hegarty *et al.* (2012), Ingram & Noltie (1995), Wigginton (1999), Wynne (1993).

H.J. KILLICK & C.A. STACE

N *Senecio eboracensis* York Ragwort
R.J. Abbott & A.J. Lowe

A fully fertile tetraploid that arose following hybridization between *S. squalidus* and *S. vulgaris* in central York (Mid-west Yorkshire) probably in the 1970s (Lowe & Abbott, 2003). It appears to be extinct in the wild but formerly occurred on disturbed ground, car park perimeters, pavement cracks, the base of street trees, and stonework on a river embankment. Lowland.

Trends *S. eboracensis* was first recognized as distinct from other 'radiate groundsels' in 1979 and was recorded sporadically until 2003 when it had almost disappeared due to city redevelopments and street cleansing. It has not been recorded since, despite repeated surveys of its historic sites. *Ex situ* plants have been grown at the University of St Andrews and seed from these plants was used to introduce it to two sites on the campus

of the University of York, but neither survived. Seed is currently stored in the Millenium Seedbank at Kew.

Biogeography Endemic.

Native	GB	IR
2000–19	0	0
1987–99	2	0
1970–86	2	0
pre-1970	0	0

	GB	IR
Long term	No trend	No trend
Short term	No trend	No trend

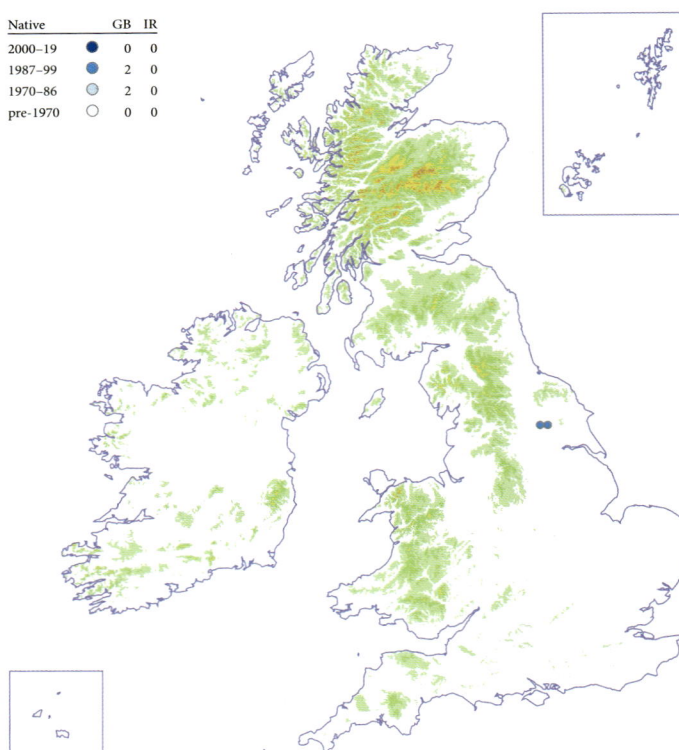

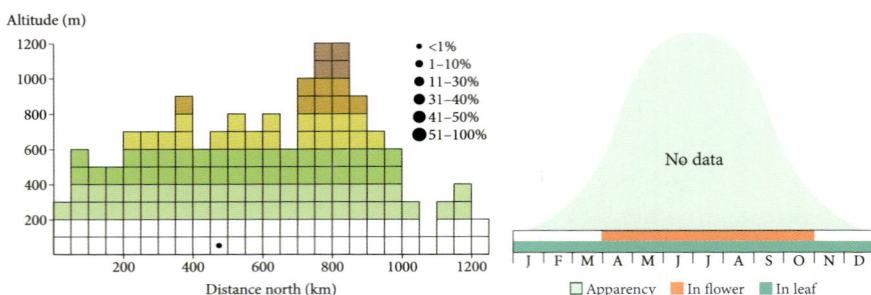

Key refs Lowe & Abbott (2003).

K.J. WALKER

Senecio vulgaris Groundsel
L.

An annual of open and disturbed ground, occurring in semi-natural habitats on sand dunes and coastal cliffs, and as a weed of waste places, roadsides, pavements, arable fields and other open habitats, often on nutrient-rich ground. The rare var. *crassifolius* is known from coastal sand and shingle in north-western Scotland and west Wales. 0–469 m (Little Cairn Table, Lanarkshire).

Trends There has been no significant change in the 10 km square distribution of *S. vulgaris* since the 1960s. The apparent decline in the Scottish Highlands, possibly due to abandoned marginal cultivations, persists. Some strains have become resistant to herbicides. The two rayed variants (subsp. *denticulatus* and var. *hibernicus*) were mapped by Perring & Sell (1968), and several county Floras have mapped the latter.

Biogeography European Southern-temperate element, but widely naturalized so that distribution is now Circumpolar Southern-temperate.

Native	GB	IR
2000–19	2554	953
1987–99	2446	885
1970–86	1508	137
pre-1970	2483	824

Key refs Chater (2010b), Grime *et al.* (2007).

H.J. KILLICK

Senecio sylvaticus Heath Groundsel
L.

A slender annual of open habitats on heathlands, often in disturbed areas, in cleared and burnt woodland, and on bushy commons; less often on railways, mine spoil, screes and sea-cliffs. It usually grows on acid, sandy, non-calcareous, sometimes eroded soils. It has a long-lived seed bank and a fairly high light requirement. 0–430 m (Llanddewi Brefi, Cardiganshire).

Trends There has been little change in the 10 km square distribution of *S. sylvaticus* since the 1960s, though it may have spread to new areas with conifers in plantations.

Biogeography European Temperate element.

Native	GB	IR
2000–19	1512	194
1987–99	1508	145
1970–86	935	36
pre-1970	1382	130

Key refs Braithwaite *et al.* (2006).

H.J. KILLICK

Ne *Senecio viscosus* Sticky Groundsel

L.

An annual herb, found on roadsides, banks, wall-tops, pavements, railway ballast, coastal shingle and dunes, in gravel-pits, and on open rough and waste ground and refuse tips. Usually growing on free-draining, disturbed substrates such as sands, gravels and cinders. Genetically dwarf variants occur on maritime shingle, where it could conceivably be native. 0–640 m (Scafell Pike, Cumberland).

Trends *S. viscosus* was first recorded in the wild in 1782 (Newhaven, East Sussex). It has spread greatly since 1900, especially in anthropogenic habitats and along roads and railways. By 2000 it had consolidated its range and had spread farther into south-western England and Ireland but since then its range has changed little, and it remains uncommon in Ireland and the Scottish Highlands.

Biogeography A European Temperate species which has spread markedly in western and northern Europe in recent centuries.

Alien	GB	IR
2000–19	1418	102
1987–99	1435	68
1970–86	965	15
pre-1970	1191	7

Key refs Akeroyd *et al.* (1978), Grime *et al.* (2007), Salisbury (1964).

H.J. KILLICK & P.A. STROH

Altitude (m) / Distance north (km) chart. Dot size key: <1%, 1–10%, 11–30%, 31–40%, 41–50%, 51–100%.

Apparency | In flower | In leaf

J F M A M J J A S O N D

Ne *Jacobaea maritima* Silver Ragwort

(L.) Pelser & Meijden

A silvery-hairy perennial herb of dry, well-drained soils, widely grown in gardens for bedding and edging and in hanging baskets and window boxes. It frequently escapes into habitats close to human habitations such as walls, pavements, refuse tips, roadside verges and waste ground. It has also been increasingly well-established on cliffs and rough ground near the sea in areas with a mild climate. Lowland.

Trends *J. maritima* was introduced into Britain by 1633, and recorded in the wild by 1891 (Lerée Bay, Guernsey), and on cliffs at Torquay in 1899. Before 1950 it was mainly recorded near to the coast in southern Britain but since then its mapped distribution has spread inland and farther north, possibly to some extent due to the more systematic recording of aliens.

Biogeography Native of the western and central Mediterranean region.

Alien	GB	IR
2000–19	311	15
1987–99	242	8
1970–86	79	0
pre-1970	49	0

Altitude (m) / Distance north (km) chart. Dot size key: <1%, 1–10%, 11–30%, 31–40%, 41–50%, 51–100%.

Apparency | In flower | In leaf

J F M A M J J A S O N D

H.J. KILLICK

Hy *Jacobaea maritima* × *vulgaris* = *J.* ×*albescens*

(Burb. & Colgan) Verloove & Lambinon

	GB	IR
Long term	No trend	No trend
Short term	No trend	No trend

A perennial herb known from coastal sand dunes, cliffs and shingle beaches, and in both coastal and inland sites from walls (a favourite habitat), old quarries, the bases of hedges, roadsides, canals and railway banks, cinder tracks and waste ground. Some populations may be persistent, but it also occurs as a casual. It arises both spontaneously and as a garden escape, is fertile, variable, and back-crosses with the parents. Lowland.

A spontaneous hybrid (native × alien).

Trends This hybrid was first noticed in 1901 at Killiney Bay (County Dublin), then in Cornwall in 1906. It is recorded in many places where *J. maritima* is not found in the wild, and occasionally is more frequent that this parent, suggesting that many wild hybrids must arise as crosses between wild *J. vulgaris* (presumably usually the female parent)

and garden plants of *J. maritima*. It appears to be spreading, though this trend may at least in part be due to fuller recording of hybrids in recent years.

Biogeography Wider distribution uncertain.

		GB	IR
2000–19	●	161	31
1987–99	●	182	5
1970–86	●	52	3
pre-1970	○	25	1

Key refs Stace *et al.* (2015).

C.A. STACE, C.D. PRESTON & D.A. PEARMAN

N *Jacobaea vulgaris* Common Ragwort

Gaertn.

	GB	IR
Long term		
Short term		

A biennial or perennial yellow-flowered herb of grasslands, and especially abundant in neglected, rabbit-infested or overgrazed pastures; it also grows on sand dunes, in scrub, open woods and along woodland rides, waste ground, road verges and waysides, and on rocks, screes and walls. Ragwort contains pyrrolizidine, toxic to the liver in humans and horses if consumed in quantity, so is specified under the Weeds Act (1959) and Ragwort Control Act (2003). Horses and livestock tend to avoid it whilst grazing, but cannot detect it in contaminated hay. Its population dynamics at Silwood Park (Berkshire), and control by exclusion of rabbits and mowing have been reported. 0–1,020 m (Stob Coire nam Beith, Glencoe, Main Argyll).

Trends *J. vulgaris* remains a ubiquitous species, found in most 10 km squares from the Channel Islands to Shetland.

Biogeography Eurosiberian Temperate element. Introduced in many countries.

Native		GB	IR
2000–19	●	2754	1002
1987–99	●	2679	953
1970–86	●	1775	186
pre-1970	○	2587	901

Key refs Bain (1991), Grime *et al.* (2007), Harper & Wood (1957), Kadereit & Sell (1986), Wardle (1987).

H.J. KILLICK

Hy *Jacobaea vulgaris × aquatica = J. ×ostenfeldii*
(Druce) B.Bock

Most records of this hybrid are from moist habitats similar to those associated with *J. aquatica*, including the edges of rivers and their associated backwaters and oxbows, lakesides, marshes, roadside ditches, damp meadows and pastures and moist woodland rides. It is recorded less frequently in rather drier sites which are the typical habitat of *J. vulgaris*. Less than 15% of the achenes ripen, but it back-crosses and very large and variable hybrid swarms can occur, particularly in the north and west. Generally lowland, but reaching *c.* 350 m at Leadgate (Cumberland).

A spontaneous hybrid (native × native).

Trends *J. ×ostenfeldii* is under-recorded in our area, perhaps sometimes having been overlooked or recorded in error as *J. vulgaris*, although the hybrid is much better recorded in

Ireland this century. Its decline in southern and eastern England appears genuine, mirroring the loss of suitable habitat and decline of *J. aquatica*.

Biogeography Widespread in western and central Europe.

	GB	IR
Long term	No trend	No trend
Short term	No trend	No trend

		GB	IR
2000–19	●	220	183
1987–99	●	166	176
1970–86	●	98	15
pre-1970	○	55	8

Key refs Stace *et al.* (2015).

C.A. STACE, C.D. PRESTON & D.A. PEARMAN

Altitude (m) histogram and phenology chart.
● <1% ● 1–10% ● 11–30% ● 31–40% ● 41–50% ● 51–100%
☐ Apparency ☐ In flower ☐ In leaf

N *Jacobaea aquatica* Marsh Ragwort
(Hill) G.Gaertn., B.Mey. & Scherb.

A yellow-flowered biennial, sometimes perennial, herb of marshes, wet meadows, fens, swamps, rush-pastures, damp woods and by streams, ponds and ditches. Its leaves are very variable in shape. Generally lowland, but reaching 482 m by Loch Lubnaig (West Perthshire).

Trends *J. aquatica* was mapped as 'all records' in the 1962 *Atlas*. Since then there has been a widespread and continuing decline in southern and eastern England. Its decline, worse than the norm for wetland habitats, is probably due to drainage of wet meadows, nutrient enrichment, re-seeding and agricultural intensification. It is likely that at least some populations have been killed off deliberately by land managers, mistaking this species for the much-derided *J. vulgaris*.

Biogeography European Temperate element.

	GB	IR
Long term	↓	↓
Short term	↓	↓

Native		GB	IR
2000–19	●	1903	898
1987–99	●	1883	864
1970–86	●	1301	161
pre-1970	○	1986	749

Alien		GB	IR
2000–19	●	1	0
1987–99	●	1	0
1970–86	●	1	0
pre-1970	○	0	0

H.J. KILLICK

Altitude (m) histogram and phenology chart.
● <1% ● 1–10% ● 11–30% ● 31–40% ● 41–50% ● 51–100%
☐ Apparency ☐ In flower ☐ In leaf

Jacobaea erucifolia Hoary Ragwort
(L.) G.Gaertn., B.Mey. & Scherb.

A yellow-flowered perennial herb
of grassland and disturbed habitats,
including hay meadows and pastures,
chalk and limestone downland, field-
borders, railway banks, roadsides, waste
places, shingle banks and fixed sand
dunes; it is usually found on neutral
or calcareous soils, especially clays
that are wet in winter but baked dry
in summer. Four varieties and a form
lacking ray-florets have been reported.
It is mostly found in lowland England
in areas with less than 800 mm rainfall.

Trends The 10 km square distribution
of *J. erucifolia* has remained largely
stable since the 1960s and it is
now better recorded in its core
areas. It is occasionally imported
in wild-flower seed mixtures.

Biogeography Eurosiberian Temperate
element; also in eastern Asia.

Native	GB	IR
2000–19	1244	29
1987–99	1129	22
1970–86	772	6
pre-1970	1046	12

Alien	GB	IR
2000–19	3	0
1987–99	3	0
1970–86	0	0
pre-1970	4	0

H.J. Killick

Jacobaea paludosa Fen Ragwort
(L.) G.Gaertn., B.Mey. & Scherb.

A long-lived perennial herb of nutrient-
rich, relatively open tall-herb fen
or reed-swamp communities. The
roadside ditch that holds the only
extant native population in our area
is usually flooded in winter but dries
out in summer. Seed-set is poor there,
but plants cultivated from material
collected from this site show improved
seed-set both in cultivation and at
transplantation sites. In continental
Europe it is primarily a plant of river
corridors and floodplains, with seeds
or fragments of rhizome capable of
regeneration if dispersed downstream
and washed up onto bare soil. Lowland.

Trends Many sites were drained in the
18th and 19th centuries, and by 1857
J. paludosa was considered to be extinct
in Britain. However, a single plant with
five flowering stems was discovered in
1972 in a recently dug Fenland roadside
ditch near Ely (Cambridgeshire), and

this original plant continues to persist,
with 33 flowering stems counted in
2019 (Stroh, 2020). Since 1992, plants
have been introduced to 33 locations
in or near to some of its historic sites
(*e.g.* Wicken Fen, Cambridgeshire), but
had been lost from all but two by 2019.
The failure of introductions is probably
due to at least three main factors:
an inability to replicate its principal
dynamic ecological niche, herbivory
by deer and slugs, and competition
from the surrounding vegetation.

Biogeography Eurosiberian Temperate
element, with a continental distribution
in western Europe.

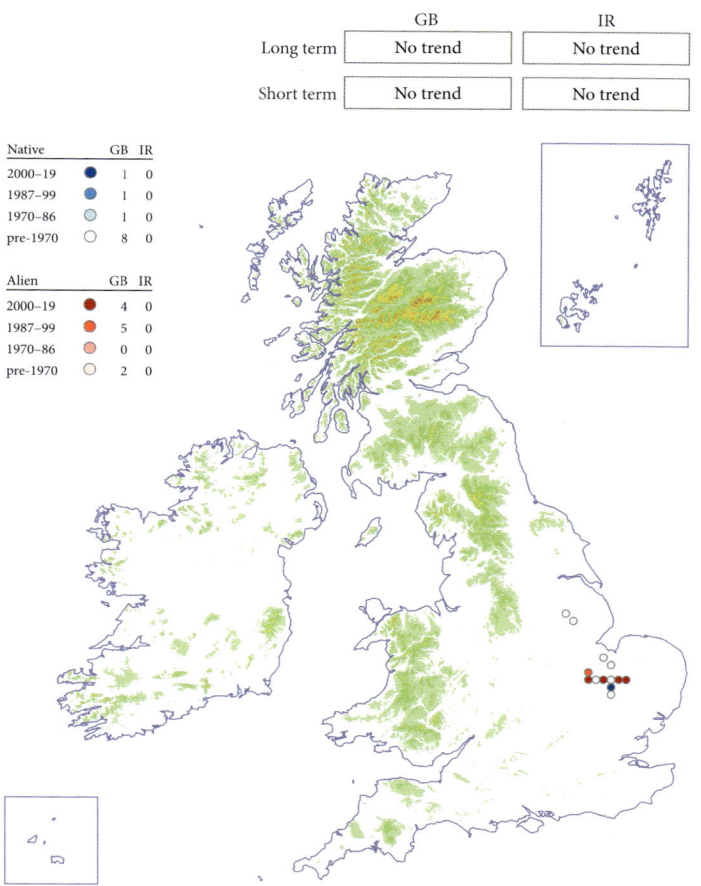

Native	GB	IR
2000–19	1	0
1987–99	1	0
1970–86	1	0
pre-1970	8	0

Alien	GB	IR
2000–19	4	0
1987–99	5	0
1970–86	0	0
pre-1970	2	0

	GB	IR
Long term	No trend	No trend
Short term	No trend	No trend

Key refs Stroh (2020), Wigginton (1999).

P.A. Stroh & M.J. Wigginton

Ne *Delairea odorata* German-ivy
Lem.

A trailing or climbing, woody perennial which grows over fences and walls and is naturalized in hedgerows and on cliff-tops. Lowland.

Trends *D. odorata* was known in cultivation in our area in 1855 and is popular in gardens, especially in coastal areas with a mild climate. It was known in the wild by 1913 (Torquay, South Devon), and can be abundant locally in the Channel Islands and the Isles of Scilly. It appears to be spreading in Ireland, where, although it was first reported in 1939, most records are from the last 20 years. It is beleived to be very invasive.

Biogeography Native of South Africa.

Alien		GB	IR
2000–19	●	28	22
1987–99	●	17	4
1970–86	●	9	0
pre-1970	○	8	0

	GB	IR
Long term	No trend	No trend
Short term		

Altitude (m) chart: ● <1% ● 1–10% ● 11–30% ● 31–40% ● 41–50% ● 51–100%

Apparency In flower In leaf

T.D. DINES & D.A. PEARMAN

N *Tephroseris integrifolia* subsp. *integrifolia* Field Fleawort
(L.) Holub

A small biennial or short-lived perennial yellow-flowered herb, occurring on shallow and infertile rendzina soils high in calcium carbonate and deficient in nitrate and phosphate. It occurs on very short, species-rich turf on downland, ancient earthworks and tracksides, and favours warm, grazed, south-facing slopes. Reproduction is mainly by seed, which are short-lived in the soil. Lowland.

Trends Declines in the 10 km square distribution of *T. integrifolia* subsp. *integrifolia* were obvious by the 1990s, with losses largely attributed to habitat destruction up till the 1970s, and undergrazing thereafter. Fertilizing, re-seeding, conifer planting and overgrazing were also implicated. Although the map appears to show stability since 2000, there continue to

be losses locally, with the main cause considered to be undergrazing (Stroh *et al.*, 2017). Two 19th century records from Westmorland have been searched for numerous times without success.

Biogeography *T. integrifolia* is a complex of taxa with a disjunct Circumpolar Wide-boreal distribution (Hultén & Fries, 1986; Meusel & Jager, 1992). Subsp. *integrifolia* is widespread in Europe but its eastern limit is unclear.

Native		GB	IR
2000–19	●	40	0
1987–99	●	48	0
1970–86	●	50	0
pre-1970	○	94	0

	GB	IR
Long term	⬇	No trend
Short term	⬇	No trend

Altitude (m) chart: ● <1% ● 1–10% ● 11–30% ● 31–40% ● 41–50% ● 51–100%

Apparency In flower In leaf

Key refs Marren (2000), Stroh *et al.* (2017), Walker *et al.* (2017).

H.J. KILLICK & P.A. STROH

Tephroseris integrifolia subsp. *maritima*
(Syme) B.Nord.

A biennial or short-lived perennial herb of mildly acidic to neutral soils (glacial drift) on grassy coastal cliff-slopes, and on ledges and in crevices on the cliff-face. Most populations occur on exposed slopes with a south-west to north-west aspect. Reproduction is mainly by seed. Lowland.

Trends *T. integrifolia* subsp. *maritima* is known only from South Stack to Porth Ruffydd in Anglesey, where it was discovered in 1800 (Pearman, 2017b). It was originally named as a variety by Syme in 1866 but was promoted to a subspecies by Chater in 1974. Populations appear to be stable. Its taxonomic position in the context of the complex variation shown in Europe by *T. integrifolia* and related species, most notably *T. helenitis*, relies on its morphology, distribution and ecology (Kadereit *et al.*, 2021),

although questions remain about the extent to which its morphology is the result of phenotypic plasticity, and recognition at subspecies level currently has no molecular support.

Biogeography Endemic.

Native	GB	IR
2000–19	2	0
1987–99	2	0
1970–86	1	0
pre-1970	2	0

	GB	IR
Long term	No trend	No trend
Short term	No trend	No trend

Key refs Kadereit *et al.* (2021), Pearman (2017b), Smith (1979), Wigginton (1999).

H.J. KILLICK & P.A. STROH

Tephroseris palustris Marsh Fleawort
(L.) Fourr.

A biennial or short-lived perennial herb of pond margins and fen ditches; in the Netherlands, it is known to be an early colonist of the bare mud on land newly reclaimed from the sea (polders). Lowland.

Trends *T. palustris* was first recorded in Britain in 1650 but had been extirpated by the end of the 19th century. It was lost from Sussex in 1725, from the Cambridgeshire and Lincolnshire fens by the early 1800s, and from the Norfolk Broads by the 1890s. Its last native record was from Dersingham (West Norfolk) in 1899. Drainage and agricultural changes probably caused its demise at most sites.

Biogeography Circumpolar Wide-boreal element.

Native	GB	IR
2000–19	0	0
1987–99	0	0
1970–86	0	0
pre-1970	26	0

	GB	IR
Long term	No trend	No trend
Short term	No trend	No trend

Key refs Marren (1999).

H.J. KILLICK & S.J. LEACH

Hy *Brachyglottis ×jubar* Shrub Ragwort
P.D.Sell

A spreading shrub frequently grown in public places, and also recorded as a persistent relic of cultivation or naturalized in rough grassland, sand dunes and waste ground, especially near the sea. Lowland.

A cultivated hybrid (alien × alien).

Trends This plant, formerly (and incorrectly) known as 'Senecio greyi' in horticulture, is now grown as the cultivar 'Sunshine' and is becoming increasingly well-established in the wild. The first naturalized occurrence in our area is from Mont Mado (Jersey, Channel Islands) in 1969; there are possibly earlier records in Cornwall, but all seem to be of plants in gardens. The map presented here does not distinguish between planted and naturalized records.

Biogeography A hybrid of garden origin and uncertain parentage.

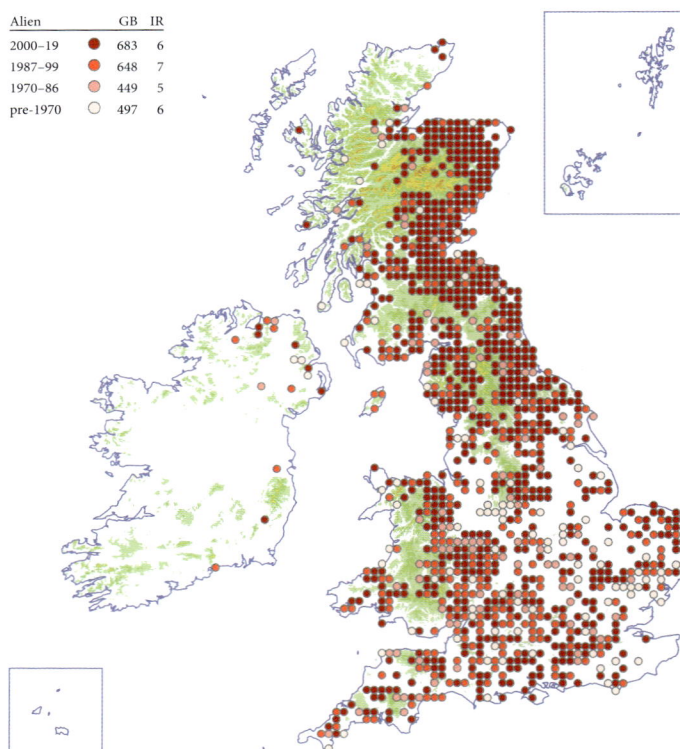

	GB	IR
2000–19	192	15
1987–99	73	2
1970–86	7	0
pre-1970	3	0

Key refs Bean (1980), Stace *et al.* (2015).

C.A. STACE, C.D. PRESTON & D.A. PEARMAN

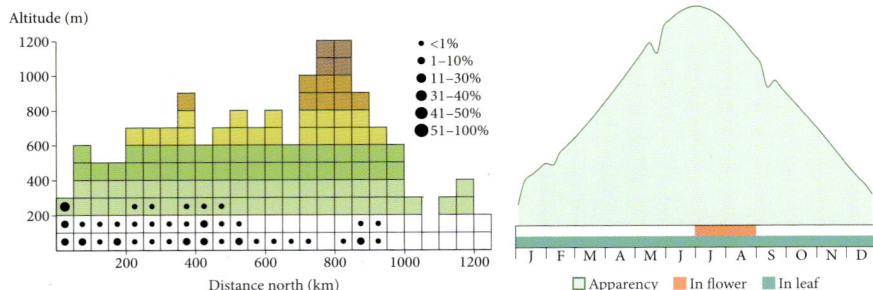

Ne *Doronicum pardalianches* Leopard's-bane
L.

A rhizomatous yellow-flowered perennial herb, well-naturalized and sometimes persistent (and occasionally invasive) in woods, plantations and hedgerows, and on streamsides and roadsides. 0–367 m (Sipton Shield, South Northumberland).

Trends This species has been cultivated in Britain since 1596 and is widely grown for ornament and formerly for medicinal purposes. It was first recorded in the wild in 1777. It has consolidated and slightly expanded its range since the 1960s, although there has been much turnover in distribution since the 2002 *Atlas*. Some mapped records may represent the hybrids *D. ×willldenowii* and *D. ×excelsum*.

Biogeography Native of western Europe, east to Germany and Italy.

Alien	GB	IR
2000–19	683	6
1987–99	648	7
1970–86	449	5
pre-1970	497	6

Key refs Leslie (1981).

H.J. KILLICK

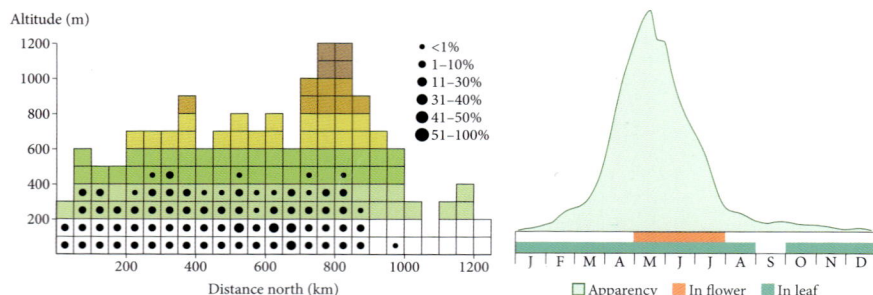

Hy *Doronicum pardalianches × plantagineum = D. ×willdenowii*
(Rouy) A.W.Hill

A perennial herb naturalized in woodland and hedges, and on shady roadsides and lane banks. Lowland.

A cultivated hybrid (alien × alien).

Trends This hybrid is often grown in gardens and was first recorded in the wild in Britain in 1800, from Widdington in North Essex, where it persisted for at least 180 years. It is often mistaken for *D. plantagineum*, and may be under-recorded.

Biogeography This hybrid is possibly a native of western Europe, but it may be of garden origin.

	GB	IR
Long term	No trend	No trend
Short term	⬇	No trend

	GB	IR
2000–19	28	0
1987–99	29	0
1970–86	3	0
pre-1970	5	0

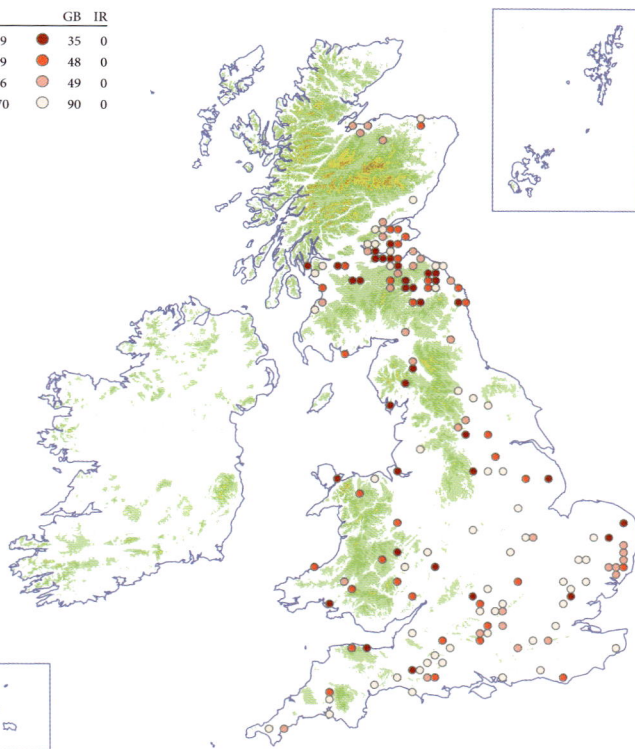

Key refs Stace *et al.* (2015).

Altitude (m)

<1%
1–10%
11–30%
31–40%
41–50%
51–100%

Distance north (km)

☐ Apparency ☐ In flower ☐ In leaf

T.D. DINES

Ne *Doronicum plantagineum* Plantain-leaved Leopard's-bane
L.

A rhizomatous perennial, occasionally naturalized in woods and shady and waste places. Although widespread it has been seen most often in south-eastern Scotland. Lowland.

Trends *D. plantagineum* was introduced into cultivation in Britain by 1571 and locally naturalized since 1799. It, and closely related taxa, are popular garden plants; its seeming decline in recent years probably reflects increasing recognition that many plants formerly identified as this species are in fact the hybrids *D. ×willdenowii* or *D. ×excelsum*.

Biogeography Native of western Europe (Iberian Peninsula, Italy, France), north to northern France.

	GB	IR
Long term	No trend	No trend
Short term	⬇	No trend

Alien	GB	IR
2000–19	35	0
1987–99	48	0
1970–86	49	0
pre-1970	90	0

Key refs Leslie (1981).

Altitude (m)

<1%
1–10%
11–30%
31–40%
41–50%
51–100%

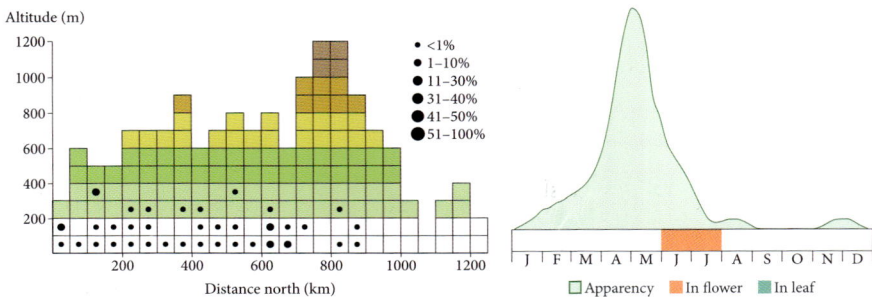

Distance north (km)

☐ Apparency ☐ In flower ☐ In leaf

H.J. KILLICK

Hy *Doronicum columnae* × *pardalianches* × *plantagineum* = *D.* ×*excelsum*
(N.E.Br.) Stace

Harpur-Crewe's Leopard's-bane

A perennial herb naturalized in woodland and shaded roadside verges, streamsides, old chalk-pits, hedges and lane banks. Lowland.

A cultivated hybrid (alien × alien).

Trends This hybrid is often grown in gardens, but like *D.* ×*willdenowii*, was probably unknown to most British botanists until Leslie's (1981) account of the British taxa, and it was treated as a variety of *D. plantagineum* (for which it may still be mistaken) until Stace's *New Flora* (1991). It would appear to be the more common of the two hybrids, but may nevertheless be under-recorded. The first record from the wild was in 1916 (Middlesex).

Biogeography A hybrid of garden origin.

	GB	IR
2000–19 ●	43	0
1987–99 ●	42	0
1970–86 ●	16	0
pre-1970 ○	2	0

Key refs Leslie (1981), Stace *et al.* (2015).

C.A. STACE, C.D. PRESTON & D.A. PEARMAN

N *Tussilago farfara* Colt's-foot
L.

A rhizomatous perennial herb, occurring, often as a pioneer, in a wide range of moist or dry, often disturbed habitats, which include heavy, poorly drained clay, sand dunes, shingle, slumping cliff-slopes, landslides, spoil heaps, seepage areas, rough grassland, crumbling riverbanks, waste places, railway ballast and roadside verges. 0–1,065 m in the Breadalbanes (Mid Perthshire).

Trends The 10 km square distribution of *T. farfara* has changed little since the 1960s, with losses in calcareous grassland being partly offset by gains on disturbed ground. It was formerly a pernicious weed of arable land on clay soils but has been much reduced by modern intensive management. It is alien in Shetland.

Biogeography Eurosiberian Boreo-temperate element; widely naturalized outside its native range.

Native	GB	IR
2000–19 ●	2581	897
1987–99 ●	2497	818
1970–86 ○	1711	115
pre-1970 ○	2476	769

Alien	GB	IR
2000–19 ●	12	0
1987–99 ●	17	0
1970–86 ●	2	0
pre-1970 ○	10	0

Key refs Braithwaite *et al.* (2006), Grime *et al.* (2007).

H.J. KILLICK

N *Petasites hybridus* Butterbur
(L.) G.Gaertn., B.Mey. & Scherb.

A very robust, dioecious rhizomatous perennial herb, with pink flower heads in spring and large leaves in summer. It grows in moist, fertile, often alluvial soils by watercourses, in wet meadows, marshes, flood plains and copses, and on roadsides. It spreads mostly vegetatively from rhizome fragments. Female plants are frequent only in northern and central England. Male-only colonies are probably single clones, many perhaps arising from deliberate plantings for a source of pollen and nectar for hive bees, but few are recorded as such. In some places the habitats of male and female plants may differ. 0–433 m at Lanehead (County Durham).

Trends The overall distribution of *P. hybridus* has not changed appreciably since the 1960s. However, 20th century records in some parts of south-eastern England have not been repeated, and where banks of rivers and canals have been hardened or tidied, some local populations have decreased.

Biogeography European Temperate element.

Native	GB	IR
2000–19	1565	508
1987–99	1587	471
1970–86	1058	65
pre-1970	1510	383

Alien	GB	IR
2000–19	26	3
1987–99	17	2
1970–86	3	0
pre-1970	18	2

Key refs Braithwaite *et al.* (2006), Greenwood (2011), Grime *et al.* (2007), Stevens (1990), Valentine (1947).

H.J. KILLICK

Ne *Petasites japonicus* Giant Butterbur
(Siebold & Zucc.) Maxim.

A large dioecious, rhizomatous perennial herb, with contrasting cream male and whitish female flowers in spring and huge leaves in summer. Planted for ornament in large gardens and well established, sometimes forming extensive colonies in shaded or open sites by rivers and other damp places, in plantations and on roadsides. Lowland.

Trends *P. japonicus* was being cultivated in Britain by 1897 and was first recorded in the wild in 1924 (Denham, Buckinghamshire). It has been used medicinally and as a vegetable (Fuki-noto) in Japan, China and Korea but has only been grown as an ornamental in our area. Most naturalized colonies appear to be single male clones that have spread vegetatively from deliberate plantings, garden escapes or throw-outs; female plants are rarely if ever naturalized. It appears to have been scarce prior to 1970 but has since increased and become invasive in some areas. It remains a scarce introduction in Ireland and much of Scotland.

Biogeography Native of Japan and Sakhalin.

Alien	GB	IR
2000–19	186	3
1987–99	113	3
1970–86	70	0
pre-1970	41	0

Key refs Desjardins *et al.* (2016).

H.J. KILLICK

Ne *Petasites albus* White Butterbur

(L.) Gaertn.

A large, dioecious rhizomatous perennial herb, with white flower heads in spring and huge leaves in summer. It is occasionally planted as an ornamental in large gardens and is found well-established in nearby woods and on waste ground, tracksides and shady riverbanks, often on nitrogen-rich soils. It occasionally forms large stands. Its spread is assumed to be mainly vegetative given the scarcity of female plants in our area. Lowland.

Trends *P. albus* was introduced to Britain by 1683, and naturalized by 1840 (Wimbotsham, West Norfolk). Its 10 km square distribution has increased steadily since the 1960s, especially in eastern and central Scotland, where it is sometimes invasive. It has spread more slowly in northern England, Wales and Ireland. In Cardiganshire, a population first reported in 1905 was recently refound. This increase in our area partly reflects more systematic recording of aliens, but also the inclusion of planted examples.

Biogeography Native of the mountains of Europe and south-western Asia.

Alien	GB	IR
2000–19	269	6
1987–99	222	6
1970–86	117	1
pre-1970	224	5

Key refs Chater (2010b), Duncan (1980).

H.J. KILLICK

Ne *Petasites pyrenaicus* Winter Heliotrope

(L.) G.López.

A dioecious perennial herb, bearing pinkish vanilla-scented male flowers in winter, attracting bees and flies. It spreads by rhizomes to form dense and very persistent patches, typically on roadsides, but also on streamsides and waste ground. Female flowers are not known from our area and so spread is entirely vegetative in soil, water or discarded garden waste. Lowland.

Trends *P. pyrenaicus* was introduced into cultivation in 1806 and the male plant has since been widely grown as an ornamental in gardens and some churchyards. It was known in the wild by at least 1835 (Bayswater, Middlesex) and, by the start of the 20th century, it appears to have been well-established in many areas. Its 10 km square distribution increased throughout the 20th century and this spread has continued since 2000 to the extent that it has become invasive in some areas. A female clone reported from a site in Sussex in 2014 was subsequently shown (using DNA analysis) to be the hybrid with *P. japonicus* (Desjardins *et al.*, 2016).

Biogeography Native of the central Mediterranean region in Europe (Italy, Sicily, Sardinia) and of northern Africa.

Alien	GB	IR
2000–19	1297	615
1987–99	1126	526
1970–86	651	38
pre-1970	855	276

Key refs Braithwaite *et al.* (2006), Desjardins *et al.* (2016).

H.J. KILLICK

Homogyne alpina Purple Colt's-foot
(L.) Cass.

A creeping perennial herb restricted as a possible native to a single broad ledge near the base of a montane cliff at the head of Glen Clova, Angus. Reproduction appears to be only by rhizomatous spread. The altitude is *c.* 600 m.

Trends This species was originally discovered in Glen Clova in *c.* 1813, but was not refound again until 1951. There is a long-standing and unresolved debate as to whether it was deliberately planted there. Plants were translocated to nearby sites in 1988. *H. alpina* was also recorded from South Uist in 1955, where it was certainly planted and is now extinct.

Biogeography A European Boreo-arctic Montane species, endemic to the mountains of western, central and eastern Europe from Spain to Bulgaria.

Key refs Marren (1999), Pankhurst & Mullin (1991), Wigginton (1999).

H.J. KILLICK

Calendula officinalis Pot Marigold
L.

An aromatic annual to perennial herb, widely grown in sunny, well-drained gardens, found as an escape in towns and villages, usually close to gardens on roadsides, bare and waste ground and also on refuse tips. It often succumbs to frost but increasingly survives in sheltered places. Lowland.

Trends *C. officinalis*, grown in British gardens by medieval times as a pot-herb, and later as a dye and medicinal and ornamental plant, is now a popular garden flower, readily self-sown and escaping. It also occurs as a birdseed and esparto alien. It was first known from the wild in County Durham (1798), later in Oxfordshire (1902), the Isles of Scilly (1939), the Channel Islands, and the Isle of Man. It began to be widely reported around 30 years ago, especially from southern Britain, and has spread greatly in the last two decades. It is treated as a cultivated archaeophyte by Stace & Crawley (2015).

Biogeography A garden plant of unknown origin.

Key refs Crawley (2005), Harvey (1981), Lousley (1971), Stace & Crawley (2015).

H.J. KILLICK

Ne *Calendula arvensis* Field Marigold

L.

An annual herb, found naturalized as a weed of cultivated ground in Guernsey and the Isles of Scilly; elsewhere it occurs as a casual on waste ground, refuse tips and pavements where it is often self-sown from window boxes or gardens nearby. It arises as a garden escape and from esparto. Lowland.

Trends *C. arvensis* was being cultivated in Britain by 1683. It was first recorded from the wild in 1796, from the shores of the harbour in Falmouth (West Cornwall). It is possible that some of the records arise from confusion with the much more common *C. officinalis*.

Biogeography Native of the Mediterranean region and south-western Asia, and naturalized elsewhere.

	GB	IR
Long term	No trend	No trend
Short term		No trend

Alien		GB	IR
2000–19	●	33	0
1987–99	●	22	0
1970–86	●	14	0
pre-1970	○	23	1

Altitude (m)

- ● <1%
- ● 1–10%
- ● 11–30%
- ● 31–40%
- ● 41–50%
- ● 51–100%

Distance north (km)

☐ Apparency ☐ In flower ☐ In leaf

T.D. DINES & D.A. PEARMAN

Ne *Osteospermum jucundum* Osteospermum

(E.Phillips) Norl.

A relatively tender sub-shrub, woody at the base, which readily roots along the stems, forming a sprawling clump, typically on walls and rocks. Lowland.

Trends *O. jucundum* was not recorded in the wild until 1974 (Penzance, West Cornwall). This late date seems unlikely to reflect the first date of its occurrence in the wild, and it was probably overlooked previously. It is an increasingly popular garden plant, and there are many cultivars available.

Biogeography Native of South Africa, now widely grown throughout the temperate world.

	GB	IR
Long term	No trend	No trend
Short term		No trend

Alien		GB	IR
2000–19	●	84	3
1987–99	●	17	0
1970–86	●	1	0
pre-1970	○	0	0

Altitude (m)

- ● <1%
- ● 1–10%
- ● 11–30%
- ● 31–40%
- ● 41–50%
- ● 51–100%

Distance north (km)

☐ Apparency ☐ In flower ☐ In leaf

D.A. PEARMAN

Ambrosia artemisiifolia Ragweed

L.

A monoecious, wind-pollinated annual herb, found as a casual on roadsides, railways, refuse tips, dockyards, construction sites, arable fields and on waste ground. It is frost-sensitive and rarely persists. It is a problematic arable weed in Europe. Lowland.

Trends *A. artemisiifolia* has been recorded as a casual since 1829, with a first record in Cobham (Surrey). Human activity is a major feature in its spread, dispersed with oil-seed, grain, other agricultural seed, animal feed and increasingly with bird-feed and on vehicles. Although many past records were not refound this century, it has in general terms become much more frequent in England and Wales, with small gains in Scotland and the first records in Ireland. Frost is an important limiting factor. A warming climate, with warmer summers and later autumn frosts, could accelerate its spread.

Biogeography Native of North America; widely naturalized elsewhere.

Alien	GB	IR
2000–19	320	13
1987–99	98	0
1970–86	39	0
pre-1970	117	1

	GB	IR
Long term	No trend	No trend
Short term	⬆	⬆

Key refs Bassett & Crompton (1975), Bullock *et al.* (2012), Essl *et al.* (2015), Rich (1994a).

H.J. KILLICK

Ambrosia trifida Giant Ragweed

L.

A tall monoecious, wind-pollinated annual herb, found on waste ground, refuse tips and around docks, as a casual or sometimes persistent alien arriving with birdseed, oil-seed, soya beans or grain. It is a serious weed in North America. Lowland.

Trends *A. trifida* arose principally as a grain contaminant and was first recorded from the wild in 1893 (Leith, Midlothian). Importation of loose cargoes at docks ceased by 1970, and seed cleaning techniques improved; it declined steeply before 2000 and our only 21st century record was in September 2000 near Southampton (South Hampshire), where a few plants were found on a wall at Marchwood Hard close to a military base serving troops from many parts of the world.

Biogeography Native of North America.

Alien	GB	IR
2000–19	1	0
1987–99	4	0
1970–86	11	0
pre-1970	70	1

	GB	IR
Long term	No trend	No trend
Short term	No trend	No trend

Key refs Rich (1994a), Wade *et al.* (1994).

H.J. KILLICK

1049

Ne *Xanthium strumarium* Rough Cocklebur
L.

An annual herb, found on estuarine shores, refuse tips, docks and waste ground, originating mainly from grain, wool, oil-seed, soya-bean waste, and also from birdseed (*e.g.* in chicken runs, pheasant cover). It is usually casual, sometimes persisting for a few years. Lowland.

Trends This species was known in the wild in Britain by 1597 (West Drayton to Iver, Middlesex). Before 1970 it was frequently introduced in wool shoddy but the use of this had almost ceased by 2000 and as a consequence there have been few recent records. More aromatic forms of *X. strumarium* with larger burs have been named *X. strumarium* subsp. *italica* and have been recorded in a few places.

Biogeography Native of both North and South America (subsp. *strumarium*), as well as eastern central and southern Europe (subsp. *italicum*).

Alien		GB	IR
2000–19	●	12	0
1987–99	●	17	0
1970–86	●	13	0
pre-1970	○	52	1

	GB	IR
Long term	No trend	No trend
Short term	No trend	No trend

Key refs Clement (1981b), Everitt *et al.* (2007), Lousley (1961), Wade *et al.* (1994), Weaver & Lechowicz (1983).

H.J. KILLICK

Ne *Xanthium spinosum* Spiny Cocklebur
L.

A spiny annual herb, found on waste ground, refuse tips, in sewage works and railway sidings. It is usually casual, sometimes persisting for a few years. It has generally arisen from wool shoddy or birdseed. Lowland.

Trends *X. spinosum* was introduced from South America via Europe, and was known in the wild in Britain by 1846 (Hertfordshire). Before 1970 it was frequently introduced in wool shoddy but its use as a fertilizer had almost ceased by 2000 and as a consequence there have been few recent records.

Biogeography Native of South America; widely naturalized elsewhere.

Alien		GB	IR
2000–19	●	7	0
1987–99	●	8	0
1970–86	●	21	0
pre-1970	○	118	0

	GB	IR
Long term	No trend	No trend
Short term	No trend	No trend

Key refs Clement (1981b).

H.J. KILLICK

Ne *Rudbeckia hirta* Black-eyed-Susan
L.

A perennial or biennial herb, which is naturalized as a garden escape in rough ground and in waste places. Some older records were from wool shoddy. Lowland.

Trends *R. hirta* was introduced into British gardens sometime before 1714 and is extremely common as a garden plant, with many cultivars. It was recorded in the wild in 1917 (near Bristol, North Somerset) and is probably increasing.

Biogeography Native of North America, but now widely naturalized elsewhere.

	GB	IR
Long term	No trend	No trend
Short term	↓ ↓ ◆ ↑ ↑	No trend

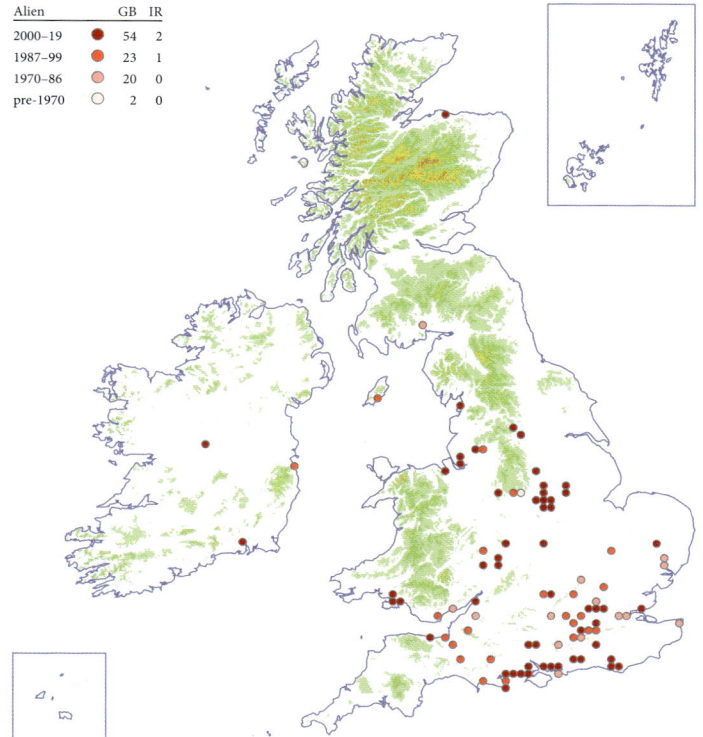

Alien	GB	IR
2000–19	54	2
1987–99	23	1
1970–86	20	0
pre-1970	2	0

Altitude (m)

Distance north (km)

☐ Apparency   ☐ In flower   ☐ In leaf

Key refs Sutton (2001).

T.D. DINES

Ne *Rudbeckia laciniata* Coneflower
L.

A perennial herb with a creeping rhizome, naturalized on riverbanks, roadsides, waste ground, refuse tips and in rough grassy places. It arises as a garden escape, throw-out, or relic of cultivation. Lowland.

Trends *R. laciniata* was already in cultivation in Britain by 1634 and is fairly popular in gardens. It was recorded from the wild in 1882, in Angus, but with no location given.

Biogeography Native of eastern North America, and invasive in parts of Europe.

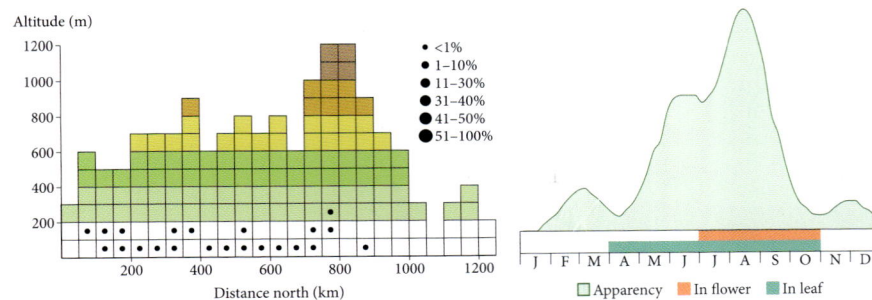

	GB	IR
Long term	No trend	No trend
Short term	↓ ↓ ◆ ↑ ↑	No trend

Alien	GB	IR
2000–19	16	0
1987–99	22	0
1970–86	23	0
pre-1970	27	0

Altitude (m)

Distance north (km)

☐ Apparency   ☐ In flower   ☐ In leaf

Key refs Sutton (2001).

T.D. DINES & D.A. PEARMAN

Ne *Helianthus annuus* Sunflower
L.

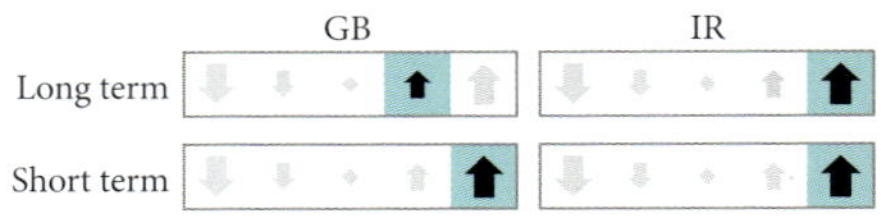

A late-flowering annual herb, widely grown for ornament, birdseed or oil-seed in gardens, allotments, arable fields and in strips along crop margins and found as a casual, or sometimes briefly persisting, on waste ground, refuse tips and roadsides, mainly on fertile, moist, well-drained soils. Lowland.

Trends *H. annuus* is a major crop worldwide, yielding cooking oil, margarine and livestock forage. It is also used as a bioremediator to remove lead and arsenic from soil. It was introduced to Britain by 1596 and first reported wild in 1891 (Warrington, South Lancashire). In the past it was grown on a small scale but was seldom recorded except as a casual on refuse tips. It is now widely and increasingly cultivated on a field scale for its oil-bearing seeds, or for birdseed. Its reported range has greatly increased in the last 30

years, especially in northern Britain, but less so in montane regions and Ireland. The records mapped include both planted and self-sown plants.

Biogeography Native of North America.

Alien	GB	IR
2000–19	897	51
1987–99	307	13
1970–86	130	3
pre-1970	139	0

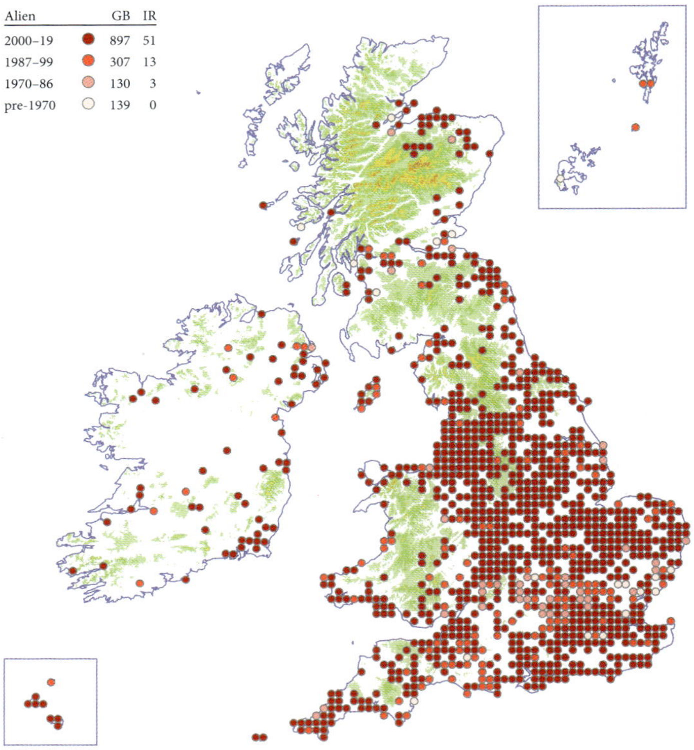

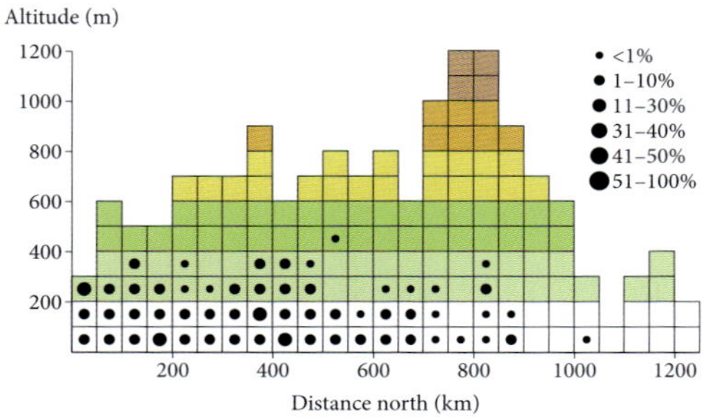

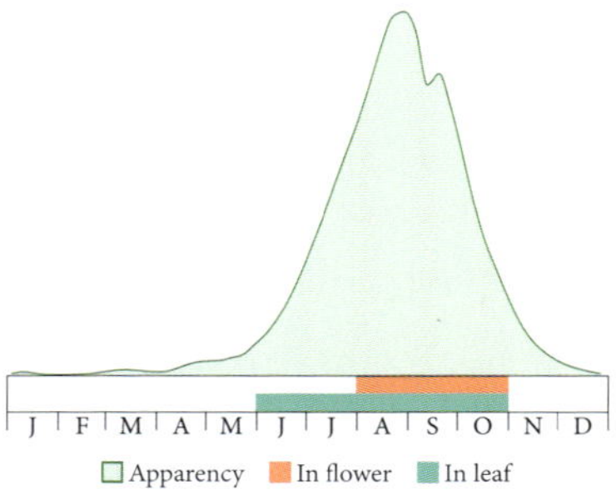

Key refs Vaughan & Geissler (2009).

H.J. KILLICK

Hy *Helianthus annuus* × *decapetalus* = *H.* ×*multiflorus*
L.

Thin-leaved Sunflower

A perennial herb which is naturalized in rough grassy places, refuse tips and on waste ground. It originates as a garden escape or throw-out. Lowland.

A cultivated hybrid (alien × alien).

Trends This hybrid was being cultivated in Britain by 1596 and was recorded from the wild by 1928 (Dagenham, South Essex).

Biogeography A hybrid of garden origin.

	GB	IR
2000–19	9	0
1987–99	12	0
1970–86	1	0
pre-1970	5	0

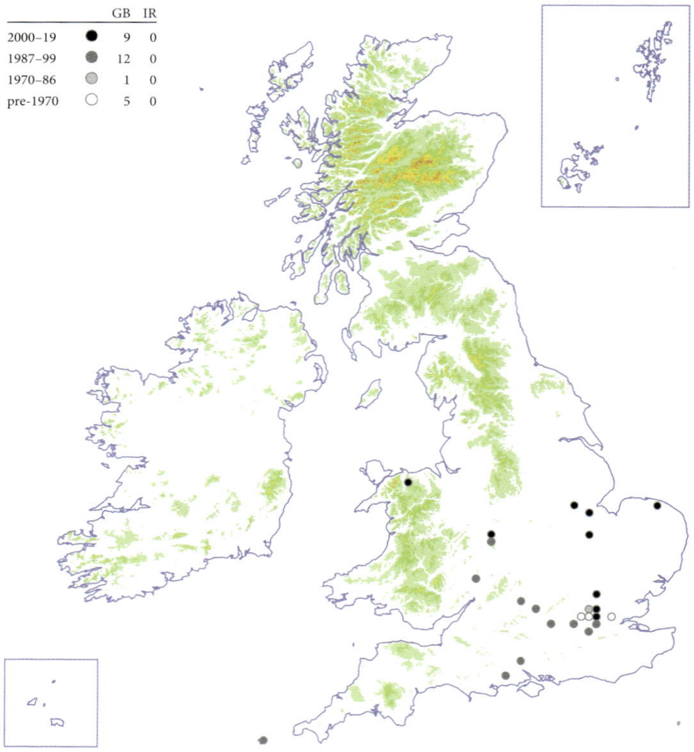

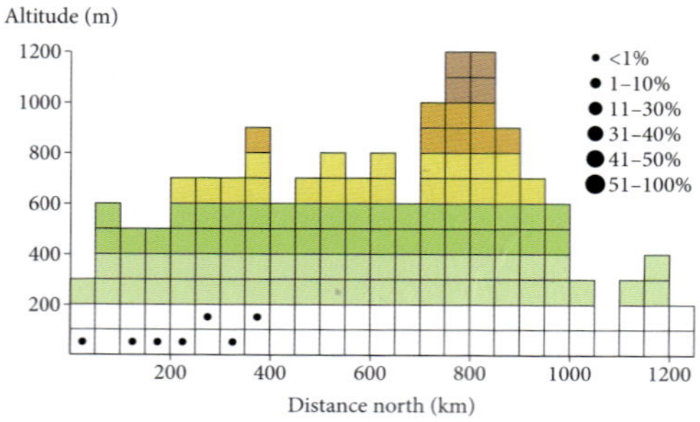

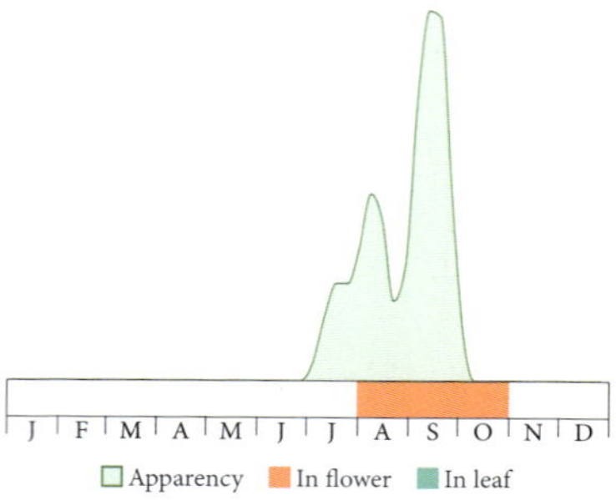

Key refs Stace *et al.* (2015).

T.D. DINES

Hy *Helianthus pauciflorus × tuberosus = H. ×laetiflorus* Perennial Sunflower
Pers.

A tall perennial hybrid occurring as a naturalized, or sometimes casual, garden escape or throw-out, and usually associated with ruderal habitats such as the towpaths of rivers and canals, roadside and tracksides, disused railways, the edges of allotments, refuse tips, piles of dumped topsoil and waste ground. It is, however, occasionally established in semi-natural habitats including sand dunes, riverbanks, streamsides and by reed-swamps and woodland. Lowland.

A cultivated hybrid (alien × alien).

Trends This hybrid was introduced to gardens in 1815 and reported from the wild (as *H. annuus*) in 1900 (Burry Port, Carmarthenshire). It is now the commonest perennial sunflower in gardens, and appears to be increasing in the wild. *H. ×laetiflorus* comprises more than one taxon, probably derived in cultivation from North American parents. Some mapped records may be misidentifications of *H. pauciflorus*.

Biogeography Probably a hybrid of garden origin.

	GB	IR
2000–19 ●	141	1
1987–99 ●	83	0
1970–86 ●	38	0
pre-1970 ○	30	0

	GB	IR
Long term	No trend	No trend
Short term	↓ ↓ ◆ ↑ ↑	No trend

Key refs Stace *et al.* (2015).

C.A. STACE, C.D. PRESTON & D.A. PEARMAN

Altitude (m) key:
- ● <1%
- ● 1–10%
- ● 11–30%
- ● 31–40%
- ● 41–50%
- ● 51–100%

Distance north (km)

□ Apparency □ In flower ■ In leaf

Ne *Helianthus tuberosus* Jerusalem Artichoke
L.

A tall, perennial herb, widely grown in gardens, allotments and on a small scale in fields as game cover or for the edible tubers on its rhizome. It is also found on refuse tips, roadsides and waste ground, often as a relic of cultivation. It flowers very late, if at all, and only after long hot summers in areas with very low rainfall; it seldom sets good seed. Lowland.

Trends *H. tuberosus* was cultivated in Britain by 1617 for its tubers, then known as 'potatoes of Canada', and is now grown in gardens and allotments. It was known to occur in the wild by 1891 (Warrington, South Lancashire). Globally it is grown as animal fodder, biomass, and as cover for gamebirds, and has become highly invasive in some countries, notably along rivers.

Biogeography Native of North America.

Alien	GB	IR
2000–19 ●	137	2
1987–99 ●	98	1
1970–86 ●	60	0
pre-1970 ○	69	0

	GB	IR
Long term	↓ ↓ ◆ ↑ ↑	No trend
Short term	↓ ↓ ◆ ↑ ↑	No trend

Key refs Swanton *et al.* (1992), Vaughan & Geissler (2009).

H.J. KILLICK

Altitude (m) key:
- ● <1%
- ● 1–10%
- ● 11–30%
- ● 31–40%
- ● 41–50%
- ● 51–100%

Distance north (km)

□ Apparency □ In flower ■ In leaf

Ne ## *Guizotia abyssinica* Niger
(L.f.) Cass.

An annual herb, found as a casual on refuse tips, sewage farms, roadsides, near oil mills, and in waste places but possibly most frequently now under bird-feeders where the seed has been used as a food to attract finches into gardens. Lowland.

Trends *G. abyssinica* has been a crop (notably oil-seed) in Ethiopia for 4,000 years and introduced to many other countries, reaching British gardens by 1806. It has been known in the wild here since 1861 (Old Hartlepool, County Durham). It was rare before 1970 but has increased markedly, especially in the last 20 years, and has spread northward, though is still scarce outside England.

Biogeography Native of eastern Africa, especially Ethiopia, and now spread by humans to much of Africa, Asia, Europe and America.

Alien	GB	IR
2000–19	239	16
1987–99	48	0
1970–86	46	0
pre-1970	45	0

Altitude (m)
- <1%
- 1–10%
- 11–30%
- 31–40%
- 41–50%
- 51–100%

Distance north (km)

Apparency In flower In leaf

Key refs Dunn (1905), Wade *et al.* (1994).

H.J. Killick

Ne ## *Galinsoga parviflora* Gallant Soldier
Cav.

An annual herb of light soils, often frequently disturbed, in cultivated fields, market gardens, nursery plots, garden centres and gardens, and in waste ground in urban areas. Usually casual, but often a persistent weed of cultivation. Lowland.

Trends This species was introduced as a garden plant to Kew Gardens by 1796, from where it had escaped by 1861 (and was known as the 'Kew Weed'). It has spread steadily since then, aided by transport from nursery gardens and occurring also as a wool alien. It is widespread as a casual, sometimes persisting, especially as a weed of cultivation. Its range and frequency has increased steadily but less so recently than that of *G. quadriradiata*.

Biogeography Native of South America; widely naturalized in other countries.

Alien	GB	IR
2000–19	343	6
1987–99	298	1
1970–86	201	1
pre-1970	245	1

Altitude (m)
- <1%
- 1–10%
- 11–30%
- 31–40%
- 41–50%
- 51–100%

Distance north (km)

Apparency In flower In leaf

Key refs Braithwaite *et al.* (2006), Warwick & Sweet (1983).

H.J. Killick

Ne *Galinsoga quadriradiata* Shaggy Soldier
Ruiz & Pav.

An annual herb of arable fields, waste ground, roadsides and refuse tips, derelict urban sites and cracks in pavements, most often occurring in the larger conurbations. Lowland.

Trends The species was first recorded from the wild in 1909 (Acton, Middlesex), perhaps being originally introduced with ornamental garden plants; it is also a birdseed alien. Early on, it may have been mistaken for *G. parviflora*, and there were records from only nine 10 km squares by 1940. Its range had doubled by the end of the 1950s and since then it has spread dramatically, becoming much more frequent than *G. parviflora*. Curiously, it has spread very little in Ireland, where it was first recorded in 1980.

Biogeography Native of Central and South America; widely naturalized in Europe and elsewhere.

Alien	GB	IR
2000–19	663	11
1987–99	384	3
1970–86	227	4
pre-1970	277	1

	<1%
	1–10%
	11–30%
	31–40%
	41–50%
	51–100%

Key refs Braithwaite *et al.* (2006), Burton (1983), Lousley (1971), Warwick & Sweet (1983).

H.J. KILLICK

N *Bidens cernua* Nodding Bur-marigold
L.

An annual herb growing on a wide range of fertile, neutral to alkaline, damp or wet substrates on the margins of slow-flowing rivers and streams, backwaters and ox-bows, by ponds and meres, often in places subject to winter flooding; also in ditches, marshes and tall-herb vegetation. A variety with ray florets (var. *radiata*) is frequent only in north-western England. 0–310 m (Heathcote, Derbyshire).

Trends *B. cernua* declined markedly in some areas before 1930. This decline, associated with drainage, lack of management, boat activity and habitat destruction, continued in some areas. Though it is probably now better recorded, it has become locally uncommon in a number of counties.

Biogeography Circumpolar Temperate element.

Native	GB	IR
2000–19	497	172
1987–99	553	198
1970–86	403	58
pre-1970	693	136

Alien	GB	IR
2000–19	1	0
1987–99	0	1
1970–86	0	0
pre-1970	0	0

	<1%
	1–10%
	11–30%
	31–40%
	41–50%
	51–100%

Key refs Braithwaite *et al.* (2006), Green *et al.* (1997), Grose (1957).

H.J. KILLICK

N *Bidens tripartita* Trifid Bur-marigold

L.

An annual herb of nutrient-rich mud or gravel by ponds, canals, slow rivers and streams, and in wet pits and wet grassland, often in areas that are inundated in winter but exposed in summer; it also occurs in ditches, peat workings and other damp places. It prefers less acidic and drier substrates than *B. cernua* though is often found with it. Generally lowland, but reaching 365 m at Pilleth (Radnorshire).

Trends *B. tripartita* had decreased by 2000, particularly in south-eastern England. Braithwaite *et al.* (2006) reported substantial declines between 1987 and 2004, and many 20th century records for Scotland, Ireland, Wales and East Anglia have not been refound this century. Drainage, the infilling of ponds and ditches, and the canalization of watercourses are all likely to have contributed to its decline.

Biogeography Eurasian Temperate element; widely naturalized outside its native range.

Native		GB	IR
2000–19	●	652	136
1987–99	●	729	137
1970–86	○	532	39
pre-1970	○	822	128

Alien		GB	IR
2000–19	●	0	0
1987–99	●	0	0
1970–86	●	1	0
pre-1970	○	1	0

Key refs Braithwaite *et al.* (2006), Clapham (1969), Green *et al.* (1997), Grose (1957).

H.J. KILLICK

Altitude (m) / Distance north (km)

• <1%
● 1–10%
● 11–30%
● 31–40%
● 41–50%
● 51–100%

J F M A M J J A S O N D
□ Apparency ■ In flower ■ In leaf

Ne *Bidens frondosa* Beggarticks

L.

An annual herb with pinnate leaves and orange disc florets (sometimes with yellow rays), found by rivers and canals, on damp, waterlogged and waste ground, and on refuse tips in urban areas and ports. The two types of achene enable it to spread by water, animals and humans. Used in herbal and modern medicine. Lowland.

Trends *B. frondosa* was first recorded as a casual in 1913 (near Micklehurst, South Lancashire), and was first known naturalized on a canal towpath near Birmingham in 1952. Its vector is unknown, but it was possibly originally introduced as a contaminant of wool products. It spread along canals in the English Midlands, and near to London, but only moderately so since 2000, and over a third of earlier records have not been refound. It is not yet invasive,

as in New Zealand, nor replacing other *Bidens*, as in parts of Europe.

Biogeography Native of North and South America; widely naturalized in temperate Europe.

Alien		GB	IR
2000–19	●	105	1
1987–99	●	75	0
1970–86	●	25	0
pre-1970	○	27	0

Key refs Cadbury *et al.* (1971), Kay (1998a), McMullen (2016).

H.J. KILLICK

Altitude (m) / Distance north (km)

• <1%
● 1–10%
● 11–30%
● 31–40%
● 41–50%
● 51–100%

J F M A M J J A S O N D
□ Apparency ■ In flower ■ In leaf

Ne *Bidens ferulifolia* Fern-leaved Beggarticks
(Jacq.) DC.

A perennial herb, grown in window boxes and hanging baskets, but frost-sensitive and thus usually grown as an annual, readily self-seeding onto pavements and waste ground but almost never persisting. Lowland.

Trends *B. ferulifolia* was introduced in 1799, and first recorded in the wild at Marston, Oxfordshire in 1915. It is now very commonly planted in hanging baskets, window boxes and containers.

Biogeography Native to Central America and southern North America.

GB		IR	
Long term	No trend	No trend
Short term	⬆	⬆

Alien	GB	IR
2000–19	73	9
1987–99	20	1
1970–86	4	0
pre-1970	0	0

Altitude (m)

<1%
1–10%
11–30%
31–40%
41–50%
51–100%

Distance north (km)

☐ Apparency ☐ In flower ☐ In leaf

D.A. PEARMAN

Ne *Cosmos bipinnatus* Mexican Aster
Cav.

An annual herb, found on waste ground and refuse tips, where it arises as a garden escape, and from birdseed, cotton refuse, and formerly, wool shoddy. It is usually casual, but some populations in southern England are naturalized. Lowland.

Trends *C. bipinnatus* was first cultivated in Britain in 1799. It was recorded from the wild in 1930 (Mitcham, Surrey), and remains a fairly frequent introduction, especially of the comparatively recently introduced dwarf cultivars.

Biogeography Native of south-western North America and Mexico, but now widely naturalized elsewhere.

GB		IR	
Long term	No trend	No trend
Short term	⬆	No trend

Alien	GB	IR
2000–19	137	0
1987–99	25	1
1970–86	22	0
pre-1970	21	0

Key refs Sutton (2001).

Altitude (m)

<1%
1–10%
11–30%
31–40%
41–50%
51–100%

Distance north (km)

☐ Apparency ☐ In flower ☐ In leaf

T.D. DINES & D.A. PEARMAN

Ne *Tagetes patula* French Marigold
L.

An annual herb, very widely grown as a bedding plant in gardens and found on waste ground and refuse tips, where it occurs as a casual escape or throw-out from gardens. It also occurs in parks and other cultivated ground as a relic of cultivation. Usually lowland, but up to 400 m at Wanlockhead (Dumfriesshire).

Trends *T. patula* was probably cultivated in Britain by 1573 or soon afterwards, and is extremely common in gardens, where it is grown as a bedding plant with a vast number of cultivars and also as an insect deterrent amongst crop plants. It was recorded in the wild in 1933 (Welwyn, Hertfordshire). Some authorities consider it to be conspecific with *T. erecta* with which it is sometimes confused.

Biogeography Native of Mexico.

Alien	GB	IR
2000–19	77	6
1987–99	33	0
1970–86	15	0
pre-1970	17	0

	GB	IR
Long term	No trend	No trend
Short term	↓ ↓ ◆ ↑ ↑	No trend

T.D. DINES & D.A. PEARMAN

Hy *Gaillardia aristata × pulchella = G. ×grandiflora* Blanketflower
hort. ex Van Houtte

An annual or short-lived perennial hybrid which is naturalized on heathland and on sand and shingle by the sea, but is more frequently casual on walls, roadsides, and in refuse tips and waste ground. It arises as a garden escape. Lowland.

A cultivated hybrid (alien × alien).

Trends This hybrid was introduced into British gardens in 1884 and is widely grown for its colourful flowers. It was first recorded in the wild at Witley Common (Surrey) in 1959, and was one of the colourful neophytes sown at the Olympic Park in Stratford (Middlesex) for the 2012 Games.

Biogeography A hybrid of garden origin.

	GB	IR
2000–19	6	0
1987–99	8	0
1970–86	4	0
pre-1970	1	0

	GB	IR
Long term	No trend	No trend
Short term	No trend	No trend

Key refs Stace *et al.* (2015).

C.A. STACE, C.D. PRESTON & D.A. PEARMAN

Hy *Helenium ×clementii* Sneezeweed
Verloove & Lambinon

A large perennial herb, widely grown in gardens and surviving where outcast on roadsides, waste ground, refuse tips, in chalk-pits and at the edge of a plantation. It also occurs as a relic of cultivation. Lowland.

A cultivated hybrid (alien × alien).

Trends The common garden ornamental *Helenium* is usually identified as the widespread North American *H. autumnale* but, according to Verloove & Limbinon (2006), it is more likely a hybrid involving extra species such as *H. bigelovii* and possibly *H. flexuosum* (*H. ×clementii*) and so that is the name we have followed here. It was being cultivated in Britain by 1729 and is very widely grown as an autumn-flowering perennial. It was recorded from the wild in 1955 (Oxfordshire). Cultivars are very variable in height and colour of flowers.

Biogeography Native of North America.

	GB	IR
2000–19	9	0
1987–99	5	0
1970–86	4	0
pre-1970	9	0

	GB	IR
Long term	No trend	No trend
Short term	No trend	No trend

Key refs Stace *et al.* (2015), Verloove & Lambinon (2006).

T.D. Dines & K.J. Walker

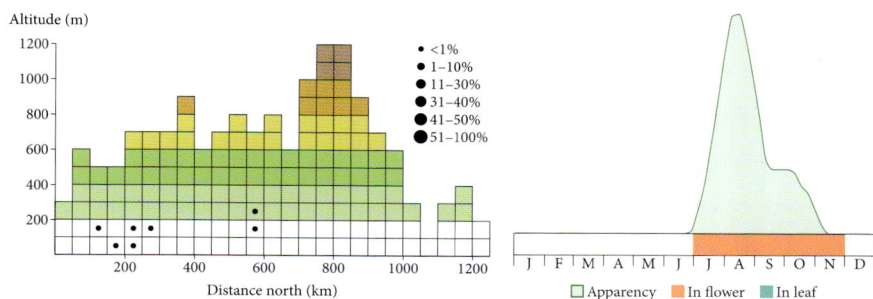

N *Eupatorium cannabinum* Hemp-agrimony
L.

A perennial herb found on base-enriched soils in a wide range of damp or wet habitats, including marginal vegetation by ponds, lakes, rivers and canals, tall-herb fen, fen-meadows, marshes, wet woodland, mires and wet heath; also flushed areas on sea-cliffs and in dune-slacks. It is infrequent in dry habitats, but is found in dry woods and on hedgebanks, on waste ground, and even on dry chalk banks. 0–410 m (Chew Road, South-west Yorkshire).

Trends Although the overall 10 km square distribution of *E. cannabinum* has changed very little since the 1960s, there has been a notable degree of turnover at the local level. This is presumably due to the loss of wetlands in areas where it has always been scarce. In other regions increases may have resulted from reduced grazing following the fencing off of ditches and other wetlands, more systematic surveys of wetland habitats, or possibly due to planting in the wild or as escapes from gardens.

Biogeography European Temperate element; also in central Asia.

Native	GB	IR
2000–19	1585	363
1987–99	1533	318
1970–86	1118	51
pre-1970	1471	235

Alien	GB	IR
2000–19	11	0
1987–99	5	0
1970–86	1	0
pre-1970	2	0

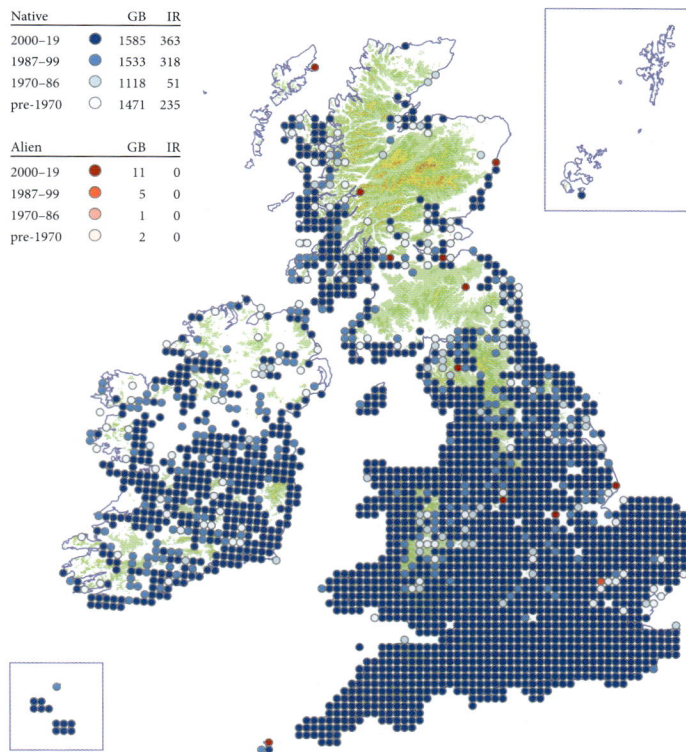

M.J. Wigginton & K.J. Walker

Ne *Escallonia rubra* var. *macrantha* Escallonia
(Hook. & Arn.) Reiche

An evergreen shrub, planted as a hedge, windbreak and wall-covering especially near to the coast and found naturalized in woodland and on cliffs, banks, roadsides and waste ground, and as a persistent relic of cultivation. Reproduction is by seed although it appears to be rarely self-sown. Lowland.

Trends *E. rubra* was introduced to Britain in 1847 and is often planted in coastal areas. It was noted as forming hedges in the Isles of Scilly in 1886, and as naturalized at Derrynane, South Kerry in 1906. It has now spread considerably in south-western Britain and Ireland, showing a marked increase since the 1960s, though it is suspected that many of the records relate to plantings and persistent relics.

Biogeography Native of South America (Argentina, Chile).

Alien	GB	IR
2000–19	323	199
1987–99	163	91
1970–86	37	7
pre-1970	38	17

	GB	IR
Long term	No trend	No trend
Short term		

Key refs Bean (1973), Coats (1963).

D.A. Pearman & J.M. Croft

N *Adoxa moschatellina* Moschatel
L.

A perennial rhizomatous herb of mesic brown earth soils on the shaded banks of rivers and streams, in deciduous woodlands and shaded hedgebanks; also occasionally in shaded base-rich sites in mountains. This is a vernal species which disappears by May or June in the lowlands. It is self-fertile, reproducing by seed and vegetatively. 0–1,065 m (Ben Lawers, Mid Perthshire).

Trends The distribution of *A. moschatellina* appears to be stable following historic losses from parts of eastern England and north-western Scotland as a result of habitat destruction. In some areas it is possibly under-recorded due to its early season. It is doubtfully native in Ireland (Hackney, 1992).

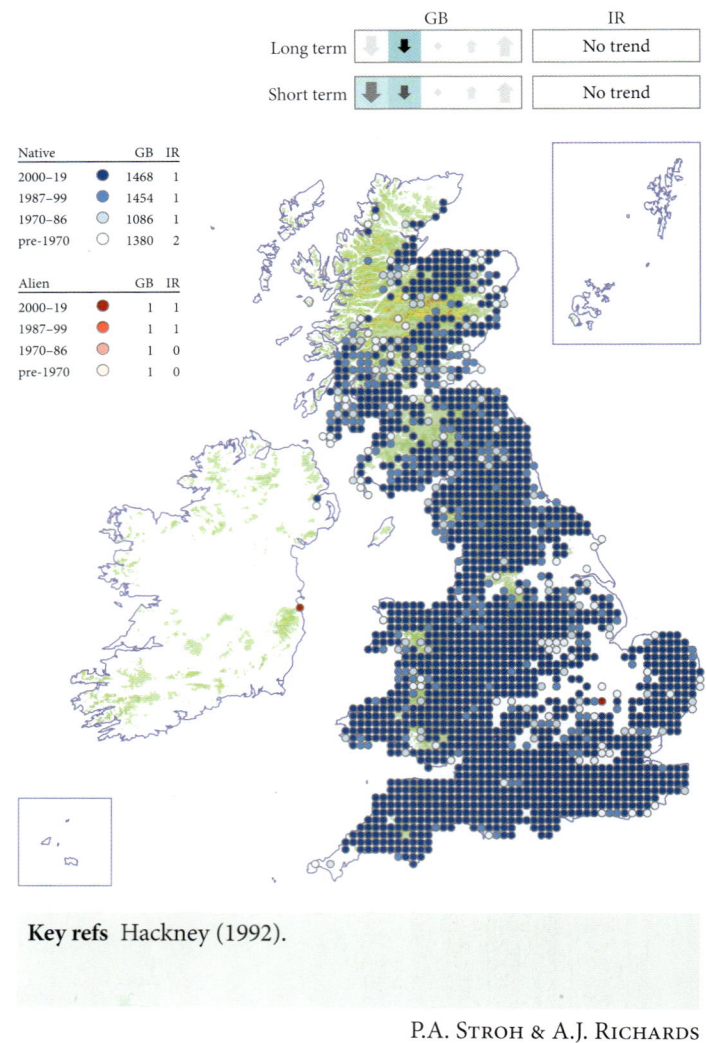

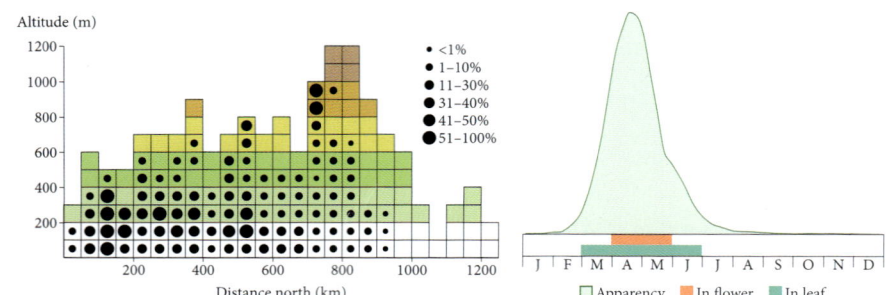

Biogeography Circumpolar Boreo-temperate element, with a disjunct distribution.

Native	GB	IR
2000–19	1468	1
1987–99	1454	1
1970–86	1086	1
pre-1970	1380	2

Alien	GB	IR
2000–19	1	1
1987–99	1	1
1970–86	1	0
pre-1970	1	0

	GB	IR
Long term		No trend
Short term		No trend

Key refs Hackney (1992).

P.A. Stroh & A.J. Richards

Ne *Sambucus racemosa* Red-berried Elder
L.

A deciduous shrub established in woodland, shrubberies, hedges and waste ground, and planted as game cover in parts of northern England and Scotland. 0–410 m (Correen Hills, North Aberdeenshire).

Trends This species was introduced in the 16th century and is quite widely cultivated for its creamy white flowers, red berries and golden pinnate foliage (*e.g.* 'Sutherland Gold'; 'Plumosa Aurea'), with a first record in the wild from Arriston, Midlothian, in 1892. Dunn (1905) described it as "occasionally noticed as a semi-wild plant near gardens and shrubberies". Most of its apparent spread as a garden escape took place in the 20th century, with much consolidation in recent decades due to a stronger focus on the recording of alien shrubs, both planted and in the wild.

Biogeography A very variable Circumpolar Boreo-temperate species, comprising several subspecies. It is absent as a native from much of northern and western Europe.

	GB	IR
Long term		No trend
Short term		No trend

Alien	GB	IR
2000–19	355	3
1987–99	283	4
1970–86	166	0
pre-1970	183	0

Key refs Bean (1980), Dunn (1905).

Altitude (m) histogram and phenology chart with legend: <1%, 1–10%, 11–30%, 31–40%, 41–50%, 51–100%. Distance north (km). Apparency, In flower, In leaf.

G.T.D. WILMORE & P.A. STROH

N *Sambucus nigra* Elder
L.

A deciduous shrub or small tree of fertile soils found in a wide range of habitats including woodland, hedgerows, grassland, scrub, waste ground, roadsides and railway banks. It is resistant to rabbit grazing and often occurs around warrens. 0–470 m (above Nenthead, Cumberland).

Trends The current 10 km square range of *S. nigra* has not changed significantly since the 1960s. It may have been introduced at some sites, and is mapped as such in northern Scotland where it is often restricted to the vicinity of human settlements; elsewhere, it is often impossible to distinguish native and alien occurrences, especially as it may spread naturally by bird-sown seeds.

Biogeography European Temperate element; widely naturalized outside its native range.

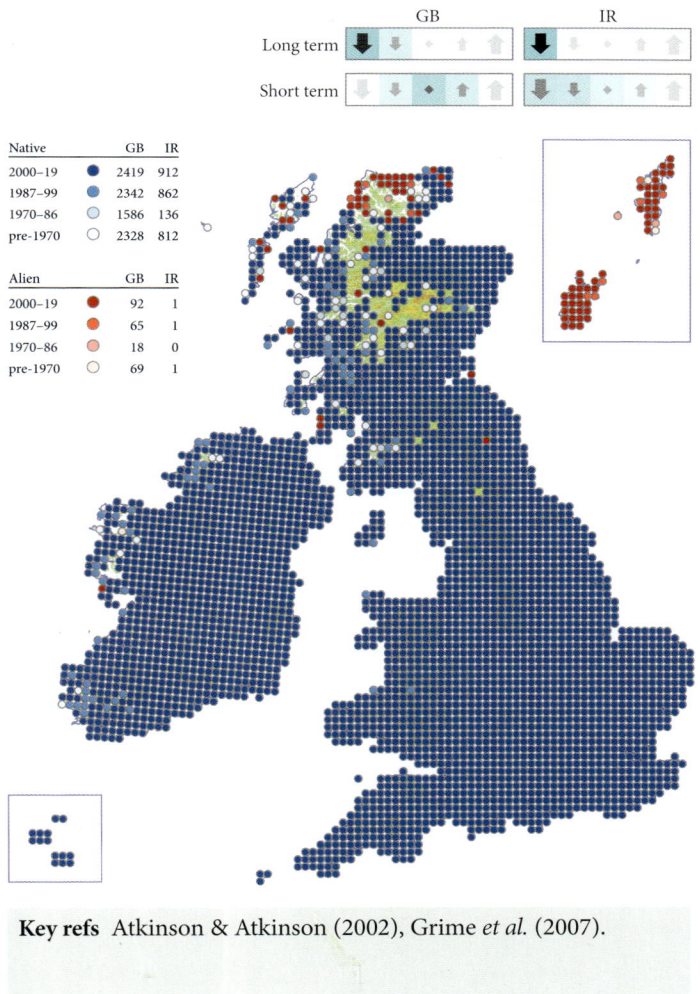

	GB	IR
Long term		
Short term		

Native	GB	IR
2000–19	2419	912
1987–99	2342	862
1970–86	1586	136
pre-1970	2328	812

Alien	GB	IR
2000–19	92	1
1987–99	65	1
1970–86	18	0
pre-1970	69	1

Key refs Atkinson & Atkinson (2002), Grime *et al.* (2007).

Altitude (m) histogram and phenology chart with legend: <1%, 1–10%, 11–30%, 31–40%, 41–50%, 51–100%. Distance north (km). Apparency, In flower, In leaf.

P.A. STROH & G.T.D. WILMORE

Ne *Sambucus canadensis* American Elder

L.

A deciduous shrub that is planted and naturalized along railway banks, hedges and roadsides, and also occurs in scrub and on waste ground. It reproduces by seed, which may be bird-sown, and vegetatively by suckering. Its altitudinal range is unknown, but is presumably almost entirely lowland.

Trends *S. canadensis* was cultivated in Britain by 1761. It was first recorded in the wild in 1946 (near Bradford, South-west Yorkshire) and it has extensively colonized the railway network in County Durham since *c.* 1974.

Biogeography Native of eastern North America.

	GB	IR
Long term	No trend	No trend
Short term	⬇⬇ ⬇ ◆ ⬆ ⬆⬆	No trend

Alien	GB	IR
2000–19	28	0
1987–99	19	0
1970–86	32	0
pre-1970	2	0

Key refs Bean (1980), Graham (1988).

T.D. DINES & D.A. PEARMAN

Ar *Sambucus ebulus* Dwarf Elder

L.

A robust herbaceous perennial, spreading vigorously by rhizomes, and formerly widely planted for medicinal use and the production of a blue dye. It occurs infrequently in hedgerows, on roadsides and waste ground, usually in small numbers but locally forming thickets (Lavin & Wilmore, 1994) where it can be very persistent (Leslie, 2019). Lowland.

Trends The distribution of *S. ebulus* shows a steady decline since the 1960s, perhaps in part due to the grubbing-out of hedgerows where it is sometimes found, but also the decline in its use as a herbal remedy (Stroh *et al.*, 2014).

Biogeography As an archaeophyte, *S. ebulus* has a European Southern-temperate distribution.

	GB	IR
Long term	⬇ ⬇ ◆ ⬆ ⬆	⬇ ⬇ ◆ ⬆ ⬆
Short term	⬇ ⬇ ◆ ⬆ ⬆	⬇ ⬇ ◆ ⬆ ⬆

Alien	GB	IR
2000–19	221	82
1987–99	261	79
1970–86	183	20
pre-1970	424	81

Key refs Lavin & Wilmore (1994), Leslie (2019), Stroh *et al.* (2014).

G.T.D. WILMORE, D.A. PEARMAN & K.J. WALKER

N *Viburnum opulus* Guelder-rose

L.

A deciduous shrub of neutral or calcareous soils favouring damp, winter-wet areas within and on the edge of woodland, scrub, plantations and hedgerows (especially well-established ones), in fen-carr, alder and willow thickets, marsh edges and on stream banks. It is also occasionally found in drier habitats such as tracksides, road verges, waste ground and in rough grassland. It is now widely planted, and bird-sown plants which spread from planted sites to the wild sometimes include yellow-fruited cultivars. 0–400 m (south of Garrigill, Cumberland).

Trends The increase in the 10 km square distribution of *V. opulus* since the 1960s is due to more intensive recording in some areas, especially Ireland this century, and deliberate planting both within and outside of its native range. It is now often very difficult to

differentiate native from alien occurrences and the native range mapped may not be accurate in some areas.

Biogeography Circumpolar Temperate element.

Native	GB	IR
2000–19	1792	613
1987–99	1635	477
1970–86	1151	80
pre-1970	1581	315

Alien	GB	IR
2000–19	113	11
1987–99	37	0
1970–86	9	0
pre-1970	20	0

Key refs Kollmann & Grubb (2002).

G.T.D. WILMORE & N. ASPEY

Ne *Viburnum trilobum* American Guelder-rose

Marshall

A small deciduous shrub, widely planted in hedgerows and amenity plantings, perhaps sometimes in error for the native *V. opulus*. Lowland.

Trends *V. trilobum* has possibly been grown here since before 1789. It was first found in the wild at Swanley and Wilmington (both West Kent) in 2005, but was probably overlooked before then as it is very similar to the native *V. opulus*. It is possible that many plants attributed to *V. trilobum* may just be vigorous variants of *V. opulus* or hybrids (Leslie, 2019).

Biogeography Native of Canada and northern United States of America, predominantly in the east, but extending west to British Columbia and Oregon.

Alien	GB	IR
2000–19	87	0
1987–99	0	0
1970–86	0	0
pre-1970	0	0

Key refs Bean (1980), Leslie (2019).

D.A. PEARMAN

N *Viburnum lantana* Wayfaring-tree
L.

A deciduous shrub of woods and wood borders, scrub, hedgerows and rough grassland on base-rich soils, especially in chalk and limestone districts. It is now frequently planted on road- and canal-sides, in parks, shrubberies, habitat creation schemes (often in areas where the species is native) and may also appear when used as a stock for other cultivated species of *Viburnum*. Bird-sown populations also occur on waste ground and in other ruderal situations and its unpalatability to rabbits allows it to invade areas of high warren densities. Lowland.

Native in Britain and a neophyte in Ireland and the Channel Islands.

Trends The native 10 km square distribution of *V. lantana* has changed very little since the 1960s, though local losses have occurred. There are now many more alien records than there were at the turn of the century and, as a result, its northern range limit has become increasingly blurred. The status of some populations within its assumed native range can also be difficult to determine.

Biogeography European Temperate element.

Native	GB	IR
2000–19	516	0
1987–99	491	0
1970–86	329	0
pre-1970	477	0

Alien	GB	IR
2000–19	512	15
1987–99	260	6
1970–86	121	3
pre-1970	154	7

Key refs Kollmann & Grubb (2002).

G.T.D. WILMORE & N. ASPEY

Ne *Viburnum tinus* Laurustinus
L.

A large, evergreen shrub, widely grown in gardens and amenity planting schemes and found on sea-cliffs, banks, woodland, rough grassland, roadsides, railway banks, waste ground and at the base of walls and fences in urban areas where it is often self or bird-sown (Leslie, 2019). Reproduction is by seed and populations can become well-established, especially on calcareous soils overlying chalk and limestone in coastal localities in southern England and north Wales. It also occurs as a relic of cultivation. Lowland.

Trends *V. tinus* has been valued in gardens for its winter flowers and its ability to withstand pollution since its introduction, which was before 1596. It was recorded from the wild in 1912 (Clifton Downs, Bristol, West Gloucestershire), and it is certainly better recorded than it was in the past.

Biogeography Native of south-western Europe and the Mediterranean region.

Alien	GB	IR
2000–19	427	48
1987–99	195	8
1970–86	36	0
pre-1970	24	2

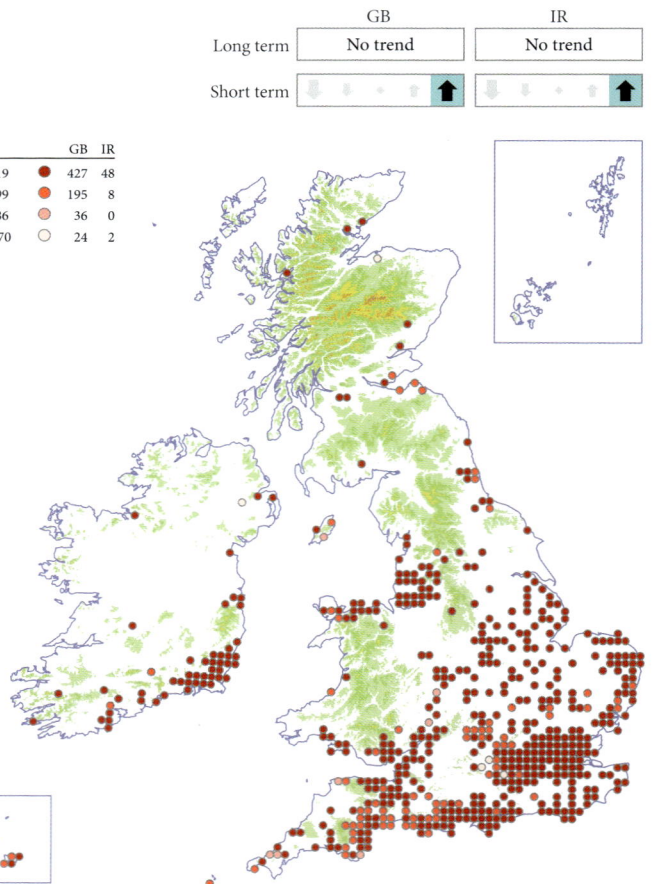

Key refs Bean (1980), Leslie (2019).

T.D. DINES & D.A. PEARMAN

Ne *Viburnum rhytidophyllum*   Wrinkled Viburnum

Hemsl.

An evergreen shrub, grown in gardens and planted in woodland, hedgerows, parkland, on roadsides and in amenity areas, from where it can become naturalized. It also occurs as a relic of cultivation. Reproduction is from seed, which can be bird-sown. Lowland.

Trends *V. rhytidophyllum* was only introduced into cultivation in 1900, but is now very popular in gardens and municipal plantings. It had been recorded as planted in the wild by 1965 (Sutton Courtney, Berkshire) and then as self-sown in Cambridge, Cambridgeshire, in 1977. It appears to be increasing, though this may be in part because it is better recorded.

Biogeography Native of China.

	GB	IR
Long term	No trend	No trend
Short term		No trend

Alien	GB	IR
2000–19	148	0
1987–99	31	0
1970–86	5	0
pre-1970	1	0

Key refs Bean (1980).

T.D. Dines & D.A. Pearman

Hy *Viburnum lantana × rhytidophyllum = V. ×rhytidophylloides*

J.V.Suringar

An evergreen shrub planted by roadsides and in other public places. There are a few records of this hybrid in the wild, growing on sandy and chalky soils in woodland and on commons and railway embankments. Lowland.

A cultivated hybrid (native × alien).

Trends This hybrid was first cultivated in Britain in 1927, and was recorded in the wild from Darenth Wood (West Kent) in 1977. It has clearly arisen from bird-sown seeds in some sites, but at least some records may be of planted shrubs. In the Cambridge area, and perhaps elsewhere, the hybrid has also been supplied as 'V. lantana' and included as a supposed native species in newly planted woodland (Kollmann & Grubb, 2002).

Biogeography A hybrid of garden origin.

	GB	IR
Long term	No trend	No trend
Short term	No trend	No trend

	GB	IR
2000–19	18	0
1987–99	4	0
1970–86	0	0
pre-1970	0	0

Key refs Kollmann & Grubb (2002), Stace *et al.* (2015).

C.A. Stace, C.D. Preston & D.A. Pearman

Ne *Symphoricarpos albus* Snowberry

(L.) S.F.Blake

A deciduous shrub, spreading by vigorous suckering, widely planted in both gardens and in the wider countryside in hedges and for game cover in woodland. It reproduces by suckering and fruits freely, but regeneration from seed is unknown. It spreads very slowly, forming thickets where initially densely planted. 0–400 m (Leadhills, Lanarkshire).

Trends *S. albus* was introduced into cultivation in Britain in 1817, and was known from the wild by 1863 (Crouch Hill, Oxfordshire). Its distribution appears to be stable.

Biogeography Native of North America; the plant naturalized here is the western var. *laevigatus*.

Alien	GB	IR
2000–19	2087	789
1987–99	1911	693
1970–86	1101	79
pre-1970	1394	427

Key refs Bean (1980), Coats (1963), Gilbert (1995).

G.T.D. WILMORE & P.A. STROH

Altitude (m) chart

- <1%
- 1–10%
- 11–30%
- 31–40%
- 41–50%
- 51–100%

Distance north (km)

Apparency — In flower — In leaf

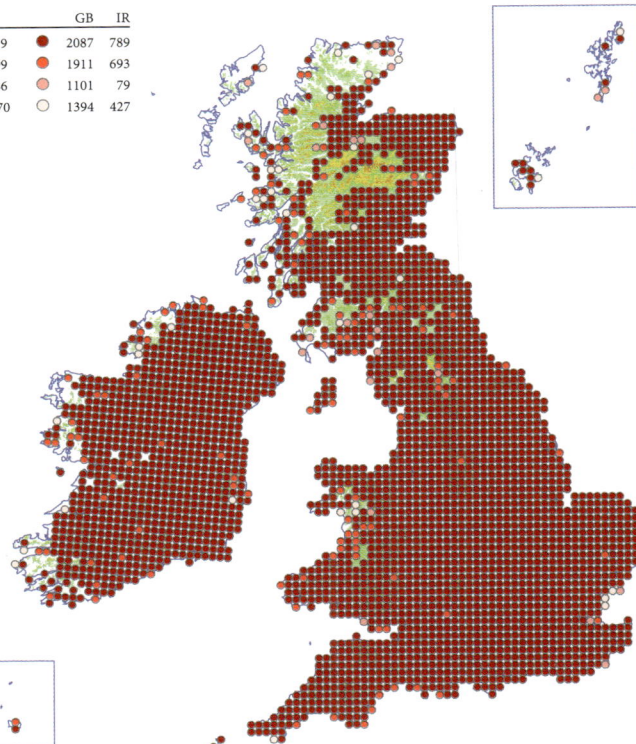

Hy *Symphoricarpos microphyllus × orbiculatus = S. ×chenaultii*

Hybrid Coralberry

Rehder

A deciduous shrub found naturalized in woodland, scrub, hedges, old quarries and by rivers, canals, roads and paths; also planted extensively in urban landscaping schemes, and sometimes arising from dumped garden material. Like *S. albus*, it reproduces by suckering, sometimes forming extensive thickets. The hybrid fruits freely but rarely regenerates from seed; there are relatively few records of apparently self-sown or bird-sown plants but some appear to originate in this way, most obviously those on walls. Lowland.

A cultivated hybrid (alien × alien).

Trends This hybrid was first recorded in the wild in 1974 (Little Abington, Cambridgeshire), but was not recognized as such until 1981. It is increasingly better recorded as botanists have become more familiar with separating the hybrid from the parent taxa. In the past, it has been mistaken for *S. orbiculatus*.

Biogeography A hybrid of garden origin.

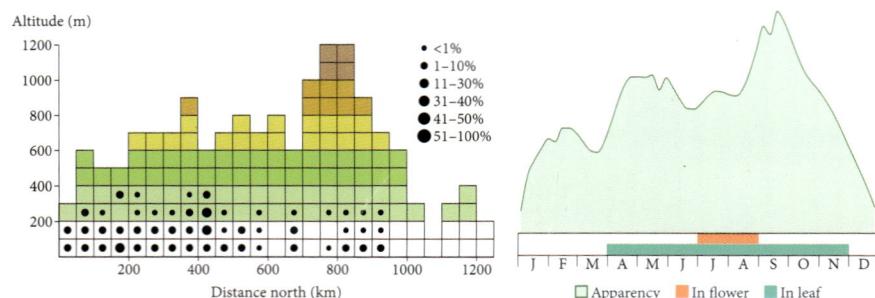

	GB	IR
2000–19	561	4
1987–99	154	0
1970–86	23	0
pre-1970	0	0

	GB	IR
Long term	No trend	No trend
Short term	No trend	No trend

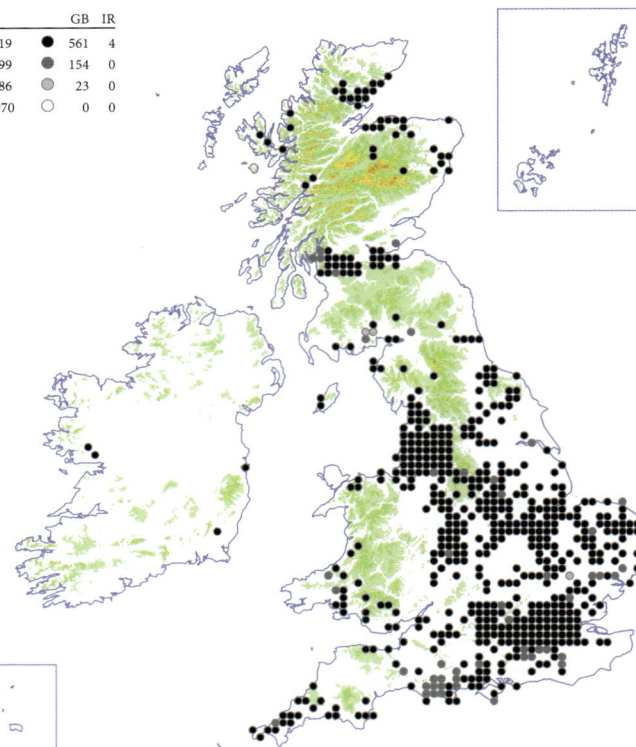

Key refs Bean (1980), Stace *et al.* (2015).

C.A. STACE, C.D. PRESTON & D.A. PEARMAN

Altitude (m) chart

- <1%
- 1–10%
- 11–30%
- 31–40%
- 41–50%
- 51–100%

Distance north (km)

Apparency — In flower — In leaf

Ne *Symphoricarpos orbiculatus* Coralberry
Moench

A deciduous shrub, spreading by suckers which grow to produce dense thickets. It is naturalized in hedges, scrub and on waste ground. Lowland.

Trends *S. orbiculatus* was being cultivated in Britain by 1730, but is not common in gardens. It was first recorded from the wild in 1968 (Box Hill, Surrey). It might on occasion be over-recorded for *S. × chenaultii*.

Biogeography Native of eastern North America.

	GB	IR
Long term	No trend	No trend
Short term		No trend

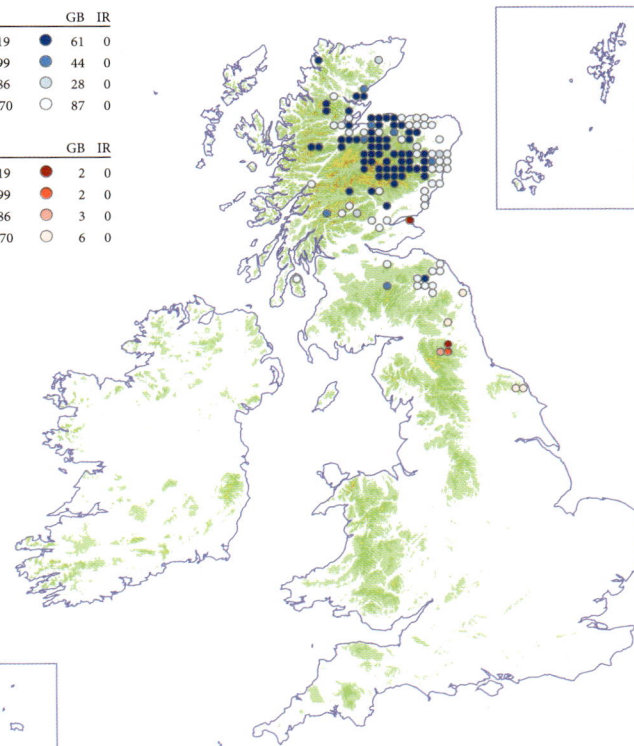

Alien	GB	IR
2000–19	73	2
1987–99	5	0
1970–86	5	0
pre-1970	0	0

Altitude (m) chart — Distance north (km)

•	<1%
•	1–10%
•	11–30%
•	31–40%
•	41–50%
•	51–100%

Apparency / In flower / In leaf

Key refs Bean (1980).

T.D. DINES

N *Linnaea borealis* Twinflower
L.

A mat-forming creeping perennial herb of native pinewoods and plantations of *Pinus sylvestris*, occasionally in birchwoods, and rarely, as a relict of former woodland cover. Populations are fragmented, as a result of loss of pinewood habitat, into a series of (mainly) self-incompatible populations. The majority of populations in its core range are sustained through vegetative reproduction in isolated patches containing one or a few clones, within which there are no immediate prospects for future seed production. A programme of artificial transplantation of clones to restore seed set within patches is underway. 0–730 m (Grampians, Easterness).

Trends The 10 km square distribution of *L. borealis* is stable within its core range, centred on the Cairngorms National Park. Here, since 2000, there has been a 38% increase in recorded 2 km squares as a result of more intensive surveying. Losses at the 10 km square scale have occurred outside this core area. Some of these populations may have derived from accidental or occasionally deliberate introductions, including all populations in northern England (Durham, South Northumberland) which were presumably introduced with tree seedlings.

Biogeography Circumpolar Boreal-montane element.

	GB	IR
Long term		No trend
Short term		No trend

Native	GB	IR
2000–19	61	0
1987–99	44	0
1970–86	28	0
pre-1970	87	0

Alien	GB	IR
2000–19	2	0
1987–99	2	0
1970–86	3	0
pre-1970	6	0

Altitude (m) chart — Distance north (km)

•	<1%
•	1–10%
•	11–30%
•	31–40%
•	41–50%
•	51–100%

Apparency / In flower / In leaf

Key refs Stewart *et al.* (1994), Swan (1993), Welch (2003), Wiberg *et al.* (2016).

A. AMPHLETT

Ne *Leycesteria formosa* Himalayan Honeysuckle
Wall.

A deciduous shrub, widely grown in gardens, and frequently established as a garden escape on walls and at the base of hedgerows, in woodland and shrubberies and on waste ground, mainly in urban areas. Most plants appear to be bird-sown but it is also planted as cover for pheasants. It frequently arises from seed, which is produced prolifically and germinates freely. Lowland.

Trends *L. formosa* was introduced into cultivation in Britain in 1824, and was first recorded from the wild in 1894 (Shute Shelve, North Somerset), where it had originally been planted as pheasant cover. It was too rare to be mapped in the 1962 *Atlas*, but since then its range has increased dramatically. Whilst this may in part be explained by better recording of alien plants, the vast majority of the increase is due to its prolific seeding and dispersal by birds.

Biogeography Native of the Himalayas, western China and Tibet. It is now classed as an invasive plant in many parts of the world.

Alien	GB	IR
2000–19	1066	347
1987–99	400	125
1970–86	110	21
pre-1970	81	17

	GB	IR
Long term		
Short term		

Key refs Bean (1973).

D.A. PEARMAN & G.T.D. WILMORE

Ne *Weigela florida* Weigelia
(Bunge) A.DC.

A deciduous shrub, grown in gardens and naturalized on railway banks, refuse tips and waste ground. Reproduction is by seed, but many occurrences are only casual. Lowland.

Trends *W. florida* was introduced into cultivation in Britain in 1845. It is extremely popular in gardens, where numerous cultivars and hybrids are grown. It was recorded from the wild in 1920 (Ballumbie Glen, Angus), and is increasingly, but erratically, recorded.

Biogeography Native of eastern Asia.

	GB	IR
Long term	No trend	No trend
Short term		No trend

Alien	GB	IR
2000–19	177	5
1987–99	24	1
1970–86	12	0
pre-1970	2	0

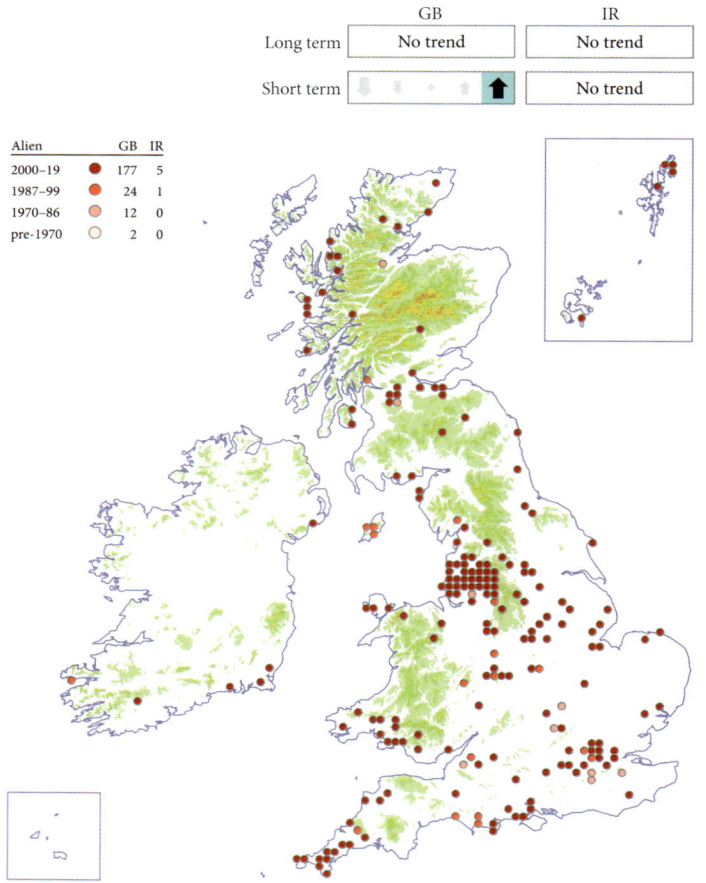

Key refs Bean (1980).

T.D. DINES & D.A. PEARMAN

Lonicera pileata Box-leaved Honeysuckle
Oliv.

An evergreen shrub, planted extensively for landscaping in urban areas (often as a low-maintenance alternative to *Buxus sempervirens*) and occasionally as game cover. Found as a garden escape on roadsides and in parks, woodland, hedges and amenity areas. It can become well-established and is sometimes self- or bird-sown. Lowland.

Trends *L. pileata* was introduced to cultivation in Britain in 1902. It was first recorded from the wild in 1959 (Ketton, Leicestershire), and is increasingly used in amenity landscape planting, often as a replacement for *L. nitida*. It is thought to be increasing in the wild, but with a more scattered distribution than *L. nitida*, although the two species are often confused. Indeed the recent *Flora of China* treated these two species as variants of *L. ligurtina* (Leslie, 2019).

Biogeography Native of China.

Alien	GB	IR
2000–19	547	43
1987–99	66	3
1970–86	4	0
pre-1970	0	0

	GB	IR
Long term	No trend	No trend
Short term		

Key refs Bean (1973), Leslie (2019).

J. Parmenter & T.D. Dines

Lonicera nitida Wilson's Honeysuckle
E.H. Wilson

An evergreen shrub, planted extensively for hedging and landscaping in urban areas (as a low-maintenance alternative to *Buxus sempervirens*) and occasionally as evergreen game cover in woodland. It is now widely naturalized in woodland, scrub, hedgerows and waste ground, where it can persist for many years. It is found self- or bird-sown but more often from dumped garden waste. Usually lowland, but up to 345 m east of Nant Bwlch-y-gwynt (Denbighshire).

Trends This species was first introduced from seed in 1908, from which the clone 'Ernest Wilson' was probably selected; this is a poor flowerer and fruiter in our area. Later, selections such as 'Fertlilis' (which won the RHS Award of Merit in 1924) became popular, as it flowers and fruits more prolifically. It was first recorded from the wild in 1950 (Rothwell Gorse, North Lincolnshire). The species is widely naturalized and is likely to be spreading, especially in southern and western Britain and also in Ireland, but there is also indication of a northward trend over recent decades. *L. pileata* appears to be replacing it in mass plantings in urban areas although the two species are often confused. Indeed the recent *Flora of China* treated these two species as variants of *L. ligustina* (Leslie, 2019).

Biogeography Native of China.

Alien	GB	IR
2000–19	1483	704
1987–99	703	429
1970–86	195	4
pre-1970	51	1

	GB	IR
Long term	No trend	No trend
Short term		

Key refs Bean (1973), Coats (1963), Leslie (2019).

J. Parmenter & G.T.D. Wilmore

Ne *Lonicera involucrata* Californian Honeysuckle

(Richardson) Banks ex Spreng.

A deciduous shrub with spreading, arching branches, widely grown in gardens and naturalized in rough grassland and waste ground. It also occurs as a relic of cultivation, and is sometimes planted in hedgerows. Reproduction is by seed, which can be bird-sown. Lowland.

Trends *L. involucrata* was introduced into cultivation in Britain in 1824. It was first recorded from the wild in 1938 (Redhall Glen, Antrim), and appears to be increasing, but remains scattered. In northern Britain its distribution is largely coastal.

Biogeography Native of western North America and east to Quebec.

	GB	IR
Long term	No trend	No trend
Short term		No trend

Alien		GB	IR
2000–19	●	60	4
1987–99	●	36	2
1970–86	●	12	0
pre-1970	○	8	0

Key refs Bean (1973), Hultén (1968).

J. PARMENTER & T.D. DINES

	<1%
●	1–10%
●	11–30%
●	31–40%
●	41–50%
●	51–100%

☐ Apparency ☐ In flower ☐ In leaf

Ne *Lonicera xylosteum* Fly Honeysuckle

L.

A deciduous shrub, formerly considered to be native in woodland on chalk in south-eastern England but also widely naturalized on free-draining basic or neutral soils in open woodland, hedgerows and scrub. Lowland.

Trends *L. xylosteum* was being cultivated in Britain by 1596. It was first recorded in the wild as a casual in 1770, it has been known from the chalk escarpment of the South Downs near Amberley (West Sussex) since 1801, where it grows in ancient woodland, hedgerows and scrub. Although arguably native there, it is considered to be an introduction given the lateness of its discovery, use as a garden plant and the frequency of introduction elsewhere (Webb, 1985; Pearman, 2007). It was lost from many sites before 1930, for reasons that are not clear, but it remains widespread.

Biogeography A Eurosiberian Temperate species; widely naturalized.

	GB	IR
Long term		
Short term		

Alien		GB	IR
2000–19	●	178	7
1987–99	●	108	6
1970–86	●	75	3
pre-1970	○	167	8

Key refs Pearman (2007), Webb (1985), Wigginton (1999).

	<1%
●	1–10%
●	11–30%
●	31–40%
●	41–50%
●	51–100%

☐ Apparency ☐ In flower ☐ In leaf

J. PARMENTER & G.T.D. WILMORE

Ne *Lonicera tatarica* Tartarian Honeysuckle
L.

A deciduous, bushy shrub widely introduced and occurring as a relic of cultivation or naturalized in hedgerows, roadsides and rough grassland. It is also capable of reproducing from seed, which can be bird-sown. Lowland.

Trends *L. tatarica* had been introduced into cultivation in Britain by 1752 and is the most commonly planted of the ornamental bush honeysuckles. It was first recorded from the wild in 1977 (Chelmondiston Tip, East Suffolk); as a relic of cultivation or naturalized species it is scattered in our area as far north as the Moray Firth.

Biogeography Native of western and central Asia.

	GB	IR
Long term	No trend	No trend
Short term		No trend

Alien	GB	IR
2000–19	65	0
1987–99	15	0
1970–86	2	0
pre-1970	0	0

Key refs Bean (1973).

J. Parmenter & T.D. Dines

Ne *Lonicera henryi* Henry's Honeysuckle
Hemsl.

A winter-green or semi-deciduous climbing shrub, naturalized on woodland margins and in hedgerows and rough grassland. It arises as a garden escape or throw-out, and is seldom found far from human habitations. It is also capable of reproducing from seed, which can be bird-sown. Lowland.

Trends *L. henryi* was not introduced to British gardens until 1908. It was recorded from the wild in 1950 (Surrey) and has since extended its range to southern Scotland and Ireland. There are many new records in London and in South Lancashire, although in some cases records may be of planted individuals in gardens.

Biogeography Native of western China.

	GB	IR
Long term	No trend	No trend
Short term		No trend

Alien	GB	IR
2000–19	84	2
1987–99	17	0
1970–86	2	0
pre-1970	1	0

Key refs Bean (1973).

J. Parmenter & T.D. Dines

Ne *Lonicera japonica* Japanese Honeysuckle

Thunb.

A partially winter-green climbing shrub, widely grown in gardens and frequently spreading to woodland margins, scrub, hedgerows and on waste ground, sometimes forming extensive thickets but seldom far from human habitations. Naturalized plants are often self- or bird-sown, but occasionally originate from dumped garden waste. Lowland.

Trends This species was introduced into Britain in 1806. Some populations are long-established, including that at Bere Ferrers in South Devon where it has been known since 1937. Its range appears to be increasing.

Biogeography Native of eastern Asia (Japan, China and Korea); naturalized in North America, where it can be a pernicious weed.

	GB	IR
Long term	No trend	No trend
Short term		

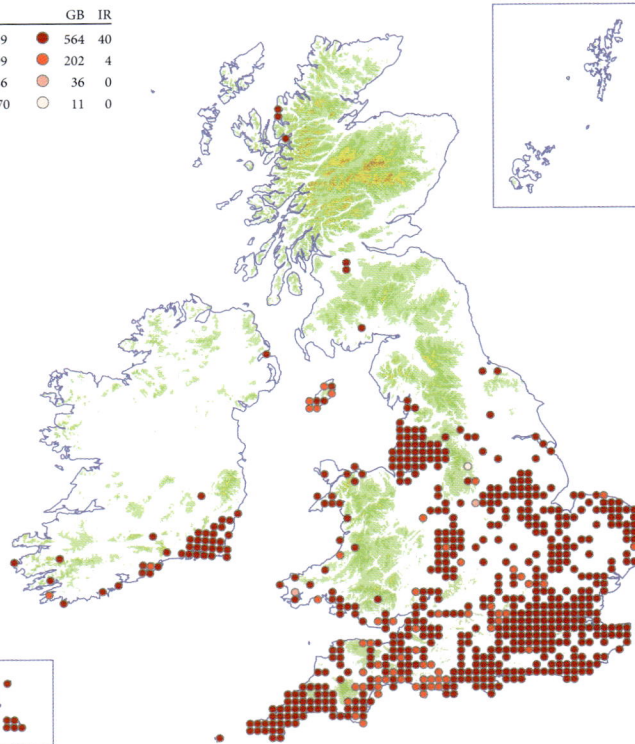

Alien	GB	IR
2000–19	564	40
1987–99	202	4
1970–86	36	0
pre-1970	11	0

Key refs Bean (1973).

J. Parmenter & G.T.D. Wilmore

Altitude (m) chart — Distance north (km)

	<1%
	1–10%
	11–30%
	31–40%
	41–50%
	51–100%

Apparency   In flower   In leaf

N *Lonicera periclymenum* Honeysuckle

L.

A perennial deciduous twining shrub or woody climber, found in woodland, scrub and hedgerows, and on shaded rocks. It prefers freely drained, moderately basic to acidic soils, but also grows on poorly drained base-rich clays. 0–610 m (Fairfield, Westmorland; Mourne Mountains in County Down).

Trends The current distribution of *L. periclymenum* has changed little since the 1960s but it may be increasing at a local scale due to escapes from gardens and a decline in woodland management.

Biogeography Suboceanic Southern-temperate element.

	GB	IR
Long term		
Short term		

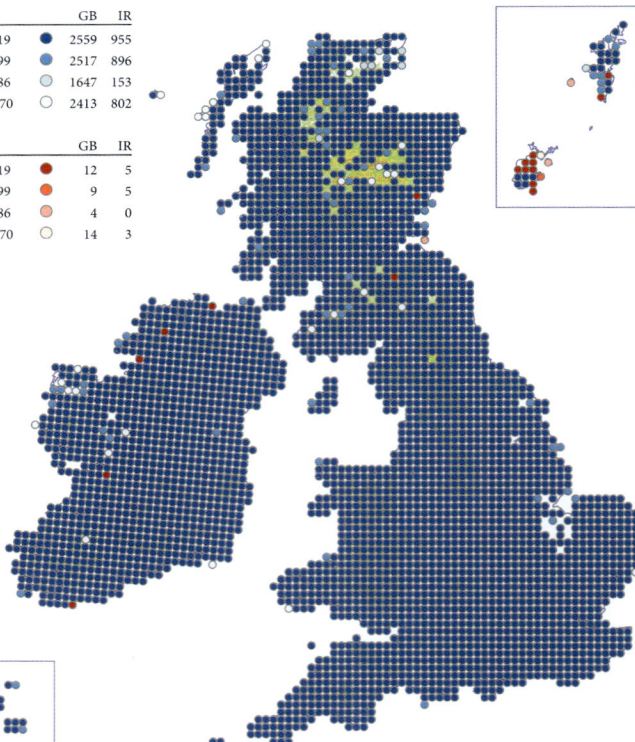

Native	GB	IR
2000–19	2559	955
1987–99	2517	896
1970–86	1647	153
pre-1970	2413	802

Alien	GB	IR
2000–19	12	5
1987–99	9	5
1970–86	4	0
pre-1970	14	3

Key refs Grime *et al.* (2007).

G.T.D. Wilmore & K.J. Walker

Altitude (m) chart — Distance north (km)

	<1%
	1–10%
	11–30%
	31–40%
	41–50%
	51–100%

Apparency   In flower   In leaf

Lonicera caprifolium Perfoliate Honeysuckle

Ne L.

A twining, deciduous climber, naturalized in woodland, scrub and hedgerows, perhaps establishing mainly from bird-sown seed from garden plants. Lowland.

Trends *L. caprifolium* has been known in cultivation in Britain since at least 1596, and was recorded in the wild by 1763 (Cherry Hinton, Cambridgeshire). However, it is less frequently cultivated now, and most modern garden plants are its hybrid with *L. etrusca* (*L. ×italica*). There are scattered records from throughout our area, but many may be misidentifications for this hybrid. As with *L. xylosteum*, it was lost from many of its sites before 1930 for reasons that are not clear.

Biogeography Native of east-central and south-eastern Europe from Italy eastwards, and of south-western Asia; widely naturalized elsewhere in Europe.

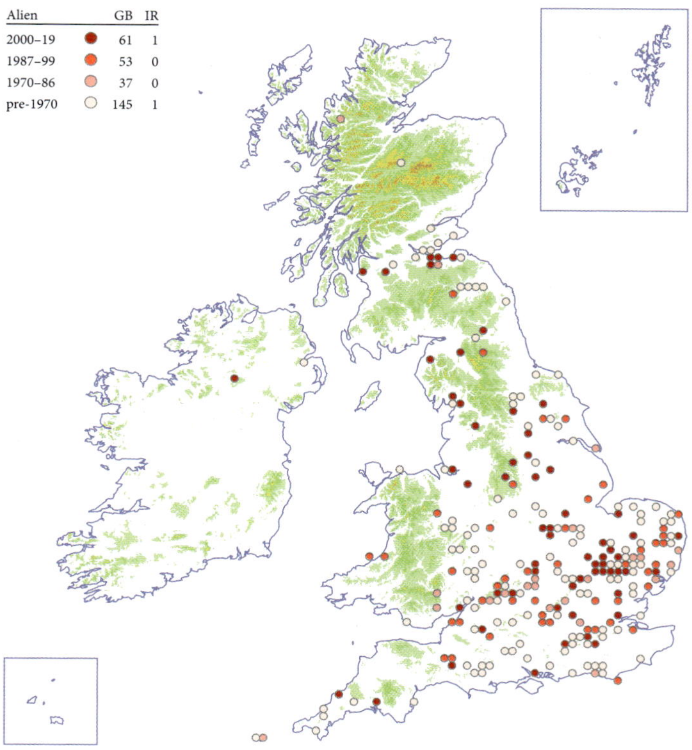

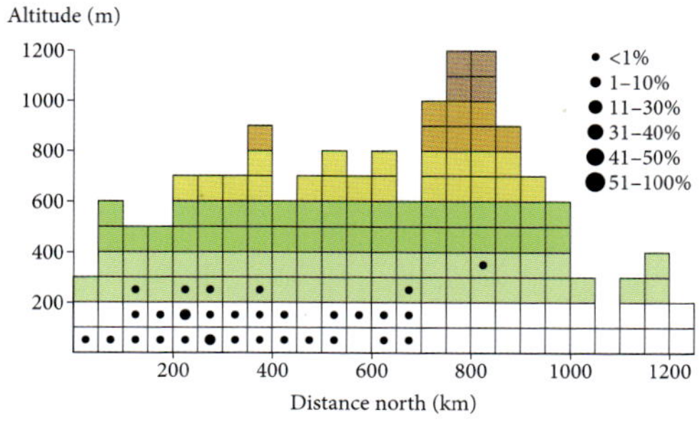

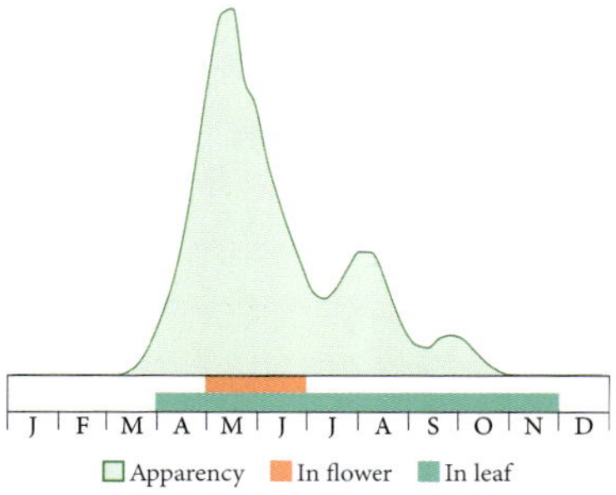

Key refs Bean (1973), Coats (1963).

J. Parmenter & G.T.D. Wilmore

Lonicera caprifolium × etrusca = L. ×italica Garden Honeysuckle

Hy Schmidt ex Tausch

A deciduous climbing shrub naturalized in scrub and hedges, churchyards, on roadsides and on waste ground. It also occurs as a relic of cultivation. Lowland.

A cultivated hybrid (alien × alien).

Trends *L. ×italica* was being grown in Britain by 1730. It was first recorded from the wild in 1967 (Juniper Hill, Oxfordshire), and may be overlooked for *L. caprifolium*. There are many more records this century due to better recording of both aliens and hybrids.

Biogeography A hybrid of garden origin.

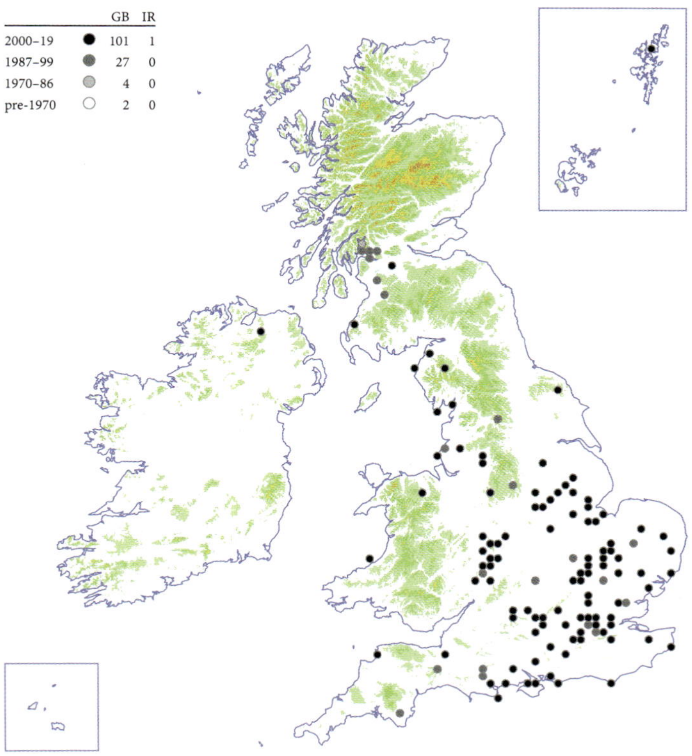

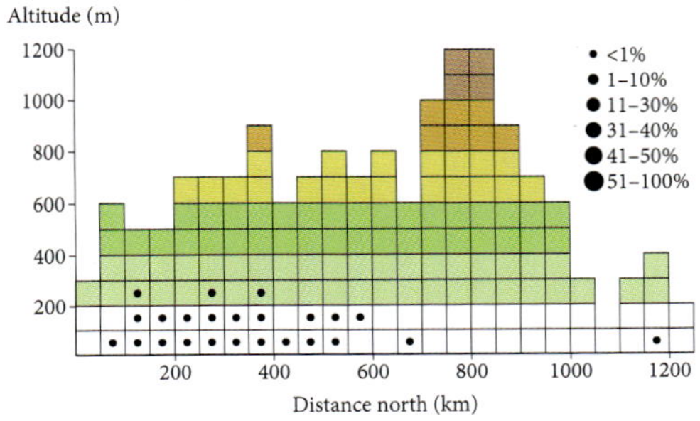

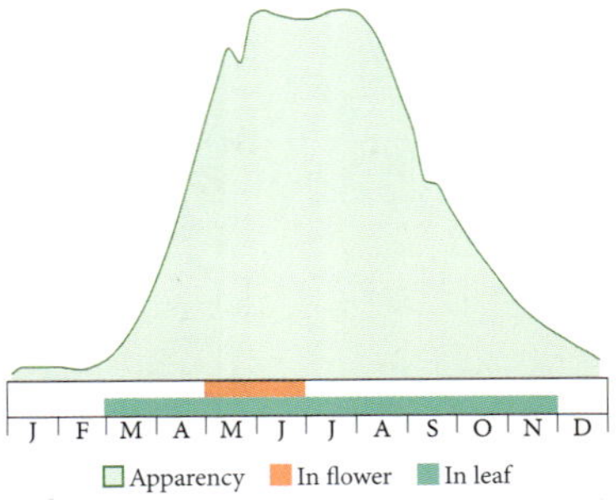

Key refs Stace *et al.* (2015).

T.D. Dines

N *Valerianella locusta* Common Cornsalad

(L.) Laterr.

A winter-annual herb of thin soils around rock outcrops and on scree, and on sand dunes and coastal shingle. It also grows in a wide range of disturbed habitats, including gravel paths, railway tracks, in paving, gardens and, rarely, on arable land. It is more frequent in semi-natural habitats and arable land than the closely related *V. carinata*, with which it is sometimes confused. Coastal populations are often the dwarf var. *dunensis*. It is grown commercially as a winter salad crop. 0–420 m (Glis Farm, Herefordshire).

Trends Overall the distribution of *V. locusta* is broadly stable, with a great deal of turnover at the hectad scale since the 1960s. It was mapped as 'all records' in the 1962 *Atlas*.

Biogeography European Temperate element; widely naturalized outside its native range.

Native	GB	IR
2000–19	1101	211
1987–99	975	188
1970–86	657	27
pre-1970	1028	98

Alien	GB	IR
2000–19	3	0
1987–99	6	0
1970–86	1	0
pre-1970	6	0

Altitude (m)

<1%
1–10%
11–30%
31–40%
41–50%
51–100%

Distance north (km)

Apparency   In flower   In leaf

P.J. Wilson

Ar *Valerianella carinata* Keeled-fruited Cornsalad

Loisel.

An autumn-germinating annual herb, almost always found in anthropogenic habitats, especially gardens, but also at the base of walls, on paths, pavements and areas of paving, in car parks, on railway platforms and tracks and on waste ground. Unlike other *Valerianella* species it is rarely found on arable land. Lowland.

Trends The 10 km square distribution of *V. carinata* has greatly increased since the 1960s, and it is now the commonest species in the genus in many areas, especially in south-western Britain. Like other southerly distributed species that have increased in recent decades, its spread began in south-western Britain, where increases are likely to have been driven by changes in climate, in particular milder winters. Its frequent association with

gardens also suggests that it may be colonizing new areas via horticulture.

Biogeography As an archaeophyte, *V. carinata* has a European Southern-temperate distribution.

Alien	GB	IR
2000–19	869	218
1987–99	476	61
1970–86	163	0
pre-1970	221	8

Altitude (m)

<1%
1–10%
11–30%
31–40%
41–50%
51–100%

Distance north (km)

Apparency   In flower   In leaf

P.J. Wilson & K.J. Walker

Ar *Valerianella rimosa* Broad-fruited Cornsalad
Bastard

An annual herb of arable land, generally found in corners and on fields margins which have escaped intensive management. It occurs on sand, calcareous clay and chalk soils, often as part of a species-rich annual community. Other habitats include quarry edges and spoil-tips. Seed longevity is unknown, but is likely to be persistent given its reappearance at some sites; germination occurs in the spring and autumn. Lowland.

Trends *V. rimosa* is known from archaeological evidence to have been present in Britain from the Iron Age. A dramatic decline was already apparent by the 1960s, and has continued since then, largely due to agricultural intensification, although several new sites have recently been discovered in southern England, in some cases due to more intensive surveys of arable habitats as a result of greater interest in the conservation of rare arable flora. Since 2000, it has been recorded in about 20 locations, although it can be sporadic at some of these sites and some populations in Suffolk are known to be deliberate introductions (Shellswell *et al.*, 2021).

Biogeography As an archaeophyte, *V. rimosa* has a European Temperate distribution.

Alien	GB	IR
2000–19	16	4
1987–99	18	0
1970–86	30	2
pre-1970	207	33

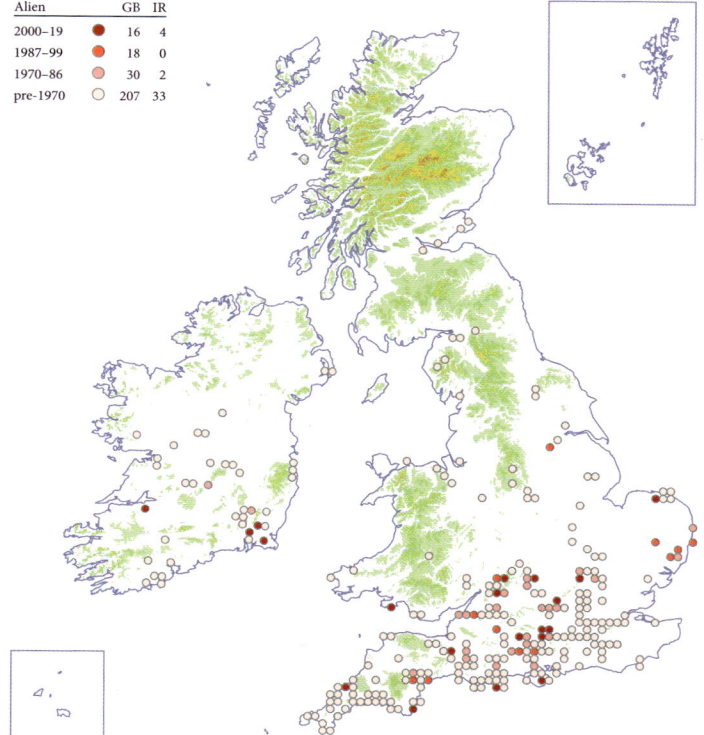

Key refs Shellswell *et al.* (2021), Wigginton (1999), Wilson (1990).

P.J. WILSON & K.J. WALKER

Ar *Valerianella dentata* Narrow-fruited Cornsalad
(L.) Pollich

An annual herb of arable land, especially on chalky soils, but locally also on sands and calcareous clays, usually in the corners of fields and along field margins which have escaped intensive management. On Salisbury Plain it occurs on disturbed track edges in areas that have been cropped in the past. It can germinate both in spring and autumn, but is most frequently found in spring-sown crops. It has moderately long-lived seeds. Lowland.

An archaeophyte in Britain and the Channel Islands and a neophyte in Ireland.

Trends There is a continuous archaeological record of this species from the Bronze Age onwards. It has decreased substantially since the 19th century with an accelerated decline during the 20th century due to the intensification of arable cropping from the 1950s onwards. It has survived only in areas with very light soils, particularly on the chalk, and in recent decades it has benefitted from the introduction of low-intensity management for weeds in these areas, as part of agri-environment schemes (Walker *et al.*, 2007).

Biogeography As an archaeophyte, *V. dentata* has a European Temperate distribution.

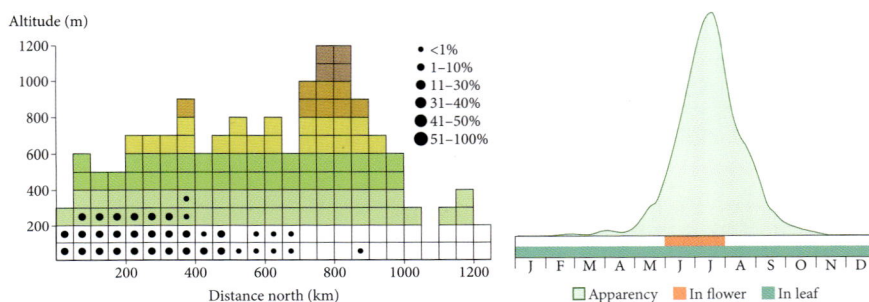

Alien	GB	IR
2000–19	177	6
1987–99	178	7
1970–86	207	3
pre-1970	578	49

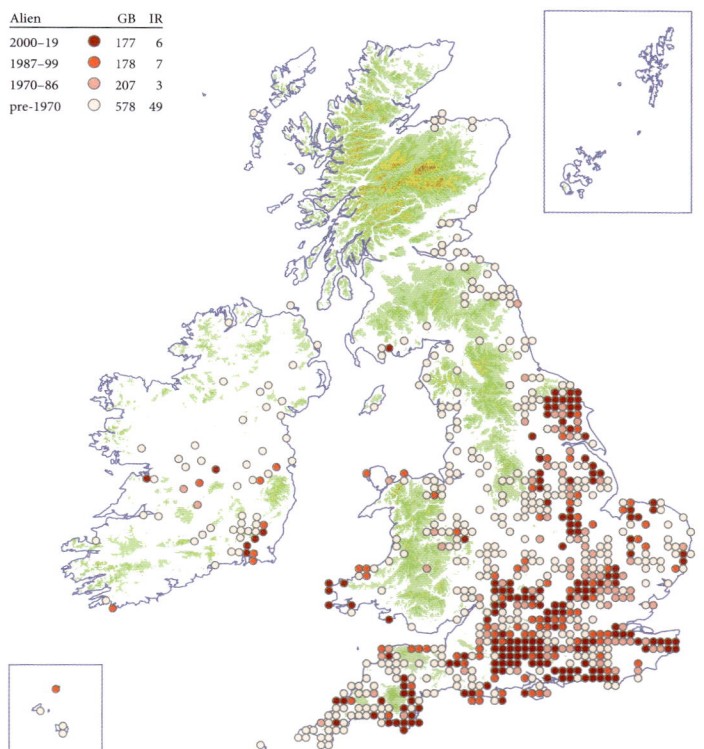

Key refs Stewart *et al.* (1994), Wilson & Aebischer (1995).

P.J. WILSON & K.J. WALKER

1075

N? *Valerianella eriocarpa* Hairy-fruited Cornsalad
Desv.

A winter-annual herb of drought-prone, stony substrates, found on cliff edges, calcareous banks, walls, quarries and other dry open habitats. It is considered to be native on thin soils over bare and disturbed limestone and hard chalk in Dorset and the Isle of Wight (Pearman & Edwards, 2002), and possibly also in parts of Cornwall and South Devon, where it grows in a similar ecological niche. Lowland.

Trends *V. eriocarpa* was being cultivated in Britain by 1821 but was not recorded in the wild until 1845. The extent of its native distribution in Dorset and the Isle of Wight was only discovered in the 1990s following intensive targeted surveying. Some older records are from arable land, where it was probably casual, or alternatively recorded in error for hairy-fruited forms of *V. dentata*.

Biogeography *V. eriocarpa* has a Submediterranean-Subatlantic distribution; it has perhaps spread northwards from the Mediterranean region as a cultivated plant or weed.

Native	GB	IR
2000–19	9	0
1987–99	10	0
1970–86	4	0
pre-1970	7	0

Alien	GB	IR
2000–19	8	0
1987–99	8	0
1970–86	12	0
pre-1970	55	0

	GB	IR
Long term		No trend
Short term	No trend	No trend

Key refs Pearman & Edwards (2002).

P.J. WILSON

Altitude (m) legend: <1%, 1–10%, 11–30%, 31–40%, 41–50%, 51–100%

Apparency — In flower — In leaf

N *Valeriana officinalis* Common Valerian
L.

A perennial herb found in a wide range of habitats. Subsp. *sambucifolia* occurs in damp grassland, marshes, fens, water margins and ditches, and wet woods throughout the country; subsp. *collina* in dry calcareous grasslands, hedgebanks and woodland rides in southern and central Britain. Lowland to 950 m at Coire an Lochain Uaine (South Aberdeenshire).

Trends *V. officinalis* was mapped as 'all records' in the 1962 *Atlas*. Although still widespread, declines have taken place in eastern and south-eastern England since the 1960s, mainly as a result of drainage, habitat destruction, and undergrazing.

Biogeography Eurasian Boreo-temperate element; widely naturalized outside its native range.

Native	GB	IR
2000–19	2266	834
1987–99	2190	740
1970–86	1450	121
pre-1970	2210	534

Alien	GB	IR
2000–19	3	2
1987–99	2	2
1970–86	1	1
pre-1970	2	2

	GB	IR
Long term		
Short term		

Key refs Grime *et al.* (2007).

P.J. WILSON

Altitude (m) legend: <1%, 1–10%, 11–30%, 31–40%, 41–50%, 51–100%

Apparency — In flower — In leaf

Ne *Valeriana pyrenaica* Pyrenean Valerian
L.

A perennial herb, grown in gardens and found naturalized in damp woodland and shady hedgebanks, often close to human habitations. Generally lowland, but reaching 305 m near Bridgend, Dufftown (Banffshire).

Trends This species has been grown in Britain since at least 1692, and was first recorded in the wild in 1782 (Blair Adam, Fifeshire) as a supposed native. Populations are often long-lived, and its distribution has changed little since the 1960s.

Biogeography Native of the Pyrenees and the Cordillera Cantabrica.

Alien	GB	IR
2000–19	147	1
1987–99	115	4
1970–86	76	3
pre-1970	142	4

P.J. Wilson

N *Valeriana dioica* Marsh Valerian
L.

A perennial herb of calcareous mires, marshy grassland, water-meadows, flushes, willow fen-carr and alder woods. 0–780 m (Cross Fell, Cumberland).

Trends *V. dioica* was lost from some areas in the late 19th and early 20th centuries, and this decline has since accelerated, particularly in central lowland areas of England in recent decades, following the degradation or loss of its wetland habitats.

Biogeography European Temperate element; also in central Asia and North America.

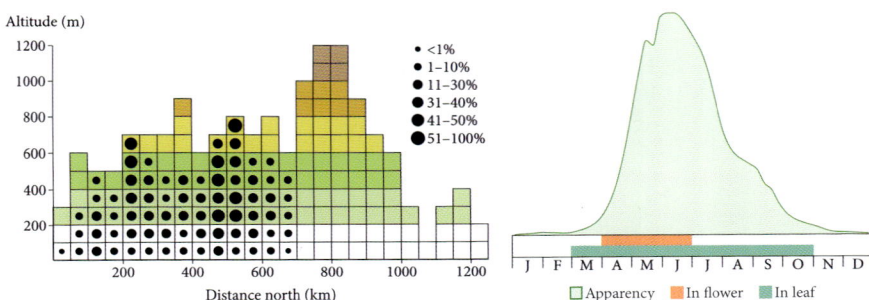

Native	GB	IR
2000–19	739	0
1987–99	814	0
1970–86	664	0
pre-1970	968	0

Alien	GB	IR
2000–19	1	0
1987–99	0	0
1970–86	0	0
pre-1970	0	0

P.J. Wilson

Ne *Centranthus ruber* Red Valerian

(L.) DC.

A partially winter-green, perennial herb, naturalized on coastal cliffs and shingle, limestone rock outcrops and pavements, in quarries, on railway banks, on old walls and buildings, at the base of walls on pavements and roadsides and in other well-drained, disturbed and open habitats including gardens, allotments and waste ground. Lowland.

Trends *C. ruber* was grown in Britain by 1596 and is a popular garden plant. It was first recorded in the wild in 1698 (Margam Abbey, Glamorganshire). There are many more records for this species since the 1960s, and in the last two decades it would appear to have consolidated its distribution, and also to have extended the edges of its range in areas of northern England and Scotland.

Biogeography Native of south-western Europe and the Mediterranean region; widely naturalized farther north in western and central Europe.

Alien	GB	IR
2000–19	1658	462
1987–99	1261	318
1970–86	630	31
pre-1970	846	135

	GB	IR
Long term	No trend	No trend
Short term		

Altitude (m)

• <1%
• 1–10%
• 11–30%
• 31–40%
• 41–50%
• 51–100%

Distance north (km)

Apparency In flower In leaf

P.J. WILSON

N? *Dipsacus fullonum* Wild Teasel

L.

A robust biennial herb, frequent in rough grassland, wood margins, thickets and hedgerows, and on roadsides and waste ground on a very wide range of soil types. It fruits prolifically, and often colonizes bare ground after disturbance. 0–365 m (Garrigill, Cumberland).

Trends *D. fullonum* has spread dramatically since the 1960s, to the north and west of its former core range in south-eastern Britain, colonizing the rest of lowland England and Wales and much of the lowlands of southern and eastern Scotland. Likewise, it has spread in many lowland regions of Ireland. It is rarely grown in gardens or introduced through other means (*e.g.* wild-flower seed mixtures) and so much of this spread must have been from native populations. Its ability to rapidly colonize, and become abundant in ruderal habitats, in particular

disturbed roadsides, has presumably been the main reason for its success, possibly assisted by dispersal in soil, the slipstreams of vehicles or by attachment to humans and livestock.

Biogeography European Temperate element.

Native	GB	IR
2000–19	1767	248
1987–99	1414	104
1970–86	812	20
pre-1970	642	30

	GB	IR
Long term		
Short term		

Altitude (m)

• <1%
• 1–10%
• 11–30%
• 31–40%
• 41–50%
• 51–100%

Distance north (km)

Apparency In flower In leaf

G.T.D. WILMORE & K.J. WALKER

Ne *Dipsacus sativus* Fuller's Teasel

(L.) Honck.

A robust biennial herb, occasionally found as an escape from cultivation or as a birdseed alien on waste ground, railway sidings and refuse tips. Lowland.

Trends *D. sativus* was formerly cultivated for use in raising the nap of woollen cloth after fulling, and was still being grown for that purpose in the late 20th century (Green *et al.*, 1997). It was first recorded from the wild in 1762. Now an occasional casual from birdseed.

Biogeography Origin uncertain; presumably derived by selection from a wild *Dipsacus* species.

	GB	IR
Long term	No trend	No trend
Short term		No trend

Alien		GB	IR
2000–19	●	22	0
1987–99	●	17	1
1970–86	●	11	0
pre-1970	○	47	1

Altitude (m) / Distance north (km)

● <1%
● 1–10%
● 11–30%
● 31–40%
● 41–50%
● 51–100%

J F M A M J J A S O N D
☐ Apparency ☐ In flower ☐ In leaf

Key refs Green *et al.* (1997).

G.T.D. Wilmore & K.J. Walker

Ne *Dipsacus laciniatus* Cut-leaved Teasel

L.

A biennial herb naturalized on refuse tips, tracks, roadsides and waste ground. It arises from birdseed or wild-flower seed mixtures. Lowland.

Trends *D. laciniatus* was cultivated in Britain by 1683. It had been recorded from the wild by 1900 (Cowley, Oxfordshire). There has been a marked increase in records this century (mainly in England), with some populations being well-established and extensive, especially on roadsides where plants can spread rapidly over long distances.

Biogeography Native of Europe (especially continental and steppic regions), north to central France, northern Germany and northern Ukraine, and south-western and central Asia.

	GB	IR
Long term	No trend	No trend
Short term		No trend

Alien		GB	IR
2000–19	●	54	0
1987–99	●	9	0
1970–86	●	1	0
pre-1970	○	1	0

Altitude (m) / Distance north (km)

● <1%
● 1–10%
● 11–30%
● 31–40%
● 41–50%
● 51–100%

J F M A M J J A S O N D
☐ Apparency ☐ In flower ☐ In leaf

T.D. Dines & J.O. Mountford

N *Dipsacus pilosus* Small Teasel
L.

A biennial herb occurring locally on woodland edges, rides and in clearings, in scrub and hedgerows, on ditch-sides and stream and riverbanks. It also grows in quarries and on waste ground. It prefers damp, calcareous soils. Lowland.

Native in Britain and a neophyte in Ireland and the Channel Islands.

Trends *D. pilosus* relies on disturbance for germination, and consequently its appearance can be very sporadic. This is likely to account for some of the losses shown on the map, although the decline in woodland management since the 1960s may account for its longer-term decline in some areas.

Biogeography European Temperate element.

Native	GB	IR
2000–19	339	0
1987–99	290	0
1970–86	215	0
pre-1970	334	0

Alien	GB	IR
2000–19	12	1
1987–99	8	0
1970–86	2	0
pre-1970	9	1

	GB	IR
Long term		No trend
Short term		No trend

G.T.D. WILMORE & K.J. WALKER

Ne *Cephalaria gigantea* Giant Scabious
(Ledeb.) Bobrov

A large perennial herb, popular in large gardens and found as a garden escape or throw-out in rough grassland and on roadsides, riverbanks, railway embankments and waste ground. It can become well established through rhizomatous growth. Lowland.

Trends *C. gigantea* was being cultivated in Britain by 1759 and is now very popular in gardens. It can easily outgrow its space, however, and is frequently discarded, being first recorded in the wild in 1915. It appears to be increasing.

Biogeography Native of the Caucasus.

Alien	GB	IR
2000–19	87	0
1987–99	51	0
1970–86	29	0
pre-1970	21	0

	GB	IR
Long term	No trend	No trend
Short term		No trend

T.D. DINES

N *Knautia arvensis* Field Scabious

(L.) Coult.

A perennial herb of calcareous and neutral grassland on well-drained, especially basic soils. It is found in chalk and limestone grassland, in rough pasture, open hedgerows and wood borders, and as a colonist on roadside verges, railway embankments and grassy waste ground. It is also a locally common weed of cultivation, especially in field-borders on the chalk. 0–500 m (grassland above Cow Green Reservoir, County Durham).

Trends *K. arvensis* was mapped as 'all records' in the 1962 *Atlas*. Losses occurred in the second half of the 20th century, and this decline appears to have continued since 2000. It is widely sown with wild-flower seed mixtures, and in some areas the distinction between native and alien records has been completely obscured.

Biogeography Eurosiberian Temperate element; widely naturalized outside its native range.

Native	GB	IR
2000–19	1489	355
1987–99	1443	372
1970–86	1056	50
pre-1970	1552	338

Alien	GB	IR
2000–19	27	0
1987–99	16	0
1970–86	6	0
pre-1970	11	0

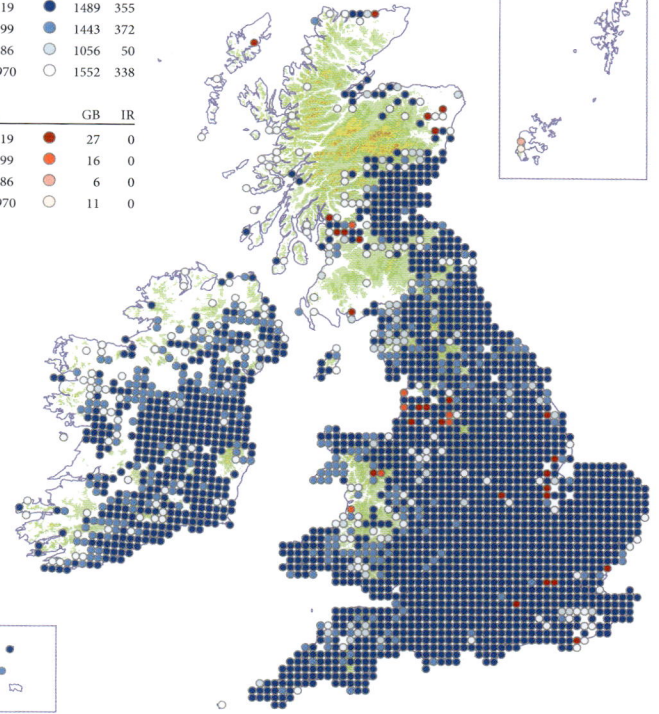

P.A. Stroh & G.T.D. Wilmore

N *Succisa pratensis* Devil's-bit Scabious

Moench

A perennial herb, growing in a wide range of moist to moderately free-draining habitats, and favouring mildly acidic soils. It occurs in woodland rides, heathland and grassland, fens and mires, and in the uplands also on cliff ledges and in ravines. 0–1,080 m (Ben Alder, Easterness).

Trends A widespread decline in lowland areas of England took place in the second half of the 20th century, with losses and the subsequent fragmentation of populations largely attributable to the destruction of grassland and heaths. Its 10 km square distribution appears to have stabilized in recent decades, albeit it is now an uncommon species locally in many areas of central and eastern England. It was mapped as 'all records' in the 1962 *Atlas*.

Biogeography Eurosiberian Temperate element.

Native	GB	IR
2000–19	2477	953
1987–99	2464	883
1970–86	1600	184
pre-1970	2422	795

Alien	GB	IR
2000–19	4	0
1987–99	3	0
1970–86	0	0
pre-1970	2	0

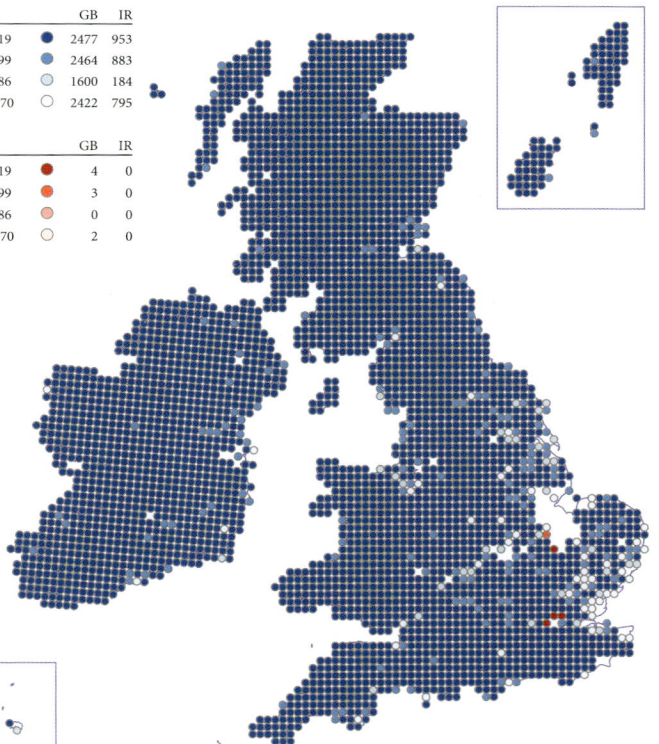

Key refs Adams (1955), Grime *et al.* (2007).

P.A. Stroh & G.T.D. Wilmore

N *Scabiosa columbaria* Small Scabious
L.

A perennial herb of dry, relatively infertile soils. Its habitats include calcareous pastures on downs, hill-slopes and banks, and it is occasionally found on cliffs and rock outcrops and in disused chalk and limestone quarries. Generally lowland, reaching 640 m on Cross Fell (Cumberland).

Native in Britain and a neophyte in Ireland.

Trends Very few losses of *S. columbaria* were evident at the 10 km scale prior to 1950, but in the second half of the 20th century decline was reported throughout its range, and particularly outside its core areas, due to the destruction of suitable grassland habitat and a lack of grazing leading to coarser swards. Its distribution appears to have stabilized since 2000, although mapping at the

10 km scale masks substantial localized declines outside of protected areas.

Biogeography European Temperate element.

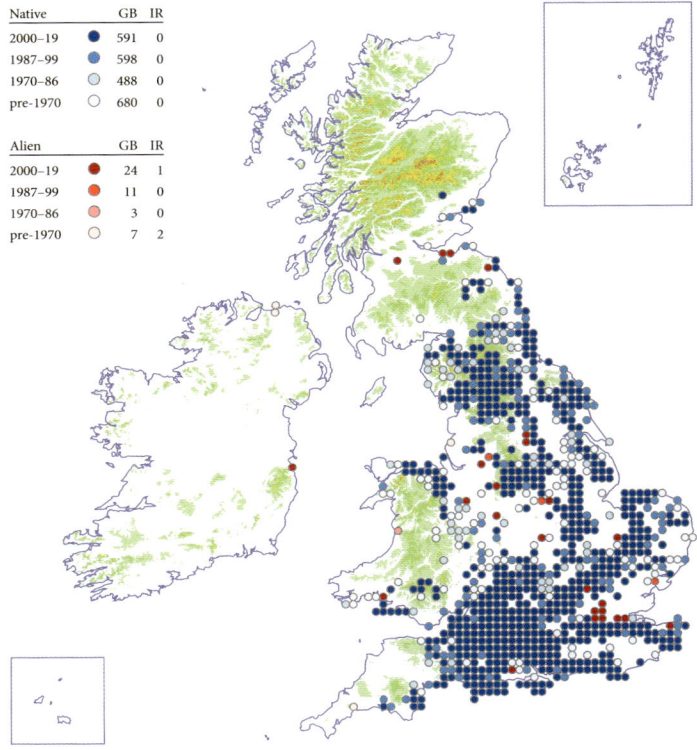

Native		GB	IR
2000–19	●	591	0
1987–99	●	598	0
1970–86	●	488	0
pre-1970	○	680	0

Alien		GB	IR
2000–19	●	24	1
1987–99	●	11	0
1970–86	●	3	0
pre-1970	○	7	2

Key refs Grime *et al.* (2007).

P.A. STROH & G.T.D. WILMORE

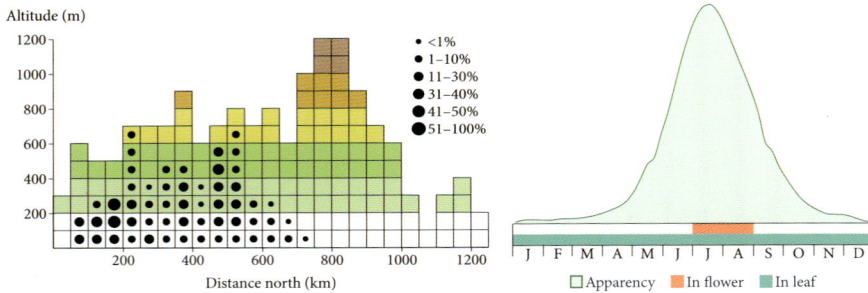

Altitude (m)

● <1%
● 1–10%
● 11–30%
● 31–40%
● 41–50%
● 51–100%

Distance north (km)

□ Apparency ■ In flower ■ In leaf

Ne *Griselinia littoralis* New Zealand Broadleaf
(Raoul) Raoul

A dioecious, salt-tolerant evergreen shrub, widely used for hedging and wind-breaks in coastal areas and found in woodland, plantations, hedges, shelter-belts, churchyards, parks and on waste ground and sea-cliffs. Although rarely fruiting in our area, it has been observed regenerating prolifically in policy woodlands on the Hebridean island of Colonsay (South Ebudes). Lowland.

Trends *G. littoralis* has been cultivated in Britain since 1857. It is popular in gardens, and frequently planted as hedges and wind-breaks in coastal areas. It was found in the wild by 1957 and by the 1990s it had been recorded from the milder coastal areas, especially in south-western Britain. Since 2000 more systematic recording of alien plants has extended this range along the full length

of the southern and western coastlines of Britain and over much of coastal Ireland.

Biogeography Native of New Zealand.

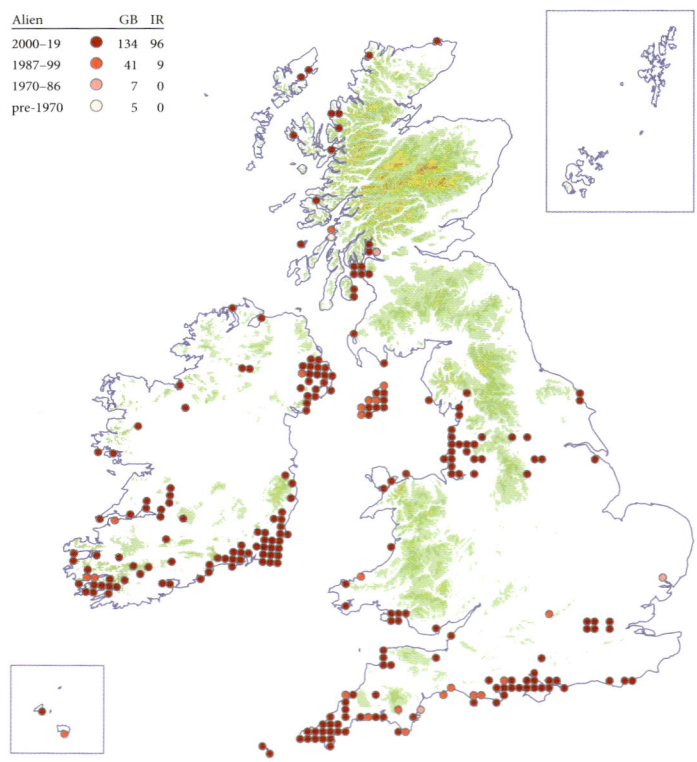

Alien		GB	IR
2000–19	●	134	96
1987–99	●	41	9
1970–86	●	7	0
pre-1970	○	5	0

Key refs Bean (1973), Pope *et al.* (2003).

H.J. KILLICK

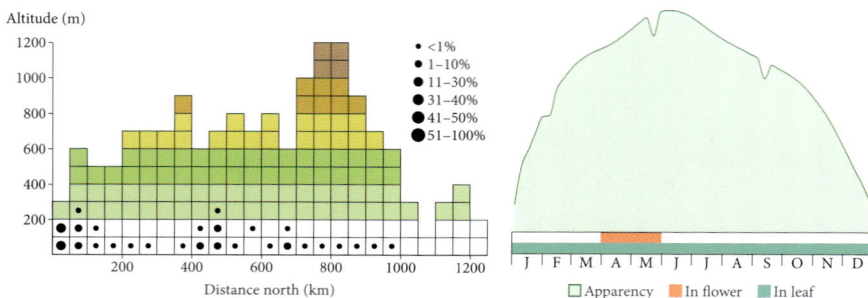

Altitude (m)

● <1%
● 1–10%
● 11–30%
● 31–40%
● 41–50%
● 51–100%

Distance north (km)

□ Apparency ■ In flower ■ In leaf

Ne *Pittosporum crassifolium* Karo

Banks & Sol. ex A.Cunn.

An evergreen shrub planted as a screen or windbreak in coastal areas and persisting or becoming naturalized in hedgerows, amongst coastal boulders and on rock outcrops, cliffs and waste ground. Reproduction is by seed, which is sticky and bird-dispersed. Lowland.

Trends *P. crassifolium* was being cultivated in British gardens by 1854 and was first recorded from the wild as planted in 1939 and as naturalized in 1952 (Isles of Scilly). The species has spread to uninhabited islands in the Isles of Scilly.

Biogeography Native of New Zealand.

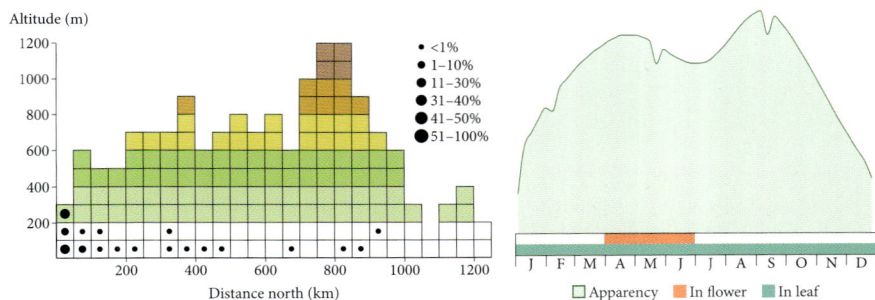

	GB	IR
Long term	No trend	No trend
Short term	No trend	No trend

Alien		GB	IR
2000–19	●	19	0
1987–99	●	7	0
1970–86	●	5	0
pre-1970	○	5	0

Key refs Bean (1976), Lousley (1971).

T.D. Dines & D.A. Pearman

Altitude (m)

● <1%
● 1–10%
● 11–30%
● 31–40%
● 41–50%
● 51–100%

Distance north (km)

☐ Apparency ☐ In flower ☐ In leaf

Ne *Pittosporum tenuifolium* Kohuhu

Gaertn.

An evergreen shrub, widely planted in mild areas, especially near the coast, and found naturalized in woodland, churchyards and as a casual on walls, along paths and in pavement cracks. Reproduction is by seed. Lowland.

Trends This species, of which many cultivars are available, was grown in Britain by 1818, and recorded from the wild as a self-sown seedling on Jethou (Channel Islands) in 1958. It is increasingly popular in gardens, and appears to be increasing in the wild although this may in part be due to better recording of alien plants in the wild.

Biogeography Native of New Zealand.

	GB	IR
Long term	No trend	No trend
Short term		

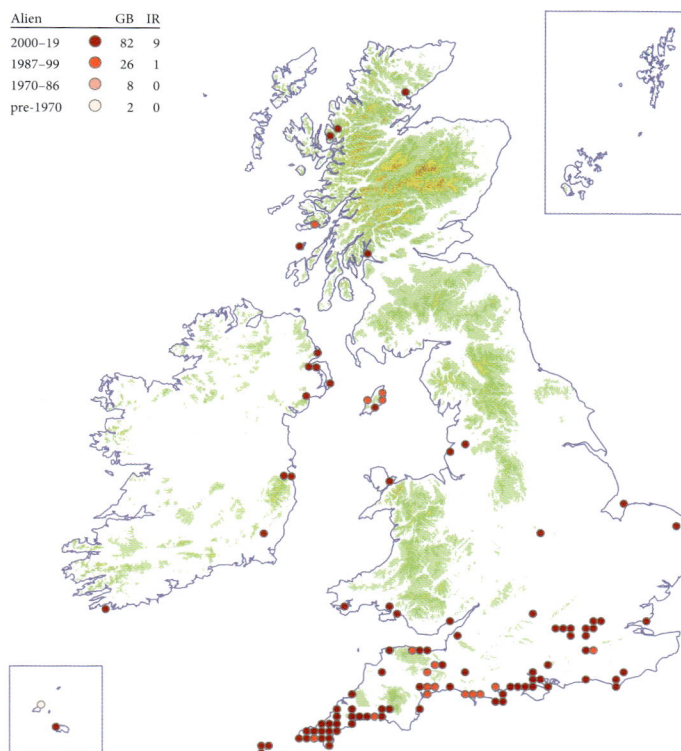

Alien		GB	IR
2000–19	●	82	9
1987–99	●	26	1
1970–86	●	8	0
pre-1970	○	2	0

Key refs Bean (1976).

Altitude (m)

● <1%
● 1–10%
● 11–30%
● 31–40%
● 41–50%
● 51–100%

Distance north (km)

☐ Apparency ☐ In flower ☐ In leaf

T.D. Dines & D.A. Pearman

Ne *Hedera colchica* Persian Ivy
(K.Koch) K.Koch

An evergreen woody climber, grown in gardens as ground cover, and found as a garden escape in woodland, hedges and scrub and on roadsides, railway banks, walls and waste ground. It reproduces vegetatively and by seed, which can be bird-sown. Lowland.

Trends *H. colchica* was known to be in cultivation in Britain in 1864, and possibly a few years earlier, and is popular in gardens and amenity plantings, where it is used for ground cover. It was first recorded in the wild in 1959 (Warley, South Essex), and is certainly under-recorded; it appears to be increasing, especially in urban areas.

Biogeography Native of northern Turkey and the Caucasus.

	GB	IR
Long term	No trend	No trend
Short term	↓ · · ↑	No trend

Alien	GB	IR
2000–19	325	3
1987–99	101	0
1970–86	35	3
pre-1970	9	0

Key refs Bean (1973), McAllister & Marshall (2017).

T.D. Dines & D.A. Pearman

Altitude (m)

- <1%
- 1–10%
- 11–30%
- 31–40%
- 41–50%
- 51–100%

Distance north (km)

☐ Apparency ■ In flower ■ In leaf

J F M A M J J A S O N D

Ne *Hedera algeriensis* Algerian Ivy
Hibberd

A woody perennial shrub with creeping and climbing stems which is found as a garden escape in hedgerows and scrub, and on waste ground and refuse tips. Discarded plants are usually casual but can become naturalized in mild climates. Lowland.

Trends *H. algeriensis* was known to be in cultivation in Britain in 1864, and possibly a few years earlier. It was first recorded in the wild in 1959 (Warley, South Essex). The concenration of records in south-east Ireland, where it has spread from gardens, especially those that have been abandoned, into ajoining hedgerows and even onto shingle beaches, reflects the interest of a botanist in that area.

Biogeography Native of northern Africa.

	GB	IR
Long term	No trend	No trend
Short term	↓ · · ↑	↓ · · ↑

Alien	GB	IR
2000–19	91	25
1987–99	13	0
1970–86	2	0
pre-1970	4	0

Key refs Bean (1973), McAllister & Marshall (2017).

D.A. Pearman & T.D. Dines

Altitude (m)

- <1%
- 1–10%
- 11–30%
- 31–40%
- 41–50%
- 51–100%

Distance north (km)

☐ Apparency ■ In flower ■ In leaf

J F M A M J J A S O N D

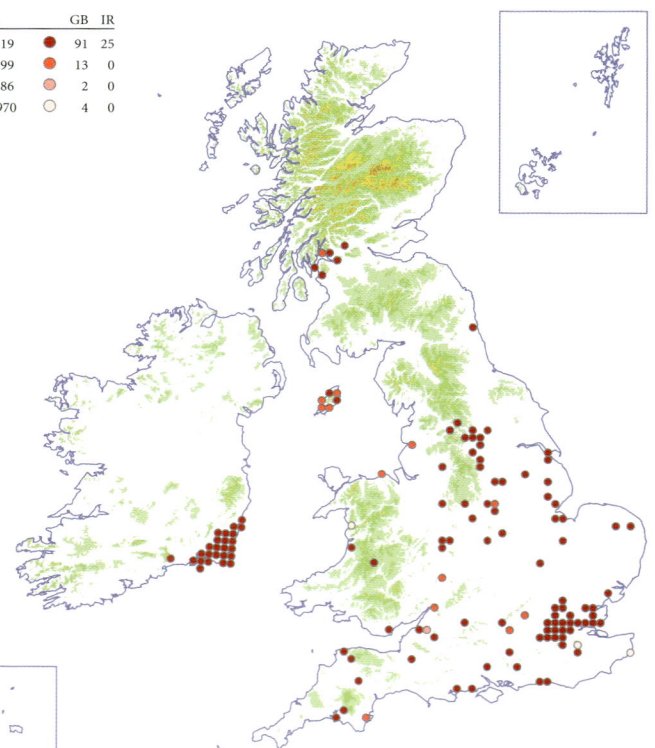

N *Hedera helix s.l.* Common & Atlantic Ivy

An evergreen woody climber most characteristic of woodland, scrub and hedgerows, but also common on walls, fences, rock outcrops and cliffs. It is shade tolerant and often carpets the ground in secondary woodland, plantations and shelter belts as well as climbing to considerable heights up trees, buildings and cliffs. It generally favours basic to moderately acidic soils. It is highly palatable, and in grazed upland areas becomes restricted to inaccessible rock outcrops. 0–610 m (Mourne Mountains, County Down).

Trends In Britain and Ireland *H. helix s.l.* includes two native species (*H. helix s.s.*, *H. hibernica*) and a large number of horticultural cultivars and varieties that are now widely established in the wild. *H. helix s.s.* (formerly *H. helix* subsp. *helix*) is a diploid taxon that occurs throughout our area but appears to be much rarer in the west, where it is largely replaced by the tetraploid *H. hibernica* (formerly

H. helix subsp. *hibernica*), and in northern Scotland where it is absent from the most mountainous areas. There have been widespread inconsistencies with the recording of both taxa, but in particular *H. helix s.s.*, with many botanists using '*Hedera helix*' as a catch-all for Ivy, and often entering records in the strict sense in error, making the separation of true *H. helix s.s.* records an intractable problem. The distribution of *H. hibernica* was better known to recorders prior to this *Atlas* survey, and we have attempted to map this species separately, though undoubtedly there will be errors. Overall the known 10 km square distribution of *H. helix s.l.* has changed very little since the 1960s except in parts of Scotland and Ireland due to more systematic recording. Frequent escapes from gardens have completely obscured the native distribution and so all hectads are mapped as presence only.

Biogeography European Southern-temperate element.

		GB	IR
2000–19	●	2567	971
1987–99	●	2455	932
1970–86	●	1832	224
pre-1970	○	2438	863

Key refs Grime *et al.* (2007).

K.J. WALKER & G.T.D. WILMORE

N *Hedera hibernica* Atlantic Ivy
(G.Kirch.) Bean

An evergreen woody climber of woodland, scrub, hedgerows, walls, rock outcrops and cliffs, which may also sprawl over the ground especially in secondary woodland, plantations and woodland strips. It is more reluctant to climb than *H. helix s.s.* and avoids only the most acidic soils.

Trends This tetraploid species is more frequent in western Britain and Ireland than *H. helix s.s.* It is much better known than when mapped by McAllister & Rutherford (1990) and for the 2002 *Atlas*, and this is reflected by the increase in distribution since 2000, particularly in Ireland. The two species (formerly treated as subsp. *hibernica* and subsp. *helix*) can be difficult to separate. It is widely grown in gardens and frequently escapes into the surrounding habitats. Many of these alien records, particularly in eastern Britain, refer to the cultivar

'Hibernica' (Irish Ivy), which is widely grown and has been found naturalized since at least 1838. Separating alien and native populations within the native range can be difficult and consequently the boundary of the native range shown on the map is somewhat arbitrary.

Biogeography Oceanic Southern-temperate element.

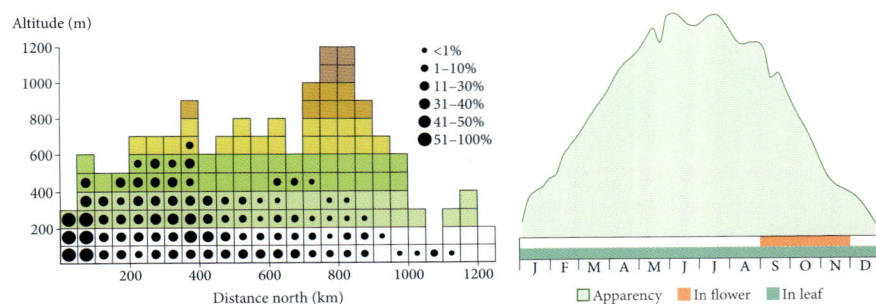

Native		GB	IR
2000–19	●	503	814
1987–99	●	312	174
1970–86	●	175	21
pre-1970	○	68	1

Alien		GB	IR
2000–19	●	866	34
1987–99	●	432	3
1970–86	●	380	15
pre-1970	○	36	0

Key refs McAllister & Rutherford (1990), Rich & Jermy (1998).

T.D. DINES & K.J. WALKER

Ne *Fatsia japonica* Fatsia
(Thunb.) Decne. & Planch.

An evergreen shrub, commonly grown in gardens, found as an escape or relic of cultivation in woodland, on roadsides and on waste ground. Reproduction by seed can occur in mild winters and there are a few reports of bird-sown plants (Leslie, 2019). Lowland.

Trends *F. japonica* was introduced into Britain in 1838, and is now extremely popular in gardens due to its ease of cultivation and bold, evergreen, often variegated, foliage. It was not recorded from the wild until 1974 (Penzance, West Cornwall) but since then it appears to have been noticed with increasing frequency, presumably primarily as discarded plants, although some records, especially in areas of London and Lancashire, may represent planted specimens within gardens.

Biogeography Native of Japan.

Alien	GB	IR
2000–19	113	3
1987–99	16	0
1970–86	0	0
pre-1970	1	0

Key refs Bean (1973), Leslie (2019).

T.D. DINES & D.A. PEARMAN

N *Hydrocotyle vulgaris* Marsh Pennywort
L.

A mat-forming perennial herb found in a wide range of damp or wet habitats, including carr, mires, fens, fen-meadows, swamps, marshes, in soakways and along spring-lines, and in dune-slacks and wet hollows in stabilized shingle. In very oceanic areas it grows in drier habitats, such as turfed wall-tops. 0–635 m (Craswall, Herefordshire).

Trends *H. vulgaris* was mapped as 'all records' in the 1962 *Atlas*. Fieldwork undertaken in the latter half of the 20th century revealed a clear decline in parts of the English Midlands and Scotland, some of which had occurred before 1950. Drainage and development have steadily eliminated many sites in southern and eastern England, notably within grazing marshes (Mountford, 1994) and this trend continues in the lowlands.

Biogeography Suboceanic Southern-temperate element.

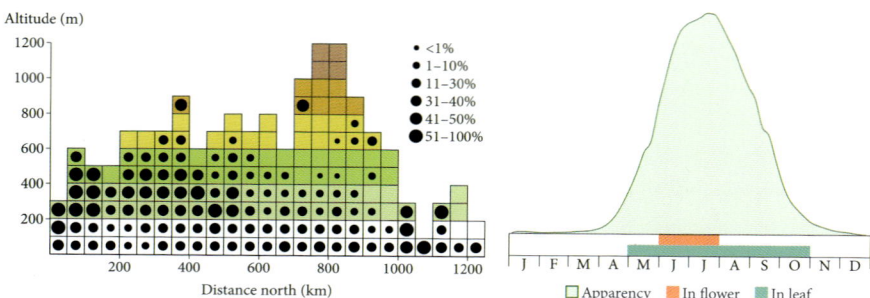

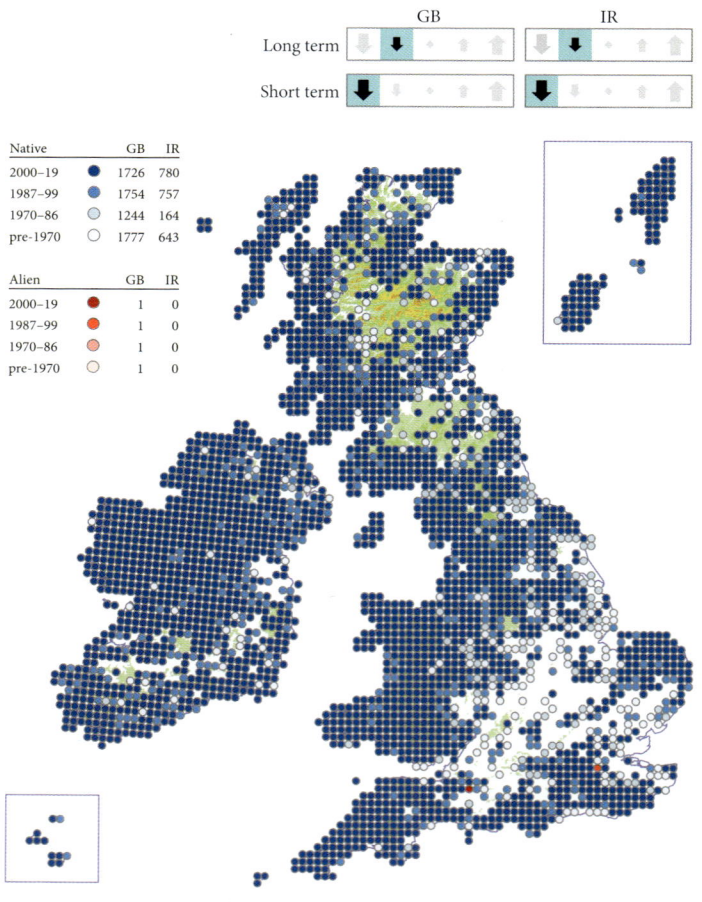

Native	GB	IR
2000–19	1726	780
1987–99	1754	757
1970–86	1244	164
pre-1970	1777	643

Alien	GB	IR
2000–19	1	0
1987–99	1	0
1970–86	1	0
pre-1970	1	0

Key refs Grime *et al.* (2007), Mountford (1994), Tutin (1980).

M. SOUTHAM & J.O. MOUNTFORD

Ne *Hydrocotyle ranunculoides* Floating Pennywort

L.f.

A robust perennial herb found rooted in mud or as a free-floating or emergent aquatic on the surface of still or slowly moving water, such as lakes, ponds, streams, ditches and canals, as well as the margins and backwaters of rivers. It can form exceptionally dense colonies very rapidly, excluding native species and causing serious restrictions to navigation by boats. Rooted plants flower and set seed; floating plants spread by rooted stem fragments, often attached to boats or as free-floating 'rafts', allowing it to spread rapidly along watercourses. Lowland.

Trends *H. ranunculoides* has been widely sold in aquatic plant nurseries and was first recorded in the wild in 1990 (Chelmsford, South Essex), soon afterward becoming a pest in the Pevensey Levels (East Sussex). From these 'bridgeheads' it has spread rapidly in the 21st century, especially in lowland England and Ulster, causing major obstacles to boats on many waterways. It continues to spread rapidly despite being banned from sale in 2014 and the significant efforts undertaken to eradicate it from many rivers and canals. It is now considered to be one of the most invasive aquatic plants in Britain, as well as an emerging threat in Ireland, with an estimated annual cost of control likely to amount to many millions of pounds.

Biogeography Native of North America; widely naturalized in Central and South America and elsewhere, as well as western Europe and Australia.

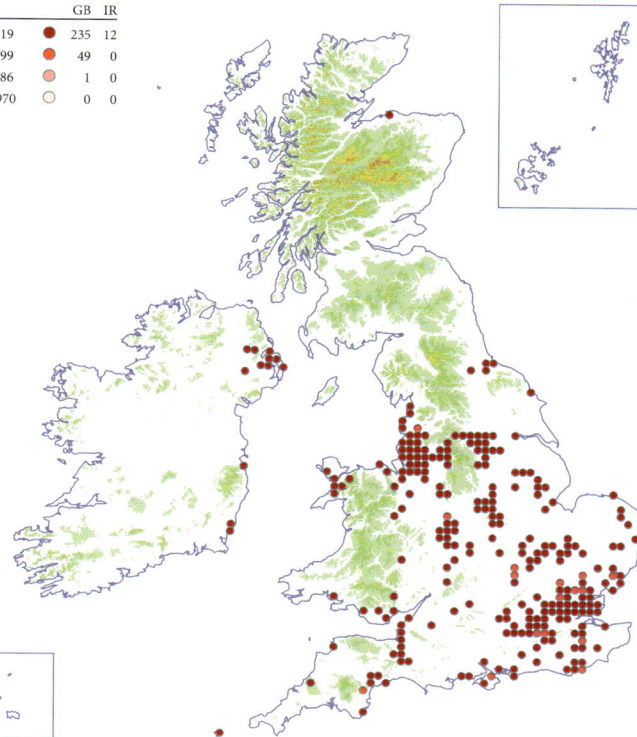

Key refs Harper (2000), Newman & Dawson (1999), Newman & Duenas (2006).

T.D. DINES, J.O. MOUNTFORD & K.J. WALKER

Ne *Turgenia latifolia* Greater Bur-parsley

(L.) Hoffm.

An annual herb, formerly a weed of arable fields, waste ground and other disturbed sites. Lowland.

Trends A grain and birdseed casual that appears to have declined by the late 19th century (Leslie, 2019). There were few 20th century records and it remains a very rare casual.

Biogeography Native of Europe and the Mediterranean region, east to central Asia. Naturalized as a weed beyond its native range.

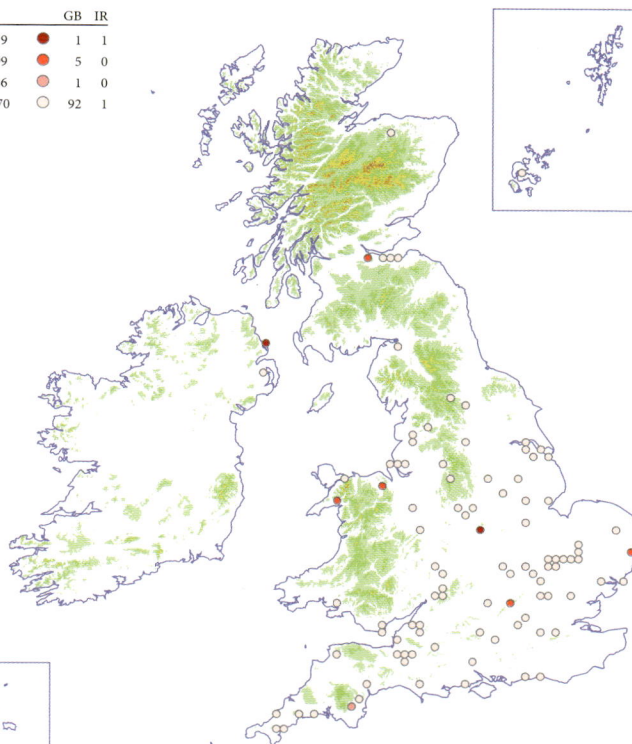

Key refs Leslie (2019), Tutin (1980).

J.O. MOUNTFORD

N *Sanicula europaea* Sanicle
L.

A perennial herb of moist soil in deciduous woodland, often where beech, ash and oaks predominate; also locally in substantial hedgebanks and on shaded roadsides. In the north and west of its range it is sometimes found in relict woodland in gorges and in sheltered stream ravines. Rarely it will colonize planted amenity or secondary woodland and the shaded parts of churchyards. The substrate is usually calcareous or otherwise base-rich, but can occasionally be neutral or mildly acidic. Generally lowland, but reaching 500 m above Malham (Mid-west Yorkshire) and possibly higher in Glencoe (Main Argyll).

Trends In the 20th century there was some decline in the frequency of this species, particularly in lowland England, through the destruction or replanting of broadleaved woodland.

Its distribution now seems stable, and is much better recorded in Ireland, with many new sites discovered. It was mapped as 'all records' in the 1962 *Atlas*.

Biogeography European Temperate element; also in central Asia.

Native	GB	IR
2000–19	1695	669
1987–99	1709	554
1970–86	1248	114
pre-1970	1839	346

Alien	GB	IR
2000–19	1	0
1987–99	1	0
1970–86	1	0
pre-1970	1	0

Key refs Grime *et al.* (2007), Tutin (1980).

M. SOUTHAM & J.O. MOUNTFORD

Ne *Astrantia major* Astrantia
L.

A long-lived and sometimes persistent perennial herb found on waste ground as an escape from cultivation or as an introduction in partially shaded habitats, most often near human habitations. Lowland.

Trends Introduced into cultivation by 1596, *A. major* is a popular garden plant and various cultivars (and three subspecies) are grown. The map in the 2002 *Atlas* was the first to show its national distribution, and there is evidence of increased frequency in the 21st century. It was first recorded in the wild in 1825 at Stokesay Castle (Shropshire).

Biogeography Native of central Europe.

Alien	GB	IR
2000–19	183	1
1987–99	65	1
1970–86	53	1
pre-1970	74	0

Key refs Tutin (1980).

M. SOUTHAM & J.O. MOUNTFORD

Ne *Eryngium planum* Blue Eryngo
L.

A perennial herb found as a naturalized or casual garden escape on grassy road verges and in waste places. Lowland.

Trends *E. planum* was being cultivated in Britain by 1596 and is very popular in gardens. It was recorded in the wild in 1951 (Hounslow Heath, Middlesex), and has been naturalized at Littlestone and Lade (West Kent) from 1965 to the present. In some areas, particularly around London, it is the most commonly recorded *Eryngium*.

Biogeography Native of central and south-eastern Europe and western and central Asia.

	GB	IR
Long term	No trend	No trend
Short term	↑	No trend

Alien	GB	IR
2000–19	93	3
1987–99	11	0
1970–86	11	0
pre-1970	6	0

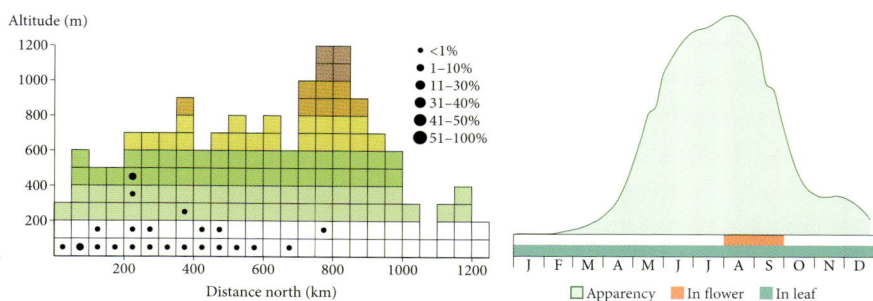

Altitude (m)

Symbol	Frequency
•	<1%
•	1–10%
●	11–30%
●	31–40%
●	41–50%
●	51–100%

Distance north (km)

Apparency   In flower   In leaf

T.D. DINES & J.O. MOUNTFORD

N *Eryngium maritimum* Sea-holly
L.

A glaucous, spiny-leaved perennial herb confined to coastal habitats, occurring mainly on incipient and mobile sand dunes and occasionally on shingle; often a little above high-tide mark. Lowland.

Trends This species disappeared from most of its sites in north-eastern England and eastern Scotland before 1930, for reasons which are unclear. There has evidently been further declines since then, and some surviving populations are quite small, but in recent decades its distribution seems fairly stable, and some new sites have been found.

Biogeography European Southern-temperate element.

	GB	IR
Long term	↓	↓
Short term	↑	↑

Native	GB	IR
2000–19	211	85
1987–99	176	72
1970–86	131	20
pre-1970	269	75

Alien	GB	IR
2000–19	3	1
1987–99	0	1
1970–86	0	0
pre-1970	4	0

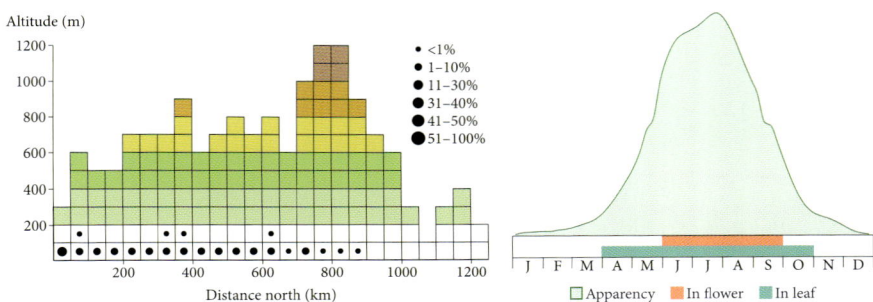

Altitude (m)

Symbol	Frequency
•	<1%
•	1–10%
●	11–30%
●	31–40%
●	41–50%
●	51–100%

Distance north (km)

Apparency   In flower   In leaf

Key refs Isermann & Rooney (2014), Tutin (1980).

M. SOUTHAM & J.O. MOUNTFORD

Ar *Eryngium campestre* Field Eryngo
L.

A perennial herb of well-drained neutral or calcareous soils in old pastures and coastal grassland in south-western England, where it is very long-established and was once considered to be native. Elsewhere, short-lived or casual populations have been reported from pastures, roadsides and rough ground. Lowland.

Trends *E. campestre* was first recorded in the wild in Devon, where it was seen by John Ray in 1662. Sites in Devon and Somerset have statutory protection and the species is persisting there with appropriate management.

Biogeography As an archaeophyte, *E. campestre* has a European Southern-temperate distribution.

Alien	GB	IR
2000–19	16	0
1987–99	12	0
1970–86	16	0
pre-1970	43	2

Key refs Stroh *et al.* (2014), Tutin (1980), Wigginton (1999).

M. Southam & J.O. Mountford

Ne *Bupleurum falcatum* Sickle-leaved Hare's-ear
L.

A biennial or short-lived perennial herb, found in hedgebanks and field-borders, on ditch-banks and on roadside verges, but only recently in the latter habitat. Plants reproduce by seed, which appears to remain viable for only one year. Lowland.

Trends This species, which was cultivated in gardens by 1739, has only been naturalized in a single locality, at Norton Heath in South Essex, where it was first recorded in 1831 and last seen in 1962. The present population there was re-established from seed taken from cultivated plants derived from the original colony. Another population in Bolton Abbey woods (Mid-West Yorkshire) was present through the 1990s but is unrecorded since 2000. It is quite widely grown in gardens.

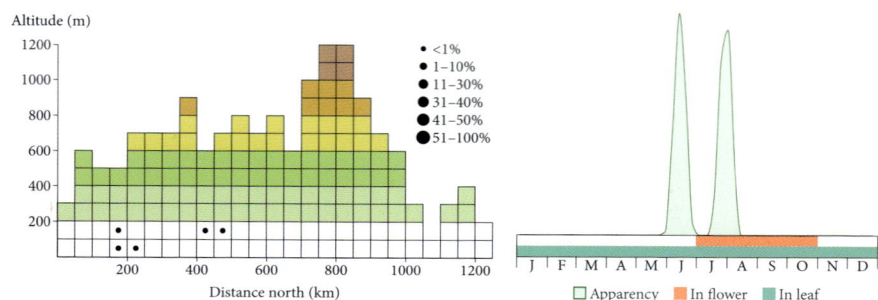

Biogeography A Eurasian Southern-temperate species.

Alien	GB	IR
2000–19	1	0
1987–99	7	0
1970–86	4	0
pre-1970	5	0

Key refs Field (1994), Sarbu *et al.* (2013), Tutin (1980), Wigginton (1999).

M. Southam & J.O. Mountford

N *Bupleurum tenuissimum* Slender Hare's-ear
L.

A slender, often diminutive, annual herb that is primarily a colonist of thinly vegetated or disturbed coastal sites, including coastal banks, sea-walls, drained estuarine marshes and the margins of brackish ditches. Inland populations grew on commons and roadsides, as well as open grassland on base-rich clays; it still grows on commons near Malvern (Worcestershire) and on a Cambridgeshire road verge. Lowland.

Trends Most of the inland sites for this species were lost before 1930, whereas its coastal distribution seems to have been largely stable since the 1970s, although there have been local declines where grassland has become coarser due to a lack of grazing. Unlike other species of the upper parts of saltmarshes, there has been little evidence of it colonizing salted roadsides other than the central reservation of the A2 near Dartford (West Kent), and road verges at Lindsell and Colchester (North Essex).

Biogeography European Southern-temperate element.

Native	GB	IR
2000–19	74	0
1987–99	71	0
1970–86	75	0
pre-1970	147	0

Alien	GB	IR
2000–19	3	0
1987–99	1	0
1970–86	0	0
pre-1970	2	0

	GB	IR
Long term	↓	No trend
Short term	↓	No trend

Key refs Coombe (1994), Leslie (2019), Stewart *et al.* (1994), Stroh *et al.* (2014), Tutin (1980), Walker *et al.* (2017).

M. Southam & J.O. Mountford

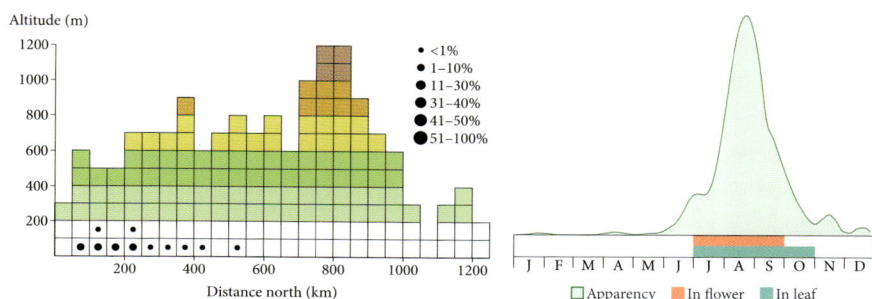

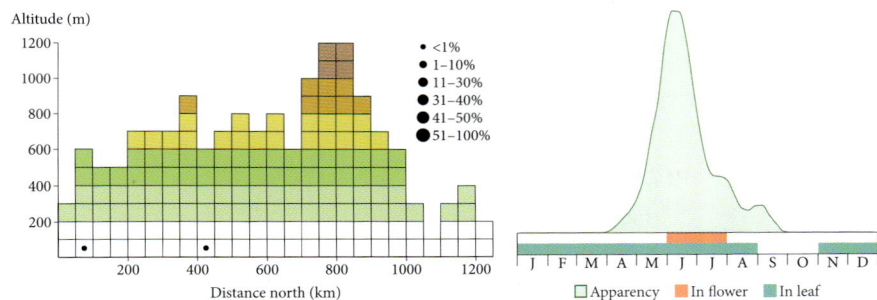

N *Bupleurum baldense* Small Hare's-ear
Turra

A diminutive annual herb of rabbit-grazed coastal grassland over calcareous substrates. Near Beachy Head (East Sussex), it occurs on bare chalk near the eroding and overhanging cliff-edge, and in Devon on made-ground as well as in cliff-top turf. In the Channel Islands it grows in open turf on consolidated sand dunes and more rarely on cliffs. Lowland.

Trends *B. baldense* was lost from all but two of its five Devon localities by the mid-20th century, and there are no records from Walls Hill near Babbacombe since 1983. There are recent records from perhaps its sole surviving site in Devon at Berry Head, where it can be very locally abundant in good seasons. The only other mainland site, near to Beachy Head (East Sussex), is perilously close to the cliff edge, and the population may have contracted somewhat in recent decades, although the number of plants fluctuates from year to year, and other populations may exist, undiscovered, nearby. Populations on the Channel Islands remain stable.

Biogeography Mediterranean-Atlantic element.

Native	GB	IR
2000–19	8	0
1987–99	8	0
1970–86	7	0
pre-1970	10	0

Alien	GB	IR
2000–19	0	0
1987–99	0	0
1970–86	0	0
pre-1970	3	0

	GB	IR
Long term	No trend	No trend
Short term	No trend	No trend

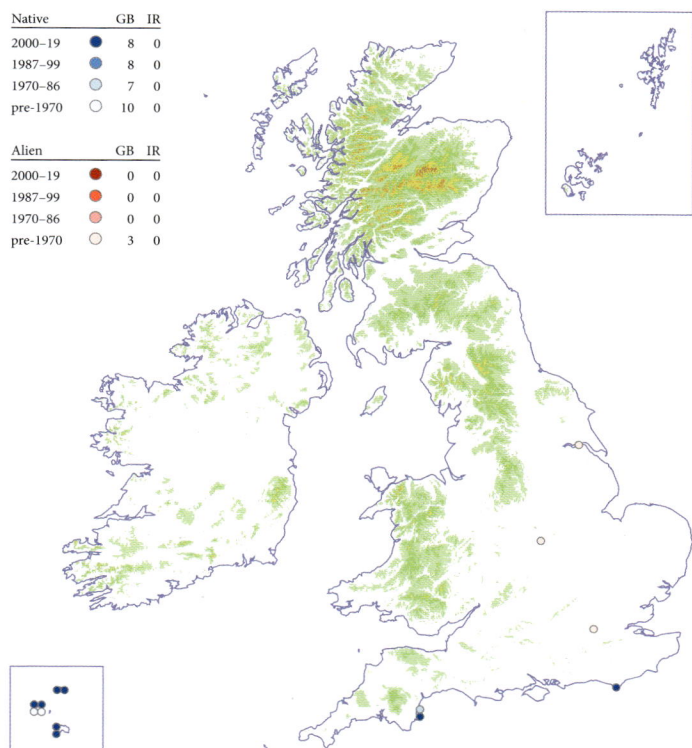

Key refs Smith *et al.* (2016), Sussex Botanical Recording Society (2018), Tutin (1980), Wigginton (1999).

M. Southam & J.O. Mountford

Ar *Bupleurum rotundifolium* Thorow-wax
L.

An archaeophyte-colonist, this annual herb was formerly a locally abundant arable weed of chalk, limestone and base-rich clay soils, but it is now an uncommon birdseed casual, especially near human habitations. Lowland.

Trends *B. rotundifolium* was frequent in the mid-19th century but, with improved seed screening, became rare by the 20th century, and has been extinct in arable habitats since the 1960s, though it continues to be a very occasional casual in waste places. Germination of its seed is affected by late frosts, and its persistence depended on repeated reintroductions, often with clover seed, from south-western Europe. It is often confused with *B. subovatum*, and some erroneous records may be included on the map. Many of the East Anglian sites are deliberate introductions.

Biogeography *B. rotundifolium* may originate in south-western Asia; it is widespread as an archaeophyte in central and southern Europe and has been introduced to many other areas worldwide.

Alien		GB	IR
2000–19	●	47	0
1987–99	●	16	0
1970–86	●	15	0
pre-1970	○	297	0

	GB	IR
Long term	⬇	No trend
Short term	⬆	No trend

Key refs Leslie (2019), Tutin (1980).

Altitude (m) · Distance north (km)
- <1%
- 1–10%
- 11–30%
- 31–40%
- 41–50%
- 51–100%

☐ Apparency ▢ In flower ▢ In leaf

M.F. Watson & J.O. Mountford

Ne *Bupleurum subovatum* False Thorow-wax
Link ex Spreng.

An annual herb, found as a casual on disturbed and waste ground, on refuse tips and in gardens where it usually originates from birdseed. Lowland.

Trends The first records of *B. subovatum* in Britain date from 1839 (Mangrove Lane, Hertfordshire). It showed a marked increase in frequency from about 1950 onwards, perhaps because of the increased availability and use of birdseed, but has been much less frequent in the late 20th and 21st centuries. It has often been confused with *B. rotundifolium*.

Biogeography Native of the Mediterranean region.

Alien		GB	IR
2000–19	●	20	0
1987–99	●	19	0
1970–86	●	101	1
pre-1970	○	97	3

	GB	IR
Long term	No trend	No trend
Short term	⬇	No trend

Key refs Tutin (1980).

Altitude (m) · Distance north (km)
- <1%
- 1–10%
- 11–30%
- 31–40%
- 41–50%
- 51–100%

☐ Apparency ▢ In flower ▢ In leaf

M.F. Watson & J.O. Mountford

N *Physospermum cornubiense* Bladderseed

(L.) DC.

A rhizomatous perennial herb often found in substantial, loose colonies in open woodland, in gorse scrub on heathlands, on rough grassy slopes (often in stream valleys), in *Molinia caerulea* grassland, and on shaded roadside banks. It also occurs rarely in the margins of arable fields. Reproduction is by seed, and the plant regenerates strongly after burning or clearance. Lowland.

Trends From the late 1970s the number of sites supporting *P. cornubiense* fell from nearly 50 to about 20, and population sizes strongly declined. This was attributed to factors rendering its habitats more densely shaded or destroying them altogether, including the lack of woodland management, afforestation, scrub clearance and the loss of grazing. There appears to have been some recovery in Cornwall since the turn of the century, although this may in part reflect more intensive recording. It was thought to have been lost from South Devon by 1977, but in 2017 one plant was found near the River Tavy, growing on a verge by woodland edge, very close to the site of the last known record. Outside its native range, *P. cornubiense* is long-established in Burnham Beeches (Buckinghamshire).

Biogeography European Temperate element.

	GB	IR
Long term	No trend	No trend
Short term	No trend	No trend

Native	GB	IR
2000–19	8	0
1987–99	10	0
1970–86	7	0
pre-1970	14	0

Alien	GB	IR
2000–19	1	0
1987–99	1	0
1970–86	1	0
pre-1970	1	0

Key refs Tutin (1980), Wigginton (1999).

M.J. WIGGINTON & J.O. MOUNTFORD

N *Oenanthe fistulosa* Tubular Water-dropwort

L.

A perennial herb of damp or wet habitats, usually in areas of winter flooding and on weakly acid to weakly basic soils. It occurs in meadows and pastures in the floodplains of rivers, where it is especially typical of grips, furrows and other depressions. It also grows in marshes and fens, and in emergent and fringing vegetation by rivers, streams, canals, ditches, lakes and ponds. It reproduces by seed, and spreads by stolons. In heavily grazed swards seed is produced virtually at ground level from secondary growth. Lowland to 415 m (Tarn Dub, North-west Yorkshire).

Trends This species, mapped as 'all records' in the 1962 *Atlas*, has declined appreciably because of drainage of wetlands, the re-seeding of old grassland or its conversion to arable, and in more recent times, neglect resulting in a tall and closed sward. Use of inorganic fertilizers and inappropriate watercourse management also pose a threat, especially where tall emergents and coarse bank species shade out populations. Many losses have occurred since 1950, and decline continues.

Biogeography European Temperate element.

	GB	IR
Long term	↓	↓
Short term	↓	↓

Native	GB	IR
2000–19	391	50
1987–99	463	53
1970–86	405	28
pre-1970	698	76

Alien	GB	IR
2000–19	2	0
1987–99	3	1
1970–86	0	0
pre-1970	1	1

Key refs Preston & Croft (1997), Stroh *et al.* (2014), Stroh *et al.* (2019), Tutin (1980), Walker *et al.* (2017).

M. SOUTHAM, M.J. WIGGINTON & J.O. MOUNTFORD

N *Oenanthe silaifolia* Narrow-leaved Water-dropwort
M.Bieb.

A perennial herb of damp grassland which receives calcareous flood-water in winter, especially where water lies for longer periods. It normally grows in hay meadows and may occur abundantly in lammas meadows, but only as depauperate individuals in more intensively farmed land. It is also found on damp streamsides and has shown some capacity to colonize wet grasslands newly created as parts of habitat restoration schemes. Lowland.

Trends Many sites were lost before 1930, but new localities for this species have been discovered since the 1960s, and its known range was extended to South-east Yorkshire in the 1980s, with new sites still being discovered in the area this century. It is eliminated by even quite modest agricultural intensification. All records from Dorset, mapped in both the 1962 *Atlas*

and in Stewart *et al.* (1994), are now regarded as errors for *O. lachenalii*. There has also been past confusion with *O. pimpinelloides*. Overall, its distribution is now considered to be stable following losses in the 20th century.

Biogeography European Southern-temperate element.

Native		GB	IR
2000–19	●	45	0
1987–99	●	38	0
1970–86	●	38	0
pre-1970	○	58	0

Alien		GB	IR
2000–19	●	2	0
1987–99	●	0	0
1970–86	●	0	0
pre-1970	○	0	0

	GB	IR
Long term	↓ ↓ ◆ ↑ ↑	No trend
Short term	↓ ↓ ◆ ↑ ↑	No trend

Key refs Stewart *et al.* (1994), Stroh *et al.* (2019), Tutin (1980).

Altitude (m) — Distance north (km)

● <1%
● 1–10%
● 11–30%
● 31–40%
● 41–50%
● 51–100%

J F M A M J J A S O N D
□ Apparency ■ In flower ■ In leaf

M. SOUTHAM & J.O. MOUNTFORD

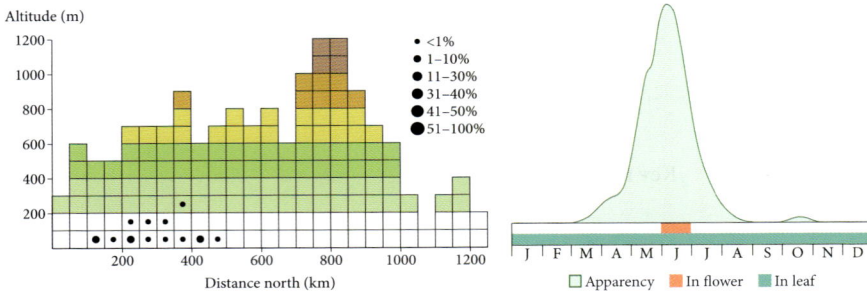

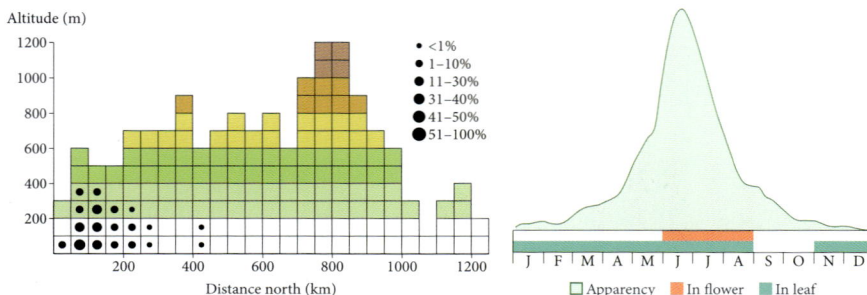

N *Oenanthe pimpinelloides* Corky-fruited Water-dropwort
L.

A tuberous perennial herb of hay meadows and pastures, especially those which are horse-grazed, and on roadsides. It grows in both damp and dry grassland, being the only British *Oenanthe* that grows in dry habitats. Lowland.

Native in Britain and a neophyte in Ireland.

Trends Despite losses last century, *O. pimpinelloides* is still present in very large numbers on some roadsides and in unimproved fields. Its range has continued to expand with the discovery of many outlying sites, which may have been either previously overlooked, and/or are a combination of recent dispersal into suitable habitat, either naturally or by fruit adhering to agricultural equipment. Climate change might also be a potential factor. A recent record in

South Lancashire (Hurst Well Valley) extends significantly its north-western range. Some earlier botanists confused *O. pimpinelloides* with either *O. lachenalii* or *O. silaifolia*, resulting in difficulty in interpreting trends. It was discovered in East Cork in the late 19th century, and much later in County Clare (1984). In recent decades further populations have been found in South Kerry (1994), County Wexford (2006), and County Waterford (2012). It is considered to be alien in Ireland, rather than a rare and overlooked native taxon.

Biogeography Mediterranean-Atlantic element.

Native		GB	IR
2000–19	●	251	0
1987–99	●	202	0
1970–86	●	143	0
pre-1970	○	171	0

Alien		GB	IR
2000–19	●	2	7
1987–99	●	2	5
1970–86	●	2	1
pre-1970	○	0	1

	GB	IR
Long term	↓ ↓ ◆ ↑ ↑	↓ ↓ ◆ ↑ ↑
Short term	↓ ↓ ◆ ↑ ↑	↓ ↓ ◆ ↑ ↑

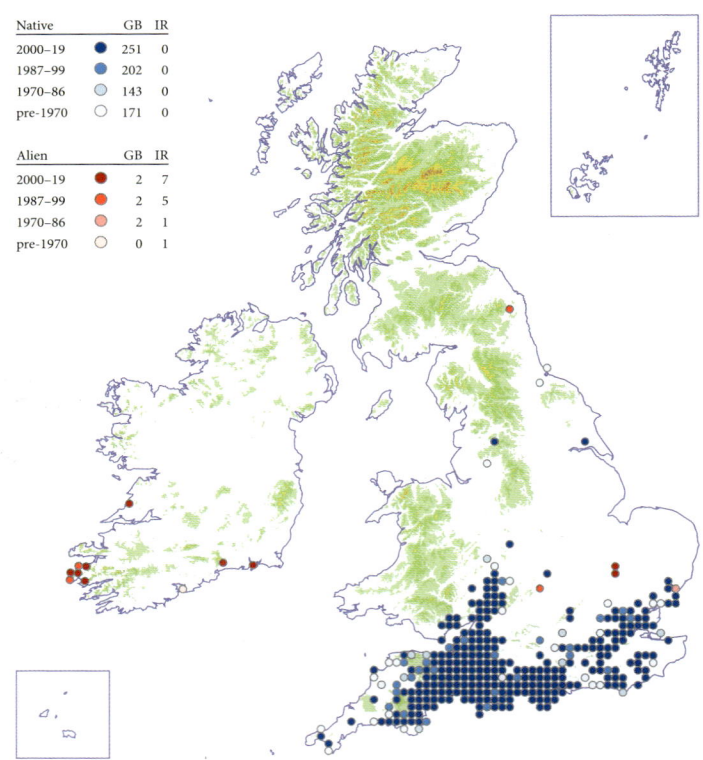

Key refs Adams (2003), Stewart *et al.* (1994), Tutin (1980).

Altitude (m) — Distance north (km)

● <1%
● 1–10%
● 11–30%
● 31–40%
● 41–50%
● 51–100%

J F M A M J J A S O N D
□ Apparency ■ In flower ■ In leaf

M. SOUTHAM & J.O. MOUNTFORD

Oenanthe lachenalii Parsley Water-dropwort

C.C.Gmel.

In coastal areas this perennial herb occurs in the uppermost parts of saltmarshes, in rough grassland in drained estuarine marshes, by brackish dykes and the lower reaches of tidal rivers. Inland, it is found in base-enriched habitats, including marshes, fen-meadows and tall-herb fen. Lowland.

Trends *O. lachenalii* is still widespread and locally plentiful, especially around the coast, although there have been losses in Essex, and in south-western England, where it was always uncommon. Many inland sites have been lost to drainage and land-fill (Leslie, 2019). It was mapped as 'all records' in the 1962 *Atlas*.

Biogeography Suboceanic Southern-temperate element.

Native	GB	IR
2000–19	333	84
1987–99	358	86
1970–86	230	27
pre-1970	444	80

Alien	GB	IR
2000–19	0	0
1987–99	0	0
1970–86	0	0
pre-1970	1	0

Key refs Leslie (2019), Tutin (1980).

M. Southam & J.O. Mountford

Oenanthe crocata Hemlock Water-dropwort

L.

A tuberous perennial herb of shallow water in ditches, the banks of streams, rivers, canals, lakes and ponds, roadside culverts, marshes and wet woodland, among boulders at the top of beaches and on dripping or flushed sea-cliffs. Reproduction is usually by seed, and it perhaps spreads when detached tuberous roots are washed downstream. Generally lowland, but reaching 415 m (Rhyd y Porthmyn Pool, Montgomeryshire).

Trends Though highly toxic to humans and animals, this species is rarely eradicated and continues to spread. The national distribution was largely stable in the 20th century but, since 2000, there has been a significant spread into East Anglia and the East Midlands, especially along rivers. This spread appears natural and may be due to waterborne seed and roots. Climate change may also be a factor, as areas of eastern England have become suitable for a plant previously typical of the milder Oceanic west.

Biogeography Suboceanic Southern-temperate element.

Native	GB	IR
2000–19	1676	641
1987–99	1465	569
1970–86	1083	112
pre-1970	1355	392

Alien	GB	IR
2000–19	3	0
1987–99	3	0
1970–86	2	0
pre-1970	0	0

Key refs Preston & Croft (1997), Tutin (1980).

M. Southam, M.J. Wigginton & J.O. Mountford

Oenanthe fluviatilis River Water-dropwort

(Bab.) Coleman

An aquatic perennial herb, most frequent in clear, meso-eutrophic water of calcareous streams and rivers; also found in canals and drainage channels (at up to 150 cm depth in fen lodes), but rarely in ponds. In flowing water, propagation is usually by plants rooting at nodes, or by vegetative fragmentation. Flowering is more frequent in still or sluggish water, but the frequency of reproduction from seed is unknown. Lowland.

Trends The decline in this species was evident by the 1960s and has continued, especially in southern and central areas of England, although some of the trends may be confounded through misrecording of *O. aquatica*. The main reasons for loss are eutrophication from agricultural run-off, dredging, and canalization of rivers, directly destroying plants or creating unsuitable turbid water. However, it was clearly under-recorded in the 1962 *Atlas* and, despite intensive recording in the latter part of the 20th century and since, it may remain locally overlooked.

Biogeography Oceanic Temperate element.

Native	GB	IR
2000–19	80	38
1987–99	135	31
1970–86	110	5
pre-1970	184	13

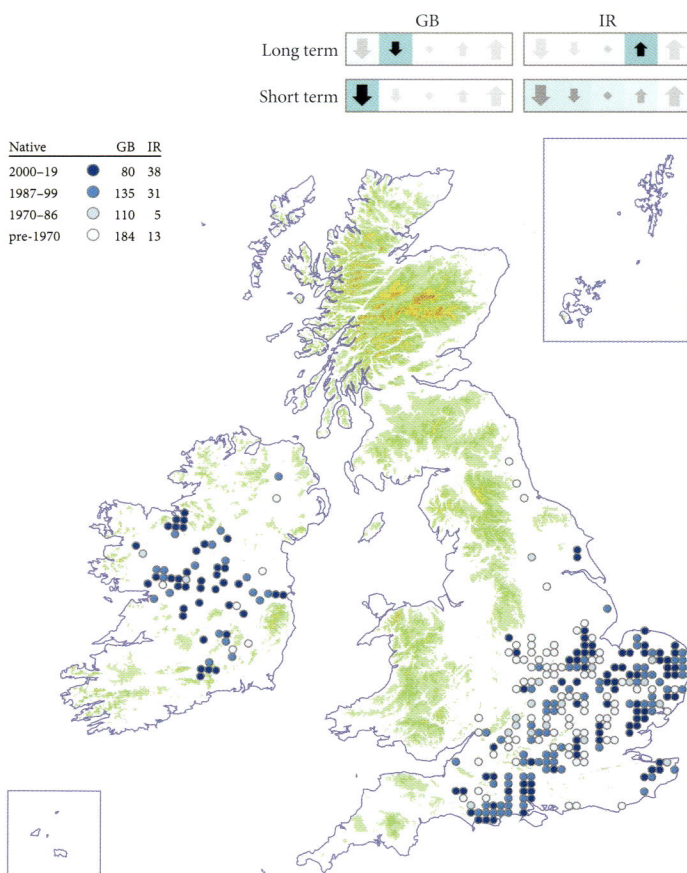

Key refs Preston & Croft (1997), Stewart *et al.* (1994), Tutin (1980).

M. Southam, M.J. Wigginton & J.O. Mountford

Oenanthe aquatica Fine-leaved Water-dropwort

(L.) Poir.

A tuberous perennial herb of still or slow-moving water, usually occurring on deep, silty, often eutrophic substrates in shallow ponds and ditches, often where water fluctuates in depth. It also grows in open vegetation by sheltered lakes, reservoirs, canals, streams and rivers, and in marshes and seasonally flooded depressions, frequently where kept open by cattle. Lowland.

Trends *O. aquatica* has declined throughout its British range, particularly in eastern England but also in the English Midlands and northern England. It is, however, better recorded now in its core areas than it was in the 1960s, including in Ireland where many new sites have been found in recent decades. The discovery of the species at a site in Carmarthenshire (Ffrwd Fen) extends significantly its western range limit in Britain. Trends are somewhat obscured through past confusion with *O. fluviatilis*.

Biogeography Eurosiberian Temperate element; also in eastern Asia.

Native	GB	IR
2000–19	276	147
1987–99	302	147
1970–86	229	46
pre-1970	415	88

Key refs Preston & Croft (1997), Tutin (1980).

M. Southam, M.J. Wigginton & J.O. Mountford

N *Sium latifolium* Greater Water-parsnip

L.

A perennial herb once typical of very wet, species-rich, tall-herb fen, which often developed as floating mats at the margins of lakes (including, on rare occasions, gravel-pits) and large rivers; now it is generally found in ditches, growing amongst other emergent species or in reedswamp, though intolerant of the deep shade of wet woodland. It prefers alkaline conditions and a peaty or alluvial soil. It is readily grazed by stock, and often restricted to inaccessible ditch-banks. Lowland.

Trends The substantial decline of *S. latifolium* was already apparent in the 1960s and has continued since then, largely due to the effects of habitat destruction, drainage, reclamation and changes in the management of water levels. Recent monitoring of populations indicates that the species benefits from management undertaken on a long rotation, with the current main threats intensive ditch-cleaning or overgrazing, although the latter may be mitigated in some instances by the presence of natural barriers, such as brim-full ditches, or a curtain of reed or willow. There have been several attempts at introducing the species to sites within the native range, some of which have proved to be successful.

Biogeography Eurosiberian Temperate element.

Native		GB	IR
2000–19	●	67	32
1987–99	●	71	26
1970–86	●	88	12
pre-1970	○	255	24

Alien		GB	IR
2000–19	●	5	0
1987–99	●	2	0
1970–86	●	2	0
pre-1970	○	4	0

Key refs Cadbury (2008), Mountford (1994), Stewart *et al.* (1994), Tutin (1980), Walker *et al.* (2017).

M. Southam & J.O. Mountford

N *Berula erecta* Lesser Water-parsnip

(Huds.) Coville

A stoloniferous perennial herb occurring as a submerged aquatic in rivers and streams with calcareous and mesotrophic water, and as an emergent species at the edges of lakes, ponds, rivers, ditches and canals, and in marshes. It is also found on seasonally flooded wet ground, and usually roots into fine silt or mud. Vegetative spread is by short-lived stolons or rhizomes, but little is known of the frequency of reproduction by seed. Lowland.

Trends *B. erecta* declined in the latter half of the 20th century, but since 2000 its distribution appears to have largely stabilized, with a number of new records found throughout its range, most notably in Ireland due to more systematic recording. However, local losses have continued into this century, caused by drainage, habitat destruction and eutrophication.

Biogeography European Temperate element; also in central Asia and North America.

Native		GB	IR
2000–19	●	914	267
1987–99	●	868	230
1970–86	●	647	45
pre-1970	○	848	139

Alien		GB	IR
2000–19	●	3	0
1987–99	●	3	0
1970–86	●	0	0
pre-1970	○	1	0

Key refs Preston & Croft (1997), Tutin (1980).

M. Southam & J.O. Mountford

N *Helosciadium nodiflorum* Fool's-water-cress
(L.) W.D.J.Koch

A perennial herb, found in shallow water in streams, ditches, swamps and marshes, and on seasonally exposed mud at the edges of ponds, lakes, rivers and canals, sometimes scrambling into nearby vegetation. It is characteristic of nutrient-enriched sites and is very palatable to cattle, which reduce its extent in grazed sites. Generally lowland, but reaching 440 m at Wild Moor (Shropshire).

Trends The 10 km square distribution of this species has been stable since the 1960s when it was mapped as 'all records' in the 1962 *Atlas*. There has been some confusion between this species and *Berula erecta*, and some older records may be in error, although the differences between the two taxa are now much better understood by recorders.

Biogeography Eurosiberian Southern-temperate element; widely naturalized outside its native range.

Native	GB	IR
2000–19	1599	797
1987–99	1553	795
1970–86	1191	113
pre-1970	1477	613

Alien	GB	IR
2000–19	1	0
1987–99	1	0
1970–86	0	0
pre-1970	0	0

Key refs Grime *et al.* (2007), Preston & Croft (1997), Tutin (1980).

M. SOUTHAM & J.O. MOUNTFORD

Hy *Helosciadium inundatum × nodiflorum = H. ×moorei*
(Syme) Warren

This perennial sterile hybrid is found in shallow water in swamps and at the edge of lakes, rivers, streams, canals and ditches, and on damp ground. Lowland.

A spontaneous hybrid (native × native).

Trends *H. ×moorei* is apparently very rare in Britain, with only one record this century. In Ireland, where it was once widely scattered, relatively few records have been made in the last 40 years, and it may be declining here, as opposed to being overlooked. Its rarity in Britain is almost certainly linked to the decline of *H. inundatum* in the lowlands.

Biogeography Apparently known only from Britain and Ireland.

	GB	IR
2000–19	1	5
1987–99	0	10
1970–86	2	9
pre-1970	7	45

	GB	IR
Long term	No trend	No trend
Short term	No trend	No trend

Key refs Stace *et al.* (2015).

M. SOUTHAM & T. O'MAHONY

Helosciadium repens Creeping Marshwort
(Jacq.) W.D.J.Koch

A slender creeping perennial herb of winter-flooded grassland subject to falling water levels in spring and summer, leaving areas of bare damp mud and short sparse vegetation. It grows on such bare areas at the classic site, Port Meadow (Oxfordshire), in neutral nutrient-rich floodplain grassland with a long history of winter inundation and summer grazing. Spread can be vegetative via the propagation of stolons, or via seed, which is long-lived in the soil. Lowland.

Trends The distribution of *H. repens* has long been uncertain because of confusion with morphologically similar forms of *H. nodiflorum* and hybrids between them. Genetic studies and a better understanding of its morphological features have produced recent confirmed records only in Port Meadow (Oxfordshire), Walthamstow Marshes (South Essex/Middlesex), and Thetford (West Suffolk). The latter site was discovered following the completion of fieldwork for this *Atlas*, in 2020, and almost certainly arose from a long-dormant seed bank (Woodward & Webster, 2021). At Port Meadow it has been known since 1900 but the population fluctuates greatly, with recent summer flooding killing many plants. At Binsey Green (Oxfordshire) it reappeared after a 48-year absence when grazing was reintroduced in 1998, but disappeared when grazing ceased after 2007. Of various attempted introductions within its historic Oxfordshire range, one at North Hinksey has thrived for over 20 years due to intensive conservation efforts. A population discovered at Walthamstow Marshes in 2002 was refound again in 2020 in a cattle-poached area. A number of historic records away from southern England are considered doubtful.

Biogeography European Temperate element.

Key refs Grassly *et al.* (1996), Stroh *et al.* (2019), Tutin (1980), Wigginton (1999), Woodward & Webster (2021).

J.P. Martin & M.F. Watson

Helosciadium inundatum Lesser Marshwort
(L.) W.D.J.Koch

A perennial herb of permanent shallow water in streams, ditches, ponds, canals and backwaters, and in sites which are subject to periodic desiccation, such as the edges of lakes, pools, reservoirs and dune-slacks. It is confined to oligotrophic or mesotrophic habitats, and most sites are base-poor. Reproduction is by seed. 0–500 m (Cronkley Fell, North-west Yorkshire).

Trends The considerable decline of *H. inundatum* in Britain, which has continued since the 1960s into the 21st century, is the result of the destruction or neglect of shallow water bodies, drainage and eutrophication, especially in the more intensively farmed lowlands. Trends in Ireland are difficult to assess; new sites have been discovered since 2000, but equally there is an absence of recent records for many historical sites.

Biogeography Suboceanic Temperate element.

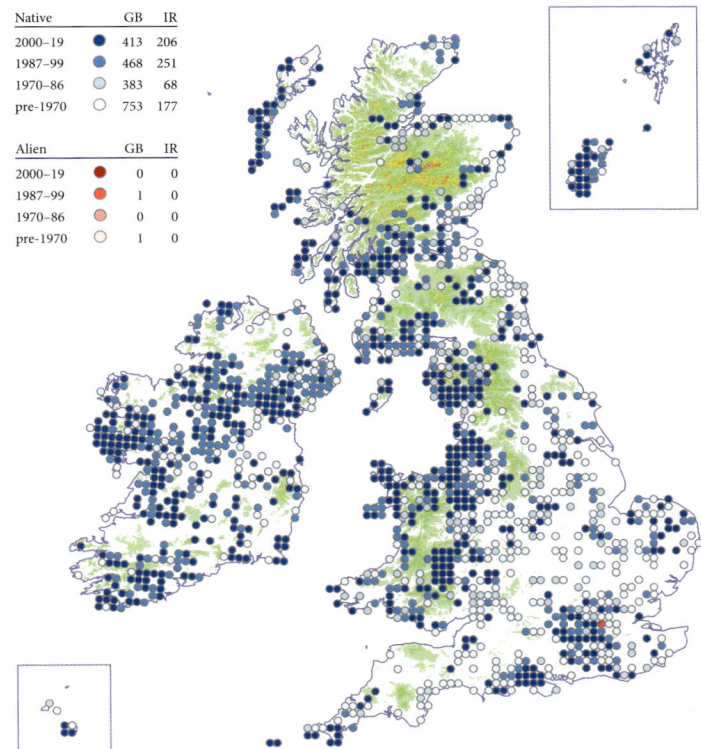

Key refs Mountford (1994), Preston & Croft (1997), Stroh *et al.* (2014), Tutin (1980).

M. Southam & J.O. Mountford

Ⓝ *Cicuta virosa* Cowbane
L.

This perennial herb grows in shallow water on the margins of standing or slowly flowing water, including lakes, ponds, rivers, streams, ditches and canals, or in deeper water on floating mats of vegetation. It also occurs in tall-herb fen, in marshy pasture and on damp mud. Lowland.

Trends Historically, many British populations of *C. virosa* were lost due to drainage, but it may have also been eradicated from some pastures because of its toxicity to cattle. Many losses occurred as early as the 18th century and it is now extinct over much of England except from its strongholds in Cheshire, Shropshire and the Norfolk Broads. It remains a rare plant in Scotland, though new discoveries continue to be made. It is much more frequent in Ireland than in Britain and its distribution since the 1960s is much better known,

largely due to more systematic recording this century. It remains locally abundant in some areas, such as County Fermanagh, where it is frequent in fen fringing the shores of larger lakes (especially around Lough Erne) although drainage continues to be a key threat (Forbes & Northridge, 2012).

Biogeography Eurasian Boreo-temperate element, with a continental distribution in western Europe.

Native	GB	IR
2000–19	78	123
1987–99	72	124
1970–86	52	44
pre-1970	123	64

Alien	GB	IR
2000–19	5	0
1987–99	1	0
1970–86	0	0
pre-1970	1	0

Key refs Forbes & Northridge (2012), Mulligan & Munro (1981), Stewart *et al.* (1994), Tutin (1980).

M.F. WATSON, J.O. MOUNTFORD & K.J. WALKER

Ⓐⓡ *Smyrnium olusatrum* Alexanders
L.

A robust perennial herb, widely naturalized in hedgebanks, on coastal cliffs, at the base of walls, and on grassy roadsides, pathsides and waste ground, most abundant near the sea but also widespread inland, especially on more base-rich or nutrient-enriched soils. Lowland.

Trends *S. olusatrum* was introduced in Roman times, and was widely cultivated until displaced by celery in the 15th century. Since the 1960s, the distribution in coastal regions has remained largely unchanged but the increase in some inland areas noted by the end of 20th century has continued. *S. olusatrum* is not salt tolerant and its predominantly coastal distribution probably reflects a preference for the frost-free mild climate of the coastal zone that is closer to that of Mediterranean and Atlantic littoral where it is native.

Nonetheless it has persisted for many decades in some inland sites.

Biogeography Native of the Mediterranean region and southern Europe, north to north-western France.

Alien	GB	IR
2000–19	912	340
1987–99	727	278
1970–86	393	46
pre-1970	545	145

Key refs Randall (2003), Salisbury (1964), Tutin (1980).

M.F. WATSON & J.O. MOUNTFORD

Ne *Smyrnium perfoliatum* Perfoliate Alexanders

L.

A biennial herb, sometimes grown in gardens and found naturalized on grassy banks and in cultivated ground. It also occurs as a casual in waste places. Lowland.

Trends *S. perfoliatum* was known in cultivation in Britain by 1596. It was recorded in the wild in 1932 (Chelsea, Middlesex), and appears to have increased in the past 50 years, especially in the London area and elsewhere in England.

Biogeography Native of south-central and southern Europe and south-western Asia.

	GB	IR
Long term	No trend	No trend
Short term	↑	No trend

Alien	GB	IR
2000–19	45	0
1987–99	19	0
1970–86	11	0
pre-1970	9	0

Key refs Tutin (1980).

Altitude (m)

- <1%
- 1–10%
- 11–30%
- 31–40%
- 41–50%
- 51–100%

Distance north (km)

☐ Apparency ■ In flower ■ In leaf

T.D. DINES & J.O. MOUNTFORD

N *Chaerophyllum temulum* Rough Chervil

L.

A biennial herb, especially characteristic of rank grassland on roadside verges, by hedges and along wood-borders and forest rides; also found on railway banks and in waste places. It tolerates light shade, but rarely occurs on damp and acidic soils. Though often described as the commonest roadside umbellifer of midsummer, it seldom if ever attains the abundance of the earlier flowering *Anthriscus sylvestris*. Reproduction is by seed. 0–465 m (Clun Forest, Shropshire).

Native in Britain and the Channel Islands and a neophyte in Ireland.

Trends There has been little appreciable change in the 10 km square distribution of *C. temulum* since the 1960s in Britain, though it seems to have declined in Ireland, where it is probably introduced (Scannell & Synnott, 1987), despite fuller recording this century.

Biogeography European Temperate element.

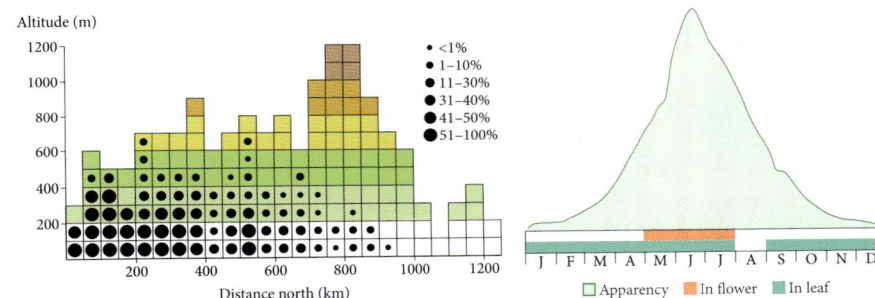

	GB	IR
Long term	↓	↓
Short term	↓	↓

Native	GB	IR
2000–19	1637	0
1987–99	1592	0
1970–86	1050	0
pre-1970	1609	0

Alien	GB	IR
2000–19	0	6
1987–99	1	12
1970–86	1	4
pre-1970	1	34

Key refs Scannell & Synnott (1987), Tutin (1980).

Altitude (m)

- <1%
- 1–10%
- 11–30%
- 31–40%
- 41–50%
- 51–100%

Distance north (km)

☐ Apparency ■ In flower ■ In leaf

M. SOUTHAM & J.O. MOUNTFORD

1101

N *Anthriscus sylvestris* Cow Parsley
(L.) Hoffm.

A robust perennial herb, characteristically abundant on roadsides and by hedgerows where it produces spectacular displays in the spring, but also occurring in abandoned pastures and under-managed hay meadows, in woodland rides and edges (especially where disturbed), on railway banks, and on waste and cultivated ground. It prefers damp, fertile soils and avoids those that are very wet or dry. Seedlings are sometimes plentiful but extension of colonies also occurs by offsets from the main stems. 0–760 m (Mt Brandon, South Kerry) and 845 m on Great Dun Fell (Westmorland).

Trends There has been no appreciable change in the distribution of *A. sylvestris* at the 10 km square scale, although it is now much better recorded in northern Scotland and western Ireland. In recent decades it has become much more abundant on roadsides due to the modern practice of leaving the cut arisings *in situ* following mowing. This, combined with increased deposition of nutrients from a variety of sources, has increased soil fertility thereby benefitting taller, more competitive herbs such as *A. sylvestris*.

Biogeography Eurasian Boreo-temperate element.

Native	GB	IR
2000–19	2461	842
1987–99	2365	760
1970–86	1594	126
pre-1970	2277	556

Alien	GB	IR
2000–19	0	0
1987–99	2	0
1970–86	0	0
pre-1970	1	0

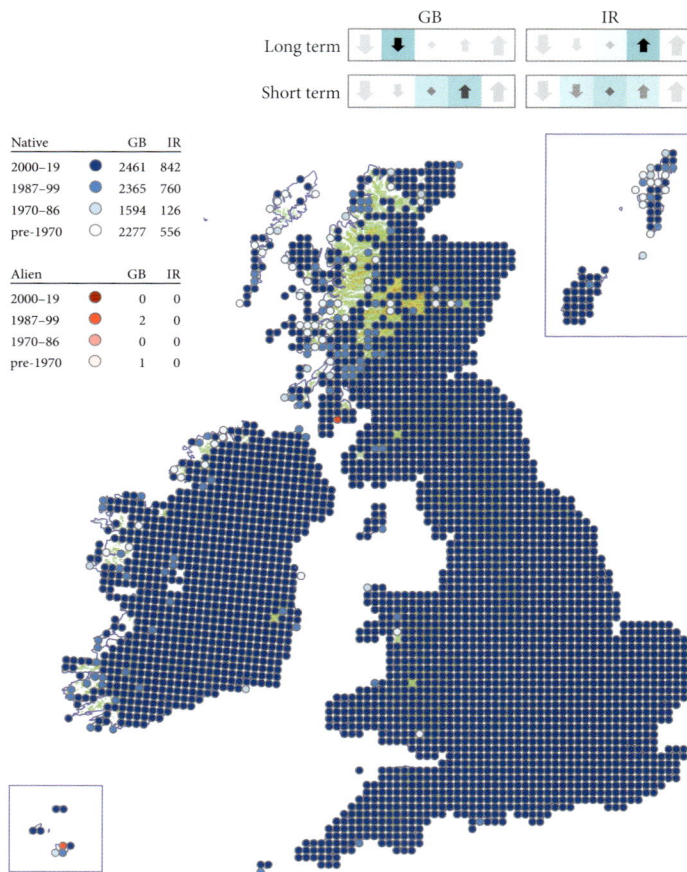

Key refs Grime *et al.* (2007), Tutin (1980).

M. Southam & J.O. Mountford

Ne *Anthriscus cerefolium* Garden Chervil
(L.) Hoffm.

An erect or spreading perennial herb, now rarely cultivated as a garden herb and found naturalized in a scattering of open and ruderal habitats, mainly in England, including a rock face in Herefordshire. It also occurs as a casual on waste ground, roadsides and rubbish tips. Lowland.

Trends *A. cerefolium* was grown in British gardens by medieval times (Harvey, 1981), but has decreased in popularity in recent years, resulting in fewer records since 2000. It was first recorded from the wild in 1775 (Worcestershire). It has been naturalized in Herefordshire since at least 1867 and persisted there into the 21st century. It is treated as a cultivated archaeophyte by Stace & Crawley (2015).

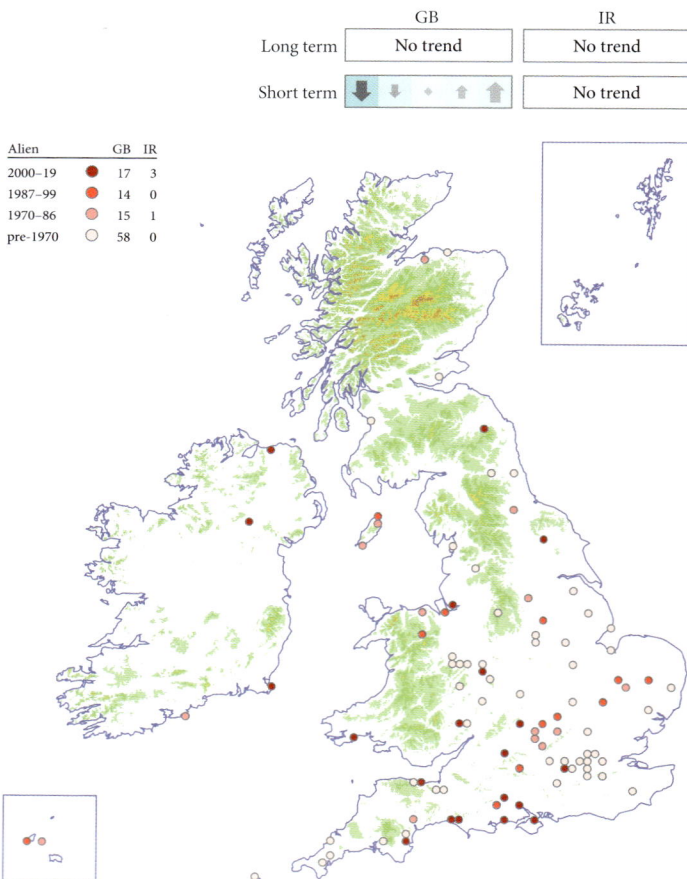

Biogeography Native of south-eastern Europe and the eastern Mediterranean region, but widely naturalized outside this area through its spread in cultivation.

Alien	GB	IR
2000–19	17	3
1987–99	14	0
1970–86	15	1
pre-1970	58	0

Key refs Harvey (1981), Stace & Crawley (2015), Tutin (1980).

M. Southam & J.O. Mountford

Anthriscus caucalis Bur Chervil

M.Bieb.

An annual herb of open habitats on well-drained, mainly sandy or gravelly soils, including dry grassland, hedgebanks, roadsides, sea-walls, waste ground, gravel-pits, arable fields and as a street weed. Lowland.

Trends Although many sites for *A. caucalis* were lost before 1930, especially in southern England, its distribution stabilized in the latter half of the 20th century. It remains frequent in East Anglia and in many coastal areas, and there have been numerous new records this century within and on the margins of its previously mapped range. Some of these records may have arisen as a result of accidental dispersal by humans, and in a few cases there is evidence to suggest that the species may have been moved in raw materials. Only the latter are mapped as alien. Most historical losses were due to changes in agricultural practices and land use.

Biogeography European Temperate element.

Native	GB	IR
2000–19	488	13
1987–99	419	16
1970–86	298	13
pre-1970	533	50

Alien	GB	IR
2000–19	27	3
1987–99	12	0
1970–86	11	0
pre-1970	13	2

Key refs Tutin (1980).

M. SOUTHAM & J.O. MOUNTFORD

Scandix pecten-veneris Shepherd's-needle

L.

An annual herb of arable fields, particularly on calcareous clay soils; occasionally on paths and banks beside current or former arable sites, and rarely on waste ground, coastal cliffs (where possibly native), and in gardens. Generally lowland, but recorded in the mid-19th century as reaching 320 m in Teesdale (County Durham).

Trends *S. pecten-veneris* was once an abundant arable weed, sufficiently so to impede harvesting, but decreased greatly after 1950 as a result of the introduction of modern farming methods, most notably inorganic herbicides. It is now on the verge of extinction (at least above-ground) in Ireland, with only a single recent record from County Waterford. It is still locally abundant in some parts of East Anglia, but its occurrence is often sporadic, depending on crop-type, use of herbicide and timing of ploughing (Leslie, 2019). It has benefitted from the introduction of conservation management as part of agri-environment schemes on some sites (Walker *et al.*, 2017).

Biogeography As an archaeophyte, *S. pecten-veneris* has a Eurosiberian Southern-temperate element; it is widely naturalized outside this range. Its spread northwards was assisted by agriculture.

Alien	GB	IR
2000–19	178	1
1987–99	175	0
1970–86	175	1
pre-1970	801	93

Key refs Leslie (2019), Stewart *et al.* (1994), Stroh *et al.* (2014), Tutin (1980), Walker *et al.* (2017).

M. SOUTHAM & J.O. MOUNTFORD

Ne *Myrrhis odorata* Sweet Cicely
(L.) Scop.

A perennial herb of hedgebanks, woodland margins, roadside verges, riverbanks and other grassy places, often close to houses or old settlements, indicating its origin in cultivation. It spreads by seed and is often dispersed over large distances along streams and rivers. Generally lowland, but reaching 500 m in East Allendale (South Northumberland).

Trends Introduced into cultivation by 1596, this species was first recorded from the wild in 1712 (near Bingley, Mid-west Yorkshire). Since the 1960s there is some evidence of increased frequency locally in the English lowlands but its overall 10 km square distribution is stable.

Biogeography Native of the mountains of central and southern Europe; widely naturalized elsewhere in temperate Europe.

Alien	GB	IR
2000–19	912	71
1987–99	916	88
1970–86	577	39
pre-1970	907	80

Key refs Grime *et al.* (2007), Tutin (1980).

M.F. WATSON & J.O. MOUNTFORD

N *Conopodium majus* Pignut
(Gouan) Loret

A perennial herb of damp or shaded meadows and pastures, hedgerows, roadside verges, copses and woodlands, and shaded riverbanks. It is especially characteristic of some types of northern hay meadow (Rodwell, 1992b), where it favours north-facing slopes, possibly due to a preference for moist conditions. It grows on a wide range of acidic and base-rich soils, but is largely absent from reclaimed land such as in Fenland and around the Thames estuary. 0–700 m (Breadalbanes, Mid Perthshire), and 845 m on Great Dun Fell (Westmorland).

Trends *C. majus* declined locally as its grassland habitats were improved during the 19th and 20th centuries (Brewis *et al.*, 1996), but its national distribution at a 10 km scale is little changed since the turn of the century, except that it is now better recorded in Ireland due to more systematic recording. It was introduced in Shetland in the 19th century, but its status in Orkney is unclear.

Biogeography Oceanic Temperate element.

Native	GB	IR
2000–19	2430	809
1987–99	2390	691
1970–86	1564	113
pre-1970	2299	424

Alien	GB	IR
2000–19	25	0
1987–99	23	0
1970–86	4	0
pre-1970	13	0

Key refs Brewis *et al.* (1996), Grime *et al.* (2007), Rodwell (1992b), Tutin (1980).

M. SOUTHAM & J.O. MOUNTFORD

Ligusticum scoticum Scots Lovage

L.

A perennial herb of coastal rock crevices and free-draining skeletal soils by the sea. Its habitats include sea-cliffs, rocky shores and platforms, spray-drenched shingle, stabilized sand dunes and stone sea-defence walls. Its palatability to sheep limits its spread into coastal grasslands. The seeds float and retain some viability even after a year in sea water. Lowland.

Trends The distribution of *L. scoticum* in Scotland and Northern Ireland is stable, following the loss of the species from some sites along the coastline of the latter last century. It is very rare in England, where there are just a handful of records this century from North Northumberland and Cumberland. Drought sensitivity and the requirement for cold, wet conditions for germination may be important in limiting the southern range of this species in our area.

Biogeography European Boreo-arctic Montane element; a coastal species also found in eastern Asia and North America.

Native	GB	IR
2000–19	319	15
1987–99	282	16
1970–86	155	4
pre-1970	299	26

Alien	GB	IR
2000–19	0	0
1987–99	0	0
1970–86	1	0
pre-1970	0	0

Key refs Palin (1988), Tutin (1980).

M.F. WATSON & J.O. MOUNTFORD

Torilis japonica Upright Hedge-parsley

(Houtt.) DC.

An annual, or rarely biennial, herb of dry neutral and basic soil, found in woodland margins, hedgerows, rough and rank grassland, and on roadside verges. 0–570 m (Hartside Quarry, Cumberland).

Trends The 10 km square distribution of *T. japonica* is little changed since the 1960s, other than more systematic recording filling apparent gaps, especially in Scotland and Ireland.

Biogeography Eurasian Temperate element; widely naturalized outside its native range.

Native	GB	IR
2000–19	2095	761
1987–99	2034	716
1970–86	1250	80
pre-1970	1958	660

Alien	GB	IR
2000–19	0	2
1987–99	1	2
1970–86	0	0
pre-1970	2	1

Key refs Grime *et al.* (2007), Tutin (1980).

M.F. WATSON & J.O. MOUNTFORD

Torilis arvensis Spreading Hedge-parsley
(Huds.) Link

An annual, rarely biennial herb, almost exclusively found as a weed of autumn-sown cereal crops, but sometimes in other arable crops; also on waste and disturbed ground. Within arable land, it is commonest in unsprayed areas such as gateways, ditch-banks and headlands. It is perhaps most frequent on calcareous clays, but is found on a wide range of soils, including sands and gravels. Lowland.

Trends Once frequent, this species had already disappeared from nearly half its 10 km grid squares by 1930, and since then its decline has been one of the most dramatic shown by any arable weed. However, this trend may possibly have been exaggerated in some regions; indeed in Fenland, there is evidence of local recovery or even spread on the banks of drainage channels disturbed by agricultural or ditch maintenance work. It is otherwise a victim of intensive crop management, being vulnerable to herbicides and unable to compete in dense crop swards. Conversion to pasture and urbanization are also factors in its long-term decline.

Biogeography As an archaeophyte, *T. arvensis* has a Eurosiberian Southern-temperate distribution.

Alien	GB	IR
2000–19	99	0
1987–99	87	0
1970–86	87	0
pre-1970	390	0

	GB	IR
Long term	↓	No trend
Short term	↓	No trend

Key refs Stewart *et al.* (1994), Stroh *et al.* (2014), Tutin (1980), Walker *et al.* (2017).

M.F. Watson & J.O. Mountford

Torilis nodosa Knotted Hedge-parsley
(L.) Gaertn.

An annual herb of dry, sparsely vegetated habitats, including open grassland, sunny banks, sea-walls, cliff-tops, arable fields, tracks, roadside verges, pavements and waste ground; occasionally in disused sand- and gravel-pits, and on refuse tips. Lowland.

Trends *T. nodosa* declined from the 1960s in many inland areas, especially as an arable weed, although it can be locally very abundant, notably on intensively grazed floodbanks, and in recent decades there has been a substantial increase of records away from arable, especially in urban areas where it is spreading on close-mown verges and in pavement cracks. Its distribution remains stable at most of its coastal sites.

Biogeography Mediterranean-Atlantic element, but naturalized north of its native range so that distribution is now Submediterranean-Subatlantic.

Native	GB	IR
2000–19	640	13
1987–99	418	18
1970–86	289	21
pre-1970	592	67

Alien	GB	IR
2000–19	2	1
1987–99	0	0
1970–86	1	0
pre-1970	5	1

	GB	IR
Long term	♦	↓
Short term	↑	↓

Key refs Tutin (1980).

M.F. Watson & J.O. Mountford

Caucalis platycarpos Small Bur-parsley

Ar

L.

An annual herb, formerly a casual in arable fields and waste places, introduced in grain, birdseed and wool. In Cambridgeshire, it showed a preference for chalky soils or boulder clay (Leslie, 2019). Lowland.

Trends An archaeophyte-colonist that, prior to the 1960s (Perring & Walters, 1962), was widely recorded in England, though very sparsely in Wales, Scotland and Ireland. It appears to have been last recorded in West Suffolk in 1968; a later record from a building site in Cambridge (1971) has been redetermined as *Orlaya daucoides* (Leslie, 2019). It probably declined through changes in cultivation, use of herbicides and the general intensification of farming. It is just possible that it could still arise on waste ground.

Biogeography Native of the Mediterranean region and south-western Asia. Widely naturalized in central Europe and elsewhere.

	GB	IR
Long term	No trend	No trend
Short term	No trend	No trend

Alien	GB	IR
2000–19	0	0
1987–99	0	0
1970–86	2	0
pre-1970	180	1

Key refs Leslie (2019), Stroh *et al.* (2014), Tutin (1980).

J.O. MOUNTFORD

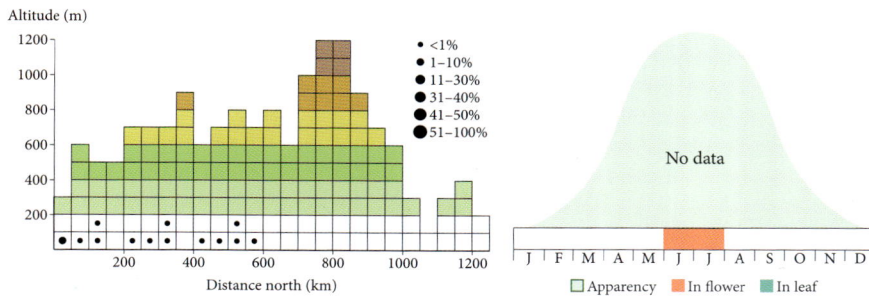

Daucus carota Carrots

N

L.

A biennial herb of fairly infertile, well-drained, often calcareous, soils. Its habitats include disturbed or open turf on chalk downs, rough grassland on roadsides, waysides and railway banks, quarries, chalk- and gravel-pits, and waste ground. In Scotland it is predominantly a coastal species. It is increasingly sown in wild-flower seed mixtures used to create 'wildlife friendly' grasslands on road verges and around arable fields. 0–400 m (Connor Hill, South Kerry).

Trends An assessment of change for this species is complicated by its widespread introduction within seed mixtures and its occurrence as a casual. Its overall distribution has increased since the 1960s presumably due to its use for landscaping, especially on road verges, but there have also been widespread losses due to the destruction

or agricultural improvement of its native grassland habitats, especially towards the fringes of its native range. Three subspecies occur in our area: the native subsp. *gummifer*, which is restricted to coastal habitats; the native subsp. *carota* (Wild Carrot), which occurs throughout the range of the species; and the cultivated subsp. *sativus* (Carrot), which occurs as an infrequent casual on refuse tips and as a relic of cultivation. Subsp. *sativus* and subsp. *gummifer* are mapped separately.

Biogeography Eurosiberian Southern-temperate element, but widely naturalized so that distribution is now Circumpolar Southern-temperate.

Native	GB	IR
2000–19	1635	708
1987–99	1511	684
1970–86	1039	89
pre-1970	1550	545

Alien	GB	IR
2000–19	149	15
1987–99	115	11
1970–86	73	4
pre-1970	113	10

Key refs Dale (1974), Grime *et al.* (2007), Tutin (1980), Zohary & Hopf (2000).

M. SOUTHAM & J.O. MOUNTFORD

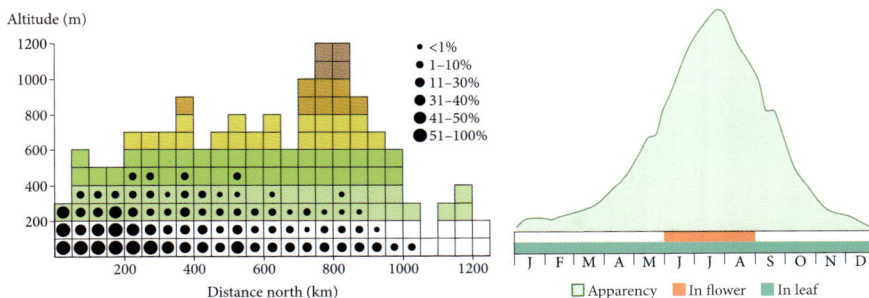

Ne *Daucus carota* subsp. *sativus* Carrot

(Hoffm.) Arcang.

	GB	IR
Long term	No trend	No trend
Short term	No trend	No trend

A biennial herb with a swollen root, which occurs on refuse tips and waste places, and as a relic of cultivation (especially extensive in the Fenland basin). Lowland.

Trends *D. carota* subsp. *sativus* has long been grown in gardens and was recorded from the wild by 1914 (Hoy, Orkney). Like many non-native species and other crops, it is being recorded with much increased frequency although this is not necessarily a sign of greater abundance in the wild.

Biogeography The origin of the cultivated plant is uncertain, as there is no archaeological evidence for its cultivation before classical times. It is clearly related to the very variable wild *D. carota* complex.

Alien	GB	IR
2000–19	66	10
1987–99	35	1
1970–86	9	0
pre-1970	11	0

Key refs Tutin (1980).

T.D. DINES & J.O. MOUNTFORD

N *Daucus carota* subsp. *gummifer* Sea Carrot

(Syme) Hook.f.

	GB	IR
Long term	No trend	No trend
Short term	No trend	No trend

A biennial herb of both open and closed maritime grassland on sea-cliffs and on stabilized sand dunes. Lowland.

Trends There has been no appreciable change in the range of subsp. *gummifer* since it was first mapped by Perring & Sell (1968), but it is now much better recorded, particularly in southern Ireland. A range of morphological intermediates exist between subsp. *gummifer* and subsp. *carota*. The most extreme form occurs in Cornwall and Devon, with the features differentiating it from subsp. *carota* becoming less obvious farther east and north (Perring & Sell, 1968). Within subsp. *gummifer*, plants in the south of the range tend to be dwarf (var. *acaulis*), whereas the taller var. *gummifer* predominates in the north.

Biogeography Oceanic Temperate element; known only from the Atlantic coast of Europe.

Native	GB	IR
2000–19	108	16
1987–99	95	2
1970–86	46	1
pre-1970	101	4

Alien	GB	IR
2000–19	3	0
1987–99	1	0
1970–86	0	0
pre-1970	1	0

Key refs Malloch & Okusanya (1979), Okusanya (1979a), Okusanya (1979b), Okusanya (1979c), Rich & Jermy (1998), Tutin (1980).

M. SOUTHAM & J.O. MOUNTFORD

N *Pimpinella major* Greater Burnet-saxifrage
(L.) Huds.

A perennial herb of basic soils derived from chalk and limestone, but also on clay, and most often found on roadsides, hedgebanks, railway banks and wood edges, sometimes persisting on roadsides when neighbouring woods have been removed and very occasionally spreading on verges where any woods were felled centuries ago, as in Fenland. Generally lowland, reaching 445 m near Lumbs Farm (Staffordshire).

Native in Britain and Ireland and a neophyte in the Channel Islands.

Trends The 1962 *Atlas* showed a few losses of *P. major* before 1930, but there is little evidence of any further decline since then; indeed, it is now much better recorded in some areas *e.g.* Cornwall and Devon. Its absence from large areas of southern England and East Anglia, despite the presence of suitable soils and habitats, is hard to explain and remains a fascinating phytogeographical puzzle.

Biogeography European Temperate element. Its scattered, mainly lowland, distribution in our area contrasts with its widespread presence in mountains in mainland Europe.

Native		GB	IR
2000–19	●	495	113
1987–99	●	453	90
1970–86	●	337	10
pre-1970	○	481	44

Alien		GB	IR
2000–19	●	10	0
1987–99	●	6	0
1970–86	●	5	0
pre-1970	○	13	1

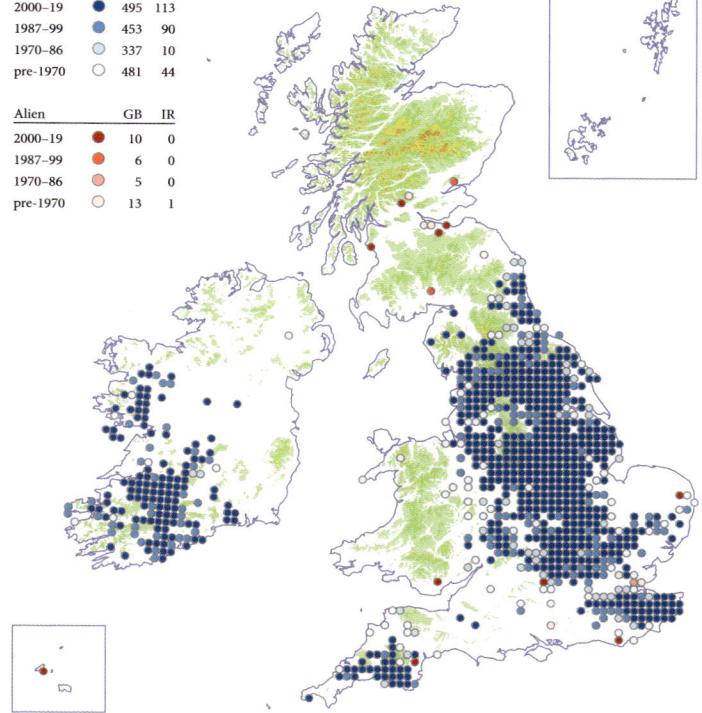

Key refs Rackham (1980), Tutin (1980).

M. Southam & J.O. Mountford

N *Pimpinella saxifraga* Burnet-saxifrage
L.

A perennial herb of grassy habitats and open rocky places on well-drained soils, favouring those which are calcareous or otherwise base-rich, but also on acidic sands. It occurs on grazed and ungrazed chalk and limestone downs, in rough pasture and other grassland, in woodland edges and open rides; less frequently on roadsides and rough ground. It regenerates from seed. Generally lowland, but reaching 810 m on Snowdon (Caernarvonshire) and Dollywagon Pike (Westmorland).

Trends At the 10 km square scale, there has been no appreciable change in the distribution of *P. saxifraga* since the 1960s, when it was mapped as 'all records'. However, there is evidence of some local decline in lowland calcareous grasslands due to habitat loss and reductions in grazing levels leading to the spread of scrub and coarse grasses.

Biogeography Eurosiberian Temperate element.

Native		GB	IR
2000–19	●	1678	309
1987–99	●	1719	296
1970–86	●	1212	55
pre-1970	○	1674	273

Alien		GB	IR
2000–19	●	0	0
1987–99	●	0	0
1970–86	●	0	0
pre-1970	○	1	0

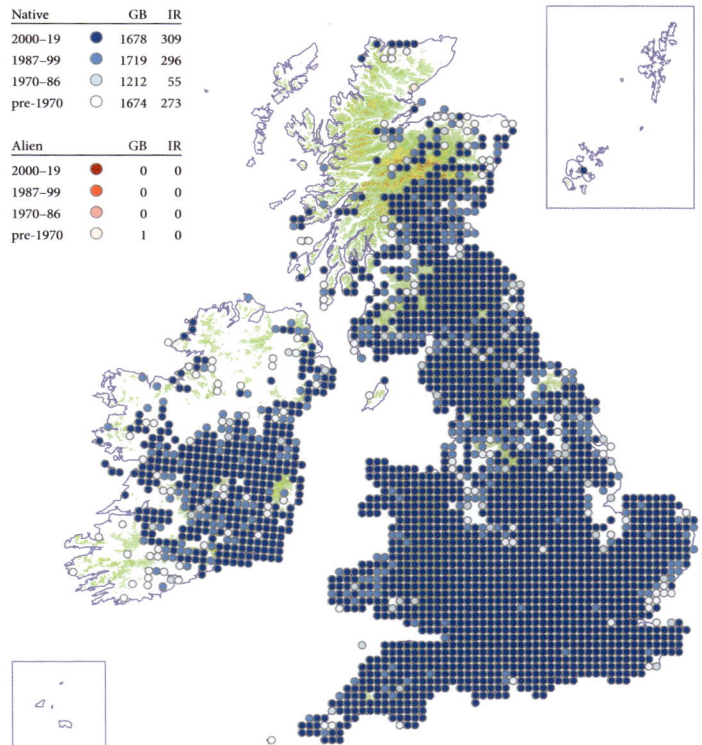

Key refs Grime *et al.* (2007), Tutin (1980).

M. Southam & J.O. Mountford

N *Silaum silaus* Pepper-saxifrage
(L.) Schinz & Thell.

A perennial herb of damp, unimproved neutral grassland, usually on clay soils. Its habitats include hay- and water-meadows, species-rich pastures and roadsides; it is occasionally found on chalk downs, railway banks and vegetated shingle. In Britain it is characteristic of the most species-rich mesotrophic communities (*e.g.* *Alopecurus pratensis*–*Sanguisorba officinalis* floodplain grassland and *Cynosurus cristatus*–*Centaurea nigra* meadows). Usually lowland, but reaching 340 m at Potrigg Scar (Westmorland).

Native in Britain and a neophyte in Ireland.

Trends The 1962 *Atlas* indicated little change in the distribution of *S. silaus* before 1930. However, since the 1960s there is evidence of a distinct decline throughout its range due to agricultural improvement, as noted in many county Floras, *e.g.* in Somerset (Green *et al.*, 1997), Oxfordshire (Killick *et al.*, 1998) and Cambridgeshire (Leslie, 2019).

Biogeography Eurosiberian Temperate element.

Native	GB	IR
2000–19	647	0
1987–99	740	0
1970–86	531	0
pre-1970	825	0

Alien	GB	IR
2000–19	1	0
1987–99	1	0
1970–86	1	0
pre-1970	1	2

Key refs Green *et al.* (1997), Killick *et al.* (1998), Leslie (2019), Rodwell (1992b), Tutin (1980).

M. SOUTHAM & J.O. MOUNTFORD

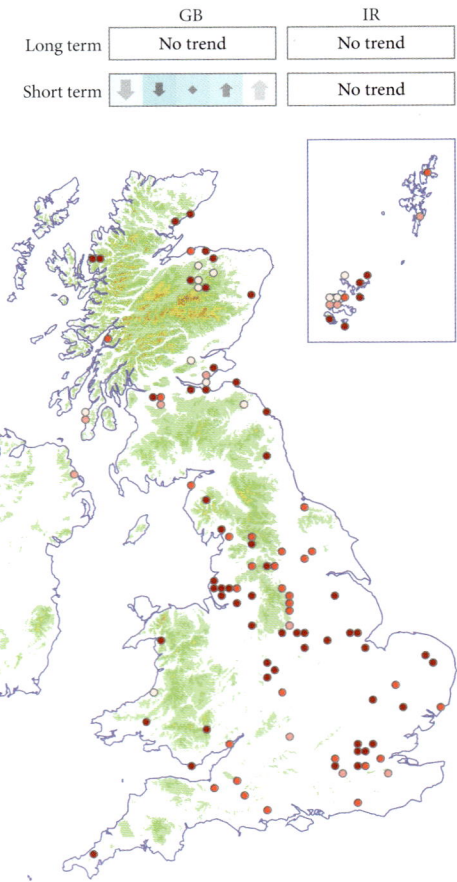

Ne *Levisticum officinale* Lovage
W.D.J.Koch

A tall clump-forming perennial, much grown as a culinary herb and found naturalized on rough ground and by walls, paths and roadsides. It also occurs as a relic of cultivation. Generally lowland but reaching 405 m at Malham Tarn Field Centre (Mid-west Yorkshire).

Trends *L. officinale* was being grown in gardens by medieval times (Harvey, 1981) and was first recorded from the wild in 1836 (Kells, Meath). Its distribution has increased since 2000, perhaps reflecting a real increase in distribution but possibly also due to recorders giving more attention to garden escapes.

Biogeography Native of Iran and Afghanistan; widely naturalized in Europe, North America and elsewhere through its use as a herb.

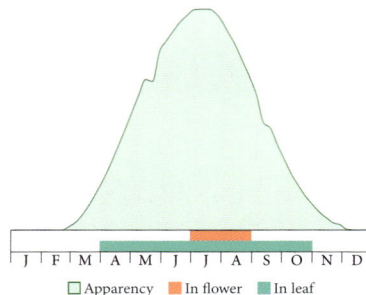

Alien	GB	IR
2000–19	60	0
1987–99	38	0
1970–86	17	1
pre-1970	18	0

Key refs Harvey (1981), Tutin (1980).

M. SOUTHAM & J.O. MOUNTFORD

Ne *Coriandrum sativum* Coriander
L.

An annual herb, cultivated in gardens and very locally at the field scale and found as a casual on refuse tips, disturbed ground, and at the edges of paths, tracks and roads, where it mainly originates from birdseed and culinary sources. It is occasionally found naturalized on roadsides as in north-western Essex. Lowland.

Trends *C. sativum* was grown in Britain by medieval times (Harvey, 1981), and is treated by Stace & Crawley (2015) as a cultivated archaeophyte. Although increasingly cultivated as a culinary herb which has resulted in a larger number of casual occurrences, its distribution in the wild is limited by the fact that young plants are very frost-tender. It was first recorded from the wild in 1762.

Biogeography Apparently native of northern Africa and western Asia; widely naturalized in southern Europe and elsewhere.

Alien	GB	IR
2000–19	120	4
1987–99	68	0
1970–86	85	0
pre-1970	131	2

	GB	IR
Long term		No trend
Short term		No trend

Key refs Harvey (1981), Stace & Crawley (2015), Tutin (1980), Vaughan & Geissler (2009), Zohary & Hopf (2000).

M. SOUTHAM & J.O. MOUNTFORD

Ne *Tordylium maximum* Hartwort
L.

An annual or biennial herb, found in neutral grassland and in grassy thorn scrub, on clayey or alluvial soils. Its extant sites are sheltered and south-facing. Its seed is apparently short-lived. Lowland.

Trends *T. maximum* was first recorded in Britain in 1672 (London, Middlesex) and it persisted in that area until 1837. It was recorded at Tilbury (South Essex), between 1875 and 1984. The current localities at Benfleet (South Essex) were discovered in 1949 and 1966, where some populations have survived development and encroaching scrub, aided by seed collection and sowing *in situ*. Although claimed as a possible native by Wigginton (1999) it is treated as a rare neophyte here following the assessment of its status by Pearman (2007).

Biogeography Native from southern and southern-central Europe and northern Turkey to the Caucasus and northern Iran.

	GB	IR
Long term	No trend	No trend
Short term	No trend	No trend

Alien	GB	IR
2000–19	2	1
1987–99	3	0
1970–86	3	0
pre-1970	11	0

Key refs Pearman (2007), Tutin (1980), Wigginton (1999).

D.A. PEARMAN

(N) *Pastinaca sativa* Parsnips
L.

The native subspecies of this biennial herb, subsp. *sylvestris*, occurs in neutral and calcareous grassland, especially in chalk and limestone districts. It is found in rank swards on downland, on roadsides, railway banks, and rough and uncultivated land. Cultivated parsnip, subsp. *sativa*, is a very occasional escape in waste ground; the eastern European subsp. *urens* is established in localities near the coast in Essex, Suffolk and parts of Norfolk, and is also reported from road verges in southern and north-western England. 0–380 m (Stainmore, Westmorland).

Native in Britain and the Channel Islands and a neophyte in Ireland.

Trends There has been no appreciable change in the 10 km square distribution of *P. sativa* since the 1960s, although there have been both losses and gains at the edges of its range. It may be increasing in some areas along new roads (Halliday, 1997; French *et al.*, 1999).

Biogeography Eurosiberian Temperate element; widely naturalized outside its native range.

Native	GB	IR
2000–19	813	0
1987–99	854	0
1970–86	597	0
pre-1970	891	0

Alien	GB	IR
2000–19	137	39
1987–99	91	18
1970–86	66	14
pre-1970	76	48

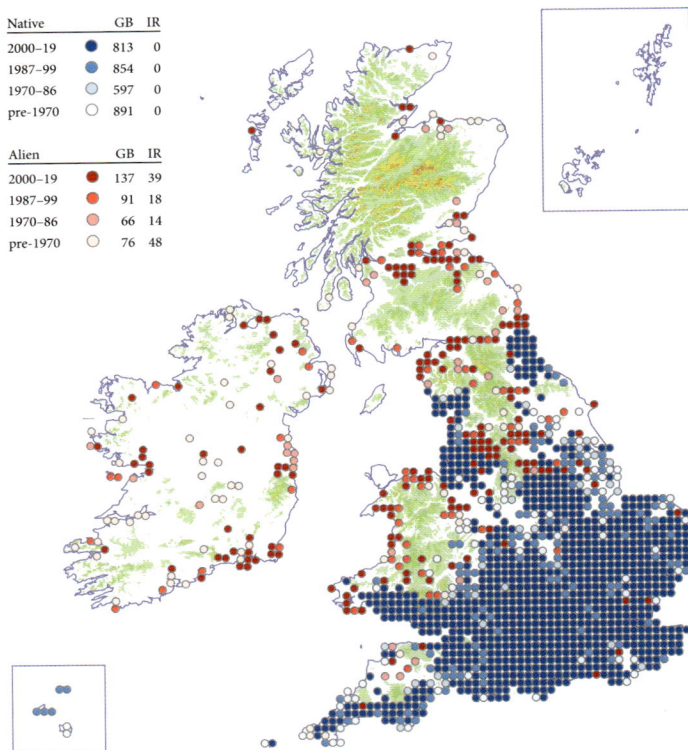

Key refs French (2020), Halliday (1997), Tutin (1980), Zohary & Hopf (2000).

M. SOUTHAM & J.O. MOUNTFORD

(N) *Heracleum sphondylium* Hogweed
L.

A robust perennial herb of dry or moist, neutral to calcareous soils. It has a wide habitat range, including rough and disturbed grassland, especially on roadsides and trackways, woodland rides, scrub, riverbanks, stabilized dunes, coastal cliffs, montane tall-herb vegetation and waste ground. 0–1,005 m (Breadalbanes, Mid Perthshire).

Trends There has been no appreciable change in the 10 km square distribution of *H. sphondylium* since the 1960s; subsp. *flavescens* from north-eastern and east-central Europe has been recorded from north-eastern Norfolk and more recently the River Conwy (Denbighshire) and may be native.

Biogeography Eurasian Boreo-temperate element; widely naturalized outside its native range.

Native	GB	IR
2000–19	2690	965
1987–99	2644	914
1970–86	1816	155
pre-1970	2545	848

Alien	GB	IR
2000–19	0	0
1987–99	1	0
1970–86	0	0
pre-1970	0	0

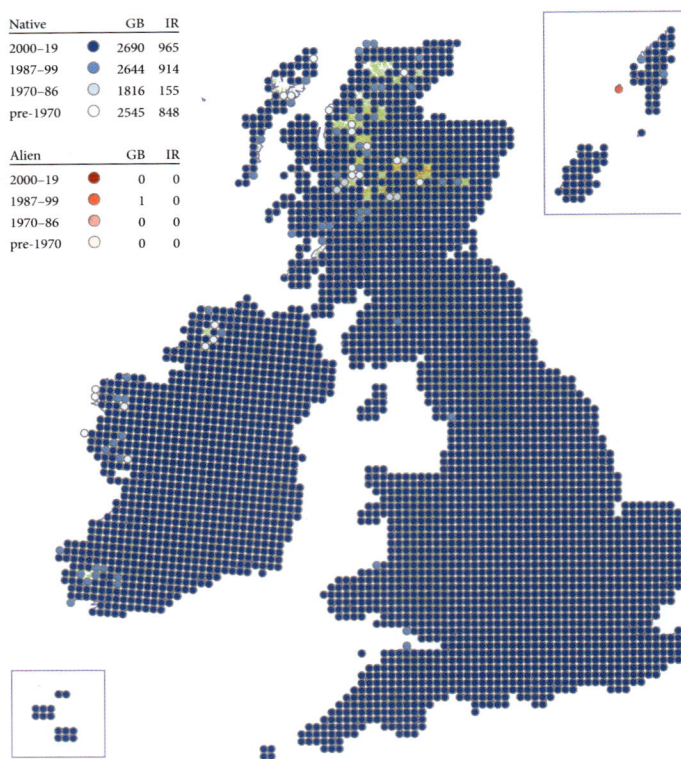

Key refs Grime *et al.* (2007), Sheppard (1991), Tutin (1980).

M.F. WATSON & J.O. MOUNTFORD

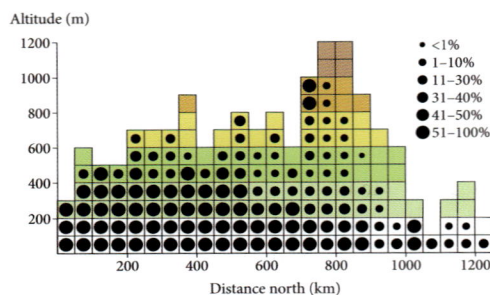

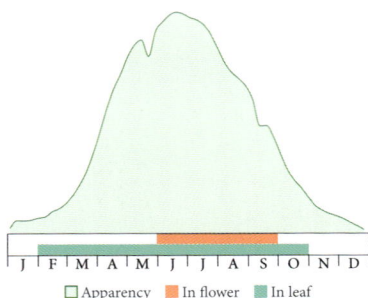

Hy ## *Heracleum sphondylium × mantegazzianum*

A tall multi-stemmed perennial herb found in open and wooded riverbanks, on the islets of large rivers and lake shores, in scrubby woodland, on roadsides, and in botanic gardens. Lowland.

A spontaneous hybrid (native × alien).

Trends According to Grace & Nelson (1981) putative hybrids occur at most places where the parents grow together, but they are not normally numerous. The hybrid must, therefore, be seriously under-recorded. It was first recorded by the River Liffey (County Dublin) by Praeger (1951) and by the River Brent (Middlesex) by M.G. Collett in 1962.

Biogeography Wider distribution uncertain.

	GB	IR
Long term	No trend	No trend
Short term	No trend	No trend

	GB	IR
2000–19	50	14
1987–99	25	4
1970–86	16	2
pre-1970	3	1

Key refs Grace & Nelson (1981), Praeger (1951), Stace *et al.* (2015).

C.A. STACE, C.D. PRESTON & D.A. PEARMAN

Ne ## *Heracleum mantegazzianum* Giant Hogweed
Sommier & Levier

A massive, often monocarpic perennial herb, mainly naturalized along rivers and streamsides but also found in derelict gardens, woodland clearings, neglected urban places, waste ground, refuse tips, roadsides, abandoned pastures and arable field margins. It spreads prolifically by seed, forming very large colonies where left to regenerate. Usually lowland but reaching 365 m on the A939 road verge near Findron (Banffshire).

Trends *H. mantegazzianum* was introduced to British gardens as a monumental curiosity by 1817. It was then deliberately planted by rivers and ponds and was first recorded in the wild in 1828 (Shelford, Cambridgeshire). It spread rapidly from the 1960s onwards, despite attempts to control it in many areas once its capacity to cause dermatitis in humans became known in the 1980s. It is now classed as one of the most invasive plant species in Europe, leading to a large body of research into its ecology, impacts and management (Psyek *et al.*, 2007). The taxonomy of 'Giant Hogweeds' has been very confused and it is likely that what has hitherto been recorded as *H. mantegazzianum* by British botanists includes a number of distinct species. Sell & Murrell (2009) recognized three species in our area whereas Denness *et al.* (2013) list five. Here we treat all the records as a single taxon, which, regardless of taxonomy, is increasing in both overall range and local abundance.

Biogeography Native of south-western Asia; widely naturalized in northern and north-western Europe.

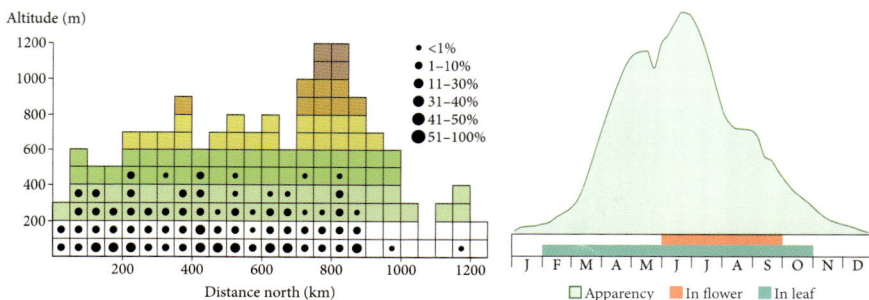

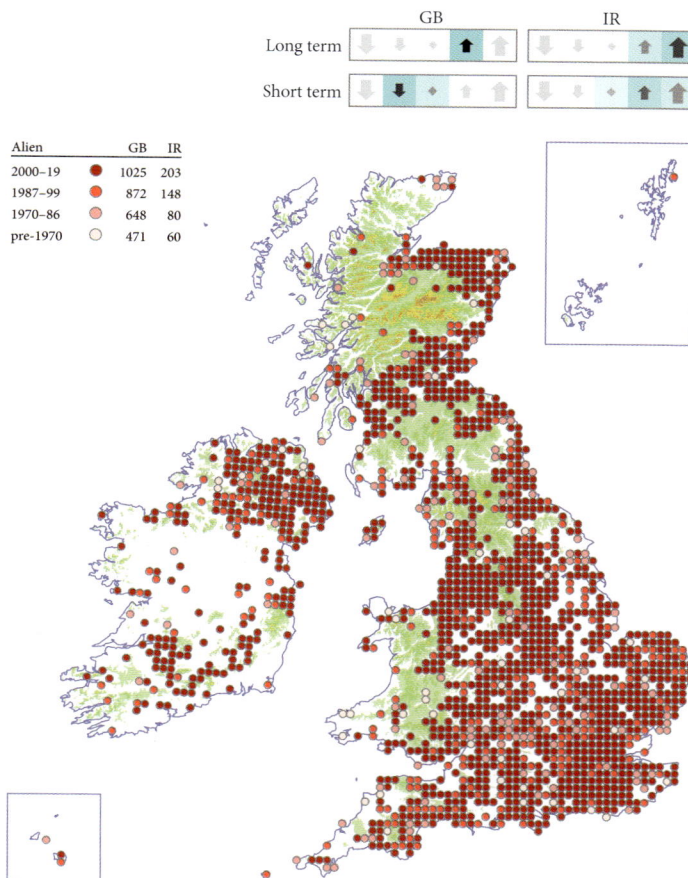

	GB		IR	
Long term				
Short term				

Alien	GB	IR
2000–19	1025	203
1987–99	872	148
1970–86	648	80
pre-1970	471	60

Key refs Denness *et al.* (2013), Pyšek *et al.* (2007), Sell & Murrell (2009), Tiley *et al.* (1996), Tutin (1980).

M. SOUTHAM & J.O. MOUNTFORD

(N) ***Bunium bulbocastanum*** Great Pignut
L.

A tuberous perennial herb of dry chalk soils, most frequent in arable fields, especially where cultivation has ceased, and sometimes dominant in arable reverting to pasture. It also grows in disturbed areas on chalk downland, field edges and green lanes, in hedgerows and scrub, on roadside verges and in quarries. Reproduction is by seed. Lowland.

Trends *B. bulbocastanum* requires open soil for seedling establishment, but mature plants can thrive in closed swards and the tubers survive shallow-ploughing. Its absence from the North and South Downs was perplexing, given its abundance in similar habitat at Boulogne (France). However, an historical record from Headley Down (North Hampshire) from 1924 has recently been confirmed, and in 2018 a small population of the species was discovered on the South Downs (West Sussex). Whilst its range otherwise remains fairly stable, populations are still locally threatened by scrub encroachment. A number of authors have questioned its native status (*e.g.* Dony, 1953; Crompton, 2001; Leslie, 2019), and the possibility remains that it was introduced as a contaminant with imported seed (Streeter, 2021).

Biogeography Suboceanic Southern-temperate element.

Native		GB	IR
2000–19	●	10	0
1987–99	●	11	0
1970–86	●	12	0
pre-1970	○	14	0

Alien		GB	IR
2000–19	●	0	0
1987–99	●	1	0
1970–86	●	0	0
pre-1970	○	2	0

	GB	IR
Long term	No trend	No trend
Short term	No trend	No trend

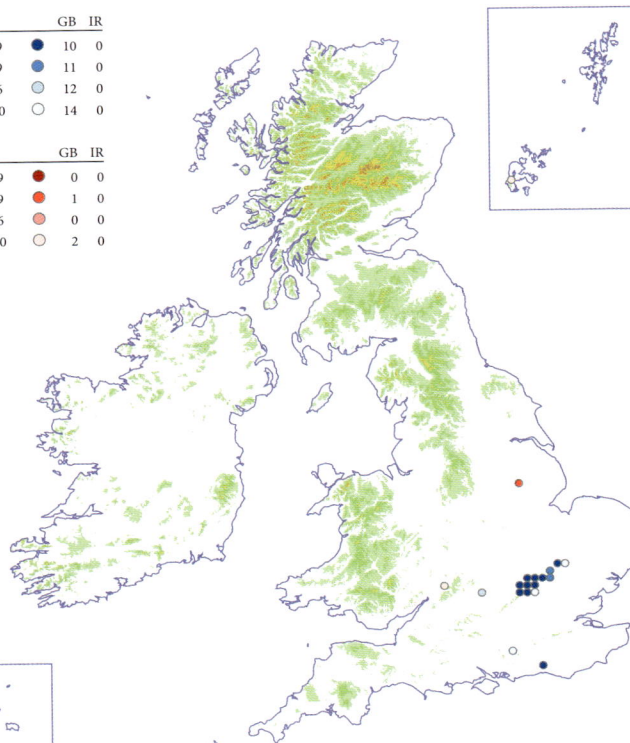

Key refs Crompton (2001), Dony (1953), Leslie (2019), Streeter (2021), Tutin (1980), Wigginton (1999).

M. SOUTHAM & J.O. MOUNTFORD

(N) ***Sison amomum*** Stone Parsley
L.

A biennial herb of sticky clay and better drained neutral to calcareous soils, found mainly in hedgerows, on banks, rough scrubby grassland, waysides and disturbed waste ground. Lowland.

Trends There was no appreciable change in the 10 km square distribution of *S. amomum* in the 20th century, although in recent years there appears to have been some expansion, mainly along the edges of its previously mapped range. Some local loss in East Anglia has been compensated to an extent by several new sites in Norfolk and local increases in Cambridgeshire, although it is possible that some of these may be through the sowing of wild-flower seed mixtures.

Biogeography Submediterranean-Subatlantic element.

Native		GB	IR
2000–19	●	747	0
1987–99	●	667	0
1970–86	●	408	0
pre-1970	○	679	0

Alien		GB	IR
2000–19	●	5	0
1987–99	●	1	0
1970–86	●	0	0
pre-1970	○	7	0

	GB	IR
Long term		No trend
Short term		No trend

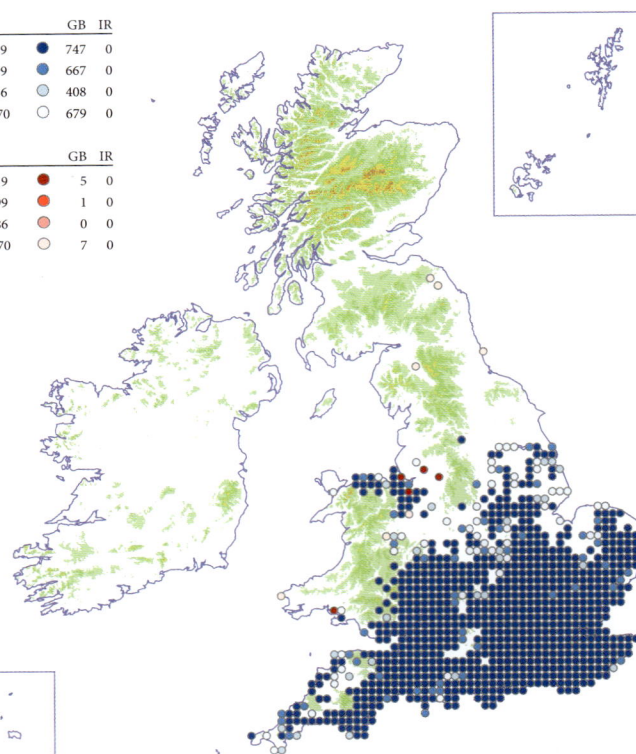

Key refs Tutin (1980).

M. SOUTHAM & J.O. MOUNTFORD

Ⓝ *Sison segetum* Corn Parsley

L.

This slender biennial herb of well-drained calcareous soils on clay or chalk is found on arable field margins, on grassy banks, roadsides, railway banks, riverbanks, by sea-walls, in drained estuarine marshes, on rough waste ground and occasionally as a garden weed. In short turf on floodbanks by the sea and rivers, it is often associated with *Torilis nodosa*. Lowland.

Native in Britain and the Channel Islands and a neophyte in Ireland.

Trends *S. segetum* was thought to be declining by the 1960s, and whilst it was undoubtedly lost from some 10 km squares, many more new records have been added since then, and its overall status appears to be stable.

Biogeography Suboceanic Southern-temperate element.

Native		GB	IR
2000–19	●	392	0
1987–99	●	316	0
1970–86	●	214	0
pre-1970	○	376	0

Alien		GB	IR
2000–19	●	5	0
1987–99	●	4	1
1970–86	●	2	0
pre-1970	○	5	0

Key refs Tutin (1980).

M. SOUTHAM & J.O. MOUNTFORD

Ⓝ *Crithmum maritimum* Rock Samphire

L.

A fleshy perennial herb of spray-drenched rock crevices and ledges on sea-cliffs, coastal rocks and on stabilized shingle; also in maritime grassland and artificial habitats such as harbour walls and stone sea defences. It appears indifferent to soil reaction, being found on many rock types from chalk and limestone to granite. Lowland.

Trends There has been a slight increase in the distribution of *C. maritimum* since the 1960s, including a number of new sites found this century in East Norfolk, East Lothian and Angus, and in south-western Ireland. This may be due to more systematic recording or possibly also an expansion in range in response to warmer winters.

Biogeography Mediterranean-Atlantic element.

Native		GB	IR
2000–19	●	327	156
1987–99	●	281	117
1970–86	●	172	23
pre-1970	○	241	90

Alien		GB	IR
2000–19	●	2	0
1987–99	●	0	0
1970–86	●	1	0
pre-1970	○	0	0

Key refs Malloch & Okusanya (1979), Okusanya (1979a), Okusanya (1979b), Okusanya (1979c), Tutin (1980).

M.J. WIGGINTON & J.O. MOUNTFORD

Ar *Carum carvi* Caraway
L.

A monocarpic perennial herb, found naturalized in meadows, on sand dunes, roadsides and railway banks, and as a casual in waste places and on rubbish tips. Generally lowland, but formerly reaching 425 m at Blair Atholl (East Perthshire).

An archaeophyte in Britain and the Channel Islands and a neophyte in Ireland.

Trends *C. carvi* was introduced from Europe by medieval times (Harvey, 1981). It was well-naturalized in Shetland and locally in England (*e.g.* around The Wash), but is now very rare in Shetland and has disappeared from most of its former strongholds. Caraway is much less frequently cultivated than formerly. Many recent occurrences have been casual, presumably arising from fruits imported as flavouring agents.

Biogeography Apparently native in Europe (especially in hilly and submontane areas), western and central Asia but its native range is obscured by spread in cultivation; now widespread in boreal and temperate zones in the Northern Hemisphere.

Alien	GB	IR
2000–19	14	5
1987–99	49	4
1970–86	50	1
pre-1970	296	28

Key refs Harvey (1981), Tutin (1980).

M. SOUTHAM & J.O. MOUNTFORD

Altitude (m) chart; ● <1%, ● 1–10%, ● 11–30%, ● 31–40%, ● 41–50%, ● 51–100%. Distance north (km).

Apparency, In flower, In leaf.

N *Trocdaris verticillata* Whorled Caraway
(L.) Raf.

A perennial, calcifugous herb of marshes, streamsides, damp meadows, rushy pastures and on wet hillsides with a pronounced soligenous influence. Especially typical of rush-pastures and mires dominated by *Molinia caerulea*. 0–465 m (Bryn Nichol, Carmarthenshire) and similar altitudes at Shalloch (Aryshire) and Lochan Beinn Damhain (Dunbartonshire).

Trends The distribution of this species is generally stable, with strongholds in the 'Rhos' pastures of south-western Wales (Pryce, 2004) and mires in western Scotland. Since the 1960s some sites have been lost, including the remaining Surrey site in 1967, and it seems to have become rarer in Devon, with the main threats associated with agricultural intensification and urbanization. However, new sites have been discovered, particularly in southern Wales, northern and western Scotland and in Ireland. In western Scotland, and perhaps elsewhere, it may be becoming more frequent in pastures where drainage is increasingly neglected. The species may also be benefitting from conservation measures introduced in recent years to conserve the Marsh Fritillary *Euphydryas aurinia* butterfly.

Biogeography Oceanic Southern-temperate element.

Native	GB	IR
2000–19	239	25
1987–99	251	26
1970–86	136	9
pre-1970	217	33

Alien	GB	IR
2000–19	0	0
1987–99	1	0
1970–86	0	0
pre-1970	1	0

Key refs ToBeS Blackstock *et al.* (1991), Kay & John (1994), Marren (1981), Pryce (2004), Stroh *et al.* (2014), Stroh *et al.* (2019), Tutin (1980). ent

M.F. WATSON & J.O. MOUNTFORD

Altitude (m) chart; ● <1%, ● 1–10%, ● 11–30%, ● 31–40%, ● 41–50%, ● 51–100%. Distance north (km).

Apparency, In flower, In leaf.

Ar *Aegopodium podagraria* Ground-elder

L.

A rhizomatous perennial herb found in a wide variety of disturbed habitats, especially hedgerows, road verges, churchyards, gardens and waste ground. It typically occurs near human habitations or in the vicinity of abandoned settlements, often in shaded habitats. It reproduces by seed and by its aggressive rhizome system. 0–470 m (Flash, Staffordshire).

Trends Archaeological evidence suggests that *A. podagraria* was introduced in Roman times, probably for medicinal and culinary use. There is little change in its range since the 1960s and the species is ubiquitous except at higher altitudes.

Biogeography A Eurosiberian Temperate species, certainly native in central and eastern Europe but with its native limits obscured by its spread in cultivation and as a weed.

Alien	GB	IR
2000–19	2481	783
1987–99	2400	736
1970–86	1452	106
pre-1970	2341	586

Key refs Tutin (1980).

M. SOUTHAM

Ne *Falcaria vulgaris* Longleaf

Bernh.

A rhizomatous perennial herb, found in a wide variety of habitats especially on calcareous soils, including pasture, arable fields, roadsides, cliff-top grassland, scrub, chalk quarries, gravel-pits, railway ballast, riverbanks and waste ground. Viable seed is only produced in warm summers in Britain and large colonies probably result from rhizomatous growth. Lowland.

Trends *F. vulgaris* was first recorded from the wild in 1858 at Preston-next-Wingham, East Kent. Some populations are well-naturalized, persistent for at least 60–80 years, but others are only transient. The distribution of naturalized populations appears to be stable.

Biogeography A Eurosiberian Temperate species, absent as a native from most of western Europe.

Alien	GB	IR
2000–19	25	0
1987–99	34	0
1970–86	24	1
pre-1970	56	1

	GB	IR
Long term	No trend	No trend
Short term		No trend

Key refs Tutin (1980).

M. SOUTHAM & J.O. MOUNTFORD

1117

(N) *Apium graveolens* Wild Celery
L.

A biennial or monocarpic perennial herb found on sea-walls, beside brackish ditches, on tidal riverbanks and drift lines, and the uppermost parts of saltmarshes. Inland it occurs locally on disturbed ground in marshes, by ponds and ditches and occasionally in gravel-pits. Lowland.

Trends Many inland sites for *A. graveolens* were lost before 1930. The coastal distribution showed a slight decline in the latter half of the 20th century, especially in Sussex and around The Wash, but now appears stable.

Biogeography Eurosiberian Southern-temperate element; widely naturalized outside its native range.

		GB	IR
Native		GB	IR
2000–19	●	282	62
1987–99	●	317	43
1970–86	●	249	8
pre-1970	○	423	63

		GB	IR
Alien		GB	IR
2000–19	●	45	0
1987–99	●	29	0
1970–86	●	16	0
pre-1970	○	48	0

Key refs Tutin (1980), Zohary & Hopf (2000).

M. Southam & J.O. Mountford

Altitude (m)

- ● <1%
- ● 1–10%
- ● 11–30%
- ● 31–40%
- ● 41–50%
- ● 51–100%

Distance north (km)

☐ Apparency   ☐ In flower   ☐ In leaf

(Ne) *Ammi majus* Bullwort
L.

An annual herb, found on waste ground, in gardens, on arable headlands, and locally in parkland and roadsides. It is sometimes sown in wild-flower seed mixes, was formerly a wool alien, but is primarily a birdseed alien which is usually casual. Lowland.

Trends Introduced by 1551 from southern Europe, *A. majus* was first recorded in the wild in 1821 (Portmarnock, Dublin). Records have increased over the past 50 years, but only as a casual. In some years it can be notably frequent *e.g.* the London area in 1993 (Wurzell, 1994b) and the Great Fen (Huntingdonshire) in 2012.

Biogeography Native of Mediterranean region.

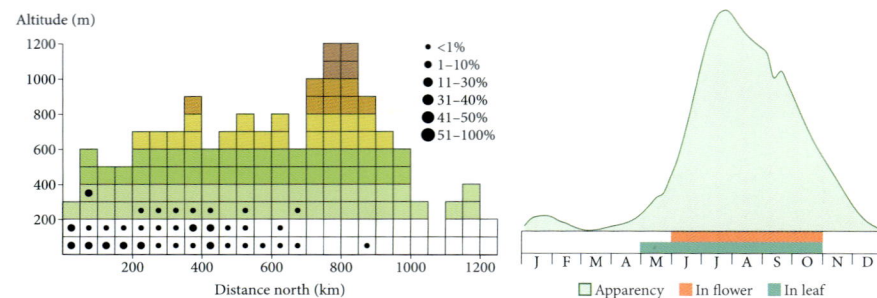

		GB	IR
Alien		GB	IR
2000–19	●	152	13
1987–99	●	119	4
1970–86	●	47	0
pre-1970	○	66	0

Long term   No trend   No trend
Short term

Key refs Tutin (1980), Wurzell (1994).

M. Southam & J.O. Mountford

Altitude (m)

- ● <1%
- ● 1–10%
- ● 11–30%
- ● 31–40%
- ● 41–50%
- ● 51–100%

Distance north (km)

☐ Apparency   ☐ In flower   ☐ In leaf

Ne *Anethum graveolens* Dill
L.

An aromatic annual thriving on light, well-drained soils, occurring as a casual in habitats associated with human activities, including in and near gardens, waste places and refuse tips. It is cultivated in market gardens and very rarely as a crop, although frost-sensitive. Sometimes included in wild-flower seed mixtures and thus established on field margins. Lowland.

Trends *A. graveolens* was grown in British gardens by medieval times (Harvey, 1981), but was not recorded from the wild until 1863 (Wandsworth, Surrey). Like other flavouring agents, it is increasingly grown in our area as culinary influences from Europe and Asia become more prevalent. It is treated as a cultivated archaeophyte by Stace & Crawley (2015).

Biogeography Native range obscure; the species perhaps originates in warm-temperate Asia but is widespread as a casual in Europe and more or less naturalized in the Mediterranean region.

Alien	GB	IR
2000–19	29	3
1987–99	19	1
1970–86	27	0
pre-1970	29	0

	GB	IR
Long term	No trend	No trend
Short term	⬇ ⬇ ◆ ⬆ ⬆	No trend

Key refs Harvey (1981), Stace & Crawley (2015), Tutin (1980), Zohary & Hopf (2000).

M. SOUTHAM & J.O. MOUNTFORD

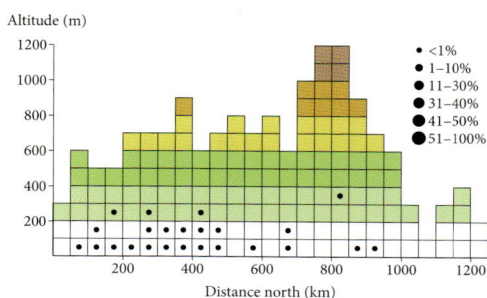

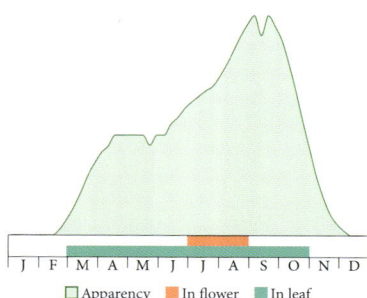

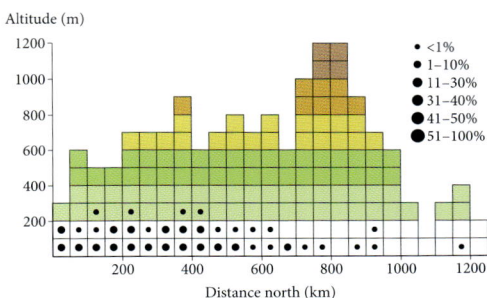

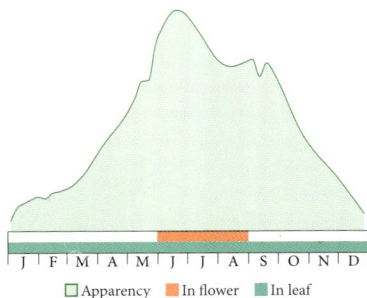

Ar *Petroselinum crispum* Garden Parsley
(Mill.) Nyman ex A.W.Hill

A biennial herb with two forms occurring in our area; the 'flat-leaved' form occurs as small but persistent colonies on coastal cliffs, banks and waste ground whereas the 'crisped-leaved' form, which is commonly grown in gardens, occurs as a casual on waste ground close to human habitations and on refuse tips. Lowland.

Trends *P. crispum* has been cultivated in British gardens since at least medieval times (Harvey, 1981). Although most records are casual, it is very persistent in many of its coastal sites. It is difficult to assess any changes in its distribution although more attention to garden escapes in recent years have led to an increased number of records in the wild.

Biogeography A cultivated species of uncertain origin which is now widely naturalized in Europe and other continents.

Alien	GB	IR
2000–19	250	27
1987–99	184	23
1970–86	118	3
pre-1970	294	28

	GB	IR
Long term	⬇ ⬇ ◆ ⬆ ⬆	⬇ ⬇ ◆ ⬆ ⬆
Short term	⬇ ⬇ ◆ ⬆ ⬆	⬇ ⬇ ◆ ⬆ ⬆

Key refs Harvey (1981), Tutin (1980).

M. SOUTHAM & J.O. MOUNTFORD

1119

Ar *Foeniculum vulgare* Fennel
Mill.

A perennial herb found on sea-walls, in gravel-pits, on roadsides and waste ground and on refuse tips. Commonest near the coast, at least some inland sites are derived from garden escapes and agricultural cultivation. It has a deep tap-root, allowing it to survive in droughted habitats and making it very persistent. It reproduces freely from seed. Lowland.

An archaeophyte in Britain and the Channel Islands and a neophyte in Ireland.

Trends Archaeological evidence suggests that *F. vulgare* has been used as a culinary herb since Roman times. It is common in gardens, where it is frequently grown as the purple-leaved cultivar 'Purpureum', but only rarely cultivated on a field scale, usually as Florence Fennel (*F. vulgare* subsp.

dulce). It has become much more frequent since the 1960s, especially inland and along roadsides.

Biogeography Subsp. *piperitum* is native to the Mediterranean region; our plant is subsp. *vulgare* which was derived from it in cultivation and is widely naturalized in Europe and elsewhere.

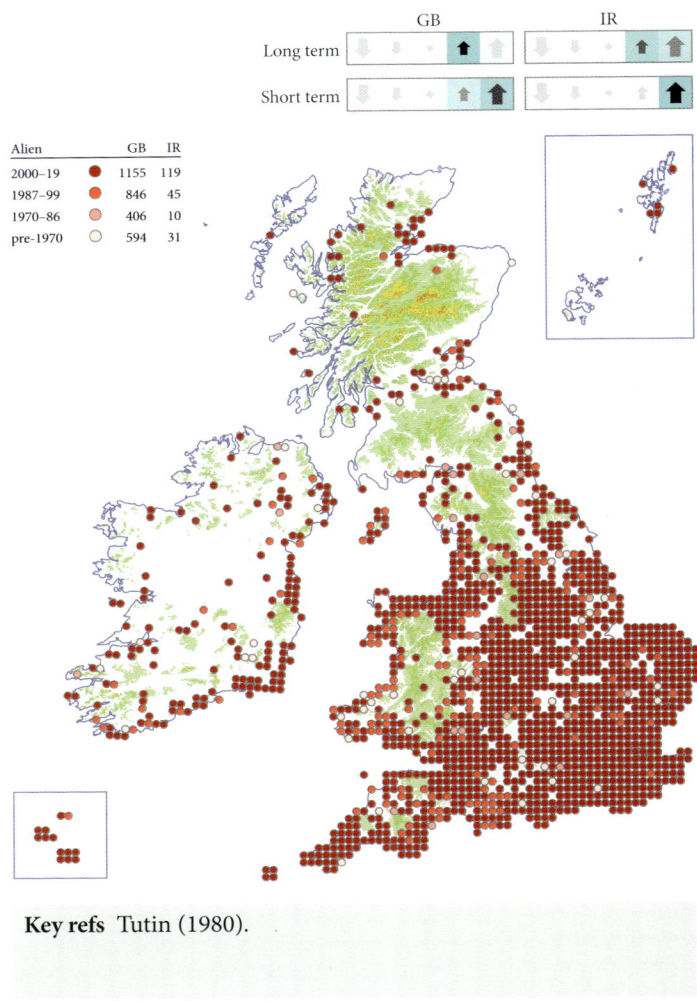

Alien		GB	IR
2000–19	●	1155	119
1987–99	●	846	45
1970–86	●	406	10
pre-1970	○	594	31

	GB	IR
Long term		
Short term		

Key refs Tutin (1980).

Altitude (m)
- <1%
- 1–10%
- 11–30%
- 31–40%
- 41–50%
- 51–100%

Distance north (km)

□ Apparency ■ In flower ■ In leaf

M. SOUTHAM & J.O. MOUNTFORD

Ar *Conium maculatum* Hemlock
L.

A biennial, winter-green herb of damp places, such as ditches and riverbanks, and of drier habitats, including rough grassland, waste ground, refuse tips and roadsides. It is a colonist of disturbed areas, particularly on dredged mud, sometimes forming large stands. Generally lowland, but reaching 371 m at Soutra Aisle (East Lothian).

Trends The distribution of *C. maculatum* is little changed since the 1960s, although there is some suggestion of local declines on the edges of its range. In addition, local increases within core areas have been reported, particularly in open habitats (Killick *et al.*, 1998) or on the banks and verges of new roads where it is likely to have been introduced in soil (Leslie, 2019).

Biogeography As an archaeophyte, *C. maculatum* has a Eurosiberian Southern-temperate distribution; it is widely naturalized outside this range.

Alien		GB	IR
2000–19	●	1631	351
1987–99	●	1634	349
1970–86	●	1092	41
pre-1970	○	1523	275

	GB	IR
Long term		
Short term		

Key refs Killick *et al.* (1998), Leslie (2019), Tutin (1980).

Altitude (m)
- <1%
- 1–10%
- 11–30%
- 31–40%
- 41–50%
- 51–100%

Distance north (km)

□ Apparency ■ In flower ■ In leaf

M. SOUTHAM & J.O. MOUNTFORD

Ne *Visnaga daucoides* Toothpick-plant
Gaertn.

An annual herb of cultivated ground in fields and gardens, and on refuse tips and waste land. It arises most frequently from birdseed and as a grain contaminant, and formerly from wool shoddy. Lowland.

Trends *V. daucoides* was cultivated in Britain by 1596. It was recorded from the wild in 1881 (Warwickshire). Like many other wool shoddy and grain aliens, it appears to have decreased, as shoddy is now scarcely used in modern agriculture, and grain cleaning techniques have improved. An apparent cluster of records in Glamorgan this century seems to reflect introduction of seed.

Biogeography Native of the Mediterranean region and south-western Asia.

	GB	IR
Long term	No trend	No trend
Short term	No trend	No trend

Alien	GB	IR
2000–19	12	0
1987–99	9	0
1970–86	19	0
pre-1970	32	0

T.D. Dines & J.O. Mountford

N *Meum athamanticum* Spignel
Jacq.

A perennial herb of deep neutral or mildly acidic brown-earth soils. Its habitats include unimproved pastures, hay meadows, mown roadside banks, woodland clearings, riverbanks and drumlins. Usually found on east-facing slopes in extensively grazed pastures with low levels of disturbance and shading. Despite being typical of mountainous regions, it is usually found below 300 m, though there are populations at 585 in White Coombe (Dumfriesshire), and at 610 m in Fealar (East Perthshire) and Melmerby High Scar (Cumberland).

Native in Britain and a neophyte in Ireland.

Trends Many sites for *M. athamanticum* were lost before 1930 as a result of agricultural improvement of grassland and probably also through deliberate destruction because it can taint cows' milk. There have been further losses since the 1960s, continuing in the latter part of the 20th century, though new sites have also been discovered in recent years within its Scottish stronghold, including a first record for Kintyre. It requires open conditions brought about by extensive grazing or a cutting regime, and so suffers from neglect that allows the spread of bracken and scrub. However, some populations have declined as a result of overgrazing.

Biogeography European Boreal-montane element, but absent from the Boreal zonobiome.

	GB	IR
Long term	↓	No trend
Short term	↓	No trend

Native	GB	IR
2000–19	86	0
1987–99	85	0
1970–86	78	0
pre-1970	142	0

Alien	GB	IR
2000–19	5	0
1987–99	2	1
1970–86	2	0
pre-1970	2	0

Key refs Stewart *et al.* (1994), Stroh *et al.* (2014), Stroh *et al.* (2019), Tutin (1980), Walker *et al.* (2017).

M.F. Watson & J.O. Mountford

N *Aethusa cynapium* Fool's Parsley
L.

An annual to winter-green biennial herb, found on the margins of arable fields and other cultivated ground, such as gardens and allotments, railway lines, pavements, road verges, soil heaps and waste ground; more rarely on open ground by hedges. Generally lowland, but reaching 435 m at Cadair Bronwen (Denbighshire).

Native in Britain and the Channel Islands and a neophyte in Ireland.

Trends *A. cynapium* was first recorded in Britain by 1597. Its overall 10 km square distribution appears to be stable with localized losses in hill areas, especially northern and western Britain, and in Ireland, where it is thought to be alien (Scannell & Synnott, 1987). Most losses have taken place since 1960 and may reflect a long-term decline in cultivation in the uplands

and agricultural intensification in the lowlands. It is a very variable species and although recent authors disagree on the number and rank of the taxa, four subspecies are now recognized in our area, although they are poorly recorded: subsp. *cynapium* is the most widespread and occurs throughout the range of the species in waste places and root crops, subsp. *agrestis* occurs amongst cereal crops and is mapped separately, whilst subsp. *elata* has been recorded in fewer than ten scattered locations and subsp. *gigantea* has only been confirmed for Cambridgeshire (Sell & Murrell, 2009).

Biogeography European Temperate element.

Native	GB	IR
2000–19	1426	0
1987–99	1415	0
1970–86	891	0
pre-1970	1374	0

Alien	GB	IR
2000–19	29	276
1987–99	26	256
1970–86	22	33
pre-1970	52	170

Key refs Scannell & Synnott (1987), Sell & Murrell (2009), Tutin (1980).

M. Southam & J.O. Mountford

Ar *Aethusa cynapium* subsp. *agrestis*
(Wallr.) Dostál

An annual of arable fields, especially cereals, as well as other cultivated ground and waste places. Lowland.

Trends Apparently common in cereal fields in East Anglia (especially Cambridgeshire), this subspecies was first mapped in the 2002 *Atlas* and remains almost certainly under-recorded; trends in its distribution are therefore difficult to assess. It was first recorded in the wild in Britain in 1924 (Addington, Surrey).

Biogeography This subspecies has a European Temperate distribution.

	GB	IR
Long term	No trend	No trend
Short term	No trend	No trend

Alien	GB	IR
2000–19	83	0
1987–99	29	0
1970–86	11	0
pre-1970	8	0

T.D. Dines & J.O. Mountford

Seseli libanotis Moon Carrot
(L.) W.D.J.Koch

A usually biennial herb, though it is sometimes a short-lived monocarpic perennial. It is mainly a plant of unimproved lightly grazed ancient chalk grassland, but in Cambridgeshire is also found on chalky roadside banks and on ledges in an abandoned chalk quarry. Reproducing by seed and long-persistent at its sites. Lowland.

Trends The 10 km square distribution of *S. libanotis* appears to be stable and all populations lie within protected Sites of Special Scientific Interest. However, despite numerous searches it has not been found at its sole Hertfordshire site (Arbury Banks) since 1976, and there was some loss in its Sussex stronghold in the 1980s, but compensated for by the discovery in 1984 of a very large colony containing many thousands of plants. The extant Sussex and Bedfordshire populations appear strong, with an increase in the number of plants in recent years, especially on Knocking Hoe (Bedfordshire) where it is now locally dominant and is spreading into adjacent grassland which has been reverting from arable since the 1990s. However, colonies in Cambridgeshire are small and vulnerable, and one has declined significantly in recent years, presumably because of unsuitable grassland management. Its capacity to spread by seed is also suggested by a casual occurrence at Chatteris (Cambridgeshire) in 1883, where it may have been accidentally introduced by a botanist.

Biogeography Eurasian Temperate element, with a continental distribution in western Europe.

	GB	IR
Long term	No trend	No trend
Short term	No trend	No trend

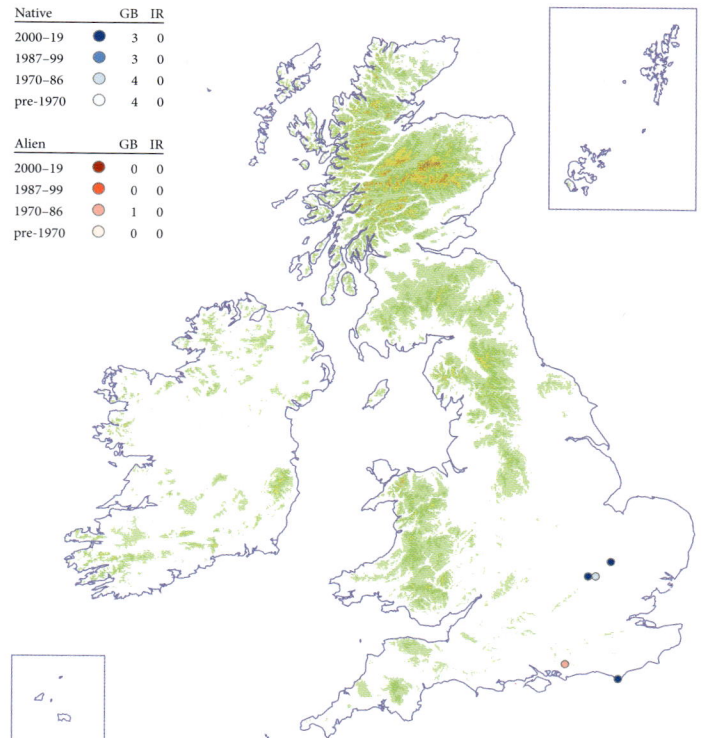

Native	GB	IR
2000–19	3	0
1987–99	3	0
1970–86	4	0
pre-1970	4	0

Alien	GB	IR
2000–19	0	0
1987–99	0	0
1970–86	1	0
pre-1970	0	0

Key refs Leslie (2019), Stroh *et al.* (2014), Stroh *et al.* (2019), Tutin (1980), Wigginton (1999).

M. SOUTHAM & J.O. MOUNTFORD

Trinia glauca Honewort
(L.) Dumort.

A monocarpic, dioecious, perennial herb restricted to dry limestone sites, typically occurring in short-grazed, open, species-rich turf on south-facing slopes. In heavily grazed turf the plant can be perennial until the opportunity arises to flower. Reproduction is by seed. Lowland.

Trends Always a very rare species, the 10 km square distribution of *T. glauca* has declined slightly since the 1960s, although it is still present at many of its South Devon and North Somerset locations, and persists at its sole site in the Avon Gorge (West Gloucestershire). In Devon it is restricted to three almost contiguous sites near to Brixham (Durl Head, Sharkham Point, Berry Head), but appears to have been lost from both Torquay locations (Petit Tor, Walls Hill) by the 1980s, possibly due to the encroachment of scrub. In Somerset it is still found at Uphill and Sand Point, and at a few sites on the western Mendips, but has been lost from five sites since the late 1980s due to a lack of grazing. It was last recorded at the introduction site at Goblin Combe (North Somerset) in 2002, with no plants found in later searches. The site is now unmanaged and shaded by trees.

Biogeography European Southern-temperate element.

	GB	IR
Long term	No trend	No trend
Short term	No trend	No trend

Native	GB	IR
2000–19	5	0
1987–99	5	0
1970–86	6	0
pre-1970	5	0

Alien	GB	IR
2000–19	1	0
1987–99	1	0
1970–86	1	0
pre-1970	1	0

Key refs Tutin (1980), Wigginton (1999).

M. SOUTHAM & J.O. MOUNTFORD

N *Selinum carvifolia* Cambridge Milk-parsley
(L.) L.

A perennial herb of fens, damp meadows and rough-grazed marshy pasture on calcareous peaty soils or fen peat overlying chalk. It does not grow on the wettest ground in fens, but prefers slightly better-drained fringe areas and low banks. Reproduction is by seed. Lowland.

Trends *S. carvifolia* was last recorded in Lincolnshire in 1931 and in Nottinghamshire by 1952. Past losses were due to drainage, ploughing or grassland improvement. Since 2000, the species has been found in three statutorily protected sites in Cambridgeshire; it continues to thrive at Chippenham Fen, but has greatly reduced in numbers at the other two and is now possibly extinct at one of these (Sawston Hall Meadows) due to a lack of management, scrub invasion and an altered water-table. It has also been introduced, using Chippenham seed, into an ex-arable wetland creation site near to Wicken Fen.

Biogeography European Temperate element.

Native	GB	IR
2000–19	2	0
1987–99	2	0
1970–86	3	0
pre-1970	3	0

Alien	GB	IR
2000–19	1	0
1987–99	1	0
1970–86	0	0
pre-1970	2	0

	GB	IR
Long term	No trend	No trend
Short term	No trend	No trend

Key refs Leslie (2019), Meade (1989), O'Leary (1989), Stroh *et al.* (2019), Tutin (1980), Wigginton (1999).

M.F. WATSON & J.O. MOUNTFORD

N *Peucedanum officinale* Hog's Fennel
L.

A perennial herb of coastal grassland occurring in rough grassland and scrubby places adjoining upper saltmarsh or brackish grazing marsh, on creek sides and on sea-walls and embankments; also on waste ground and, rarely, on roadsides. Plants have a very large and long taproot, and spread by rhizomatous growth and perhaps also by seed, but seed ripens only in warm years. Lowland.

Trends This species was first recorded in 1666 in Sussex, but has not been seen there subsequently. It appears to have become more common in North Essex since 1960, though some outlying populations have been lost. It has been planted intentionally near to native populations in Essex to increase suitable habitat for Fisher's Estuarine Moth *Gortyna borelii* subsp. *lunata*, as *P. officinale* is the main foodplant for its larvae. It is thriving in its core Kent localities, and continues to persist in Southwold (East Suffolk), where its discovery in 1990 was a significant extension of its known range.

Biogeography European Southern-temperate element.

Native	GB	IR
2000–19	8	0
1987–99	7	0
1970–86	6	0
pre-1970	6	0

Alien	GB	IR
2000–19	2	0
1987–99	0	0
1970–86	0	0
pre-1970	1	0

	GB	IR
Long term	No trend	No trend
Short term	No trend	No trend

Key refs Kitchener (2022), Randall & Thornton (1996), Tutin (1980), Wigginton (1999).

M. SOUTHAM & J.O. MOUNTFORD

Thysselinum palustre Milk-parsley

(L.) Hoffm.

A biennial or short-lived perennial herb of permanently damp peat, often in sites flooded in winter. It is most characteristic of tall-herb fen, being found in both cut and uncut stands. It can survive in fen scrub and alder-carr, and it occurs rarely in marshes and damp pasture. Lowland.

Trends Many sites of *T. palustre* were destroyed in the 19th century, following drainage and reclamation. Since 1930, further sites have been lost in East Anglia, principally to scrub invasion. Most extant sites are now in nature reserves, where occasional mowing favours its survival and spread. It is now most frequent in the Norfolk Broads, where it has also been introduced to a few sites, and in Breckland. Discovery of the species in 2008 by a tarn margin in Westmorland (near Newby Bridge) is a significant extension to the previously accepted native range, and would appear to confirm an 1885 record noting the possible presence of *T. palustre* in the county. The species is an important food plant for the Swallowtail butterfly *Papilio machaon*, currently restricted to the Norfolk Broads.

Biogeography Eurosiberian Boreo-temperate element, with a continental distribution in western Europe.

Native	GB	IR
2000–19	21	0
1987–99	25	0
1970–86	24	0
pre-1970	44	0

Alien	GB	IR
2000–19	4	0
1987–99	2	0
1970–86	2	0
pre-1970	3	0

Key refs Harvey & Meredith (1981), Meredith & Grubb (1993), Porter & Halliday (2014), Stewart *et al.* (1994), Tutin (1980).

M.F. WATSON & J.O. MOUNTFORD

Imperatoria ostruthium Masterwort

L.

A perennial herb naturalized in moist or damp grassy areas, including marshy pasture, on hillsides and by streams and rivers, and sometimes established around farm buildings. Generally lowland, but reaching 385 m at Langdon Beck and reportedly much higher near Cow Rake Rig (both County Durham).

Trends *I. ostruthium* was formerly cultivated as a pot-herb or for veterinary purposes. It was first recorded in Ireland in 1746 at Knockroe (County Waterford) and in Britain in 1777 (Dunbartonshire and Peebleshire). It is very persistent and shows no sign of a change in its distribution since the 1960s.

Biogeography Native of the mountains of central and south-western Europe.

Alien	GB	IR
2000–19	85	7
1987–99	77	12
1970–86	63	8
pre-1970	138	12

Key refs Tutin (1980).

M.F. WATSON & J.O. MOUNTFORD

N *Angelica sylvestris* Wild Angelica
L.

A perennial herb, occurring on base-rich soils in a wide variety of habitats, including damp woods and carr, damp neutral grassland, marshes, mires, swamps and tall-herb fens, river- and ditch-banks, sea-cliffs, ungrazed montane grassland and mountain ledges. Reproduction is by seed. 0–1,000 m (Sgurr nan Conbhairean, Easterness).

Trends *A. sylvestris* is ubiquitous at the 10 km square resolution and its distribution has changed little since the 1960s, though there have been localized declines in intensively managed lowland landscapes.

Biogeography Eurosiberian Boreo-temperate element.

Native	GB	IR
2000–19	2708	980
1987–99	2660	941
1970–86	1879	188
pre-1970	2590	873

Key refs Grime *et al.* (2007), Tutin (1980).

M. Southam & J.O. Mountford

N *Angelica archangelica* Garden Angelica
L.

A robust monocarpic perennial herb that, as a presumed native plant, occurs as a sporadic colonist of beaches in Shetland. However, it occurs much more widely as a naturalized garden escape on riversides and by canals, roadsides and in waste places. It is otherwise seen only in small numbers in gardens or as an escaped casual. Lowland.

Trends *A. archangelica* subsp. *littoralis* is believed to have arrived naturally from Norway, possibly more than once, and established temporarily in remote coastal locations on Shetland in the late 20th and early 21st centuries (Stroh & Scott, 2017). It has not been recorded since 2002, but could potentially recolonize. All other records are of subsp. *archangelica* which was being cultivated in Britain by 1568 and was first recorded from the wild in *c.*1700 (Middlesex). It is still grown in herb gardens and although its overall range has not increased markedly since the 1960s, it has clearly expanded its frequency within its core areas of London, the middle and lower Trent and the Manchester-Liverpool conurbation. General greater attention to garden-escapes and alien species is reflected in a wide scattering of casual records.

Biogeography A Eurasian Boreal-montane species; a rare example of a northern species which has spread south in Europe as a result of cultivation.

Native	GB	IR
2000–19	1	0
1987–99	2	0
1970–86	0	0
pre-1970	0	0

Alien	GB	IR
2000–19	144	6
1987–99	94	8
1970–86	41	1
pre-1970	69	0

Key refs Scott & Palmer (1987), Stroh & Scott (2017), Tutin (1980), Vaughan & Geissler (2009).

M. Southam & J.O. Mountford

Ne *Acorus calamus* Sweet-flag

L.

A rhizomatous perennial herb, planted in gardens and naturalized along the margins of streams, slow-flowing rivers, canals, ponds and lakes in shallow, nutrient-rich calcareous water. The European plant is a sterile triploid. It does not set fruit in the British Isles and so its dispersal must depend on fragments of rhizome moved by water and deliberate planting by man. Lowland.

Trends *A. calamus* was introduced into England by 1582 and was established in the wild by 1656 (Witton Fens, East Norfolk). It continues to be more widespread than in the 1960s with some evidence of spread around its earlier strongholds, probably due to better recording as the plant flowers shyly in our area and may well have been overlooked in the past.

Biogeography Native plants are diploid (Siberia, North America) or tetraploid (southern and eastern Asia); the origin of the triploid is unknown but it is naturalized in Europe and western Asia, the Himalayas and eastern North America.

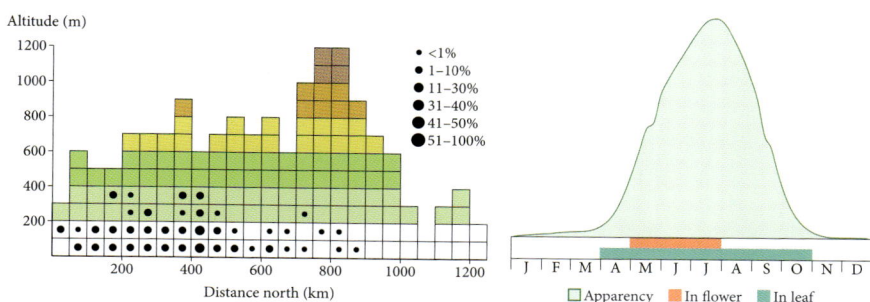

Alien		GB	IR
2000–19	●	458	7
1987–99	●	401	10
1970–86	●	244	3
pre-1970	○	332	12

Key refs Preston & Croft (1997).

R. WILSON

Ne *Lysichiton americanus* American Skunk-cabbage

Hultén & H.St.John

A perennial herb, spreading by erect rhizomes, widely planted as an ornamental beside ponds and streams in parks and gardens, where it reproduces by seed and quickly becomes established downstream in wet woodland, swamps and marshes. Mainly lowland, but up to 425 m in Kielder Forest (South Northumberland).

Trends *L. americanus* was introduced into cultivation in 1901 and was known in the wild by 1947 (Surrey). Since 2000 it has been recorded in roughly 1,000 new sites (an eight-fold rate of increase compared with the previous 40 years), and the record shows that a larger proportion of these are in the wider countryside. It is now considered invasive on ecological grounds, particularly in swampy woodland where it can dominate large areas, making removal of rhizomes very laborious. In

the past it has been more widespread in western Britain than elsewhere but with continuing spread this geographical distinction is now less well marked.

Biogeography Native of western North America.

Alien		GB	IR
2000–19	●	518	67
1987–99	●	176	22
1970–86	●	72	10
pre-1970	○	23	2

Key refs Alberternst & Nawrath (2002), Flora of North America Editorial Committee (2000).

R. WILSON & M.W. RAND

Ne *Calla palustris* Bog Arum
L.

A rhizomatous perennial herb which grows as floating mats at the edges of lakes and ponds, or rooted in marshes and wet alder-carr. Reproduction is vegetative by rhizome fragments; seeds are produced in Britain (and avidly eaten by ducks) but details of germination are unknown. Lowland.

Trends *C. palustris* was cultivated in Britain by 1738. It was planted at Black Pond (Surrey) in 1861, and persisted for at least 30 years. Another population in Surrey, at Bolder Mere, persisted for over 60 years. It is better recorded now than when mapped by Preston & Croft (1997). Its range in the last 20 years has changed little but recorded sites have increased. It has been deemed invasive in high-quality stream habitat in the New Forest and targeted for eradication.

Biogeography *C. palustris* has a Circumpolar Boreal-montane distribution; it is, however, virtually absent as a native from the Oceanic zone in Europe.

Alien	GB	IR
2000–19	45	0
1987–99	29	1
1970–86	21	0
pre-1970	13	0

	GB	IR
Long term	No trend	No trend
Short term	↓ ↓ ◆ ↑ ↑	No trend

Key refs Preston & Croft (1997).

T.D. Dines & M.W. Rand

Ne *Zantedeschia aethiopica* Altar-lily
(L.) Spreng.

A tuberous perennial herb, widely grown in gardens and found naturalized in ditches, damp hedgerows and scrub, and in neglected fields where it arises as a garden escape or throw-out. Reproduction is vegetative and populations can be very persistent; seed is very rarely, if ever, produced. Lowland.

Trends *Z. aethiopica* was being cultivated in British gardens by 1731 and is very widely grown, especially in areas with a mild climate. It was first recorded from the wild in 1952 (Kenmare River, West Kerry), and has increased considerably since then, particularly in the last two decades in Ireland and the milder parts of western Britain. It readily spreads vegetatively along even small watercourses, and is considered invasive in parts of its introduced range including Spain, where it also spreads by seed (Galán & Castroviejo, 2007).

Given its hardiness, it is potentially invasive in areas with a mild climate especially as winters become less severe as a result of climate change.

Biogeography Native of South Africa.

Alien	GB	IR
2000–19	117	34
1987–99	28	3
1970–86	11	0
pre-1970	7	1

	GB	IR
Long term	No trend	No trend
Short term	↓ ↓ ◆ ↑ ↑	↓ ↓ ◆ ↑ ↑

Key refs Galán & Castroviejo (2007), Sing *et al.* (1996).

T.D. Dines & M.W. Rand

Ⓝ *Arum maculatum* Lords-and-Ladies

L.

A rhizomatous perennial herb of woodlands, hedgerows and other shaded habitats on moist, well-drained and reasonably fertile, often base-rich, soils. Generally lowland, but reaching 425 m at Ystradfellte (Breconshire).

Trends The distribution of *A. maculatum* has shown little change since the 1960s. There have undoubtedly been some localized losses caused by hedgerow removal, but this has been compensated for by its ability to establish itself quickly in new areas of suitable habitat, such as on roadside banks, and in scrub, regenerating woodlands and plantations. Local Floras suggest that it is introduced north of South Northumberland and Cumbria, presumably in topsoil and garden waste, although the precise limits of its native range are now impossible to discern and so it as mapped as native throughout England, Wales, Ireland and the Channel Islands and as alien in Scotland and the Isle of Man.

Biogeography European Temperate element.

Native	GB	IR
2000–19	1614	677
1987–99	1574	603
1970–86	1176	110
pre-1970	1495	387

Alien	GB	IR
2000–19	239	0
1987–99	190	0
1970–86	120	0
pre-1970	170	0

Key refs Boyce (1993), Grime *et al.* (2007), Prime (1954), Prime (1960), Sowter (1949).

R. WILSON & J.O. MOUNTFORD

Ⓝ *Arum italicum* Italian Lords-and-Ladies

Mill.

A rhizomatous perennial herb that occurs as a native in woodlands, hedgebanks, scrub and field-borders where it has a preference for shaded, humid environments and deep, well-drained soils reasonably rich in nutrients. Reproduction is by division of the rootstock; only the alien subsp. *italicum* sets abundant seed. This subspecies is more frequently grown in gardens and as a consequence is much more widespread than subsp. *neglectum* as a garden escape. Lowland.

Native in Britain and the Channel Islands and a neophyte in Ireland.

Trends The native distribution of *A. italicum* is probably stable, although alien occurrences, especially of the non-native subsp. *italicum*, are increasing. The two subspecies found in our area, the native subsp. *neglectum* and the alien subsp. *italicum*, are mapped separately.

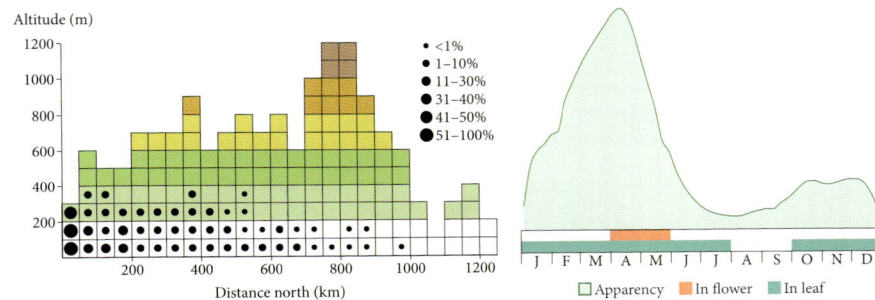

Biogeography Mediterranean-Atlantic element.

Native	GB	IR
2000–19	65	0
1987–99	63	0
1970–86	44	0
pre-1970	61	0

Alien	GB	IR
2000–19	901	122
1987–99	276	25
1970–86	106	4
pre-1970	75	3

Key refs Boyce (1993).

R. WILSON

Ⓝ *Arum italicum* subsp. *neglectum*

(F. Towns.) Prime

A rhizomatous perennial found in hedgebanks, scrub and stony field-borders close to the coast and in hanger woodlands at inland sites. It thrives at sites where there is a shaded, humid environment (often growing on the north side of walls), and a deep, well-drained soil reasonably rich in nutrients. It reproduces by natural division of the rootstock, but little seed is set because the flowers are often eaten by animals. Lowland.

Trends The distribution of this subspecies as a native plant appears to be stable. It is increasing as a garden throw-out or escape, but it is much less frequently grown than subsp. *italicum*.

Biogeography Oceanic Temperate element; found in western Europe from northern Spain to Britain.

	GB	IR
Long term	No trend	No trend
Short term	No trend	No trend

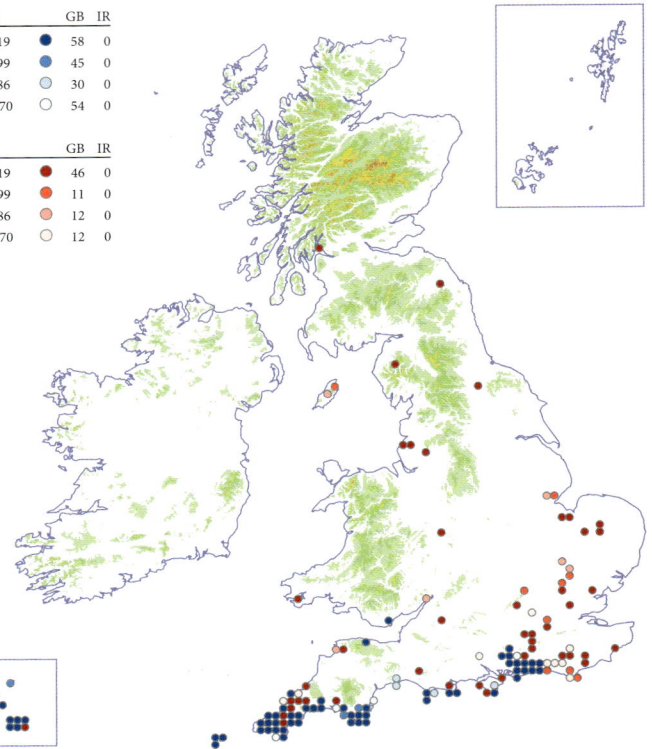

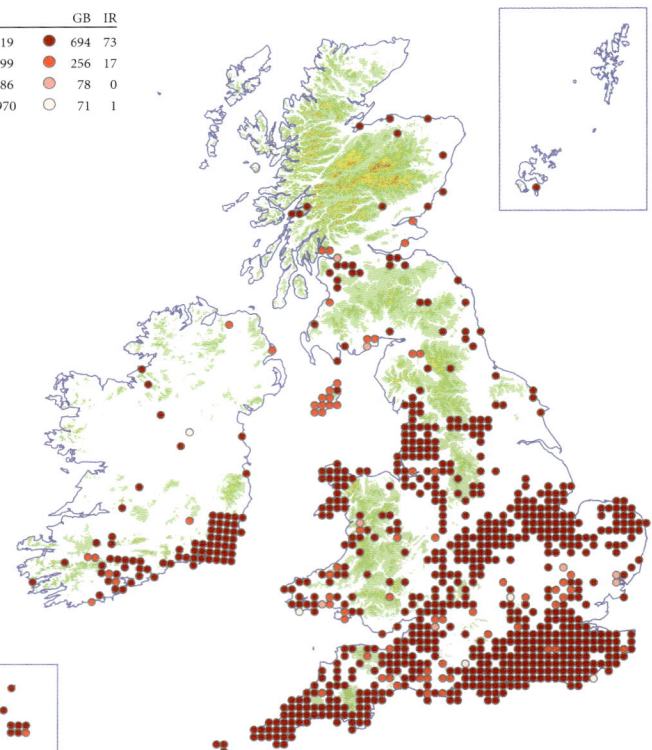

Native	GB	IR
2000–19	58	0
1987–99	45	0
1970–86	30	0
pre-1970	54	0

Alien	GB	IR
2000–19	46	0
1987–99	11	0
1970–86	12	0
pre-1970	12	0

Altitude (m) — Distance north (km)

<1% · 1–10% · 11–30% · 31–40% · 41–50% · 51–100%

Apparency · In flower · In leaf

Key refs Boyce (1993), Prime (1954), Prime (1960), Stewart *et al.* (1994).

R. Wilson & J.O. Mountford

Ⓝⓔ *Arum italicum* subsp. *italicum*

Mill.

A rhizomatous perennial herb, widely grown in gardens and found as a garden escape in scrub and shaded hedgebanks, often in places where garden waste has been dumped or in the wilder parts of churchyards. It sets abundant seed which is often bird-sown, sometimes at considerable distance from human habitations. Lowland.

Trends This subspecies was cultivated in Britain by 1683 and was known from the wild by 1902 (Ponsanooth, West Cornwall). It is popular in gardens, and its distribution has markedly expanded since 2000, notably in County Wexford, Lancashire, the West Midlands, Norfolk and the Fenland basin.

Biogeography *A. italicum* subsp. *italicum* has a Mediterranean-Atlantic distribution.

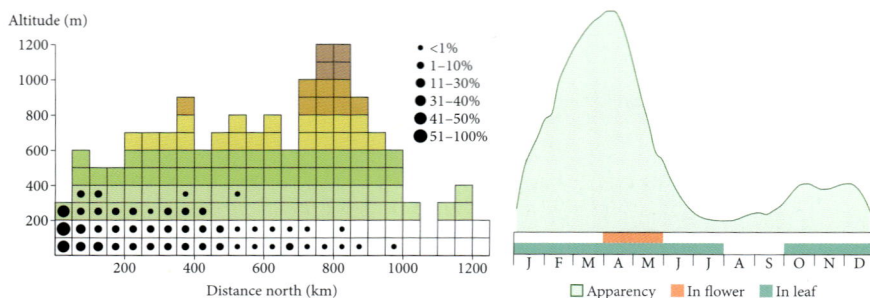

	GB	IR
Long term	No trend	No trend
Short term	No trend	No trend

Alien	GB	IR
2000–19	694	73
1987–99	256	17
1970–86	78	0
pre-1970	71	1

Altitude (m) — Distance north (km)

<1% · 1–10% · 11–30% · 31–40% · 41–50% · 51–100%

Apparency · In flower · In leaf

Key refs Boyce (1993), Prime (1954), Prime (1960).

R. Wilson & J.O. Mountford

Ne *Dracunculus vulgaris* Dragon Arum

Schott

A tuberous perennial herb which is naturalized in rough grassland, on grassy banks, in hedgerows and on waste ground. It also occurs as a relic of cultivation. Lowland.

Trends *D. vulgaris* was being grown in British gardens by 1200 (Harvey, 1981), and is widely cultivated for its dramatic leaves and flowers. It was recorded from the wild by 1918 (Perranporth, West Cornwall), and is almost certainly increasing around London and elsewhere in southern England.

Biogeography Native of the central and eastern Mediterranean region.

Alien	GB	IR
2000–19	33	3
1987–99	29	0
1970–86	22	0
pre-1970	17	0

	GB	IR
Long term	No trend	No trend
Short term	↓ ↓ ◆ ↑ ↑	No trend

Key refs Harvey (1981).

T.D. Dines & J.O. Mountford

N *Spirodela polyrhiza* Greater Duckweed

(L.) Schleid.

S. polyrhiza grows in base-rich water in ponds, ditches, canals and slowly flowing rivers. It is particularly frequent in grazing marshes. It tolerates high nutrient levels and in cultivation it flourishes when grown on diluted cattle slurry (Stadtlander *et al.*, 2019). Flowers have only been reported once in our area (in 1906) and reproduction is by vegetative budding. Lowland.

Trends In many British areas there has been a long-term decline resulting from habitat loss or the unsympathetic management of remaining water bodies. However, it has increased greatly in recent decades in some areas where suitable habitats persist, such as the Ouse Washes (Cambridgeshire), almost certainly as a result of its tolerance of hypertrophic conditions (Newbold, 2003a). It has spread greatly in Ireland in recent decades, and Forbes & Northridge

(2012) concluded that it must be a recent colonist, but it may also be responding there to nutrient enrichment.

Biogeography Circumpolar Southern-temperate element.

Native	GB	IR
2000–19	412	130
1987–99	333	78
1970–86	191	33
pre-1970	423	39

Alien	GB	IR
2000–19	19	0
1987–99	3	0
1970–86	5	0
pre-1970	5	0

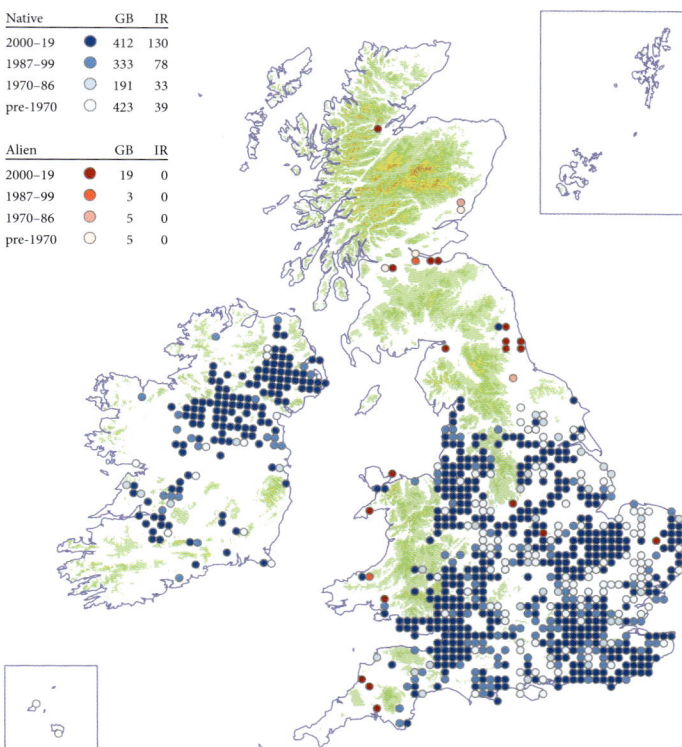

	GB	IR
Long term	↓ ↓ ◆ ↑ ↑	↓ ↓ ◆ ↑ ↑
Short term	↓ ↓ ◆ ↑ ↑	↓ ↓ ◆ ↑ ↑

Key refs Forbes & Northridge (2012), Newbold (2003a), Preston & Croft (1997), Stadtlander *et al.* (2019).

C.D. Preston

Lemna gibba Fat Duckweed
L.

This buoyant duckweed is a plant of still or slowly flowing, eutrophic water in ponds, canals, ditches or the quiet backwaters of rivers; it can also grow in brackish water. In very eutrophic sites it may form dense masses which exclude other aquatics. It reproduces by vegetative budding, though it flowers slightly more freely than our other Lemnaceae. Lowland.

Trends *L. gibba* is not easily separated from *L. minor* and this makes the map difficult to interpret. The density of recent records in some areas of England probably reflects the fact that variants of *L. gibba* with flat fronds are now recognized, rather than overlooked as *L. minor*. In these areas the map is consistent with Rumsey & Lansdown's (2012) contention that *L. gibba* is the most abundant duckweed in parts of southern and eastern Britain.

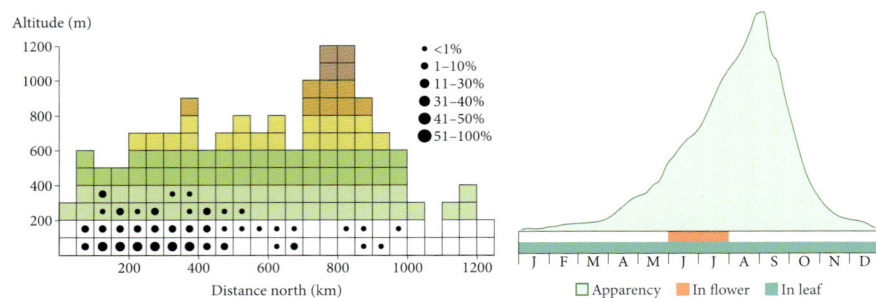

Biogeography European Southern-temperate element; also in central Asia and North America.

Native	GB	IR
2000–19	569	51
1987–99	458	34
1970–86	320	9
pre-1970	474	32

Key refs Preston & Croft (1997), Rumsey & Lansdown (2012).

C.D. PRESTON

Lemna minor Common Duckweed
L.

This is our most widespread and frequent floating aquatic plant, often abundant on a wide variety of still or slowly flowing, mesotrophic or eutrophic waters. It also occurs terrestrially on exposed mud, or damp stonework and rocks. Plants rarely flower and reproduction is by vegetative budding. 0–530 m (Brown Clee, Shropshire).

Trends Although *L. minor* is undoubtedly widespread, it is probably over-recorded because variants of *L. gibba* with flat fronds may be mistaken for it. Whether or not this affects the map at the hectad scale is unclear, and the relative frequency of the two species requires detailed and critical study, especially in southern and eastern England.

Biogeography Circumpolar Southern-temperate element; widely naturalized outside its native range.

Native	GB	IR
2000–19	2171	770
1987–99	2057	763
1970–86	1398	138
pre-1970	1745	478

Alien	GB	IR
2000–19	1	0
1987–99	2	0
1970–86	2	0
pre-1970	1	0

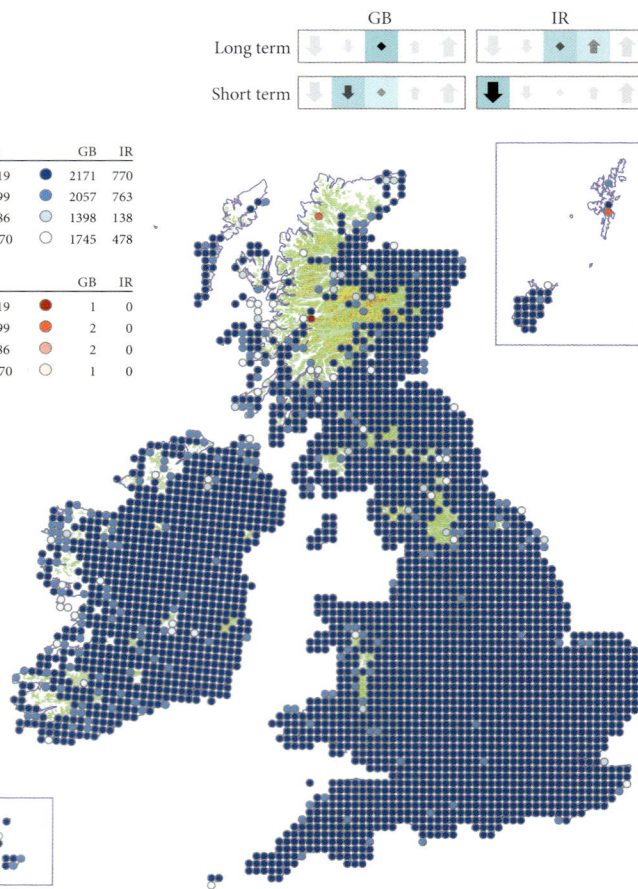

Key refs Grime *et al.* (2007), Preston & Croft (1997).

C.D. PRESTON

Ne *Lemna turionifera* Red Duckweed
Landolt

An annual free-floating aquatic herb, primarily of ditches in grazing marshes with occasional records from artificial ponds. Lowland.

Trends *L. turionifera* is known mainly from grazing marshes. It was first recorded near to Wareham (Dorset) in 2007, and is almost certainly under-recorded.

Biogeography Scattered in northern Europe, also occurs in North America.

	GB	IR
Long term	No trend	No trend
Short term		No trend

Alien	GB	IR
2000–19	44	0
1987–99	0	0
1970–86	0	0
pre-1970	0	0

Altitude (m)

	<1%
	1–10%
	11–30%
	31–40%
	41–50%
	51–100%

Distance north (km)

Apparency / In flower / In leaf

Key refs Lansdown (2008).

R.V. LANSDOWN

Ne *Lemna minuta* Least Duckweed
Kunth

A perennial herb, often found in abundance as a floating aquatic on the surface of lakes, ponds, slowly flowing rivers, streams, canals and ditches. It is sufficiently shade-tolerant to occur on ponds shaded by marginal trees or woodland. Reproduction is by vegetative budding. Lowland.

Trends This species was first recorded in Britain in 1977, when it was discovered in Cambridge, and it spread rapidly in Britain. It was already widespread in southern England by 2000 and records since then indicate a further spread northwards. It has spread equally rapidly in Ireland since it was first found at three widely separated sites in 1993 (Reynolds, 2002).

Biogeography Native to temperate and subtropical North and South America. It has become widely naturalized in

Europe since it was first discovered in France in 1965 and at least two earlier herbarium specimens, from Hungary and Portugal, have subsequently come to light.

	GB	IR
Long term	No trend	No trend
Short term		

Alien	GB	IR
2000–19	1198	207
1987–99	584	7
1970–86	100	0
pre-1970	10	0

Altitude (m)

	<1%
	1–10%
	11–30%
	31–40%
	41–50%
	51–100%

Distance north (km)

Apparency / In flower / In leaf

Key refs Cotton (1999), Flora of North America Editorial Committee (2000), Preston & Croft (1997), Reynolds (2002).

C.D. PRESTON

Lemna trisulca Ivy-leaved Duckweed

L.

The only submerged species of *Lemna* in our area, *L. trisulca* is frequent in mesotrophic to eutrophic, still to slowly flowing waters where low nutrient levels or exposure prevent the development of a dense blanket of floating *Lemna* species. Reproduction is by vegetative budding; flowering is very rare. Generally lowland, but reaching 360 m at Forest Lodge (Breconshire) and Kingside Loch (Selkirkshire).

Trends The distribution of *L. trisulca* appears to be broadly stable, though there have been some local losses. Several new sites have been discovered since 2000 in north-eastern Scotland, where it is now known to extend north to Caithness.

Biogeography Circumpolar Temperate element.

Native		GB	IR
2000–19	●	1071	348
1987–99	●	914	321
1970–86	●	631	85
pre-1970	○	918	152

Alien		GB	IR
2000–19	●	3	0
1987–99	●	3	0
1970–86	●	1	0
pre-1970	○	2	0

Key refs Preston & Croft (1997).

C.D. PRESTON

Wolffia arrhiza Rootless Duckweed

(L.) Horkel ex Wimm.

This tiny rootless plant floats on ponds and ditches as small, pure patches or scattered amongst other floating Lemnaceae. The largest populations are in grazing marsh ditches. Reproduction is by vegetative budding; flowers have never been seen either in our area or elsewhere in western Europe. Lowland.

Trends The range of *W. arrhiza* was contracting until the late 20th century, when it was thought to have been discovered in the Gwent Levels, Monmouthshire (1982) and the Pevensey Levels, East Sussex (1994) and rediscovered in the London area at the London Wetland Centre, Surrey (2000). However, fieldwork by Lansdown *et al.* (2022) has shown that *W. columbiana* is widespread within the British range of *W. arrhiza*. In 2021 *W. columbiana* was the only *Wolffia* that they could

find in the Pevensey Levels, and the only species in the Gwent Levels were this and another alien, *W. globosa*. The historic and current distributions of the native and alien *Wolffia* species clearly need to be disentangled, and all records here are mapped without status. *W. columbiana* was discovered in Germany and the Netherlands in 2013, and Schmitz *et al.* (2014) refer to the possible "clandestine replacement" of *W. arrhiza* by *W. columbiana*.

Biogeography Eurosiberian Southern-temperate element.

	GB	IR
2000–19	30	0
1987–99	27	0
1970–86	28	0
pre-1970	36	0

Key refs Lansdown *et al.* (2022), Preston & Croft (1997), Schmitz *et al.* (2014), Stewart *et al.* (1994).

C.D. PRESTON

N *Tofieldia pusilla* Scottish Asphodel
(Michx.) Pers.

A rhizomatous, perennial herb of streamsides and calcareous flushes, requiring constant moisture but not waterlogged conditions. Mainly upland, but from near sea level at Durness (West Sutherland) to 1,020 m on Meall Garbh (Mid Perthshire).

Trends The distribution of *T. pusilla* appears to be broadly stable at the 10 km square scale. More systematic recording in the Scottish Highlands has resulted in a small increase in its known range but there are a number of hectads, especially around the fringes of its distribution, where the species has not been recorded in recent decades. The relatively small English population in Teesdale is intensively monitored and appears to be declining due to a reduction in grazing levels. It was discovered new to science in 1671 close to the Scottish border (see Braithwaite, 2004), and recorded from Charnwood Forest (Leicestershire) in 1828.

Biogeography Circumpolar Arctic-montane element.

Native		GB	IR
2000–19	●	121	0
1987–99	●	107	0
1970–86	●	109	0
pre-1970	○	122	0

Alien		GB	IR
2000–19	●	0	0
1987–99	●	0	0
1970–86	●	1	0
pre-1970	○	0	0

Key refs Stewart *et al.* (1994).

I. TAYLOR

N *Sagittaria sagittifolia* Arrowhead
L.

A perennial herb of shallow, still or slowly flowing, calcareous and eutrophic water. In major rivers it may be present only as submerged leaves, but in ditches, lakes, ponds and canals it often produces emergent leaves and flowers. It perennates as tubers produced on stolons in the leaf axils. Lowland.

Native in Britain and Ireland and a neophyte in the Channel Islands.

Trends The overall British range of *S. sagittifolia* is stable, though in some areas the plant has been lost from ditches and is now restricted to larger rivers (Tarpey & Heath, 1990). In Ireland it has spread through canals. It rarely colonizes new habitats, but is sometimes deliberately introduced to ponds.

Biogeography Eurosiberian Boreo-temperate element.

Native		GB	IR
2000–19	●	473	97
1987–99	●	495	86
1970–86	●	348	33
pre-1970	○	554	71

Alien		GB	IR
2000–19	●	74	1
1987–99	●	32	0
1970–86	●	12	0
pre-1970	○	31	0

Key refs Preston & Croft (1997), Tarpey & Heath (1990).

C.D. PRESTON

Ne *Sagittaria latifolia* Duck-potato
Willd.

A tuberous and stoloniferous perennial herb found growing in shallow water in lakes, ponds, canals, ditches, streams and rivers, where it has usually originally been planted. It appears to be spreading in some rivers. Reproduction is by seed and vegetative spread. Lowland.

Trends *S. latifolia* was introduced into cultivation in Britain in 1819, and was first recorded in the wild in 1941 (Epsom Common, Surrey). It is now much better recorded than when mapped by Preston & Croft (1997) and its range has increased considerably, with numerous new records from the English Midlands and northern England, though it is still commonest in Surrey.

Biogeography Native of North, Central and South America; naturalized in several European countries.

	GB	IR
Long term	No trend	No trend
Short term		No trend

Alien	GB	IR
2000–19	51	0
1987–99	17	0
1970–86	10	0
pre-1970	7	0

Key refs Flora of North America Editorial Committee (2000), Preston & Croft (1997).

T.D. Dines & J.O. Mountford

N *Baldellia ranunculoides* Lesser Water-plantain
(L.) Parl.

A perennial herb that usually grows as an emergent or on damp ground at the edge of water bodies such as lakes and pools, marshes, fens, ditches, dune-slacks and saltmarsh pools, always in places where potential competitors are restricted by fluctuating water levels, disturbance or moderate exposure. It is adapted to grow in infertile habitats and is usually found in mildly to strongly calcareous or brackish waters, over a range of organic or inorganic substrates. 0–399 m (Loch Ossian, Westerness).

Trends *B. ranunculoides* is in long-term decline both in our area and throughout its European range, for a number of reasons including habitat destruction, succession following reduced disturbance or grazing, and eutrophication. The decline is especially marked in the eastern part

of its range, and Ireland is now one of the strongholds of the species. The stoloniferous, self-incompatible subsp. *repens* is much rarer in Britain and Ireland than subsp. *ranunculoides* and is perhaps found in less calcareous waters. Intermediates occur and are probably of hybrid origin.

Biogeography Suboceanic Southern-temperate element; the subspecies have broadly sympatric ranges.

	GB	IR
Long term		
Short term		

Native	GB	IR
2000–19	203	239
1987–99	212	242
1970–86	198	70
pre-1970	506	196

Alien	GB	IR
2000–19	1	0
1987–99	2	0
1970–86	0	0
pre-1970	0	0

Key refs Arrigo *et al.* (2011), Jones (2015), Kozlowski *et al.* (2008), Kozlowski & Vallelian (2009), Kozlowski *et al.* (2009), Preston & Croft (1997), Walker *et al.* (2017).

C.D. Preston

Luronium natans Floating Water-plantain

(L.) Parl.

A stoloniferous perennial of mesotrophic or oligotrophic lakes, pools and slow-flowing rivers, and abandoned or little-used canals. In deep or fast-flowing water it persists as a carpet of plants with rosettes of linear-lanceolate submerged leaves, and sometimes with cleistogamous flowers, but it produces expanded floating leaves and flowers freely in quieter or shallower water or on exposed mud. Freely fruiting populations may have a persistent seed bank (Nielsen *et al.*, 2006). 0–500 m (Llyn Cerrigllwydion Isaf, Radnorshire).

Trends There is clear evidence for the long-term decline of *L. natans* in England (where most surviving populations are in canals) and at the periphery of its Welsh range – notably in Anglesey and Glamorgan (Lansdown & Wade, 2003). The major factor has been habitat loss, with eutrophication a possible subsidiary cause. Known populations have been well-surveyed since 2000, but further populations, especially those of submerged plants, may still await discovery in both Britain and Ireland.

Biogeography Suboceanic Temperate element; it is a European endemic, most frequent in the Temperate zone, extending east to Poland.

Native		GB	IR
2000–19	●	52	3
1987–99	●	56	1
1970–86	●	38	0
pre-1970	○	74	0

Alien		GB	IR
2000–19	●	7	0
1987–99	●	8	0
1970–86	●	6	0
pre-1970	○	4	0

Key refs Kay *et al.* (1999), Lansdown & Wade (2003), Nielsen *et al.* (2006), Preston & Croft (1997).

C.D. PRESTON

Alisma plantago-aquatica Water-plantain

L.

A perennial herb growing on exposed mud at the shallow edge of still or slow-flowing waters, or in marshes and swamps. It is confined to mesotrophic or eutrophic habitats. Plants fruit prolifically, and the species is a frequent colonist of newly created ponds, recently cleaned ditches and flooded mineral workings. Generally lowland, but reaching 460 m at Brown Clee (Shropshire).

Trends A well-recorded species which has a stable distribution in Britain and Ireland and remains frequent in areas of suitable habitat. Any losses must be balanced by its capacity to colonize newly created water bodies.

Biogeography Circumpolar Wide-temperate element; widely naturalized outside its native range.

Native		GB	IR
2000–19	●	1607	586
1987–99	●	1596	572
1970–86	●	1188	109
pre-1970	○	1508	387

Alien		GB	IR
2000–19	●	15	1
1987–99	●	10	0
1970–86	●	4	0
pre-1970	○	4	0

Key refs Grime *et al.* (2007), Preston & Croft (1997).

C.D. PRESTON

(N) *Alisma lanceolatum* Narrow-leaved Water-plantain
With.

An emergent perennial herb, found in shallow water or on exposed mud at the edge of a wide range of water bodies, although in many areas it is particularly frequent in canals. It is most frequent in eutrophic, calcareous water and rooted in a fine substrate. Lowland.

Trends *A. lanceolatum* was not consistently recognized by British botanists as a distinct species until 1952, so distributional trends are difficult to assess. It might still be overlooked as *A. plantago-aquatica*, but the map may also include erroneous records, as narrow-leaved plants of that species are sometimes misidentified as *A. lanceolatum*. Hybrids may be present and add to the identification problems, but cytological confirmation is lacking (Stace *et al.*, 2015).

Biogeography Eurosiberian Southern-temperate element; introduced in western North America (Oregon, California) and as a weed of rice fields in Australia.

Native	GB	IR
2000–19	324	40
1987–99	297	27
1970–86	203	17
pre-1970	300	11

Alien	GB	IR
2000–19	18	0
1987–99	6	0
1970–86	3	0
pre-1970	5	0

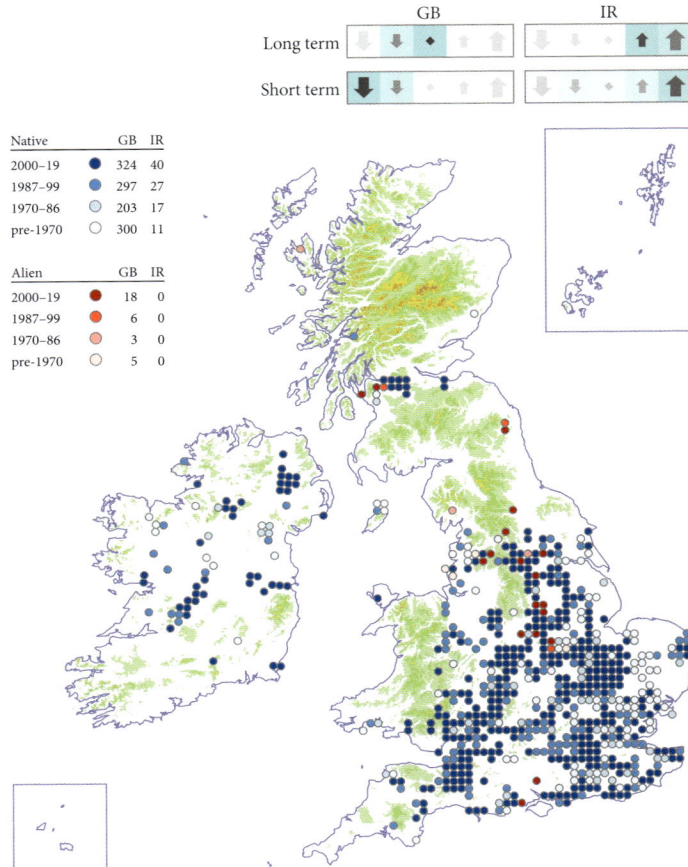

Key refs Ash *et al.* (2004), Preston & Croft (1997), Stace *et al.* (2015).

C.D. PRESTON

(N) *Alisma gramineum* Ribbon-leaved Water-plantain
Lej.

An annual or perennial herb which grows as a submerged aquatic, an emergent or a terrestrial plant in or alongside lakes, rivers and fenland drains and ditches. Submerged plants may flower but the most freely flowering populations are those exposed by temporary falls in water level. Plants may arise from a dormant seed bank after disturbance. Lowland.

Trends This species maintains a precarious presence in Britain, with persistent populations only known from Westwood Great Pool, Worcestershire, (first found 1920) and the Spalding area, South Lincolnshire (first found 1955). Short-lived populations were known at Welches Dam, Cambridgeshire (1972–76), and Langmere, West Norfolk (1960, 1972). It has not persisted at other sites to which it has been introduced.

Biogeography Circumpolar Temperate element, with a continental distribution in western Europe and a disjunct distribution elsewhere.

	GB	IR
Long term	No trend	No trend
Short term	No trend	No trend

Native	GB	IR
2000–19	4	0
1987–99	2	0
1970–86	4	0
pre-1970	3	0

Alien	GB	IR
2000–19	0	0
1987–99	3	0
1970–86	0	0
pre-1970	0	0

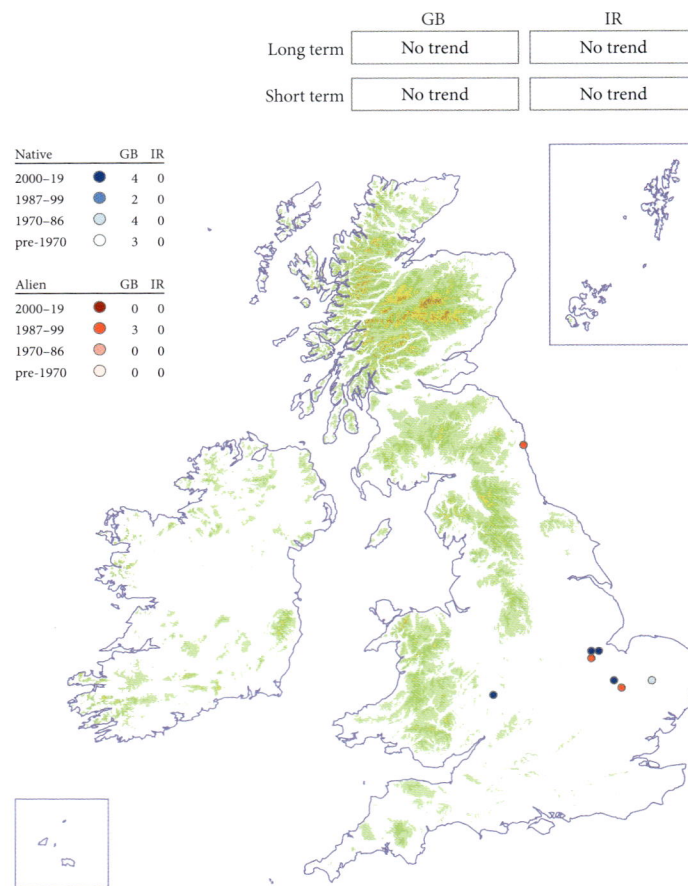

Key refs Lansdown (2011), Wigginton (1999).

C.D. PRESTON

N *Damasonium alisma* Starfruit
Mill.

This phenotypically plastic annual herb grows in small ponds where the habitat is kept open by fluctuating water levels and disturbance by grazing animals or conservation management. Its sites are usually flooded in winter but may be wet or dry in summer. Plants germinate in water in autumn and flower the following summer in shallow water or terrestrially on mud. The species is confined to inorganic, acidic substrates but the water is sometimes more base-rich. The seeds persist in a long-lived seed bank from which plants may arise after disturbance. Lowland.

Trends Though formerly widespread, there is no evidence that *D. alisma* was ever common. It declined catastrophically in the 19th and early 20th centuries following the decline of traditional grazing regimes. Most sites have become filled in, overgrown or

reduced to suburban duck-ponds. The three sites known to Birkinshaw (1994) increased to six in the 1990s following conservation management to restore open conditions, but it failed to persist at most and has occurred naturally in only two ponds in 2000–19. However, it has also regenerated following reintroduction to three more ponds and introduction to four more in the same period (Lansdown & McVeigh, 2019).

Biogeography Mediterranean-Atlantic element; declining throughout its world range.

	GB	IR
Long term	No trend	No trend
Short term	No trend	No trend

Native	GB	IR
2000–19	2	0
1987–99	4	0
1970–86	3	0
pre-1970	54	0

Alien	GB	IR
2000–19	4	0
1987–99	3	0
1970–86	0	0
pre-1970	4	0

Key refs Birkinshaw (1994), Lansdown (2015), Lansdown & McVeigh (2019), Preston & Croft (1997), Wigginton (1999).

C.D. Preston

N *Butomus umbellatus* Flowering-rush
L.

A submerged or emergent rhizomatous perennial herb which grows in calcareous, often eutrophic, water at the edges of rivers, lakes, canals, ditches and in swamps. Both diploid and triploid populations occur, and the fertile diploid appears to have a more restricted range than the triploid, which rarely sets seed but reproduces by lateral buds on the rhizome (Bailey & Preston, 2011). Lowland.

Native in Britain and a neophyte in Ireland and the Channel Islands.

Trends *B. umbellatus* remains frequent in suitable habitats within its core range, although there is evidence for a decline in some areas (Sanford & Fisk, 2010). Since 1950 it has spread in northern England and southern Scotland, as in the Tweed catchment, where it was first recorded in 1956, and along the

River Eden (Cumbria). In Ireland Webb & Scannell (1983) suggest that it is native in some areas, including County Clare, although it is treated here as an alien. It initially spread along canals and more recently from cultivated material into numerous catchments such as Lough Neagh and Lough Erne (Forbes & Northridge, 2012).

Biogeography Eurosiberian Temperate element; widely naturalized outside its native range.

Native	GB	IR
2000–19	480	0
1987–99	507	0
1970–86	373	0
pre-1970	519	0

Alien	GB	IR
2000–19	158	111
1987–99	80	75
1970–86	49	38
pre-1970	80	47

Key refs Bailey & Preston (2011), Forbes & Northridge (2012), Preston & Croft (1997), Sanford & Fisk (2010), Webb & Scannell (1983).

C.D. Preston

N *Hydrocharis morsus-ranae* Frogbit
L.

The floating rosettes of this perennial herb are found in shallow, calcareous, mesotrophic or eutrophic water in the sheltered bays of lakes or in ponds, canals and ditches, and very rarely in rivers. Lakes are the main habitat in Ireland whereas in England and Wales it is most frequent in grazing marsh ditches. The main Scottish population is in the Forth and Clyde Canal, where it has been established since 1983 (Watson, 1988). Reproduction is primarily vegetative; viable seed is sometimes set, but seedlings are probably rare. Lowland.

Trends In England and Wales the contraction of the range of *H. morsus-ranae* was already apparent by the mid-20th century, and was primarily the result of habitat loss (especially the conversion of grazing marshes to arable). Since then it has persisted in its core areas of grazing marshes. Although it has declined in some such areas in recent decades it has increased in others, notably the Ouse Washes, Cambridgeshire, where it was extinct by 1978 but had recolonized by 2003 (Cadbury *et al.*, 1994; Leslie, 2019). There is less evidence for a historic decline in Ireland, where the habitat is less vulnerable to destruction. It is sometimes planted or discarded into the wild.

Biogeography Eurosiberian Temperate element; widely naturalized outside its native range.

Native	GB	IR
2000–19	159	70
1987–99	158	58
1970–86	136	19
pre-1970	300	41

Alien	GB	IR
2000–19	78	0
1987–99	31	0
1970–86	12	0
pre-1970	28	0

Key refs Cadbury *et al.* (1994), Catling *et al.* (2003), Leslie (2019), Preston & Croft (1997), Stewart *et al.* (1994), Watson (1988).

C.D. PRESTON

N? *Stratiotes aloides* Water-soldier
L.

Native populations of this perennial herb are found in calcareous, meso-eutrophic lakes, ponds and ditches. Alien colonies occur in a range of other habitats, including canals and flooded gravel-pits. Plants sink in autumn and usually (but not always) float to the surface in summer, producing dense floating stands. All our plants are female, reproducing vegetatively. Lowland.

Native or alien in Britain and a neophyte in Ireland.

Trends As elsewhere in western Europe, the native range of *S. aloides* has been obscured by introductions. In Britain it was first recorded in 1626, and is generally regarded as native in eastern England, although the presence of only one sex suggests that this may not be so (Cook & Urmi-König, 1983). In Britain, apparently native populations have been in long-term decline, probably due to eutrophication. The population in County Fermanagh, which Forbes & Northridge (2012) regard as native, has expanded since 1980. Some undoubtedly alien populations are well-established and expanding, as in Lough Derg (Minchin *et al.*, 2021a), whereas others have proved to be short-lived.

Biogeography Eurosiberian Boreo-temperate element; widely naturalized outside its native range.

Native	GB	IR
2000–19	31	0
1987–99	17	0
1970–86	16	0
pre-1970	61	0

Alien	GB	IR
2000–19	277	10
1987–99	196	7
1970–86	74	2
pre-1970	114	6

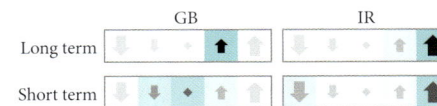

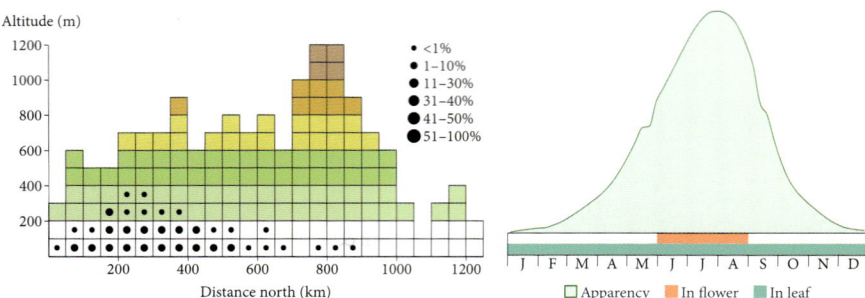

Key refs Cook & Urmi-König (1983), Forbes & Northridge (2012), Harpenslager *et al.* (2015), Minchin *et al.* (2021a), Preston & Croft (1997), Snyder *et al.* (2016), Stewart *et al.* (1994).

C.D. PRESTON

Ne *Egeria densa* Large-flowered Waterweed
Planch.

An evergreen perennial herb which grows submerged in rivers and canals, where it is often naturalized, and in ponds and pools, where it may only be casual. The water at some sites is (or was formerly) subject to warming from cotton mills and glass works, although *E. densa* is less frequent in such sites than formerly. All our plants may be male; reproduction is by vegetative spread. Lowland.

Trends *E. densa* is grown by aquarists and this may be the source of all our plants. It was first recorded in the wild in Britain in 1953 (Ashton Canal, South Lancashire). Although possibly declining in its former stronghold of urban canals, it appears more numerous in artificial water-bodies in the Midlands and especially in Cornwall.

Biogeography Native of South America; widely found in the wild in North and Central America, Europe, eastern Africa, Japan and Australasia, but only truly naturalized in warm-temperate and subtropical areas.

Alien	GB	IR
2000–19	34	1
1987–99	20	1
1970–86	13	0
pre-1970	4	0

Key refs Preston & Croft (1997).

T.D. Dines & J.O. Mountford

Ne *Elodea canadensis* Canadian Waterweed
Michx.

This aquatic perennial herb has a broad habitat range, growing in mesotrophic to eutrophic waters from the shallows to depths of 3 metres or more. It favours still or slowly flowing sites where silt accumulates. All plants in our area are female and reproduce vegetatively. 0–505 m Brown Clee (Shropshire).

Trends This species was first recorded in Britain in 1842 and in Ireland in 1854, subsequently spreading very rapidly. However, by the 1860s its excessive abundance in its first British sites had begun to decline although it persisted in reduced quantity. In the late 20th century it disappeared from some areas, often being replaced in eutrophic waters by *E. nuttallii*.

Biogeography Native of temperate North America; widely naturalized in Europe and Australasia.

Alien	GB	IR
2000–19	1273	423
1987–99	1431	387
1970–86	1063	89
pre-1970	1194	186

Key refs Barrat-Segretain *et al.* (2002), Flora of North America Editorial Committee (2000), Grime *et al.* (2007), Preston (2002), Preston & Croft (1997), Spicer & Catling (1988).

C.D. Preston

Ne *Elodea nuttallii* Nuttall's Waterweed
(Planch.) H.St.John

Like *E. canadensis*, this perennial herb is found in still or slowly flowing, shallow or deep water. It appears to be more restricted to eutrophic water than its congener, and it may be frequent even in highly disturbed canals and rivers. Unlike many submerged aquatics, it is able to persist under a blanket of floating *Azolla filiculoides* or *Lemna minuta*. It is an effective colonizer of new habitats, despite the fact that it must spread vegetatively as all plants in our area are female. 0–505 m (Brown Clee, Shropshire).

Trends This species is grown by aquarists and pondkeepers. It was first recorded as naturalized in Britain in 1966 (Oxfordshire), and has since spread rapidly. It was first found in Ireland in 1984, at Lough Neagh (Tyrone). By 2000 it had occupied much of its current British range, though it has since spread at the edges of that range in south-western England, Wales, north-eastern England and eastern Scotland. In Ireland it has spread extensively from the eastern sites in which it was recorded by 2000.

Biogeography Native of temperate North America; naturalized in Europe since 1939 and in Japan since the 1960s.

	GB	IR
Long term	No trend	No trend
Short term		

Alien	GB	IR
2000–19	1023	156
1987–99	842	24
1970–86	319	3
pre-1970	56	1

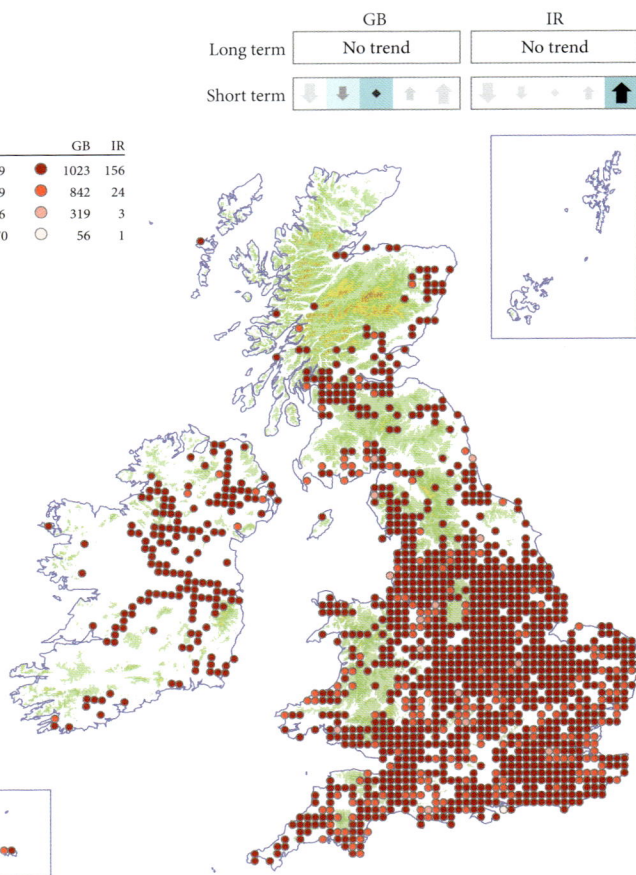

Key refs Barrat-Segretain *et al.* (2002), Flora of North America Editorial Committee (2000), Janes *et al.* (1996), Preston & Croft (1997).

C.D. PRESTON

N *Hydrilla verticillata* Esthwaite Waterweed
(L.f.) Royle

In Britain and Ireland, *H. verticillata* grows in relatively deep water in mesotrophic lakes, only occasionally extending into the shallows. The Irish population is known to be female, but flowers have never been seen in Britain. Reproduction is by turions. Lowland.

Trends Although this species was first discovered in Britain at Esthwaite Water (Westmorland) in 1914 it has not been seen at this site since 1941, and may have been eliminated by eutrophication. It survives at Lough Rusheenduff (West Galway), where it was discovered in 1935, and it was found at a single site in Kirkcudbrightshire in 1999.

Biogeography Eurasian Southern-temperate element, with a continental distribution in western Europe; widely naturalized outside its native range.

	GB	IR
Long term	No trend	No trend
Short term	No trend	No trend

Native	GB	IR
2000–19	1	2
1987–99	1	1
1970–86	0	1
pre-1970	1	1

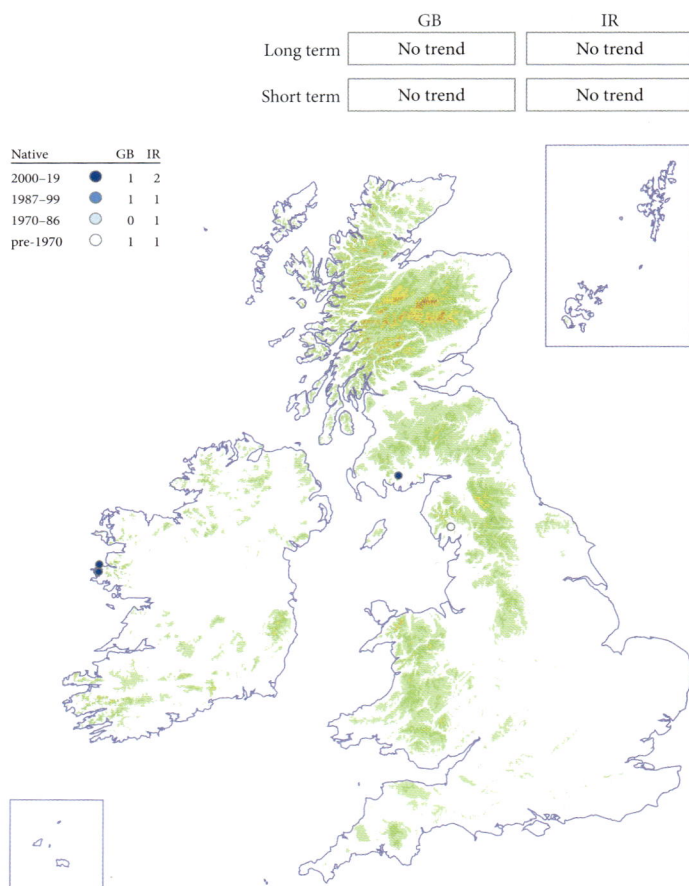

Key refs Langeland (1996), Preston & Croft (1997), Scannell & Webb (1976).

C.D. PRESTON

Ne *Lagarosiphon major* Curly Waterweed
(Ridl.) Moss ex V.A.Wager

A winter-green, perennial herb that grows as a submerged aquatic in standing waters, including lakes, ponds and flooded mineral workings, and in canals. It may be abundant in both small ponds and large lakes. In Lough Corrib, Galway, the most vigorous growth takes place in winter and by the spring it forms a dense canopy at the water surface that excludes most of the native macrophytes found elsewhere in the lake (Caffrey *et al.*, 2011). Only female plants have been recorded outside the native range, and reproduction is by vegetative fragmentation. Generally lowland, but reaching 470 m at Titterstone Clee (Shropshire).

Trends This commonly cultivated aquatic was first recorded as naturalized in Britain in 1944. Although it was not common enough to map in the 1962 *Atlas*, it was widespread by 2000 and has been recorded in many more sites since then. It almost certainly owes its spread to the release of discarded material from garden ponds or aquaria into the wild and subsequent vegetative reproduction.

Biogeography Native of southern Africa; widely established in western and central Europe and extensively naturalized in New Zealand.

GB	IR
Long term	No trend	No trend

Alien	GB	IR
2000–19	521	54
1987–99	426	13
1970–86	137	0
pre-1970	62	1

Key refs Caffrey *et al.* (2011), Preston & Croft (1997).

C.D. Preston

N *Najas flexilis* Slender Naiad
(Willd.) Rostk. & W.L.E.Schmidt

An aquatic annual herb that is usually rooted in fine, silty sediments in deep, clear, oligo-mesotrophic or mesotrophic lakes. These lakes are typically situated in acidic catchments but receive some base-enrichment from nearby basalt, limestone or calcareous dune-sand. Colonies characteristically grow at depths of 1·5 m or more, and extend into shallower water only in the most sheltered situations. Populations fluctuate in numbers from year to year, but the causes of such fluctuations are unknown. Lowland.

Trends *N. flexilis* formerly had a much wider distribution in Europe but its range contracted during the post-glacial period. It is an elusive species which has been recorded at an increasing number of British and Irish sites in recent decades as a result of intensive surveys. However, it was last seen at its only English site, Esthwaite Water (Westmorland), in 1982, and its loss there is clearly attributable to eutrophication (Bishop *et al.*, 2019). Eutrophication is also the main cause of the severe decline in mainland Scotland, combined with the spread of *Elodea* species. It now appears to have been lost from some sites where it was last recorded after 2000, including Loch of Butterstone and Loch of the Lowes, East Perthshire (Gunn & Carvallo, 2020).

Biogeography Circumpolar Boreal-montane element, with a disjunct distribution.

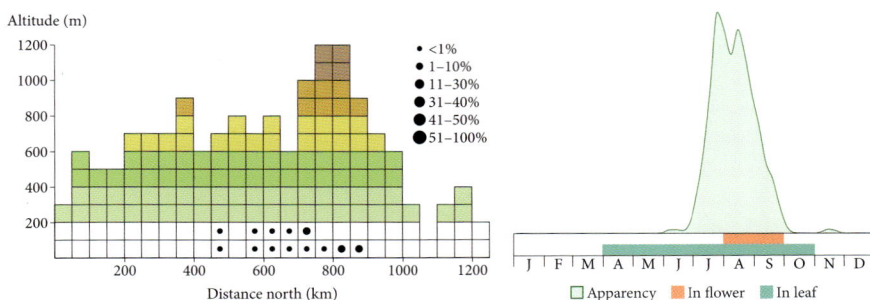

Native	GB	IR
2000–19	20	36
1987–99	19	22
1970–86	14	21
pre-1970	14	17

Alien	GB	IR
2000–19	0	0
1987–99	0	0
1970–86	0	0
pre-1970	1	0

Key refs Bishop *et al.* (2019), Gunn & Carvallo (2020), Preston & Croft (1997), Stewart *et al.* (1994), Wingfield *et al.* (2004).

C.D. Preston

Ⓝ *Najas marina* Holly-leaved Naiad
L.

An annual aquatic herb of meso-eutrophic water over deep substrates of peat or silty mud in the Norfolk Broads, including the mildly brackish Thurne Broads. It is also known from an ornamental lake and a marl-pit pond elsewhere in East Norfolk, in an artificial lake at Arundel, West Sussex, and in Darwell Reservoir, East Sussex. It is a dioecious annual; both sexes occur in Norfolk, but Handley & Davey (2000) found that female plants greatly outnumbered males in Hickling Broad. It is possible that some seed is produced apomictically. Lowland.

Trends First discovered in Britain in 1883 (Hickling Broad, East Norfolk), *N. marina* decreased in the late 1960s as a result of pollution, but has since responded to action which has been taken to reduce nutrient levels in the Norfolk Broads. It was first recorded outside the Broads system near Cawston in Norfolk in 2010, then found in Sussex at Arundel in 2015 (Lansdown *et al.*, 2016) and at Darwell Reservoir in 2019.

Biogeography Circumpolar Southern-temperate element, with a continental distribution in western Europe.

	GB	IR
Long term	No trend	No trend
Short term	No trend	No trend

Native	GB	IR
2000–19	7	0
1987–99	3	0
1970–86	4	0
pre-1970	4	0

Key refs Handley & Davy (2000), Lansdown *et al.* (2016), Preston & Croft (1997), Wigginton (1999).

C.D. PRESTON

Ⓝ *Scheuchzeria palustris* Rannoch-rush
L.

A rhizomatous perennial herb of deep blanket bogs, typically occurring along the edges of runnels, pools or semi-submerged *Sphagnum* lawns at pool edges. Although it formerly occurred close to sea level at Thorne Moors (South-west Yorkshire), its extant sites on Rannoch Moor are all at *c.* 300 m (Mid Perthshire and Main Argyll). It was found at 460 m near Coire Daingean, Westerness, in 2018.

Trends All English sites for *S. palustris* were lost before 1900 due to drainage and eutrophication of lowland mosses and mires. Its distribution in Scotland is probably stable; new sites have been found on Rannoch Moor and in 2018 for the first time in Westerness. This gives hope for further discoveries in remote upland bogs. It was discovered in County Offaly in 1951, but the original site was lost to peat extraction by 1960, and a nearby transplant did not survive.

Biogeography Circumpolar Boreal-montane element, with a continental distribution in western Europe.

	GB	IR
Long term	No trend	No trend
Short term	No trend	No trend

Native	GB	IR
2000–19	8	0
1987–99	5	0
1970–86	4	0
pre-1970	12	1

Alien	GB	IR
2000–19	0	0
1987–99	0	0
1970–86	0	0
pre-1970	1	0

Key refs Godwin (1975), Smith *et al.* (2021a), Wigginton (1999).

F.J. RUMSEY

Ne *Aponogeton distachyos* Cape-pondweed

L.f.

A tuberous-rooted perennial herb which grows as an emergent aquatic in water up to 2 m deep. It may persist for many years in lakes and ponds as a relic of cultivation, or at sites where it is introduced into the wild. It has been known to reproduce by seed in Britain, but shows little sign of spreading to new sites without human assistance. Lowland.

Trends This species was first cultivated in Britain in 1788 and is now popular in water gardens for its hawthorn-scented white flowers. It was recorded from the wild by 1889 (Middlesex) and it has persisted at Keston, West Kent, since 1909. It has been recorded with increasing frequency since 2000.

Biogeography Native of South Africa (Cape Province); established as an alien elsewhere in Africa and in western Europe, California, South America, Australia and New Zealand.

Long term	GB	IR
	No trend	No trend
Short term		No trend

Alien		GB	IR
2000–19	●	87	4
1987–99	●	48	0
1970–86	●	21	0
pre-1970	○	23	0

Key refs Flora of North America Editorial Committee (2000), Pemberton (2000), Preston & Croft (1997).

C.D. PRESTON

N *Triglochin palustris* Marsh Arrowgrass

L.

A slender, perennial, rhizomatous herb of open, damp, grassy or marshy places, often on calcareous substrates. Its habitats include wet meadows and rush-pastures, heaths, fens, springs and flushes, saltmarsh fringes flushed with fresh water, and river shingle in upland areas. 0–970 m (Beinn Heasgarnich, Mid Perthshire).

Trends *T. palustris* is inconspicuous, rarely present in quantity and may accordingly be overlooked. A marked decline in southern England has taken place since the 1960s, owing to the loss of its habitat through drainage, agricultural intensification and a lack of grazing or disturbance. In recent decades this decline has slowed, though the same damaging factors still account for losses locally, and there are fewer records than in previous atlas surveys in many lowland 10 km squares.

Biogeography Circumpolar Boreo-temperate element.

	GB					IR				
Long term	↓	↓	◆	↑	↑	↓	↓	◆	↑	↑
Short term	↓	↓	↑	↑	↑	↓	↓	↑	↑	↑

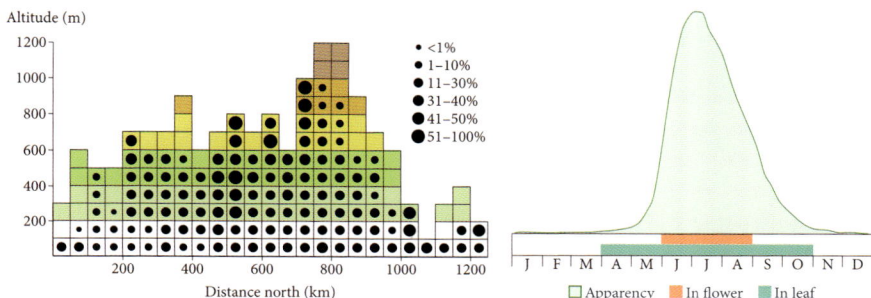

Native		GB	IR
2000–19	●	1588	569
1987–99	●	1685	602
1970–86	○	1195	124
pre-1970	○	1733	433

F.J. RUMSEY

N *Triglochin maritima* Sea Arrowgrass
L.

A rhizomatous perennial herb of saline habitats. It is abundant in coastal and estuarine saltmarshes, flushed coastal rocks and cliff edges subject to sea spray, and the banks of tidal rivers. Inland, it occurs in brackish pastures as, for example, over saline Keuper beds in Cheshire, and at one site in Hampshire in flushed turf on calcareous clay. Very rarely it grows alongside salt-treated roads. Usually lowland, but found at 380 m at Dirdhu (Moray), and at 575 m by the Hartside cafe in Cumberland.

Trends This species shows no appreciable change to its range since the 1990s. Losses from its few inland sites through habitat destruction are largely historical and the species distribution is stable.

Biogeography Circumpolar Boreo-temperate element.

Native	GB	IR
2000–19	778	257
1987–99	708	224
1970–86	422	92
pre-1970	690	168

Alien	GB	IR
2000–19	1	0
1987–99	0	0
1970–86	0	0
pre-1970	0	0

Key refs Davy & Bishop (1991), Lee (1977).

F.J. RUMSEY

Altitude (m) / Distance north (km)

<1% / 1–10% / 11–30% / 31–40% / 41–50% / 51–100%

Apparency / In flower / In leaf

N *Zostera marina* Eelgrass
L.

A rhizomatous perennial of tidal mudflats, in estuaries and coastal lagoons and in the subtidal zone, on substrates of gravel, sand, sandy mud and mud. It is usually found below the half-tide mark and descends to depths of about 4 metres. Plants with narrower leaves, often found in shallower, more turbid water in the upper parts of the tidal range, were formerly treated as *Z. angustifolia* and mapped as such in the 2002 *Atlas* but are now regarded as conspecific with *Z. marina*. Lowland.

Trends Populations of *Z. marina* all along the Atlantic coasts of Europe and North America were devastated in the 1930s by a wasting disease, caused by a protist, *Labyrinthula zosterae*, that was eventually described in 1991 (Ralph & Short, 2002). The species has never fully recovered and has later been affected by further, small-scale outbreaks of the disease. There are obvious difficulties in recording this marine species and many old and recent records are based on stranded plants. However, sea-grass beds in Britain and Ireland are believed to have declined since 1990 (Jones & Unsworth, 2016; Green *et al.*, 2021). Jones & Unsworth's biometrical survey in 2013 concluded that surviving beds of *Z. marina* are in a perilous state, and in particular stressed by nitrogen enrichment, even in sites such as Skomer, Pembrokeshire. Only in sites remote from large population centres, such as the Isles of Scilly and Mannin Bay, West Galway, are they in a healthy condition.

Biogeography Circumpolar Wide-temperate element.

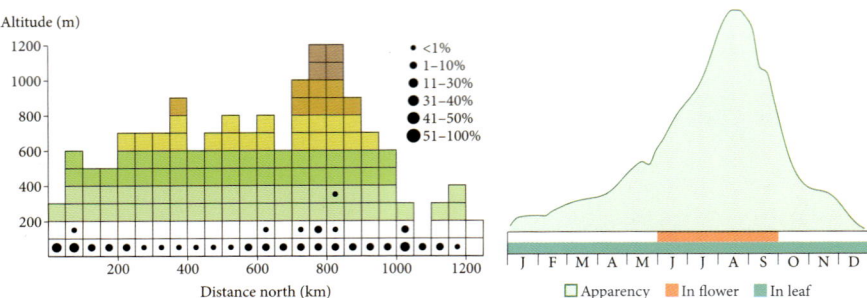

Native	GB	IR
2000–19	203	72
1987–99	182	53
1970–86	148	24
pre-1970	301	45

Key refs Borum *et al.* (2004), den Hartog (1970), Green *et al.* (2021), Jones & Unsworth (2016), Ralph & Short (2002), Stewart *et al.* (1994), Tutin (1942).

C.D. PRESTON

Altitude (m) / Distance north (km)

<1% / 1–10% / 11–30% / 31–40% / 41–50% / 51–100%

Apparency / In flower / In leaf

N *Zostera noltei* Dwarf Eelgrass

Hornem.

Although a coastal species, this rhizomatous perennial is found at higher levels of the shore than *Z. marina*. It grows in the inter-tidal zone in sheltered estuaries, bays and harbours, where it is found on mixed substrates of sand and mud. Plants are often concentrated in pools or runnels on the shore. Compared with other European seagrasses, it is a small, rapidly growing species producing shoots with a short lifespan and small fruits; it is thus well adapted to withstand disturbance and to respond to improving environmental conditions (Borum *et al.*, 2004). Lowland.

Trends *Z. noltei* is less vulnerable to poor water quality than *Z. marina*, although it is adversely affected by heavy urban and industrial pollution. Detailed surveys this century in Milford Haven, Pembrokeshire, have shown that the larger populations are robust

and thriving and have even expanded in area (Bertelli *et al.*, 2018). The reason for the lack of recent records from many sites away from the main estuaries requires further research. *Z. noltei* may be under-recorded, though it is easier to survey than *Z. marina* as long as recorders are prepared to devote time to its otherwise unrewarding habitat. However, small populations in Milford Haven are more transient than larger colonies and the map may reflect similar fluctuations elsewhere.

Biogeography Eurasian Southern-temperate element.

Native	GB	IR
2000–19	84	23
1987–99	71	21
1970–86	95	19
pre-1970	123	26

Alien	GB	IR
2000–19	0	0
1987–99	0	0
1970–86	0	0
pre-1970	1	0

Key refs Bertelli *et al.* (2018), Borum *et al.* (2004), den Hartog (1970), Stewart *et al.* (1994).

C.D. PRESTON

N *Potamogeton natans* Broad-leaved Pondweed

L.

This rhizomatous perennial herb is frequent as a floating-leaved aquatic in still or slowly flowing waters, and more rarely found as plants with submerged phyllodes in more rapid streams and rivers. It has a very wide ecological tolerance, growing in oligotrophic to eutrophic and base-poor to base-rich water over a wide range of substrates. Although it may be found in shallow swamps, or in water over 5 m deep, it is most frequent at moderate depths of 1–2 metres. It is sometimes deliberately introduced in ponds. 0–760 m (below Stob Ban, Westerness).

Trends There is no evidence for any overall change in the 10 km square distribution of *P. natans* since systematic recording at the hectad scale began in the 1950s.

Biogeography Circumpolar Boreo-temperate element.

Native	GB	IR
2000–19	2144	649
1987–99	2065	615
1970–86	1396	135
pre-1970	1426	108

Key refs Grime *et al.* (2007), Preston (1995b), Preston & Croft (1997).

C.D. PRESTON

N *Potamogeton polygonifolius* Bog Pondweed
Pourr.

This rhizomatous perennial herb may grow as an aquatic in shallow water in lakes, pools, the backwaters of rivers, streams and ditches, or in a dwarf, subterrestrial state in wet *Sphagnum* lawns or 'brown moss' communities. It is usually restricted to acidic water, only rarely occurring in highly calcareous but nutrient-poor sites. Plants fruit freely in most habitats. 0–780 m (Lochan an Tairbh-uisge, Mid Perthshire).

Trends This species has been lost from areas of south-eastern England where suitable habitats have always been rare, and have been gradually reduced over recent centuries by habitat destruction, drainage or falling water-tables. It remains a frequent species in the more acidic areas of Britain and Ireland. The dramatic increase in 10 km squares since the 1960s is attributable to caution in

accepting unlocalized pre-1970 records of *Potamogeton* taxa (Preston, 1995).

Biogeography Suboceanic Temperate element; also in North America.

Native	GB	IR
2000–19	1681	650
1987–99	1588	545
1970–86	1059	115
pre-1970	1130	120

Alien	GB	IR
2000–19	1	0
1987–99	0	0
1970–86	1	0
pre-1970	0	0

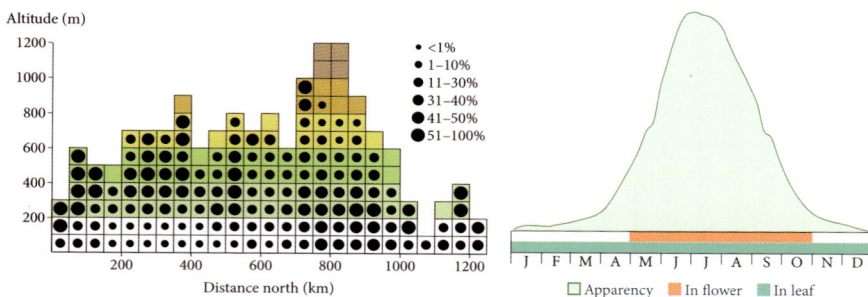

Key refs Preston (1995b), Preston & Croft (1997).

C.D. PRESTON

N *Potamogeton coloratus* Fen Pondweed
Hornem.

This winter-green, rhizomatous perennial aquatic herb is found in shallow, calcium-rich but nutrient-poor waters in lakes, pools, clay-pits, shallow streams and ditches. It grows over a range of substrates, including peat, marl, sand and clay. It is self-compatible and typically sets copious amounts of seed; there is some evidence that the seeds can persist in a seed bank for over 30 years (Kaplan *et al.*, 2014). Lowland.

Trends *P. coloratus* has declined over much of its British range, having been lost from many sites because of drainage or eutrophication. Many remaining localities are in nature reserves. It has, however, also colonized some new habitats since 1930, such as abandoned brickfields in Peterborough. In Ireland it is almost certainly still more frequent in the central plain than the map suggests.

Biogeography European Southern-temperate element.

Native	GB	IR
2000–19	76	74
1987–99	74	101
1970–86	63	46
pre-1970	118	42

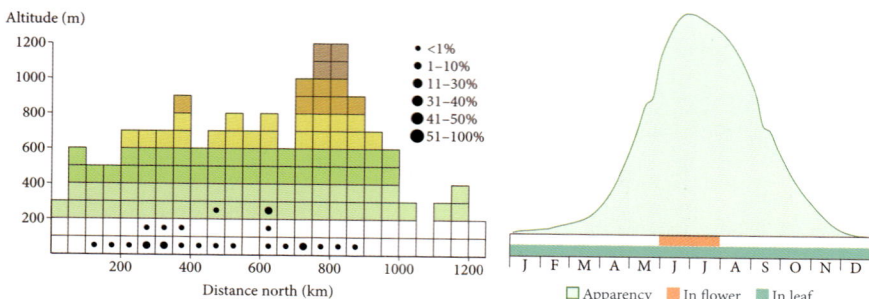

Key refs Kaplan *et al.* (2014), Preston (1995b), Preston & Croft (1997), Stewart *et al.* (1994).

C.D. PRESTON

N *Potamogeton nodosus* Loddon Pondweed

Poir.

This rhizomatous perennial herb is confined to a few calcareous and moderately eutrophic rivers, where it grows in shallow or fairly deep water. In the River Stour (Dorset) it is found over gravelly substrates and avoids soft muds and clays (Preston, 1995b), though in the Thames it grows over silt in slow-flowing stretches and sheltered backwaters (R.V. Lansdown, pers. comm.). It reproduces vegetatively but it has not been found with fruits in Britain. Lowland.

Trends *P. nodosus* has a relatively stable distribution in the Bristol Avon, the Dorset Stour and the River Loddon (Berkshire). In the late 20th century it was thought to be extinct in the Thames, perhaps eliminated in the 1950s by eutrophication and increasing pleasure-boat traffic, but it was rediscovered in 2009 and is now known from several sites in the river. The record from the Warwickshire Stour is based on a single, 19th century specimen.

Biogeography Circumpolar Southern-temperate element.

Long term	GB					IR
						No trend
Short term						No trend

Native	GB	IR
2000–19	16	0
1987–99	9	0
1970–86	11	0
pre-1970	13	0

Alien	GB	IR
2000–19	0	0
1987–99	1	0
1970–86	0	0
pre-1970	0	0

Altitude (m) chart; Distance north (km)

- <1%
- 1–10%
- 11–30%
- 31–40%
- 41–50%
- 51–100%

☐ Apparency   ☐ In flower   ☐ In leaf

Key refs Preston (1995a), Preston (1995b), Preston & Croft (1997), Wigginton (1999).

C.D. PRESTON

N *Potamogeton lucens* Shining Pondweed

L.

A rhizomatous perennial herb with submerged but no floating leaves, *P. lucens* grows in relatively deep, calcareous water in lakes, larger rivers, canals, flooded chalk- and gravel-pits and major fenland drains. It is found in clear, nutrient-poor, unpolluted waters as well as more eutrophic and turbid sites. 0–380 m (Malham Tarn, Mid-west Yorkshire).

Trends *P. lucens* is a conspicuous and easily identified species. A decline at the fringes of its range was already apparent by the late 20th century, especially in eastern Scotland where some of the lakes in which it grew were particularly vulnerable to eutrophication (Preston & Croft, 1995). The failure of recorders to refind it in many of the English hectads in which it was recorded between 1970 and 1999 suggests a further reduction in range. It remains frequent in the calcareous waters of central Ireland.

Biogeography Eurosiberian Temperate element.

	GB					IR
Long term						
Short term						

Native	GB	IR
2000–19	218	160
1987–99	284	126
1970–86	221	52
pre-1970	365	68

Altitude (m) chart; Distance north (km)

- <1%
- 1–10%
- 11–30%
- 31–40%
- 41–50%
- 51–100%

☐ Apparency   ☐ In flower   ☐ In leaf

Key refs Preston (1995b), Preston & Croft (1997).

C.D. PRESTON

Hy *Potamogeton gramineus × lucens = P. ×angustifolius*
Long-leaved Pondweed
J.Presl

This rhizomatous perennial is found in a range of waters including lakes, rivers, streams, fenland lodes and large ditches. It is usually found in at least moderately deep water (>0·5 m), although it does sometimes occur in places where water levels fluctuate, such as the Breckland meres in West Norfolk. It may survive periods when water levels are low as dwarf terrestrial plants, but it is much less frequent than *P. gramineus* in shallow, fluctuating waters. In Scotland it is characteristically found in mesotrophic lakes with at least slight base-enrichment, often in the absence of *P. lucens*, sometimes in the absence of both parents. It is morphologically variable and some populations are sterile whereas others set well-formed fruit. 0–395 m (Loch na Craige, Mid Perthshire).

A spontaneous hybrid (native × native).

Trends There is little evidence for the decline of this hybrid in north-western Ireland and western Scotland, where it is probably under-recorded. In eastern Ireland, eastern Scotland and England there is a clear decline, probably because of eutrophication coupled with the loss of sympathetic management of drains and ditches. Such decline matches that of *P. lucens* in eastern Scotland and *P. gramineus* in England and eastern Scotland.

Biogeography Widespread in temperate Europe.

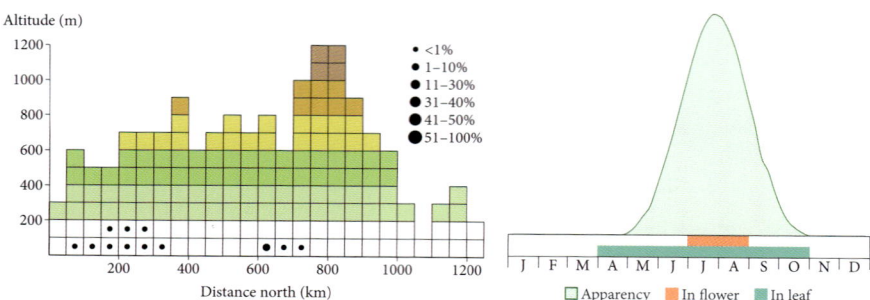

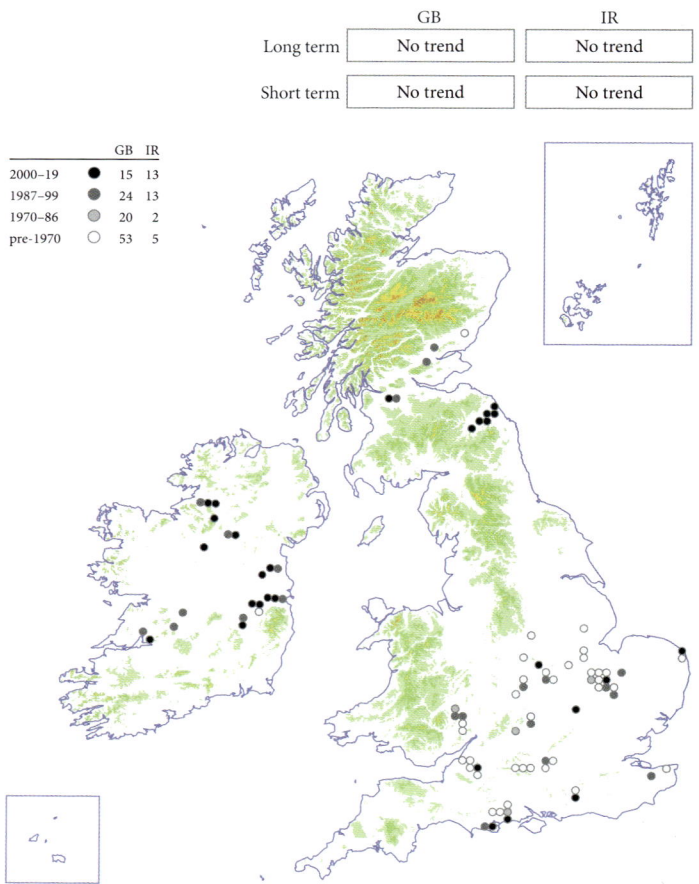

		GB	IR
2000–19	●	29	66
1987–99	●	43	56
1970–86	●	24	13
pre-1970	○	74	59

	GB	IR
Long term		
Short term	No trend	No trend

Altitude (m)

<1%
1–10%
11–30%
31–40%
41–50%
51–100%

Distance north (km)

J F M A M J J A S O N D
☐ Apparency ■ In flower ■ In leaf

Key refs Stace *et al.* (2015).

C.D. Preston

Hy *Potamogeton lucens × perfoliatus = P. ×salicifolius*
Willow-leaved Pondweed
Wolfg.

This rhizomatous perennial is well-established and locally frequent in slowly flowing rivers, canals and deep fenland drains; it is also recorded from a few lakes. It requires relatively deep, moderately or strongly calcareous, meso-eutrophic or eutrophic water. Lowland.

A spontaneous hybrid (native × native).

Trends *P. ×salicifolius* has become extinct in some lakes because of eutrophication, and it appears to be less frequent than formerly in canals. However, it is similar in morphology to *P. lucens* and is probably under-recorded. Some populations are well established and long persistent, notably those in the River Tweed and River Wye, where the hybrid was first collected in 1830 and 1854 respectively.

Biogeography Widespread in temperate Europe.

		GB	IR
2000–19	●	15	13
1987–99	●	24	13
1970–86	●	20	2
pre-1970	○	53	5

	GB	IR
Long term	No trend	No trend
Short term	No trend	No trend

Altitude (m)

<1%
1–10%
11–30%
31–40%
41–50%
51–100%

Distance north (km)

J F M A M J J A S O N D
☐ Apparency ■ In flower ■ In leaf

Key refs Stace *et al.* (2015).

C.D. Preston

Potamogeton gramineus Various-leaved Pondweed
L.

This variable rhizomatous perennial herb is found in relatively shallow water in a variety of water bodies, including lakes, reservoirs, rivers, streams, canals and ditches. It tolerates a wide range of water quality, although it is absent both from the most acidic and oligotrophic sites and from the most eutrophic. It withstands fluctuating water levels and can even survive occasional, short-term desiccation. 0–915 m (Meall nan Tarmachan, Mid Perthshire).

Trends Like some other broad-leaved *Potamogeton* species and hybrids, *P. gramineus* has gradually been lost from many sites in the southern part of its British range. It has suffered from habitat loss and has been eliminated from surviving habitats by processes such as the conversion of grassland landscapes to arable, reduced ditch management, falling water tables and eutrophication.

Biogeography Circumpolar Boreo-temperate element.

Native	GB	IR
2000–19	219	132
1987–99	266	112
1970–86	217	55
pre-1970	325	90

Key refs Preston (1995b), Preston & Croft (1997).

C.D. PRESTON

Potamogeton gramineus × perfoliatus = P. ×nitens
Bright-leaved Pondweed
Weber

This rhizomatous perennial is the most frequent pondweed hybrid in our area, found in more or less mesotrophic water in lakes, reservoirs, streams, canals, fenland lodes and ditches, and occasionally in flooded sand- and gravel-pits. It may be present in abundance, growing in large beds in smoothly flowing rivers, lakes and reservoirs. Plants are most luxuriant in water 0·5–1·5 m deep, but like *P. gramineus* this hybrid will also grow as small plants in very shallow water in streams and at the edges of lakes and reservoirs. It can persist as terrestrial plants on mud at times when water levels are very low. 0–640 m (Loch Oss, West Perthshire).

A spontaneous hybrid (native × native).

Trends *P. ×nitens* is a sterile hybrid which can resemble *P. gramineus* very closely, and is almost certainly under-recorded. Like *P. gramineus* and *P. ×angustifolius*, it has declined in south-eastern England and East Anglia.

Biogeography Widespread in boreal and temperate regions of Europe and also recorded elsewhere in the Northern Hemisphere.

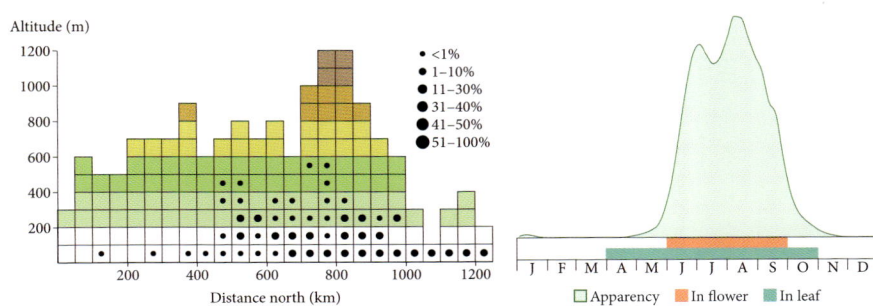

	GB	IR
2000–19	83	64
1987–99	148	73
1970–86	71	19
pre-1970	121	46

Key refs Stace *et al.* (2015).

C.D. PRESTON

(N) *Potamogeton alpinus* Red Pondweed
Balb.

A rhizomatous perennial aquatic herb of still or slow-flowing water in lakes, rivers, canals, ditches and flooded mineral workings. *P. alpinus* is often found in sites where silt accumulates, such as lake inflows or backwaters in rivers. It characteristically grows in mesotrophic, often neutral or mildly acidic water. 0–945 m (Meall nan Tarmachan, Mid Perthshire).

Trends Many of the sites from which *P. alpinus* has been lost in England are small ponds, pits and ditches where it was last seen in the 19th century. Evidence from recent recording suggests that this retreat northwards and westwards continues, even if allowance is made for the inadequate recording of aquatic plants in some areas. Many recent losses have been ascribed to eutrophication.

Biogeography Circumpolar Boreal-montane element.

Native		GB	IR
2000–19	●	187	102
1987–99	●	247	101
1970–86	○	214	30
pre-1970	○	362	60

Alien		GB	IR
2000–19	●	0	0
1987–99	●	0	0
1970–86	●	1	0
pre-1970	○	0	0

Key refs Preston (1995b), Preston & Croft (1997).

C.D. PRESTON

(N) *Potamogeton praelongus* Long-stalked Pondweed
Wulfen

This winter-green, rhizomatous perennial herb is the most characteristic pondweed of deep water in Britain and Ireland, usually growing at depths greater than 1 m in clear, mesotrophic water in lakes, rivers, canals and major drains. It has only rarely been recorded from shallow water. 0–800 m (Loch Coire Cheap, Mid Perthshire).

Trends *P. praelongus* appears to have been lost from many waters in the southern half of its range since 1930. The most likely cause of this decline is eutrophication. However, there has been a minor resurgence in the East Midlands (Northamptonshire, Cambridgeshire) since 2010. As a species of deeper water it can be inconspicuous; it was well-recorded in the Scottish loch surveys in the 1980s

and 1990s but has been less intensively surveyed in Scotland since 2000.

Biogeography Circumpolar Boreal-montane element.

Native		GB	IR
2000–19	●	114	93
1987–99	●	117	59
1970–86	○	82	27
pre-1970	○	192	34

Key refs Preston (1995b), Preston & Croft (1997), Stewart *et al.* (1994).

C.D. PRESTON

Potamogeton perfoliatus Perfoliate Pondweed
L.

An aquatic herb characteristically found in larger water bodies, occasionally growing in oligotrophic sites but more often found in mesotrophic or eutrophic conditions. It is a rhizomatous perennial that grows in shallow water in sites which are not prone to occasional desiccation, but is most vigorous at depths of 1 m or more. It fruits freely in still water. 0–780 m (Loch an Tairbh-uisge, Mid Perthshire).

Trends An initial decline of *P. perfoliatus* was noted in some areas of lowland England in the 2002 *Atlas*, and the 21st century records, if taken at face value, suggest that it has now suffered a much more serious contraction of range. Further studies are needed to test whether this decline is as bad as it appears, or whether it is in part attributable to the under-recording of an easily identified aquatic. In Scotland and

Northern Ireland many records were made during intensive lake surveys in the 1980s and 1900s, so under-recording is a more obvious explanation of apparent losses there.

Biogeography Circumpolar Boreo-temperate element, with a disjunct distribution.

Native	GB	IR
2000–19	571	308
1987–99	738	249
1970–86	550	88
pre-1970	700	85

Key refs Preston (1995b), Preston & Croft (1997).

C.D. Preston

Potamogeton epihydrus American Pondweed
Raf.

In the Outer Hebrides, this rhizomatous perennial herb grows in a few peaty lochans, in oligotrophic and base-poor water less than 1 m deep. It is also established in the mesotrophic Rochdale Canal (South Lancashire) and the Calder & Hebble Navigation (Southwest Yorkshire). Plants from Loch na Creitheach, Skye (North Ebudes) have been tentatively identified as this species; it is known only from washed-up submerged leaves, and repeated attempts to find adequate material or a rooted colony have been unsuccessful. Lowland.

Trends This species was first discovered in England near Halifax (South-west Yorkshire) in 1907; although it must be an introduction there, the manner of its arrival from North America is unclear. It was not found in the Outer Hebrides,

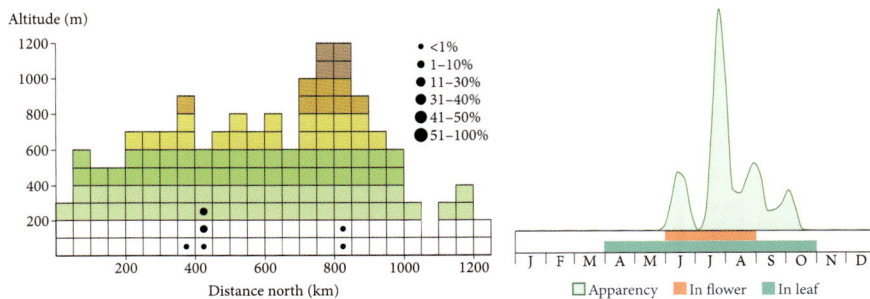

where it is native, until 1943, and there is no evidence for any subsequent change in its distribution or abundance there.

Biogeography Oceanic Boreo-temperate element; in Europe restricted to Britain but widespread in North America.

Native	GB	IR
2000–19	2	0
1987–99	3	0
1970–86	1	0
pre-1970	2	0

Alien	GB	IR
2000–19	4	0
1987–99	8	0
1970–86	4	0
pre-1970	4	0

Key refs Flora of North America Editorial Committee (2000), Preston (1995b), Preston & Croft (1997), Wigginton (1999).

C.D. Preston

N *Potamogeton friesii* Flat-stalked Pondweed
Rupr.

An aquatic herb of calcareous and often rather eutrophic, still or very slowly flowing waters. These include lakes, sluggish rivers and streams, canals, fenland lodes and flooded mineral workings. Plants fruit rather rarely and the normal mode of reproduction is by turions. Lowland.

Trends *P. friesii* expanded through the canal network, and subsequently declined as canals became disused or dominated by pleasure-boat traffic. It may be even more under-recorded than other linear-leaved pondweeds as it tends to die down earlier in the season than many aquatics, so that the extent of any decline in other habitats is difficult to assess.

Biogeography Circumpolar Boreo-temperate element, with a disjunct distribution.

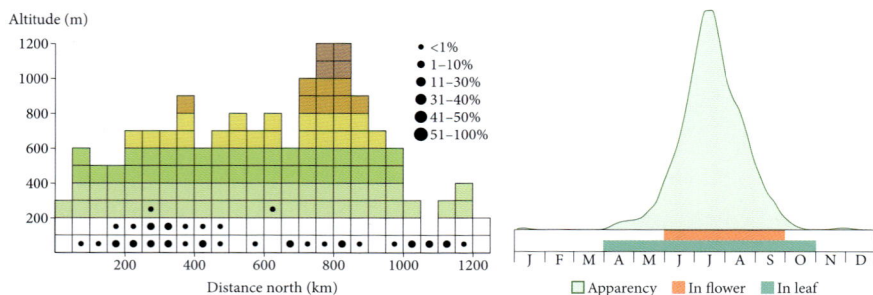

		GB	IR
Long term		↓	↑
Short term		↓	↓

Native		GB	IR
2000–19	●	107	35
1987–99	●	100	25
1970–86	○	107	12
pre-1970	○	225	13

Altitude (m) chart — x-axis Distance north (km); dot-size key: <1%, 1–10%, 11–30%, 31–40%, 41–50%, 51–100%

Phenology chart: J F M A M J J A S O N D — Apparency, In flower, In leaf

Key refs Preston (1995b), Preston & Croft (1997), Stewart *et al.* (1994).

C.D. PRESTON

N *Potamogeton rutilus* Shetland Pondweed
Wolfg.

This aquatic herb grows submerged in unpolluted, more or less mesotrophic lochs and adjoining streams, usually where there is some base-enrichment. It has only rarely been found with fruit in Scotland, and normally reproduces by turions. 0–350 m (Drumore Loch, Angus).

Trends In 1962 *P. rutilus* was regarded as a very rare species, known only from the Outer Hebrides and Shetland. Intensive surveys of aquatic habitats have gradually revealed more colonies, and others perhaps remain to be discovered. It has been lost from at least one site, Loch Flemington (Easterness), because of eutrophication.

Biogeography European Boreal-montane element.

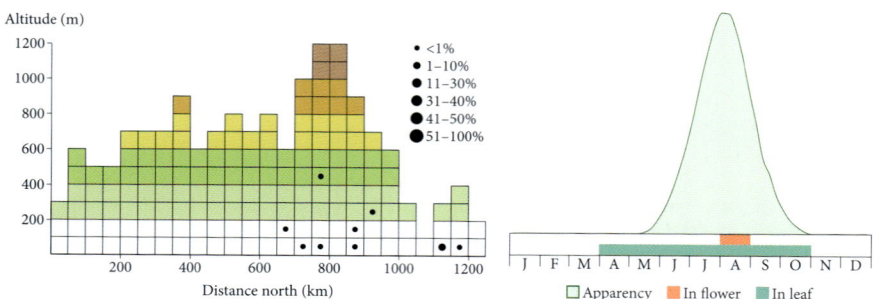

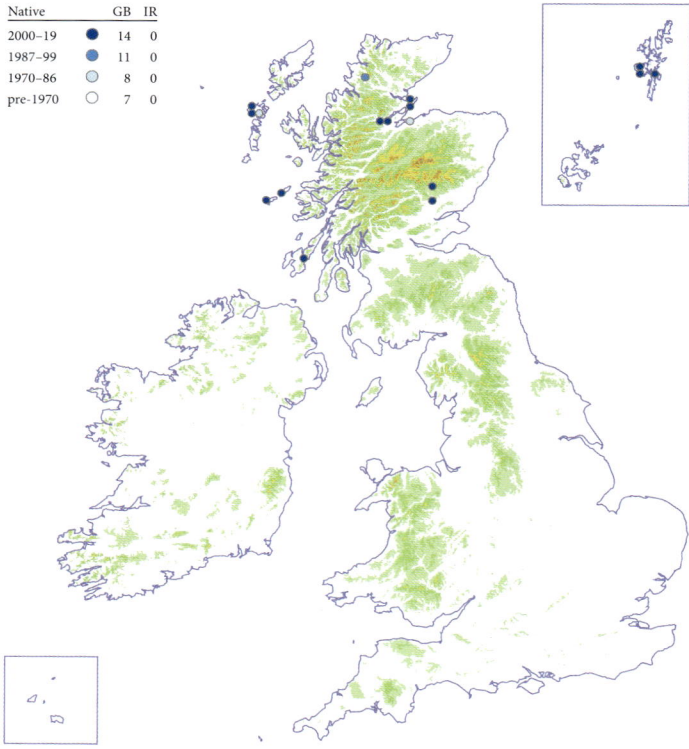

	GB	IR
Long term	No trend	No trend
Short term	No trend	No trend

Native		GB	IR
2000–19	●	14	0
1987–99	●	11	0
1970–86	○	8	0
pre-1970	○	7	0

Altitude (m) chart — x-axis Distance north (km); dot-size key: <1%, 1–10%, 11–30%, 31–40%, 41–50%, 51–100%

Phenology chart: J F M A M J J A S O N D — Apparency, In flower, In leaf

Key refs Preston (1995b), Preston & Croft (1997), Wallace (2005), Wigginton (1999).

C.D. PRESTON

N *Potamogeton obtusifolius* Blunt-leaved Pondweed
Mert. & W.D.J.Koch

An aquatic herb characteristically found in mesotrophic or meso-eutrophic, acidic or neutral standing waters in lakes, ponds and flooded mineral workings, or in canals and the backwaters of rivers. It may, however, occupy a broader habitat range in areas such as Northern Ireland where it is especially frequent. It fruits freely, and also reproduces by turions. 0–480 m (Angle Tarn, Patterdale, Westmorland).

Trends In the 2002 *Atlas* it was suggested that *P. obtusifolius* had declined throughout much of its British range and this is supported by the results of later recording, although the picture is complicated by the possibility that populations may come and go, at least in smaller water bodies, and by the vagaries of aquatic recording. The last records from hectads with no recent records span a notably wide range from the mid-19th century to the 1990s. There is less evidence of decline in Ireland.

Biogeography Circumpolar Boreo-temperate element, with a disjunct distribution.

Native	GB	IR
2000–19	298	175
1987–99	345	127
1970–86	303	46
pre-1970	354	55

Alien	GB	IR
2000–19	1	0
1987–99	0	0
1970–86	1	0
pre-1970	0	0

Key refs Preston (1995b), Preston & Croft (1997).

C.D. PRESTON

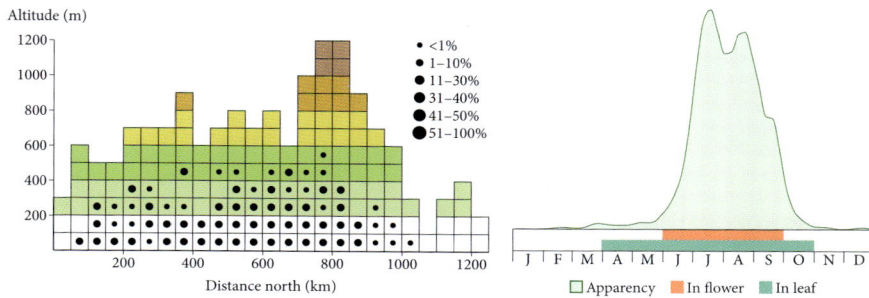

N *Potamogeton pusillus* Lesser Pondweed
L.

An aquatic herb of standing or slowly flowing water in sheltered lakes and reservoirs, ponds, rivers, canals, ditches and flooded mineral workings. It favours mesotrophic to eutrophic water and tolerates slightly brackish conditions. Plants are self-compatible and easily self-pollinated; they produce seeds freely and also reproduce by turions. The species often colonizes new sites. 0–320 m (Stony Middleton, Derbyshire).

Trends *P. pusillus* and *P. berchtoldii* were confused in our area until 1938 and many recorders still struggle to identify them, so the records are difficult to interpret. However, there is increasing evidence that *P. pusillus* has replaced *P. berchtoldii* as the more common of the two species in the eutrophic English lowlands.

Biogeography Circumpolar Southern-temperate element.

Native	GB	IR
2000–19	632	103
1987–99	545	135
1970–86	384	24
pre-1970	498	32

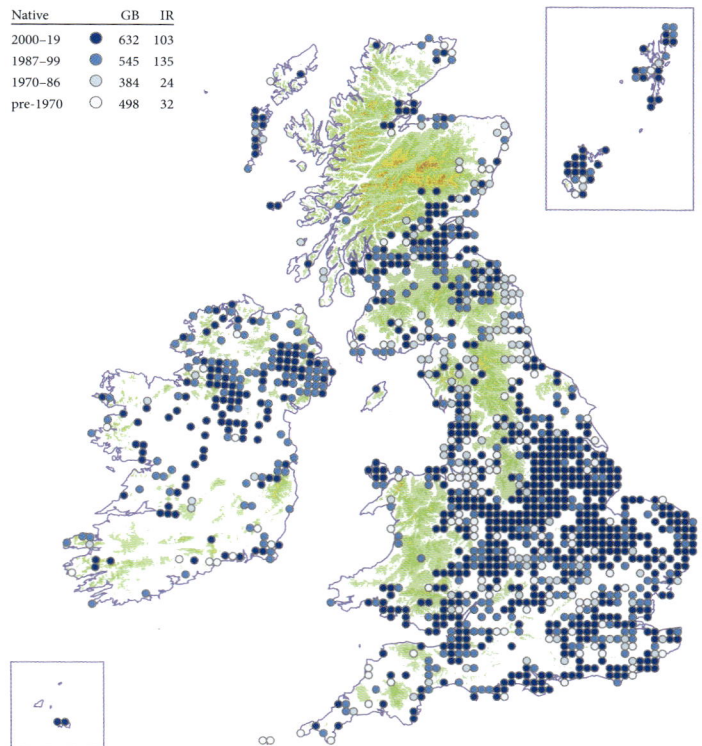

Key refs Kaplan & Štěpánek (2003), Preston (1995b), Preston & Croft (1997).

C.D. PRESTON

N *Potamogeton berchtoldii* Small Pondweed
Fieber

A variable aquatic herb which occurs in a wide range of still or slowly flowing waters, which may be base-rich or base-poor, oligotrophic, mesotrophic or eutrophic, and exposed or sheltered. *P. berchtoldii* is sometimes found in brackish sites, but is usually replaced in such habitats by *P. pusillus*. The species is self-compatible and easily self-pollinated; populations in shallow water produce seeds freely and all populations reproduce by turions. The species often colonizes new sites. 0–710 m (Lochan nan Cat, Mid Perthshire).

Trends Until 1938, *P. berchtoldii* was confused with *P. pusillus* in our area. It is under-recorded by botanists who neglect linear-leaved pondweeds but may be over-recorded by others who assume that linear-leaved species are *P. berchtoldii* and fail to identify material microscopically. The maps, although difficult to interpret, are consistent with the view that *P. pusillus* has replaced *P. berchtoldii* as the more frequent taxon in the eutrophic lowlands, although the latter remains frequent in the north and west. In Scotland and Northern Ireland many records were made by lake surveys in the late 20th century and recording has been less intensive since 2000.

Biogeography Circumpolar Boreo-temperate element.

Native		GB	IR
2000–19	●	990	335
1987–99	●	1004	265
1970–86	○	660	87
pre-1970	○	799	111

Key refs Kaplan & Štěpánek (2003), Preston (1995b), Preston & Croft (1997).

C.D. PRESTON

N *Potamogeton trichoides* Hairlike Pondweed
Cham. & Schltdl.

An aquatic herb found in a range of still or slowly flowing, mesotrophic or eutrophic waters including lakes, ponds, rivers, canals, ditches and flooded mineral workings. It often colonizes disturbed sites such as recently cleared canals and ditches. Reproduction is by seed and by turions. Lowland.

Trends This linear-leaved pondweed is very easily overlooked, especially when growing with *P. pusillus*, and it is only likely to be recognized by experienced recorders. However, botanists have gradually become more conscious of it in recent decades. This makes trends in its distribution hard to assess, but there is evidence of a genuine increase in frequency since 1960 in the Somerset Levels and a more recent increase in the Ouse Washes (Cadbury *et al.*, 2003), perhaps because of eutrophication. This is probably also true of other areas of England, and increases have also been reported from the Netherlands (Bruinsma, 1996, Mesters, 1995) and north-western Germany (Wiegleb *et al.*, 1991).

Biogeography Eurosiberian Southern-temperate element.

Native		GB	IR
2000–19	●	185	0
1987–99	●	120	0
1970–86	○	76	0
pre-1970	○	106	0

Alien		GB	IR
2000–19	●	0	0
1987–99	●	1	0
1970–86	●	0	0
pre-1970	○	0	0

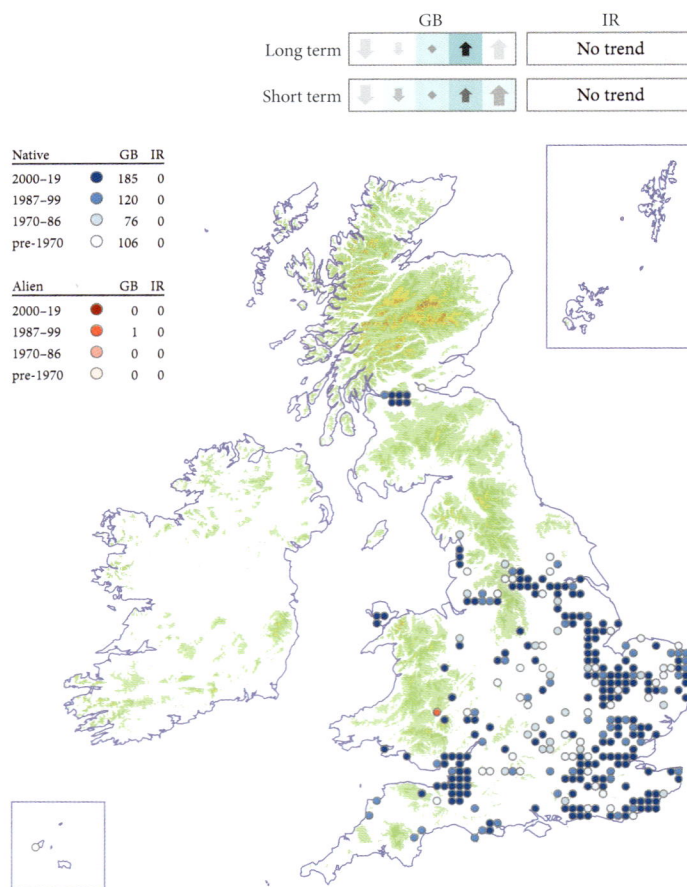

Key refs Bruinsma (1996), Cadbury *et al.* (2003), Mesters (1995), Preston (1995b), Preston & Croft (1997), Stewart *et al.* (1994), Wiegleb *et al.* (1991).

C.D. PRESTON

N *Potamogeton compressus* Grass-wrack Pondweed

L.

This aquatic herb has been recorded from a wide range of habitats: lakes, sluggish rivers, ditches, canals and flooded mineral workings. Its sites share a tendency to be still or slowly flowing, mesotrophic to eutrophic and slightly to moderately base-rich. Plants rarely fruit and the normal mode of reproduction is by the rather large turions. Lowland.

Trends This species appears to have been in gradual decline for over 150 years. By 2000 it was almost extinct in lakes and rivers and declining in grazing marsh ditches but there were some flourishing populations in canals, especially the Montgomery branch of the Shropshire Union Canal. However, it has subsequently undergone an unexpected resurgence in the eastern part of its range in the English Midlands, recolonizing Cambridgeshire from the River Nene in Northamptonshire and now known in numerous sites in this area.

Biogeography Eurasian Boreo-temperate element; declining throughout its European range.

Native		GB	IR
2000–19	●	35	0
1987–99	●	38	0
1970–86	○	43	0
pre-1970	○	125	0

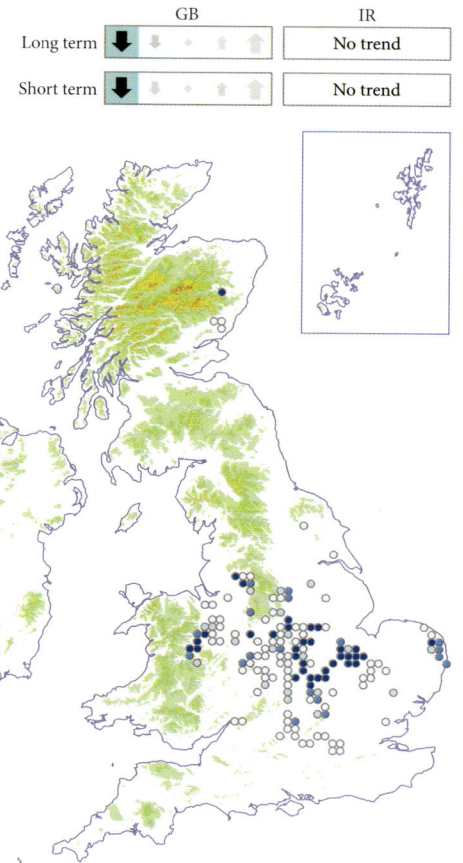

Key refs Birkinshaw *et al.* (2013), Graham & Preston (2012), Preston (1995b), Preston & Croft (1997), Stewart *et al.* (1994).

C.D. Preston

N *Potamogeton acutifolius* Sharp-leaved Pondweed

Link

This submerged aquatic herb has a very narrow habitat niche, being confined to shallow, species-rich drainage ditches in lowland grazing marshes, where it typically grows in calcareous, mesotrophic or meso-eutrophic water. It tends to be most abundant in the second to fourth years after ditches are slubbed out, and declines thereafter (Newbold, 2003b). Although it fruits relatively freely and also produces turions, it shows little or no propensity to colonize new localities. Lowland.

Trends *P. acutifolius* has suffered a gradual, long-term decline. Since 1960 it has decreased in Norfolk, become extinct in the London area and been reduced to a single population in Dorset. However, the range now appears to have stabilized and several vigorous populations survive in Sussex.

Biogeography European Temperate element; scarce and declining throughout its European range.

Native		GB	IR
2000–19	●	10	0
1987–99	●	14	0
1970–86	○	14	0
pre-1970	○	30	0

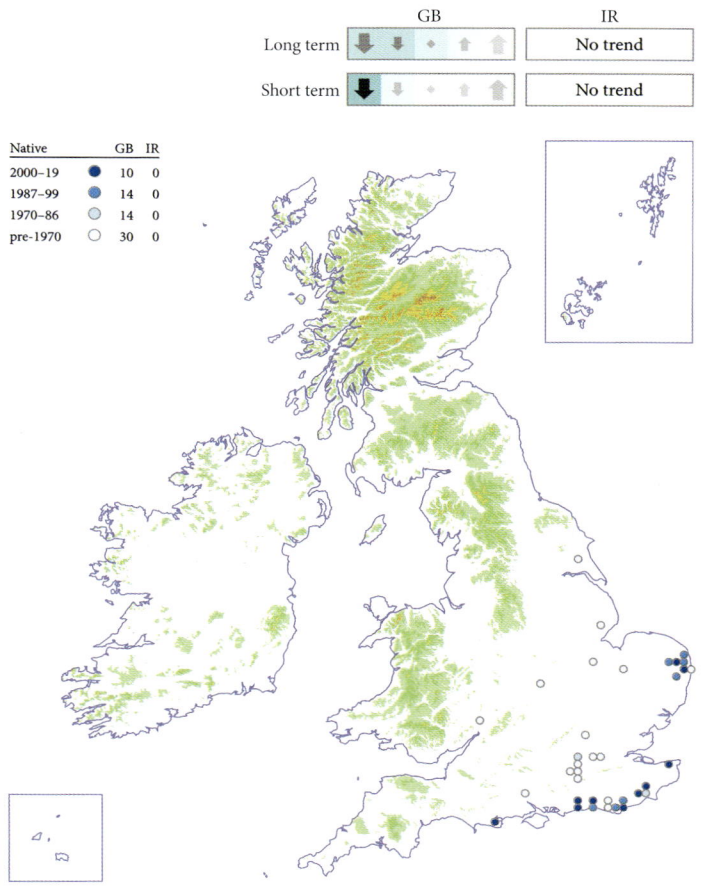

Key refs Lansdown (2021a), Newbold (2003b), Preston (1995b), Preston & Croft (1997), Preston & Pearman (1998), Wigginton (1999).

C.D. Preston

N *Potamogeton crispus* Curled Pondweed

L.

A winter-green, rhizomatous perennial aquatic herb which grows in a wide range of mesotrophic or eutrophic waters. These include lakes, ponds, rivers, streams, canals, ditches and disused mineral workings. It is more tolerant of eutrophication than most British pondweeds. Although fruit production is not uncommon, the usual mode of reproduction is probably by turions. Generally lowland, but reaching 400 m at Loch Kennard (Mid Perthshire).

Trends This is the most distinctive *Potamogeton* species in our area, and it is therefore relatively well recorded. There is little evidence for any change in its overall British or Irish distribution since the 1960s although it now appears to be more common in many areas, possibly as a result of more systematic recording.

Biogeography Eurasian Southern-temperate element, but naturalized in North America so distribution is now Circumpolar Southern-temperate.

Native	GB	IR
2000–19	1225	271
1987–99	1237	322
1970–86	937	91
pre-1970	1024	95

Alien	GB	IR
2000–19	3	0
1987–99	3	0
1970–86	2	0
pre-1970	2	0

Key refs Catling & Dobson (1985), Grime *et al.* (2007), Preston (1995b), Preston & Croft (1997).

C.D. PRESTON

N *Stuckenia filiformis* Slender-leaved Pondweed

(Pers.) Börner

This rhizomatous aquatic herb usually grows in open vegetation at the shallow edges of lakes. It is typically found over gravel, sand, silt or mud in sites where the water is base-rich, eutrophic or slightly brackish. It also occasionally grows in rivers, streams and ditches. Plants fruit freely and also perennate by tubers. 0–390 m at Drumore Loch (East Perthshire), formerly at 735 m at Coire Dhubh-chlair (Mid Perthshire).

Trends *S. filiformis* was last collected in Anglesey in 1826, and it has almost certainly decreased in the southern part of its Scottish range, as it can no longer be found at some of its former sites in Fife.

Biogeography Circumpolar Boreal-montane element.

Native	GB	IR
2000–19	86	64
1987–99	104	50
1970–86	83	22
pre-1970	111	33

Alien	GB	IR
2000–19	0	0
1987–99	0	0
1970–86	0	0
pre-1970	1	0

Key refs Preston (1995b), Preston & Croft (1997), Stewart *et al.* (1994).

C.D. PRESTON

Stuckenia pectinata Fennel Pondweed

(L.) Börner

This rhizomatous, linear-leaved aquatic herb is a characteristic species of eutrophic or brackish waters, where it may form dense stands in lakes, reservoirs, rivers, streams, canals, ditches, ponds and flooded mineral workings. It is tolerant of disturbance in canals and navigable rivers. It is occasionally found in highly calcareous but nutrient-poor lakes. Plants fruit freely in still waters and perennate by tubers in all habitats. Lowland, but with a historical record of 500 m from Llyn Anafon (Caernarvonshire).

Trends *S. pectinata* remains frequent through much of its range. Its tolerance of eutrophic waters allows it to persist in areas from which other aquatics have been lost. Losses from habitat destruction have often been compensated for by the ability of the species to colonize newly available habitats such as flooded sand- and gravel-pits. It is likely that it has been overlooked in many of the hectads with no recent record.

Biogeography Circumpolar Wide-temperate element.

Native	GB	IR
2000–19	908	208
1987–99	958	209
1970–86	701	67
pre-1970	783	102

Alien	GB	IR
2000–19	0	1
1987–99	2	1
1970–86	0	0
pre-1970	1	0

Key refs Preston (1995b), Preston & Croft (1997).

C.D. PRESTON

Groenlandia densa Opposite-leaved Pondweed

(L.) Fourr.

A perennial herb of shallow, clear, base-rich water which may grow in lakes and rivers, but is more frequent in smaller waters such as streams, canals, ditches and ponds. In many ditch sites it requires regular clearance to prevent the open water communities becoming overgrown by emergents. It rarely colonizes newly available habitats, although it is sometimes found as an introduction in ponds. Generally lowland, but reaching 380 m at Malham Tarn (Mid-west Yorkshire).

Trends *G. densa* has declined in Britain owing to urbanization, which has led to its loss from the London area, the drying-up of spring-fed streams and ditches because of falling water tables, eutrophication and the lack of ditch management. This decline began before 1930, but is still continuing. It was refound at just 23% of a sample of post-1970 sites revisited between 2008 and 2013, a very low refind rate, although it may have been missed at some sites if they were visited at a stage in the management cycle when the plant was not apparent (Walker *et al.*, 2017).

Biogeography European Temperate element.

Native	GB	IR
2000–19	157	22
1987–99	214	20
1970–86	221	7
pre-1970	546	31

Alien	GB	IR
2000–19	2	0
1987–99	2	0
1970–86	1	0
pre-1970	3	0

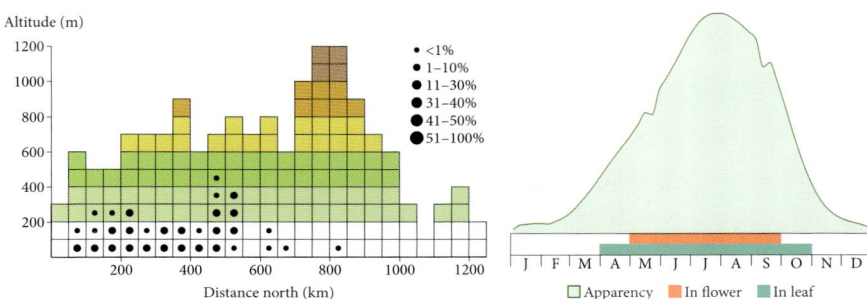

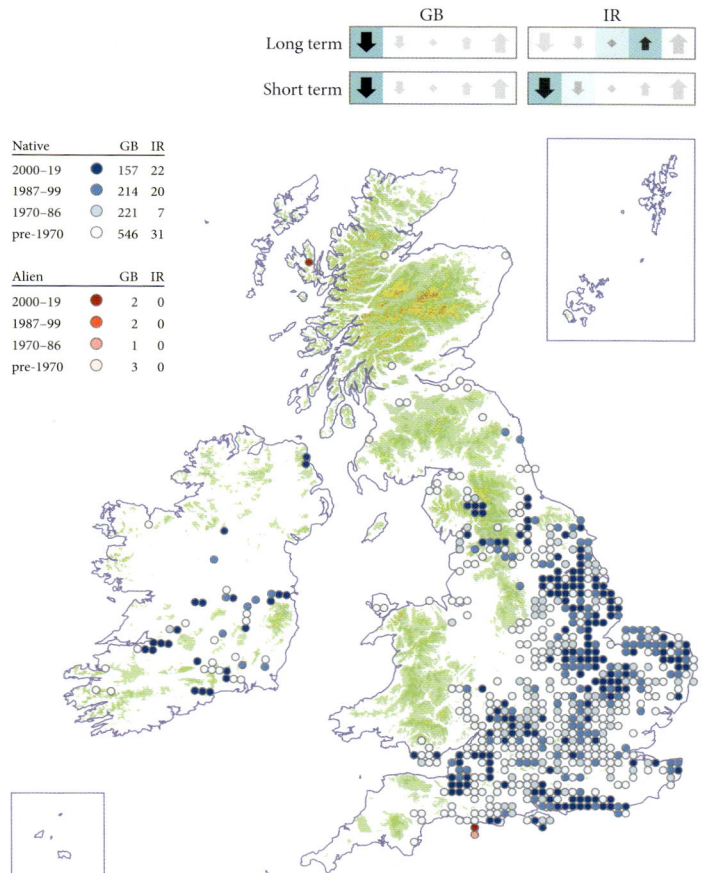

Key refs Preston (1995b), Preston & Croft (1997), Walker *et al.* (2017).

C.D. PRESTON

N

Zannichellia palustris Horned Pondweed

L.

This submerged, perennial aquatic grows in a range of shallow-water habitats. The most characteristic include clear chalk streams, eutrophic lakes and ponds, including sites with high wildfowl numbers and turbid water, and brackish lagoons, ponds and ditches. It is a frequent colonist of disused mineral workings. *Z. palustris* subsp. *palustris* is the more common of the two subspecies whereas most records of subsp. *pedicellata* are from coastal sites, but there are few records of either taxon. 0–380 m (Llynheilyn, Radnorshire).

Trends *Z. palustris* is easily overlooked by botanists without a specialist interest in aquatics, especially when it grows with other fine-leaved aquatics. It has certainly been lost from some areas in which small water bodies such as ponds and ditches have disappeared, but the loss may not be as serious as the map suggests. By contrast, there is evidence for an increase in the species in shallow, base-rich lakes in northern England in the last 150–200 years in response to eutrophication (Bennion *et al.*, 2018). It may also have increased in frequency in lowland Scotland since the 1960s.

Biogeography Circumpolar Southern-temperate element.

Native		GB	IR
2000–19		682	90
1987–99		773	146
1970–86		645	56
pre-1970		904	84

Alien		GB	IR
2000–19		0	0
1987–99		1	0
1970–86		0	0
pre-1970		1	0

Key refs Bennion *et al.* (2018), Preston & Croft (1997).

C.D. PRESTON

N?

Zannichellia obtusifolia Thin-leaved Horned-pondweed

Talavera, García-Mur. & H.Smit

A submerged, perennial aquatic discovered in 2016 in a brackish borrow-dyke behind a sea-wall in North Essex. Lowland.

Trends *Z. obtusifolia* is currently known from only a single site in North Essex where it is presumed to be native, and possibly arrived on migratory wildfowl, with the closest wild and native populations in south-western France.

Biogeography Native to the Mediterranean from Morocco to France and Sardinia (although differences in the interpretation of species in the genus *Zannichellia* make the overall distribution difficult to define).

	GB	IR
Long term	No trend	No trend
Short term	No trend	No trend

Native		GB	IR
2000–19		1	0
1987–99		0	0
1970–86		0	0
pre-1970		0	0

Key refs Adams (2017).

J.O. MOUNTFORD

Ruppia maritima Beaked Tasselweed
L.

A submerged, annual or perennial aquatic of brackish waters, growing in shallow water in coastal lakes, pools on saltmarshes, rock pools, creeks and ditches near the sea. It is also found as a dwarf variant on tidal mud-flats, especially in north-eastern Scotland. Records from inland sites in Cheshire are from areas of natural salt deposits. Lowland.

Trends Although *R. maritima* is doubtless under-recorded in some coastal areas, it had been lost from many sites before 1930 and this loss has continued in the southern part of its range around expanding coastal settlements.

Biogeography Circumpolar Wide-temperate element, but this requires reassessment as it is becoming clear that the species has a much more restricted range than has hithero been assigned to it (den Hartog and Triest, 2020).

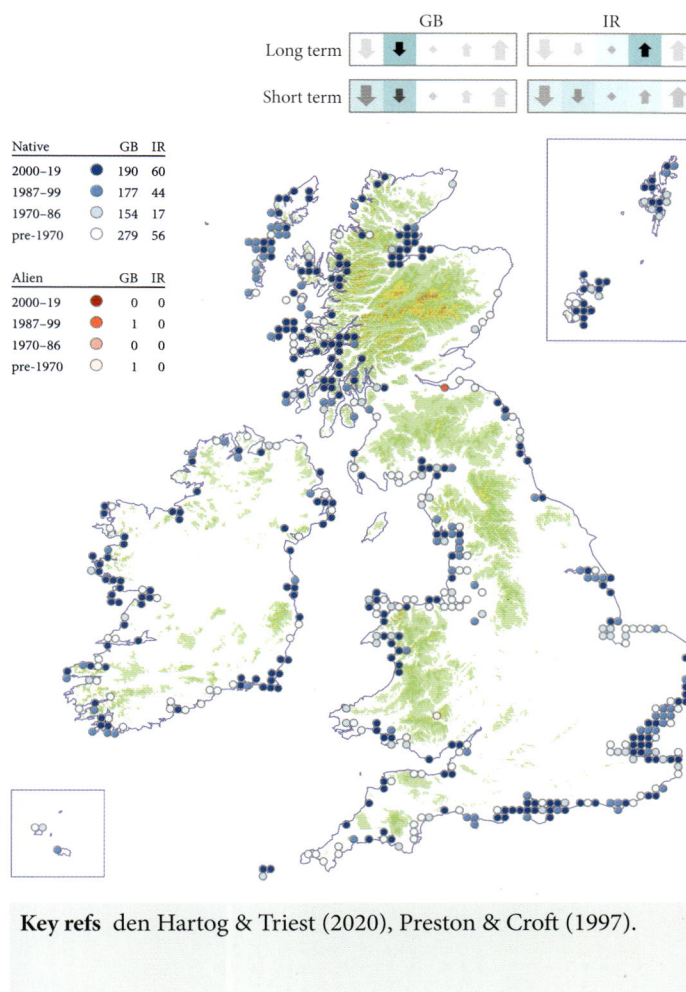

Native	GB	IR
2000–19	190	60
1987–99	177	44
1970–86	154	17
pre-1970	279	56

Alien	GB	IR
2000–19	0	0
1987–99	1	0
1970–86	0	0
pre-1970	1	0

Key refs den Hartog & Triest (2020), Preston & Croft (1997).

C.D. PRESTON

Ruppia spiralis Spiral Tasselweed
L. ex Dumort.

A perennial aquatic which occurs in similar habitats to *R. maritima*, including coastal lakes, tidal inlets, creeks and brackish ditches. It usually grows in deeper water than that species and tolerates more saline conditions, even growing with *Zostera* species. Lowland.

Trends Records of *R. spiralis* need to be based on flowering or fruiting material, but the species flowers less freely than *R. maritima* and trends in its distribution are therefore difficult to assess. It has not been seen since 1930 at some of the sites without recent records, but it might well be refound in those in which it was last seen in the late 20th century.

Biogeography Circumpolar Wide-temperate element, but absent from eastern North America. The taxonomy of the genus is in a state of flux and there are clearly more species with narrower ranges than has been recognized in the past (den Hartog and Triest, 2020). The distribution of *R. spiralis* will need to be reassessed once its taxonomy has been clarified.

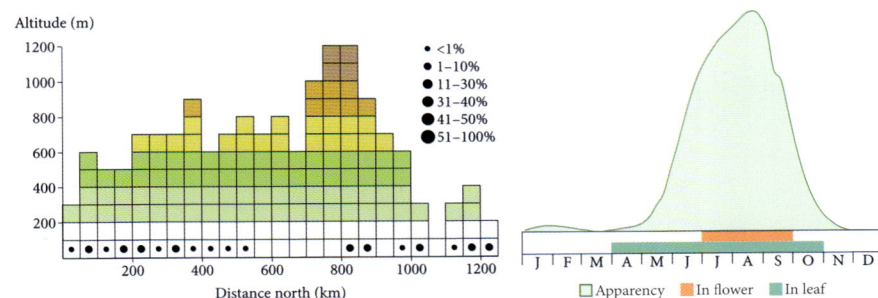

Native	GB	IR
2000–19	57	17
1987–99	57	11
1970–86	50	4
pre-1970	99	17

Key refs den Hartog & Triest (2020), Preston & Croft (1997), Stewart *et al.* (1994).

C.D. PRESTON

Narthecium ossifragum Bog Asphodel
(L.) Huds.

A rhizomatous perennial herb of wet, moderately basic to strongly acidic mineral soils and peats, in a wide range of raised, valley and blanket mire communities, and in wet heaths and flushes, especially where there is some surface water flow. It is intolerant of over-topping by rank vegetation or scrub which may develop on richer sites in the absence of grazing but, despite its toxicity, plants may also be suppressed by heavy grazing. 0–1,005 m (Beinn Heasgarnich, Mid Perthshire) but reportedly to 1,130 m elsewhere in Scotland.

Trends *N. ossifragum* experienced a significant range contraction, especially from the more readily drained areas of lowland England, between the 17th and 19th centuries, continuing in some counties until the late 20th century. Even in upland areas where wholesale loss did not occur, some populations were reduced through intensive sheep grazing as evidenced by recovery and expansion where grazing pressure has subsequently been eased. Its distribution now appears to be generally stable although many of the surviving populations in south-eastern England are very small and vulnerable to localized drainage, vegetational succession, woodland establishment or urban development.

Biogeography Oceanic Boreo-temperate element.

Key refs Chater (2010b), Crawley (2005), Dupont (1962), Greenwood (2012), Hawksford & Hopkins (2011), Summerfield (1974), Sussex Botanical Recording Society (2018).

I. TAYLOR

Native	GB	IR
2000–19	1481	685
1987–99	1428	621
1970–86	916	140
pre-1970	1414	528

Tamus communis Black Bryony
L.

A dioecious, tuberous climber, found mostly on neutral to calcareous, well-drained soils, particularly those overlying chalk and limestone, but also on clay. It can be luxuriant in hedgerows, woodland edges and along paths and in waste land, but is often found in a depauperate, non-flowering state in woodland. It possesses a very large tuber and therefore avoids shallow or waterlogged soil. It is bird-sown, but is a slow colonist. Generally lowland, but reaching 350 m near to Mynydd Troed (Breconshire).

Native in Britain and the Channel Islands and a neophyte in Ireland.

Trends There has been very little change in the overall distribution of *T. communis* since the 1960s.

Biogeography Submediterranean-Subatlantic element.

Key refs Burkill (1944), Grime *et al.* (2007).

A.J. RICHARDS

Native	GB	IR
2000–19	1370	0
1987–99	1356	0
1970–86	955	0
pre-1970	1317	0

Alien	GB	IR
2000–19	5	5
1987–99	2	5
1970–86	1	6
pre-1970	4	3

(N) *Paris quadrifolia* Herb-Paris
L.

A rhizomatous, perennial herb of moist, calcareous, usually ancient ash woodland, and occasionally in the grikes on open limestone pavement. It flowers and fruits most freely in the early open stages of a traditional coppice cycle, but persists in deep shade, and is well adapted to such conditions in managed woodland. It disappears following clear-felling, probably mainly through desiccation. Seedling recruitment and colonization of new sites appear to be rare. Generally lowland, but reaching 360 m at Great Asby Scar (Westmorland) and Garrigill (Cumberland), and reportedly up to 470 m at Settle Scar, above Stockdale Farm (Mid-west Yorkshire).

Trends Many populations of *P. quadrifolia* were lost across its range in Britain before 1930, especially in northern England and central Scotland.

Since then there has been more limited, though continuing, decline, especially in south-eastern England, through the destruction and coniferization of ancient woodland with very limited gains to offset the losses, due to inherently poor dispersive abilities.

Biogeography Eurosiberian Boreo-temperate element.

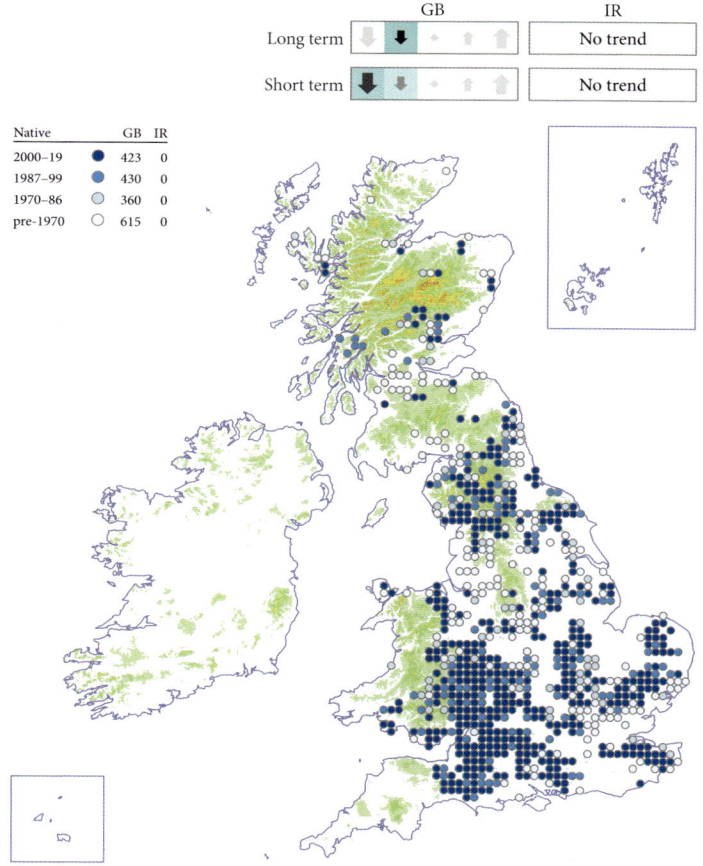

Native	GB	IR
2000–19	423	0
1987–99	430	0
1970–86	360	0
pre-1970	615	0

Key refs Jacquemyn *et al.* (2008), Kirby (2020), Leslie (2019), Mabey (1996), Sussex Botanical Recording Society (2018).

I. Taylor

(Ne) *Alstroemeria aurea* Peruvian Lily
Graham

A tuberous perennial herb which occurs as a naturalized garden escape on damp ground, in grassy and rough places, in an urban nature reserve, a recreation ground and as a relic of commercial cultivation. Lowland.

Trends *A. aurea* was introduced into cultivation in Britain in 1830 and is increasingly popular in gardens. It was first recorded in the wild in 1916 (Edinburgh, Midlothian) and appears to be increasing.

Biogeography Native of Chile.

Alien	GB	IR
2000–19	45	0
1987–99	36	0
1970–86	16	0
pre-1970	8	0

Key refs Measures & Thomas (2011).

T.D. Dines & N. Aspey

N *Colchicum autumnale* Meadow Saffron

L.

An autumn-flowering, cormous perennial herb of damp grassland, including damp meadows and riverbanks, but now most frequently encountered in clearings and rides within woodland, as it is toxic to livestock and often destroyed when growing in farmland. It is increasingly also naturalized when discarded from gardens or deliberately planted in churchyards, estate woodlands and amenity grasslands. Mainly lowland, but up to 420 m at Horseditch (Shropshire).

Native in Britain and Ireland and a neophyte in the Channel Islands.

Trends *C. autumnale* was lost from many of its grassland sites before 1930 though drainage, ploughing or targeted destruction because of its toxicity to livestock. Further losses have occurred since then, especially from meadows, but it remains frequent within woodland clearings and rides in its core areas in south-western Britain. This showy flower, which is popular in gardens, readily becomes naturalized when planted or discarded into suitable habitats and there are indications this may be increasing, most notably in eastern Scotland.

Biogeography European Temperate element.

Native	GB	IR
2000–19	137	2
1987–99	163	3
1970–86	130	1
pre-1970	261	9

Alien	GB	IR
2000–19	161	2
1987–99	79	0
1970–86	43	0
pre-1970	59	1

Key refs Butcher (1954), Crawley (2005), Grey-Wilson *et al.* (2020), Mabey (1996), Stroh *et al.* (2019).

I. TAYLOR

N *Gagea lutea* Yellow Star-of-Bethlehem

(L.) Ker Gawl.

A bulbous perennial herb of moist, base-rich, shady habitats including woods, hedgerows, limestone pavements, pastures, riversides and stream banks. In northern Britain many populations are confined to alluvium in riverine woodland subject to seasonal flooding. Mainly lowland, but to 340 m on wooded limestone pavement near to Ribblehead (Mid-west Yorkshire), where it rarely flowers.

Trends *G. lutea* is often shy-flowering, especially in its shadier localities, and many populations are small, widely scattered and often transient where subject to seasonal flooding by rivers. These factors undoubtedly have led to it being under-recorded in the past. It is, therefore, difficult to assess trends, but the overall distribution appears to be relatively stable with an increase in its known range in some areas due to more systematic recording. However, in northern England localized declines have been reported due to competition with the alien *Allium paradoxum* which is increasingly becoming naturalized on riverbanks, and in other areas (*e.g.* Worcestershire) expanding populations of *A. ursinum* have been implicated in driving local losses.

Biogeography European Temperate element, with a continental distribution in western Europe; also in central and eastern Asia.

Native	GB	IR
2000–19	142	0
1987–99	121	0
1970–86	118	0
pre-1970	170	0

Alien	GB	IR
2000–19	3	1
1987–99	1	0
1970–86	2	0
pre-1970	5	0

Key refs Stewart *et al.* (1994).

I. TAYLOR & K.J. WALKER

N *Gagea bohemica* Early Star-of-Bethlehem

(Zauschn.) Schult. & Schult.f.

A bulbous perennial herb of shallow pockets of soil in crevices, on ledges and in small, grazed patches of turf on south- and east-facing slopes overlying dolerite. Between 210 and 330 m at Stanner Rocks (Radnorshire).

Trends *G. bohemica* flowers infrequently in Britain, reproducing almost exclusively by bulbils. This, coupled with its very early flowering season and a long summer dormancy, led to the species remaining undetected until 1965 (and unrecognized as *G. bohemica* until 1975). However, the sole population is large and appears to be stable.

Biogeography European Southern-temperate element, with a continental distribution in western Europe.

	GB	IR
Long term	No trend	No trend
Short term	No trend	No trend

Native	GB	IR
2000–19	1	0
1987–99	1	0
1970–86	1	0
pre-1970	1	0

Key refs Kay & John (1995), Slater (1990), Wigginton (1999), Woods & Rix (1981).

I. TAYLOR

N *Gagea serotina* Snowdon Lily

(L.) Ker Gawl.

A bulbous perennial herb confined to damp ledges and crevices of mildly acidic rocks, usually on north- to north-east-facing cliffs, frequently in shaded sites and often sheltered by overhangs. Seeds are rarely produced, most reproduction being effected by rhizome-like structures. 550–760 m (Snowdonia, Caernarvonshire).

Trends *G. serotina* appears to be a glacial relic in Britain. Populations have long been restricted to relatively inaccessible ground, perhaps because of centuries of overgrazing by sheep, and have been further reduced by collection since its discovery in the late 17th century. The surviving populations appear to be stable.

Biogeography Circumpolar Arctic-montane element, but absent from the European Arctic and from eastern North America.

	GB	IR
Long term	No trend	No trend
Short term	No trend	No trend

Native	GB	IR
2000–19	2	0
1987–99	2	0
1970–86	2	0
pre-1970	2	0

Key refs Jones & Gliddon (1999), Wigginton (1999), Woodhead (1951a).

I. TAYLOR

Ne *Erythronium dens-canis* Dog's-tooth-violet
L.

A bulbous perennial herb which
is naturalized in woodland, parks
and rough grassland, where it is
originally planted or occurs as a
relic of cultivation. Reproduction
by seed can be prolific. Lowland.

Trends *E. dens-canis* was grown
in British gardens by 1596. It
was recorded from the wild in
1965 (Frilford, Berkshire).

Biogeography Native of Eurasia.

	GB	IR
Long term	No trend	No trend
Short term		No trend

Alien	GB	IR
2000–19	35	1
1987–99	15	1
1970–86	4	0
pre-1970	4	1

Altitude (m)

<1%
1–10%
11–30%
31–40%
41–50%
51–100%

Apparency   In flower   In leaf

J F M A M J J A S O N D

T.D. DINES & D.A. PEARMAN

Ne *Tulipa sylvestris* Wild Tulip
L.

A perennial herb with a stoloniferous
bulb, occasionally grown in gardens
and found naturalized in open
woodlands, orchards, hedgerows, on
riverbanks, in damp meadows and
pastures, chalk-pits, grassy banks and
waste ground. Populations arise from
discarded bulbs, deliberate planting
or as relics of former cultivation. It
sometimes fails to flower or set seed
but established populations can be very
long-lived as at Aubert Ings (Mid-west
Yorkshire), for example, where it has
been known since 1864. Lowland.

Trends *T. sylvestris* was in cultivation
in Britain by 1629. It was formerly very
popular as a garden plant, and was
recorded from the wild by 1792 (Bury
St Edmunds, West Suffolk). It appears
to have been widely naturalized by the
late 18th and 19th centuries but it had
already declined dramatically by the

1960s. Although tulips have remained
almost ubiquitous in gardens, the
popularity of *T. sylvestris* has waned
in favour of more showy species
and cultivars. As a result, new wild
populations are rarely established and
the species appears to be continuing its
inexorable decline as long-established
populations succumb to changes in
land management and development.

Biogeography Native range uncertain;
present in Europe, northern Africa and
south-western Asia.

	GB	IR
Long term	No trend	No trend
Short term		No trend

Alien	GB	IR
2000–19	55	0
1987–99	68	0
1970–86	49	0
pre-1970	175	1

Altitude (m)

<1%
1–10%
11–30%
31–40%
41–50%
51–100%

Apparency   In flower   In leaf

J F M A M J J A S O N D

Key refs Everett (2013), Leslie (2019), Mabey (1996), Wilford
(2006).

I. TAYLOR

Ne *Tulipa gesneriana* Garden Tulip
L.

A bulbous perennial herb, much grown in gardens and municipal plantings as spring bedding and frequently found on waste ground, roadsides, refuse tips, disused quarries and railways, and tipped soil where they originate from discarded bulbs in garden waste. Deliberate planting of cultivars away from flower-beds has also increased significantly in recent years. Most cultivars rarely persist but some forms survive for many years in favourable, generally warm, sunny and well-drained locations. Lowland.

Trends *T. gesneriana* was cultivated in Britain by 1596 and is very common in gardens with many forms and cultivars available, developed and selected in Europe since the Renaissance from stock imported from the gardens of the Ottoman Empire. It was not recorded from the wild until 1955 (Frilford,

Berkshire). Since then its 10 km square distribution has increased markedly although this is likely to include many occurrences that can scarcely be considered 'wild'. Well-adapted variants in favoured locations can slowly increase over time, primarily by vegetative means.

Biogeography *T. gesneriana* is of uncertain, and probably garden, origin.

Alien	GB	IR
2000–19	567	13
1987–99	184	0
1970–86	22	0
pre-1970	13	0

	GB	IR
Long term	No trend	No trend
Short term	↑	↑

Key refs Everett (2013), Grey-Wilson & Mathew (1981), Leslie (2019), Wilford (2006).

I. TAYLOR

Ne *Fritillaria meleagris* Fritillary
L.

A bulbous perennial herb, which has long been popular as a garden plant, frequently planted in gardens, parkland, churchyards, nature reserves, roadsides and other grassy places where it readily becomes naturalized from seed. Long-established populations, often originating from seed dispersed from large gardens or sometimes originally planted, occur in damp, sometimes winter-flooded hay-meadows with aftermath grazing. Lowland.

Trends This species was cultivated in Britain by 1596 but was not recorded in the wild until 1736 (Ruislip, Middlesex). Large populations in floodplain meadows in the River Thames basin and East Anglia, with a few outliers in the English Midlands, were mapped as native in the 2002 *Atlas* but are now considered to be long-established introductions in view of the very late year of discovery and

rapid population growth in meadows where the species is known to have been introduced (Pearman, 2007; Walker, 2021). Many of these meadow populations have been lost through habitat destruction and management intensification since the 1960s although the extent of these losses has, to some extent, been limited by conservation protection (Horton & Jefferson, 2006). *F. meleagris* is now far more common as a planted ornamental or garden escape, especially in urban areas, parks and gardens, churchyards and country parks, and on nature reserves (Walker, 2021) and its 10 km square distribution appears to have increased dramatically over the past 20 years.

Biogeography European Temperate element. Native from central Russia southwards to the southern Alps and central Balkans; naturalized elsewhere in Europe.

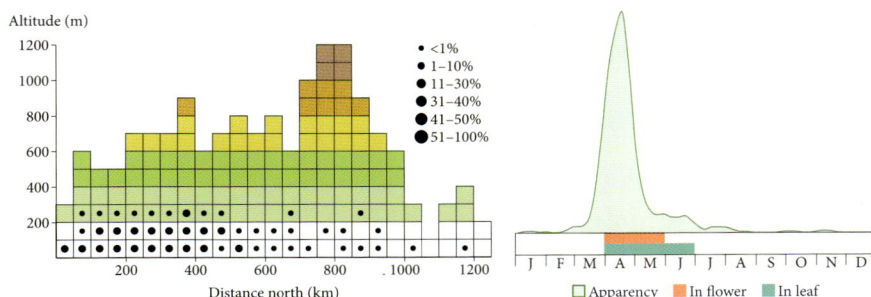

Alien	GB	IR
2000–19	383	4
1987–99	162	0
1970–86	100	0
pre-1970	175	0

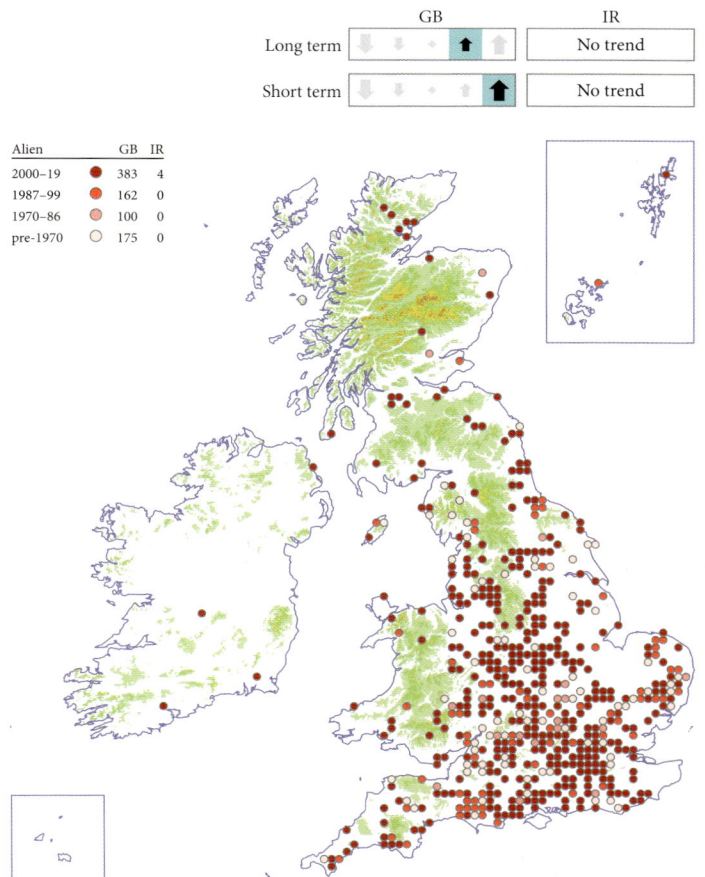

	GB	IR
Long term	↑	No trend
Short term	↑	No trend

Key refs Horton & Jefferson (2006), Killick *et al.* (1998), Mabey (1996), Pearman (2007), Stewart *et al.* (1994), Stroh *et al.* (2019), Walker (2021).

I. TAYLOR & K.J. WALKER

Ne *Lilium martagon* Martagon Lily

L.

A bulbous perennial herb, widely grown in gardens and found, usually as single plants or small clumps, in lightly shaded areas in woodlands by streams, on woodland edges or in coppiced woodland where it may have originally been deliberately planted, discarded in garden waste or possibly escaped from nearby gardens. It may become abundant in regularly coppiced areas. It also occurs in old orchards, on road and tracksides, on waste ground and as a relic of cultivation. The seeds are wind-dispersed and bulbs may also be dispersed by jays, or along watercourses. Lowland.

Trends *L. martagon* was introduced into British gardens by 1596. It was first recorded in the wild in 1782, but not until 1883 in the Wye Valley, where it was once considered to be native in ancient woodland. There

is some evidence of an expansion in its British range in recent decades, perhaps most notably in northern England and in southern and central Scotland, although this may be due, in part, to the more systematic recording of garden escapes. Its distribution appears to be increasing in Ireland, where it was first recorded in 1985 (Knockballymore Lough, Fermanagh).

Biogeography A Eurosiberian Temperate species; naturalized in northern Europe north of its native range.

Alien		GB	IR
2000–19	●	230	10
1987–99	●	172	1
1970–86	●	162	1
pre-1970	○	156	0

Key refs Harvey (1996), Lousley (1976).

I. TAYLOR

Ne *Lilium pyrenaicum* Pyrenean Lily

Gouan

A bulbous perennial herb, widely grown in gardens and often found close to human habitations in lightly shaded areas in woodlands, wood-borders, churchyards, hedgerows, road and tracksides, old ruins, and disused railway lines, usually as single plants or isolated clumps and arising from discarded or deliberately planted garden material. Relatively large, long-established and naturally regenerating populations are known from a few sites in south-western England, south-western Wales and eastern Scotland. 0–365 m (near Llanfair Clydogau, Cardiganshire).

Trends *L. pyrenaicum* has been cultivated in Britain since before 1596 and was recorded from the wild by 1853. As with *L. martagon* there is evidence of an expansion of its British range in recent decades, most strikingly in north-eastern Scotland where it is now

locally frequent on road and tracksides, often close to human habitations. The recording of garden escapes has improved considerably in recent decades and so it is difficult to assess the true extent of the increase but it would appear to be genuine in many areas.

Biogeography Native of the Pyrenees.

Alien		GB	IR
2000–19	●	277	25
1987–99	●	177	2
1970–86	●	107	1
pre-1970	○	92	0

Key refs Chater (2010b), Dupont (1962).

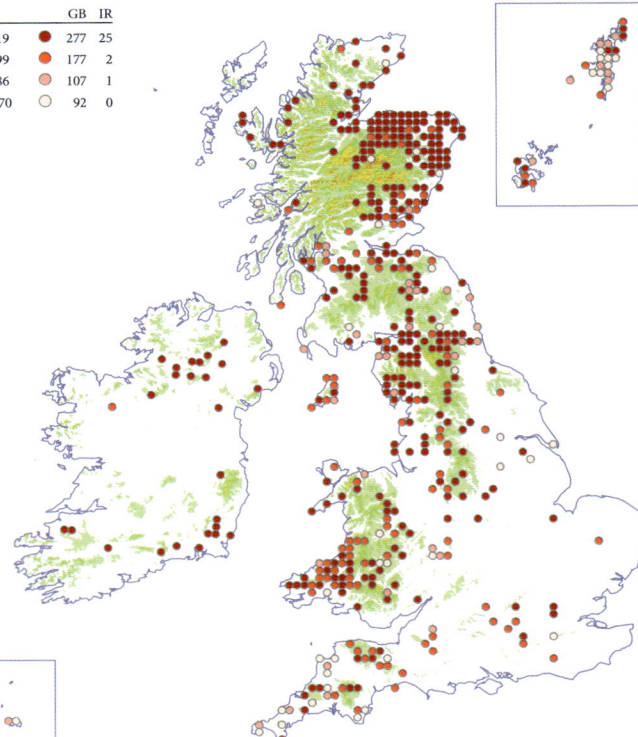

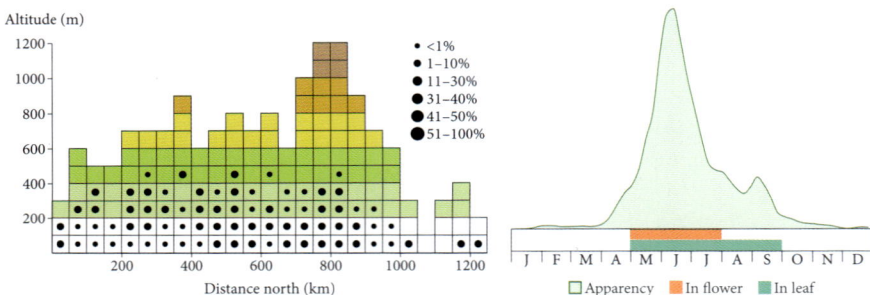

I. TAYLOR

Cypripedium calceolus Lady's-slipper

L.

A rhizomatous perennial herb found on well-drained calcareous soils derived from limestone, in herb-rich grassland, shallow grykes of limestone pavement and open woodland. Plants are long-lived but seed-set is poor. Generally lowland, but planted, and surviving, at 420–460 m near to Malham Tarn (Mid-west Yorkshire).

Trends This species suffered many losses due to collecting for both gardens and herbaria, mostly during the 19th century, and was thought to be extinct by the early 20th century. The single surviving native colony, rediscovered by two brothers in 1930, remained a closely guarded secret for many years and, since the 1970s, has been heavily protected, primarily from human interference, but also from grazing by sheep, rabbits, rodents, slugs and snails. A large-scale, long-term recovery programme centred

on captive breeding has proved to be a qualified success, allowing (re)establishment of the species in around a dozen new and former sites within its historic range in Cumbria, Durham, Lancashire, Yorkshire and Derbyshire. Seedlings are difficult to establish as they are favoured by slugs and snails.

Biogeography Circumpolar Boreo-temperate element, with a continental distribution in western Europe.

Native	GB	IR
2000–19	1	0
1987–99	1	0
1970–86	1	0
pre-1970	13	0

Alien	GB	IR
2000–19	11	0
1987–99	11	0
1970–86	2	0
pre-1970	13	0

Key refs Cheffings & Farrell (2005), Fay *et al.* (2009), Harrap & Harrap (2009), Kull (1999), Ramsey & Stewart (1998), Wigginton (1999).

R.M. Bateman & K.J. Walker

Cephalanthera damasonium White Helleborine

(Mill.) Druce

A shade-loving rhizomatous perennial herb usually found in woods, especially those dominated by *Fagus sylvatica* with little ground cover but also extending into chalk scrub, abandoned quarries and occasionally north-facing grassland. It is restricted to well-drained soils on chalk and oolitic limestone. It has a genetic profile consistent with self-pollination; flowers open little if at all. It is a more effective colonist than other *Cephalanthera* species, rapidly invading juvenile beech plantations. Lowland.

Trends Historically, many sites for *C. damasonium* have been lost due to the clearfelling or coniferization of lowland woodland, particularly since 1930. Almost all former outlying sites north of a line from the Severn to The Wash appear to have been lost prior to 2000, confining this species to south-eastern England, where its ability to colonize

young *Fagus sylvatica* plantations means that new populations are occasionally found. It remains plentiful in suitable habitats, though flowering appears strongly influenced by annual rainfall patterns. This has become a model species for the study of mycorrhizal fungi in facultative mycoheterotrophs.

Biogeography European Temperate element.

Native	GB	IR
2000–19	170	0
1987–99	143	0
1970–86	128	0
pre-1970	211	0

Alien	GB	IR
2000–19	1	0
1987–99	0	0
1970–86	0	0
pre-1970	0	0

Key refs Bateman *et al.* (2005), Harrap & Harrap (2009), Micheneau *et al.* (2010), Shefferson *et al.* (2016).

P.D. Carey, T.D. Dines & R.M. Bateman

Ⓝ *Cephalanthera longifolia* Narrow-leaved Helleborine
(L.) Fritsch

A long-lived rhizomatous perennial herb occupying a variety of woodland types, most commonly of *Fagus sylvatica* or *Quercus robur–Fraxinus excelsior*, on calcareous soils, usually on chalk and hard limestone but also on calcareous schist in Scotland. It prefers permanent patches of light and is most frequent on steep, rocky slopes with an open tree canopy, but is also found along woodland edges and rides, in scrub and along roadside verges. In Ireland it favours periodically inundated lough-side woodlands, but also occurs rarely in machair. Lowland.

Trends Formerly widespread and locally frequent throughout our area, *C. longifolia* declined markedly in the 19th and early 20th centuries, inland sites being at greater risk. Its decline has slowed during the last three decades. Although this species remains widely distributed, with concentrations in Hampshire and the mid-western coast of Scotland, most surviving populations are small. The achilles heel of *C. longifolia* is its narrow range of tolerance of light (and thus of both desiccation and competition), which makes it vulnerable to cessation of woodland management or coniferization; it is also prone to browsing by deer.

Biogeography European Temperate element; also in central Asia.

Native		GB	IR
2000–19	●	57	11
1987–99	●	40	9
1970–86	○	43	5
pre-1970	○	119	26

Alien		GB	IR
2000–19	●	0	0
1987–99	●	0	0
1970–86	●	0	0
pre-1970	○	1	0

Key refs Byfield (1993), Curtis & Thompson (2009), Hedley (1998), Micheneau *et al.* (2010), Stewart *et al.* (1994), Walker *et al.* (2017), Wheeler (1998).

P.D. CAREY, T.D. DINES & R.M. BATEMAN

Ⓝ *Cephalanthera rubra* Red Helleborine
(L.) Rich.

A long-lived rhizomatous perennial herb of well-drained sloping sites on calcareous soils, most commonly in the dappled shade of clearings within mature beechwoods. It is a poor competitor and does not form large colonies in Britain, where dormancy appears to be frequent, flowering stems are rarely produced and seed-set is low. Lowland.

Trends This elusive species has always been very rare. Sparsely distributed across southern England in the 19th and early 20th centuries, it is now confined to small populations at single sites in the Cotswolds, Chilterns and Hampshire downs, where a new site was discovered in 2018, compensating for a nearby locality where plants have not been recorded since 2007. Its intolerance of both shade and light-assisted competition mean that its survival requires careful, well-informed management of the habitat, and fencing is needed to discourage grazing by deer and rabbits.

Biogeography European Temperate element.

	GB	IR
Long term	No trend	No trend
Short term	No trend	No trend

Native		GB	IR
2000–19	●	4	0
1987–99	●	3	0
1970–86	○	5	0
pre-1970	○	9	0

Key refs Cheffings & Farrell (2005), Gilián *et al.* (2019), Harrap & Harrap (2009), Micheneau *et al.* (2010), Newman *et al.* (2007), Stroh *et al.* (2014).

P.D. CAREY, T.D. DINES & R.M. BATEMAN

Epipactis palustris Marsh Helleborine
(L.) Crantz

A rhizomatous perennial herb of neutral to calcareous fens, marshes, damp pastures, meadows and dune-slacks, where it can become abundant through vegetative reproduction. It prefers flushed or seasonally inundated areas where competition from other vegetation is limited. Other habitats include slumped terraces of wet, calcareous sea-cliffs and flooded quarries and gravel-pits; a few transient populations have appeared in chalk grassland. It is phylogenetically distinct from other native *Epipactis* taxa. Lowland.

Trends Drainage of fens and marshes has caused a considerable decline in this species, most losses occurring before 1930. It is vulnerable to changes in water-level and to nutrient enrichment, as well as cessation of grazing. The pattern in England and Wales shows a general retreat to areas where fens and dune-slacks remain extensive and healthy. Only five populations currently occur in Scotland, whereas more systematic recording gives the impression of increased frequency in central Ireland.

Biogeography Eurosiberian Temperate element.

Native	GB	IR
2000–19	169	150
1987–99	197	105
1970–86	167	36
pre-1970	406	77

Alien	GB	IR
2000–19	2	0
1987–99	2	0
1970–86	0	0
pre-1970	1	0

Key refs Allan *et al.* (1993), Bateman *et al.* (2005), Curtis & Thompson (2009), Jacquemyn *et al.* (2014).

R.M. BATEMAN, P.D. CAREY & T.D. DINES

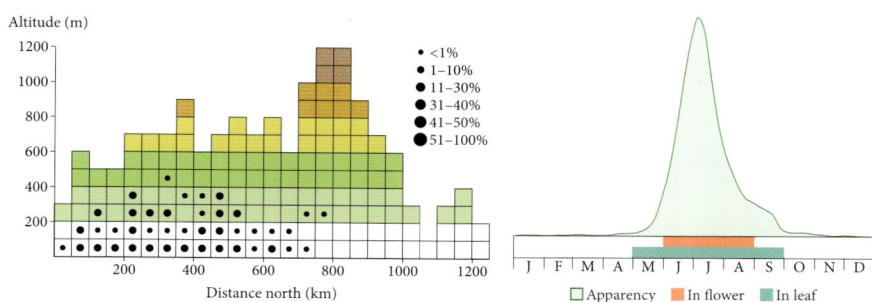

Epipactis atrorubens Dark-red Helleborine
(Hoffm.) Besser

A rhizomatous perennial herb found mostly on bare rock or well-drained skeletal soils overlying limestone. Habitats include exposed scree slopes, open grassy banks, shaded grikes of limestone pavements and ledges on cliff and quarry faces; less often, open woodland and stabilized sand dunes. Most populations are small and often include many non-flowering plants. 0–610 m (Gleann Beag, East Perthshire).

Trends Its exacting habitat requirements confine this species to isolated areas in northern England, north Wales, Scotland, and the Burren region of western Ireland. The overall distribution of *E. atrorubens* is stable. It is now recorded from more sites than ever before, but some populations have been lost as a result of quarrying activities. Cessation of grazing is an additional threat, as is overgrazing by deer and rabbits.

Biogeography Eurosiberian Boreo-temperate element.

Native	GB	IR
2000–19	39	11
1987–99	44	9
1970–86	40	9
pre-1970	46	8

Key refs Hollingsworth *et al.* (2006), Sramkó *et al.* (2019), Stewart *et al.* (1994), Walker (2015a).

R.M. BATEMAN, P.D. CAREY & T.D. DINES

N *Epipactis purpurata* Violet Helleborine
Sm.

A rhizomatous perennial herb occurring in a wide range of woodland types. It is most characteristic of densely shaded *Fagus sylvatica* woods, particularly those on 'clay-with-flints' deposits, but is also frequent in neutral to mildly acidic, usually clay-rich soils that support mixed woodland and coppices of *Corylus avellana* and *Carpinus betulus*. Deep shade is typical but not essential. Lowland.

Trends Confined to south-eastern and central England. Outliers in Yorkshire and Lincolnshire appear to have been lost, leaving a single population in Shropshire as the most northerly outpost of this species. Woodland clearances have for long eliminated populations, but in compensation, its tolerance of deep shade means that *E. purpurata* is one of very few species to have benefitted from declining woodland management during the 20th century, particularly cessation of coppicing. This species is often described as easily overlooked, but any residual under-recording is better attributed to the botanical tedium of its preferred low-diversity habitats. It is best sought during wet summers.

Biogeography European Temperate element.

Native	GB	IR
2000–19	173	0
1987–99	161	0
1970–86	140	0
pre-1970	195	0

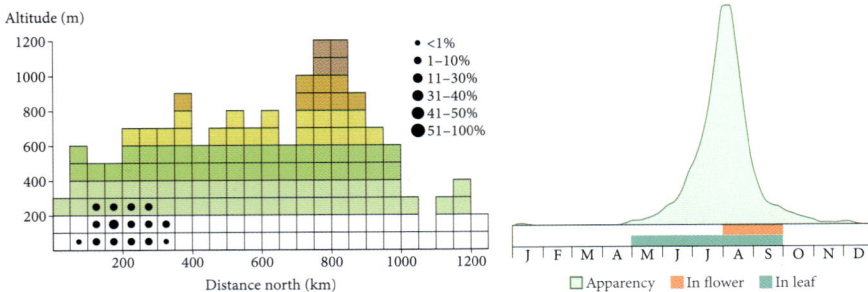

Key refs Bateman (1981), Bateman (2020c), Harrap & Harrap (2009), Hollingsworth *et al.* (2006), Jakubska-Busse *et al.* (2017), Sramkó *et al.* (2019).

R.M. Bateman, P.D. Carey & T.D. Dines

N *Epipactis helleborine* Broad-leaved Helleborine
(L.) Crantz

A highly adaptable rhizomatous perennial herb of calcareous to slightly acidic soils that ideally prefers dappled shade but occupies a wide range of habitats; these include deciduous (typically beech or oak) and coniferous woodland, hedgerows, scrub, shady banks, streamsides, roadsides, railways, spoil heaps, alder-carr, dunes and dune-slacks, limestone pavement, screes and even open grassland. It can invade secondary woodland and also occurs in urban habitats, particularly abandoned gardens where it can become invasive. 0–380 m (Llaneglwys, Breconshire).

Native in Britain and Ireland and a neophyte in the Channel Islands.

Trends By far the most frequent British *Epipactis* species, thanks to its broad ecological tolerance and higher frequency of cross-pollination, although it is more sporadic in southern Ireland, upland Scotland and East Anglia.

It appears to be declining slowly in central and northern England. The 2002 *Atlas* mapped as a separate species 'E. youngiana', occupying heavy metal waste and bings in ten hectads in the north of England and southern Scotland, but this has since been shown through DNA analyses to be a minor variant of *E. helleborine*. In compensation, recent DNA evidence confirmed earlier reports that populations in the Kenfig and Oxwich dune systems of south Wales are assignable to *E. helleborine* subsp. *neerlandica*, a taxon otherwise known only from the coastal dunes of the Netherlands, Germany and Denmark. Subsp. *neerlandica* evolved from within subsp. *helleborine*, which is also the ancestor of *E. dunensis* and probably *E. leptochila*.

Biogeography Eurasian Temperate element; widely naturalized outside its native range.

Native	GB	IR
2000–19	1026	181
1987–99	904	108
1970–86	694	43
pre-1970	970	90

Alien	GB	IR
2000–19	1	1
1987–99	2	0
1970–86	0	0
pre-1970	0	0

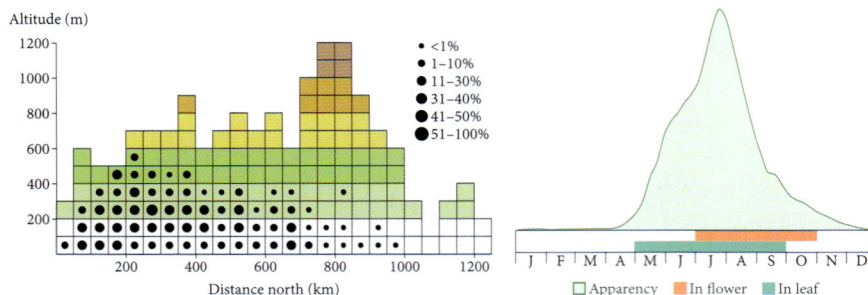

Key refs Bateman (2006), Bateman (2020c), Brys & Jacquemyn (2016), Hollingsworth *et al.* (2006), Jacquemyn *et al.* (2018), Kreutz (2008), Lewis (2003), Squirrell *et al.* (2001).

R.M. Bateman, P.D. Carey & T.D. Dines

Epipactis leptochila Narrow-lipped Helleborine

(Godfery) Godfery

A rhizomatous perennial herb typically found in the deep shade of *Fagus sylvatica* woods on calcareous substrates, particularly on slopes and embankments where soils are especially thin. Lowland.

Trends Despite excellent taxonomic work on British and Irish *Epipactis* throughout the last 100 years, *E. leptochila* has previously been mapped together with *E. dunensis*. It is now clear from detailed molecular research that, despite their morphological similarity, they are not only distinct species but also fairly distantly related. This insight helps to explain their contrasting habitat preferences and mutually exclusive distributions within Britain and Ireland, *E. leptochila* being confined to the area south of a line from the Llŷn Peninsula to The Wash. This apparent disparity may be simplistic, as the distributions of these two species overlap extensively in mainland Europe, where *E. leptochila* encompasses *E. neglecta*, *E. peitzii* and *E. futakii*. In contrast, *E. muelleri* remains a distinct species that occurs immediately beyond the English Channel, and therefore should continue to be sought in the British Isles. Conclusively circumscribing *E. leptochila* has crucial consequences for determining its conservation status. Populations are sporadic in appearance, but most are small and declining, even in the heartland of the species in the Cotswolds and Chilterns; there are no recent records from its former outliers in Shropshire, Devon or Kent. Changes in woodland management alone appear insufficient to explain its decline; increasingly dry summers represent a more credible explanation.

Biogeography European Temperate element.

Native	GB	IR
2000–19	23	0
1987–99	30	0
1970–86	37	0
pre-1970	44	0

Key refs Bateman (2020c, 2021a), Brys & Jacquemyn (2016), Delforge & Gévaudan (2002), Hollingsworth *et al.* (2006), Richards & Squirrell (2009), Sramkó *et al.* (2019).

R.M. Bateman, P.D. Carey & T.D. Dines

Epipactis dunensis Dune Helleborine

(T.Stephenson & T.A.Stephenson) Godfery

A rhizomatous perennial herb that is dominantly self-pollinated and does not tolerate severe competition. The most natural habitat of this species is the margins of coastal dune-slacks where it grows among *Salix repens*, although it spreads readily into any neighbouring conifer plantations. Inland populations probably formed later, as they favour anthropogenic substrates, typically occurring in open *Betula* woods on well-drained, neutral to mildly acidic stony soils sometimes polluted with zinc and lead metals, including spoil heaps and bings. Remarkably, it was recently discovered growing in municipal flower-beds in central Harrogate (Mid-west Yorkshire). Lowland.

Trends Most inland populations were ascribed to *E. leptochila* until molecular analyses demonstrated their affinity to *E. dunensis*; the two species were mapped together as *E. leptochila* agg. in the 2002 *Atlas*. A further infraspecific taxon was established for a single population on the Northumbrian island of Lindisfarne, and briefly enjoyed fame as an endemic species, *E. sancta*, although current evidence suggests that the population is more appropriately treated as a subspecies or variety of *E. dunensis*. The combination of uncertain circumscription and challenging identification has left *E. dunensis* under-recorded, although the documented increase in 10 km square records probably reflects a genuine expansion, including a first record for Ireland, near Dublin.

Biogeography European Temperate element. Often cited as endemic to our area, this species actually extends eastward across Europe at least as far as Hungary, where it is often referred to as *E. bugacensis* and *E. rhodanensis*.

Native	GB	IR
2000–19	46	2
1987–99	26	0
1970–86	24	0
pre-1970	12	0

Key refs Bateman (2020c), Delforge (1995), Harrap & Harrap (2009), Richards (1994), Richards & Squirrell (2009), Santos & Sayers (2020), Sramkó *et al.* (2019), Young (1948), Young (1962).

R.M. Bateman, P.D. Carey & T.D. Dines

Ⓝ *Epipactis phyllanthes* Green-flowered Helleborine
G.E.Sm.

A rhizomatous perennial herb with an exceptionally broad ecological tolerance, from deep shade to full sun in soils that range from mildly acidic to strongly alkaline and from exceptionally dry and humus-poor to ever-wet and humic. Arguably most typical of sparsely vegetated, shaded woodland, its habitats include *Fagus sylvatica* woods among ivy on chalk, flinty clays or sandstones, *Pinus* and *Betula* scrub, *Corylus avellana* coppice, shaded roadside verges, riverside and lakeside willow-carr (including brackish water), and on stabilized sand dunes. It is predominantly self-pollinating. Overall, this species survives better in challenging habitats than competitive vegetation, rendering many of its populations comparatively transient. Lowland.

Trends Distributional change is especially difficult to assess in *E. phyllanthes*. Losses in its heartland of Hampshire and the Chilterns, presumably due to habitat change, appear to have been more than offset by 21st century discoveries in East Anglia, northern England and Ireland, together with the first Scottish records in 2012, adjacent to the Moray Firth. Northward migration might reasonably be inferred from this pattern, but the sporadic and often transient occurrence of populations, combined with the gradual realization that identification of this species is easier than generally supposed, could simply suggest improved recording in regions where *E. phyllanthes* has in the past been relatively unfamiliar.

Biogeography European Temperate element.

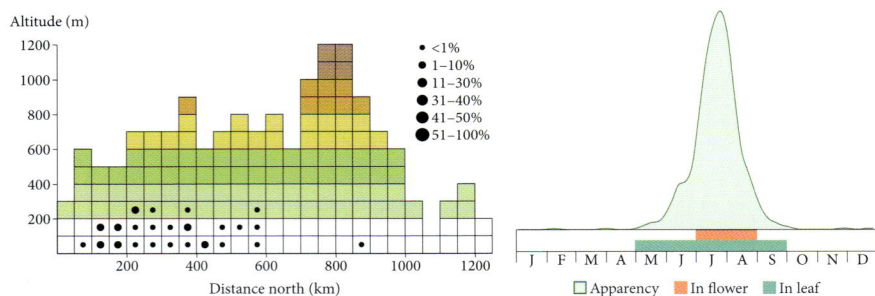

Native		GB	IR
2000–19	●	124	16
1987–99	●	91	5
1970–86	○	82	4
pre-1970	○	85	5

Alien		GB	IR
2000–19	●	1	0
1987–99	●	0	0
1970–86	●	0	0
pre-1970	○	0	0

Key refs Bateman (2020c), Curtis & Thompson (2009), Hollingsworth *et al.* (2006), Lewis (2017), Lewis & Spencer (2005), Sramkó *et al.* (2019), Stewart *et al.* (1994).

R.M. BATEMAN, P.D. CAREY & T.D. DINES

Ⓝ *Neottia ovata* Common Twayblade
(L.) Bluff & Fingerh.

A rhizomatous perennial herb found on a wide range of calcareous to neutral or, less often, mildly acidic soils. Its habitats span a range from full sun to deep shade; they encompass grasslands (including hay meadows), woodland, hedgerows, scrub, sand dunes, dune-slacks, fens, limestone pavement and heathland. It frequently occurs, often as large colonies, on railway embankments and in disused quarries, sand-pits and spoil heaps. 0–670 m (Ben Lawers, Mid Perthshire).

Trends Although this cosmopolitan species is widespread throughout much of our area, there are many 10 km squares without recent records. Some lowland sites have been lost to agricultural activities, including ploughing of grassland and hedgerow removal. The majority of losses, however, may be a result of long-term neglect or a lack of suitable grassland management,

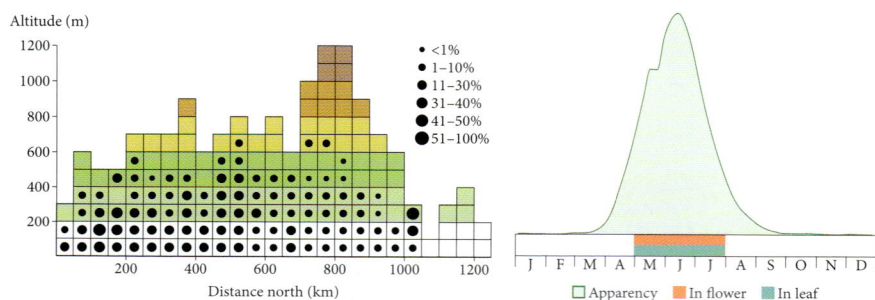

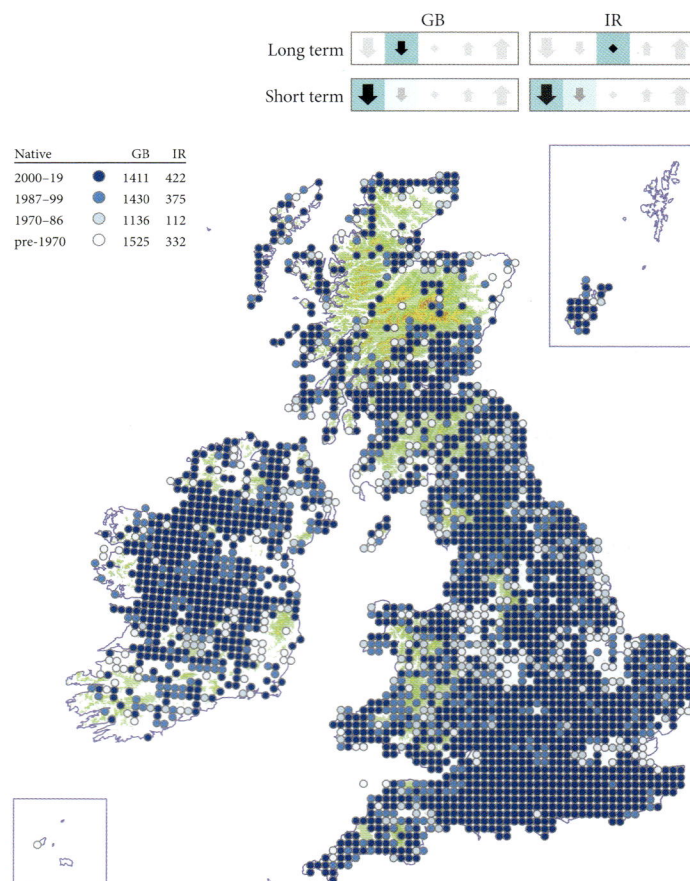

as well as the piecemeal destruction of suitable habitat for development.

Biogeography Eurosiberian Boreo-temperate element.

Native		GB	IR
2000–19	●	1411	422
1987–99	●	1430	375
1970–86	○	1136	112
pre-1970	○	1525	332

Key refs Allan *et al.* (1993), Harrap & Harrap (2009), Jenkinson (1991), Kotlinek *et al.* (2015), Sanford (1991), Zhou & Jin (2018).

P.D. CAREY, T.D. DINES & R.M. BATEMAN

Neottia cordata Lesser Twayblade
(L.) Rich.

A perennial rhizomatous herb of wet heath and blanket bog, often growing in *Sphagnum* or in the moss layer beneath dense *Calluna vulgaris* and *Vaccinium myrtillus*, usually in deep shade in humid, acidic conditions. It also grows in moss in damp, heavily shaded carr woodland, and occasionally under *Pinus*. Reproduction is by root-buds and seed, though most plants in any population are non-flowering. 0–1,065 m (Stob Coire an Easain, Westerness).

Trends The strongly boreal distribution of *N. cordata* means that it is frequent in the more oceanic parts of northern Scotland and only occasional in northern England, north Wales and Northern Ireland. It has declined outside these core areas, losses being greatest from lowland sites due to drainage of swamps, cutting of wet forests and burning of grouse moors where it

usually only survives in pockets of wet heath or bog that are too wet to burn. It appears to have been lost from the New Forest and Dorset heaths. However, it is an exceptionally inconspicuous plant and therefore undoubtedly remains under-recorded, even in its core areas.

Biogeography Circumpolar Boreal-montane element, with a disjunct distribution.

Native	GB	IR
2000–19	643	116
1987–99	496	52
1970–86	378	16
pre-1970	596	69

Key refs Allan *et al.* (1993), Kotlinek *et al.* (2018), Lallemand *et al.* (2019), Stroh *et al.* (2014), Zhou & Jin (2018).

P.D. CAREY, T.D. DINES & R.M. BATEMAN

Neottia nidus-avis Bird's-nest Orchid
(L.) Rich.

A perennial herb, spreading by short rhizomes, typically found in the deep, moist humus of densely shaded *Fagus sylvatica* woods on chalky soils with little associated vegetation. Less commonly it occurs in mixed deciduous woodland, mature *Corylus avellana* coppices and avenues of *Tilia* species, on soils derived from limestones and base-rich clays and sands. *N. nidus-avis* is an obligate mycoheterotroph that is entirely dependent on mycorrhizal fungi from the family Sebacinaceae for its nutrition. Generally lowland but reaching 345 m at Slit Wood (County Durham).

Trends *N. nidus-avis* suffered a considerable decline throughout the 20th century. Most losses are probably due to deforestation and successional changes associated with radical changes in woodland management, although its especially rapid decline from apparently

suitable habitats in south-eastern England and East Anglia suggests an additional cause, possibly decreased spring and summer rainfall coupled with increased atmospheric deposition of nitrogen and other pollutants. Many of its historic sites are also now heavily browsed by deer, including non-native species introduced during the mid-20th century (*e.g.* Reeves's Muntjac *Muntiacus reevesi*). Apparent increases in southern and western Ireland and the Outer Hebrides are probably the result of more systematic recording in recent decades.

Biogeography Eurosiberian Temperate element; also in eastern Asia.

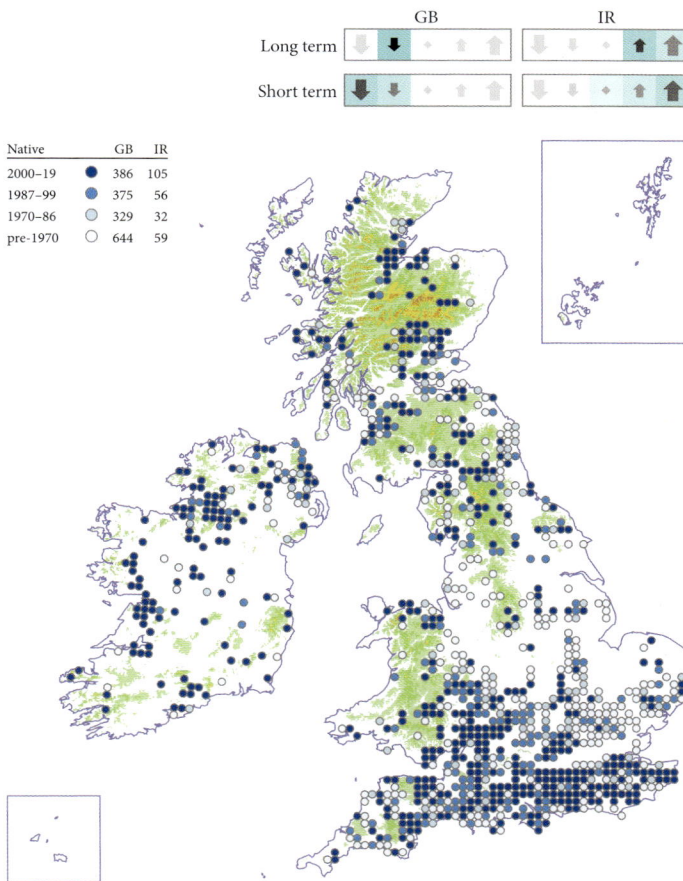

Native	GB	IR
2000–19	386	105
1987–99	375	56
1970–86	329	32
pre-1970	644	59

Key refs Allan *et al.* (1993), Bateman *et al.* (2005), Curtis & Thompson (2009), Harrap & Harrap (2009), Selosse *et al.* (2002).

P.D. CAREY, T.D. DINES & R.M. BATEMAN

(N) *Epipogium aphyllum* Ghost Orchid

Sw.

An obligately mycoheterotrophic herb usually growing in deep leaf-litter, and historically confined to two small areas: *Fagus sylvatica* woods on chalk in the mid-Chiltern dipslope, and oakwoods on clay between Hereford and Ludlow. The extensive underground rhizomes produce bulbils and can show considerable longevity, but flowering stems are produced only sporadically and rarely set seed. Lowland.

Trends Now the most arduously sought British plant, the appropriately named Ghost Orchid appeared in most years in at least one of its Chilterns sites between 1953 and 1987, but not since. 19th century records from Herefordshire were followed by observations of single flowering stems in Herefordshire in 1982, 1991 and (soon after the species had been declared extinct in Britain by some authorities) in 2009. There

are many theories of the impact of various climatic factors on flowering and/or seed-set in this species, which appears vulnerable to drought, habitat degradation (including soil compaction), and predation by slugs and snails.

Biogeography Eurasian Boreal-montane element.

	GB	IR
Long term	No trend	No trend
Short term	No trend	No trend

Native	GB	IR
2000–19	1	0
1987–99	1	0
1970–86	4	0
pre-1970	9	0

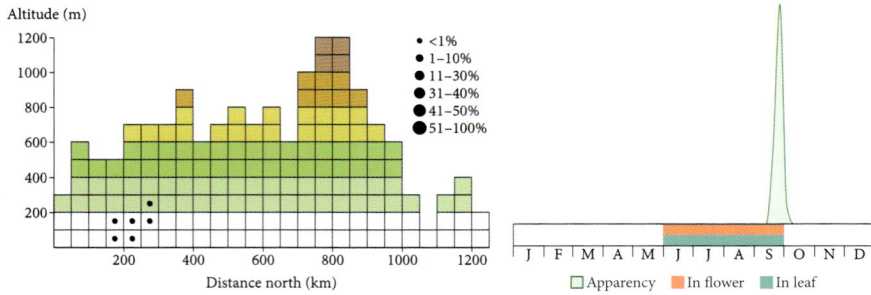

Altitude (m) histogram / distance north (km); apparency, in flower, in leaf phenology chart.

Dot size key: <1%, 1–10%, 11–30%, 31–40%, 41–50%, 51–100%

Key refs Bateman (2006, 2010), Claessens & Kleynen (2011), Cole (2014), Jannink & Rich (2010), Stroh *et al.* (2014), Taylor & Roberts (2011).

R.M. BATEMAN, P.D. CAREY & T.D. DINES

(N) *Liparis loeselii* Fen Orchid

(L.) Rich.

L. loeselii is a pseudobulbous perennial herb restricted to two regions of Britain that feature contrasting habitats, both requiring some bare ground and perennial neutral or calcareous groundwater. In East Anglia it is restricted to species-rich fens on infertile soils, mainly old peat cuttings, among *Phragmites australis* and *Cladium mariscus*. Along the south Wales coast it grows in recently disturbed dune-slacks, where it will tolerate prolonged submersion (it also occupied a similar habitat in North Devon from 1966 to 1987). Both Welsh and East Anglian populations are dependent on occupying a 'goldilocks' zone where disturbance is neither too little nor too great. Lowland.

Trends This species declined greatly throughout the 19th and 20th centuries due to habitat destruction, scrub encroachment and the cessation of peat

cutting. Today, the main threat to the three remaining, closely spaced East Anglian populations is groundwater extraction. Similarly, only three populations remain in the south Wales dune-slacks, where coastal management and undergrazing have stabilized dunes and so reduced the number of young slacks available for colonization. Recently, deliberate reversal of the stabilization process at the largest Welsh population has proved highly successful, while conservation management at one of the East Anglian sites has similarly greatly expanded the population size.

Biogeography Eurosiberian Temperate element, with a continental distribution in western Europe; also in eastern Asia and North America.

	GB	IR
Long term	No trend	No trend
Short term	No trend	No trend

Native	GB	IR
2000–19	6	0
1987–99	8	0
1970–86	9	0
pre-1970	29	0

Alien	GB	IR
2000–19	2	0
1987–99	0	0
1970–86	1	0
pre-1970	2	0

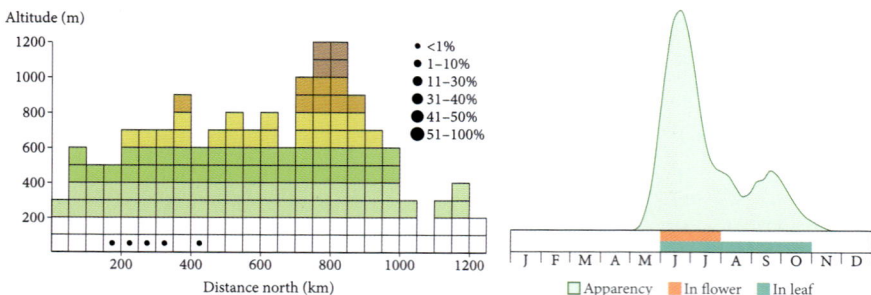

Altitude (m) histogram / distance north (km); apparency, in flower, in leaf phenology chart.

Dot size key: <1%, 1–10%, 11–30%, 31–40%, 41–50%, 51–100%

Key refs Cameron (2005), Jones (1998), Luer (1975), Pillon *et al.* (2006), Stroh *et al.* (2014), Wheeler *et al.* (1998).

R.M. BATEMAN, P.D. CAREY & T.D. DINES

Hammarbya paludosa Bog Orchid

(L.) Kuntze

A pseudobulbous herb of bogs and valley mires where the water is usually very acidic but perpetually subject to some lateral movement. Typically it grows amongst saturated *Sphagnum*, but also on peaty mud and among grasses on the edges of runnels and flushes. 0–600 m (Ben Gulabin, East Perthshire).

Trends *H. paludosa* is an extremely inconspicuous species that requires focused surveys to relocate it even in areas where its distribution is well known. Some large populations have been discovered recently in the more remote and under-explored parts of its range, and others surely remain overlooked. Surprisingly for a pseudobulbous species, it is extremely vulnerable to desiccation. Drainage of bogs, particularly in the lowlands, caused a dramatic decline of this species, especially in England before 1930. Overgrazing may have caused losses in some upland areas, particularly through poaching.

Biogeography Circumpolar Boreal-montane element, with a disjunct distribution.

Native		GB	IR
2000–19	●	160	23
1987–99	●	129	16
1970–86	○	91	8
pre-1970	○	221	33

Alien		GB	IR
2000–19	●	0	0
1987–99	●	0	0
1970–86	●	1	0
pre-1970	○	0	0

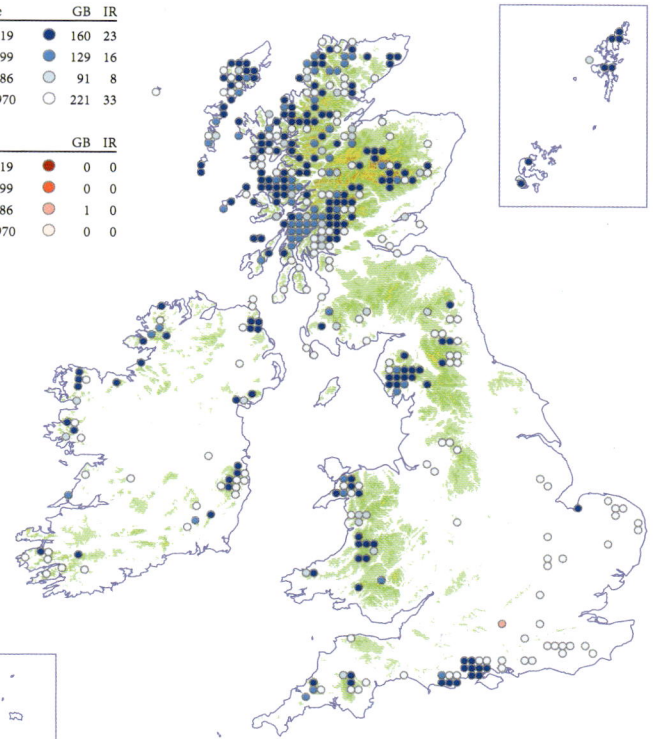

Key refs Allan *et al.* (1993), Harrap & Harrap (2009), Stewart *et al.* (1994), Stroh (2015d).

P.D. CAREY, T.D. DINES & R.M. BATEMAN

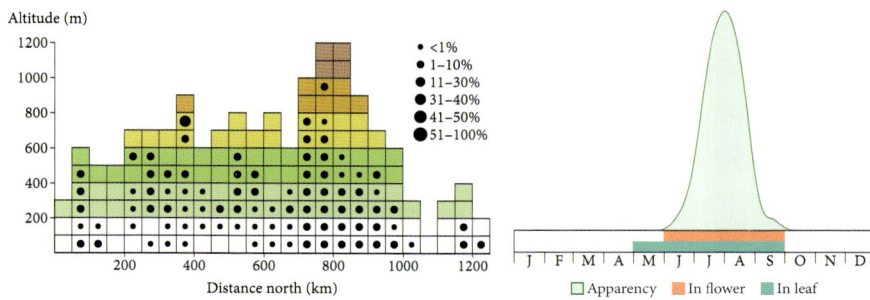

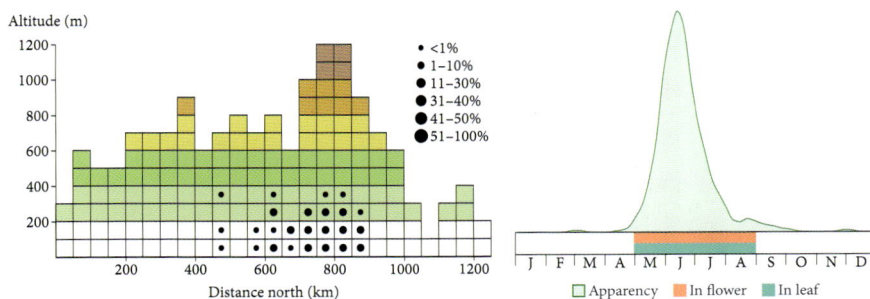

Corallorhiza trifida Coralroot Orchid

Châtel.

This rhizomatous herb, an obligate mycoheterotroph, is usually found in shaded, damp alder- and willow-carr on raised mires and lake margins, but also occurs in dune-slacks with *Salix repens*. More rarely, it grows in tall-herb fen, in *Betula* and *Pinus sylvestris* woods (amongst *Sphagnum*) and on moorland. It occasionally colonizes secondary habitats, including plantations and quarries. 0–365 m (Braemar, South Aberdeenshire).

Trends As *C. trifida* is easily overlooked, recent discoveries of new sites cannot readily be translated into assumptions of improved performance by the orchid, especially as the boundaries of its distribution appear unchanged; it remains concentrated in eastern Scotland. It has probably been lost from its southern outliers, near Settle in Mid-west Yorkshire (Salt Lake Quarry, Lawkland Moss), where it was last reported in 1990 and 1988 respectively.

Biogeography Circumpolar Boreal-montane element, with a continental distribution in western Europe.

Native		GB	IR
2000–19	●	82	0
1987–99	●	62	0
1970–86	●	64	0
pre-1970	○	54	0

Key refs Allan *et al.* (1993), Harrap & Harrap (2009), Stewart *et al.* (1994).

P.D. CAREY, T.D. DINES & R.M. BATEMAN

(N) *Spiranthes spiralis* Autumn Lady's-tresses
(L.) Chevall.

A tuberous herb of unimproved, well-grazed or mown grassland (including lawns and roadside verges) on dry calcareous soils, especially on chalk and limestone, and on cliff-tops and sand dunes; also on mildly acidic heathlands. It can persist undetected for many years, flowering profusely when late-summer grazing or mowing ceases. Lowland.

Trends This species declined considerably, particularly before 1930, when many pastures were re-sown or converted to arable. Subsequent losses are more likely to reflect improvement of grasslands with herbicides and fertilizers or, conversely, undergrazing. Always absent from Scotland and Northern Ireland, this species has experienced a striking retreat to the south and west, leaving only scattered remnants in central England, East Anglia and southern Ireland. Losses from habitats that still appear suitable for this species suggest that climate change – specifically, increased continentality – may have contributed to its decline.

Biogeography European Southern-temperate element.

Native		GB	IR
2000–19	●	329	45
1987–99	●	323	36
1970–86	●	222	21
pre-1970	○	626	96

Alien		GB	IR
2000–19	●	2	0
1987–99	●	1	0
1970–86	●	0	0
pre-1970	○	1	0

Key refs Dueck *et al.* (2014), Jacquemyn & Hutchings (2010), Stroh (2014b), Stroh *et al.* (2019), Wells (1967).

P.D. CAREY, T.D. DINES & R.M. BATEMAN

(N) *Spiranthes aestivalis* Summer Lady's-tresses
(Poir.) Rich.

A tuberous perennial herb formerly occurring amongst *Sphagnum* mosses in several valley bogs in the New Forest (South Hampshire), in a *Sphagnum* bog on Guernsey, and on wet, sandy ground beside St. Ouen's Pond on Jersey. Lowland.

Trends This species has been extirpated from Britain. The last record was in 1959 from the New Forest (South Hampshire), where five populations, some large, were progressively lost to a combination of drainage, afforestation and, most notably, serious over-collecting. It was eliminated from the Channel Islands for the same reasons, last flowering in Guernsey in 1914 and in Jersey in the late 1920s.

Biogeography European Temperate element.

	GB	IR
Long term	No trend	No trend
Short term	No trend	No trend

Native		GB	IR
2000–19	●	0	0
1987–99	●	0	0
1970–86	●	0	0
pre-1970	○	3	0

Key refs Brewis *et al.* (1996), Dueck *et al.* (2014), Foley (2004), Le Sueur (1984), McClintock (1975), Summerhayes (1968).

P.D. CAREY, T.D. DINES & R.M. BATEMAN

N *Spiranthes romanzoffiana* Irish Lady's-tresses

Cham.

A tuberous herb of neutral or acidic, nutrient poor, often peaty soils amongst periodically flooded or flushed vegetation, most commonly by rivers, streams and lake margins; also in machair–moorland ecotones. It often occurs amongst *Molinia caerulea* in pastures grazed (and therefore poached) by cattle or ponies. Arguments that its reproduction is mostly vegetative appear inconsistent with its wide yet scattered distribution; this may be explained by recent observations of limited vegetative spread but also limited seed production in apparently abortive capsules. Lowland.

Trends Sporadic flowering makes this species difficult to detect. Nonetheless, a deliberate recording effort has revealed far more new sites than have been lost to drainage and reclamation. Its remarkable distribution shows concentrations in

south-western Ireland (declining), the lake district of west-central Ireland, around Lough Neagh in north-eastern Ireland, and throughout the southern Hebrides. An extraordinary genetic boundary separates populations north of Mull from all those located farther south. Outlying populations are known from Dartmoor (although it has not been seen here since 1993) and west Wales (discovered in 2019).

Biogeography Oceanic Boreal-montane element; in Europe restricted to Britain and Ireland but widespread in North America.

Native	GB	IR
2000–19	27	31
1987–99	18	16
1970–86	14	18
pre-1970	11	29

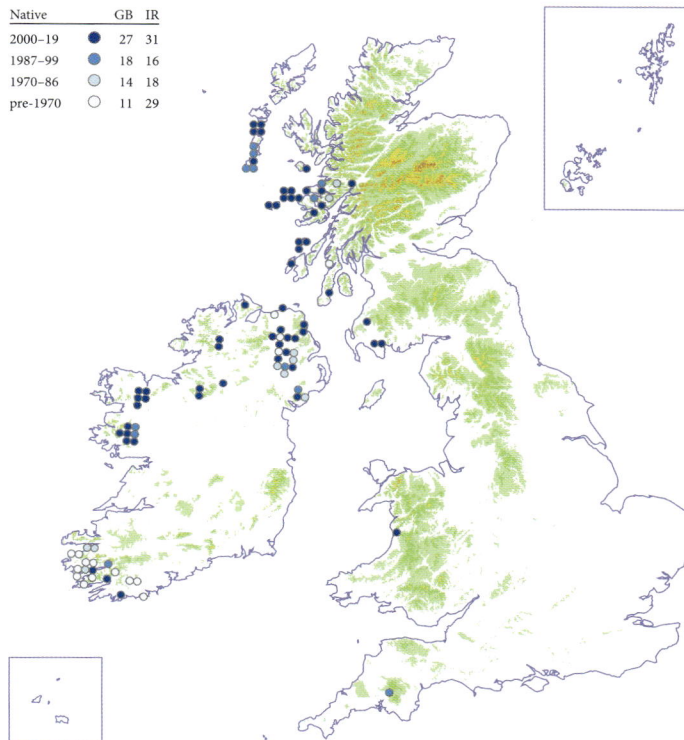

Key refs Curtis & Thompson (2009), Dueck *et al.* (2014), Forrest *et al.* (2004), Gulliver (1996), Horsman (2005), Pearman & Preston (2000), Scobie (2007), Stroh *et al.* (2019).

P.D. Carey, T.D. Dines & R.M. Bateman

N *Goodyera repens* Creeping Lady's-tresses

(L.) R.Br.

A creeping, stoloniferous evergreen perennial herb of semi-natural and planted coniferous woodland, usually of *Pinus sylvestris*, where it prefers slight to moderate shade in moist layers of moss and pine-needles. It also occurs under planted *Pinus* on stabilized sand dunes. 0–335 m (Morinsh, Banffshire), but with an exceptional record at 740 m from Ben Rinnes (Banffshire).

Trends Although core populations in the Caledonian pine forests of north-eastern Scotland remain strong, outlying populations are gradually being lost, particularly in south-eastern Scotland and on the Norfolk coast, where extant populations occur under pines on stabilized sand dunes at Holkham (West Norfolk). The most frequent cause is decreased shading and scrub encroachment following felling and replanting of *Pinus sylvestris*, though

increased shading is also damaging. Detailed genetic studies are needed to select among three hypotheses for the origin of the East Anglian outlier: transplanting from Scotland alongside *P. sylvestris* seedlings, subsequent natural colonization of the pine plantations by wind-blown seed, or (less likely) preceding the pine plantations as natural populations that initially occupied open heathland.

Biogeography Circumpolar Boreal-montane element.

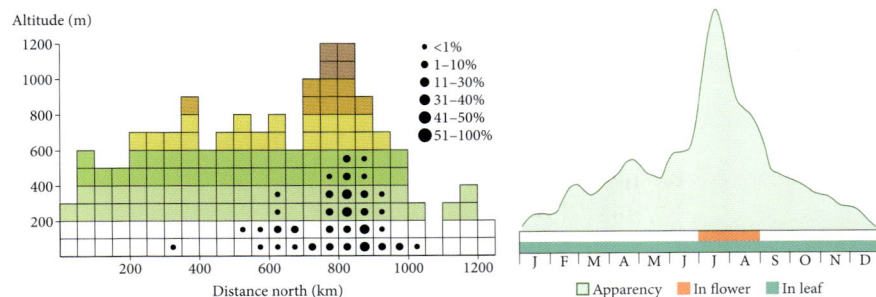

Native	GB	IR
2000–19	146	0
1987–99	108	0
1970–86	94	0
pre-1970	158	0

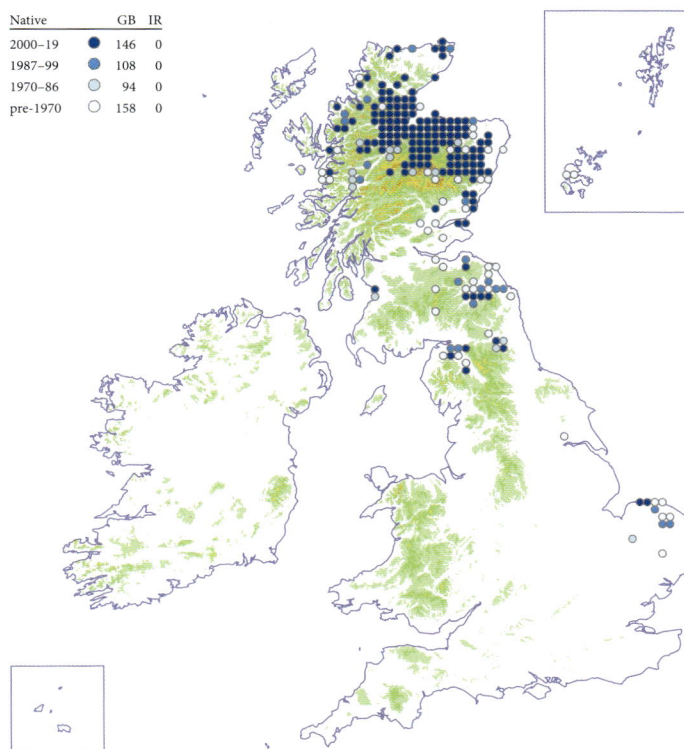

Key refs Allan *et al.* (1993), Brzosko *et al.* (2013), Groom (2013), Harrap & Harrap (2009), Hill & Preston (2015), Stewart *et al.* (1994), Summerhayes (1968).

P.D. Carey, T.D. Dines & R.M. Bateman

N *Herminium monorchis* Musk Orchid
(L.) R.Br.

A tuberous perennial herb of short turf on calcareous soils overlying chalk or oolitic limestone, particularly on the small terracettes of steep slopes. It also grows on quarry floors and on old lime-kiln spoil heaps. Lowland.

Trends This species declined throughout the 20th century, through ploughing and increased grazing. Losses have continued, mostly due to a lack of grazing and consequent scrub encroachment, though they have been partly offset by its ability to colonize new sites, notably abandoned quarries. *H. monorchis* is surprisingly vulnerable to prolonged drought, despite its preference for exposed, well-drained soils on south-facing slopes; it may therefore prove especially vulnerable to climate change. Former sites in Wales and East Anglia have all been lost, this species now being confined to south-eastern and south-central England. Massive fluctuations in numbers of flowering plants between years make population size difficult to assess, but most populations appear to be decreasing in size.

Biogeography Eurasian Temperate element, with a continental distribution in western Europe.

Native		GB	IR
2000–19	●	26	0
1987–99	●	33	0
1970–86	○	46	0
pre-1970	○	100	0

Key refs Bateman *et al.* (2003), Rudall *et al.* (2013), Stewart *et al.* (1994), Stroh *et al.* (2019), Walker *et al.* (2017), Wells *et al.* (1998).

R.M. BATEMAN, P.D. CAREY & T.D. DINES

N *Platanthera chlorantha* Greater Butterfly-orchid
(Custer) Rchb.

This tuberous perennial herb is found in a wide variety of habitats, usually on well-drained calcareous soils. Typical habitats include downland, rough pasture, hay meadows, scrub and well-established deciduous woodland, where it prefers dappled sunlight. It occurs less often on sand dunes and railway embankments. Rarely, it grows on slightly acidic soils in moorland and wet, heathy pasture. 0–460 m (Harwood Dale, South Northumberland).

Trends *P. chlorantha* has suffered gradual but protracted decline across Britain and Ireland; recent losses have been greatest in areas of more intensive agriculture. Reasons include destruction, coniferization or altered management of woodland, and the agricultural improvement of pastures and hay meadows.

Biogeography European Temperate element.

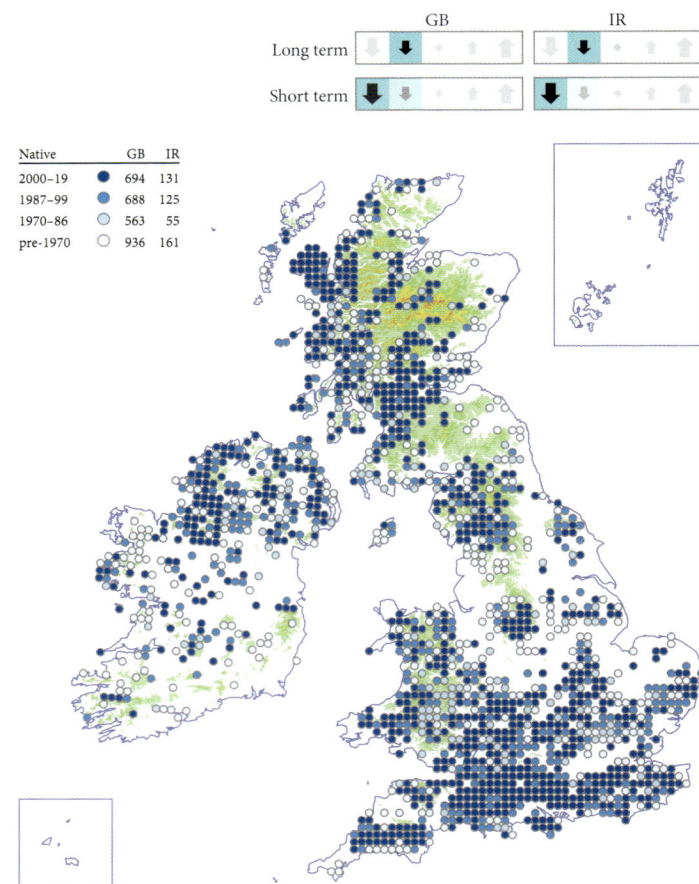

Native		GB	IR
2000–19	●	694	131
1987–99	●	688	125
1970–86	○	563	55
pre-1970	○	936	161

Key refs Bateman *et al.* (2012), Bateman *et al.* (2014), Harrap & Harrap (2009), Stroh *et al.* (2019).

R.M. BATEMAN, P.D. CAREY & T.D. DINES

Ⓝ *Platanthera bifolia* Lesser Butterfly-orchid
(L.) Rich.

A perennial herb of heathy pastures, damp and dry grassland, fens, mires, open scrub, woodland edges and rides, and on moorland, often amongst *Erica tetralix* and *Pteridium aquilinum*; it is found on a wide variety of acidic and calcareous soils overlying sands, gravels, clays, chalks and limestones. It tolerates considerable soil moisture, also occupying marginal zones of acidic bogs, flushes and calcareous fens. 0–520 m (north of Gleann Fionnlighe, Westerness).

Trends The considerable long-term decline suffered by this species is continuing, most severely in England; in East Anglia, historical records from approximately 40 hectads now appear to be represented by just two populations, both on the Norfolk coast. Only the heartlands of *P. bifolia* in western and northern Scotland and Ireland appear

relatively unchanged. In the lowlands it has been lost through drainage, woodland disturbance and agricultural intensification, whereas some upland populations have suffered due to altered grazing regimes. The losses appear to have disproportionately affected the ecotypes of calcareous grassland and of woodland relative to that occupying acid heathland. Detailed molecular comparison of these three ecotypes could potentially yield taxonomic decisions comparable to those recently applied to the three native ecotypes of *Gymnadenia*. Also, the larger flowered *P. muelleri* or *P. fornicata*, recently segregated from *P. bifolia* in continental Europe, should be sought in Britain, as populations occur as close as Belgium.

Biogeography Eurasian Boreo-temperate element.

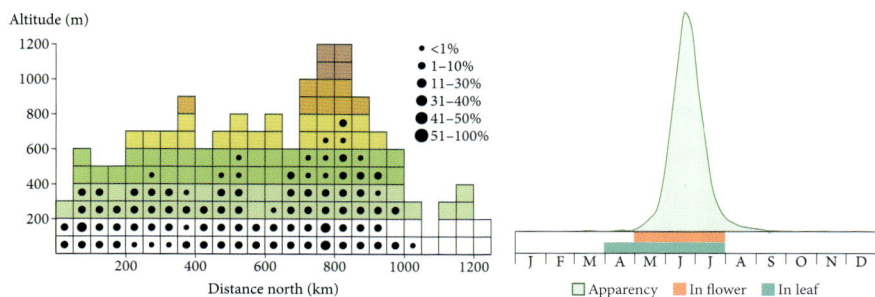

Native	GB	IR
2000–19	413	210
1987–99	382	168
1970–86	370	64
pre-1970	857	196

Key refs Bateman *et al.* (2012), Bateman *et al.* (2014), Baum & Baum (2017), Durka *et al.* (2017), Stroh *et al.* (2019), Tyteca & Esposito (2018), Tyteca *et al.* (2018b).

R.M. Bateman, P.D. Carey & T.D. Dines

Ⓝ *Pseudorchis albida* Small-white Orchid
(L.) Á.Löve & D.Löve

A tuberous perennial herb of well-drained hill pastures, streamside mires, mountain grasslands and cliff ledges on infertile (often glacial) soils that range from mildly acidic to calcareous. *P. albida* also occurs on recently burnt moorland, but does not persist when *Calluna vulgaris* and/ or *Pteridium aquilinum* regrows. Rarely, it occurs in acidic *Quercus* woodland and stabilized coastal dunes. 0–550 m (Ben Chaisteil, Main Argyll), but reportedly higher in the Cairngorms at the head of Caenlochan Glen (Angus).

Trends This is a species of particular conservation concern, as the majority of recorded populations have been lost and most of those that remain are small, offsetting the supposed benefits of high fruit-set. Although it is easily overlooked, *P. albida* nonetheless appears to be declining rapidly throughout our area with the exception of the uplands of northern Scotland.

This species has long been lost from the Weald of south-eastern England and, more recently, from much of northern England other than the Yorkshire and Cumbria Dales. It may soon be lost to Wales and appears to be declining especially rapidly in Ireland, though the large number of comparatively recent records from the Sligo region suggest that it may be under-recorded elsewhere. Early phases of this decline were likely due mainly to habitat destruction, afforestation or agricultural improvement, but it is also a poor competitor; grazing by livestock or deer must be neither absent nor too intense.

Biogeography European Boreal-montane element; also in North America.

Native	GB	IR
2000–19	136	21
1987–99	144	32
1970–86	122	16
pre-1970	315	90

Key refs Allan *et al.* (1993), Bateman *et al.* (2017a), Bateman *et al.* (2018b), Duffy *et al.* (2008), Duffy *et al.* (2011), Jersákova *et al.* (2011), Reinhammar *et al.* (2002).

R.M. Bateman, P.D. Carey & T.D. Dines

(N) *Gymnadenia conopsea s.l.* Fragrant-orchids

A taxonomically contentious aggregate of tuberous perennial herbs. Its constituent taxa have radically different habitat preferences that stretch from chalk downland through calcareous marshes and fens to acidic heathlands, and consequently show contrasting geographical and altitudinal distributions.

Trends *G. conopsea s.l.* is well-distributed across Britain and Ireland, but less frequent in areas dominated by intensive agriculture. Recent discussions regarding whether this aggregate is best treated as one, two or three species have focused on the contrast between strongly divergent molecular signatures, genome sizes, flowering periods and habitat preferences versus a relatively low degree of morphological divergence that renders near-cryptic the three taxa. Here, these taxa have

been elevated to species level from the subspecific status that they were awarded previously. Optimised morphological circumscriptions are leading to much-improved, though still far from perfect, mapped distributions for the three species. However, the relatively high proportion of uncertain identifications makes trends of gain or loss especially difficult to discern within this aggregate, and more appropriately considered at the level of individual species. Mixed populations are uncommon, though at least one locality in Cumbria supports all three *Gymnadenia* species.

Biogeography Eurosiberian temperate element.

Native	GB	IR
2000–19	845	249
1987–99	850	253
1970–86	672	67
pre-1970	1069	251

Alien	GB	IR
2000–19	1	0
1987–99	1	0
1970–86	0	0
pre-1970	0	0

Altitude (m) chart:
- <1%
- 1–10%
- 11–30%
- 31–40%
- 41–50%
- 51–100%

Apparency / In flower / In leaf

Key refs Bateman (2006, 2021c), Bateman & Denholm (2019), Bateman *et al.* (2021b), Brandrud *et al.* (2019), Campbell *et al.* (2007), Chapurlat *et al.* (2020), Meekers *et al.* (2012).

R.M. Bateman & I. Denholm

(N) *Gymnadenia conopsea* Chalk Fragrant-orchid
(L.) R.Br.

A tuberous perennial herb of chalk downland and limestone pastures and pavement, occasionally found on stabilized dunes and along the margins of base-rich fens. It also occasionally invades artificial habitats, including abandoned quarries, industrial waste, roadside verges and railway banks. 0–415 m (Harwood Beck, County Durham).

Trends Although *G. borealis* and *G. densiflora* have been relatively well recorded this century, this is less true of *G. conopsea*, which is morphologically intermediate between the other two species and thus is less easily identified with confidence. Although sparse records persist on the map, it has yet to be conclusively demonstrated that *G. conopsea s.s.* occurs in Scotland. Despite the far from perfect mapping, there is evidence that this species has

declined throughout its range, due mainly to ploughing and agricultural improvement of its grassland habitats, as well as altered management leading to scrub encroachment.

Biogeography Eurasian Boreo-temperate element.

Native	GB	IR
2000–19	264	141
1987–99	155	53
1970–86	115	30
pre-1970	186	41

Alien	GB	IR
2000–19	1	0
1987–99	1	0
1970–86	0	0
pre-1970	0	0

	GB	IR
Long term	No trend	No trend
Short term	No trend	No trend

Altitude (m) chart:
- <1%
- 1–10%
- 11–30%
- 31–40%
- 41–50%
- 51–100%

Apparency / In flower / In leaf

Key refs Bateman (2006, 2021c), Bateman & Denholm (2019), Bateman *et al.* (2021b), Brandrud *et al.* (2019), Campbell *et al.* (2007), Lönn *et al.* (2006), Sark *et al.* (2011).

R.M. Bateman & I. Denholm

N *Gymnadenia densiflora* Marsh Fragrant-orchid
(Wahlenb.) A.Dietr.

A tuberous perennial herb of base-rich wet meadows, fens, ditches and flushes. Occasionally it is recorded from dune-slacks, clay undercliffs and north-facing chalk and limestone grassland. Mainly lowland, but reaching 380 m (Hermitage, Roxburghshire).

Trends Long distinguished from *G. conopsea s.s.* but at varietal or subspecies level, this species remains under-recorded in Scotland and also in Ireland, where it may eventually be shown to be the most frequent species of *Gymnadenia*. Losses appear most frequent in England, but this may simply reflect more attentive recording in other countries. It is very sensitive to eutrophication, drainage and lowering of the water table, and so has declined, particularly in the East Anglian fens. Ploughing of grassland has also reputedly eliminated some populations.

Late-flowering populations occurring in dune-slacks at Kenfig (Glamorganshire), and on at least two chalk downland localities in Sussex were recently shown to resemble molecularly, but nonetheless differ from, *G. densiflora*; they have been equated tentatively with *G. densiflora* subsp. *friesica* (formerly a variety) of the Frisian Islands in the Netherlands.

Biogeography European Temperate element.

	GB	IR
Long term	No trend	No trend
Short term	No trend	No trend

Native		GB	IR
2000–19	●	158	63
1987–99	●	85	10
1970–86	○	54	0
pre-1970	○	103	5

Key refs Bateman (2006), Bateman & Denholm (2019), Bateman *et al.* (2021b), Brandrud *et al.* (2019), Campbell *et al.* (2007), Kreutz (2008), Sark *et al.* (2011).

R.M. BATEMAN & I. DENHOLM

N *Gymnadenia borealis* Heath Fragrant-orchid
(Druce) R.M.Bateman, Pridgeon & M.W.Chase

A tuberous perennial herb of mildly base-rich to mildly acidic grasslands, machair, heathlands, moors, and on tussocks in flushes on soils derived from substrates including sands, limestones and clays. It is also frequently encountered on roadside verges and in abandoned quarries. 0–610 m (Ben Lawers, Mid Perthshire).

Trends Although this species remains under-recorded, its distribution across Britain and Ireland has become much clearer over the last two decades; this is the dominant *Gymnadenia* species in Cornwall, western Wales, Northern Ireland, northern England and Scotland, where *G. borealis* and *Dactylorhiza maculata* are the most frequent orchids in the uplands. Sporadic heathland populations in southern England are declining, where both altered management regimes and increased

periods of drought are suspected causes. Rare records of this species from chalk downland have been discounted as depauperate plants of *G. conopsea s.s.*

Biogeography Possibly a boreal endemic, though populations of similar morphology that occur in Norway and Portugal may ultimately cause this species to be recategorized as a member of the Boreal element.

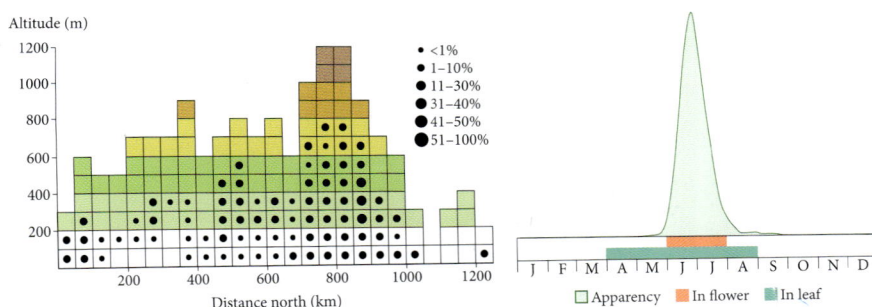

	GB	IR
Long term	No trend	No trend
Short term	No trend	No trend

Native		GB	IR
2000–19	●	385	27
1987–99	●	100	5
1970–86	○	47	0
pre-1970	○	37	0

Key refs Bateman (2006), Bateman & Denholm (2019), Bateman *et al.* (2021b), Brandrud *et al.* (2019), Campbell *et al.* (2007), Meekers *et al.* (2012), Tyteca *et al.* (2018a).

R.M. BATEMAN & I. DENHOLM

Hy *Dactylorhiza fuchsii* × *Gymnadenia conopsea s.l.*

	GB	IR
Long term	No trend	No trend
Short term	No trend	No trend

Due to the past use of the hybrid binomial ×*Dactylodenia st-quintinii* as a 'catch-all' to cover these hybrids when all the fragrant-orchids were considered to be a single species, it has proved impossible to map separately with any confidence hybrid records of *D. fuchsii* with the three *Gymnadenia* parent species currently recognized (*G. conopsea s.s.*, *G. borealis*, *G. densiflora*). The hybrid of *D. fuchsii* with *G. conopsea s.s.* (×*Dactylodenia heinzeliana*) is probably the most common intergeneric hybrid orchid in our area, often found in chalk or limestone grassland where the parents occur together. The hybrid of *D. fuchsii* with *G. borealis* (×*Dactylodenia st-quintinii*) is almost certainly widespread in northern England and Scotland, most likely to be found in heathland, upland pastures and hay meadows. Confirmed records of hybrids of *D. fuchsii* with *G. densiflora* are surprisingly rare, given that the parents occur frequently together, most commonly in calcareous marshes and flooded quarries but also occasionally in calcareous flushes on limestone grassland (Lang, 2001). Populations are usually small, and often consist of a single plant. 0–410 m (Ben Lawers, Mid Perthshire).

A spontaneous hybrid (native × native).

Trends The distribution and range for all three ×*Dactylodenia* hybrid taxa subsumed into *D. fuchsii* × *G. conopsea s.l.* are under-recorded, and these hybrids should be searched for wherever the parent species occur together.

Biogeography Hybrids between *D. fuchsii* and fragrant orchids are also known on the mainland of western Europe.

		GB	IR
2000–19	●	24	1
1987–99	●	34	1
1970–86	●	20	1
pre-1970	○	17	0

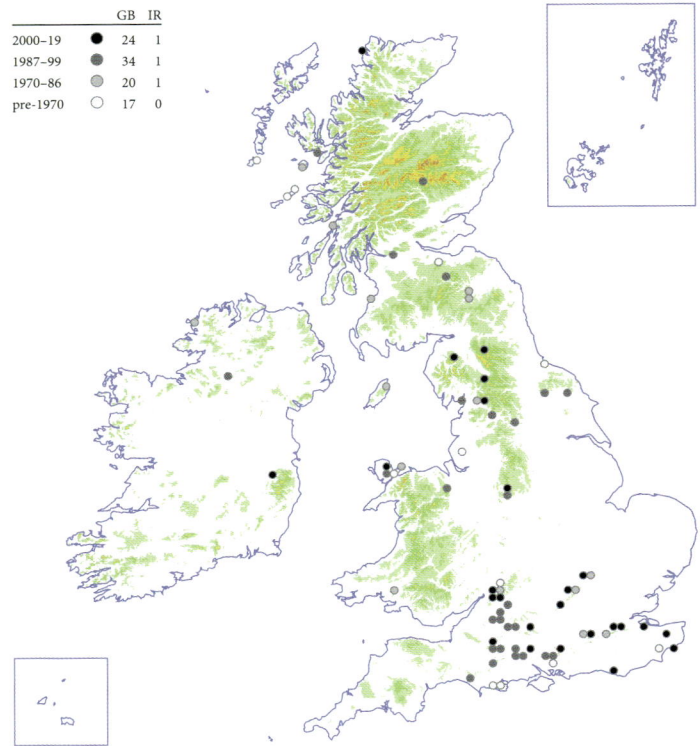

Key refs Lang (2001), Stace *et al.* (2015).

P.A. STROH & R.M. BATEMAN

Altitude (m) chart — legend: <1%, 1–10%, 11–30%, 31–40%, 41–50%, 51–100%. Distance north (km). Apparency / In flower / In leaf.

Hy *Dactylorhiza maculata* × *Gymnadenia conopsea s.l.*

	GB	IR
Long term	No trend	No trend
Short term	No trend	No trend

All records of *G. conopsea s.l.* (inclusive of *G. conopsea s.s.*, *G. borealis*, *G. densiflora*) × *D. maculata* are included on the map, although most if not all are likely to represent hybrids involving *G. borealis* (×*Dactylodenia evansii*). The latter is the most calcifugous of the British and Irish *Gymnadenia* species and *D. maculata* is a consistent calcifuge; there is thus an overlap in their habitat requirements. *G. borealis* tends to grow in slightly drier soils than *D. maculata* and hybrids occur most often in ecotones of intermediate soil moisture.

A spontaneous hybrid (native × native).

Trends This hybrid concept is mapped in an atlas for the first time. All *G. conopsea s.l.* hybrids with *D. maculata* are likely to be under-recorded, but most especially ×*Dactylodenia evansii*.

Biogeography Limited evidence suggests that this aggregate hybrid occurs sporadically across Europe, typically in small numbers wherever the two parental species co-occur, although its distribution is uncertain due to differing views amongst continental botanists on the taxonomy of its parent species.

		GB	IR
2000–19	●	24	0
1987–99	●	15	0
1970–86	●	17	2
pre-1970	○	18	2

Key refs Stace *et al.* (2015).

R.M. BATEMAN

Altitude (m) chart — legend: <1%, 1–10%, 11–30%, 31–40%, 41–50%, 51–100%. Distance north (km). Apparency / In flower / In leaf.

Dactylorhiza fuchsii Common Spotted-orchid
(Druce) Soó

This tuberous perennial herb grows on neutral or base-rich soils in a wide range of habitats, including deciduous woodland, scrub, roadsides, chalk grassland, meadows, marshes, dune-slacks, fens and, more rarely, mildly acidic heaths. It can become abundant in artificial habitats such as waste ground, abandoned gravel-pits, quarries and railway embankments. 0–825 m (Great Dun Fell, Westmorland).

Trends *D. fuchsii* is the most widespread orchid species across our area; occasional losses have probably been balanced by its ability to colonize newly available, often man-made, habitats. The apparent substantial decreases this century in the extreme south-west of Britain and Ireland and the Scottish Highlands are perplexing; one possible explanation is greater skill among the botanical community in distinguishing

D. fuchsii from the morphologically similar *D. maculata*, which is relatively common in these areas. This species hybridizes readily with all other dactylorchids, and may have played a role in the origin of all of the British and Irish allotetraploid dactylorchids other than *D. kerryensis*. Some authorities still maintain that some plants from the machair of north-western Ireland and western Scotland merit subspecific status as subsp. *hebridensis*, whereas in Scandinavia the diploid *D. fuchsii* is still widely regarded as a subspecies of the tetraploid *D. maculata*.

Biogeography Eurosiberian Temperate element.

Native	GB	IR
2000–19	2025	763
1987–99	1975	679
1970–86	1440	140
pre-1970	1743	487

Key refs Bateman (2021b), Bateman & Denholm (1989), Pillon *et al.* (2007), Stahlberg & Hedrén (2008), Stahlberg & Hedrén (2010).

R.M. BATEMAN & I. DENHOLM

Dactylorhiza fuchsii × maculata = D. ×transiens
(Druce) Soó

A tuberous perennial herb occasionally found where base-rich and base-poor soils coexist, allowing the parents to grow together, such as where sandstones are interbedded with limestones or where limestones are overlain by acidic peaty deposits. It has been reported from coastal dunes, lowland and upland meadows, marshes, heathland, roadside embankments and disused quarries. Even where large numbers of each species are found together, convincing hybrid plants can be few in number, and any introgressed plants are impossible to identify morphologically with confidence. It is triploid, and sterile. Lowland.

A spontaneous hybrid (native × native).

Trends An uncommon hybrid which may sometimes be recorded in error for variants of either parent. Some

losses are due to habitat destruction, but most are probably due to the transient nature of the hybrid.

Biogeography This hybrid is also recorded from several countries in mainland Europe, though the frequent inclusion there of *D. fuchsii* within *D. maculata* has tended to obscure the occurrence of the hybrid (Bateman & Denholm, 2003).

	GB	IR
2000–19	97	18
1987–99	71	5
1970–86	47	3
pre-1970	44	4

	GB	IR
Long term	No trend	No trend
Short term	No trend	No trend

Key refs Bateman & Denholm (2003), Stace *et al.* (2015).

C.A. STACE, C.D. PRESTON & D.A. PEARMAN

Hy *Dactylorhiza fuchsii × incarnata* = *D. ×kernerorum*
(Soó) Soó

A tuberous perennial herb of neutral or mildly acidic damp heathland or heathy grassland where the relatively calcifugous *D. incarnata* subsp. *pulchella* is one parent, and in coastal dune-slacks and machair and moist, base-rich grassland and calcareous flushes, marshes and fens inland where the *D. incarnata* parent is usually one of the more calcicolous subspecies. It may persist in the absence of *D. incarnata* if drainage has caused the loss of this species from the site. Although both parents are diploid, this hybrid is usually sterile and populations usually consist of only a few plants. Lowland.

A spontaneous hybrid (native × native).

Trends Given the frequency of the parents in suitable habitat, this is a surprisingly uncommon hybrid, although it is probably under-recorded.

Populations tend to be naturally transient, disappearing even if the habitat remains unaltered, and this probably accounts for most of the losses.

Biogeography Widespread in temperate Europe.

	GB	IR
Long term	No trend	No trend
Short term	No trend	No trend

	GB	IR
2000–19	29	9
1987–99	35	3
1970–86	21	5
pre-1970	26	1

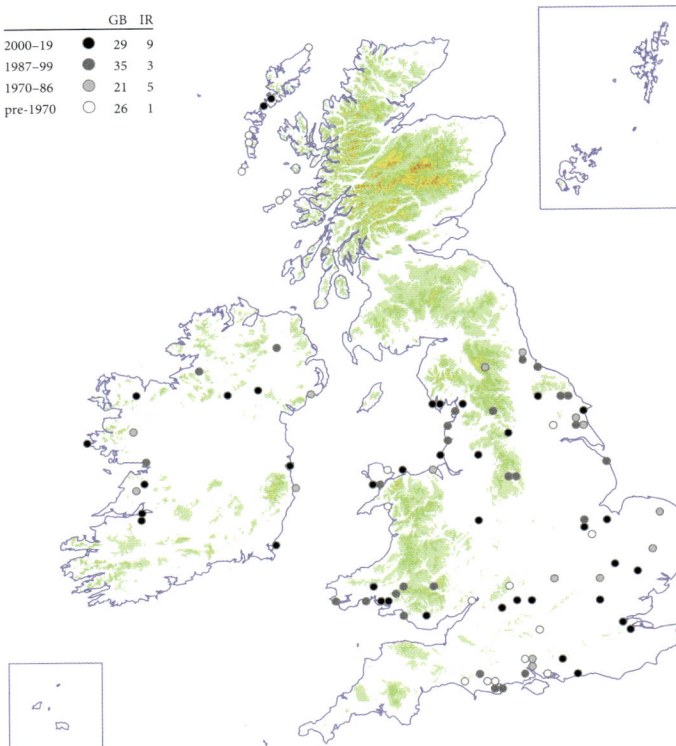

Key refs Stace *et al.* (2015).

C.A. STACE, C.D. PRESTON & D.A. PEARMAN

Hy *Dactylorhiza fuchsii × praetermissa* = *D. ×grandis*
(Druce) P.F.Hunt

A tall tuberous perennial herb commonly found where the parents grow together, typically in habitats such as damp pasture, marshes, base-rich fens and wet meadows, consolidated dunes, dune-slacks and flushed slopes on the coast, and on damp chalk grassland, lawns and roadside verges. It is especially frequent in man-made habitats such as disused brickworks, quarries, railway cuttings and industrial waste land, and although normally found with both parents, the hybrid may persist in the absence of *D. praetermissa* in chalk grassland, and in the absence of *D. fuchsii* in marshes. This hybrid is triploid, partially fertile and frequently back-crosses with the parents, creating long-lived hybrid swarms. Generally lowland, but reaching 380 m at Buxton (Derbyshire).

A spontaneous hybrid (native × native).

Trends Although this is the most frequent *Dactylorhiza* hybrid, it is still probably under-recorded. Its overall distribution is likely to be increasing, especially in central and northern England, due to the spread of *D. praetermissa* into new areas as a result of climate change.

Biogeography This hybrid is also recorded from mainland Europe within the limited distribution of *D. praetermissa* (northern France and the Low Countries).

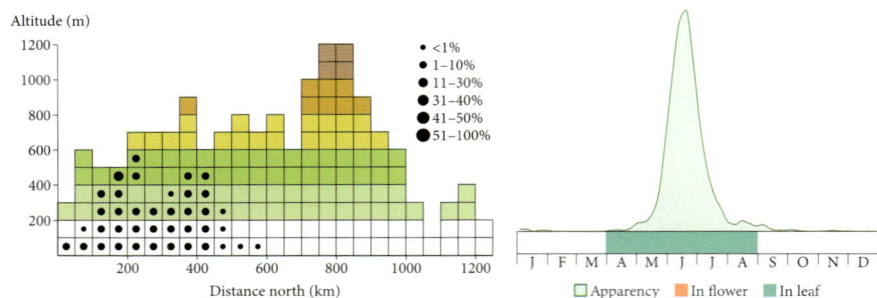

	GB	IR
Long term	No trend	No trend
Short term	No trend	No trend

	GB	IR
2000–19	411	0
1987–99	235	0
1970–86	148	0
pre-1970	108	0

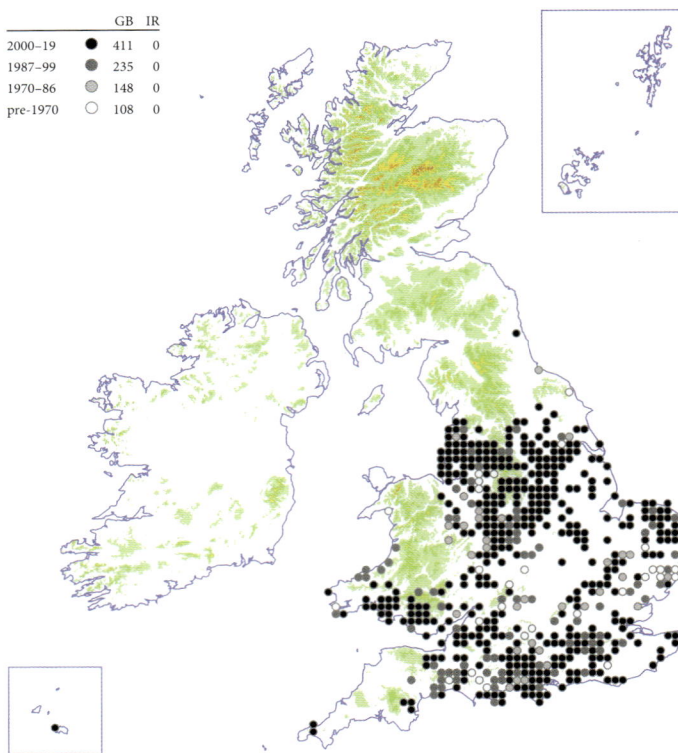

Key refs Stace *et al.* (2015).

C.A. STACE, C.D. PRESTON & D.A. PEARMAN

Hy *Dactylorhiza fuchsii × purpurella = D. ×venusta*

(T.Stephenson & T.A.Stephenson) Soó

		GB	IR
Long term		No trend	No trend
Short term		No trend	No trend

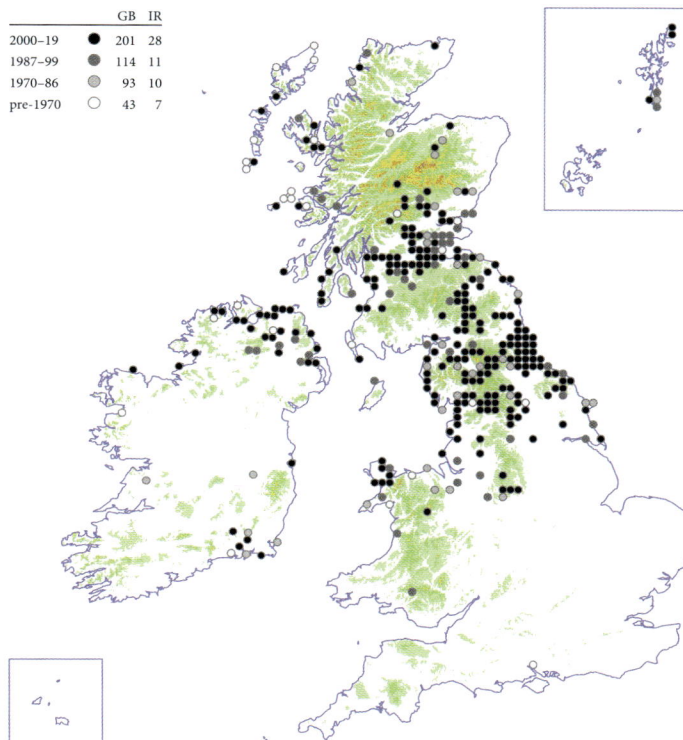

This tuberous perennial herb is frequent wherever the parents grow together, and is found in consolidated sand dune grassland and dune-slacks, calcareous fens, marshes, wet pastures and damp scrub. It also occurs amongst *Dactylorhiza* populations which have colonized old gravel-pits and disused limestone quarries, colliery slag heaps and tips of calcareous industrial waste. It may persist in the absence of *D. purpurella* if drainage has caused the loss of this species from the site. This partially fertile triploid hybrid can back-cross with its parents, and is often present in long-lived hybrid swarms. 0–360 m (Nenthead, Cumberland).

A spontaneous hybrid (native × native).

Trends A frequent *Dactylorhiza* hybrid, but probably still under-recorded. Its overall distribution is likely to be stable. The hybrid record from the outlying and now extinct population of *D. purpurella* in Hampshire may instead represent a morphologically extreme form of *D. praetermissa*.

Biogeography Described from Britain; in mainland Europe *D. purpurella* is confined to south-western Scandinavia, but no record of the hybrid is known.

	GB	IR
2000–19	201	28
1987–99	114	11
1970–86	93	10
pre-1970	43	7

Key refs Stace *et al.* (2015).

C.A. STACE, C.D. PRESTON & D.A. PEARMAN

Altitude (m) / Distance north (km)

Apparency | In flower | In leaf

N *Dactylorhiza maculata* Heath Spotted-orchid

(L.) Soó

	GB	IR
Long term		
Short term		

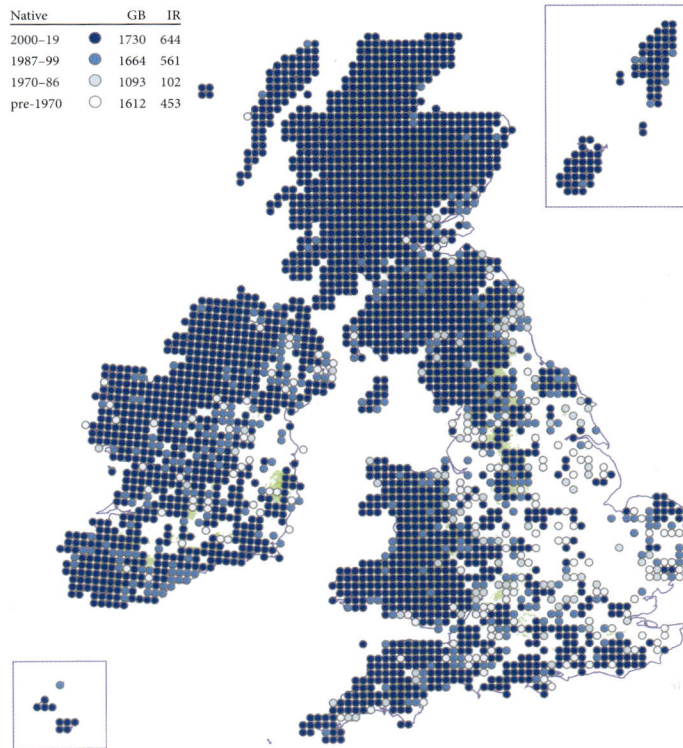

This tuberous perennial herb is found on a range of damp to wet, typically mildly acidic soils in a wide variety of habitats, including unimproved grasslands, dry and wet heathlands, flushes and the margins of blanket bogs. It also occurs in pockets of peat on limestone and, more rarely, in open woodland. 0–915 m (Ben Lawers, Mid Perthshire).

Trends *D. maculata* is sporadic over much of southern and central England and central Ireland but is ubiquitous elsewhere; it remains extremely abundant in heathlands and moorlands in northern and western parts of Britain and Ireland, and may be the most numerous orchid in our area. The more isolated inland-lowland populations in central and eastern England and central Ireland are gradually being eliminated through destruction, drainage or changed management of their habitats, particularly of heathlands. The species is an autopolyploid that probably originated in eastern Europe; British and Irish populations are relatively young but are not evolutionarily cohesive, leading to the rejection of any idea that they might better be treated as a separate species, *D. ericetorum*.

Biogeography Eurosiberian Boreo-temperate element.

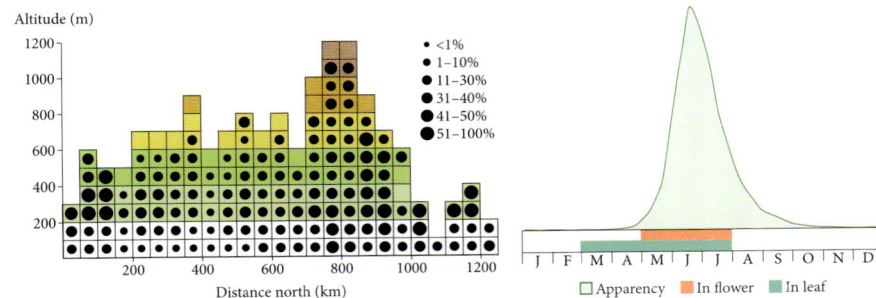

Native	GB	IR
2000–19	1730	644
1987–99	1664	561
1970–86	1093	102
pre-1970	1612	453

Key refs Allan *et al.* (1993), Bateman (2021b), Bateman & Denholm (1989, 2003), Brandrud *et al.* (2020), Dufrene *et al.* (1991), Eccarius (2016), Pillon *et al.* (2007).

R.M. BATEMAN & I. DENHOLM

Altitude (m) / Distance north (km)

Apparency | In flower | In leaf

Hy *Dactylorhiza maculata × praetermissa = D. ×hallii*
(Druce) Soó

A tuberous perennial herb of calcareous to mildly acidic soils, found on flushed cliff slopes, heathland over serpentine and gabbro, base-rich fens, acidic marshes, moist meadows and pastures, and roadside verges. Since the parents differ markedly in their tolerance to calcium, they do not meet frequently, and the hybrid, which is tetraploid, is therefore uncommon. It is, however, relatively fertile and hybrid swarms can be formed through back-crossing with the parents. Lowland.

A spontaneous hybrid (native × native).

Trends Although uncommon, this hybrid is likely to be under-recorded. Its overall distribution is probably stable.

Biogeography This hybrid is also recorded from the Netherlands.

	GB	IR
Long term	No trend	No trend
Short term	No trend	No trend

	GB	IR
2000–19	68	0
1987–99	52	0
1970–86	27	0
pre-1970	36	0

Key refs Stace *et al.* (2015).

C.A. STACE, C.D. PRESTON & D.A. PEARMAN

Altitude (m) / Distance north (km)
<1%, 1–10%, 11–30%, 31–40%, 41–50%, 51–100%

Apparency / In flower / In leaf

J F M A M J J A S O N D

Hy *Dactylorhiza maculata × purpurella = D. ×formosa*
(T.Stephenson & T.A.Stephenson) Soó

A tuberous perennial herb of calcareous to mildly acidic soils, typically occurring in habitats such as moist sea-cliffs, the sides of streams and ditches and in bogs, lakeside marshes, flushes, marshy fields, damp meadows and lawns. Usually, but not always, it occurs in the presence of the parents. It is tetraploid, fully fertile and frequently back-crosses with the parents, creating long-lived hybrid swarms. 0–410 m (Ben Lawers, Mid Perthshire).

A spontaneous hybrid (native × native).

Trends A frequent hybrid, but almost certainly still under-recorded. Its overall distribution is likely to be stable.

Biogeography This hybrid is also recorded from Norway.

	GB	IR
Long term	No trend	No trend
Short term	No trend	No trend

	GB	IR
2000–19	172	17
1987–99	87	5
1970–86	65	5
pre-1970	81	3

Key refs Stace *et al.* (2015).

C.A. STACE, C.D. PRESTON & D.A. PEARMAN

Altitude (m) / Distance north (km)
<1%, 1–10%, 11–30%, 31–40%, 41–50%, 51–100%

Apparency / In flower / In leaf

J F M A M J J A S O N D

Dactylorhiza incarnata Early Marsh-orchid
(L.) Soó

Tuberous perennial herbs that together constitute an aggregate of ecotypes that collectively span a remarkable range of habitats; this species is constrained mainly by a need for ever-wet soils. The majority of the ecotypes prefer calcareous substrates, occurring in water-meadows, marshes, fens, flushes, lough-sides and dune-slacks, though subsp. *pulchella* has a preference for *Sphagnum* bogs and damp heaths developed on acidic soils. 0–610 m (Atholl, East Perthshire, and Caenlochan, Angus).

Trends Occurring throughout the British Isles, *D. incarnata* has declined gradually but continually due to drainage and agricultural improvement, as well as lowered water tables; it is often the first *Dactylorhiza* to be lost when a habitat begins to dry out. Losses have therefore occurred throughout its range but have been most severe in the more agriculturally intensive

and urbanized areas. Mapping of the subspecies has improved greatly, but detailed molecular comparison is urgently required; the peculiar impoverished genome of this species seems incongruent with its ability to evolve a wide spectrum of more narrowly focused ecotypes, and these remain in need of reliable explanation. Among the five subspecies mapped separately, a narrow circumscription of subsp. *ochroleuca* has been adopted and ongoing nomenclatural controversies surrounding subsp. *cruenta* have been sidelined pending stronger data. In addition, subsp. *gemmana* is omitted because it is viewed as a 'category of convenience' for unusually vigorous populations and *D. incarnata* subsp. *lobbii*, recently suggested to occur in a Welsh dune system, is doubtfully distinct from *D. incarnata* subsp. *incarnata*.

Biogeography Eurosiberian Boreo-temperate element.

Native	GB	IR
2000–19	784	295
1987–99	715	210
1970–86	536	76
pre-1970	825	180

Key refs Bateman & Denholm (1985), Cole & Waller (2020), Haggar (2004a), Hedrén & Nordström (2009a), Pillon *et al.* (2007).

R.M. Bateman & I. Denholm

Dactylorhiza incarnata subsp. *incarnata*

A tuberous perennial herb of calcareous fens, ditches, marshes, wet meadows and upland flushes on base-rich or calcareous soils. It can be a robust plant, especially in the south, and may be abundant in suitable habitats. 0–585 m (High Cup Nick, Westmorland), and possibly higher in Scotland.

Trends This is the most widespread and variable subspecies of *D. incarnata*; plants in the north and west tend to be smaller and darker-flowered than those farther south. Improved recording probably explains increases in apparent frequency in Scotland, Ireland and East Anglia, but also increases confidence in the evidence of a substantial decline across much of England and Wales. Fen and marsh populations have suffered losses due to agricultural improvement, drainage and depleted water tables, whereas water-meadow populations are

vulnerable to changes in grazing regime.

Biogeography Eurosiberian Boreo-temperate element; subsp. *incarnata* occurs throughout much of the range of the species.

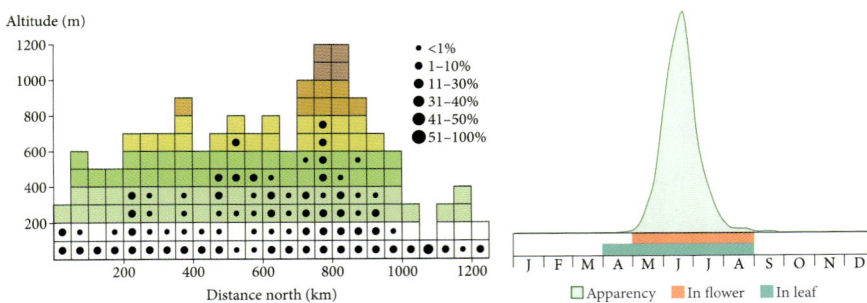

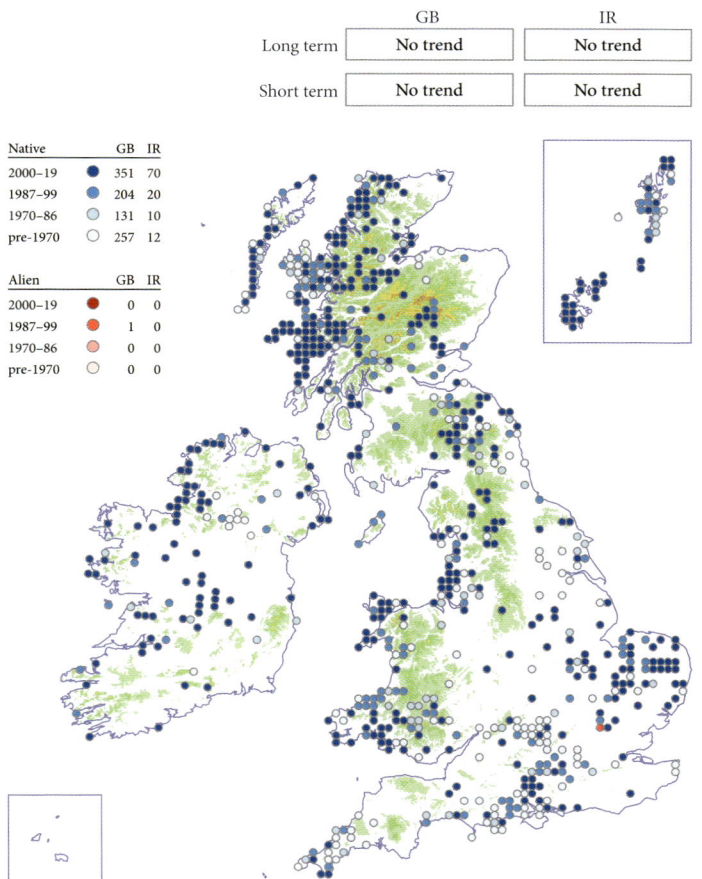

	GB	IR
Long term	No trend	No trend
Short term	No trend	No trend

Native	GB	IR
2000–19	351	70
1987–99	204	20
1970–86	131	10
pre-1970	257	12

Alien	GB	IR
2000–19	0	0
1987–99	1	0
1970–86	0	0
pre-1970	0	0

Key refs Bateman & Denholm (1985), Pillon *et al.* (2007).

R.M. Bateman & I. Denholm

Ⓝ *Dactylorhiza incarnata* subsp. *coccinea*

(Pugsley) Soó

A tuberous perennial herb of machair grassland and especially damp dune-slacks, where it can be abundant. It also occasionally grows on the wet terraces of slumped sea-cliffs, and inland in calcareous fens, flushes and peat cuttings in central Ireland where buried lake deposits have been exposed. More recently, it has become admixed with other subspecies of *D. incarnata* on fly-ash waste from power stations. Lowland.

Trends Subsp. *coccinea* occurs sporadically across Britain and Ireland, concentrated in coastal areas that feature extensive dune systems. Mapping has much improved since the first map was published in 1968, particularly in western Scotland, though morphological boundaries can be difficult to discern between subsp. *incarnata* in dunes and subsp. *pulchella* on fly-ash waste. The putatively endemic status of this subspecies has not yet been tested through comparative DNA-based analyses, though populations of *D. incarnata* occupying identical dune habitats along the Netherlands coast do not achieve even vaguely similar depths of red pigmentation. Most populations are sufficiently large to survive coastal development; scrubbing over following stabilization of dunes is probably the greater threat.

Biogeography Probably endemic.

	GB	IR
Long term	No trend	No trend
Short term	No trend	No trend

Native	GB	IR
2000–19	119	62
1987–99	88	13
1970–86	37	20
pre-1970	54	2

Key refs Allan *et al.* (1993), Bateman & Denholm (1985), Curtis & Thompson (2009), Haggar (2005a), Pedersen (2001), Pillon *et al.* (2007).

R.M. Bateman & I. Denholm

Ⓝ *Dactylorhiza incarnata* subsp. *pulchella*

(Druce) Soó

A tuberous perennial herb of acidic valley bogs, marshes and damp heathland, typically growing with *Sphagnum*. However, similar purple-flowered plants also occur in marshes and fens on more neutral substrates, sometimes co-occurring with subsp. *incarnata*. 0–530 m (Beinn Heasgarnich, Mid Perthshire).

Trends Mapping of this subspecies has improved greatly during the 21st century in Scotland and especially Ireland. It is becoming increasingly evident that it suffered substantial losses across southern and central England and the Welsh Borders during the 19th and 20th centuries, presumably primarily through drainage and desiccation of its preferred *Sphagnum* bog habitats.

Biogeography Subsp. *pulchella* has been reported from mainland Europe, but assessing its distribution is complicated by the fact that the purple-flowered fen-dwelling form is regarded by many authorities as assignable to, and in some opinions typical of, subsp. *incarnata*.

	GB	IR
Long term	No trend	No trend
Short term	No trend	No trend

Native	GB	IR
2000–19	233	165
1987–99	136	18
1970–86	97	17
pre-1970	92	11

Alien	GB	IR
2000–19	0	0
1987–99	1	0
1970–86	0	0
pre-1970	0	0

Key refs Allan *et al.* (1993), Bateman & Denholm (1985), Haggar (2004a), Pillon *et al.* (2007).

R.M. Bateman & I. Denholm

ⓝ *Dactylorhiza incarnata* subsp. *cruenta*
(O.F.Müll.) P.D.Sell

A tuberous perennial herb of gently sloping, lightly grazed, neutral to slightly alkaline flushed grassland (Wester Ross), a *Carex lasiocarpa* mire (West Sutherland) and *Schoenus nigricans* flushes (Hoy, Orkney). It is more widespread in Ireland where it favours more strongly alkaline lough-side marshes, mainly in the west. Lowland but growing at up to 450 m in Wester Ross.

Trends A popular taxonomic football, this subspecies (or species, or variety) was mapped for Scotland but not the longer-standing Irish populations in the 2002 *Atlas*; these were instead assigned to subsp. *pulchella*. However, molecular analyses have demonstrated that, in both countries, the spotted-leaved plants of subsp. *cruenta* reliably differ genetically from associated unspotted plants formerly attributed to subsp. *pulchella*.

Unfortunately, the necessary geographically broader molecular study needed to compare in detail populations assigned to subsp. *cruenta* in Ireland and Scotland with those in Scandinavia has yet to be conducted. The most pragmatic interim solution is to continue referring both the Irish and Scottish populations to subsp. *cruenta*. There is little evidence that it is declining in either Scotland or Ireland; it seems more likely that it is under-recorded in both countries.

Biogeography Eurosiberian Boreal-montane element.

	GB	IR
Long term	No trend	No trend
Short term	No trend	No trend

Native		GB	IR
2000–19	●	3	15
1987–99	●	2	1
1970–86	●	1	4
pre-1970	○	0	0

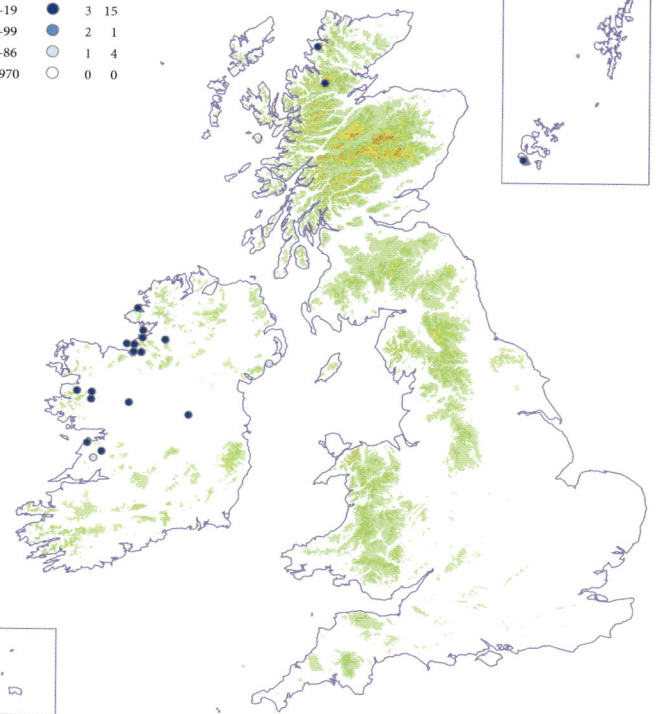

Key refs Bateman (2006), Eccarius (2016), Haggar (2004b), Hedrén *et al.* (2011b), Kenneth & Tennant (1987), Pillon *et al.* (2007), Wigginton (1999).

R.M. BATEMAN & I. DENHOLM

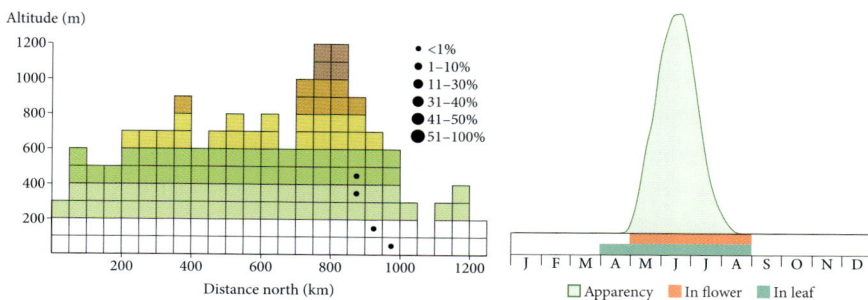

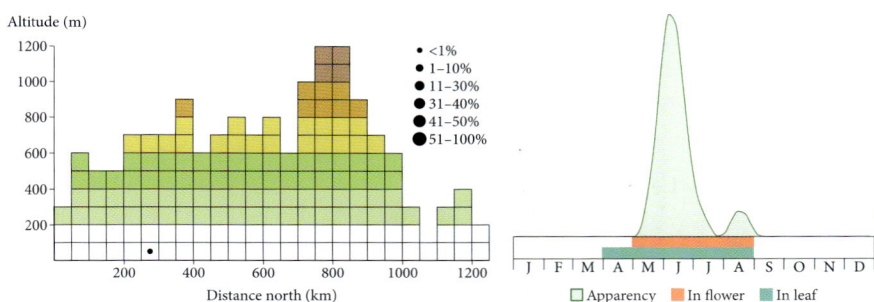

Altitude (m) / Distance north (km)

	<1%
●	1–10%
●	11–30%
●	31–40%
●	41–50%
●	51–100%

J F M A M J J A S O N D

Apparency   In flower   In leaf

ⓝ *Dactylorhiza incarnata* subsp. *ochroleuca*
(Wüstnei ex Boll) P.F.Hunt & Summerh.

A tuberous perennial herb restricted to moist, periodically inundated calcareous fens, preferring open mossy areas of low competition. Lowland.

Trends Until recently, subsp. *ochroleuca* was often confused with albino variants of other subspecies of *D. incarnata*, which exaggerated its apparent distribution. The distribution of this uncommon subspecies has steadily declined since the 1960s, reaching a point where it appears to have been lost from Cambridgeshire and reduced to just two adjacent fens in Suffolk. The plant has proven vulnerable to changes in water level, cessation of reed-cutting, and to consequent scrub encroachment.

Biogeography European Temperate element.

	GB	IR
Long term	No trend	No trend
Short term	No trend	No trend

Native		GB	IR
2000–19	●	2	0
1987–99	●	3	0
1970–86	●	3	0
pre-1970	○	2	0

Key refs Bateman & Denholm (1983b), Bateman & Denholm (1985), Filippov *et al.* (2017), Foley (2000b), Haggar (2005b), Hedrén & Nordström (2009a), Stroh *et al.* (2014).

R.M. BATEMAN & I. DENHOLM

Altitude (m) / Distance north (km)

	<1%
●	1–10%
●	11–30%
●	31–40%
●	41–50%
●	51–100%

J F M A M J J A S O N D

Apparency   In flower   In leaf

N *Dactylorhiza praetermissa* Southern Marsh-orchid
(Druce) Soó

A tuberous perennial herb of calcareous and neutral marshes, fens, damp meadows, roadsides and dune-slacks, avoiding areas that are inundated for long periods. It occurs less frequently in less acidic bogs and wet heathland, and is occasionally found in small numbers in drier sites such as chalk downland and cliff ledges. It also readily colonizes roadside verges and artificial habitats such as quarries, gravel-pits and industrial waste ground. Generally lowland, but to 510 m at Alport Moor (Derbyshire).

Trends The geographical antithesis of *D. purpurella*, this species is widespread and locally abundant across southern and central England and south Wales, together with the Channel Islands, but more sporadic in northern England and north Wales. In recent decades its range has expanded rapidly northward

to include Anglesey, Cumberland and Northumberland. These changes, which could be a direct response to climate change, are resulting in a wider zone of co-occurrence with *D. purpurella*, thereby increasing opportunities for hybridization and genetic introgression. Although there have been local losses to drainage and habitat destruction, *D. praetermissa* subsp. *praetermissa* is still frequent in suitable habitats in many areas and has increased considerably in man-made habitats. *D. praetermissa* subsp. *schoenophila* is mapped separately.

Biogeography Oceanic Temperate element.

Native		GB	IR
2000–19	●	1041	0
1987–99	●	865	0
1970–86	○	611	0
pre-1970	○	663	0

Alien		GB	IR
2000–19	●	0	0
1987–99	●	1	0
1970–86	●	1	0
pre-1970	○	1	0

Key refs Bateman (2006, 2011b, 2019, 2020b), Bateman & Denholm (2012), Brandrud *et al.* (2020), Hedrén *et al.* (2011a), Pedersen (2010), Pillon *et al.* (2007).

R.M. BATEMAN & I. DENHOLM

N *Dactylorhiza praetermissa* subsp. *schoenophila*
R.M.Bateman & Denholm

A tuberous perennial herb of calcareous and neutral fens, some extensive in East Anglia but elsewhere confined to open *Schoenus*-dominated areas in the wettest centres of small isolated marshes. Lowland.

Trends This controversial subspecies was established in 2012 to encompass dactylorchid populations in south-eastern England that previously were erroneously assigned to *D. traunsteinerioides*. Although these populations resemble in some characters *D. traunsteinerioides*, they have DNA profiles typical of *D. praetermissa*, and at most localities *D. praetermissa* subsp. *praetermissa* occurs in immediately adjacent habitats. Whether subsp. *schoenophila* merits varietal rather than subspecies status should in the future be determined by whether or not its morphological deviation from

subsp. *praetermissa* largely reflects ecophenotypy rather than genetic divergence. This taxon is frequent in East Anglia (where it may prove to have been over-recorded, in most cases as *D. traunsteineri*), with outliers in Hampshire, Oxfordshire and Somerset.

Biogeography On current evidence, this subspecies is endemic to England, though this recently established taxon should be sought throughout the distribution of *D. praetermissa* (including northern France and the Low Countries).

Native		GB	IR
2000–19	●	16	0
1987–99	●	26	0
1970–86	○	11	0
pre-1970	○	9	0

Key refs Bateman (2011b), Bateman (2020b), Bateman & Denholm (2012), Cole & Waller (2020), Eccarius (2016).

R.M. BATEMAN & I. DENHOLM

N *Dactylorhiza purpurella* Northern Marsh-orchid
(T.Stephenson & T.A.Stephenson) Soó

A tuberous perennial herb of neutral or, less often, base-rich soils, occurring in dune-slacks, machair, meadows, fens, marshes, flushes, ditches and on roadside verges, as well as open woodland. It is also frequently encountered on cliffs, in old quarries and urban wasteland, where it can colonize drier sites such as rubble, and it occasionally occurs in gardens. 0–610 m (Creag Dhuba, Loch Ericht, Westerness).

Trends The distribution of this species approximates to the last glacial maximum, with reports south of a line linking the Severn to the Humber representing known or suspected introductions. In Ireland, this species is still often confused with *D. kerryensis*, with which it hybridizes in mixed populations. A more accurate distribution is gradually emerging that shows this species to be concentrated

in the north with an outlier in the south-east of Ireland. Populations of *D. purpurella* var. *cambrensis* showing substantial leaf-spotting from the coasts of Wales and Scotland were wrongly attributed to *D. majalis* in the 2002 *Atlas*; similar plants also occur inland in Cumbria. Its overall distribution is stable in Britain, although there have been limited losses due to habitat destruction and drainage.

Biogeography Formerly regarded as endemic to the British Isles, this species has since been shown to occur along the Scandinavian coasts and on the Faroe Islands. Oceanic Boreal-montane element.

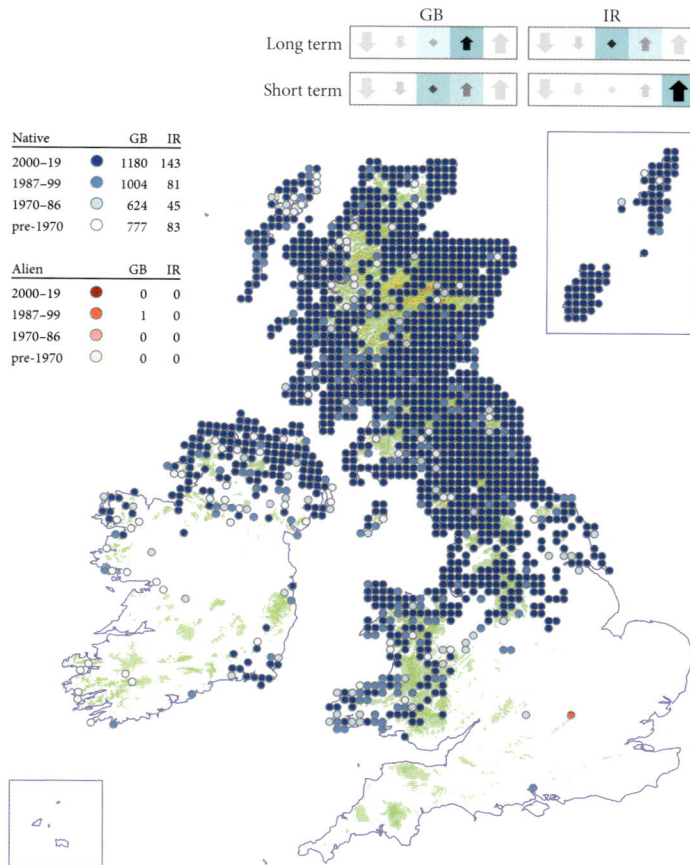

Native	GB	IR
2000–19	1180	143
1987–99	1004	81
1970–86	624	45
pre-1970	777	83

Alien	GB	IR
2000–19	0	0
1987–99	1	0
1970–86	0	0
pre-1970	0	0

Key refs Bateman (2006), Bateman & Denholm (1983a, 2012), Brandrud *et al.* (2020), Hedrén *et al.* (2011a), Pedersen (2007), Pillon *et al.* (2007).

R.M. BATEMAN & I. DENHOLM

N *Dactylorhiza traunsteinerioides* Narrow-leaved Marsh-orchid
(Pugsley) R.M.Bateman & Denholm

A tuberous perennial herb occupying specific habitats that are usually fed by the active upwelling of lime-rich but nutrient-poor groundwater, creating low-competition environments rich in *Schoenus nigricans*; these include fens, where the tubers can develop within moss rather than soil layers, water-meadows or, more rarely, dune-slacks and machair. Many populations occupy more localized flushes that form islands within contrasting surrounding vegetation such as heathland. Mostly Lowland, but rising to 405 m at Glen Chorainn (Wester Ross), and possibly higher elsewhere.

Trends This controversial taxon has become the most intensively researched British and Irish orchid species. In the 2002 *Atlas* the majority of populations in Scotland were mapped separately as *D. lapponica*, but molecular data suggest that this is a species confined to Scandinavia. All populations from south of a line connecting the Severn

Estuary to The Wash that were mapped as *D. traunsteinerioides* (under the name *D. traunsteineri*) in the 2002 *Atlas* are now assigned to *D. praetermissa* subsp. *schoenophila*. *D. traunsteinerioides* is molecularly distinct from the continental *D. traunsteineri* of the Alps and Scandinavia, although at least one molecularly distinct population near Stavanger on the Norwegian coast now challenges the claim of *D. traunsteinerioides* to be endemic to our area. Improved understanding of this species is facilitating the regular discovery of new populations in Ireland and Scotland, where its documented distribution has therefore expanded greatly. It is usually accompanied by several other dactylorchid species, encouraging frequent hybridization that can seriously introgress small populations.

Biogeography European Boreo-temperate element; possibly endemic to the British Isles.

Native	GB	IR
2000–19	56	43
1987–99	39	18
1970–86	26	21
pre-1970	19	22

Long term | No trend | No trend

Key refs Balao *et al.* (2016), Bateman (2011b, 2019, 2020b), Bateman & Denholm (2012), Hedrén & Nordström (2009b), Hedrén *et al.* (2011a), Pillon *et al.* (2007).

R.M. BATEMAN & I. DENHOLM

(N) *Dactylorhiza kerryensis* Irish Marsh-orchid
(Wilmott) P.F.Hunt & Summerh.

A tuberous perennial herb that prefers soils that are moist and often humic, ranging from slightly alkaline to fairly acid and often glacially derived. It favours meadows, pastures, coastal grasslands, roadside verges, marshes, bog margins and dune-slacks; along limestone lough shores and pavements it tends to inhabit pockets of peat. It tolerates a degree of disturbance and can rapidly invade newly formed habitats, including industrial waste. Lowland.

Trends This species is endemic to, and presumably originated in, Ireland; it is the product of allopolyploid speciation between *D. maculata* and *D. incarnata*. Preston *et al.* (2002a), following Stace (1997), incorrectly synonymized this species with the exclusively continental *D. majalis* (which is actually more closely related to *D. praetermissa*), and also included in the map a minority of Scottish

populations of *D. traunsteinerioides* and some Scottish and Welsh populations of *D. purpurella* var. *cambrensis*. Confusion with these two species, and with hybrids, continues to hamper mapping of *D. kerryensis*, particularly towards the northern and eastern margins of its range. It has become clearer that populations are concentrated close to the western and southern coasts, and only sporadic across much of the interior and the north. Although uncertain identifications preclude accurate assessment of expansion or contraction, serious recent decline seems unlikely in this ecologically relatively flexible species.

Biogeography Endemic to Ireland; possibly the only orchid species endemic to the British Isles (*cf.* treatments of *D. traunsteinerioides* and *Gymnadenia borealis*).

	GB	IR
Long term	No trend	No trend
Short term	No trend	↓↓◆↑↑

Native	GB	IR
2000–19	0	172
1987–99	0	126
1970–86	0	30
pre-1970	0	26

Altitude (m) chart with legend: <1%, 1–10%, 11–30%, 31–40%, 41–50%, 51–100%. "No data".

Phenology legend: Apparency, In flower, In leaf

Key refs Bateman (2006), Bateman & Denholm (1983a), Bateman & Denholm (2012), Brandrud *et al.* (2020), Eccarius (2016), Hedrén *et al.* (2011a), Pillon *et al.* (2007).

R.M. BATEMAN & I. DENHOLM

(N) *Dactylorhiza viridis* Frog Orchid
(L.) R.M.Bateman, Pridgeon & M.W.Chase

A tuberous perennial herb restricted in southern Britain to dry, well-grazed, base-rich grassland such as chalk downland and dunes; disturbed soils of ancient earthworks and quarries are particularly favoured. Elsewhere it is less constrained to calcareous soils and grows in a wider range of grasslands, machair and associated coastal golf-courses, flushes, limestone pavement, quarries, scree, clifftops, rocky ledges and roadsides. 0–1,055 m (Cairn Toul, South Aberdeenshire).

Trends *D. viridis* has been subject to long-term decline, particularly in central England and East Anglia. Initial losses were greatest in lowland pastures of England, from which it is now almost extirpated; ploughing, agricultural improvement and undergrazing appear the most likely culprits, as it is especially intolerant of shade or competition. More

recently, chalk downland populations have suffered, apparently due to summer drought. Difficult to detect, it may nonetheless be at present the most rapidly declining orchid in our area, showing an overall pattern of northward retreat. Although it was formerly placed in its own monotypic genus, *Coeloglossum*, numerous molecular studies have shown that this species is more appropriately viewed as an early divergent member of the genus *Dactylorhiza*. Although most populations are diploid, evidence is accumulating that a minority of comparatively vigorous populations may be tetraploid.

Biogeography Circumpolar Boreal-montane element.

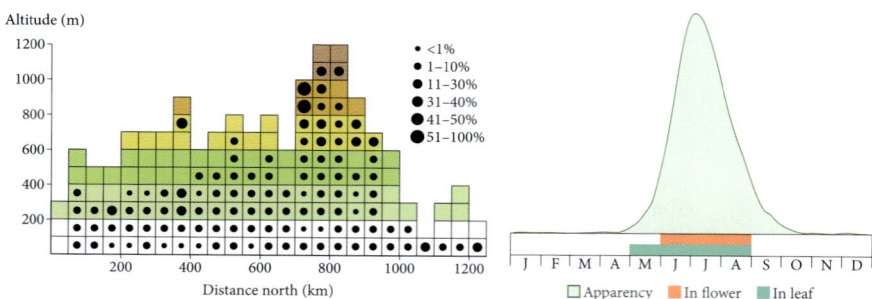

	GB	IR
Long term	↓	↓◆
Short term	↓	↓

Native	GB	IR
2000–19	392	95
1987–99	419	101
1970–86	346	32
pre-1970	857	157

Altitude (m) chart with legend: <1%, 1–10%, 11–30%, 31–40%, 41–50%, 51–100%.

Phenology legend: Apparency, In flower, In leaf

Key refs Bateman (2009), Bateman & Rudall (2018), Bateman *et al.* (2018b), Brandrud *et al.* (2020), Devos *et al.* (2006), Pillon *et al.* (2007), Stroh *et al.* (2019).

R.M. BATEMAN & I. DENHOLM

N *Orchis mascula* Early-purple Orchid

(L.) L.

This tuberous perennial herb grows on a variety of neutral and calcareous soils. It is most frequent in ancient broad-leaved woodland, coppices and calcareous grassland, but also occurs in floodplain grasslands (often with other ancient woodland indicators), hedgerows, scrub, on roadside verges and railway banks, and on limestone pavement and moist cliff ledges. Mainly lowland; it is rare only in regions that are unusually mountainous, boggy or intensively cultivated, and in urban centres. 0–880 m (Caenlochan, Angus).

Trends It is unfortunate that *O. mascula* is under-researched relative to other species of *Orchis s.s.* as it is a particularly good indicator of established woodland. This species has gradually declined in some areas, particularly central England and parts of Scotland. Most losses are due to woodland felling and coniferization, cessation of coppicing, intensification of grassland management and ploughing.

Biogeography European Temperate element.

Native		GB	IR
2000–19	●	1477	486
1987–99	●	1496	382
1970–86	●	1192	88
pre-1970	○	1602	225

Alien		GB	IR
2000–19	●	2	0
1987–99	●	4	0
1970–86	●	2	0
pre-1970	○	3	0

Key refs Bateman (2009), Bateman (2012a), Bateman *et al.* (2003), Jacquemyn *et al.* (2009a), Jacquemyn *et al.* (2009c), Jacquemyn *et al.* (2009b), Kretzschmar *et al.* (2007).

P.D. CAREY, T.D. DINES & R.M. BATEMAN

N *Orchis purpurea* Lady Orchid

Huds.

This long-lived tuberous perennial herb is found on thin calcareous soils, typically over chalk but also on clay, ragstone and Carboniferous limestone. It grows in open woodland dominated by *Corylus avellana*, *Fagus sylvatica* or *Fraxinus excelsior* and scrub and also increasingly in open grassland. Lowland.

Trends This species suffered losses in its core area in the North Downs of Kent, largely before 1930, but now appears to be stable there. Losses in West Sussex have been compensated for by a few new records spread across much of southern England, this species progressively appearing in Oxfordshire (1961), Herefordshire (1967), West Gloucestershire (1991), North Hampshire (2003), Berkshire (2005) and East Sussex (2008).

Biogeography European Temperate element.

Native		GB	IR
2000–19	●	17	0
1987–99	●	16	0
1970–86	●	19	0
pre-1970	○	34	0

Alien		GB	IR
2000–19	●	1	0
1987–99	●	0	0
1970–86	●	0	0
pre-1970	○	1	0

Key refs Bateman *et al.* (2008), Rose (1948), Stewart *et al.* (1994), Stroh *et al.* (2019).

P.D. CAREY, T.D. DINES & R.M. BATEMAN

(N) *Orchis militaris* Military Orchid

L.

A tuberous perennial herb typically found on chalk in grassland, scrub and woodland glades, together with a chalk-pit and a gravel-pit. Lowland.

Trends Populations in the Chilterns and Suffolk are only subtly distinct. Formerly frequent in the Chilterns, habitat destruction and collecting caused a decline in this species until it was considered extinct in the 1920s. It was refound in Buckinghamshire in 1947, Suffolk in 1954 and Oxfordshire in 1972; all three populations are now large and stable. Other sites are more sporadic; most are deliberate introductions, though a single clump appearing in a Hertfordshire gravel-pit between 2016 and 2019 may have been native.

Biogeography Eurosiberian Temperate element, with a continental distribution in western Europe.

		GB	IR
Long term		No trend	No trend
Short term		No trend	No trend

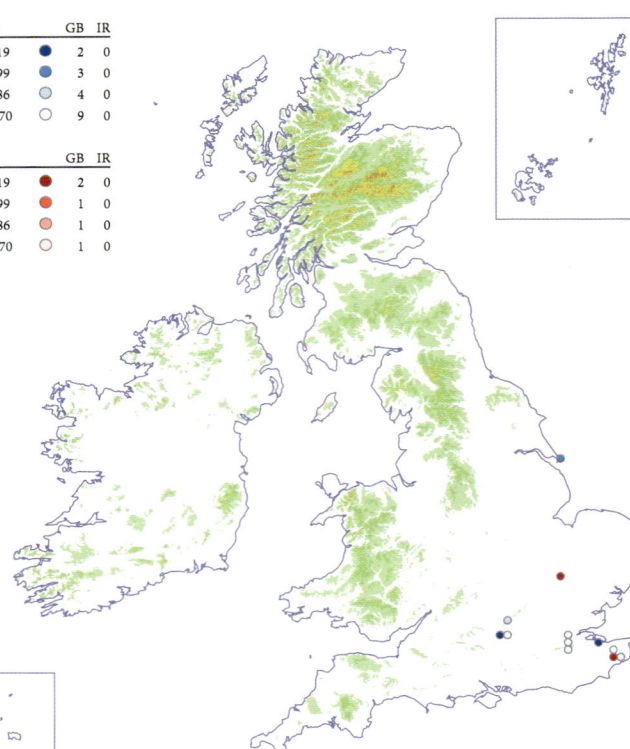

Native		GB	IR
2000–19		5	0
1987–99		4	0
1970–86		4	0
pre-1970		19	0

Alien		GB	IR
2000–19		1	0
1987–99		3	0
1970–86		1	0
pre-1970		1	0

Altitude (m)

- <1%
- 1–10%
- 11–30%
- 31–40%
- 41–50%
- 51–100%

Distance north (km)

J F M A M J J A S O N D

☐ Apparency ▮ In flower ▮ In leaf

Key refs Bateman & Rudall (2011, 2014), Farrell (1985), Hutchings *et al.* (1998), Stroh (2016), Sumpter *et al.* (2004), Waite & Farrell (1998).

P.D. Carey, T.D. Dines & R.M. Bateman

(N) *Orchis simia* Monkey Orchid

Lam.

This perennial, tuberous herb is found on south-facing banks in grazed chalk grassland. It is tolerant of some degree of shade from scrub, and can also grow on woodland edges. Lowland.

Trends *O. simia* was first recorded in 1777 in Kent and declined in the 19th century through the ploughing of downland and intensive botanical collecting. Following ploughing of its last Oxfordshire site, it was briefly thought to have been extirpated from Britain until the extant native Kent population at Ospringe Down was found in 1955. Seed from this site was used to establish a second population in Kent at Parkgate Down. Kentish and Chilterns plants are readily distinguished, the latter revealing genetic evidence of past hybridization with *O. militaris*. In 1974, a few plants appeared at Spurn Point (South-east Yorkshire), but their dune habitat was washed away in 1983. There have also been sporadic sightings elsewhere in the Chilterns. The extant Oxfordshire and Kent populations have expanded since management began, initially assisted by artificial pollination but more recently only by management of grazing. The populations appear stable, albeit at a low level at Ospringe Down.

Biogeography European Southern-temperate element.

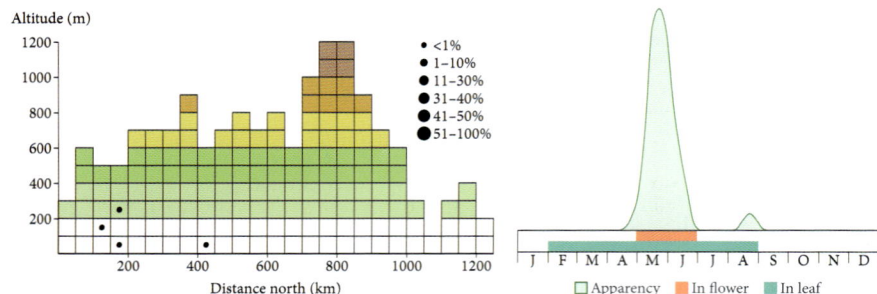

		GB	IR
Long term		No trend	No trend
Short term		No trend	No trend

Native		GB	IR
2000–19		2	0
1987–99		3	0
1970–86		4	0
pre-1970		9	0

Alien		GB	IR
2000–19		2	0
1987–99		1	0
1970–86		1	0
pre-1970		1	0

Altitude (m)

- <1%
- 1–10%
- 11–30%
- 31–40%
- 41–50%
- 51–100%

Distance north (km)

J F M A M J J A S O N D

☐ Apparency ▮ In flower ▮ In leaf

Key refs Bateman & Farrington (1989), Bateman *et al.* (2008), Harrap & Harrap (2009), Stroh *et al.* (2014), Stroh *et al.* (2019).

P.D. Carey, T.D. Dines & R.M. Bateman

Orchis anthropophora Man Orchid

(L.) All.

This tuberous perennial herb is found in old chalk-pits and limestone quarries, calcareous grassland (often towards the foot of a slope where soils are deeper) and on road verges. It tolerates considerable shade and is often found at the edge of scrub amongst coarse grasses such as *Bromopsis erecta* and *Brachypodium pinnatum*. Lowland.

Trends Molecularly determined incorporation of the former monotypic genus *Aceras* into *Orchis* is now universally accepted. By 1930, most East Anglian populations of this species had been destroyed by ploughing. Similar fates have since eliminated more sites, and others have been lost to scrub encroachment, fertilizer spray drift and inappropriate roadside cutting regimes. Continuous heavy grazing is detrimental, eventually causing its demise. Nonetheless, it is tempting to attribute to climate change the precipitous retreat of this species to its heartland in the North Downs. Given this context, the discovery in 2007 of a small population at High Barn SSSI (North Lincolnshire) is remarkable, and extends the known global northern limit for this species.

Biogeography Mediterranean-Atlantic element.

Native		GB	IR
2000–19	●	57	0
1987–99	●	55	0
1970–86	●	52	0
pre-1970	○	106	0

Alien		GB	IR
2000–19	●	2	0
1987–99	●	1	0
1970–86	●	2	0
pre-1970	○	2	0

Key refs Bateman (2009), Bateman *et al.* (2003), Jacquemyn *et al.* (2011), Kretzschmar *et al.* (2007), Stewart *et al.* (1994), Stroh *et al.* (2019), Walker *et al.* (2017).

P.D. Carey, T.D. Dines & R.M. Bateman

Anacamptis pyramidalis Pyramidal Orchid

(L.) Rich.

A tuberous perennial herb of well-drained calcareous soils, this species is found in grazed downland, limestone pavement, dune-slacks, machair and on cliff-tops, but is particularly well adapted to the longer grass of semi-stable dunes, scrub and churchyards. It often acts as a pioneer orchid, colonizing the disturbed ground of abandoned quarries, filled-in gravel pits, industrial waste land, roadside verges, tracksides and railway embankments. 0–375 m Blaenavon (Monmouthshire).

Trends This under-researched species is largely coastal in northern and western Britain and Ireland, and is absent from much of Scotland outside the Hebrides. Other than modest losses in Ireland attributed largely to agricultural improvement, the overall distribution of this species was judged stable through much of the 20th century. However, since 1990 it has increased considerably in numbers of both plants and populations, as well as consolidating its foothold along the western and eastern coasts of northern England and Scotland. Autotetraploid populations have recently been identified in continental Europe and should now be sought in Britain and Ireland.

Biogeography European Southern-temperate element.

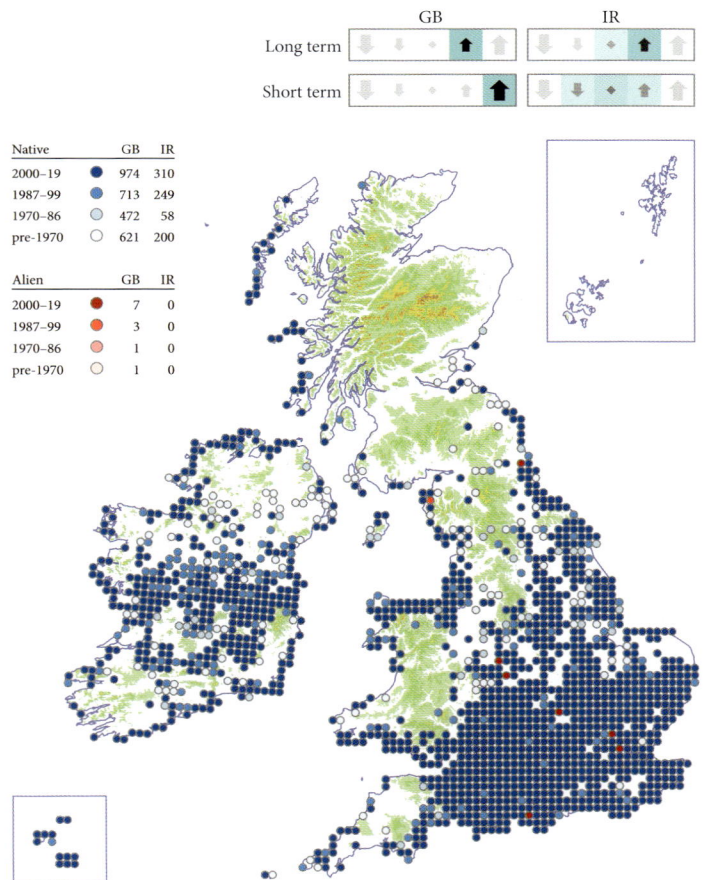

Native		GB	IR
2000–19	●	974	310
1987–99	●	713	249
1970–86	●	472	58
pre-1970	○	621	200

Alien		GB	IR
2000–19	●	7	0
1987–99	●	3	0
1970–86	●	1	0
pre-1970	○	1	0

Key refs Allan *et al.* (1993), Bateman (2004), Bateman *et al.* (1997), Braithwaite *et al.* (2006), Pegoraro *et al.* (2019), Scopece *et al.* (2010).

P.D. Carey, T.D. Dines & R.M. Bateman

Anacamptis laxiflora Loose-flowered Orchid

(Lam.) R.M.Bateman, Pridgeon & M.W.Chase

A tuberous perennial herb of base-rich wet meadows and marshy fields. Lowland.

Native in the Channel Islands and a neophyte in Britain.

Trends Formerly placed in *Orchis* but transferred to *Anacamptis* following molecular studies, *A. laxiflora* is confined to the Channel Islands. It has decreased there since the early 20th century due to the intensification of agriculture (including groundwater extraction) and to urban development. Most sites are now better protected and some populations have reached a considerable size, particularly on Guernsey.

Biogeography Eurosiberian Southern-temperate element, with a continental distribution in western Europe.

		GB	IR
	Long term	No trend	No trend
	Short term	No trend	No trend

Native		GB	IR
2000–19	●	6	0
1987–99	●	7	0
1970–86	●	4	0
pre-1970	○	7	0

Alien		GB	IR
2000–19	●	1	0
1987–99	●	1	0
1970–86	●	0	0
pre-1970	○	0	0

Altitude (m)

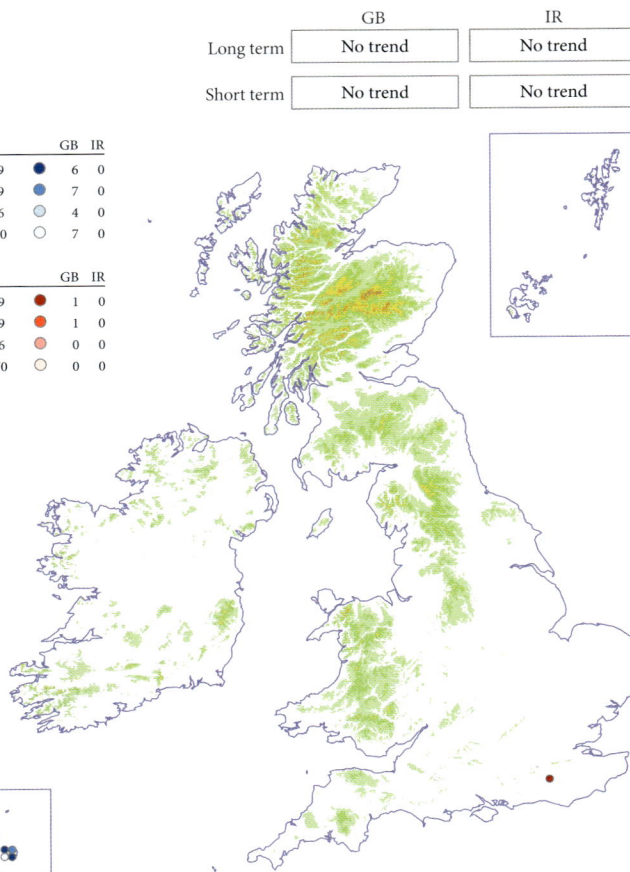

●	<1%
●	1–10%
●	11–30%
●	31–40%
●	41–50%
●	51–100%

Distance north (km)

▢ Apparency ▮ In flower ▮ In leaf

Key refs Bateman *et al.* (1997), Harrap & Harrap (2009), Le Sueur (1984), McClintock (1975), Wood & Ramsay (2004).

P.D. CAREY, T.D. DINES & R.M. BATEMAN

Anacamptis morio Green-winged Orchid

(L.) R.M.Bateman, Pridgeon & M.W.Chase

A tuberous perennial herb occurring on damp to fairly dry and base-rich to mildly acidic soils. It is most frequent in hay meadows and pastures, but it also grows on sand dunes, heathlands and roadsides, and in quarries, sand- and gravel-pits, churchyards and lawns. In both Scotland and Northern Ireland it is confined to only one small area. Mostly lowland; 0–395 m (Pennerley Meadows, Shropshire).

Trends This species declined steadily throughout the 19th and 20th centuries, primarily due to ploughing and improvement of grasslands. A good indicator of unimproved grassland (and often associated with ancient ridge and furrow), it is often present in only small numbers in hectads where it was once common, especially in northern and central England. It is sensitive to use of both herbicides and fertilizers, and

intolerant of competition from coarse grasses; this orchid now fares best in meadows that are actively managed to ensure its ongoing success. Beneath its general decline appear to be retreats southward and toward coastlines.

Biogeography European Temperate element.

	GB	IR
Long term		
Short term		

Native		GB	IR
2000–19	●	489	36
1987–99	●	513	53
1970–86	●	470	19
pre-1970	○	809	96

Alien		GB	IR
2000–19	●	5	0
1987–99	●	2	0
1970–86	●	1	0
pre-1970	○	1	0

Altitude (m)

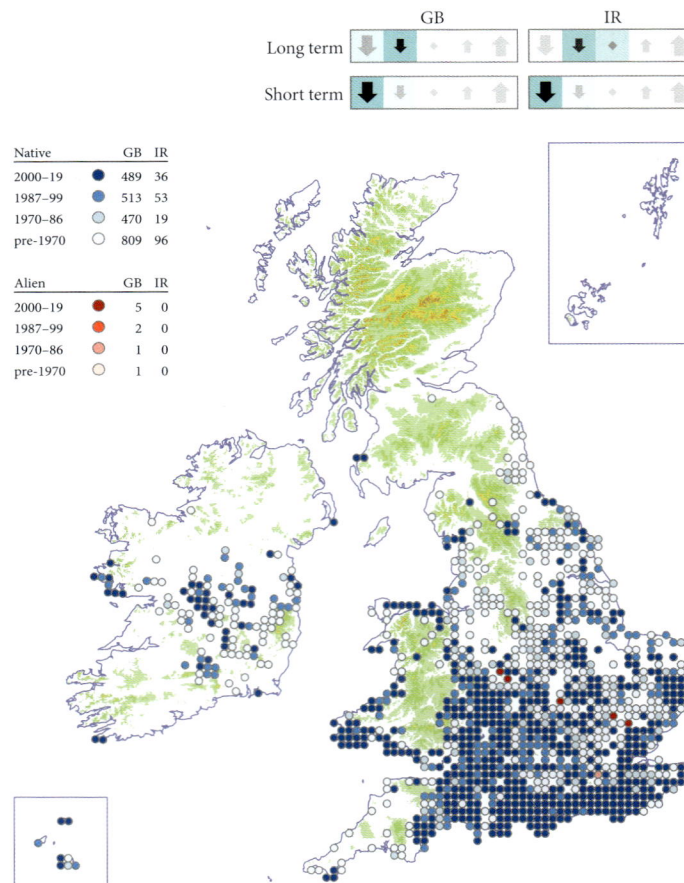

●	<1%
●	1–10%
●	11–30%
●	31–40%
●	41–50%
●	51–100%

Distance north (km)

▢ Apparency ▮ In flower ▮ In leaf

Key refs Bateman (2004), Hornemann *et al.* (2012), Silvertown *et al.* (1993), Stewart *et al.* (1994), Stroh (2015a), Wells *et al.* (1998).

P.D. CAREY, T.D. DINES & R.M. BATEMAN

Neotinea ustulata Burnt Orchid

(L.) R.M.Bateman, Pridgeon & M.W.Chase

This tuberous perennial herb requires warm, dry conditions and is often found in tightly grazed chalk and limestone grassland on south-facing slopes, showing a particular association with ancient earthworks. It occurs less often on sandy and gravelly soils in riverside meadows, where it is often sporadic in occurrence, and on sand dunes. Mainly lowland, but reaching 355 m at Middleton Moor (Derbyshire), and reportedly higher in County Durham.

Trends Molecular studies demonstrate conclusively that this species is most appropriately treated under *Neotinea* rather than *Orchis*. The majority of populations flower in late May and early June, but the trans-European segregate *N. ustulata* var. *aestivalis* flowers so much later (July) that it could readily be mapped separately, though it is at best only subtly distinct both

morphologically and genetically; within the British Isles it appears to be confined to southern England. The spectacular decline of this species has been well-documented. Losses have been largely due to changes in agricultural practices, such as ploughing and the cessation of grazing, and through habitat destruction by building and quarrying. This species remains frequent in its headquarters on Salisbury Plain, and 1993 brought the welcome discovery of a population along the south Wales coastline.

Biogeography European Temperate element.

Native	GB	IR
2000–19	47	0
1987–99	57	0
1970–86	66	0
pre-1970	255	0

Key refs Bateman (2007), Bateman (2009), Bateman (2012a), Bateman *et al.* (2003), Foley (1992), Stewart *et al.* (1994), Stroh *et al.* (2019), Tali *et al.* (2004), Tali *et al.* (2006), Walker *et al.* (2017).

P.D. CAREY, T.D. DINES & R.M. BATEMAN

Neotinea maculata Dense-flowered Orchid

(Desf.) Stearn

This tuberous perennial herb grows in a wide range of habitats on base-rich rocky or gravelly substrates. It can be found in the crevices of limestone pavement, in old pastures, hill grasslands, dunes and on road verges. Occasionally, it occurs on peat overlying more acidic rocks, and in *Corylus avellana–Fraxinus excelsior* woodland. Lowland.

Trends Although *N. maculata* has been lost from many sites in Ireland, it has recently been found at several new sites, extending its overall distribution eastwards. However, this species is in decline overall, a conclusion reinforced by mathematical modelling of its current distribution. It was also found regularly at its sole former locality on the Isle of Man between 1967 and 1985 but has not been seen since.

Biogeography Mediterranean-Atlantic element. This species is routinely autogamous, yet molecular analyses have shown only subtle distinction from Mediterranean populations, despite the much greater frequency of pale-flowered morphs.

Native	GB	IR
2000–19	0	22
1987–99	0	16
1970–86	1	17
pre-1970	1	10

Key refs Allen (1968), Allen (1984), Duffy *et al.* (2008), Duffy *et al.* (2009), Webb & Scannell (1983).

P.D. CAREY, T.D. DINES & R.M. BATEMAN

N *Himantoglossum hircinum* Lizard Orchid
(L.) Spreng.

A tuberous, winter-green perennial herb of chalk and, less often, limestone in open calcareous grassland or light scrub, on roadsides and in quarries; rarely on heathland or lawns. It tolerates coarse grasses and has a particular association with golf courses. Most of the few larger, robust populations occupy calcareous sand dunes. Lowland.

Trends This species was restricted to Kent until the early 1900s, when it underwent a remarkable expansion, reaching as far north as Yorkshire and becoming a pioneer subject for the use of phytogeography to study climate change (Good, 1936; Pfeifer *et al.*, 2006). After 1934, it declined rapidly but maintained much of the expanded range. *H. hircinum* returned to Yorkshire in 2011, reflecting a steady rise in post-1999 colonization events that has most benefitted south-eastern England and the Channel Islands. Although many occurrences appear monocarpic, Although flowering is erratic, an increasing number of populations are becoming self-sustaining.

Biogeography Submediterranean-Subatlantic element.

Native	GB	IR
2000–19	52	0
1987–99	23	0
1970–86	22	0
pre-1970	118	0

Alien	GB	IR
2000–19	4	0
1987–99	1	0
1970–86	1	0
pre-1970	1	0

	GB	IR
Long term	↓	No trend
Short term	↑	No trend

Key refs Bateman *et al.* (2013), Bateman *et al.* (2017b), Carey (1998), Carey (1999), Carey & Farrell (2002), Good (1936), Pfeifer *et al.* (2006), Sramkó *et al.* (2014), Stroh *et al.* (2019).

P.D. CAREY, T.D. DINES & R.M. BATEMAN

N? *Serapias parviflora* Lesser Tongue-orchid
Parl.

A tuberous perennial herb that in the Mediterranean occupies an exceptional range of habitats other than strongly acidic soils or deep shade; its colonizing ability is enhanced by routine autogamy. Here, it has been found at just one locality, growing in rabbit-grazed grassland among *Ulex europaeus* and *Rubus fruticosus* agg. scrub on south-facing coastal cliffs in East Cornwall. Lowland.

Trends The Cornish population survived from 1989 to 2008, peaking at five flowering plants in 1991. Attempts to augment the population in 1998 with plants raised *ex situ* from seed collected at the site failed, and unfortunately in 2009 the habitat was devastated by overgrazing and poaching by cattle. As with all occurrences of this genus in southern England, the origin of this population has been much debated.

This seems an unlikely choice of site for deliberate introduction, and natural populations occur as close as Brittany. Also, most *Serapias* are strong colonizers and likely to benefit from the development of a more continental climate in southern England.

Biogeography Mediterranean-Atlantic element.

Native	GB	IR
2000–19	1	0
1987–99	1	0
1970–86	0	0
pre-1970	0	0

	GB	IR
Long term	No trend	No trend
Short term	No trend	No trend

Key refs Bateman (2006), Bournérias & Prat (2005), Cheffings & Farrell (2005), Cole & Waller (2020), Harrap & Harrap (2009), Madge (1994), Murphy (1994), Rich (2003), Stroh *et al.* (2014).

R.M. BATEMAN & I. DENHOLM

(N?) *Serapias lingua* Tongue-orchid
L.

A tuberous perennial herb, found in rough grassland at three sites in our area. In its Mediterranean heartland it tolerates a wide range of soil pH and moisture but avoids deep shade and intense competition; it can rapidly colonize disturbed ground. Lowland.

Trends *S. lingua* is questionably native in Britain and has been found in three separate sites where it may have been a natural colonist and a fourth where a small population has been established in the grounds of a botanical garden (Wakehurst Place, East Sussex). In Guernsey, a single plant flowered on the margin of a golf course in 1992 but has not been recorded since. The first mainland occurrence consisted of three plants discovered in a coastal hay meadow in South Devon in 1998; the population survived until at least 2003, peaking at nine plants. The third and largest population of around 60 plants was discovered in rough grassland in North Essex in 2017; it survives at this site but is under threat of development. *S. lingua* is perhaps the most persistent of three groups of this classic Mediterranean genus that appear to be attempting to colonize southern England from north-western France, presumably via wind-blown dust-seed, but unfortunately it is also increasingly widely grown as a specialist garden plant and so deliberate or accidental introduction cannot be ruled out (that is how *S. lingua* recently became naturalized in the hills above Adelaide, Australia).

Biogeography Mediterranean-Atlantic element.

	GB	IR
Long term	No trend	No trend
Short term	No trend	No trend

Native	GB	IR
2000–19	2	0
1987–99	1	0
1970–86	0	0
pre-1970	0	0

Alien	GB	IR
2000–19	1	0
1987–99	0	0
1970–86	0	0
pre-1970	0	0

Key refs Bateman (2006), Cheffings & Farrell (2005), Cole & Waller (2020), Conran *et al.* (2011), Harrap & Harrap (2009), Rich (2003).

R.M. BATEMAN & I. DENHOLM

(N) *Ophrys insectifera* Fly Orchid
L.

A shade-tolerant tuberous herb usually found on chalk and limestone soils in open deciduous woodland, particularly beech, but also recorded from scrub, hazel coppice, grassland, chalk-pits, limestone pavement, disused railways, spoil heaps and, rarely, unstable coastal cliffs. By contrast, in Ireland and Anglesey it occurs in open calcareous flushes, lough-sides and fens – the preferred habitat of *O. insectifera* in Scandinavia. 0–390 m (Helbeck Wood, Westmorland).

Trends *O. insectifera* is most frequent in our area on the English chalk and in the Burren region of western Ireland, but sporadic and uncommon elsewhere. Although losses have been few this century, viewed in the longer term they have proven extreme in some areas, most notably East Anglia where records from approximately 40 historical 10 km squares have diminished to just two localities. Losses in woodland are due to scrub encroachment, the closing of canopies and clearance, together with increased grazing by deer, whereas losses from fens are due mainly to drainage or lowering of the water table.

Biogeography European Temperate element.

Native	GB	IR
2000–19	120	20
1987–99	124	17
1970–86	132	14
pre-1970	268	18

Key refs Bateman *et al.* (2018a), Devey *et al.* (2008), Stroh (2015b), Walker *et al.* (2017).

R.M. BATEMAN, P.D. CAREY & T.D. DINES

Ⓝ *Ophrys sphegodes* Early Spider-orchid
Mill.

A winter-green, often short-lived perennial tuberous herb, most typical of ancient, species-rich, heavily grazed grassland on chalk and Purbeck limestone, but also capable of colonizing disturbed ground in limestone quarries, spoil heaps and tracksides. Lowland.

Trends Formerly widespread if sporadic across southern and eastern England during the 19th century, this species soon retreated to three strongholds: on limestone in Purbeck (Dorset), and on chalk on the South Downs of East Sussex and North Downs of East Kent. Fortunately, some populations are large in each of these areas. *O. sphegodes* occurs only sporadically and transiently inland and on the Channel Islands. In continental Europe it can be a rapid colonizer of disturbed calcareous soils, and demonstrated this ability in Kent during the 1990s by colonizing the main spoil generated through excavation of the Channel Tunnel. Reduced by the ploughing or improvement of grasslands, or by changes in grazing regime, this species might be predicted to expand northward in response to warmer drier summers, but so far it has not done so, thereby raising concerns about the timing of its flowering relative to the emergence of likely pollinators. However, detailed monitoring of a population in Sussex between 1975–2005 showed that peak flowering advanced by around two weeks over that period (Hutchings, 2010). This species has become a popular model for evolutionary research, and sufficient morphological variation has been detected among English populations to match several continental microspecies.

Biogeography Submediterranean-Subatlantic element.

Native		GB	IR
2000–19	●	19	0
1987–99	●	18	0
1970–86	●	13	0
pre-1970	○	61	0

Alien		GB	IR
2000–19	●	2	0
1987–99	●	1	0
1970–86	●	0	0
pre-1970	○	0	0

	GB	IR
Long term	⬇ ⬇ ・ ⬆ ⬆	No trend
Short term	⬇ ⬇ ・ ⬆ **⬆**	No trend

Key refs Bateman (2018b), Bateman *et al.* (2011), Bateman *et al.* (2018a), Breitkopf *et al.* (2013), Hutchings (2010), Jacquemyn & Hutchings (2015), Robbirt *et al.* (2014).

R.M. Bateman, P.D. Carey & T.D. Dines

Ⓝ *Ophrys apifera* Bee Orchid
Huds.

A facultatively autogamous, tuberous perennial herb of calcareous, well-drained soils. Its diverse habitats include mesotrophic and calcareous grasslands, scrub, railway banks, roadsides, lawns, sand dunes and limestone pavement; rarer occurrences occupy dense beechwoods or fens. It favours disturbed sites such as quarries, gravel-pits, undercliffs, car-parks, amenity turf and industrial waste ground, where it can become at least transiently abundant. 0–435 m (Bradwell Moor, Derbyshire).

Trends The range of this species has increased dramatically in Britain since the 1960s, especially this century, with newly colonized sites more than compensating for any losses caused by ploughing or improvement of grassland, cessation of grazing and the in-filling of quarries. Its known distribution in Ireland would also appear to have increased in the last two decades, probably due to a combination of a more favourable climate, and more systematic recording. Previously absent from Scotland, since 2003 it has been found in eight Scottish 10 km squares, bypassing the Southern Uplands and thus presenting the hallmarks of a species that is migrating northward via dust-like seeds, and likely benefitting from climate change.

Biogeography Submediterranean-Subatlantic element.

Native		GB	IR
2000–19	●	1101	205
1987–99	●	838	95
1970–86	●	529	43
pre-1970	○	652	116

	GB		IR	
Long term	・ **⬆** ⬆		・ **⬆** ⬆	
Short term	**⬆**		**⬆**	

Key refs Bateman *et al.* (2018a), Braithwaite *et al.* (2006), Devey *et al.* (2008), Harrap & Harrap (2009), Wells & Cox (1989), Wells & Cox (1991).

R.M. Bateman, P.D. Carey & T.D. Dines

Ⓝ *Ophrys fuciflora* Late Spider-orchid
(Crantz) Moench

This long-lived, tuberous perennial herb grows on well-drained chalk soil in species-rich, closely grazed grassland; it cannot compete in longer grassland. Some colonies occupy previously disturbed areas, but rarely spread to adjacent sites. Lowland.

Trends Historically recorded for eight 10 km squares but recently only from four contiguous squares spanning 18 km of short chalk grassland along the south-facing North Downs escarpment in East Kent. A survey conducted in 2002 revealed ten localities, of which eight have been reconfirmed during the last decade. Surprisingly, these few populations, most of which are small, encompass sufficient variation, both morphological and molecular, to represent several microspecies as widely recognized among continental *Ophrys*. Victorian records from nearby hectads

are suspect, making it difficult to assess the true degree of range contraction, which presumably reflected ploughing, agricultural improvement or altered grazing regimes in its chalk grassland habitats. Hybridization with larger admixed populations of *O. apifera* has also been demonstrated as a threat at three localities. Most sites are now carefully managed, and protection is given against rabbit grazing. Given that East Kent represents the northernmost extent of the European distribution of this species, a warming climate could potentially encourage range expansion provided that pseudo-copulatory pollination remains feasible.

Biogeography Submediterranean-Subatlantic element.

Native	GB	IR
2000–19	4	0
1987–99	4	0
1970–86	4	0
pre-1970	8	0

	GB	IR
Long term	No trend	No trend
Short term	No trend	No trend

Altitude (m)

• <1%
• 1–10%
• 11–30%
● 31–40%
● 41–50%
● 51–100%

☐ Apparency ☐ In flower ☐ In leaf

Key refs Bateman (2018b), Bateman *et al.* (2011), Bateman *et al.* (2018a), Devey *et al.* (2008), Devey *et al.* (2009), Stone & Russell (2000), Stroh *et al.* (2019).

R.M. Bateman, P.D. Carey & T.D. Dines

Ⓝⓔ *Libertia formosa* Chilean-iris
Graham

A rhizomatous perennial herb naturalized on rough ground, roadside verges, waysides, lake shores and coasts. It usually originates as a garden escape or throw-out. Lowland.

Trends *L. formosa* was probably introduced into British gardens in 1830, and is increasingly popular in areas with a milder climate. It was first recorded from the wild in 1916 (Hartland, North Devon) and is increasing.

Biogeography Native of Chile and Argentina.

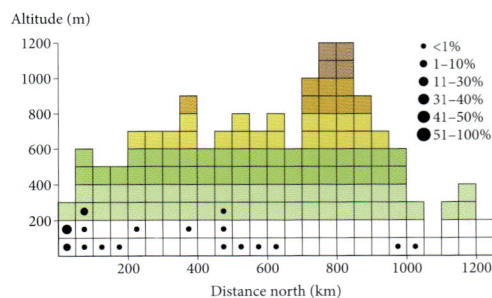

	GB	IR
Long term	No trend	No trend
Short term		

Alien	GB	IR
2000–19	42	31
1987–99	27	6
1970–86	14	0
pre-1970	3	1

Altitude (m)

• <1%
• 1–10%
• 11–30%
● 31–40%
● 41–50%
● 51–100%

☐ Apparency ☐ In flower ☐ In leaf

D.A. Pearman & T.D. Dines

Sisyrinchium bermudiana Blue-eyed-grass
L.

A perennial herb of wet meadows, ditch-sides and lake-shores. It is thought to be native in western Ireland and recorded as a naturalized alien in similar habitats and on waste ground throughout Britain. Lowland.

Native in Ireland and a neophyte in Britain.

Trends There has been a notable increase in records across the native range of this species in western Ireland during the last 20 years, although this probably represents more extensive and diligent recording rather than a significant increase in population and range. Naturalized plants have been reported throughout Britain, but *S. bermudiana* has long been confused with the more commonly cultivated *S. montanum* and some records mapped may be errors for the latter.

Biogeography Oceanic Wide-temperate element; in Europe restricted to Ireland as a native but widespread in North America.

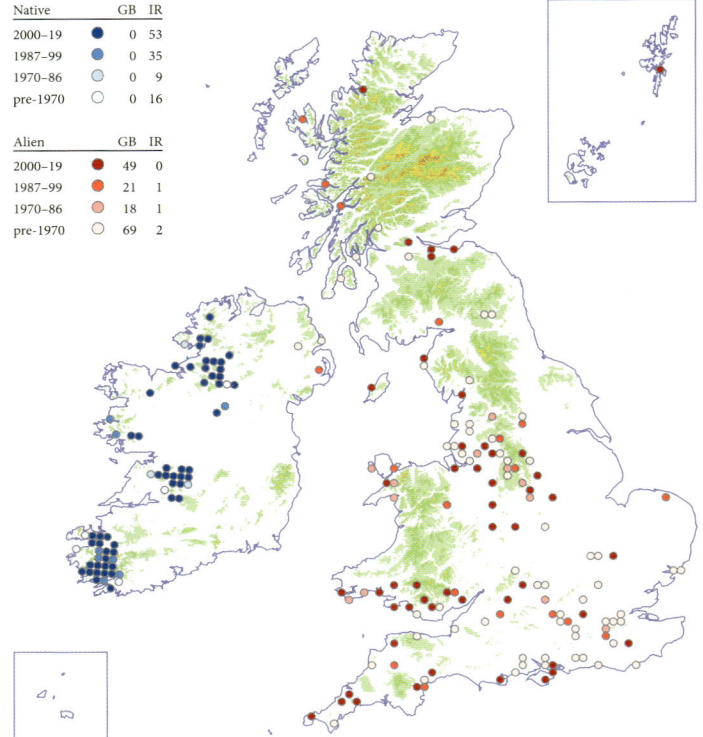

Native	GB	IR
2000–19	0	53
1987–99	0	35
1970–86	0	9
pre-1970	0	16

Alien	GB	IR
2000–19	49	0
1987–99	21	1
1970–86	18	1
pre-1970	69	2

Key refs Leslie (2019).

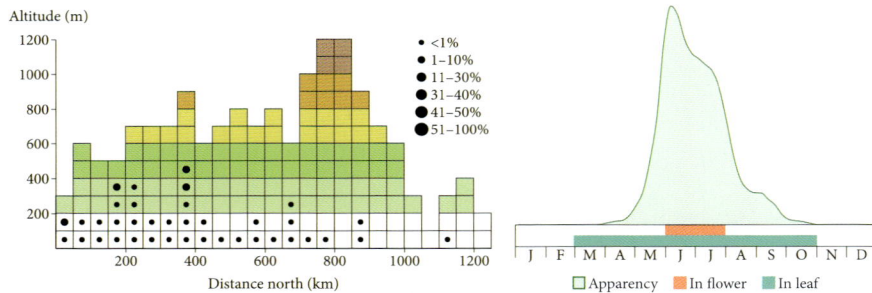

I. TAYLOR

Sisyrinchium montanum American Blue-eyed-grass
Greene

A perennial herb, commonly grown in gardens and found on open waste ground, rough grassland, spoil, pond margins, crevices in pavements and gutters and at the base of walls. Spreading freely by seed where discarded in suitable habitats. Lowland.

Trends *S. montanum* has been cultivated since 1693 and was known in the wild by 1871 (Christchurch, South Hampshire). It appears to have increased in recent decades possibly, in part, due to the more systematic recording of garden escapes. It is likely that some if not all British records of *S. bermudiana*, which is much less frequently cultivated, may refer to this species.

Biogeography Native of North America; widely naturalized in central Europe.

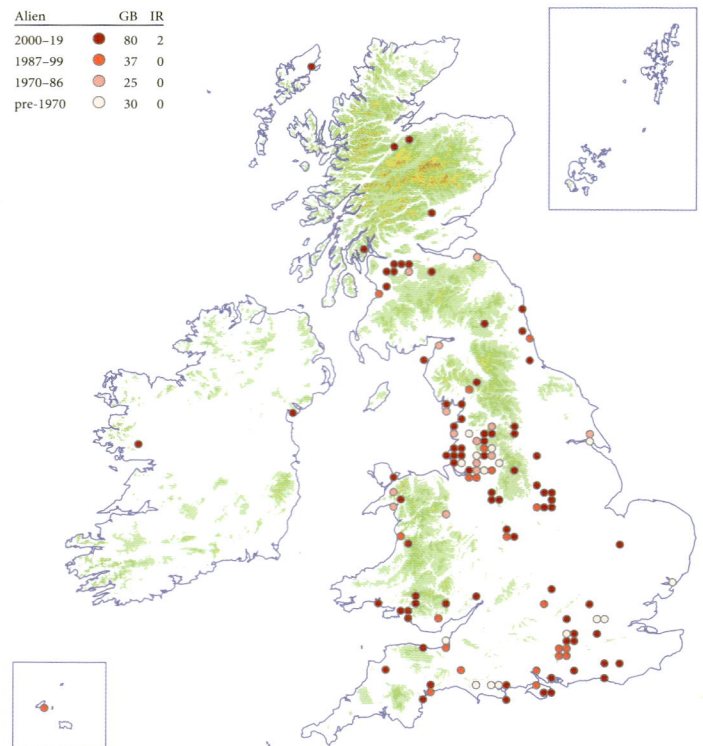

Alien	GB	IR
2000–19	80	2
1987–99	37	0
1970–86	25	0
pre-1970	30	0

Key refs Leslie (2019).

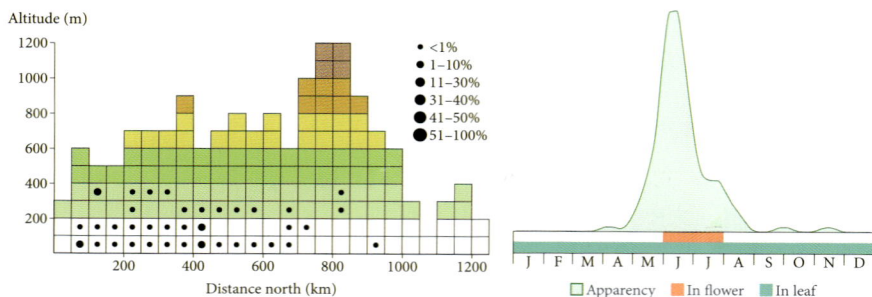

I. TAYLOR

Ne *Sisyrinchium californicum* Yellow-eyed-grass

(Ker Gawl.) W.T.Aiton

A short-lived, semi-evergreen perennial herb, widely grown in gardens and naturalized on lake shores, in marshy meadows, and in other damp, grassy places. It freely reproduces by seed and some populations are very large. Lowland.

Trends *S. californicum* was introduced into cultivation in Britain in 1796 and is widely grown in gardens. It was first recorded from the wild in 1896, when it was found in great quantity near Rosslare Station, County Wexford; it still persists in the area. It appears to be increasing.

Biogeography Native of coastal western North America.

Alien		GB	IR
2000–19	●	55	15
1987–99	●	25	1
1970–86	●	7	1
pre-1970	○	6	2

T.D. Dines & D.A. Pearman

Ne *Sisyrinchium striatum* Pale Yellow-eyed-grass

Sm.

A winter-green, perennial herb, widely grown in gardens and found on waste ground, roadsides, paths, pavements, dumped soil, and at the base of walls and in cemeteries. It often originates from discarded garden waste. Populations are usually short-lived but it can be persistent in southern and eastern England where it may self-sow prolifically, sometimes directly from gardens. Lowland.

Trends *S. striatum* has been cultivated in Britain since 1788 and has gained popularity as a garden plant in recent years. It was recorded from the wild by 1919 (Christchurch, South Hampshire) and over the past few decades its 10 km square distribution has increased significantly, especially in south-eastern England.

Biogeography Native of South America.

Alien		GB	IR
2000–19	●	251	7
1987–99	●	56	0
1970–86	●	10	0
pre-1970	○	3	0

Key refs Crawley (2005), Leslie (2019).

I. Taylor

Ne *Iris germanica* Bearded Iris
L.

A rhizomatous perennial herb, very commonly cultivated and found in rough grassland, sand dunes, roadsides, railway banks, refuse tips, waste ground and abandoned fields. It sometimes occurs as a relic of cultivation or establishes from rhizomes discarded in garden waste. It rarely produces seed in Britain, but can spread vegetatively, although it rarely persists. Lowland.

Trends *I. germanica* has been grown in gardens since at least 995 (Harvey, 1981). It is frequently cultivated and becomes naturalized when deliberately planted or discarded in suitable, open, free-draining habitats. It has been known in the wild since at least 1905. Its 10 km square distribution has increased since the 1960s but is unevenly recorded.

Biogeography This cultivated species is probably a hybrid of garden origin, but if so its parentage is very obscure.

Alien		GB	IR
2000–19	●	251	4
1987–99	●	185	1
1970–86	●	80	0
pre-1970	○	57	0

Key refs Harvey (1981).

I. TAYLOR

Ne *Iris sibirica* Siberian Iris
L.

A rhizomatous perennial herb of moisture-retentive rough grassland, open damp woodland and waste ground. It is often long-lived when discarded from gardens into suitable habitats, where it sometimes spreads by seed. Lowland.

Trends *I. sibirica* was being cultivated in British gardens by 1596, and was recorded from the wild by 1928. Commonly cultivated in gardens where it can become invasive and is therefore often discarded in garden waste. This appears to be the main factor driving the steady increase in its 10 km square distribution that has occurred in recent decades, although it has also been deliberately planted during wetland restoration or creation schemes.

Biogeography Native of central and eastern Europe and western Asia.

Alien		GB	IR
2000–19	●	124	2
1987–99	●	58	0
1970–86	●	22	0
pre-1970	○	6	0

I. TAYLOR

N *Iris pseudacorus* Yellow Iris
L.

A rhizomatous perennial herb of wet meadows, wet woods, fens, the margins of lakes, ponds and watercourses, wet dune-slacks, and, in northern and western Britain, also of coastal streams, shingle, upper saltmarshes and raised beaches. It reproduces by seed and by vegetative spread. It is often planted in the wild and may occasionally escape from cultivation. Generally lowland, but reaching 480 m at Nenthead (Cumberland), and 570 m in Hartside Quarry (Cumberland).

Trends *I. pseudacorus* is almost ubiquitous in the lowlands of Britain and Ireland and its 10 km square distribution and range appear to be broadly stable. There is some evidence of recent localized increases, which may be due to more systematic recording of wetland ecosystems but is perhaps more likely due to an increase in deliberate introductions around restored or newly created waterbodies.

Biogeography European Southern-temperate element; widely naturalized outside its native range.

Native	GB	IR
2000–19	2538	950
1987–99	2457	919
1970–86	1668	159
pre-1970	2309	816

Alien	GB	IR
2000–19	8	1
1987–99	4	0
1970–86	1	0
pre-1970	3	0

Key refs Boon & Outen (2011), Hawksford & Hopkins (2011), Killick *et al.* (1998), Preston & Croft (1997), Sussex Botanical Recording Society (2018), Sutherland (1990).

I. TAYLOR

Ne *Iris versicolor* Purple Iris
L.

A rhizomatous perennial herb which is naturalized in wetland habitats including reed-swamps and lakesides. It arises from deliberate planting, or as a garden escape or throw-out. Mainly lowland, but up to 385 m on the Totley Moss Verge (Derbyshire).

Trends *I. versicolor* was being cultivated in Britain by 1732 and grown in water- and bog-gardens. It was first recorded from the wild in 1893 (South-west Yorkshire) and is now found scattered throughout much of Britain.

Biogeography Native of eastern North America.

Alien	GB	IR
2000–19	68	0
1987–99	29	0
1970–86	14	0
pre-1970	14	0

J. PARMENTER & T.D. DINES

Hy *Iris versicolor × virginica = I. ×robusta* Windermere Iris
E.S.Anderson

A rhizomatous perennial herb rarely naturalized in wet meadows, lake shores and riversides, and occasionally intentionally planted in similar habitats. It is sterile and reproduces vegetatively by rhizome fragments. Lowland.

A cultivated hybrid (alien × alien).

Trends This attractive hybrid is grown in water- and bog-gardens and was first recorded in Windermere (Westmorland) in 1965, by which time it was well established.

Biogeography Native of eastern North America and also a hybrid of garden origin.

	GB	IR
Long term	No trend	No trend
Short term	No trend	No trend

	GB	IR
2000–19 ●	3	1
1987–99 ●	1	0
1970–86 ●	1	0
pre-1970 ○	1	0

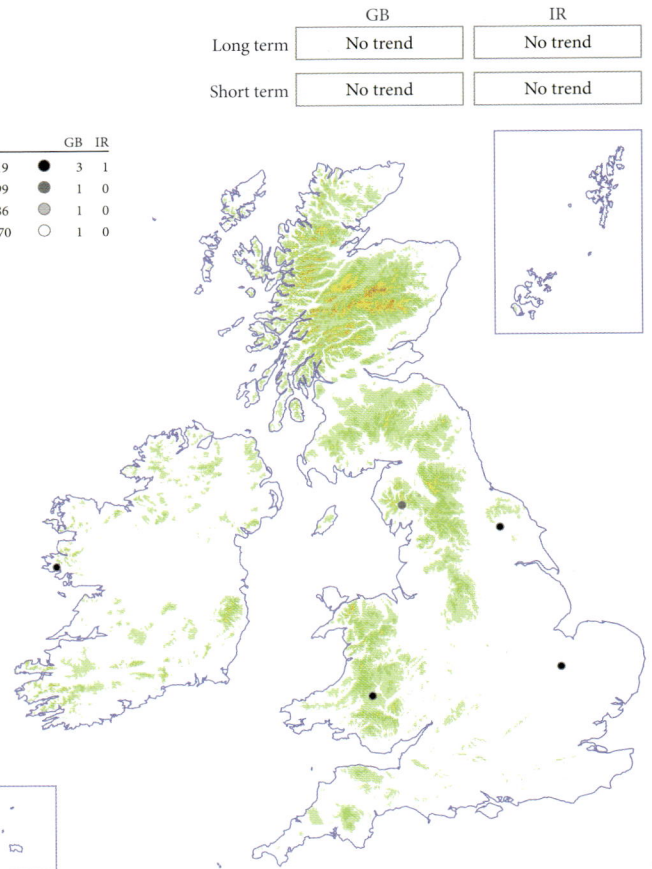

Key refs Stace *et al.* (2015).

T.D. Dines

Altitude (m)
- ● <1%
- ● 1–10%
- ● 11–30%
- ● 31–40%
- ● 41–50%
- ● 51–100%

Distance north (km)

☐ Apparency   ☐ In flower   ☐ In leaf

Ne *Iris orientalis* Turkish Iris
Mill.

A rhizomatous perennial herb which is grown in gardens and is naturalized in scrub, rough grassland, banks, roadside verges and on cliffs. It also occurs as a relic of cultivation. Lowland.

Trends *I. orientalis* was introduced into cultivation in 1790 and is often grown in gardens, especially in areas with a mild climate. It was first recorded from the wild in 1959 (Sand Point, North Somerset), and is extending its range, although the majority of records are from coastal areas in southern England.

Biogeography Native of Turkey.

	GB	IR
Long term	No trend	No trend
Short term		No trend

Alien	GB	IR
2000–19 ●	100	1
1987–99 ●	34	0
1970–86 ●	5	0
pre-1970 ○	0	0

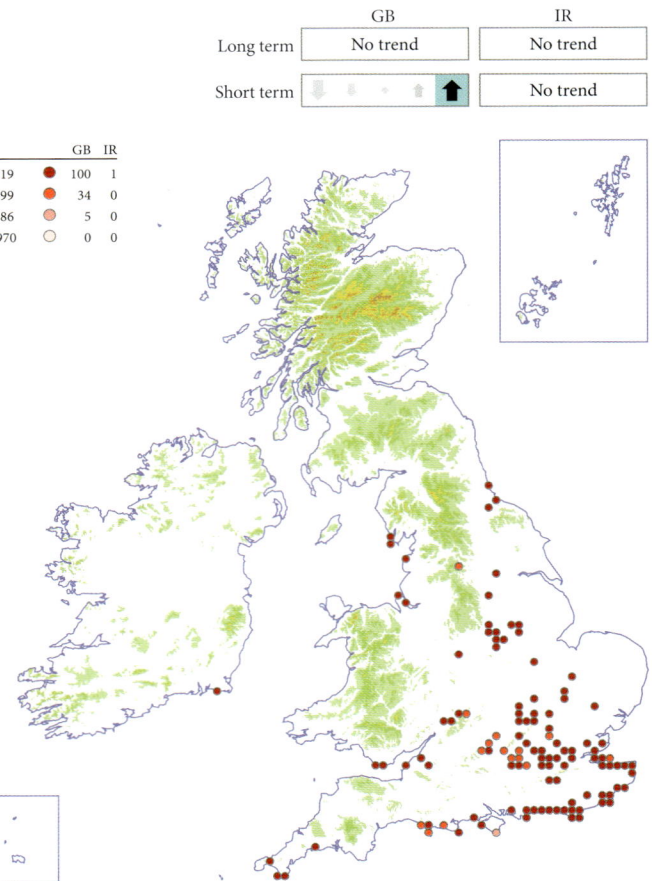

Altitude (m)
- ● <1%
- ● 1–10%
- ● 11–30%
- ● 31–40%
- ● 41–50%
- ● 51–100%

Distance north (km)

☐ Apparency   ☐ In flower   ☐ In leaf

J. Parmenter & T.D. Dines

N *Iris foetidissima* Stinking Iris

L.

A perennial herb, highly tolerant of drought and shade, found in hedgebanks and woods, and on sheltered scrubby sea-cliffs, mostly on calcareous substrates. In many areas it is especially associated with churchyards and cemeteries. Reproduction is by bird-dispersed seed and by rhizomatous extension. Lowland.

Native in Britain and the Channel Islands and a neophyte in Ireland.

Trends The native range of *I. foetidissima* is much obscured by garden throw-outs, bird-sown escapes from cultivated stock and deliberate introductions. It is treated here as alien throughout Ireland, the Isle of Man, Scotland and northern England, including much of the north Midlands, although the limits of its native range in Britain are now very obscure. It appears to be increasing steadily throughout Britain and Ireland though interpretation of the extent of this is complicated by more diligent recording of the species in marginally wild environments. Superficially the data suggest some range expansion to northern Britain and also a population-level increase within the native range, where many of the newly documented populations are suspected of having originated from garden sources.

Biogeography Suboceanic Southern-temperate element.

Native		GB	IR
2000–19	●	758	0
1987–99	●	678	0
1970–86	○	423	0
pre-1970	○	493	0

Alien		GB	IR
2000–19	●	588	121
1987–99	●	205	49
1970–86	●	89	15
pre-1970	○	95	39

Key refs Boon & Outen (2011), Chater (2010b), Crawley (2005), Hawksford & Hopkins (2011), Leslie (2019).

I. TAYLOR

Hy *Iris filifolia* × *tingitana* = *I.* ×*hollandica* Dutch Iris

H.R.Wehrh.

A bulbous perennial herb known from abandoned gardens, old bulb fields, roadside verges, disused clay-pits and refuse tips. It either persists as a relict of cultivation, or as a discard from gardens. Lowland.

A cultivated hybrid (alien × alien).

Trends This hybrid was introduced into cultivation in 1909. A wide variety of cultivars are available and these are now very popular in gardens. It was recorded in the wild by 1970 (Jersey).

Biogeography A hybrid of garden origin.

	GB	IR
Long term	No trend	No trend
Short term		No trend

		GB	IR
2000–19	●	22	1
1987–99	●	9	0
1970–86	●	0	0
pre-1970	○	0	0

Key refs Stace *et al.* (2015).

T.D. DINES

N **Romulea columnae** Sand Crocus
Sebast. & Mauri

A cormous perennial herb of short, open turf on freely draining sandy ground and cliff-slopes near the sea. Reproduction is mostly by seed, with division of the corm being less significant. Lowland.

Trends The overall 10 km square distribution of *R. columnae* has changed very little since the 1960s and the populations in the Channel Islands (where it is common in suitable habitats) and at Dawlish Warren (South Devon) appear to be stable. In 2002, following an absence of over 120 years, it was rediscovered at Polruan in Cornwall where it was reported as very locally abundant in short, cliff-top turf (French, 2020). There appears to have been some decline in the population since, due to changes in habitat management.

Biogeography Mediterranean-Atlantic element.

	GB	IR
Long term	No trend	No trend
Short term	No trend	No trend

Native	GB	IR
2000–19	15	0
1987–99	15	0
1970–86	5	0
pre-1970	12	0

Key refs French (2020), Wigginton (1999).

I. Taylor

Ne **Crocus vernus agg.** Spring Crocuses

A cormous perennial herb, flowering in the spring and very variable in colour but usually purple or strongly striped. It is widely planted in gardens and a variety of grassy habitats, especially in churchyards and amenity grasslands, and on roadside verges, where it readily naturalizes. The taxonomy of this species has changed in recent years: *C. vernus s.s.* now represents the small, often white-flowered, high mountain crocus of the Alps, which is rarely seen in cultivation, whereas the taxon formerly known as *C. vernus* is now referable to *C. neapolitanus* of which there are many cultivars, some polyploid and known as 'Large Dutch' crocuses; it is these cultivars that are most likely to be found naturalized in our area. Lowland.

Trends *C. vernus* agg. was introduced into cultivation in Britain before 1600 and was first recorded in the wild in 1763 (Battersea Mill, Surrey). It has been very widely planted including as a substitute for saffron (*C. sativus*), and it is still found in great abundance at a few long-established sites such as at Inkpen (Berkshire). The known distribution has increased dramatically since the 1960s although this is partly due to the more systematic recording of alien species. However, it remains unevenly recorded.

Biogeography *C. vernus s.s.* is a native of southern Europe, found in lowland to submontane grassy habitats, to 1,500 m. *C. neapolitanus* is known from Italy and the north-western Balkans.

	GB	IR
Long term	No trend	No trend
Short term		

Alien	GB	IR
2000–19	699	17
1987–99	296	0
1970–86	81	0
pre-1970	94	1

Key refs Mabey (1996), Mathew (1982), Ruksans (2017).

I. Taylor

Ne *Crocus tommasinianus* Early Crocus

Herb.

A cormous perennial herb, flowering in the spring, found in open deciduous woodland, churchyards and cemeteries, on roadsides and in parks and amenity grasslands. Although many populations originate from corms deliberately planted in the wild, it can become invasive in gardens and is frequently discarded onto road- and track-sides and waste ground. Whether deliberately planted, discarded or self-sown from garden populations, it readily becomes naturalized, spreading prolifically both vegetatively and by seed. Lowland.

Trends *C. tommasinianus* has been cultivated in Britain since 1847. It was probably under-recorded in the past when there was a general reluctance to record ornamental species in amenity areas. It may also have been confused with *C. neapolitanus* and both of these factors make assessment of changes in its distribution difficult. It was not recorded in the wild in Britain until 1963. However, its popularity as a garden plant, its ease of cultivation and a considerable increase in records over the past 20 years seem to reflect a genuine expansion of its range.

Biogeography Native of the Balkan Adriatic coastal mountains, southern Hungary and north-western Bulgaria.

		GB	IR
Long term		No trend	No trend
Short term		⬆	No trend

Alien		GB	IR
2000–19	●	560	2
1987–99	●	176	0
1970–86	●	37	0
pre-1970	○	10	0

Key refs Mathew (1982).

I. Taylor & B. Mathew

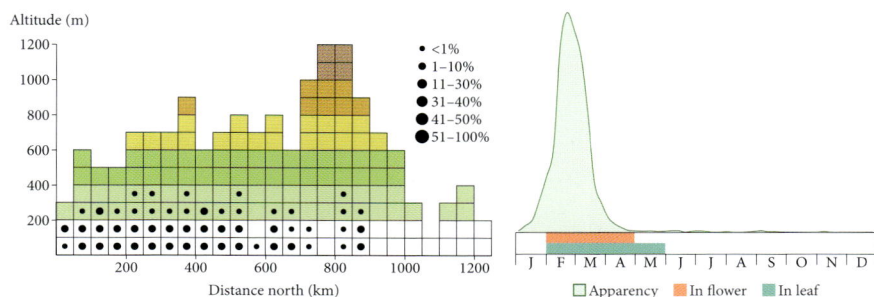

Ne *Crocus chrysanthus* Golden Crocus

(Herb.) Herb.

A spring flowering cormous perennial herb with yellow flowers which is naturalized in grassland, churchyards and on roadside verges. It also occurs as a relic of cultivation. Lowland.

Trends This species was introduced into cultivation in Britain around 1868, and is widely grown in gardens. It was first recorded from the wild in 1959 (Fletcher Moss, Didsbury, South Lancashire) and is being recorded with increasing frequency.

Biogeography Native of the Balkans and western, central and southern Turkey.

		GB	IR
Long term		No trend	No trend
Short term		⬆	No trend

Alien		GB	IR
2000–19	●	95	0
1987–99	●	44	0
1970–86	●	6	0
pre-1970	○	3	0

Key refs Mathew (1982), Wurzell (1992a).

T.D. Dines & D.A. Pearman

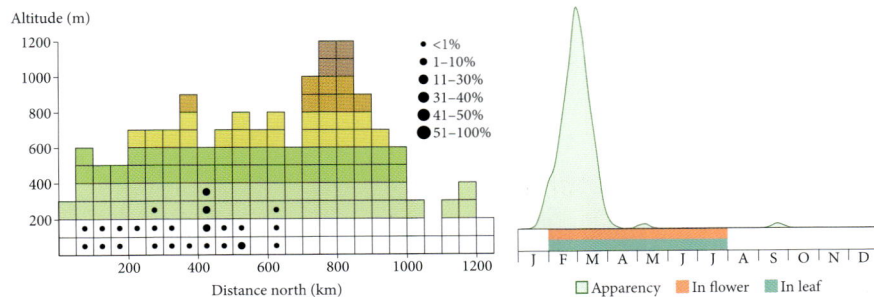

Hy *Crocus chrysanthus × biflorus = C. ×hybridus*
Petrovič

		GB	IR
Long term		No trend	No trend
Short term		No trend	No trend

A cormous perennial herb which is widely grown and is rarely naturalized in grassy places, including roadsides and churchyards, where it mainly arises as a relic of cultivation. Lowland.

A cultivated hybrid (alien × alien).

Trends It is uncertain when this hybrid was introduced into cultivation, but it was recorded as well naturalized in the wild by 1992 in Tottenham (Middlesex). It is the parentage of many garden hybrids and could occur spontaneously in mixed populations of the parent species in our area. It is almost certainly under-recorded.

Biogeography A hybrid of garden origin; the parents are very closely related and might be colour variants of the same species, although they very rarely occur together in their native ranges. Intermediate plants occur where they do occur together as natives (Mathew, 1982).

	GB	IR
2000–19	7	0
1987–99	4	0
1970–86	0	0
pre-1970	1	0

Altitude (m)

- <1%
- 1–10%
- 11–30%
- 31–40%
- 41–50%
- 51–100%

Distance north (km)

Apparency · In flower · In leaf

Key refs Mathew (1982), Stace *et al.* (2015).

T.D. DINES

Hy *Crocus angustifolius × flavus = C. ×luteus*
Lam.

		GB	IR
Long term		No trend	No trend
Short term			No trend

A cormous perennial herb of churchyards, roadsides, parks and other amenity grasslands. It is often long-lived when discarded into suitable habitats, where it spreads vegetatively. Lowland.

A cultivated hybrid (alien × alien).

Trends *C. ×stellaris* is commonly grown in gardens as the sterile cultivar 'Golden Yellow' (also known as 'Dutch Yellow' or 'Yellow Giant'). This cultivar was raised over two hundred years ago and its parent species have been cultivated in Britain since the 16th century. It was first recorded in the wild in 1848 and appears to be steadily increasing, but it is very unevenly recorded and has been confused with other taxa, especially cultivars of its parent species and of *C. chrysanthus*, making changes in distribution difficult to assess.

Biogeography A hybrid of garden origin.

	GB	IR
2000–19	133	1
1987–99	97	0
1970–86	6	0
pre-1970	6	0

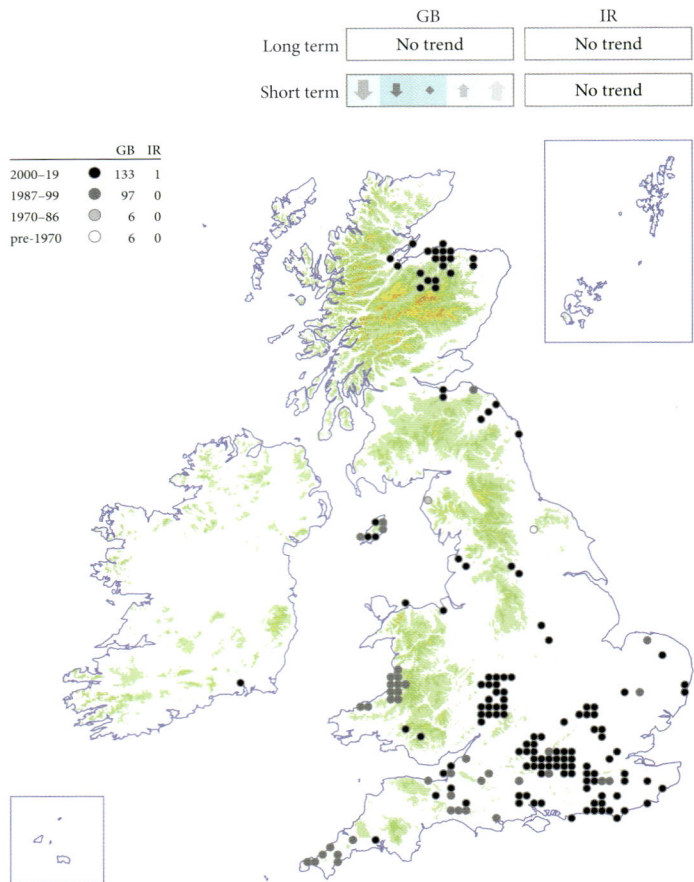

Altitude (m)

- <1%
- 1–10%
- 11–30%
- 31–40%
- 41–50%
- 51–100%

Distance north (km)

Apparency · In flower · In leaf

Key refs Mathew (1982), Stace *et al.* (2015).

I. TAYLOR

Ne *Crocus nudiflorus* Autumn Crocus
Sm.

A cormous perennial herb, flowering in the autumn and found naturalized in moist meadows, pastures, amenity grasslands and on roadsides, often where originally planted and where it spreads vegetatively by means of rhizomes forming uniform, sometimes extensive populations. Lowland.

Trends This species was introduced into cultivation before 1600, possibly as a substitute for saffron (*C. sativus*). It is grown in gardens and is still found as a relic of cultivation. *C. nudiflorus* was first recorded in the wild in 1738 and its British distribution appears to be gradually expanding. However, its long-established concentration in north-western England and the Midlands continues to be evident (the type locality for the species is in Nottinghamshire) and it remains a scarce alien elsewhere.

Biogeography Native of south-western France and northern Spain.

Alien		GB	IR
2000–19	●	104	0
1987–99	●	73	0
1970–86	●	46	0
pre-1970	○	69	0

	GB	IR
Long term	No trend	No trend
Short term	⬇ ⬇ ◆ ⬆ ⬆	No trend

Altitude (m)

200 400 600 800 1000 1200
Distance north (km)

● <1%
● 1–10%
● 11–30%
● 31–40%
● 41–50%
● 51–100%

J F M A M J J A S O N D
☐ Apparency ▮ In flower ▮ In leaf

Key refs Mathew (1982).

I. Taylor & B. Mathew

Ne *Crocus speciosus* Bieberstein's Crocus
M.Bieb.

An autumn-flowering cormous perennial herb which has violet-blue flowers with dissected orange stigma branches. It is naturalized in churchyards and rough grassland and on roadsides and grassy tracksides. It also occurs as a relic of cultivation. Lowland.

Trends This is perhaps the most widely grown of the autumn-flowering *Crocus* species, and was being grown in British gardens by 1839. It was recorded from the wild in 1964 (Keston, West Kent) but was apparently known a few years before that. Like many crocuses it is being much more widely recorded.

Biogeography Native of south-western Asia. The cultivated plants are all referable to *C. speciosus* subsp. *speciosus*.

Alien		GB	IR
2000–19	●	49	0
1987–99	●	27	0
1970–86	●	11	0
pre-1970	○	4	0

	GB	IR
Long term	No trend	No trend
Short term	⬇ ⬇ ◆ ⬆ ⬆	No trend

Altitude (m)

200 400 600 800 1000 1200
Distance north (km)

● <1%
● 1–10%
● 11–30%
● 31–40%
● 41–50%
● 51–100%

J F M A M J J A S O N D
☐ Apparency ▮ In flower ▮ In leaf

Key refs Mathew (1982).

T.D. Dines & D.A. Pearman

(N) *Gladiolus illyricus* Wild Gladiolus

W.D.J.Koch

A cormous perennial herb of acidic, brown-earth soils, found in grass-heaths, usually in association with *Pteridium aquilinum* which may afford the plant some protection from grazing, although excessive accumulation of bracken litter appears to lead to population decline. It presumably reproduces primarily by offsets, as flowering and seed production seem to be very limited. Lowland.

Trends *G. illyricus* was first recorded in the wild in 1856. Babington (1863) regarded it as native to our area, though Townsend (1904) suggested that bulbs may have arrived with young fir trees imported from Landes in France, subsequently spreading into the New Forest (South Hampshire). There has been little recent change in the overall 10 km square distribution of this species, but populations have declined locally, probably as a result of changes in management such as the introduction of summer control of bracken rather than the traditional harvesting in the autumn for animal bedding. Excessive or poorly managed burning might also be implicated on some sites.

Biogeography Mediterranean-Atlantic element. Our plant would appear to fall within *G. gallaecicus*, a taxon otherwise restricted to west-central France and north-western Iberia.

Long term	No trend	No trend
Short term	No trend	No trend

Native	GB	IR
2000–19	5	0
1987–99	6	0
1970–86	6	0
pre-1970	7	0

Alien	GB	IR
2000–19	0	0
1987–99	1	0
1970–86	0	0
pre-1970	0	0

	<1%
	1–10%
	11–30%
	31–40%
	41–50%
	51–100%

Key refs Babington (1863), Rand (2005), Tison & Girod (2014), Townsend (1904), Wigginton (1999).

I. TAYLOR

(Ne) *Gladiolus communis* Eastern Gladiolus

L.

A cormous perennial herb, grown in gardens and commercially in fields and found as a relic in old bulb fields and on field margins where originally cultivated. It also persists where garden waste has been discarded on roadsides, in hedges, on rough ground and clifftops but only in areas with a mild climate as the corm is susceptible to winter frost. Lowland.

Trends *G. communis* was introduced from southern Europe by 1596. It was first recorded in the wild in 1862. By the 1960s it was largely confined to the Isles of Scilly (where it was grown commercially) and West Cornwall; since then it has spread along the coast of southern Britain, as well as inland, often arising from garden waste. As with many garden escapes, it is difficult to assess whether this is a genuine increase or a reflection of more systematic recording of alien species.

Biogeography Native of the Mediterranean region.

Alien	GB	IR
2000–19	190	15
1987–99	167	3
1970–86	36	0
pre-1970	26	1

	<1%
	1–10%
	11–30%
	31–40%
	41–50%
	51–100%

Key refs French (2020), Lousley (1971), Sussex Botanical Recording Society (2018).

I. TAYLOR

Ne ***Schizostylis coccinea*** Kaffir Lily
Backh. & Harv. ex Hook.

A late-summer to autumn flowering
perennial herb, spreading by short
rhizomes, grown in a multiplicity of
cultivars, and becoming increasingly
popular in gardens. It is found as
a garden discard on road verges
and in waste places. Lowland.

Trends *S. coccinea* was introduced to
Britain just before 1863, and was first
recorded in the wild in 1979 (Silwood
Park, Berkshire) where it survives. It
was originally thought to be a tender
plant but is increasing in the wild where
it can be astonishingly persistent and
often almost ineradicable. It is now
commonly sold as *Hesperantha coccinea*.

Biogeography Native in southern Africa
(eastern provinces of South Africa north
to Zimbabwe).

	GB	IR
Long term	No trend	No trend
Short term		No trend

Alien	GB	IR
2000–19	46	2
1987–99	3	0
1970–86	0	0
pre-1970	0	0

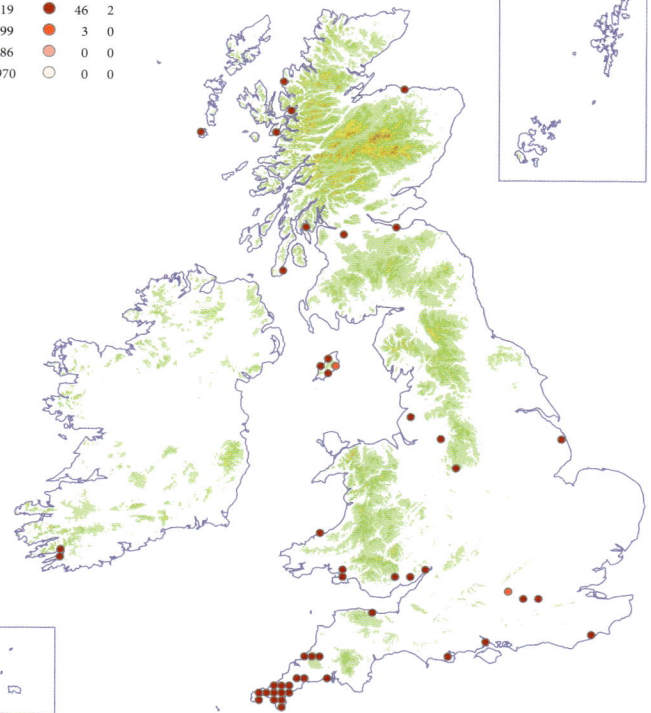

Altitude (m)

- <1%
- 1–10%
- 11–30%
- 31–40%
- 41–50%
- 51–100%

Distance north (km)

☐ Apparency ☐ In flower ☐ In leaf

D.A. Pearman

Hy ***Freesia* × *hybrida*** Freesia
L.H.Bailey

A cormous perennial herb which is
grown in bulb-fields and occurs as a
relic of cultivation in and by old fields on
Tresco and St Mary's (Isles of Scilly), and
as a casual on waste ground in Guernsey
(Channel Islands), where plants are
grown under glass. It is also recorded
as a casual on waste ground at Thorpe
Salvin (South-west Yorkshire). Lowland.

A cultivated hybrid (alien × alien).

Trends *F. ×hybrida* was introduced
into cultivation in Britain by 1911. It
is very popular as a cut-flower but is
only grown in gardens in areas with
very mild climates. The first record in
the wild is from St Mary's in 1961.

Biogeography A hybrid of garden
origin.

	GB	IR
Long term	No trend	No trend
Short term	No trend	No trend

	GB	IR
2000–19	6	0
1987–99	3	0
1970–86	0	0
pre-1970	1	0

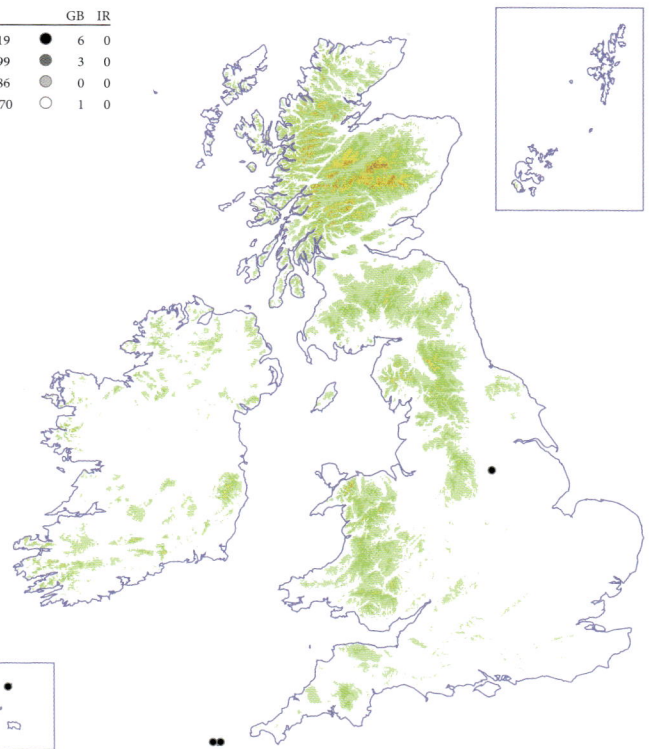

Altitude (m)

- <1%
- 1–10%
- 11–30%
- 31–40%
- 41–50%
- 51–100%

Distance north (km)

☐ Apparency ☐ In flower ☐ In leaf

Key refs Stace *et al.* (2015).

C.A. Stace, C.D. Preston & D.A. Pearman

Hy *Crocosmia paniculata × pottsii*

A cormous perennial herb, grown in gardens and naturalized on moist soils on roadsides, woodland margins, quarries, waste ground and refuse tips. It persists and spreads vegetatively when discarded into suitable habitats. Generally lowland, but reaching 390 m north of Carter Bar (Roxburghshire).

A cultivated hybrid (alien × alien).

Trends This hybrid was mapped as *C. paniculata* in the 2002 *Atlas* but all records under that name are now thought referable to its hybrid with *C. pottsii* which is very widely grown in gardens (Stace, 2010; Stace *et al.*, 2015). It was cultivated in Britain by 1881 and first recorded in the wild as an outcast in 1907 (Musselburgh, Midlothian). It appears to be gradually increasing its range across our area, especially in north-western England and eastern Scotland, and most notably throughout Ireland. However, any assessment of trends is complicated by past taxonomic confusion, and also with tall, vigorous cultivars which are often of complex hybrid origin, frequently also involving *C. masoniorum*.

Biogeography *C. paniculata* is native of South Africa but the hybrid probably arose in gardens by accident and clones were propogated without regard to their parentage (Stace *et al.*, 2015). Most plants grown today as *C. paniculata* are referable to this sterile hybrid (Goldblatt *et al.*, 2004).

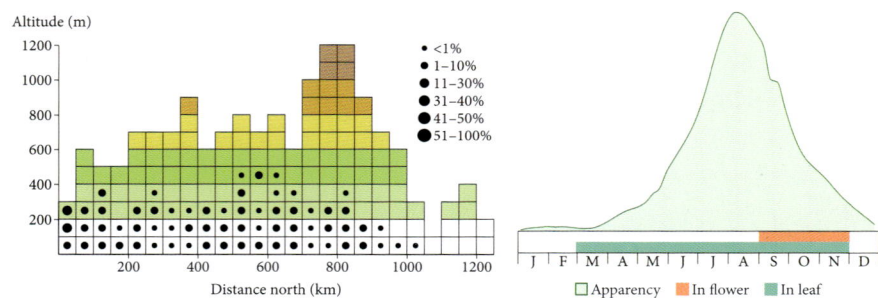

	GB	IR
Long term	No trend	No trend
Short term		

		GB	IR
2000–19	●	392	124
1987–99	●	119	12
1970–86	●	16	1
pre-1970	○	8	0

Key refs Chater (2010b), Goldblatt *et al.* (2004), Stace *et al.* (2015).

I. Taylor

Ne *Crocosmia masoniorum* Giant Montbretia
(L.Bolus) N.E.Br.

A cormous perennial herb, grown in gardens and naturalized on roadsides and waste ground. It reproduces vegetatively through the production of stolons, but most of the records in the wild must be of garden throwouts. Generally lowland, but up to 345 m as a planted specimen at Mar Lodge (South Aberdeenshire).

Trends It is thought that *C. masoniorum* was introduced into cultivation in Britain before 1954, and was first recorded from the wild in 1982 (Garelochhead, Dunbartonshire). It is now commonly grown in gardens, particularly as the cultivar 'Lucifer', and is becoming frequent in the wild.

Biogeography Native of South Africa.

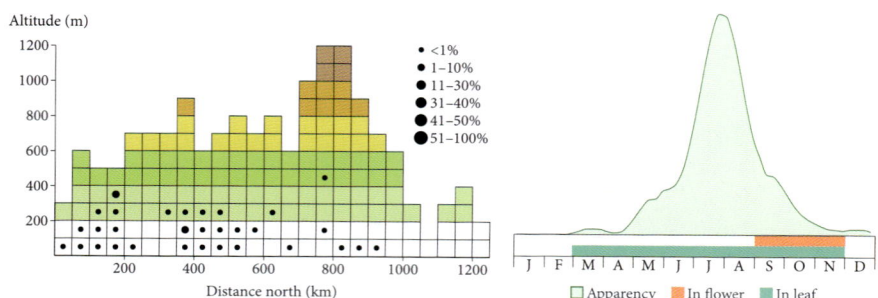

	GB	IR
Long term	No trend	No trend
Short term		

Alien		GB	IR
2000–19	●	74	8
1987–99	●	7	3
1970–86	●	4	8
pre-1970	○	0	0

Key refs Goldblatt *et al.* (2004).

D.A. Pearman & T.D. Dines

Ne *Crocosmia pottsii* Potts' Montbretia

(Macnab ex Baker) N.E.Br.

A cormous perennial herb, grown in gardens and naturalized beside roads, rivers and lakes, and on waste ground, where it arises as a garden escape. It mainly reproduces vegetatively through the production of stolons, but most of the records in the wild must be of garden throw-outs. Lowland.

Trends *C. pottsii* was introduced into cultivation in 1882 and is commonly grown in gardens. It was first recorded from the wild in 1961 in a disused quarry (Bellanoch, Kintyre). This species is very similar to *C. ×crocosmiiflora* and the uneven coverage shown on the map suggests that it may be overlooked for the hybrid in some areas.

Biogeography Native of South Africa.

Alien	GB	IR
2000–19	86	48
1987–99	42	2
1970–86	7	1
pre-1970	0	0

Key refs Goldblatt *et al.* (2004).

D.A. Pearman & T.D. Dines

Hy *Crocosmia aurea × pottsii = C. ×crocosmiiflora* Montbretia

(Lemoine) N.E.Br.

A cormous perennial herb spreading vegetatively by means of rhizomes to form dense clumps in woods and hedgebanks, the sides of lakes, rivers and streams, on coastal cliffs and slopes, sand dunes, quarries, churchyards, by roadsides and on waste ground. Although some viable seed is produced, most wild populations have probably arisen from discarded garden plants and subsequent vegetative spread. Generally lowland, but reaching 500 m at Garn Goch (Glamorganshire).

A cultivated hybrid (alien × alien).

Trends This hybrid, which is extremely common in gardens, was raised in France in 1880 and reached Britain the same year. It was first recorded from the wild by the River Esk (Midlothian) in 1907. Since the 1960s it has dramatically extended its range eastwards and considerably consolidated its distribution in western Britain and Ireland, where it is now one of the most frequent established aliens, sometimes forming dense stands for hundreds of metres on riverbanks and lanesides.

Biogeography A hybrid of garden origin between two South African parents.

	GB	IR
2000–19	2029	876
1987–99	1312	672
1970–86	555	63
pre-1970	510	349

Key refs Nelson (1993), Stace *et al.* (2015).

C.A. Stace, C.D. Preston & D.A. Pearman

Ne *Simethis mattiazzii* Kerry Lily

(Vand.) Sacc.

A rhizomatous, perennial herb found only in dry, rocky, maritime heath near Derrynane on the coast of South Kerry and on the Béarra Peninsula, West Cork. It was formerly naturalized near the coast in southern England. Lowland.

Trends The Irish population of *S. mattiazzii* has declined in recent decades, mainly due to a lack of grazing. Uncontrolled fires have affected some populations, though these may actually favour the species. The Irish populations appear to be genetically uniform and it is now thought that the species was brought to Ireland in goods or packaging, through trade or smuggling locally, perhaps one or two centuries ago (Lupton & Sheehy Skeffington, 2020). The English plants may have been imported with *Pinus pinaster*. They were known in Dorset from 1847 until *c.* 1914, and in South Hampshire in 1915.

Biogeography Native of south-western Europe, Morocco, Algeria and Tunisia.

	GB	IR
Long term	No trend	No trend
Short term	No trend	No trend

Alien	GB	IR
2000–19	0	4
1987–99	0	4
1970–86	0	1
pre-1970	2	3

Key refs Dupont (1962), Lupton & Sheehy Skeffington (2020).

I. TAYLOR & M. SHEEHY SKEFFINGTON

Ne *Hemerocallis fulva* Orange Day-lily

(L.) L.

A perennial herb, with short, thick rhizomes, widely grown in gardens and often persisting where discarded or deliberately planted in open woodlands, dune-slacks, amenity grasslands and hedgerows, on roadsides, streamsides and riverbanks, alongside railways and paths and on waste ground. Usually closely associated with human settlements and thriving especially in damp or shady locations. Lowland.

Trends *H. fulva* was introduced into cultivation in Britain before 1596. It is very commonly grown in gardens, and readily persists when discarded into suitable habitats. It was known to occur in the wild by at least 1905; most early records are from southern England. There has been a notable range expansion in the last 30 years with many more records in northern England (especially Lancashire), the Isle of Man

and Scotland. It remains relatively rare in Wales but is increasing and was first recorded in the wild in Ireland in 2000. As with many cultivated aliens, it is inconsistently recorded and almost certainly under-recorded in many areas.

Biogeography A cultivated plant of uncertain origin; most garden plants are reported to be a sterile triploid.

	GB	IR
Long term	No trend	No trend
Short term		

Alien	GB	IR
2000–19	309	7
1987–99	177	0
1970–86	50	0
pre-1970	14	0

Key refs Crawley (2005), French (2020), Leslie (2019), Sussex Botanical Recording Society (2018).

I. TAYLOR

Ne *Hemerocallis lilioasphodelus* Yellow Day-lily
L.

A perennial herb naturalized in woodland and on roadsides, railway banks and waste ground, where it arises as a garden escape. It may also occur as a relic of cultivation. The plant is self-sterile and in mainland Europe it spreads extensively by clonal growth, so seed is rarely set. Lowland.

Trends *H. lilioasphodelus* was being grown in British gardens by 1596, and is now widely cultivated. It was first recorded in the wild in 1894 (Belfast, County Antrim). Some populations are long-lived; it persisted at Charterhouse (North Somerset) from 1957 to at least 2008.

Biogeography Native of China; naturalized in Europe.

Alien	GB	IR
2000–19	43	1
1987–99	21	0
1970–86	9	0
pre-1970	9	0

	GB	IR
Long term	No trend	No trend
Short term	↓ ↓ ◆ ↑ ↑	No trend

T.D. Dines & D.A. Pearman

Ne *Kniphofia uvaria* Red-hot-poker
(L.) Oken

A shortly rhizomatous perennial herb, widely grown in gardens and found on sand dunes, riverbanks, roadsides, quarries and waste ground, usually occurring as persistent isolated clumps arising from discarded or deliberately planted garden stock. Seed is occasionally set and large populations can form in this way, especially on well-drained soils in southern and coastal localities. Lowland.

Trends *K. uvaria* has been cultivated in Britain since 1705, but was not recorded from the wild until 1950. Its 10 km square distribution has increased since 2000, especially in England and eastern Scotland, although this is likely to reflect the more systematic recording of garden escapes then a genuine increase. Most plants grown in gardens are complex hybrids and it is very likely that some of these will have been recorded in error as *K. uvaria*.

Biogeography Native of South Africa.

Alien	GB	IR
2000–19	217	5
1987–99	126	0
1970–86	29	1
pre-1970	5	0

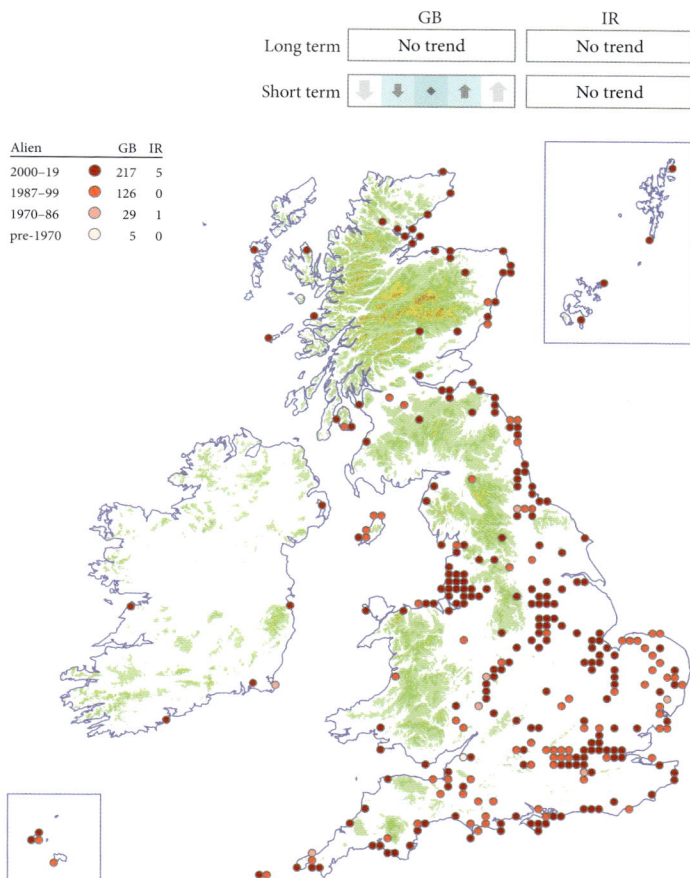

	GB	IR
Long term	No trend	No trend
Short term	↓ ↓ ◆ ↑ ↑	No trend

Key refs Leslie (2019), Stace *et al.* (2015), Whitehouse (2016).

I. Taylor

Hy *Kniphofia* ×*praecox* Greater Red-hot-poker
Baker

A rhizomatous perennial herb that is well naturalized on sand dunes or survives where planted or discarded in garden waste in scrub on sea-shores, and on streamsides, roadside banks and verges, grassy slopes, by farm tracks, in disused quarries and on waste ground. Lowland.

A cultivated hybrid (alien × alien).

Trends *K.* ×*praecox* was described by Baker (1870) from material cultivated in England, although apparently recently imported from South Africa, and is very widely grown in gardens. It was recorded in the wild by 1957 (Jersey). This taxon is probably a hybrid complex involving *K. uvaria* and *K. bruceae* as parents. The hybrid is much confused with *K. uvaria*, and the true distribution of the hybrid is imperfectly known.

Biogeography A hybrid of garden origin.

	GB	IR
Long term	No trend	No trend
Short term	No trend	No trend

		GB	IR
2000–19	●	90	8
1987–99	●	38	0
1970–86	●	3	0
pre-1970	○	6	0

Key refs Baker (1870), Stace *et al.* (2015).

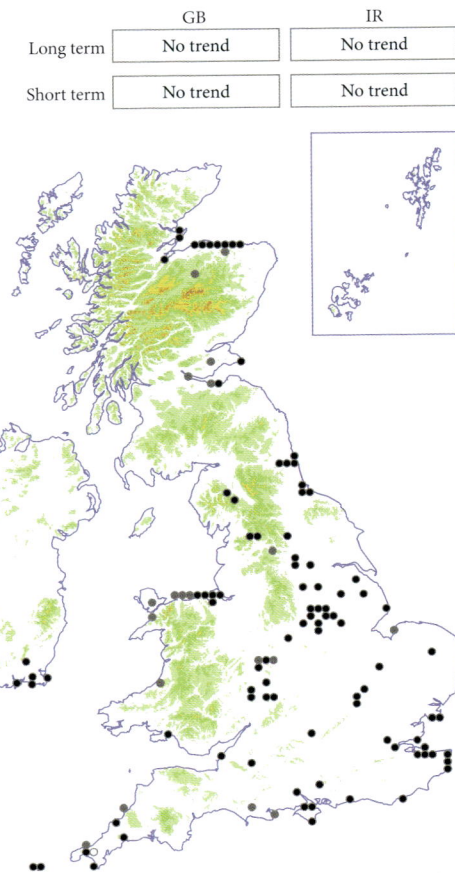

C.A. STACE, C.D. PRESTON & D.A. PEARMAN

Ne *Phormium tenax* New Zealand Flax
J.R.Forst. & G.Forst.

A large, long-lived, evergreen perennial herb, widely grown in gardens and planted as a windbreak in coastal areas and found on coastal cliffs, rocks and sand dunes and more rarely on waste ground inland. Plants reproduce by seed and can become naturalized in suitable areas. Lowland.

Trends *P. tenax* was introduced into cultivation in 1789 and is now very popular in gardens. It was formerly grown in the Isles of Scilly and Isle of Man as a fibre crop. It was first recorded in the wild in 1898 (Tresco, Isles of Scilly), and has increased in the last two decades through deliberate plantings, the discarding of garden material and self-seeding.

Biogeography Native of New Zealand and Norfolk Island.

	GB	IR
Long term	No trend	No trend
Short term	↑	↑

Alien		GB	IR
2000–19	●	171	133
1987–99	●	39	37
1970–86	●	14	2
pre-1970	○	19	15

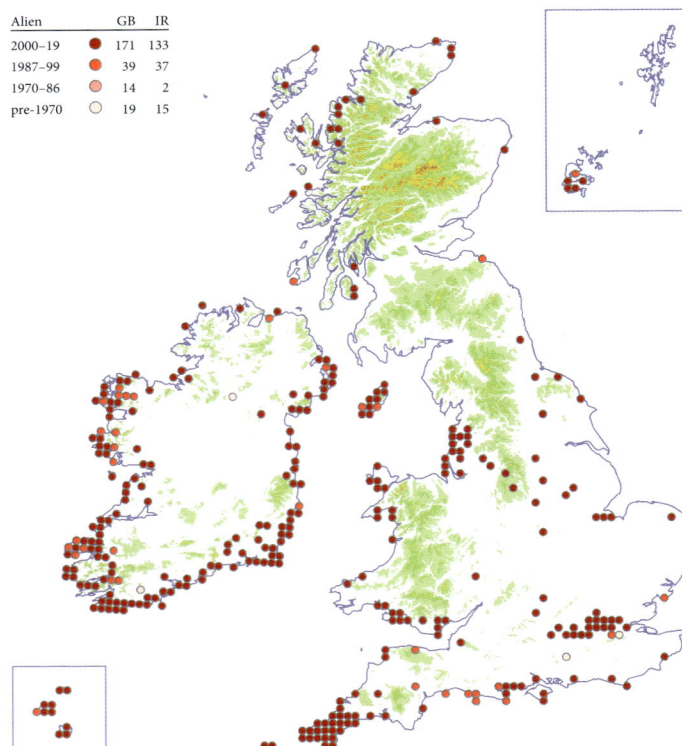

T.D. DINES

Ⓝ *Allium schoenoprasum* Chives
L.

A bulbous perennial herb found as a native on thin soils over limestone, serpentine and basic igneous rocks; it sometimes grows in rank grass on deeper soils, and in crevices of riverside bedrock. As an alien it grows on road verges, tracksides, in paving-cracks, at the base of walls, in gutters and on waste ground and is usually self-sown from nearby gardens or from discarded garden waste. Most alien populations appear to remain small with limited evidence of dispersal in the wild. Mainly lowland, but reaching 395 m at Simonsbath (South Somerset).

Trends The native distribution of this species appears stable, but alien occurrences, mainly as a direct result of material discarded in garden waste, continue to increase. It is treated as unquestionably native in Cornwall and possibly also in similar habitats in Pembrokeshire but the native status of other populations mapped here (Wye Valley, Carmarthenshire, Northumberland) has been questioned due to their close proximity to monasteries and castles (Pearman, 2013). It is regarded as probably introduced in Ireland (Scannell & Synnott, 1987) but is mapped as a native here in seasonally flooded hollows on limestone pavement at Lough Mask (East Mayo) (Curtis & McGough, 1988).

Biogeography Assigned to the Circumpolar Boreo-arctic Montane element, but with an anomalous distribution; widely naturalized outside its native range.

Native	GB	IR
2000–19	16	1
1987–99	14	2
1970–86	13	2
pre-1970	18	2

Alien	GB	IR
2000–19	317	15
1987–99	115	3
1970–86	41	3
pre-1970	52	0

Key refs French (2020), Maskew (2014), Pearman (2013), Scannell & Synnott (1987), Stewart *et al.* (1994).

I. TAYLOR

Ⓝₑ *Allium cepa* Onion
L.

A bulbous perennial herb, widely grown in gardens and also in fields and found as a relic of cultivation or a throw-out on refuse tips, waysides and waste ground, derelict sites and neglected allotments. This species is a fertile diploid. Lowland.

Trends *A. cepa* was being cultivated in British gardens by medieval times and remains a widely grown vegetable crop. It was recorded from the wild by 1896 (Chigwell, South Essex) though probably has a long unrecorded history as a casual before that. It is treated as a cultivated archaeophyte by Stace & Crawley (2015). Increases are probably due to better recording of aliens rather than a genuine spread. Since 2000 records are concentrated in areas that reflect commercial production.

Biogeography Origin uncertain; known from tomb paintings to have been cultivated by the Ancient Egyptians and now widespread as a crop.

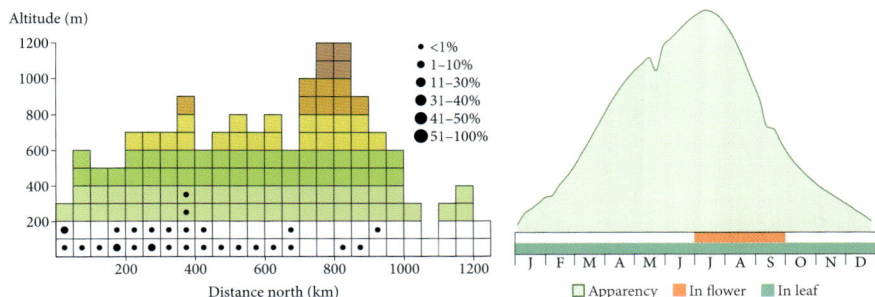

Alien	GB	IR
2000–19	101	7
1987–99	34	1
1970–86	9	0
pre-1970	12	0

Key refs Stace & Crawley (2015), Zohary & Hopf (2000).

T.D. DINES & N. ASPEY

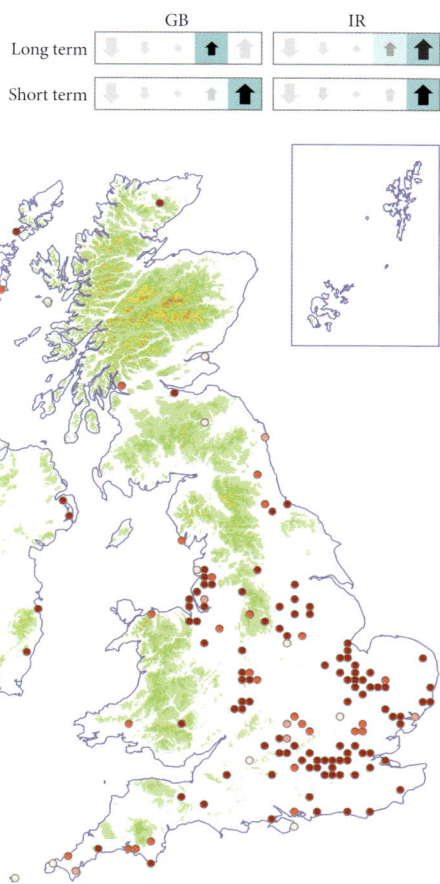

Ne *Allium roseum* Rosy Garlic
L.

A bulbous perennial herb, grown in gardens and found naturalized on rough and waste ground, open rocky slopes, hedgebanks, pavements, churchyards and roadsides. Lowland.

Trends *A. roseum* was introduced into cultivation by 1752, and first recorded in the wild in 1837. Both var. *bulbiferum* and var. *roseum* are commonly cultivated in gardens; var. *bulbiferum*, in which some of the flowers in the umbel are replaced by bulbils, is particularly likely to be naturalized when planted or discarded in suitable habitats. The distribution of *A. roseum* has increased since the 1960s, especially along the southern coast of England as well as inland, although many of the inland populations have been short-lived, presumably due to the severity of winter frosts.

Biogeography A variable species, native of the Mediterranean region.

Alien	GB	IR
2000–19	286	10
1987–99	132	0
1970–86	50	0
pre-1970	39	0

Key refs Stace & Crawley (2015), Zohary & Hopf (2000).

I. Taylor

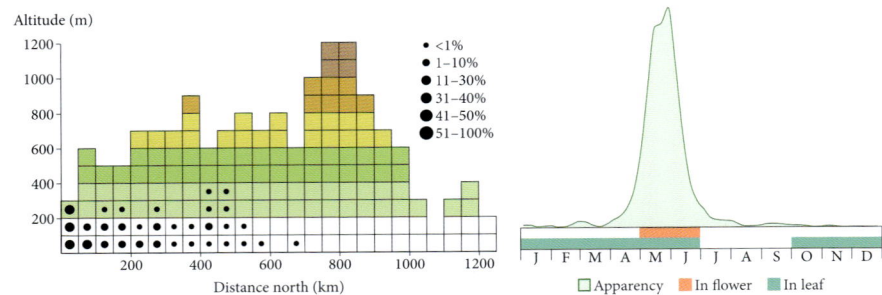

Ne *Allium neapolitanum* Neapolitan Garlic
Cirillo

A bulbous perennial herb grown in gardens and naturalized in fields, hedgerows, on roadsides and on waste ground. It also occurs as a relic of cultivation. Some populations are very long-lived. Lowland.

Trends *A. neapolitanum* was introduced into cultivation in Britain in 1781 and is popular in gardens. It was recorded from the wild by 1864 (Guernsey) and is probably increasing, especially in southern England, but with records now reaching as far north as Northern Ireland, the Isle of Man and West Lancashire.

Biogeography Native of south-western Europe and the Mediterranean region.

Alien	GB	IR
2000–19	99	2
1987–99	40	0
1970–86	11	0
pre-1970	15	0

	GB	IR
Long term	No trend	No trend
Short term		No trend

T.D. Dines & N. Aspey

Ne *Allium subhirsutum* Hairy Garlic

L.

A bulbous perennial herb grown in gardens and naturalized in fields, hedgerows and on roadsides, banks and waste ground. It also occurs as a relic of cultivation. Lowland.

Trends This species was being cultivated in British gardens by 1596. It was recorded from the wild by 1954 (Teignmouth, South Devon) and is increasing.

Biogeography Native of the Mediterranean region.

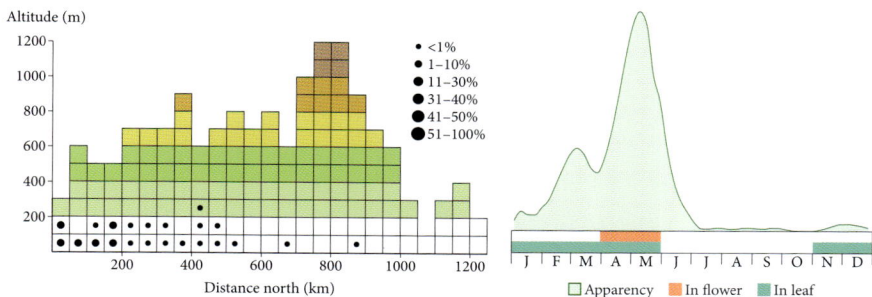

		GB	IR
	Long term	No trend	No trend
	Short term	↑	No trend

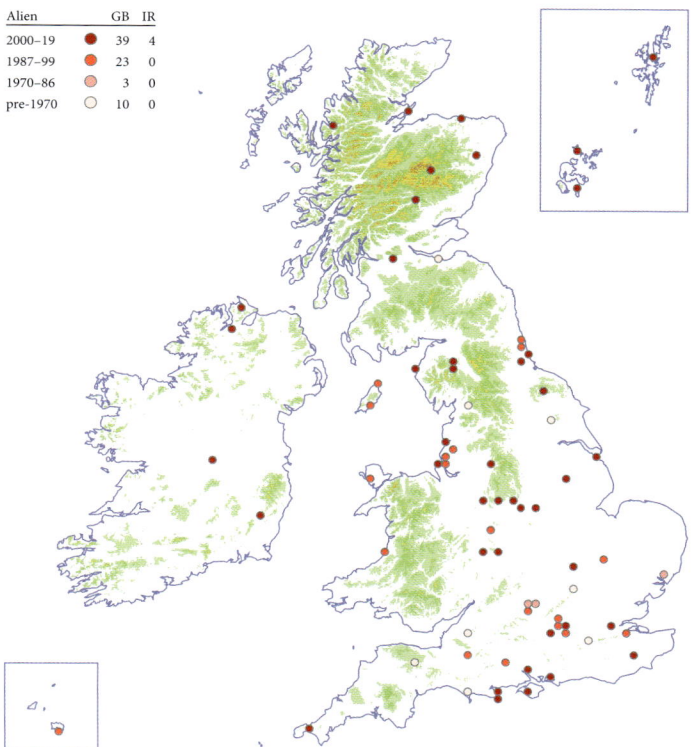

Alien		GB	IR
2000–19	●	142	1
1987–99	●	31	0
1970–86	●	5	0
pre-1970	○	7	0

Altitude (m)

●	<1%
●	1–10%
●	11–30%
●	31–40%
●	41–50%
●	51–100%

Distance north (km)

☐ Apparency ▮ In flower ▮ In leaf

T.D. Dines & N. Aspey

Ne *Allium moly* Yellow Garlic

L.

A bulbous perennial herb, grown in gardens and naturalized in fields and hedgerows and on roadsides, banks, tracksides and derelict land, especially in warm, sunny sites. Lowland.

Trends *A. moly* was introduced into cultivation in Britain by 1596 and is very popular in gardens. It was first recorded from the wild in 1838 (Surrey) and appears to be increasing with records doubling since 2000, albeit from a very low base, and now noted in Scotland and Ireland.

Biogeography Native of shaded mountain rocks in eastern Spain and south-western France.

		GB	IR
	Long term	No trend	No trend
	Short term	↑	No trend

Alien		GB	IR
2000–19	●	39	4
1987–99	●	23	0
1970–86	●	3	0
pre-1970	○	10	0

Altitude (m)

●	<1%
●	1–10%
●	11–30%
●	31–40%
●	41–50%
●	51–100%

Distance north (km)

☐ Apparency ▮ In flower ▮ In leaf

T.D. Dines & N. Aspey

Ne *Allium triquetrum* Three-cornered Garlic

L.

A bulbous perennial herb, occasionally grown in gardens and found naturalized on roadsides, hedgebanks, field margins, coastal cliff-tops, rough grassland, pavements, car parks and waste ground. Its spreads readily by ant-dispersed seed. Lowland.

Trends *A. triquetrum* was introduced into cultivation by 1759 and noted as established here by 1849, initially in Guernsey. By the 1960s it was well established in south-western Britain and southern Ireland and since then it has spread rapidly eastwards and northwards to colonize the milder regions of England, coastal Wales and Ireland with scattered, though sometimes short-lived, populations in northern England and western Scotland. It has become invasive in some habitats in more oceanic climates and it may be increasing elsewhere due to milder winters.

Biogeography Native of the western and central Mediterranean region.

Alien	GB	IR
2000–19	802	305
1987–99	316	116
1970–86	102	12
pre-1970	96	26

Key refs Chater (2010b), French (2020), Leslie (2019).

I. TAYLOR & K.J. WALKER

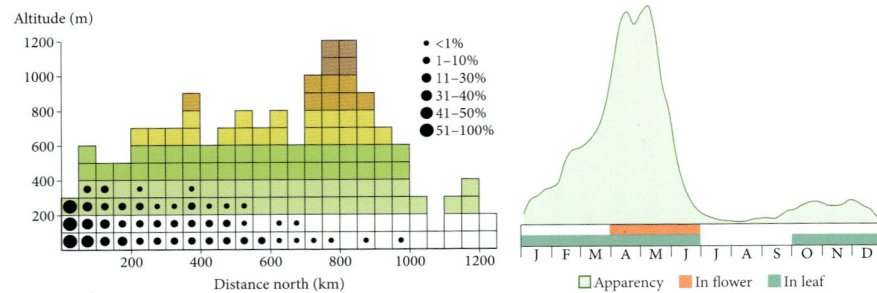

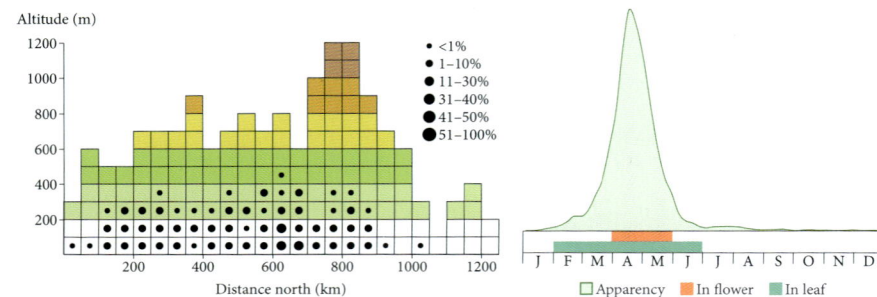

Ne *Allium paradoxum* Few-flowered Garlic

(M.Bieb.) G.Don

A bulbous perennial herb, spreading by means of inflorescence bulbils in a wide variety of, usually ungrazed, situations such as riverbanks, parks and gardens, roadsides, field margins, other rough and waste ground, and woodland. Generally lowland, but reaching 375 m at Carter Bar (Roxburghshire).

Trends *A. paradoxum* was introduced into cultivation in 1823 and first recorded in the wild near Edinburgh in 1863. It can be very invasive when discarded into disturbed habitats, and is increasingly abundant throughout its rapidly expanding range, especially in south-eastern Scotland and north-eastern England where the bulbils are widely dispersed along river valleys during floods. In some of these areas it is now as abundant as *A. ursinum* and swamps other spring flowers in woodlands (Braithwaite, 2014), most notably *Gagea lutea*. Its distinctly eastern distribution contrasts with that of *A. triquetrum*.

Biogeography Native of the Caucasus and Iran.

Alien	GB	IR
2000–19	554	27
1987–99	271	8
1970–86	161	3
pre-1970	113	3

Key refs Braithwaite (2014), Oswald (1993).

I. TAYLOR & K.J. WALKER

(N) *Allium ursinum* Ramsons
L.

A bulbous perennial herb, growing in moist woodlands, on the shady banks of watercourses, along hedgebanks and in the grikes of limestone pavement. It is occasionally found in more open situations such as rock crevices, scree and coastal cliff ledges. Regeneration is primarily by seed. It is perhaps also occasionally deliberately planted. Generally lowland, but reaching 570 m at Glen Glass (East Ross).

Native in Britain and Ireland and a neophyte in the Channel Islands.

Trends The known 10 km square distribution of *A. ursinum* has increased since the 1960s in parts of eastern England, Ireland and Scotland due to more systematic recording. Some populations, however, especially those on wooded riverbanks and streamsides prone to occasional inundation, appear to be expanding.

Biogeography European Temperate element.

Native		GB	IR
2000–19	●	2017	514
1987–99	●	1840	326
1970–86	○	1175	68
pre-1970	○	1662	146

Alien		GB	IR
2000–19	●	25	2
1987–99	●	13	0
1970–86	●	4	0
pre-1970	○	7	0

Key refs Grime *et al.* (2007), Hawksford & Hopkins (2011), Leslie (2019), Mabey (1996), Tutin (1957).

I. TAYLOR

Altitude (m) / Distance north (km)

☐ Apparency ☐ In flower ☐ In leaf

(N) *Allium oleraceum* Field Garlic
L.

A bulbous perennial herb of dry, usually steeply sloping, calcareous grasslands, and open sunny banks in river floodplains. Many populations grow on road verges and tracksides. Reproduction is primarily from inflorescence bulbils, although seed production can be significant following warm, moist summers. Floodplain populations are able to disperse widely during the winter through flood-borne bulbils although some fail to flower due to hay-cutting. 0–365 m (Dovedale, Derbyshire).

Native in Britain and a neophyte in Ireland.

Trends Recording may have been hindered by confusion with both *A. scorodoprasum* and *A. vineale*, and the species can be difficult to locate from early summer onwards in ranker swards, making trends difficult to interpret. Nonetheless, significant decline is evident, particularly during the early part of the 20th century although this appears to have slowed in recent decades. Causes of loss include agricultural intensification or abandonment and the conversion of marginal grasslands to other uses, including tree planting. Some roadside populations have succumbed to competition from unmown coarse grasses or have been lost due to shading from adjacent hedges and scrub.

Biogeography European Temperate element; widely naturalized outside its native range.

Native		GB	IR
2000–19	●	178	0
1987–99	●	158	0
1970–86	○	107	0
pre-1970	○	255	0

Alien		GB	IR
2000–19	●	7	4
1987–99	●	6	7
1970–86	●	2	3
pre-1970	○	8	7

Key refs Leslie (2019), Maskew (2014), Stewart *et al.* (1994), Stroh (2014a), Stroh *et al.* (2019).

I. TAYLOR

Altitude (m) / Distance north (km)

☐ Apparency ☐ In flower ☐ In leaf

Ne *Allium carinatum* Keeled Garlic
L.

A bulbous perennial herb, widely grown in gardens and found naturalized in churchyards, rough and waste ground and on roadsides, where it may originate from seed or, perhaps more frequently, from inflorescence bulbils in discarded garden waste. Lowland.

Trends *A. carinatum* was cultivated in Britain by 1789 and is frequently grown in gardens. It has been naturalized in our area since at least 1806. There is little evidence of any significant increase in range since the 1960s.

Biogeography Native of central and south-eastern Europe; naturalized north and west of its native range.

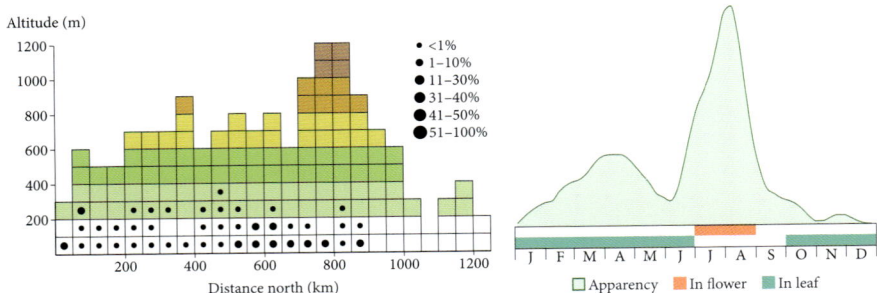

Alien	GB	IR
2000–19	124	12
1987–99	88	10
1970–86	61	8
pre-1970	77	9

Altitude (m) legend:
- <1%
- 1–10%
- 11–30%
- 31–40%
- 41–50%
- 51–100%

Distance north (km)

Apparency · In flower · In leaf

Key refs Oswald (1993).

I. TAYLOR

Ne *Allium sativum* Garlic
L.

A bulbous perennial herb which is naturalized on the sea-shore at Porth Dinllaen (Caernarvonshire) and in a saltmarsh beside the River Lune (West Lancashire). Elsewhere, it occurs as a relic of cultivation or a food-waste alien on refuse tips and waste ground. It is diploid but most cultivars are sterile. Lowland.

Trends *A. sativum* was being grown in British gardens by medieval times (Harvey, 1981) and is widely grown as a flavouring and for a medicinal oil. It was recorded from the wild by 1837 (Rochester, West Kent). Records have greatly increased from a low baseline since 2000, probably connected to greater agricultural and horticultural use, but also as a result of the better recording of aliens. It is treated as a cultivated archaeophyte by Stace & Crawley (2015).

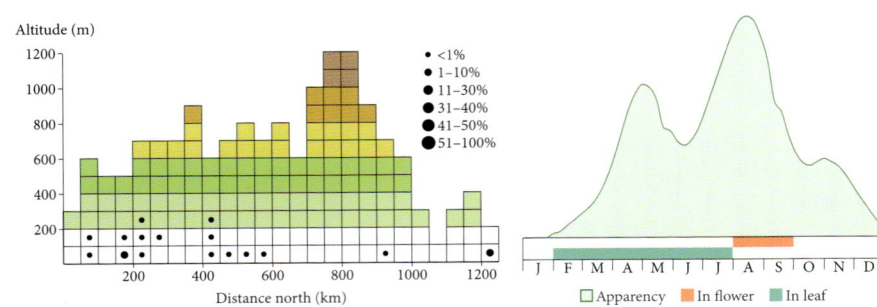

Biogeography Origin uncertain; possible ancestral species have been identified from Turkey and the Near East. Like other cultivated *Allium* species, the first evidence for its domestication comes from Ancient Egypt.

Alien	GB	IR
2000–19	38	9
1987–99	6	2
1970–86	3	0
pre-1970	4	0

	GB	IR
Long term	No trend	No trend
Short term		

Altitude (m) legend:
- <1%
- 1–10%
- 11–30%
- 31–40%
- 41–50%
- 51–100%

Distance north (km)

Apparency · In flower · In leaf

Key refs Harvey (1981), Mathew (1996), Stace & Crawley (2015), Zohary & Hopf (2000).

T.D. DINES & N. ASPEY

Allium ampeloprasum Wild Leek

Ar

L.

A bulbous perennial herb, found naturalized in rank vegetation in sandy and rocky places near the sea where it is usually associated with man-made habitats such as old fields, roadsides, hedgebanks, ruined settlements, paths and tracks, bulbfields and drainage ditches, and often spreading from there onto sheltered cliff-slopes and streamsides. Elsewhere it grows a casual garden escape on pavements, waste ground and other disturbed places. *A. ampeloprasum* var. *ampeloprasum* reproduces mainly by seed, whereas var. *bulbiferum* and var. *babingtonii* spread mainly by inflorescence bulbils. Lowland.

Trends This species is an ancient introduction with three distinct varieties recorded in our area: var. *babingtonii*, thought by some authorities to be an endemic, is widespread in south-western

Britain and western Ireland and has greatly extended its range since the 1960s; var. *bulbiferum* is confined to the Channel Islands (and possibly a few sites on mainland Britain) where it is relatively stable; and var. *ampeloprasum* occurs scattered throughout the range of the species and may be declining. The species may occasionally be misrecorded for *A. sativum* or *A. scorodoprasum*.

Biogeography As an archaeophyte, *A. ampeloprasum* has a Mediterranean-Atlantic distribution.

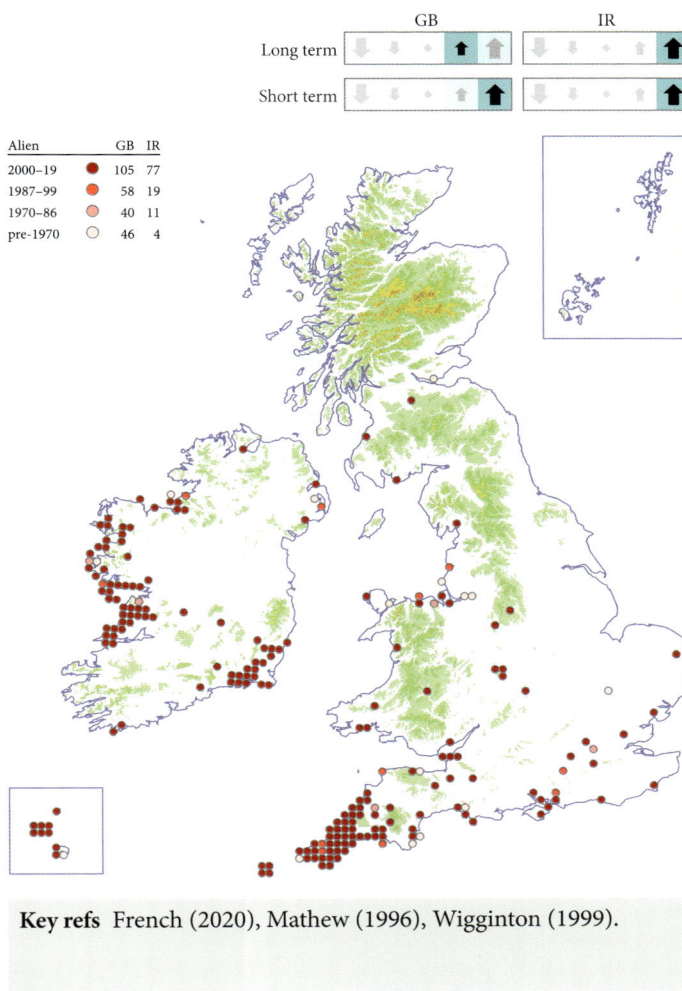

Alien	GB	IR
2000–19	105	77
1987–99	58	19
1970–86	40	11
pre-1970	46	4

Key refs French (2020), Mathew (1996), Wigginton (1999).

I. TAYLOR

Allium porrum Leek

Ne

L.

A bulbous perennial herb, widely grown in gardens and as an agricultural crop, and found as a relic of cultivation or a throw-out on refuse tips, derelict allotments, by canals, on waysides and waste ground. This species is fertile and usually tetraploid. Lowland.

Trends *A. porrum* was being grown in British gardens by medieval times (Harvey, 1981) and is very widely grown as a vegetable crop. It was recorded from the wild by 1931 (Henfield, East Sussex). The recent increase in records this century is almost certainly due to better recording of aliens rather than a genuine increase in the wild. It is treated as a cultivated archaeophyte by Stace & Crawley (2015).

Biogeography *A. porrum* was almost certainly derived by selection from *A. ampeloprasum*. Vegetables are rarely

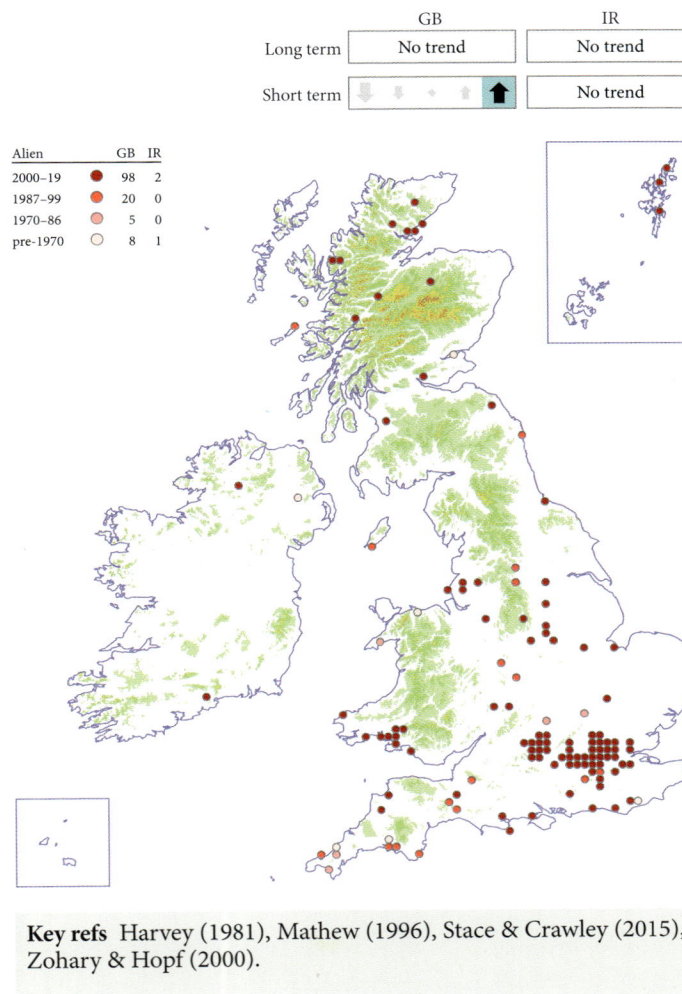

preserved in archaeological contexts, so the first evidence for its cultivation comes from Ancient Egyptian illustrations.

Alien	GB	IR
2000–19	98	2
1987–99	20	0
1970–86	5	0
pre-1970	8	1

Key refs Harvey (1981), Mathew (1996), Stace & Crawley (2015), Zohary & Hopf (2000).

T.D. DINES & N. ASPEY

N *Allium scorodoprasum* Sand Leek
L.

A bulbous, perennial herb, spreading mainly by bulbils in rough grassland and on road verges, tracksides, railway embankments and waste ground. It also occurs on sandy riverbanks and in open woodlands on well-drained soils and in a variety of coastal habitats. Generally lowland, but up to 440 m near to Black Brook nature reserve (Staffordshire).

Native in Britain and a neophyte in Ireland.

Trends The distribution of *A. scorodoprasum* appears to be stable in Britain, both as a native in northern England and Scotland and as an introduction in Wales and southern England. There are signs of a slight expansion in Ireland although this may reflect more systematic recording in recent decades.

Biogeography European Temperate element, with a continental distribution in western Europe; widely naturalized outside its native range. Our plant is sometimes considered to be a horticulturally derived variant of the southern European *A. scorodoprasum* subsp. *rotundum*.

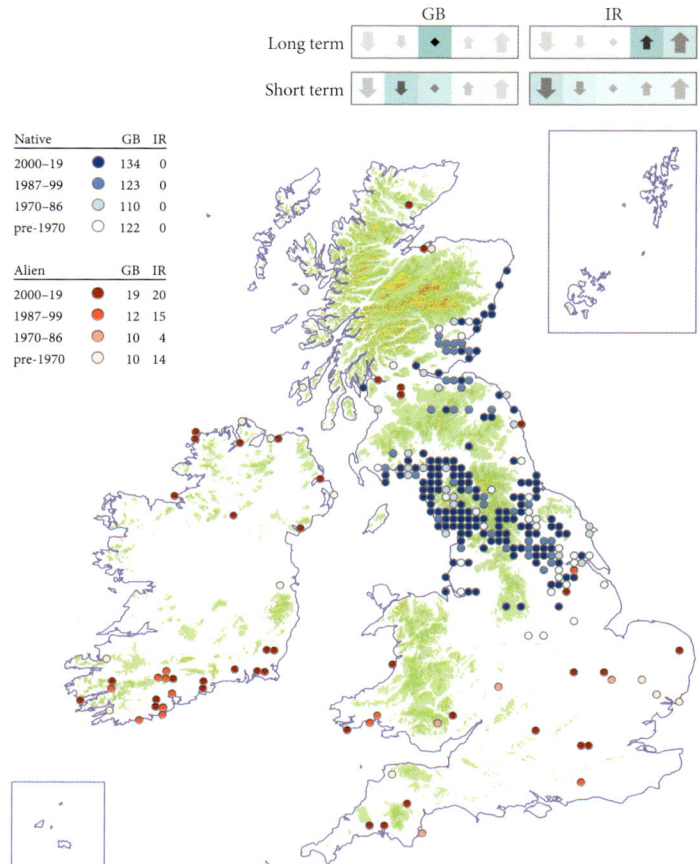

Native		GB	IR
2000–19	●	134	0
1987–99	●	123	0
1970–86	●	110	0
pre-1970	○	122	0

Alien		GB	IR
2000–19	●	19	20
1987–99	●	12	15
1970–86	●	10	4
pre-1970	○	10	14

Altitude (m) chart; key:
● <1%
● 1–10%
● 11–30%
● 31–40%
● 41–50%
● 51–100%

Distance north (km)

J F M A M J J A S O N D
☐ Apparency ☐ In flower ☐ In leaf

Key refs Mathew (1996), Stewart *et al.* (1994).

I. TAYLOR

N? *Allium sphaerocephalon* Round-headed Leek
L.

A bulbous perennial herb found as a possible native on dry, rocky south- and west-facing slopes in the Avon Gorge (West Gloucestershire), and on rough, sandy ground by the sea at St. Aubin's Bay, Jersey. Both populations are very small. Lowland.

Native or alien in Britain and the Channel Islands and a neophyte in Ireland.

Trends *A. sphaerocephalon* was first cultivated in Britain in 1759, and was first recorded in the wild in Jersey in 1836 and in the Avon Gorge in 1847, where it has long been treated as a native plant (Lovatt, 1982). Recreational pressure and safety works within the Avon Gorge have contributed to a decline in recent decades. It appears to be stable in Jersey. It is being increasingly grown in gardens, and seems to be increasing as an escape.

Biogeography European Southern-temperate element.

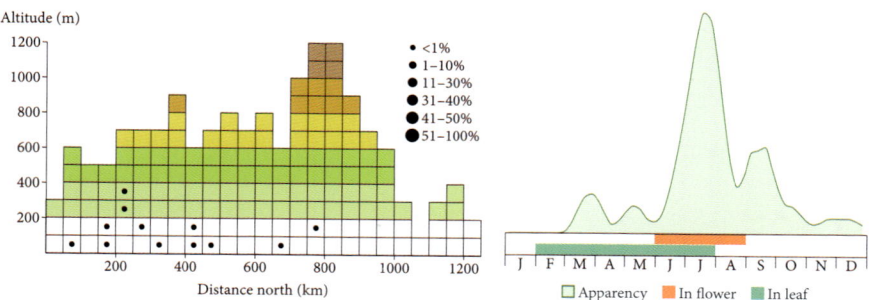

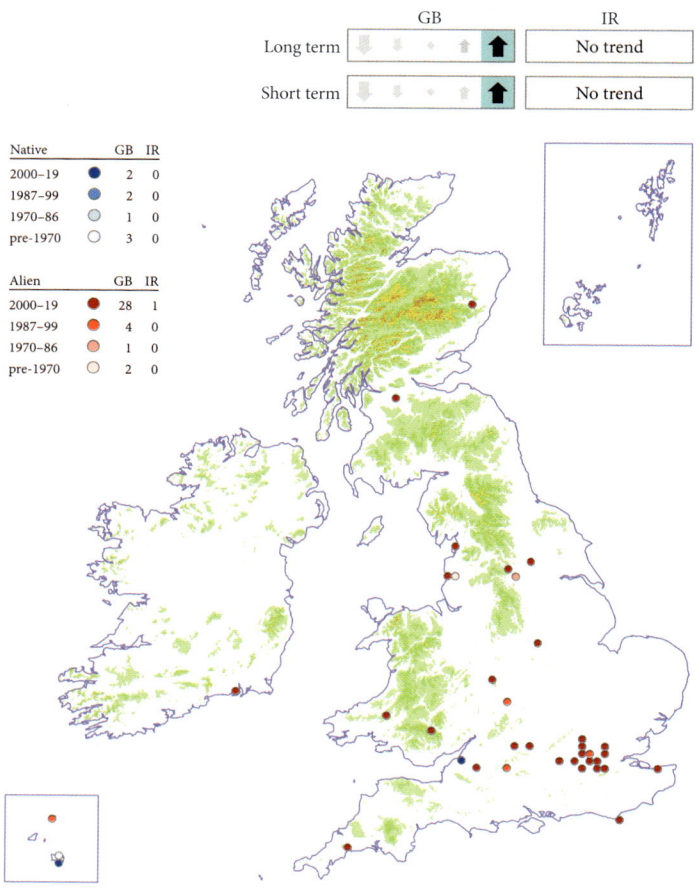

Native		GB	IR
2000–19	●	2	0
1987–99	●	2	0
1970–86	●	1	0
pre-1970	○	3	0

Alien		GB	IR
2000–19	●	28	1
1987–99	●	4	0
1970–86	●	1	0
pre-1970	●	2	0

Long term GB / IR No trend
Short term GB / IR No trend

Altitude (m) chart; key:
● <1%
● 1–10%
● 11–30%
● 31–40%
● 41–50%
● 51–100%

Distance north (km)

J F M A M J J A S O N D
☐ Apparency ☐ In flower ☐ In leaf

Key refs Lovatt (1982), Mathew (1996), Wigginton (1999).

I. TAYLOR

N *Allium vineale* Wild Onion
L.

A bulbous perennial herb of well-drained, neutral or calcareous soils, generally occurring in summer-dry grasslands, hedgerows, roadsides, wood borders and cultivated ground, and formerly a serious weed of cereal crops in south-eastern England. Also found on coastal cliff ledges in western Scotland. Generally lowland, but reaching 455 m in Wensleydale (North-west Yorkshire).

Trends Trends for *A. vineale* present a complex picture of considerable expansion of populations in some areas, most dramatically though not exclusively in south-western Britain, with contrasting, localized distributional losses in others, particularly in northern Britain. Increases appear to be related to episodic ground disturbance followed by interludes of little or no management intervention. There are few available data to assess the relative abundance of the bulbiliferous, floriferous and mixed inflorescence variants although the exclusively floriferous form appears to be rare.

Biogeography European Temperate element; widely naturalized outside its native range.

Native	GB	IR
2000–19	1137	114
1987–99	1016	82
1970–86	644	12
pre-1970	800	28

Alien	GB	IR
2000–19	4	0
1987–99	4	3
1970–86	3	0
pre-1970	1	0

Key refs Braithwaite *et al.* (2006), Mathew (1996), Richens (1947).

I. TAYLOR

Ne *Allium siculum* Honey Garlic
Ucria

A bulbous perennial herb naturalized in woodland, under *Pteridium aquilinum* and on roadsides and waste ground, where it originates as a garden escape or throw-out. Lowland.

Trends *A. siculum* was introduced into cultivation in Britain in 1832 or a little earlier and is increasingly popular in gardens. It is still present in the Avon Gorge (Bristol, West Gloucestershire), where it was sown along with other *Allium* species, and first recorded in 1906; it is increasing elsewhere.

Biogeography Native of southern Europe, just extending into Asia in north-west Turkey.

Alien	GB	IR
2000–19	128	1
1987–99	25	0
1970–86	14	0
pre-1970	5	0

	GB	IR
Long term	No trend	No trend
Short term		No trend

Key refs Houston *et al.* (1991).

T.D. DINES & D.A. PEARMAN

Ne *Agapanthus praecox* African Lily
Willd.

A perennial herb with tuber-like rhizomes forming dense clumps; naturalized on sandy ground in the Isles of Scilly and in coastal towns, and on waste ground and roadsides in Cornwall, but perhaps only casual elsewhere. It is planted or arises as a garden escape. Lowland.

Trends *A. praecox* was introduced into Britain in 1687, and is very popular in gardens for its large umbels of blue flowers. It was first recorded from the wild in 1886 (Tresco, Isles of Scilly). Records are concentrated in the south-west of England, with disparate records elsewhere, some of which are probably of planted garden plants.

Biogeography Native of South Africa.

Alien		GB	IR
2000–19	●	60	3
1987–99	●	14	0
1970–86	●	5	0
pre-1970	○	4	0

	GB	IR
Long term	No trend	No trend
Short term	↑	No trend

Altitude (m)
- ● <1%
- ● 1–10%
- ● 11–30%
- ● 31–40%
- ● 41–50%
- ● 51–100%

Distance north (km)

☐ Apparency ☐ In flower ☐ In leaf

T.D. DINES & N. ASPEY

Ne *Tristagma uniflorum* Spring Starflower
(Lindl.) Traub

A bulbous perennial herb, widely grown in gardens and found naturalized, where discarded, on waste ground or where planted in churchyards, on road verges and in amenity grasslands, especially on sandy soils in regions with a mild climate. It also occurs as a garden escape as it is capable of spreading by seed and can establish small populations in pavement cracks, in roadside gutters and along the base of walls, usually close to human habitations. Lowland.

Trends *T. uniflorum* was first cultivated in 1832 and is frequently grown in gardens. It was first recorded in the wild in 1921 (Jersey), and was known in the Isles of Scilly by 1952. Its range has increased in recent decades due to many more records of self-sown plants in the vicinity of gardens, but also because of the more systematic recording of garden escapes.

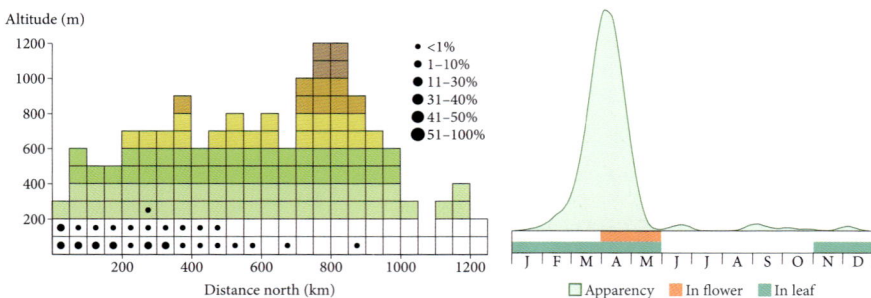

Biogeography Native of South America.

Alien		GB	IR
2000–19	●	196	1
1987–99	●	77	2
1970–86	●	28	0
pre-1970	○	10	0

	GB	IR
Long term	No trend	No trend
Short term	↑	No trend

Altitude (m)
- ● <1%
- ● 1–10%
- ● 11–30%
- ● 31–40%
- ● 41–50%
- ● 51–100%

Distance north (km)

☐ Apparency ☐ In flower ☐ In leaf

Key refs Chater (2010b), Crawley (2005), Hawksford & Hopkins (2011), Leslie (2019), Lousley (1971), Sussex Botanical Recording Society (2018).

I. TAYLOR

Hy *Crinum bulbispermum × moorei = C. ×powellii* Powell's Cape-lily
Baker

A bulbous perennial herb found as
a naturalized garden escape on sand
dunes on Jersey and Alderney, and rarely
on the mainland on a roadside verge
(Isle of Wight), in dumped soil (North
Somerset), in a paddock close to a tidal
river (East Sussex), and at the edge of
cliffs near to human habitations (Isle of
Wight and South Hampshire). Lowland.

A cultivated hybrid (alien × alien).

Trends *C. ×powellii* was cultivated
in British gardens by 1887, is often
grown in areas with a mild climate,
and was first recorded in the wild at
La Seline (Jersey). Only naturalized
records have been mapped.

Biogeography A hybrid of garden
origin.

		GB	IR
Long term		No trend	No trend
Short term		No trend	No trend

		GB	IR
2000–19	●	12	0
1987–99	●	3	0
1970–86	●	0	0
pre-1970	○	0	0

Altitude (m)

● <1%
● 1–10%
● 11–30%
● 31–40%
● 41–50%
● 51–100%

☐ Apparency ☐ In flower ☐ In leaf

Key refs Stace *et al.* (2015).

T.D. Dines & P.A. Stroh

Ne *Leucojum aestivum* Summer Snowflake
L.

A bulbous perennial herb, widely grown
in gardens and found naturalized in
winter-flooded riverside alder- or
willow-carr, meadows and woodland
rides. It is also frequently naturalized
where discarded in garden waste or
deliberately planted in woodlands,
cemeteries, churchyards, railway
embankments, amenity grasslands,
hedgerows, roadsides and waste ground,
usually, though not exclusively, near
to human habitations. Lowland.

Trends This species was in cultivation by
1596 and was first recorded in the wild
in 1788 (Greenwich, West Kent). Two
subspecies have been recorded in our
area: subsp. *pulchellum* is an undoubted
alien which is widely grown in gardens
whereas subsp. *aestivum* was formerly
considered to be a rare native in
southern England and Ireland (Preston
et al., 2002a). However, the late year of

its discovery, long use as a garden plant
and disjunct distribution with respect
to its core range in Europe all point to it
being a modern introduction (Pearman,
2013). The two subspecies have often
been confused and so the identity of
many records is either unknown or in
doubt. Both subspecies readily become
naturalized where discarded or, less
commonly, deliberately planted in
suitable situations and their ranges are
expanding in both Britain and Ireland.

Biogeography *L. aestivum* subsp.
aestivum is native over much of Europe
(except the north), extending east to the
Caucusus and Iran; subsp. *pulchellum*
is native of the western Mediterranean
islands.

		GB	IR
Long term		↑	↑
Short term		↑	↑

Alien		GB	IR
2000–19	●	575	65
1987–99	●	277	33
1970–86	●	123	19
pre-1970	○	110	13

Altitude (m)

● <1%
● 1–10%
● 11–30%
● 31–40%
● 41–50%
● 51–100%

☐ Apparency ☐ In flower ☐ In leaf

Key refs Chater (2010b), Crawley (2005), Farrell (1979), Gillam
(1993), Killick *et al.* (1998), Pearman (2013), Wigginton (1999).

I. Taylor & K.J. Walker

Ne *Leucojum vernum* Spring Snowflake
L.

A bulbous perennial herb, grown in gardens and found naturalized on damp soils in woodland, scrub, cemeteries, churchyards, streamsides and riversides, hedgerows, roadsides and other grassy places where planted or discarded in garden waste. Lowland.

Trends This species was being cultivated in Britain by 1596 and was first recorded in the wild in 1834 (Bicester, Oxfordshire). The majority of populations appear to have originated from bulbs planted or discarded in suitable habitats. Its 10 km square distribution has increased, possibly due to the more systematic recording of garden escapes. It is perhaps sometimes recorded in error for early flowering, depauperate plants of *L. aestivum*.

Biogeography A European Temperate species, absent as a native from much of western Europe.

Alien	GB	IR
2000–19	133	0
1987–99	51	1
1970–86	39	1
pre-1970	22	0

Key refs Bowen (2000), Crawley (2005), Killick *et al.* (1998).

I. TAYLOR

Ne *Galanthus nivalis* Snowdrop
L.

A bulbous perennial herb frequently naturalized from discarded or deliberately planted bulbs in moist woodland, parkland and churchyards, but also on road verges, by rivers and streams and in damp grassland. Viable seed is produced in the wild but seedlings are infrequently recorded, and spread away from planted sites is probably mainly by soil disturbance and subsequent dispersal of bulbs (*e.g.* along watercourses during floods). 0–510 m (Rookhope Head, County Durham).

Trends This species was known in cultivation in Britain in 1597 but was not recorded in the wild until 1778. It has been regarded as a native in the past, but is now generally accepted as an alien in our area (Preston *et al.*, 2002a). There has been a substantial increase in the 10 km square distribution since the 1960s, reflecting the more diligent recording of aliens in recent decades but possibly also a genuine spread in some areas.

Biogeography A European Southern-temperate species; widely naturalized outside its native range.

Alien	GB	IR
2000–19	2003	148
1987–99	1626	34
1970–86	934	5
pre-1970	814	2

Key refs Chater (2010b), Crawley (2005), Davis (1999), Leslie (2019), Mabey (1996), Sussex Botanical Recording Society (2018).

I. TAYLOR

Hy *Galanthus nivalis* × *plicatus* = *G.* ×*valentinei*
Beck

A fertile hybrid recorded from churchyards, cemeteries, hedgebanks and secondary woodland, and on riverbanks and roadside verges. It sometimes occurs as large, naturalized populations, often with its parents but sometimes in the absence of one or both. Colonies may include double-flowered variants (Chater, 2010b). It is apparently fertile, but vegetative reproduction via the expansion of clumps and the dispersal of bulbs is almost certainly the main means of spread in the wild. Lowland.

A cultivated hybrid (alien × alien).

Trends This hybrid is well recorded in counties where botanists have examined snowdrops critically; elsewhere it is probably overlooked as either *G. nivalis* or *G. plicatus*. The first naturalized records are from Great and Little Bealings (East Suffolk) in 1947.

Biogeography Hybrid swarms have been recorded from European Turkey, which lies in the overlap of the confirmed distributions of both parents.

	GB	IR
Long term	No trend	No trend
Short term	No trend	No trend

		GB	IR
2000–19	●	150	2
1987–99	●	49	0
1970–86	●	7	0
pre-1970	○	1	0

Key refs Chater (2010b), Stace *et al.* (2015).

C.A. STACE, C.D. PRESTON & D.A. PEARMAN

Altitude (m) / Distance north (km) / Apparency / In flower / In leaf

---

Ne *Galanthus plicatus* Pleated Snowdrop
M.Bieb.

A bulbous perennial herb of deciduous woodland, hedgerows, roadsides, churchyards, cemeteries and parkland which is also occasionally found as a relic of cultivation. The majority of established populations are clearly derived from deliberate plantings although some have arisen from discarded garden stock. It often produces abundant seedlings and populations can be maintained and may spread by this means. Two subspecies are found in our area: subsp *byzantinus* is an uncommon taxon naturalized in southern England; subsp. *plicatus* is mapped separately. Lowland.

Trends *G. plicatus* has been grown in British gardens since 1818, but was not recorded from the wild until 1947 (East Suffolk). It is less commonly cultivated than *G. nivalis* and remains much less frequent in the wild. However, as with other snowdrops, it is often planted in churchyards and cemeteries and on verges close to human habitations and it appears to be increasing, particularly on the chalk of southern and eastern England. It was recorded for the first time in Wales in 2004 (Cwm Ivy Wood, Glamorganshire) and from Ireland in 2016 (County Wexford). It is often found growing with *G. nivalis* and in such situations it readily produces fertile hybrids.

Biogeography Native of Romania and north-western Turkey and the Crimean Peninsula.

	GB	IR
Long term	No trend	No trend
Short term	↓ ↓ · ↑ ⬆	No trend

Alien		GB	IR
2000–19	●	209	4
1987–99	●	68	0
1970–86	●	15	0
pre-1970	○	2	0

Key refs Chater (2010b), Crawley (2005), Davis (1999), Leslie (2019), Sussex Botanical Recording Society (2018).

I. TAYLOR

Altitude (m) / Distance north (km) / Apparency / In flower / In leaf

Ne *Galanthus plicatus* subsp. *plicatus* Pleated Snowdrop
M.Bieb.

A bulbous perennial herb of deciduous woodland, hedgerows, roadsides, churchyards, cemeteries and parkland, where it is usually originally planted; it is also found as a relic of cultivation. This subspecies often produces abundant seedlings and populations can be maintained in this way. Lowland.

Trends *G. plicatus* has been grown in British gardens since 1818. It is uncertain when this subspecies was introduced into cultivation, but its first record from the wild was not until 1993, at Leith Hill, Surrey; it is probably under-recorded.

Biogeography Native of eastern Romania, north-western Turkey and the Crimean Peninsula.

	GB	IR
Long term	No trend	No trend
Short term	No trend	No trend

Alien	GB	IR
2000–19	63	4
1987–99	13	0
1970–86	0	0
pre-1970	0	0

T.D. Dines & P.A. Stroh

Hy *Galanthus elwesii* × *plicatus*

A bulbous perennial hybrid which is grown in gardens and rarely occurs as an escape. Lowland.

A cultivated hybrid (alien × alien).

Trends It is not known whether this plant was introduced into cultivation as a hybrid, or whether it arose spontaneously in gardens or in the wild. In one Cambridgeshire site, however, a clump of this hybird was found growing with both parents and is thought to have almost certainly arisen *in situ* where plants had been clearly self-sowing. It was first reported from Britain by Sell & Murrell (1996) on the basis of plants collected in Cambridgeshire in 1992. It may be more widespread than the map suggests.

Biogeography Wider distribution uncertain.

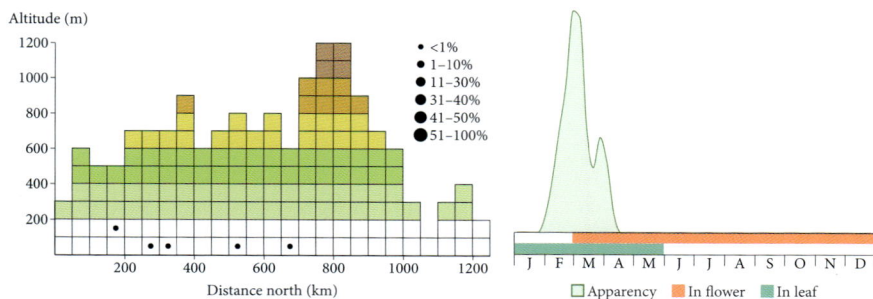

	GB	IR
Long term	No trend	No trend
Short term	No trend	No trend

	GB	IR
2000–19	8	0
1987–99	2	0
1970–86	0	0
pre-1970	0	0

Key refs Stace *et al.* (2015).

C.A. Stace, C.D. Preston & D.A. Pearman

Ne *Galanthus elwesii* Greater Snowdrop

Hook.f.

A bulbous perennial herb, widely planted in gardens, churchyards, open woodland, roadsides and parkland, generally in sunnier, warmer and drier situations than *G. nivalis* and *G. plicatus*. As with *G. plicatus*, most populations encountered in the wild are likely to have been planted although it can arise from bulbs discarded in garden waste or washed down streams. Despite limited seed set, some populations may be slowly expanding by this means. Lowland.

Trends *G. elwesii* has been grown in British gardens since 1875 and is now frequently planted in wild locations, usually close to human habitations. It was first recorded in the wild in about 1957 (Surrey) and is now very widespread, especially across southern, central and eastern England. The increase in the known distribution is in part due to a growing interest in the genus as well as the more systematic recording of garden escapes in wild locations.

Biogeography Native of the mountains of south-eastern Europe and Turkey.

Alien		GB	IR
2000–19	●	296	1
1987–99	●	109	0
1970–86	●	13	0
pre-1970	○	8	0

	GB	IR
Long term	No trend	No trend
Short term	↑	No trend

Key refs Chater (2010b), Crawley (2005), Davis (1999), Leslie (2019), Sussex Botanical Recording Society (2018).

I. Taylor

Ne *Galanthus woronowii* Green Snowdrop

Losinsk.

A bulbous perennial herb, now widely grown and distinctive for its broad fresh green leaves, with scattered records from churchyards, parks and other places. Lowland.

Trends *G. woronowii* was long treated as synonymous with *G. ikariae* from the Aegean. It is not yet known when it was introduced into this country, but it was probably just after 1880. The first record in the wild is 1984 at Bayfordbury, Hertfordshire.

Biogeography Native of western Georgia, southern Russia and north-eastern Turkey.

Alien		GB	IR
2000–19	●	230	1
1987–99	●	39	0
1970–86	●	2	0
pre-1970	○	0	0

	GB	IR
Long term	No trend	No trend
Short term	↑	No trend

Key refs Bishop *et al.* (2006).

D.A. Pearman

Narcissus Daffodils
L.

A taxonomically difficult genus of bulbous perennial herbs that are extremely widely planted in wild locations in the lowlands, most notably in vast ranks alongside roads in urban and rural locations as well in woodlands, pastures, parks, churchyards, amenity grasslands and pathsides; also occurring as relics of cultivation in abandoned gardens or in waste places where thrown out in garden waste. The sole native taxon (*N. pseudonarcissus* subsp. *pseudonarcissus*) has a restricted natural distribution although this has been largely obscured by planting. There is a bewildering array of naturalized cultivars and hybrids creating inherent identification difficulties. There remains a legacy of inconsistent recording although there have been significant improvements in assigning naturalized populations to cultivars and hybrids in the last 15 years. 0–545 m (Hartside, Cumberland).

Native in Britain and the Channel Islands and alien in Ireland.

Trends Although planted daffodils have been grossly under-recorded in the past there is no doubt that the dramatic increase shown on the map is real and reflects the increasing trend to plant (or discard) them in the wild since the 1960s. Plants readily become naturalized in these circumstances and variable levels of recording (to species, hybrids or cultivars), often only as closest approximations, complicates the interpretation of apparent trends for individual taxa, but taken as a whole they are evidently increasing.

Biogeography A genus centred on the Mediterranean region and most diverse in south-western Europe.

Key refs Blanchard (1990), Chater (2010b), Crawley (2005), French (2020), Leslie (2019), Nunez *et al.* (2003), Sussex Botanical Recording Society (2018).

I. TAYLOR & K.J. WALKER

Narcissus tazetta Bunch-flowered Daffodil
L.

A bulbous perennial herb, widely grown in gardens and found principally as a naturalized relic of cultivation, especially in bulb-fields in the Channel Islands. It is also planted on roadsides, and is occasionally found as a casual garden throw-out on refuse tips and waste ground. Lowland.

Trends This species was being cultivated in Britain by 1596, and is very popular in gardens. It was recorded from the wild by 1876 (Penarth, Glamorganshire). Its distribution is now much better known in Cornwall, South Hampshire and south-eastern Ireland; it is probably under-recorded elsewhere.

Biogeography Native of south-western Europe, the Mediterranean region and south-western Asia; widespread as an introduction elsewhere in Asia.

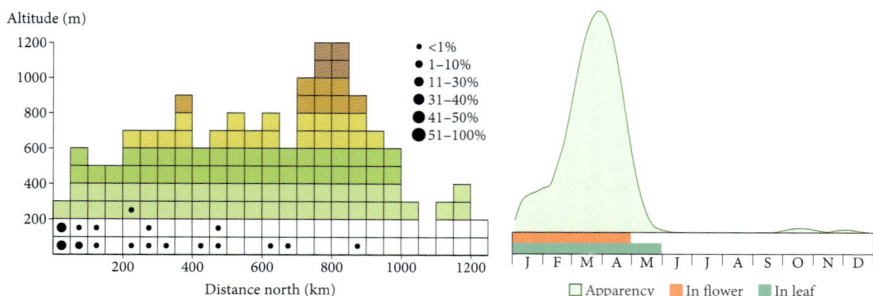

Key refs Blanchard (1990).

T.D. DINES & P.A. STROH

Hy *Narcissus poeticus × tazetta = N. ×medioluteus* Primrose-peerless
Mill.

A bulbous perennial herb found in old bulb-fields as a relic of commercial cut-flower production, and also grown in gardens and readily becoming naturalized from discarded bulbs in woodland, scrub, hedgerows, orchards, churchyards, on roadsides, by tracks and paths and on waste ground. Lowland.

A cultivated hybrid (alien × alien).

Trends This hybrid was known by Ray (1677) as an occasional garden relic or escape on field margins. This taxon includes a variety of mono- and bi-coloured, single- and double-flowered cultivars which are collectively known to gardeners as the 'Poetaz' narcissi. As with all alien *Narcissus* taxa, they are under-recorded.

Biogeography This hybrid occurs naturally in France but the naturalized plants are of garden origin.

	GB	IR
Long term	No trend	No trend
Short term	No trend	No trend

		GB	IR
2000–19	●	73	13
1987–99	●	75	1
1970–86	●	24	1
pre-1970	○	83	10

Key refs Ray (1677), Stace *et al.* (2015).

I. TAYLOR

Altitude (m) histogram. Legend: ● <1%, ● 1–10%, ● 11–30%, ● 31–40%, ● 41–50%, ● 51–100%. Distance north (km).

Apparency / In flower / In leaf — J F M A M J J A S O N D

Ne *Narcissus poeticus* Pheasant's-eye Daffodil
L.

A bulbous perennial herb, frequently planted in hedgerows and cemeteries, on roadsides, by tracks and alongside paths and often naturalizing. It is also regularly found on rough and waste ground where it is arises from discarded garden waste, and occasionally also as a relic of cultivation in old fields and gardens. This is the traditional May-flowering daffodil with white tepals and a short, usually red-rimmed, yellow, cup-shaped corona. 0–325 m (Bauminich, Moray).

Trends *N. poeticus* was cultivated in Britain by 1538 and is commonly grown in gardens. It is frequently planted or discarded, usually close to human habitations and was known from the wild by 1779 (Woodbastwick, East Norfolk). The taxonomy of *N. poeticus* and its close allies is complex, but most records are probably referable to subsp. *poeticus*. In some areas

records may also encompass the closely related *N. radiiflorus* and other subspecies, variants and cultivars, especially the widely cultivated 'Actaea', which occurs throughout the range of the species shown on the map. As with all garden daffodils it is likely to be very unevenly recorded.

Biogeography Native of the mountains of southern Europe.

	GB	IR
Long term	No trend	No trend
Short term		

Alien		GB	IR
2000–19	●	515	9
1987–99	●	296	0
1970–86	●	97	0
pre-1970	○	84	0

Key refs Blanchard (1990), Boon & Outen (2011), Chater (2010b), Crawley (2005), Leslie (2019), Sussex Botanical Recording Society (2018).

I. TAYLOR

Altitude (m) histogram. Legend: ● <1%, ● 1–10%, ● 11–30%, ● 31–40%, ● 41–50%, ● 51–100%. Distance north (km).

Apparency / In flower / In leaf — J F M A M J J A S O N D

Hy *Narcissus poeticus × pseudonarcissus = N. ×incomparabilis*
Mill.

Nonesuch Daffodil

A bulbous perennial herb widely planted and established in churchyards and cemeteries and in woodland, scrub, hedgerows, coastal dunes, and on stream banks, village greens, roadsides, tracksides and waste ground, usually from discarded or deliberately planted stock. It is sometimes found on field margins as a relic of commercial cut-flower production. 0–370 m (Hengwm Annedd, Cardiganshire).

A cultivated hybrid (native × alien).

Trends This taxon, which has been grown in British gardens since the 16th century, was first recorded in the wild in 1711 (Hornsey, Middlesex). Further hybridization with other introduced taxa and back-crossing with *N. pseudonarcissus* may occur

in the wild. The patchy nature of its mapped distribution geographically and over time reflects the interests of botanists recording within a particular county. It is sometimes mistaken for cultivars of *N. pseudonarcissus*.

Biogeography This hybrid probably occurs naturally in France but the naturalized plants are of garden origin.

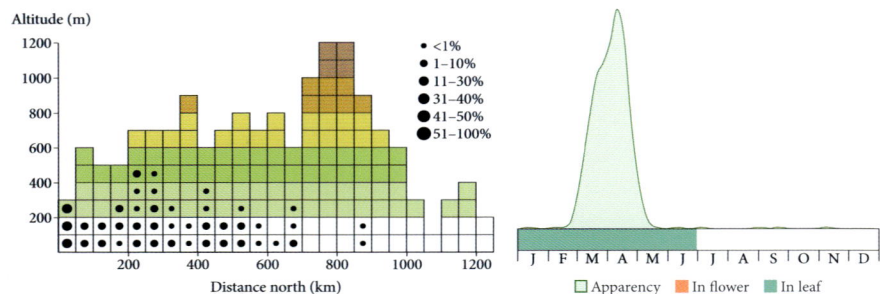

		GB	IR
2000–19	●	206	20
1987–99	●	166	0
1970–86	●	7	0
pre-1970	○	39	0

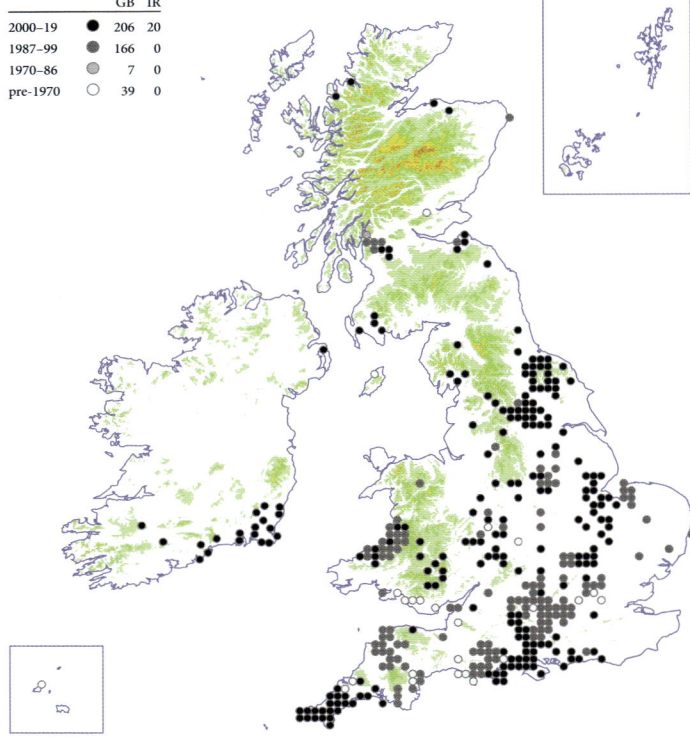

Altitude (m) chart, distance north (km); apparency / in flower / in leaf phenology chart.

Key percentage legend:
● <1%
● 1–10%
● 11–30%
● 31–40%
● 41–50%
● 51–100%

Key refs Stace *et al.* (2015).

I. TAYLOR

Hy *Narcissus jonquilla × pseudonarcissus = N. ×odorus*
L.

Campernelle Jonquil

A bulbous perennial herb grown in gardens and occasionally naturalized in woodland, hedgebanks and on roadsides and waste ground. Lowland.

A cultivated hybrid (native × alien).

Trends It is uncertain when *N. ×odorus* was introduced into cultivation in Britain, but it is known to have been naturalized in a field near St Austell (West Cornwall) in 1903, where thousands of plants in a damp meadow were reported, though the field was ploughed soon after. It would appear to be genuinely uncommon in our area.

Biogeography A hybrid of garden origin.

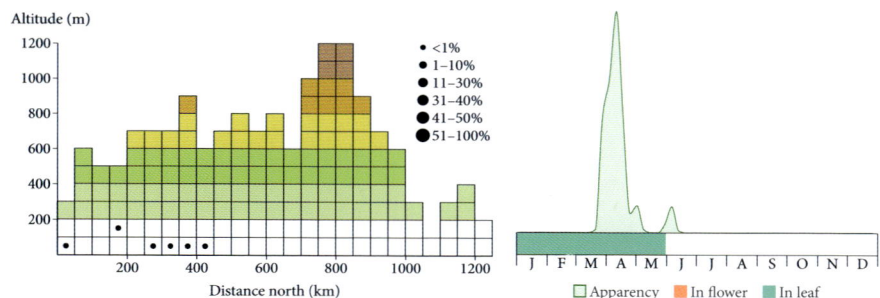

		GB	IR
2000–19	●	15	0
1987–99	●	1	0
1970–86	●	4	0
pre-1970	○	3	0

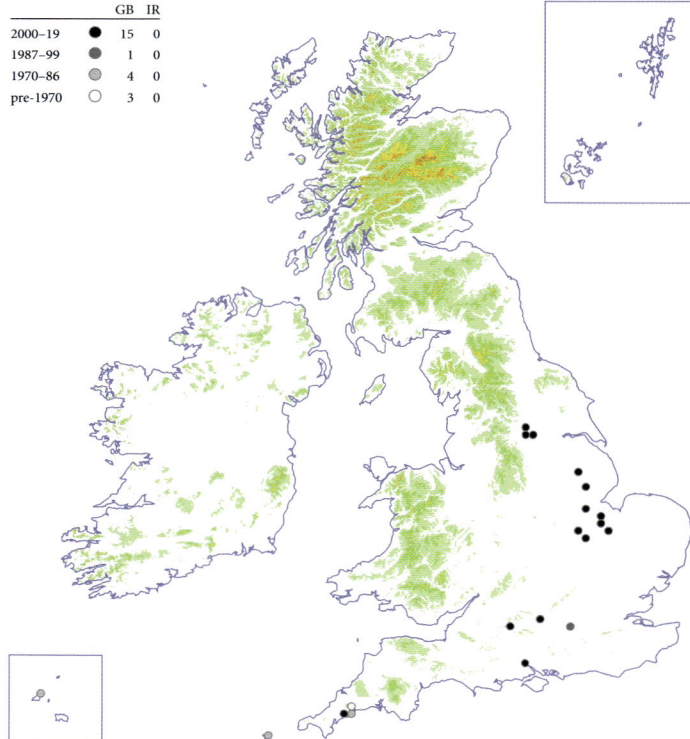

Altitude (m) chart, distance north (km); apparency / in flower / in leaf phenology chart.

Key percentage legend:
● <1%
● 1–10%
● 11–30%
● 31–40%
● 41–50%
● 51–100%

Key refs Stace *et al.* (2015).

C.A. STACE, C.D. PRESTON & D.A. PEARMAN

N *Narcissus pseudonarcissus* subsp. *pseudonarcissus* Daffodil

A bulbous perennial herb occurring as a native in ash and oak woodlands, bracken stands, scrubby banks and old pastures, and widely planted in parks, churchyards, amenity grasslands, and on road verges and pathsides; occurring as a throw-out on waste ground and as a relic of cultivation in abandoned gardens. Short, small-flowered plants which are relatively uniform in flower, with pale yellow, often twisted tepals and narrow, deeper yellow, trumpet-shaped coronas may be the only truly native daffodils in Britain and may be attributable to var. *humilis*. Lowland.

Native in Britain and the Channel Islands and alien in Ireland.

Trends *N. pseudonarcissus* subsp. *pseudonarcissus* suffers, as do most members of this genus, from inconsistent recording: some garden selections, cultivars and even hybrids may be assigned to this taxon on the basis of a "closest fit" approach and under-recording continues to be an issue in situations where plants appear to have been deliberately planted, even when they may have persisted for many years. However, there are indications that there has been some increase in alien occurrences in widely scattered parts of both Britain and Ireland whilst there may have been some recent losses of native populations, especially around the fringes of core areas in south-western England, the West Midlands and north-western England. The extent of its native range in our area is probably now intractable given the extent of planting; populations in semi-natural habitats in England and Wales are generally mapped as native unless evidence points to the contrary. It is indisputably alien in Ireland and usually regarded as such in Scotland.

Biogeography Suboceanic Temperate element; naturalized in Europe outside its native range.

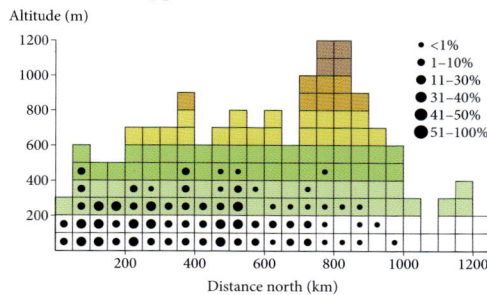

Native	GB	IR
2000–19	370	0
1987–99	465	0
1970–86	281	0
pre-1970	442	0

Alien	GB	IR
2000–19	245	15
1987–99	255	1
1970–86	137	0
pre-1970	196	6

	GB		IR	
Long term				
Short term				

Key refs Hawksford & Hopkins (2011), Leslie (2019), Mabey (1996), Nunez *et al.* (2003), Sussex Botanical Recording Society (2018).

I. TAYLOR

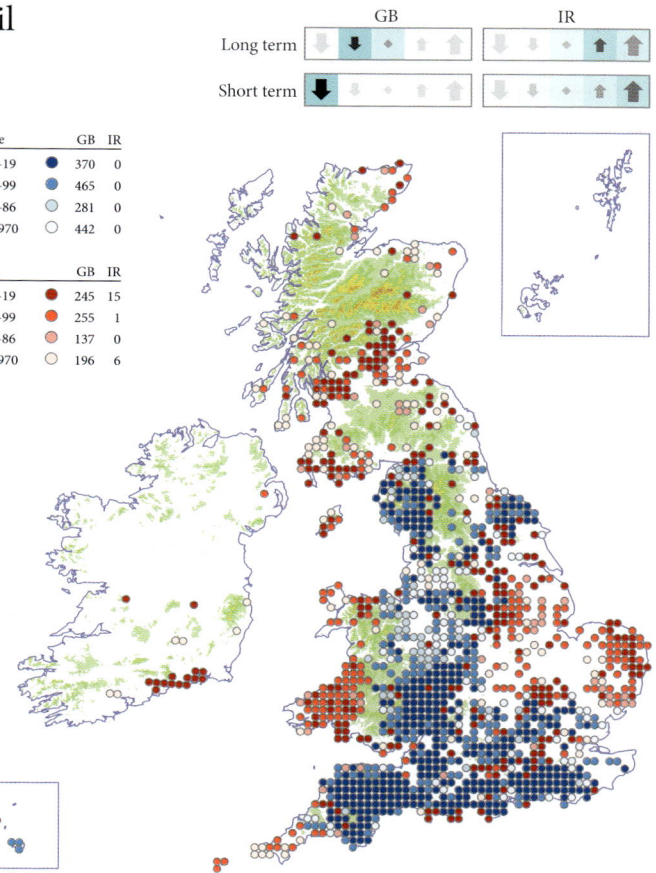

Hy *Narcissus cyclamineus* × *pseudonarcissus* = *N.* ×*monochromus*
P.D.Sell

Reflexed Daffodil

A bulbous perennial herb; as the cultivar 'February Gold' it is commonly planted in towns and villages, and frequent in churchyards throughout the country, occasionally found as an outcast on waste ground and local or rare in woodland. The less frequently encountered cultivar 'Peeping Tom' is occasionally planted in parkland and churchyards, and rare as an outcast. Lowland.

A cultivated hybrid (native × alien).

Trends Many garden cultivars of *Narcissus* are referable to this hybrid. They are very widely grown and are certainly under-recorded. The lack of any recent records in Berkshire reflects differing intensities of recording between the last two atlas periods, rather than real loss.

Biogeography A hybrid of garden origin.

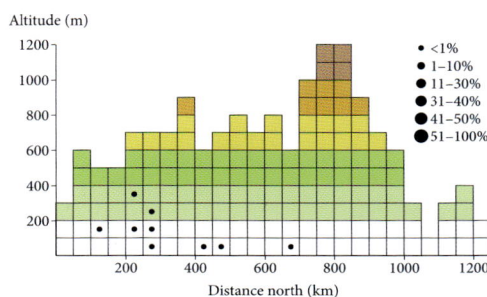

	GB	IR
Long term	No trend	No trend
Short term	No trend	No trend

	GB	IR
2000–19	13	0
1987–99	29	0
1970–86	0	0
pre-1970	0	0

Key refs Stace *et al.* (2015).

C.A. STACE, C.D. PRESTON & D.A. PEARMAN

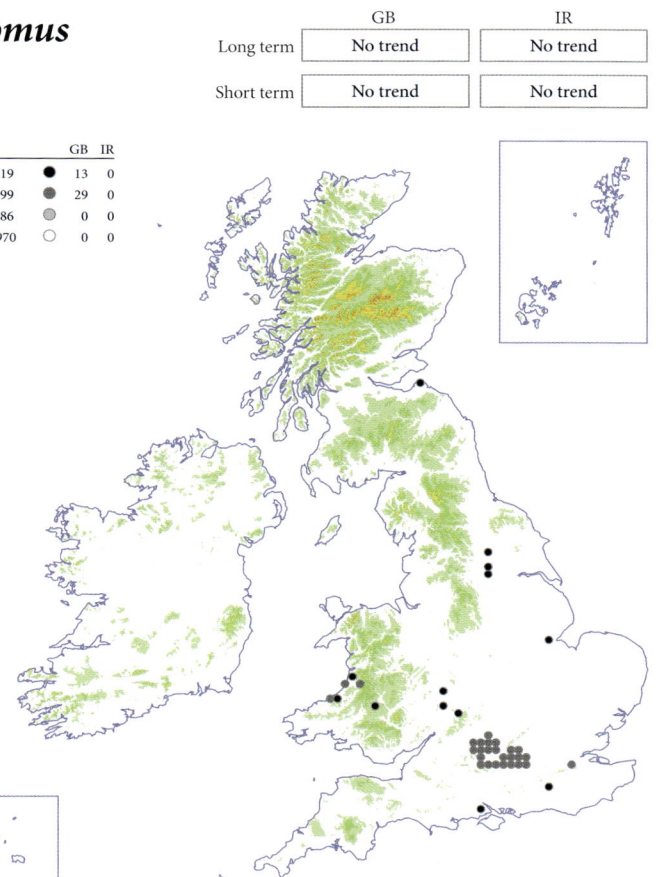

Ne *Narcissus obvallaris* Tenby Daffodil
Salisb.

A bulbous perennial herb, found in hedgerows, churchyards, roadsides and other, generally open, grassy places. It is occasionally found as a persistent, deliberately planted or discarded clump or small colony in parts of Britain other than south-western Wales. Lowland.

Trends A puzzling taxon now thought to have been derived from wild forms of *N. hispanicus* brought into cultivation by Medieval times. It was named in 1786 and was first recorded in the wild, near to Tenby (Pembrokeshire), in 1829. The vast majority of records come from south-western Wales (Pembrokeshire, Carmarthenshire, Cardiganshire) where it is frequently encountered close to human habitations. The Welsh population was much reduced by commercial bulb collectors in the early 19th century but it remains widespread with no evidence of a

change in distribution in recent decades, despite more systematic recording of garden escapes. It is very similar to some wild forms of *N. hispanicus* and so is treated as a subspecies of Spanish Daffodil by some authorities (*N. hispanicus* subsp. *hispanicus*).

Biogeography A plant of uncertain origin.

	GB	IR
Long term	No trend	No trend
Short term	⬇ ⬇ ◆ ⬆ ⬆	No trend

Alien	GB	IR
2000–19	57	0
1987–99	50	0
1970–86	9	0
pre-1970	14	0

Altitude (m) / Distance north (km)
Key: <1%, 1–10%, 11–30%, 31–40%, 41–50%, 51–100%
Apparency / In flower / In leaf

Key refs Blanchard (1990), Chater (2010b), Crawley (2005), Mabey (1996), Nunez *et al.* (2003).

I. TAYLOR

Ne *Narcissus hispanicus* Spanish Daffodil
Gouan

A bulbous perennial herb frequently naturalized from discarded or deliberately planted bulbs in woodlands, churchyards, amenity grasslands, hedgerows, on roadsides, alongside tracks and paths and on waste ground. It is also found as a relic of commercial cut-flower production and in abandoned gardens. Generally lowland, but reaching 425 m at Princeton Church (South Devon).

Trends This taxon was cultivated in British gardens by 1596, and was recorded in the wild in 1813 (Hornsey, Middlesex). Hybridization with other daffodils, especially *N. pseudonarcissus* subsp. *pseudonarcissus*, complicates recording but cultivars of *N. hispanicus* are the most widespread daffodils deliberately planted or discarded in the wild across most areas of Britain and Ireland. Despite improvements

in the recording of daffodils since 2000, the large, single-flowered, yellow trumpet varieties continue to be the most intractable. Confusion also exists between this taxon and the larger single-coloured cultivars of *N. ×incomparabilis*. As a consequence, *N. hispanicus* tends to be recorded only in areas where there are enthusiasts identifying Daffodils.

Biogeography Native of southern France and the Iberian Peninsula.

	GB	IR
Long term	No trend	No trend
Short term	⬇ ⬇ ◆ ⬆ ⬆	⬇ ⬇ ◆ ⬆ ⬆

Alien	GB	IR
2000–19	336	8
1987–99	178	0
1970–86	24	0
pre-1970	46	0

Altitude (m) / Distance north (km)
Key: <1%, 1–10%, 11–30%, 31–40%, 41–50%, 51–100%
Apparency / In flower / In leaf

Key refs Blanchard (1990), Chater (2010b), Crawley (2005), French (2020).

I. TAYLOR

Ne *Pancratium maritimum* Sea Daffodil
L.

A bulbous perennial herb, naturalized on coastal shingle and sand dunes. Lowland.

Trends *P. maritimum* was cultivated in Britain by 1579, and is occasionally grown in gardens in areas with a very mild climate. The first documented record in the wild is from Strete, near Slapton (South Devon) in 1993, though anecdotal evidence supports a much earlier date of discovery at this location, perhaps as early as the 1960s. Subsequently, it has been found on sand dunes at Dawlish Warren (South Devon), Marazion (West Cornwall), and Sandbanks (Dorset). There is no certain evidence of the mode of introduction but it occurs in similar habitats along the western coasts of Portugal, Spain and France, north to southern Brittany, and it is possible that bulbs were carried on currents and colonized British beaches naturally. However, in at least two of the sites it grows alongside established garden throw-outs, the Strete site is close to houses with large gardens on the cliff top above, and the site at Dawlish Warren is situated on the footprint of an old chalet garden. The current consensus is that it has either been deliberately planted, or is naturalized from nearby gardens.

Biogeography Native of south-western Europe and the Mediterranean region.

	GB	IR
Long term	No trend	No trend
Short term	No trend	No trend

Alien	GB	IR
2000–19	4	0
1987–99	1	0
1970–86	0	0
pre-1970	0	0

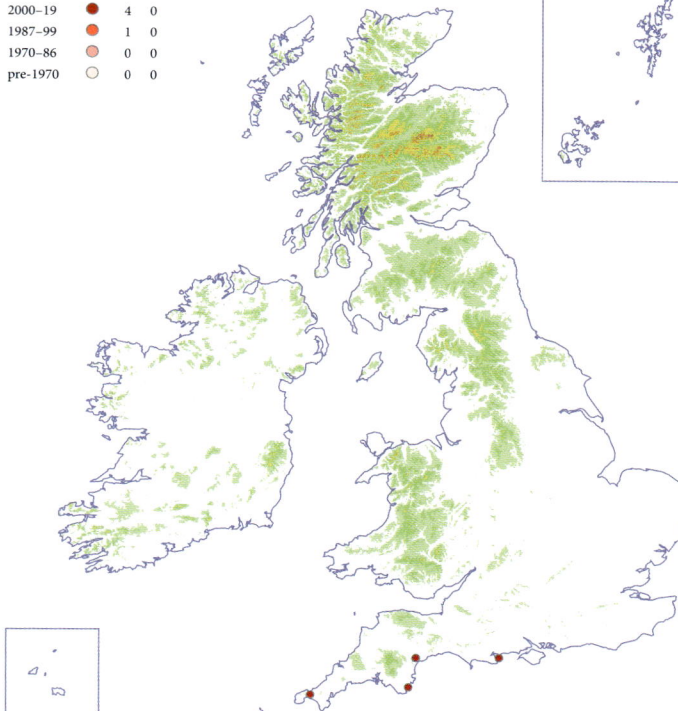

Key refs Pearman (2022).

Altitude (m)

Distance north (km)

• <1%
• 1–10%
• 11–30%
• 31–40%
• 41–50%
• 51–100%

J F M A M J J A S O N D
☐ Apparency ☐ In flower ☐ In leaf

P.A. STROH

N *Convallaria majalis* Lily-of-the-valley
L.

A rhizomatous perennial herb of freely draining, nutrient-poor soils. It can be abundant in woods dominated by *Fraxinus excelsior* on limestone in northern and western Britain, in the grikes of limestone pavements and in a wide variety of woodland types, mostly on acidic soils, in southern and eastern England. It also grows in a fen in Cumbria. It is increasingly found as an established garden escape or discard in a variety of situations such as woodland edges, roadsides, along railways, in cemeteries and churchyards, and on dumped soil. 0–490 m (Ogof Ffynnon Ddu, Breconshire).

Native in Britain and a neophyte in Ireland and the Channel Islands.

Trends Following a period of significant decline prior to the 1930s, the native distribution of *C. majalis* now appears to be broadly stable, although this is obscured by the widespread occurrence of naturalized plants. Across much of England and Wales it is particularly difficult to distinguish native and alien populations and the map must be regarded as an approximation in this regard. The scale of the recent increase in non-native records is made especially apparent outside the native range such as in northern Scotland, Northern Ireland and in the Channel Islands.

Biogeography European Boreo-temperate element; also in eastern Asia and widely naturalized outside its native range.

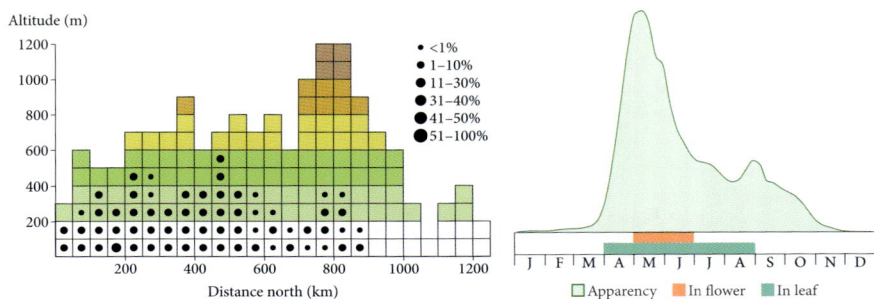

	GB	IR
Long term		
Short term		

Native	GB	IR
2000–19	260	0
1987–99	255	0
1970–86	226	0
pre-1970	341	0

Alien	GB	IR
2000–19	308	9
1987–99	219	2
1970–86	91	2
pre-1970	168	1

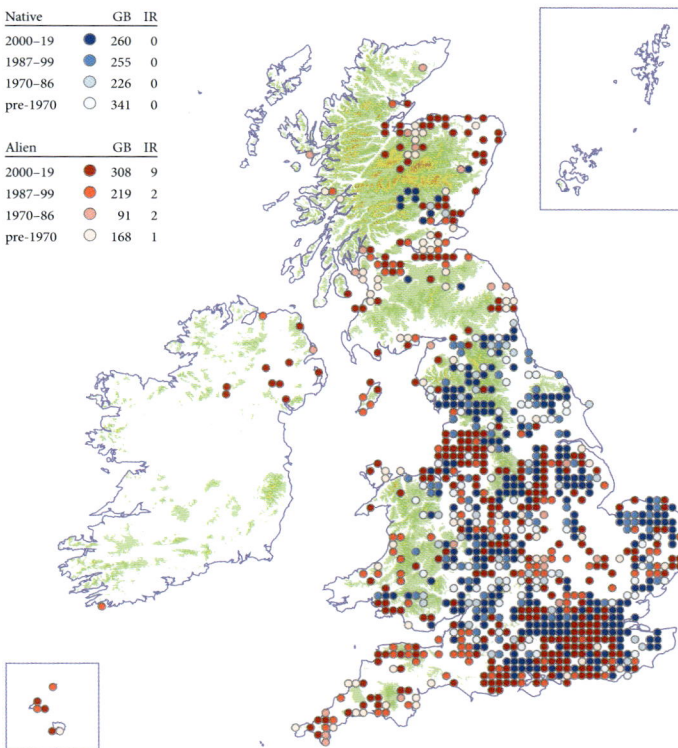

Key refs Crawley (2005), Leslie (2019), Mabey (1996), Peterken (1981), Sussex Botanical Recording Society (2018).

Altitude (m)

Distance north (km)

• <1%
• 1–10%
• 11–30%
• 31–40%
• 41–50%
• 51–100%

J F M A M J J A S O N D
☐ Apparency ☐ In flower ☐ In leaf

I. TAYLOR

Polygonatum multiflorum Solomon's-seal

(L.) All.

A rhizomatous perennial herb, thought to be native only in ashwoods and thickets over chalk and limestone, and less frequently over other non-acidic substrates. It is widely planted in cemeteries, churchyards and parkland and widespread as a garden outcast in a variety of situations such as woodland margins, road verges and dumped soil. Lowland.

Native in Britain and a neophyte in Ireland and the Channel Islands.

Trends *P. multiflorum* is frequently planted or discarded into the wild and therefore its native range is difficult to define with any certainty. Alien populations remain over-recorded for the hybrid *P. ×hybridum* which is the more commonly cultivated of the two taxa. The increase in records in some areas over the past 20 years

or so probably represents some real increase in populations originating from introduced or discarded plants combined with a greater enthusiasm on the part of recorders to document persistent non-native occurrences of ornamental garden taxa such as this.

Biogeography European Temperate element; also in central and eastern Asia.

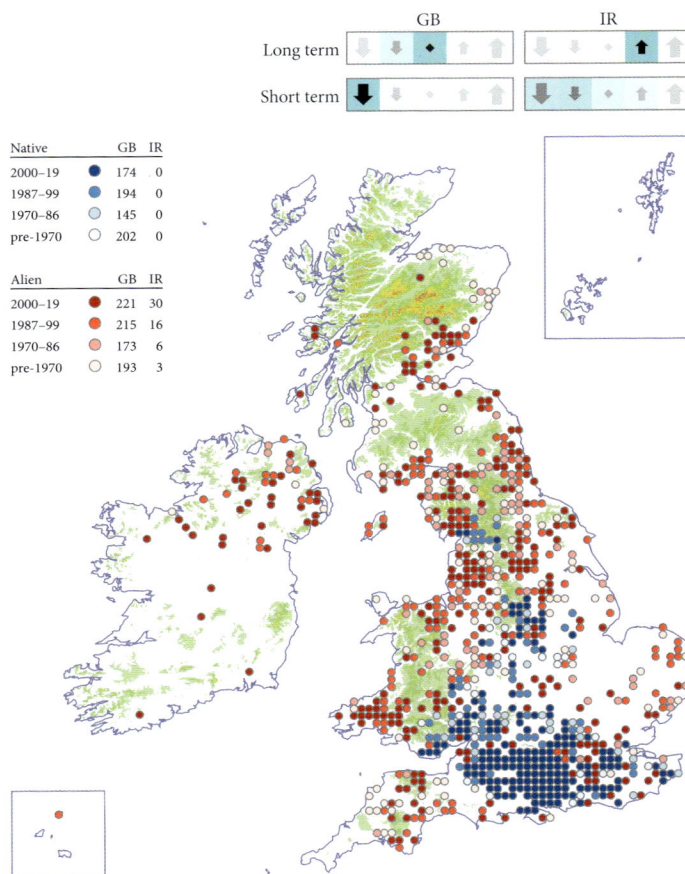

Native	GB	IR
2000–19	174	0
1987–99	194	0
1970–86	145	0
pre-1970	202	0

Alien	GB	IR
2000–19	221	30
1987–99	215	16
1970–86	173	6
pre-1970	193	3

Key refs Chater (2010b), Crawley (2005), Greenwood (2012), Stace *et al.* (2015), Sussex Botanical Recording Society (2018).

I. TAYLOR

Polygonatum multiflorum × odoratum = P. ×hybridum

Brügger

Garden Solomon's-seal

A rhizomatous perennial herb of woodland margins, riversides, railway embankments, churchyards, hedgerows, roadsides and rough ground. It is usually sterile. Lowland.

A spontaneous hybrid (native × native).

Trends *P. ×hybridum* is by far the most frequently grown *Polygonatum* in gardens, and is often discarded in garden waste due to its vigour in cultivation. It does, however, occur naturally with both parents at a few sites in woodland on Oolitic limestone in North Wiltshire. It has been recorded in the wild since at least 1864 (Flitwick Wood, Bedfordshire). Many records of naturalized plants previously identified as *P. multiflorum* are probably referable to this hybrid.

Biogeography Wild hybirds and garden escapes are recorded in northern and central Europe, and garden escapes are recorded from New Zealand.

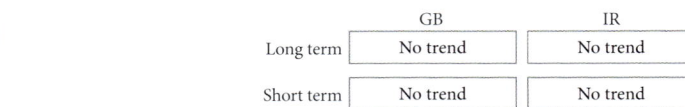

	GB	IR
2000–19	883	50
1987–99	469	33
1970–86	182	4
pre-1970	135	3

	GB		IR	
Long term	No trend		No trend	
Short term	No trend		No trend	

Key refs Stace *et al.* (2015).

C.A. STACE, C.D. PRESTON & D.A. PEARMAN

N *Polygonatum odoratum* Angular Solomon's-seal
(Mill.) Druce

A rhizomatous, perennial herb of ancient *Fraxinus excelsior* woods, often growing in the crevices of limestone rock outcrops or the grikes of limestone pavement. It is sometimes naturalized in shaded habitats, such as wood margins and hedgerows when planted or discarded from gardens. Generally lowland, but reaching 485 m on Craig y Cilau (Breconshire).

Native in Britain and a neophyte in Ireland.

Trends Some populations of *P. odoratum* have been lost to quarrying of limestone and, in the north of its range, through the destruction of limestone pavement, but the latter threat is now much reduced. It is sometimes grown in gardens, and is occasionally naturalized when discarded or deliberately planted in suitably shady, base-rich situations.

Biogeography Eurasian Temperate element.

Native	GB	IR
2000–19	20	0
1987–99	27	0
1970–86	29	0
pre-1970	39	0

Alien	GB	IR
2000–19	8	0
1987–99	12	1
1970–86	8	1
pre-1970	19	2

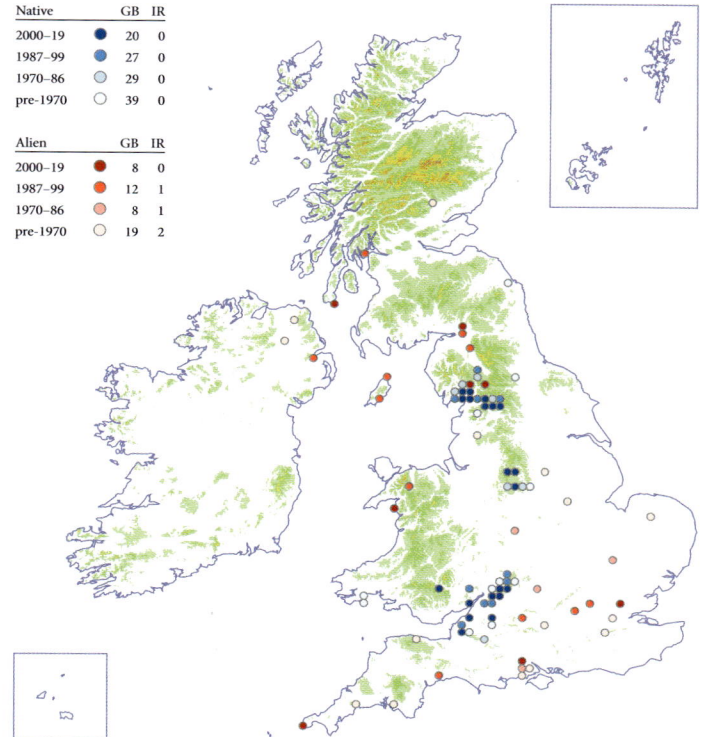

	GB	IR
Long term		No trend
Short term		No trend

Key refs Stewart *et al.* (1994).

I. TAYLOR

N *Polygonatum verticillatum* Whorled Solomon's-seal
(L.) All.

A rhizomatous, perennial herb usually found on moist, nutrient-rich, usually basic soils in wooded gorges and on a wooded riverbank. Plants reproduce vegetatively, by rhizomatous spread, whilst fruiting is generally poor, with recruitment from seed apparently very infrequent. Lowland.

Trends The distribution of *P. verticillatum* is broadly stable. Flowering appears to be restricted by excessive shading at a number of localities and limited opportunities for cross-pollination further restrict seed production.

Biogeography European Boreal-montane element.

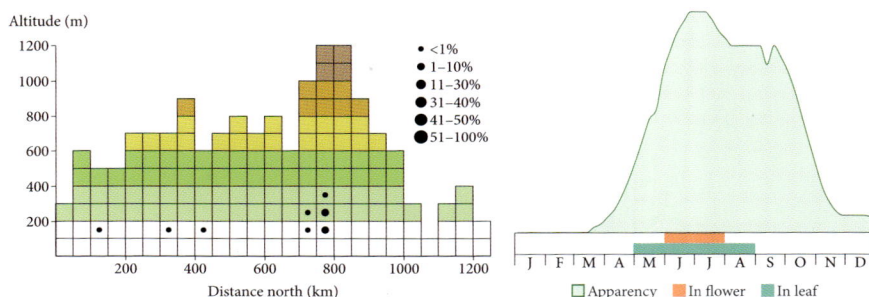

	GB	IR
Long term	No trend	No trend
Short term	No trend	No trend

Native	GB	IR
2000–19	8	0
1987–99	8	0
1970–86	6	0
pre-1970	10	0

Alien	GB	IR
2000–19	2	0
1987–99	2	0
1970–86	1	0
pre-1970	1	0

Key refs Wigginton (1999).

I. TAYLOR

Maianthemum bifolium May Lily
(L.) F.W.Schmidt

A rhizomatous, perennial herb of free-draining acidic soils in birch and oak woodlands, but also persisting at presumed native sites replanted with conifers. It is also introduced into a variety of other woodland types and to localities outside its probable native range, where it is generally short-lived. Flowering and seed-set is poor. Lowland.

Native or alien in Britain and a neophyte in Ireland.

Trends *M. bifolium* was known in both cultivation and the wild by 1597. Records from the 17th century suggest that it was formerly more abundant and widespread, but extant populations tend to be isolated and very small. Its native status is debatable and the three extant native hectads mapped are simply locations where it has persisted since the 19th century – Fulsby Wood

(North Lincolnshire), Forge Valley (North-east Yorkshire) and Blanchland (Durham). The fourth mapped native site, in Ken Wood on Hampstead Heath (Middlesex), was last recorded in 1929. It is usually short-lived at all other sites mapped as alien. For example, the largest British population (Swanton Novers, Norfolk), once estimated to comprise over 50,000 plants, only persisted from 1955 to the late 1990s. Some records mapped may be errors for *M. kamtschaticum* which appears to be increasing as a garden escape.

Biogeography Eurasian Boreo-temperate element, with a continental distribution in western Europe.

Native	GB	IR
2000–19	3	0
1987–99	3	0
1970–86	3	0
pre-1970	4	0

Alien	GB	IR
2000–19	6	1
1987–99	9	1
1970–86	9	0
pre-1970	14	0

	GB	IR
Long term	↓	No trend
Short term	No trend	No trend

Key refs Wigginton (1999).

I. Taylor & K.J. Walker

Ornithogalum pyrenaicum Spiked Star-of-Bethlehem
L.

A bulbous perennial herb of *Fraxinus excelsior–Ulmus* woodland, hedgerows, road verges and rough grassy banks on calcareous soils, and a notable feature of road verges and green lanes in Somerset and Wiltshire. It is very occasionally found as a persistent survivor when deliberately planted or discarded from gardens into similar habitats outside the native range. Lowland.

Native in Britain and a neophyte in Ireland.

Trends There has been no significant change in the native range of *O. pyrenaicum* since the 1960s, although some woodland populations have gradually succumbed to ecological changes following the loss of mature elms. It was formerly harvested, sometimes on a commercial scale, as a native substitute for asparagus, hence the

vernacular name Bath Asparagus, and it is occasionally grown in gardens, from which it may be discarded or planted in the wild and become naturalized.

Biogeography Submediterranean-Subatlantic element.

Native	GB	IR
2000–19	22	0
1987–99	27	0
1970–86	21	0
pre-1970	26	0

Alien	GB	IR
2000–19	20	1
1987–99	13	0
1970–86	10	0
pre-1970	31	0

	GB	IR
Long term	◆	No trend
Short term	↓	No trend

Key refs Boon & Outen (2011), Crawley (2005), Gillam (1993), Hill & Price (2000), Stewart *et al.* (1994), Sussex Botanical Recording Society (2018).

I. Taylor

Ne *Ornithogalum umbellatum s.l.* Star-of-Bethlehem

A bulbous spring-flowering perennial herb, widely grown in gardens and naturalized in grassy places, rough ground, arable margins, roadsides, tracksides, old meadows and pastures and in open woodlands. It reproduces primarily by bulblets which are likely to be dispersed in soil or garden waste. It is found also as a persistent relic of cultivation. Lowland.

Trends *O. umbellatum s.l.* is an aggregate of different cytotypes which have variously been treated as species or subspecies. The triploid subsp. *campestre* (formerly *O. angustifolium*) has been treated as a native in Breckland and elsewhere in eastern England (Trist, 1979; Petch & Swann, 1968) but it is treated here as an introduction. It was first recorded by the River Thames (Surrey) 1598. The larger-flowered hexaploid subsp. *umbellatum* is a more obvious ornamental and was first recorded in the wild in 1968 (Fleam Dyke, Cambridgeshire). The relative abundance and distribution of the two subspecies is uncertain but the overall 10 km square distribution of the aggregate is increasing.

Biogeography Native of southern and southern-central Europe but widely naturalized farther north.

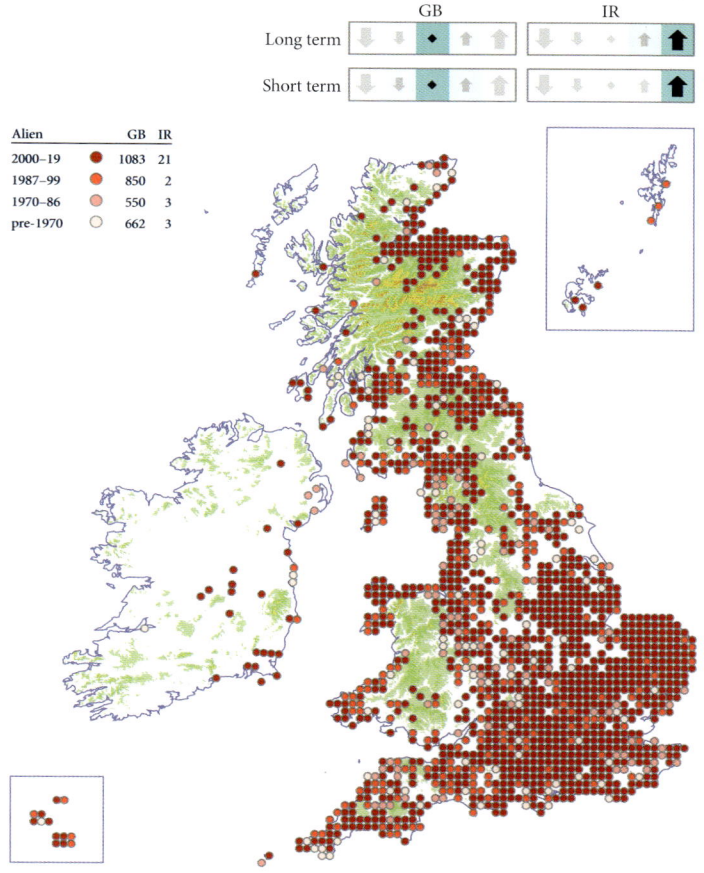

Alien		GB	IR
2000–19	●	1083	21
1987–99	●	850	2
1970–86	●	550	3
pre-1970	○	662	3

Key refs Petch & Swann (1968), Trist (1979).

F.J. RUMSEY

Ne *Ornithogalum nutans* Drooping Star-of-Bethlehem

L.

A bulbous perennial herb, grown in gardens and found naturalized on the edges of woodland, in scrub, in cemeteries and churchyards, along hedgerows, on roadsides and in rough grassy places. It is often planted deliberately, but also arises from discarded garden waste. Lowland.

Trends *O. nutans* was cultivated in Britain by 1629 and is frequently grown in gardens. It was recorded from the wild by 1805 (Eaton Ford, Bedfordshire). Populations are usually small and short-lived though a few are persistent and extensive, such as at Hoarstone Farm, near Bewdley (Worcestershire) where it was first collected in 1852. It appears to have been more common in the past but its modern distribution appears to be relatively stable.

Biogeography Native of the Balkans (Bulgaria, Greece) and Turkey.

Alien		GB	IR
2000–19	●	84	0
1987–99	●	78	0
1970–86	●	66	0
pre-1970	○	137	0

Key refs Boon & Outen (2011), Leslie (2019), Mabey (1996).

I. TAYLOR

Ne *Scilla bifolia* Alpine Squill

L.

A bulbous perennial herb naturalized in churchyards, on roadsides, riverbanks and other grassy banks. It originates as a garden escape or from deliberate planting, and also occurs as a relic of cultivation. Populations on riverbanks presumably originate from waterborne dispersal of seeds or bulbs. Lowland.

Trends *S. bifolia* was already grown by Gerard in 1596 and is very widely cultivated in gardens. It was first recorded from the wild in 1869 (Teignmouth, South Devon) and is probably increasing, or is now better recorded.

Biogeography Native of central and southern Europe and south-western Asia.

Alien		GB	IR
2000–19	●	70	0
1987–99	●	40	0
1970–86	●	6	0
pre-1970	○	2	0

	GB	IR
Long term	No trend	No trend
Short term		No trend

Altitude (m)

- <1%
- 1–10%
- 11–30%
- 31–40%
- 41–50%
- 51–100%

Apparency | In flower | In leaf

T.D. DINES & D.A. PEARMAN

Ne *Scilla bithynica* Turkish Squill

Boiss.

A bulbous perennial herb naturalized on riverbanks, in churchyards, in open woodland and on grassy banks. It originates as a garden escape or from deliberate planting, and also occurs as a relic of cultivation. Lowland.

Trends *S. bithynica* was being cultivated in British gardens by 1924 or shortly before, and is now quite commonly grown. It was first recorded in the wild in 1982 (Milford, South Wiltshire), and was found in a long-derelict garden in South Essex in 1989 and by a river in West Kent in 1990.

Biogeography Native of Bulgaria and northern Turkey.

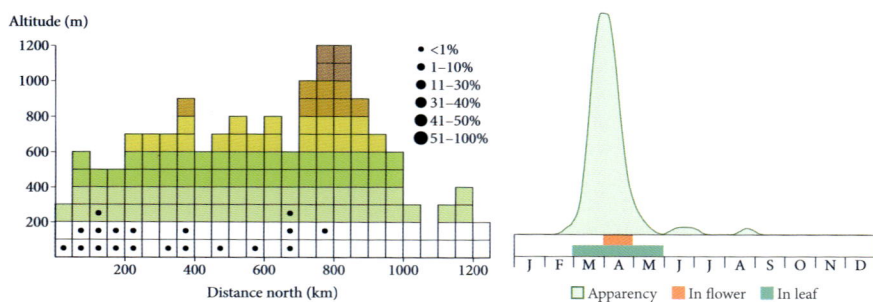

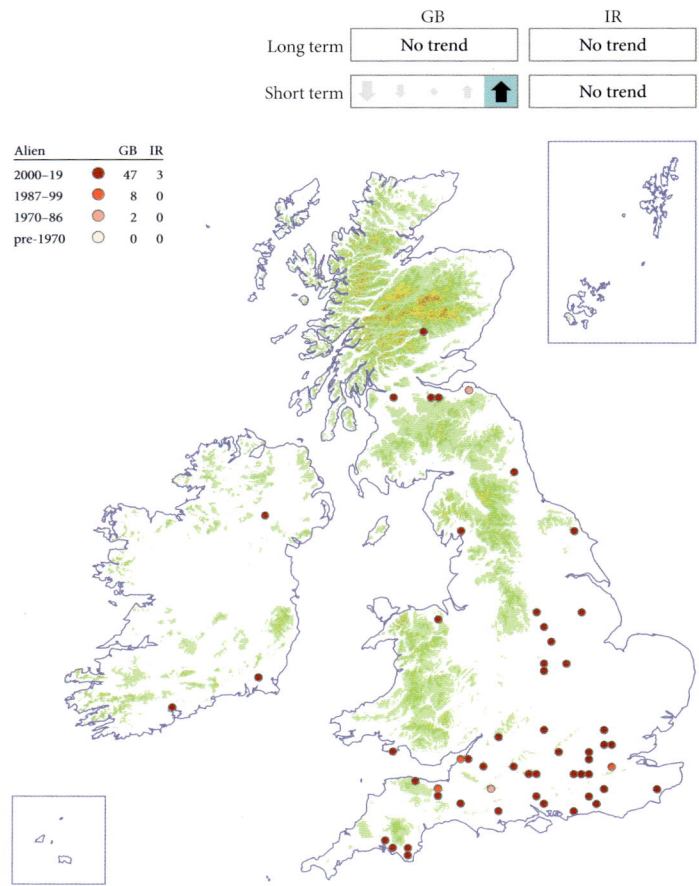

Alien		GB	IR
2000–19	●	47	3
1987–99	●	8	0
1970–86	●	2	0
pre-1970	○	0	0

	GB	IR
Long term	No trend	No trend
Short term		No trend

Altitude (m)

- <1%
- 1–10%
- 11–30%
- 31–40%
- 41–50%
- 51–100%

Apparency | In flower | In leaf

Key refs Nicolle (1991).

T.D. DINES & D.A. PEARMAN

Ne *Scilla siberica* Siberian Squill

Haw.

A bulb-forming perennial herb of free-draining, often sandy soils in coastal grasslands, churchyards and open woodland, and on heaths, roadsides and waste ground, rarely far from human habitations. It regenerates freely in abandoned gardens or where discarded or planted in suitable habitats. Lowland.

Trends *S. siberica* was introduced in 1796 and is now commonly cultivated. However, it was not formally recorded from the wild until 1968 (Lesnes Abbey, West Kent). The large increase in records since the 1960s may, in part, reflect an increase in planting of this species, especially in churchyards and cemeteries, but also the more systematic recording of garden escapes.

Biogeography Native of southern Russia, Turkey and the Caucasus.

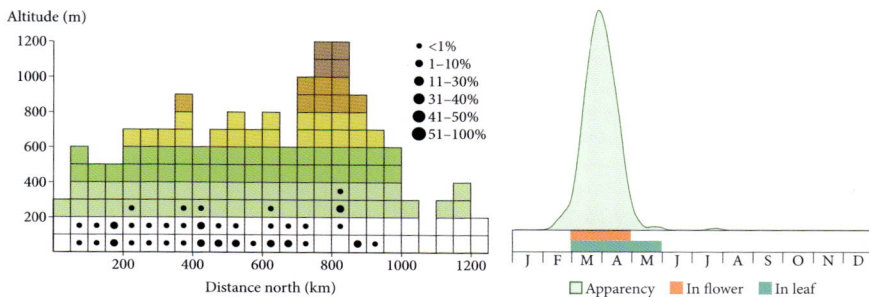

Alien	GB	IR
2000–19	204	3
1987–99	80	0
1970–86	27	0
pre-1970	9	0

Key refs Abbott (2005), Burton (1983), Leslie (2019).

I. TAYLOR

N *Scilla verna* Spring Squill

Huds.

A bulb-forming perennial herb of short turf and maritime heath on exposed cliff-tops and on rocky slopes near the sea, sometimes within the zone regularly affected by sea-water spray. In areas with a pronounced oceanic climate (*e.g.* Anglesey and the Northern Isles) it can occur on heathland well inland. Also on very sparsely vegetated serpentine fellfield in Shetland. Generally lowland, but reaching 415 m on Foula (Shetland).

Trends There is no evidence of any significant recent change in the distribution of *S. verna*. Within its highly restricted habitat, the species is often present in large numbers, and its sites are usually too exposed for any major threat from vegetational succession or land-use changes.

Biogeography Oceanic Temperate element.

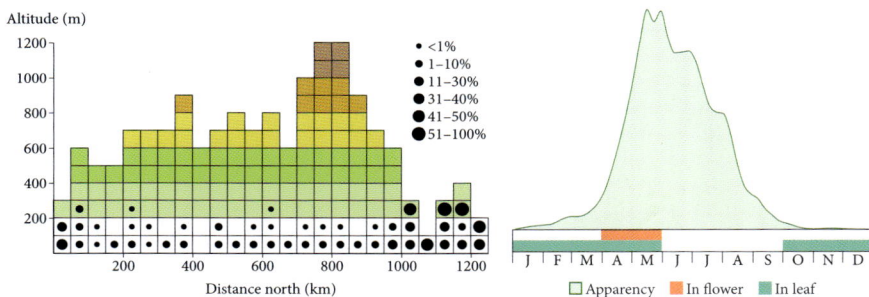

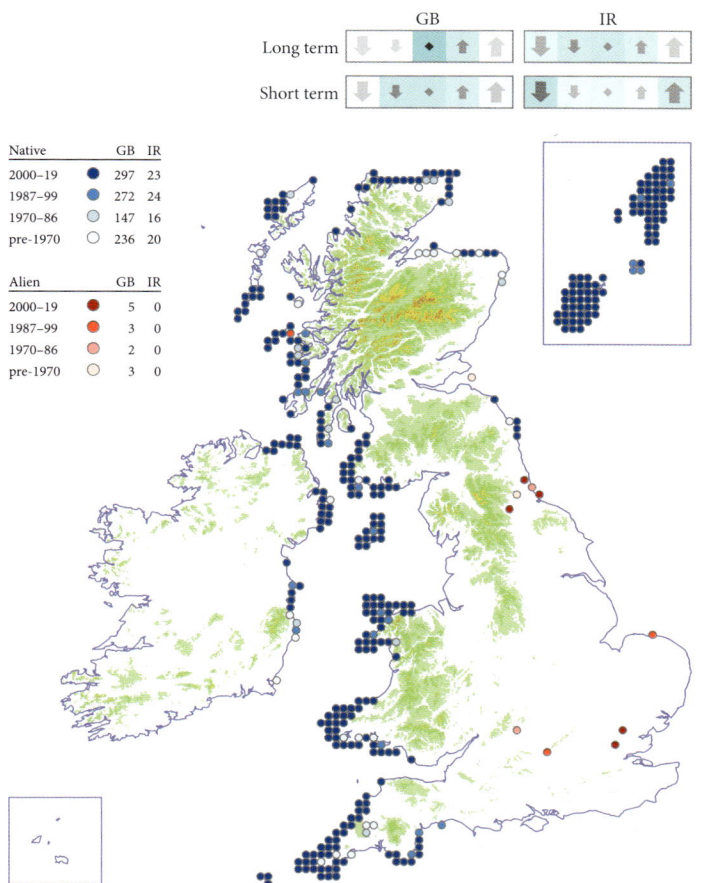

Native	GB	IR
2000–19	297	23
1987–99	272	24
1970–86	147	16
pre-1970	236	20

Alien	GB	IR
2000–19	5	0
1987–99	3	0
1970–86	2	0
pre-1970	3	0

Key refs Chater (2010b), Dupont (1962), French (2020), Hepburn (1952), Scott & Palmer (1987).

I. TAYLOR

N ***Scilla autumnalis*** Autumn Squill

L.

A bulb-forming perennial herb of open, drought-prone grasslands and heathy vegetation in rocky or sandy places near the sea; also on terrace gravels in the lower Thames valley. Lowland.

Trends There is little evidence of significant change in distribution or abundance of *S. autumnalis* since the 1960s. It is tetraploid almost throughout its British range, the exception being on the south coast of Cornwall and on Guernsey where a hexaploid form occurs.

Biogeography Mediterranean-Atlantic element.

	GB				IR	
Long term					No trend	
Short term					No trend	

Native	GB	IR
2000–19	46	0
1987–99	45	0
1970–86	39	0
pre-1970	55	0

Altitude (m)	
	<1%
	1–10%
	11–30%
	31–40%
	41–50%
	51–100%

Apparency   In flower   In leaf

Key refs French (2020), Stewart *et al.* (1994).

I. TAYLOR

Ne ***Scilla forbesii*** Glory-of-the-snow

(Baker) Speta

A bulb-forming perennial herb, very widely planted in parks, gardens and churchyards on free-draining soils where it seeds freely and readily becomes naturalized. It also arises from discarded material on roadsides, rough grassland and waste ground and occasionally on riverbanks where it presumably originates from waterborne seed dispersed from gardens. Lowland.

Trends *S. forbesii* has been cultivated in British gardens since 1877, but plants were not recorded from the wild until 1968 (Mickley, Mid-west Yorkshire). Any assessment of change is complicated by former confusion with *S. luciliae* although this species is much less commonly cultivated. However, there has been a significant increase in the 10 km square distribution since the 1960s reflecting a genuine increase in the numbers of introductions, as

well as re-assessments of previously misnamed populations and the more systematic recording of garden escapes.

Biogeography Native of the mountains of western and south-western Turkey.

	GB				IR	
Long term	No trend				No trend	
Short term					No trend	

Alien	GB	IR
2000–19	318	0
1987–99	125	0
1970–86	28	0
pre-1970	5	0

Altitude (m)	
	<1%
	1–10%
	11–30%
	31–40%
	41–50%
	51–100%

Apparency   In flower   In leaf

Key refs Abbott (2005), Killick *et al.* (1998), Leslie (2019).

I. TAYLOR

Ne *Scilla luciliae* Boissier's Glory-of-the-snow
(Boiss.) Speta

A bulbous perennial herb naturalized
on roadsides and waste ground, and
in churchyards and other rough grassy
places. It arises as a garden escape or
persists as a relic of cultivation. Lowland.

Trends *S. luciliae* was introduced into
cultivation in Britain around 1889,
and is often grown in gardens. It was
first recorded from the wild in 1995
(Hackney, Middlesex), though a 1965
record from Hayes Common (West
Kent) might be this species. Its true
distribution is difficult to assess as it
is often confused with *S. forbesii*.

Biogeography Native of western
Turkey (an endemic of very restricted
distribution).

	GB	IR
Long term	No trend	No trend
Short term		No trend

Alien	GB	IR
2000–19	78	0
1987–99	17	0
1970–86	7	0
pre-1970	5	0

Altitude (m)

	<1%
	1–10%
	11–30%
	31–40%
	41–50%
	51–100%

Distance north (km)

☐ Apparency   ☐ In flower   ☐ In leaf

T.D. Dines & D.A. Pearman

Ne *Scilla sardensis* Lesser Glory-of-the-snow
(Whittall ex Barr) Speta

A bulbous perennial herb naturalized
on roadsides and waste ground, and
in churchyards and other rough grassy
places. It arises as a garden escape or
persists as a relic of cultivation. Lowland.

Trends *S. sardensis* was introduced
into cultivation in Britain in 1883,
and is often grown in gardens. It
was first recorded from the wild in
1981 (Epping Forest, South Essex)
and appears to be increasing.

Biogeography Native of western Turkey.

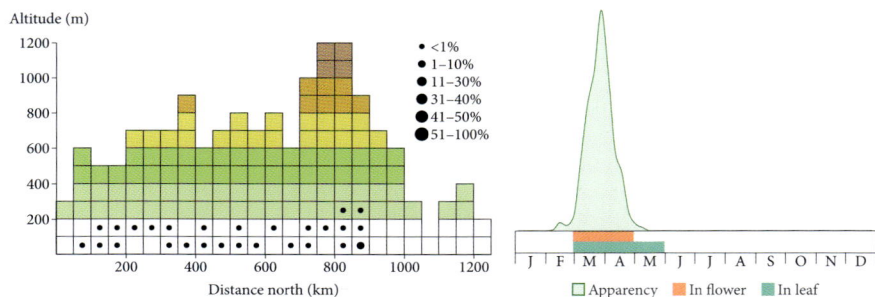

	GB	IR
Long term	No trend	No trend
Short term		No trend

Alien	GB	IR
2000–19	86	0
1987–99	22	0
1970–86	9	0
pre-1970	0	0

Altitude (m)

	<1%
	1–10%
	11–30%
	31–40%
	41–50%
	51–100%

Distance north (km)

☐ Apparency   ☐ In flower   ☐ In leaf

T.D. Dines & D.A. Pearman

N *Hyacinthoides non-scripta* Bluebell

(L.) Chouard ex Rothm.

A bulb-forming perennial herb occurring, often abundantly, in a wide variety of deciduous woodland types, in hedgerows, on shady banks and, especially in western and upland areas, in hay meadows and pastures, under *Pteridium aquilinum* and on coastal cliffs. It is also occasionally found as a naturalized garden escape. Generally lowland, but reaching 685 m on Craig-yr-Ysfa (Caernarvonshire).

Trends The overall 10 km square distribution of *H. non-scripta* appears stable and it remains abundant in suitable habitats throughout its range, with increases in some regions since the 1960s due to more systematic recording (*e.g.* Ireland, parts of Scotland). Prior to being afforded legal protection in 1998 a few populations (*e.g.* in Norfolk) were damaged by large-scale commercial collection for sale in horticulture.

Populations may sometimes be locally depleted by repeated trampling and, despite a degree of toxicity, it also appears to be sensitive to long-term grazing, with flowering in particular much reduced by deer (especially Reeves's Muntjac *Muntiacus reevesi*) in parts of southern England. Recent research in Scotland has, to a large extent, alleviated fears that this species might be in imminent threat of depletion through hybridization and introgression with *H. hispanica* and *H. ×massartiana*. The work found significantly lower reproductive success in the non-natives which, when combined with the considerably greater abundance of *H. non-scripta*, suggests the risk of genetic swamping is highly unlikely.

Biogeography Oceanic Temperate element.

Native	GB	IR
2000–19	2421	850
1987–99	2314	702
1970–86	1607	161
pre-1970	2236	435

Alien	GB	IR
2000–19	17	2
1987–99	10	1
1970–86	6	0
pre-1970	11	0

Key refs Chater (2010b), Crawley (2005), Grime *et al.* (2007), Kohn *et al.* (2009), Kohn *et al.* (2019).

I. TAYLOR

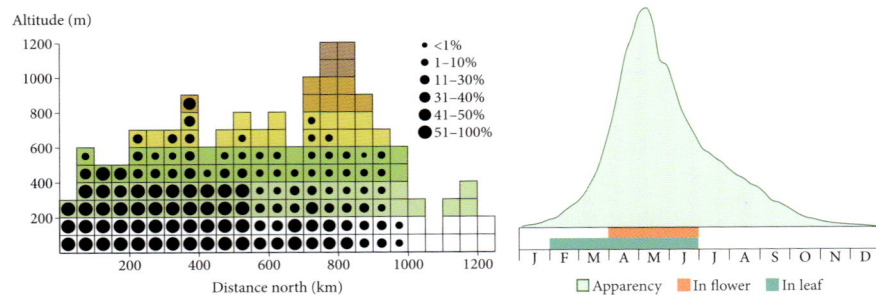

Hy *Hyacinthoides non-scripta × hispanica = H. ×massartiana*

Geerinck

Hybrid Bluebell

A bulbous perennial herb occurring where garden waste is dumped, typically found on the edges of woodland in urban areas and by roadsides, shelter-belts, hedgerows, churchyards, coastal grassland and sand dunes, and on riverbanks, railway embankments, tracksides and waste ground. The hybrid is rarely found in deep shade. In a few sites it appears to have arisen by spontaneous hybridization in the wild between *H. hispanica* and *H. non-scripta*, but the vast majority of occurrences are of plants spreading from gardens or arising from bulbs discarded in garden waste, often in the absence of both parents. Generally lowland, but up to 390 m at Ramshaw Rocks (Staffordshire).

A spontaneous hybrid (native × alien).

Trends This fertile hybrid is the commonest cultivated bluebell. Discarded bulbs readily become

naturalized and though hybridization and introgression with *H. non-scripta* is possible, as yet it does not appear to be threatening our native Bluebell (Kohn *et al.*, 2009; 2019). First recorded in the wild in 1923 (London, Middlesex), its presence was only widely appreciated from the late 1980s onwards after Page (1987) and Rich & Rich (1988) drew it to the attention of botanists. Its recorded range and frequency have increased dramatically since then, presumably due to its greater familiarity to recorders, but possibly also due to a genuine increase in the incidence of escapes and throw-outs. It is still unevenly recorded.

Biogeography This hybrid arises spontaneously where the native ranges of the parents meet, suggesting that the latter are only subspecifically distinct (Sell & Murrell, 1996); it is naturalized elsewhere in western Europe.

	GB	IR
2000–19	1976	315
1987–99	1083	93
1970–86	232	1
pre-1970	57	0

Key refs Kohn *et al.* (2009), Kohn *et al.* (2019), Page (1987), Rich & Jermy (1998), Rich & Rich (1988), Stace (1975), Stace *et al.* (2015).

C.A. STACE, C.D. PRESTON & D.A. PEARMAN

Ne *Hyacinthoides hispanica* agg. Spanish & Hybrid Bluebells

Bulbous perennial, spring-flowering herbs, naturalized where planted or cast out of gardens, on road verges, amenity areas, parklands and in woodlands. Pure examples of the variable Iberian *H. hispanica* are uncommon in cultivation and rarely escape. Much of the seed set by these plants is hybrid, as pollen is preferentially carried from the more numerous native *H. non-scripta*. In urban areas there is almost complete introgression with these native populations rendering accurate identification problematic. Triploid broad-leaved plants, believed to have been derived in cultivation more than 150 years ago, which for many years were equated to *H. hispanica*, may be of complex, probably hybrid origin. This aggregate thus encompasses all those Bluebells which are not of the pure native species. Lowland.

Trends Considerable confusion has surrounded the identity of the numerous horticultural forms now planted widely or escaping via garden material into the landscape, not least through changing views on naming and the growing awareness of hybridization and its consequences. Although mapping shows the aggregate to be almost ubiquitous in lowland areas at a hectad level, there has been only very limited encroachment into the core ancient woodland areas occupied by *H. non-scripta* (Kohn *et al.*, 2019) despite widespread fears that these garden plants would eventually replace the native species (Kohn *et al.*, 2009).

Biogeography *H. hispanica* is an endemic of south and central Iberia, hybridizing with the more northerly *H. non-scripta* where naturally sympatric and in cultivation elsewhere, giving rise to abundant fertile introgressants.

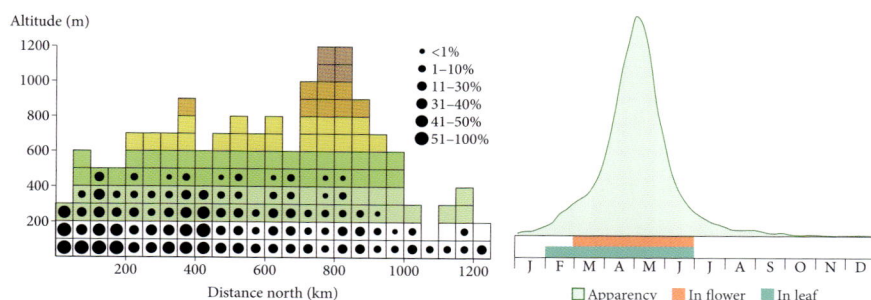

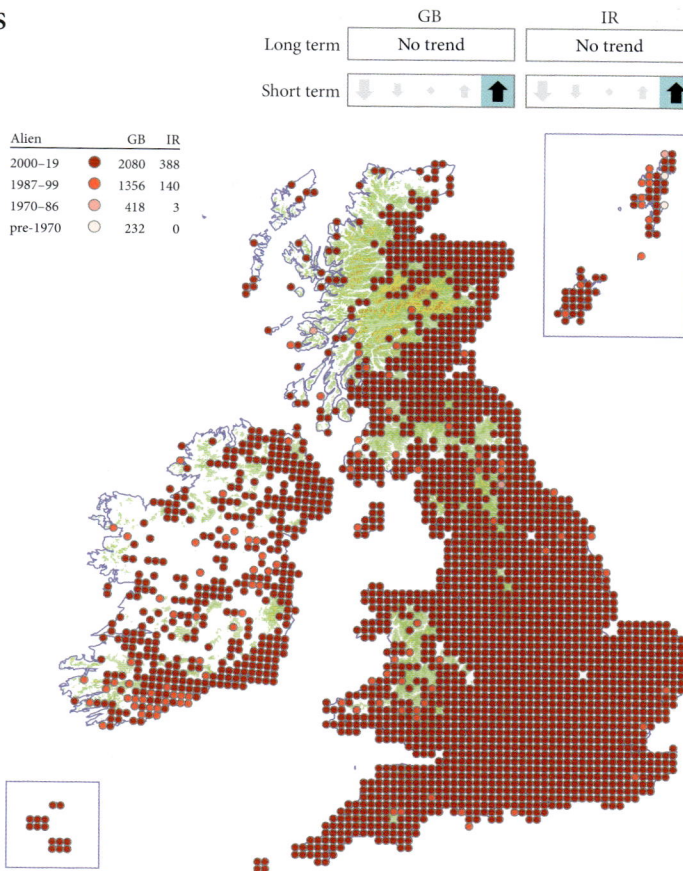

	GB	IR
Long term	No trend	No trend
Short term		

Alien		GB	IR
2000–19	●	2080	388
1987–99	●	1356	140
1970–86	●	418	3
pre-1970	○	232	0

Key refs Kohn *et al.* (2009), Kohn *et al.* (2019).

F.J. RUMSEY

Ne *Hyacinthus orientalis* Hyacinth

L.

A bulbous perennial herb, widely planted in gardens and public spaces, found on roadsides, hedgebanks, in churchyards and cemeteries, in open woodland, on waste ground and sand dunes, usually occurring as isolated clumps arising from discarded or deliberately planted garden stock. Plants can be persistent, especially in warm sites subject to summer drought. Lowland.

Trends *H. orientalis* was being cultivated in Britain by 1596 and is very commonly grown as a winter-flowering house-plant or as spring bedding. Bulbs are sometimes discarded or planted in the wild following flowering, and it was known from the wild by 1957. The number of records has increased significantly since 2000 and, whilst some of this increase is due to more

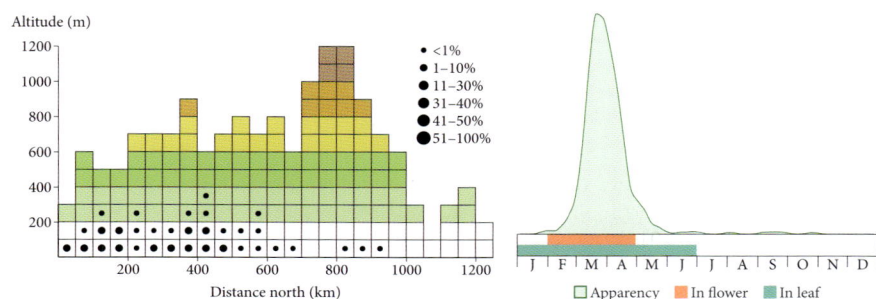

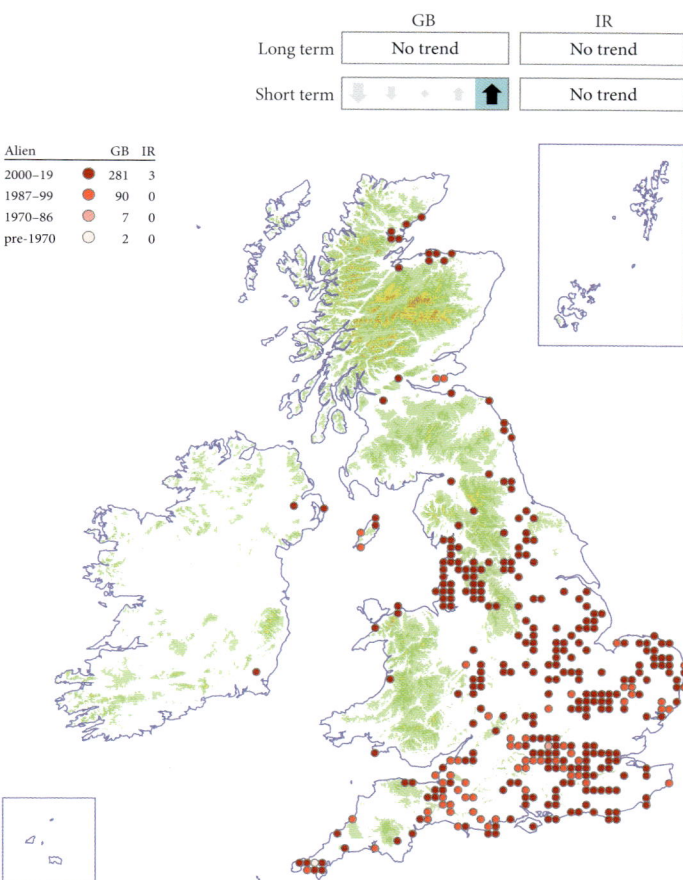

systematic recording of aliens, its range does appear to be slowly expanding.

Biogeography Native of south-western Asia, but modified in cultivation.

	GB	IR
Long term	No trend	No trend
Short term		No trend

Alien		GB	IR
2000–19	●	281	3
1987–99	●	90	0
1970–86	●	7	0
pre-1970	○	2	0

Key refs Crawley (2005), Leslie (2019), Sussex Botanical Recording Society (2018).

I. TAYLOR

Ⓝ *Muscari neglectum* Grape-hyacinth
Guss. ex Ten.

A bulbous perennial herb, sometimes grown in gardens and found naturalized on free-draining, often sandy, nutrient-poor soils in eastern England where its main habitats include short, open acid grasslands, hedgerows, pine plantations, rough ground and roadsides. Elsewhere, it is found as a garden escape or outcast, often close to human habitations, on roadsides, tracksides, pavements, allotments and waste ground, where it is generally short-lived. It spreads by seed and the production of vast quantities of small bulblets (Leslie, 2019). Lowland.

Trends *M. neglectum* was in cultivation by 1596 and was first recorded in the wild in 1776 (Hengrave and Cavenham, Suffolk). In the past, populations in sandy habitats in eastern England (as described above) were treated as native (Preston *et al.*, 2002a), but are now thought to be long-established introductions, possibly originating from agricultural seed imported from Europe (Pearman, 2013). These populations have declined over recent decades, mainly as a result of development pressures and vegetational succession. Elsewhere, it is without doubt an increasing garden alien, although some of this increase may be accounted for by more systematic recording over recent decades. It has has long been confused with, and over-recorded for, *M. armeniacum*, which is more common both in gardens and as an escape in the wild.

Biogeography Eurosiberian Southern-temperate element. Native in Europe to northern France and south-central Russia, also in northern Africa.

Alien	GB	IR
2000–19	258	4
1987–99	134	0
1970–86	112	1
pre-1970	117	0

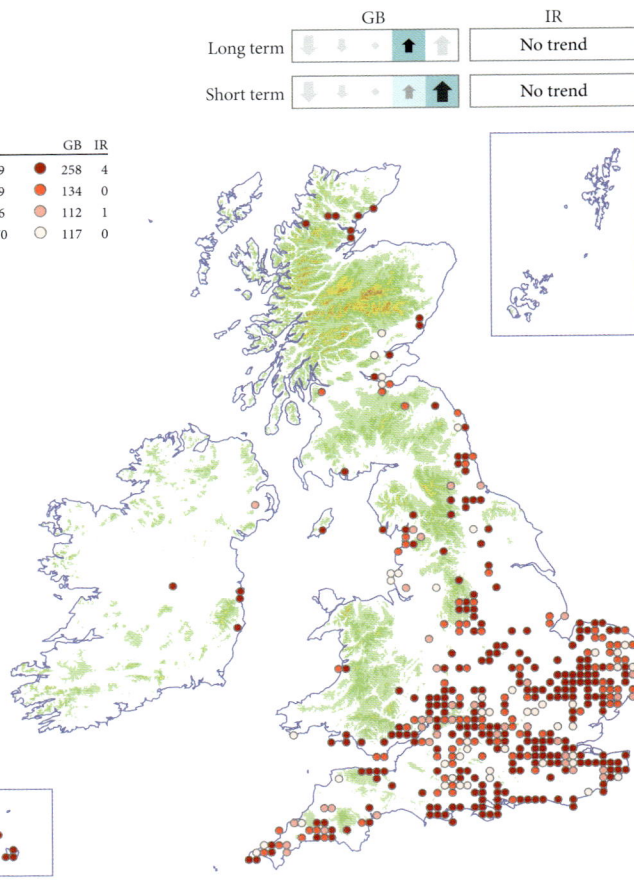

	GB	IR
Long term		No trend
Short term		No trend

Key refs Beckett & Bull (1999), Killick *et al.* (1998), Leslie (2019), Pearman (2013), Sanford & Fisk (2010), Stroh *et al.* (2019), Wigginton (1999).

I. TAYLOR & K.J. WALKER

Ⓝ *Muscari armeniacum* Garden Grape-hyacinth
Leichtlin ex Baker

A bulbous perennial herb, commonly grown in gardens and found on free-draining soils in grasslands, hedgerows, sand dunes, roadsides, walls, refuse tips, active and disused railways, pavements and waste ground. It often becomes invasive in gardens and so is frequently discarded into the wild where it readily becomes naturalized. It is sometimes deliberately planted in churchyards and cemeteries and along roadsides. Populations can rapidly spread vegetatively and by seed in suitable habitats. Lowland.

Trends This species has been cultivated in Britain since 1878 and was recorded in the wild by 1892. It has long been confused with *M. neglectum* and, to a lesser extent, *M. botryoides*, and has therefore been under-recorded in some areas. It is now by far the commonest grape-hyacinth grown in gardens and encountered in the wild, with a huge increase in 10 km square records since the 1960s, a trend that has continued over the last 20 years, in part due to the more systematic recording of ornamental plants. It is certainly increasing due to repeated introduction and frequent regeneration in the wild.

Biogeography Native of the Balkans, Turkey and the Caucasus.

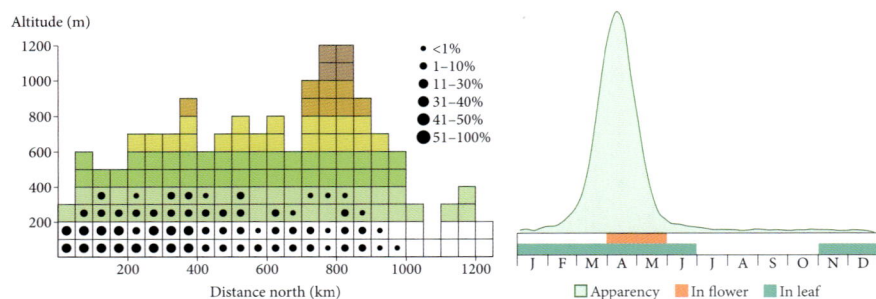

Alien	GB	IR
2000–19	1258	40
1987–99	596	6
1970–86	142	0
pre-1970	33	0

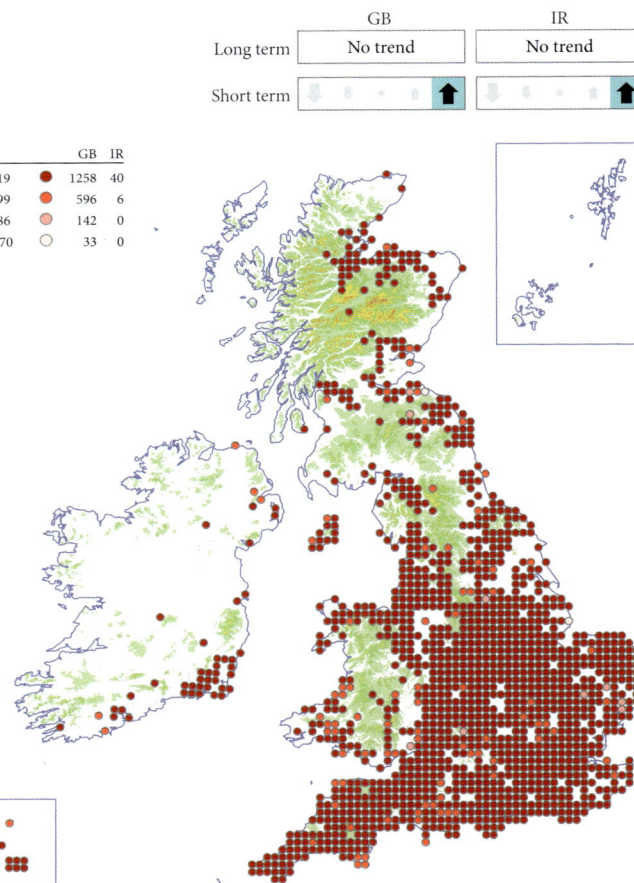

	GB	IR
Long term	No trend	No trend
Short term		

Key refs Boon & Outen (2011), Crawley (2005), Greenwood (2012), Leslie (2019), Rich & Jermy (1998), Sussex Botanical Recording Society (2018).

I. TAYLOR

Ne *Muscari comosum* Tassel Hyacinth
(L.) Mill.

A bulbous perennial herb, grown in
gardens and found in sand dunes,
sandy grasslands and cultivated and
waste ground. Populations are usually
short-lived when discarded into the
wild, but those on dunes and in short,
open turf, especially in the warmer
parts of Britain, can occasionally
become established. Lowland.

Trends *M. comosum* has been cultivated
in Britain since 1596 and was known
in the wild by 1888. It remains a very
scarce alien with few naturalized
populations, including on the Channel
Islands where it might conceivably be
native given its occurrence as a native in
northern France (McClintock, 1975).

Biogeography A European Southern-
temperate species. Native of much of
Europe, north to northern France and
east to the Caucasus and Iran.

Alien	GB	IR
2000–19	25	0
1987–99	31	0
1970–86	19	0
pre-1970	42	0

Key refs McClintock (1975).

I. TAYLOR

N *Asparagus prostratus* Wild Asparagus
Dumort.

A dioecious, rhizomatous perennial
herb of free-draining coastal cliffs, cliff-
tops and slopes, and sand dunes. On
coastal cliffs, plants often grow through
a dense mat of *Festuca rubra*, usually in
very rocky soils. On sand dunes, they
can be found in either open or closed
turf, frequently by paths. Lowland.

Trends *A. prostratus* remains a very
localized plant with around 1,200
individuals in 28 populations in Britain
(Rich *et al.*, 2002) and fewer than 250
individuals in only six populations in
Ireland (Wyse-Jackson *et al.*, 2016).
Natural recruitment is often poor and
there have been some recent losses.
On the other hand, intensive surveys
over the last 20 years in both Britain
and Ireland have revealed previously
unknown populations. Overall the range
is roughly stable and whilst populations
are scattered and frequently very small

and single-sexed, work is underway, as
on the Lizard Peninsula (Cornwall), to
reinforce populations, particularly to
redress sex imbalances where they occur.

Biogeography Oceanic Temperate
element.

Native	GB	IR
2000–19	17	8
1987–99	17	5
1970–86	12	4
pre-1970	21	7

Key refs French (2020), Kay & John (1995), Rich *et al.* (2002),
Wigginton (1999), Wyse Jackson *et al.* (2016).

I. TAYLOR & K.J. WALKER

Ar *Asparagus officinalis* Garden Asparagus
L.

A dioecious, shortly rhizomatous perennial herb, widely grown in gardens and fields for its edible shoots. Naturalized on free-draining sandy soils on grassy heathlands, dunes, road verges, hedgerows and railways, in pavement cracks and at the foot of walls and fence-lines and in dry waste places. Arising as either a relic of cultivation or via bird-dispersed seed. Lowland.

Trends *A. officinalis* has been cultivated in Britain since Roman times. It is now widely grown commercially and on a small scale in gardens. Its recorded 10 km distribution has expanded considerably since the 1960s, reflecting its increased cultivation and the more systematic documentation of aliens in recent years.

Biogeography A Eurosiberian Temperate taxon; native over much of Europe, eastwards to central Asia, widely naturalized outside its native range.

Alien	GB	IR
2000–19	500	6
1987–99	499	4
1970–86	240	2
pre-1970	293	4

Key refs Leslie (2019), Zohary & Hopf (2000).

I. TAYLOR

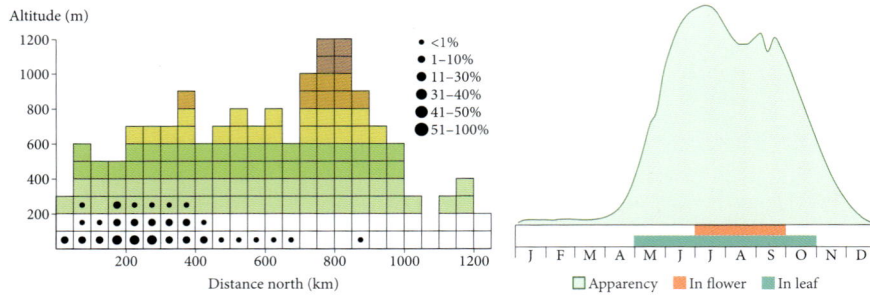

N *Ruscus aculeatus* Butcher's-broom
L.

A dioecious, evergreen, rhizomatous shrub, found as a native in dry woods and hedgerows, and on cliffs and rocky ground near the sea in southern England, the Channel Islands and on the Gower in Wales. It is occasionally planted for game cover or for ornament and is naturalized in habitats similar to those in which it is native, particularly in churchyards and near human habitations. It reproduces vegetatively by creeping rhizomes, and by seed, which is bird-dispersed. Lowland.

Native in Britain and the Channel Islands and a neophyte in Ireland.

Trends *R. aculeatus* is frequently grown in gardens and readily becomes established where discarded, deliberately planted or bird-sown in suitable habitats. There has been a significant increase in records outside the assumed native range over the last two to three decades, especially in Ireland, and whilst this may in part be due to ongoing introductions, it is probably also a result of increased diligence in reporting non-natives. The overall distribution appears relatively stable. The line between native and alien occurrences is becoming ever more blurred and even within the mapped native range, it is undoubtedly much planted and bird-dispersed from populations of garden origin.

Biogeography Submediterranean-Subatlantic element.

Native	GB	IR
2000–19	230	0
1987–99	224	0
1970–86	127	0
pre-1970	217	0

Alien	GB	IR
2000–19	546	52
1987–99	446	12
1970–86	296	2
pre-1970	322	6

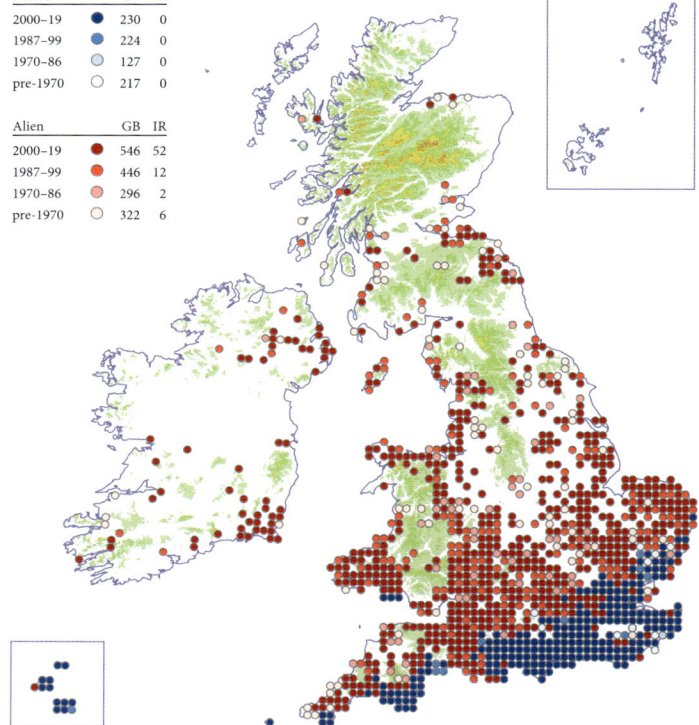

Key refs Crawley (2005), Leslie (2019), Mabey (1996), Sussex Botanical Recording Society (2018), Thomas & Mukassabi (2014).

I. TAYLOR

Ne *Yucca gloriosa* Spanish-dagger

L.

An evergreen perennial with impressive sword-like leaves, increasingly grown in gardens and found on sand dunes and in gravel-pits and waste places where originally planted or arising from garden waste. Some coastal populations are very persistent and appear to be regenerating. Lowland.

Trends *Y. gloriosa* was grown by Gerard by 1596 and is popular in gardens, especially in mild, coastal areas. It was recorded from the wild in 1842 (Crymlyn Burrows, Glamorganshire) as a well-established plant on the seashore, and is increasingly recorded in waste places. The majority of British records appear to be var. *recurvifolia* although var. *gloriosa* also occurs. The taxonomy of *Yucca* is confused and so the map may include records for other species within the genus. Some records for Greater London may be of garden plants, rather than naturalized escapes

Biogeography Native of south-eastern North America.

Alien		GB	IR
2000–19	●	214	3
1987–99	●	24	0
1970–86	●	6	0
pre-1970	○	4	0

	GB	IR
Long term	No trend	No trend
Short term	⬆	No trend

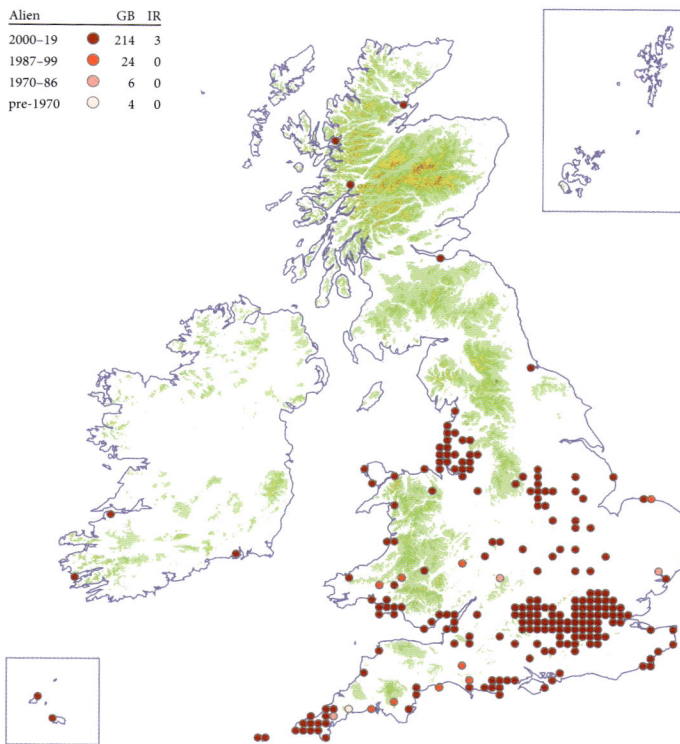

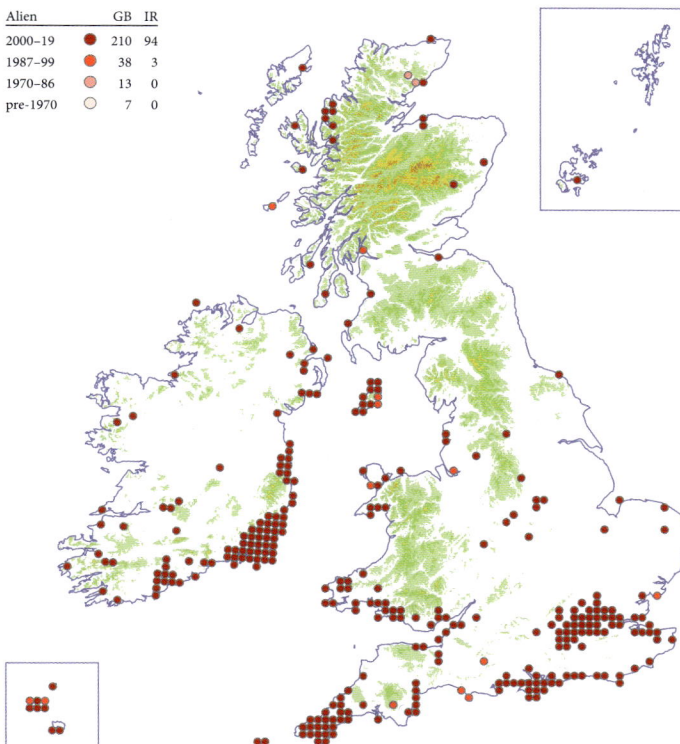

Key refs Irish & Irish (2000).

T.D. Dines, D.A. Pearman & K.J. Walker

Ne *Cordyline australis* Cabbage-palm

(G.Forst.) Endl.

An evergreen perennial, eventually with a woody tree-like stem. It is grown in gardens and planted in parks and amenity areas where the climate is mild. Perhaps mostly surviving where dumped but seedlings have been reported in many areas where it occurs. Lowland.

Trends *C. australis* was cultivated in Britain by 1823, and is increasingly popular in gardens in suitable areas. It was first recorded from the wild in 1965 (Redruth, West Cornwall). There are now very many more records, but whether these originate from plantings, garden waste or are self-sown is unclear.

Biogeography Native of New Zealand.

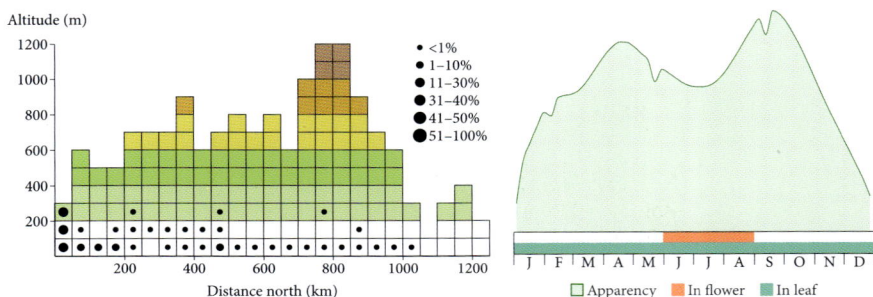

Alien		GB	IR
2000–19	●	210	94
1987–99	●	38	3
1970–86	●	13	0
pre-1970	○	7	0

	GB	IR
Long term	No trend	No trend
Short term	⬆	⬆

Key refs Bean (1970).

D.A. Pearman & T.D. Dines

Ne *Tradescantia virginiana* Spiderwort
L.

A shortly rhizomatous, tufted perennial herb, widely grown in gardens and found on refuse tips and waste ground, where it arises as a garden throw-out. It is usually casual but can be naturalized. Lowland.

Trends *T. virginiana* was being cultivated in Britain by 1629, and is very popular in gardens. It was first recorded from the wild in 1965 (Berkshire and West Kent, and also in Middlesex, where it was noted to have been established on waste ground for around a decade). It must be more frequent than the map suggests. Some or most garden plants are hybrids with other species and it is certain that many records refer to these.

Biogeography Native of eastern North America.

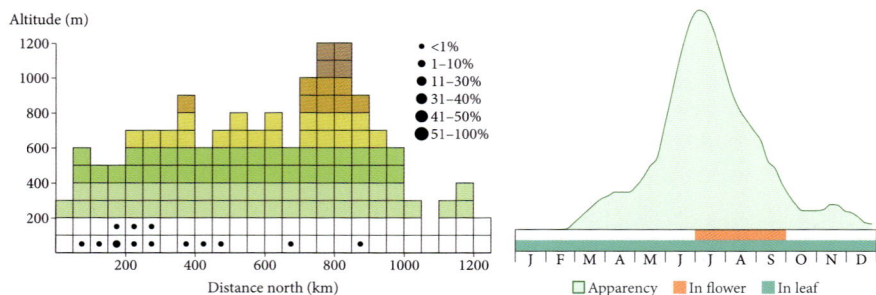

	GB	IR
Long term	No trend	No trend
Short term	↓	No trend

Alien		GB	IR
2000–19	●	26	0
1987–99	●	23	0
1970–86	●	8	0
pre-1970	○	6	0

Altitude (m)

●	<1%
●	1–10%
●	11–30%
●	31–40%
●	41–50%
●	51–100%

Apparency   In flower   In leaf

Key refs Flora of North America Editorial Committee (2000).

D.A. PEARMAN & T.D. DINES

Ne *Pontederia cordata* Pickerelweed
L.

A rhizomatous perennial herb which grows in shallow water around ponds and gravel-pits, usually where originally planted but occasionally as a garden escape. Lowland.

Trends *P. cordata* was cultivated in Britain by 1751, and is popular in water gardens for its cordate leaves and spikes of blue flowers. It was recorded from the wild in Britain in 1949 (Wimborne, Dorset) and in Ireland in 1958. Its 10 km square distribution increased slowly during the 20th century but since 2000 this increased dramatically, mostly in southern Britain but with a range now extending to the Inner Hebrides. Although it appears to be transient in many sites, it can rapidly build large stands leading to it being categorized as invasive in several European countries.

Biogeography Native of North and South America.

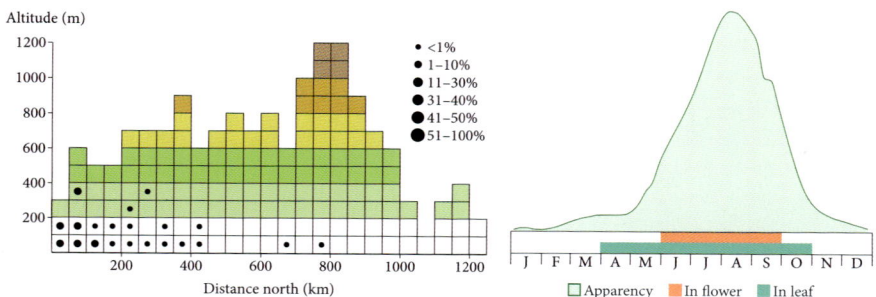

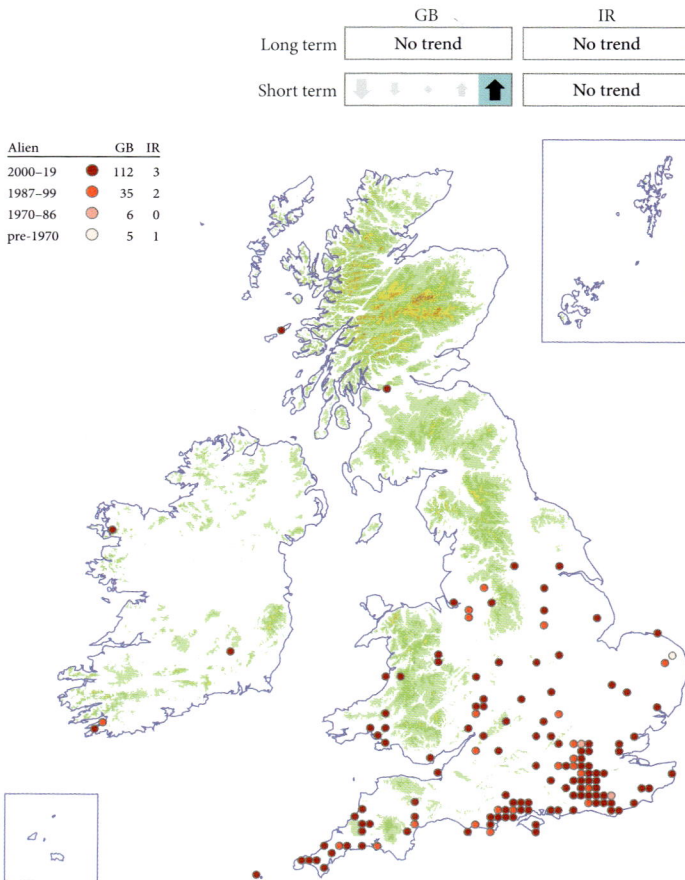

	GB	IR
Long term	No trend	No trend
Short term	↑	No trend

Alien		GB	IR
2000–19	●	112	3
1987–99	●	35	2
1970–86	●	6	0
pre-1970	○	5	1

Altitude (m)

●	<1%
●	1–10%
●	11–30%
●	31–40%
●	41–50%
●	51–100%

Apparency   In flower   In leaf

Key refs Green (2000), Meerts (1988), Verloove (2015).

T.D. DINES & M.W. RAND

Ⓝ *Sparganium erectum* Branched Bur-reed
L.

A rhizomatous perennial emergent which grows in shallow water in lakes, rivers, streams, canals and ditches. Although it usually occurs in a narrow band at the water's edge, it is sometimes found as larger stands in swamps. It grows in mesotrophic or eutrophic habitats, and is very tolerant of eutrophication. Cattle will eat it readily, and it is often absent or rare on grazed lake shores. 0–510 m (Brown Clee, Shropshire).

Trends The distribution of this species is essentially similar to that mapped in earlier atlases, and it appears to be broadly stable at the hectad scale. Braithwaite *et al.* (2006) suggested that it was increasing at the tetrad scale, perhaps a result of the increasing tendency to restrict the access of livestock to water margins. Four suspecies are present in our area:

subsp. *erectum*, subsp. *microcarpum*, subsp. *neglectum* and subsp. *oocarpum*. Of these, subsp. *neglectum* would appear to be the most frequent, and subsp. *oocarpum* the rarest, although all are under-recorded

Biogeography Circumpolar Temperate element, but absent from eastern North America.

Native		GB	IR
2000–19	●	2082	738
1987–99	●	1980	689
1970–86	○	1464	113
pre-1970	○	1711	434

Alien		GB	IR
2000–19	●	2	0
1987–99	●	3	0
1970–86	○	0	0
pre-1970	○	0	0

Key refs Braithwaite *et al.* (2006), Cook (1962), Grime *et al.* (2007), Preston & Croft (1997).

C.D. PRESTON

Ⓝ *Sparganium emersum* Unbranched Bur-reed
Rehmann

A perennial herb of still or slowly flowing, mesotrophic or eutrophic waters in lakes, ponds, rivers, streams, canals and ditches. Like *S. erectum*, it is a rhizomatous perennial but it usually grows in deeper water. It is tolerant of disturbance and may be frequent even in heavily managed rivers. 0–500 m (Crook Burn, Cumberland).

Trends *S. emersum* is often overlooked when growing as non-flowering populations with "rather anonymous strap-shaped leaves" (Braithwaite *et al.*, 2006) and this may be the explanation for the absence of recent records from many of the hectads in which it was recorded in the late 20th century. This is a particularly likely scenario in Scotland, where aquatic habitats were particularly well recorded in the earlier period and where recorders face the additional

problem of distinguishing this species from *S. angustifolium* and their hybrid.

Biogeography Circumpolar Boreo-temperate element.

Native		GB	IR
2000–19	●	1006	372
1987–99	●	1021	334
1970–86	○	722	46
pre-1970	○	930	152

Alien		GB	IR
2000–19	●	2	0
1987–99	●	0	0
1970–86	○	1	0
pre-1970	○	1	0

Key refs Braithwaite *et al.* (2006), Preston & Croft (1997).

C.D. PRESTON

N *Sparganium angustifolium* Floating Bur-reed
Michx.

A perennial herb of clear, oligotrophic water, only rarely extending into mesotrophic conditions. It is most frequent in upland lakes but also grows in pools, rivers, streams, canals and ditches. Many sites are exposed to strong winds, but it prefers water 0·3–1·5 m deep, away from the most exposed shallows. 0–1,005 m (Beinn Heasgarnich, Mid Perthshire).

Trends *S. angustifolium* was well recorded by lake surveys in Scotland and Northern Ireland in the 1980s and 1990s and the intensity of this fieldwork has not been matched since 2000. However, some populations in north-eastern Ireland and along the eastern edge of the Scottish range have certainly been lost, possibly owing to eutrophication.

Biogeography European Boreal-montane element; also in eastern Asia and North America.

Native	GB	IR
2000–19	575	94
1987–99	557	141
1970–86	263	26
pre-1970	322	96

Alien	GB	IR
2000–19	0	0
1987–99	1	0
1970–86	1	0
pre-1970	1	0

Key refs Preston & Croft (1997).

C.D. PRESTON

N *Sparganium natans* Least Bur-reed
L.

A rhizomatous perennial emergent that grows in shallow, sheltered waters at the edges of lakes, or in ponds, slowly flowing streams and drainage ditches. It is found in mesotrophic, highly calcareous to acidic waters. Its rhizomes are short and it usually reproduces by seed. 0–670 m (Slioch, West Ross).

Trends The contraction of the range of *S. natans*, with the loss of most populations in lowland England, Wales and south-eastern Ireland, had already taken place by 1950, and since then the species has persisted in these areas as a few scattered populations. These losses were caused by the drainage of wetlands and perhaps by the eutrophication of surviving sites. The species is more frequent in upland Scotland, where it may have been overlooked in many of the hectads in which it was recorded between 1987 and 1999.

Biogeography Circumpolar Boreo-temperate element.

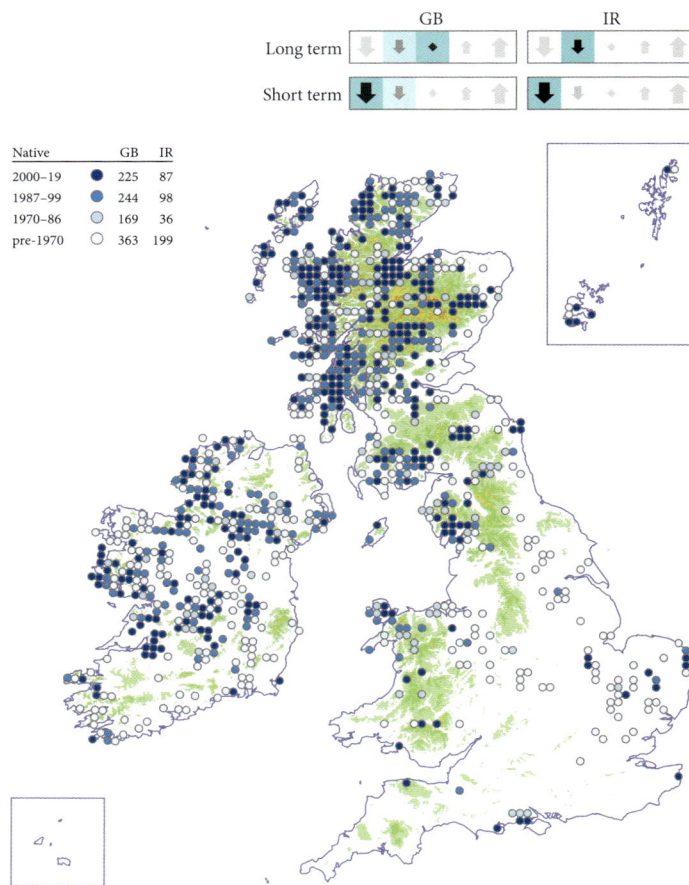

Native	GB	IR
2000–19	225	87
1987–99	244	98
1970–86	169	36
pre-1970	363	199

Key refs Preston & Croft (1997).

C.D. PRESTON

Typha latifolia Bulrush

L.

A rhizomatous perennial growing as an emergent in shallow water or on exposed mud at the edge of lakes, ponds, canals and ditches and (less frequently) by streams and rivers. It favours nutrient-rich sites. It spreads by wind-dispersed fruits, often colonizing newly excavated ponds and ditches and subsequently spreading by vegetative growth. 0–500 m (Brown Clee Hill, Shropshire).

Trends In the second half of the 20th century *T. latifolia* increased in frequency in its core range, and spread westwards and northwards in Britain into new areas of south-western England, Wales, northern England and Scotland. Since 2000 it has consolidated its range in eastern Scotland and the number of scattered populations in north-western and northern Scotland has increased. It has also increased its 10 km square range throughout Ireland since the 1960s,

although this may partly reflect more intensive recording. The reasons for its increase are unknown but may reflect its ability to rapidly colonize and then dominate a wide range of newly created nutrient-rich water-bodies, including those associated with new road, housing and industrial developments.

Biogeography Circumpolar Southern-temperate element.

Native	GB	IR
2000–19	1944	749
1987–99	1788	613
1970–86	1213	118
pre-1970	1390	340

Alien	GB	IR
2000–19	82	1
1987–99	34	0
1970–86	13	0
pre-1970	22	0

	GB	IR
Long term	↑	↑
Short term	↑	↑

Key refs Grace & Harrison (1986), Grime *et al.* (2007), Preston & Croft (1997).

C.D. Preston & K.J. Walker

Typha angustifolia × latifolia = T. ×glauca Hybrid Reedmace

Godr.

This vigorous rhizomatous perennial may form extensive clones in shallow water at the edge of eutrophic standing waters. It is recorded by rivers only infrequently. The hybrid may grow with one or both parents, or with neither of them. Research in North America suggests that it is particularly successful in disturbed habitats with fluctuating water levels. F$_1$ hybrids are highly sterile. Lowland.

A spontaneous hybrid (native × native).

Trends Although this hybrid was clearly described by Lousley (1947), Tutin (1947) and Stace (1975) it was not mentioned by Clapham *et al.* (1952, 1962) and overlooked by most British botanists until Leslie (1984) drew attention to it. Records have increased gradually since then, but it must still be under-recorded.

Biogeography Widespread in Europe and North America.

	GB	IR
2000–19	119	1
1987–99	87	2
1970–86	15	0
pre-1970	13	0

	GB	IR
Long term	No trend	No trend
Short term	No trend	No trend

Key refs Leslie (1984), Lousley (1947), Stace (1975), Stace *et al.* (2015), Tutin (1947).

C.D. Preston

N *Typha angustifolia* Lesser Bulrush
L.

This tall, rhizomatous perennial grows as an emergent in mesotrophic or eutrophic water in lakes, ponds, ditches and flooded mineral workings. It tends to grow in deeper water than *T. latifolia*, and tolerates mesotrophic as well as eutrophic conditions. It also grows as floating rafts at some sites. Lowland.

Trends The 10 km square distribution of *T. angustifolia* has increased markedly since the 1960s with a notable number of new records since 2000. It is often cultivated as an ornamental aquatic, and the vast majority of these new populations are likely to have arisen as garden escapes. These introductions have now almost completely obscured its native range and consequently all records are mapped without status.

Biogeography Eurosiberian Temperate element; also in North America.

		GB	IR
2000–19	●	817	36
1987–99	●	650	38
1970–86	●	424	21
pre-1970	○	594	36

Key refs Grace & Harrison (1986), Preston & Croft (1997).

C.D. PRESTON

N *Eriocaulon aquaticum* Pipewort
(Hill) Druce

The perennial rosettes of *E. aquaticum* grow on peat or on inorganic substrates at the edge of oligotrophic lakes and pools. It ranges from levels which are often exposed above the water to those which are permanently submerged. Little is known about its reproductive ecology. Generally lowland, but reaching 300 m in Glen Lough (West Cork).

Trends The distribution of this distinctive species seems to be both well-documented and stable. Its habitat is so widespread in western Scotland that it is difficult to explain its limited occurrence there, but there have been no significant changes since its discovery in mainland Scotland in 1967 and extensive loch surveys in the late 20th century resulted in only minor extensions of its known range.

Biogeography Oceanic Boreal-montane element; in Europe restricted to Britain and Ireland but widespread in North America.

Native		GB	IR
2000–19	●	8	57
1987–99	●	10	45
1970–86	●	9	17
pre-1970	○	7	60

Key refs Flora of North America Editorial Committee (2000), Preston & Croft (1997), Wigginton (1999).

C.D. PRESTON

Ne *Juncus planifolius* Broad-leaved Rush
R.Br.

A tufted perennial herb, resembling a species of *Luzula*, found on base-poor peaty soil by streams, on lake-shores, in runnels through wet meadows, on tracks and on mineral soil in quarries. It thrives in shallow running water. Its mode of introduction is unknown. Lowland.

Trends *J. planifolius* was first found in Ireland in 1971, new to the Northern Hemisphere, is now established in suitable habitats throughout West Galway, where it is locally abundant and spreading. It was first recorded in East Mayo in 2015 and West Mayo in 2017.

Biogeography Native of Australasia and southern South America.

	GB	IR
Long term	No trend	No trend
Short term	No trend	No trend

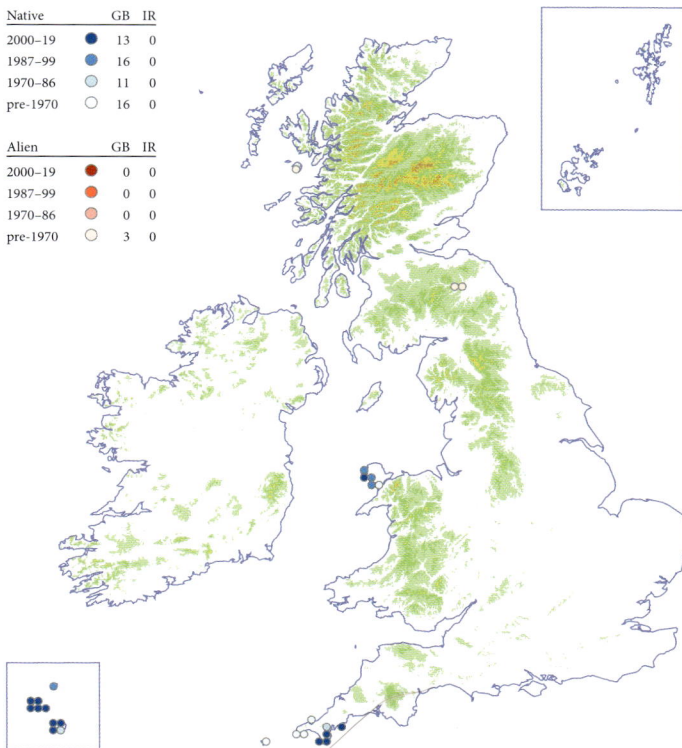

Alien	GB	IR
2000–19	0	20
1987–99	0	3
1970–86	0	4
pre-1970	0	0

Key refs Scannell (1973), Scannell (1975).

C.A. STACE & J.O. MOUNTFORD

N *Juncus capitatus* Dwarf Rush
Weigel

A tiny, autumn-germinating annual rush of barish ground often kept open by standing water in winter and always droughted in summer. It grows around serpentine rock outcrops and winter-wet erosion pans, on ledges and crevices of granite sea-cliffs, in dune-slacks and sometimes in quarries. Lowland.

Trends British populations of *J. capitatus* vary greatly in size from year to year, and reports of extinction have sometimes proved to be premature, notably on Anglesey where it was rediscovered in 1995, although in recent years succession and a lack of disturbance at its sole extant Welsh site (Cymyran) have almost completely eliminated the areas of open damp peaty sand that it favours. The main threat to the Cornish sites is the cessation of grazing, but there is some suggestion of a recent eastward spread. Discoveries at The Blouth and Nare Head (East Cornwall) following the Foot and Mouth epidemic of 2001 were attributed to more intensive sheep grazing due to restrictions on animal movement, and the creation of a very short, open turf.

Biogeography European Southern-temperate element; widely naturalized outside its native range.

	GB	IR
Long term	No trend	No trend
Short term	No trend	No trend

Native	GB	IR
2000–19	13	0
1987–99	16	0
1970–86	11	0
pre-1970	16	0

Alien	GB	IR
2000–19	0	0
1987–99	0	0
1970–86	0	0
pre-1970	3	0

Key refs French (2020), Wigginton (1999).

C.A. STACE & J.O. MOUNTFORD

(N) *Juncus subnodulosus* Blunt-flowered Rush
Schrank

A strongly rhizomatous perennial rush growing in dense stands in fens and fen-meadows, marshes, wet meadows, dune-slacks, ditches and by water, usually in more base-rich conditions than any of the other jointed-rushes (sect. *Septati*) and often on peaty soil; it also sometimes occurs in brackish water. It can become dominant in the absence of grazing, especially in abandoned fen-meadows. Lowland.

Trends *J. subnodulosus* has been lost from many sites in southern England both before 1930 and subsequently, because of drainage of its habitat. However, surveys in the late 20th century showed that it was more frequent in Wales than was suspected, and new sites have been found this century, notably in central areas of England and in Ireland, although it appears to have declined in the south-

west, where it was always rare. This species is very distinct from other jointed-rushes and the map should indicate its true distribution.

Biogeography European Southern-temperate element.

Native		GB	IR
2000–19	●	465	138
1987–99	●	489	143
1970–86	○	348	48
pre-1970	○	480	118

Alien		GB	IR
2000–19	●	1	0
1987–99	●	0	0
1970–86	●	0	0
pre-1970	○	0	0

Key refs Richards & Clapham (1941c).

C.A. STACE & J.O. MOUNTFORD

(N) *Juncus alpinoarticulatus* Alpine Rush
Chaix

A montane, rhizomatous rush of rather open wet turf or bare gravels in marshes and flushes and by lakes and streams, usually on base-rich soil and often over limestone. It is often found with a range of other less common montane calcicoles in bryophyte-rich habitats. The nominate subspecies occurs from 128 m (Tulach Hill, Mid Perthshire) to 1,015 m on Meall Garbh (Mid Perthshire), but subsp. *rariflorus* has been recorded almost entirely at 130 m by Loch Ussie (East Ross & Cromarty).

Trends *J. alpinoarticulatus* has been much confused with variants of *J. articulatus*, and sometimes grows and hybridizes with them. New finds in recent years are a result of better identification skills rather than natural range extension.

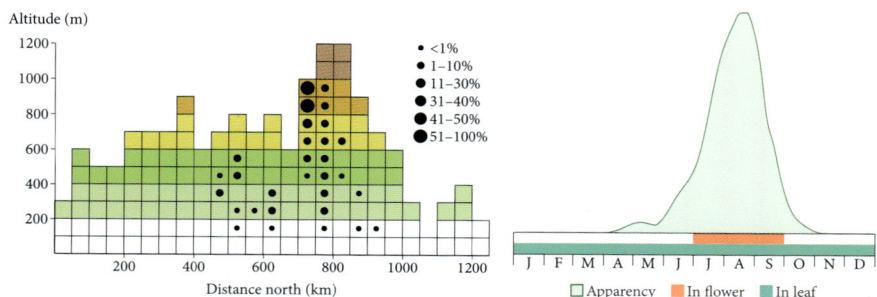

Biogeography Circumpolar Boreal-montane element.

Native		GB	IR
2000–19	●	33	0
1987–99	●	29	0
1970–86	○	34	0
pre-1970	○	34	0

Key refs Stewart *et al.* (1994).

C.A. STACE & J.O. MOUNTFORD

N *Juncus articulatus* Jointed Rush
L.

A very variable, erect to decumbent, clumped to extensively rhizomatous rush of a wide range of wet or damp habitats, both freshwater and brackish. It is characteristic of damp grasslands, marshes, ditches, flushes, rutted woodland rides, margins of ponds, lakes and streams and dune-slacks, avoiding only the most acid soils. 0–930 m (Aonach Beag, Westerness).

Trends There has been no appreciable change in the overall 10 km square range of *J. articulatus* since the 1960s, and its ability to colonize wet disturbed habitats means that any local losses are compensated by new populations.

Biogeography Eurosiberian Southern-temperate element, but widely naturalized so that distribution is now Circumpolar Southern-temperate.

	GB	IR
Long term		
Short term		

Native	GB	IR
2000–19	2743	981
1987–99	2681	912
1970–86	1781	180
pre-1970	2492	781

Altitude (m)

<1%
1–10%
11–30%
31–40%
41–50%
51–100%

Distance north (km)

Apparency In flower In leaf

Key refs Grime *et al.* (2007).

C.A. STACE & J.O. MOUNTFORD

Hy *Juncus acutiflorus × articulatus = J. ×surrejanus*
Druce ex Stace & Lambinon

J. acutiflorus and *J. articulatus* frequently grow together in areas of moderate acidity, and hybrids can occur in varying quantity in a wide range of damp and wet habitats. The hybrid is sometimes more common than either parent (as in parts of central Wales). It is usually highly sterile, but a small proportion of flowers can produce viable seed. Lowland to 425 m at Pont Crugnant (Montgomeryshire).

A spontaneous hybrid (native × native).

Trends This hybrid is frequently misidentified as one or other parent, and though there are many new records this century, it is almost certainly still under-recorded. Areas of concentrated records in Wales, south-eastern and north-western England reflect the activities of recorders familiar with the hybrid.

Biogeography This hybrid is also recorded from western and central Europe.

	GB	IR
Long term	No trend	No trend
Short term	No trend	No trend

	GB	IR
2000–19	261	74
1987–99	157	34
1970–86	71	16
pre-1970	68	64

Altitude (m)

<1%
1–10%
11–30%
31–40%
41–50%
51–100%

Distance north (km)

Apparency In flower In leaf

Key refs Stace *et al.* (2015).

C.A. STACE, C.D. PRESTON & D.A. PEARMAN

N *Juncus acutiflorus* Sharp-flowered Rush
Ehrh. ex Hoffm.

A usually tall and erect rush, more extensively rhizomatous than *J. articulatus*. It occurs in wet or damp habitats on acidic soils, frequently at a lower pH than is tolerated by *J. articulatus*, particularly in damp meadows and pastures, marshes, bogs, wet heathland, and by ditches and ponds. This preference for acidic soils and permanent grassland is reflected in its being almost absent from the mainly calcareous and arable Fenland basin. 0–800 m (Glencoe, Main Argyll) and perhaps higher on Ben Lawers (Mid Perthshire).

Trends *J. acutiflorus* was under-recorded in the first half of the 20th century. It often closely resembles the more robust growth-forms of *J. articulatus* and this might have produced some inaccuracies in the records of both species. However, they are both so frequent that this would be unlikely to affect the distributions shown on the maps. Nonetheless, there is evidence of localized decline where grassland is being replaced by arable farming and where the soils are highly calcareous, as in Cambridgeshire (Leslie, 2019).

Biogeography European Temperate element; also in North America.

Native	GB	IR
2000–19	2385	920
1987–99	2299	781
1970–86	1633	159
pre-1970	1950	578

Alien	GB	IR
2000–19	9	0
1987–99	12	0
1970–86	4	0
pre-1970	4	0

Key refs Leslie (2019), McVean & Ratcliffe (1962).

C.A. STACE & J.O. MOUNTFORD

N *Juncus bulbosus* Bulbous Rush
L.

A very variable rush, ranging from tufted, terrestrial plants to submerged, floating aquatics, often rooting at the nodes and with proliferating flowers. It occurs in or by water and in open, often seasonally wet habitats, in acidic to neutral soils *e.g.* moist heaths, wheel-ruts and woodland rides. Unusually, it grows in some calcareous turloughs in the Burren. 0–1,040 m (Carrauntoohill, South Kerry).

Trends Although the 10 km square distribution of *J. bulbosus* appears to be stable throughout much of our area, there have been declines at the margins of its range, especially in the more intensively farmed regions of the English Midlands and eastern England. Some authorities divide the species into *J. bulbosus* and *J. kochii*, but opinions differ widely on their taxonomic merit and distribution. For example, Stace (2019) recognizes subsp. *kochii* whereas Sell & Murrell (1996) include all variants within a broadly defined *J. bulbosus*.

Biogeography European Boreo-temperate element; also in North America.

Native	GB	IR
2000–19	2086	811
1987–99	2026	722
1970–86	1332	142
pre-1970	1838	551

Key refs Grime *et al.* (2007), Preston & Croft (1997), Webb & Scannell (1983).

C.A. STACE & J.O. MOUNTFORD

(N) *Juncus pygmaeus* Pigmy Rush
Rich. ex Thuill.

A tiny, loosely tufted, spring-germinating annual rush of winter-wet, compacted open ground on serpentine heathland, such as in gateways and on wheel tracks, less often in natural areas of erosion and in quarries. On these sites there is a thin layer of loess, laid down at the end of the last glaciation, which overlies the hard rock geology. Lowland.

Trends The overall 10 km square distribution of *J. pygmaeus* is stable on the Lizard Peninsula. Populations vary greatly in size from year to year, and there was a strong decline during the 1980s and 1990s, mainly due to tracks becoming abandoned and vegetated over, or infilled with hardcore. However, a targeted programme of mechanical scraping of old trackways this century has resulted in the reappearance of this species at many historical, 'lost' sites.

Biogeography Mediterranean-Atlantic element.

	GB	IR
Long term	No trend	No trend
Short term	No trend	No trend

Native		GB	IR
2000–19	●	3	0
1987–99	●	3	0
1970–86	●	3	0
pre-1970	○	4	0

Altitude (m) / Distance north (km)

● <1%
● 1–10%
● 11–30%
● 31–40%
● 41–50%
● 51–100%

J F M A M J J A S O N D
☐ Apparency ■ In flower ■ In leaf

Key refs Wigginton (1999).

C.A. STACE & J.O. MOUNTFORD

(N) *Juncus biglumis* Two-flowered Rush
L.

A tiny, tufted perennial rush of damp rocky or gravelly places, ranging from well-watered rock faces and gravelly flushes to marshes with short open vegetation. It is confined to base-rich, but relatively competition-free, habitats in species-rich localities. From 370 m on Rum (North Ebudes) to 1,100 m in the Breadalbanes (Mid Perthshire) and Aonach Beag (Westerness).

Trends The distribution of *J. biglumis* appears stable, and is probably still present in remote sites discovered in north-western Scotland in the late 20th century. Old records for Upper Teesdale are considered doubtful in the absence of convincing herbarium material, and are not mapped.

Biogeography Circumpolar Arctic-montane element.

	GB	IR
Long term		No trend
Short term		No trend

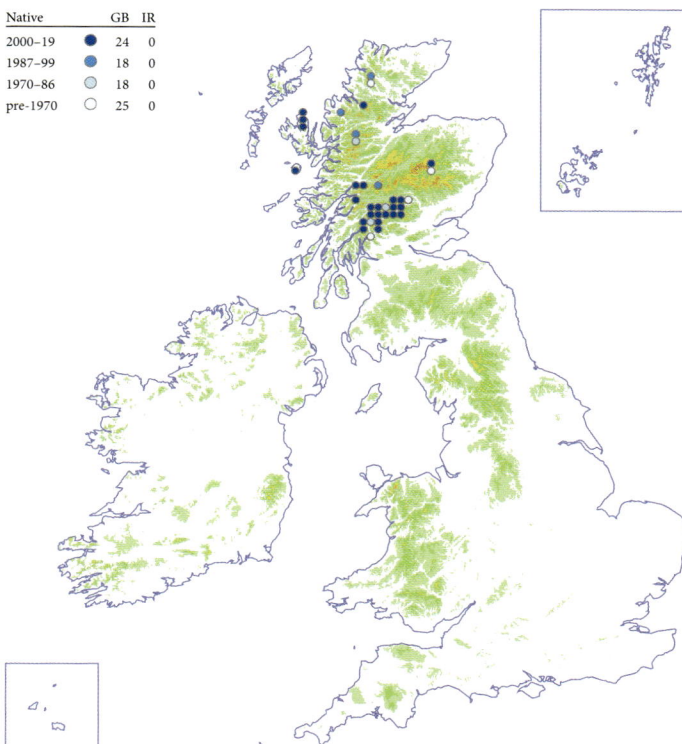

Native		GB	IR
2000–19	●	24	0
1987–99	●	18	0
1970–86	●	18	0
pre-1970	○	25	0

Altitude (m) / Distance north (km)

● <1%
● 1–10%
● 11–30%
● 31–40%
● 41–50%
● 51–100%

J F M A M J J A S O N D
☐ Apparency ■ In flower ■ In leaf

Key refs Stewart *et al.* (1994).

C.A. STACE & J.O. MOUNTFORD

N *Juncus triglumis* Three-flowered Rush
L.

A short, tufted, montane perennial rush of base-rich damp rocky or gravelly places, flushes and small marshes with little competing vegetation. It occupies the same habitats as the rarer *J. biglumis*, and often grows near or with it, but is less restricted to high altitudes, descending from 1,065 m on Snowdon (Caernarvonshire) to 60 m on Unst (Shetland).

Trends *J. triglumis* was lost from Orkney before 1914 but survives on the Hill of Colvadale (Shetland). The overall 10 km square distribution elsewhere has changed little since the 1960s, although more intensive recording within its core range in Scotland has resulted in a number of new locations, and many populations that were not refound in the late 20th century have been recorded for the current survey.

Biogeography Circumpolar Arctic-montane element.

Native		GB	IR
2000–19	●	143	0
1987–99	●	140	0
1970–86	○	106	0
pre-1970	○	156	0

C.A. Stace & J.O. Mountford

N *Juncus castaneus* Chestnut Rush
Sm.

A short, tufted perennial rush of species-rich localities, often growing with one or both of *J. biglumis* and *J. triglumis*, although it is more characteristic of wetter and more calcareous habitats, such as the margins of flushes where it can better withstand competition from grasses. From 610 m on Sgurr na Lapaich (Easterness) to 1,015 m on Beinn Heasgarnich (Mid Perthshire).

Trends Whilst surveys this century suggest that *J. castaneus* might have been overlooked in some sites where it was not found in the 1990s, there is some cause for concern as many populations are small and often in locations where there is heavy grazing by sheep and deer. Conversely, the species was found in three new 10 km squares during the current survey, with all sites supporting small numbers of

plants, and it is possible that it may persist, overlooked, elsewhere.

Biogeography Circumpolar Arctic-montane element.

Native		GB	IR
2000–19	●	28	0
1987–99	●	18	0
1970–86	○	20	0
pre-1970	○	38	0

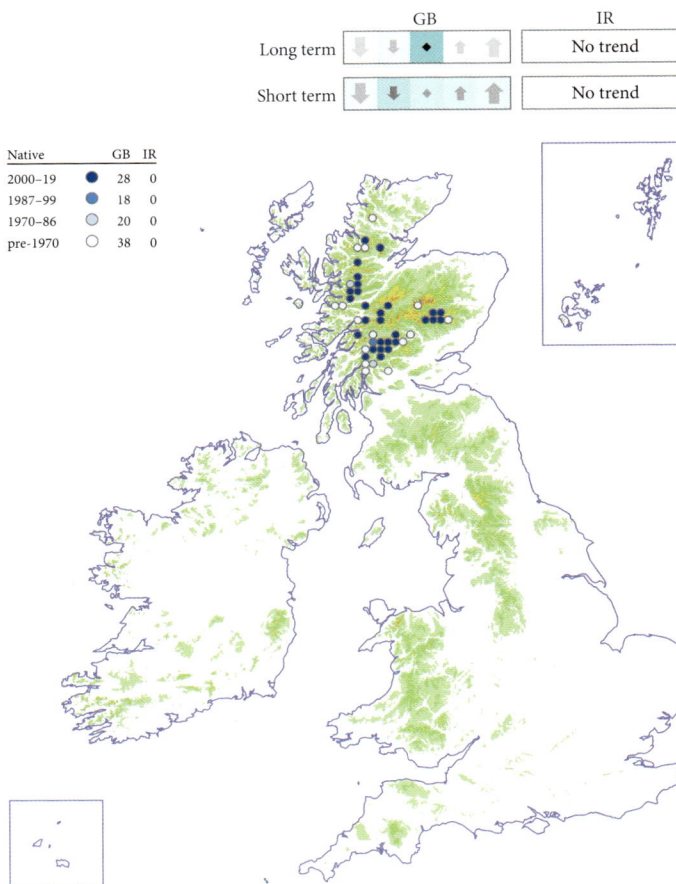

C.A. Stace & J.O. Mountford

(N) *Juncus maritimus* Sea Rush

Lam.

A rhizomatous, clump-forming perennial rush of saltmarshes and saline dune-slacks. It also occurs in areas subject to freshwater seepage on low, exposed rocky cliff-tops and stony sea-loch shores. It is tolerant of a wide range of salinity and soil moisture, occurring at all levels in saltmarshes and in both silty and sandy substrates. Lowland.

Trends *J. maritimus* has been lost since the 1960s from a number of sites on the coasts of southern and eastern England, as well as eastern Scotland, but the distribution is stable elsewhere. *J. maritimus* var. *atlanticus* is confined to the Isles of Scilly.

Biogeography European Southern-temperate element; widely naturalized outside its native range.

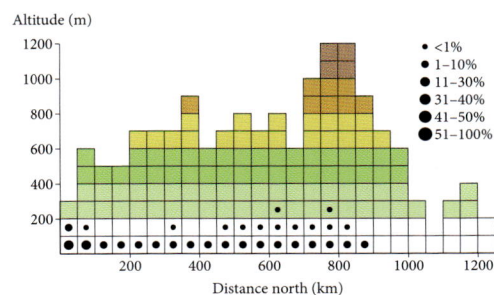

Native	GB	IR
2000–19	323	187
1987–99	306	170
1970–86	193	59
pre-1970	317	119

Alien	GB	IR
2000–19	0	0
1987–99	0	0
1970–86	0	0
pre-1970	1	0

Key refs Snogerup (1993).

C.A. STACE & J.O. MOUNTFORD

(N) *Juncus acutus* Sharp Rush

L.

A tall, tussock-forming perennial rush of saline or brackish dune-slacks, in the uppermost levels of dry saltmarsh and on shingle banks. In Pembrokeshire it also occurs on cliff-tops. There is often little competing vegetation. Lowland.

Trends *J. acutus* seems to be an efficient colonizer and, in Britain, sometimes quickly appears in newly available sites including, very rarely, wet sandy depressions inland. There have been very few 10 km square losses since the 1960s, and the distribution is now better known in southern Ireland. Local losses have resulted from sea-defence works or changing coastlines.

Biogeography Mediterranean-Atlantic element; also in western North America.

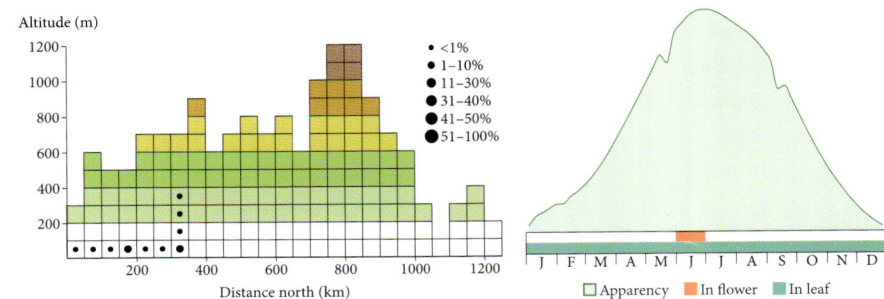

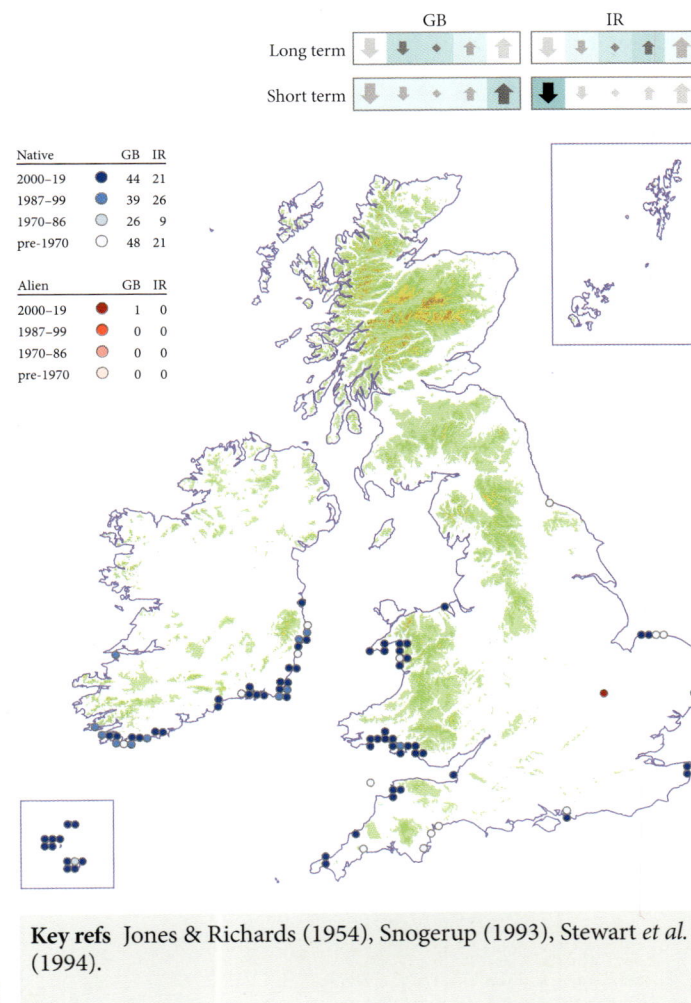

Native	GB	IR
2000–19	44	21
1987–99	39	26
1970–86	26	9
pre-1970	48	21

Alien	GB	IR
2000–19	1	0
1987–99	0	0
1970–86	0	0
pre-1970	0	0

Key refs Jones & Richards (1954), Snogerup (1993), Stewart *et al.* (1994).

C.A. STACE & J.O. MOUNTFORD

(N) *Juncus squarrosus* Heath Rush
L.

A wiry, tufted perennial rush which is characteristic of wet peaty heathland and moorland, raised and valley mires and upland flushes on acidic substrates. It is highly unpalatable to livestock and this has favoured its spread in the uplands. 0–1,190 m (Ben Lawers, Mid Perthshire).

Trends *J. squarrosus* has been lost from many sites in southern and eastern England, due to drainage and agricultural improvement. This decline began in the late 19th century as lowland wet heaths were drained and converted to farmland (Mountford, 1994). Its distribution elsewhere appears to be stable, and it has undoubtedly increased in abundance in upland regions where it has been favoured by the drainage and burning of wet heaths and blanket bogs, and subsequent overgrazing by sheep.

Biogeography Suboceanic Temperate element; also in Greenland.

Native	GB	IR
2000–19	1709	467
1987–99	1654	430
1970–86	993	64
pre-1970	1299	223

Key refs Dupont (1962), Grime *et al.* (2007), Mountford (1994), Welch (1966).

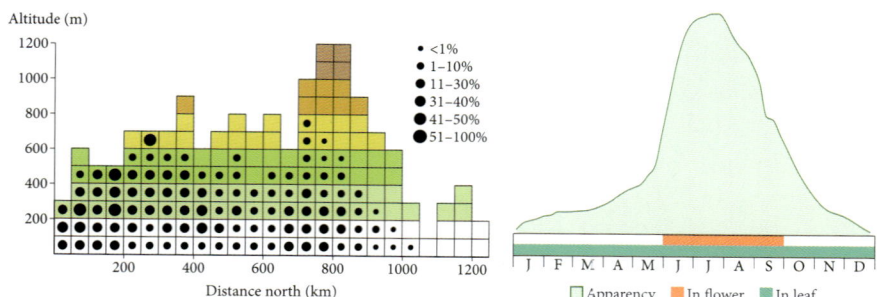

C.A. STACE & J.O. MOUNTFORD

(Ne) *Juncus tenuis* Slender Rush
Willd.

A winter-green, densely tufted perennial herb found on damp open ground on or by roads, tracks and paths, especially along tracks in woodlands, plantations, heathlands and fens, and by lake and pond margins, disused railways, river shingle and on waste ground. Usually on acid soils though not confined to them. Spreading prodigiously by seed. 0–430 m (above Dent station, North-west Yorkshire, and in the Caulderbeck Fells, Cumberland), exceptionally to 680 m (Pumlumon Fawr, Cardiganshire).

Trends This species was first recorded from Angus in 1796, but did not begin to spread widely until the late 19th century. It has never been cultivated in our area and was probably originally introduced in fodder for livestock or soil attached to trees, timber or other raw materials imported from North America. Claims for native status in Ireland are unproven. Since the 1960s it has consolidated its range in northern and western Britain, and markedly expanded its range in Ireland, the English Midlands, East Anglia and southern and eastern Scotland. Both *J. dudleyi* and *J. anthelatus* have been treated as varieties of *J. tenuis* in the past.

Biogeography Native of North and South America.

Alien	GB	IR
2000–19	1294	266
1987–99	828	122
1970–86	470	9
pre-1970	627	59

Key refs Flora of North America Editorial Committee (2000), Richards (1943a), Salisbury (1974).

C.A. STACE & J.O. MOUNTFORD

Juncus compressus Round-fruited Rush

Jacq.

A compact to spreading, rhizomatous perennial rush of marshes, wet meadows and pastures, usually where the sward is kept short by mowing or grazing. Some populations are close to the sea where conditions are brackish, and in these habitats it occasionally grows with *J. gerardii*. It occurs less frequently on the shores of ponds and lakes, on seasonally wet fields recently reverted from arable (as in wetland creation schemes) and on salted roadsides, usually on the very edge of the carriageway. *J. compressus* prefers weakly acid to weakly basic soils. 0–370 m (above Dent station, North-west Yorkshire).

Trends *J. compressus* has always been confused with *J. gerardii*, especially near the sea; in coastal areas it could well be under- or over-recorded. Many recent county Floras record a decline because of drainage and the loss of permanent pastures. Conversely, it has appeared in new sites on the edges of reservoirs, newly created grasslands with livestock and on salted roadsides. It is mapped as native in Ireland, but its status there is uncertain (Scannell & Synnott, 1987). Overall, it appears to be declining, with the main cause a lack of management, especially undergrazing (Walker *et al.*, 2017). However, for at least some of these sites loss could be reversed via a long-lived seed bank if suitable conditions were reinstated.

Biogeography Eurosiberian Temperate element; widely naturalized outside its native range.

Native	GB	IR
2000–19	219	3
1987–99	192	1
1970–86	206	2
pre-1970	335	1

Alien	GB	IR
2000–19	0	0
1987–99	1	0
1970–86	0	0
pre-1970	1	0

Key refs Scannell & Synnott (1987), Stroh *et al.* (2014), Stroh *et al.* (2019), Walker *et al.* (2017).

C.A. STACE & J.O. MOUNTFORD

Juncus gerardii Saltmarsh Rush

Loisel.

A perennial rush of saline habitats, mostly in the uppermost parts of coastal saltmarshes, but also around coastal rock pools, in spray-drenched cliff-top turf and at saline sites inland, including (as a probable native) in ditchsides and pits in Fenland and as an introduction on disturbed ground. Recently it has also colonized salted road verges inland in parts of northern England and Scotland. Lowland, although unintentionally but successfully introduced with other halophytes on a bank below a roadside car park at 575 m at the Hartside Cafe, Cumberland (Corner, 1997) and still present in 2018.

Trends There is little change in the overall 10 km square distribution of *J. gerardii* since the 1960s, although the number of inland records on saline sites has increased. Those on inland road verges have been mapped as native.

Biogeography Circumpolar Wide-temperate element.

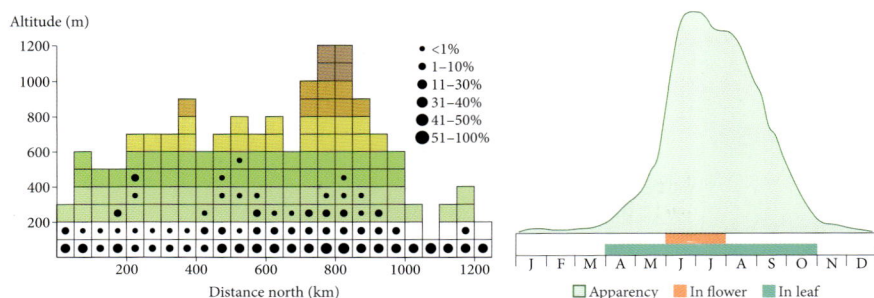

Native	GB	IR
2000–19	859	270
1987–99	792	228
1970–86	454	101
pre-1970	732	177

Alien	GB	IR
2000–19	15	0
1987–99	18	0
1970–86	17	0
pre-1970	9	0

Key refs Corner (1997).

C.A. STACE & J.O. MOUNTFORD

N *Juncus trifidus* Three-leaved Rush
L.

A small, densely tufted perennial rush found in gravelly or bryophyte- or lichen-rich places on mountains on shallow soil or in rock crevices, on both acidic and calcareous substrata. *J. trifidus* is one of the principal angiosperms of wind-swept, often almost snow-free plateau edges over *c.* 1,000 m and less exposed areas that are snow-covered for several months. In Britain this vegetation has been described as *Juncus trifidus–Racomitrium lanuginosum* rush-heath (Rodwell, 1992b). From 240 m on Ronas Hill (Shetland) to 1,305 m on Ben Macdui (South Aberdeenshire).

Trends A number of new populations have been discovered this century within the known range, and the distribution of *J. trifidus* remains stable.

Biogeography Eurosiberian Arctic-montane element; also in North America.

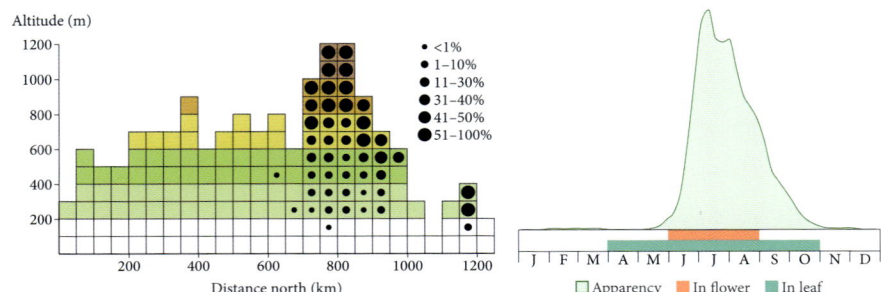

Native	GB	IR
2000–19	141	0
1987–99	138	0
1970–86	87	0
pre-1970	146	0

Key refs Ingram (1958), McVean & Ratcliffe (1962), Rodwell (1992b).

C.A. STACE & J.O. MOUNTFORD

N *Juncus bufonius s.l.*

These annual rushes are found in a wide variety of habitats which are moist or flooded in winter, and where there is some disturbance and little or no competition. This includes the edges of ponds, lakes and marshes, dune-slacks, estuaries, saltmarshes, sandy seashores, and tracks and gateways. 0–650 m Stob na Cruaiche (Main Argyll).

Trends The overall 10 km square range of *J. bufonius s.l.* appears to be stable. The taxonomy of the British and Irish species included in the *J. bufonius* complex (*J. ranarius*, *J. bufonius s.s.* and *J. foliosus*) was elucidated in the 1970s and 1980s, and the many new records this century for these segregates reflects a better understanding by recorders of the distinguishing characters, although in a few areas

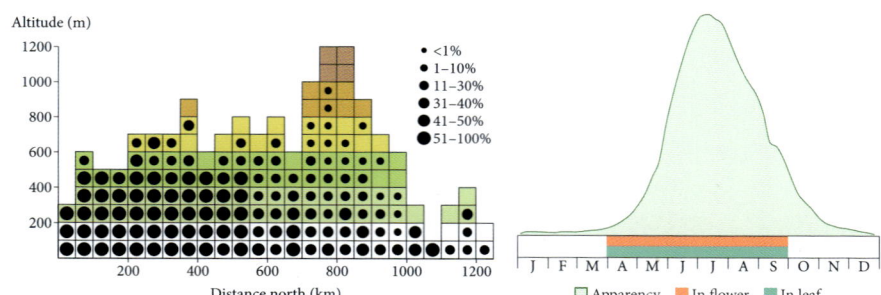

they remain under-recorded where botanists only record the aggregate.

Biogeography The distribution of the segregate species is given in the relevant accounts.

Native	GB	IR
2000–19	2724	945
1987–99	2632	866
1970–86	1724	150
pre-1970	2440	671

Key refs Cope & Stace (1978), Cope & Stace (1983), Cope & Stace (1985), Grime *et al.* (2007).

C.A. STACE & J.O. MOUNTFORD

Ⓝ *Juncus foliosus* Leafy Rush

Desf.

A spring-germinating annual rush and the most robust member of the *J. bufonius* aggregate, occurring in wet fields, marshes and ditches and on the muddy margins of lakes and ponds, sometimes with *J. bufonius s.s.* Although often found near the coast, it appears not to tolerate brackish conditions. 0–410 m (south of Elan, Breconshire).

Trends *J. foliosus* was recognized in Britain as a subspecies in 1959 but did not become widely known until Cope & Stace (1978) treated it as a species. Although almost certainly still under-recorded, there are considerably more records since 2000, both within its core distribution and farther east. The current map indicates a predominantly south-western distribution which fits in with its wider European range and is almost certainly a true reflection of reality.

Biogeography Suboceanic Southern-temperate element.

	GB	IR
Long term	No trend	No trend
Short term	↓	

Native	GB	IR
2000–19	173	144
1987–99	184	59
1970–86	75	13
pre-1970	37	26

Key refs Cope & Stace (1978), Cope & Stace (1983), Cope & Stace (1985), Grime *et al.* (2007).

C.A. STACE & J.O. MOUNTFORD

Ⓝ *Juncus bufonius* Toad Rush

L.

An annual rush of habitats where the water-table is at least seasonally high and there is little competition, including the margins of ponds, lakes, streams and rivers, marshes and dune-slacks, and rarely acid bogs. It also grows around brackish lakes and on estuarine mud- and sand-flats, and is often a weed of disturbed ground, including tracks and roadsides, especially in ruts. 0–650 m Stob na Cruaiche (Main Argyll).

Trends *J. bufonius s.s.* was not separated from other members of the *J. bufonius* aggregate until 1978, and was under-recorded in some areas in the 20th century. It is, however, the most frequent species of the aggregate, and systematic recording since 2000 has confirmed that it occurs throughout the range of the aggregate.

Biogeography Circumpolar Wide-temperate element; widely naturalized outside its native range.

	GB	IR
Long term	No trend	No trend
Short term	↑	◆

Native	GB	IR
2000–19	2626	875
1987–99	2183	730
1970–86	865	79
pre-1970	688	51

Key refs Cope & Stace (1978), Cope & Stace (1983), Cope & Stace (1985), Grime *et al.* (2007).

C.A. STACE & J.O. MOUNTFORD

N *Juncus ranarius* Frog Rush
Songeon & E.P.Perrier

A dwarf, annual, spring-germinating rush of bare damp brackish places near the coast and sometimes inland, often with *J. bufonius s.s.* It is typical of coastal mud- and sand-flats above the high-water mark and of the margins of saline and brackish lakes, and is also found on bare mud and waste ground associated with inland salt-flashes and salt-workings, and on highly basic lime-waste tips. Generally lowland, but up to 525 m on Buttertubs Pass (North-west Yorkshire).

Trends *J. ambiguus* was not separated from *J. bufonius* in Britain until 1978 and is often confused with variants of *J. bufonius s.s.* Although probably still under-recorded in more remote areas of Scotland and western Ireland, the map reflects improved recognition of the taxon and a truer depiction of its distribution.

Biogeography European Southern-temperate element; also in North America.

Key refs Cope & Stace (1978), Cope & Stace (1983), Cope & Stace (1985), Grime *et al.* (2007).

C.A. STACE & J.O. MOUNTFORD

Ne *Juncus subulatus* Somerset Rush
Forssk.

A rhizomatous perennial herb forming large patches in brackish marshes in its native Mediterranean range. In North Somerset it was naturalized in brackish reed-swamp in a dune system for many years; in Stirlingshire, it occurred in a pool on reclaimed dockland. Lowland.

Trends This species was first recorded in Britain in 1954 (Berrow, North Somerset) and its mode of introduction is uncertain. It may have arrived with shipping, and is therefore treated here as a neophyte, but could have been introduced by birds (its closest native localities are on the coast of northern Spain), in which case it would be native to Britain (Willis & Davies, 1960). A second site was found in Scotland in 1983 (Stirlingshire). It showed no sign of spreading beyond its immediate points of entry. *J. subulatus* has not been recorded in Somerset since 1998 though it was well established prior to that; it is presumed extinct in Stirlingshire.

Biogeography A Mediterranean-Atlantic species.

Key refs Stewart (1987), Willis & Davies (1960).

C.A. STACE & J.O. MOUNTFORD

Juncus balticus Baltic Rush
Willd.

A slender perennial rush of dune-slacks and other damp areas in maritime sand, mud or peat, frequently beside river estuaries, in open or closed vegetation. It is also found on bare or grassy upland river terraces, and increasingly along road verges and tracksides. It also occurs inland in north-eastern Scotland on river-terraces or floodplains or in marshes. The plant is rhizomatous, sometimes forming conspicuous lines of stems and rarely forming dense patches. Generally sea level, but reaching 405 m on Slochd Mor (Easterness).

Trends The distribution of *J. balticus* appears to be stable, and is now better recorded throughout its Scottish range, with a notable and continuing expansion of its distribution along road corridors and tracksides, to the extent that it is now more widespread in these habitats than along inland riversides (Amphlett, 2019a). An increase in abundance in its very restricted sites in South Lancashire was reported in the late 20th century and although it has maintained its presence in the core of this population, there is evidence of decline in the outliers. A recent find in South Hampshire is likely to be an accidental introduction.

Biogeography Circumpolar Boreo-arctic Montane element.

Native	GB	IR
2000–19	67	0
1987–99	59	0
1970–86	42	0
pre-1970	75	0

Alien	GB	IR
2000–19	1	0
1987–99	1	0
1970–86	0	0
pre-1970	0	0

	GB	IR
Long term		No trend
Short term		No trend

Key refs Amphlett (2019a), Smith (1984), Stace (1972), Stewart *et al.* (1994).

C.A. STACE & J.O. MOUNTFORD

Juncus filiformis Thread Rush
L.

A rhizomatous perennial rush of stony or silty margins of lakes and reservoirs, mostly in a narrow fringing zone of periodically inundated wet marshy pasture or more open ground. Mainly lowland, but reaching 410 m at Burnhope Reservoir (County Durham).

Trends *J. filiformis* is evidently very effectively dispersed, presumably by wildfowl, as it can appear in newly available habitats far from known sites. It is, however, very easily overlooked due to its thin, often short (and heavily grazed) stems rather sparsely distributed on extended rhizomes, and for this reason may have been somewhat under-recorded. It was known from only five 10 km squares outside the Lake District in the 1950s, but a probable combination of more intensive recording and natural dispersal has resulted in numerous new records in Scotland, from Peeblesshire to the Outer Hebrides, and a first record for Ireland (Lough Allen, County Leitrim).

Biogeography Circumpolar Boreal-montane element.

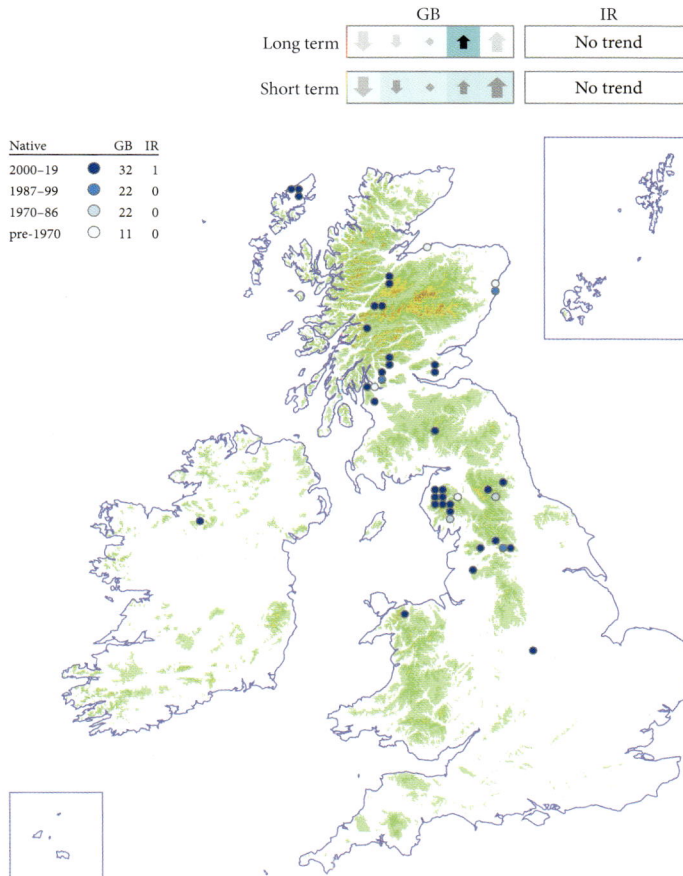

Native	GB	IR
2000–19	32	1
1987–99	22	0
1970–86	22	0
pre-1970	11	0

	GB	IR
Long term		No trend
Short term		No trend

Key refs Blackstock (1981), Richards (1943b), Stewart *et al.* (1994).

C.A. STACE & J.O. MOUNTFORD

(N) *Juncus inflexus* Hard Rush
L.

A clump-forming perennial rush of wet places by rivers, ponds and lakes, and in marshes, wet fields, ditches and occasionally dune-slacks and fens. It is almost always on base-rich soils, frequently on heavy clays, where it replaces *J. effusus*. 0–550 m (Mattergill Sike, Westmorland).

Trends There has been no appreciable change in the 10 km square distribution of this species since the 1960s, although its range is now better known in Ireland due to more systematic recording in recent decades. The absence of *J. inflexus* from parts of England, Wales and Ireland indicates an absence of base-rich substrates whereas most of Scotland lies beyond its northern limit in Europe.

Biogeography Eurosiberian Southern-temperate element; widely naturalized outside its native range.

Native	GB	IR
2000–19	1719	654
1987–99	1692	576
1970–86	1271	75
pre-1970	1506	455

Alien	GB	IR
2000–19	1	0
1987–99	3	0
1970–86	1	0
pre-1970	1	0

Key refs Richards & Clapham (1941a).

C.A. STACE

(Hy) *Juncus effusus* × *inflexus* = *J.* ×*diffusus*
Hoppe

J. effusus and *J. inflexus* often occur together in lowland habitats, but their hybrid is uncommon and usually only present as one or few plants in a population, though it has been recorded as frequent in a marshy pasture at Llechryd (Cardiganshire) where the parents occur (Chater, 2010b). *J. inflexus* normally flowers later than *J. effusus*, and this appears to be a largely effective isolating mechanism. The hybrid is, however, not fully sterile and second or back-cross generations might occur. Lowland to 305 m (Gilcambon Beck, Cumberland).

Trends The majority of pre-1970 records shown here are those mapped by Perring & Sell (1968). The range of the hybrid has not changed since then, but it is easily overlooked and the lack of recent records probably indicates under-recording.

Biogeography Widespread in Europe.

	GB	IR
Long term	No trend	No trend
Short term	No trend	No trend

	GB	IR
2000–19	112	13
1987–99	85	8
1970–86	47	2
pre-1970	215	17

Key refs Chater (2010b), Stace *et al.* (2015).

C.A. STACE, C.D. PRESTON & D.A. PEARMAN

Juncus effusus Soft-rush

L.

A clump-forming perennial rush that grows by the sides of rivers, streams, lakes and ponds, and in marshes, wet grassland, ditches and open wet woodland. It avoids base-rich soils and is most characteristic of sandy and peaty substrates, especially open heathlands and hill-pastures, where it can be dominant and is frequently 'controlled' using herbicides and mowing. It is strongly favoured by disturbance of the soil in wet grassland, regenerating profusely from a very long-lived seed bank. 0–870 m (Meall a'Bhuiridh, Main Argyll).

Trends *J. effusus* is ubiquitous at the 10 km square scale and as such its range has not changed since the 1960s.

Biogeography European Southern-temperate element; also disjunctly in central and eastern Asia and North America and widely naturalized outside its native range.

Native	GB	IR
2000–19	2784	989
1987–99	2742	949
1970–86	2039	213
pre-1970	2628	888

Key refs Grime *et al.* (2007).

C.A. STACE & J.O. MOUNTFORD

Juncus conglomeratus × *effusus* = *J.* ×*kern-reichgeltii*

Jansen & Wacht. ex Reichg.

This hybrid occurs on the shores of lakes and reservoirs and in dune-slacks, wet woodland rides, felled plantations, marshes, fens, wet meadows, damp heathland, flushed hillside slopes and blanket bogs; it also extends into drier acid grassland. Generally lowland, but to 390 m in Carmarthenshire, and up to 520 m at Grafea Elan (Cardiganshire).

A spontaneous hybrid (native × native).

Trends The problems with identifying this hybrid are reflected in the distribution map, which shows numerous records for Carmarthenshire and Cardiganshire, where R.D. Pryce and A.O. Chater have learnt to recognize it, but relatively few records elsewhere. It is often found where the two parents grow together and is, therefore, likely to be greatly under-recorded.

Biogeography Temperate Europe and Newfoundland.

GB	IR
Long term	No trend	No trend
Short term	No trend	No trend

	GB	IR
2000–19	164	11
1987–99	42	6
1970–86	8	1
pre-1970	7	0

Key refs Stace *et al.* (2015).

C.A. STACE, C.D. PRESTON & D.A. PEARMAN

Ⓝ *Juncus conglomeratus* Compact Rush
L.

A clump-forming perennial rush of slightly drier habitats than *J. effusus*, avoiding the wetter places and more acidic soils, being characteristic of damp fields, ditches, open woodland and margins of still or running water. It behaves as a calcifuge in East Anglia (Leslie, 2019) and generally appears less efficient than *J. effusus* at colonizing disturbed sites, such as abandoned arable and degraded pasture. 0–840 (Breadalbanes, Mid Perthshire), and 845 m on Great Dun Fell (Westmorland).

Trends Despite the well-documented morphological differences between *J. effusus* and *J. conglomeratus*, they are still frequently confused. *J. conglomeratus* appears to be genuinely better recorded in Ireland in recent years, but might be somewhat over-recorded throughout its mapped range. Generally, however, the present map indicates a stable

distribution, with Fenland being the only significant region where it appears to be largely absent.

Biogeography European Temperate element; widely naturalized outside its native range.

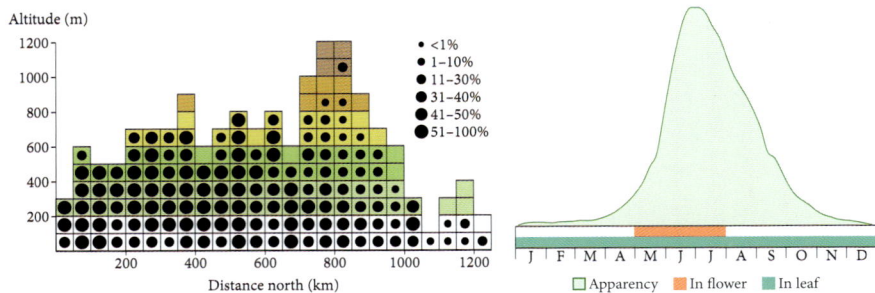

Native	GB	IR
2000–19	2573	868
1987–99	2465	713
1970–86	1540	127
pre-1970	2225	459

Key refs Agnew (1968), Leslie (2019), Richards & Clapham (1941b).

C.A. STACE & J.O. MOUNTFORD

Ⓝ *Luzula forsteri* Southern Wood-rush
(Sm.) DC.

A tufted, grass-like perennial wood-rush of woodlands and other moist but well-drained shaded places, often on roadside banks and in hedgerows. It is most frequent on acidic soils, but avoids the most acidic. Competition is rarely tolerated, and plants usually occur in leaf-litter or moss-dominated sites. It often grows with *L. pilosa*, and appears to have very similar ecological requirements in southern England. Lowland.

Trends There were local losses of *L. forsteri* in the latter part of the 20th century, particularly in south-eastern England, but the overall 10 km square distribution is generally stable, and new records within its core areas have to some extent offset losses. It has recently been recorded in a few native sites outside of its core range, including single localities in Cardiganshire,

where it had not been known since the early 1800s, and Merionethshire. The record from a churchyard near Ullswater (Cumberland) is considered to be an introduction.

Biogeography Submediterranean-Subatlantic element.

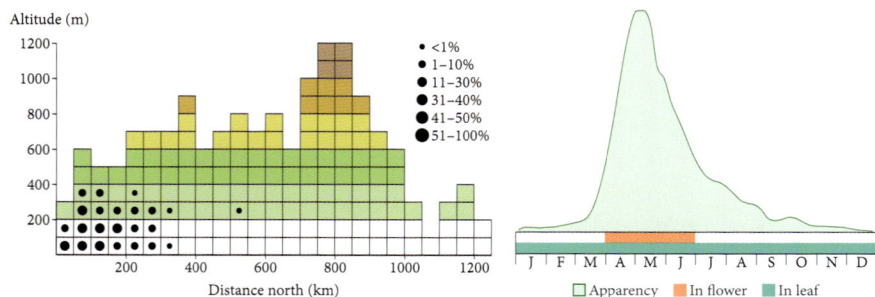

Native	GB	IR
2000–19	264	0
1987–99	251	0
1970–86	158	0
pre-1970	252	0

Alien	GB	IR
2000–19	1	0
1987–99	0	0
1970–86	0	0
pre-1970	0	0

C.A. STACE & J.O. MOUNTFORD

Hy *Luzula forsteri × pilosa = L. ×borreri*
Bromf. ex Bab.

Throughout its range *L. forsteri* is usually found growing with *L. pilosa*, and hybrids are not infrequent since there appear to be no ecological differences between the parents. The hybrids are usually sterile, but some seed is formed and back-crossing is suspected. Lowland.

A spontaneous hybrid (native × native).

Trends The current distribution of this hybrid is probably stable. Though there is a notable lack of records in south-western England, where recent county Floras have been published, it is easily overlooked, and may still be present in 10 km squares for which there are only pre-2000 records. Its discovery at Trefor (Denbighshire) in 2004, and its former presence in Ireland, are remarkable given that both areas lie well outside the range of *L. forsteri*.

Biogeography An uncommon hybrid, recorded in mainland Europe from France and Germany.

	GB	IR
Long term	No trend	No trend
Short term	No trend	No trend

		GB	IR
2000–19	●	40	0
1987–99	●	51	0
1970–86	●	10	0
pre-1970	○	90	1

Key refs Stace *et al.* (2015).

C.A. STACE, C.D. PRESTON & D.A. PEARMAN

N *Luzula pilosa* Hairy Wood-rush
(L.) Willd.

A tufted, grass-like perennial wood-rush of woodlands and other moist but well-drained shaded places, often on roadside-banks and in hedgerows, generally on fairly acidic soils but not confined to them. *L. pilosa* is also found under heather and bracken in upland heathlands. Plants usually occur in leaf-litter or moss-dominated sites, and competition is rarely tolerated. In upland areas, more exposed sites such as quarries, pastures and rough ground are occupied. 0–670 m (Ben Lawers, Mid Perthshire) and possibly higher at Caenlochan (Angus).

Trends This species was mapped as 'all records' in the 1962 *Atlas*. Some decline was noted in the latter half of the 20th century, especially in central and eastern England, but recent intensive recording efforts have to some extent balanced previous losses.

Biogeography Eurosiberian Boreo-temperate element.

Native		GB	IR
2000–19	●	1899	292
1987–99	●	1782	228
1970–86	○	1205	78
pre-1970	○	1747	90

Alien		GB	IR
2000–19	●	1	0
1987–99	●	1	0
1970–86	●	0	0
pre-1970	○	1	0

Key refs Grime *et al.* (2007).

C.A. STACE & J.O. MOUNTFORD

(N) *Luzula sylvatica* Great Wood-rush
(Huds.) Gaudin

A rhizomatous patch-forming perennial wood-rush of damp, acidic, usually shaded habitats, including oak and birch woodlands where it often grows beside running water, on open, peaty heathlands and moorlands, and on rock ledges and rocky streamsides in the mountains. It is intolerant of grazing and is often confined to woods or, in the uplands, rocky outcrops beyond the reach of sheep and deer. In Scotland, it is the favoured nest material of Golden Eagles *Aquila chrysaetos*. 0–1,040 m (Carrauntoohill, South Kerry).

Trends *L. sylvatica* has declined in central and eastern England since the 1960s but its distribution elsewhere appears to be stable and even increasing in some areas, although this may reflect more systematic recording. In some cases it has been difficult for recorders to ascertain the status of a new occurrence, as it may also be found as a garden escape.

Biogeography European Temperate element.

Native	GB	IR
2000–19	1954	666
1987–99	1876	554
1970–86	1135	116
pre-1970	1744	342

Alien	GB	IR
2000–19	21	0
1987–99	5	0
1970–86	0	0
pre-1970	3	0

Key refs McVean & Ratcliffe (1962).

C.A. Stace & J.O. Mountford

(Ne) *Luzula luzuloides* White Wood-rush
(Lam.) Dandy & Wilmott

A tufted, perennial herb, spreading by rhizomes, grown for ornament in large estate gardens and policy woodlands and found naturalized in woodland and other moist shady places, often by streams, but sometimes in open peaty places in upland areas. Generally lowland, but reaching 365 m at Garsdale Head (Westmorland), and exceptionally at 845 m on Great Dun Fell (Westmorland).

Trends *L. luzuloides* was introduced into Britain by 1829 and was recorded from the wild by 1879 (Bletchingley, Surrey). Dunn (1905) described it as "recorded two or three times in England" but since then it has spread or been more systematically recorded, especially in Scotland and northern England.

Biogeography Native of central Europe particularly in the mountains; naturalized farther north, especially in the Nordic countries, and in North America.

Alien	GB	IR
2000–19	71	3
1987–99	57	1
1970–86	57	0
pre-1970	63	1

Key refs Dunn (1905).

C.A. Stace & J.O. Mountford

N *Luzula campestris* Field Wood-rush
(L.) DC.

An early flowering, low-growing, tufted but shortly rhizomatous wood-rush characteristic of short, unshaded, relatively infertile grassland. It is found in a range of grazed or mown, often trampled, grasslands, particularly pastures, meadows, grassy verges and lawns which are moderately acidic to slightly alkaline. Taller grassland, rocky ledges and slopes, and quarries and spoil heaps are also colonized. 0–1,005 m (Carnedd Dafydd, Caernarvonshire).

Trends There has been little change in the 10 km square distribution of this species since the 1960s, save for a better understanding of the distribution in Ireland and northern Scotland due to more systematic recording this century.

Biogeography European Temperate element.

Native	GB	IR
2000–19	2679	893
1987–99	2549	761
1970–86	1645	136
pre-1970	2456	513

Key refs Grime *et al.* (2007).

C.A. STACE & J.O. MOUNTFORD

N *Luzula multiflora* Heath Wood-rush
(Ehrh.) Lej.

An early flowering tufted wood-rush found in a variety of grasslands, preferring more acidic soils and more shaded places than *L. campestris*. It occurs on heathlands and moors and in the drier parts of bogs and mires, in fen-meadows and other grassy places, and in open birchwoods and on wood margins. 0–1,170 m (Ben More, Mid Perthshire).

Trends Although formerly confused with *L. campestris*, this species appears to have declined in central and eastern England since the 1960s due to the loss of lowland heathand and bog communities. Its distribution appears to be stable elsewhere. Three subspecies are recognized in our area: both subsp. *multiflora* and subsp. *congesta* occur throughout the range of the species and often grow together. They are very unevenly recorded and so are not mapped separately here. The recently recognized subsp. *hibernica* is mapped separately.

Biogeography Circumpolar Wide-boreal element; widely naturalized outside its native range.

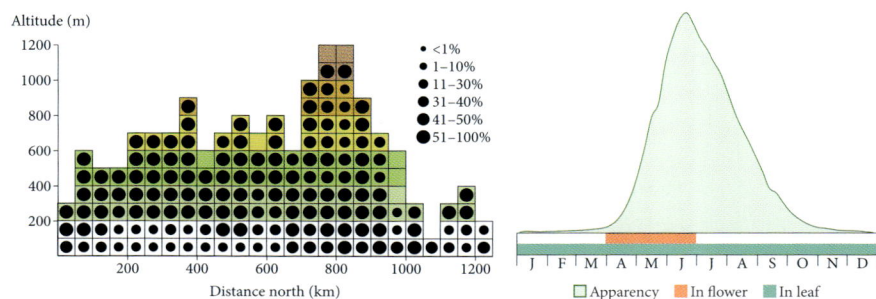

Native	GB	IR
2000–19	2329	857
1987–99	2255	767
1970–86	1438	125
pre-1970	2080	540

Alien	GB	IR
2000–19	2	0
1987–99	2	0
1970–86	1	0
pre-1970	2	0

Key refs Kirschner & Rich (1996).

C.A. STACE & J.O. MOUNTFORD

N *Luzula multiflora* subsp. *hibernica*
Kirschner & T.C.G.Rich

A tetraploid perennial wood-rush of acidic grasslands amongst blanket bogs as well as tracks, road verges, disturbed edges of bogs, open conifer plantations, woodland clearings and secondary woodland. Lowland.

Trends This subspecies has not been mapped previously but appears to be widespread in western Ireland, partly replacing *L. multiflora* subsp. *multiflora*. As it was only recently recognized, it is almost certainly under-recorded. It is possibly derived from the hybrid between *L. campestris* and *L. pallescens*.

Biogeography Endemic to Ireland.

	GB	IR
Long term	No trend	No trend
Short term	No trend	No trend

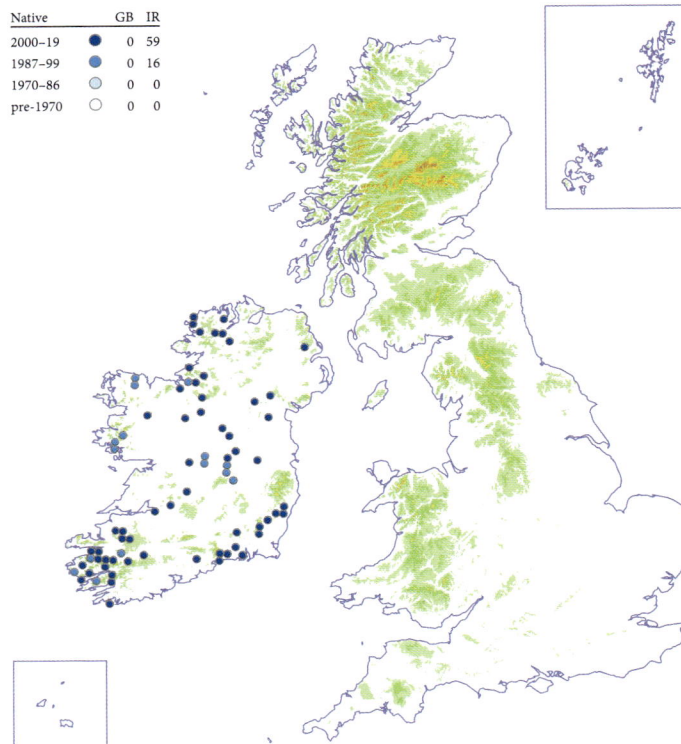

Native		GB	IR
2000–19	●	0	59
1987–99	●	0	16
1970–86	○	0	0
pre-1970	○	0	0

Key refs Kirschner & Rich (1996).

J.O. MOUNTFORD

N *Luzula pallescens* Fen Wood-rush
Sw.

A tufted but shortly rhizomatous wood-rush of drier grassy parts of fens, open peat, and banks, rides and glades in damp peaty woodland, particularly in disturbed ground. Lowland.

Trends *L. pallescens* was discovered in our area in 1907, and is extant at both of its Huntingdonshire sites, with recent records from Holme Fen (2018) and Woodwalton Fen (2011), though it has been feared extinct several times. It is probable that a persistent soil seed bank gives rise to populations following renewed peat disturbance; the most recent sighting at Holme Fen, for example, was on peat recently cleared of *Salix* scrub. A 1970 record from Lough Neagh (County Antrim) is plausible, although no specimen was taken for critical examination. A subsequent search of the site in an attempt to relocate the species found that the habitat had been destroyed (Hackney, 1992).

Biogeography Eurasian Boreo-temperate element, with a continental distribution in western Europe; also in North America and widely naturalized outside its native range.

	GB	IR
Long term	No trend	No trend
Short term	No trend	No trend

Native		GB	IR
2000–19	●	2	0
1987–99	●	2	0
1970–86	○	2	1
pre-1970	○	2	0

Alien		GB	IR
2000–19	●	0	0
1987–99	●	0	0
1970–86	●	0	0
pre-1970	○	1	0

Key refs Hackney (1992), Rich (1994b), Wigginton (1999).

C.A. STACE & J.O. MOUNTFORD

Ⓝ *Luzula arcuata* Curved Wood-rush
(Wahlenb.) Sw.

A dwarf, tufted, shortly rhizomatous and stoloniferous wood-rush of bare windswept rocky summit ridges and plateaux that are mostly kept free of winter snow, where it often grows with *Juncus trifidus*. In high-altitude corries it can occur in areas of snow-lie with greater vegetation cover. From 760 m (Slioch, West Ross) to 1,305 m (Ben Macdui, South Aberdeenshire).

Trends As remote terrain became more accessible to botanists in the 20th century, so *L. arcuata* was found at new sites, but it seems likely there was little change in its overall distribution. Whilst northern Scotland has been broadly well-recorded in recent times, a lack of records this century from West Sutherland reflects the challenges of repeat recording in remote and mountainous terrain, rather than the actual loss of populations.

In general terms, its survival in Britain may be threatened by climate change as Scottish populations are at the absolute southern limit of its European range (Preston, 2007).

Biogeography European Arctic-montane element, but absent from mountains of central Europe; also in eastern Asia and western North America.

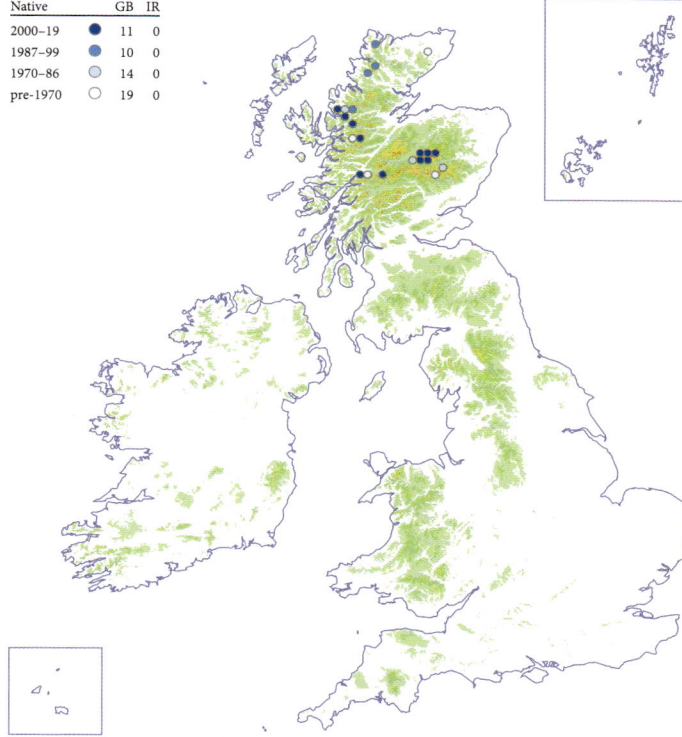

Native	GB	IR
2000–19	11	0
1987–99	10	0
1970–86	14	0
pre-1970	19	0

Key refs Preston (2007), Stewart *et al.* (1994), Wigginton (1999).

J.O. Mountford & C.A. Stace

Altitude (m) chart — legend:
• <1%
• 1–10%
● 11–30%
● 31–40%
● 41–50%
● 51–100%

Distance north (km)

☐ Apparency ■ In flower ■ In leaf

Ⓝ *Luzula spicata* Spiked Wood-rush
(L.) DC.

A dwarf, tufted, shortly rhizomatous and stoloniferous calcifugous wood-rush of barish, open stony ground on mountains, both on flat areas and slopes, cliffs and rock ledges, occasionally washed down rivers and on bulldozed hill tracks. It usually occurs in species-poor localities. From 275 m (Ronas Hill, Shetland) to 1,305 m (Ben Macdui, South Aberdeenshire).

Trends There is little change in the 10 km square distribution of *L. spicata*. The absence of records this century in some previously occupied localities in north-western Scotland is likely to reflect the difficulties in recording in remote and mountainous terrain, rather than actual loss. Two 19th century records from the Lake District shown in the 1962 *Atlas* are not supported by any herbarium material, are now considered dubious and are not mapped.

Biogeography European Arctic-montane element; also in central Asia and North America.

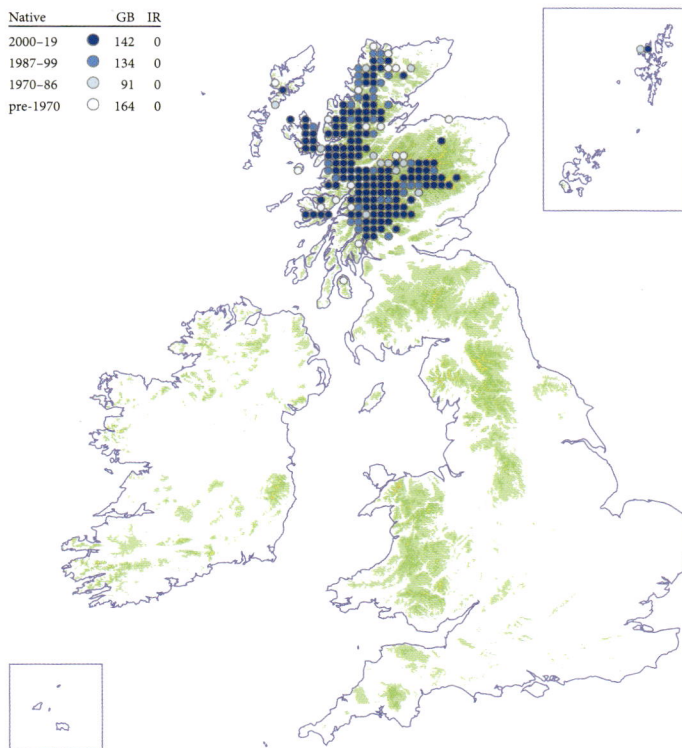

Native	GB	IR
2000–19	142	0
1987–99	134	0
1970–86	91	0
pre-1970	164	0

Altitude (m) chart — legend:
• <1%
• 1–10%
● 11–30%
● 31–40%
● 41–50%
● 51–100%

Distance north (km)

☐ Apparency ■ In flower ■ In leaf

J.O. Mountford

(N) *Eriophorum angustifolium* Common Cottongrass
Honck.

A rhizomatous perennial of open, wet, peaty ground, usually acidic but also occurring in calcareous flushes, sometimes colonizing peat-cuttings and often growing in standing water. Its habitats range from upland blanket bogs and hillside flushes to wet heaths and marshy meadows in the lowlands. 0–1,230 m (Ben Macdui, South Aberdeenshire).

Trends *E. angustifolium* continues to be widespread and abundant in suitable habitat in most of Ireland, Scotland and upland areas of England, even in heaths and bogs that have been degraded by centuries of overgrazing and pollution. However, its range has been considerably reduced in the English lowlands as a result of drainage, groundwater extraction and the cessation of grazing; populations continue to be lost in the 21st century.

Biogeography Circumpolar Wideboreal element.

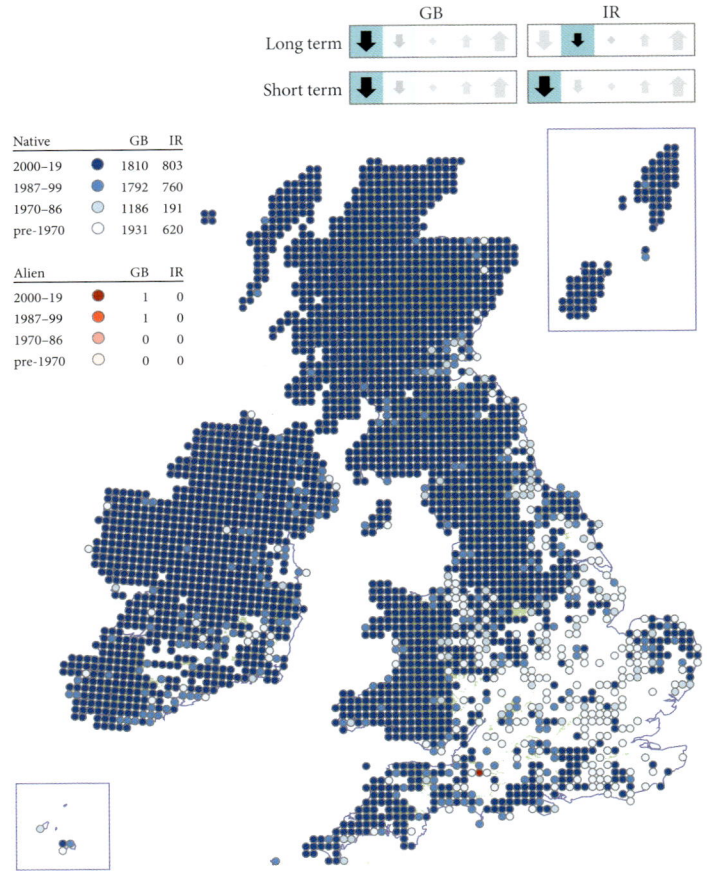

Native	GB	IR
2000–19	1810	803
1987–99	1792	760
1970–86	1186	191
pre-1970	1931	620

Alien	GB	IR
2000–19	1	0
1987–99	1	0
1970–86	0	0
pre-1970	0	0

Key refs Grime *et al.* (2007), Jermy *et al.* (2007), Phillips (1954).

M.S. PORTER & M.J.Y. FOLEY

(N) *Eriophorum latifolium* Broad-leaved Cottongrass
Hoppe

A rhizomatous perennial herb of open sites, growing in wet, base-rich lowland meadows and mires, and in fens and calcareous flushes and mires in the uplands. 0–715 m (Breadalbanes, Mid Perthshire).

Trends *E. latifolium* has suffered a steady decline since early in the 20th century, and losses have continued up until the present day, most notably in lowland areas of England due to drainage, afforestation and agricultural intensification. However, the situation is markedly different in upland areas of Britain, and in Ireland, where many new sites have been discovered in recent decades as a result of more systematic recording.

Biogeography European Boreo-temperate element.

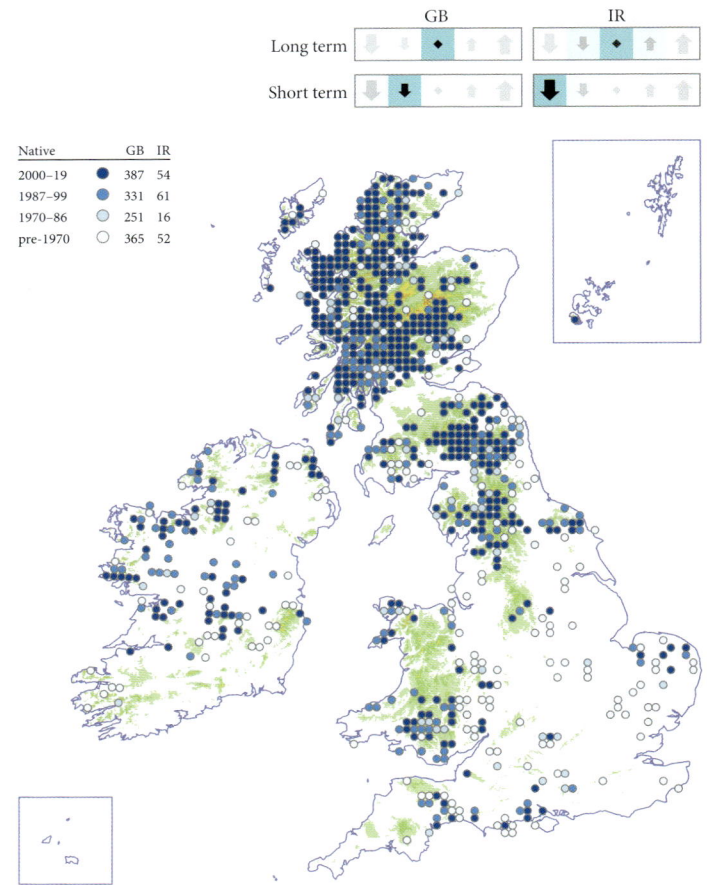

Native	GB	IR
2000–19	387	54
1987–99	331	61
1970–86	251	16
pre-1970	365	52

Key refs Jermy *et al.* (2007).

M.S. PORTER & M.J.Y. FOLEY

Eriophorum gracile Slender Cottongrass

W.D.J.Koch ex Roth

A rhizomatous perennial found in the wettest parts of valley bogs, transitional mires, poor fens, on the edge of alder-carr, typically over liquid peats and, in County Galway, floating rafts of vegetation. Its sites are calcareous or moderately acidic, and have some water movement. Lowland.

Trends In England *E. gracile* formerly occurred in Dorset, Northamptonshire, South Somerset, North-west Yorkshire, Norfolk and North Hampshire but now only survives at one location in Surrey (Peatmoor Pond, where it is still abundant) and three sites in South Hampshire, with plants at one of these locations (Holmsley Bog) appearing in 2004 after an absence of 50 years following scrub removal. In Wales, where it was always a rare species, it persists at a single site in

Glamorganshire (Pant y Sais Fen) and at two sites on the Llŷn Peninsula. In Ireland, where it was first discovered in 1966, its distribution is now much better known, with a number of new sites discovered in recent decades. Drainage, eutrophication, afforestation and infilling are the main factors associated with the loss of this species (Walker, 2003).

Biogeography Circumpolar Boreo-temperate element, with a continental distribution in western Europe; rare and declining in Europe and Fennoscandia.

Native	GB	IR
2000–19	7	13
1987–99	8	14
1970–86	6	9
pre-1970	14	8

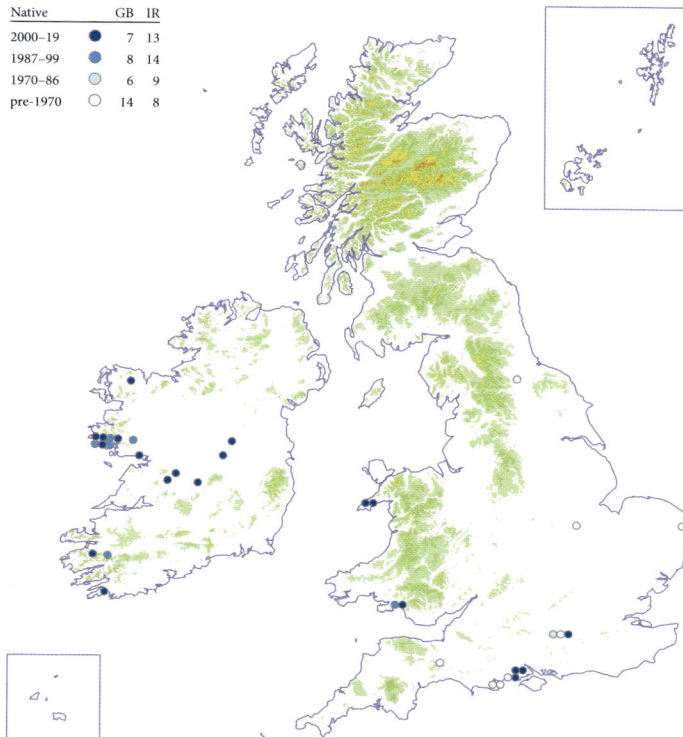

Key refs Conaghan & Sheehy Skeffington (2009), Jermy *et al.* (2007), Kay & John (1995), Walker (2003), Wigginton (1999).

M.S. PORTER & M.J.Y. FOLEY

Eriophorum vaginatum Hare's-tail Cottongrass

L.

A tussock-forming rhizomatous perennial herb of wet heaths and mires, including blanket- and raised bogs. It is characteristic of wet peaty moorlands, often dominant or co-dominant with *Calluna vulgaris*, where it survives, or even increases, after burning. Its sites are always open and almost always acidic. 0–1,070 m (Ben Heasgarnich, Mid Perthshire).

Trends Many lowland sites for *E. vaginatum* had been lost by the early 20th century, and since then, further losses have occurred in England, especially in the north Midlands. The species remains abundant in many areas of northern and western Britain and in Ireland, and it is almost exclusively in these areas that new sites have been discovered this century.

Biogeography Circumpolar Boreo-arctic Montane element.

Native	GB	IR
2000–19	1386	567
1987–99	1305	471
1970–86	757	113
pre-1970	1283	338

Alien	GB	IR
2000–19	1	0
1987–99	0	0
1970–86	1	0
pre-1970	1	0

Key refs Grime *et al.* (2007), Jermy *et al.* (2007), Wein (1973).

M.S. PORTER & M.J.Y. FOLEY

N *Trichophorum alpinum* Cotton Deergrass
(L.) Pers.

		GB	IR
Long term		No trend	No trend
Short term		No trend	No trend

A perennial herb, formerly known from the drier parts of a single bog in Angus. Lowland.

Trends In Britain, *T. alpinum* has only been recorded from the Moss of Restennet (Angus), where it was first discovered in 1791. It was last recorded in 1888, being lost shortly after this, probably as a result of the extraction of marl from the site.

Biogeography Circumpolar Boreal-montane element, with a continental distribution in western Europe.

Native		GB	IR
2000–19	●	0	0
1987–99	●	0	0
1970–86	○	0	0
pre-1970	○	1	0

Key refs Ingram & Noltie (1981), Jermy *et al.* (2007), Lusby (1998), Marren (1999).

M.S. PORTER & M.J.Y. FOLEY

Altitude (m)

Distance north (km)

< 1%
1–10%
11–30%
31–40%
41–50%
51–100%

No data

Apparency   In flower   In leaf

N *Trichophorum cespitosum s.l.* Deergrass
Palla

		GB			IR		
Long term							
Short term							

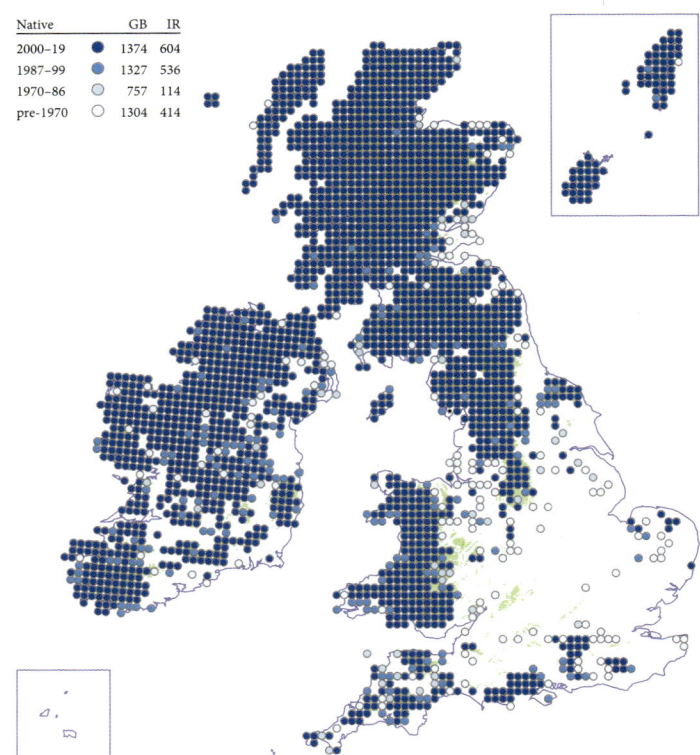

A densely tufted perennial herb of peaty moors and bogs over acidic soils, persisting in burnt and even heavily deer-grazed areas. It is also local on open ground on wet lowland heaths, where it often avoids the wettest sites and favours grazed, burnt and trampled areas. 0–1,190 m (above Caenlochan, Angus).

Trends The map presented here includes *T. cespitosum s.s.*, *T. germanicum* and their hybrid. *T. germanicum* was widely recognized as distinct from *T. cespitosum* subsp. *cespitosum* by the end of the 20th century (Swan, 1999), and the vast majority of historical records shown here are likely to refer to *T. germanicum*. Whilst declines have continued on the lowland heaths of southern and eastern England, mainly because of drainage, numbers have been maintained in all upland areas of Britain and in much of Ireland. In these damper upland areas and in southern lowland bogs it remains common and widespread.

Biogeography Native of north-western Europe as far east as the island of Bornholm in the Baltic Sea.

Native		GB	IR
2000–19	●	1374	604
1987–99	●	1327	536
1970–86	○	757	114
pre-1970	○	1304	414

Key refs Hollingsworth & Swan (1999), Jermy *et al.* (2007), Swan (1999).

M.S. PORTER & F.J. ROBERTS

Altitude (m)

Distance north (km)

< 1%
1–10%
11–30%
31–40%
41–50%
51–100%

Apparency   In flower   In leaf

(N) *Trichophorum cespitosum* Northern Deergrass
(L.) Hartm.

A perennial herb of stony, calcareous springs and flushes, mineral-rich seepage areas around basin mires and on the deep peat of basin and valley mires. From near to sea level (Fish House Moss, Westmorland) to 620 m (Scotsman's Knowe, North Northumberland).

Trends This taxon was traditionally included in national Floras as *T. cespitosum* subsp. *cespitosum*, and has only more recently been recognized as distinct from *T. germanicum* at specific level (Swann, 1999). It has, therefore, only recently become better known to British and Irish botanists and thus its distribution is not yet fully established. Many sites have been added since 2000 in northern England, Scotland and Ireland. The hybrid with *T. germanicum* often occurs with *T. cespitosum* s.s. but is more widespread.

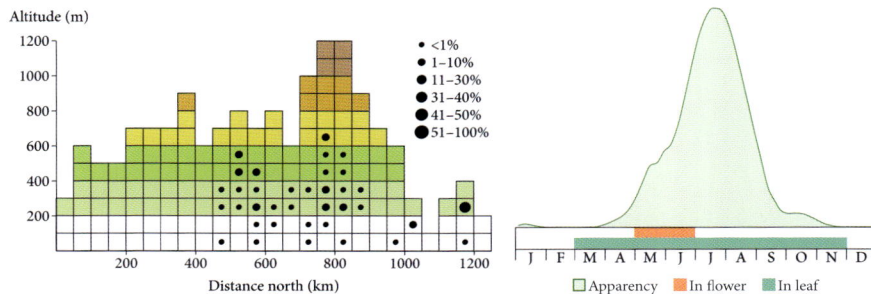

Biogeography *T. cespitosum* s.s. occurs throughout the Circumpolar Boreal-montane range of the species, except in those areas of north-western Europe where it is replaced by *T. germanicum*. It also occurs in the Himalayas, North America and Greenland.

	GB	IR
Long term	No trend	No trend
Short term		

Native		GB	IR
2000–19	●	47	21
1987–99	●	6	0
1970–86	●	1	0
pre-1970	○	6	4

Key refs Hollingsworth & Swan (1999), Jermy *et al.* (2007), Swan (1999).

M.S. PORTER & F.J. ROBERTS

(Hy) *Trichophorum cespitosum × germanicum = T. ×foersteri*
(Swan) D.A.Simpson

This hybird occupies the full spectrum of damp habitats between those of the parent species (Roberts, 2009a), including intact raised mires, basin and valley bog communities, seepages, whether over deep peat or rock, and base-rich flushes. At the calcareous extreme, it is found in the mires of Widdybank Fell (County Durham), growing in open vegetation on residual peaty hummocks and the sides of runnels with several rare Arctic-montane calcicoles, with *T. cespitosum* often just below in the more obvious seepages. It has a wide altitudinal range, reaching 1,050 m on Ben Lawers (Mid Perthshire), well above the known maximum for *T. cespitosum* (620 m) but approaching that for *T. germanicum* (1,190 m).

A spontaneous hybrid (native × native).

Trends *T. cespitosum* was a poorly understood taxon in our area until Swan (1999) clarified its taxonomy and described the hybrid as *T. cespitosum* nothosubsp. *foersteri*. Our knowledge of the distribution of both parent taxa and the hybrid is still very incomplete, but it is clear that the hybrid is much more frequent and widespread than *T. cespitosum*.

Biogeography Known from Norway, Belgium, the Netherlands and Germany.

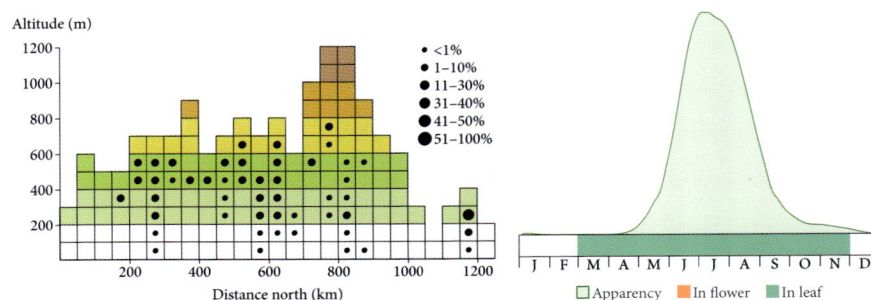

	GB	IR
Long term	No trend	No trend
Short term	No trend	No trend

		GB	IR
2000–19	●	68	18
1987–99	●	52	0
1970–86	●	3	0
pre-1970	○	36	4

Key refs Roberts (2009a), Stace *et al.* (2015), Swan (1999).

C.A. STACE, C.D. PRESTON & D.A. PEARMAN

N *Bolboschoenus maritimus* Sea Club-rush

(L.) Palla

A rhizomatous perennial herb mainly of saline ground or in shallow brackish water, usually rooted in mud but sometimes in gravel and shingle. Coastal habitats include pools in saltmarshes, tidal riverbanks, creeks, ditches, lakes, ponds, borrow-pits, and also marshes and damp pastures. It is occasionally found in freshwater habitats inland, including reservoirs, flooded riversides, and clay- and gravel-pits where it has sometimes been introduced. It reproduces by rhizomatous spread, tubers and seed. Lowland.

Trends The overall distribution of *B. maritimus* is stable, and numbers are being maintained in coastal sites. It appears to have been lost from some of its inland sites, although at some locations plants have recently been redetermined as

B. laticarpus. It is sometimes planted deliberately in lakes and ponds.

Biogeography Eurosiberian Southern-temperate element; widely naturalized outside its native range.

Native	GB	IR
2000–19	700	222
1987–99	638	193
1970–86	411	59
pre-1970	592	117

Alien	GB	IR
2000–19	46	0
1987–99	27	0
1970–86	11	0
pre-1970	16	0

Key refs Jermy *et al.* (2007), Preston & Croft (1997).

M.S. PORTER & M.J.Y. FOLEY

N? *Bolboschoenus laticarpus* Inland Club-rush

Marhold, Hroudová, Ducháček & Zákr.

A perennial herb found in a range of inland wetlands, including rivers and watercourses, meres, ponds, ornamental lakes, reservoirs and gravel-pits. Lowland.

Trends Although *B. laticarpus* has been present in Britain for more than 150 years it has only recently been described, and the differences between it and *B. maritimus* clearly delineated. Consequently, its range is still imperfectly known but, in its continental range, it is increasing in abundance and colonizing a wider range of habitats and this may also be occurring here. Due to uncertainty over its origin, all records are mapped as 'present', without status assigned.

Biogeography Native of western, central and southern Europe, extending

northwards to the Baltic Sea and to the Urals in the east.

	GB	IR
2000–19	31	0
1987–99	2	0
1970–86	2	0
pre-1970	8	0

	GB	IR
Long term	No trend	No trend
Short term	No trend	No trend

Key refs Rumsey *et al.* (2019).

M.S. PORTER

N *Scirpus sylvaticus* Wood Club-rush

L.

A robust rhizomatous perennial herb which may form extensive stands in swampy valley woodlands and similar shady places; also in wet pastures bordering woods and streams, and on the margins of rivers, streams, lakes and ponds. It typically grows over thick, rather eutrophic silts which are often iron-enriched (Rodwell, 1991). Lowland, reaching 315 m at Bellcrag Flow (South Norhtumberland).

Trends This species has suffered a steady and continuing general decline since the 1960s Although new records made since the turn of the century have gone some way to redressing the balance, losses from known sites have continued, though perhaps at a lesser rate. In some areas it may suffer from heavy grazing by cattle or competition from rank vegetation on riverbanks.

Biogeography Eurosiberian Temperate element.

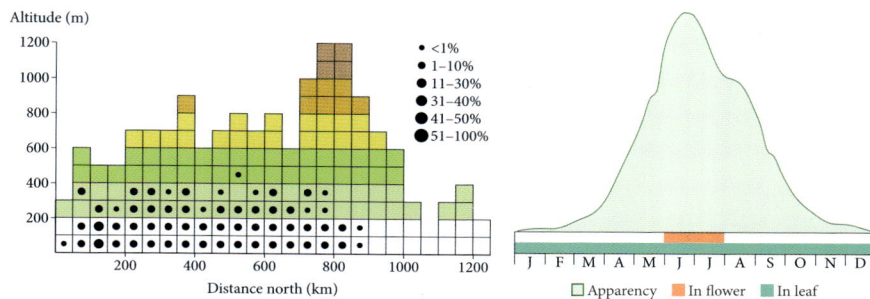

Native		GB	IR
2000–19	●	598	34
1987–99	●	552	56
1970–86	●	469	36
pre-1970	○	614	56

Alien		GB	IR
2000–19	●	7	0
1987–99	●	0	0
1970–86	●	0	0
pre-1970	○	0	0

Key refs Jermy *et al.* (2007), Rodwell (1991).

M.S. PORTER & M.J.Y. FOLEY

N *Schoenoplectus lacustris* Common Club-rush

(L.) Palla

A rhizomatous perennial herb of standing or flowing fresh water, in conditions ranging from eutrophic and base-rich to oligotrophic and base-poor. Substrates include silt, clay, peat or gravel. It occurs in ponds, lakes, canals, dykes and slow-moving rivers, usually in water 0·3–1·5 m deep, but it can also be found at greater depths. Generally lowland, but reaching 405 m at Dock Tarn (Cumberland).

Trends The distribution of *S. lacustris* is very similar to that shown in the 1962 *Atlas*, where it was mapped as 'all records'. Although there were local losses during the second half of the 20th century, particularly in south-eastern England, many of these have been balanced by discoveries made since 2000, although some of these new records may have resulted from planting.

Biogeography Eurosiberian Wide-temperate element.

Native		GB	IR
2000–19	●	965	492
1987–99	●	979	469
1970–86	●	634	118
pre-1970	○	841	304

Alien		GB	IR
2000–19	●	27	1
1987–99	●	16	0
1970–86	●	2	0
pre-1970	○	5	0

Key refs Jermy *et al.* (2007), Preston & Croft (1997).

M.J.Y. FOLEY & M.S. PORTER

N ***Schoenoplectus tabernaemontani*** Grey Club-rush
(C.C.Gmel.) Palla

A rhizomatous perennial herb, most frequent in coastal sites where it grows in brackish water in rivers, dykes, tidal channels, lagoons and dune-slacks; also in depressions in saltmarsh and in wet pasture. Inland, it occurs by lakes, ponds, slow-flowing rivers, streams and canals, and in flooded quarries and pits. Lowland.

Trends The marked increase in inland sites noted in the second half of the 20th century has continued, perhaps in part due to better recording now that its ability to grow inland is appreciated more widely. There are also new records from coastal sites, especially in south-eastern Ireland. It may have been planted at some of its inland sites.

Biogeography Eurasian Southern-temperate element.

Native		GB	IR
2000–19	●	649	164
1987–99	●	539	165
1970–86	●	369	42
pre-1970	○	437	96

Alien		GB	IR
2000–19	●	23	0
1987–99	●	10	0
1970–86	●	1	0
pre-1970	○	7	0

	GB	IR
Long term		
Short term		

Key refs Jermy *et al.* (2007), Preston & Croft (1997).

M.S. PORTER & M.J.Y. FOLEY

Altitude (m) / Distance north (km) histogram with dot-size legend (<1%, 1–10%, 11–30%, 31–40%, 41–50%, 51–100%); Apparency / In flower / In leaf phenology chart.

N ***Schoenoplectus triqueter*** Triangular Club-rush
(L.) Palla

A tussock-forming, rhizomatous perennial herb of mud-banks along the lower reaches of tidal rivers, where it may become submerged at the highest tides. It may be associated with freshwater seepage lines. Lowland.

Trends Populations of *S. triqueter* have been lost to land reclamation and as a result of bank construction. Plants on the Thames were last seen in 1939 and the last surviving English population on the River Tamar (South Devon) finally disappeared in 2010. At this site, contributing factors to its loss are thought to include the absence of open muddy riverbank habitat, nutrient enrichment leading to an expansion of reedswamp, and erosion. However, in the 1980s a few plants from the Tamar were taken into cultivation as a precaution, and in 1997/8 stock derived from this source was introduced at five locations. Only one of these populations survived, and in 2010 a further five sites were planted out. *S. triqueter* is still present in Ireland by the River Shannon (County Limerick) and its tributaries, where populations are considerably larger than in Britain, though some are threatened by development.

Biogeography Eurasian Temperate element.

	GB	IR
Long term	No trend	No trend
Short term	No trend	No trend

Native		GB	IR
2000–19	●	1	4
1987–99	●	1	4
1970–86	●	1	2
pre-1970	○	8	3

Alien		GB	IR
2000–19	●	2	0
1987–99	●	0	0
1970–86	●	0	0
pre-1970	○	0	0

Key refs French (2020), Jermy *et al.* (2007), Preston & Croft (1997), Rich & Fitzgerald (2002), Smith *et al.* (2016), Wigginton (1999).

M.S. PORTER & M.J.Y. FOLEY

Altitude (m) / Distance north (km) histogram with dot-size legend (<1%, 1–10%, 11–30%, 31–40%, 41–50%, 51–100%); Apparency / In flower / In leaf phenology chart.

N? *Schoenoplectus pungens* Sharp Club-rush
(Vahl) Palla

A rhizomatous perennial herb that was formerly known from the margin of a coastal lake in Jersey, where it was thought to be native, and from a wet, coastal dune-slack near Ainsdale (South Lancashire) where it is likely to have been introduced. Lowland.

Native or alien in the Channel Islands and a neophyte in Britain.

Trends *S. pungens* was first recorded in our area in 1724 in Jersey. It declined there and was last seen in the early 1970s. It was first collected at Ainsdale in 1909, and in 1928 a large patch occurred in a dune-slack. Its origin there is obscure and it became extinct by 1978. Ainsdale stock survived in cultivation, however, and in 1990 was planted at four suitable sites at Birkdale on the same area of coast. At two of these it thrived and subsequently spread naturally to adjacent areas.

Biogeography European Temperate element; widespread in North America.

	GB	IR
Long term	No trend	No trend
Short term	No trend	No trend

Native	GB	IR
2000–19	0	0
1987–99	0	0
1970–86	1	0
pre-1970	1	0

Alien	GB	IR
2000–19	1	0
1987–99	1	0
1970–86	3	0
pre-1970	2	0

Key refs Jermy *et al.* (2007), Preston & Croft (1997), Smith (2005).

M.S. PORTER & M.J.Y. FOLEY

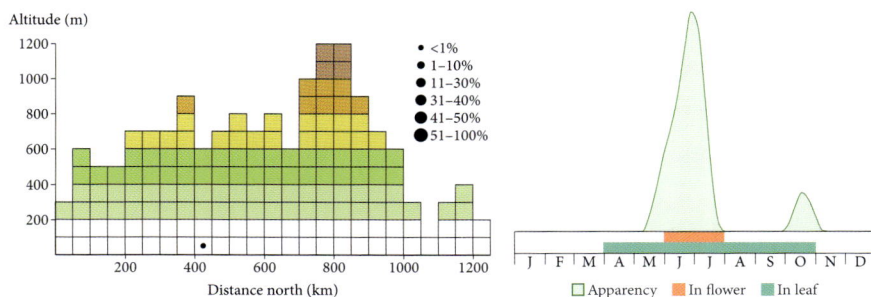

N *Eleocharis palustris* Common Spike-rush
(L.) Roem. & Schult.

An emergent rhizomatous perennial herb, found on the margins of ponds, lakes, slow-flowing rivers and streams, in fens, marshes, swamps and wet meadows, and in ditches, dune-slacks and saltmarshes. It grows in a wide range of organic and mineral soils, but rarely on acidic peat. It spreads by rhizomes and reproduces by seed. 0–585 m at Loch Fender (Mid Perthshire).

Trends The distribution of *E. palustris* is stable, and many sites thought to be lost in the latter half of the 20th century have been refound since 2000. Subsp. *vulgaris* is found throughout the range of the species. Subsp. *palustris* is mapped separately.

Biogeography Eurasian Wide-temperate element.

Native	GB	IR
2000–19	2404	758
1987–99	2384	675
1970–86	1559	147
pre-1970	2055	440

Alien	GB	IR
2000–19	3	0
1987–99	4	0
1970–86	0	0
pre-1970	4	0

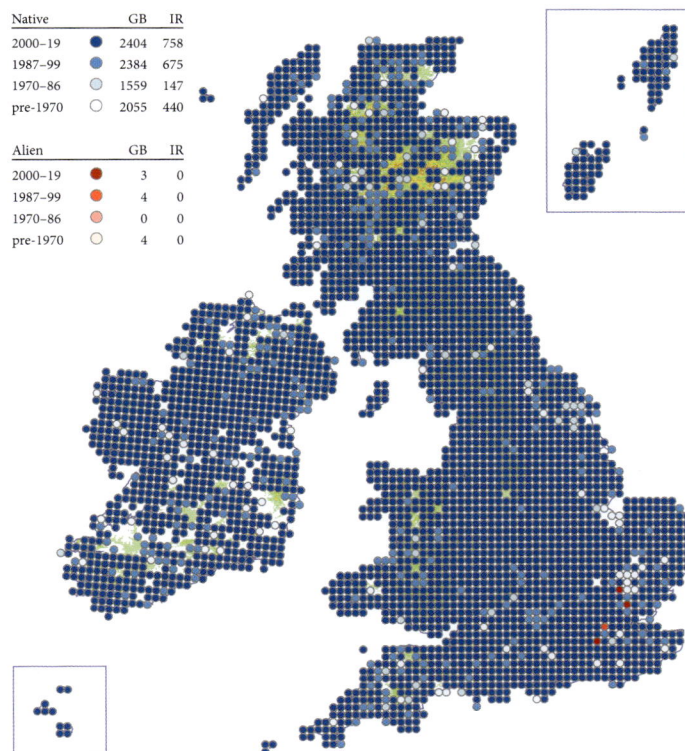

Key refs Grime *et al.* (2007), Jermy *et al.* (2007), Preston & Croft (1997).

M.S. PORTER & F.J. ROBERTS

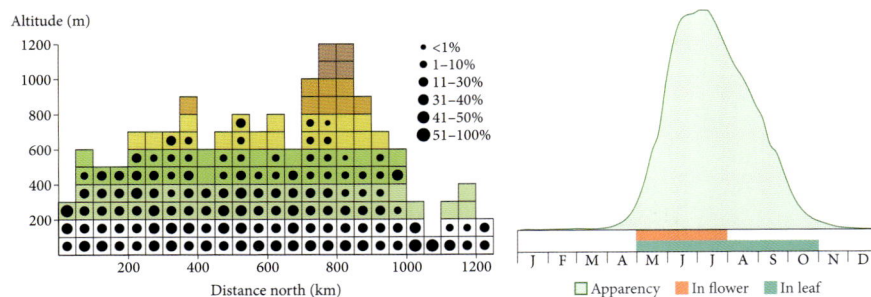

N *Eleocharis palustris* subsp. *palustris*

	GB	IR
Long term	No trend	No trend
Short term	No trend	No trend

A rhizomatous perennial herb found on the margins of ponds, lakes and rivers, and in fens, marshes, wet meadows and ditches. It does not appear to be ecologically distinct from subsp. *vulgaris* and, indeed, is often found growing with it. Lowland.

Trends Both subspecies of *E. palustris* are very poorly recorded. Subsp. *palustris* was mapped by Perring & Sell (1968) using records collected by S.M. Walters, and there have been very few new records since then. It has apparently been lost from some sites where it was known to Walters, and a detailed survey is required to establish its current distribution.

Biography Subsp. *palustris* is more widespread than subsp. *vulgaris* in Europe, extending from northern Scandinavia to the Mediterranean region.

Native	GB	IR
2000–19	2	0
1987–99	3	0
1970–86	1	0
pre-1970	23	0

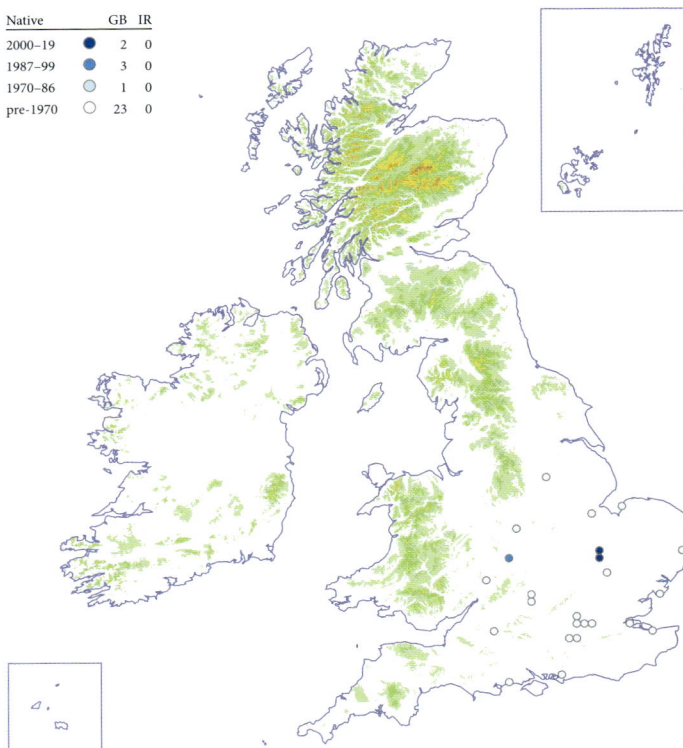

Altitude (m)

- <1%
- 1–10%
- 11–30%
- 31–40%
- 41–50%
- 51–100%

Key refs Jermy *et al.* (2007), Preston & Croft (1997), Walters (1949a).

M.S. PORTER, D.A. PEARMAN & F.J. ROBERTS

☐ Apparency ☐ In flower ☐ In leaf

N *Eleocharis mamillata* subsp. *austriaca* Northern Spike-rush
(Hayek) Strandh.

	GB	IR
Long term	No trend	No trend
Short term	⬇	No trend

A rhizomatous perennial herb found in the middle reaches of upland rivers, usually in slacker water in places which are to some extent protected from spates, such as in shallow bays. It also grows in ditches, pools, runnels, springs and flooded areas of abandoned quarries. The substrate is usually gravel with some silt deposition. It has two centres of population: the Scottish and English Borders, and the valleys of the Rivers Wharfe and Ribble in the Yorkshire Dales. 60–375 m (near Bewcastle, Cumbria).

Trends *E. mamillata* subsp. *austriaca* was discovered near Buckden in Wharfedale (Mid-west Yorkshire) in 1947, but not recognized until 1960. A number of new sites were subsequently discovered, some only to be lost again as the plant responded to changed conditions. The greater frequency of

spates due to altered land-use and climate change threatens its survival in its riverine habitat. Since 2000, seven new locations have been found, all within or close to the known range.

Biogeography European Boreal-montane element.

Native	GB	IR
2000–19	13	0
1987–99	12	0
1970–86	11	0
pre-1970	9	0

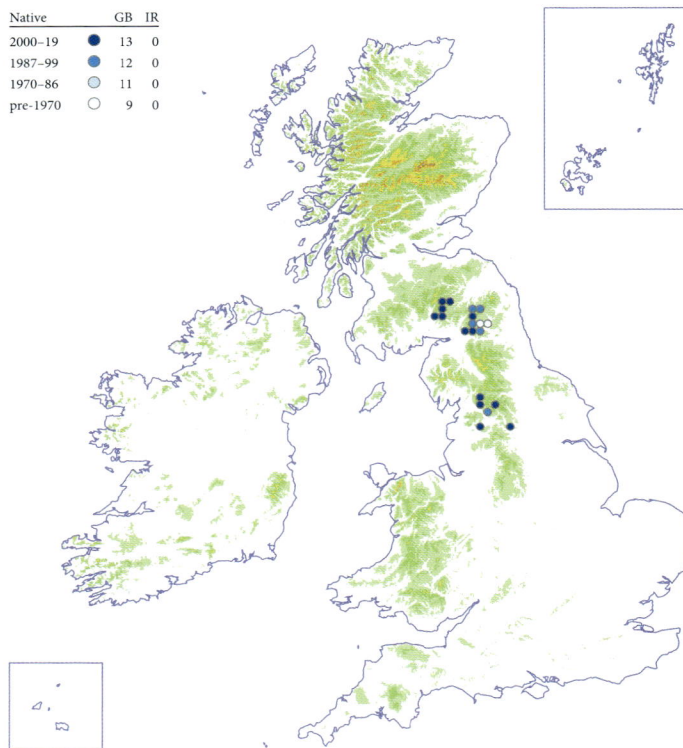

Altitude (m)

- <1%
- 1–10%
- 11–30%
- 31–40%
- 41–50%
- 51–100%

Key refs Jermy *et al.* (2007), Walters (1963), Wigginton (1999).

☐ Apparency ☐ In flower ☐ In leaf

M.S. PORTER & F.J. ROBERTS

Eleocharis uniglumis Slender Spike-rush
(Link) Schult.

A rhizomatous perennial herb, predominantly of coastal habitats, growing in damp dune-slacks, saltmarshes, short, brackish grassland and pools in the spray zone. It also occurs inland in base-rich wet meadows and upland calcareous marshes, and locally, as in Oxfordshire, by springs with higher than normal sodium content. Generally lowland, but reaching 325 m at Ponterwyd (Cardiganshire), and 420 m at Malham Tarn (Mid-west Yorkshire).

Trends The coastal distribution of *E. uniglumis* has probably remained stable, although it is much better recorded in recent years. It was lost from many of its inland sites during the 20th century, and although there have been some new inland sites discovered this century, or populations refound,

the majority of new records since 2000 have been from coastal locations.

Biogeography Circumpolar Temperate element.

Native	GB	IR
2000–19	461	112
1987–99	383	82
1970–86	230	19
pre-1970	312	41

Alien	GB	IR
2000–19	0	0
1987–99	1	0
1970–86	0	0
pre-1970	0	0

Key refs Jermy *et al.* (2007), Walters (1949a).

M.S. PORTER & F.J. ROBERTS

Eleocharis multicaulis Many-stalked Spike-rush
(Sm.) Desv.

A densely tufted perennial herb mainly of acid bogs, wet heath, valley mires, pools, seepages and wet hollows over peat, and at the edge of acidic lakes; also occurring in coastal dune-slacks. 0–610 m (Macgillycuddy's Reeks, South Kerry) and potentially higher on Ben Lawers (Mid Perthshire).

Trends Many sites for *E. multicaulis* were lost in the 19th century, due to drainage and changes in land use, and losses continued throughout the 20th century, most notably in eastern England and eastern Scotland. However, this rather inconspicuous species continues to be much better recorded in the uplands. In the late 1980s and 1990s, for example, it was known from over six times as many 10 km squares in Wales as it was in the first half of that century, and this trend appears to be

continuing across its range, especially in western regions, with numerous new sites found since 2000 in Ireland, Wales, south-western England and Scotland.

Biogeography Suboceanic Temperate element.

Native	GB	IR
2000–19	688	292
1987–99	687	261
1970–86	379	44
pre-1970	646	207

Key refs Jermy *et al.* (2007).

M.S. PORTER & F.J. ROBERTS

1291

Eleocharis quinqueflora Few-flowered Spike-rush

(Hartmann) O.Schwarz

A perennial herb of base-rich marshes and fens, calcareous mires on peaty soils, gravelly and muddy calcareous flushes with seeping water and by wet paths; also in coastal cliff-flushes, dune-slacks and in the upper parts of saltmarshes. It requires open sites and is often dependent on grazing, cutting or disturbance. 0–975 m (Meall Garbh, East Perthshire).

Trends Many lowland sites for this species were lost in the 19th century and 20th century due to the drainage of wetland sites and a lack of grazing. Since 2000 numerous new records have been made, but these are almost all in areas where the species was already well-represented. It remains very sparse in much of eastern and southern England and southern Ireland.

Biogeography European Boreo-temperate element; also in central and eastern Asia and North America.

Native	GB	IR
2000–19	982	179
1987–99	882	178
1970–86	554	60
pre-1970	883	147

Altitude (m)	
•	<1%
•	1–10%
●	11–30%
●	31–40%
●	41–50%
●	51–100%

Distance north (km)

Apparency | In flower | In leaf

Key refs Jermy *et al.* (2007).

M.S. Porter & F.J. Roberts

Eleocharis acicularis Needle Spike-rush

(L.) Roem. & Schult.

A rhizomatous perennial herb growing on the margins of lakes, ponds, reservoirs, lodes, canals and rivers, in sites subject to winter flooding, and fully aquatic in shallow, still or slow-moving mesotrophic to eutrophic water. It roots into sand, gravel, mud or silt, often forming extensive lawns, but flowering only when exposed by falling water levels. Generally lowland but reaching 405 m at Loch Beanie (East Perthshire).

Trends Submerged populations of *E. acicularis* are often overlooked. Furthermore, this species can reappear in former sites when conditions become suitable, and can colonize newly flooded sand- and gravel-pits. However, although under-recording may make the situation seem worse than it is, there can be no doubt that *E. acicularis* has been lost from many sites, probably as a result of ponds drying out or becoming

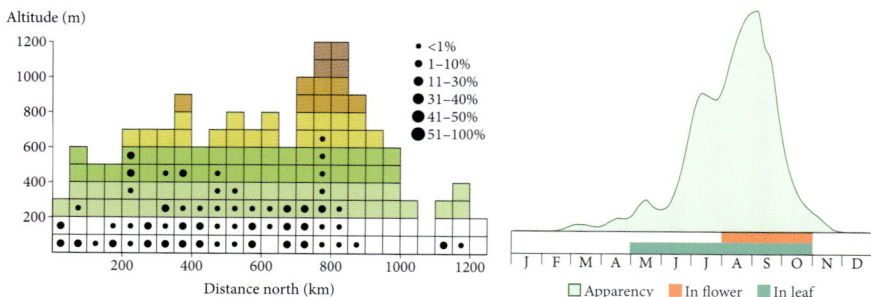

overgrown, or the destruction of sites by agricultural and urban developments.

Biogeography Circumpolar Boreo-temperate element.

Native	GB	IR
2000–19	156	56
1987–99	150	43
1970–86	123	26
pre-1970	292	65

Altitude (m)	
•	<1%
•	1–10%
●	11–30%
●	31–40%
●	41–50%
●	51–100%

Distance north (km)

Apparency | In flower | In leaf

Key refs Jermy *et al.* (2007), Preston & Croft (1997), Stewart *et al.* (1994).

M.S. Porter & F.J. Roberts

N *Eleocharis parvula* Dwarf Spike-rush

(Roem. & Schult.) Link ex Bluff, Nees & Schauer

A diminutive rhizomatous perennial growing on firm estuarine mud by tidal rivers and in tidal pans in brackish grazing marshes. It occurs close to the upper limit of tidal influence, avoiding strongly saline areas. It reproduces vegetatively by turions, and by seed, but flowering and fruiting are very poor in many localities. Lowland.

Trends Colonies of *E. parvula* have been lost due to dredging and the cessation of grazing, which allows the development of taller vegetation. It appears to have gone from some of its sites in north Wales and southern England, and there have been no records in Ireland since 1992. However, the discovery of sites in northern Scotland (East Ross in 1999 and West Sutherland in 2016) suggests that it may be present in other northern sites, particularly as it is very small and easily overlooked.

Biogeography European Temperate element; also in eastern Asia and North America.

	GB	IR
Long term	No trend	No trend
Short term	No trend	No trend

Native	GB	IR
2000–19	8	0
1987–99	8	2
1970–86	7	1
pre-1970	15	5

Key refs Dines & Preston (2000), Jermy *et al.* (2007), Kay & John (1995), Wigginton (1999).

M.S. PORTER & F.J. ROBERTS

N *Scirpoides holoschoenus* Round-headed Club-rush

(L.) Soják

A rhizomatous perennial herb that occurs as a native in only two sites in Britain; at Braunton Burrows (North Devon) a large population is found in damp dune-slacks and on adjacent low dunes, while the very much smaller population at Berrow Dunes (North Somerset) is in a damp sandy hollow on a coastal golf course. Elsewhere, it occurs as an alien, especially in dockland and industrial areas, mainly in south Wales. Substantial ripening of fruit and seed set appear to occur only after a long, hot summer. Lowland.

Trends The native 10 km distribution of this species is stable, though native populations are at risk from scrub encroachment, which requires careful management, and hydrological changes. It may be increasing as an introduction although some colonies in industrial areas have been lost to development.

Biogeography Eurosiberian Southern-temperate element.

	GB	IR
Long term	↓ ↓ ◆ ↑ ↑	No trend
Short term	No trend	No trend

Native	GB	IR
2000–19	2	0
1987–99	2	0
1970–86	2	0
pre-1970	4	0

Alien	GB	IR
2000–19	9	0
1987–99	7	0
1970–86	3	0
pre-1970	4	0

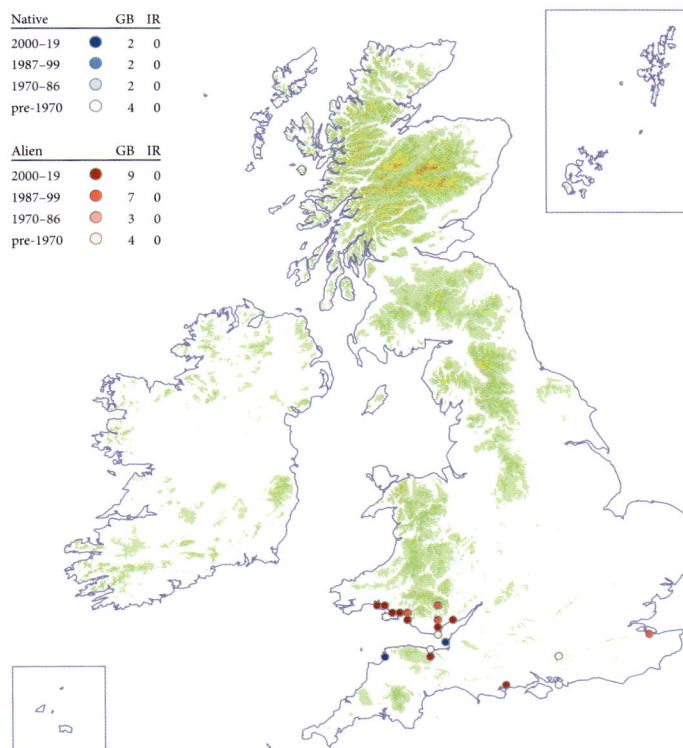

Key refs Jermy *et al.* (2007), Wigginton (1999).

M.S. PORTER & M.J.Y. FOLEY

Isolepis setacea Bristle Club-rush
(L.) R.Br.

An annual to short-lived perennial herb of open, damp, generally acidic sites, especially those subject to winter flooding. It occurs on sandy or gravelly tracks, on the shores of lakes or ponds, in short grassland on wet peaty rides, on eroding streamsides and occasionally on the coast in sand dunes or in turf in the upper zones of saltmarshes. 0–590 m (High Cup Nick, Westmorland) and 595 m on Ben Lawers (Mid Perthshire).

Trends *I. setacea* was mapped as 'all records' in the 1962 *Atlas*. A large proportion of the lowland losses occurred between the 1950s and 1970s due to drainage resulting from changed farming practices. However, its distribution appears to have stabilized in recent years, and many more records have been made this century, with the species now known to be common in many parts of Britain and Ireland. As a

pioneer species of disturbed ground, it may still be overlooked in some areas.

Biogeography Eurosiberian Temperate element; widely naturalized outside its native range.

Native	GB	IR
2000–19	1767	660
1987–99	1588	531
1970–86	992	71
pre-1970	1405	303

Alien	GB	IR
2000–19	1	0
1987–99	1	0
1970–86	0	0
pre-1970	1	0

Key refs Jermy *et al.* (2007).

M.S. PORTER & M.J.Y. FOLEY

Isolepis cernua Slender Club-rush
(Vahl) Roem. & Schult.

An annual to short-lived perennial herb of wet, coastal grassland, in bare or open sites over damp sand, peat and mud, in short turf and sometimes in flushes and trickles on rocky cliffs. In the New Forest (South Hampshire), where it is locally common, it occurs inland in flushed acidic or base-rich turf and in old marl-pits. Lowland.

Trends Some sites for *I. cernua* were lost before 1930, but the distribution appears to have undergone a marked increase since then, especially in its stronghold along the Irish coast, and western Scotland and Wales, almost certainly due to a combination of more systematic recording and a wider understanding of the differences between this species and *I. setacea*.

Biogeography Mediterranean-Atlantic element; also in North America.

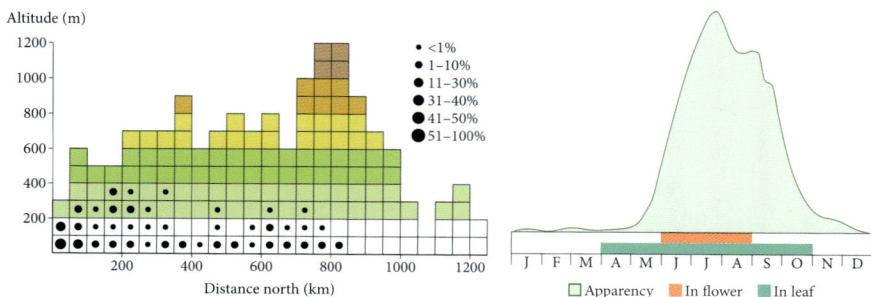

Native	GB	IR
2000–19	249	209
1987–99	177	158
1970–86	82	13
pre-1970	185	121

Alien	GB	IR
2000–19	1	0
1987–99	0	0
1970–86	0	0
pre-1970	0	0

Key refs Jermy *et al.* (2007).

M.S. PORTER & M.J.Y. FOLEY

N *Eleogiton fluitans* Floating Club-rush
(L.) Link

A perennial herb found mainly on peaty, acidic substrates in, or on the margins of slow-flowing streams, ditches, pools and the sheltered shores of some larger lakes and tarns, often in seasonally flooded sites. It also occurs in muddy hollows in grasslands and heaths, and the wet floors of disused quarries, sand- and gravel-pits. 0–490 m (Loch Hoil, Mid Perthshire) and potentially higher on Schiehallion (Mid Perthshire).

Trends Many of the losses of *E. fluitans* occurred before 1930, following drainage or the loss of lowland heathland. This decline has to some extent continued inland, in north-eastern England and in eastern Scotland, although many new records have been made since the turn of the century, for example in the Fenland region of East Anglia, western parts of Britain and in Ireland.

Biogeography Oceanic Southern-temperate element, with a disjunct distribution.

Native	GB	IR
2000–19	586	178
1987–99	566	174
1970–86	337	37
pre-1970	625	184

Alien	GB	IR
2000–19	0	0
1987–99	1	0
1970–86	1	0
pre-1970	1	0

Key refs Jermy *et al.* (2007), Preston & Croft (1997).

M.S. PORTER & M.J.Y. FOLEY

N *Cyperus longus* Galingale
L.

A rhizomatous perennial herb of marshes and wet pastures near the coast, and sometimes in base-rich flushes on sea-cliffs. It also occurs on pond margins and in ditches inland, where it is usually planted. As a native it is southern and western in distribution. Reproduction is through vigorous rhizomatous spread, and it may not set seed in Britain. Lowland.

Native in Britain and the Channel Islands and a neophyte in Ireland.

Trends The native distribution of *C. longus* has declined since the 1960s due to agricultural changes, including the cessation of grazing, although new native sites have been discovered, most notably in north Wales. In comparison, it has increased very considerably as an alien, particularly this century, and it now occurs widely as a naturalized garden escape or planted ornamental throughout lowland England and Wales.

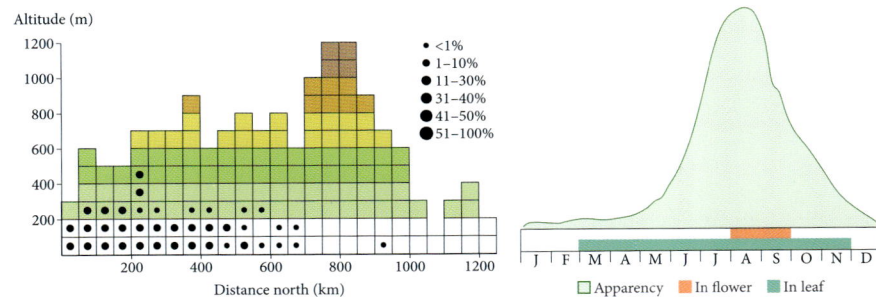

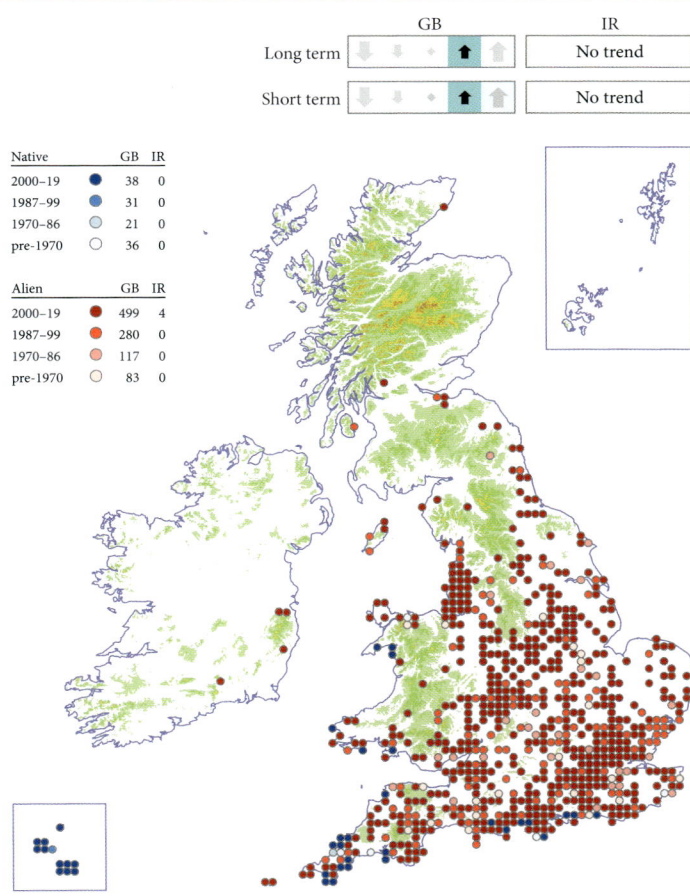

Biogeography European Southern-temperate element.

Native	GB	IR
2000–19	38	0
1987–99	31	0
1970–86	21	0
pre-1970	36	0

Alien	GB	IR
2000–19	499	4
1987–99	280	0
1970–86	117	0
pre-1970	83	0

Key refs Jermy *et al.* (2007), Stewart *et al.* (1994).

M.S. PORTER & M.J.Y. FOLEY

Ne *Cyperus eragrostis* Pale Galingale
Lam.

A perennial sedge, found on roadsides, riverbanks and pond margins, in ditches and on ballast and rough ground, where it occurs as a grass-seed alien and sometimes as a garden escape. It has become well naturalized in some places, especially in the Channel Islands, but is more often only casual. Lowland.

Trends *C. eragrostis* was possibly introduced to cultivation in Britain in 1790. It was first recorded in the wild in 1876 (Penarth Ferry, Glamorganshire). Although some populations have been lost in the London area, the overall distribution has increased substantially.

Biogeography Native of tropical America.

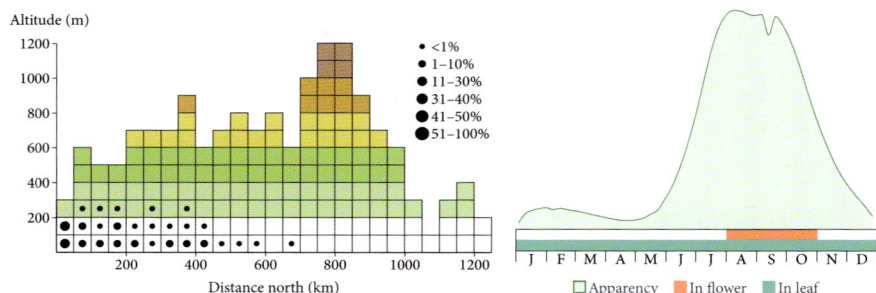

		GB	IR
Long term		No trend	No trend
Short term		↑	↑

Alien		GB	IR
2000–19	●	346	22
1987–99	●	67	3
1970–86	●	18	0
pre-1970	○	14	0

Key refs Jermy *et al.* (2007).

M.S. PORTER & M.J.Y. FOLEY

N *Cyperus fuscus* Brown Galingale
L.

An annual sedge of moist, open, disturbed ground around the margins of ponds and by ditches, often on ground subject to flooding in the winter. The substrate may be peaty, muddy or stony but needs to be humus-rich. Seed may not ripen in cool summers. Lowland.

Trends The conditions favoured by *C. fuscus* were traditionally maintained by grazing animals, but cessation of grazing, encroachment by scrub and lowering of the water-tables have all contributed to an appreciable decline which began before 1930. It is also threatened by the spread of the invasive *Ludwigia gradiflora* subsp. *hexapetala* at one of its most important sites in South Hampshire (Braemore Marsh). However, all its extant sites now benefit from statutory protection, and since seed appears to be long-lived,

populations may be revived with suitable conservation management.

Biogeography Eurosiberian Southern-temperate element.

		GB	IR
Long term		No trend	No trend
Short term		No trend	No trend

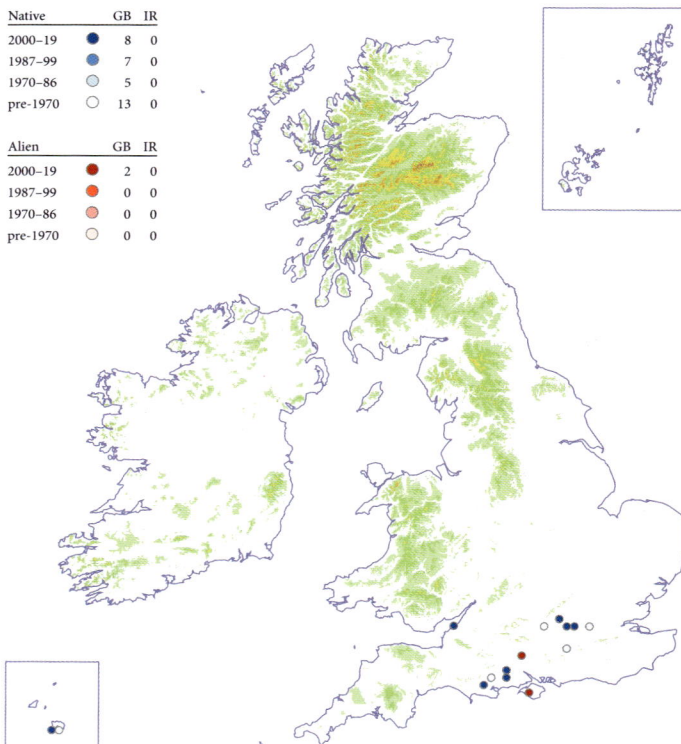

Native		GB	IR
2000–19	●	8	0
1987–99	●	7	0
1970–86	●	5	0
pre-1970	○	13	0

Alien		GB	IR
2000–19	●	2	0
1987–99	●	0	0
1970–86	●	0	0
pre-1970	○	0	0

Key refs Jermy *et al.* (2007), Rich (1999c), Wigginton (1999).

M.S. PORTER & M.J.Y. FOLEY

Blysmus compressus Flat-sedge
(L.) Panz. ex Link

A rhizomatous perennial herb, found in open areas in marshes and fens, and in short, sedge-rich, damp grassland, calcareous flushes and stream borders which are subject to flooding with base-rich water. It also occurs, very occasionally, on the fringes of saltmarshes and on salted roadsides. 0–490 m (County Durham).

Trends Although still locally abundant in the uplands of northern England and the Scottish Borders, *B. compressus* has declined severely over much of its range. Many sites were lost in the 19th century, but this decline continued throughout the 20th and into the 21st century due to drainage, the loss of unimproved damp grasslands, falling water-tables, eutrophication and the reduction or cessation of grazing.

Biogeography European Temperate element, with a continental distribution in western Europe; also in central Asia.

Native	GB	IR
2000–19	120	0
1987–99	144	0
1970–86	155	0
pre-1970	343	0

Key refs Jermy *et al.* (2007), Stroh *et al.* (2019), Walker *et al.* (2017).

M.S. PORTER & M.J.Y. FOLEY

Blysmus rufus Saltmarsh Flat-sedge
(Huds.) Link

A rhizomatous perennial herb, found in sandy or gravelly wet runnels and depressions in saltmarshes, and in brackish ditches and dune-slacks. It also occurs in freshwater seepages, beside streams where they debouch onto the beach and, occasionally, on rocky shores. Lowland.

Trends Most of the losses of *B. rufus* around the Irish Sea and in eastern Scotland took place before 1930, and the distribution now appears to be generally stable. However, recent losses from saltmarshes in Cumbria show that it can be vulnerable to prolonged overgrazing. During the current survey the species was found in many of the more remote 10 km squares in which it had not been seen since the 1970s, suggesting that it is still overlooked in some regions.

Biogeography European Boreal-montane element; also in central Asia and North America.

Native	GB	IR
2000–19	282	52
1987–99	208	38
1970–86	133	17
pre-1970	298	60

Key refs Jermy *et al.* (2007).

M.S. PORTER & M.J.Y. FOLEY

Schoenus nigricans Black Bog-rush
L.

A tussock-forming perennial herb of calcareous and other base-rich fens (especially near to springs), and of peaty flushes, marshes, bogs, dune-slacks, sea-cliff flushes, and the upper fringes of saltmarshes where there is base-rich flushing. In western Ireland, it is frequent on acid blanket-bog. Generally lowland, but reaching 550 m in the Mourne Mountains (County Down).

Trends *S. nigricans* had widely declined in the lowlands by the end of the 19th century, and such losses continued in these areas for much of the 20th century. In its core areas near the western coasts of Britain and in Ireland, however, its distribution remains stable, and a small number of new sites have been found this century.

Biogeography Eurosiberian Southern-temperate element; also in North America.

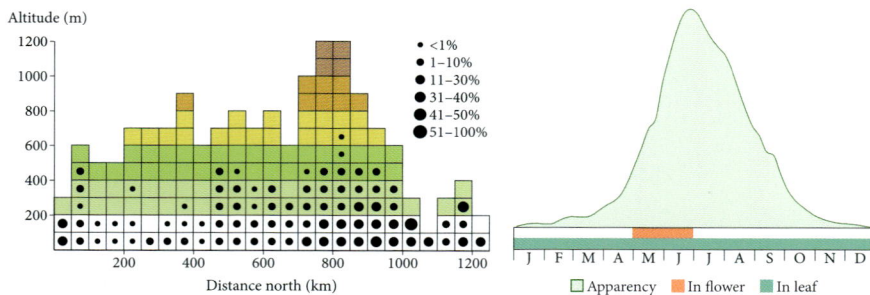

Native	GB	IR
2000–19	598	412
1987–99	543	398
1970–86	313	96
pre-1970	641	322

Alien	GB	IR
2000–19	1	0
1987–99	1	0
1970–86	1	0
pre-1970	0	0

Key refs Sparling (1968).

M.S. PORTER & M.J.Y. FOLEY

Schoenus ferrugineus Brown Bog-rush
L.

A tussock-forming perennial herb of base-rich, often stony, flushes within calcareous grassland, usually adjacent to unimproved heathland. Seed production is low, and dispersal is restricted as the seed is retained in the inflorescence for up to a year. From 200 m above Loch Tummel (Mid Perthshire) to 422 m on Ben Vrackie (East Perthshire).

Trends *S. ferrugineus* was thought to have become extinct in Scotland when, in 1950, its original site on the edge of Loch Tummel was flooded after water-levels were raised. Two transplants from here to Ben Vrackie survived. However, since 1970 over ten previously unknown native sites have been discovered, including three new populations this century, all near Blair Atholl, Perthshire. All sites have some form of statutory protection, as this species is vulnerable to drainage and intensive grazing.

Biogeography European Boreal-montane element.

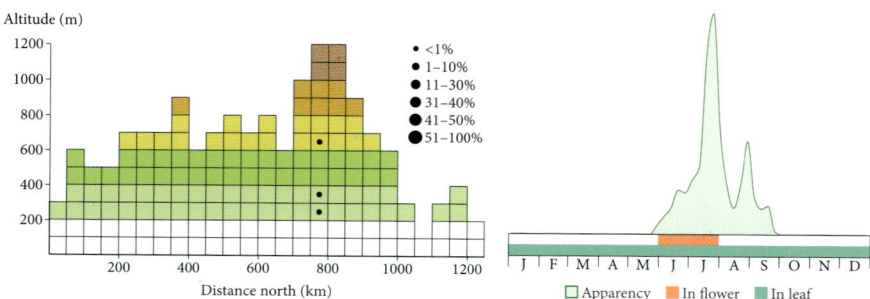

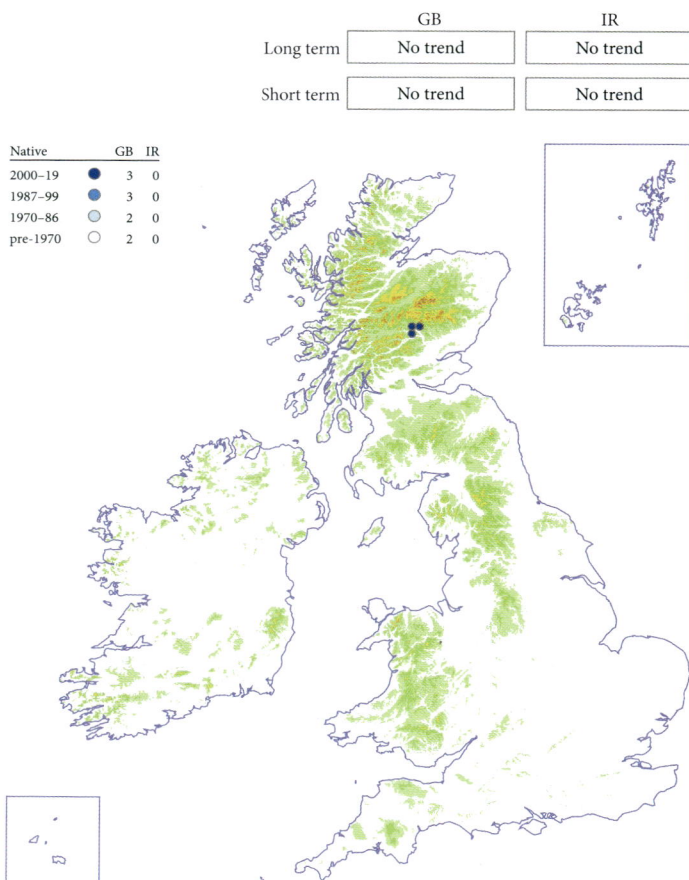

	GB	IR
Long term	No trend	No trend
Short term	No trend	No trend

Native	GB	IR
2000–19	3	0
1987–99	3	0
1970–86	2	0
pre-1970	2	0

Key refs Jermy *et al.* (2007), Wigginton (1999).

M.S. PORTER & M.J.Y. FOLEY

N *Cladium mariscus* Great Fen-sedge
(L.) Pohl

A rhizomatous perennial sedge of oligotrophic to mesotrophic habitats, usually growing on peat, and found in swamps at the margins of lakes and ponds and along streams, in tall-herb fens and open fen-carr. In England and Wales it is largely restricted to calcareous sites, whereas on Hebridean Islands and in western Ireland it also occurs in acidic areas. Generally lowland but occurring at 255 m at Sunbiggin Tarn (Westmorland), and 320 m at Traeth Mawr (Breconshire).

Trends *C. mariscus* declined throughout the 20th century, largely as a result of mechanization and more efficient drainage technology, and some lowland sites are still threatened by eutrophication and scrub invasion. It is locally common in East Anglia, on the western coast of Scotland and in western and central areas of Ireland, where many new records reflect a greater intensity of recording since 2000. Elsewhere its distribution now appears to be stable.

Biogeography Eurosiberian Southern-temperate element; also in North America.

Native	GB	IR
2000–19	144	181
1987–99	148	194
1970–86	103	62
pre-1970	194	154

Alien	GB	IR
2000–19	12	0
1987–99	6	0
1970–86	3	0
pre-1970	2	0

Key refs Conway (1942), Jermy *et al.* (2007), Preston & Croft (1997).

M.S. Porter & M.J.Y. Foley

N *Rhynchospora alba* White Beak-sedge
(L.) Vahl

A perennial sedge of base-poor acidic bogs, wet heaths and mires, often in association with *Sphagnum* species. It is intolerant of competition, preferring open sites, and is frequently found on bare wet peat, sometimes in shallow standing water. It is characteristic of western areas of Britain and Ireland where annual rainfall exceeds 1,200 mm. Generally lowland, but reaching 850 m (Clogwyn y Garnedd, Caernarvonshire).

Trends Many former lowland sites of *R. alba* were lost in the 19th century as a result of drainage, peat extraction and afforestation, and losses continued in southern and central England for much of the 20th century. Its distribution elsewhere has remained largely stable, and new locations have been found since 2000 within its core range due to more intensive recording.

Biogeography Circumpolar Boreo-temperate element, with a disjunct distribution.

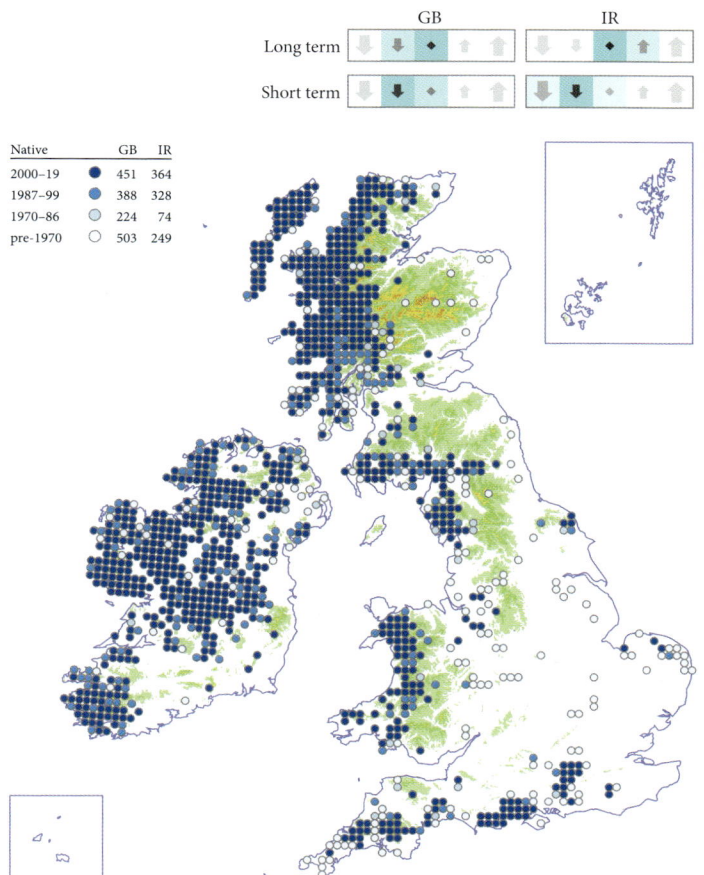

Native	GB	IR
2000–19	451	364
1987–99	388	328
1970–86	224	74
pre-1970	503	249

Key refs Jermy *et al.* (2007).

M.S. Porter & M.J.Y. Foley

Rhynchospora fusca Brown Beak-sedge

(L.) W.T.Aiton

A rhizomatous perennial sedge of wet heaths, acidic mires, shallow pools and soakaways in blanket bogs and mires, favouring bare peat where competition is limited. In parts of Scotland it is characteristic of 'ladder pools' on watersheds. It spreads vegetatively, and may reproduce by seed. Lowland.

Trends Although most English sites for *R. fusca* outside its core area had already been destroyed before 1930, more were lost throughout the 20th century, sometimes as a result of drainage but more frequently because of invading carr following a reduction or cessation of grazing. Surviving populations in England are now confined to the New Forest and Dorset heaths, and a single site in Surrey (Thursley Common National Nature Reserve). In Wales, where it was always a rare species, *R. fusca* is now known from just one locality, Cors Fochno (Cardiganshire). However, in Scotland its distribution has remained largely unchanged since the turn of the century, with many new sites discovered since the 1960s, and in Ireland, the apparent widespread decline before 2000 has been partially redressed by recent discoveries due to fuller recording.

Biogeography Suboceanic Boreo-temperate element; also in North America.

Native	GB	IR
2000–19	30	40
1987–99	29	32
1970–86	26	18
pre-1970	35	72

Key refs Jermy *et al.* (2007), Stewart *et al.* (1994).

M.S. PORTER & M.J.Y. FOLEY

Carex paniculata Greater Tussock-sedge

L.

A large, tussock-forming perennial sedge of wetland habitats, usually somewhat base-enriched, including swamps and fens, the edges of lakes, ponds, canals and ditches, open fen-carr and swampy woodland. It usually grows in the open, where it fruits freely, but tolerates moderate shade, although then it can become smaller and less vigorous, flowering only sparsely. Generally lowland, but to over 600 m on Gylchedd (Denbighshire).

Trends *C. paniculata* was lost from many sites during the 20th century and declined in some of its former strongholds, such as the Norfolk Broads, where 'tussock-fens' ceased to develop. However, such declines appear to have slowed, and many new locations have been discovered across its range during recent decades as a result of more systematic recording, especially in the Scottish borders, northern Scotland, and Ireland.

Biogeography European Temperate element.

Native	GB	IR
2000–19	1198	493
1987–99	1175	402
1970–86	928	101
pre-1970	1117	226

Alien	GB	IR
2000–19	8	1
1987–99	1	0
1970–86	1	0
pre-1970	0	0

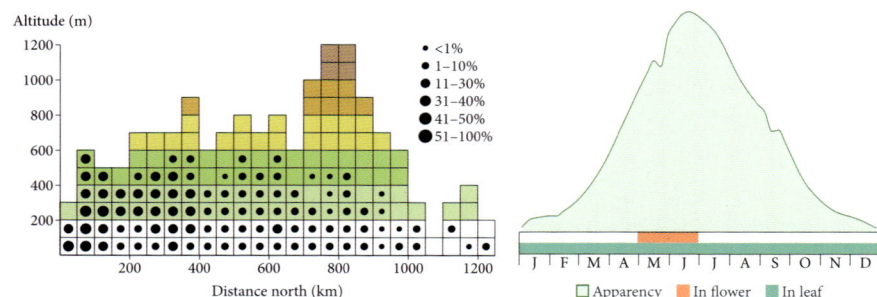

Key refs Jermy *et al.* (2007), Preston & Croft (1997).

M.S. PORTER & M.J.Y. FOLEY

Hy *Carex paniculata × remota = C. ×boenninghausiana*
Weihe

One of the more frequent sedge hybrids, found in damp shady habitats such as wet woodland, including woodland flushes, alder swamps and willow-carr, the edges of lakes and reservoirs, ponds, streams, canals and ditches, reed-swamp and wet grassland. It often grows in close association with *C. paniculata*. It seems to be totally sterile and tolerates shade. Lowland.

A spontaneous hybrid (native × native).

Trends Whilst many new populations of this hybrid have been found this century, there are few records from north Wales, and it has not been recorded since 1970 at many of its known sites in southern England. It is not clear whether the high proportion of older records simply reflects the gradual accumulation of records of short-lived

hybrid populations, or whether the hybrid is now rarer that it once was.

Biogeography Widespread in temperate Europe.

	GB	IR
Long term	No trend	No trend
Short term	No trend	No trend

		GB	IR
2000–19	●	43	12
1987–99	●	40	9
1970–86	●	25	3
pre-1970	○	79	8

Key refs Stace *et al.* (2015).

M.J.Y. FOLEY & M.S. PORTER

Altitude (m) — Distance north (km)

Apparency — In flower — In leaf

N *Carex appropinquata* Fibrous Tussock-sedge
Schumach.

A tussock-forming perennial sedge, mainly occurring in open fenland and mires but also in willow-carr where, however, its numbers may sometimes be reduced by shading and drying out. Although its preference is for moderately base-rich habitat, it can grow well in more acid fens. Generally lowland, but reaches 380 m at Malham Tarn (Mid-west Yorkshire).

Trends The current distribution of *C. appropinquata* presents a mixed picture. It is no longer present in southern England and has experienced some decline in its East Anglian stronghold as a result of drainage and drought and the subsequent encroachment of scrub. It is absent from three of its five historical sites in lowland Yorkshire, and has not been recorded since 2000 at many of its Irish localities. However, at the

two remaining locations in Yorkshire and at its sites in the Scottish Borders *C. appropinquata* appears to be thriving.

Biogeography Eurosiberian Boreo-temperate element, with a continental distribution in western Europe.

Native		GB	IR
2000–19	●	22	5
1987–99	●	25	8
1970–86	●	28	12
pre-1970	○	29	7

Alien		GB	IR
2000–19	●	0	0
1987–99	●	0	0
1970–86	●	0	0
pre-1970	○	1	0

	GB	IR
Long term		
Short term		

Key refs Corner (1969), Jermy *et al.* (2007), Stewart *et al.* (1994).

M.S. PORTER & M.J.Y. FOLEY

Altitude (m) — Distance north (km)

Apparency — In flower — In leaf

Carex diandra Lesser Tussock-sedge

Schrank

A perennial sedge of wet, peaty areas, tolerating both acidic soils and those flushed by calcareous springs. It is often found on the margins of pools and in swamps, though it can also thrive on the edges of wet woods, among scattered trees or in fen-carr. Generally lowland, but reaching 370 m near Malham Tarn (Mid-west Yorkshire), and 518 m on Ben Vrackie (East Perthshire).

Trends *C. diandra* was lost from many lowland sites as a result of drainage and scrub encroachment, especially in southern and eastern England, during the 20th century. Though most losses occurred before 1930, sites are still being lost in England. It is much better recorded in Scotland and Ireland where an encouraging number of new records have been made since the turn of the century due to more systematic recording.

Biogeography Circumpolar Boreo-temperate element.

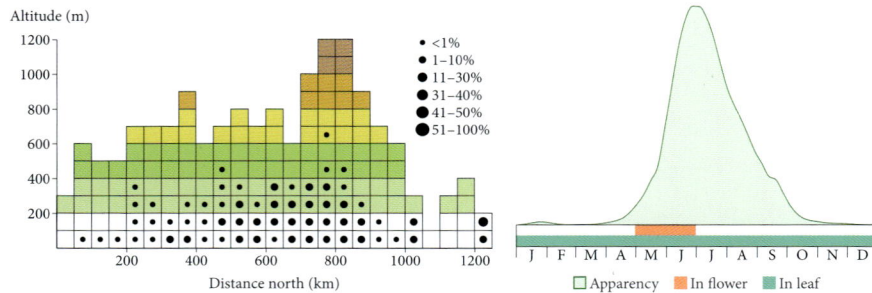

Native	GB	IR
2000–19	174	201
1987–99	188	209
1970–86	165	63
pre-1970	268	158

Alien	GB	IR
2000–19	1	0
1987–99	0	0
1970–86	0	0
pre-1970	0	0

Key refs Jermy *et al.* (2007).

M.S. PORTER & M.J.Y. FOLEY

Carex vulpina True Fox-sedge

L.

A perennial sedge of wet, open habitats, usually over chalk or limestone including ditches, meadows and beside ponds and rivers. It prefers heavy clay soils that are flooded in winter and therefore sometimes grows in standing water. Plants fruit freely but it rarely flowers under shade. Lowland.

Trends *C. vulpina* was not distinguished from *C. otrubae* until 1939 and, even with careful examination, the two species are still confused, making any assessment of trends difficult. It appears that many colonies were lost in the 20th century, largely due to water extraction, ditch clearing, the filling of ponds and shading. Since 2000 there appear to be fewer losses and some new sites have been found, but the plant remains vulnerable in our area. The most northerly site (Norton-on-Derwent, North-east Yorkshire) was

lost in the 1960s but in 2004 it was re-introduced using plants originating from East Sussex (although it is not known whether they have survived). The only other confirmed northern site is near to Fishlake (South-west Yorkshire) where it occurs in ditches around a series of flood-meadows by the River Don.

Biogeography Eurosiberian Temperate element, with a continental distribution in western Europe.

Native	GB	IR
2000–19	13	0
1987–99	12	0
1970–86	13	0
pre-1970	23	0

Alien	GB	IR
2000–19	1	0
1987–99	0	0
1970–86	1	0
pre-1970	1	0

Key refs Jermy *et al.* (2007), Porley (1999), Stewart *et al.* (1994), Wigginton (1999).

M.S. PORTER, R.D. PORLEY & K.J. WALKER

N *Carex otrubae* False Fox-sedge
Podp.

A perennial sedge of wetlands, usually on heavy soils. It is found on the sides of streams and ponds, in ditches, swamps, wet lowland meadows and pastures, at the upper edge of saltmarshes, strandlines on beaches and shingle, and, less commonly, on damp roadsides and hedgebanks. In northern England and Scotland it is essentially a coastal plant. It usually grows in slightly drier conditions than the much rarer *C. vulpina*, tending to avoid standing water. Generally a lowland plant and decidedly less common in mountainous or upland areas, but it has been recorded at an altitude of 465 m near Flash (Staffordshire).

Trends The overall distribution of *C. otrubae* is little changed since the early 20th century, though loss of habitat through drainage has resulted in some local declines. Encouragingly, many new sites have been discovered since the turn of the century.

Biogeography Eurosiberian Southern-temperate element.

Native		GB	IR
2000–19	●	1544	398
1987–99	●	1476	307
1970–86	●	1000	69
pre-1970	○	1336	242

Alien		GB	IR
2000–19	●	0	0
1987–99	●	1	0
1970–86	●	0	0
pre-1970	○	1	0

Key refs Jermy *et al.* (2007), Pearman (1994).

M.S. Porter & M.J.Y. Foley

Hy *Carex otrubae × remota = C. ×pseudoaxillaris*
K.Richt.

A generally sterile hybrid, found near both parents in a range of damp or seasonally wet habitats, including woodland rides and clearings, hedgerows and ditch-sides, by streams, canals, reservoirs, pits and ponds, in wet meadows, on roadside banks and disused railways. In northern Britain, where it is a mainly coastal plant, it may grow on wet cliff ledges and on muddy shores, just above the strandline. Lowland.

A spontaneous hybrid (native × native).

Trends The mapped 10 km square distribution of this hybrid is similar to that shown in the 2002 *Atlas*. There is no evidence for long-term persistence in many sites, and so the fact that records over the past 50 years are much less numerous than pre-1970 ones may simply reflect the gradual accumulation of records of short-lived populations, rather than a decline in frequency.

Biogeography Outside our area *C. ×pseudoaxillaris* is recorded from Germany and the Netherlands.

		GB	IR
2000–19	●	72	2
1987–99	●	50	5
1970–86	●	35	3
pre-1970	○	273	13

	GB	IR
Long term	No trend	No trend
Short term	No trend	No trend

Key refs Stace *et al.* (2015).

M.J.Y. Foley & M.S. Porter

(N) *Carex spicata* Spiked Sedge

Huds.

A perennial sedge of rough grasslands, roadsides, railway embankments, hedgebanks, woodland rides and clearings, open scrub and waste ground. It is a plant of moist, neutral or slightly base-rich, heavy soils, and cannot withstand much competition. Generally lowland, but reaching 370 m at Beaufort (Breconshire).

Trends This species was previously confused with *C. muricata* subsp. *pairae*, but a clear account of the differences was provided by Jermy *et al.* (1982). Since then it has been recorded much more frequently and in many more areas of Britain and Ireland, and its known range has steadily expanded, although it remains rare in Ireland and is absent from Cornwall and upland regions of Britain.

Biogeography European Temperate element; widely naturalized outside its native range.

Native		GB	IR
2000–19	●	1054	32
1987–99	●	874	22
1970–86	○	610	19
pre-1970	○	582	23

Alien		GB	IR
2000–19	●	5	0
1987–99	●	1	0
1970–86	●	0	0
pre-1970	○	1	0

Key refs David & Kelcey (1985), Jermy *et al.* (1982), Jermy *et al.* (2007).

M.S. PORTER & M.J.Y. FOLEY

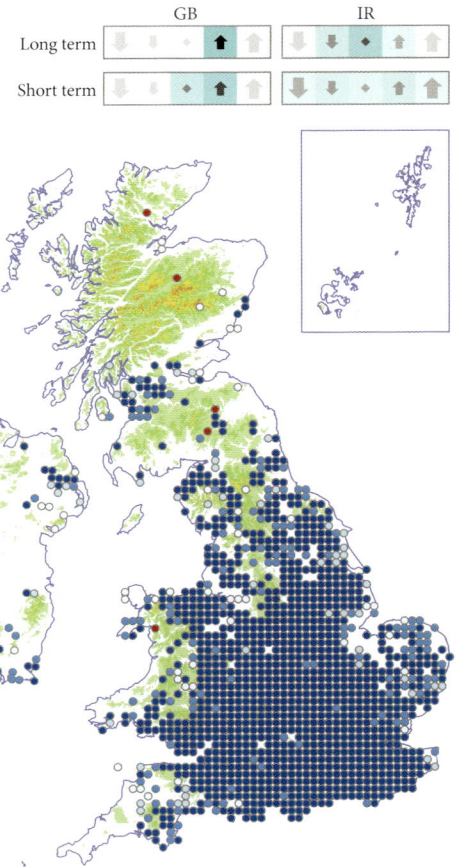

(N) *Carex muricata* subsp. *muricata* Large-fruited Prickly-sedge

L.

A perennial sedge of dry habitats over chalk and limestone, being found on limestone pavements, ledges, grassy slopes and scree; some sites are shaded. Generally lowland, but reaching 340 m at Colt Park Wood (Mid-west Yorkshire).

Trends *C. muricata* subsp. *muricata* has been recorded from around 20 sites in England and a single site in Scotland (Thirlestaine Castle, Berwickshire) where it was last found in the 1870s. All its English sites are still extant with the exception of one site in Gloucestershire, last recorded in 1983 and lost through overgrowth of surrounding vegetation. Plants were re-introduced to the same site, but these died out by 1989. A large population was discovered in Shropshire in 1999 and an extension to it confirmed in 2000. Since then a number of new sites have been found in the Chiltern Hills (Oxfordshire,

Buckinghamshire), usually in woodland or on the edge of woodland, extending its known southern and eastern range. The three populations in the Yorkshire Dales in northern England are all very small and therefore highly sensitive to changes in management.

Biogeography European Boreo-temperate element; introduced to North America.

Native		GB	IR
2000–19	●	9	0
1987–99	●	6	0
1970–86	○	5	0
pre-1970	○	5	0

	GB	IR
Long term	No trend	No trend
Short term	No trend	No trend

Key refs David & Kelcey (1985), Foley & Porter (2000), Jermy *et al.* (2007), Wigginton (1999).

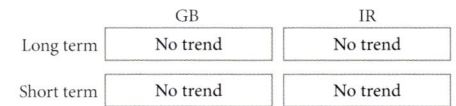

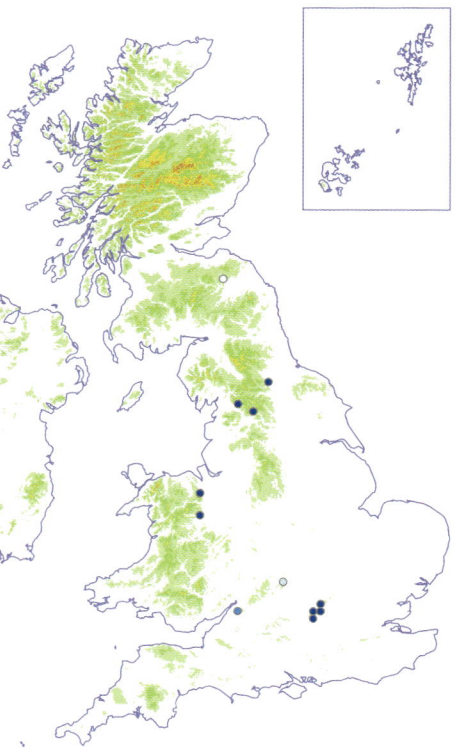

M.S. PORTER, M.J.Y. FOLEY & K.J. WALKER

(N) *Carex muricata* subsp. *pairae* Small-fruited Prickly-sedge
(F.W.Schultz) Čelak.

A tufted perennial sedge of well-drained, light, sometimes sandy soils, preferring rather acidic substrates and thus usually avoiding limestone areas. It is found on hedgebanks, earth-filled walls and roadsides, in rough meadows, heathland and on rocky slopes, and is somewhat intolerant of shade. Generally lowland, but reaching 410 m Black Mountain (Radnorshire).

Trends The current taxonomic treatment of the *C. muricata* aggregate was set out by Jermy *et al.* (1982). Since then *C. muricata* subsp. *pairae* has been much better recorded but is still overlooked in some areas, largely as a result of confusion with *C. spicata*. Nevertheless, many new records have been made, especially in East Anglia, south-western England, Wales and southern Scotland.

Biogeography European Southern-temperate element.

Native	GB	IR
2000–19 ●	827	57
1987–99 ●	643	36
1970–86 ○	476	7
pre-1970 ○	365	22

Alien	GB	IR
2000–19 ●	0	0
1987–99 ●	0	0
1970–86 ●	1	0
pre-1970 ○	0	0

	GB	IR
Long term	No trend	No trend
Short term		

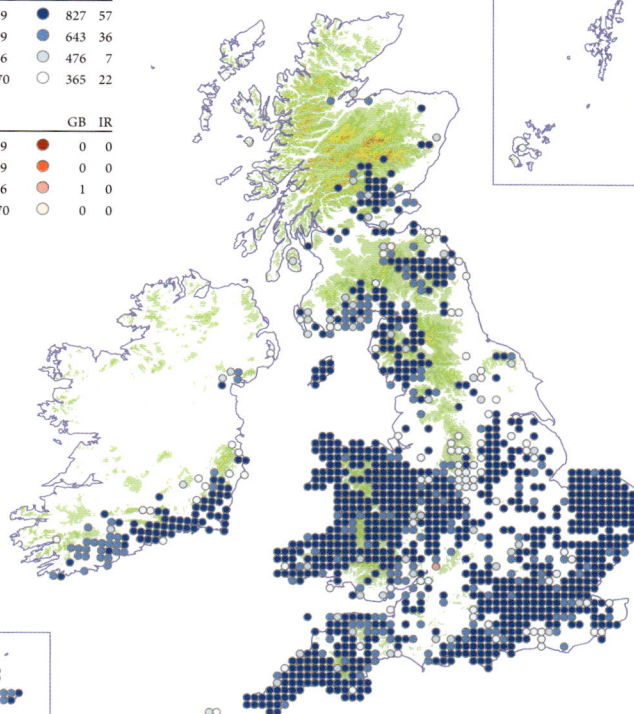

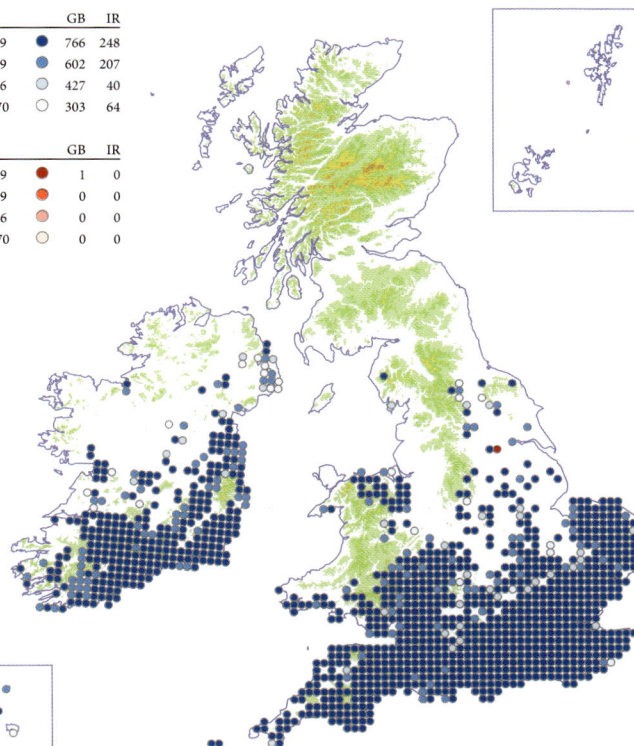

Key refs David & Kelcey (1985), Jermy *et al.* (1982), Jermy *et al.* (2007).

M.S. PORTER & M.J.Y. FOLEY

Altitude (m) chart — Distance north (km)

Apparency · In flower · In leaf

(N) *Carex divulsa* subsp. *divulsa* Grey Sedge
Stokes

A tufted perennial sedge tolerating a wide range of soil fertility and pH, except soils which are markedly acidic, and typically found in hedgebanks, scrub, along woodland borders and paths, on roadsides and in rough, open grassland. Mainly lowland, but reaching 400 m at Waen Ganol (Denbighshire).

Trends This subspecies was mapped as *C. divulsa* in the 1962 *Atlas*, as records for subsp. *leersii* were mapped separately as *C. polyphylla*. Since then its range has expanded markedly northwards in both Britain and Ireland. This spread has continued since 2000, filling in many of the gaps within its previously mapped range. Although some of this increase must be due to better recording of taxa within the *C. muricata* aggregate and more systematic recording, it also appears to be genuinely expanding

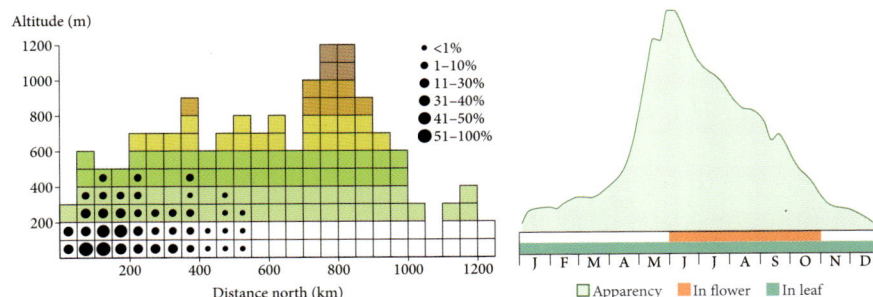

its range, possibly as a result of climate change and changes to the management of boundary habitats.

Biogeography European Southern-temperate element; the species is mapped by Hultén & Fries (1986).

Native	GB	IR
2000–19 ●	766	248
1987–99 ●	602	207
1970–86 ○	427	40
pre-1970 ○	303	64

Alien	GB	IR
2000–19 ●	1	0
1987–99 ●	0	0
1970–86 ●	0	0
pre-1970 ●	0	0

	GB	IR
Long term	No trend	
Short term		

Key refs David & Kelcey (1985), Jermy *et al.* (2007).

M.S. PORTER, M.J.Y. FOLEY & K.J. WALKER

Altitude (m) chart — Distance north (km)

Apparency · In flower · In leaf

N *Carex divulsa* subsp. *leersii* Many-leaved Sedge
(F.W.Schultz) W.Koch

A tufted perennial sedge of roadsides, woodland rides, hedgebanks and open grassland, mainly on chalk or limestone but occasionally on more acidic soils. Lowland, reaching an altitude of 220 m in Wensleydale (North-west Yorkshire).

Trends This subspecies was mapped as *C. polyphylla* in the 1962 *Atlas*. Increased understanding of the taxonomy of this subspecies, as well as other taxa in the *C. muricata* aggregate, has led to many new records since the 1960s, both within and beyond its original range. However, the two subspecies of *C. divulsa* are linked by a range of intermediates which can make identification challenging in some areas (*e.g.* Leslie, 2019). Like subsp. *divulsa* its range may be increasing due to climate change although ultimately any future expansion will be more limited due to its restriction to calcareous soils.

Biogeography Eurosiberian Southern-temperate element; this subspecies extends farther north in Europe than subsp. *divulsa*.

	GB	IR
Long term	↑	No trend
Short term	↑	No trend

Native	GB	IR
2000–19	297	0
1987–99	172	0
1970–86	125	0
pre-1970	113	0

Alien	GB	IR
2000–19	0	0
1987–99	1	0
1970–86	1	0
pre-1970	0	0

Key refs David & Kelcey (1985), Jermy *et al.* (2007), Leslie (2019).

M.S. PORTER & M.J.Y. FOLEY

N *Carex arenaria* Sand Sedge
L.

A rhizomatous perennial sedge of sandy habitats, where it can be a dominant plant of fixed dunes, dune-slacks, sandy flats and on tracksides or other ruderal habitats. Though predominantly coastal, it can be locally common on dunes and heaths inland, particularly on the Lincolnshire coversands and paleo-dune systems in Breckland. It can be a rapid colonizer, spreading by far-creeping rhizomes. It is occasionally found as an alien on railway clinker or in sites associated with new developments where it has probably arrived with imported sands and gravels. Lowland.

Trends There has been little change in the coastal 10 km square distribution of this species since the 1960s. Whilst *C. arenaria* has not been refound at some inland sites, such losses have been balanced by new records made since the turn of the century.

Biogeography European Temperate element.

	GB	IR
Long term	↓	↑
Short term	↓	↓

Native	GB	IR
2000–19	625	187
1987–99	600	166
1970–86	375	44
pre-1970	577	124

Alien	GB	IR
2000–19	27	1
1987–99	17	0
1970–86	13	0
pre-1970	14	0

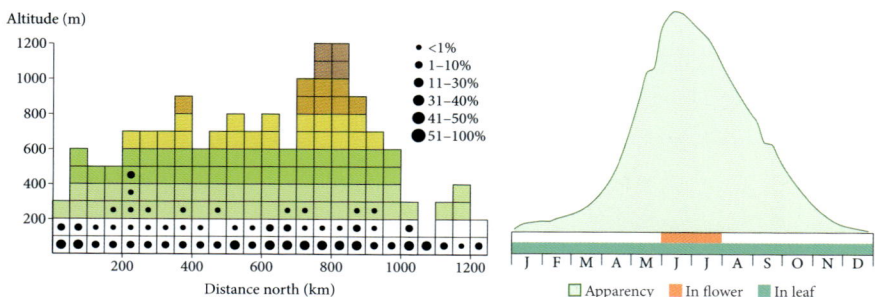

Key refs Jermy *et al.* (1982), Jermy *et al.* (2007), Noble (1982).

M.S. PORTER & M.J.Y. FOLEY

N *Carex disticha* Brown Sedge

Huds.

A rhizomatous perennial sedge of wet meadows and marshes, fens, by ditches and streams, on the margins of lakes and ponds, and occasionally in dune-slacks. It almost invariably grows in sunny sites, particularly on base-enriched substrates, and favours areas with a fluctuating water table. Although it grows at an altitude of 470 m on Windburgh Hill (Roxburghshire), it is generally a lowland species and is absent or scarce in the mountainous regions of Britain and Ireland.

Trends *C. disticha* has declined throughout the southern half of its British range since the 1960s due to drainage or changes in land use, although it can be easily overlooked, especially when it is present only as scattered non-flowering shoots. This decline has been much less marked in Scotland and Ireland, and has been more than compensated by new discoveries, largely due to more systematic recording towards the end of the last century and during this century.

Biogeography Eurosiberian Temperate element.

Native	GB	IR
2000–19	973	480
1987–99	952	412
1970–86	692	82
pre-1970	873	237

Key refs Jermy *et al.* (2007).

M.S. PORTER & M.J.Y. FOLEY

N *Carex chordorrhiza* String Sedge

L.f.

A rhizomatous perennial sedge of fens and very wet base-poor mires, where it usually grows in standing water. Propagation appears to be mainly vegetative by long trailing runners, although genetic variation within its populations suggests that it also reproduces by seed. Lowland.

Trends *C. chordorrhiza* may be a late glacial relic in our area. It was known from Altnaharra (West Sutherland) from the end of the 19th century but a larger population was later discovered much farther south at Insh Marshes (East Inverness) in 1978, where it is now known to be much more frequent than was first supposed. *C. chordorrhiza* is susceptible to both drainage and, apparently, to prolonged submergence but, under current management, both populations are thriving.

Biogeography Circumpolar Boreo-arctic Montane element, with a continental distribution in western Europe.

Native	GB	IR
2000–19	3	0
1987–99	3	0
1970–86	4	0
pre-1970	1	0

	GB	IR
Long term	No trend	No trend
Short term	No trend	No trend

Key refs Jermy *et al.* (2007), Wigginton (1999).

M.S. PORTER & M.J.Y. FOLEY

N *Carex divisa* Divided Sedge
Huds.

A rhizomatous perennial sedge of brackish ditches, marshes and damp grasslands near the sea, usually growing in inorganic soils. It avoids areas of standing water. Although largely a coastal plant, it still occurs in a small number of inland sites. Lowland.

Trends By the start of the 20th century *C. divisa* had already suffered a marked decline on the coast, particularly in south-western England as well as inland. It remains locally frequent in suitable areas in southern and eastern England, and there has been little change in its overall 10 km square distribution since the 1960s, with local losses due to coastal development and the widespread conversion of coastal grazing marshes to arable land somewhat compensated by the discovery of new locations this century. In Ireland, populations in County Dublin were lost to development and it was considered to be extinct in County Kilkenny and County Wexford until rediscovered in 1990, where it still persists.

Biogeography Submediterranean-Subatlantic element.

Native		GB	IR
2000–19	●	95	2
1987–99	●	96	2
1970–86	○	81	0
pre-1970	○	138	5

Alien		GB	IR
2000–19	●	1	0
1987–99	●	2	0
1970–86	●	1	0
pre-1970	○	4	0

Key refs Curtis & FitzGerald (1994), Jermy *et al.* (2007), Stewart *et al.* (1994).

M.S. PORTER & M.J.Y. FOLEY

N *Carex maritima* Curved Sedge
Gunnerus

A rhizomatous perennial sedge of coastal sites, found in short vegetation in damp dune-slacks, in saltmarshes and on open sand, often close to freshwater seepages or where streams debouch onto the shore. It is mobile and can colonize new sites with suitable habitat. Populations can be very large. Lowland.

Trends *C. maritima* appears to have suffered a considerable decline before 1930. Assessments of more recent trends are difficult to interpret because more systematic surveys since 2000 have resulted in the discovery of many presumably overlooked populations in northern Scotland, the Outer Hebrides and in Orkney. Historical losses have occurred due to the construction of coastal leisure facilities and such activities continue to remain a threat. It no longer occurs on St. Andrews Golf Course (Fife), where it was abundant in 1984, or in England, having not been seen on Holy Island (North Northumberland) since 1984, despite intensive searches.

Biogeography Circumpolar Arctic-montane element.

Native		GB	IR
2000–19	●	51	0
1987–99	●	25	0
1970–86	○	43	0
pre-1970	○	73	0

Alien		GB	IR
2000–19	●	0	0
1987–99	●	1	0
1970–86	●	0	0
pre-1970	○	0	0

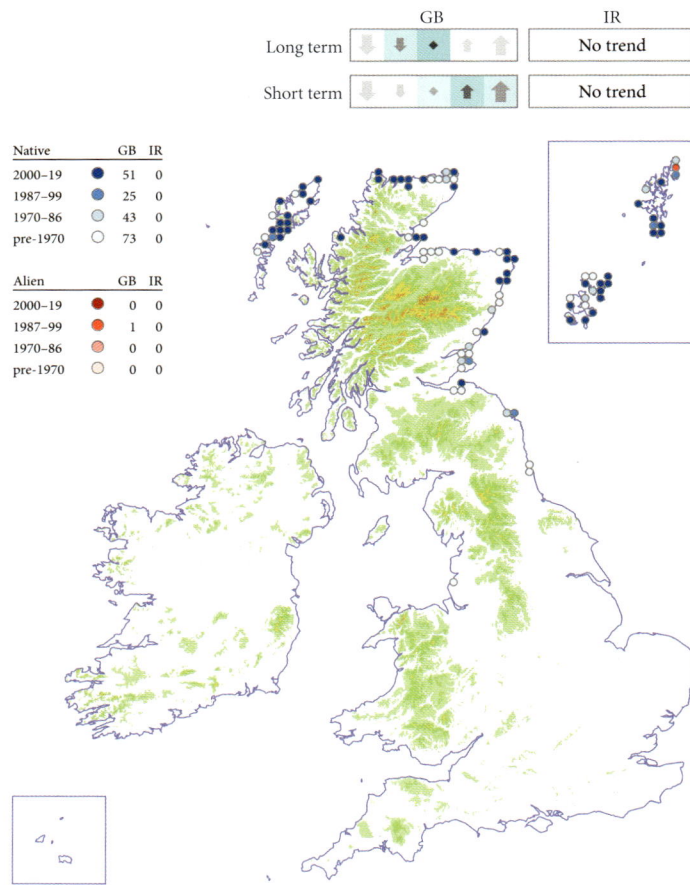

Key refs Jermy *et al.* (2007), Leach (1986), Stewart *et al.* (1994).

M.S. PORTER & M.J.Y. FOLEY

Carex remota Remote Sedge

L.

A tufted perennial sedge of damp, usually bare neutral or acidic soil in woodland and woodland rides, often growing in considerable shade. It can become dominant in favoured habitats, such as in woods that are seasonally flooded. Generally lowland, but reaching 440 m in Neuadd House (Breconshire) and possibly higher on Cadair Idris (Merionethshire).

Trends The overall distribution of *C. remota* is stable and it remains a very common sedge of damp woodlands in many parts of Britain and Ireland. More systematic recording in recent decades has led to many new records, particularly in central areas of Ireland and northern and eastern Scotland.

Biogeography European Temperate element; also in central and eastern Asia.

Native	GB	IR
2000–19	1905	771
1987–99	1719	616
1970–86	1227	117
pre-1970	1560	369

Key refs Jermy *et al.* (2007).

M.S. PORTER & M.J.Y. FOLEY

Carex leporina Oval Sedge

L.

A tufted perennial sedge, especially of acidic grassland, frequent in upland pastures, *Nardus stricta* grassland and *Calluna vulgaris* moorland. It is also common on lowland heaths, in damp meadows, woodland rides and edges, in ruderal habitats, and sometimes in moderately base-rich flushes and dune-slacks. It tolerates trampling and is often found along paths and tracks. It can also tolerate high fertility and can be frequent in semi-improved meadows. 0–1,005 m (Lochnagar, South Aberdeenshire).

Trends *C. leporina* was mapped as 'all records' in the 1962 *Atlas*. It remains widespread and common throughout Britain and Ireland despite localized declines in parts of southern and eastern England in the latter half of the 20th century due to habitat loss. Its overall 10 km square distribution appears to be stable and since 2000 it has been recorded in many new localities, especially in Ireland, due to more systematic recording.

Biogeography Eurosiberian Boreo-temperate element; widely naturalized outside its native range.

Native	GB	IR
2000–19	2274	781
1987–99	2141	622
1970–86	1352	98
pre-1970	2056	473

Key refs Jermy *et al.* (2007).

M.S. PORTER & M.J.Y. FOLEY

(N) *Carex echinata* Star Sedge
Murray

A perennial sedge of seasonally or permanently waterlogged habitats on acidic to base-rich substrates. It is found in a wide range of wetland habitats including mires, wet heaths, upland flushes and springs; also in rush-pastures, wet meadows, flushed grassland on hill-slopes and, rarely, in wet woodland rides. 0–1,166 m (Ben More, Mid Perthshire).

Trends *C. echinata*, which was mapped as 'all records' in the 1962 *Atlas*, was lost from many 10 km squares in lowland England in the 19th century through drainage and improvement of wetlands for agriculture. These losses continued throughout lowland England for much of the 20th century. However, suitable habitat still occurs in upland regions throughout the rest of Britain and Ireland and in these areas it remains abundant.

Biogeography European Boreo-temperate element; also in North America.

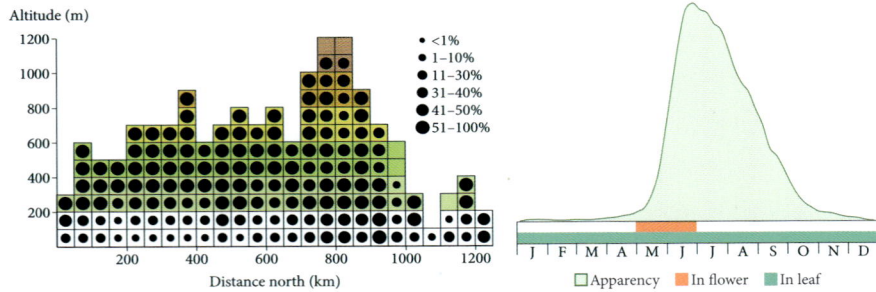

Native		GB	IR
2000–19	●	1796	777
1987–99	●	1773	694
1970–86	○	1165	161
pre-1970	○	1874	579

Alien		GB	IR
2000–19	●	1	0
1987–99	●	0	0
1970–86	●	0	0
pre-1970	○	0	0

Key refs Jermy *et al.* (2007).

M.S. PORTER & M.J.Y. FOLEY

Altitude (m) chart; Distance north (km)
● <1%
● 1–10%
● 11–30%
● 31–40%
● 41–50%
● 51–100%

☐ Apparency ▮ In flower ▮ In leaf

(N) *Carex dioica* Dioecious Sedge
L.

A shortly rhizomatous dioecious perennial sedge of very wet, neutral to base-rich mires. It grows particularly well in silty, calcareous mud and by the edges of lime-rich flushes and springs. Although it occurs at sea level, many sites are at moderate or high altitudes, ascending to about 1,066 m on Ben Lawers (Mid Perthshire).

Trends *C. dioica* had already declined dramatically in lowland England and southern and eastern Ireland by the turn of the 20th century, due to drainage, agricultural improvement and possibly changes in hydrology due to water abstraction for agriculture and drinking water. There continued to be further losses, most notably in England south of the Severn-Humber line, but a very substantial number of new records have been found in northern and western Britain this century, and in Ireland, due to more systematic recording.

Biogeography Circumpolar Boreo-arctic Montane element.

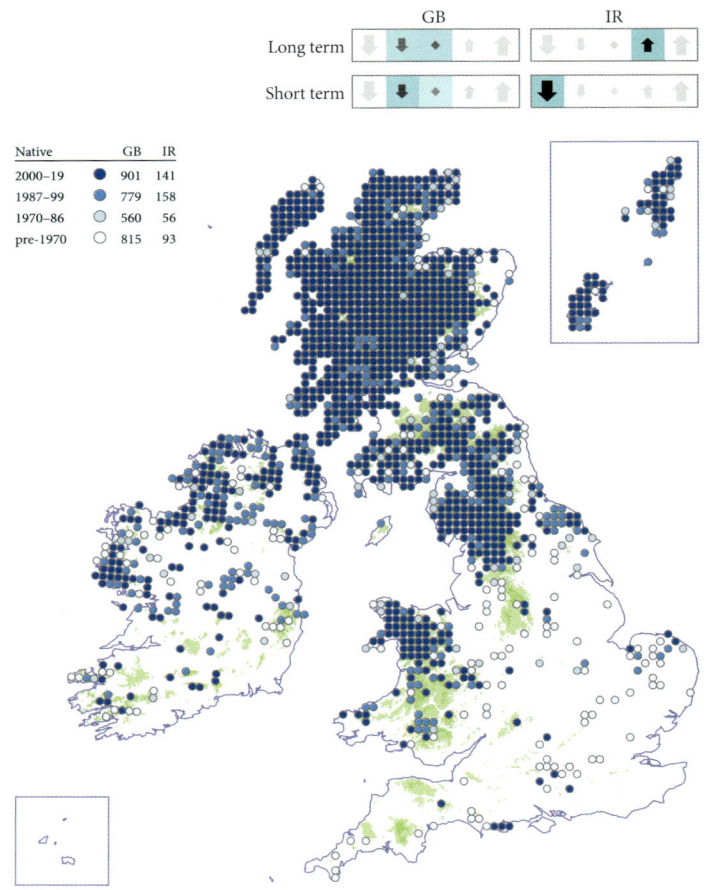

Native		GB	IR
2000–19	●	901	141
1987–99	●	779	158
1970–86	○	560	56
pre-1970	○	815	93

Key refs Jermy *et al.* (2007).

M.S. PORTER & M.J.Y. FOLEY

Altitude (m) chart; Distance north (km)
● <1%
● 1–10%
● 11–30%
● 31–40%
● 41–50%
● 51–100%

☐ Apparency ▮ In flower ▮ In leaf

Carex davalliana Davall's Sedge
Sm.

A perennial dioecious sedge, formerly found in a calcareous mire in North Somerset. Lowland.

Trends *C. davalliana* was known from a single site at Lansdown near to Bath where it was present until the 1830s. The site was drained and subsequently built on, and there was no trace of the plant in 1852. Other records of this species in Britain have proved to be forms of *C. dioica*.

Biogeography European Temperate element, with a continental distribution in western Europe.

	GB	IR
Long term	No trend	No trend
Short term	No trend	No trend

Native	GB	IR
2000–19	0	0
1987–99	0	0
1970–86	0	0
pre-1970	1	0

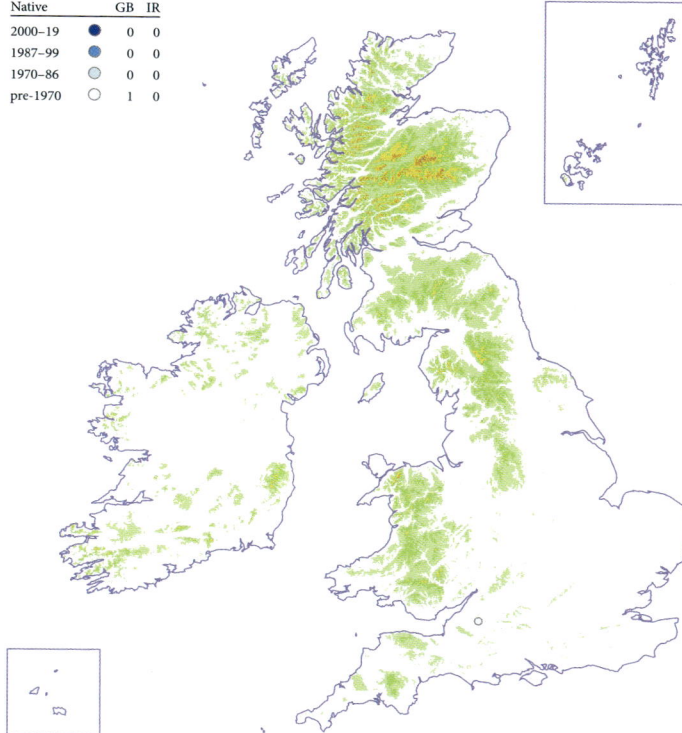

Key refs Jermy *et al.* (1982), Marren (1999), White (1912).

M.S. PORTER & M.J.Y. FOLEY

Carex elongata Elongated Sedge
L.

A perennial sedge of very wet woodlands, especially those dominated by *Alnus glutinosa* and those on lake shores, but also found on pond margins, on canal sides, in ditches and seasonally flooded areas, and in wet meadows. In favourable conditions it can form large, loose tussocks, sometimes rooted in the decorticated logs of fallen trees. It flowers freely in more open situations but it appears that the seed is seldom viable. Lowland.

Trends Many populations of *C. elongata* were lost as a result of drainage and habitat destruction before 1930, especially in Yorkshire and Lancashire. Since then its distribution has remained relatively stable in Britain, with a slight extension of the previously known range in Ireland due to more systematic recording. The number of tussocks in some colonies seems to have increased markedly in recent decades, and at some sites at least – as at Roudsea Wood (Westmorland) and Askham Bog (Mid-west Yorkshire) – it appears to be thriving. Indeed, at Askham Bog the population has increased from 250 tussocks in 1978 to over 6,000 today, making it possibly the largest population in Britain (Fitter *et al.*, 2021).

Biogeography Eurosiberian Boreal-montane element, with a continental distribution in western Europe.

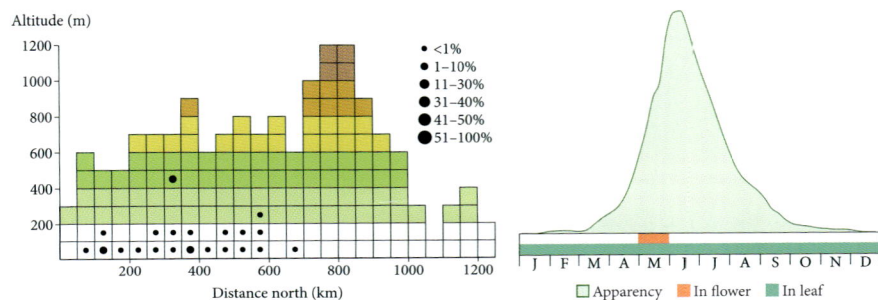

Native	GB	IR
2000–19	39	15
1987–99	32	11
1970–86	34	15
pre-1970	64	7

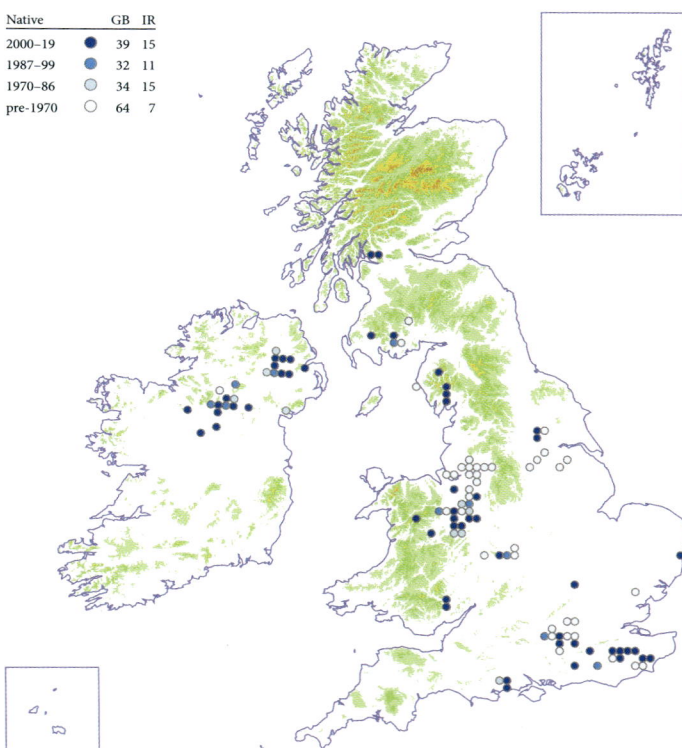

Key refs David (1978b), Fitter *et al.* (2021), Jermy *et al.* (2007), Stewart *et al.* (1994).

M.S. PORTER & M.J.Y. FOLEY

(N) *Carex lachenalii* Hare's-foot Sedge
Schkuhr

A perennial sedge of wet, acidic, north-facing slopes and rock ledges, and in nutrient-poor flushes, especially in areas where snow lies late into the spring. Montane, from 950 m on Cairn Toul (South Aberdeenshire), but formerly lower in Glen Coe, to 1,150 m on Ben Macdui (South Aberdeenshire).

Trends The distribution of *C. lachenalii* appears to be stable. Since the turn of the century additional colonies have been found close to known sites and a large new colony was found on Ben Nevis (Westerness). Some sites are very remote and, as it is a difficult sedge to recognize when not in fruit, it is probably still present in some areas for which there are no recent records. Rockfalls or landslips are potential threats.

Biogeography Circumpolar Arctic-montane element.

	GB	IR
Long term	No trend	No trend
Short term	No trend	No trend

Native		GB	IR
2000–19	●	6	0
1987–99	●	6	0
1970–86	○	5	0
pre-1970	○	7	0

Key refs Jermy *et al.* (2007), Wigginton (1999).

M.S. PORTER & M.J.Y. FOLEY

(N) *Carex canescens* White Sedge
L.

A perennial sedge of lowland bogs, *Sphagnum* swamps in lowland basin mires, nutrient-poor mires in the mountains (where it may be the dominant sedge), and wet, acidic, occasionally sandy heaths. 0–1,100 m (Ben Alder, Westerness).

Trends *C. canescens* suffered a steady decline during much of the 20th century, especially in lowland England, mainly as a result of drainage and changes in farming practices. In recent years, however, many more sites have been discovered, particularly in north-western Scotland and in Ireland due to more systematic recording.

Biogeography Circumpolar Boreal-montane element.

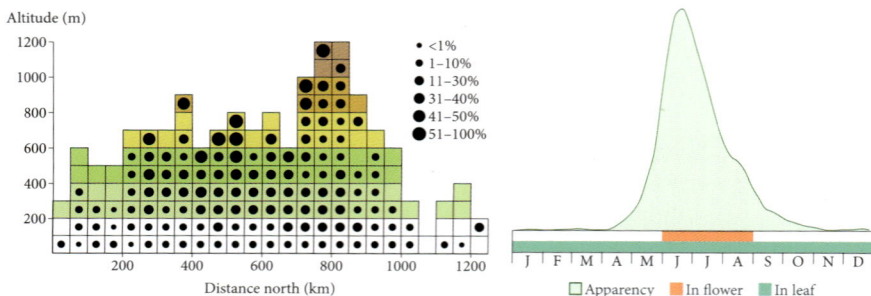

	GB	IR
Long term		
Short term		

Native		GB	IR
2000–19	●	917	136
1987–99	●	886	161
1970–86	○	652	66
pre-1970	○	790	111

Key refs Jermy *et al.* (2007).

M.S. PORTER & M.J.Y. FOLEY

N *Carex hirta* Hairy Sedge
L.

A perennial sedge found in a wide variety of damp, grassy habitats, particularly in areas influenced by human activities such as waste ground, tracksides, roadside verges and hedgebanks. It is also frequent in rough grassland, hayfields, and occasionally sand dunes, marshes and damp, open woods. It avoids highly acidic, infertile soils. Generally lowland but reaching 580 m at Darngill Bridge (Cumberland).

Trends *C. hirta* is one of the most widespread sedges in our area. Its distribution appears to be stable; localized losses have been more than compensated by new discoveries, especially in Ireland, due to more systematic recording.

Biogeography European Temperate element; widely naturalized outside its native range.

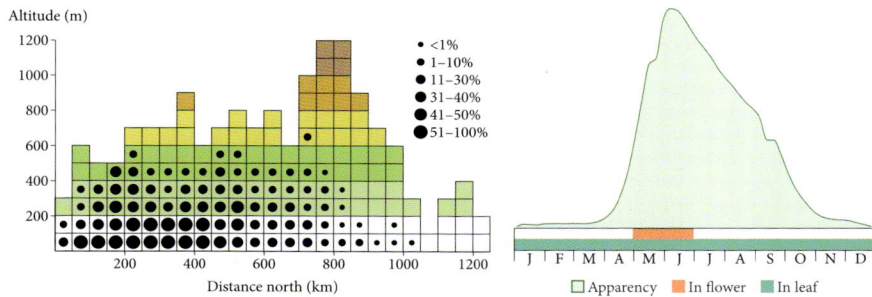

Native		GB	IR
2000–19	●	1900	629
1987–99	●	1790	500
1970–86	○	1262	116
pre-1970	○	1580	302

Alien		GB	IR
2000–19	●	1	0
1987–99	●	1	0
1970–86	●	1	0
pre-1970	○	0	0

Altitude (m) chart: x-axis Distance north (km); dot size legend: <1%, 1–10%, 11–30%, 31–40%, 41–50%, 51–100%

Apparency | In flower | In leaf

Key refs Jermy *et al.* (2007).

M.S. Porter & M.J.Y. Foley

N *Carex lasiocarpa* Slender Sedge
Ehrh.

A rhizomatous perennial sedge of reed-swamps and other marginal vegetation around lakes, pools and slow-flowing streams and rivers, and in flushes and wet hollows in fens; it can also colonize old peat workings and drainage channels. It generally occurs in nutrient-poor water, which may be base-rich or base-poor. 0–650 m (east of Beinn Heasgarnich, Mid Perthshire).

Trends Some populations of *C. lasiocarpa* were lost as a result of drainage by the start of the 20th century and, up to the present day, there have been further declines, particularly in East Anglia and in other parts of lowland England and eastern Ireland where it is now absent or rare. These losses have been compensated to some extent by new discoveries as a result of more systematic recording over the last 20 years.

Biogeography Circumpolar Boreal-montane element.

Native		GB	IR
2000–19	●	324	88
1987–99	●	313	116
1970–86	○	197	35
pre-1970	○	273	104

Altitude (m) chart: x-axis Distance north (km); dot size legend: <1%, 1–10%, 11–30%, 31–40%, 41–50%, 51–100%

Apparency | In flower | In leaf

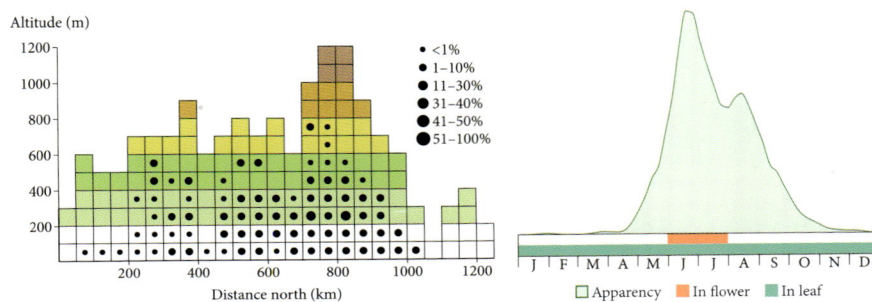

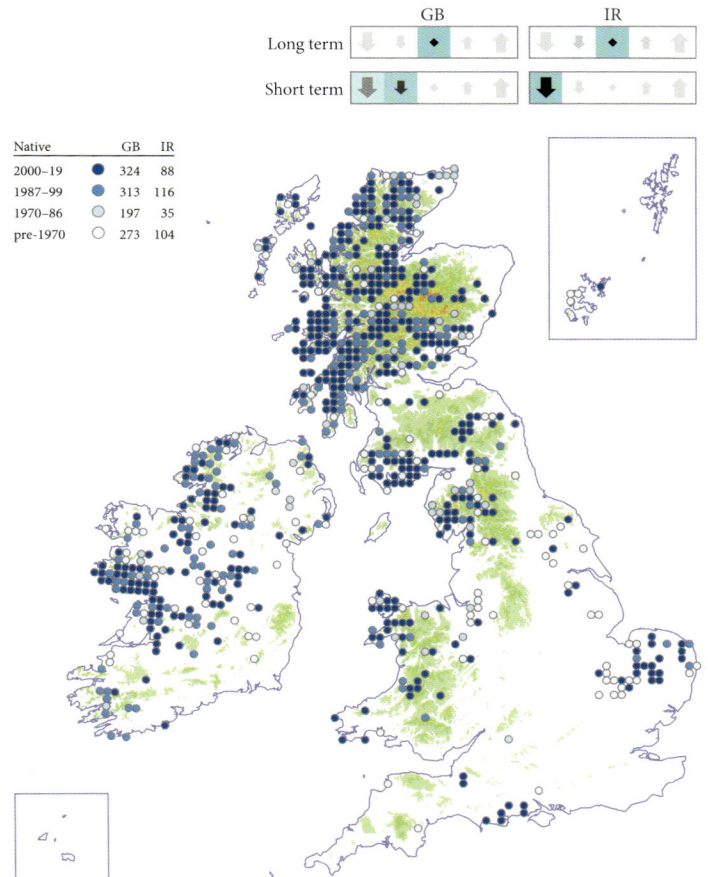

Key refs Jermy *et al.* (2007), Preston & Croft (1997).

M.S. Porter & M.J.Y. Foley

(N) *Carex acutiformis* Lesser Pond-sedge
Ehrh.

A rhizomatous perennial sedge of base-rich, mesotrophic and eutrophic water, often occurring in extensive stands by the sides of rivers, lakes and ponds, and in marshy areas near streams, fen-meadows and tall-herb fen, and carr; it is notably shade-tolerant. It avoids sites subject to marked fluctuations in water level. Reproduction by seed is poor. 0–485 m Dale Head (County Durham).

Trends Apart from some local declines, the 10 km square distribution of *C. acutiformis* appears to be stable, with some new sites discovered since the turn of the century, particularly on the edges of its range, presumably due to more systematic recording. *C. acutiformis* was mapped as 'all records' in the 1962 *Atlas*.

Biogeography Eurosiberian Temperate element.

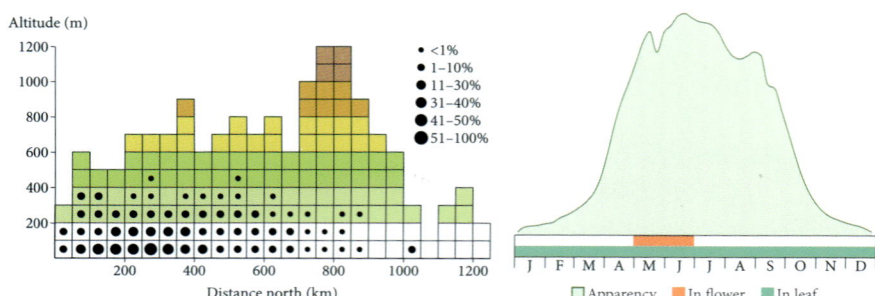

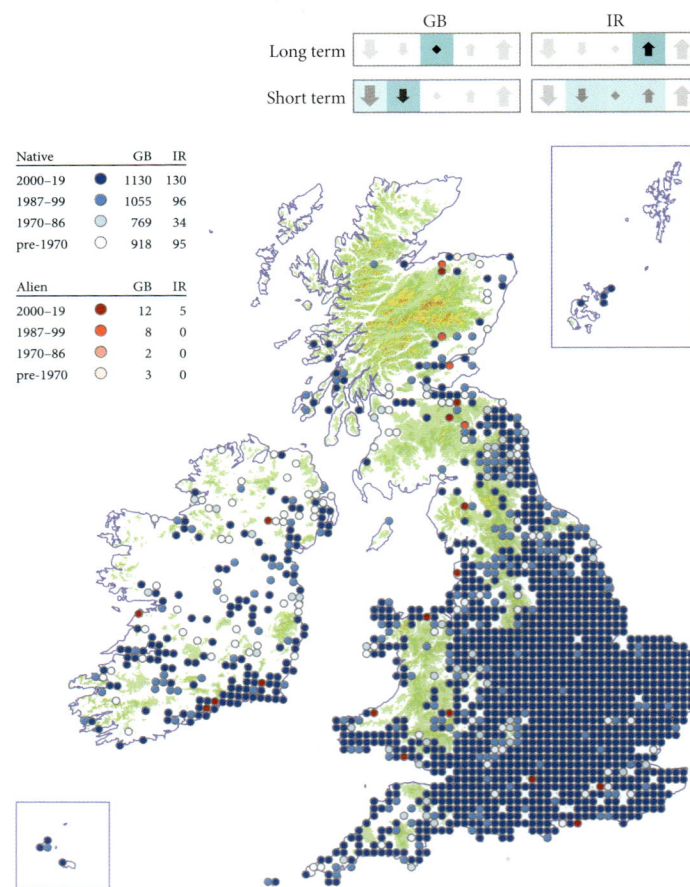

Native	GB	IR
2000–19	1354	181
1987–99	1292	110
1970–86	919	40
pre-1970	1133	122

Alien	GB	IR
2000–19	2	0
1987–99	4	0
1970–86	2	0
pre-1970	1	0

Altitude (m) chart — Distance north (km); dot size legend: <1%, 1–10%, 11–30%, 31–40%, 41–50%, 51–100%

Apparency / In flower / In leaf

Key refs Grime *et al.* (2007), Jermy *et al.* (2007), Preston & Croft (1997).

M.S. PORTER & M.J.Y. FOLEY

(N) *Carex riparia* Greater Pond-sedge
Curtis

A rhizomatous perennial sedge of reed-swamps, the edges of pools and lakes, in marshy areas and wet woodland, and along the banks of slow-flowing rivers and canals. It is a species of base-rich, mesotrophic or eutrophic sites. Reproduction is mainly vegetative, but new colonies can arise from seed. Generally lowland but reaching 390 m at Bettws-y-Crwyn, near Bishop's Castle (Shropshire).

Trends The overall 10 km square distribution of *C. riparia* appears to be gradually extending northwards and westwards, and its frequency in Ireland is now better known due to more systematic recording in recent decades. It is sometimes planted by ponds, and some records mapped as native may refer to such introductions.

Biogeography Eurosiberian Temperate element.

Native	GB	IR
2000–19	1130	130
1987–99	1055	96
1970–86	769	34
pre-1970	918	95

Alien	GB	IR
2000–19	12	5
1987–99	8	0
1970–86	2	0
pre-1970	3	0

Altitude (m) chart — Distance north (km); dot size legend: <1%, 1–10%, 11–30%, 31–40%, 41–50%, 51–100%

Apparency / In flower / In leaf

Key refs Jermy *et al.* (2007), Preston & Croft (1997).

M.S. PORTER & M.J.Y. FOLEY

Carex pseudocyperus Cyperus Sedge
L.

A pioneer sedge of wet mud and shallow water, found in a wide variety of habitats including the edges of lakes, ponds, reservoirs, rivers, ditches, canals and backwaters. It also occurs in reedswamps and tall-herb fens, and readily colonizes sand-, gravel-, clay- and marl-pits. It is shade-tolerant, and is found in swampy alder woods and willow-carr. Reproduction is by seed. Lowland.

Trends During the 20th century *C. pseudocyperus* was lost from many 10 km squares in our area, particularly in south-eastern and eastern England and the southern half of Ireland. Recently, however, this decline seems to have slowed and perhaps even reversed; since 2000 it has extended its range in northern and western Britain and more sites have been refound or discovered throughout its range,

although introductions and garden escapes may account for some of these.

Biogeography Eurosiberian Temperate element; also in eastern Asia and North America.

Key refs Jermy *et al.* (2007), Preston & Croft (1997).

M.S. PORTER & M.J.Y. FOLEY

Carex rostrata Bottle Sedge
Stokes

A rhizomatous perennial sedge forming emergent stands on the edges of lakes and ponds, rivers and streams, in ditches, swamps, fens and bog pools, wet meadows, flush-bogs on hillsides, sea-cliff flushes, wet dune-slacks, and alder- and willow-carr. It usually grows in oligotrophic or mesotrophic, acidic waters, though it also occurs in nutrient-poor calcareous conditions. 0–1,040 m (Creag Meagaidh, Westerness).

Trends The distribution of *C. rostrata* is stable except in south-eastern England and the English Midlands where it has been declining for over a century due to the drainage of wetlands and habitat destruction. Nevertheless, it remains widespread and often frequent in Scotland, Wales, northern England and Ireland.

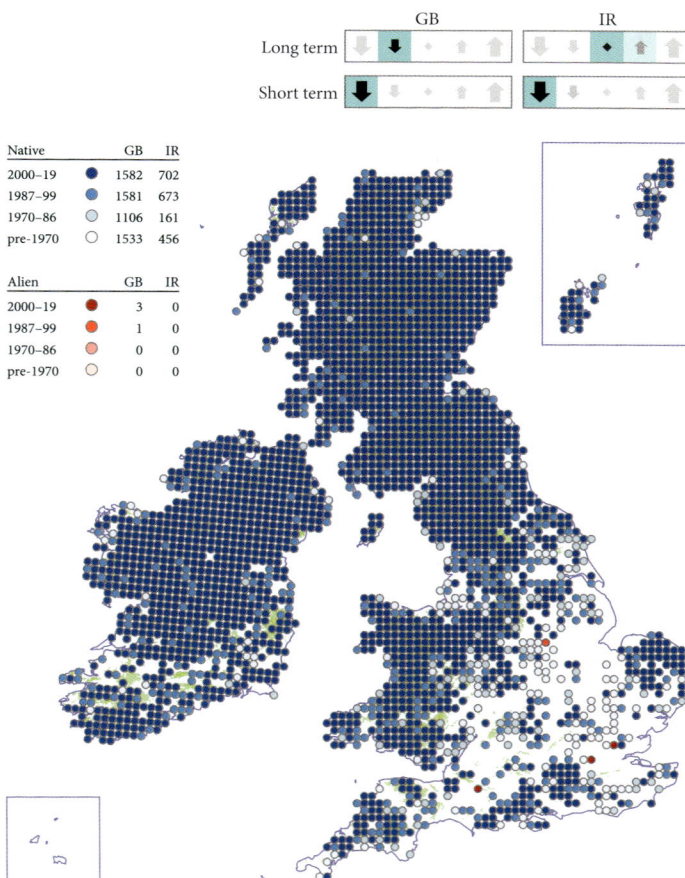

Biogeography Circumpolar Boreo-temperate element.

Key refs Jermy *et al.* (2007), Preston & Croft (1997).

M.S. PORTER & M.J.Y. FOLEY

Hy *Carex rostrata × vesicaria = C. ×involuta*
(Bab.) Syme

		GB	IR
Long term		No trend	No trend
Short term		No trend	No trend

A hybrid sedge of wet places, especially in marshes and fens by rivers, streams, lakes, reservoirs and ponds, often in sedge-dominated communities, and usually with both parents. It is, however, present in Shetland in the apparent absence of *C. vesicaria*, and a single tussock of the hybrid found in 1983 at Llwyn-y-celyn (Monmouthshire) grew in the absence of both parents, perhaps because they had been eliminated by drainage. It is highly sterile, but may spread to form large stands. Generally lowland, but the presise upper altitudinal limit is unknown.

A spontaneous hybrid (native × native).

Trends This hybrid is probably under-recorded; it is very variable and many forms closely resemble one or other of the parents. There is no evidence for any significant change in its 10 km square distribution, though the drainage and destruction of sites at a local level have led to the loss of some populations.

Biogeography It is widespread in western, central and northern Europe, and is also recorded from North America.

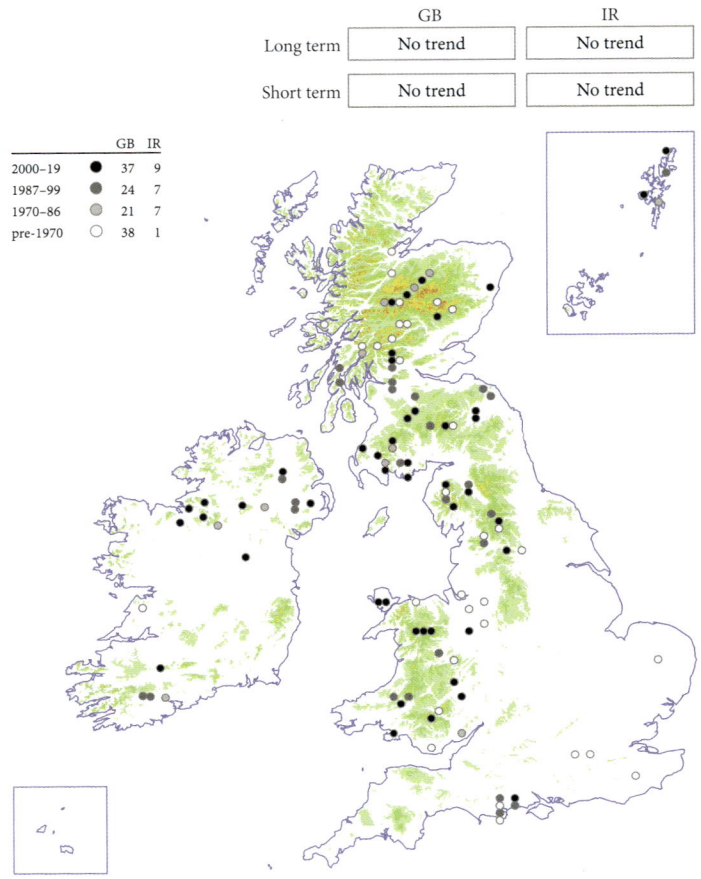

		GB	IR
2000–19	●	37	9
1987–99	●	24	7
1970–86	●	21	7
pre-1970	○	38	1

Key refs Stace *et al.* (2015).

M.J.Y. FOLEY & M.S. PORTER

N *Carex vesicaria* Bladder-sedge
L.

		GB		IR	
Long term		↓		↑	
Short term		↓		↓	

A perennial sedge of wetlands, mainly mesotrophic and at least slightly basic, occurring where the water table lies close to or above the soil surface. It is found by lakes, reservoirs, rivers, streams, ponds and canals, in marshes and swamps, ditches, wet meadows and depressions in pasture, and in wet woodland. It also colonizes wet hollows in disused sand-, gravel- and clay-pits. 0–480 m (source of Nant Tadarn, Breconshire) but potentially higher in Dumfriesshire and East Ross.

Trends *C. vesicaria* was lost from many sites in England and south-eastern Ireland in the 20th century as a result of drainage, falling water tables, ditch cleaning and eutrophication. Whilst losses are still occurring, there have been many new finds throughout its range since 2000, and overall the distribution is now more or less stable.

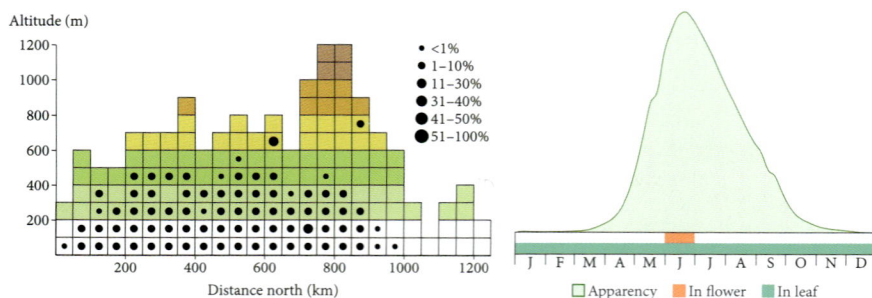

Biogeography Circumpolar Boreo-temperate element.

Native		GB	IR
2000–19	●	573	202
1987–99	●	540	160
1970–86	○	446	54
pre-1970	○	648	127

Alien		GB	IR
2000–19	●	4	0
1987–99	●	2	0
1970–86	●	0	0
pre-1970	○	0	0

Key refs Jermy *et al.* (2007), Preston & Croft (1997).

M.S. PORTER & M.J.Y. FOLEY

Carex saxatilis Russet Sedge

L.

A rhizomatous perennial sedge of mountain plateaus, saddles and gentle slopes, and in damp flushes and hollows where snow lies late in the spring. It tolerates a wide range of soil pH. In our area it is mainly confined to the mountains of western Scotland where rainfall levels are high. From 460 m in Glen Clunie (South Aberdeenshire) to 1,164 m on Ben Lawers (Mid Perthshire).

Trends The distribution of *C. saxatilis* appears to be stable and it is probably still present in most of the 10 km squares lacking recent records, especially in the north of its range. It is under little threat, and is now better recorded than it was when mapped by Stewart *et al.* (1994), with at least eight new locations discovered since 2000.

Biogeography Circumpolar Arctic-montane element; absent from the mountains of central Europe.

Native	GB	IR
2000–19	54	0
1987–99	43	0
1970–86	41	0
pre-1970	57	0

Key refs Jermy *et al.* (2007), Stewart *et al.* (1994).

M.S. PORTER & M.J.Y. FOLEY

Carex pendula Pendulous Sedge

Huds.

A perennial sedge of damp base-rich, heavy (often clay) soils, in shaded habitats. It is found in deciduous woodland, by ditches, ponds, streams, in hedgerows and on tracksides. Reproduction by seed can be prolific and this sedge is becoming ubiquitous and locally invasive in many parts of Britain and Ireland, often originating as a garden escape. Additionally, seeds appear able to survive for many years in the soil (D.A. Pearman, pers. comm.). Usually lowland, but reaching 490 m at Cerrigydrudion (Denbighshire), where it appears to be a naturalized plant.

Trends *C. pendula* has shown a marked consolidation and northward expansion of its range in the lowlands of Britain and Ireland since the 1960s. It is locally abundant in many woodlands on heavy soils where it appears to be outcompeting other ground flora

species. It is widely grown in gardens as an ornamental plant, and escapes may account for much of this spread, although it may have also been favoured by atmospheric deposition of nutrients, increased deer grazing and distubance events such as deconiferization. The limits of its native range are now obscured by garden escapes and so all records are mapped without status.

Biogeography European Southern-temperate element.

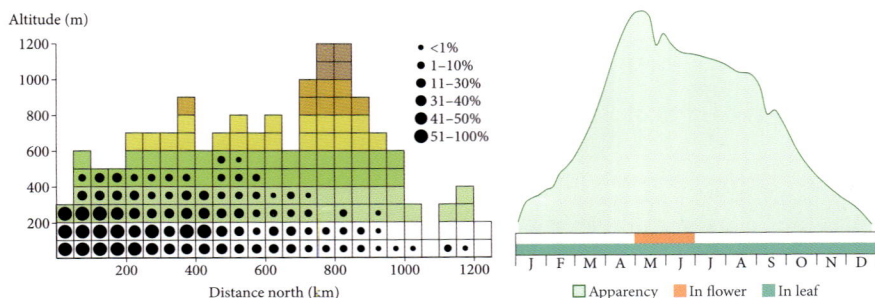

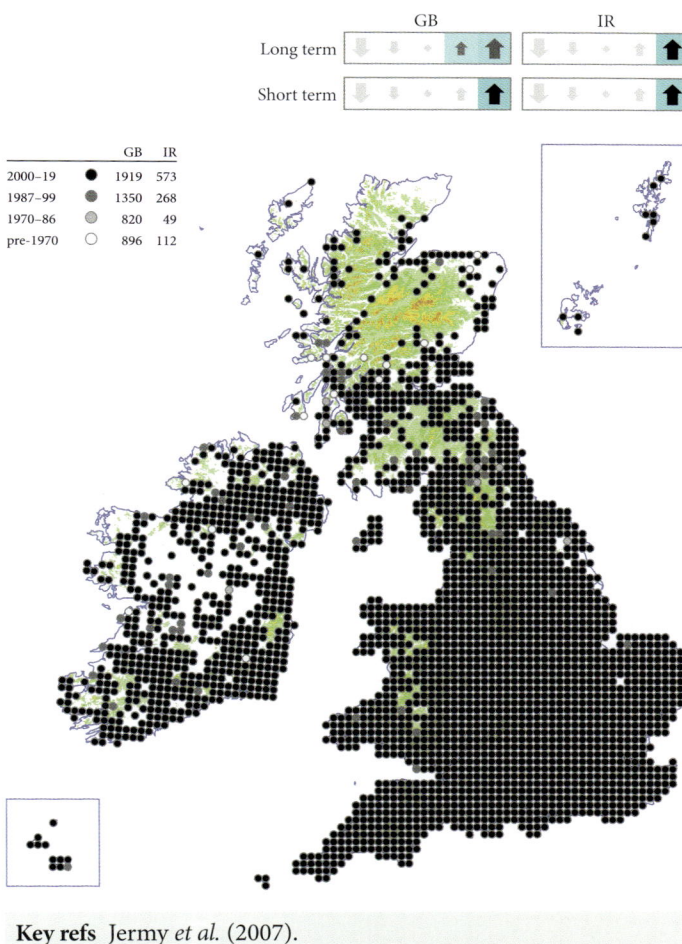

	GB	IR
2000–19	1919	573
1987–99	1350	268
1970–86	820	49
pre-1970	896	112

Key refs Jermy *et al.* (2007).

M.S. PORTER, M.J.Y. FOLEY & K.J. WALKER

Ⓝ *Carex sylvatica* Wood-sedge
Huds.

A perennial sedge of woodlands, generally preferring heavy, moist soils where there is some base-enrichment. In many woods it is particularly frequent along the sides of paths or in rutted tracks. It is occasionally found in open scrub, on limestone pavements, coastal slopes and in damp grassland, but it is likely to be a woodland relic in such places. Generally lowland, but reaching 565 m on Ben Bulben (County Sligo), and reportedly at 640 m in the Scottish Highlands, and with an exceptional altitude of 845 m on Great Dun Fell (Westmorland), where it was unintentionally introduced with a seed mix sown in the mid-1980s.

Trends *C. sylvatica* is one of the most frequent sedges throughout lowland Britain and Ireland, except in northern Scotland. There has been no appreciable change in its distribution except in north-eastern Scotland and Ireland, where the number of records has increased since the turn of the century due to more systematic recording.

Biogeography Eurasian Temperate element.

Native	GB	IR
2000–19	1892	734
1987–99	1707	542
1970–86	1198	119
pre-1970	1529	273

Alien	GB	IR
2000–19	6	0
1987–99	6	0
1970–86	3	0
pre-1970	2	0

Key refs Jermy *et al.* (2007).

M.S. Porter & M.J.Y. Foley

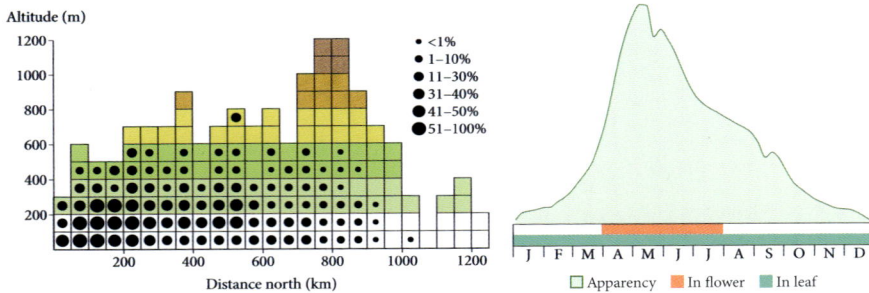

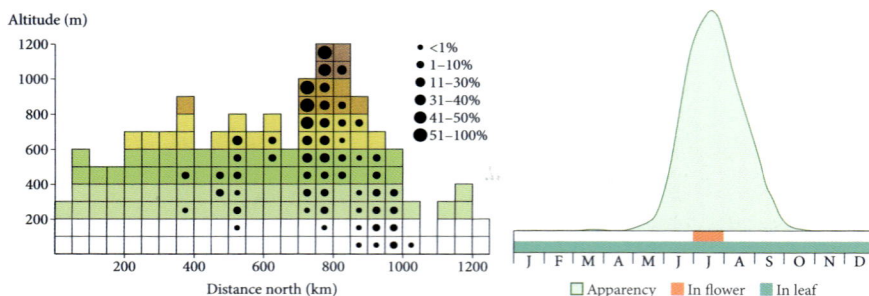

Ⓝ *Carex capillaris* Hair Sedge
L.

A small perennial sedge of base-rich upland grasslands, particularly those flushed by calcareous spring-water, and moist limestone or mica-schist crags, slopes and ledges. Though it can tolerate some shading, it is generally found in open situations and short vegetation, often in species-rich communities. It is usually found at moderate or high altitudes, reaching 1,150 m on Ben Lawers (Mid Perthshire), but it descends to sea level in northern Scotland.

Trends *C. capillaris* appears to be stable in its main strongholds in Scotland and Upper Teesdale but there appears to have been a recent decline at some of its more peripheral sites, notably in Caithness and especially in Mid-west Yorkshire where it has only been recorded at one of its historical sites (Sulber Pasture) since the turn of the century. An outlying record from the Hebridean island of Rum is now thought to have been a deliberate introduction (Pearman & Walker, 2004b).

Biogeography Circumpolar Boreo-arctic Montane element.

Native	GB	IR
2000–19	90	0
1987–99	87	0
1970–86	79	0
pre-1970	94	0

Alien	GB	IR
2000–19	0	0
1987–99	0	0
1970–86	1	0
pre-1970	1	0

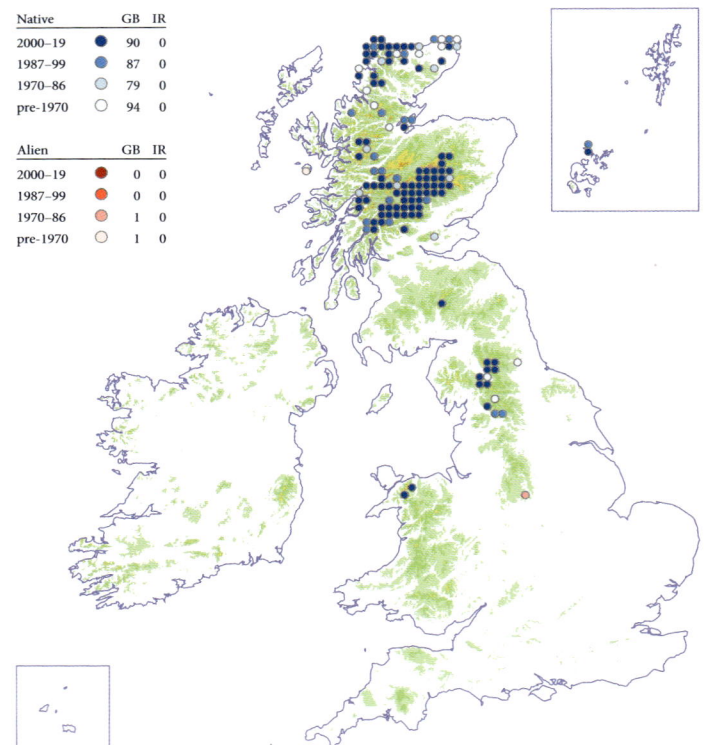

Key refs Jermy *et al.* (2007), Pearman & Walker (2004b), Stewart *et al.* (1994).

M.S. Porter & M.J.Y. Foley

(N) *Carex strigosa* Thin-spiked Wood-sedge

Huds.

A perennial sedge of moist, base-rich, sometimes clayey, soils in deciduous or mixed woodlands, often forming dense patches near streams or in flushes and seepages emanating from springs. It occurs most frequently in clearings and along tracks, but is sometimes found in considerable shade. Lowland.

Trends *C. strigosa* is easily overlooked, and has been considerably better recorded since the 1980s, with many new records having been made throughout its range. It was rediscovered in Scotland in 2016 (Loch Fern, Kirkcudbrightshire).

Biogeography Suboceanic Temperate element.

Native		GB	IR
2000–19	●	413	114
1987–99	●	328	66
1970–86	○	236	33
pre-1970	○	273	47

Alien		GB	IR
2000–19	●	1	0
1987–99	●	0	0
1970–86	●	0	0
pre-1970	○	0	0

Key refs Jermy *et al.* (2007).

M.S. PORTER & M.J.Y. FOLEY

(N) *Carex flacca* Glaucous Sedge

Schreb.

A rhizomatous perennial sedge of unshaded neutral and calcareous grasslands over a wide range of substrates including chalk, limestone, sand and clay, and a frequent pioneer of disturbed bare areas. It is tolerant of both damp and dry conditions, and also occurs in wet meadows, on spray-drenched sea-cliffs, on the uppermost parts of saltmarshes, in base-rich mountain flushes and on rock ledges. Found at most altitudes, reaching 925 m on Stob Binnein (Mid Perthshire).

Trends *C. flacca* is the most widespread sedge in our area with a near-ubiquitous distribution at the 10 km square resolution. Its overall distribution is stable with recent increases in Ireland and northern Scotland resulting from more systematic recording.

Biogeography European Southern-temperate element; widely naturalized outside its native range.

Native		GB	IR
2000–19	●	2699	966
1987–99	●	2557	911
1970–86	○	1712	167
pre-1970	○	2363	716

Key refs Grime *et al.* (2007), Jermy *et al.* (2007), Taylor (1956).

M.S. PORTER & M.J.Y. FOLEY

N *Carex panicea* Carnation Sedge

L.

A perennial sedge of damp or wet habitats including marshy grassland, swamps, upland calcareous grassland, hay- and water-meadows, mesotrophic to oligotrophic mires, sea-cliff grassland, heaths and calcareous flushes and springs in montane grassland; also, in northern and western Britain and Ireland, in the uppermost parts of saltmarshes. It appears to be largely indifferent to soil pH, occurring on calcareous, neutral or moderately acidic soils. 0–1,125 m (Cairngorms).

Trends *C. panicea* was mapped as 'all records' in the 1962 *Atlas*. It has declined markedly in lowland regions of eastern and south-eastern England, particularly in the latter half of the last century, due to the drainage and improvement of its wetland habitats for agriculture. Elsewhere its distribution appears to be stable and it remains

common in many upland regions. Its distribution is now much better understood in Ireland due to more systematic recording in recent decades.

Biogeography European Boreo-temperate element; also in central Asia.

Native	GB	IR
2000–19	2281	892
1987–99	2302	845
1970–86	1513	195
pre-1970	2208	668

Alien	GB	IR
2000–19	1	0
1987–99	1	0
1970–86	0	0
pre-1970	0	0

Key refs Grime *et al.* (2007), Jermy *et al.* (2007).

M.S. PORTER & M.J.Y. FOLEY

N *Carex vaginata* Sheathed Sedge

Tausch

A rhizomatous perennial sedge of flushed, moderately basic to slightly acidic mountain grassland; also found in flush-bogs and on rock ledges. In northern England it often grows in damp, flushed grassland below limestone escarpments. It can be locally abundant and form large patches by rhizomatous growth, but is shy-flowering and for that reason may often be overlooked. From 380 m at Tulach Hill (Mid Perthshire) to 1,150 m on Cairn Toul (South Aberdeenshire), but usually found above 700 m.

Trends There has been a considerable extension in the range of *C. vaginata* over recent decades, largely as a result of more systematic recording of suitable habitats rather than a genuine increase. The most notable extension occurred in northern England where it was first discovered flowering in 2002 (Green

and Dufton Fells, Westmorland and Cumberland) as a result of the relaxation of sheep-grazing following the 2001 Foot and Mouth epidemic. Further finds were made in subsequent years and DNA analyses suggests that these English plants have been present for some considerable time (French *et al.*, 2005).

Biogeography Circumpolar Boreo-arctic Montane element.

Native	GB	IR
2000–19	86	0
1987–99	55	0
1970–86	59	0
pre-1970	57	0

Key refs French *et al.* (2005), Jermy *et al.* (2007), Robinson (2003), Stewart *et al.* (1994).

M.S. PORTER & M.J.Y. FOLEY

N *Carex depauperata* Starved Wood-sedge
Curtis ex With.

A perennial sedge of dry, base-rich, free-draining soils. At its two extant native sites in England it grows in semi-shade on laneside banks at the edge of deciduous woodland; in Ireland it grows in a partially shaded, wooded limestone area. It cannot tolerate deep shade but responds well to coppicing and periodic disturbance. Lowland.

Trends The destruction of woodland and cessation of woodland management are probably the main reasons for the decline of this species in Britain, although it has always been rare. It is now known from five sites in our area: at one of these (Gofynne, Breconshire) it is considered to be an escape from cultivation; it has been planted as part of a species recovery programme near Cranborne (Dorset), in an area where it occurred historically. One English site has been augmented with reintroductions. The species has been added to the Scottish flora recently as a result of the discovery and determination of old herbarium specimens.

Biogeography Submediterranean-Subatlantic element; also in central Asia.

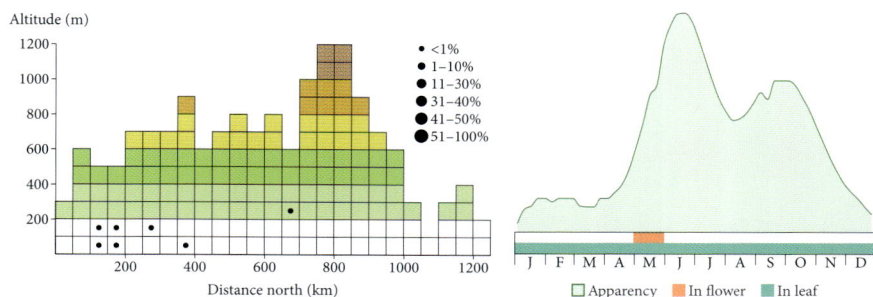

Native	GB	IR
2000–19	2	1
1987–99	2	1
1970–86	2	1
pre-1970	8	0

Alien	GB	IR
2000–19	2	0
1987–99	0	0
1970–86	0	0
pre-1970	1	0

	GB	IR
Long term	No trend	No trend
Short term	No trend	No trend

Altitude (m)
- <1%
- 1–10%
- 11–30%
- 31–40%
- 41–50%
- 51–100%

Distance north (km)

☐ Apparency ☐ In flower ☐ In leaf

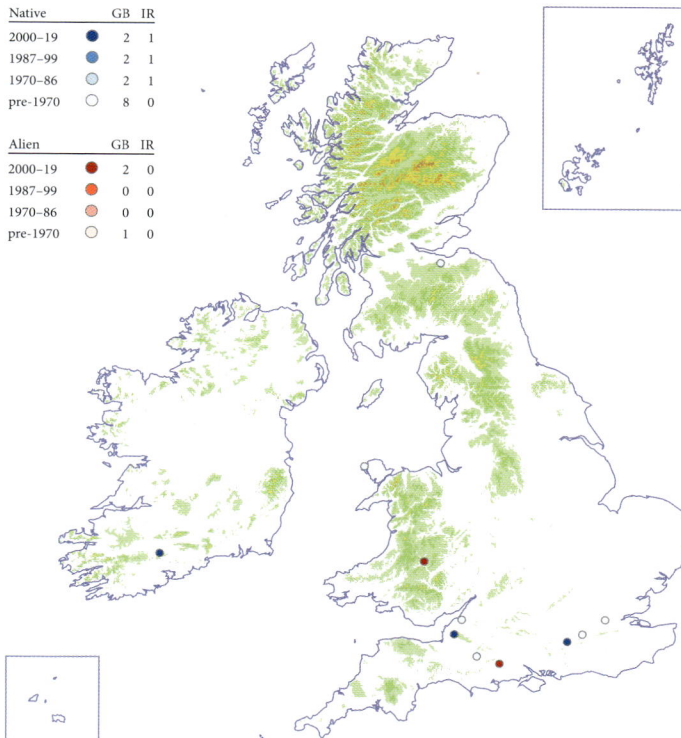

Key refs Jermy *et al.* (2007), O'Mahony (1976), Wigginton (1999).

M.S. PORTER & M.J.Y. FOLEY

N *Carex laevigata* Smooth-stalked Sedge
Sm.

A perennial sedge of moist woodlands on heavy clay soils, often where there is some flushing with base-rich water. Although most frequent in shaded sites, it is sometimes found in more open situations, such as on the edges of reedbeds, in open woodland on hillsides, or occasionally in open grassy flushes and damp meadows. It is a plant of low or moderate altitudes, in hilly or mountainous areas where the annual rainfall exceeds 750 mm, and ascends to about 410 m in the Slaheny Valley (County Kerry), and 760 m at Coire Laogh (Easterness).

Trends The 10 km square distribution of *C. laevigata* appears to be stable, and is now much better known in Scotland and Ireland as a result of more systematic recording. However, there would seem to have been some decline in the drier lowland regions in Britain and Ireland where it is always likely to have been rare.

Biogeography Oceanic Temperate element.

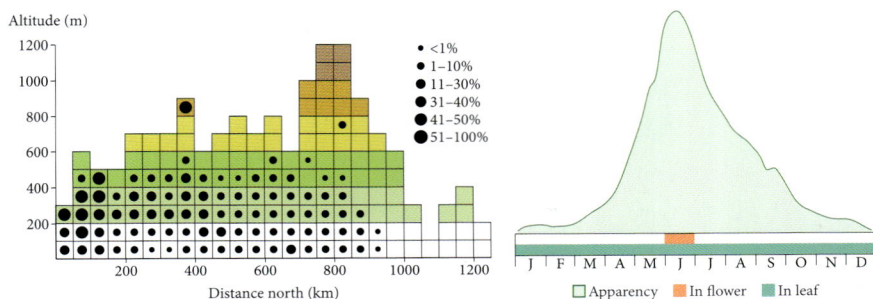

Native	GB	IR
2000–19	818	296
1987–99	739	225
1970–86	565	55
pre-1970	699	137

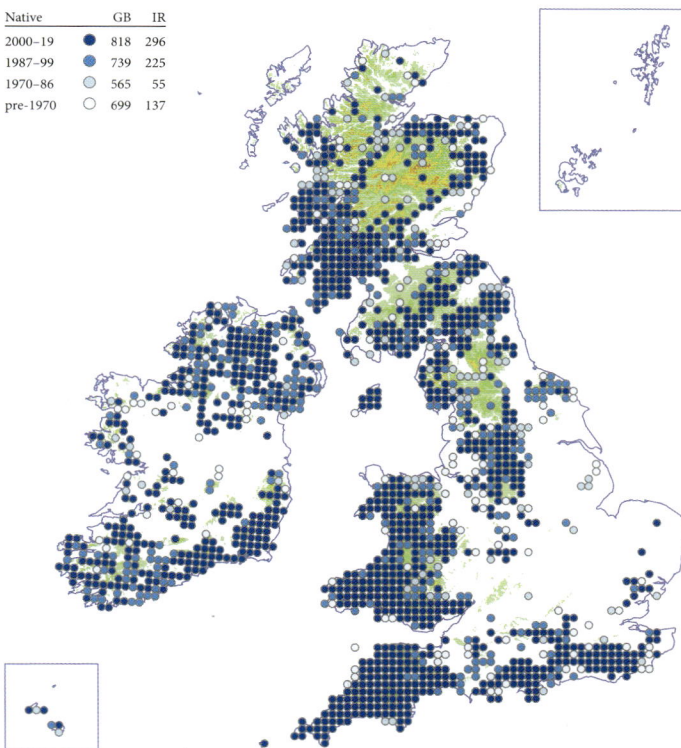

	GB	IR
Long term		
Short term		

Altitude (m)
- <1%
- 1–10%
- 11–30%
- 31–40%
- 41–50%
- 51–100%

Distance north (km)

☐ Apparency ☐ In flower ☐ In leaf

Key refs Jermy *et al.* (2007).

M.S. PORTER & M.J.Y. FOLEY

N *Carex binervis* Green-ribbed Sedge
Sm.

A perennial sedge of both wet and dry acidic soils, found in a wide range of habitats from sandy lowland heaths and *Nardus stricta* grassland to heather moorland, rocky hillsides and mountain summits. Its preferred sites are generally open but it also occurs in shady places, including deciduous and mixed woodlands. It is also occasionally found on coastal cliffs. 0–930 m (Glyder Fach, Caernarvonshire) and reportedly higher in the Scottish Highlands.

Trends *C. binervis* is common in suitable habitats, and its 10 km square distribution appears to be stable in upland areas of Britain and Ireland. There has been some small-scale decline in drier lowland regions and where arable farming dominates, but such losses in our area have been balanced by new finds in Ireland. It was mapped as 'all records' in the 1962 *Atlas*.

Biogeography Oceanic Temperate element.

Native	GB	IR
2000–19	1799	648
1987–99	1678	556
1970–86	1022	87
pre-1970	1595	401

Alien	GB	IR
2000–19	0	0
1987–99	0	1
1970–86	0	0
pre-1970	0	0

Altitude (m)
• <1%
• 1–10%
• 11–30%
• 31–40%
• 41–50%
• 51–100%

Distance north (km)

Apparency   In flower   In leaf

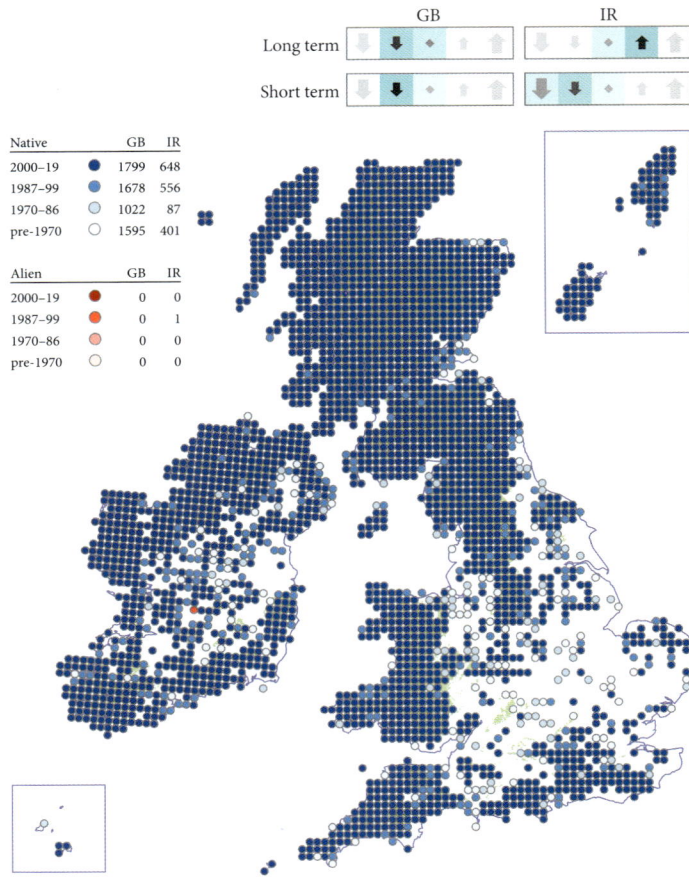

Key refs ToB Dupont (1962), Jermy *et al.* (2007). eSent

M.S. PORTER & M.J.Y. FOLEY

N *Carex distans* Distant Sedge
L.

A perennial sedge of sea-cliffs, rocky shores, coastal grasslands and the uppermost parts of saltmarshes; usually growing in bare rock-crevices or on free-draining sandy or gravelly substrates, but also in flushes and seepage zones on cliffs, and where streams debouch onto the shore. In northern and western Britain and in Ireland it is largely a coastal plant but in southern and eastern England and occasionally elsewhere it also grows inland in wet meadows, marshes and fens on mineral-rich soils and roadsides. Lowland, but formerly occurring at 575 m as an established accidental introduction at Hartside summit (Cumberland).

Trends There has been little change in the overall 10 km square distribution of *C. distans* at its coastal sites since the 1960s, save for Ireland and northern and western Scotland where many gaps have been filled thanks to more systematic recording over the past two decades. Throughout much of the 20th century there was a steady decline inland due to the drainage and destruction of its wetland habitats, although a handful of new records made since the turn of the century, mainly in old ditchbanks or small fragments of flushed grassland, suggest that it may have been overlooked in at least some areas previously, particularly in England.

Biogeography European Southern-temperate element.

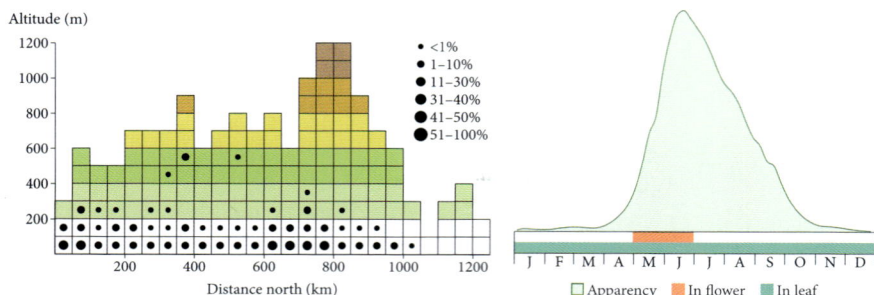

Native	GB	IR
2000–19	596	200
1987–99	539	159
1970–86	379	36
pre-1970	615	122

Alien	GB	IR
2000–19	2	0
1987–99	0	0
1970–86	0	0
pre-1970	0	0

Altitude (m)
• <1%
• 1–10%
• 11–30%
• 31–40%
• 41–50%
• 51–100%

Distance north (km)

Apparency   In flower   In leaf

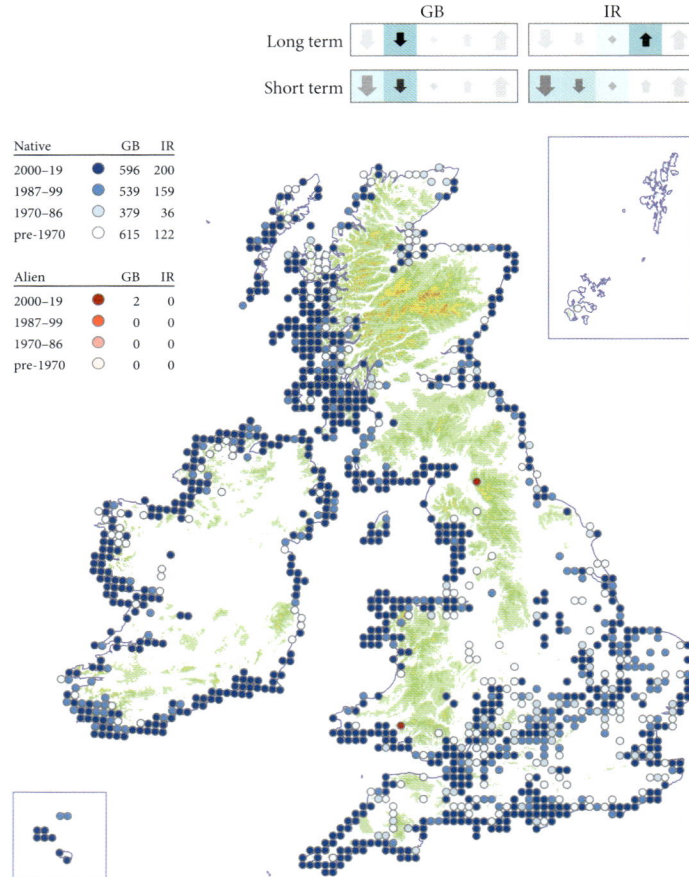

Key refs Jermy *et al.* (2007).

M.S. PORTER & M.J.Y. FOLEY

N ***Carex punctata*** Dotted Sedge

Gaudin

A perennial sedge of sheltered rock ledges and clefts on sea-cliffs, invariably in seepage zones where freshwater trickles down the cliff-face. It is also found on wet sandy patches in saltmarshes, and amongst rocks or on sand where streams debouch onto the shore. It occurs in similar habitats to *C. distans*, with which it is often confused. Lowland.

Trends *C. punctata* has a limited distribution on the coasts of Britain and Ireland, occurring mostly in the milder southern and western regions with obvious gaps in its distribution. It tends to be rather mobile and is often present in small populations. Although some sites have been lost, the overall 10 km square distribution appears to be stable, and more systematic recording has led to the discovery of new sites and the filling of gaps within its known range in recent decades.

Biogeography Suboceanic Southern-temperate element.

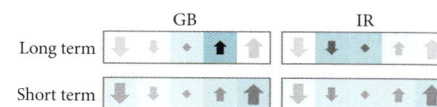

Native	GB	IR
2000–19	54	25
1987–99	38	15
1970–86	37	25
pre-1970	48	30

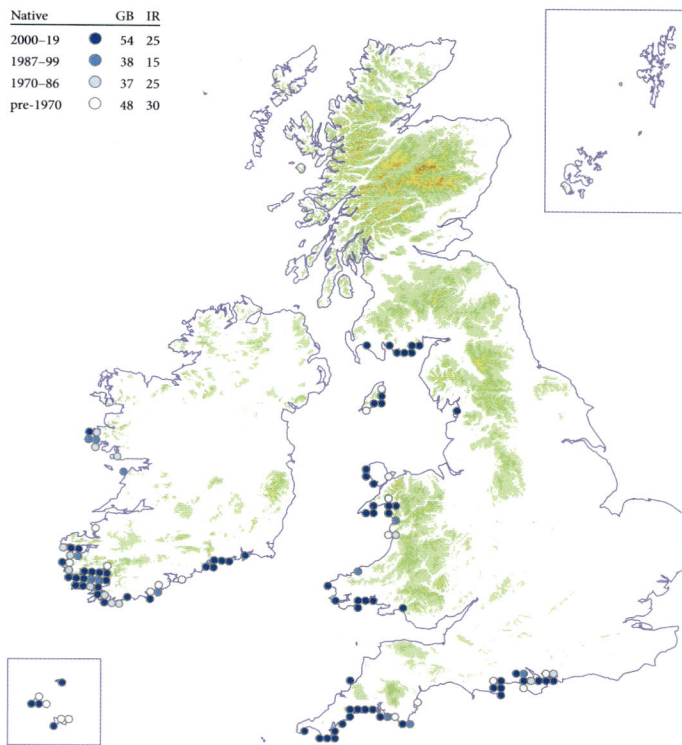

Key refs Jermy *et al.* (2007), Stewart *et al.* (1994).

M.S. Porter & M.J.Y. Foley

N ***Carex extensa*** Long-bracted Sedge

Gooden.

A perennial sedge, mainly confined to areas within reach of sea water or spray. It is found on muddy or sandy estuarine flats, at the uppermost levels of saltmarshes, and the edges of brackish ditches and in crevices on moist coastal rocks and low cliffs. It often grows with *C. distans*. Lowland.

Trends There has been little overall change in the 10 km square distribution of *C. extensa*, save for increases in parts of northern and western Scotland and western Ireland due to more systematic recording since 2000.

Biogeography European Southern-temperate element.

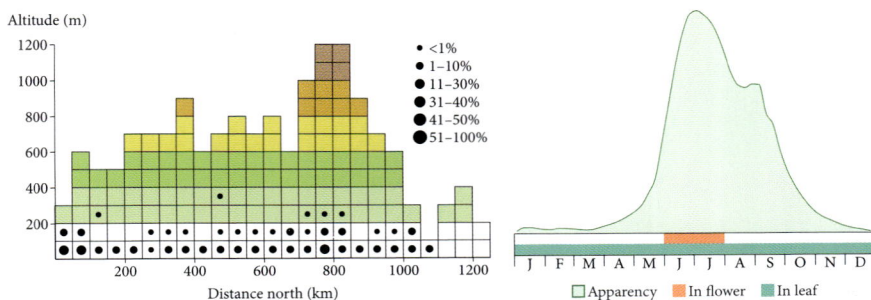

Native	GB	IR
2000–19	442	205
1987–99	306	144
1970–86	189	60
pre-1970	335	116

Key refs Jermy *et al.* (2007).

M.S. Porter & M.J.Y. Foley

N *Carex hostiana* Tawny Sedge
DC.

A perennial sedge of damp, base-rich grassland and flushes. It occurs in fens, flushed valley bogs and mires, wet meadows, marshes, rock flushes and dune-slacks. In lowland regions of Ireland it tolerates more acidic conditions. 0–995 m on the saddle between Ben Lawers and Beinn Ghlas, and potentially higher on Ben Lawers (all Mid Perthshire.

Trends *C. hostiana* was mapped as 'all records' in the 1962 *Atlas*. There has been an appreciable decline in its overall 10 km square distribution since the 1960s, particularly in lowland regions of southern England and south-western Ireland, due to the loss and modification of its wetland habitats. Many new sites have also been recorded in Ireland since 2000, due to fuller

recording. Its distribution appears to be much more stable in upland regions where it remains locally abundant.

Biogeography European Temperate element; also in North America.

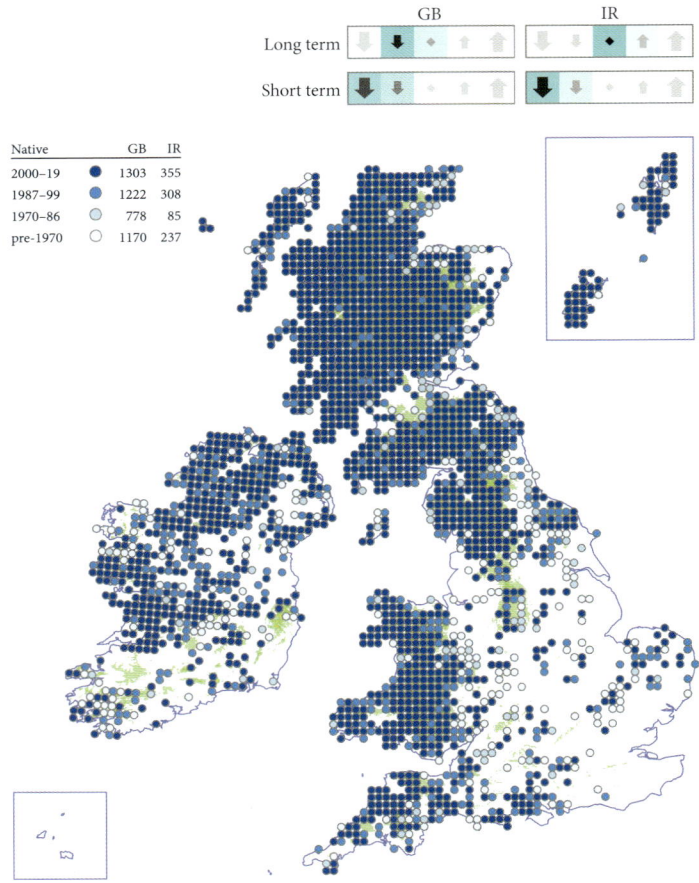

Native		GB	IR
2000–19	●	1303	355
1987–99	●	1222	308
1970–86	●	778	85
pre-1970	○	1170	237

Key refs Jermy *et al.* (2007).

M.S. PORTER & M.J.Y. FOLEY

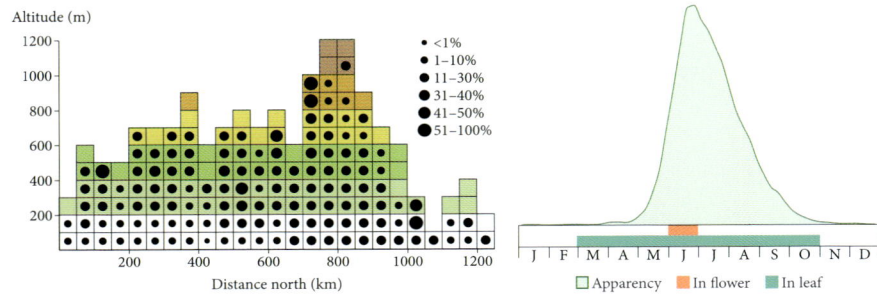

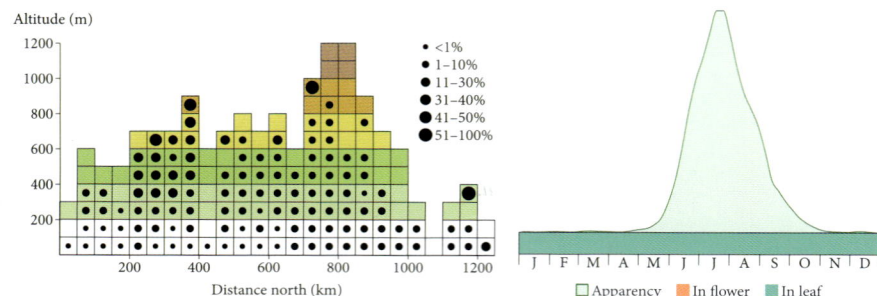

Hy *Carex hostiana* × *viridula s.l.*

C. hostiana forms sterile hybrids with *C. lepidocarpa*, *C. demissa* and *C. viridula*. These yellow sedge parents have a turbulent taxonomic history, and have been treated as subspecies of the *C. viridula* aggregate in recent years. Their hybrids with *C. hostiana* may be found in fens, wet meadows, heathland and moorland, and on the margins of lakes, especially where there is flushing with base-rich water. *C. demissa* is the most frequent of the species within *C. viridula s.l.*, has the greatest ecological range, and its hybrid with *C. hostiana* occurs most frequently, sometimes in the absence of *C. hostiana*. *C. lepidocarpa* has a more calcicolous habitat than either *C. demissa* or *C. viridula*, occurring in base-rich wetlands and sometimes coastal marshes; it is, therefore, closer than the latter two in its ecology to *C. hostiana*, and its hybrid with *C. hostiana* may be

frequent in such habitat. The hybrid with *C. viridula*, much the rarest of the three, has been confirmed from only four sites. 0–1,073 m on Ben Lawers (Mid Perthshire).

A spontaneous hybrid (native × native).

Trends Due to difficulties in determining the parents, many of the available records simply refer to *C. hostiana* × *viridula s.l.*, or alternatively are erroneously named as *C. ×fulva* as a 'catch-all'. It has become increasingly difficult to disentangle the distribution of the three hybrids with any degree of confidence and they are, therefore, not included as individual maps. In the broad sense, and as individual taxa, they are almost certainly still under-recorded.

Biogeography Widespread in temperate Europe.

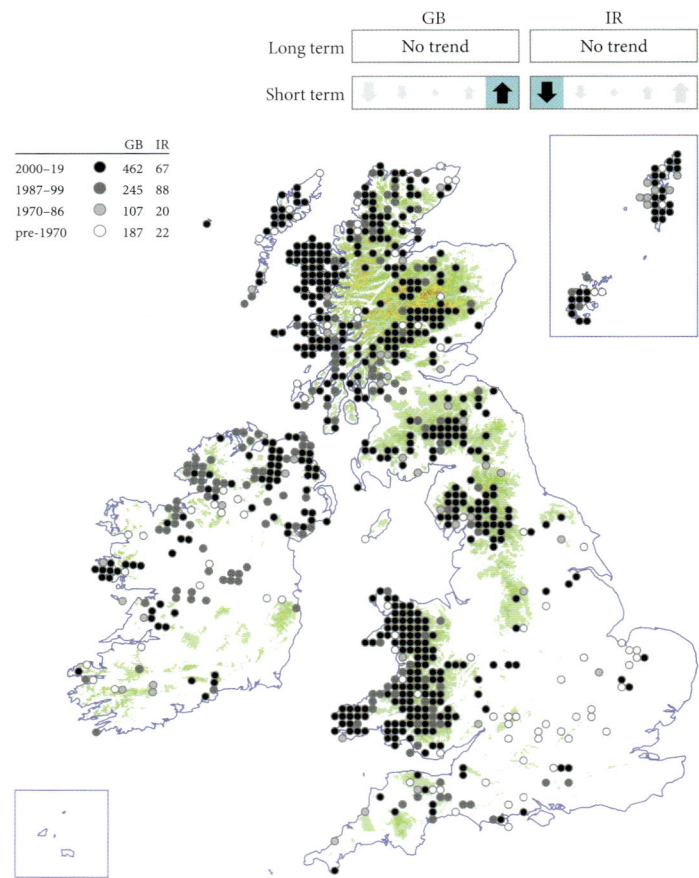

		GB	IR
2000–19	●	462	67
1987–99	●	245	88
1970–86	●	107	20
pre-1970	○	187	22

Key refs Stace *et al.* (2015).

M.S. PORTER & M.J.Y. FOLEY

N *Carex flava* Large Yellow-sedge

L.

A perennial sedge of calcareous mires and in damp woodland on peaty soil flushed by calcareous water from adjacent limestone outcrops. Growing at near sea level at Roudsea Wood (Westmorland) and at 380 m at Malham Tarn (Mid-west Yorkshire).

Trends In our area *C. flava* has been confirmed as a native from only two sites. A large and thriving population occurs at Roudsea Wood (Westmorland) where it has been known since the early 20th century and favours areas of dappled shade maintained by judicious thinning of the tree canopy. Its presence at Malham Tarn (Mid-west Yorkshire) had long been suspected but was only confirmed following a detailed morphological study published in 2001 (Blackstock & Ashton, 2001). The most recent survey in 2013 revealed a population of around 40

plants. Allozyme analysis of a colony of *C. lepidocarpa* at Greywell Fen (North Hampshire) suggests the historic presence of *C. flava*. It was also recorded at one site in Ireland, in County Clare in 1968 (not mapped), growing with hybrids with *C. lepidocarpa*. On subsequent visits only the hybrid has been found. In 2018 a previously unrecorded population was discovered in a fen adjacent to Gaitbarrows (West Lancashire) which subsequently turned out to be an occurrence resulting from the experimental introduction of plants grown on from seed collected from Gaitbarrows. In addition, some plants have been translocated from the Roudsea Wood site to suitable areas nearby.

Biogeography European Boreo-temperate element; also in central Asia and North America.

		GB	IR
Long term		No trend	No trend
Short term		No trend	No trend

Native	GB	IR
2000–19	2	0
1987–99	1	0
1970–86	1	0
pre-1970	3	0

Alien	GB	IR
2000–19	1	0
1987–99	0	0
1970–86	0	0
pre-1970	0	0

Key refs Blackstock & Ashton (2001), Blackstock & Jermy (2001), Jermy *et al.* (2007), Wigginton (1999).

M.S. Porter, M.J.Y. Foley & K.J. Walker

N *Carex lepidocarpa* Long-stalked Yellow-sedge

Tausch

A perennial sedge of fens and calcareous mires, especially in areas of winter flooding. It is also frequent in base-rich flushes and on wet ledges on sea-cliffs, hills and mountainsides, usually in short, open vegetation. 0–992 m (Beinn Heasgarnich, Mid Perthshire)

Trends Historically, *C. lepidocarpa* declined in lowland England, presumably due to drainage and agricultural improvements, and succession following undergrazing or neglect. Surviving populations in many lowland areas are now very small. Populations in upland regions appear to be more stable with many new discoveries in northern England, Scotland and Ireland as a result of fuller recording this century. Intermediates with *C. demissa* occur and can cause taxonomic difficulties in some areas.

Biogeography European Temperate element; also in eastern North America.

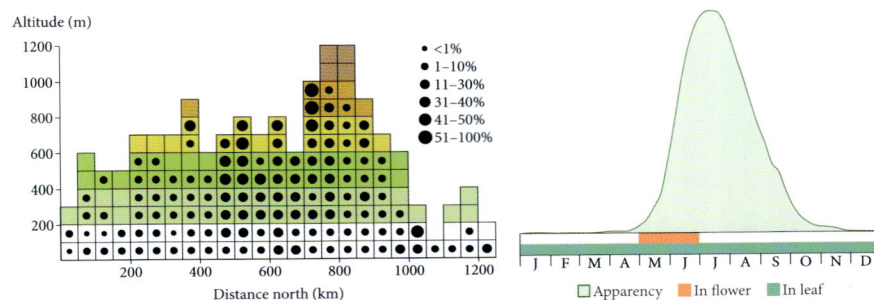

Native	GB	IR
2000–19	974	316
1987–99	879	354
1970–86	672	105
pre-1970	661	196

Key refs Jermy *et al.* (2007).

M.S. Porter & M.J.Y. Foley

N *Carex demissa* Common Yellow-sedge

Hornem.

A perennial sedge of wet substrates ranging from acidic to neutral or occasionally mildly alkaline. It is found in a wide variety of open habitats, including sandy shores, tracks, streamsides, wet fields and heathland, the margins of ponds and lakes, wet rocky hillsides, flushes and seepage areas. 0–1,155 m (Ben Lawers, Mid Perthshire).

Trends *C. demissa* is the most widespread of the yellow-sedges due to its wide tolerance of soil pH. Its distribution is now much better known than when mapped (as 'all records') in the 1962 *Atlas*, due to more systematic recording. It remains frequent over much of Britain and Ireland but has experienced some decline at the edges of its range in southern England, in the English Midlands and in central areas of Ireland, almost certainly due to drainage and loss of wetland habitats. However, new records made in these areas since the turn of the century have gone some way to redressing the balance. Its morphology is very variable with a number of distinct forms approaching *C. lepidocarpa*, leading to confusion in some regions.

Biogeography Suboceanic Boreo-temperate element; also in eastern North America.

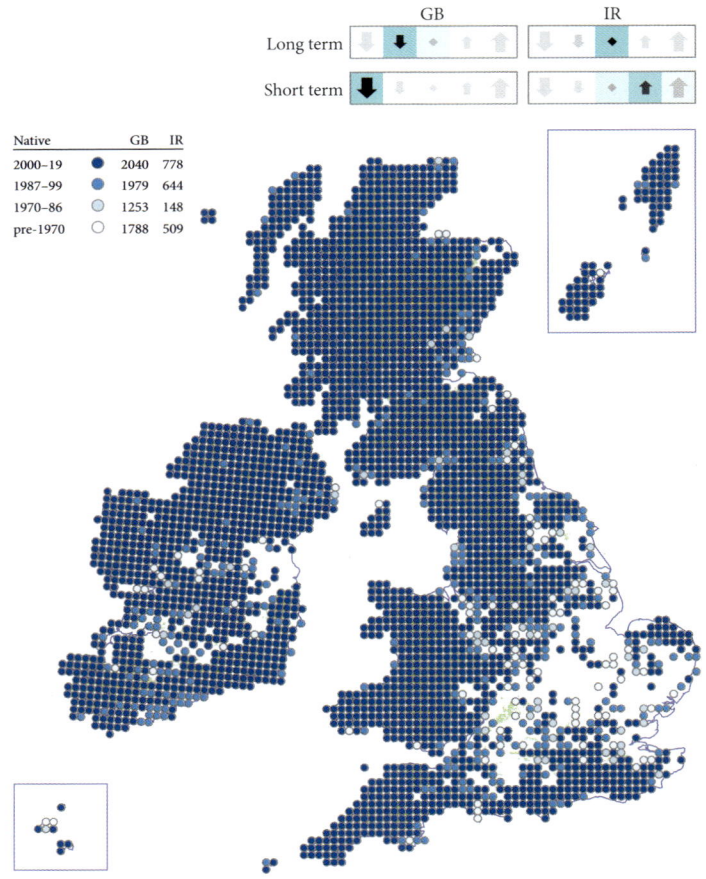

Native	GB	IR
2000–19	2040	778
1987–99	1979	644
1970–86	1253	148
pre-1970	1788	509

Key refs Jermy *et al.* (2007).

M.S. PORTER, M.J.Y. FOLEY & K.J. WALKER

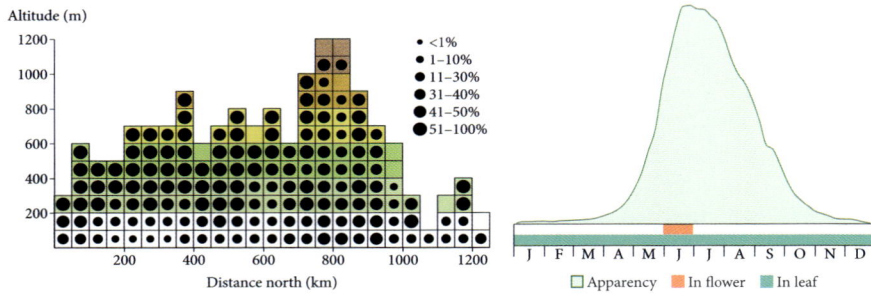

N *Carex viridula* Yellow-sedge

Michx.

A perennial sedge of open, damp or wet habitats, including dune-slacks, the upper edges of saltmarshes, on the stony margins of lakes or pools, and in open fens and marshes. It usually occurs on flushed acidic soils, but also locally on base-rich substrates. Usually lowland, but in the Scottish Highlands it has been recorded at 930 m on Beinn Heasgarnich (Mid Perthshire).

Trends *C. viridula* is a diminutive sedge which is easily overlooked and as a result under-recorded in the past. Its distribution is now much better known, with a considerable number of new records made since 2000 from coastal areas of northern and western Britain and Ireland. It has, however, experienced decline in some areas, and notably from inland sites in southern and eastern England and from central Ireland.

Biogeography European Boreo-temperate element; also in eastern Asia and widespread in North America.

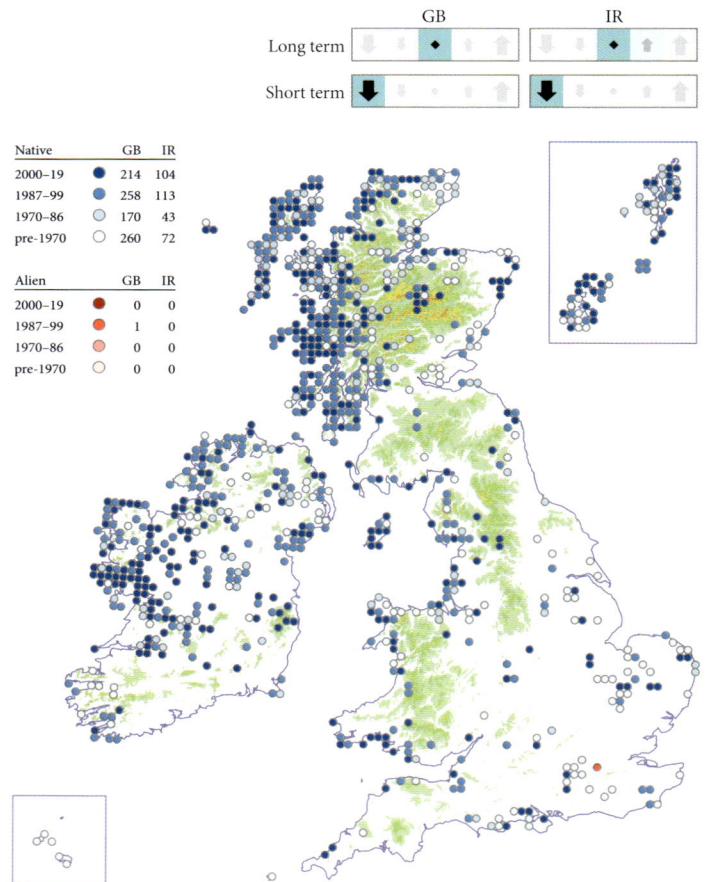

Native	GB	IR
2000–19	214	104
1987–99	258	113
1970–86	170	43
pre-1970	260	72

Alien	GB	IR
2000–19	0	0
1987–99	1	0
1970–86	0	0
pre-1970	0	0

Key refs Jermy *et al.* (2007).

M.J.Y. FOLEY & M.S. PORTER

(N) *Carex pallescens* Pale Sedge
L.

A perennial sedge of damp grassland, woodland rides and clearings and stream banks; usually on moist, mildly acidic to neutral soils. In the Scottish mountains and some of the hills of northern England it is found on acidic, wet grassy slopes. Lowland to 855 m at Craig Derry (South Aberdeenshire).

Trends *C. pallescens* was mapped as 'all records' in the 1962 *Atlas*. It has declined historically but less so since 2000 and it remains widespread and locally common in parts of northern, southern and western Britain, particularly in upland regions. In Ireland there have been appreciably more records for southern and central areas since the turn of the century due to more systematic recording.

Biogeography Eurosiberian Boreo-temperate element; also in North America.

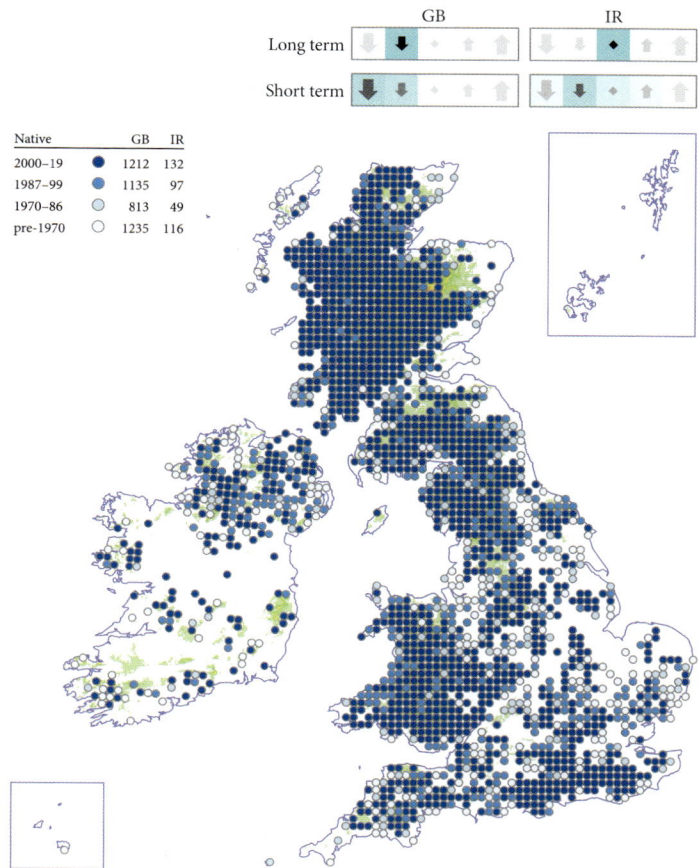

Native		GB	IR
2000–19	●	1212	132
1987–99	●	1135	97
1970–86	●	813	49
pre-1970	○	1235	116

Key refs Jermy *et al.* (2007).

M.J.Y. FOLEY & M.S. PORTER

(N) *Carex digitata* Fingered Sedge
L.

A perennial sedge of open deciduous woodland over limestone, but also found on adjacent areas of scree, rock outcrops, and sheltered limestone pavement. It seeds freely in lightly shaded habitats but ceases to flower and dies out if the canopy becomes too closed or the site overgrown. New plants can appear from dormant seed following disturbance. Lowland.

Trends *C. digitata* is still locally abundant on limestone in the Wye Valley, Avon Gorge, Cotswolds, Derbyshire Dales and around Morecambe Bay. After losses during the much of the last century its distribution appeared to have stabilized by the 1990s, and new locations have been found in the last decade in Westmorland and West Lancashire.

Biogeography European Boreo-temperate element, with a continental distribution in western Europe; also in eastern Asia.

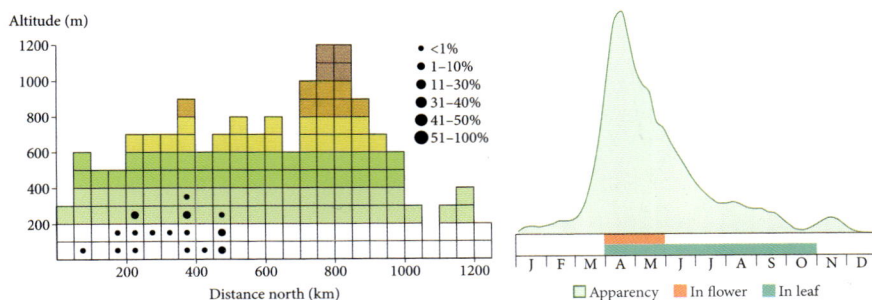

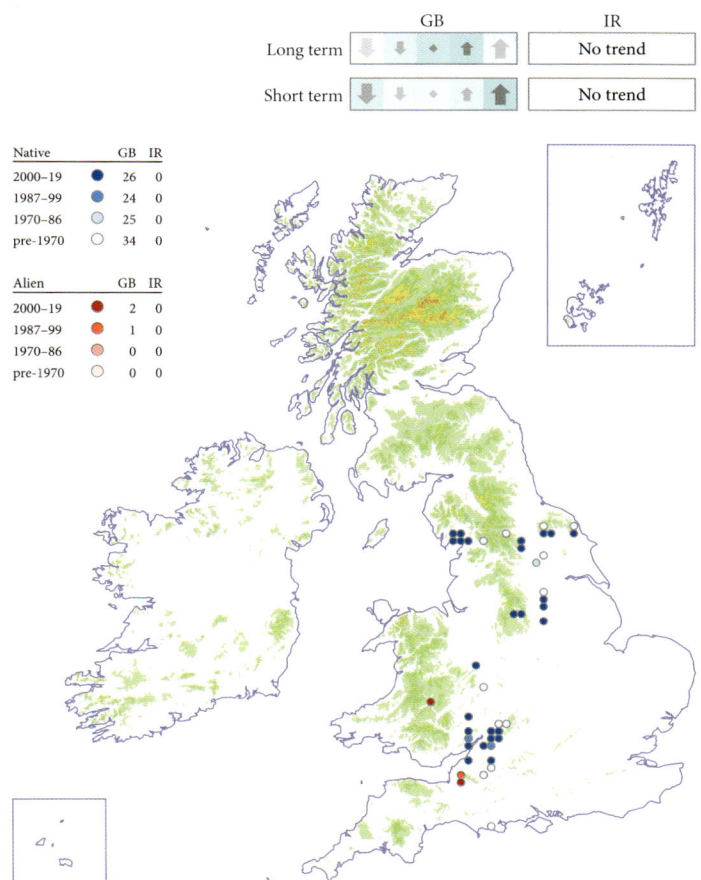

Native	GB	IR
2000–19	26	0
1987–99	24	0
1970–86	25	0
pre-1970	34	0

Alien	GB	IR
2000–19	2	0
1987–99	1	0
1970–86	0	0
pre-1970	0	0

Key refs David (1978a), Jermy *et al.* (2007), Stewart *et al.* (1994).

M.J.Y. FOLEY & M.S. PORTER

N ***Carex ornithopoda*** Bird's-foot Sedge
Willd.

A perennial sedge of skeletal, well-drained soils on south-facing slopes overlying Carboniferous limestone. It grows in open grassland, on rocky outcrops, screes, crags and limestone pavements, and occasionally also in partial shade in open limestone woodland. Lowland, ascending to 600 m on Long Fell, Warcop (Westmorland).

Trends *C. ornithopoda* has a very localized distribution centered on the limestones around Morecambe Bay and near Orton in Westmorland, with outlying populations in the Derbyshire Dales. Its distribution is stable and is now much better known after the discovery of new sites in Cumberland and Mid-west Yorkshire in the 1980s, and two new sites in Westmorland since 2000. However, many populations remain vulnerable to intensive grazing by sheep, and it

has not been seen at two Yorkshire sites since the end of the 19th century.

Biogeography European Boreal-montane element.

	GB	IR
Long term	No trend	No trend
Short term	No trend	No trend

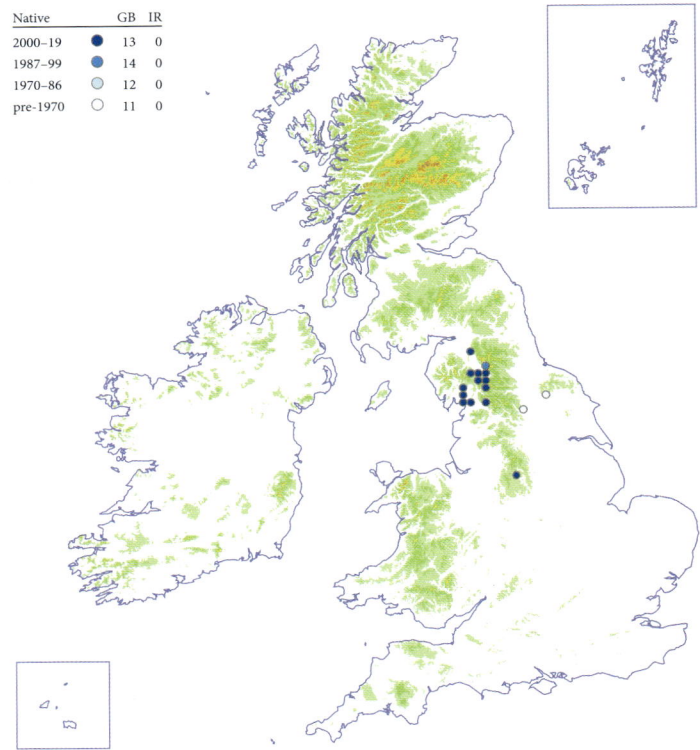

Native	GB	IR
2000–19	● 13	0
1987–99	● 14	0
1970–86	◐ 12	0
pre-1970	○ 11	0

Key refs Corner & Roberts (1989), David (1980), Jermy *et al.* (2007), Porter & Roberts (1997), Wigginton (1999).

M.S. PORTER & M.J.Y. FOLEY

N ***Carex humilis*** Dwarf Sedge
Leyss.

A perennial sedge of closely grazed calcareous grassland, especially on chalk downland in Dorset, Wiltshire and Hampshire where it is strongly associated with ancient earthworks (*e.g.* boundary dykes, tumuli). In limestone areas it also occurs locally in grazed pastures as well as on field margins, tracksides and rock outcrops. It fruits freely, but regeneration from seed and spread into new areas have only rarely been reported. Lowland.

Trends The overall 10 km square distribution of *C. humilis* appears to be reasonably stable, but detailed studies in Dorset revealed that over 10% of its recorded sites had been ploughed up while others had been lost or reduced due to relaxation in grazing pressure (Pearman, 1997), a trend which has continued since the turn of the century. It was discovered on the

Isle of Wight in 2006. The majority of extant sites have some form of statutory protection, but even here undergrazing is proving deleterious on some sites.

Biogeography Eurasian Temperate element, with a continental distribution in western Europe.

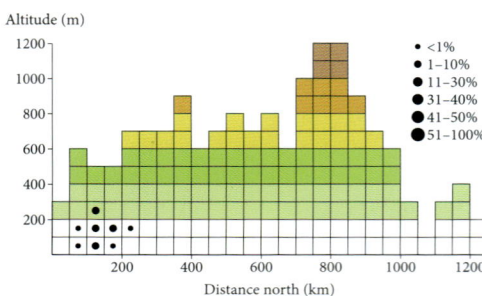

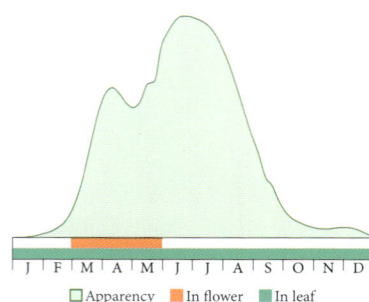

	GB	IR
Long term	⬇ ⬇ ◆ ⬆ ⬆	No trend
Short term	⬇ ⬇ ◆ ⬆ ⬆	No trend

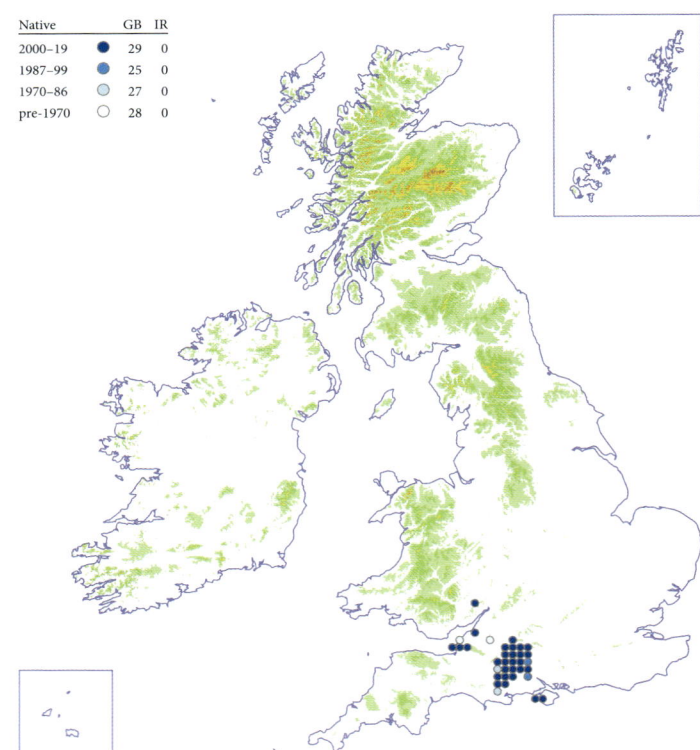

Native	GB	IR
2000–19	● 29	0
1987–99	● 25	0
1970–86	◐ 27	0
pre-1970	○ 28	0

Key refs Jermy *et al.* (2007), Pearman (1997), Stewart *et al.* (1994).

M.S. PORTER & M.J.Y. FOLEY

Carex caryophyllea Spring-sedge

Latourr.

A shortly rhizomatous perennial sedge, typically found in meadows and pastures on dry, calcareous or base-rich soils but also in grasslands and heaths on mildly acidic soils, and in well-drained grassland and ledges and flushes in the uplands. It also occurs in maritime sites such as on the tops of sea cliffs and in sand dune grasslands. 0–913 m (Stuchd an Lochain, Mid Perthshire).

Trends Though there is evidence of decline, especially in the English Midlands and south-eastern England, with most losses having occurred since 1950, over much of the range of *C. caryophyllea* it appears to be stable, and there are numerous new records since the turn of the century, most notably in Ireland where its distribution is now much better known than it was in the latter half of the 20th century. It was mapped as 'all records' in the 1962 *Atlas*.

Biogeography Eurosiberian Temperate element.

Native	GB	IR
2000–19	1576	349
1987–99	1520	327
1970–86	988	84
pre-1970	1420	226

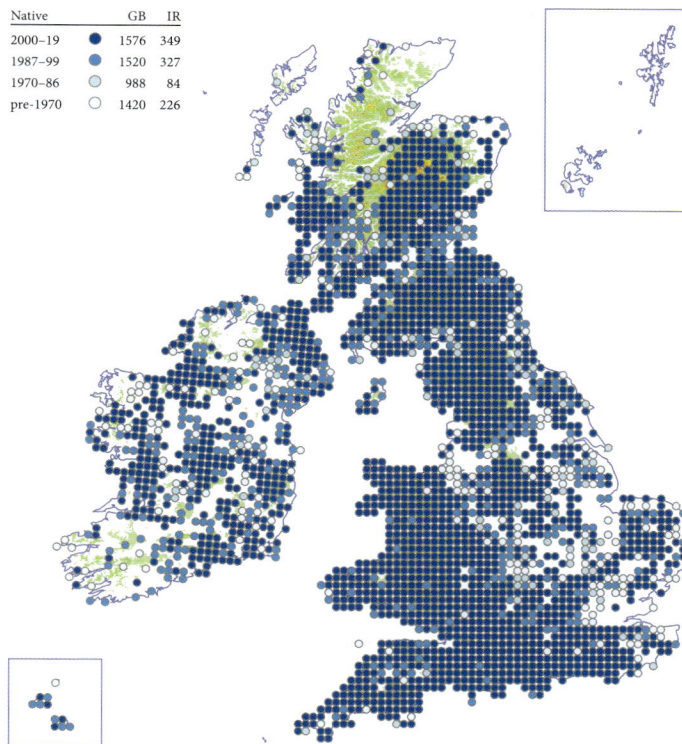

Key refs Grime *et al.* (2007), Jermy *et al.* (2007).

M.S. PORTER & M.J.Y. FOLEY

Carex filiformis Downy-fruited Sedge

L.

A rhizomatous perennial sedge of calcium-rich soils in a wide range of habitats but, despite this, it has a very limited distribution in our area. It is most characteristic of damp meadows, but is also found in dry grassland, grassy woodland rides and along roadsides. Lowland.

Trends Although a few populations of *C. filiformis* were lost to agricultural improvement and pesticide spraying along roadsides in the latter half of the 20th century, its overall distribution now appears to be stable and all of its extant sites have some degree of protection (as Sites of Special Scientific Interest). New populations were discovered in Somerset in 2003 and in Essex in 2018, suggesting that it may be overlooked elsewhere as it is a difficult plant to detect when not in flower.

Biogeography Eurosiberian Temperate element, with a continental distribution in western Europe.

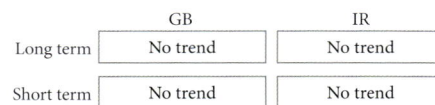

Native	GB	IR
2000–19	13	0
1987–99	12	0
1970–86	11	0
pre-1970	14	0

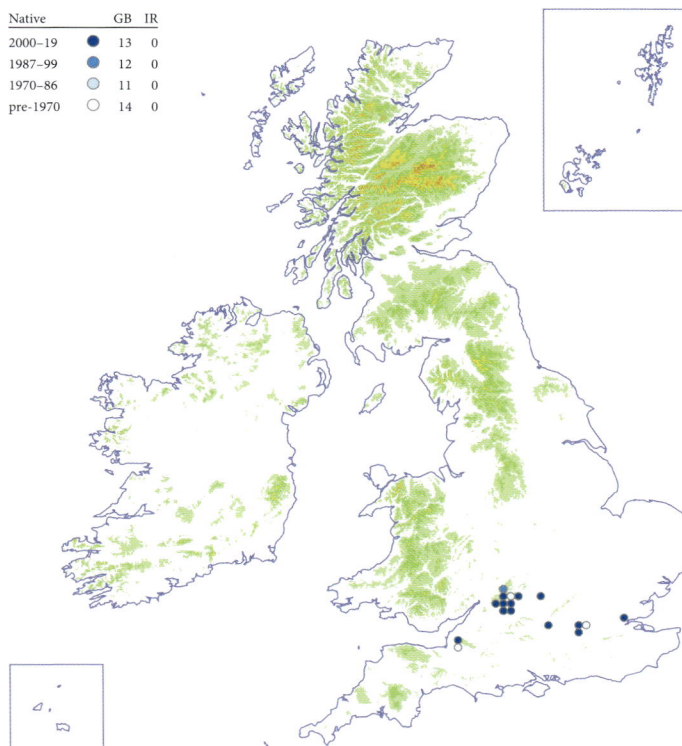

	GB	IR
Long term	No trend	No trend
Short term	No trend	No trend

Key refs David (1983), Jermy *et al.* (2007), Wigginton (1999).

M.S. PORTER & M.J.Y. FOLEY

N *Carex ericetorum* Rare Spring-sedge
Pollich

A perennial sedge of short grassland on infertile soils overlying limestone, chalk or chalky boulder-clay. It is a poor competitor and soon disappears if grazing is relaxed and the sward becomes too tall. It reproduces vegetatively and by seed, albeit sparingly. Lowland in East Anglia, eastern England and around Morecambe Bay, extending up to 540 m on Cronkley Fell in Upper Teesdale (North-west Yorkshire).

Trends Historically, around 40% of British populations of *C. ericetorum* have been lost due to ploughing-up of grasslands, lack of grazing, agricultural intensification and quarrying, mainly in East Anglia and eastern England (Walker & Stroh, 2021). Populations in north-western England are much larger and more stable, although it has declined in numbers at a few sites where stocking levels have been reduced over the last

20 years (*e.g.* Widdybank Fell, Orton Scar). Although the majority of extant sites receive statutory protection (as Sites of Special Scientific Interest) many continue to be at risk from reductions in grazing levels. It is easy to overlook due to its erratic flowering and similarity to *C. caryophyllea*, and this presumably accounts for the discovery of a new site in Mid-west Yorkshire (Ledsham Banks) as well as its rediscovery at two other sites after an absence of many years.

Biogeography Eurosiberian Boreal-montane element, with a continental distribution in western Europe.

Native	GB	IR
2000–19	19	0
1987–99	20	0
1970–86	27	0
pre-1970	28	0

Key refs David (1981), Jermy *et al.* (2007), Stewart *et al.* (1994), Stroh *et al.* (2019), Walker *et al.* (2017), Walker & Stroh (2020).

M.S. PORTER, M.J.Y. FOLEY & K.J. WALKER

N *Carex montana* Soft-leaved Sedge
L.

A perennial sedge originally thought to be confined to rough, open grassland on limestone. However, recent studies have shown that it grows only where non-calcareous drift overlays the calcareous bedrock, and it can in fact thrive in neutral to acidic grassland, on heathland and in woodland rides, often in partial shade. Generally lowland, but reaching 560 m at Carreg yr Ogof (Carmarthenshire).

Trends The recognition of the wider ecological amplitude of *C. montana* has led to its discovery in many new 10 km squares since the 1960s, particularly in southern Wales and Hampshire. The most striking extension to its range came with the discovery of new sites in Cornwall, where it was growing in some quantity, although this is balanced somewhat by its disappearance from Sussex (last seen in 1974) and Berkshire

(destroyed by roadworks in 1973) and by a reduction in numbers at its outlying site in Derbyshire in recent years.

Biogeography European Temperate element, with a continental distribution in western Europe; also in central and eastern Asia.

Native	GB	IR
2000–19	36	0
1987–99	40	0
1970–86	35	0
pre-1970	29	0

Alien	GB	IR
2000–19	2	0
1987–99	2	0
1970–86	1	0
pre-1970	0	0

Key refs Jermy *et al.* (2007), Kay & John (1994), Stewart *et al.* (1994).

M.S. PORTER & M.J.Y. FOLEY

N

Carex pilulifera Pill Sedge
L.

A perennial sedge of base-poor, usually acidic soils; its habitats include sandy heaths, dune grassland, open woodlands, acid grassland and dry heathland. Although it favours free-draining soils it can be abundant in damp pastures. It is most frequent in upland and mountainous regions. 0–1,170 m (Ben More, Mid Perthshire).

Trends *C. pilulifera* was mapped as 'all records' in the 1962 *Atlas*. There seems to have been little change in its overall distribution and frequency in upland regions where it remains relatively common in suitable habitats. In comparison, it is now scarce in central and eastern England due to the loss of lowland heathlands and acid pastures, although there have been many new discoveries as a result of more systematic recording in recent decades, especially in Ireland.

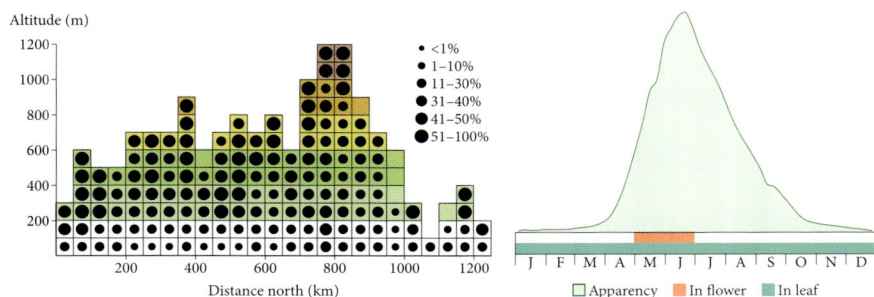

Biogeography European Temperate element.

Native		GB	IR
2000–19	●	1971	462
1987–99	●	1780	353
1970–86	○	1099	75
pre-1970	○	1631	184

Key refs Grime *et al.* (2007), Jermy *et al.* (2007).

M.S. PORTER & M.J.Y. FOLEY

N

Carex atrofusca Scorched Alpine-sedge
Schkuhr

A perennial sedge of stony, calcareous, usually micaceous flushes, especially at the point of emergence of springs, and bogs. It also occurs on steep rock-flushes where it may be protected by rocks or tufts of grass. Formerly recorded below 600 m, it is currently known from five localities between 680 m (Ben Lawers, Mid Perthshire) and 1,000 m (Beinn Heasgarnich, Mid Perthshire).

Trends There has been little change in either the 10 km square distribution or the abundance of this species, and a survey carried out in 2013 showed no sign of a decline. A record from Beinn an Dothaidh (Main Argyll) in 1976 has not been confirmed and is now regarded as doubtful. An outlying record from the Hebridean island of Rum is now thought to have been a deliberate introduction (Pearman & Walker, 2004b).

Biogeography Circumpolar Arctic-montane element.

Native		GB	IR
2000–19	●	4	0
1987–99	●	4	0
1970–86	○	5	0
pre-1970	○	5	0

Alien		GB	IR
2000–19	●	0	0
1987–99	●	0	0
1970–86	●	0	0
pre-1970	○	1	0

	GB	IR
Long term	No trend	No trend
Short term	No trend	No trend

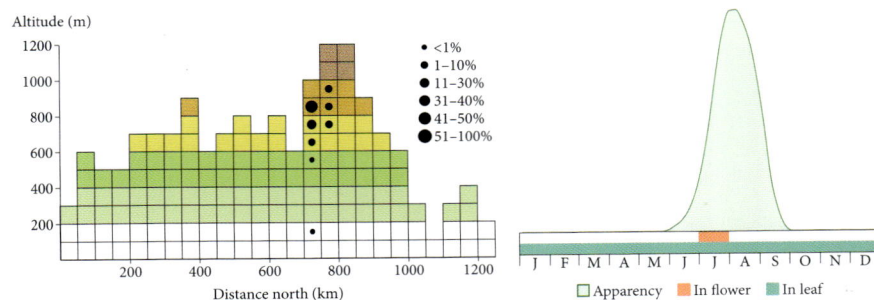

Key refs Jermy *et al.* (2007), Pearman & Walker (2004b), Wigginton (1999).

M.S. PORTER & M.J.Y. FOLEY

N *Carex limosa* Bog-sedge
L.

A perennial sedge of deep *Sphagnum* mires and the wet, peaty margins of pools, often growing in standing water. Most of its sites are acidic and oligotrophic, but unlike *C. magellanica*, with which it shares a similar ecology, it tends to occur in areas subject to some mineral enrichment. *C. limosa* usually occurs below 300 m but reaches 830 m on Meall nan Tarmachan (Mid Perthshire).

Trends *C. limosa* has a very restricted range in our area, being absent from much of southern and eastern England and south-eastern Ireland. It is still locally abundant in Dorset and Hampshire but has been lost from East Anglia where it was last recorded in 1974. It is most frequent in north-western Scotland and north-western Ireland but even in these strongholds it appears to be gradually declining, probably as a result of drainage, afforestation and, in Ireland, peat extraction. However, the recent discovery of a site on Bodmin Moor (East Cornwall) is a welcome and significant extension to its range, and new sites have been found in Scotland, Wales and Ireland in the past 20 years due to more systematic recording.

Biogeography Circumpolar Boreal-montane element.

Native	GB	IR
2000–19	296	119
1987–99	272	140
1970–86	158	52
pre-1970	273	111

Key refs Jermy *et al.* (2007), Preston & Croft (1997).

M.S. PORTER & M.J.Y. FOLEY

N *Carex rariflora* Mountain Bog-sedge
(Wahlenb.) Sm.

A perennial sedge of wet, base-poor peats, mainly occurring in flush-bogs on gentle slopes, often in areas of late snow-lie or by streams flowing from them. It also occurs by pools, and on terraces by the side of incised burns. From 790 m in Drumochter Forest (Westerness) and Meikle Kilrannoch (Angus) to 1,125 m at Lochan Bhuidhe and Ben Macdui (both Banffshire).

Trends *C. rariflora* has been discovered in many new sites within its known range since the 1980s, some of them very extensive. Around 30 populations are currently known, including seven discovered since 2000. Climate change is possibly the only major threat to this species.

Biogeography Circumpolar Arctic-montane element; absent from mountains of central Europe.

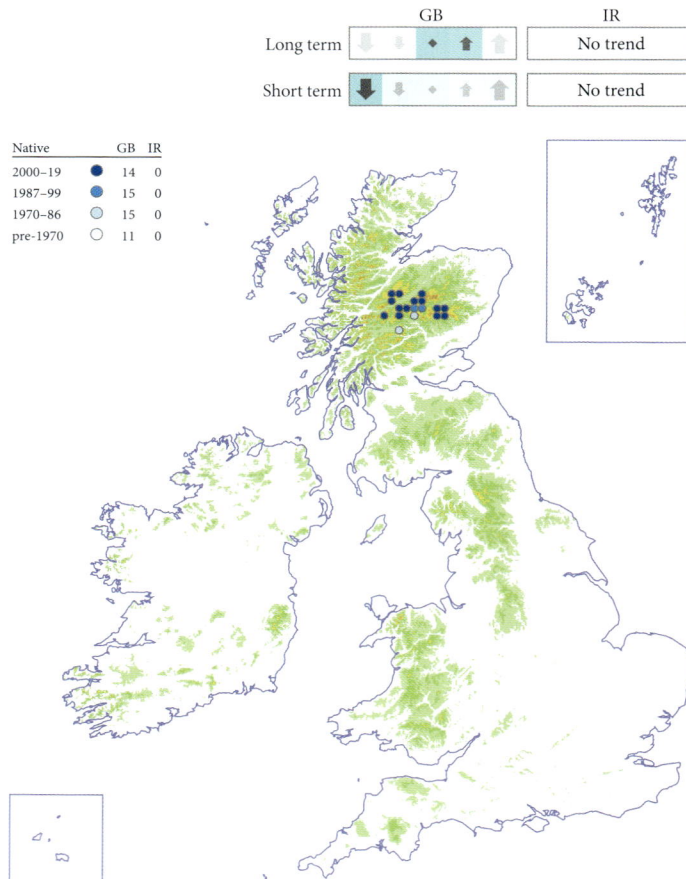

Native	GB	IR
2000–19	14	0
1987–99	15	0
1970–86	15	0
pre-1970	11	0

Key refs Jermy *et al.* (2007), Wigginton (1999).

M.S. PORTER & M.J.Y. FOLEY

N *Carex magellanica* Tall Bog-sedge

Lam.

A perennial sedge of wet ground, pools and hummocks in *Sphagnum* bogs, or at the edges of gently sloping mires where there is slight lateral water movement, but seldom in standing water; consequently often found along watersheds. It generally occurs in open ground, but sometimes persists in carr. From 30 m (Shian, Mid Perthshire), but generally upland, reaching 685 m (Ben Lui, Main Argyll).

Trends *C. magellanica* is very sparsely scattered in suitable habitats in upland regions of northern and western Britain and Ireland. Many new sites were found during systematic surveys in the 1990s, particularly in Wales (where it was originally collected around 1835 but not refound again until 1963), Cumbria, Main Argyll and Northern Ireland, and new sites have continued to be found since 2000 throughout

its known range in Scotland and Northern Ireland (County Tyrone). However, many sites were lost in the 20th century as a result of drainage or afforestation, and during the current survey a number of populations that were recorded in the previous atlas survey have not been refound.

Biogeography Circumpolar Boreal-montane element.

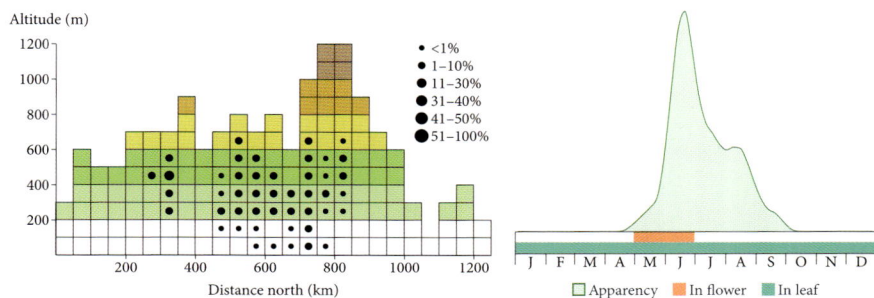

Native		GB	IR
2000–19	●	76	7
1987–99	●	71	6
1970–86	○	70	4
pre-1970	○	82	4

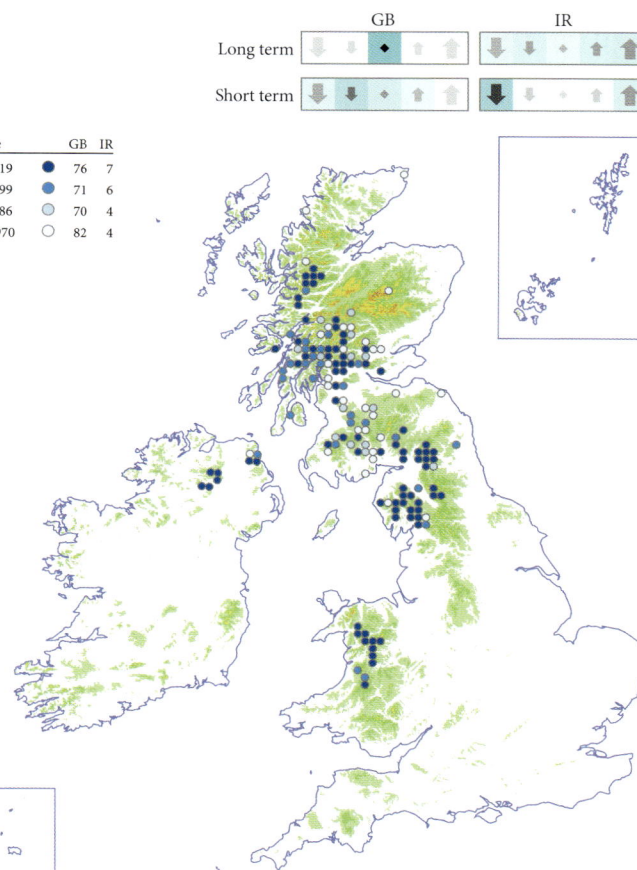

Key refs Jermy *et al.* (2007), Stewart *et al.* (1994).

M.S. PORTER & M.J.Y. FOLEY

N *Carex atrata* Black Alpine-sedge

L.

A perennial sedge of ungrazed mountain rock-faces and ledges of both wet and dry calcareous cliffs, or cliffs where there is calcareous veining. It grows in short vegetation or amongst tall herbs, and in dwarf *Salix* scrub. Populations are probably maintained by vegetative growth. From 550 m in Coire Ghamhnain (Main Argyll) and usually above 700 m, reaching 1,095 m on Ben Lawers (Mid Perthshire).

Trends The distribution of *C. atrata* is reasonably stable, although in a number of Scottish sites it has not been recorded this century. In Snowdonia, the Lake District and southern Scotland in particular some populations are small and thus vulnerable, but the plant has been remarkably persistent. An outlying record from the Hebridean island of Rum is now thought to

have been a deliberate introduction (Pearman & Walker, 2004b).

Biogeography Circumpolar Boreo-arctic Montane element.

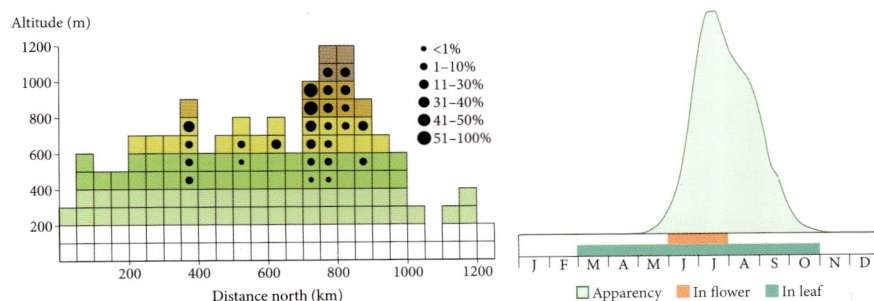

Native		GB	IR
2000–19	●	31	0
1987–99	●	36	0
1970–86	○	38	0
pre-1970	○	44	0

Alien		GB	IR
2000–19	●	0	0
1987–99	●	0	0
1970–86	○	0	0
pre-1970	○	1	0

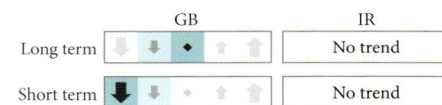

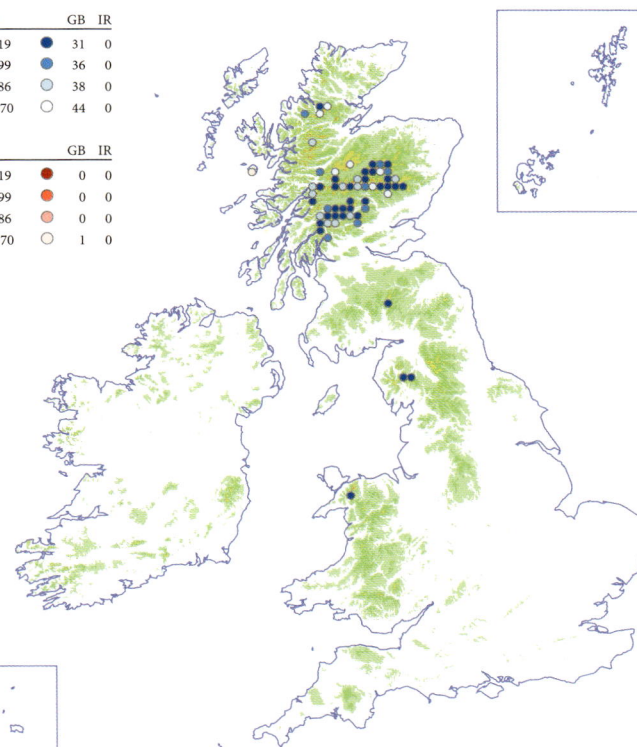

Key refs Jermy *et al.* (1982), Jermy *et al.* (2007), Pearman & Walker (2004b), Stewart *et al.* (1994).

M.S. PORTER & M.J.Y. FOLEY

N *Carex buxbaumii* Club Sedge

Wahlenb.

	GB	IR
Long term	No trend	No trend
Short term	No trend	No trend

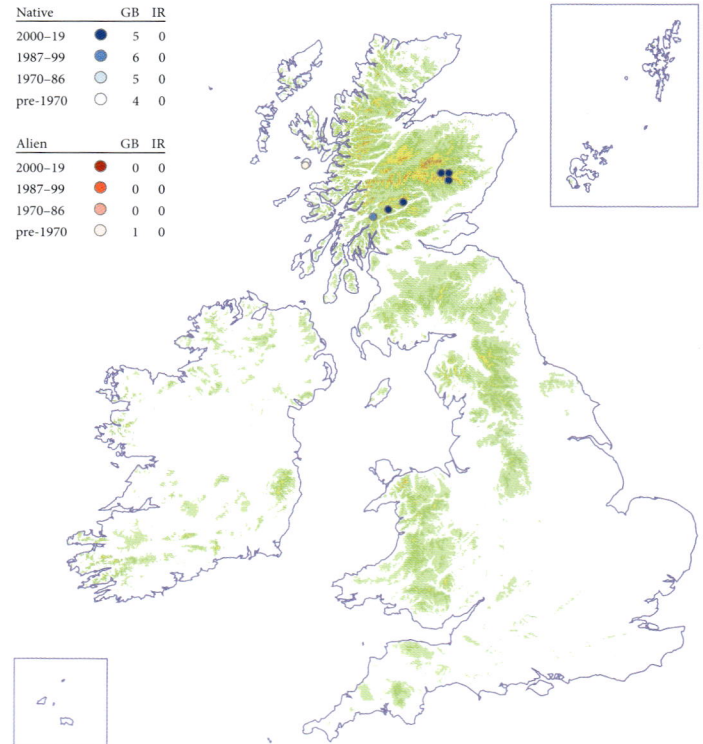

A perennial sedge of mesotrophic fens and mires, on or near the margins of lakes, often bordering outflow streams, and always in areas which are periodically inundated. It can survive in the company of low shrubs but does less well when *Myrica gale* invades. It is often subject to light grazing by cattle. Lowland.

Trends *C. buxbaumii* is known from four sites in Scotland, two of which were first discovered in the 1980s. All known colonies appear to be thriving. In Ireland it was only ever known from one location, a small island in Lough Neagh (County Antrim), where it was last recorded in 1886. Shortly afterwards the 'almost impenetrable thicket of scrubby wood' in which it grew was cleared, the area grazed by cattle, and the plant lost.

Biogeography Eurosiberian Boreal-montane element, with a continental distribution in western Europe; also in eastern Asia and North America.

Native	GB	IR
2000–19	3	0
1987–99	3	0
1970–86	3	0
pre-1970	2	1

Key refs Harron (1986), Jermy *et al.* (2007), Wigginton (1999).

M.S. PORTER & M.J.Y. FOLEY

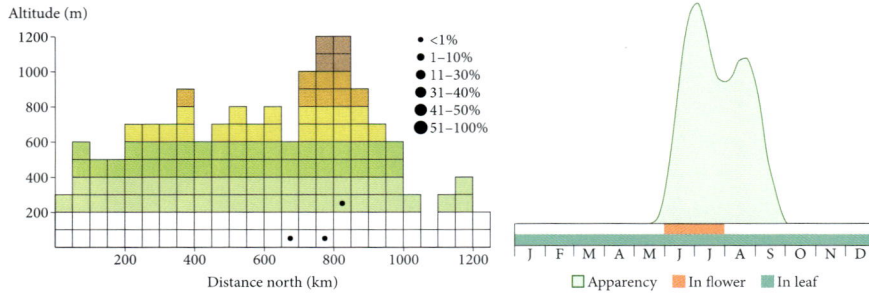

Altitude (m)

• <1%
• 1–10%
• 11–30%
• 31–40%
• 41–50%
• 51–100%

Distance north (km)

☐ Apparency ■ In flower ■ In leaf

N *Carex norvegica* Close-headed Alpine-sedge

Retz.

	GB	IR
Long term	No trend	No trend
Short term	No trend	No trend

A perennial sedge of wet, stony slopes, ledges and turf over basic rock, often mica-schist, and with base-rich run-off. All the sites have a mainly north-facing aspect, and occur in places where snow lies late in the spring. Populations are usually quite small and of very limited extent. From 700 m at Corrie Fee (Angus) to 975 m on Beinn Heasgarnich (Mid Perthshire).

Trends *C. norvegica* is a highly localized sedge confined to a small number of mountains in the central and eastern highlands of Scotland. Although it has not been found at one site (Ben Oss, Mid Perthshire) since 1987, its distribution is generally stable. Recent counts of two populations suggest that both are very healthy, with one producing the highest ever count of fruiting stems. An outlying

record from the Hebridean island of Rum is now thought to have been a deliberate introduction (Pearman & Walker, 2004b).

Biogeography Circumpolar Arctic-montane element.

Native	GB	IR
2000–19	5	0
1987–99	6	0
1970–86	5	0
pre-1970	4	0

Alien	GB	IR
2000–19	0	0
1987–99	0	0
1970–86	0	0
pre-1970	1	0

Key refs Jermy *et al.* (2007), Pearman & Walker (2004b), Wigginton (1999).

M.J.Y. FOLEY & M.S. PORTER

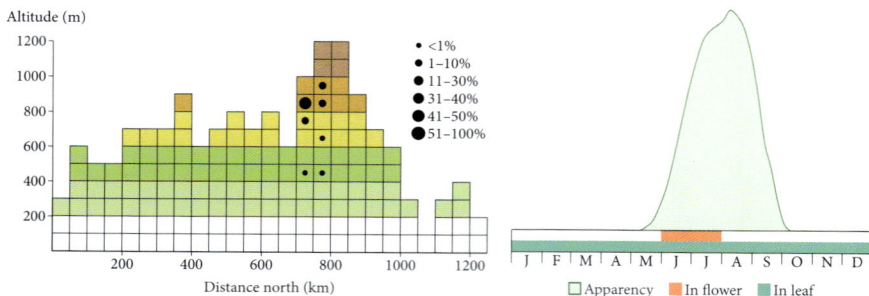

Altitude (m)

• <1%
• 1–10%
• 11–30%
• 31–40%
• 41–50%
• 51–100%

Distance north (km)

☐ Apparency ■ In flower ■ In leaf

N *Carex recta* Estuarine Sedge
Boott

A rhizomatous perennial sedge of marshes along the lower reaches of rivers and estuaries, growing in places where silt is periodically deposited or where the water-table fluctuates. It sets few viable seeds and reproduction is mostly vegetative. Lowland.

Trends *C. recta* is known from three rivers in north-eastern Scotland: the Wick River (Caithness), the River Beauly (Easterness) and the Kyle of Sutherland (East Ross & East Sutherland). Although River Beauly populations have declined considerably since the 1980s, new sites have since been found on the Kyle of Sutherland where colonies can be extensive, and the population on the Wick River appears to be stable. *C. recta* is thought to have arisen through hybridization between *C. aquatilis* and the Scandinavian species *C. paleacea* (Faulkner, 1972).

Biogeography Oceanic Boreal-montane element; also in North America.

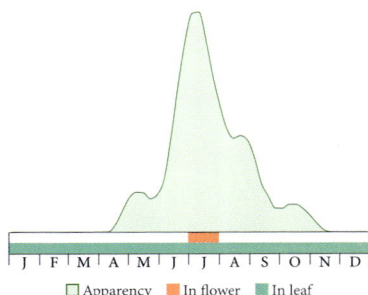

	GB	IR
Long term	No trend	No trend
Short term	No trend	No trend

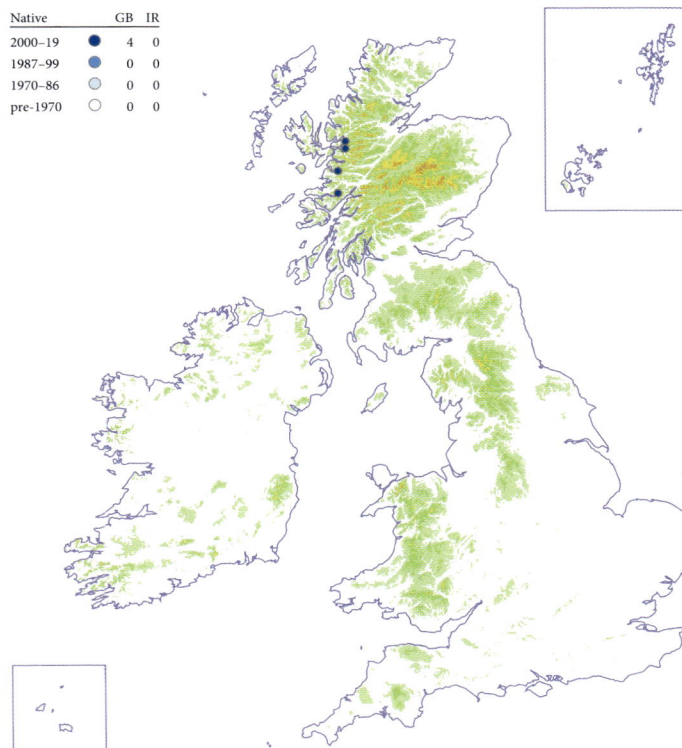

Native	GB	IR
2000–19	6	0
1987–99	4	0
1970–86	4	0
pre-1970	3	0

Key refs Faulkner (1972), Jermy *et al.* (2007), Preston & Croft (1997), Wigginton (1999).

M.S. PORTER & M.J.Y. FOLEY

N *Carex salina* Saltmarsh Sedge
Wahlenb.

A rhizomatous perennial sedge of the mid-lower region of saltmarshes, growing in silt along creeks or in the saltmarsh sward in situations where it is often inundated by high tides. Lowland.

Trends *C. salina* is thought to be a stabilized hybrid but neither of its parents (*C. paleacea* and *C. subspathacea*) have been recorded in our area. It was first recorded in Britain in 2004 at the head of Loch Duich, Morvich (West Ross) (Dean *et al.*, 2005). Since then saltmarsh surveys have revealed further records, all in the same general area in western Scotland, and it is now known from four 10 km squares. The fact that it flowers early and has very short stems means that it is easily overlooked in saltmarsh vegetation.

Biogeography Native to northern and north-eastern Europe, and subarctic North America to eastern Canada.

	GB	IR
Long term	No trend	No trend
Short term	No trend	No trend

Native	GB	IR
2000–19	4	0
1987–99	0	0
1970–86	0	0
pre-1970	0	0

Key refs Dean *et al.* (2005), Jermy *et al.* (2007).

M.S. PORTER

N *Carex aquatilis* Water Sedge
Wahlenb.

A morphologically variable, rhizomatous perennial sedge. In the lowlands, robust plants grow on riverbanks and the margins of lakes and in mires, muddy estuaries and reed-swamps. In its upland sites, it is a smaller plant and often grows on deep, wet, gently sloping peat. 0–1,030 m (Beinn Heasgarnich, Mid-Perthshire).

Trends Because of better recognition and recording, *C. aquatilis* is now known from many more 10 km squares than formerly and new sites continue to be recorded throughout its range. Even so, it is easy to overlook and may have been missed in more remote, rarely visited, areas; this may also account for some apparent losses.

Biogeography Circumpolar Boreo-arctic Montane element; absent from the mountains of central Europe.

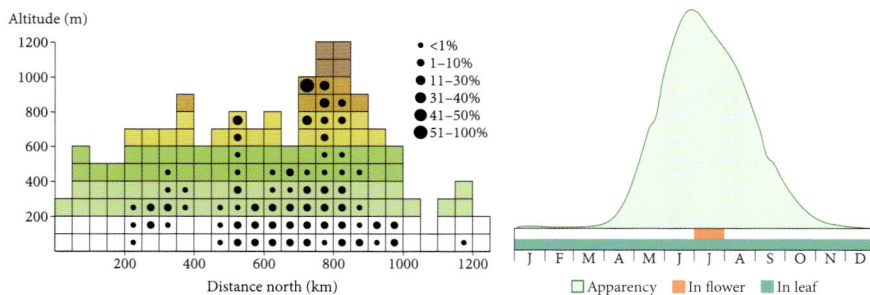

Native	GB	IR
2000–19	179	28
1987–99	152	19
1970–86	133	9
pre-1970	130	19

Altitude (m)
• <1%
• 1–10%
● 11–30%
● 31–40%
● 41–50%
● 51–100%

Distance north (km)

Apparency In flower In leaf

Key refs Jermy *et al.* (2007), Preston & Croft (1997), Stewart *et al.* (1994).

M.S. PORTER & M.J.Y. FOLEY

N *Carex acuta* Slender Tufted-sedge
L.

A rhizomatous perennial of shallow water or wet ground found at the edges of rivers, streams, canals, lakes and ponds, in swamps, ditches and unimproved flood-meadows, and in marshland. It usually grows in calcareous and mesotrophic or eutrophic conditions, in areas subject to frequent flooding. It is shade-tolerant and is sometimes present under riverside trees or in wet woodland. Generally lowland, but up to 420 m by Afon Amnodd-bwll (Merionethshire).

Native in Britain and Ireland and a neophyte in the Channel Islands.

Trends *C. acuta* has declined in many areas, principally because of drainage and the canalization of rivers and streams. Since the turn of the century, however, this decline appears to have slowed and its discovery in new areas throughout its range is some compensation for earlier losses.

Biogeography Eurosiberian Boreo-temperate element.

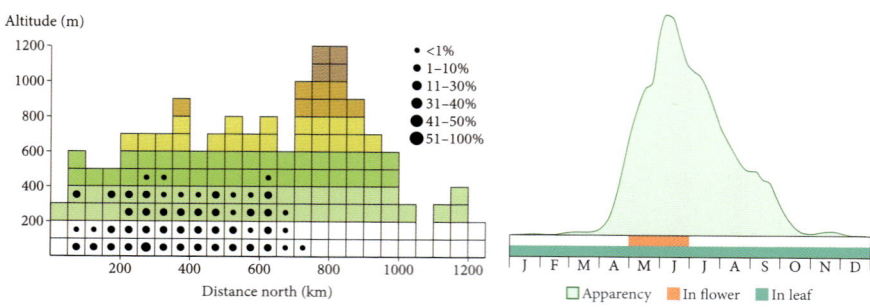

Native	GB	IR
2000–19	431	29
1987–99	419	28
1970–86	384	13
pre-1970	510	44

Alien	GB	IR
2000–19	0	0
1987–99	2	0
1970–86	1	0
pre-1970	1	0

Altitude (m)
• <1%
• 1–10%
● 11–30%
● 31–40%
● 41–50%
● 51–100%

Distance north (km)

Apparency In flower In leaf

Key refs Jermy *et al.* (2007), Preston & Croft (1997).

M.S. PORTER & M.J.Y. FOLEY

N *Carex trinervis* Three-nerved Sedge
Degl.

	GB	IR
Long term	No trend	No trend
Short term	No trend	No trend

A perennial sedge known in our area only from Ormesby (East Norfolk). Precise details of the habitat are unknown but in western Europe it grows in dune-slacks and upper saltmarsh communities The Ormesby site is 8 km from the sea but was coastal in Romano-British times and some sandy hollows may have remained until comparatively recent times. Lowland.

Trends The Ormesby specimens were collected by H.G. Glasspoole in 1869; the species has never been refound there. Some of the specimens are morphologically close to *C. nigra*, with which *C. trinervis* is known to hybridize freely. Their identification as *C. trinervis* is not absolutely certain.

Biogeography Oceanic Temperate element.

Native	GB	IR
2000–19	0	0
1987–99	0	0
1970–86	0	0
pre-1970	1	0

Key refs Dupont (1962), Jermy *et al.* (2007).

M.S. Porter & M.J.Y. Foley

N *Carex nigra* Common Sedge
(L.) Reichard

	GB	IR
Long term		
Short term		

A perennial sedge of wetland habitats, avoiding only those which are extremely basic or extremely acidic. It is found in fens, fen-meadows, bogs, streamsides, lakesides and flushes, wet grassland and, on the coast, in dune-slacks and saltmarshes. This sedge is morphologically highly variable, ranging from tussocky forms in stagnant, acidic sites with fluctuating water-levels to rhizomatous tufted variants in calcareous mires. 0–1,005 m (Beinn Heasgarnich, Mid Perthshire).

Trends The overall 10 km square distribution of *C. nigra* appears to be stable except in south-eastern England and the English Midlands where it has declined, presumably due to the drainage of wetlands for agriculture. It is now much better recorded in Ireland, especially in the south, due to more systematic recording.

Biogeography Eurosiberian Boreo-temperate element; also in North America.

Native	GB	IR
2000–19	2429	899
1987–99	2389	800
1970–86	1669	177
pre-1970	2265	639

Key refs Grime *et al.* (2007), Jermy *et al.* (2007).

M.S. Porter & M.J.Y. Foley

(N) *Carex elata* Tufted-sedge

All.

A tussock-forming perennial sedge of oligotrophic, mesotrophic or sometimes eutrophic marshy habitats, often with a calcareous influence, including fens, the margins of lakes, ponds, rivers and canals, ditches prone to seasonal flooding, and wet *Alnus* or *Salix* woodland. Lowland.

Trends Historically, many populations of *C. elata* were lost as a result of drainage and ditch widening, particularly in East Anglia and other parts of eastern England. Its core 10 km square distribution now appears to be stable, although extremely localized. In Scotland it is present on the margins of three lochs, the northernmost near to Oban (Black Lochs). Recent records from the Hebridean islands of Colonsay and Oronsay are likely to be errors for tussocky forms of *C. nigra*, although there is a single confirmed record

for Tiree (Loch Bhasapol) based on a specimen collected in 1940. However, it was not refound during a recent survey of the island (Pearman & Preston, 2000).

Biogeography Eurasian Temperate element.

Native		GB	IR
2000–19	●	186	181
1987–99	●	166	166
1970–86	●	168	68
pre-1970	○	232	119

Alien		GB	IR
2000–19	●	23	0
1987–99	●	0	0
1970–86	●	0	0
pre-1970	○	3	0

Altitude (m) / Distance north (km) chart with legend:
● <1%
● 1–10%
● 11–30%
● 31–40%
● 41–50%
● 51–100%

Phenology chart: J F M A M J J A S O N D — □ Apparency ■ In flower ■ In leaf

Key refs Jermy *et al.* (2007), Pearman & Preston (2000), Preston & Croft (1997), Stewart *et al.* (1994).

M.S. PORTER & M.J.Y. FOLEY

(N) *Carex cespitosa* Scarce Tufted-sedge

L.

The only known site for *C. cespitosa* in Britain and Ireland is in a boggy section of a damp, neutral, alluvial pasture on gravels in the floodplain of the River Rib (Hertfordshire), where it is fed by a fairly strong spring. Lowland.

Trends *C. cespitosa* is confined to a single site in Britain where it was discovered in 1985, although it was not correctly identified and described until 2011 (James *et al.*, 2012). It is morphologically very similar to *C. elata* and some forms of *C. nigra* and so may be overlooked in other sites. Elsewhere in Europe it is said to be under threat, presumably from drainage. Its Hertfordshire site is on the very western edge of its global distribution.

Biogeography Native throughout much of northern and central Europe, extending to northern Spain in the

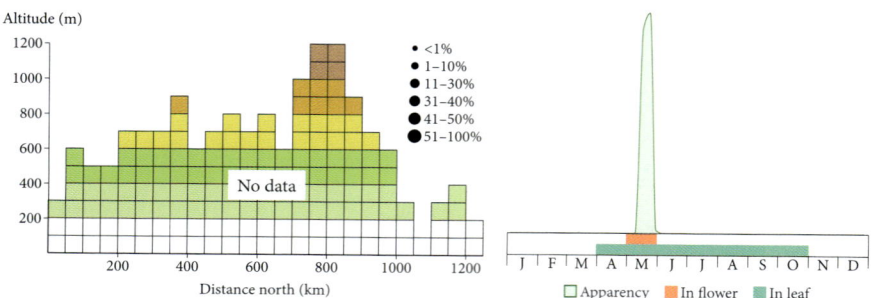

south; western, central and eastern Asia as far east as Japan and north-eastern Russia.

	GB	IR
Long term	No trend	No trend
Short term	No trend	No trend

Native		GB	IR
2000–19	●	1	0
1987–99	●	0	0
1970–86	●	0	0
pre-1970	○	0	0

Altitude (m) / Distance north (km) chart with "No data" label and legend:
● <1%
● 1–10%
● 11–30%
● 31–40%
● 41–50%
● 51–100%

Phenology chart: J F M A M J J A S O N D — □ Apparency ■ In flower ■ In leaf

Key refs James *et al.* (2012).

M.S. PORTER

N *Carex bigelowii* Stiff Sedge
Torr. ex Schwein.

A perennial sedge of base-poor, well-drained grassland and sedge-heaths on mountain tops, plateaus and ridges, open stony ground in corries where snow lies late, and on ledges in gullies. Where such gullies are subject to flushing it can be a robust plant. From 15 m at Tressa Ness (Shetland), but generally an upland species, usually occurring above 600 m, and reaching 1,305 m on Ben Macdui (South Aberdeenshire).

Trends The 10 km square distribution of *C. bigelowii* is generally stable, with the discovery of new sites since 2000 balancing historical losses, most of which have not been seen for over a century.

Biogeography Circumpolar Arctic-montane element.

Native	GB	IR
2000–19	368	41
1987–99	309	19
1970–86	221	7
pre-1970	296	38

Key refs Callaghan *et al.* (2001), Jermy *et al.* (2007).

M.S. PORTER & M.J.Y. FOLEY

N *Carex microglochin* Bristle Sedge
Wahlenb.

A shortly rhizomatous perennial sedge of base-rich flushes on gently sloping or 'stepped' ground on micaceous silt or gravel. Also, occasionally, on steep burn-sides downstream of large colonies. Reproduction appears to be mainly vegetative. Restricted to between 610 m and 975 m on Ben Lawers (Mid Perthshire).

Trends Regular monitoring of *C. microglochin* since the 1980s has shown very little change in the overall size of the colonies on Ben Lawers. A survey carried out in 2014 showed the plant to be thriving.

Biogeography European Arctic-montane element; also in central Asia and North and South America.

	GB	IR
Long term	No trend	No trend
Short term	No trend	No trend

Native	GB	IR
2000–19	1	0
1987–99	1	0
1970–86	1	0
pre-1970	1	0

Key refs Jermy *et al.* (2007), Wigginton (1999).

M.S. PORTER & M.J.Y. FOLEY

N *Carex pauciflora* Few-flowered Sedge
Lightf.

A perennial sedge of very wet, acidic, oligotrophic raised and blanket bogs, often growing on and around hummocks and usually in association with *Sphagnum* species. Lowland to 650 m (Beinn Heasgarnich, Mid Perthshire) and potentially higher in the Cairngorms.

Trends The overall distribution of *C. pauciflora* appears to be stable, with numerous new sites discovered within the known range in central and north-western Scotland since 2000. It was discovered at its most southerly British site in Montgomeryshire in 2000. It is a very inconspicuous species and is easily overlooked, so it may well still be present in many 10 km squares for which there are no recent records. However, it has not been recorded at its sole Yorkshire site (Derwent Head, North-east Yorkshire) since 1992, and there are very few records this century for South Northumberland.

Biogeography Circumpolar Boreal-montane element.

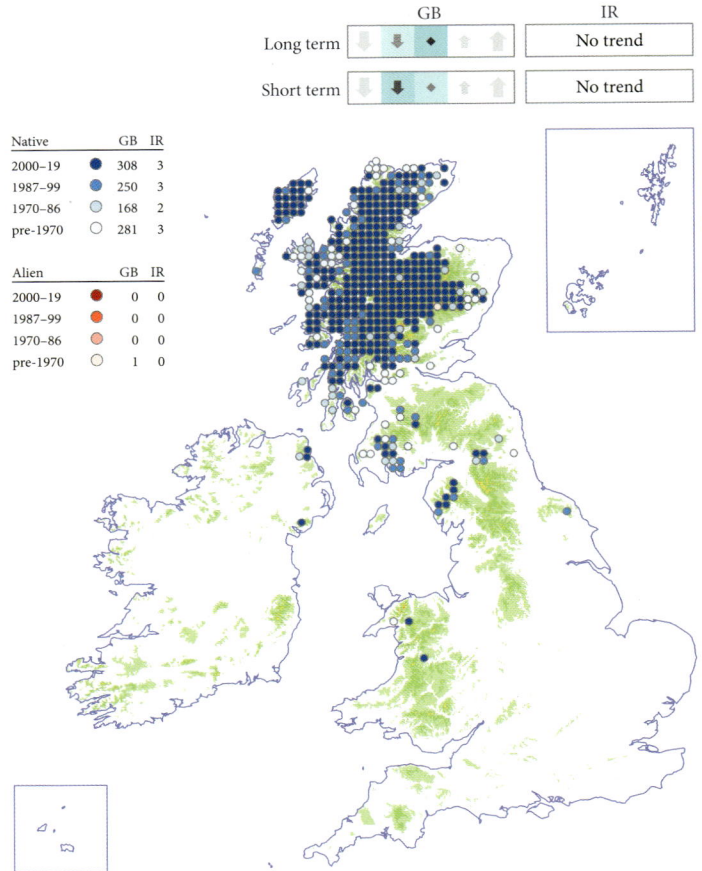

Native	GB	IR
2000–19	308	3
1987–99	250	3
1970–86	168	2
pre-1970	281	3

Alien	GB	IR
2000–19	0	0
1987–99	0	0
1970–86	0	0
pre-1970	1	0

Key refs Jermy *et al.* (2007).

M.S. PORTER & M.J.Y. FOLEY

N *Carex rupestris* Rock Sedge
Bellardi ex All.

A perennial sedge of basic substrates on cliff ledges and crevices, and on broken rocky or grassy slopes, always on base-rich rocks or rocks subject to calcareous flushing; also in dwarf shrub heath over limestone. It is often shy to flower, and it sometimes grows with *C. pulicaris* with which it can be easily confused. Found near sea level in north-western Scotland, but usually from 600 m, to 935 m on Ben Fin, Glen Lawers (Mid Perthshire).

Trends *C. rupestris* is a very localized plant in Scotland, confined to the Grampian mountains, the north-western Highlands, the northern coast and the Isle of Skye. Although it has not been recorded recently in ten hectads where it was originally known, this is unlikely to indicate a decline as it can be a very difficult plant to find even when in flower. Since 2000 it has been discovered at three new localities, including several hundred flowering spikes on Beinn na Socaich (Westerness).

Biogeography Circumpolar Arctic-montane element.

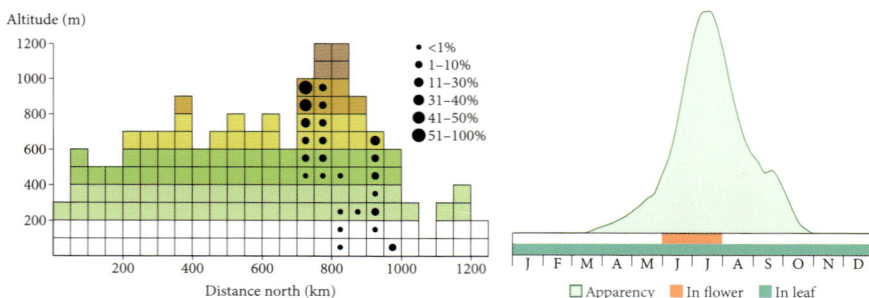

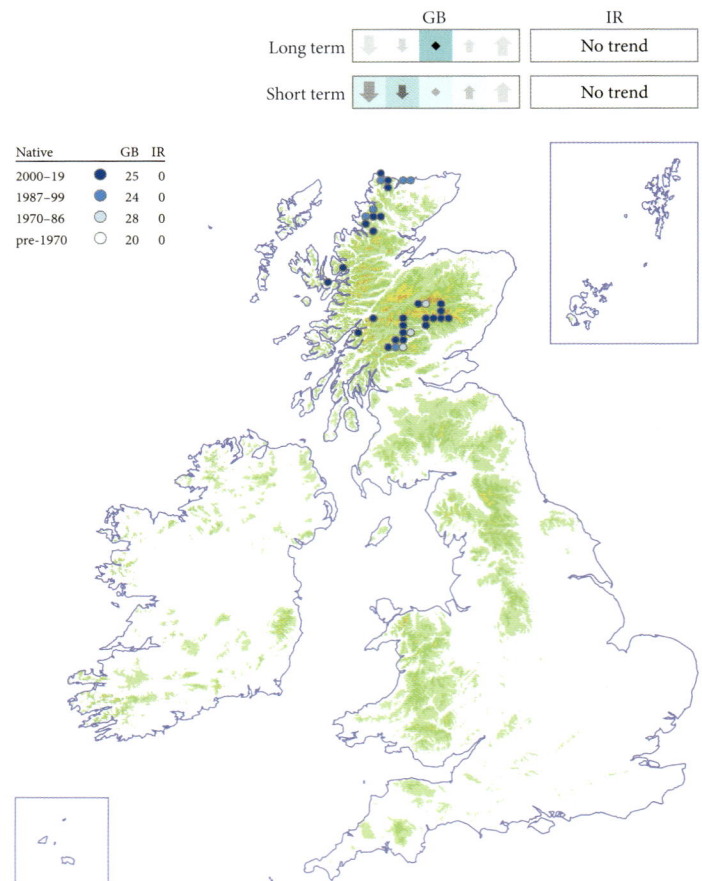

Native	GB	IR
2000–19	25	0
1987–99	24	0
1970–86	28	0
pre-1970	20	0

Key refs Jermy *et al.* (2007), Stewart *et al.* (1994).

M.S. PORTER & M.J.Y. FOLEY

N *Carex pulicaris* Flea Sedge
L.

A perennial sedge of damp neutral or calcareous soils, and of more acidic soils where these are flushed by mineral-enriched groundwater. Typical habitats include short-sedge mires, damp meadows and pastures, fen-meadows, wet heaths, flushes and springs, montane rock ledges and *Dryas* heath. It also sometimes occurs in drier situations on north-facing slopes in chalk or limestone grassland. 0–1,035 m (Beinn Heasgarnich, Mid Perthshire).

Trends The 10 km square distribution of *C. pulicaris* is largely unchanged in upland regions of northern and western Britain and Ireland, whereas marked declines in the lowlands, already apparent in the 1960s, have continued, particularly in the English Midlands and south-eastern England, through the depletion of the water-table, drainage and the destruction of damp meadows and pastures. Since 2000, more systematic recording in Ireland and, to a lesser extent in Scotland, has produced many new records.

Biogeography Suboceanic Temperate element.

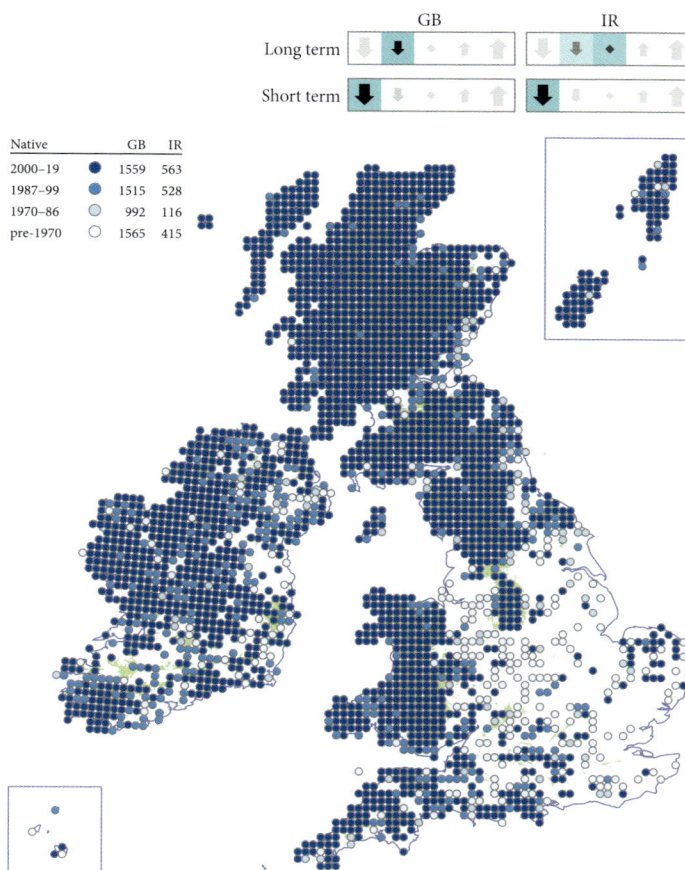

Native		GB	IR
2000–19	●	1559	563
1987–99	●	1515	528
1970–86	○	992	116
pre-1970	○	1565	415

Key refs Jermy *et al.* (2007).

M.S. Porter & M.J.Y. Foley

N *Carex simpliciuscula* False Sedge
Wahlenb.

A densely tufted perennial sedge of open, stony flushes, base-rich mires and wet, grassy or sedge-rich turf on limestone or calcareous mica-schist. Generally montane, occurring as low as 525 m in Upper Teesdale (North-west Yorkshire) but reaching 1,065 m on Meall Garbh (Mid Perthshire).

Trends The 10 km square distribution of *C. simpliciuscula* is stable within its very limited range of Perthshire, Main Argyll and Upper Teesdale (County Durham and North-west Yorkshire). It is easily overlooked, and new populations continue to be discovered throughout its Scottish range, and also in Upper Teesdale, with a record at Holmwath flushes in 2017 extending its known southern limits. In addition, sites where the species was not refound during fieldwork for the 2002 *Atlas* have been recorded this century.

Some populations are very extensive, with tens of thousands of plants.

Biogeography Circumpolar Arctic-montane element.

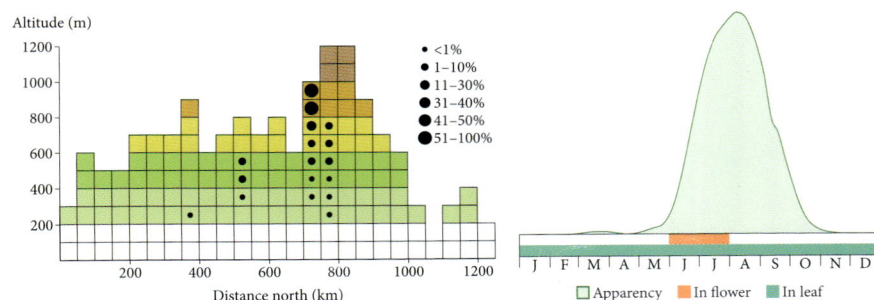

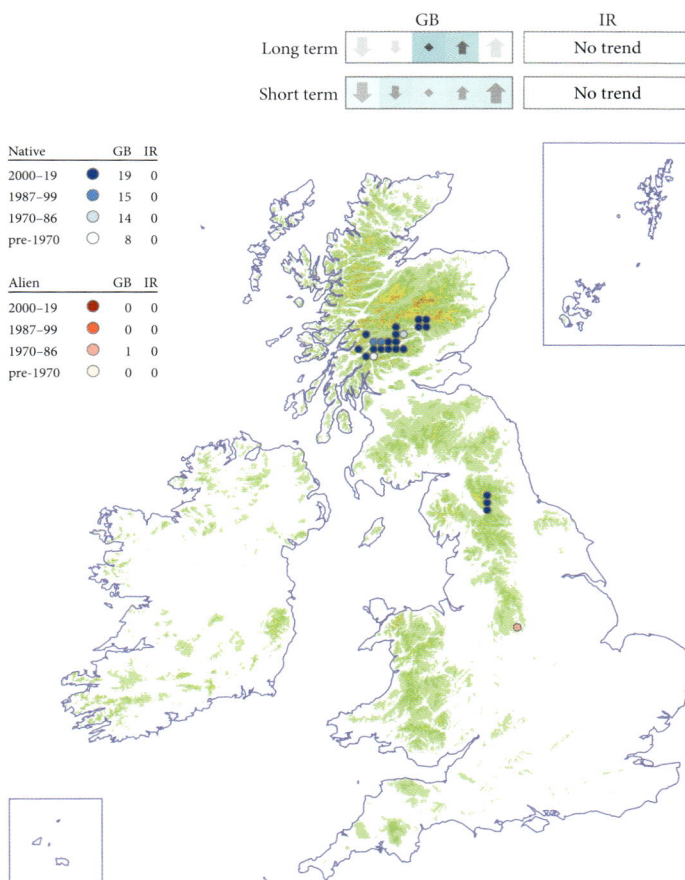

Native		GB	IR
2000–19	●	19	0
1987–99	●	15	0
1970–86	○	14	0
pre-1970	○	8	0

Alien		GB	IR
2000–19	●	0	0
1987–99	●	0	0
1970–86	●	1	0
pre-1970	○	0	0

Key refs Jermy *et al.* (2007), Wigginton (1999).

M.S. Porter & M.J.Y. Foley

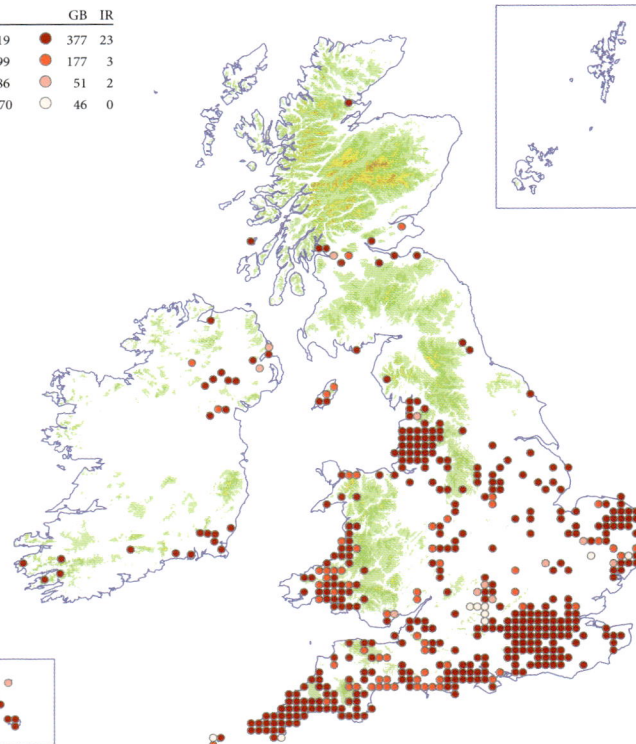

Ne *Pseudosasa japonica* Arrow Bamboo
(Siebold & Zucc. ex Steud.) Makino ex Nakai

A winter-green, woody bamboo, forming a slowly expanding clump, widely grown in gardens and found as a relic in old gardens and along wooded streamsides in the grounds of country houses, and now becoming well-established in the wild in a variety of usually moist, shaded habitats. Lowland.

Trends *P. japonica* has been grown in British gardens since 1850, and was first recorded in the wild in 1955 (Headington, Oxfordshire). It is now the most frequently grown bamboo in our area. Flowering is frequent, and this often, but not always, results in the death of the plant. It is certainly increasing, mostly due to deliberate planting, but is unevenly recorded. It may well be over-recorded for other bamboo species.

Biogeography Native of Japan and Korea.

		GB	IR
Long term		No trend	No trend
Short term			

Alien		GB	IR
2000–19	●	377	23
1987–99	●	177	3
1970–86	●	51	2
pre-1970	○	46	0

Key refs Bell (2000), Ryves *et al.* (1996).

S.J. LEACH & D.A. PEARMAN

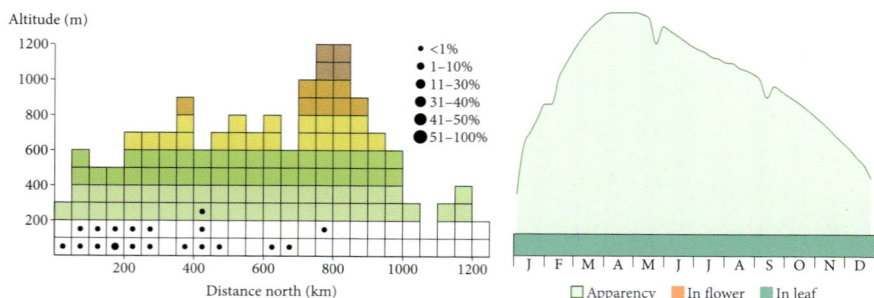

Altitude (m) / Distance north (km) — histogram legend: <1%, 1–10%, 11–30%, 31–40%, 41–50%, 51–100%

Apparency In flower In leaf

Ne *Sasaella ramosa* Hairy Bamboo
(Makino) Makino

A woody, rhizomatous perennial bamboo which is planted and naturalized in woodland and rough grassland, and on commons and roadsides; it also occurs as a relic of cultivation. Lowland.

Trends *S. ramosa* was introduced into cultivation in Britain in 1892, and it is increasingly popular in gardens. It was recorded from the wild by 1971 (Cliveden, Buckinghamshire). It is uncertain whether the increased number of records, particularly in Surrey and Sussex, is due to better recording there than elsewhere or a genuine spread of the species.

Biogeography Native of Japan.

		GB	IR
Long term		No trend	No trend
Short term			No trend

Alien		GB	IR
2000–19	●	60	1
1987–99	●	33	0
1970–86	●	15	0
pre-1970	○	6	0

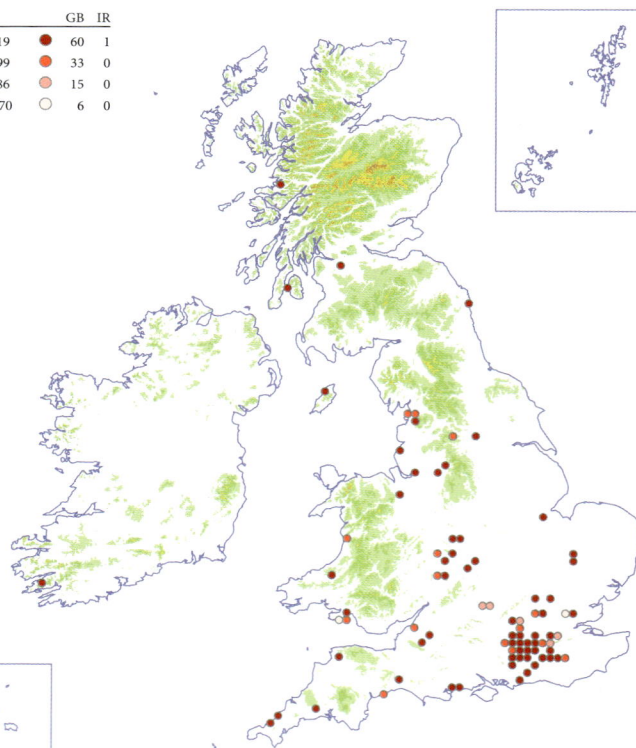

Key refs Bell (2000), Ryves *et al.* (1996).

T.D. DINES & D.A. PEARMAN

Altitude (m) / Distance north (km) — histogram legend: <1%, 1–10%, 11–30%, 31–40%, 41–50%, 51–100%

Apparency In flower In leaf

Ne *Sasa palmata* Broad-leaved Bamboo
(Burb.) E.G.Camus

An extensively rhizomatous, winter-green woody bamboo, widely grown in gardens and estates and increasingly naturalized in abandoned gardens, damp woodlands and along shaded, overgrown stream banks. Rarely flowering and so probably only ever established through vegetative spread. Lowland.

Trends *S. palmata* is the widest-leaved of all our bamboos and was introduced to Britain in about 1889. It is commonly grown in gardens and the grounds of country houses and was recorded from the wild by 1946 (Tunbridge Wells, West Kent). It is very persistent and in milder counties can spread over long distances – one area of the Lizard Peninsula (West Cornwall) has a population nearly 1 km long. It is certainly increasing, almost certainly due to deliberate planting and vegetative spread.

Biogeography Native of Japan and Sakhalin.

Alien	GB	IR
2000–19	277	71
1987–99	142	13
1970–86	35	4
pre-1970	17	0

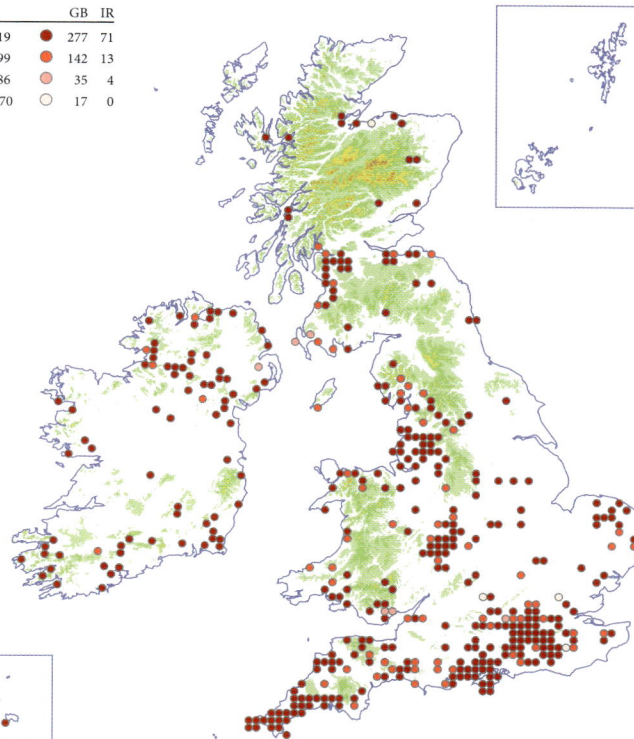

Key refs Bell (2000), Ryves *et al.* (1996).

S.J. LEACH & D.A. PEARMAN

Ne *Yushania anceps* Indian Fountain-bamboo
(Mitford) W.C.Lin

A large, woody perennial bamboo, planted and naturalized in woodlands, by rivers, in parks and estates, and also occurring as a relic of cultivation. It spreads vegetatively to form dense thickets, and (unusually for a bamboo) reproduction by seed has been reported. Lowland.

Trends *Y. anceps* was introduced into cultivation in Britain in 1896, and is increasingly popular in gardens. It was first recorded from the wild in 1960 (Crab Apple Copse, Surrey) and may be increasing, or, more likely, is better recorded.

Biogeography Native of the central and north-western Himalayas.

Alien	GB	IR
2000–19	36	0
1987–99	26	0
1970–86	11	0
pre-1970	5	0

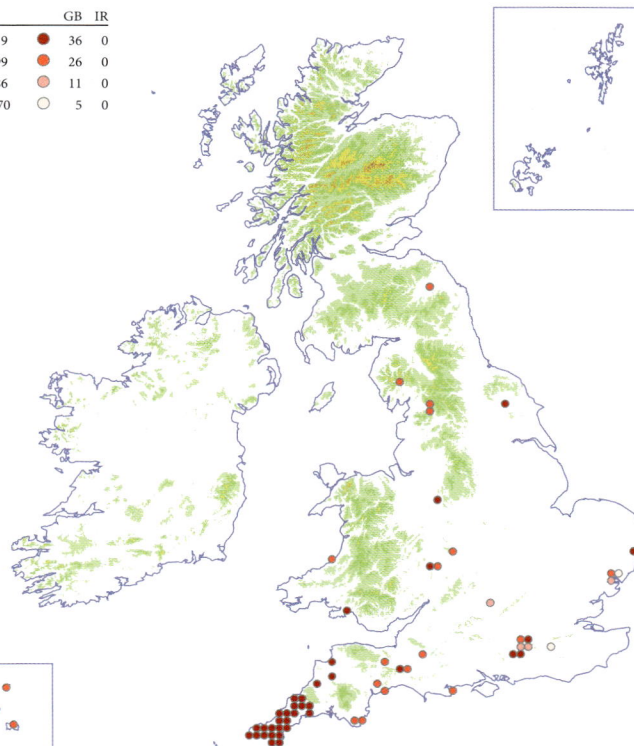

Key refs Bell (2000), Ryves *et al.* (1996).

T.D. DINES & D.A. PEARMAN

Leersia oryzoides Cut-grass

(L.) Sw.

A rhizomatous perennial herb of nutrient-rich mud around the cattle-trampled margins of lakes and ponds, in ditches, on canal banks and riversides; also formerly in wet meadows. Lowland.

Trends *L. oryzoides* has declined since the 1960s, and several populations have been lost in the last 20 years, including those in Somerset which were last seen in the early 1990s. It is now apparently restricted to several sites in West Sussex, and a recently discovered (2002) site at Richmond, Surrey. The Sussex sites are centered around Amberley Wild Brooks, but there are outliers, and since 2000 it has been recorded in 13 tetrads. It has been reintroduced into two other locations, in Surrey and the New Forest, South Hampshire. The drainage and infilling of ponds and ditches, and possibly the over-zealous maintenance of canal banks, are thought to have contributed to its decline, yet appropriate management in Sussex has led to rediscoveries. The Cambridgeshire record is assumed to be an unintentional introduction, arriving with other planted aquatic and marginal species.

Biogeography European Temperate element; also in central and eastern Asia and North America.

Native	GB	IR
2000–19	5	0
1987–99	5	0
1970–86	6	0
pre-1970	23	0

Alien	GB	IR
2000–19	2	0
1987–99	2	0
1970–86	1	0
pre-1970	3	0

	GB	IR
Long term	No trend	No trend
Short term	No trend	No trend

Key refs Cope & Gray (2009), Wigginton (1999).

S.J. LEACH & D.A. PEARMAN

Nardus stricta Mat-grass

L.

A densely tufted, shortly rhizomatous perennial found on winter-wet, base-poor, infertile and peaty soils, occurring in great quantity on upland hill-slopes, moorland and mountains, including snow-bed communities, but also found on lowland mires, heaths and acidic grasslands, and even sometimes in the upper reaches of saltmarsh turf. 0–1,305 m (Ben Macdui, South Aberdeenshire).

Trends *N. stricta* has declined in lowland Britain due to the loss of infertile, acidic habitats. Its distribution in the uplands appears to be more stable at the 10 km scale but, like *Juncus squarrosus*, it is highly unpalatable to sheep but can withstand heavy grazing, and so it has probably increased dramatically in abundance over recent centuries.

Biogeography European Boreo-temperate element; also in central Asia and widely naturalized outside its native range.

Native	GB	IR
2000–19	1803	490
1987–99	1798	427
1970–86	1140	82
pre-1970	1869	419

Key refs Chadwick (1960), Cope & Gray (2009), Grime *et al.* (2007).

F.H. PERRING, D.A. PEARMAN & K.J. WALKER

Ne *Nassella tenuissima* Argentine Needle-grass

(Trin.) Barkworth

A tufted, relatively short-lived perennial grass, recently popular in ornamental plantings where it readily self-seeds along paths, pavements, hedgerows, roadsides and in waste ground. Formerly also a crop impurity. Lowland.

Trends *N. tenuissima* was formerly found only as a grain casual, first recorded in Worcestershire in 1958, but it is now very widely grown in gardens, where it seeds prolifically. Its distribution appears to be increasing, especially in urban areas.

Biogeography Native of South America, northwards to Texas.

Alien	GB	IR
2000–19	161	11
1987–99	0	0
1970–86	0	0
pre-1970	0	0

	GB	IR
Long term	No trend	No trend

Key refs Ryves *et al.* (1996).

D.A. PEARMAN

Ne *Anemanthele lessoniana* Pheasant's-tail

(Steud.) Veldkamp

A densely tufted perennial, spreading very freely by seed. A popular ornamental grass that is now extensively grown in gardens and in amenity planting schemes, and is spreading from there along wall bases, road gutters, pavements, hedges, on track and road verges and on waste ground. Often only casual as plants get sprayed or weeded out in urban locations. Lowland.

Trends *A. lessoniana* was first recognized at Trengwainton (West Cornwall) in 1974, but, probably because it was not described in Stace (1991, 1997), remained unreported until 2006, when it was described as a pavement weed in South Somerset, and then in Cambridgeshire. Since that time it has been widely, but very unevenly, reported.

Biogeography A native of New Zealand.

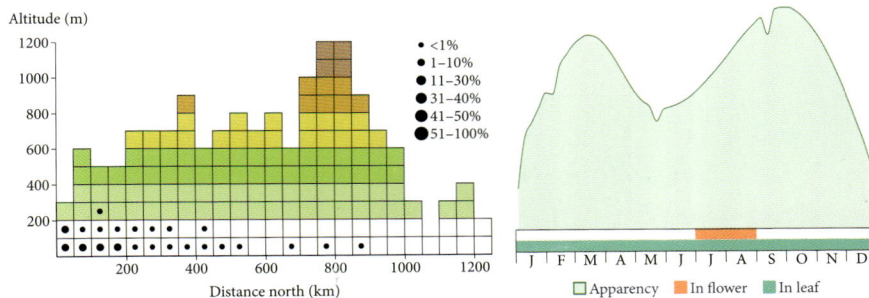

Alien	GB	IR
2000–19	149	20
1987–99	5	0
1970–86	1	0
pre-1970	0	0

	GB	IR
Long term	No trend	No trend

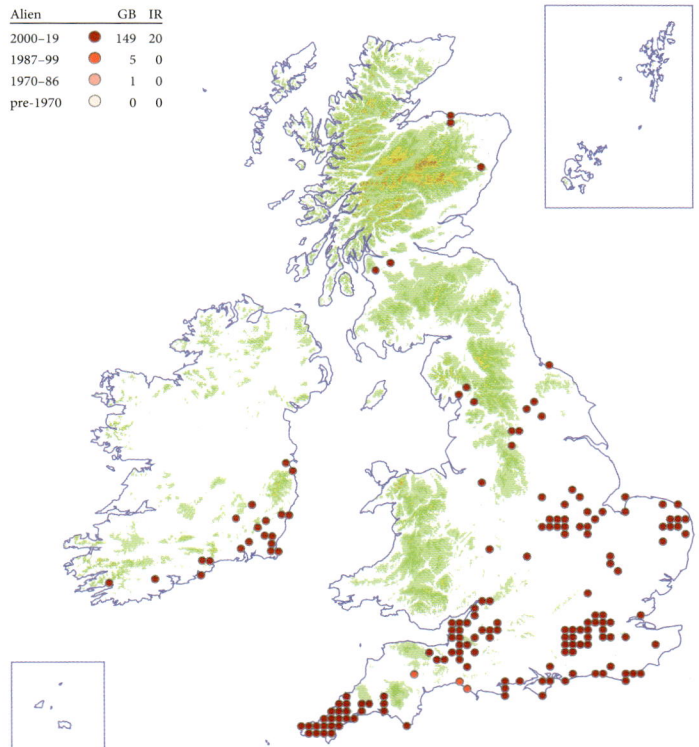

D.A. PEARMAN & K.J. WALKER

Ⓝ *Glyceria maxima* Reed Sweet-grass
(Hartm.) Holmb.

A rhizomatous perennial herb growing in ditches, canals, lakes and ponds, either rooted on the bank or in the water, and often forming floating rafts; also in seasonally flooded grasslands. It was formerly cultivated as a fodder crop, and is much planted in ponds. Generally lowland, but reaching 600 m at Sprinkling Tarn (Cumberland).

Native in Britain and Ireland and a neophyte in the Channel Islands.

Trends *G. maxima* has increased since the 1960s, particularly in northern Britain. Many of these records are likely to be deliberate introductions, as it is a frequent (and aggressive) constituent of new ponds, sometimes in its lurid form var. *variegata*, the taxon frequently sold in garden centres.

Biogeography Circumpolar Temperate element; widely naturalized outside its native range.

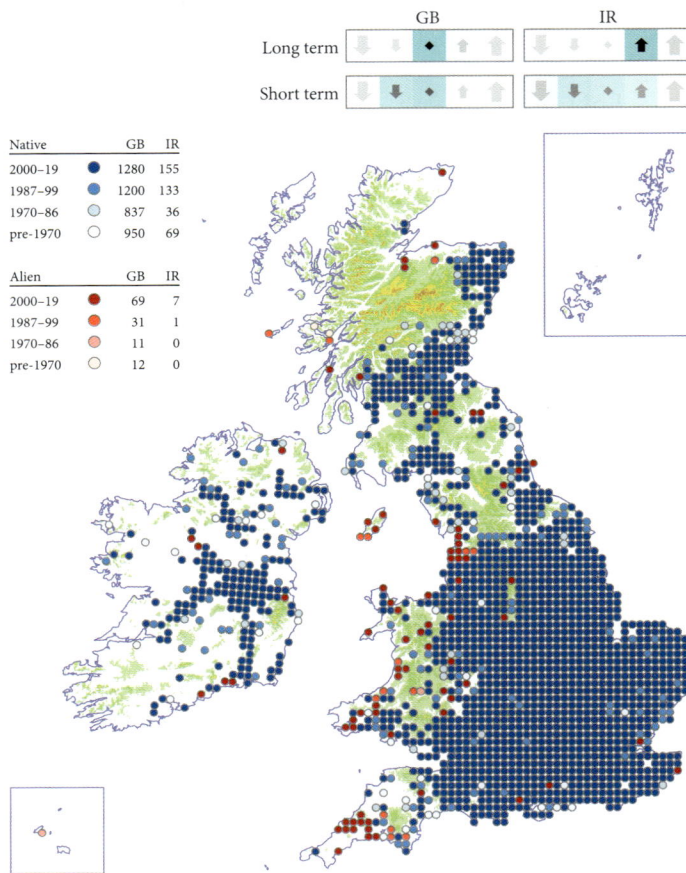

Native	GB	IR
2000–19	1280	155
1987–99	1200	133
1970–86	837	36
pre-1970	950	69

Alien	GB	IR
2000–19	69	7
1987–99	31	1
1970–86	11	0
pre-1970	12	0

Key refs Cope & Gray (2009), Grime *et al.* (2007), Lambert (1947), Preston & Croft (1997).

S.J. LEACH & D.A. PEARMAN

Ⓝ *Glyceria fluitans* Floating Sweet-grass
(L.) R.Br.

A perennial grass of marshes, swamps and muddy pond margins, and forming floating rafts in shallow water in ditches, rivers, ponds and lakes; tolerant of high levels of disturbance and nutrient-enrichment. 0–720 m (Knock Fell, Westmorland).

Trends *G. fluitans* remains common and widespread in our area at the 10 km square scale; although there has been no appreciable change in range since the 1960s, to some extent this masks losses at a more local scale following the infilling or neglect of ponds, and the piecemeal loss of small areas of other suitable wetland habitats.

Biogeography European Temperate element; widely naturalized outside its native range.

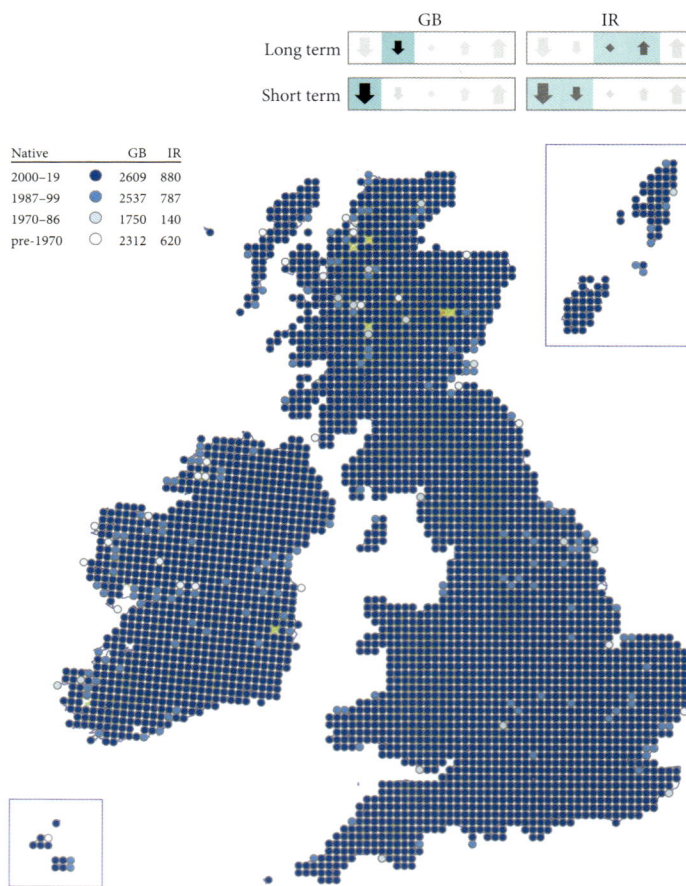

Native	GB	IR
2000–19	2609	880
1987–99	2537	787
1970–86	1750	140
pre-1970	2312	620

Key refs Cope & Gray (2009), Grime *et al.* (2007), Preston & Croft (1997).

S.J. LEACH & D.A. PEARMAN

Hy *Glyceria fluitans × notata = G. ×pedicellata* Hybrid Sweet-grass
F. Towns.

A stoloniferous perennial grass forming small colonies or large and persistent stands in reservoirs, on damp mud at the edges of lakes, reservoirs, ponds, rivers, streams and ditches, in marshes, wet meadows and roadside verges, and on rutted tracks. It may outnumber its parents, or occur in the absence of one or both of them. It is completely sterile, but spreads vegetatively and detached ramets may be carried by water to new sites. 0–550 m (Moor House, Westmorland).

A spontaneous hybrid (native × native).

Trends The map in Perring & Sell (1968) under-estimated the distribution of this taxon, and it is now relatively well recorded. The apparent extension of range, particularly in Ireland, is attributable to better recording in recent decades, but it is probably still under-recorded in some areas.

Biogeography Widespread in temperate Europe.

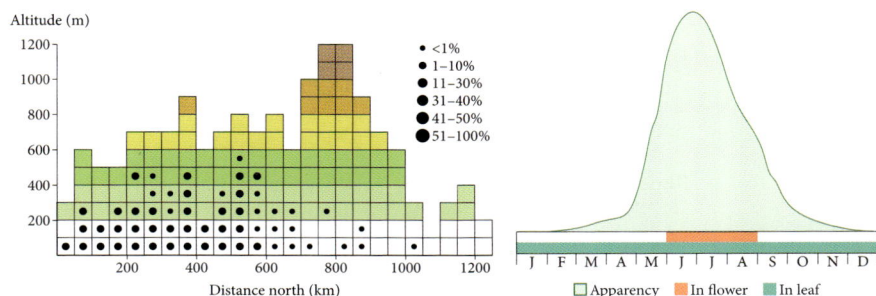

		GB	IR
2000–19	●	172	16
1987–99	●	328	45
1970–86	●	288	9
pre-1970	○	436	17

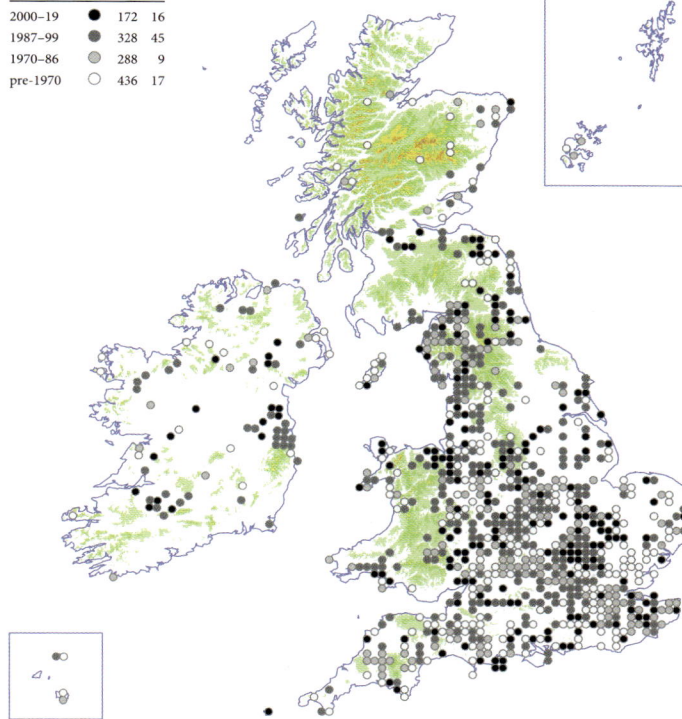

Key refs Stace *et al.* (2015).

S.J. Leach

N *Glyceria declinata* Small Sweet-grass
Bréb.

A perennial grass of muddy pond margins, cattle-trampled ditches and marshy fields; also in shallow water by ponds, rivers and canals, but apparently less frequently in the permanently waterlogged habitats favoured by other *Glyceria* species. 0–690 m (Green Castle, Knock Ore Gill, Westmorland).

Trends This species is easily overlooked, but its small stature and glaucous leaves give it a distinctive appearance. It was under-recorded in the 1960s and this is possibly still true in some areas, though Ireland is now much better recorded. It has evidently declined in some parts of eastern England, presumably due to the loss of wetland habitats.

Biogeography Suboceanic Temperate element.

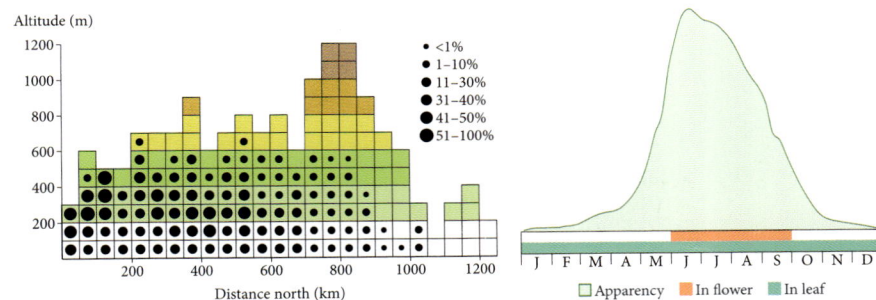

Native		GB	IR
2000–19	●	1638	461
1987–99	●	1536	256
1970–86	●	945	45
pre-1970	○	944	103

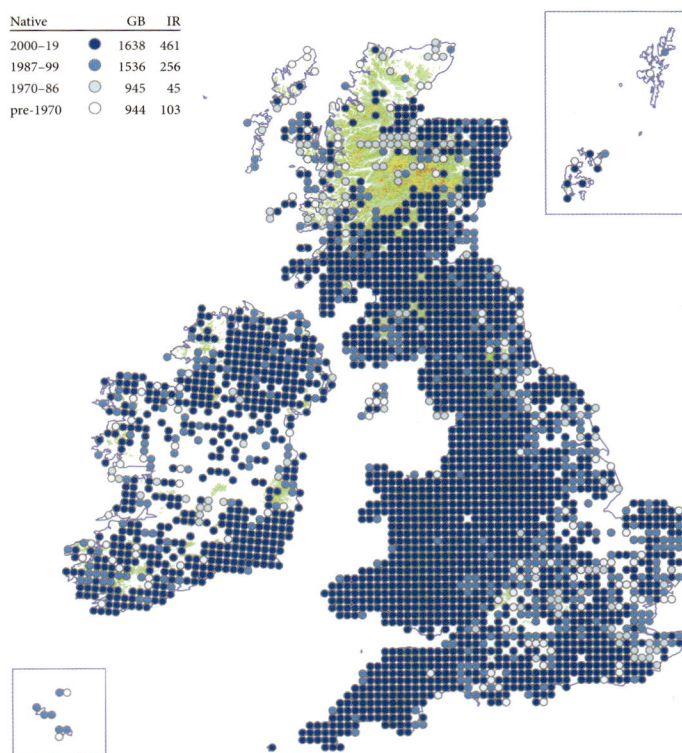

Key refs Cope & Gray (2009), Preston & Croft (1997).

S.J. Leach & D.A. Pearman

N *Glyceria notata* Plicate Sweet-grass
Chevall.

A stoloniferous perennial grass of ditches, streams and muddy pond margins, occurring on more calcareous substrates than other British *Glyceria* species. It reproduces by seed, which appears to be persistent, and by detached stolons. 0–450 m (Cefn Hill plantation, Herefordshire).

Trends Although *G. notata* has been patently better recorded since the 1960s, there are sufficient older records to suggest that it has declined in parts of southern England because of drainage and other damaging activities.

Biogeography European Temperate element; also in central Asia.

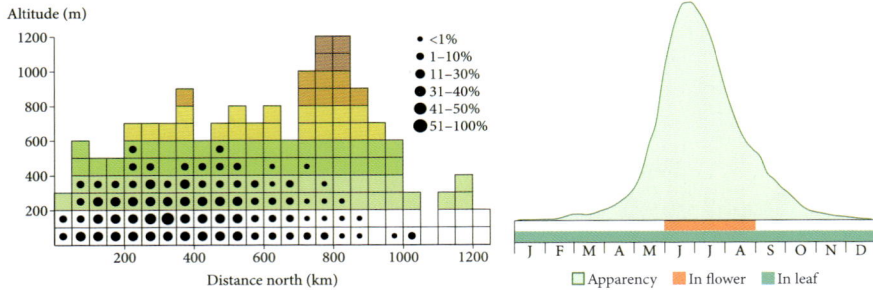

Native	GB	IR
2000–19	1157	281
1987–99	1110	278
1970–86	823	52
pre-1970	1001	132

Alien	GB	IR
2000–19	2	0
1987–99	2	0
1970–86	0	0
pre-1970	2	0

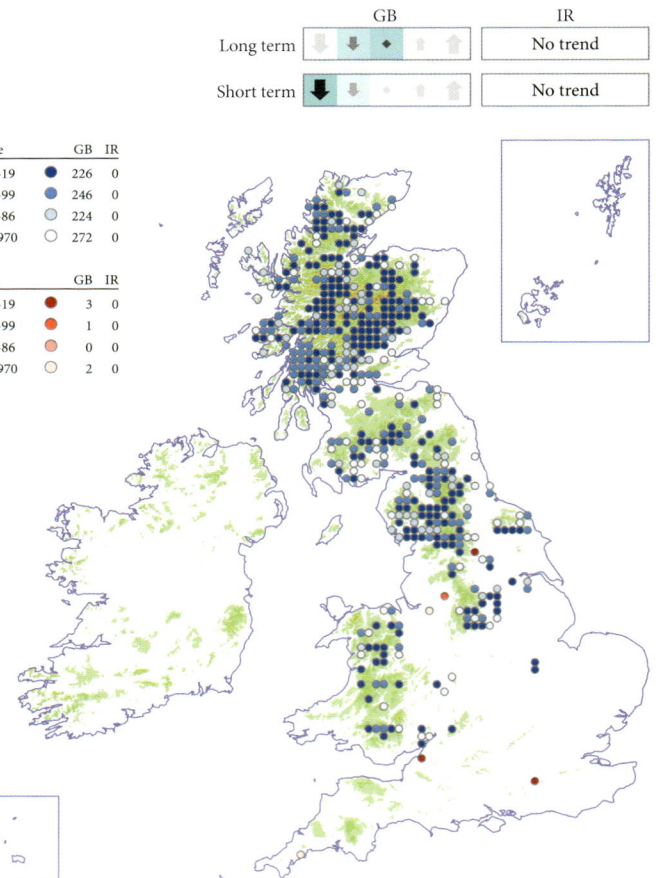

Key refs Cope & Gray (2009), Preston & Croft (1997).

S.J. LEACH & D.A. PEARMAN

N *Melica nutans* Mountain Melick
L.

A rhizomatous, perennial grass of basic infertile soils over limestone and other base-rich rocks, occurring in shady places in deciduous woodland, on woodland margins, in the grikes of limestone pavement and on rock ledges. Lowland to 820 m in Glen Isla (Angus).

Trends There is some evidence of a decline before 1930, especially in southern Scotland, but other than local losses the distribution of *M. nutans* is unchanged. It is now much better recorded, and it is likely that it is still present in the bulk of the squares for which the 1987–99 record is the latest available.

Biogeography Eurasian Boreo-temperate element, with a continental distribution in western Europe.

Native	GB	IR
2000–19	226	0
1987–99	246	0
1970–86	224	0
pre-1970	272	0

Alien	GB	IR
2000–19	3	0
1987–99	1	0
1970–86	0	0
pre-1970	2	0

Key refs Cope & Gray (2009).

F.H. PERRING & D.A. PEARMAN

N *Melica uniflora* Wood Melick
Retz.

A rhizomatous perennial grass of woodland rides and margins, of shady hedgebanks and rock ledges, mainly on free-draining, base-rich soils. It often grows in localized patches, suggesting that regeneration is mainly by rhizomatous spread. 0–395 m (Ysbyty Ifan, Denbighshire), and up to 485 m in the Scottish Highlands.

Trends There seems to have been little change in the distribution of *M. uniflora* since the 1960s, although the increase in records from Ireland is a remarkable example of more systematic recording.

Biogeography European Temperate element.

Native	GB	IR
2000–19	1287	238
1987–99	1319	198
1970–86	960	74
pre-1970	1218	99

Alien	GB	IR
2000–19	2	0
1987–99	1	0
1970–86	0	0
pre-1970	2	0

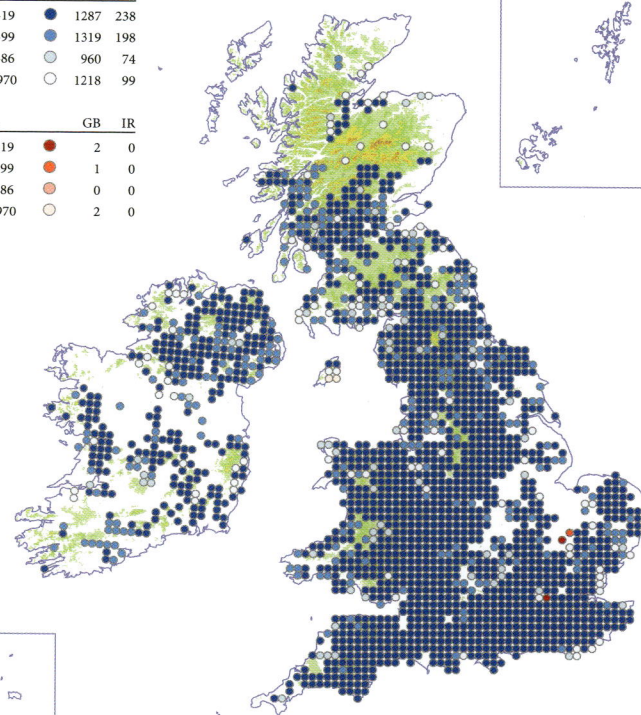

Altitude (m)

• <1%
• 1–10%
• 11–30%
• 31–40%
• 41–50%
• 51–100%

Distance north (km)

J F M A M J J A S O N D
☐ Apparency ☐ In flower ☐ In leaf

Key refs Cope & Gray (2009), Grime *et al.* (2007).

F.H. Perring & D.A. Pearman

N *Brachypodium pinnatum s.l.* Heath False-bromes

Strongly rhizomatous perennial grasses found on dry, relatively infertile calcareous soils. In chalk and limestone grassland it can become a dominant constituent over large areas. It also occurs on arable field borders, in scrub, quarries, and on railway banks and roadsides, where it may be accidentally introduced. It spreads by rhizomes and has a poor seed-set. Generally lowland, but reaching 380 m at South House Pavement Nature Reserve (Mid-west Yorkshire).

Trends *B. pinnatum s.l.* includes two taxa that have only been differentiated relatively recently by British and Irish botanists. *B. pinnatum* is considered to be the more widespread and shade-tolerant plant of marginal sites on clay soils. In contrast, *B. rupestre* appears to be restricted to more calcareous soils over chalk and limestone. However, the two species are very difficult to separate reliably in the field (Leslie, 2019), and Cope & Gray (2009) suggest that a distinction should not be attempted until better discriminating characters are found. *B. pinnatum s.l.* has spread in and around its core areas since the 1960s due to a relaxation of grazing by livestock and rabbits. Once established it can form dense species-poor stands, and is extremely difficult to eliminate; attempts to control it by burning and herbicides have largely failed. As in Europe, elevated levels of soil nitrogen from atmospheric and agricultural sources are likely to have favoured its growth in recent decades, meaning that where it is present as a minor constituent of the sward the timing and levels of grazing previously considered appropriate to maintain species-rich grassland may now need to be revised. It also appears to be increasing as an alien.

Biogeography Eurosiberian Temperate element.

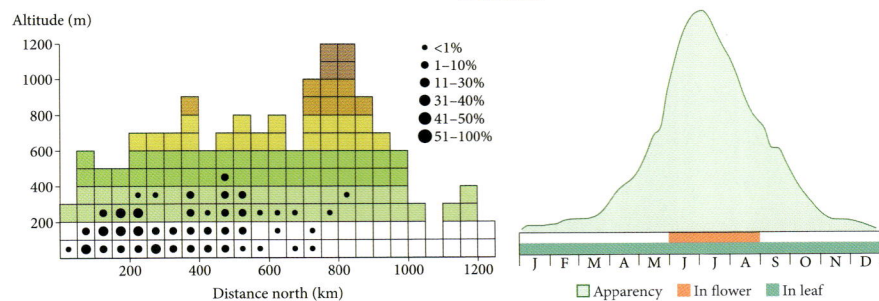

Native	GB	IR
2000–19	349	16
1987–99	482	11
1970–86	256	5
pre-1970	466	13

Alien	GB	IR
2000–19	19	0
1987–99	30	0
1970–86	15	0
pre-1970	13	0

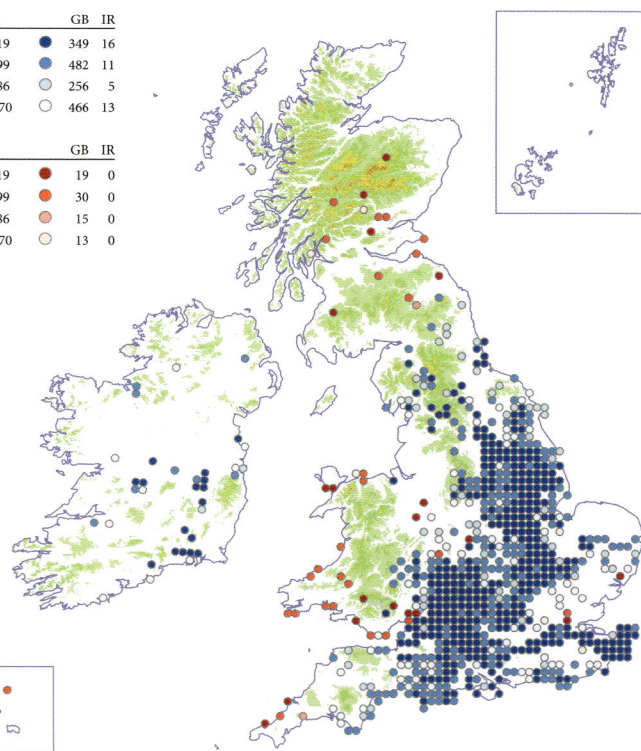

Altitude (m)

• <1%
• 1–10%
• 11–30%
• 31–40%
• 41–50%
• 51–100%

Distance north (km)

J F M A M J J A S O N D
☐ Apparency ☐ In flower ☐ In leaf

Key refs Cope & Gray (2009), Grime *et al.* (2007), Leslie (2019).

D.A. Pearman & K.J. Walker

Brachypodium sylvaticum False Brome

(Huds.) P.Beauv.

A tufted perennial grass of well-drained neutral to calcareous soils. In the lowlands, it is predominantly a plant of woodland and other shady habitats, including hedgerows, railway banks and roadsides, and it has colonized chalk and limestone downland following scrub invasion. It can persist in areas of former woodland or scrub. Above c. 200 m, it can occur in more open situations including limestone grassland and pavements, cliffs and screes. 0–505 m (Creag Dhubh, Easterness) and probably higher on Ben Nevis (Westerness).

Trends The 10 km square distribution of *B. sylvaticum* is stable, with small increases in some regions due to more systematic recording.

Biogeography European Temperate element; also in central and eastern Asia and widely naturalized outside its native range.

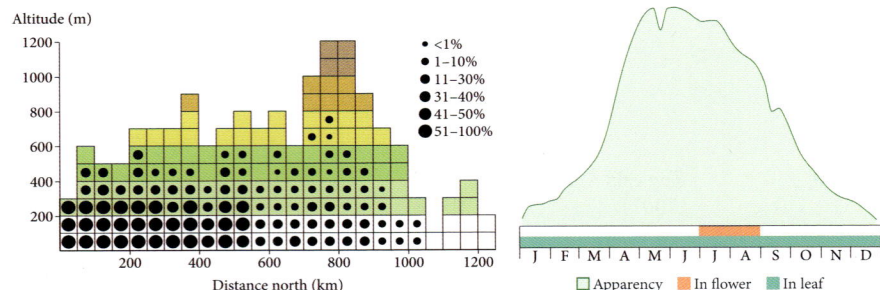

Native	GB	IR
2000–19	2282	823
1987–99	2154	724
1970–86	1438	140
pre-1970	2024	558

Key refs Cope & Gray (2009), Grime *et al.* (2007).

D.A. PEARMAN

Schedonorus pratensis Meadow Fescue

(Huds.) P.Beauv.

A short-lived perennial grass of a wide range of neutral grasslands, usually on fertile soils, including pastures, hay- and water-meadows. It is often sown for fodder and has become naturalized on roadsides, railway banks and waste ground. 0–575 m (Hartside, Cumberland) and exceptionally at 845 m on Great Dun Fell (Westmorland).

Trends The native distribution of *S. pratensis* has been obscured by sowing, and it may only occur in northern and western Britain and western Ireland as a relic of cultivation. It has declined as a result of the loss of wet meadows and a downturn in its popularity in grass mixtures.

Biogeography Eurosiberian Boreo-temperate element, but widely naturalized so that distribution is now Circumpolar Boreo-temperate.

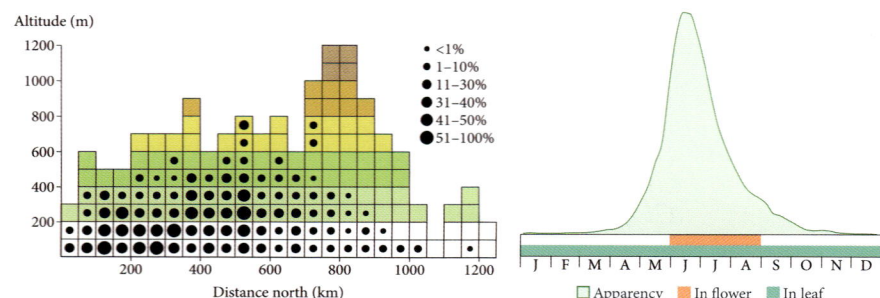

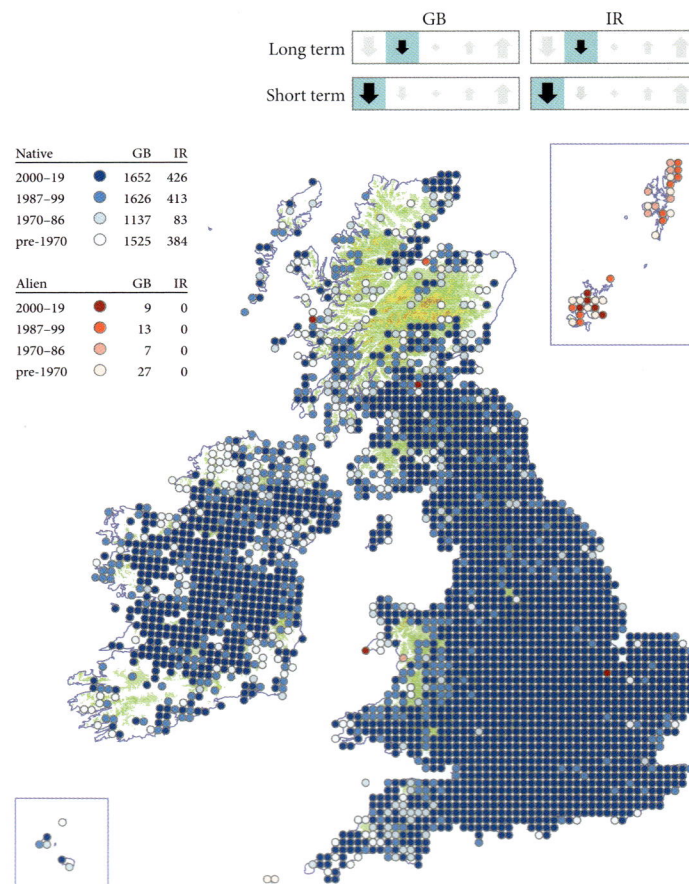

Native	GB	IR
2000–19	1652	426
1987–99	1626	413
1970–86	1137	83
pre-1970	1525	384

Alien	GB	IR
2000–19	9	0
1987–99	13	0
1970–86	7	0
pre-1970	27	0

Key refs Cope & Gray (2009), Grime *et al.* (2007).

F.H. PERRING

Schedonorus arundinaceus Tall Fescue

(Schreb.) Dumort.

A robust perennial grass of scrub and woodland margins, hedgerows, pastures and meadows, river gravel, roadsides, railway banks and waste ground, on neutral or basic soils. It is also found along the banks of tidal rivers in places liable to inundation by brackish or sea water, and on slumping sea-cliffs. 0–430 m (north of Alston, Cumberland) and, presumably as an introduction, at 570 m at Hartside Summit (Cumberland).

Trends *S. arundinaceus* was formerly used in seed mixtures and is only a relic of cultivation in some areas. However, it appears to have become much more frequent since the 1960s, and in recent decades may have benefitted from changes to the management of marginal grassland, as it can persist in swards that are mown infrequently. A bulbous variety appears to be spreading, possibly because of mechanized hedge-trimming or wider vehicles disturbing banks.

Biogeography Eurosiberian Southern-temperate element; widely naturalized outside its native range.

Native	GB	IR
2000–19	2075	596
1987–99	1900	472
1970–86	1189	87
pre-1970	1396	256

Alien	GB	IR
2000–19	27	0
1987–99	17	0
1970–86	8	0
pre-1970	17	0

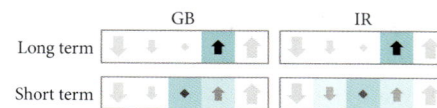

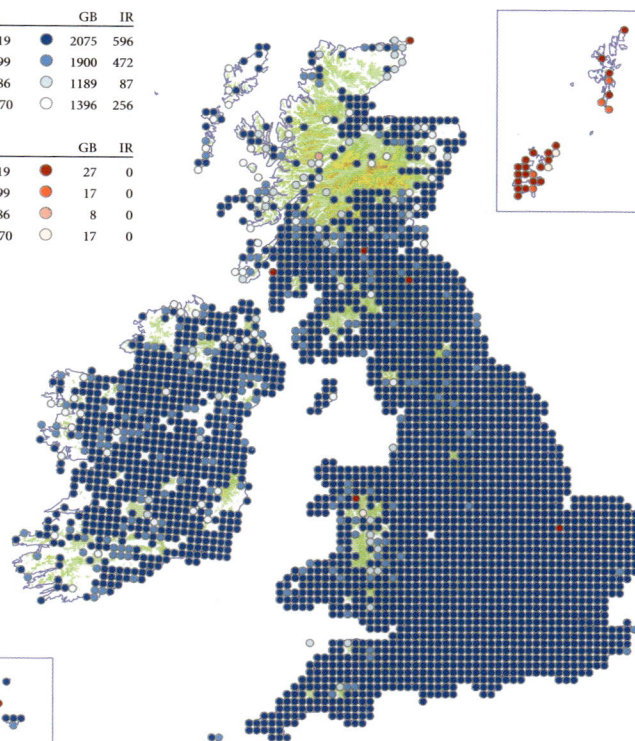

Key refs Cope & Gray (2009), Gibson (2001), Gibson & Newman (2001).

F.H. Perring & D.A. Pearman

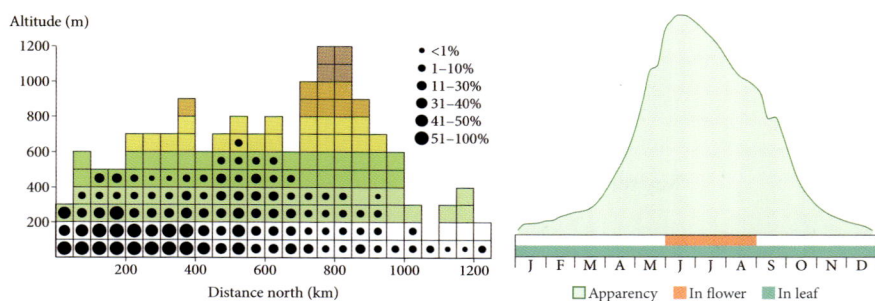

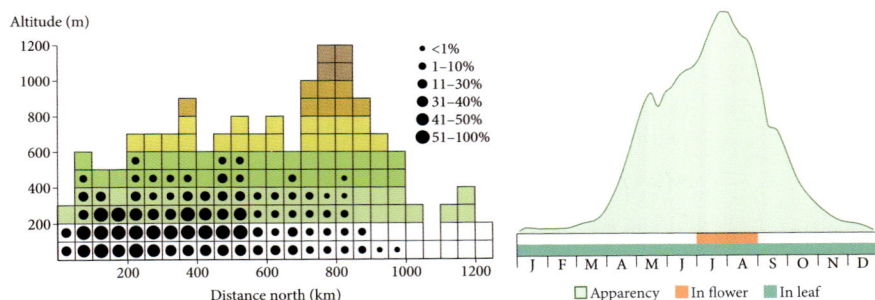

Schedonorus giganteus Giant Fescue

(L.) Holub

A tufted perennial grass of moist woodland on neutral to base-rich soils, often associated with *Brachypodium sylvaticum* and *Bromopsis ramosa*. It is particularly frequent beside streams, along rides, in disturbed areas in clearings and on woodland margins, and as a colonist of secondary woodland. It is dispersed by its fruits, which adhere to fur and clothing. 0–370 m (near Nenthead, Cumberland).

Trends The distribution of *S. giganteus* is stable, and is now much better recorded in Ireland.

Biogeography European Temperate element; also in central Asia.

Native	GB	IR
2000–19	1777	414
1987–99	1726	268
1970–86	1163	80
pre-1970	1461	151

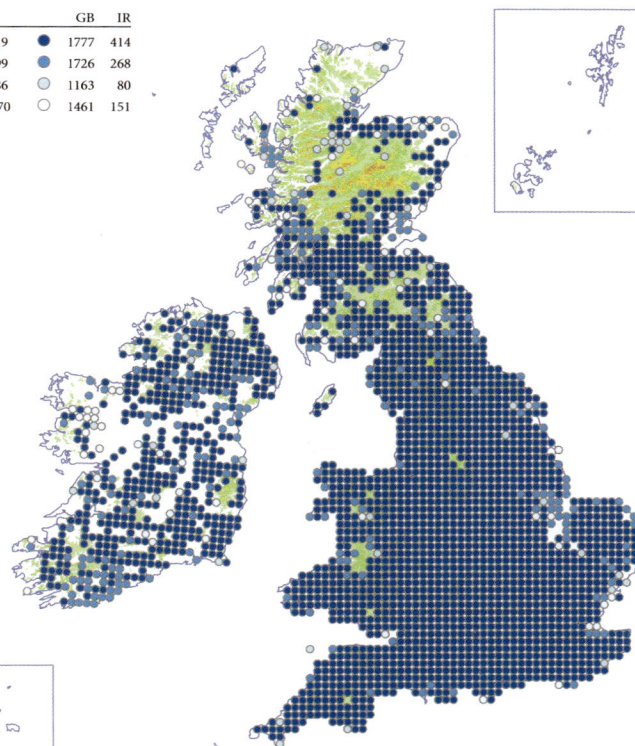

Key refs Cope & Gray (2009), Grime *et al.* (2007), Peterken (1981).

F.H. Perring & D.A. Pearman

Hy *Schedonorus pratensis* × *Lolium perenne* = ×*Schedolium loliaceum*
(Huds.) Holub

Hybrid Fescue

This rather variable hybrid grass is most frequent in damp grassland on heavy, fertile soils. It grows in meadows and pastures, including water-meadows, marshy grassland by streams and ponds, on riversides and muddy ditchsides, in churchyards, reseeded grassland and on roadsides and tracksides. Generally lowland, but reaching 470 m at Tyne Head (Cumberland).

A spontaneous hybrid (native × native).

Trends This is the most widespread of the hybrids between *Schedonorus* and *Lolium*, and has long been known to botanists, having been described as a species by Hudson (1762) from roadsides and pastures near Vauxhall (Surrey), though it is almost certainly under-recorded. It may sometimes have been recorded erroneously for other ×*Schedolium* hybrids or even

for variants of *Lolium perenne*. It is unclear whether the absence of recent records in many squares reflects a lack of recording or a genuine decline.

Biogeography Widespread in temperate Europe.

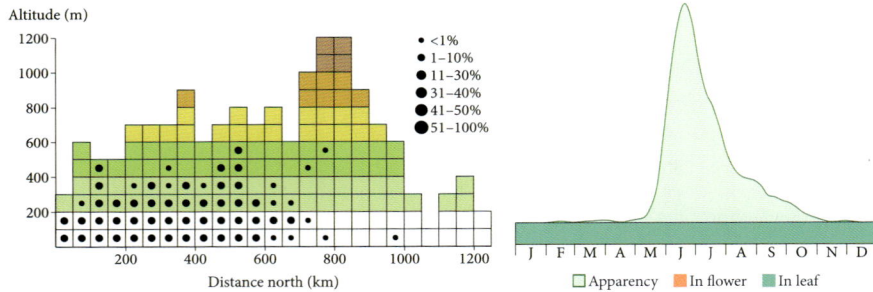

		GB	IR
2000–19	●	352	35
1987–99	●	442	55
1970–86	●	307	15
pre-1970	○	490	22

Key refs Stace *et al.* (2015).

C.A. Stace, C.D. Preston & D.A. Pearman

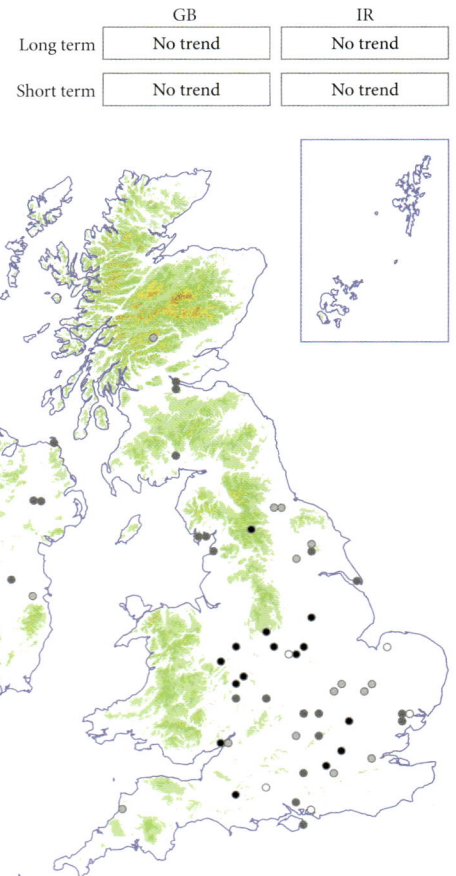

Hy *Schedonorus pratensis* × *Lolium multiflorum* = ×*Schedolium braunii*
(K.Richt.) Stace

This largely sterile hybrid grass is known from meadows, damp roadsides and pathsides, the edges of *Lolium* leys, reseeded roadside verges, field margins and waste ground. Lowland.

A spontaneous hybrid (native × alien).

Trends ×*S. braunii* was first recorded by C.E. Hubbard from Appleton (West Norfolk) in 1933, and has a thinly scattered distribution in England, Wales and Ireland. There are very few records from Scotland, and none this century. This hybrid lacks the long-recorded history of ×*S. loliaceum* in our area, and as a result is probably under-recorded. It has not been mapped in a distribution atlas previously.

Biogeography Known from temperate Europe.

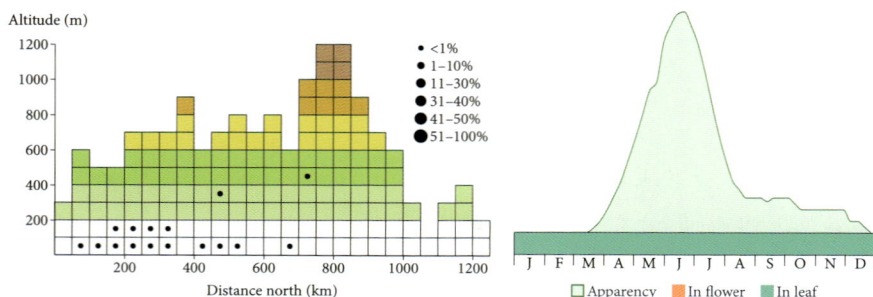

		GB	IR
2000–19	●	15	0
1987–99	●	18	5
1970–86	●	16	1
pre-1970	○	7	1

	GB	IR
Long term	No trend	No trend
Short term	No trend	No trend

Key refs Stace *et al.* (2015).

C.A. Stace, C.D. Preston & D.A. Pearman

Lolium perenne Perennial Rye-grass
L.

A perennial grass, now mainly a species of re-seeded lowland leys that are heavily treated with inorganic fertilizers, but it is also found in hay-meadows, downland, rush-pastures, wet grasslands, amenity grasslands, lawns, and road verges; also in a range of open ruderal habitats. As a native, it favours fertile, heavy, neutral soils, but is also found on those which are mildly acidic or basic. 0–755 m (Great Dun Fell, Westmorland) and probably higher in the Scottish Highlands.

Trends As a native, *L. perenne* was probably primarily a grass of wet grasslands on heavy soils, from where a number of variants were selected for breeding in the early 19th century. Since then highly productive and palatable forage varieties, able to withstand trampling, mowing and heavy grazing, have become an almost ubiquitous

feature of the farmed landscape throughout our area, so much so that its original native distribution has been completely obscured. Consequently all records are mapped without status.

Biogeography European Southern-temperate element; widely naturalized outside its native range.

		GB	IR
2000–19	●	2747	985
1987–99	●	2666	932
1970–86	●	1704	164
pre-1970	○	2604	885

Key refs Beddows (1967), Cope & Gray (2009), Grime *et al.* (2007).

F.H. PERRING, D.A. PEARMAN & K.J. WALKER

Lolium multiflorum × perenne = L. ×boucheanum Hybrid Rye-grass
Kunth

An annual or short-lived perennial grass hybrid, commonly sown by itself or in mixtures in short-term grass leys. It is also found in meadows and old pastures, as a weed in fields of cereals, root crops and on field margins, and in habitats that are less closely associated with agricultural land, such as species-rich chalk grassland, on riverside flood banks, on roadsides (including newly sown verges), on sandy ground by the sea and in gravel-pits inland. The parents are completely inter-fertile, and many cultivars of the hybrid have been developed. Lowland.

A cultivated hybrid (native × alien).

Trends *L. ×boucheanum* was, up to about 1980, probably the most commonly sown *Lolium* but is often mistaken for one of its parents. The map shows clearly the areas where

botanists are familiar with this very widespread but under-recorded hybrid. It was first collected at Poulton (North Wiltshire) in 1875 but not recorded systematically until long after this date.

Biogeography Widespread in temperate Europe.

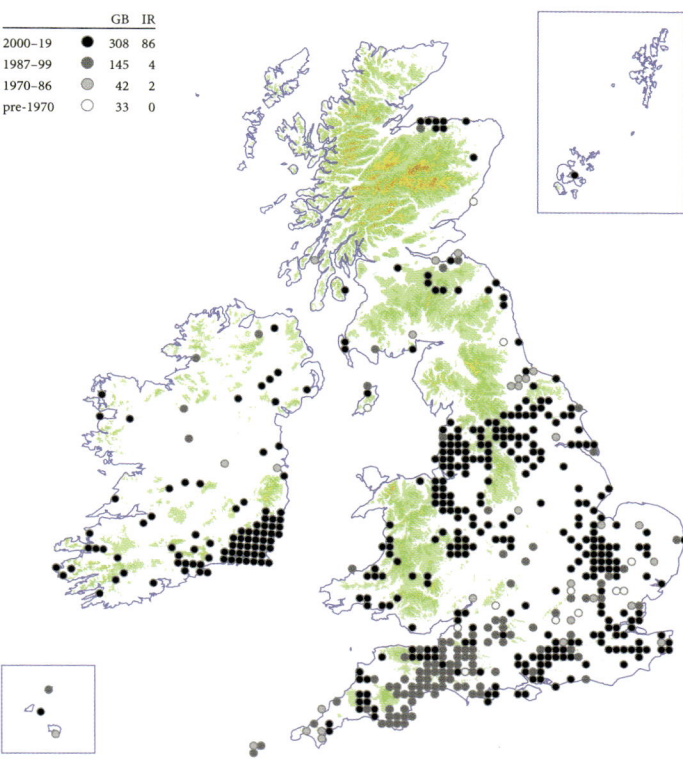

		GB	IR
2000–19	●	308	86
1987–99	●	145	4
1970–86	●	42	2
pre-1970	○	33	0

Key refs Stace *et al.* (2015).

C.A. STACE, C.D. PRESTON & D.A. PEARMAN

Ne *Lolium multiflorum* Italian Rye-grass

Lam.

An annual or short-lived perennial grass, mainly found in re-seeded leys, but also on field margins, in gateways, along farm tracks, on roadsides and rough ground. It often persists for a few years, but rarely becomes naturalized. Generally lowland, but reaching 410 m above Garrigill (Cumberland).

Trends *L. multiflorum* was introduced for use in agriculture in the 1830s, and has since been widely cultivated as a fodder plant in temporary grass-leys. It is probably under-recorded, or confused with the hybrid *L. ×boucheanum*. It was known from the wild by 1840. Its range is stable in Britain, but it is more frequent in Ireland than previously thought.

Biogeography Probably native of the Mediterranean region, but widely used for fodder and now widespread in Europe and other temperate regions.

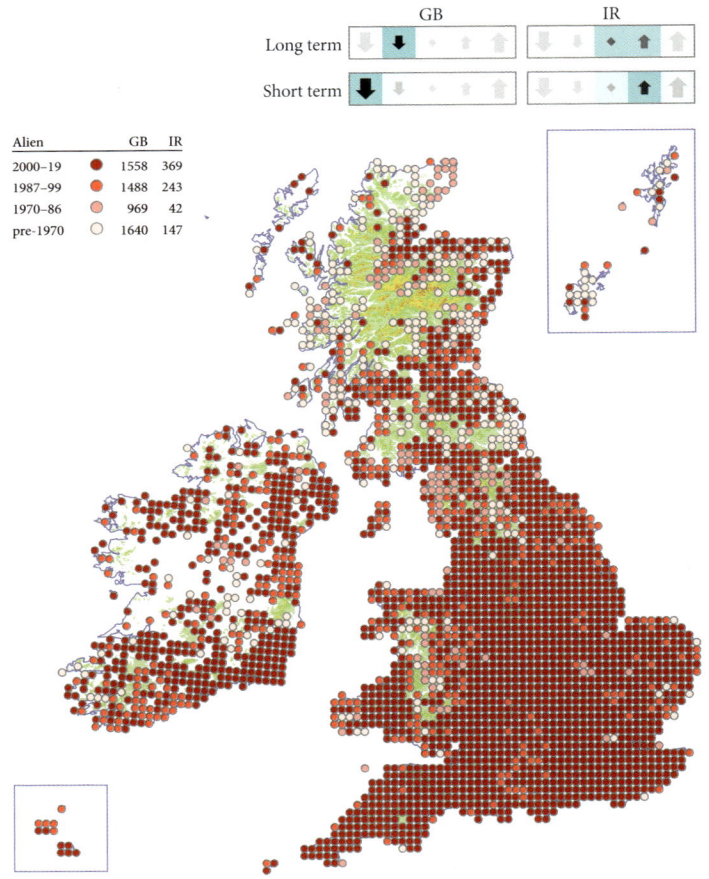

Alien	GB	IR
2000–19	1558	369
1987–99	1488	243
1970–86	969	42
pre-1970	1640	147

Key refs Beddows (1973), Cope & Gray (2009), Rich & Jermy (1998), Ryves *et al.* (1996).

F.H. PERRING & D.A. PEARMAN

Ar *Lolium temulentum* Darnel

L.

An annual grass, formerly occurring as a persistent weed of cereal crops or on refuse tips. It has disappeared from both these habitats (except in western Ireland or as a deliberate introduction at a few sites in England) and is now an extremely rare casual of waste places, originating from grain, birdseed and wool shoddy. Lowland.

Trends *L. temulentum*, first recorded in Britain by 1548, was formerly a serious weed of cereal crops, but had almost disappeared from this habitat by the 1940s. In Britain it continues to be recorded as a casual, but much less frequently now than in the 1950s and 1960s. It is probably extinct as an archaeophyte in Britain as recent records were deliberate introductions to help conserve the species. In Ireland it survives in a few fields on the Aran Islands where it occurs as a contaminant of rye crops (*Secale cereale*) grown for thatching for houses and barns (Bleasdale, 1994). It is sometimes toxic to humans and livestock (Cooper & Johnson, 1988).

Biogeography Perhaps native of the Mediterranean region and south-western Asia, but native range obscured by its spread with cultivation; once widespread in Europe and naturalized in Japan, North and South America, Australasia and elsewhere.

Alien	GB	IR
2000–19	3	2
1987–99	20	2
1970–86	95	0
pre-1970	344	38

Key refs Bleasdale (1994), Cooper & Johnson (1988), Cope & Gray (2009).

D.A. PEARMAN & K.J. WALKER

N *Drymochloa sylvatica* Wood Fescue

(Pollich) Holub

A long-lived, shallow-rooted perennial grass of moist, ancient wooded valleys, on near-vertical cliffs, rocky slopes, deciduous wood margins and streamsides, especially on seepage lines or by waterfalls. Subsidiary habitats include vegetated talus below cliffs if above flood level, and wooded limestone pavement. It grows on coal measure sandstones which often are quite high in carbonates, and other soils of a moderate base status, often growing with *Luzula sylvatica*. As it requires continuous levels of high humidity and is shallow-rooted, the grass tends to survive in sites which are too unstable for the woodrush, but never dry out. 0–400 m (Nant Ysgolion gorge, Talerddig, Montgomeryshire).

Trends A greater knowledge of its ecological niche, together with more systematic recording in the late 20th century of areas where the species happens to be frequent (northern England and Scotland) revealed that *D. sylvatica* was much more widespread than previously thought. This species grows in habitats which are sometimes virtually inaccessible, and its absence since 2000 from some 10 km squares may in part reflect difficulties in recording rather than actual loss, particularly in Scotland, although recent targeted surveys in north-eastern England have shown a real decline in population frequency at many sites, with rockfall and landslides the primary threats. Being evergreen, it is best searched for (with binoculars) in the winter, when tree leaves have fallen.

Biogeography European Temperate element.

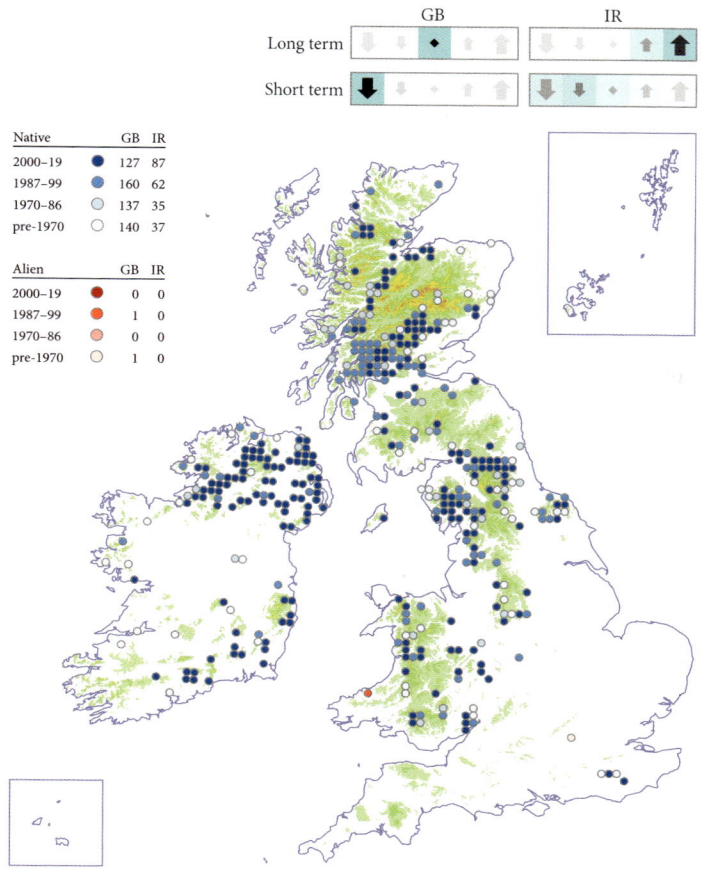

Native	GB	IR
2000–19	127	87
1987–99	160	62
1970–86	137	35
pre-1970	140	37

Alien	GB	IR
2000–19	0	0
1987–99	1	0
1970–86	0	0
pre-1970	1	0

Key refs Cope & Gray (2009), Richards (2015b), Stewart *et al.* (1994).

A.J. RICHARDS, D.A. PEARMAN & P.A. STROH

Ne *Festuca heterophylla* Various-leaved Fescue

Lam.

A rather tall, densely tufted perennial grass, widely naturalized in woods, spinneys and wood-borders on light soils. Lowland.

Trends This species became available in Britain in 1812 and was originally planted for ornament or ground cover and possibly for fodder. It was a constituent of Victorian grass-seed mixtures and was frequently sown on woodland rides, beneath tree-belts and in parks and gardens. It was first recorded in the wild in 1874 (Kelso, Roxburghshire). More recently, it has occurred as a contaminant of grass-seed mixtures. There has been a steady decline over the last 50 years, though it may have been overlooked in some of its old sites.

Biogeography A European Temperate species.

	GB	IR
Long term	No trend	No trend
Short term	No trend	No trend

Alien	GB	IR
2000–19	36	3
1987–99	43	2
1970–86	35	1
pre-1970	48	0

Key refs Cope & Gray (2009), Ryves *et al.* (1996).

S.J. LEACH & D.A. PEARMAN

N *Festuca arenaria* Rush-leaved Fescue
Osbeck

An extensively rhizomatous perennial grass of sand dunes and open sandy shingle; also, more rarely, on cliff-tops, ledges and rough ground near the sea. On sand dunes it typically occurs on semi-mobile foredunes dominated by *Ammophila arenaria* or *Leymus arenarius*. Lowland.

Trends This account encompasses both subspecies, subsp. *arenaria* and subsp. *oraria* (*F. juncifolia*). Its overall distribution appears to be stable, with slight increases in some regions, presumably due to more systematic recording. It is difficult to explain the relative lack of recent records from the western coasts of Britain.

Biogeography Oceanic Temperate element.

	GB	IR
Long term	No trend	No trend
Short term	↓ ↓ • ↑ ⬆	No trend

Native		GB	IR
2000–19	●	102	1
1987–99	●	70	0
1970–86	○	55	4
pre-1970	○	97	3

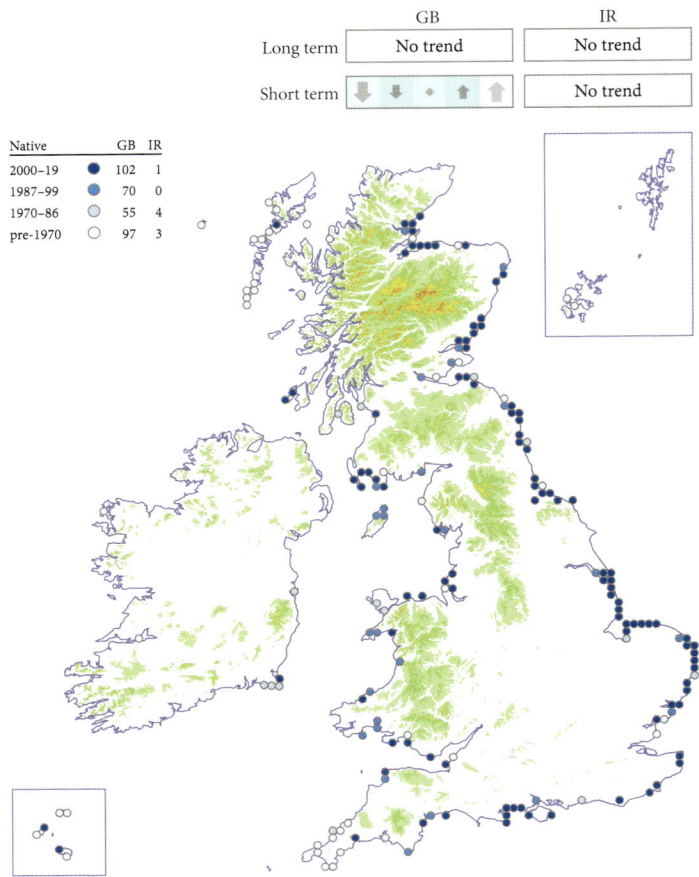

Key refs Auquier (1971b), Cope & Gray (2009), Freijsen & Heeres (1972), Stewart *et al.* (1994).

S.J. LEACH & D.A. PEARMAN

N *Festuca rubra* agg. Red Fescues

Extremely morphologically variable tufted or rhizomatous perennial grasses of all kinds of grassy habitats, including lowland meadows and pastures, saltmarshes, cliff-top grassland, sand dunes, upland pastures, mountain grasslands and rock ledges. Some of these taxa are also frequently sown for agriculture, landscaping and amenity. 0–1,080 m (Snowdon, Caernarvonshire).

Trends *F. rubra* agg. has a near-ubiquitous distribution at the 10 km square resolution and there appears to have been very little change in its overall distribution since the 1960s. The aggregate includes *F. arenaria* and *F. rubra*, the latter divided into seven subspecies. Of these, *F. rubra* subsp. *rubra* occurs throughout the range of the species. The other taxa are mapped separately, but note that Cope & Gray (2009) are very sceptical

as to the worth (or practicality) of separating some of these subspecies.

Biogeography Circumpolar Wide-boreal element; widely naturalized outside its native range.

	GB	IR
Long term	↓ ↓ • ↑ ⬆	↓ ↓ • ↑ ⬆
Short term	↓ ↓ • ↑ ⬆	↓ ↓ • ↑ ⬆

Native		GB	IR
2000–19	●	2837	1002
1987–99	●	2772	941
1970–86	○	1954	249
pre-1970	○	2519	689

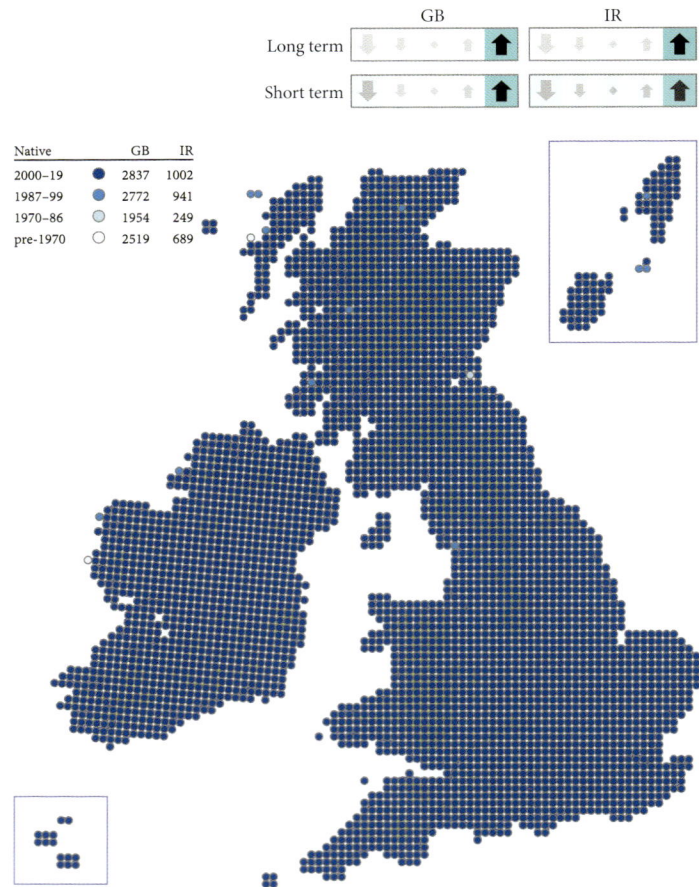

Key refs Al-Bermani (1991), Cope & Gray (2009), Grime *et al.* (2007), Stace *et al.* (1992).

S.J. LEACH & D.A. PEARMAN

N *Festuca rubra* subsp. *juncea*
(Hack.) K.Richt.

A densely tufted, shortly rhizomatous perennial grass of sea-cliffs and coastal rock outcrops, occasionally found inland in rocky places. Lowland.

Trends This subspecies, as presently delimited, incorporates coastal populations previously assigned to subsp. *pruinosa*, though this amalgamation is not accepted by Cope & Gray (2009). Neither taxon was mapped in the 1962 *Atlas*, and there are insufficient data available to allow an assessment of long-term changes in distribution. In common with other subspecies of *F. rubra*, subsp. *juncea* is probably under-recorded. Non-pruinose populations, in particular, can be easily overlooked, or assigned to the separate subspecies if the taxonomy in Cope & Gray (2009) is adopted.

Biogeography Widespread in Europe; wider distribution uncertain.

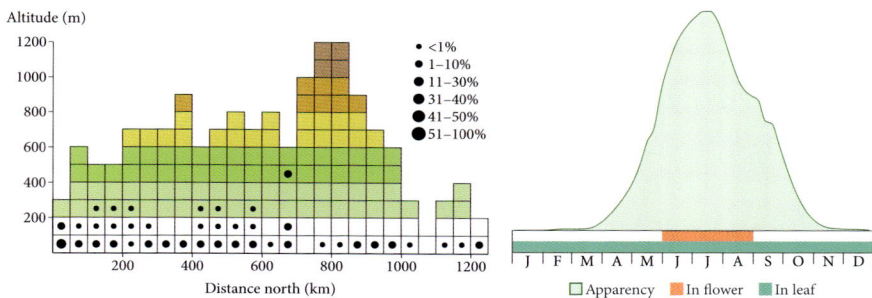

Native	GB	IR
2000–19	232	16
1987–99	182	13
1970–86	33	7
pre-1970	35	0

Alien	GB	IR
2000–19	4	0
1987–99	2	0
1970–86	0	0
pre-1970	0	0

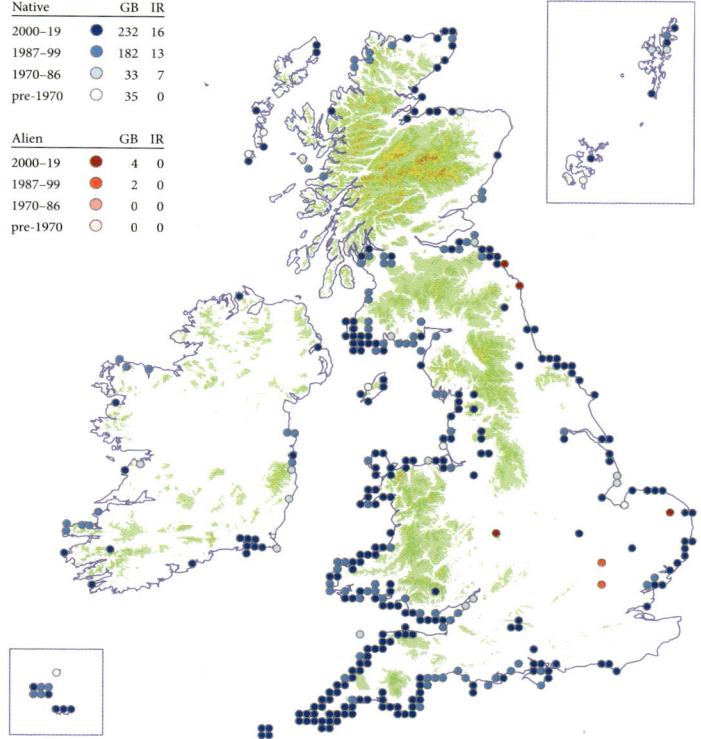

Key refs Auquier (1971a), Cope & Gray (2009).

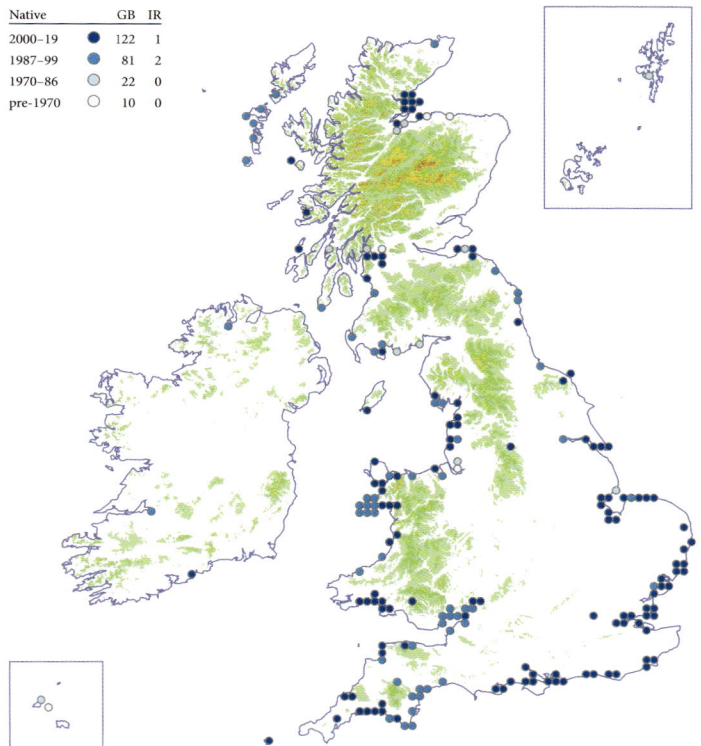

S.J. Leach & D.A. Pearman

N *Festuca rubra* subsp. *litoralis*
(G.Mey.) Auquier

A shortly rhizomatous, mat-forming perennial grass of saltmarshes, often dominating large areas in the middle and upper marsh; also found in brackish grazing marshes and other sandy or muddy saline areas. Lowland.

Trends This taxon was first mapped in the 2002 *Atlas*. The present map shows a wider distribution, though with some localized losses in areas where it is still likely to occur, reinforcing the view that it is still widely under-recorded. Apparently, it has been used as 'sea-washed' turf of the highest quality for tennis courts and bowling greens.

Biogeography European Boreo-temperate element; recorded from the Atlantic coast of Europe and the Baltic region.

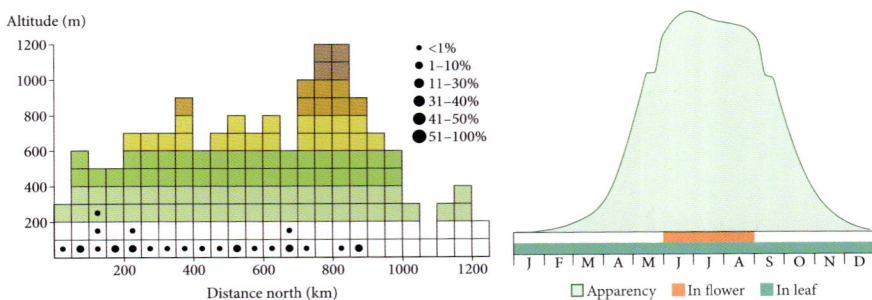

Native	GB	IR
2000–19	122	1
1987–99	81	2
1970–86	22	0
pre-1970	10	0

S.J. Leach & D.A. Pearman

N *Festuca rubra* subsp. *commutata* Chewing's Fescue
Gaudin

A densely tufted perennial grass of all kinds of grassy places, especially on well-drained soils. Under the name of Chewing's Fescue, this taxon is an important constituent of grass-seed mixtures and this may account for the many records of subsp. *commutata* from roadsides, amenity grasslands and garden lawns. Mainly lowland; its precise upper altitudinal limit is unknown.

Native in Britain and a neophyte in Ireland.

Trends The difficulty in identifying this subspecies combined with its widespread introduction makes it almost impossible to assess trends in its distribution. It is certainly under-recorded in most areas, as systematic recording in a few areas has shown it to be frequent there. It is not feasible to distinguish between native and introduced populations

with any accuracy, and consequently all records are mapped without status.

Biogeography European Temperate element.

		GB	IR
2000–19	●	195	1
1987–99	●	96	0
1970–86	●	40	0
pre-1970	○	61	0

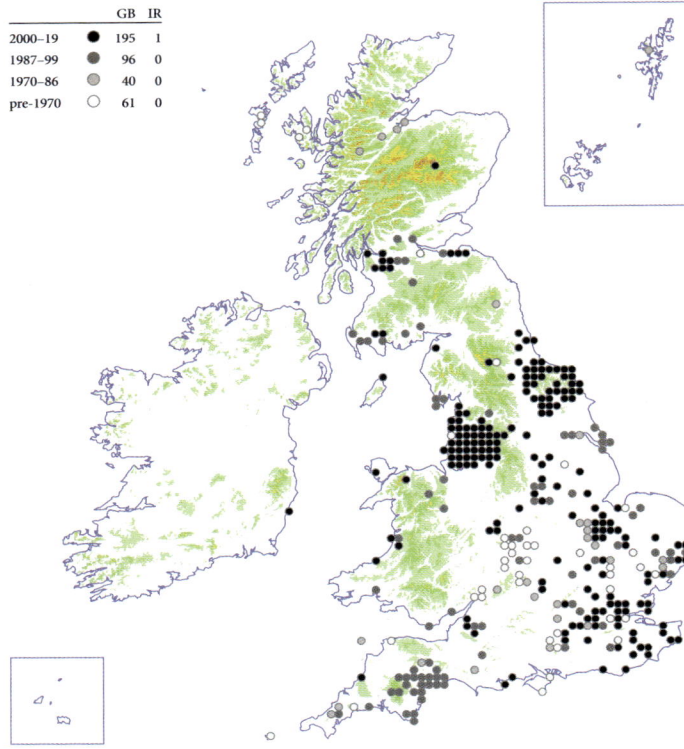

Key refs Cope & Gray (2009).

S.J. Leach & D.A. Pearman

N *Festuca rubra* subsp. *arctica*
(Hack.) Govor.

A rhizomatous perennial grass of wet mountain slopes and gullies, rock ledges and flushes, and also on serpentine at lower altitudes. 0–915 m (Meall nan Tarmachan, Mid Perthshire).

Trends *F. rubra* subsp. *arctica* (formerly named *F. richardsonii*) is under-recorded. With the exception of northern England and the Outer Hebrides, there are very few recent records and so it is not possible to accurately ascertain trends in distribution. The almost complete absence of recent records on the Scottish mainland is a symptom of the difficulty recorders have in distinguishing this taxon.

Biogeography Circumpolar Arctic-montane element.

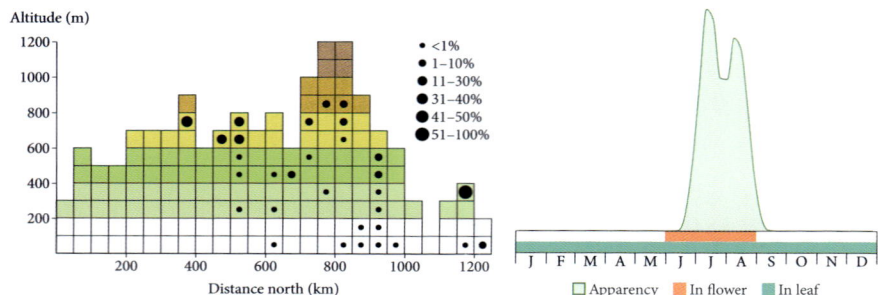

Native		GB	IR
2000–19	●	19	0
1987–99	●	24	0
1970–86	●	4	0
pre-1970	○	6	0

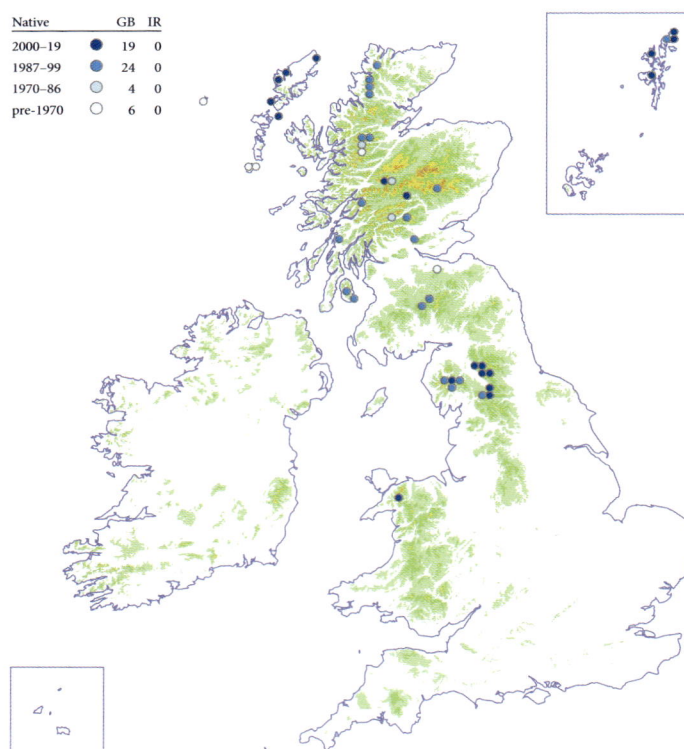

Key refs Cope & Gray (2009).

S.J. Leach & D.A. Pearman

Ⓝ *Festuca rubra* subsp. *scotica*
S.Cunn. ex Al-Bermani

A rhizomatous perennial grass of wet, grassy turf around rock outcrops and on cliff ledges. From sea level to at least 825 m in the Scottish Highlands.

Trends *F. rubra* subsp. *scotica* was first recognized by C.E. Hubbard from an unnamed location in the Cairngorms but was not formally named until 1991 (Al-Bermani & Stace, 1991). The fact that there is only one recent record strongly suggests that this species is grossly under-recorded, since both the original describers and Cope & Gray (2009) characterize it as being widespread in northern Britain.

Biogeography Its European range is uncertain; the 2002 *Atlas* states that it is known from Scandinavia and Iceland as well as Scotland, whereas Cope & Gray (2009) claim that this variant is unknown outside our area.

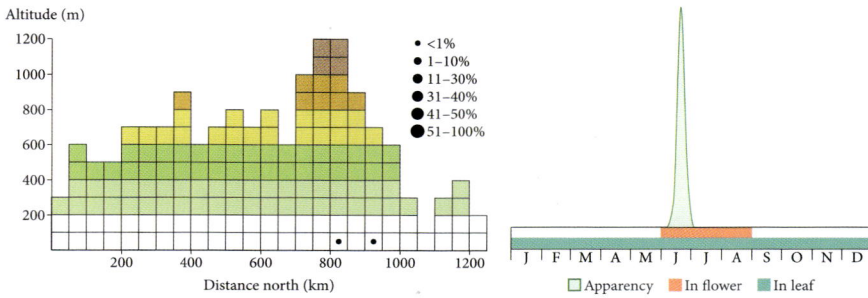

		GB	IR
Long term		No trend	No trend
Short term		No trend	No trend

Native		GB	IR
2000–19	●	1	0
1987–99	●	3	0
1970–86	◔	4	0
pre-1970	○	5	0

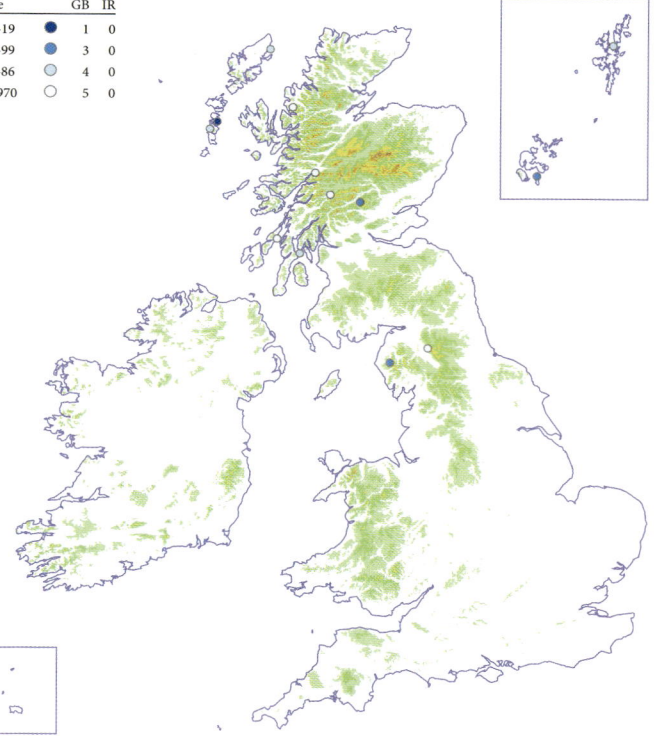

Key refs Cope & Gray (2009), Halliday (1995).

S.J. Leach & D.A. Pearman

Altitude (m) chart with markers: <1%, 1–10%, 11–30%, 31–40%, 41–50%, 51–100%; Distance north (km).

Apparency, In flower, In leaf

Ⓝ̲ₑ *Festuca rubra* subsp. *megastachys*
Gaudin

A rhizomatous, patch-forming perennial grass of waysides and other grassy places, including re-seeded grasslands and garden lawns. Lowland, but reaching 310 m on the A44, west of Bwlch Nantyrarian (Cardiganshire).

Trends This taxon was not mapped in the 1962 *Atlas*. It has been much introduced as an amenity grass but Cope & Gray (2009) suggest that native populations have been known since the late 18th century. However, the first record we have traced was made in 1831 (Woodbury, South Devon). Whilst there are conflicting opinions about the status of this species in our area, it is certainly under-recorded, having been ignored, or not recognized, by recorders in many counties.

Biogeography Wider native distribution uncertain.

		GB	IR
Long term		No trend	No trend
Short term		No trend	No trend

Alien		GB	IR
2000–19	●	124	0
1987–99	●	120	1
1970–86	◔	21	0
pre-1970	○	14	0

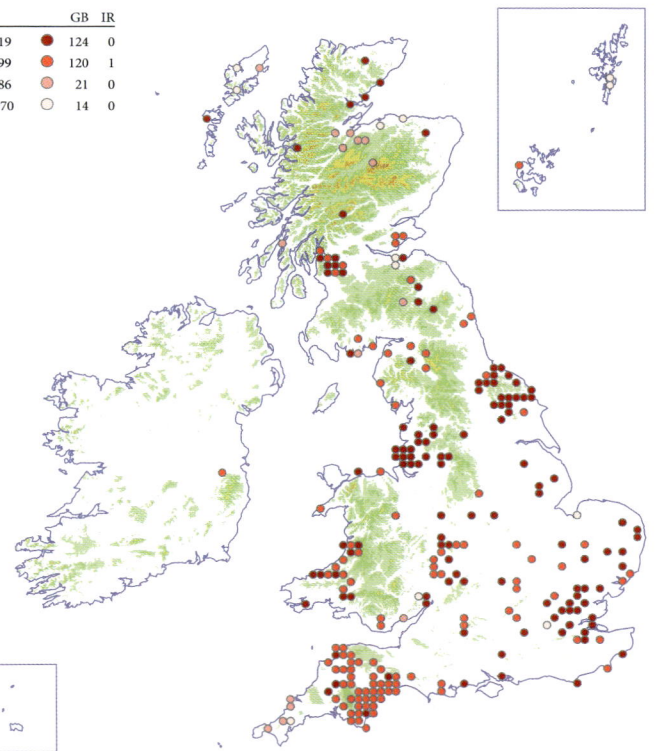

Key refs Cope & Gray (2009).

S.J. Leach & D.A. Pearman

Altitude (m) chart with markers: <1%, 1–10%, 11–30%, 31–40%, 41–50%, 51–100%; Distance north (km).

Apparency, In flower, In leaf

Festuca ovina agg. Sheep's-fescues

These perennial grasses grow in a variety of well-drained acidic and basic, usually infertile, habitats, including open woodland, grasslands, sand dunes, heathlands, moorlands, rock ledges and sea-cliffs. Some species are now frequently sown in grass-seed and wild-flower seed mixtures. 0–1,305 m (Ben Macdui, South Aberdeenshire).

Trends The distribution of *F. ovina* agg. is stable. All eight species forming this aggregate are mapped separately. Some of these are poorly known and many botanists, although distinguishing *F. vivipara*, otherwise record only *F. ovina* agg.

Biogeography This aggregate includes *F. vivipara* and a complex of other taxa which have a Eurasian Boreo-temperate distribution but have been widely introduced elsewhere.

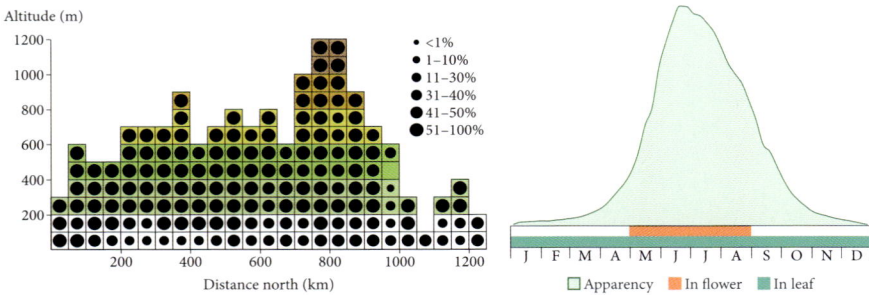

	GB	IR
Long term	No trend	No trend
Short term	No trend	No trend

Native	GB	IR
2000–19	2627	679
1987–99	2580	577
1970–86	1732	133
pre-1970	2483	534

Alien	GB	IR
2000–19	8	1
1987–99	8	1
1970–86	5	0
pre-1970	7	0

Key refs Cope & Gray (2009), Grime *et al.* (2007), Stace *et al.* (1992), Wilkinson & Stace (1991).

S.J. LEACH

Festuca ovina Sheep's-fescue
L.

A morphologically variable, densely tufted perennial grass of a wide range of infertile, well-drained habitats, including both lowland and upland calcareous and acid grasslands and dry heathlands, rocky mountain slopes and rock ledges, and sea-cliffs. 0–1,305 m (Ben Macdui, South Aberdeenshire).

Trends The 10 km square distribution of *F. ovina* appears to be stable, and is now much better known. The map includes records of the species and its three component subspecies: subsp. *ovina*, subsp. *hirtula* and subsp. *ophiolíticola*. This grass is of enormous agricultural and socio-economic importance, being one of the predominant constituents of pastures across great swathes of upland Britain and Ireland. No information is available on the spread or trends of the subspecies.

Biogeography Eurasian Boreo-temperate element; widely naturalized outside its native range.

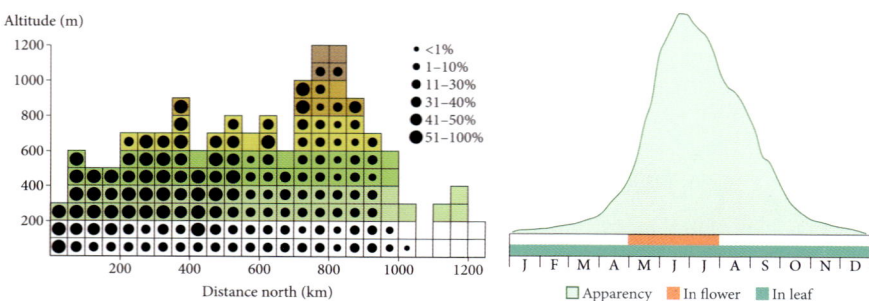

Native	GB	IR
2000–19	2041	544
1987–99	1717	400
1970–86	702	106
pre-1970	603	437

Alien	GB	IR
2000–19	5	1
1987–99	3	1
1970–86	4	0
pre-1970	2	1

Key refs Cope & Gray (2009), Grime *et al.* (2007), Wilkinson & Stace (1991).

S.J. LEACH & D.A. PEARMAN

Festuca vivipara Viviparous Sheep's-fescue
(L.) Sm.

A tufted perennial grass of upland heathy pastures, open *Betula* and *Quercus* woodland, rock ledges and crevices, and a wide range of mountain slope and plateau communities including areas of late snow-lie; also found in the drier parts of bogs and on stream banks. It grows on both basic and acidic substrates. From sea level in western Scotland and Ireland, to 1,335 m on Ben Nevis (Westerness).

Trends The overall 10 km square range of *F. vivipara* has remained relatively stable since the 1960s. It is now better recorded in England, Wales and Ireland.

Biogeography Circumpolar Boreo-arctic Montane element.

Key refs Cope & Gray (2009), Wilkinson & Stace (1991).

F.H. PERRING & D.A. PEARMAN

Festuca filiformis Fine-leaved Sheep's-fescue
Pourr.

A densely tufted perennial grass of heathlands, moorlands and infertile grasslands, sometimes also found in open woodland, parkland and other grassy places. It appears to be more drought-resistant than *F. ovina* and as a consequence it is often more abundant on drier, more acidic and infertile, well-drained soils. 0–1,035 m (Meall Ghaordie, Mid Perthshire).

Trends The map in Perring & Sell (1968) was based on material seen by C.E. Hubbard or other reliable recorders. Since then *F. filiformis* has become more widely known, and this explains its apparent increase, especially in northern Britain and Ireland. There has, however, been much confusion between it and other taxa within the *F. ovina* complex (especially short-awned variants), and it has probably been over-recorded in some areas (which might explain the lack of recent records in south-western England and elsewhere) and overlooked in others. The status of the records in southern Ireland is unclear.

Biogeography Suboceanic Temperate element.

Key refs Cope & Gray (2009), Wilkinson & Stace (1991).

S.J. LEACH & D.A. PEARMAN

N *Festuca armoricana* Breton Fescue

Kerguélen

A densely tufted perennial grass apparently restricted to fixed sand dunes at St Ouen's and St Brelade's Bays, Jersey. Lowland.

Trends This species, a member of the *F. ovina* complex, appears to be stable in Jersey. It may have been overlooked elsewhere in the Channel Islands, and possibly also in southern England.

Biogeography Oceanic Temperate element.

	GB	IR
Long term	No trend	No trend
Short term	No trend	No trend

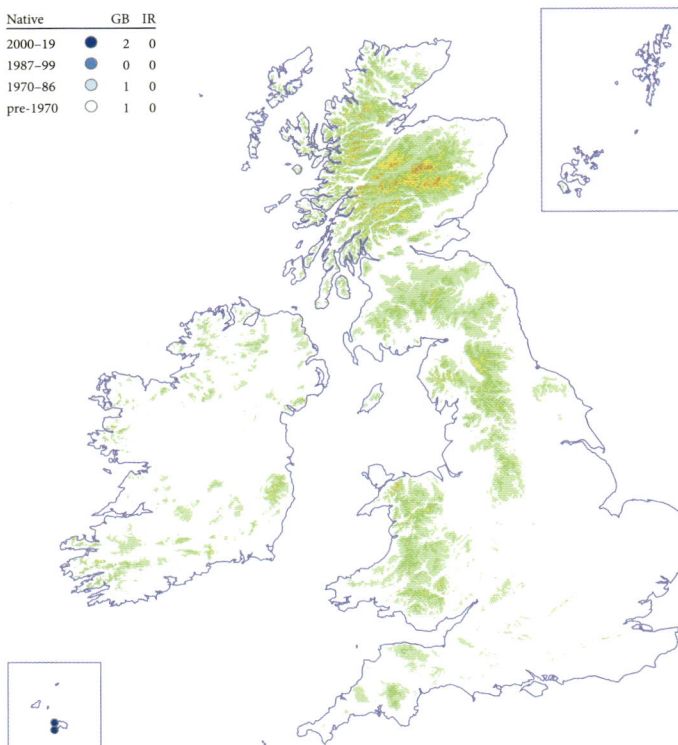

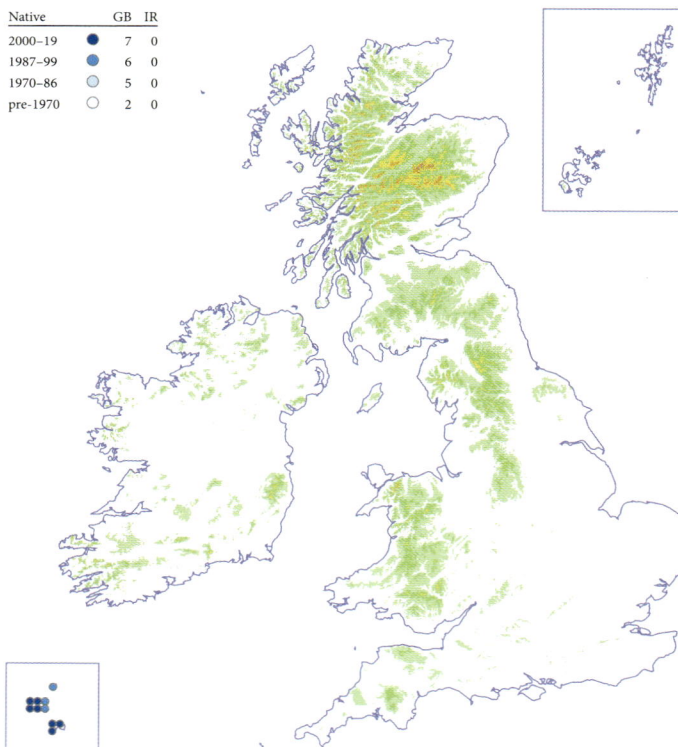

Native	GB	IR
2000–19	2	0
1987–99	0	0
1970–86	1	0
pre-1970	1	0

Key refs Cope & Gray (2009), Wilkinson & Stace (1991).

S.J. LEACH & D.A. PEARMAN

N *Festuca huonii* Huon's Fescue

Auquier

A densely tufted perennial grass of grassy cliff-tops and ledges and screes on acid rocks in the Channel Islands. Lowland.

Trends This member of the *F. ovina* complex is frequent within its restricted range and there are no indications of any recent change in its distribution. It was reported from near Prawle Point, South Devon, in 1992 (Takagi-Arigho, 1995), but recent opinion is that it may have been a depauperate specimen of *F. longifolia*.

Biogeography Oceanic Temperate element; confined to Brittany and the Channel Islands.

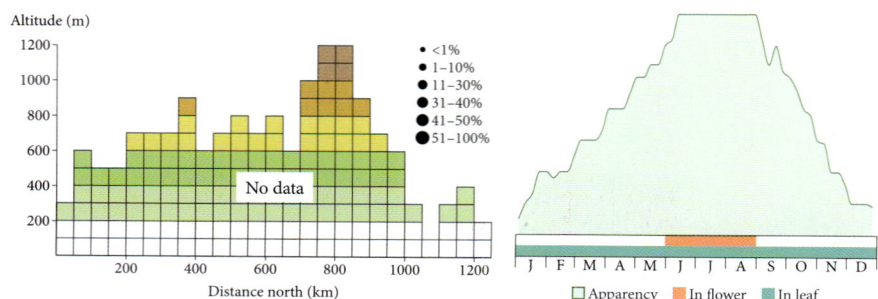

	GB	IR
Long term	No trend	No trend
Short term	No trend	No trend

Native	GB	IR
2000–19	7	0
1987–99	6	0
1970–86	5	0
pre-1970	2	0

Key refs Auquier (1973), Cope & Gray (2009), Takagi-Arigho (1995), Wilkinson & Stace (1991).

S.J. LEACH & D.A. PEARMAN

N? *Festuca lemanii* Confused Fescue

Bastard

A tufted perennial grass of grassy places on well-drained, acidic or calcareous soils, often occurring with *F. ovina*. Lowland.

Trends This species was not separately mapped in the 1962 *Atlas*. At that time, *F. lemanii* and the alien *F. trachyphylla* were collectively known by the misapplied name *F. longifolia*, and there continues to be much confusion between *F. lemanii* and other taxa within the *F. ovina* complex, including *F. ovina* itself. It is little known to British botanists, with the first record only in 1982 (Seven Sisters, Herefordshire), can easily be overlooked and is probably still much under-recorded.

Biogeography Oceanic Temperate element.

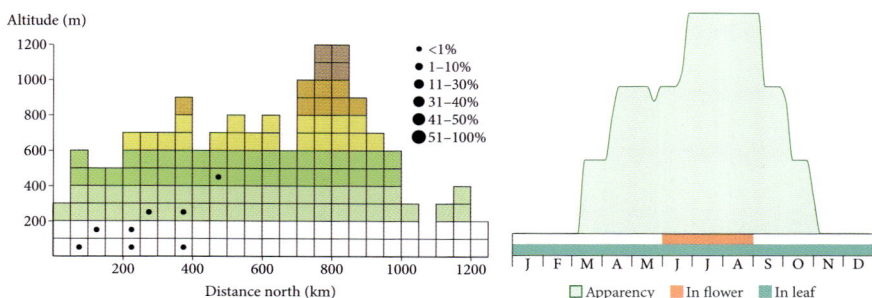

	GB	IR
Long term	No trend	No trend
Short term	↓	No trend

Native	GB	IR
2000–19	7	0
1987–99	9	0
1970–86	3	0
pre-1970	1	0

Alien	GB	IR
2000–19	0	0
1987–99	1	0
1970–86	0	0
pre-1970	0	0

Altitude (m)

• <1%
• 1–10%
● 11–30%
● 31–40%
● 41–50%
● 51–100%

Apparency   In flower   In leaf

Key refs Cope & Gray (2009), Stace & Wilkinson (1989), Wilkinson & Stace (1991).

S.J. LEACH & D.A. PEARMAN

Ne *Festuca trachyphylla* Hard Fescue

(Hack.) R.P.Murray

A tufted perennial herb, introduced in turf-grass and seed mixtures (as *F. duriuscula*) and frequently naturalized on roadsides, railway banks, commons, golf courses and other amenity grasslands, especially on well-drained, acidic soils. Generally lowland, but reaching 365 m at Taddington (Derbyshire).

Trends *F. trachyphylla* and *F. lemanii* were collectively mapped under the misapplied name *F. longifolia* in the 1962 *Atlas*, and there continues to be much confusion between *F. trachyphylla* and other 'blue-leaved' taxa within the *F. ovina* species-complex. It has been known in the wild since 1825 (Cambridgeshire), and though there are now many more records than there were in the latter decades of the 20th century, it is probably much under-recorded.

Biogeography Native of central Europe.

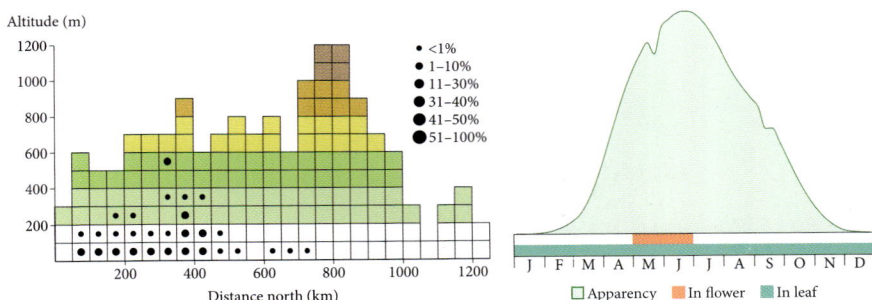

	GB	IR
Long term	No trend	No trend
Short term	↑	No trend

Alien	GB	IR
2000–19	226	2
1987–99	84	0
1970–86	40	0
pre-1970	74	0

Altitude (m)

• <1%
• 1–10%
● 11–30%
● 31–40%
● 41–50%
● 51–100%

Apparency   In flower   In leaf

Key refs Cope & Gray (2009), Ryves *et al.* (1996), Stace & Wilkinson (1989), Wilkinson & Stace (1991).

S.J. LEACH & D.A. PEARMAN

N *Festuca longifolia* Blue Fescue

Thuill.

A densely tufted perennial grass of dry, rabbit-grazed heathlands, sandy roadside banks and maritime cliff-tops and ledges. Lowland.

Trends Past confusion between *F. longifolia* and other glaucous *Festuca* taxa, and a consequent lack of reliable historical data, means that changes in distribution remain unclear. It was discovered in East Cornwall in 2004 in similar maritime habitats to the sites in South Devon, and on the Isle of Wight in 2007. Several colonies in Breckland have been lost since the early 1980s. Most surviving populations there, and in Nottinghamshire and Lincolnshire, are small and at risk of being outcompeted by taller grasses or shaded out by trees. Coastal populations are less threatened, although those in Lincolnshire have not been seen since the 1980s.

Biogeography Oceanic Temperate element.

Native	GB	IR
2000–19	18	0
1987–99	19	0
1970–86	11	0
pre-1970	9	0

Alien	GB	IR
2000–19	2	0
1987–99	1	0
1970–86	0	0
pre-1970	0	0

	GB	IR
Long term	No trend	No trend
Short term		No trend

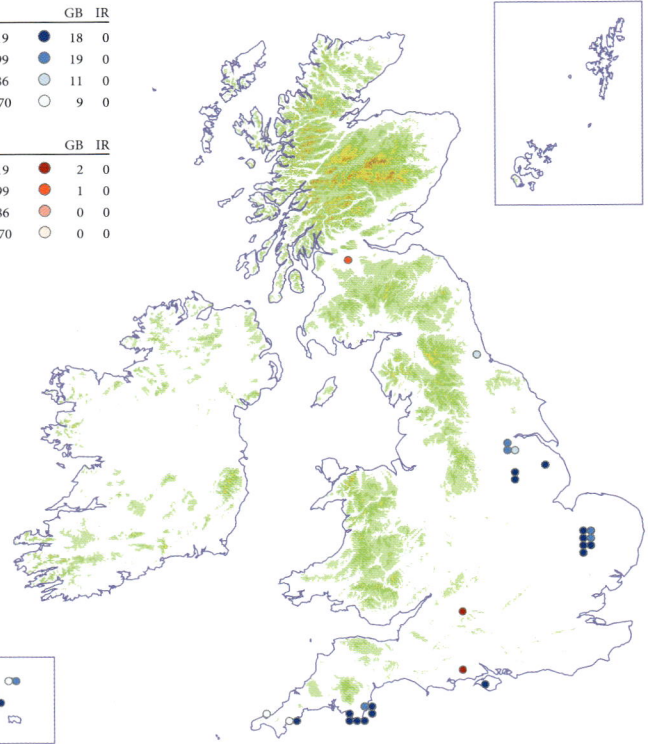

Key refs Cope & Gray (2009), Gibson & Taylor (2005), Stace & Wilkinson (1989), Trist (1973), Wigginton (1999).

S.J. LEACH & D.A. PEARMAN

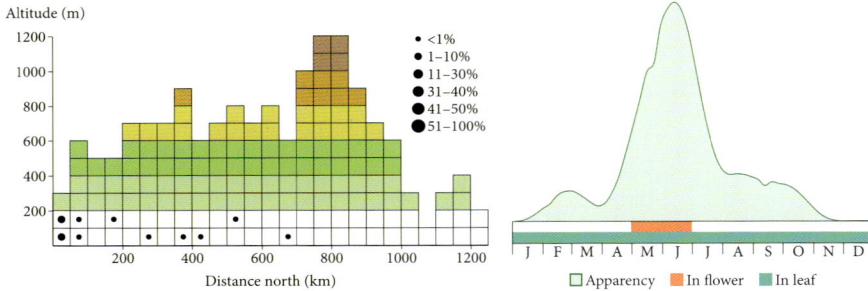

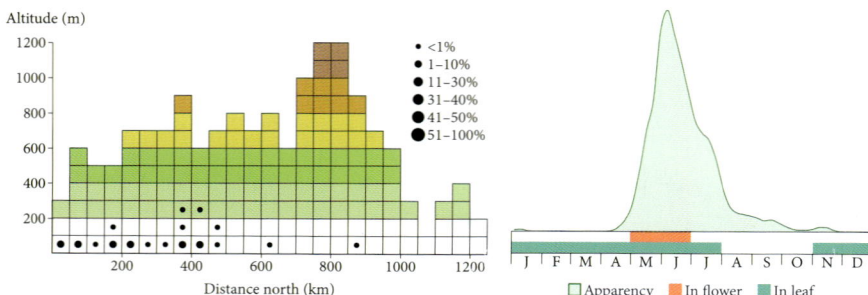

N *Vulpia fasciculata* Dune Fescue

(Forssk.) Fritsch

An annual grass of sand dunes, particularly open, disturbed areas on fixed dunes, and sandy shingle, and frequently associated with other winter-annuals. Lowland.

Trends The overall 10 km square distribution of *V. fasciculata* appears to be stable and is better known due to fuller recording in the latter half of the 20th century, and since 2000. Its abundance on some sites increased following the reduction of rabbit populations due to the spread of myxomatosis in the mid-1950s. In 2004 a population was discovered on sand dunes at Findhorn (Moray), significantly extending northwards its known British range. It may be confused with stunted plants of *V. bromoides*.

Biogeography Mediterranean-Atlantic element.

Native	GB	IR
2000–19	100	21
1987–99	93	14
1970–86	64	7
pre-1970	84	13

Alien	GB	IR
2000–19	2	1
1987–99	1	0
1970–86	1	0
pre-1970	6	0

	GB	IR
Long term		
Short term		

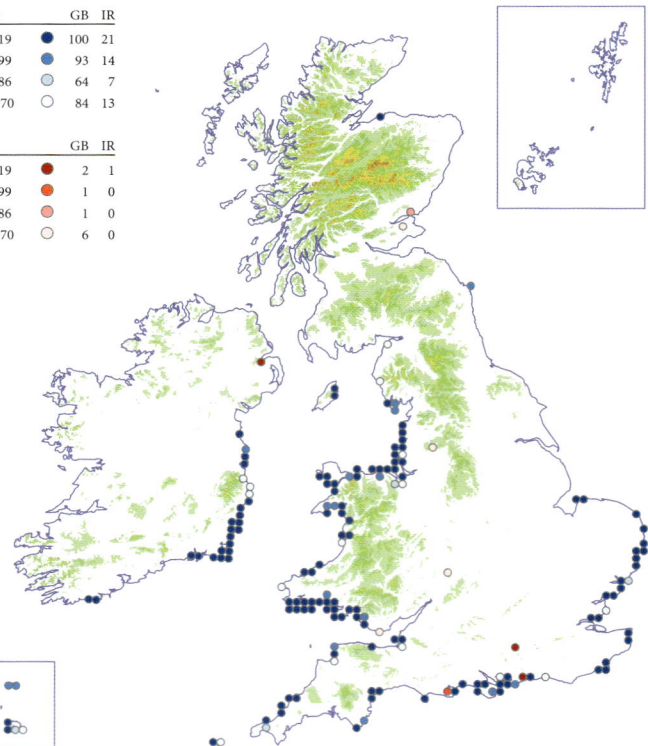

Key refs Cope & Gray (2009), Stewart *et al.* (1994), Watkinson (1978).

S.J. LEACH & D.A. PEARMAN

N *Vulpia bromoides* Squirreltail Fescue
(L.) Gray

An annual of open grasslands, heaths, cliff-tops and sand dunes. It also grows in artificial habitats such as quarries, wall-tops, pavements, railways and rough and waste ground in built-up areas. It was formerly a frequent introduction from wool shoddy. It favours well-drained soils, often growing abundantly on drought-prone south-facing banks and slopes, but appears to be indifferent to soil pH. 0–490 m (Fanna Hill, Roxburghshire).

Trends *V. bromoides* is our most common and widespread species of *Vulpia* and its 10 km square distribution has increased since the 1960s, largely due to its spread in artificial habitats and more intensive recording in some regions.

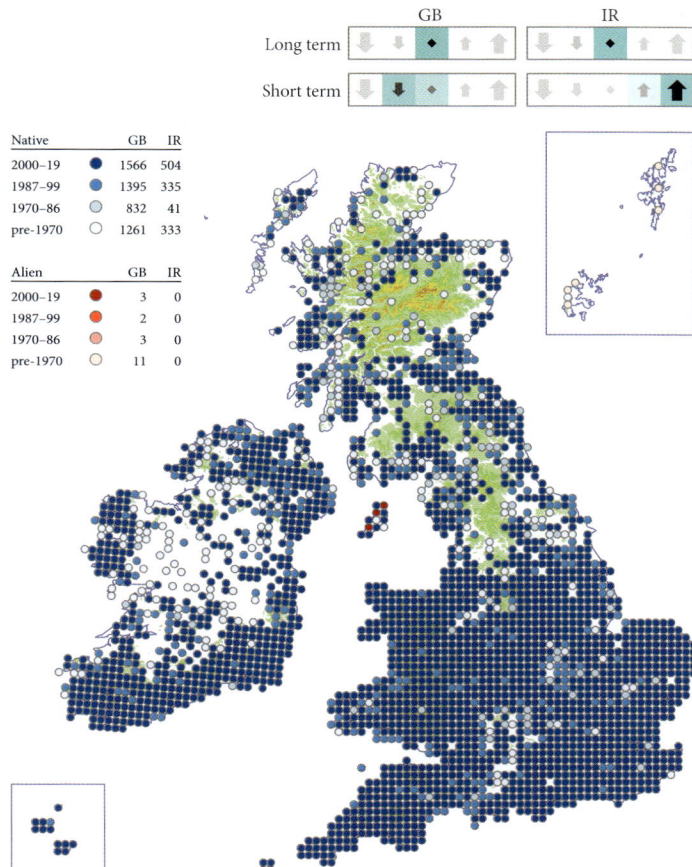

Biogeography Submediterranean-Subatlantic element; widely naturalized outside its native range.

Native		GB	IR
2000–19	●	1566	504
1987–99	●	1395	335
1970–86	●	832	41
pre-1970	○	1261	333

Alien		GB	IR
2000–19	●	3	0
1987–99	●	2	0
1970–86	●	3	0
pre-1970	○	11	0

Key refs Cope & Gray (2009).

S.J. Leach

Ar *Vulpia myuros* Rat's-tail Fescue
(L.) C.C.Gmel.

An annual grass, found naturalized on active and disused railways, tracks and roadsides, as well as an urban weed on pavements, walls, waste ground and in car parks. Occasionally found as a weed of cultivation and as an introduction from wool shoddy, grain and grass-seed mixtures. Mainly lowland, but reaching 450 m at Forest Quarry, Nant-y-Mynydd (Glamorganshire).

Trends Even allowing for the possibility that this species was under-recorded in the past, it is clear that *V. myuros* has become more frequent across much of its range since the 1960s, especially in central, western and northern Britain and in Ireland. It is likely that the plant had colonized many areas via the rail network.

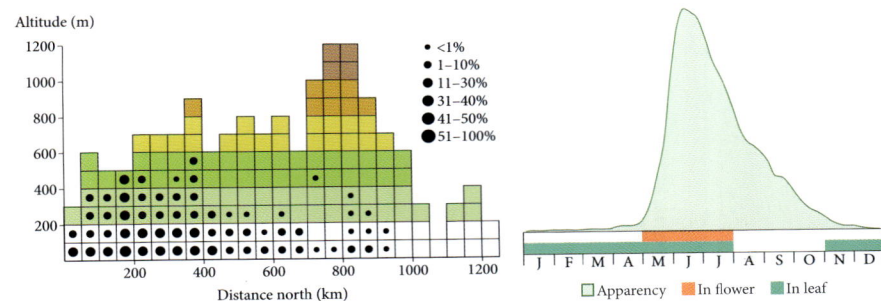

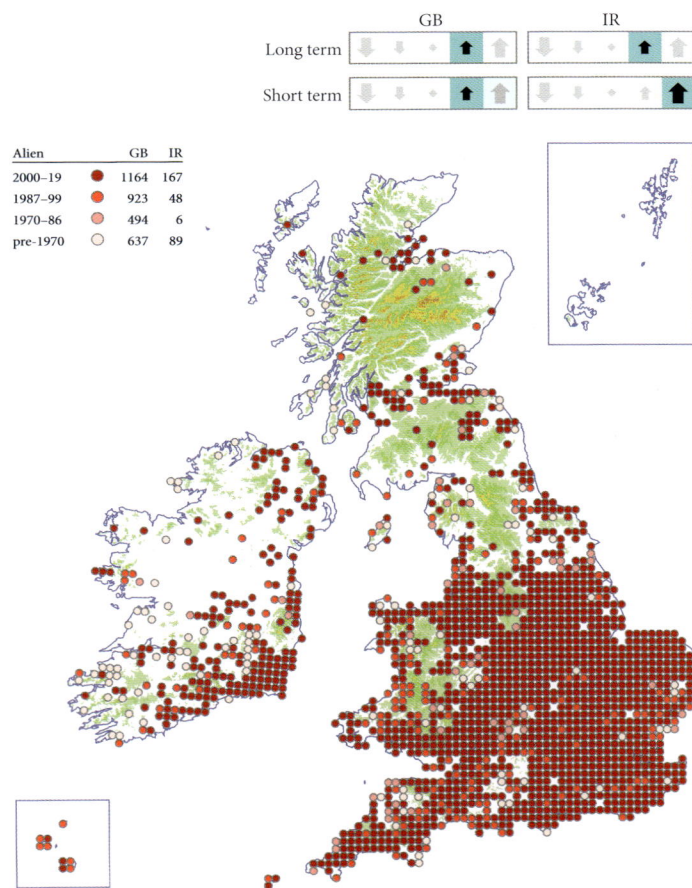

Biogeography As an archaeophyte, *V. myuros* has a Eurosiberian Southern-temperate distribution; it is widely naturalized outside this range.

Alien		GB	IR
2000–19	●	1164	167
1987–99	●	923	48
1970–86	●	494	6
pre-1970	○	637	89

Key refs Cope & Gray (2009).

S.J. Leach & D.A. Pearman

N *Vulpia ciliata* Bearded Fescue
Dumort.

An annual grass of disturbed sandy ground. The native subsp. *ambigua* is found on tracks and paths through coastal dunes, and inland on sandy heaths, along roadsides and in patches of open grassland. The non-native subsp. *ciliata* is a very rare casual, formerly associated with grain and with wool shoddy. Lowland.

Trends The 10 km square distribution of *V. ciliata* is probably stable overall, with a number of gains and losses since the 1960s. It is probably under-recorded rather than absent in some areas where there have been no records made since 2000. It might be being dispersed by aggregate lorries, as are other coastal species such as *Erodium maritimum*.

Biogeography Mediterranean-Atlantic element; subsp. *ambigua* is restricted to Britain, Belgium and northern France.

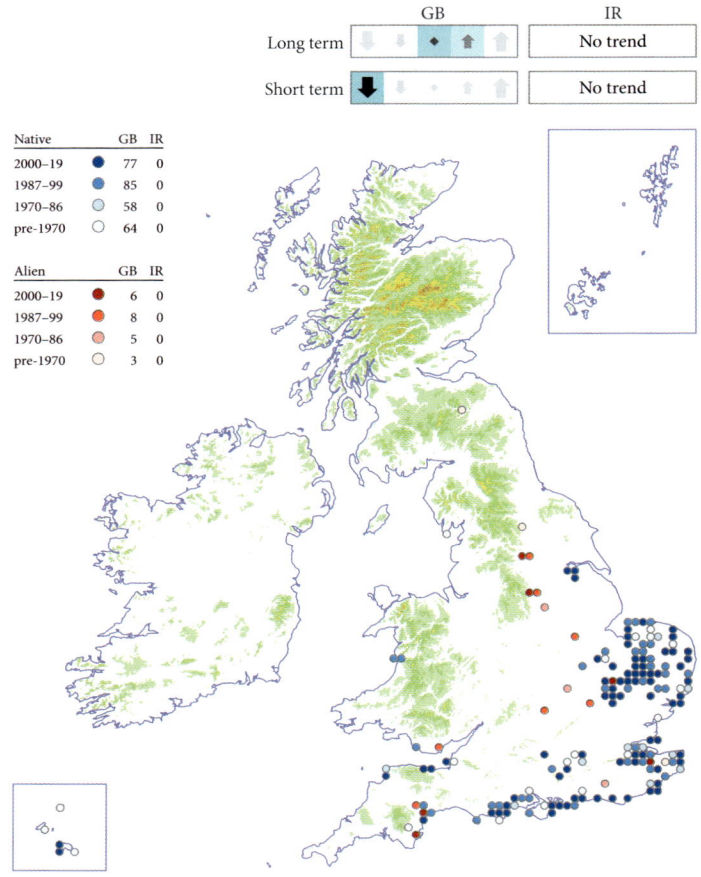

Native	GB	IR
2000–19	77	0
1987–99	85	0
1970–86	58	0
pre-1970	64	0

Alien	GB	IR
2000–19	6	0
1987–99	8	0
1970–86	5	0
pre-1970	3	0

	GB	IR
Long term		No trend
Short term		No trend

Key refs Carey *et al.* (1995), Cope & Gray (2009), Stewart *et al.* (1994), Watkinson *et al.* (1998).

S.J. LEACH & D.A. PEARMAN

Ne *Vulpia unilateralis* Mat-grass Fescue
(L.) Stace

An annual grass of bare stony ground, dry banks and grassy tracks on chalk and limestone; also on railway ballast, walls and refuse tips. Lowland.

Biogeography A Submediterranean-Subatlantic species; also recorded in central Asia.

Trends This inconspicuous species was first recorded in our area in 1903 (Carlby, South Lincolnshire). It was discovered in a few new sites in the latter half of the 20th century, and more locations have been found in the last 20 years, though whether this means the species is increasing, or had been previously overlooked, is uncertain. There is little consensus on its status in Britain. It was mapped as a neophyte in the 2002 *Atlas*, whilst others (*e.g.* Stace, 2019) argue that it is probably native. Given its habitats and behaviour it is probably best treated as a rare casual that is persistent in a few sites, and is mapped as an alien here.

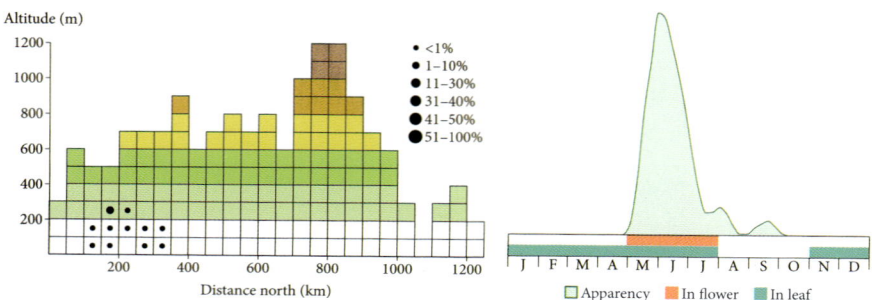

	GB	IR
Long term		No trend
Short term	No trend	No trend

Alien	GB	IR
2000–19	16	0
1987–99	17	0
1970–86	20	0
pre-1970	27	0

Key refs Cope & Gray (2009), Stace (1961), Stewart *et al.* (1994).

S.J. LEACH & D.A. PEARMAN

Ⓝ *Dactylis glomerata* Cock's-foot
L.

A tufted perennial grass of a wide variety of habitats including woodlands, meadows and pastures, chalk and limestone downland, upland hill-slopes, maritime grasslands, fixed sand dunes, arable field margins, roadsides and waste ground on a wide range of fertile, neutral and basic soils. 0–685 (Breadalbanes, Mid Perthshire) and exceptionally at 845 m on Great Dun Fell (Westmorland).

Trends *D. glomerata* is near-ubiquitous at the 10 km square level and there has been no appreciable change in its distribution since the 1960s. It is well adapted to human-modified habitats and quickly dominates undergrazed pastures, yet can be brought under control by grazing or mowing. It has long been a common constituent of grass-seed mixtures for agricultural leys, with much seed coming from Denmark, and more recently in seed

sown to create 'tussocky' grassland to benefit wildlife on agricultural land. It is often a relic of cultivation in the extreme north and west of Britain.

Biogeography Eurosiberian Southern-temperate element, but widely naturalized so that distribution is now Circumpolar Southern-temperate.

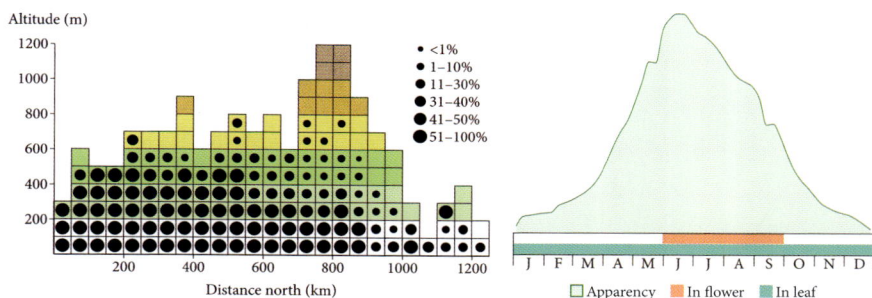

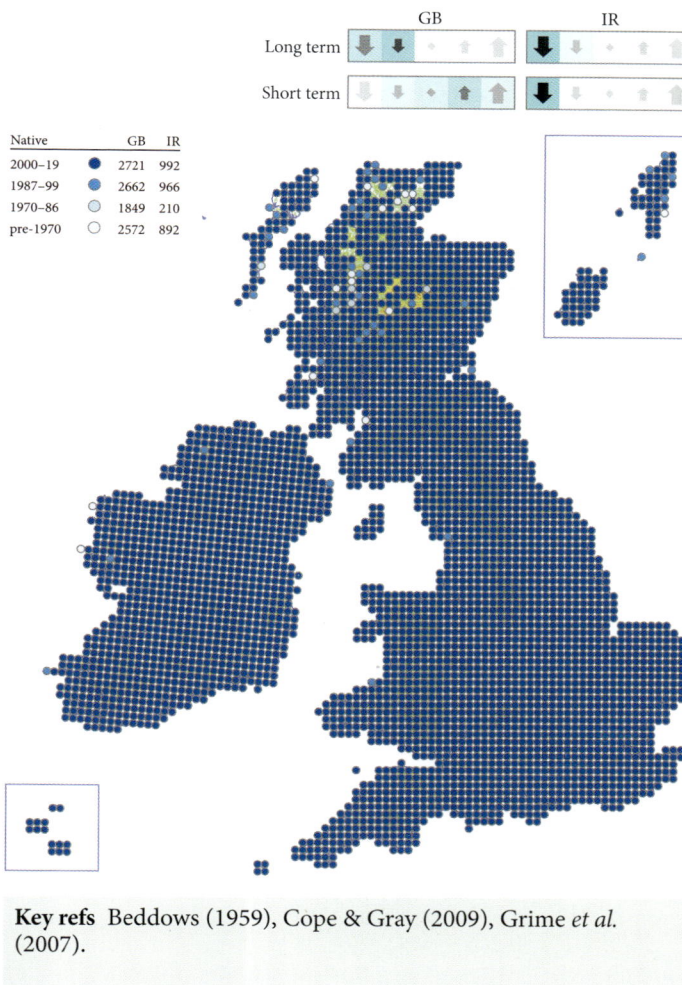

Native		GB	IR
2000–19	●	2721	992
1987–99	●	2662	966
1970–86	○	1849	210
pre-1970	○	2572	892

Key refs Beddows (1959), Cope & Gray (2009), Grime *et al.* (2007).

F.H. Perring & D.A. Pearman

Ⓝ *Cynosurus cristatus* Crested Dog's-tail
L.

A short-lived perennial grass of a wide variety of grasslands, particularly short and heavily grazed pastures that have had some agricultural improvement in the past. It grows in a range of neutral to base-rich, fairly well-drained or damp soils, avoiding only the extremes of base-status, waterlogging, drought and disturbance. It does not form a persistent seed bank. Generally below 500 m, but reaching 780 m near Great Dun Fell (Westmorland), as well as at 845 m on the access track to the summit of that hill.

Trends *C. cristatus* is near-ubiquitous at the 10 km square resolution. There has been no overall change in its known distribution since the 1960s except for slight increases in northern Scotland and Ireland due to more systematic recording. It was a major constituent of agricultural seed mixtures until

the 1940s, and is still used in amenity sowings, in seed mixtures for meadow restoration projects, and possibly in upland leys on poor soils. The scale of these introductions has been so great that its natural (native) distribution is now completely obscured and so all records are mapped as 'presence only'.

Biogeography European Temperate element; widely naturalized outside its native range.

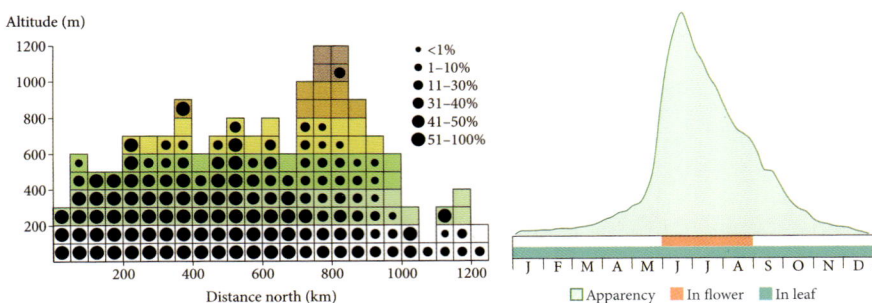

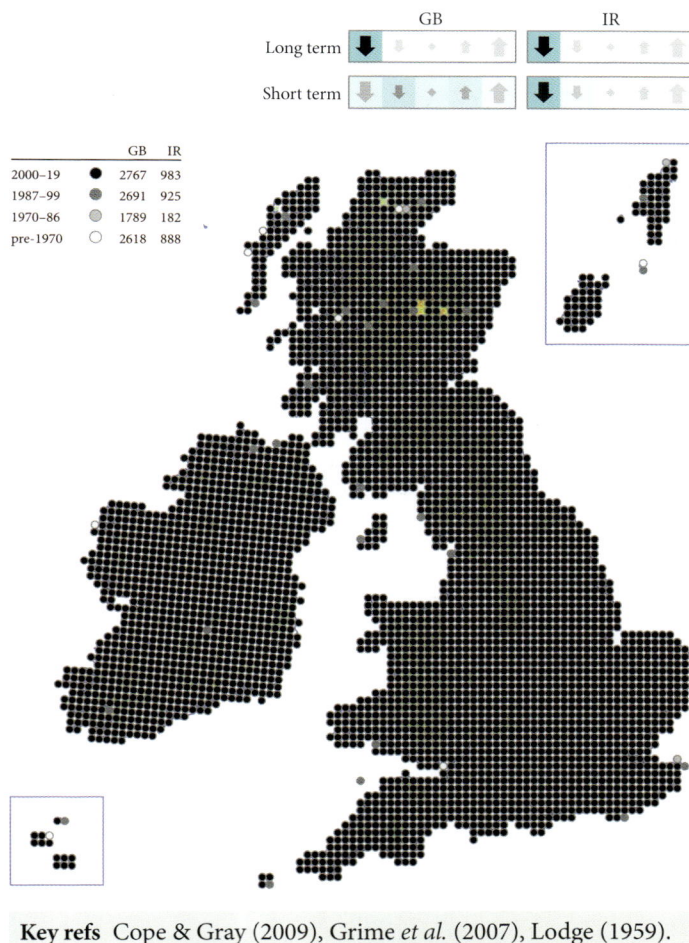

		GB	IR
2000–19	●	2767	983
1987–99	●	2691	925
1970–86	○	1789	182
pre-1970	○	2618	888

Key refs Cope & Gray (2009), Grime *et al.* (2007), Lodge (1959).

D.A. Pearman & K.J. Walker

Ne *Cynosurus echinatus* Rough Dog's-tail

L.

An annual grass naturalized on open sandy soils in the Channel Islands and the Isles of Scilly where it can sometimes be an abundant weed in bulb fields, and in a few localities in similar habitats in southern England. Elsewhere, it is found as a grain and wool shoddy casual on waste ground, refuse tips and occasionally on arable land. Lowland.

Trends *C. echinatus* was first recorded in the wild in 1778 (Sandwich, East Kent), but it has declined as a casual over the last 50 years, mirroring decline in the use of wool shoddy. It is sometimes grown as an ornamental grass for drying.

Biogeography Native of southern Europe, the Mediterranean region and south-west Asia; widely naturalized farther north in Europe and in other continents.

	GB	IR
Long term	No trend	No trend
Short term	↓	No trend

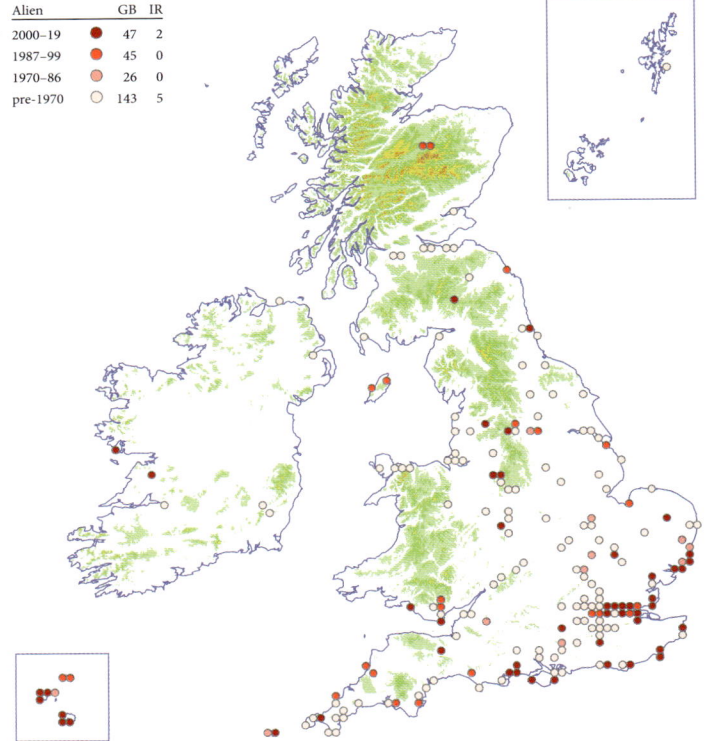

Alien		GB	IR
2000–19	●	47	2
1987–99	●	45	0
1970–86	●	26	0
pre-1970	○	143	5

●	<1%
●	1–10%
●	11–30%
●	31–40%
●	41–50%
●	51–100%

Key refs Cope & Gray (2009).

D.A. Pearman

N *Catapodium rigidum* Fern-grass

(L.) C.E.Hubb.

A winter-annual grass of dry, barish places on sandy banks, stabilized shingle, in chalk grassland and around rock outcrops, usually preferring calcareous substrates; also in artificial habitats such as quarries, walls, pavements and railway ballast. 0–490 m (Cwar yr Hendre, Breconshire).

Trends There has been little change in the distribution of *C. rigidum* since the 1960s, though some inland sites have been lost. The more strictly coastal subsp. *majus*, which was mapped by Perring & Sell (1968), is mainly confined to south-western Britain, Ireland and the Channel Islands. Interestingly, this subspecies appears to be spreading as a pavement weed in some urban areas (*e.g.* Taunton, Cambridge, London, Dublin, Leeds) but is very unevenly recorded as so is not mapped separately here.

Biogeography Submediterranean-Subatlantic element.

	GB	IR
Long term	◆	◆
Short term	◆	↑

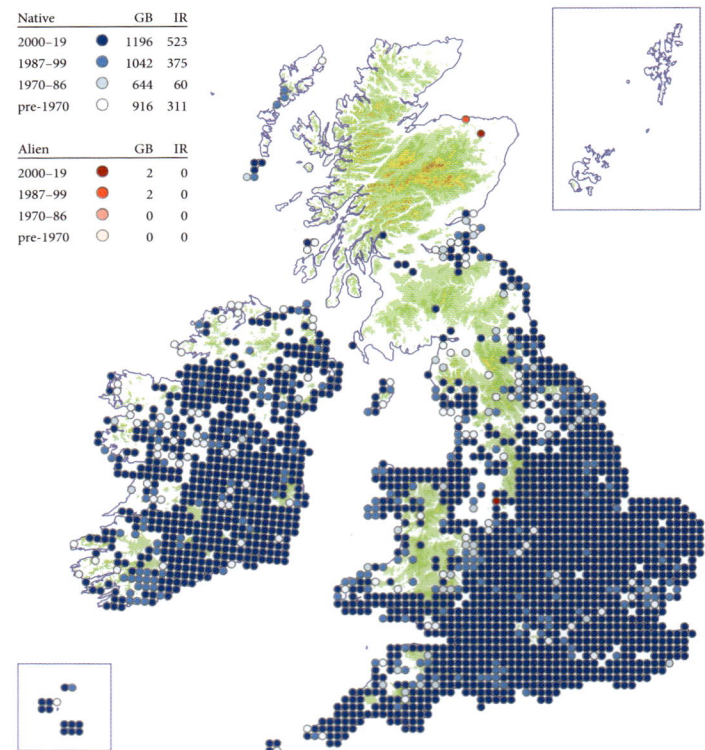

Native		GB	IR
2000–19	●	1196	523
1987–99	●	1042	375
1970–86	●	644	60
pre-1970	○	916	311

Alien		GB	IR
2000–19	●	2	0
1987–99	●	2	0
1970–86	●	0	0
pre-1970	○	0	0

●	<1%
●	1–10%
●	11–30%
●	31–40%
●	41–50%
●	51–100%

Key refs Clark (1974), Cope & Gray (2009), Grime *et al.* (2007).

S.J. Leach & D.A. Pearman

(N) *Catapodium marinum* Sea Fern-grass
(L.) C.E.Hubb.

An annual grass of dry bare places by the sea including rock crevices, grassy banks, cliff-tops, sand dunes and stabilized shingle; also in artificial habitats such as walls and pavements, and increasingly inland by salt-treated roads. Lowland, but up to 385 m on a roadside near Hafod Dinbych (Denbighshire).

Trends There has been little change in the coastal distribution of *C. marinum* since the 1960s, other than small extensions of its range as a result of more systematic recording in some areas. However, it has recently been increasingly recorded inland on salt-treated roadsides; it was first noticed in that habitat in the mid-1980s, though only since the mid-1990s has it begun to spread appreciably, especially in eastern England.

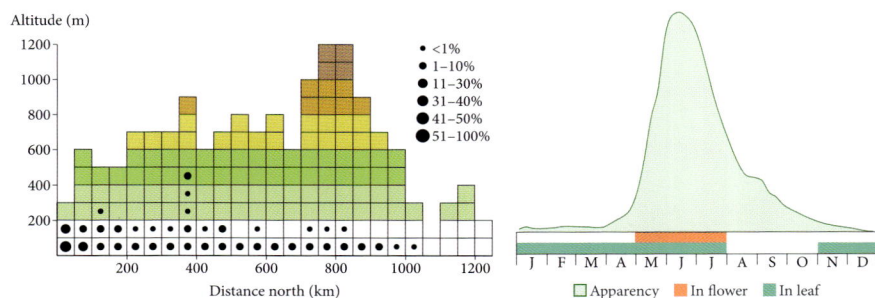

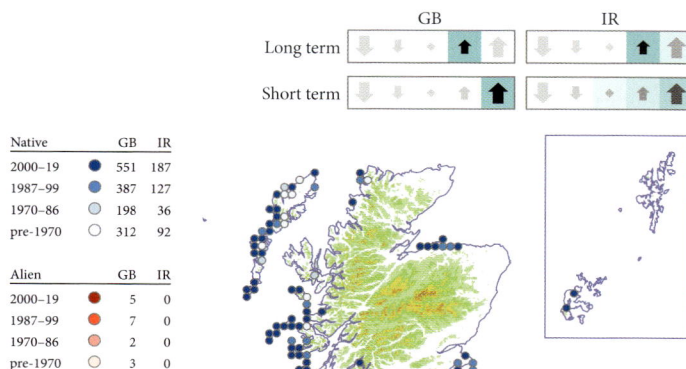

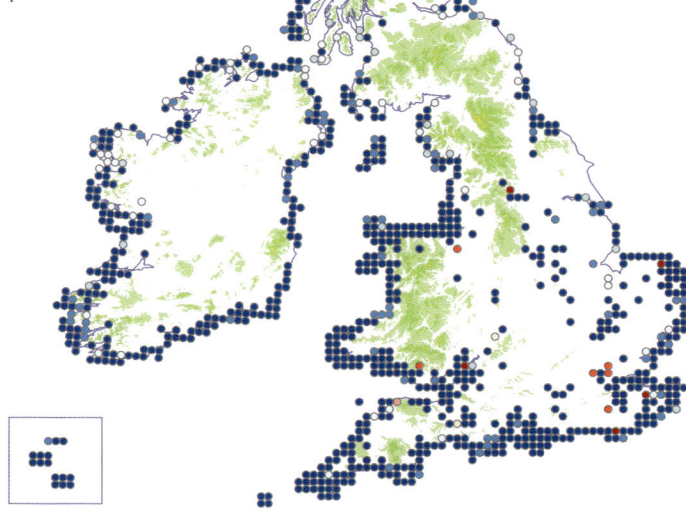

Biogeography Mediterranean-Atlantic element.

Native		GB	IR
2000–19	●	551	187
1987–99	●	387	127
1970–86	●	198	36
pre-1970	○	312	92

Alien		GB	IR
2000–19	●	5	0
1987–99	●	7	0
1970–86	●	2	0
pre-1970	○	3	0

Key refs Cope & Gray (2009).

S.J. Leach & D.A. Pearman

(N) *Parapholis strigosa* Hard-grass
(Dumort.) C.E.Hubb.

An annual grass of damp barish places by the sea; especially characteristic of the upper parts of grazed *Festuca rubra–Puccinellia maritima* saltmarshes, but also on mud banks, shingle ridges, saltmarsh-sand dune transitions and sea-walls. In western Britain and Ireland it occurs along rocky coasts in beach-head saltmarshes. Rarely, it grows inland by salt-treated roads. Lowland.

Trends The known distribution of *P. strigosa* appears to be relatively stable overall. Although it has not been refound at some coatal hectads this century, new locations have been recorded in East Anglia on the margins of salted road verges. It would also appear to be better recorded in Ireland since the 2002 *Atlas*. The species is inconspicuous and is probably still somewhat under-recorded.

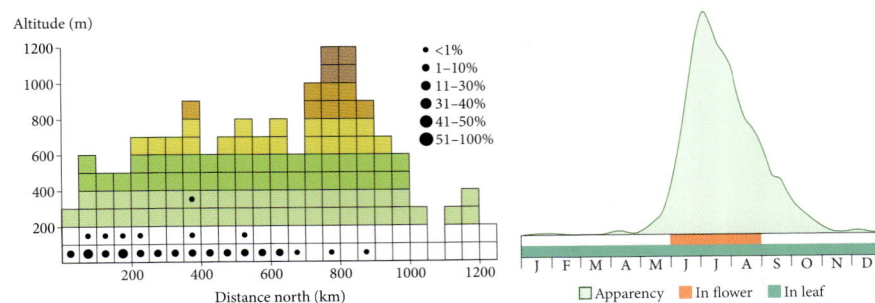

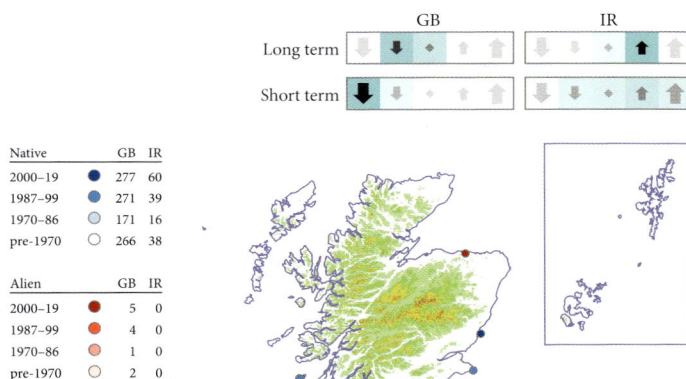

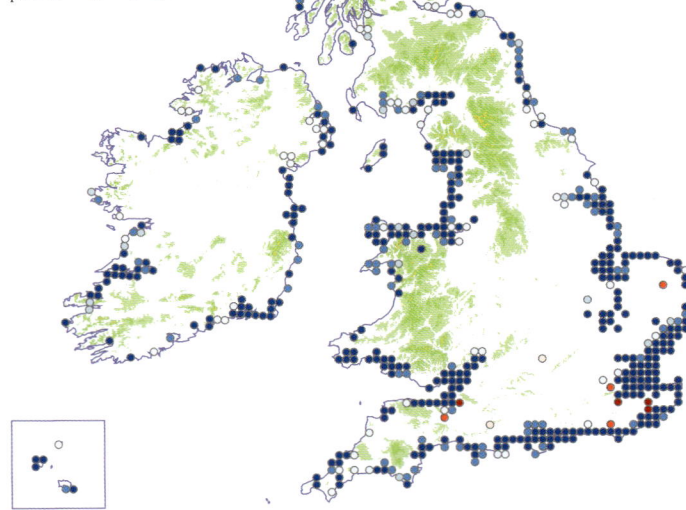

Biogeography Suboceanic Southern-temperate element.

Native		GB	IR
2000–19	●	277	60
1987–99	●	271	39
1970–86	●	171	16
pre-1970	○	266	38

Alien		GB	IR
2000–19	●	5	0
1987–99	●	4	0
1970–86	●	1	0
pre-1970	○	2	0

Key refs Cope & Gray (2009).

S.J. Leach & D.A. Pearman

Parapholis incurva Curved Hard-grass

(L.) C.E.Hubb.

An annual of bare places by the sea, including gravelly mud banks, shingle ridges, rock ledges and cliff-tops, and the uppermost parts of saltmarshes; also in artificial habitats such as sea-walls and wooden mooring stays. There are rare occurrences around docks and inland as a wool and ballast alien and more recently along salt-treated road verges. Lowland.

Trends *P. incurva* is an extremely inconspicuous grass which is much better recorded now than in the past, though it is still confused with *P. strigosa*, from which it can only really be reliably separated by its tiny anthers. In Ireland it is confined to a single site near to Dublin (Howth Head) where it was discovered in 1979 (Akeroyd, 1984). It has been lost from some sites due to coastal reclamation and the upgrading of sea defences.

Biogeography Mediterranean-Atlantic element.

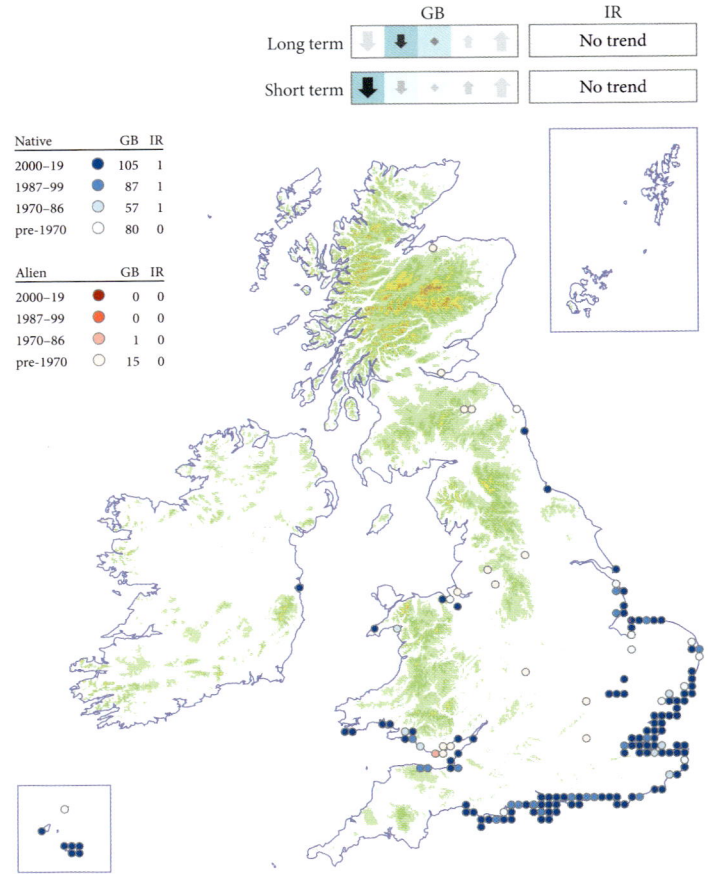

Native	GB	IR
2000–19	105	1
1987–99	87	1
1970–86	57	1
pre-1970	80	0

Alien	GB	IR
2000–19	0	0
1987–99	0	0
1970–86	1	0
pre-1970	15	0

Key refs Akeroyd (1984), Cope & Gray (2009), Stewart *et al.* (1994).

S.J. LEACH & D.A. PEARMAN

Catabrosa aquatica Whorl-grass

(L.) P.Beauv.

A stoloniferous perennial grass of muddy pond margins, cattle-poached ditches, canals and sluggish streams; also, as var. *uniflora*, on wet open sand by the sea, including where streams run out onto beaches, where it is often the only plant species present. Almost entirely lowland, but recorded in flushes at 735 m on Mickle Fell (North-west Yorkshire) and Knock Fell (Westmorland).

Trends *C. aquatica* has declined appreciably since the 1960s due to the drainage and infilling of ponds and marshes and the canalization of lowland watercourses. It is highly palatable to livestock, but this in itself would not have contributed to the observed scale of decline, unless stock numbers were heavier. However, var. *uniflora* remains widespread in western and north-western Scotland, perhaps also in western Ireland, and is now much better recorded than in 20th century.

Biogeography European Boreo-temperate element; also in central Asia and North America.

Native	GB	IR
2000–19	398	166
1987–99	494	177
1970–86	358	39
pre-1970	727	175

Alien	GB	IR
2000–19	0	0
1987–99	0	1
1970–86	0	0
pre-1970	0	1

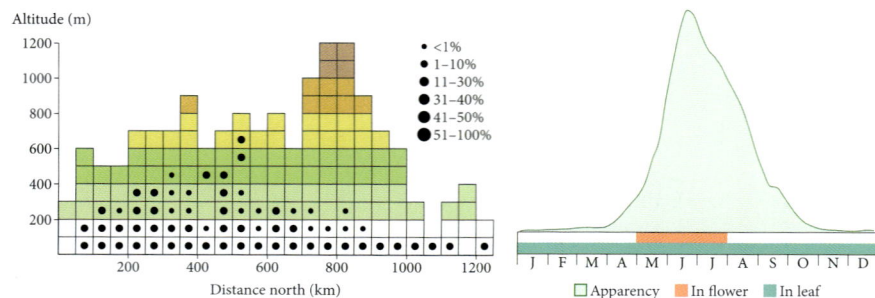

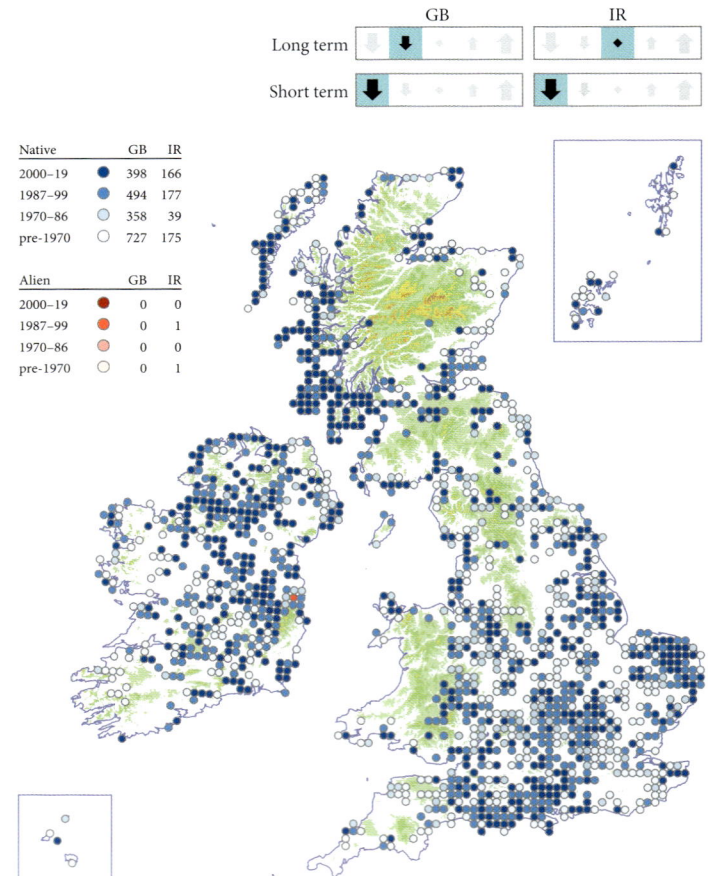

Key refs Cope & Gray (2009), Preston & Croft (1997).

S.J. LEACH & D.A. PEARMAN

N *Puccinellia maritima* Common Saltmarsh-grass
(Huds.) Parl.

A stoloniferous perennial grass of saltmarshes, often dominant over large areas in the lower and middle marsh, and in saline pans and depressions in the upper marsh; also locally on bare saline soils above the tidal limit, on sea-walls and beside grazing marsh ditches. It occurs in both grazed and ungrazed marshes. Rarely, it occurs in saline areas inland, and as a colonist by salt-treated roads. Lowland.

Trends The coastal distribution of *P. maritima* has remained largely unchanged since the 1960s, although it is now better recorded in north-western Scotland and Ireland. Since the early 1970s it has been recorded occasionally alongside salt-treated roads in England.

Biogeography Oceanic Boreo-temperate element; also in North America.

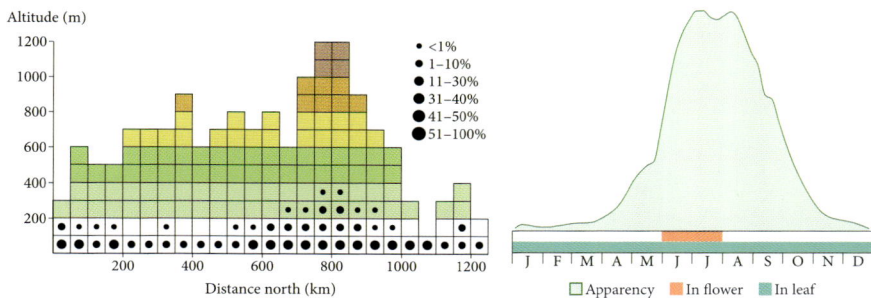

Native		GB	IR
2000–19	●	726	207
1987–99	●	605	170
1970–86	◐	389	86
pre-1970	○	613	127

Alien		GB	IR
2000–19	●	1	0
1987–99	●	0	0
1970–86	◑	0	0
pre-1970	○	0	0

Key refs Cope & Gray (2009), Gray & Scott (1977), Matthews & Davison (1976).

S.J. Leach

N *Puccinellia distans* Reflexed Saltmarsh-grass
(Jacq.) Parl.

A perennial grass of barish muddy saline ground near to the sea, along the upper edges of saltmarshes, on sea-walls and amongst coastal rocks; also in saline areas inland in Britain, and as a colonist by salt-treated roads. It favours compacted, poorly drained, heavy soils. Lowland, but with a number of roadside records in upland areas, up to an altitude of 625 m at Bealach nan Ba (West Ross).

Trends As in the 2002 *Atlas*, this map includes records of subsp. *distans* and subsp. *borealis*; the latter is also mapped separately. The coastal distribution of *P. distans* has changed very little in our area since the 1960s. In Britain it has spread rapidly inland along salted roadsides since 1970, colonizing much of western Britain and eastern Scotland since 2000; it continues to spread to new regions via both major and minor roads. It has not spread in the same way in Ireland due to the use of grit rather than salt to de-ice roads.

Biogeography Eurosiberian Boreo-temperate element; widely naturalized outside its native range.

Native		GB	IR
2000–19	●	1338	43
1987–99	●	870	22
1970–86	◐	418	19
pre-1970	○	366	19

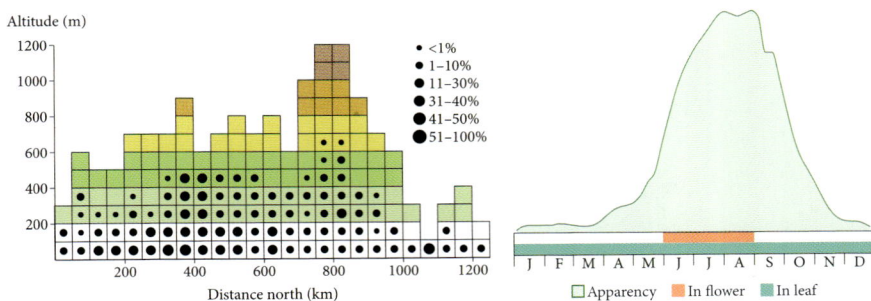

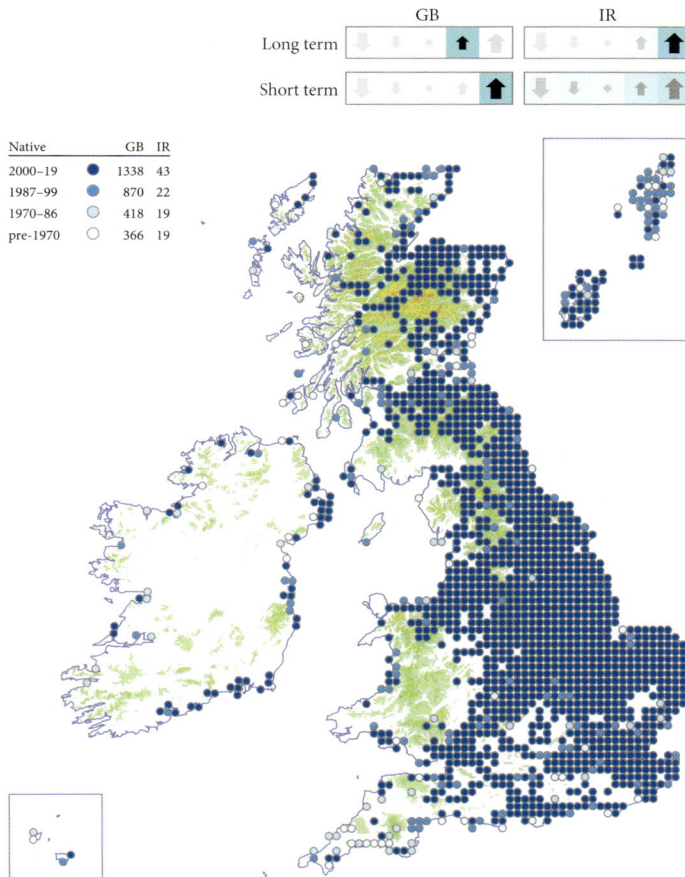

Key refs Coombe (1994), Cope & Gray (2009), Scott (1985), Scott & Davison (1982).

S.J. Leach

Puccinellia distans subsp. *borealis* Northern Saltmarsh-grass

(Holmb.) W.E.Hughes

A tufted perennial grass of rocky shores, growing on low cliffs and amongst rocks and boulders on pebble beaches, on the stonework of harbour walls and slipways, and only rarely in saltmarshes. Lowland.

Trends This taxon, at one time regarded as a species in its own right (*P. capillaris*), has only relatively recently had its taxonomy and distribution clearly defined (Trist & Butler, 1995). Because there are few historical records, changes in its distribution cannot be assessed with any confidence. It was first recorded in Ireland in 2001. It has also been found, but rarely, on salt-treated roads.

Biogeography European Boreo-arctic Montane element; restricted to the coasts of northern Europe.

	GB	IR
Long term	No trend	No trend
Short term	No trend	No trend

Native	GB	IR
2000–19	66	2
1987–99	86	0
1970–86	38	0
pre-1970	34	0

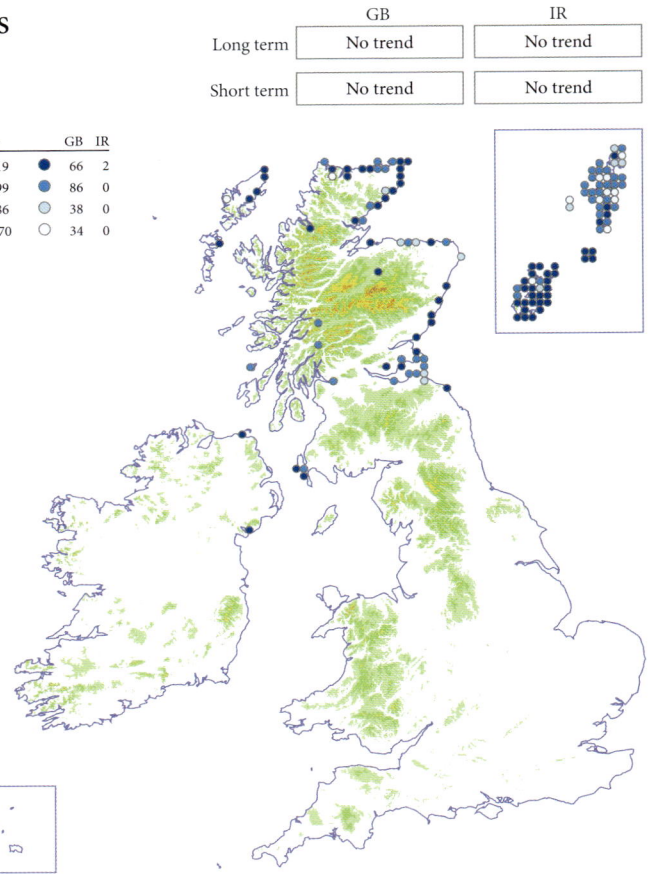

Key refs Cope & Gray (2009), Trist & Butler (1995).

S.J. Leach & D.A. Pearman

Altitude (m) / Distance north (km)

<1%
1–10%
11–30%
31–40%
41–50%
51–100%

Apparency In flower In leaf

Puccinellia fasciculata Borrer's Saltmarsh-grass

(Torr.) E.P.Bicknell

A tufted short-lived perennial grass of bare places by the sea, in grazing marshes around cattle-poached pools and depressions, on earthen sea-walls, vehicle tracks and the mud dredged from ditches. It also occurs rarely beside salt-treated roads inland. Lowland.

Trends This species is slowly decreasing, even in its core areas, as a result of the infilling of pools and ditches, the upgrading of sea-walls and the conversion of coastal grazing marshes to arable. Since 2000 only three populations, with a total of six plants, have been recorded west of Bournemouth (South Hampshire). It now includes *P. pseudodistans* (as *P. fasciculata* var. *pseudodistans*), which was mapped separately in the 1962 *Atlas*.

Biogeography Suboceanic Southern-temperate element; also in North America.

	GB				IR			
Long term	↓					↓		↑
Short term	↓				↓			↑

Native	GB	IR
2000–19	53	9
1987–99	64	7
1970–86	50	2
pre-1970	85	11

Alien	GB	IR
2000–19	1	0
1987–99	1	0
1970–86	5	0
pre-1970	2	0

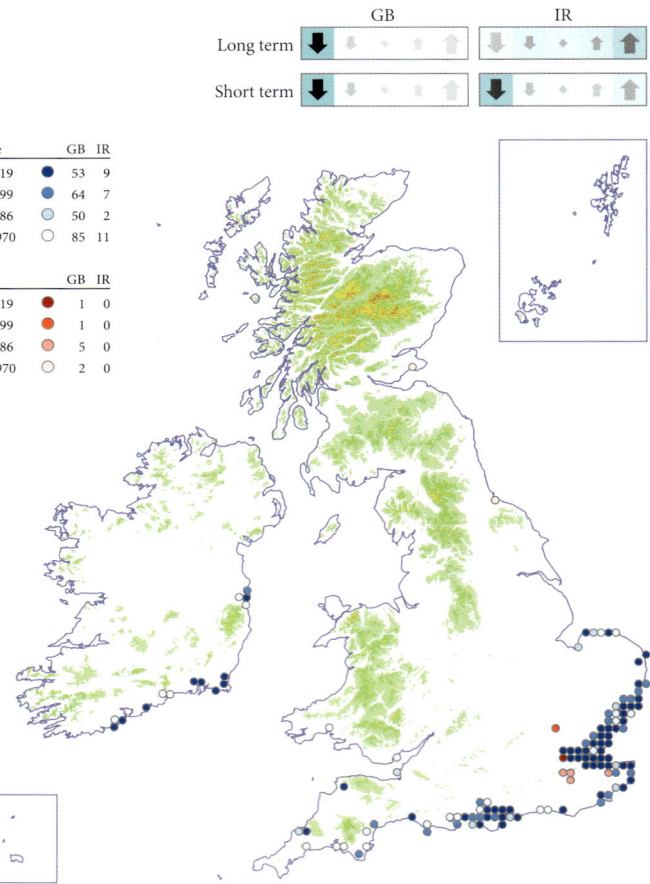

Key refs Cope & Gray (2009), Kitchener (1983), Stewart *et al.* (1994).

S.J. Leach & D.A. Pearman

Altitude (m) / Distance north (km)

<1%
1–10%
11–30%
31–40%
41–50%
51–100%

Apparency In flower In leaf

Ⓝ *Puccinellia rupestris* Stiff Saltmarsh-grass
(With.) Fernald & Weath.

An annual or biennial grass of bare saline soils above the tidal limit, behind sea-walls, on tracks and in grazing marshes around cattle-trodden pools and depressions, and sometimes on firm muddy shingle and in rock crevices. *P. rupestris* occurs rarely inland by saline springs and salt-treated roads. Lowland.

Native in Britain and the Channel Islands and a neophyte in Ireland.

Trends *P. rupestris* was declining in northern England before 1930, and is now practically extinct north of The Wash. It has also declined in southern England, probably due to the infilling of pools and ditches, upgrading of sea-walls and the conversion of coastal grazing marshes to arable. Away from its main centres it often persists in only very small numbers, but seems to have a long-lived seed bank. It was recorded

before 1930 in south-eastern Scotland and probably elsewhere as a ballast alien.

Biogeography Oceanic Southern-temperate element.

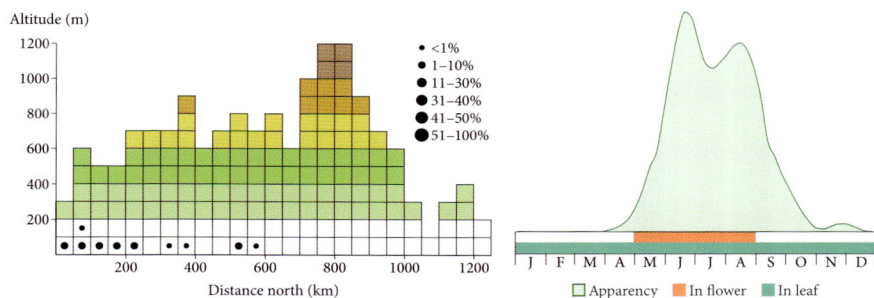

Native	GB	IR
2000–19	70	0
1987–99	76	0
1970–86	65	0
pre-1970	132	0

Alien	GB	IR
2000–19	0	0
1987–99	0	0
1970–86	0	0
pre-1970	4	1

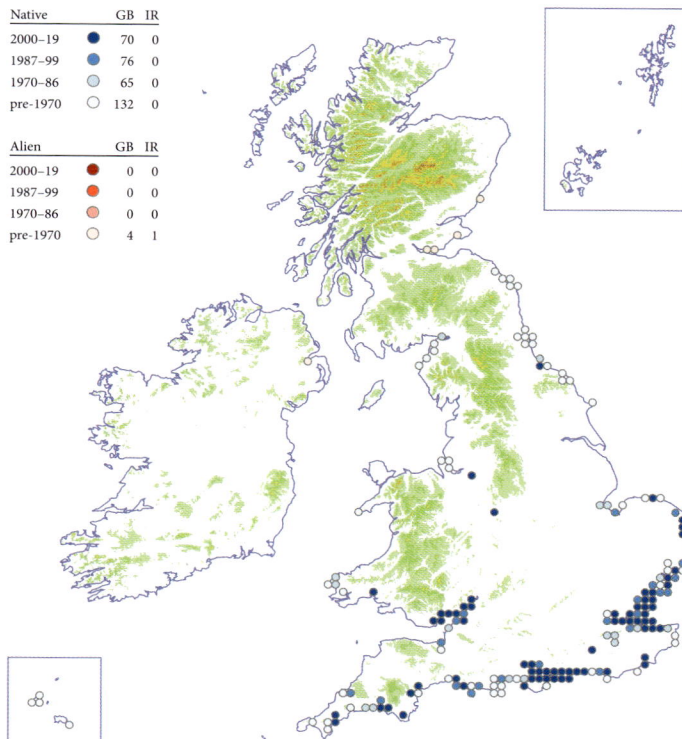

Key refs Cope & Gray (2009), Kitchener (1983), Stewart *et al.* (1994).

S.J. LEACH & D.A. PEARMAN

Ⓝ *Sesleria caerulea* Blue Moor-grass
(L.) Ard.

A tufted, rhizomatous perennial grass of well-drained, mainly open habitats on limestone, including grassland and heath, screes and cliffs, and the grikes and clint-hollows of limestone pavement. It extends locally into open woodland in Ireland and northern England, and is found on sandy loams over micaceous schists in Perthshire. 0–1,005 m (Ben Lawers, Mid Perthshire).

Trends Because *S. caerulea* is not very palatable to sheep, it becomes dominant in heavily grazed pastures, forming a species-poor turf. With the widespread replacement of sheep with beef cattle it is increasing in areas of Carboniferous limestone in northern England and the Burren, and is becoming a threat to some rare plants associated with short, open swards (*e.g. Carex ericetorum*). It was discovered in the Derbyshire Dales in 1989, and has recently been

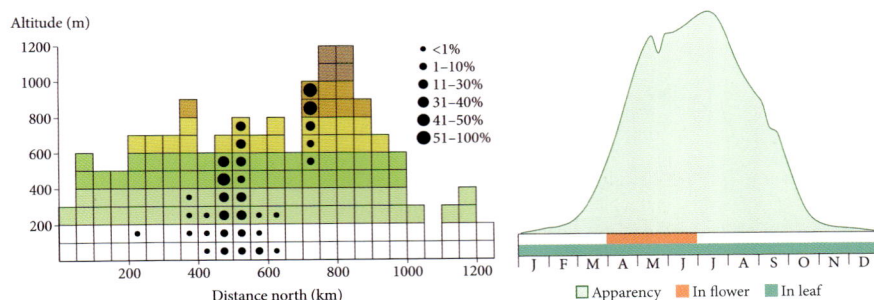

recorded in a quarry in Herefordshire, presumably as an alien arrival.

Biogeography European Boreo-temperate element.

Native	GB	IR
2000–19	58	85
1987–99	64	71
1970–86	64	27
pre-1970	67	57

Alien	GB	IR
2000–19	3	0
1987–99	2	0
1970–86	1	0
pre-1970	1	0

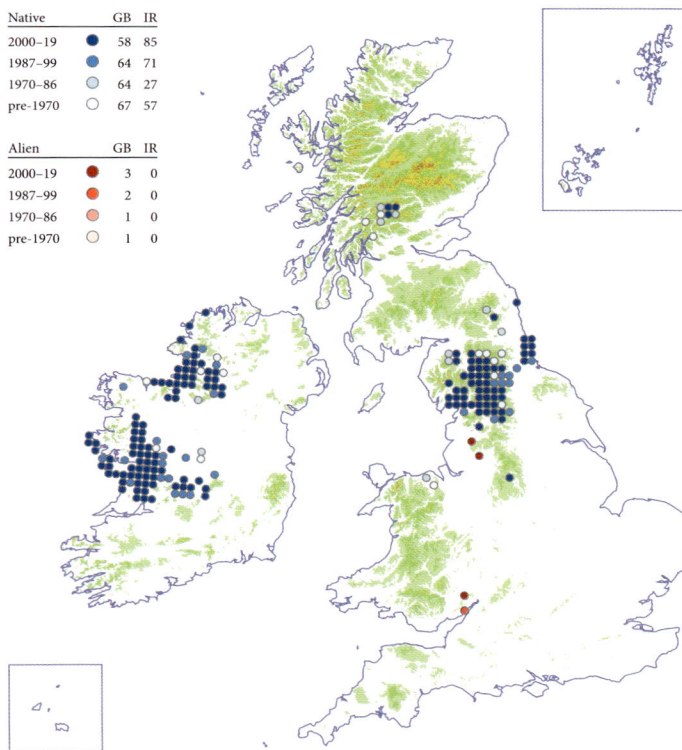

Key refs Cope & Gray (2009), Dixon (1982), Halliday (1997), Stewart *et al.* (1994).

F.H. PERRING & D.A. PEARMAN

Mibora minima Early Sand-grass

(L.) Desv.

A diminutive winter-annual grass of coastal sand dunes. In Wales it is found on open nutrient-poor substrates which are free-draining but damp in winter; in the Channel Islands, on sand dunes and barish gravelly cliff-slopes. It is recorded at other sand dune sites in England, Scotland, and now Ireland, as well as inland as a rare casual plant in nurseries and gardens. Lowland.

Trends *M. minima* has been known on Anglesey since 1762, and from the Channel Islands for 200 years, and has been assumed to be native in both areas. Since the 1960s it has also been found on sand dunes in Glamorganshire (1964), Dorset (1993), South Lancashire (1996), West Cork (2005), West Lancashire (2007), the Outer Hebrides (2015), and County Dublin (2019). The late date of discovery introduces a degree of doubt about their native status, but it is entirely plausible that it had simply been overlooked, as it is tiny and breaks up very early in the season; alternatively, it may have dispersed there 'naturally' on the feet of livestock or humans. Most coastal records are therefore mapped as native. The population on sand dunes in Lothian (Weaklaw Rocks), discovered in the early 19th century, is known to have been sown there (Smith *et al.*, 2002). The status of the population in Studland (Dorset) is more contentious; it occurred on sand dunes close to a track near to a car park and was mapped as alien in the 2002 *Atlas*, but a native occurrence seems equally likely given its distribution, habitats and pattern of colonization elsewhere.

Biogeography Suboceanic Southern-temperate element.

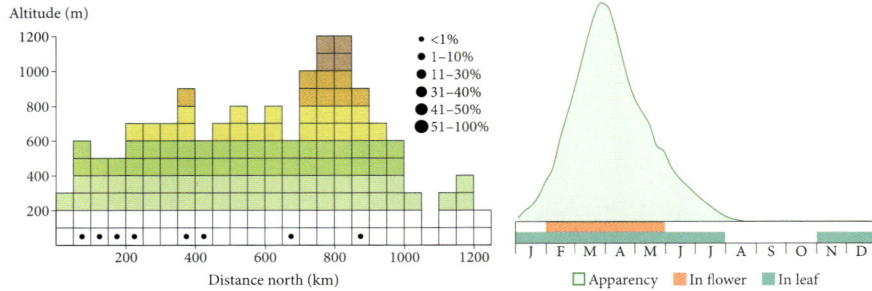

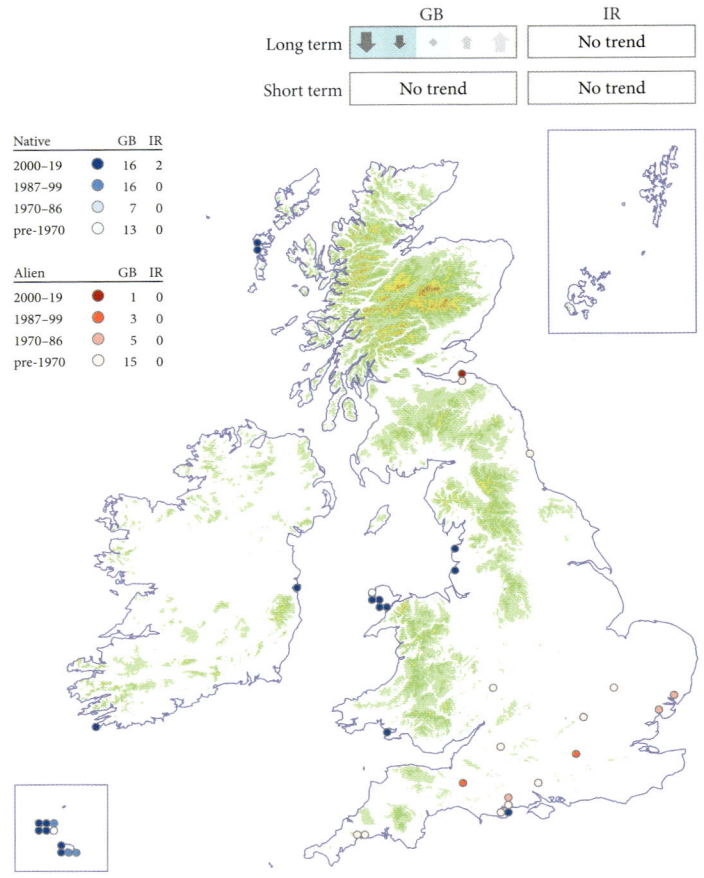

Native	GB	IR
2000–19	16	2
1987–99	16	0
1970–86	7	0
pre-1970	13	0

Alien	GB	IR
2000–19	1	0
1987–99	3	0
1970–86	5	0
pre-1970	15	0

Key refs Cope & Gray (2009), O'Mahony (2006), Smith *et al.* (2002), Wigginton (1999).

S.J. Leach, D.A. Pearman & K.J. Walker

Arrhenatherum elatius False Oat-grass

(L.) P.Beauv. ex J.Presl & C.Presl

A tufted perennial grass found on a wide range of neutral to base-rich soils. It is frequent in grasslands that are not or only lightly managed, especially on road verges, hedgebanks, field margins, riverbanks, woodland rides, waste ground and in meadows, pastures and grasslands reverting back from arable cultivation. It is also an important stabilizer of limestone scree, and a colonizer of bare, muddy, calcareous cliffs and maritime shingle. Var. *bulbosum* is found as an arable weed on light soils and is widely distributed on roadside banks; indeed it is the dominant form in western parts of Britain and Ireland. 0–705 m (near Broad Cairn, Angus).

Trends *A. elatius* is almost ubiquitous at the 10 km square level, except for the most mountainous regions of Scotland, and its overall distribution has changed very little since the 1960s. Var. *bulbosum* is found in arable fields, particularly in southern and central England, and also in semi-natural habitats, mainly in the west of our area. There are anecdotal reports of it being encouraged by direct drilling practices, and it also appears to be spread by ground disturbance during the mechanical trimming of hedges.

Biogeography European Temperate element; widely naturalized outside its native range.

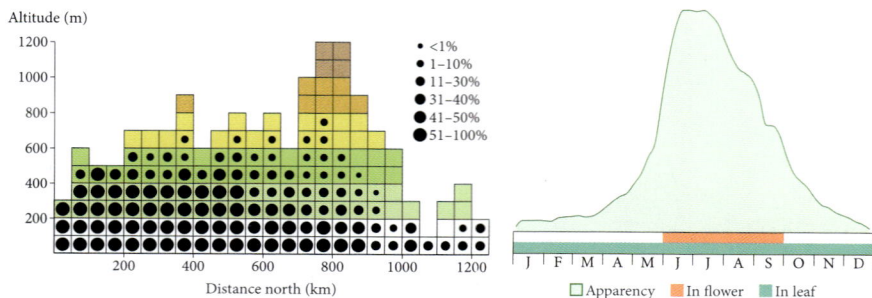

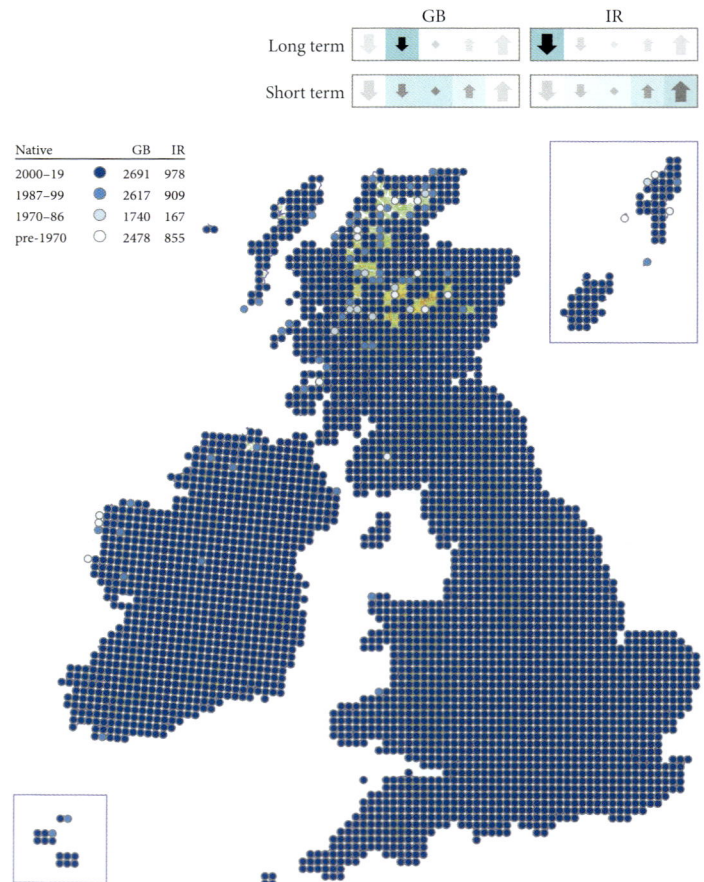

Native	GB	IR
2000–19	2691	978
1987–99	2617	909
1970–86	1740	167
pre-1970	2478	855

Key refs Cope & Gray (2009), Grime *et al.* (2007), Pfitzenmeyer (1962).

D.A. Pearman

(Ar) *Avena fatua* Wild-oat
L.

An annual grass, found most often as a weed of arable land, especially in wheat crops, seeding before the crop. It is also found in set-aside, along the disturbed margins of paths, tracks and roads, on dumped soil and waste ground, and as a weed of gardens and allotments where it usually arises from birdseed. Less often a serious weed. Generally lowland, but reaching 345 m by the A483 near Dolfor (Montgomeryshire).

Trends *A. fatua* has expanded northwards and westwards in Britain and in Ireland over the last 60 years. Within its former range it has dramatically increased in frequency since 1945, and has proved resistant to some herbicides, although specific controls are now available. However, weeding by hand ('rogueing') is still practiced in parts of the country. In some areas it is no longer a serious weed of crops and now is usually confined to crop margins (Leslie, 2019).

Biogeography Perhaps native to the eastern Mediterranean region and the Near East, but it has spread with cultivation and now has a virtually worldwide distribution outside the tropics.

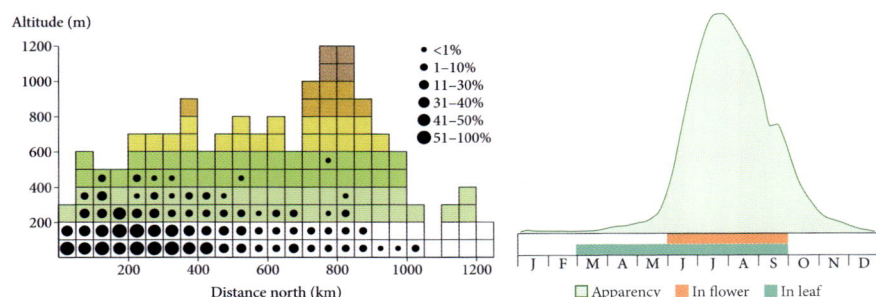

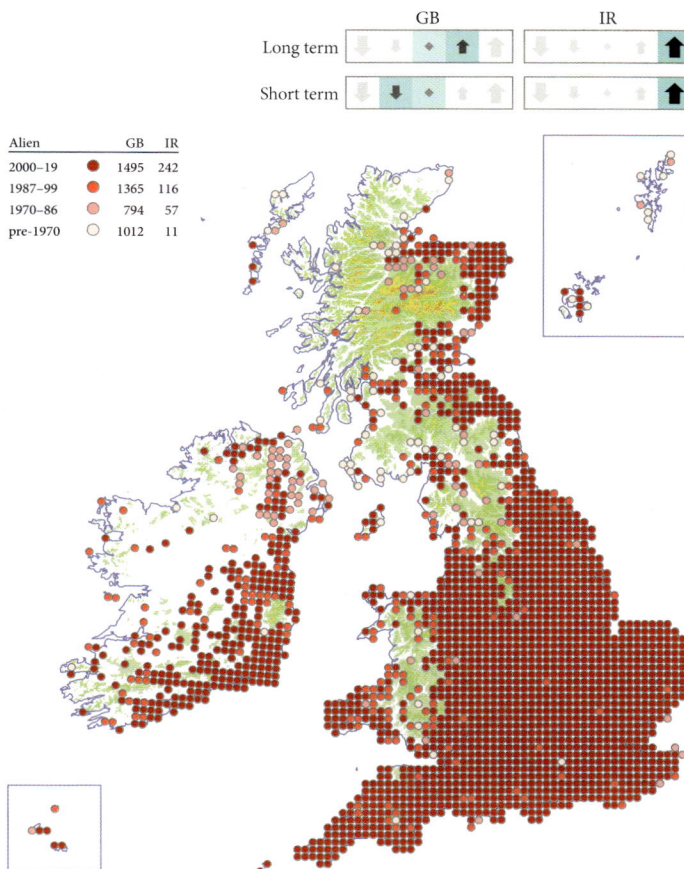

Alien	GB	IR
2000–19	1495	242
1987–99	1365	116
1970–86	794	57
pre-1970	1012	11

Key refs Cope & Gray (2009), Leslie (2019), Sharma & Vanden Born (1978).

D.A. Pearman & K.J. Walker

(Ne) *Avena sterilis* Winter Wild-oat
L.

An annual grass, usually found in or around the margins of arable fields, especially winter wheat on heavy clays. It also occurs on disturbed track and road verges, on waste ground, refuse tips, gardens and allotments and formerly as a wool shoddy alien. Lowland.

Trends *A. sterilis*, which was cultivated in Britain by 1640, was first recorded in the wild as a casual in 1903 (Leith, Midlothian) and then in 1910 as a crop weed (Port Meadow, Oxfordshire), and has apparently spread from Oxfordshire to neighbouring counties. It is now much less frequent than 40 years ago, but because it often grows with *A. fatua*, it may still be overlooked. Almost all of the records are for subsp. *ludoviciana*; subsp. *sterilis* is a rare casual, occasionally cultivated for ornamental use.

Biogeography Native of the Mediterranean region, south-western and central Asia; widely naturalized north of its native range in Europe.

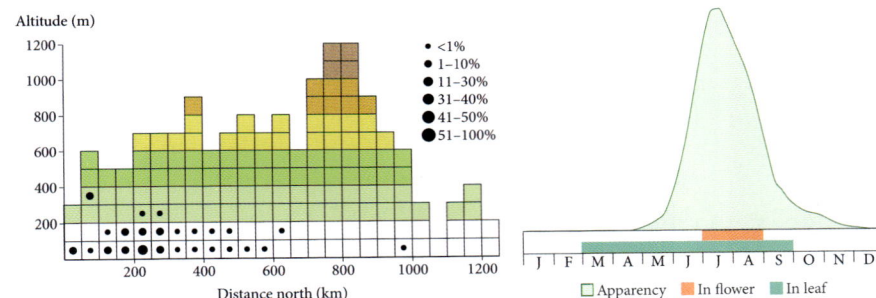

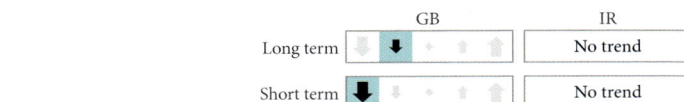

Alien	GB	IR
2000–19	141	4
1987–99	174	0
1970–86	81	0
pre-1970	205	0

Key refs Cope & Gray (2009), Thurston (1954).

D.A. Pearman & K.J. Walker

N? *Gaudinia fragilis* French Oat-grass

(L.) P.Beauv.

An annual or short-lived perennial grass of meadows, pastures and waysides on calcareous clay soils; also an occasional casual around docks and on refuse tips. Lowland.

Native or alien in Britain and the Channel Islands and a neophyte in Ireland.

Trends *G. fragilis* was cultivated in Britain by 1770 and was first recorded in the wild, as an introduction, in 1902 (Leith Docks, Midlothian). Its distribution since 1980 is much better known, following the discovery of what were clearly overlooked populations in grasslands in south-western England, and intensive surveys of suitable habitats nearby (Leach & Pearman, 2003); new populations have continued to be found this century, slightly extending its possibly native range. It

has a strikingly similar distribution to *Oenanthe pimpinelloides* and this, together with its preference for old meadows, has led some to consider that it is native, at least in its core areas. Alternatively, it may have been introduced in the late 19th and early 20th centuries with grass seed imported from southern Europe, subsequently spreading as a result of hay-making.

Biogeography Submediterranean-Subatlantic element.

Native	GB	IR
2000–19	48	0
1987–99	46	0
1970–86	16	0
pre-1970	10	0

Alien	GB	IR
2000–19	7	4
1987–99	3	4
1970–86	4	0
pre-1970	12	8

Key refs Cope & Gray (2009), Leach & Pearman (2003), Marren (1999), McClintock (1972).

S.J. Leach & D.A. Pearman

N *Trisetum flavescens* Yellow Oat-grass

(L.) P.Beauv.

A perennial grass of well-drained neutral and calcareous grassland, found in lowland pasture and hay meadows (where it was at one time included in agricultural seed mixtures), on downland, banks and roadsides, and occasionally rocks. It is most abundant in old, ungrazed hay meadows. It is highly palatable to stock and susceptible to damage by heavy trampling. It is the classic 'subordinate' grass, always occurring in low abundance and never dominant. 0–560 m (Hartside, Cumberland).

Trends The distribution of *T. flavescens* appears to have declined, although it is frequently overlooked when not in flower. It is alien in Orkney and Shetland and its status is doubtful in other areas of northern and western Scotland, and in north Wales and

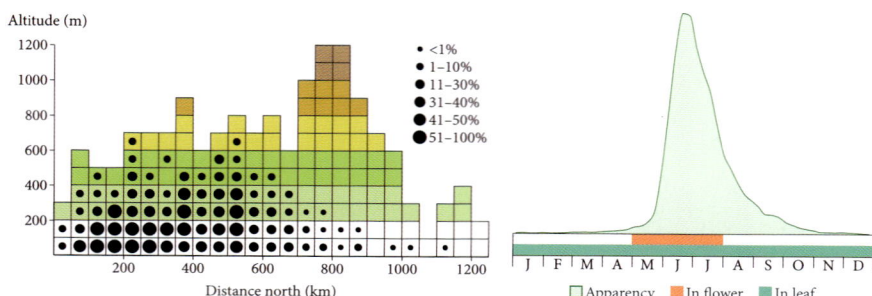

parts of south-western England. The tall alien subsp. *purpurascens* appears to have been widely sown in seed mixtures on verges and in grassland recreation schemes in recent decades.

Biogeography European Temperate element; widely naturalized outside its native range.

Native	GB	IR
2000–19	1546	235
1987–99	1577	246
1970–86	1060	42
pre-1970	1480	232

Alien	GB	IR
2000–19	1	0
1987–99	2	0
1970–86	1	0
pre-1970	6	0

Key refs Cope & Gray (2009), Dixon (1995), Grime *et al.* (2007).

F.H. Perring & D.A. Pearman

Koeleria vallesiana Somerset Hair-grass
(Honck.) Gaudin

A tufted perennial grass of open, sheep- and cattle-grazed grassland around rock outcrops on south-facing Carboniferous limestone slopes. Its sites are characterized by high levels of insolation and summer drought. Lowland.

Trends *K. vallesiana* is restricted to the Mendip Hills in North Somerset where it was first collected in 1726, but not recognized until it was rediscovered by G.C. Druce in 1904. Its distribution at the 10 km square scale is stable, but it has been lost from some 1 km squares due to lack of grazing and spread of scrub. It was deliberately planted in Goblin Combe (North Somerset) by the University of Bristol in 1955, where it still persists on rock outcrops on a steep south-facing slope.

Biogeography Suboceanic Southern-temperate element.

	GB	IR
Long term	No trend	No trend
Short term	No trend	No trend

Native		GB	IR
2000–19	●	4	0
1987–99	●	4	0
1970–86	◐	4	0
pre-1970	○	4	0

Alien		GB	IR
2000–19	●	1	0
1987–99	●	1	0
1970–86	◐	0	0
pre-1970	○	1	0

Key refs Cope & Gray (2009), Green *et al.* (1997), Stroh *et al.* (2019), Wigginton (1999).

S.J. Leach & D.A. Pearman

Koeleria macrantha Crested Hair-grass
(Ledeb.) Schult.

A perennial grass of infertile grasslands, mainly on calcareous substrates; also around rock outcrops, screes, quarry heaps and old lead workings. In many areas it is most frequent in dry, sandy, base-rich grassland on cliff-tops and dunes. Generally lowland, but reaching 710 m on Little Fell (Westmorland).

Trends There has been a gradual decline in the range of *K. macrantha* since the 1960s, especially in the lowlands, due to habitat destruction and intensification of grassland management. However, it is easily overlooked and so new discoveries continue to be made due to more systematic recording. It is an extremely variable species but the numerous entities have not been thoroughly explored or described.

Biogeography Circumpolar Temperate element.

Native		GB	IR
2000–19	●	852	230
1987–99	●	985	196
1970–86	◐	614	44
pre-1970	○	956	171

Alien		GB	IR
2000–19	●	0	0
1987–99	●	1	0
1970–86	◐	1	0
pre-1970	○	0	0

Key refs Cope & Gray (2009), Dixon (2000), Grime *et al.* (2007), Looman (1978).

S.J. Leach & D.A. Pearman

Ne *Lagurus ovatus* Hare's-tail
L.

An annual grass, naturalized on sand dunes in the Channel Islands and in England as far north as Teesside. Elsewhere it occurs as a casual garden escape on walls, pavements, roadsides, refuse tips and in car parks, or formerly, as an introduction from wool shoddy or grain. Lowland.

Trends *L. ovatus* was introduced to cultivation in Britain by 1640 and is widely grown in gardens. It was first recorded in the wild by 1787 in Guernsey, where it has long been naturalized. Deliberate attempts to establish it in Jersey were eventually successful in the 1860s. It appears to be increasing as an established alien on sand dunes in England.

Biogeography A Mediterranean-Atlantic species; widely naturalized in North and South America, southern Africa, Australia and elsewhere.

Long term	GB	IR
	No trend	No trend

Alien	GB	IR
2000–19	130	7
1987–99	88	4
1970–86	52	1
pre-1970	47	0

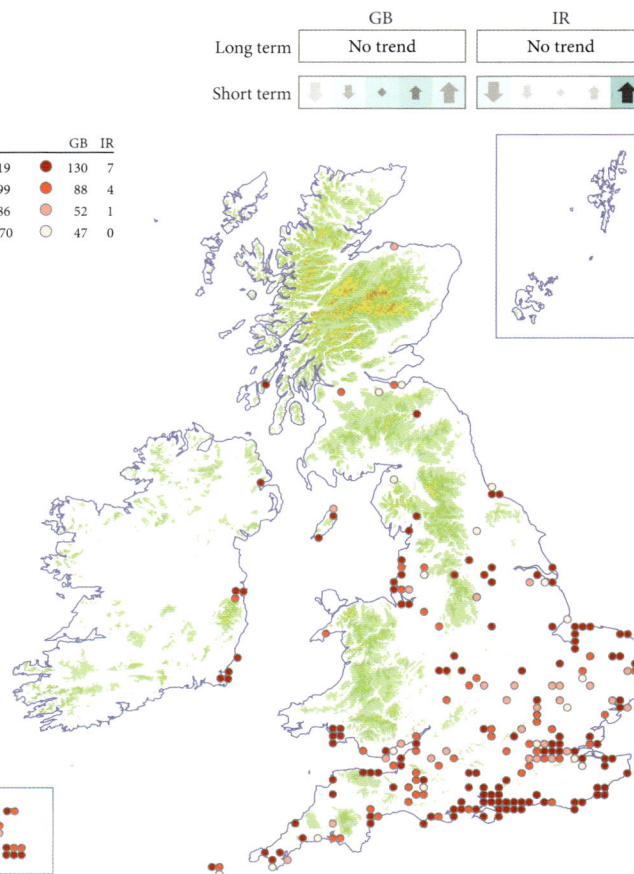

Key refs Cope & Gray (2009), McClintock (1975), Ryves *et al.* (1996).

S.J. Leach & D.A. Pearman

N *Hierochloe odorata* Holy-grass
(L.) P.Beauv.

A rhizomatous perennial grass of wetland habitats, including lakeside reedbeds, sedge swamps, willow-carr, riverbanks and wet meadows; also, in south-western Scotland, at the base of coastal cliffs where streams emerge and along the upper edge of fringing saltmarshes. 0–300 m (Clearburn Loch, Selkirkshire).

Trends There has been an increase in the number of sites recorded for *H. odorata* since 2000, presumably as a result of more systematic recording rather than genuine spread. It is now known to be frequent in Orkney, where it was first recorded in 1980, and where all sites are near Norse church sites. It has been lost from its only site in Ireland, on Lough Neagh, because of the water levels being lowered artificially.

Biogeography Circumpolar Boreal-montane element, with a continental distribution in western Europe.

	GB	IR
Long term		No trend
Short term		No trend

Native	GB	IR
2000–19	22	0
1987–99	15	1
1970–86	14	1
pre-1970	10	1

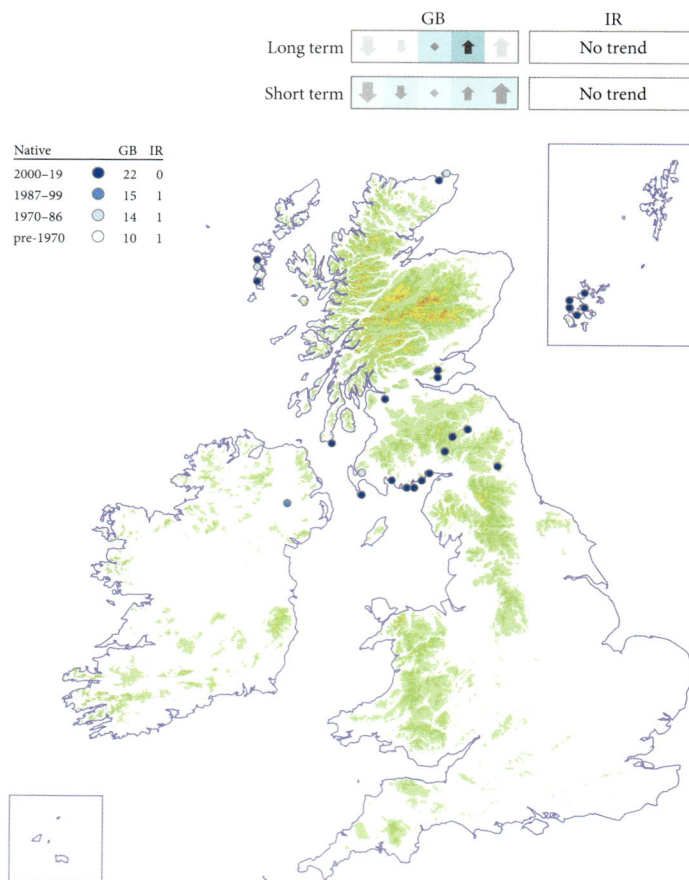

Key refs Cope & Gray (2009), Wigginton (1999).

S.J. Leach & D.A. Pearman

N *Anthoxanthum odoratum* Sweet Vernal-grass
L.

A short-lived, winter-green perennial grass which occurs in a wide variety of habitats, including floodplain hay meadows, damp pastures throughout the lowlands and uplands, blanket bog and wet heaths, fen grassland and mires, rush-pastures, sand dunes, roadsides, and woodland rides. It is most frequent on damp, acidic soils, and avoids those that are drought-prone or waterlogged. It is occasionally found in calcareous grassland but usually where soils are deepest. Reproduction is by seed, from a persistent seed bank. 0–1,276 m (Ben Nevis, Westerness).

Trends *A. odoratum* was, until the 1920s, a component of grass-seed mixtures but has since been lost from many pastures that have been improved. Nonetheless it is still ubiquitous at the 10 km square scale and its distribution appears to be stable.

Biogeography Eurosiberian Wide-temperate element, but widely naturalized so that distribution is now Circumpolar Wide-temperate.

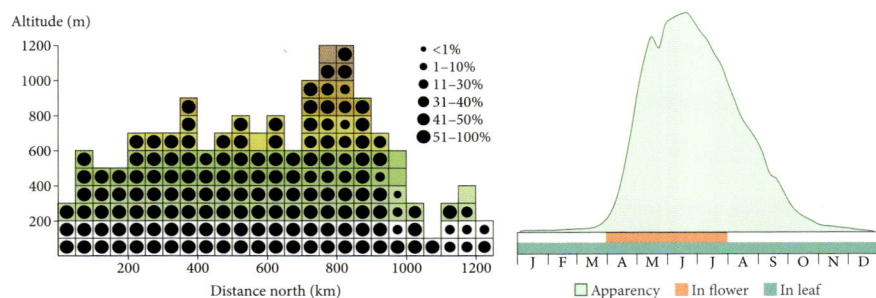

Native		GB	IR
2000–19	●	2804	1001
1987–99	●	2757	940
1970–86	○	1919	249
pre-1970	○	2656	887

Key refs Cope & Gray (2009), Grime *et al.* (2007), Wu & Jain (1980).

D.A. PEARMAN

● <1%
● 1–10%
● 11–30%
● 31–40%
● 41–50%
● 51–100%

Apparency   In flower   In leaf

Ne *Anthoxanthum aristatum* Annual Vernal-grass
Boiss.

An annual grass, formerly a persistent weed of cereal crops on sandy or gravelly soils in south-eastern England and East Anglia, but recently found only as a rare casual in disturbed soils at RAF Lakenheath (West Suffolk). Lowland.

Trends *A. aristatum* is thought to have been introduced from France in the latter half of the 19th century as an impurity in fodder-plant seed. It was first recorded in the wild in 1872 (Knutsford, Cheshire). Its decline was noticeable by the 1962 *Atlas*, with many losses before 1930, probably due to improved grain-cleaning techniques, which reduced its incidence as an arable weed.

Biogeography Native of southern Europe; widespread as a naturalized or casual introduction farther north.

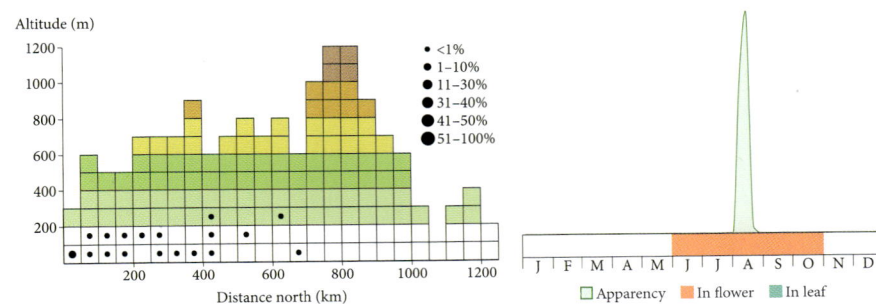

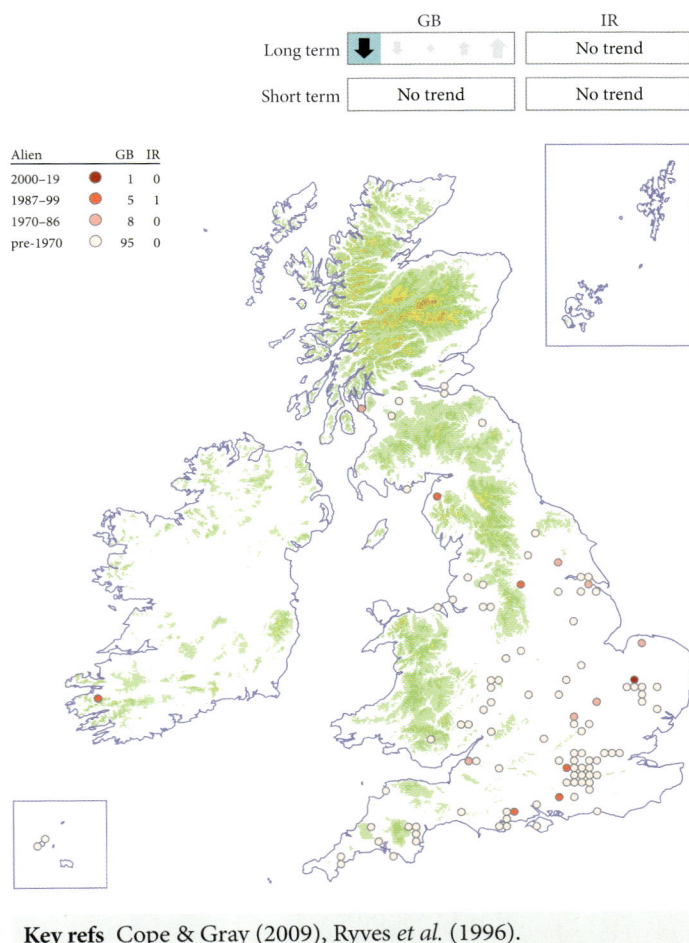

Alien		GB	IR
2000–19	●	1	0
1987–99	●	5	1
1970–86	●	8	0
pre-1970	○	95	0

Key refs Cope & Gray (2009), Ryves *et al.* (1996).

S.J. LEACH & D.A. PEARMAN

● <1%
● 1–10%
● 11–30%
● 31–40%
● 41–50%
● 51–100%

Apparency   In flower   In leaf

N *Phalaris arundinacea* Reed Canary-grass
L.

A rhizomatous perennial grass of ditches, riverbanks, alder/willow-carr and the margins of canals, reservoirs, lakes and ponds, growing especially well where the water-table fluctuates widely. It prefers slightly drier sites than *Glyceria maxima* and *Phragmites australis*, and can occur on roadsides. A variegated form, var. *picta*, known as 'Gardener's Garters', occurs not infrequently as a garden throw-out. 0–475 m (Cwar yr Hendre, Breconshire), and exceptionally at 845 m on Great Dun Fell (Westmorland).

Trends There is no evidence of any change in the distribution of this species since the 1960s. Its ability to tolerate summer-dry conditions has enabled it to survive, and even thrive, in the modern landscape.

Biogeography Circumpolar Boreo-temperate element; widely naturalized outside its native range.

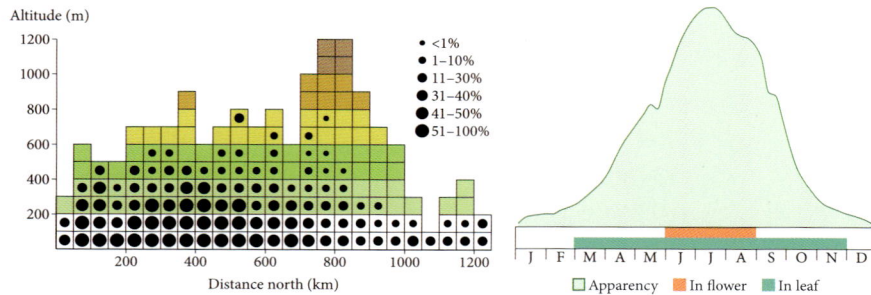

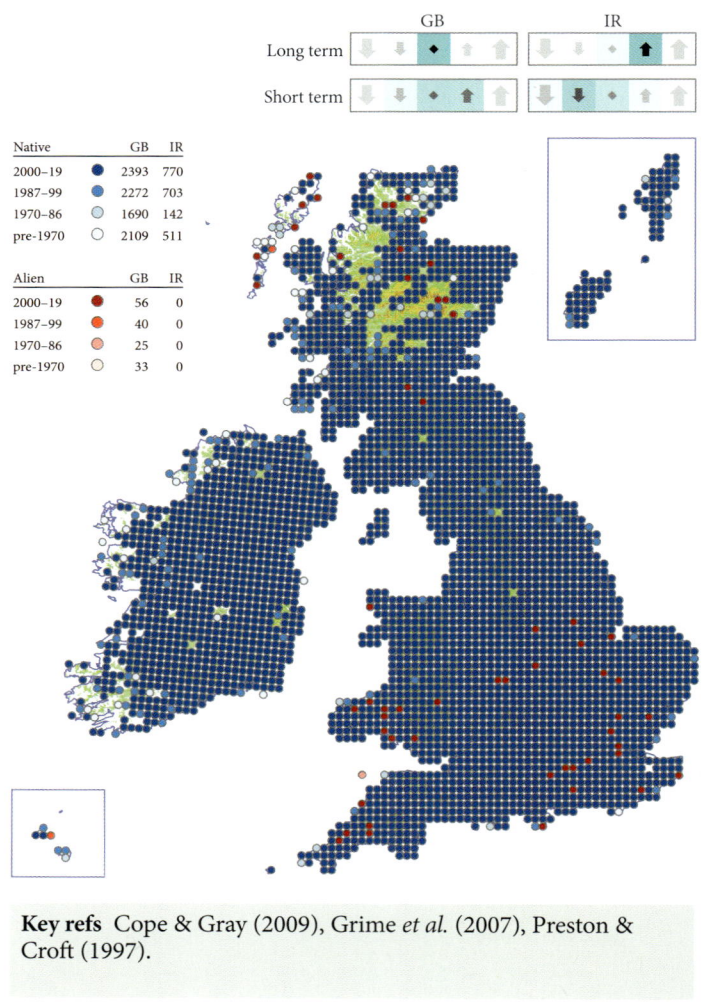

Native	GB	IR
2000–19	2393	770
1987–99	2272	703
1970–86	1690	142
pre-1970	2109	511

Alien	GB	IR
2000–19	56	0
1987–99	40	0
1970–86	25	0
pre-1970	33	0

Altitude (m)

- <1%
- 1–10%
- 11–30%
- 31–40%
- 41–50%
- 51–100%

J F M A M J J A S O N D

☐ Apparency ☐ In flower ☐ In leaf

Key refs Cope & Gray (2009), Grime *et al.* (2007), Preston & Croft (1997).

S.J. LEACH

Ne *Phalaris aquatica* Bulbous Canary-grass
L.

A shortly rhizomatous, perennial herb, naturalized in woodland glades, field-borders, roadsides and waste places. It also occurs as a casual on refuse tips and waste ground as a wool, esparto and birdseed alien, and as a contaminant of grass-seed. Lowland.

Trends *P. aquatica* is sown as cover and food for pheasants, more rarely for grazing or silage, sometimes as robust Australian strains. It was first recorded in the wild in 1900 (Falmouth, West Cornwall) and seems to be slowly increasing, especially in East Anglia and south-eastern England.

Biogeography Native of the Mediterranean region and south-western Asia; widely introduced by cultivation elsewhere.

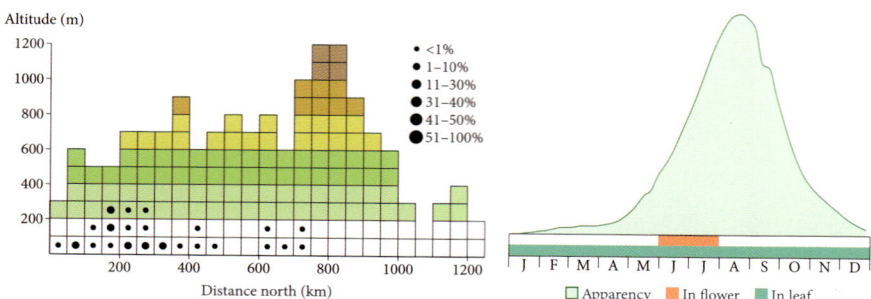

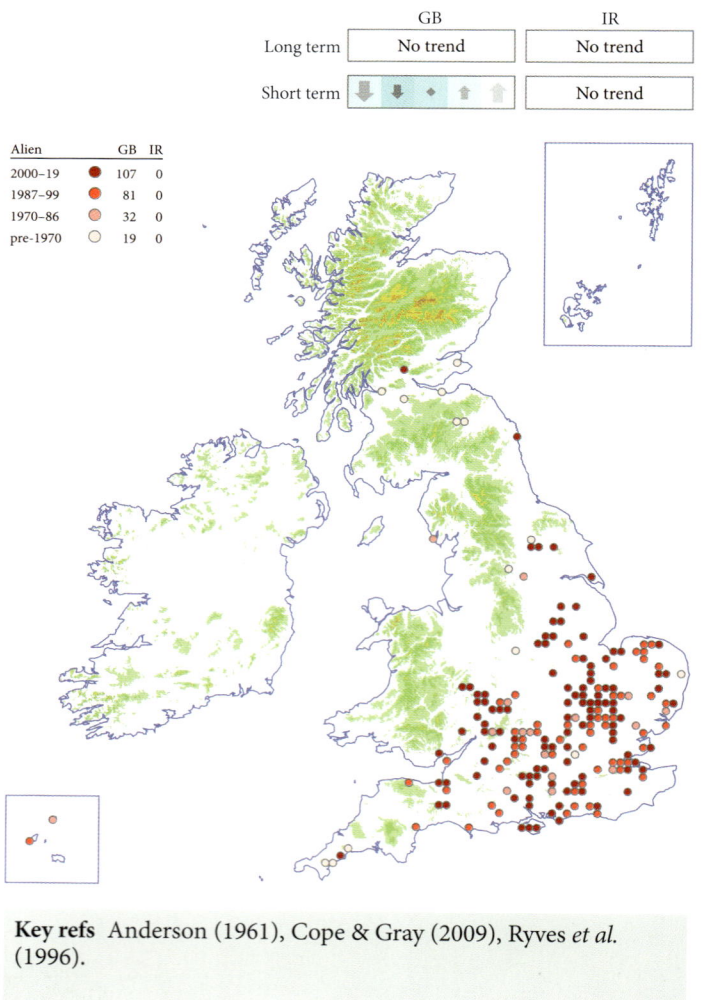

	GB	IR
Long term	No trend	No trend
Short term		No trend

Alien	GB	IR
2000–19	107	0
1987–99	81	0
1970–86	32	0
pre-1970	19	0

Altitude (m)

- <1%
- 1–10%
- 11–30%
- 31–40%
- 41–50%
- 51–100%

J F M A M J J A S O N D

☐ Apparency ☐ In flower ☐ In leaf

Key refs Anderson (1961), Cope & Gray (2009), Ryves *et al.* (1996).

S.J. LEACH & D.A. PEARMAN

Ne *Phalaris canariensis* Canary-grass
L.

An annual grass of waste ground, refuse tips, walls, roadsides and pavement cracks, especially in built-up areas. It is a casual from birdseed, grain, and possibly wool shoddy, but rarely persists. Generally lowland, but reaching 430 m at Nenthead (Cumberland).

Trends *P. canariensis* was known as a cultivated grass to William Turner by 1562. The first record from the wild was on Thomas Johnson's trip to East Kent in 1632. In the 19th century it was grown as a speciality crop for birdseed in south-eastern England, and reaped and bound in sheaves like wheat. Whilst there have been many new records this century, there are also many 10 km squares where this casual species has not been refound, making an assessment of change difficult.

Biogeography Perhaps native to north-western Africa and the Canary Islands; widely naturalized in the Mediterranean region and in other continents.

Alien	GB	IR
2000–19	701	71
1987–99	655	41
1970–86	421	13
pre-1970	789	20

Key refs Anderson (1961), Cope & Gray (2009).

S.J. Leach & D.A. Pearman

Ne *Phalaris minor* Lesser Canary-grass
Retz.

An annual grass, usually found as a casual on refuse tips and waste ground, but sometimes established amongst arable crops, including bulb-fields in the Isles of Scilly and carrot fields in East Anglia. It mainly originates from grain, birdseed, wool and esparto. Lowland.

Trends *P. minor* was noted by Ryves *et al.* (1996) as possibly native in the Channel Islands, where it was known in the wild as early as 1791, but most *Phalaris* species were spreading by then and it is probably alien there. There has been an extraordinary increase of records from south-eastern Ireland, where, beginning in 1993, it has spread and is sometimes now found as an abundant species in arable crops.

Biogeography A Mediterranean-Atlantic species; very widely naturalized outside its native range.

Alien	GB	IR
2000–19	43	59
1987–99	30	5
1970–86	20	0
pre-1970	63	0

Key refs Anderson (1961), Cope & Gray (2009), McClintock (1975), Mhic Daeid & Reynolds (1999), Ryves *et al.* (1996).

S.J. Leach & D.A. Pearman

Ne *Phalaris paradoxa* Awned Canary-grass
L.

An annual grass, originating from birdseed, grain, wool, esparto and other sources and widely planted as a constituent of gamebird seed mixtures. It is found as a casual on refuse tips and waste ground, and as a weed in arable fields and newly sown grass leys. Lowland.

Trends *P. paradoxa* was recorded as a casual on heaps of ballast by 1831 (Durham) and appears to be an increasing species, becoming well-established as an arable weed in southern Britain.

Biogeography Native of the Mediterranean region and south-western Asia; widely naturalized or present as a casual elsewhere.

	GB	IR
Long term	No trend	No trend
Short term	↑	No trend

Alien	GB	IR
2000–19	157	1
1987–99	66	0
1970–86	30	0
pre-1970	66	1

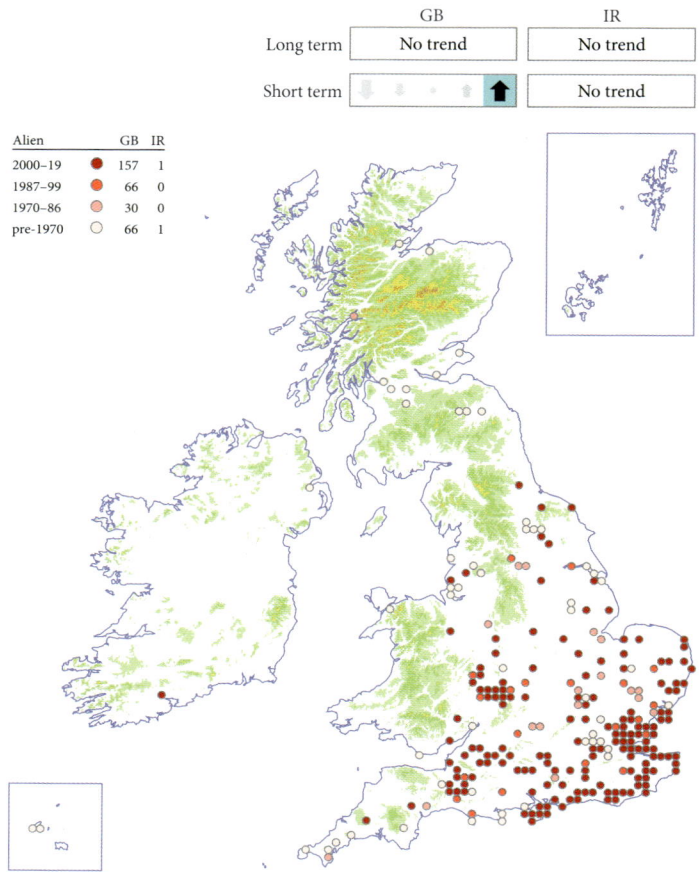

Key refs Anderson (1961), Cope & Gray (2009), Ryves *et al.* (1996).

S.J. LEACH & D.A. PEARMAN

Altitude (m) / Distance north (km)
- <1%
- 1–10%
- 11–30%
- 31–40%
- 41–50%
- 51–100%

J F M A M J J A S O N D
☐ Apparency ☐ In flower ☐ In leaf

N *Holcus lanatus* Yorkshire-fog
L.

A short-lived, tufted perennial grass of a wide range of grasslands, including hay meadows, fen pastures, hill pastures, acid grassland, chalk and limestone downland, as well as hedgebanks, open woodland, moorland, rough grassland and waste ground. It grows in dry to winter-wet, acidic to calcareous soils, and is most vigorous in moist but not waterlogged habitats. It tolerates mowing and grazing, but not heavy trampling. Mainly found below 500 m, but up to 845 m on Great Dun Fell (Westmorland), and with an exceptional record at 980 m on Carnedd Llewelyn (Caernarvonshire).

Trends *H. lanatus* is near-ubiquitous at the 10 km square scale and there has been no appreciable change in this range since the 1960s. It is of little value for grazing and consequently it is rarely sown for hay or silage production.

Biogeography European Southern-temperate element; widely naturalized outside its native range.

	GB				IR			
Long term	↓	↓	·	↑	↑	↓	↓	·	↑	↑
Short term	↓	↓	·	↑	↑	↓	↓	·	↑	↑

Native	GB	IR
2000–19	2829	1005
1987–99	2793	958
1970–86	1985	239
pre-1970	2669	899

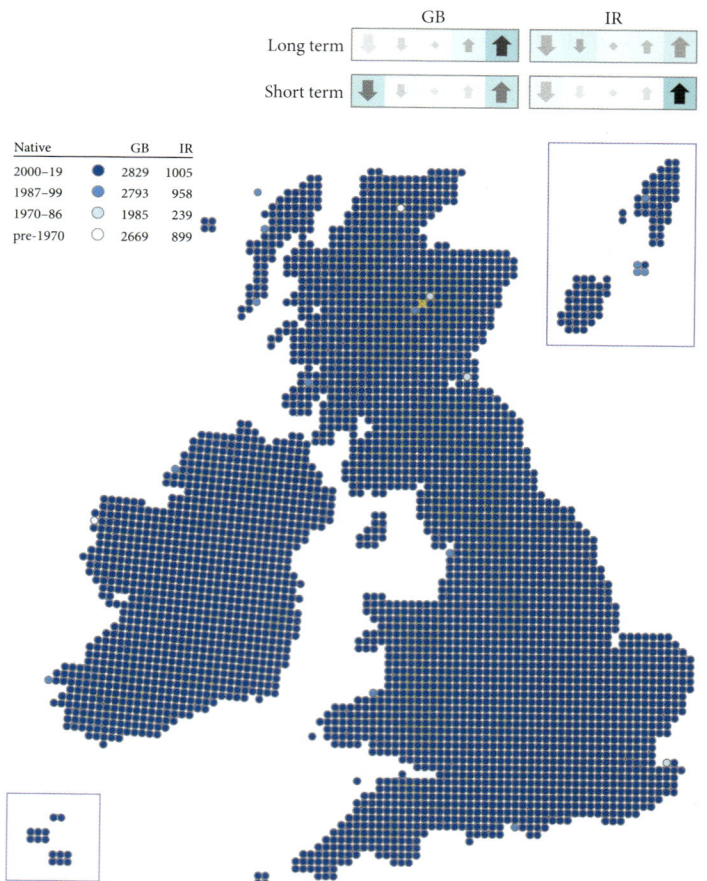

Key refs Beddows (1961), Cope & Gray (2009), Grime *et al.* (2007), Thompson & Turkington (1988).

F.H. PERRING & D.A. PEARMAN

Altitude (m) / Distance north (km)
- <1%
- 1–10%
- 11–30%
- 31–40%
- 41–50%
- 51–100%

J F M A M J J A S O N D
☐ Apparency ☐ In flower ☐ In leaf

Holcus mollis Creeping Soft-grass
L.

A creeping, rhizomatous perennial grass of well-drained acidic or neutral soils, found in *Quercus* and *Betula* woods, fen woodland, open conifer plantations, hedgebanks, on heathland, and under *Pteridium aquilinum*. It is capable of spreading into damper grassland and is locally a troublesome weed of arable land. *H. mollis* tolerates occasional mowing or light grazing but is a poor competitor with more vigorous grasses. 0–735 m (Cross Fell, Cumberland).

Trends *H. mollis* is a very widespread species but much more localized than *H. lanatus* due to its more exacting ecological requirements. There has been no appreciable change in its known distribution since the 1960s, although it is now better recorded in some regions.

Biogeography European Temperate element.

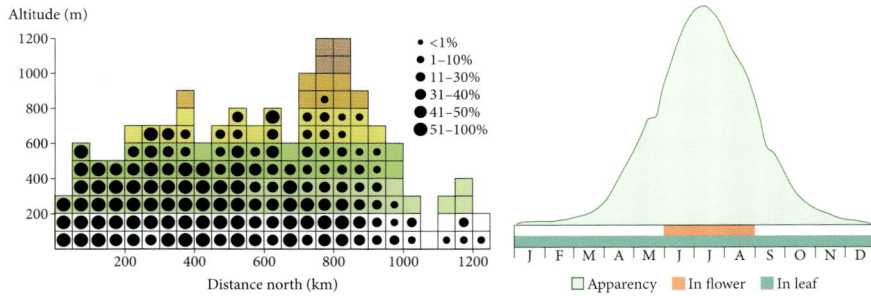

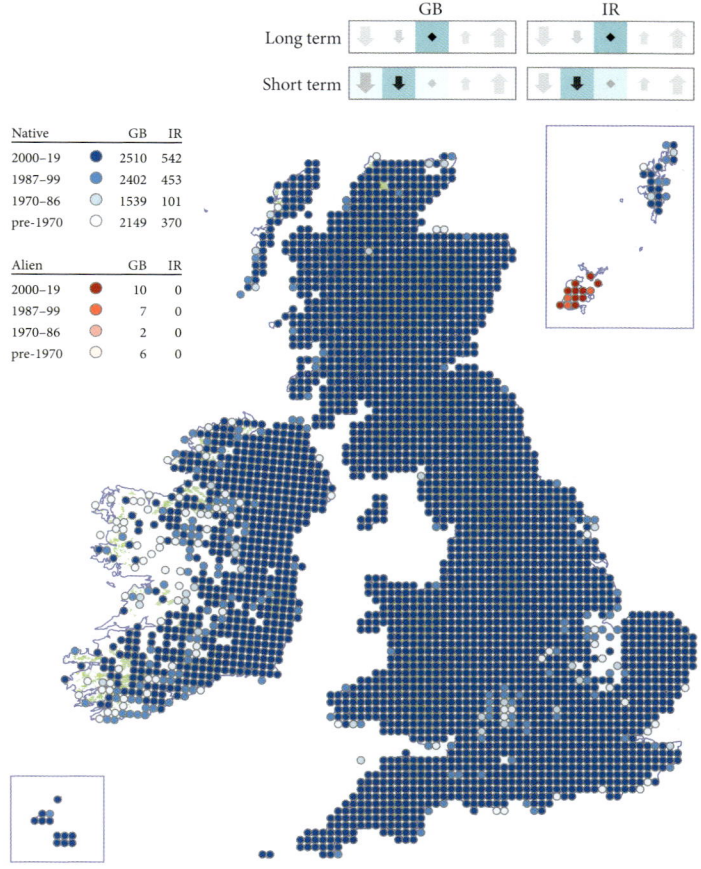

Native	GB	IR
2000–19	2510	542
1987–99	2402	453
1970–86	1539	101
pre-1970	2149	370

Alien	GB	IR
2000–19	10	0
1987–99	7	0
1970–86	2	0
pre-1970	6	0

Key refs Cope & Gray (2009), Grime *et al.* (2007), Ovington & Scurfield (1956).

F.H. PERRING & D.A. PEARMAN

Deschampsia cespitosa Tufted Hair-grass
(L.) P.Beauv.

A tufted perennial grass of poorly drained, mildly acidic, neutral or basic soils in woodland, rough and marshy grasslands, fen-meadows, grass-heath, and a wide range of montane habitats. It can rapidly colonize bare ground and tolerates some disturbance. It is morphologically and cytologically variable and either proliferates or sets copious seed. 0–1,335 m (Ben Nevis, Westerness).

Trends The known 10 km square distribution of *D. cespitosa* appears to be stable. It often persists in overgrazed pasture because its unpalatable leaves have a high silica content. It persists in woodlands and amongst invading scrub where the shade is not too dense. Subsp. *cespitosa* occurs throughout the range of the species; subsp. *alpina* and subsp. *parviflora* are mapped separately.

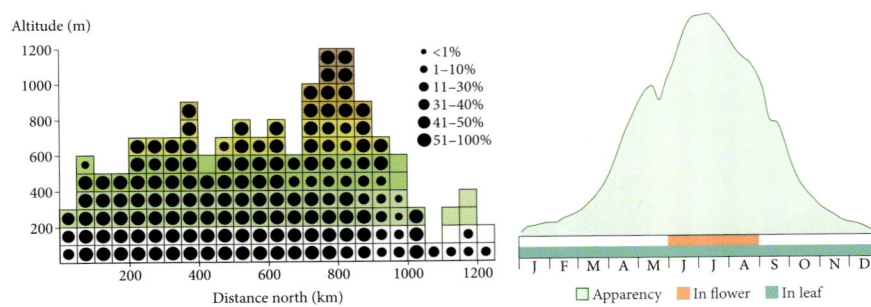

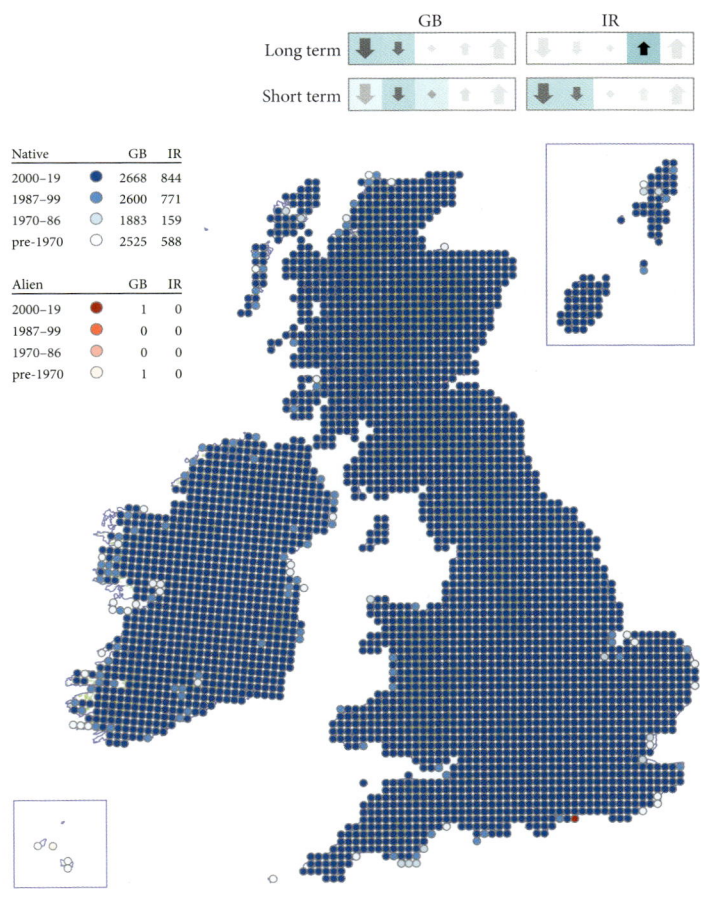

Biogeography Circumpolar Wide-boreal element; widely naturalized outside its native range.

Native	GB	IR
2000–19	2668	844
1987–99	2600	771
1970–86	1883	159
pre-1970	2525	588

Alien	GB	IR
2000–19	1	0
1987–99	0	0
1970–86	0	0
pre-1970	1	0

Key refs Cope & Gray (2009), Davy (1980), Grime *et al.* (2007).

D.A. PEARMAN

Deschampsia cespitosa subsp. *parviflora*

(Thuill.) Dumort.

A tufted perennial grass of damp woodland and woodland rides on poorly drained, heavy soils. The persistent seed bank allows it to survive the cycle of dense shade of mature coppice. Predominantly lowland.

Trends The presence of this taxon in our area was only recently brought to the attention of British and Irish botanists (Rich & Rich, 1988), although it was mentioned briefly in earlier works (*e.g.* Hubbard, 1954). Although its range and distribution are better known now than they were 20 years ago, it is still very unevenly recorded and therefore likely to still be under-recorded in many areas.

Biogeography Also recorded from central Europe.

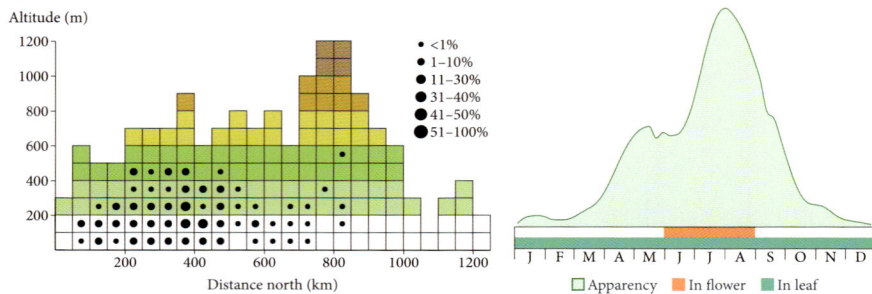

	GB	IR
Long term	No trend	No trend
Short term	No trend	No trend

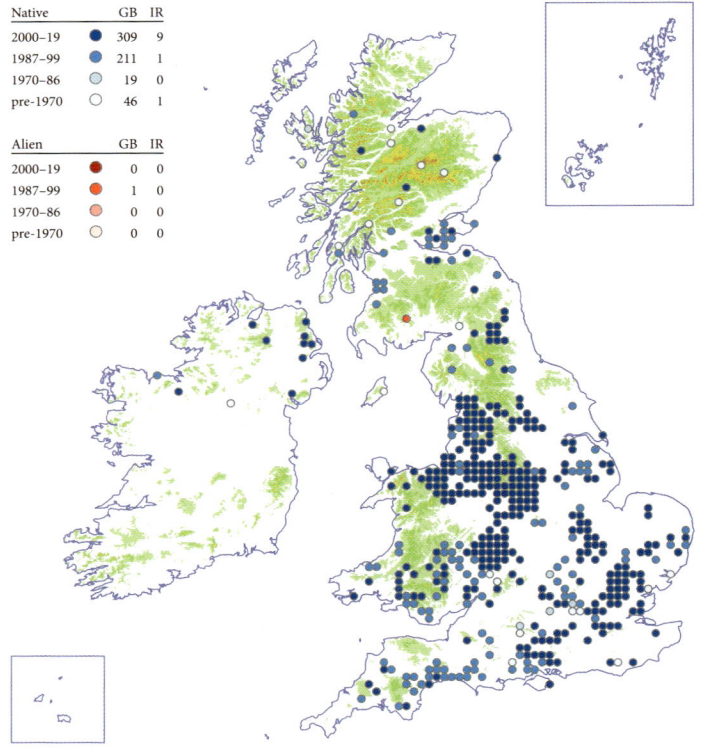

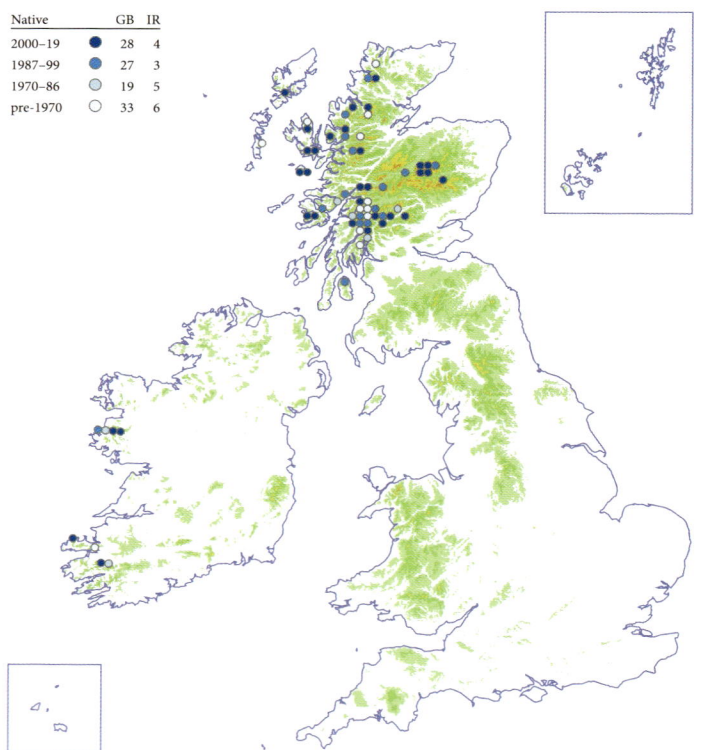

Native	GB	IR
2000–19	309	9
1987–99	211	1
1970–86	19	0
pre-1970	46	1

Alien	GB	IR
2000–19	0	0
1987–99	1	0
1970–86	0	0
pre-1970	0	0

Key refs Chiapella (2000), Cope & Gray (2009), Hubbard (1954), Rich & Rich (1988).

D.A. Pearman

Deschampsia cespitosa subsp. *alpina*

(L.) Hook.f.

A tufted perennial grass of very open montane habitats, growing on rock ledges, slumped soil and level gravelly flushes, often in sheltered areas where the snow lies late in the spring. It reproduces vegetatively by proliferous spikelets. From 800 m to 1,335 m (Ben Nevis, Westerness).

Trends This subspecies is poorly known and as such is likely to be much under-recorded. It is sometimes confused with proliferous forms of subsp. *cespitosa*, as in north Wales. There are also numerous unmapped records from the Scottish Highlands that may represent either subsp. *alpina* or proliferous subsp. *cespitosa*. It appears to be very rare in Ireland although further research and surveying is needed to clarify its distribution there. As a consequence, the map should be treated as provisional.

Biogeography European Arctic-montane element; also recorded from Greenland, eastern Canada and eastern Asia but absent from the mountains of central Europe.

	GB	IR
Long term	No trend	No trend
Short term	No trend	No trend

Native	GB	IR
2000–19	28	4
1987–99	27	3
1970–86	19	5
pre-1970	33	6

Key refs Cope & Gray (2009), Stewart *et al.* (1994).

D.A. Pearman

N *Aristavena setacea* Bog Hair-grass
(Huds.) F. Albers & Butzin

A densely tufted perennial grass of peaty or stony margins of lochs, shallow pools and seasonally inundated depressions on heaths, and blanket bogs. It appears to be very exacting in its ecological requirements, favouring bare areas that are flooded in winter but dry in summer, and possibly where there is some lateral water movement. 0–320 m (Loch Morlich, Easterness), with an exceptional record of 420 m (Mullach Bhiogadail, Outer Hebrides).

Native in Britain and Ireland and a neophyte in the Channel Islands.

Trends *A. setacea* was lost from many lowland sites in England and Scotland by the mid-20th century through habitat destruction or undergrazing of heathland, and whilst localized declines have continued, since 2000 its distribution would seem to have been generally stable, with new locations discovered in core areas of north-western Scotland, and populations refound elsewhere at remote sites for which there were no records for at least 50 years.

Biogeography Oceanic Temperate element.

Native	GB	IR
2000–19	71	7
1987–99	69	8
1970–86	39	7
pre-1970	91	10

Alien	GB	IR
2000–19	0	0
1987–99	0	0
1970–86	0	0
pre-1970	1	0

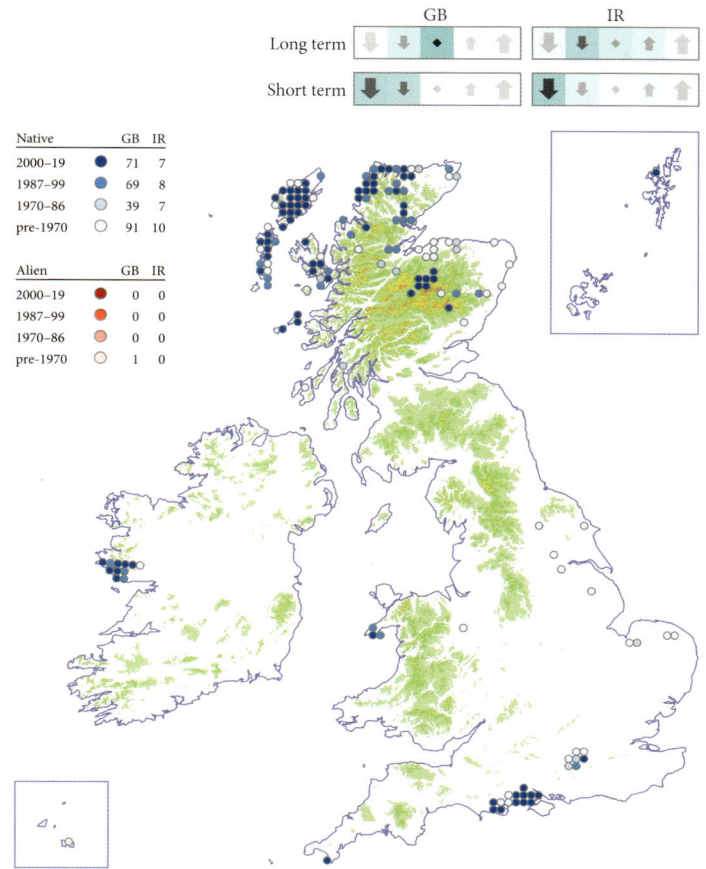

Key refs Cope & Gray (2009), Dupont (1962), Stewart *et al.* (1994).

F.H. PERRING & D.A. PEARMAN

N *Avenella flexuosa* Wavy Hair-grass
(L.) Drejer

A loosely to densely tufted, clump or carpet-forming perennial grass of lowland acidic grasslands and grass-heaths, moorland, hill-pasture, exposed mountain grass-, sedge- and moss-heaths, and open woodland, usually of *Betula* or *Quercus*, where it is often dominant. It grows on a wide range of freely draining base-poor substrates, including leached soils over basic rocks. It can survive in sheep-grazed woodland and degraded upland pastures. 0–1,305 m (on the summit of Ben Macdui, Banffshire).

Trends Although the overall 10 km square distribution of *A. flexuosa* has changed little since the 1960s, it is now much better known in Ireland as a result of more systematic recording and it has declined locally in lowland areas due to the destruction of heathland and acidic grassland. However, recent research has shown that this species has increased in abundance on lowland dry heaths in recent decades as a result of atmospheric deposition of nutrients, leading to a decline in threatened heathland communities (Marrs, 1993; Britton *et al.*, 2003). It also appears to have increased in the uplands, possibly for the same reasons, especially in montane communities (Britton *et al.*, 2009).

Biogeography European Boreo-temperate element; also in northern Asia and North and South America.

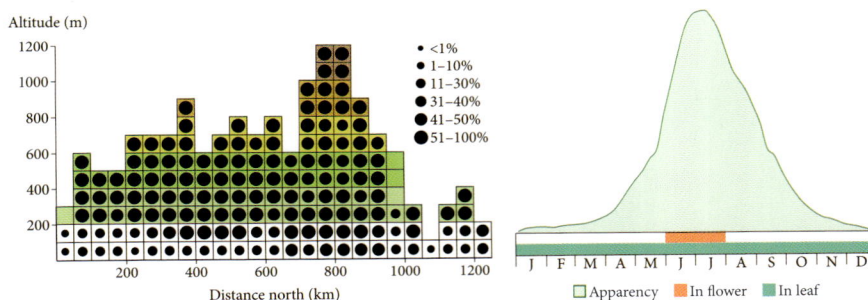

Native	GB	IR
2000–19	2130	455
1987–99	2104	355
1970–86	1326	85
pre-1970	2018	229

Alien	GB	IR
2000–19	0	0
1987–99	1	0
1970–86	1	0
pre-1970	1	0

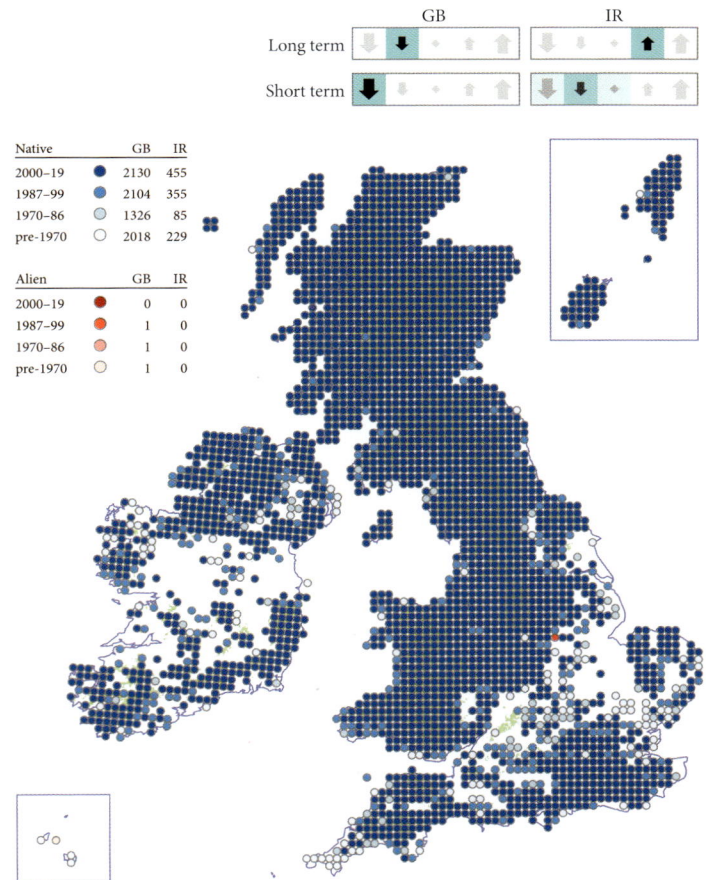

Key refs Britton *et al.* (2003), Britton *et al.* (2009), Cope & Gray (2009), Grime *et al.* (2007), Marrs (1993), Scurfield (1954).

F.H. PERRING, D.A. PEARMAN & K.J. WALKER

N *Corynephorus canescens* Grey Hair-grass
(L.) P.Beauv.

A perennial grass of open areas on consolidated sand dunes, sandy shingle and open sand by the sea. It also occurs on paleo-dunes and sandy heathland on acidic soils inland. It requires mobile sand for its survival; mature tufts are reinvigorated by partial burial. Lowland.

Native in Britain and the Channel Islands and a neophyte in Ireland.

Trends The overall distribution of *C. canescens* is probably stable, following losses before 1930. It is still locally frequent in coastal habitats in East Anglia, Lancashire and the Channel Islands and inland in Breckland and Worcestershire. Its status is uncertain in some areas. In Lancashire, Savidge *et al.* (1963) regard it as native but Sell & Murrell (1996) treat it as probably introduced. In north-eastern Scotland, where it has been known since at least

1900, both Webster (1978) and Trist (1998) describe it as alien, but Ryves *et al.* (1996) suggest that its recent arrival may be an expansion of its natural range. The Worcestershire sites were only discovered in 1981, but it grows with several other species of open, inland sandy heath, such as *Silene conica* and *Teesdalia nudicaulis*, and Trist (1998) regards it as a relict native here, as does Chatters (2020a).

Biogeography European Southern-temperate element.

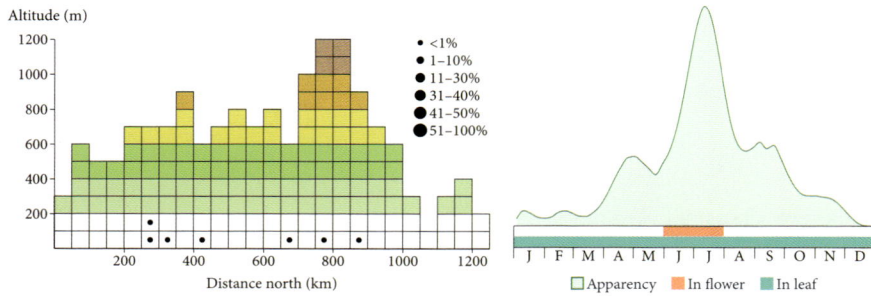

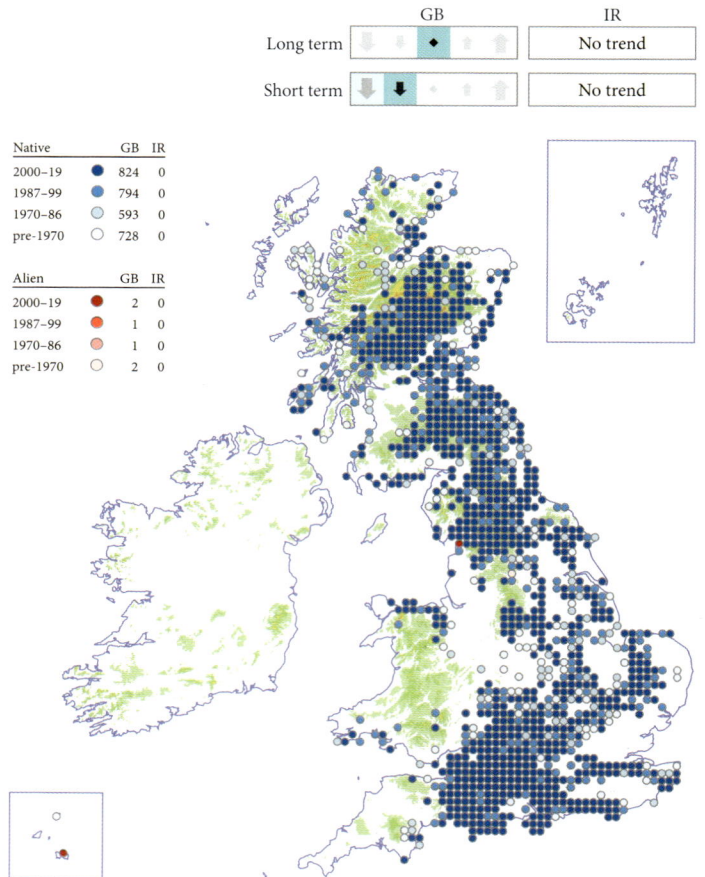

Native	GB	IR
2000–19	18	0
1987–99	19	0
1970–86	18	0
pre-1970	24	0

Alien	GB	IR
2000–19	4	0
1987–99	4	1
1970–86	3	0
pre-1970	7	0

Key refs Chatters (2020a), Cope & Gray (2009), Marshall (1967), Ryves *et al.* (1996), Savidge *et al.* (1963), Stewart *et al.* (1994), Trist (1998), Webster (1978), Wigginton (1999).

S.J. LEACH & D.A. PEARMAN

N *Helictochloa pratensis* Meadow Oat-grass
(L.) Romero Zarco

A perennial herb of calcareous rendzina and brown earth soils, usually over chalk or limestone, but also over glacial deposits and basic igneous rocks. It is characteristic of well-grazed chalk and limestone downland, but is also found on screes, cliffs and limestone pavements, and occasionally in open *Fraxinus* woods, on sand dunes and on montane ledge communities with *Dryas octopetala*. 0–835 m (Breadalbanes, Mid Perthshire).

Trends The distribution of *H. pratensis* is stable throughout much of its range, though many of the 10 km squares in south-eastern England where it was once common now have records only from a single locality, indicating substantial localized and ongoing decline in some lowland areas. Montane populations with larger spikelets may be taxonomically distinct.

Biogeography European Temperate element.

Native	GB	IR
2000–19	824	0
1987–99	794	0
1970–86	593	0
pre-1970	728	0

Alien	GB	IR
2000–19	2	0
1987–99	1	0
1970–86	1	0
pre-1970	2	0

Key refs Cope & Gray (2009), Dixon (1991), Grime *et al.* (2007).

F.H. PERRING & D.A. PEARMAN

Avenula pubescens Downy Oat-grass

(Huds.) Dumort.

A perennial grass growing in a wide range of moist or dry, neutral and calcareous grasslands. It is found in meadows and pastures, on roadsides and railway banks, in open woodland and rides, on coastal cliffs, fixed dunes, and in mildly acidic grassland over gravel, and on some less acidic heaths. It tolerates modest mowing, grazing and manuring, but not artificial fertilizers or competition from vigorous fodder-grasses. 0–745 m (Coire Lochain, Westerness).

Trends Although there are many new 10 km square records for *A. pubescens* this century, presumably as a result of more systematic recording, its distribution has declined in some regions, especially central and eastern areas of lowland England, which presumably reflects the loss or modification of infertile grasslands and other habitats in these regions.

Biogeography European Temperate element; also in central Asia and widely naturalized outside its native range.

Native	GB	IR
2000–19	1364	374
1987–99	1287	327
1970–86	914	69
pre-1970	1128	194

Alien	GB	IR
2000–19	1	0
1987–99	0	0
1970–86	0	0
pre-1970	0	0

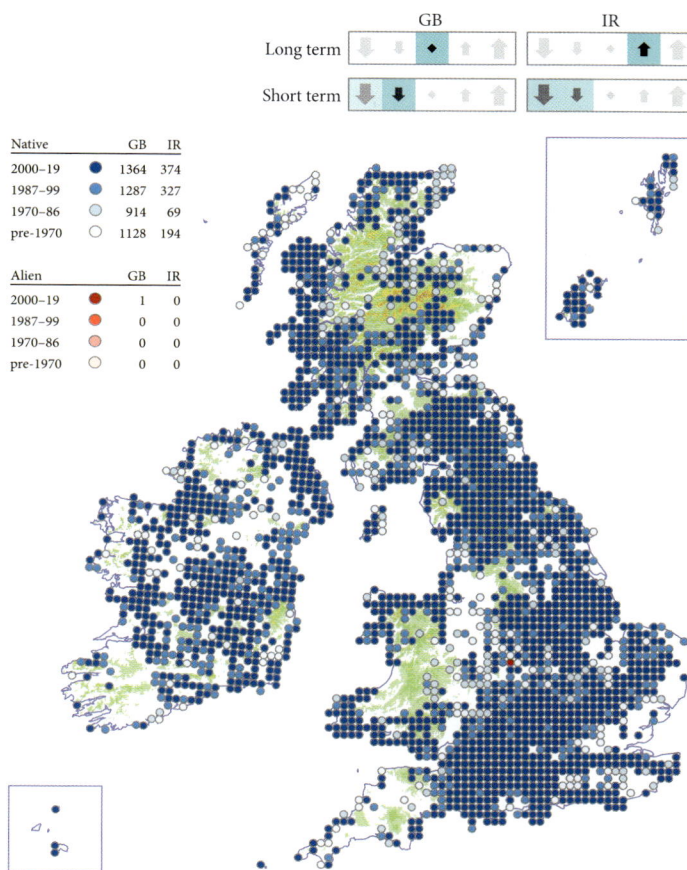

Key refs Cope & Gray (2009), Dixon (1991), Grime *et al.* (2007).

F.H. PERRING & D.A. PEARMAN

Aira caryophyllea Silver Hair-grass

L.

An annual grass of well-drained sandy and rocky places, cliff-tops, heaths, summer-parched grasslands, anthills and stabilized sand dunes; also on stone walls and railway ballast. Rarely, it is recorded as a wool casual. 0–560 m (Mourne Mountains, County Down).

Trends During the 20th century *A. caryophyllea* declined throughout its range, especially in south-eastern England. Losses would appear to have continued since 2000. The reasons for this are unclear but are possibly due to a general decline in the area of open, infertile, dry habitats supporting rich assemblages of short-lived plants, including grass and lichen-heaths and lowland heathlands (Cope & Gray, 2009).

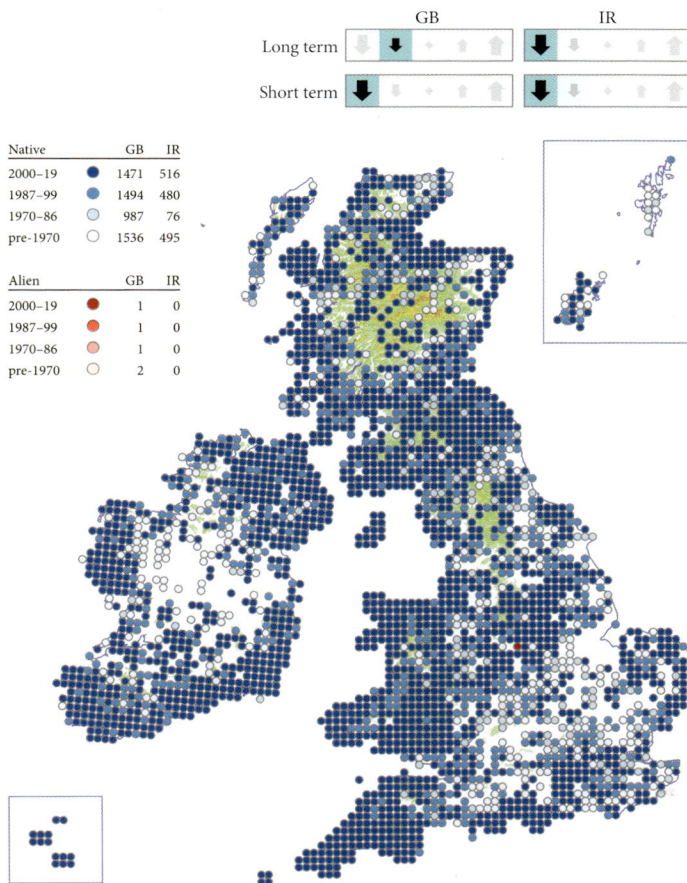

Biogeography European Southern-temperate element; widely naturalized outside its native range.

Native	GB	IR
2000–19	1471	516
1987–99	1494	480
1970–86	987	76
pre-1970	1536	495

Alien	GB	IR
2000–19	1	0
1987–99	1	0
1970–86	1	0
pre-1970	2	0

Key refs Cope & Gray (2009).

S.J. LEACH & D.A. PEARMAN

N *Aira praecox* Early Hair-grass
L.

An annual grass of sandy, gravelly and rocky places, commonly on thin acidic soils around rock outcrops, on walls, cliff-tops, heathlands and sand dunes. It is now rarely recorded as a wool casual. Generally lowland, but reaching 685 m on Mangerton Mountain (South Kerry).

Trends There seems to have been some decline in the distribution of *A. praecox* since the 1960s, both in England and in central Ireland, but not to the same extent as *A. caryophyllea* (Cope & Gray, 2009). These losses have presumably been due to a general decline in the extent of of open, infertile, dry habitats supporting rich assemblages of short-lived plants, including grass and lichen-heaths and lowland heathlands.

Biogeography Suboceanic Southern-temperate element; widely naturalized outside its native range.

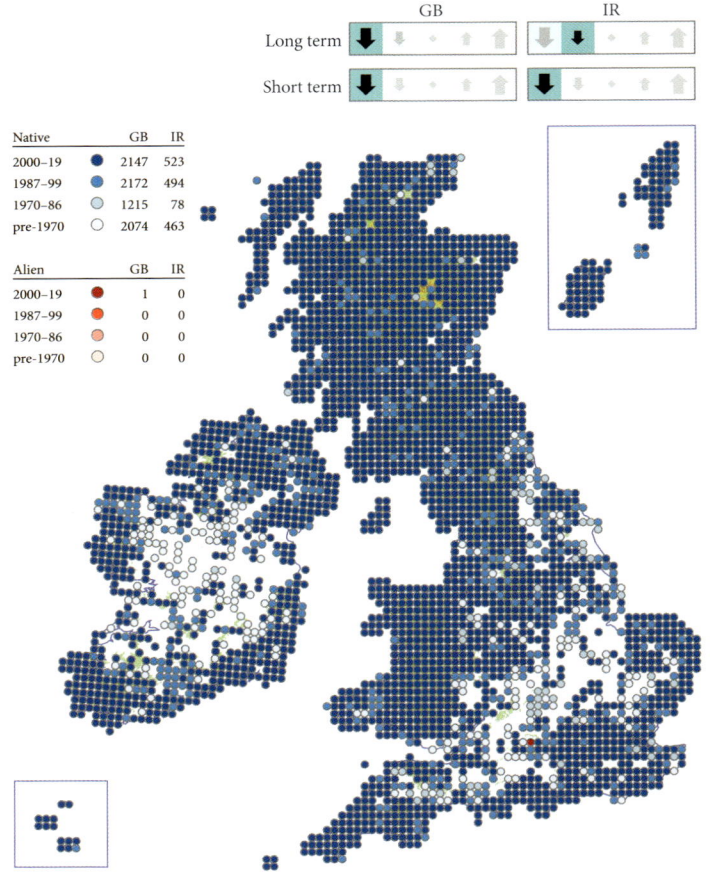

Native	GB	IR
2000–19	2147	523
1987–99	2172	494
1970–86	1215	78
pre-1970	2074	463

Alien	GB	IR
2000–19	1	0
1987–99	0	0
1970–86	0	0
pre-1970	0	0

Key refs Cope & Gray (2009), Grime *et al.* (2007), Rich & Woodruff (1990).

S.J. Leach & D.A. Pearman

N *Briza media* Quaking-grass
L.

A shortly rhizomatous perennial grass, most frequently found in unimproved, species-rich, well-grazed grassland on infertile, calcareous soils and favouring well-drained slopes. However, it also occurs in old meadows and pastures on neutral and sometimes acidic soils, in the drier parts of fens, and occasionally in soligenous mires and on roadbanks and tracksides in otherwise acidic habitats. 0–875 m (Ben Lawers, Mid Perthshire).

Trends There has been little change in the 10 km square distribution of *B. media* since the 1960s. However, more locally, the destruction, neglect or undergrazing of grasslands have led to localized losses and a decline in frequency in many areas, particularly in lowland regions of England. For example, in Kent there has been a 34% decline at the 2 km square resolution since the 1980s.

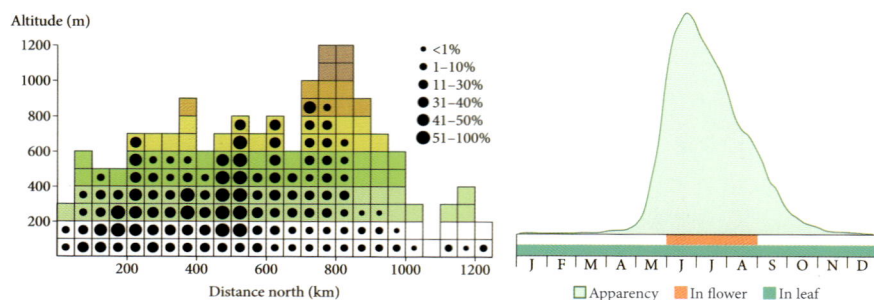

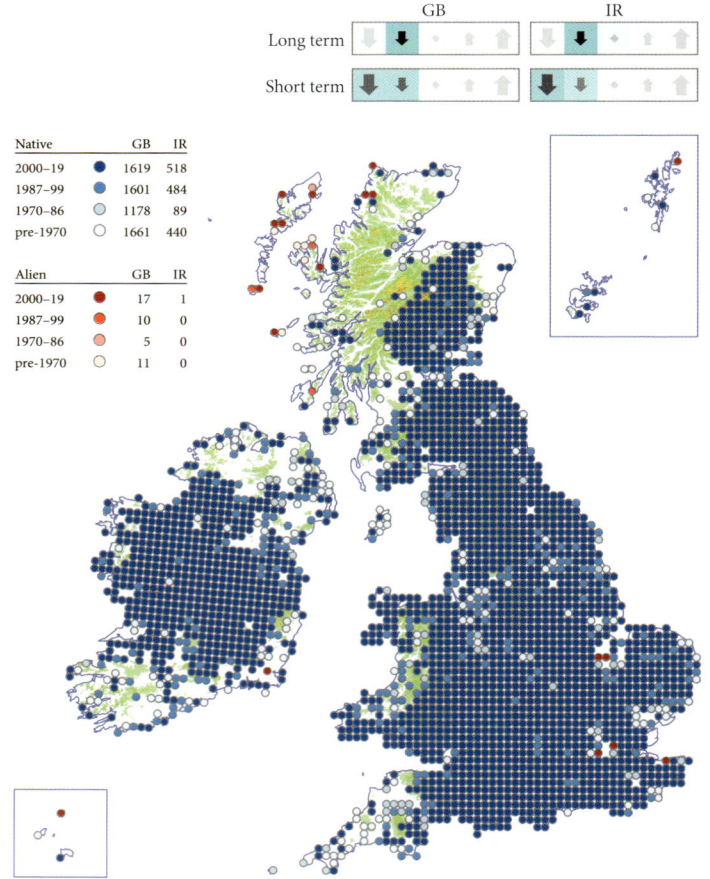

Biogeography European Temperate element.

Native	GB	IR
2000–19	1619	518
1987–99	1601	484
1970–86	1178	89
pre-1970	1661	440

Alien	GB	IR
2000–19	17	1
1987–99	10	0
1970–86	5	0
pre-1970	11	0

Key refs Cope & Gray (2009), Dixon (2002), Grime *et al.* (2007), Kitchener (2022).

D.A. Pearman

(Ar) *Briza minor* Lesser Quaking-grass
L.

An annual grass, found mainly on light, base-poor cultivated soils, including bulb-fields. It also occurs as a casual on roadsides, walls and, more rarely, on waste ground and refuse tips. Lowland.

An archaeophyte in Britain and the Channel Islands and a neophyte in Ireland.

Trends *B. minor* was first recorded from the wild in Britain in 1696 (Jersey). It is susceptible to herbicides and is unable to survive in highly fertilized crops, but persists in favourable, open habitats, such as on arable headlands under low intensity farming regimes. It is still frequent in Cornwall, especially in the Isles of Scilly, but continues to decline elsewhere.

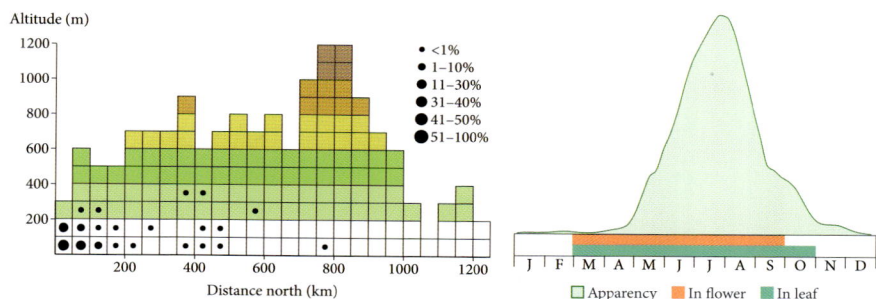

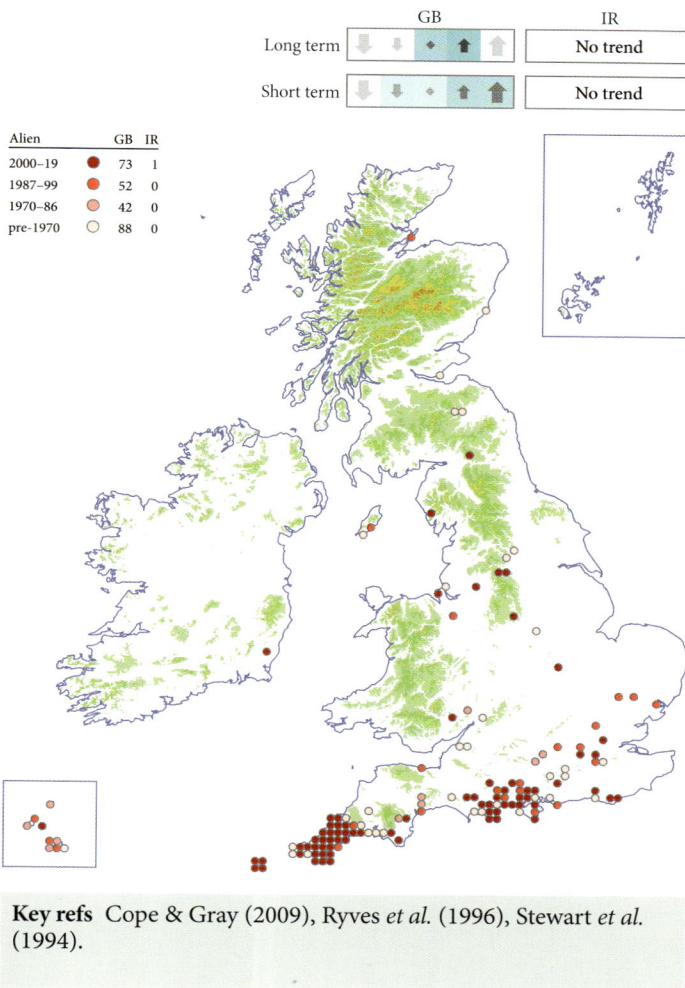

Biogeography A Mediterranean-Atlantic species. It was introduced with cultivation in the northern part of this range and is widely naturalized in warm-temperate regions throughout the world.

Alien	GB	IR
2000–19	73	1
1987–99	52	0
1970–86	42	0
pre-1970	88	0

Key refs Cope & Gray (2009), Ryves *et al.* (1996), Stewart *et al.* (1994).

D.A. PEARMAN

(Ne) *Briza maxima* Greater Quaking-grass
L.

An annual grass, naturalized or occurring casually on dry, bare banks and field margins, in cultivated ground including gardens, bulb-fields, on sand dunes, sea-cliffs, refuse tips, waste ground and wall-tops, and in pavement cracks. Lowland.

Trends *B. maxima* was grown in Britain by 1621 and first recorded in the wild in 1859 (Jersey). It is now very frequent in south-western England and the Channel Islands, and increasingly found elsewhere. Seeds germinate *en masse* very soon after dropping, and once established it is difficult to eradicate. It is frequently grown for ornamental purposes, and is increasing as a garden escape. It was also formerly introduced with wool shoddy and esparto.

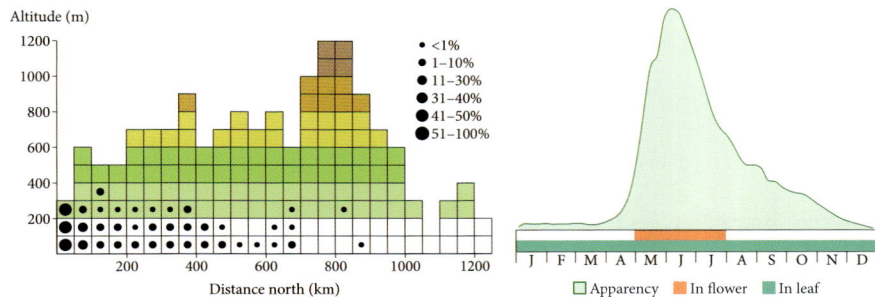

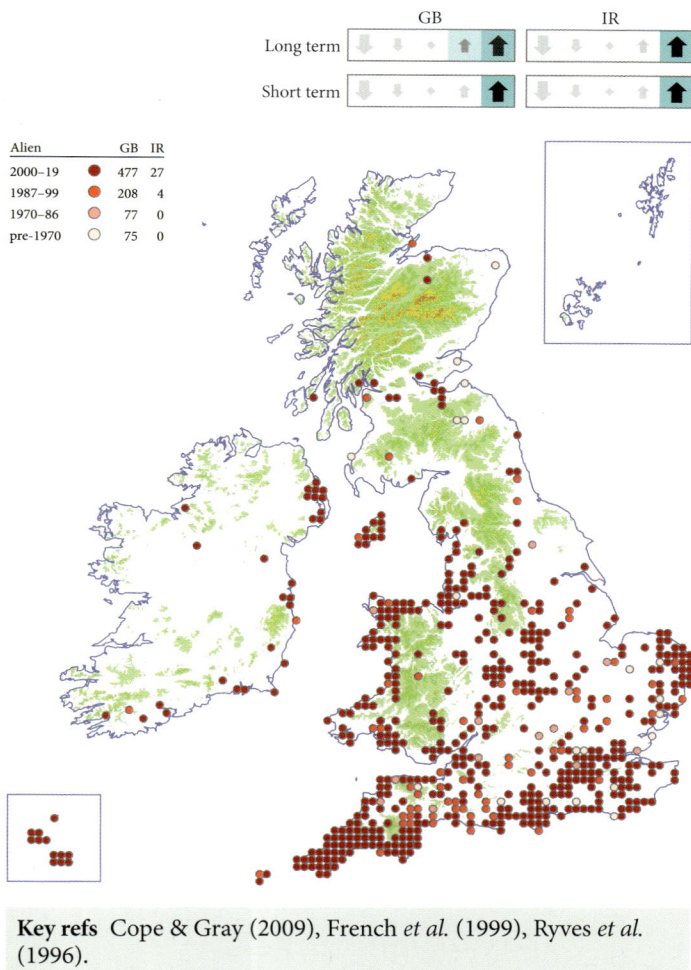

Biogeography Native of the Mediterranean region; widely naturalized in warm-temperate regions throughout the world.

Alien	GB	IR
2000–19	477	27
1987–99	208	4
1970–86	77	0
pre-1970	75	0

Key refs Cope & Gray (2009), French *et al.* (1999), Ryves *et al.* (1996).

S.J. LEACH & D.A. PEARMAN

N *Agrostis capillaris* Common Bent
L.

A rhizomatous, occasionally stoloniferous, perennial herb occurring mainly on dry or damp, neutral to moderately acidic soils; its habitats include lowland pastures, hay meadows, upland hill-pasture, heathlands, montane grass-heaths, open woodland and scrub, sand dunes and a range of ruderal habitats including soils contaminated by heavy metals. It is extensively sown as a lawn and amenity grass, on its own or with other species. 0–1,233 m (Aonach Beag, Westerness).

Trends There has been no appreciable change in the range of *A. capillaris* since the 1960s, save for a scattering of records this century in previously under-recorded areas of Scotland and Ireland.

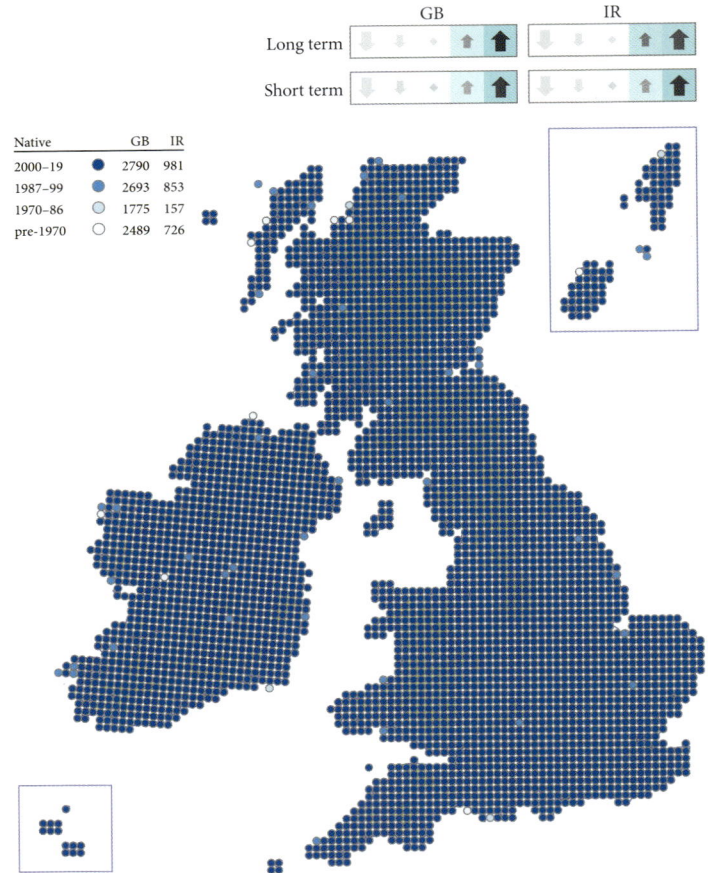

Biogeography Eurosiberian Boreo-temperate element; widely naturalized outside its native range.

Native		GB	IR
2000–19	●	2790	981
1987–99	●	2693	853
1970–86	◔	1775	157
pre-1970	○	2489	726

Key refs Cope & Gray (2009), Grime *et al.* (2007).

D.A. PEARMAN

Hy *Agrostis capillaris* × *stolonifera* = *A.* ×*murbeckii*
Fouill.

A naturally occurring hybrid between two of the commonest species of *Agrostis* in our area, potentially occurring wherever the two parents meet, particularly in damp neutral pastures, hay meadows on moist clay or alluvial soils, and in old acidic grassland. Hybrids appear better adapted to withstand grazing as they combine the spreading ability of *A. stolonifera* with the density of *A. capillaris*. Lowland.

A spontaneous hybrid (native × native).

Trends This hybrid was first mapped in Stace *et al.* (2015). The paucity of records is a graphic illustration of the under-recording of *Agrostis* hybrids.

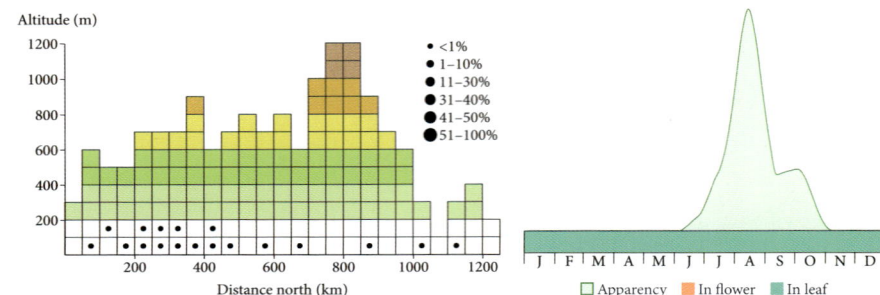

Biogeography Widespread in central and northern Europe. In eastern Fennoscandia it is primarily a coastal plant. It is also recorded from some areas (*e.g.* New Zealand) where both parents are introduced.

		GB	IR
2000–19	●	25	0
1987–99	●	16	0
1970–86	◐	18	0
pre-1970	○	34	0

	GB	IR
Long term	No trend	No trend
Short term	No trend	No trend

Key refs Stace *et al.* (2015).

C.A. STACE, C.D. PRESTON & D.A. PEARMAN

Ar *Agrostis gigantea* Black Bent
Roth

A rhizomatous perennial grass, mostly found in and around arable fields, in set-aside and other cultivated areas, especially where recently abandoned. Also along tracks and ditches and in ploughed fields and damp pastures, on waste ground, pavements and along active and disused railways. *A. gigantea* spreads by seeds and by rhizomes. Lowland, but reaching c. 400 m at Nantypyllau and elsewhere in Clun Forest (Shropshire).

Trends *A. gigantea* may have been overlooked in the past, or confused with *A. stolonifera*. Despite being vulnerable to herbicides, the species' distribution appears to have been relatively stable since the 1960s, although it is almost certainly still under-recorded.

Biogeography As an archaeophyte, *A. gigantea* has a Eurasian Southern-temperate distribution, but it is naturalized in North America so its distribution is now Circumpolar Southern-temperate.

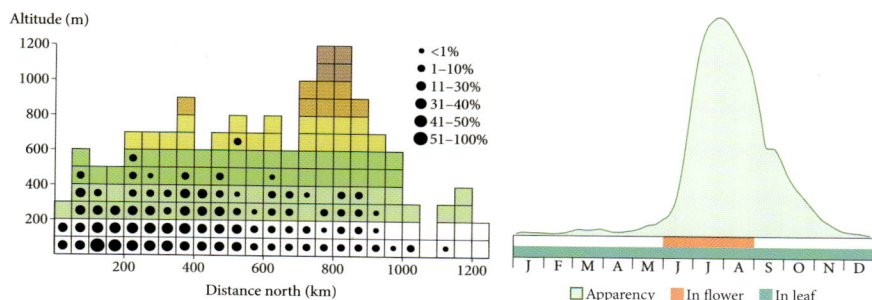

Alien	GB	IR
2000–19	1361	125
1987–99	1299	81
1970–86	832	14
pre-1970	906	28

Key refs Cope & Gray (2009).

D.A. PEARMAN & K.J. WALKER

Ne *Agrostis castellana* Highland Bent
Boiss. & Reut.

A shortly rhizomatous perennial of roadsides, amenity grassland, temporary leys and cultivated land. It is often sown in grass-seed as a cheap substitute for *A. capillaris*, and in wild-flower mixtures, and was formerly introduced in wool shoddy. Lowland.

Trends This species was first recorded in Britain, as a casual, in 1924 (Clifton, West Gloucestershire). It is not known when it was first imported as an intentional constituent of grass-seed mixtures but it has certainly been sown in many locations, sometimes as part of habitat creation schemes. Its distribution is uncertain and it may be under-recorded in some areas (Stace, 2019) or over-recorded in others (Cope & Gray, 2009), possibly for the hybrid with *A. capillaris* which is reported to be a common constituent of amenity

plantings. The only record from Ireland is from County Limerick in 2007.

Biogeography Native of the Mediterranean region.

Alien	GB	IR
2000–19	87	1
1987–99	62	0
1970–86	17	0
pre-1970	8	0

Key refs Cope & Gray (2009), Ryves *et al.* (1996).

D.A. PEARMAN & K.J. WALKER

1391

Agrostis stolonifera Creeping Bent
L.

A stoloniferous perennial grass, found in a wide variety of habitats due to its wide tolerance of soil moisture, fertility, salinity and reaction. It occurs in permanent grassland (including inundation and brackish communities), in upper saltmarsh and dune-slacks, on sand dunes and sandy flats, on cliffs and in mires, springs, flushes and ditches. It also grows on spoil heaps and a wide range of open and disturbed habitats, and is a weed in arable sites. 0–1,169 m (Ben Nevis, Westerness).

Trends There has been no appreciable change in the distribution of *A. stolonifera* since the 1960s. It is very variable in form, and distinct ecotypes have evolved in response to newly available habitats.

Biogeography Circumpolar Wide-temperate element; widely naturalized outside its native range.

Native	GB	IR
2000–19	2820	994
1987–99	2760	950
1970–86	1949	277
pre-1970	2355	745

Key refs Cope & Gray (2009), Grime *et al.* (2007).

D.A. PEARMAN

Agrostis curtisii Bristle Bent
Kerguélen

A tufted perennial grass of the drier parts of infertile, sandy and peaty lowland heathlands, especially those with impeded drainage, occasionally extending to more consistently waterlogged ground. In closed communities it occurs as scattered plants, but it can seed prolifically into burnt or disturbed ground and rapidly form an almost continuous cover. It also occurs in open acidic woodland over gravel and sand. Generally lowland, but reaching 615 m on High Willhays, Dartmoor (South Devon).

Trends Since the 1960s *A. curtisii* has been lost from a few 10 km squares on the margins of its range due to habitat destruction. However, these losses have been compensated to some extent by its ability to colonize open ground rapidly, for example following disturbances to heathlands and moorlands such as fire and following the removal of pine plantations on former heathlands where it re-colonized from long-buried seed banks (Pywell *et al.*, 2002). New populations discovered in Oxfordshire this century may have been introduced from Berkshire on machinery.

Biogeography Oceanic Southern-temperate element.

Native	GB	IR
2000–19	173	0
1987–99	177	0
1970–86	135	0
pre-1970	181	0

Key refs Cope & Gray (2009), Dupont (1962), Erskine *et al.* (2018), Ivimey-Cook (1959), Pywell *et al.* (2002).

D.A. PEARMAN

N *Agrostis canina* Velvet Bent

L.

A stoloniferous, perennial grass of wet, infertile, acidic (often peaty) soils in marshy grasslands, rush-pastures, fens, mires, heathlands, fen-meadows, springs and soakaways, swamps and water margins. It may exploit vegetation gaps or act as a dominant. It spreads by seed and by stolon fragments. 0–1,035 m (Macgillycuddy's Reeks, South Kerry) and possibly higher in Glencoe (Main Argyll).

Trends The map of *A. canina s.l.* in the 1962 *Atlas* included *A. canina s.s.* and *A. vinealis*. Although these taxa have long been recognized at varietal or subspecific rank, they have only recently been treated as species (Clapham *et al.*, 1987). The distribution of *A. canina s.s.* is now much better understood, especially in southern Ireland, but it is still under-recorded in areas for which only records of the aggregate are available. Its distribution in northern Scotland remains unclear, with some grass experts even suggesting that it may be absent north of Inverness. Its overall distribution appears stable although it has suffered localized declines in southern England, presumably due to the drainage of wetland habitats.

Biogeography Circumpolar Boreo-temperate element, with a disjunct distribution.

Native	GB	IR
2000–19	1893	682
1987–99	1686	417
1970–86	724	58
pre-1970	383	32

Key refs Cope & Gray (2009), Grime *et al.* (2007).

D.A. Pearman

N *Agrostis vinealis* Brown Bent

Schreb.

A shortly rhizomatous perennial grass, mainly of dry or free-draining, acidic, sandy or peaty soils in upland and montane regions including heathlands, acidic grassland, open woodland and plantations (especially those dominated by birch, pine and oak), woodland clearings and on rides and montane rock outcrops. It is much less widespread in the lowlands. On some lowland heaths *A. vinealis* may grow in damp situations, but unlike *A. canina* it avoids waterlogged soils. It is also widely sown as a drought-resistant lawn grass. 0–845 m (Little Dun Fell, Westmorland) and 1,100 m on Aonach Mor (Westerness).

Trends Until fairly recently (Clapham *et al.*, 1987) this species was treated as a variety or subspecies of *A. canina*; though it is now much better recorded across Britain and Ireland, it remains under-recorded in many areas and so the mapped distribution should be treated as provisional.

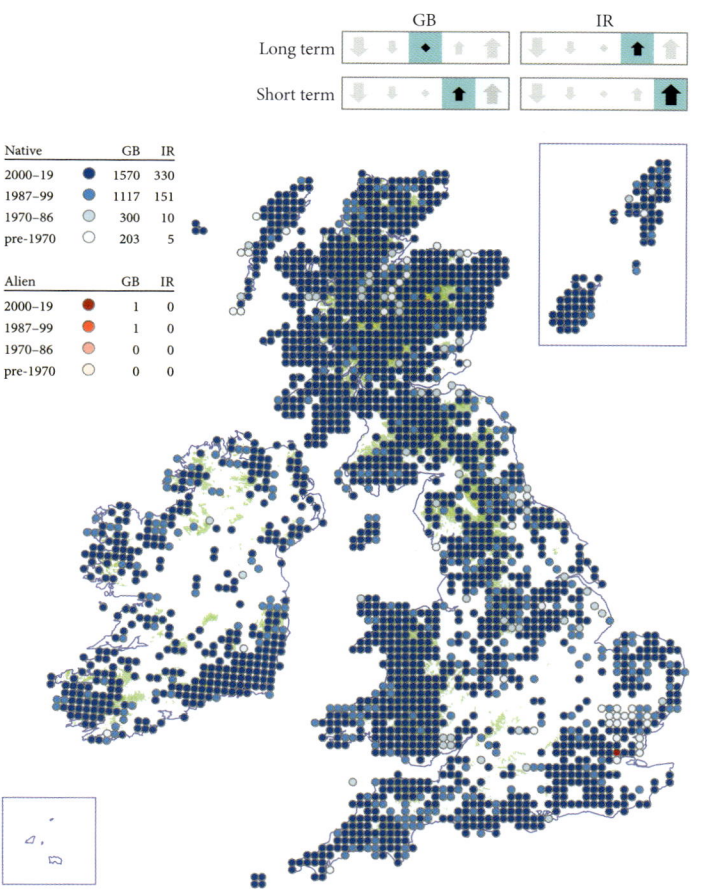

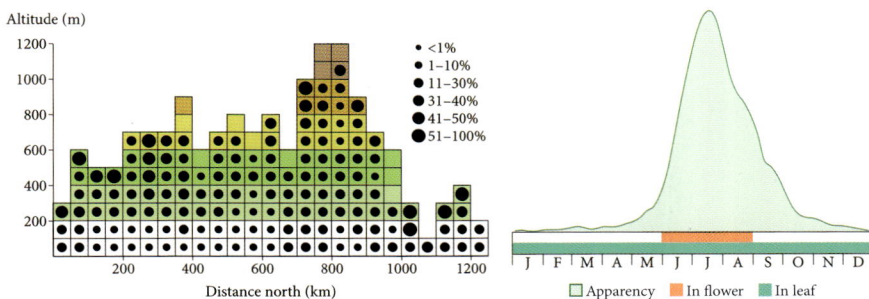

Biogeography European Temperate element; also in North America.

Native	GB	IR
2000–19	1570	330
1987–99	1117	151
1970–86	300	10
pre-1970	203	5

Alien	GB	IR
2000–19	1	0
1987–99	1	0
1970–86	0	0
pre-1970	0	0

Key refs Cope & Gray (2009), Grime *et al.* (2007).

D.A. Pearman & K.J. Walker

N *Calamagrostis epigejos* Wood Small-reed
(L.) Roth

A tufted rhizomatous perennial grass, occurring in damp woods, ditches, fens, ungrazed or lightly grazed grasslands, and on sheltered sea-cliffs and sand dunes; also as a colonist of artificial habitats such as old quarries, roadsides, railway banks and brownfield sites. It usually grows on light sands or heavy clays. 0–455 m (Mar Forest, South Aberdeenshire).

Trends *C. epigejos* has increased its range since the 1960s. Counties in which local Floras recorded it rarely in the past now find it frequently, and report too that it has become more invasive locally. Such spread, and at some sites dominance, is in many areas likely to be linked to a relaxation of grazing or cutting, possibly in combination with the effects of increased atmospheric deposition of nitrogen from anthropogenic sources (*e.g.* vehicles, livestock, fertilizers).

Biogeography Eurasian Boreo-temperate element.

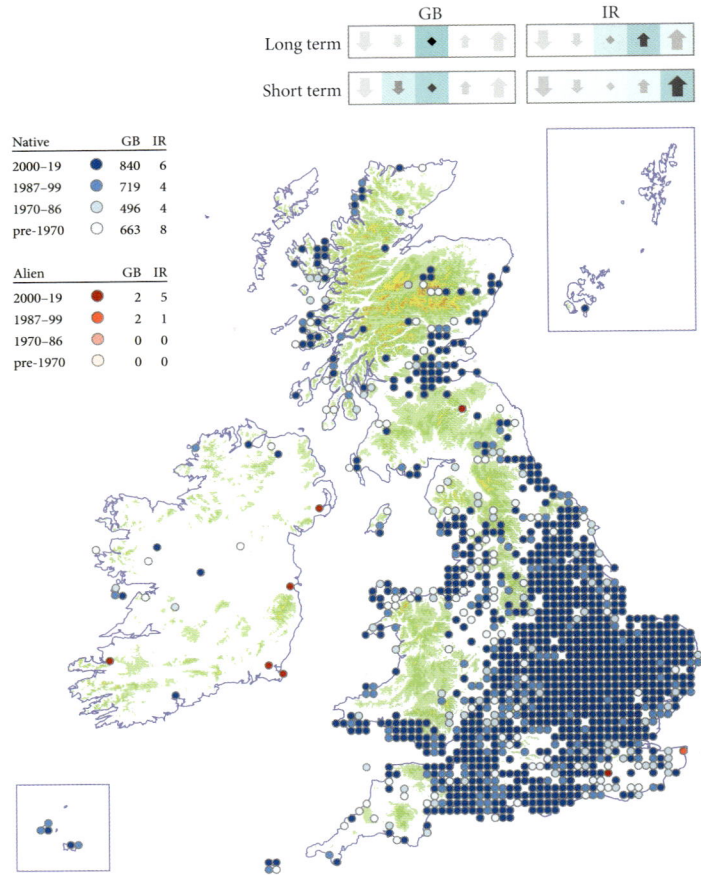

Native	GB	IR
2000–19	840	6
1987–99	719	4
1970–86	496	4
pre-1970	663	8

Alien	GB	IR
2000–19	2	5
1987–99	2	1
1970–86	0	0
pre-1970	0	0

Key refs Cope & Gray (2009), Holub *et al.* (2012), Rebele & Lehmann (2001).

S.J. LEACH & D.A. PEARMAN

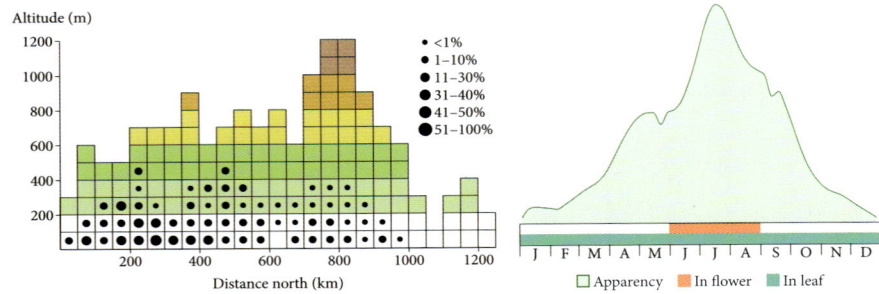

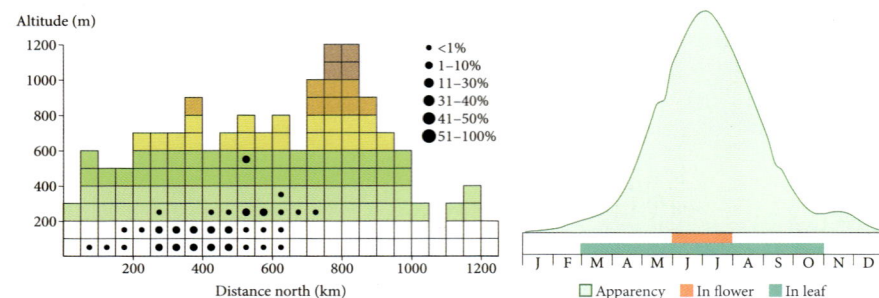

N *Calamagrostis canescens* Purple Small-reed
(F.H.Wigg.) Roth

A perennial grass of lakeside marshes, fen-meadows, tall-herb fens, alder- or willow-carr, and rides and clearings in damp woodland, often in species-rich vegetation and sometimes forming extensive stands. Generally lowland, but reaching 335 m on Malham Moor (Mid-west Yorkshire).

Trends The retreat of *C. canescens* from its peripheral localities was apparent by the 1960s, and has continued in some areas, though in general its rate of decline appears to have slowed in recent decades. Even within its core range, succession and falling water tables may be reducing the extent of wetland habitats available for this species. On the other hand, all records in the Scottish Borders have been made since 1962 and this suggests that it may continue to be overlooked in other areas.

Biogeography Eurosiberian Boreo-temperate element, with a continental distribution in western Europe.

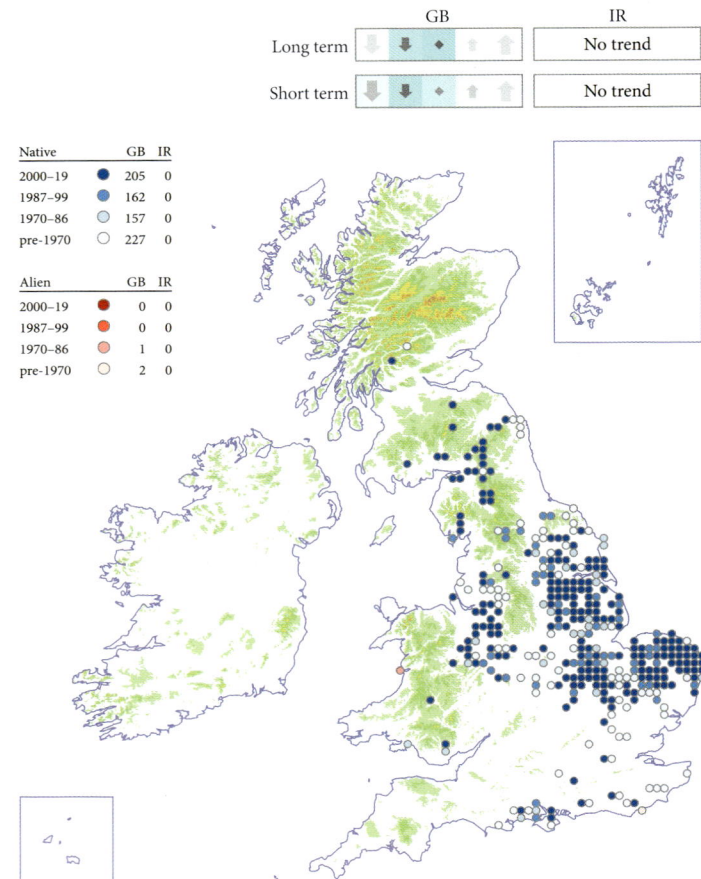

Native	GB	IR
2000–19	205	0
1987–99	162	0
1970–86	157	0
pre-1970	227	0

Alien	GB	IR
2000–19	0	0
1987–99	0	0
1970–86	1	0
pre-1970	2	0

Key refs Cope & Gray (2009).

S.J. LEACH & D.A. PEARMAN

Calamagrostis purpurea Scandinavian Small-reed
(Trin.) Trin.

	GB	IR
Long term	No trend	No trend
Short term	No trend	No trend

An apomictic rhizomatous perennial grass of wet willow-carr, especially in areas that are flooded in winter, usually forming large and dominant stands. It also occurs in marshes, ditches and old peat diggings. Generally lowland, but reaching 340 m at Braemar (South Aberdeenshire) and possibly higher elsewhere.

Trends The presence of this taxon in Britain was not recognized until 1980, although it had been collected before that date (such as from near Braemar, South Aberdeen, in 1941). It may still be under-recorded, and though no new sites have been found in Britain since 2000, it was discovered, new to Ireland, in County Meath in 2018.

Biogeography Eurosiberian Boreal-montane element.

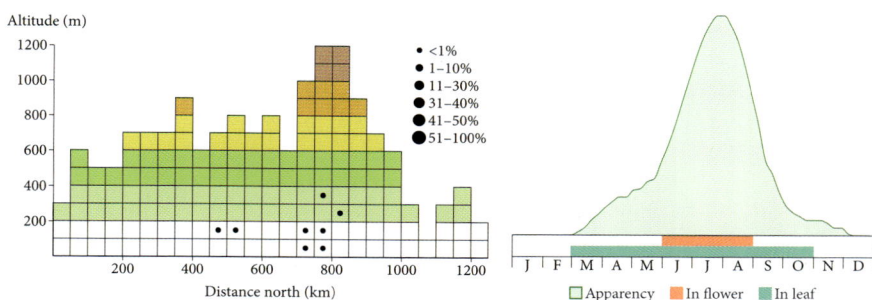

Native	GB	IR
2000–19	9	2
1987–99	9	0
1970–86	7	0
pre-1970	4	0

Key refs Cope & Gray (2009), Norton & Roberts (2020).

S.J. Leach & D.A. Pearman

Calamagrostis stricta Narrow Small-reed
(Timm) Koeler

	GB		IR
Long term			No trend
Short term			No trend

A tufted rhizomatous perennial grass of near-neutral mires and lake margins, often forming stands that are locally dominant. 0–380 m (Malham, Mid-west Yorkshire).

Trends It is hard to assess trends in the distribution of *C. stricta* as it has been confused in the past with *C. scotica*, *C. purpurea* and hybrids of *C. canescens* (including *C. canescens* × *C. stricta*). It has certainly been lost from some lowland sites through drainage, and is less common now in the Breckland region of East Anglia, in eastern Yorkshire and around Lough Neagh in Northern Ireland. It is easily overlooked and may still be present in several upland squares for which there are no records this century. Tellingly, it has been found in three new areas since 2000 – in Peeblesshire, Mid Perthshire and Easterness – and at a new site in Caithness, due to more systematic recording. Some plants in north-eastern Scotland appear to be intermediate with the closely related *C. scotica*, suggesting that hybridization or introgression has occurred there in the past.

Biogeography Circumpolar Boreo-arctic Montane element.

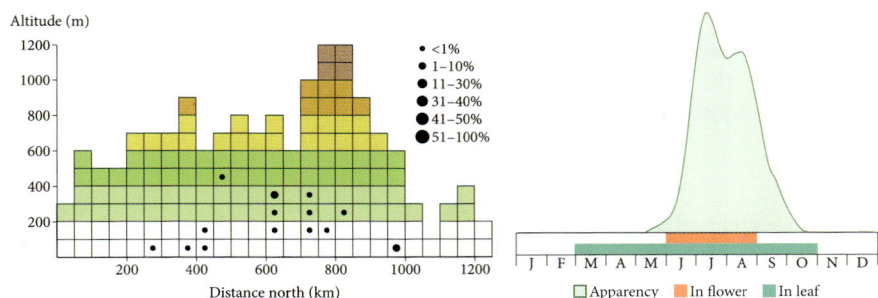

Native	GB	IR
2000–19	15	1
1987–99	12	1
1970–86	15	4
pre-1970	21	5

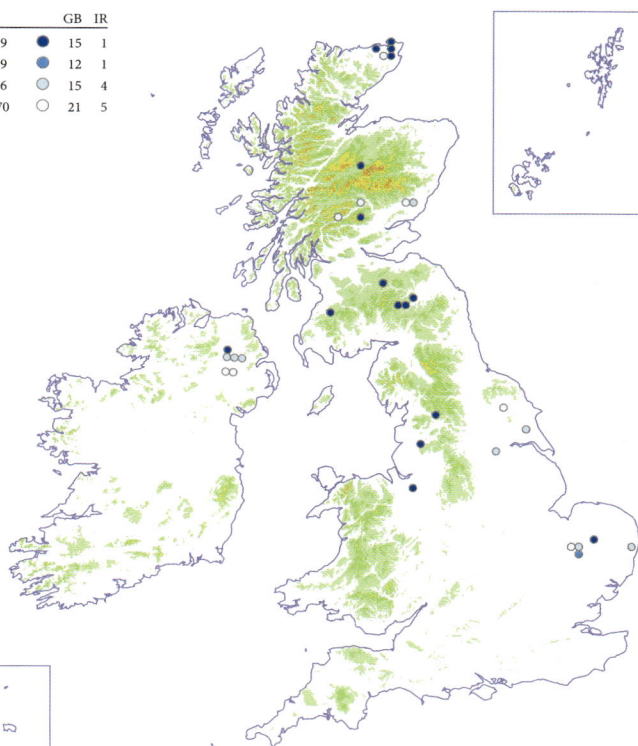

Key refs Cope & Gray (2009), Crackles (1995), Crackles (1997), Stewart *et al.* (1994), Strachan (2019), Wigginton (1999).

S.J. Leach, K.J. Walker & D.A. Pearman

Ⓝ *Calamagrostis scotica* Scottish Small-reed
(Druce) Druce

A tufted rhizomatous perennial grass, restricted to a single drained loch basin, where it occurs amongst *Juncus*-dominated pasture, along drainage channels and in willow-carr and tall-herb fen, that are all usually flooded during the winter months. Lowland.

Trends This taxon was not mapped separately in the 1962 *Atlas*, being grouped with *C. stricta* as *C. neglecta* agg. It has been known from Loch of Durran (Caithness) since 1863 and, despite the loch being drained in the 1870s and recent changes in management, the population seems relatively stable, at around 4,000 culms across six hectares (Strachan, 2019). Reports of *C. scotica* occurring elsewhere in northern Scotland and in Roxburghshire have never been substantiated and may reflect past hybridization and introgression with the very closely related *C. stricta*.

Biogeography Endemic.

	GB	IR
Long term	No trend	No trend
Short term	No trend	No trend

Native		GB	IR
2000–19	●	1	0
1987–99	●	1	0
1970–86	○	1	0
pre-1970	○	1	0

Key refs Cope & Gray (2009), Foley & Porter (2006), Strachan (2019), Wigginton (1999).

S.J. Leach, K.J. Walker & D.A. Pearman

Ⓝ *Ammophila arenaria* Marram
(L.) Link

A rhizomatous perennial grass of coastal sand dunes where it is a key species, stabilizing mobile dunes and blow-outs. It is widely planted as a sand binder on the coast. Inland, it is a rare casual, although several attempts have been made in recent years to establish it on golf courses and on an army range. Lowland.

Trends There is no evidence of appreciable change in the 10 km square distribution of *A. arenaria* over the last 60 years. There have been some local losses, but introductions inland and the widespread planting on eroding dunes have had little impact on its overall distribution.

Biogeography European Southern-temperate element; widely naturalized outside its native range.

	GB	IR
Long term		
Short term		

Native		GB	IR
2000–19	●	494	163
1987–99	●	471	150
1970–86	○	281	33
pre-1970	○	446	104

Alien		GB	IR
2000–19	●	9	0
1987–99	●	7	1
1970–86	●	7	1
pre-1970	○	6	0

Key refs Cope & Gray (2009), Huiskes (1979).

S.J. Leach & D.A. Pearman

N? *Gastridium ventricosum* Nit-grass

(Gouan) Schinz & Thell.

A winter-annual grass of well-drained grasslands on calcareous soils, especially on shallow soils on south-facing slopes where the turf is broken by patches of crumbling soil. It used to be a locally frequent weed of cornfields, and is an occasional wool and grain casual. Lowland.

Trends *G. ventricosum* was first recorded in 1688 (Tunbridge Wells, West Kent) and is possibly only native in semi-natural grassland in the Channel Islands and in south-western Britain, where it has been found to be much more widespread than shown in the 1962 *Atlas*. Formerly it was regarded as an arable weed, but it had largely vanished from cultivated ground by 1930 and now just hangs on in this habitat in one area of South Hampshire. The current distribution appears stable. As habitat details are not available for many old records, they are mapped as if they were native.

Biogeography Mediterranean-Atlantic element.

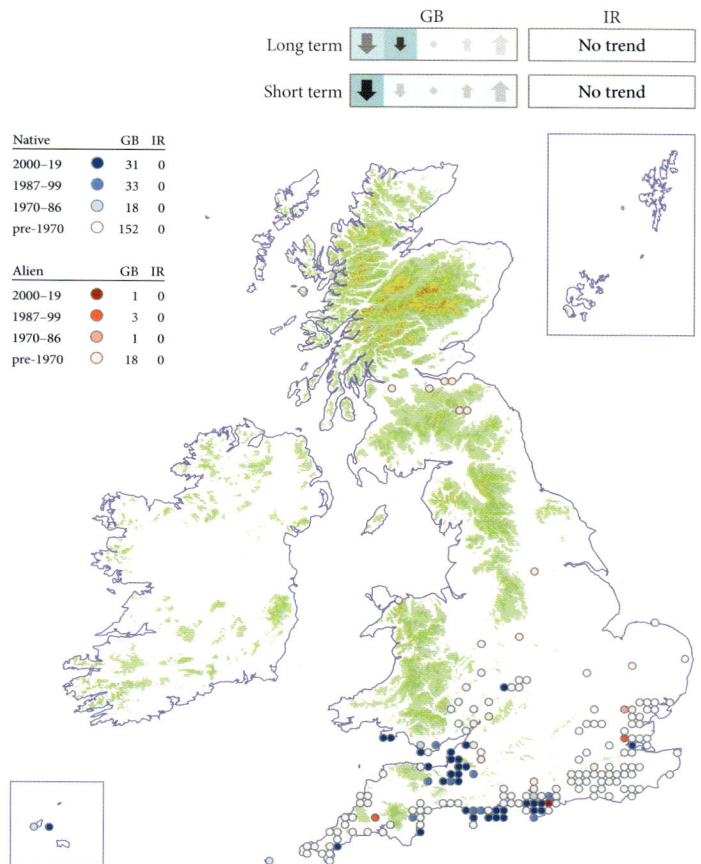

Native	GB	IR
2000–19	31	0
1987–99	33	0
1970–86	18	0
pre-1970	152	0

Alien	GB	IR
2000–19	1	0
1987–99	3	0
1970–86	1	0
pre-1970	18	0

Key refs Cope & Gray (2009), Ryves *et al.* (1996), Trist (1986), Wigginton (1999).

S.J. Leach & D.A. Pearman

Ne *Polypogon viridis* Water Bent

(Gouan) Breistr.

An annual or perennial grass of wall-bases, pavements, gravel drives, roadsides and waste ground; commonly occurring as a persistent weed in nurseries and garden centres, and now a very familiar alien in many urban centres. Generally lowland, but reaching 520 m by a roadside over Axe Edge Moor (Derbyshire).

Trends *P. viridis* was first noted in the wild in St Sampson, Guernsey, in 1860. It was recorded in Jersey in 1906, and for a long while the Channel Islands was considered to be its stronghold in our area. Its 10 km square distribution increased only gradually during the 20th century, with a first record for Ireland in 1998. Its subsequent spread has been remarkable, starting mainly in south-western England and moving northwards. It now ranks as one of the most rapidly increasing aliens in our area, with a 10 km square distribution increasing 15-fold in just 20 years. Although it is possible that this grass and its urban habitats were somewhat under-recorded in past decades, the main factors in the considerable increase of records and range this century would seem to be associated with human-mediated dispersal in building material and on vehicles, its long flowering period and dispersal potential once established in a locality, and more favourable environmental conditions for persistence as a consequence of milder winters.

Biogeography Native of southern Europe, south-western and central Asia and northern Africa; widely naturalized elsewhere.

Alien	GB	IR
2000–19	865	81
1987–99	75	1
1970–86	22	0
pre-1970	31	0

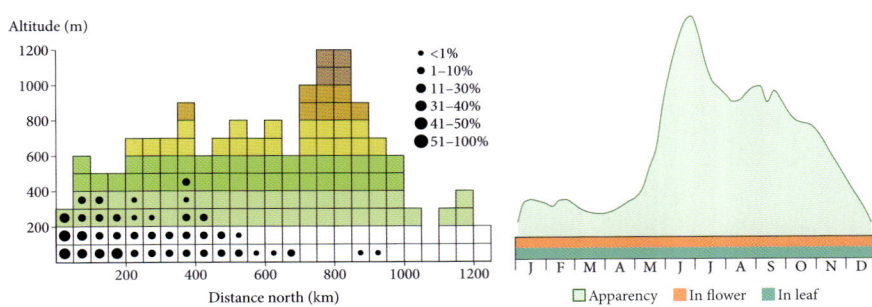

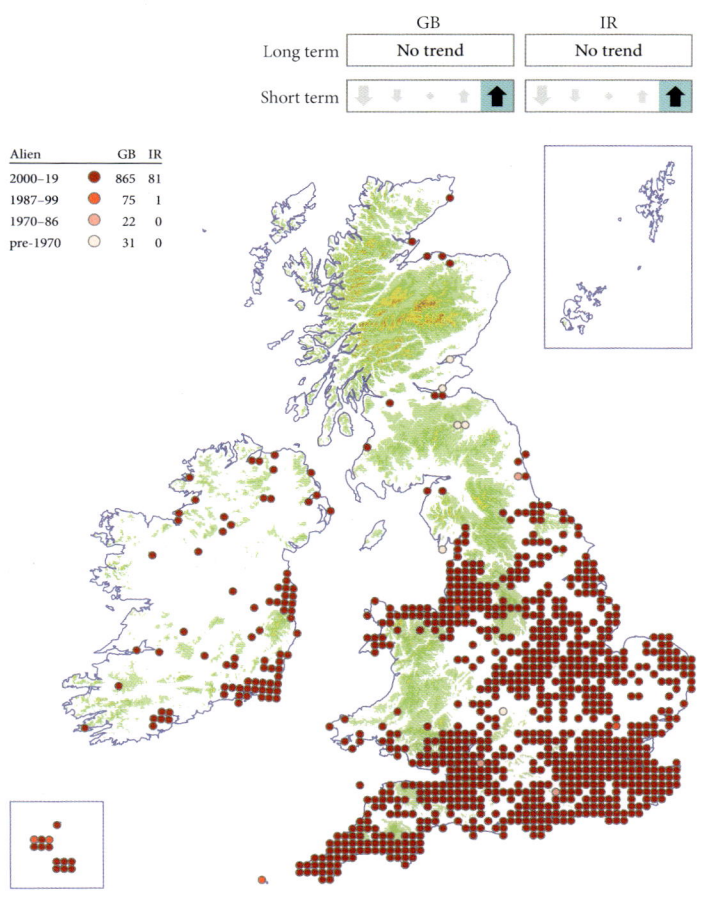

Key refs Baker & Pescott (2014), Cope & Gray (2009), Le Sueur (1984), McClintock (1975), McClintock (1987).

S.J. Leach & D.A. Pearman

N *Polypogon monspeliensis* Annual Beard-grass
(L.) Desf.

A native annual grass of barish places by the sea, in damp, cattle-trodden grazing marshes, at the edges of dried-up brackish pools and ditches, and in the uppermost parts of saltmarshes. It is also found around docks and inland as an introduction from birdseed and grass-seed, and formerly from wool shoddy when used as an agricultural fertilizer. Seeds may also be dispersed by birds and vehicles. Lowland.

Native in Britain and a neophyte in Ireland and the Channel Islands.

Trends The native distribution of *P. monspeliensis* is assumed to be broadly similar to that mapped in the 2002 *Atlas*, although the very substantial increase inland this century has greatly obscured the distinction between native and alien occurrences. New populations seem to be almost entirely ruderal (*e.g.* found in waste ground, railway lines, quarries,

newly constructed habitats, *etc.*), and we have chosen to map all such occurrences as introductions, though plants found on salted roadsides with other halophytes could conceivably represent an extension of the native range. Pond and ditch infilling, and the drainage and conversion of coastal marshes to arable, have led to declines in native populations in some areas, although those along the Thames estuary and Dungeness (West and East Kent respectively) have increased in recent decades, perhaps due to disturbance of the long-lived seed bank following cattle grazing, ditch clearance and the construction of new sea-walls (Kitchener, 2021).

Biogeography Mediterranean-Atlantic element; widely naturalized outside its native range.

Native	GB	IR
2000–19	51	0
1987–99	30	0
1970–86	20	0
pre-1970	31	0

Alien	GB	IR
2000–19	359	14
1987–99	67	0
1970–86	35	0
pre-1970	98	5

Key refs Cope & Gray (2009), Kitchener (2022), Stewart *et al.* (1994).

S.J. Leach, D.A. Pearman & P.A. Stroh

Altitude (m) — histogram with point-size key: <1%, 1–10%, 11–30%, 31–40%, 41–50%, 51–100%. Distance north (km).

Apparency / In flower / In leaf (J F M A M J J A S O N D)

N *Milium effusum* Wood Millet
L.

An evergreen perennial grass of damp, deciduous woods and shaded banks, where it grows on winter-wet, calcareous to mildly acidic clay and loam soils, and also over rocks in western Scotland. It is regarded as an indicator of ancient woodland in some parts of eastern England. However, it is able to colonize open sites which are disturbed by felling or fire, and there is evidence of spread to more recent secondary woodland in some upland areas. 0–380 m (west of Dockray, Cumberland).

Trends This species was mapped as 'all records' in the 1962 *Atlas*. It is quite an inconspicuous species with a relatively dynamic life-cycle tied to disturbance events (*e.g.* tree-falls, clear-felling, *etc.*); there have beeen many new discoveries since the 1960s, presumably as a result of more systematic recording.

Biogeography Circumpolar Boreo-temperate element, with a disjunct distribution.

Native	GB	IR
2000–19	1199	64
1987–99	1159	45
1970–86	812	19
pre-1970	1017	46

Alien	GB	IR
2000–19	8	0
1987–99	4	0
1970–86	0	0
pre-1970	3	0

Key refs Cope & Gray (2009), De Frenne *et al.* (2017), Grime *et al.* (2007).

F.H. Perring & D.A. Pearman

Altitude (m) — histogram with point-size key: <1%, 1–10%, 11–30%, 31–40%, 41–50%, 51–100%. Distance north (km).

Apparency / In flower / In leaf (J F M A M J J A S O N D)

(N) *Milium vernale* Early Millet
M.Bieb.

An inconspicuous, early flowering, annual grass growing in small patches in the short, nearly closed turf of fixed sand dunes. Lowland.

Trends This species is restricted to two localities on the north coast of Guernsey (Channel Islands), where it was first recorded in 1899 but then remained unrecorded for 50 years. The Guernsey plant is a genetically distinct, prostrate form which was described as subsp. *sarniense* by McClintock (1986).

Biogeography Mediterranean-Atlantic element; it reaches its northern limit on the island of Terschelling, Netherlands.

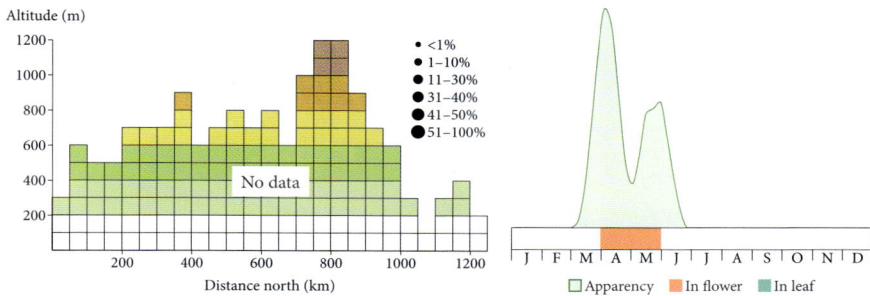

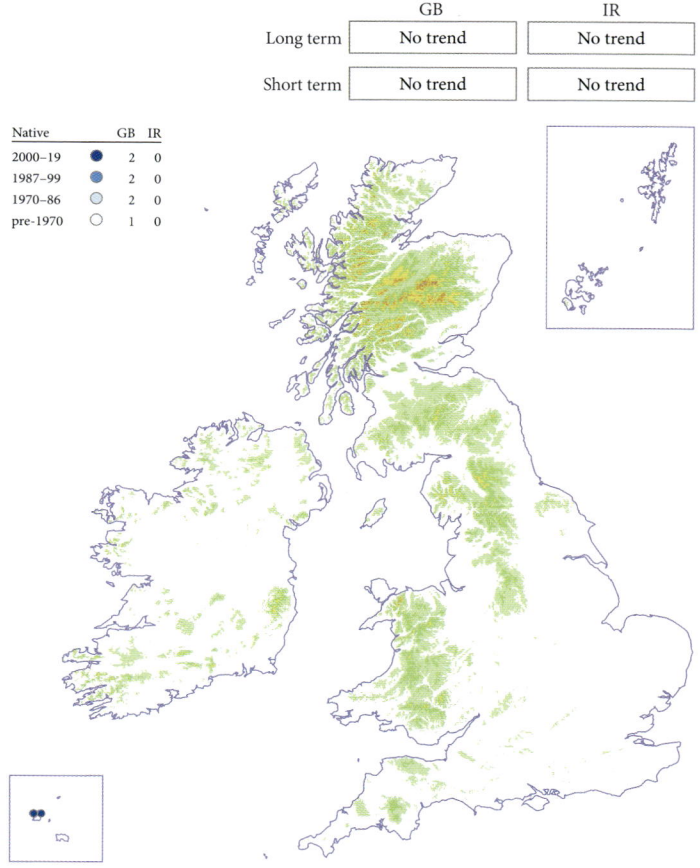

	GB	IR
Long term	No trend	No trend
Short term	No trend	No trend

Native	GB	IR
2000–19	2	0
1987–99	2	0
1970–86	2	0
pre-1970	1	0

Key refs Cope & Gray (2009), McClintock (1975), McClintock (1986), Tutin (1950).

F.H. PERRING & D.A. PEARMAN

(Ar) *Apera spica-venti* Loose Silky-bent
(L.) P.Beauv.

An annual herb of open habitats, mostly on the margins of arable fields, where it can be a troublesome weed, but also in ruderal habitats, such as sandy tracks, old sand- and gravel-pits, refuse tips, railway sidings, roadsides and pavements. Lowland, but casual at 690 m on Ingleborough (Mid-west Yorkshire) where it was introduced during footpath maintenance.

An archaeophyte in Britain and the Channel Islands and a neophyte in Ireland.

Trends *A. spica-venti* has been treated as a native by some authors, but its artificial habitat and the transient nature of its populations suggests that it is an ancient introduction. It appears to be slowly declining in arable habitats due the increased use of herbicides. It was grown in the London area in the early 19th century as an ornamental grass for drying.

Biogeography As an archaeophyte *A. spica-venti* has a Eurosiberian Boreo-temperate distribution; it is widely naturalized outside this range.

	GB	IR
Long term		No trend
Short term		No trend

Alien	GB	IR
2000–19	134	2
1987–99	155	1
1970–86	141	0
pre-1970	240	0

Key refs Cope & Gray (2009), Stewart *et al.* (1994), Warwick *et al.* (1985).

D.A. PEARMAN & K.J. WALKER

Ne *Apera interrupta* Dense Silky-bent
(L.) P.Beauv.

An annual herb, mainly found on the margins of dry, sandy arable fields, but also recorded from the disturbed edges of tracks and roads, disused railways and in old sand- and gravel-pits and abandoned quarries. It has a more permanent niche in some tightly grazed grassy or grass-heath habitats. It occurs in waste ground as a casual from imported aggregates, and as a seed impurity. Lowland.

Trends The core distribution of *A. interrupta*, which was first recorded in the wild in 1843 (Marks Tey, North Essex), seems to be stable although there have been losses due to intensification of arable cropping in many areas. However, its seed is long-lived and as a consequence it remains locally abundant, especially on the very dry, infertile soils of East Anglia.

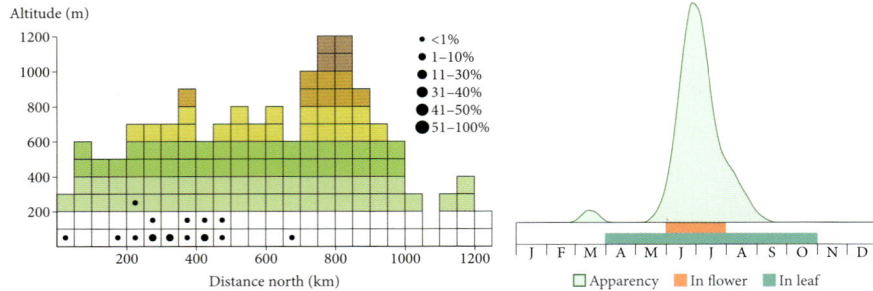

Biogeography A Eurosiberian Southern-temperate species.

Alien	GB	IR
2000–19	41	0
1987–99	65	0
1970–86	54	0
pre-1970	53	0

Key refs Cope & Gray (2009), Stewart *et al.* (1994).

D.A. Pearman & K.J. Walker

N *Alopecurus pratensis* Meadow Foxtail
L.

A tufted perennial herb of a wide range of grasslands, particularly those with moist, fertile soils. It also occurs on roadsides and woodland margins. It avoids waterlogged habitats, and is absent from light and dry soils, including arable fields. Generally lowland, but reaching 675 m on Ousby Fell (Cumberland) and exceptionally at 845 m on Great Dun Fell (Westmorland).

Trends *A. pratensis* was frequently sown in seed mixtures up to the 1950s. Many local strains still occur, particularly in pastures that have not been re-sown recently. In recent years it has become a regular component of wild-flower seed mixtures used for the creation of meadows in lowland areas. Its 10 km square distribution appears to be stable and it is now better recorded in Scotland and Ireland due to more systematic surveys.

Biogeography Eurosiberian Boreo-temperate element, but widely naturalized so that distribution is now Circumpolar Boreo-temperate.

Native	GB	IR
2000–19	2374	792
1987–99	2247	674
1970–86	1409	92
pre-1970	2096	420

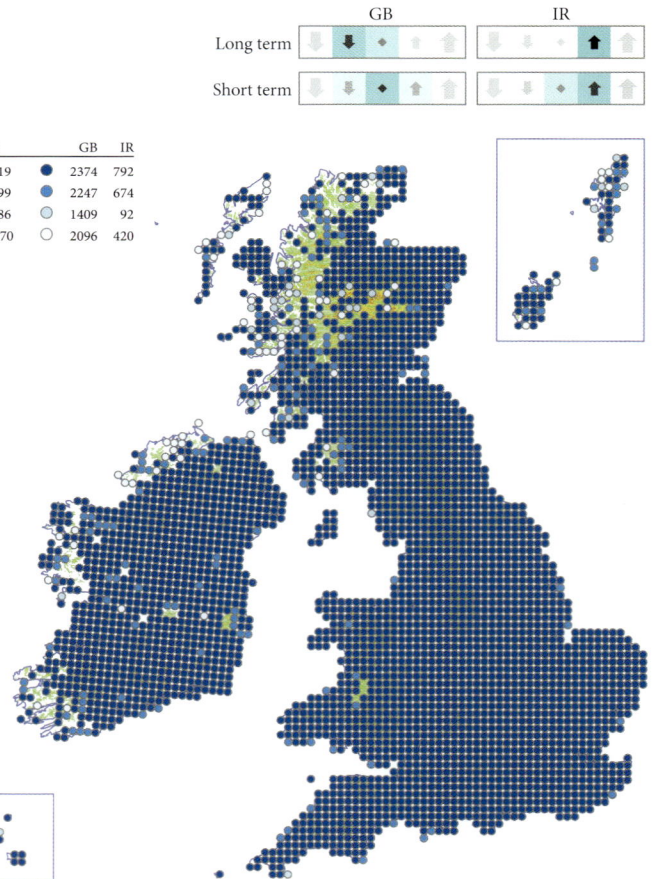

Key refs Cope & Gray (2009), Grime *et al.* (2007).

D.A. Pearman

Hy *Alopecurus geniculatus × pratensis = A. ×brachystylus*
Peterm.

A perennial grass of damp meadows and pastures, roadside verges, the sides of ditches and ponds and the banks of streams and rivers, usually where the parents grow together. It is almost invariably sterile. Its formation is facilitated by the fact that flowers of the parents are always markedly protogynous, and may therefore be cross-pollinated in the period before self-pollination is possible. Generally lowland, but reaching 425 m at Mole's Chamber (North Devon).

A spontaneous hybrid (native × native).

Trends This hybrid is almost certainly under-recorded. Hybrid material was first collected in 1854 at Albourne Place (West Sussex), but did not become known to British botanists until it was found in 1899, growing in "considerable abundance" in a low-lying meadow by the River Avon at Chesford Bridge (Warwickshire).

Biogeography Widespread in boreal and temperate Europe.

	GB	IR
Long term	No trend	No trend
Short term	No trend	No trend

	GB	IR
2000–19	19	1
1987–99	34	0
1970–86	20	0
pre-1970	27	0

Altitude (m) — <1%, 1–10%, 11–30%, 31–40%, 41–50%, 51–100%

Apparency · In flower · In leaf

Key refs Stace *et al.* (2015).

C.A. STACE, C.D. PRESTON & D.A. PEARMAN

N *Alopecurus geniculatus* Marsh Foxtail
L.

A perennial grass, rooting at the nodes, which is frequent on fertile soils that are flooded in winter, such as muddy ditches, wet arable fields, pond margins and grazing marshes. It readily colonizes bare mud and disturbed areas, where it can become very abundant, but avoids very acidic and very basic soils. Generally lowland, but reaching 595 m on Highfield (South Northumberland), and exceptionally at 845 m on Great Dun Fell (Westmorland).

Trends The range of *A. geniculatus* has not changed significantly since the 1960s, although it is now better recorded in parts of Scotland and Ireland.

Biogeography European Boreo-temperate element; widely naturalized outside its native range.

	GB	IR
Long term		
Short term		

Native	GB	IR
2000–19	2516	856
1987–99	2403	721
1970–86	1567	99
pre-1970	2155	478

Altitude (m) — <1%, 1–10%, 11–30%, 31–40%, 41–50%, 51–100%

Apparency · In flower · In leaf

Key refs Cope & Gray (2009), Grime *et al.* (2007).

D.A. PEARMAN

Ⓝ *Alopecurus bulbosus* Bulbous Foxtail
Gouan

A perennial grass of periodically flooded brackish grassland in unimproved coastal grazing marshes, at the edges of coastal ditches and in trampled ground at the base of sea-walls; also locally abundant in the uppermost parts of saltmarshes. Lowland.

Trends *A. bulbosus* was much under-recorded until the 1980s, and is now known to be still present (and sometimes abundant) at many sites from which it was thought to have been lost. Its 10 km square distribution appears reasonably stable since 2000, although locally some populations have declined due to drainage and improvement of its grassland habitat. Where salinity is reduced by sea-defence schemes it readily hybridizes with *A. geniculatus*, and eventually disappears. It has been found at several

new sites this century, including two locations in Pembrokeshire, slightly extending its known western limits.

Biogeography Suboceanic Southern-temperate element.

Native	GB	IR
2000–19	52	0
1987–99	59	0
1970–86	44	0
pre-1970	76	0

Alien	GB	IR
2000–19	0	0
1987–99	0	0
1970–86	1	0
pre-1970	2	0

Key refs Cope & Gray (2009), Stewart *et al.* (1994).

D.A. Pearman

Ⓝ *Alopecurus aequalis* Orange Foxtail
Sobol.

An annual, occasionally biennial or perennial grass most frequently found on bare mud in areas that are wet in winter but dry out in the summer, including the margins of ponds, ditches, reservoirs, turloughs, and flooded gravel-pits and on bare mud in winter-flooded arable fields and pastures. It has also been found as a weed in aquatic garden centres. Lowland, but reaching 540 m at Brown Clee Hill (Shropshire).

Trends Although *A. aequalis* has been lost from many suitable sites since the 1960s, it readily colonizes new open habitats, and this has resulted in many new 10 km square records this century. Population sizes are very variable, and it may not appear when water levels remain high, resulting in sporadic appearances over time and the potential for under-recording. It is often overlooked as,

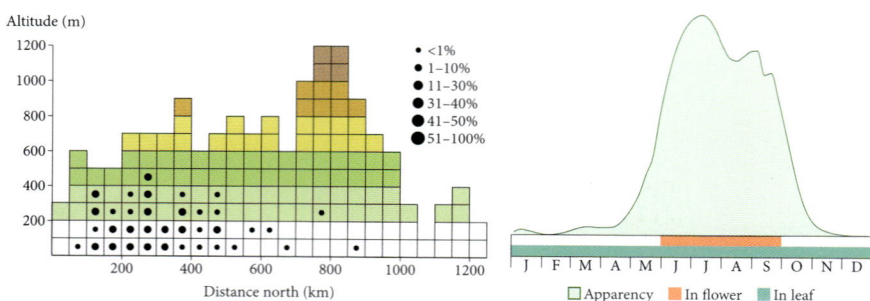

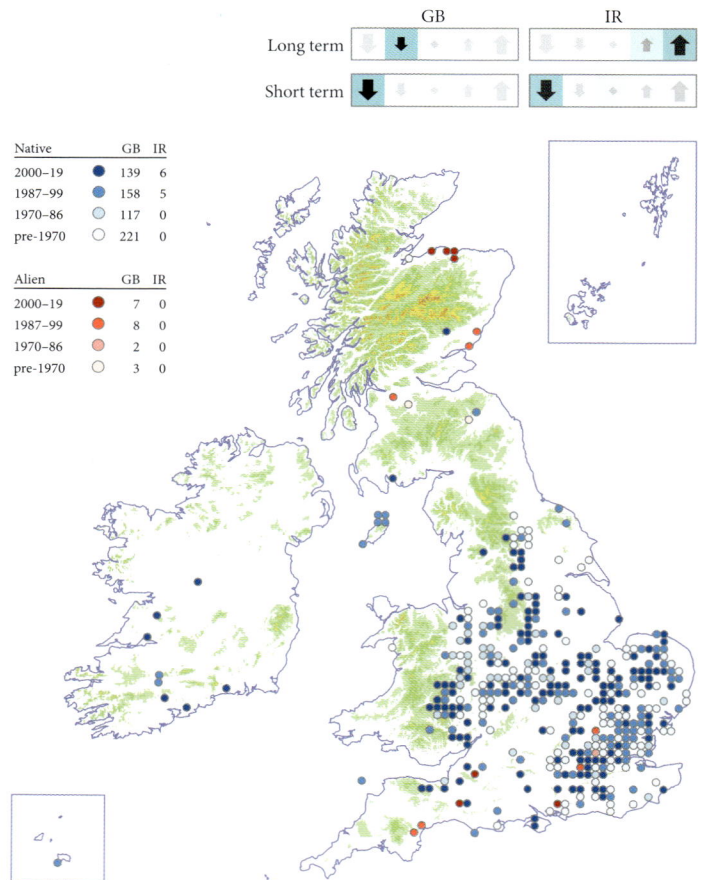

or mistaken for, *A. geniculatus*. It was not discovered in Ireland until 1992.

Biogeography Circumpolar Boreo-temperate element.

Native	GB	IR
2000–19	139	6
1987–99	158	5
1970–86	117	0
pre-1970	221	0

Alien	GB	IR
2000–19	7	0
1987–99	8	0
1970–86	2	0
pre-1970	3	0

Key refs Cope & Gray (2009), Goodwillie (1999b), Stewart *et al.* (1994).

D.A. Pearman

N *Alopecurus magellanicus* Alpine Foxtail
Lam.

A shortly rhizomatous perennial grass, found on the margins of (or in) oligotrophic springs and flushes, often associated with late snow-beds. It occurs on a wide range of acidic or slightly basic rocks. From around 460 m on Widdybank Fell (Durham) to 1,220 m on Braeriach (South Aberdeenshire).

Trends *A. magellanicus* has been recorded at several new localities within its existing range since the 1960s, and has also been found in new areas of central and north-western Scotland. In 2007 it was discovered on Great Shunner Fell (North-west Yorkshire) in flushed grassland close to a site for *Saxifraga hirculus*, extending the southern limits of its global range by 26 km. It is an inconspicuous grass, especially as it is shy-flowering and any inflorescences produced are often eaten off, but observations have been greatly assisted by the general relaxation of sheep-grazing that has taken place since the outbreak of Foot and Mouth Disease in 2001.

Biogeography Circumpolar Arctic-montane element; in Europe restricted to Britain, Svalbard, arctic Russia and the Urals.

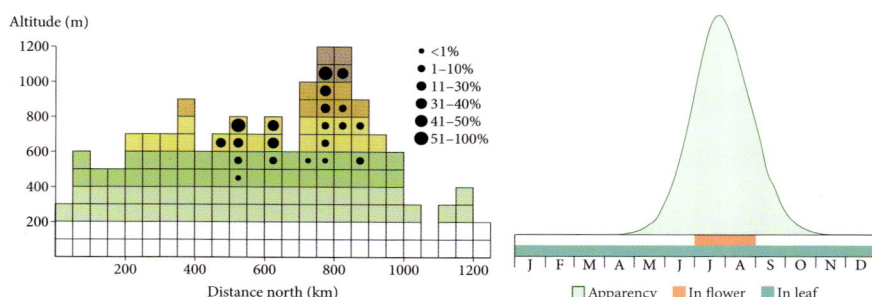

Native		GB	IR
2000–19	●	26	0
1987–99	●	18	0
1970–86	○	21	0
pre-1970	○	28	0

Alien		GB	IR
2000–19	●	0	0
1987–99	●	0	0
1970–86	●	0	0
pre-1970	○	1	0

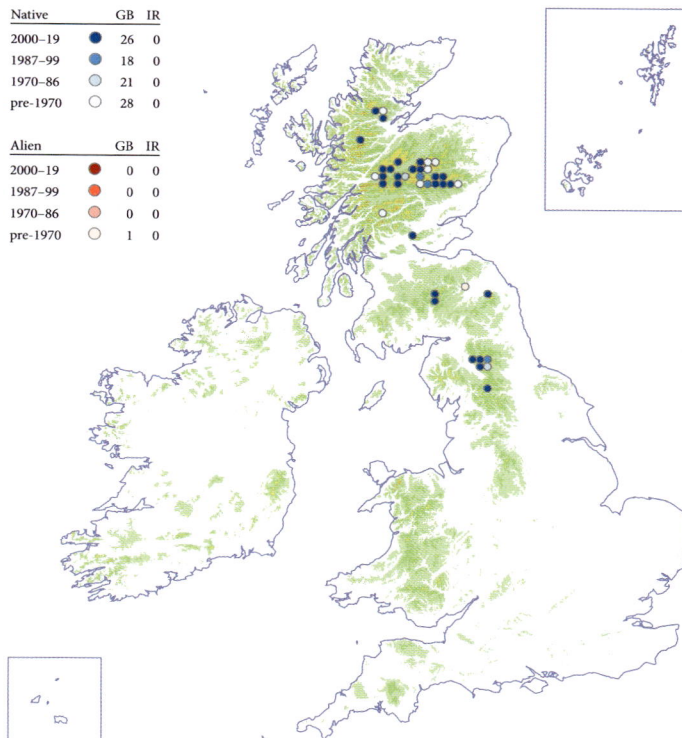

Key refs Cope & Gray (2009), Robinson (2007), Stewart *et al.* (1994), Walker (2014b).

D.A. PEARMAN

Ar *Alopecurus myosuroides* Black-grass
Huds.

An annual herb found in and on the margins of cereal crops and rapidly increasing as an abundant weed, particularly of winter-sown wheat on heavy clays. It also occurs in rank and neglected grassland, set-aside, waste ground and on the disturbed edges of tracks and roads. It grows on both light and heavy soils. Predominantly lowland.

An archaeophyte in Britain and the Channel Islands and a neophyte in Ireland.

Trends *A. myosuroides* has increased in its core range and spread northwards and westwards since the 1960s, despite significant advances in weed control within arable crops. This has been largely due to the spread of strains that have evolved specific resistance to several commonly used herbicides, combined with the increased planting of winter cereal crops and the decline of stubble burning (Hicks *et al.*, 2020).

Biogeography As an archaeophyte, *A. myosuroides* has a European Southern-temperate distribution; it is widely naturalized outside this range.

Alien		GB	IR
2000–19	●	1055	19
1987–99	●	895	5
1970–86	●	564	1
pre-1970	○	787	2

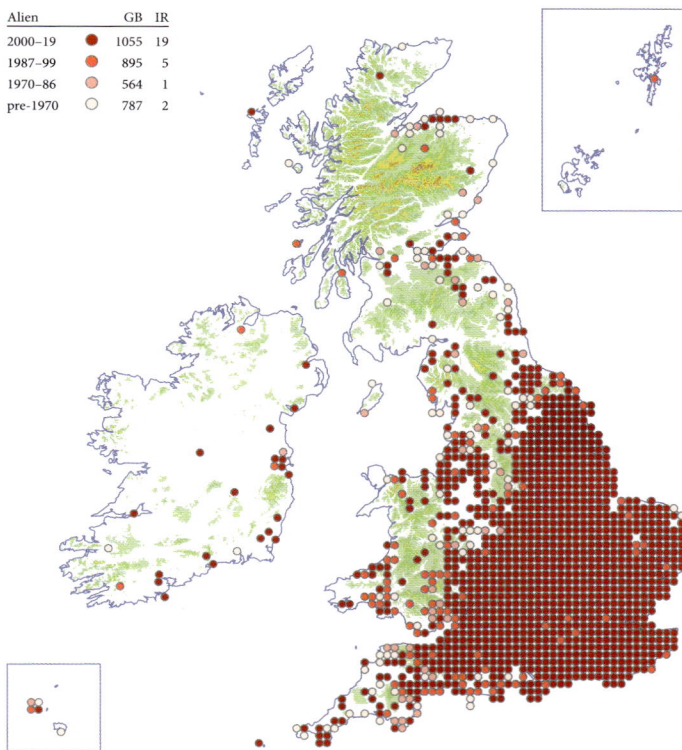

Key refs Cope & Gray (2009), Hicks *et al.* (2020), Moss *et al.* (2007), Naylor (1972).

D.A. PEARMAN & K.J. WALKER

N *Phleum pratense s.l.*

P. pratense and *P. bertolonii* are perennial grasses that grow in a wide range of grassland habitats, such as meadows and pastures, rough grassland, field margins, verges and waste places. They are frequently sown in grasslands (*P. bertolonii* less so) and also occur as casuals from birdseed, wool shoddy and other sources. 0–620 m (Killhope Cross, County Durham), and exceptionally at 845 m on Great Dun Fell (Westmorland).

Trends This aggregate comprises *P. pratense s.s.* and *P. bertolonii*. There has been little change in its distribution since the 1960s. Much seed sown as leys comes from North America, whence it was first imported around 1720 by Timothy Hanson. It has not been possible to distinguish native and introduced records, except perhaps in south-western

Ireland and the Northern Isles.

Biogeography The distributions of the two component species are given in the relevant accounts.

Native	GB	IR
2000–19	2344	717
1987–99	2278	611
1970–86	1565	105
pre-1970	2208	518

Alien	GB	IR
2000–19	89	4
1987–99	70	10
1970–86	16	0
pre-1970	62	2

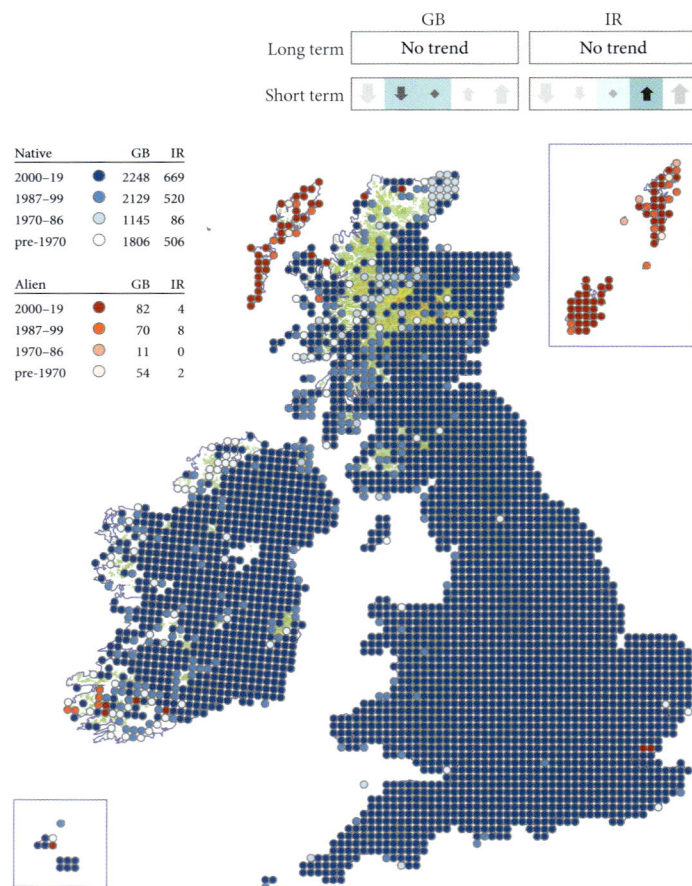

Key refs Cope & Gray (2009), Grime *et al.* (2007), Ryves *et al.* (1996).

S.J. LEACH & D.A. PEARMAN

N *Phleum pratense* Timothy
L.

A perennial grass growing in a wide range of grassy habitats, including meadows, pastures, rough grassland, field margins and waysides; it is widely sown in many of these grasslands and it occurs as a casual from wool shoddy, birdseed and other sources. *P. pratense s.s.* tends to occur on rather heavier, damper soils than *P. bertolonii*. 0–620 m (Killhope Cross, County Durham).

Trends *P. pratense s.s.* was not mapped in the 1962 *Atlas*, being included with *P. bertolonii* within the map of *P. pratense s.l.* These two taxa are still much confused. Native and alien records have seldom been distinguished, though the latter must be considerable. There appears to be no change in its overall 10 km distribution.

Biogeography Eurosiberian Temperate element, but widely naturalized so that distribution is now Circumpolar Temperate.

Native	GB	IR
2000–19	2248	669
1987–99	2129	520
1970–86	1145	86
pre-1970	1806	506

Alien	GB	IR
2000–19	82	4
1987–99	70	8
1970–86	11	0
pre-1970	54	2

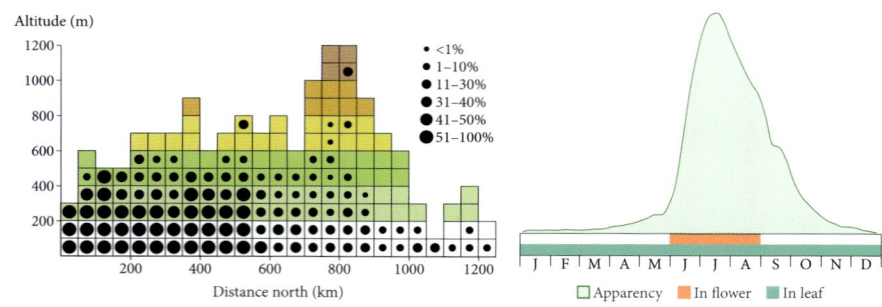

Key refs Cope & Gray (2009), Grime *et al.* (2007), Ryves *et al.* (1996).

S.J. LEACH & D.A. PEARMAN

N *Phleum bertolonii* Smaller Cat's-tail
DC.

A perennial grass of old meadows and pastures, downs, roadside-banks and waste places; often with *P. pratense*, but showing a preference for slightly thinner swards and drier, less fertile soils. It occasionally occurred as a wool-alien, on shoddy fields and refuse tips. Generally lowland, but reaching 420 m at Mynydd Bach (Denbighshire).

Trends This taxon seems to have a greater persistence than *P. pratense*, has a long-lived seed bank and as a native is probably more widespread than that species. It was not separately mapped in the 1962 *Atlas* and there remains much confusion between it and *P. pratense*. Robust agricultural strains of *P. bertolonii* are distinguishable from small *P. pratense* only by their differing chromosome number (Halliday, 1997). It must still be under-recorded in Ireland.

Biogeography European Southern-temperate element; widely naturalized outside its native range.

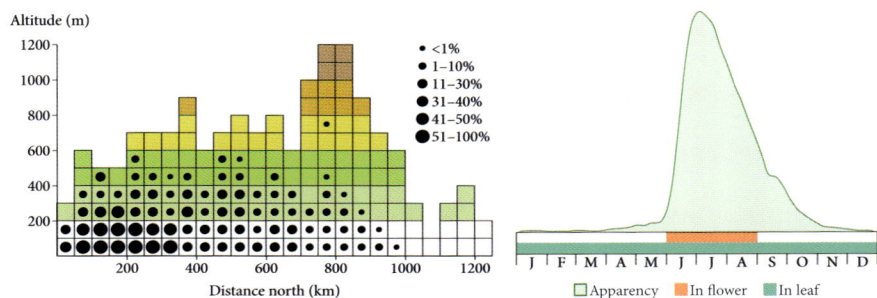

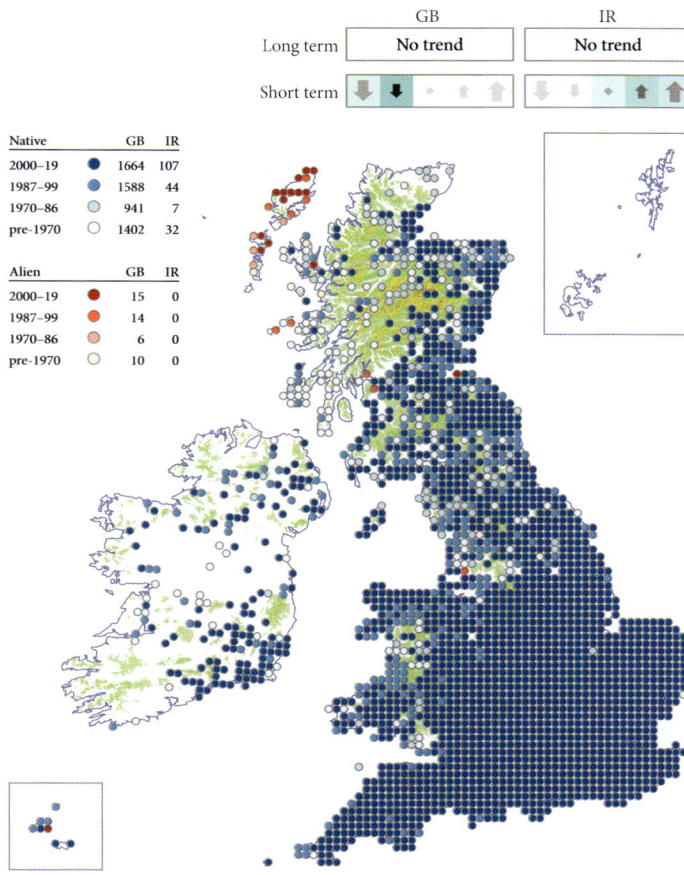

Native	GB	IR
2000–19	1664	107
1987–99	1588	44
1970–86	941	7
pre-1970	1402	32

Alien	GB	IR
2000–19	15	0
1987–99	14	0
1970–86	6	0
pre-1970	10	0

	GB	IR
Long term	No trend	No trend
Short term		

Altitude (m)

- <1%
- 1–10%
- 11–30%
- 31–40%
- 41–50%
- 51–100%

Distance north (km)

Apparency In flower In leaf

Key refs Cope & Gray (2009), Grime *et al.* (2007), Halliday (1997), Ryves *et al.* (1996).

S.J. Leach & D.A. Pearman

N *Phleum alpinum* Alpine Cat's-tail
L.

A loosely tufted perennial grass of damp, calcareous or base-enriched substrates in the mountains. It occurs in a variety of habitats, including moist or dry cliff-faces, corrie rock ledges and wet grassy slopes. From 610 m on Braeriach (South Aberdeenshire) to 1,220 m on Cairntoul (South Aberdeenshire).

Trends *P. alpinum* normally occurs in lightly grazed or ungrazed habitats, and heavy grazing may be partly responsible for its present restriction in some areas. However, there is no evidence of widespread decline, and it probably still persists undetected in some 10 km squares for which there are only pre-2000 records. In northern England it survives precariously at two sites on Cross Fell (Cumberland), but it has not been seen in recent years on Helvellyn,

the only other station recorded south of the Scottish Highlands (Halliday, 1997).

Biogeography Circumpolar Boreo-arctic Montane element, as well as high mountains in Chile and Argentina

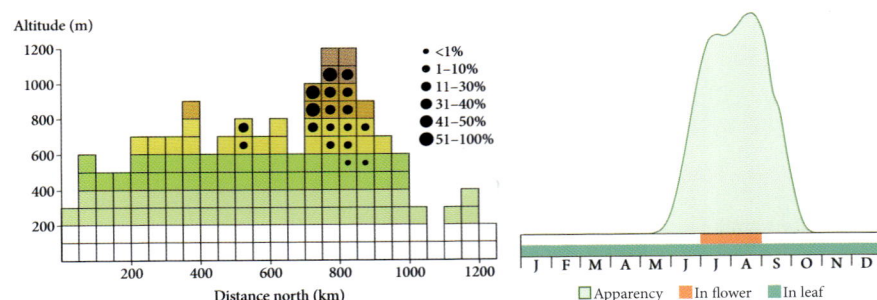

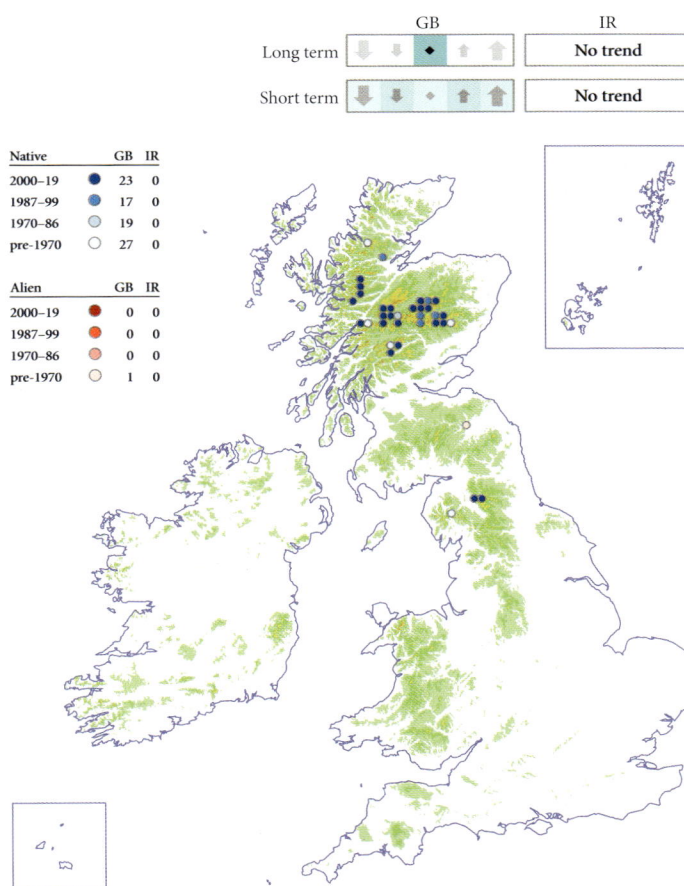

	GB	IR
Long term		No trend
Short term		No trend

Native	GB	IR
2000–19	23	0
1987–99	17	0
1970–86	19	0
pre-1970	27	0

Alien	GB	IR
2000–19	0	0
1987–99	0	0
1970–86	0	0
pre-1970	1	0

Altitude (m)

- <1%
- 1–10%
- 11–30%
- 31–40%
- 41–50%
- 51–100%

Distance north (km)

Apparency In flower In leaf

Key refs Cope & Gray (2009), Halliday (1997), Ryves *et al.* (1996), Stewart *et al.* (1994).

S.J. Leach & D.A. Pearman

N *Phleum phleoides* Purple-stem Cat's-tail

(L.) H.Karst.

A perennial grass of open habitats on free-draining sandy or chalky soils, especially in Breckland (East Anglia) where it occurs on grazed grass-heaths, road verges and trackside banks, and on exposed chalk in the vicinity of pits, rabbit warrens and other disturbed places. Lowland.

Trends Most losses of *P. phleoides* occurred before 1930. Since then, its known range has extended eastwards; its easternmost site, at Stuston Common (East Suffolk), was first discovered in 1991 but it did not persist there. It is thriving in open habitats in Breckland, sometimes with huge populations (>100,000) at one site, though the seedlings are very susceptible to spring droughts.

Biogeography Eurosiberian Temperate element, with a continental distribution in western Europe.

Native	GB	IR
2000–19	11	0
1987–99	12	0
1970–86	16	0
pre-1970	24	0

Alien	GB	IR
2000–19	0	0
1987–99	0	0
1970–86	0	0
pre-1970	3	0

	GB				IR
Long term					No trend
Short term		No trend			No trend

Key refs Cope & Gray (2009), Wigginton (1999).

S.J. Leach & D.A. Pearman

N *Phleum arenarium* Sand Cat's-tail

L.

An annual grass of coastal sand dunes and sandy shingle, usually on mobile or semi-fixed *Ammophila arenaria* dunes and frequently associated with winter-annuals such as *Aira praecox*, *Myosotis ramosissima* and *Vulpia fasciculata*; it also occurs inland in Breckland (East Anglia), on open grass-heaths, wind-blown sand banks and other disturbed, open, sandy areas. Elsewhere, it is a rare casual inland, sometimes arriving with imported sea-sand. Lowland.

Trends The distribution of *P. arenarium* has declined since the 1960s, most notably inland in the East Anglian Brecklands due to the loss of, sandy habitats.

Biogeography European Southern-temperate element.

Native	GB	IR
2000–19	137	42
1987–99	149	54
1970–86	100	16
pre-1970	193	53

Alien	GB	IR
2000–19	2	0
1987–99	0	0
1970–86	1	0
pre-1970	5	0

	GB				IR
Long term					
Short term					

Key refs Cope & Gray (2009), Ernst & Malloch (1994).

S.J. Leach & D.A. Pearman

(N) *Poa infirma* Early Meadow-grass
Kunth

An annual grass growing in a variety of habitats close to the sea in trampled grassland, on cliff-top paths, tracksides, picnic sites, lawns, car parks, road verges and stabilized sand dunes, and increasingly on open ground in urban areas and, as an erect form, under trees. Lowland.

Native in Britain and the Channel Islands and a neophyte in Ireland.

Trends Historically, *P. infirma* was restricted to West Cornwall, the Isles of Scilly and the Channel Islands but in recent decades there has been a considerable expansion of range eastwards and northwards in Britain. Milder winters and dispersal by humans are likely to have contributed to its spread. Its frequent association with

man-made habitats has led to doubts about its native status in Britain, with a first record as recently as 1876. In Ireland, where it is considered to be an alien, it was first found in a garden in 1987 (County Londonderry) and in the wild in West Cork in 2000.

Biogeography Mediterranean-Atlantic element.

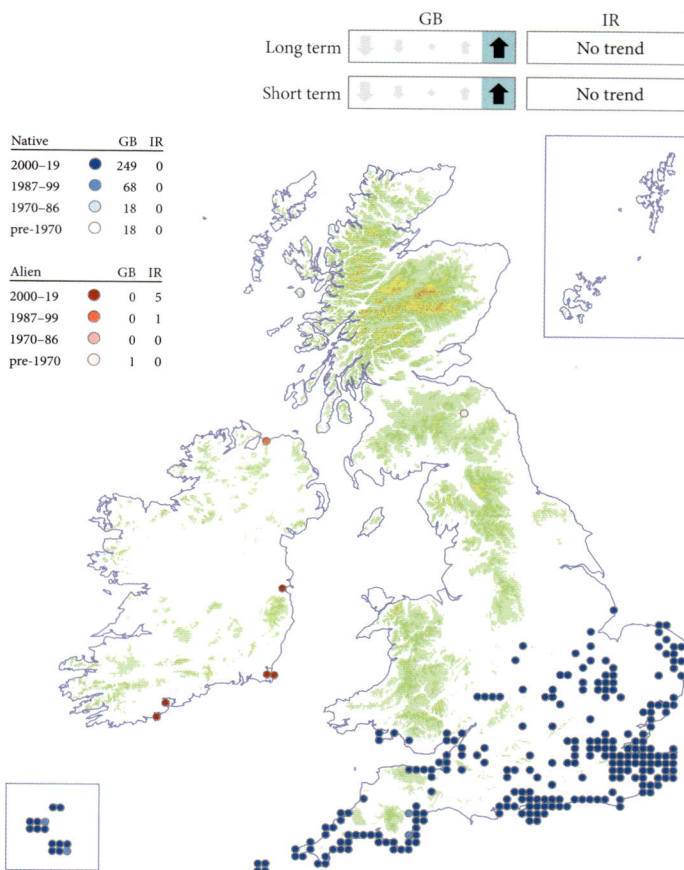

Native	GB	IR
2000–19	249	0
1987–99	68	0
1970–86	18	0
pre-1970	18	0

Alien	GB	IR
2000–19	0	5
1987–99	0	1
1970–86	0	0
pre-1970	1	0

	GB	IR
Long term	↑	No trend
Short term	↑	No trend

Altitude (m) / Distance north (km) chart; legend: <1%, 1–10%, 11–30%, 31–40%, 41–50%, 51–100%

Apparency / In flower / In leaf

Key refs Cope & Gray (2009), Wigginton (1999).

S.J. Leach, D.A. Pearman & K.J. Walker

(N) *Poa annua* Annual Meadow-grass
L.

An annual grass that is an almost ubiquitous weed of a wide range of disturbed and man-made habitats, including overgrazed and trampled grasslands, lawns, arable fields, road sides, waste ground, paths, waysides and wall-tops. Perennial biotypes occur throughout our area. *P. annua* is also a common birdseed alien, formerly a wool alien, and a familiar garden weed throughout our area. 0–1,214 m (Ben Lawers, Mid Perthshire).

Trends *P. annua* is ubiquitous at the 10 km square level and its range has not changed since the 1960s.

Biogeography Eurosiberian Wide-temperate element, but widely naturalized so that its distribution is now Circumpolar Wide-temperate.

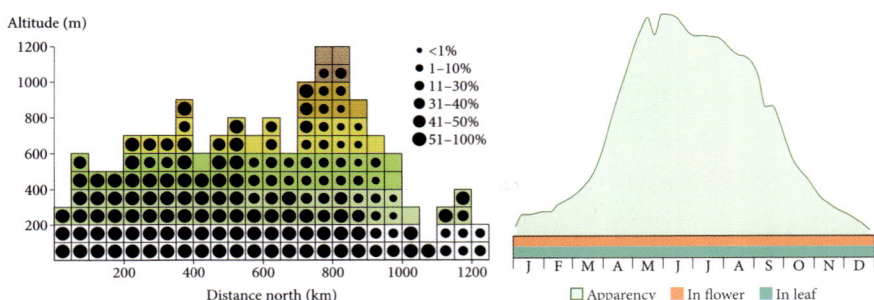

Native	GB	IR
2000–19	2811	999
1987–99	2753	954
1970–86	1767	182
pre-1970	2639	899

Alien	GB	IR
2000–19	0	1
1987–99	0	1
1970–86	0	0
pre-1970	0	1

	GB	IR
Long term		↓
Short term	↑	↑

Altitude (m) / Distance north (km) chart; legend: <1%, 1–10%, 11–30%, 31–40%, 41–50%, 51–100%

Apparency / In flower / In leaf

Key refs Cope & Gray (2009), Grime *et al.* (2007), Hutchinson & Seymour (1982), Warwick (1979).

S.J. Leach & D.A. Pearman

N *Poa trivialis* Rough Meadow-grass
L.

A stoloniferous perennial grass often indicative of disturbance and high fertility in a wide range of habitats including open woodland, meadows, pastures, walls, waste ground, waysides and cultivated land; it also grows in marshes and beside ponds, ditches and streams. It was formerly included in commercial grass-seed mixtures, and is still used in amenity and wild-flower grasslands. It was a common wool alien. Generally below 500 m, but reaching 1,065 m on Carn Eige, Glen Affric (Easterness).

Trends There has been no change in the 10 km square range of *P. trivialis* since the 1960s. It is a very widespread plant of ruderal situations throughout Britain and Ireland, being absent only from the most mountainous regions.

Biogeography Eurosiberian Wide-temperate element, but widely naturalized so that its distribution is now Circumpolar Wide-temperate.

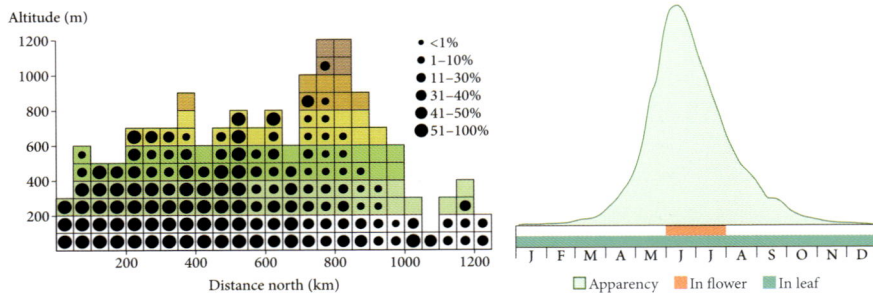

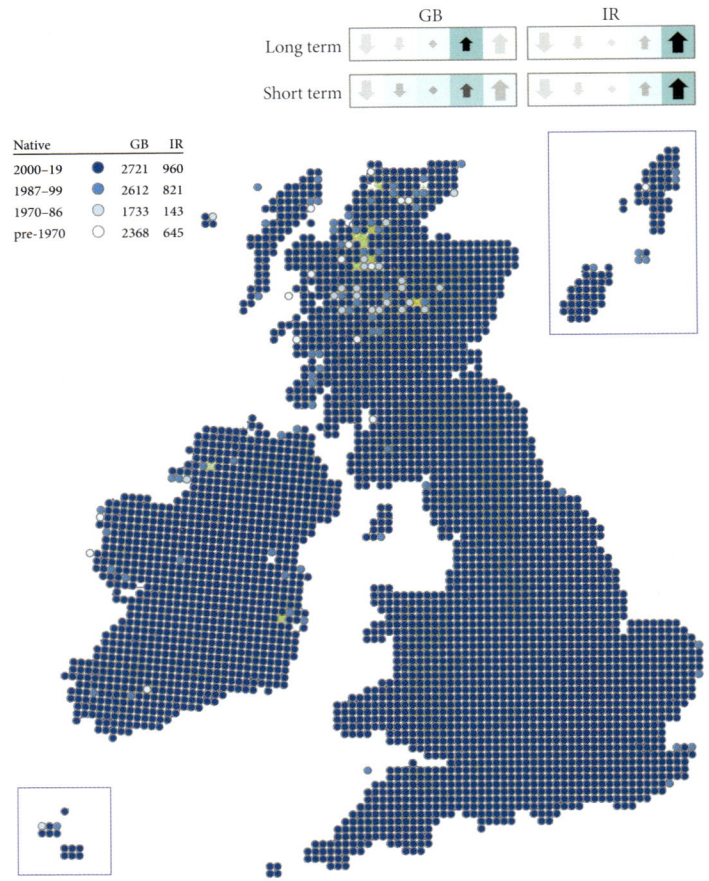

Native	GB	IR
2000–19	2721	960
1987–99	2612	821
1970–86	1733	143
pre-1970	2368	645

Key refs Cope & Gray (2009), Grime *et al.* (2007).

S.J. Leach & D.A. Pearman

N *Poa pratensis s.l.*

These rhizomatous perennial grasses are found in a wide range of grassland habitats, on soils that are wet to dry, infertile to fertile, somewhat acidic to strongly calcareous. They grow in all sorts of grasslands, on sand dunes, riverbanks, mountain slopes, roadsides, waste ground and wall-tops. 0–1,070 m (Beinn a'Bhuird, South Aberdeenshire).

Trends There is no evidence of any change in the range of *P. pratensis s.l.* since the 1960s. The aggregate includes three species (*P. pratensis s.s.*, *P. humilis* and *P. angustifolia*), all of which are mapped separately. Cope & Gray (2009) prefer to treat the segregates as subsp. *pratensis*, subsp. *irrigata*, and subsp. *angustifolia*. *P. pratensis s.s.* is likely to have been widely sown in pastures in the past and possibly vastly over-recorded for *P. humilis*.

Biogeography The three species in our area have a Circumpolar Wide-temperate distribution; the fourth European species, *P. alpigena*, extends the range to the high Arctic.

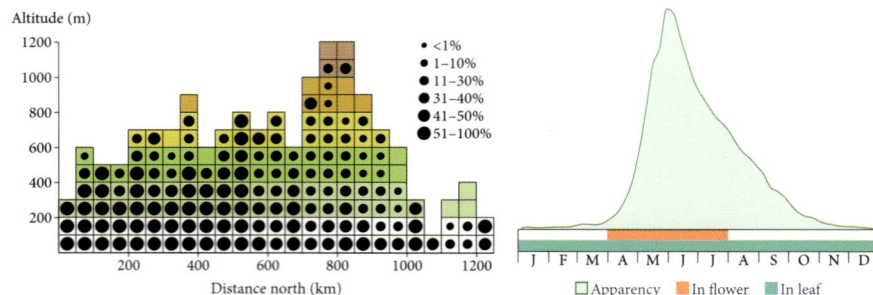

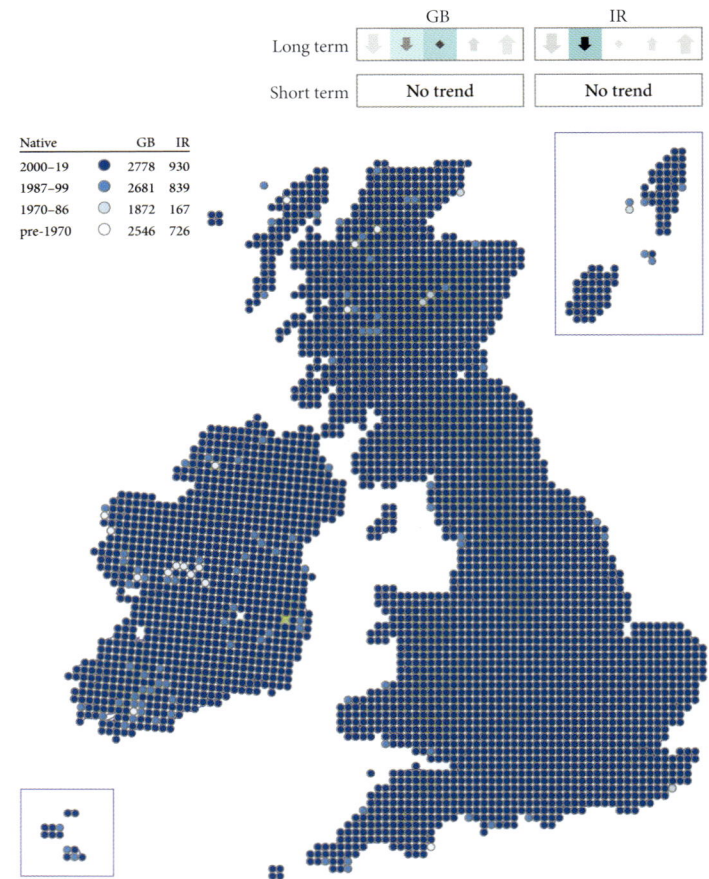

Native	GB	IR
2000–19	2778	930
1987–99	2681	839
1970–86	1872	167
pre-1970	2546	726

Key refs Barling (1959), Barling (1962), Barling (1967), Cope & Gray (2009), Grime *et al.* (2007).

S.J. Leach & D.A. Pearman

Ⓝ *Poa humilis* Spreading Meadow-grass
Ehrh. ex Hoffm.

A rhizomatous perennial grass found in a wide variety of grassland habitats, including neutral meadows, damp pastures, calcareous grassland, sand dunes, roadsides, wall-tops, riverbanks and mountain slopes, including rock outcrops and screes. Morphologically and cytologically this is a highly variable species; some of its variants are apomictic, and its ecological requirements appear to be very broad. 0–1,194 m (Ben Lawers, Mid Perthshire) and possibly higher elsewhere.

Trends In the 1962 *Atlas*, *P. humilis* was not distinguished from other taxa within the *P. pratensis* group, but it was mapped by Perring & Sell (1968). It is better recorded in recent decades, and although it is still confused with other *Poa* species and the paucity of reliable historical data makes distributional trends difficult to assess,

its distribution is likely to be stable. This taxon is recognized in Cope & Gray (2009) as *P. pratensis* subsp. *irrigata*.

Biogeography World distribution uncertain, but it is predominately a species of northern latitudes, and the British Isles is probably at its southern limit.

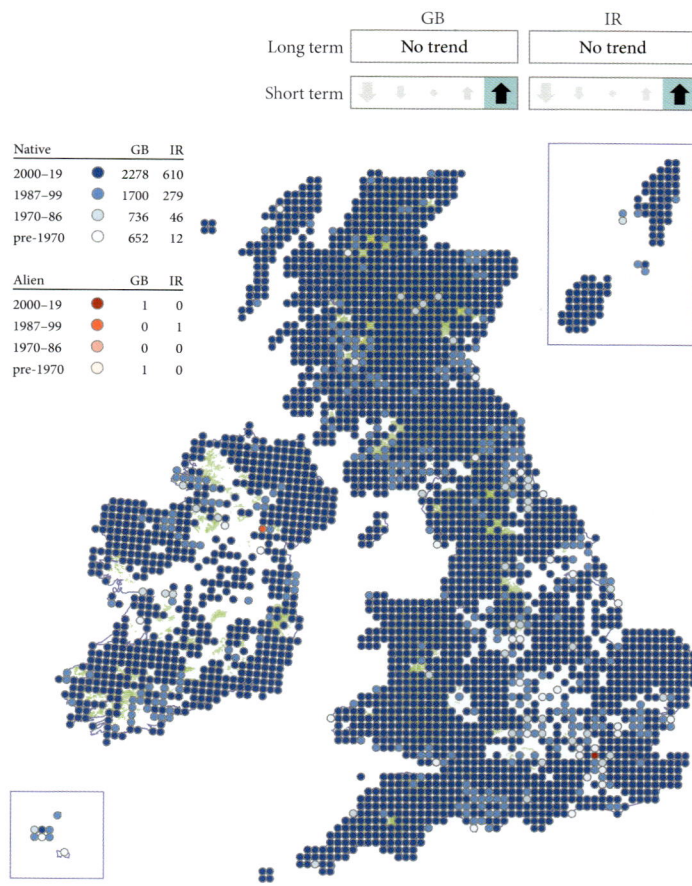

Native		GB	IR
2000–19	●	2278	610
1987–99	●	1700	279
1970–86	●	736	46
pre-1970	○	652	12

Alien		GB	IR
2000–19	●	1	0
1987–99	●	0	1
1970–86	●	0	0
pre-1970	○	1	0

Key refs Barling (1962), Cope & Gray (2009), Trist (1989).

S.J. Leach, D.A. Pearman & K.J. Walker

Ⓝ *Poa pratensis* Smooth Meadow-grass
L.

A rhizomatous perennial grass of meadows, pastures, waysides, lawns and amenity grasslands (including sports pitches) and waste places; formerly an important constituent of agricultural seed mixtures, and still used in the sowing of amenity and wild-flower grasslands. It is a versatile grass, preferring well-drained, neutral soils of moderate to high fertility, and tolerant of grazing and trampling. Generally lowland, but with an exceptional record of 1,070 m from Beinn a'Bhuird (South Aberdeenshire).

Trends There are no reliable historical data to allow an assessment of whether the distribution of this taxon is changing. Its native status is questionable in large parts of our area and has been hopelessly obscured by sowing as an agricultural and amenity grass, and so is mapped here without status. It is still

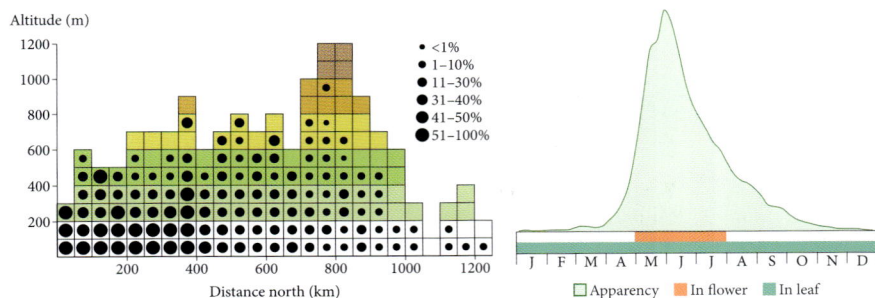

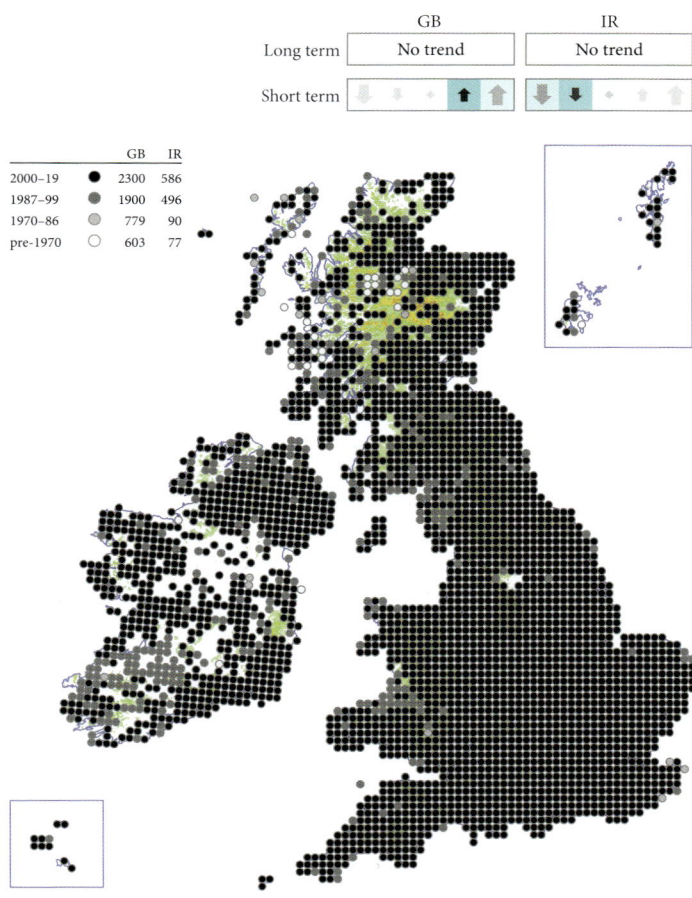

unevenly reported and probably vastly over-recorded for *P. humilis* which seems much more likely to be a native taxon given its distribution and habitats.

Biogeography Circumpolar Wide-temperate element; widely naturalized outside its native range.

		GB	IR
2000–19	●	2300	586
1987–99	●	1900	496
1970–86	●	779	90
pre-1970	○	603	77

Key refs Barling (1967), Cope & Gray (2009), Grime *et al.* (2007).

S.J. Leach, D.A. Pearman & K.J. Walker

N *Poa angustifolia* Narrow-leaved Meadow-grass
L.

A rhizomatous perennial grass of dry grassland, wall-tops, rough ground and railway embankments, typically on relatively infertile chalky, sandy or gravelly soils, but also clays that dry out in the summer, and thus able to persist in very xerophytic habitats. In parts of southern England it often occurs in partial shade under beech trees. It flowers and sets seed earlier than other members of the *P. pratensis* group. Predominantly lowland.

Trends Historically, *P. angustifolia* has been confused with other members of the *P. pratensis* group. Its distribution was mapped by Perring & Sell (1968) and investigated by Sargent *et al.* (1986). It is possibly decreasing in semi-natural habitats, but trends are difficult to assess given the lack of historical data and it is likely to be still under-recorded, particularly in Scotland and northern England. There are, however, many new records within its core range since 2000 and the map is probably a reasonable reflection of its distribution here. It appears to be genuinely much rarer than *P. humilis*, with which it is sometimes confused, and the two taxa can grow together in calcareous grassland. This taxon is recognized in Cope & Gray (2009) as *P. pratensis* subsp. *angustifolia*.

Biogeography Circumpolar Southern-temperate element.

	GB	IR
Long term	No trend	No trend
Short term	↓ **↓** ◆ ↑ ↑	No trend

Native	GB	IR
2000–19	643	1
1987–99	536	0
1970–86	460	0
pre-1970	388	0

Alien	GB	IR
2000–19	2	0
1987–99	2	0
1970–86	2	0
pre-1970	1	0

Key refs Barling (1959), Barling (1967), Cope & Gray (2009), Sargent *et al.* (1986).

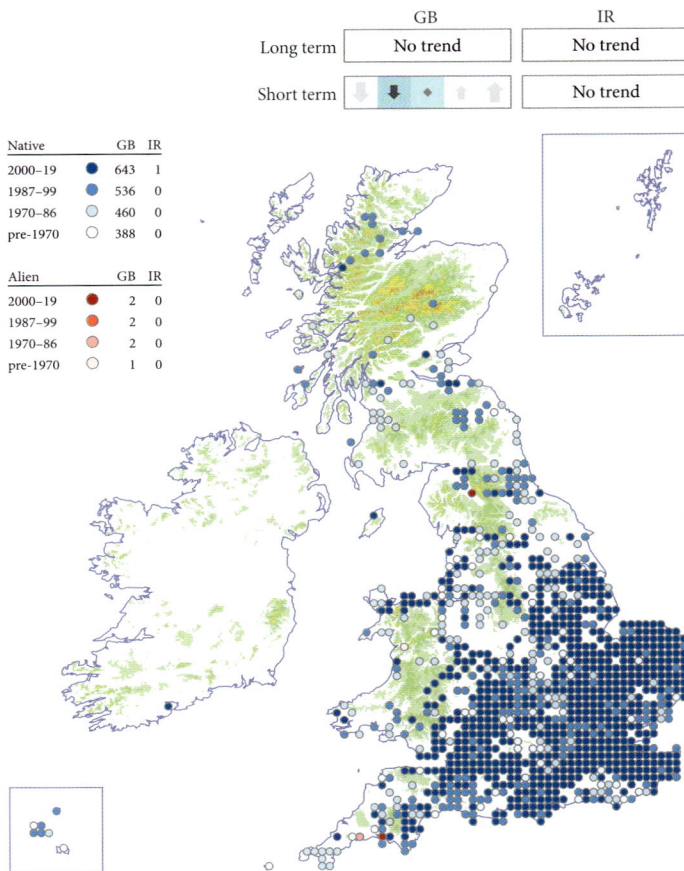

S.J. LEACH & D.A. PEARMAN

Altitude (m) — Distance north (km)

● <1%
● 1–10%
● 11–30%
● 31–40%
● 41–50%
● 51–100%

☐ Apparency ■ In flower ■ In leaf
J F M A M J J A S O N D

Ne *Poa chaixii* Broad-leaved Meadow-grass
Vill.

A stout, densely tufted perennial grass, found naturalized in copses and open woodland, occasionally growing with *Festuca heterophylla*, another ornamental species admired by Victorian gardeners. Generally lowland, but reaching 395 m (The Quiraing, North Ebudes).

Trends *P. chaixii* has been grown in gardens for ornament or ground cover since before 1802, and was much planted in the 19th century in the grounds of large estates, especially in Scotland. It was first recorded in the wild in 1851 (Chelsea Hospital, Middlesex). There has been a decline in its 10 km square distribution since the 1960s, probably because it is less frequently planted, but it is possibly still overlooked in some areas.

Biogeography Native of montane woods in central and southern Europe; widely naturalized farther north.

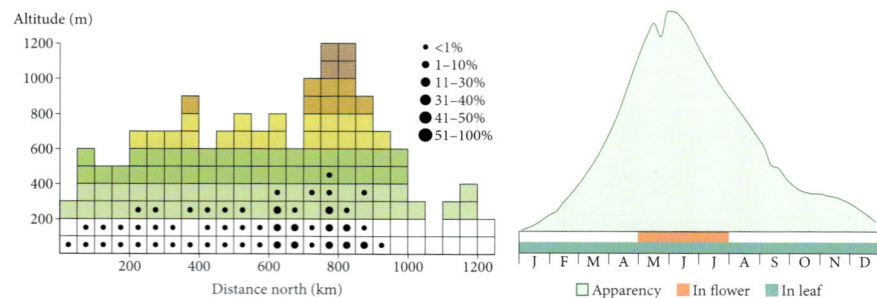

	GB	IR
Long term	↓ ↓ ◆ ↑ ↑	No trend
Short term	↓ **↓** ◆ ↑ ↑	No trend

Alien	GB	IR
2000–19	98	1
1987–99	87	3
1970–86	77	1
pre-1970	109	0

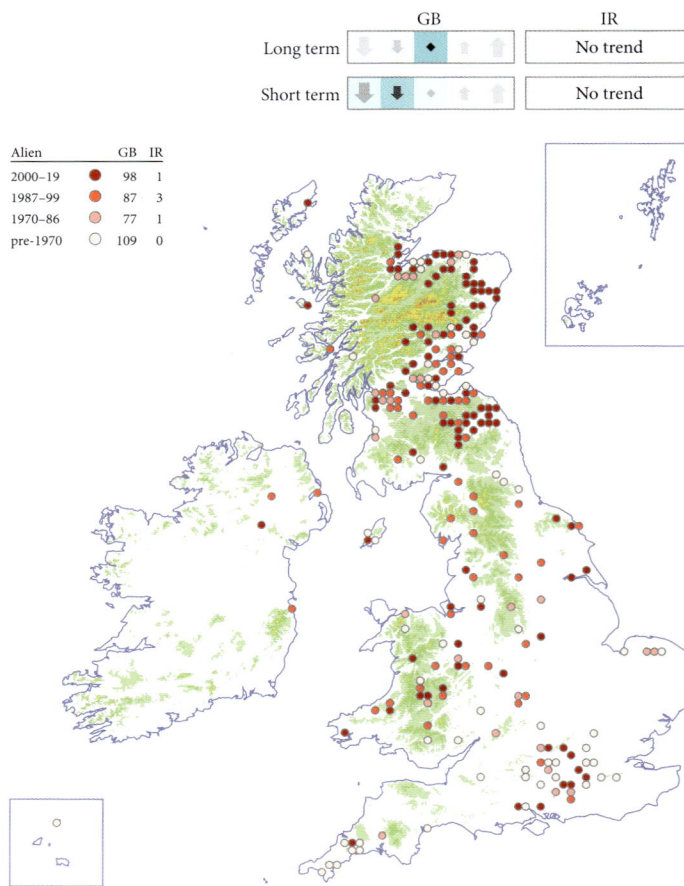

Key refs Cope & Gray (2009), Ryves *et al.* (1996).

S.J. LEACH & D.A. PEARMAN

Altitude (m) — Distance north (km)

● <1%
● 1–10%
● 11–30%
● 31–40%
● 41–50%
● 51–100%

☐ Apparency ■ In flower ■ In leaf
J F M A M J J A S O N D

Poa flexuosa Wavy Meadow-grass
Sm.

A tufted perennial grass of acidic rock ledges, screes and stony mountain plateaux. From 760 m to 1,210 m (Ben Nevis, Westerness).

Trends Since 1970 *P. flexuosa* has been recorded from about a dozen sites, in six 10 km squares. This number appears to have remained constant though most of these sites support only very small populations. Its hybrid with *P. alpina* (*P.* ×*jemtlandica*) occurs with it at some sites, and may perhaps have given rise to some misidentifications.

Biogeography European Arctic-montane element; also in North America.

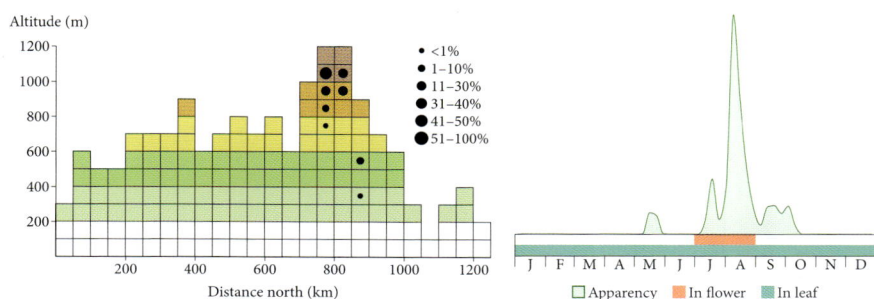

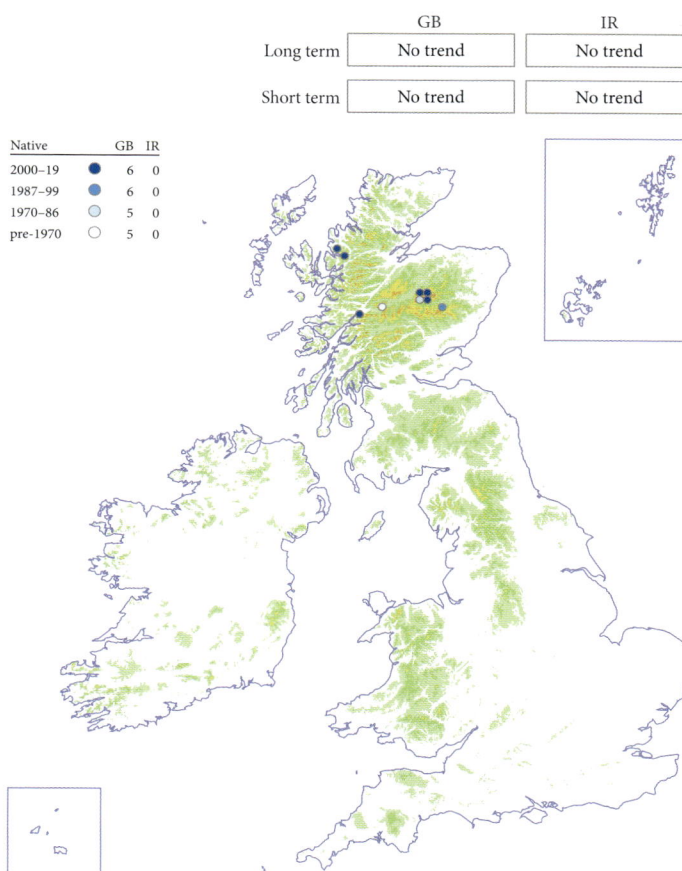

Native	GB	IR
2000–19	6	0
1987–99	6	0
1970–86	5	0
pre-1970	5	0

Key refs Cope & Gray (2009), Wigginton (1999).

S.J. Leach & D.A. Pearman

Poa compressa Flattened Meadow-grass
L.

A rhizomatous perennial grass of rough or stony ground, cinders, dry grassy banks, waysides and walls. Some populations on refuse tips and waste ground are probably introductions from wool shoddy and other sources. Generally lowland, but reaching 420 m on the Stiperstones and on Titterstone Clee (both Shropshire).

Native in Britain and the Channel Islands and a neophyte in Ireland.

Trends The 10 km square distribution of *P. compressa* appears to have declined, although the species is sometimes confused with other *Poa* species, particularly *P. humilis*, and is still unevenly recorded. It is not possible to make a clear distinction between native and introduced populations, particularly in Scotland. It is regarded as alien in Ireland (Scannell & Synnott, 1987).

Biogeography European Temperate element; widely naturalized outside its native range.

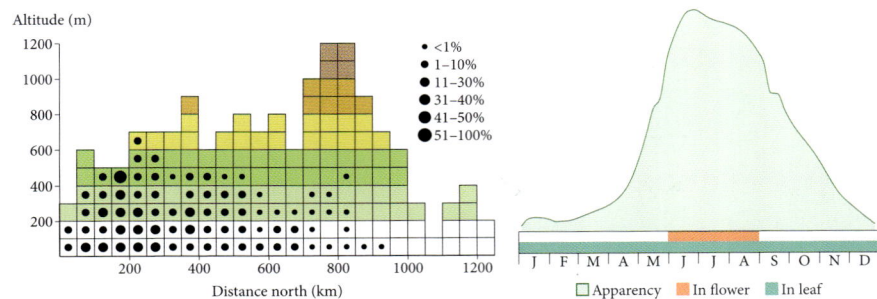

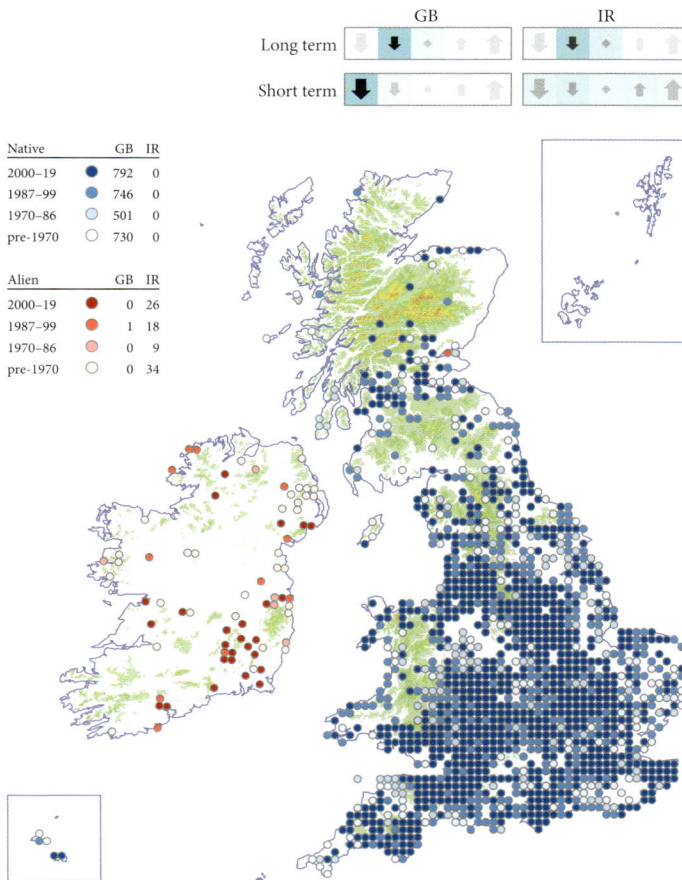

Native	GB	IR
2000–19	792	0
1987–99	746	0
1970–86	501	0
pre-1970	730	0

Alien	GB	IR
2000–19	0	26
1987–99	1	18
1970–86	0	9
pre-1970	0	34

Key refs Cope & Gray (2009), Scannell & Synnott (1987).

S.J. Leach & D.A. Pearman

Ne *Poa palustris* Swamp Meadow-grass
L.

A short-lived tufted perennial grass, found in marshes, fens, ditches, willow-carr and at the edges of rivers, canals, lakes and ponds; occasionally around docks, by railways and on waste ground. Generally lowland, but the precise upper altitudinal limit is unknown.

Trends *P. palustris* is thought to have been introduced as a fodder grass by 1814, and was recorded from the wild in 1879 (Kew, Surrey). The map suggests a substantial decline since the 1960s, although at many old localities its occurrence was probably only transient. It is easily overlooked.

Biogeography A Circumpolar Boreo-temperate species, but absent as a native from much of western Europe.

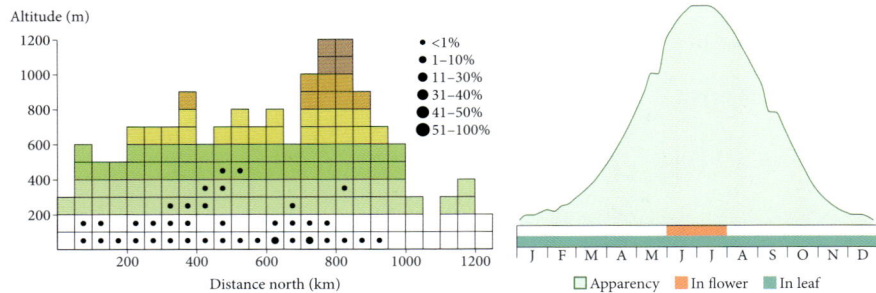

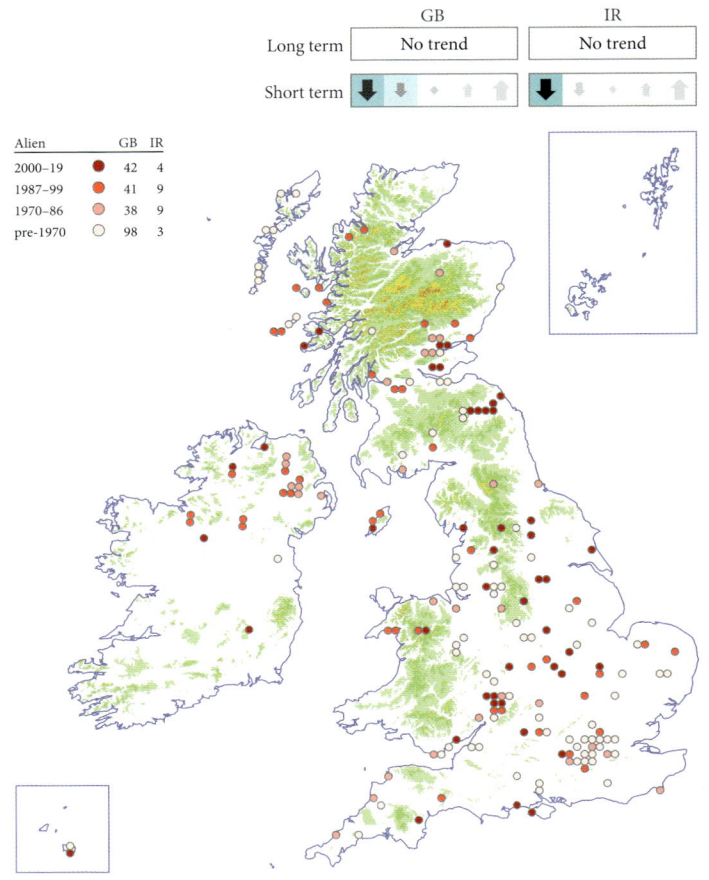

	GB	IR
Long term	No trend	No trend
Short term	↓	↓

Alien	GB	IR
2000–19	42	4
1987–99	41	9
1970–86	38	9
pre-1970	98	3

Key refs Cope & Gray (2009), Stewart *et al.* (1994).

S.J. Leach & D.A. Pearman

N *Poa glauca* Glaucous Meadow-grass
Vahl

A tufted perennial grass of damp mountain rock faces, open ledges, screes and rocky slopes on calcareous substrates, often with *P. alpina*. It is also known as a casual by a disused railway in Cardiganshire. From 125 m on Ben Lawers (Mid Perthshire) to 1,110 m on Lochnagar (South Aberdeen) and Ben Lawers (Mid Perthshire).

Trends It is possible that *P. glauca* has declined since the 1960s, in part due to overgrazing, though it might still persist at some sites in remote or mountainous areas where there are no recent records. Cope & Gray (2009) confirm what many botanists have suspected in the past, namely that it is barely tenable to separate this species from *P. nemoralis*.

Biogeography Circumpolar Boreo-arctic Montane element.

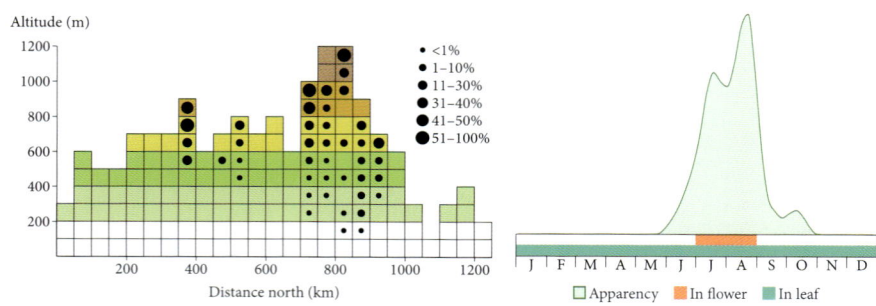

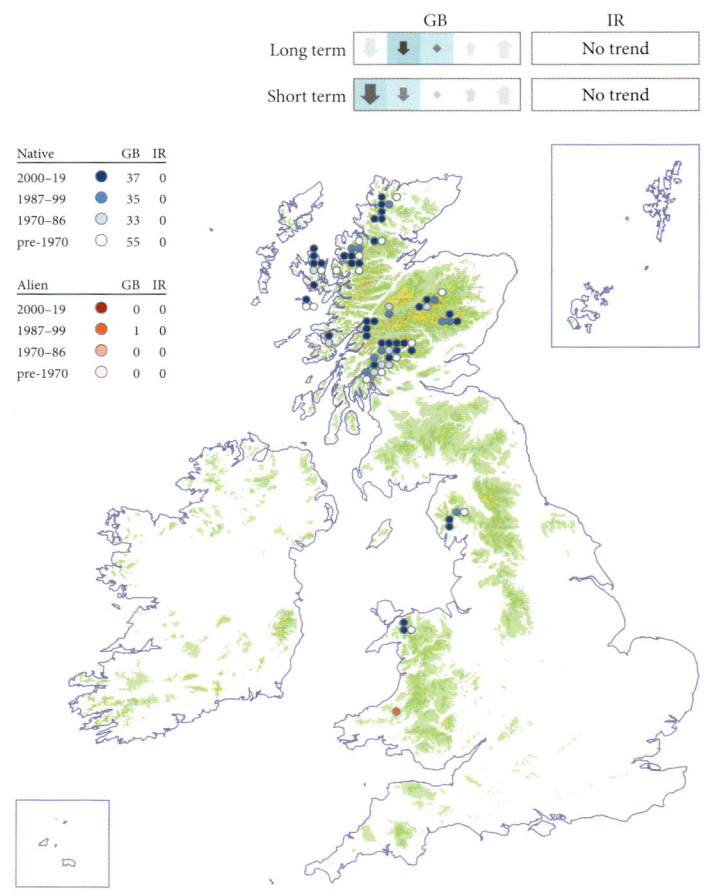

	GB	IR
Long term	↓	No trend
Short term	↓	No trend

Native	GB	IR
2000–19	37	0
1987–99	35	0
1970–86	33	0
pre-1970	55	0

Alien	GB	IR
2000–19	0	0
1987–99	1	0
1970–86	0	0
pre-1970	0	0

Key refs Cope & Gray (2009), Stewart *et al.* (1994).

S.J. Leach & D.A. Pearman

N *Poa nemoralis* Wood Meadow-grass
L.

A tufted perennial grass of woodland rides and glades, hedgerows and other shaded places; also locally on walls, and in the mountains on dry rock ledges. It was occasionally sown in woodlands and parks for its ornamental value, while in some areas it may have been introduced with wool shoddy, grass-seed or soil. Generally lowland, but reaching 940 m (Coire Gabhail, Glencoe, Main Argyll).

Native in Britain and the Channel Islands and a neophyte in Ireland.

Trends The native distribution of *P. nemoralis* is impossible to delimit with any degree of certainty. It is probably native throughout most of Britain, though it has been introduced in many places. In Ireland, where it was probably originally introduced, it is unclear whether it is spreading or better recorded. In the uplands it can be confused with *P. glauca* which some consider to just be a form of *P. nemoralis*.

Biogeography Circumpolar Boreo-temperate element.

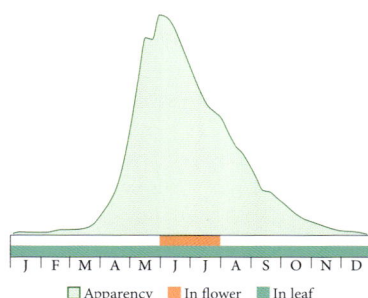

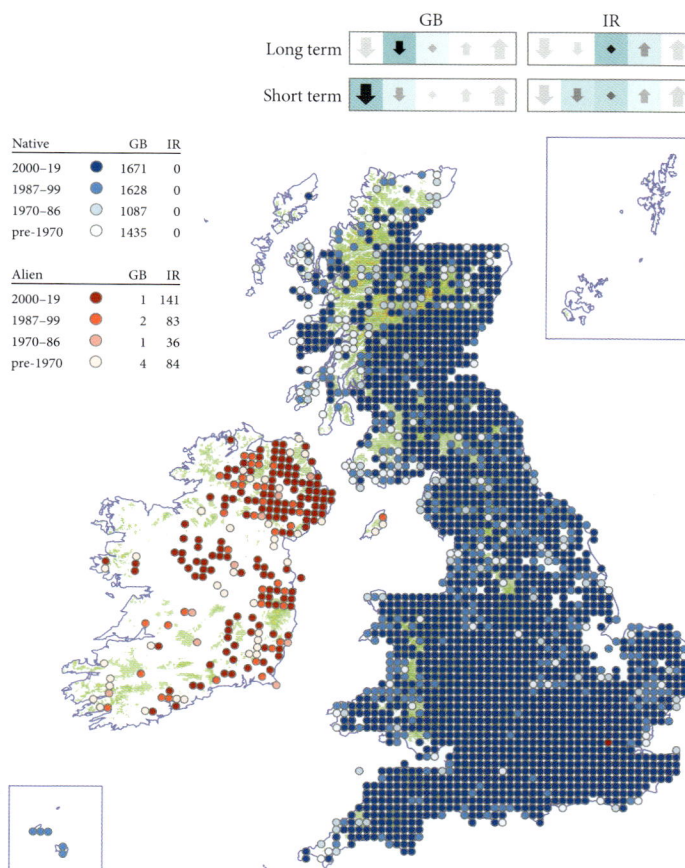

Native	GB	IR
2000–19	1671	0
1987–99	1628	0
1970–86	1087	0
pre-1970	1435	0

Alien	GB	IR
2000–19	1	141
1987–99	2	83
1970–86	1	36
pre-1970	4	84

Key refs Cope & Gray (2009), Plue *et al.* (2020), Scannell & Synnott (1987).

S.J. Leach & D.A. Pearman

N *Poa bulbosa* Bulbous Meadow-grass
L.

A tufted bulbous-based perennial grass of open grassland and barish sandy or rocky places near the sea; mainly on sand dunes and stabilized shingle, but also on bare chalk and limestone. Inland, it is found on compacted, often sandy or gravelly verges, in closely mown turf and on gravelly or concrete tracks (Leslie, 2019). Some populations are wholly or partially proliferous. Lowland.

Native in Britain and the Channel Islands and a neophyte in Ireland.

Trends The 10 km square distribution of *P. bulbosa* has increased since the 1960s. New records in some coastal areas such as Lincolnshire, East Kent, Isle of Wight, and southern Wales may represent recent spread or previously overlooked populations. The origins of the inland colonies, which have increased, are uncertain: they could be previously overlooked native populations, recent arrivals as a result of a natural extension of range, or introductions with sand and ballast. Those around Cambridge, where it was first found in 2003 and is now known to be frequent, may be of long-standing (Leslie, 2019). It was first found in Ireland in 1997 (Rosslare, County Wexford), where it persists. It is tempting to suggest that this species may be benefitting from climate change, as well as human-assisted dispersal in raw materials and in soil attached to vehicles and humans.

Biogeography Eurosiberian Southern-temperate element; widely naturalized outside its native range.

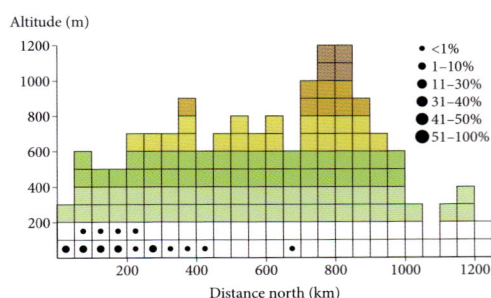

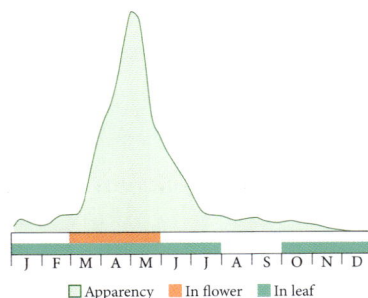

Native	GB	IR
2000–19	105	0
1987–99	65	0
1970–86	54	0
pre-1970	54	0

Alien	GB	IR
2000–19	3	1
1987–99	4	1
1970–86	3	0
pre-1970	5	0

Key refs Cope & Gray (2009), Leslie (2019), Stewart *et al.* (1994).

S.J. Leach & D.A. Pearman

N *Poa alpina* Alpine Meadow-grass
L.

A perennial grass of damp mountain rock faces, open ledges and rocky slopes on calcareous substrates, sometimes growing with *P. glauca*. Most populations are wholly or partially proliferous. From 350 m on Coir an t'Seasgaich (North Ebudes) to 1,275 m on Ben Nevis (Westerness).

Trends The overall 10 km square distribution of *P. alpina* has not changed appreciably since the 1960s. It has not been refound in a number of squares since 2000, though many are remote locations seldom visited by botanists and so it is likely to be still present in many, if not all, of these. It is sensitive to overgrazing, and injudicious collecting was blamed for some losses in the past, but it is difficult to believe that this still applies. Populations outside Scotland are small and vulnerable with England, Wales and Ireland each supporting fewer than a few hundred plants in a handful of locations.

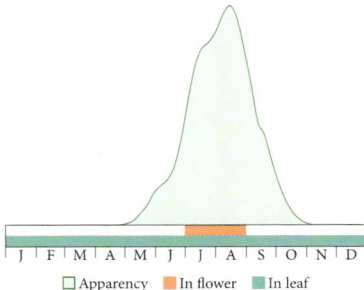

Biogeography Circumpolar Arctic-montane element, with a disjunct distribution.

Native	GB	IR
2000–19	40	3
1987–99	46	2
1970–86	41	1
pre-1970	61	2

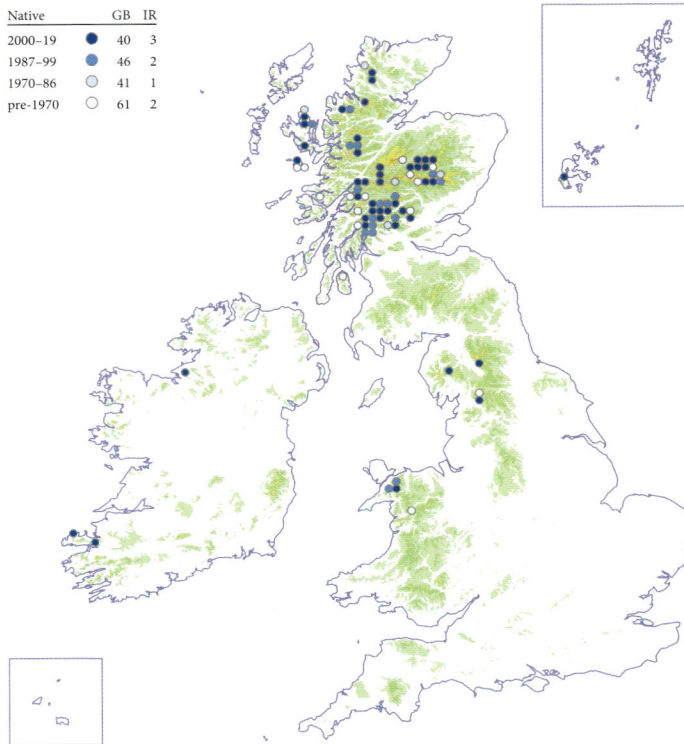

Key refs Cope & Gray (2009), Stewart *et al.* (1994).

S.J. Leach & D.A. Pearman

Ne *Bromus arvensis* Field Brome
L.

A winter-annual grass, found in arable and cultivated fields and on tracksides, docks and waste ground, mostly on nutrient-poor, light or sandy soils. It is usually casual or shortly persistent and arises from wool, grain and agricultural seed. Lowland.

Trends *B. arvensis* may originally have been sown as a hay-crop, on its own or with other fodder plants. It was first recorded in the wild in 1763 (Gravesend, West Kent) and was formerly frequent (being cultivated at Kew, Surrey, by 1768), but underwent a dramatic decline during the 20th century, probably due to improved seed cleaning methods, increased use of herbicide and the decline in wool shoddy. Most records were made before 1930.

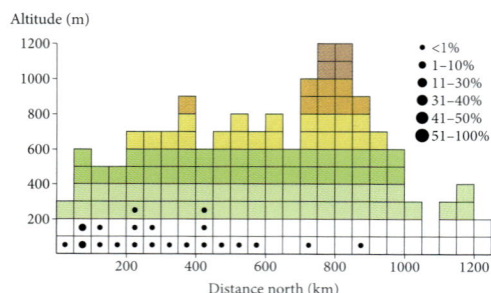

Biogeography Native range uncertain; *B. arvensis* has spread with cultivation to attain a European Temperate distribution.

Alien	GB	IR
2000–19	23	0
1987–99	13	0
1970–86	12	0
pre-1970	216	0

Key refs Cope & Gray (2009), Ryves *et al.* (1996).

S.J. Leach & D.A. Pearman

Bromus racemosus s.l. Smooth Brome

L.

An annual grass of unimproved hay- and water-meadows, usually on damp, periodically flooded alluvial soils. It is most frequent on the drier margins of fields, sometimes growing on the dredgings from the ditches bordering them. It is increasingly a persistent weed of arable land, especially winter wheat. Predominantly lowland.

Trends *B. racemosus* and the closely related *B. commutatus* were mapped separately by Perring & Walters (1962) and in the 2002 *Atlas* but the latter is now considered to be a variety of *B. racemosus* (Cope & Gray, 2009; Stace, 2019). Records for both taxa are shown on the map. *B. racemosus s.l.* is now much better recorded than it was before the 1960s. It has declined in some areas through the drainage and improvement of grasslands for intensive agriculture, but as with other species of

Bromus, it has developed tolerance to herbicides and has benefitted too from the cessation of burning after harvest, and from direct drilling techniques.

Biogeography European Temperate element; widely naturalized outside its native range.

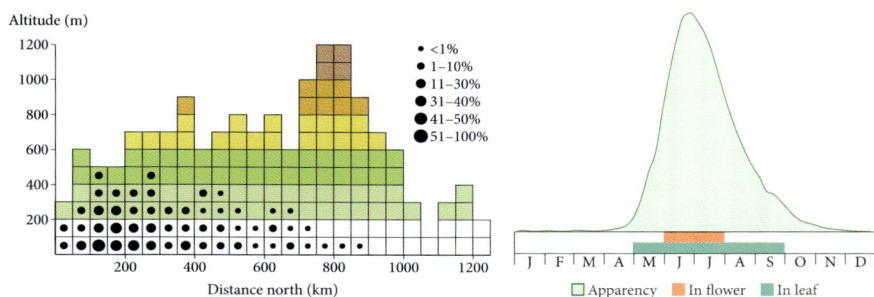

Native		GB	IR
2000–19	●	880	61
1987–99	●	663	31
1970–86	○	364	7
pre-1970	○	574	83

Alien		GB	IR
2000–19	●	41	0
1987–99	●	15	0
1970–86	●	15	0
pre-1970	○	100	0

Key refs Cope & Gray (2009).

D.A. Pearman

Bromus hordeaceus Soft-brome

L.

A winter-annual grass of moderately fertile neutral soils, particularly favouring disturbed or open habitats. It occurs on coastal cliffs, in pastures and hay meadows; also introduced as an impurity in grass-seed to arable fields, tracksides and waste ground. It does not form a persistent seed bank, and is intolerant of heavy grazing or frequent mowing. It tends to avoid wet or very acidic sites. 0–550 m (Kilhope, County Durham).

Trends The 10 km square distribution of this very variable species is largely unchanged since the 1960s, although it is now much better recorded in Ireland and Scotland due to more systematic recording. Subsp. *hordeaceus* is by far the commonest of the taxa that occur throughout the range of the species shown on the map. Subsp. *divaricatus* is a rare casual with a

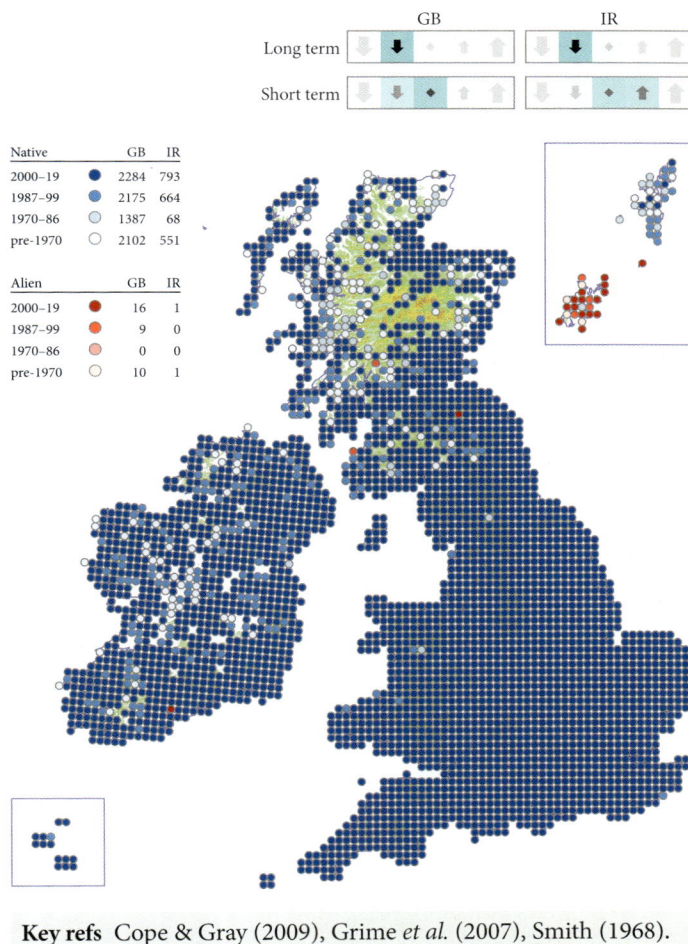

scattered distribution. Subsp. *ferronii*, subsp. *longipedicellatus* and subsp. *thominei* are mapped separately.

Biogeography European Southern-temperate element; widely naturalized outside its native range.

Native		GB	IR
2000–19	●	2284	793
1987–99	●	2175	664
1970–86	○	1387	68
pre-1970	○	2102	551

Alien		GB	IR
2000–19	●	16	1
1987–99	●	9	0
1970–86	●	0	0
pre-1970	○	10	1

Key refs Cope & Gray (2009), Grime *et al.* (2007), Smith (1968).

D.A. Pearman

(N) *Bromus hordeaceus* subsp. *ferronii* Least Soft-brome
(Mabille) P.M.Sm.

A winter-annual grass of shallow, drought-prone soils on exposed coastal cliff-tops, shingle beaches and banks, and occasionally sand dunes. It flowers and sets seed in the spring, well before its habitats become severely droughted. Lowland.

Trends The distribution of subsp. *ferronii* is generally stable, and with several new sites discovered within its core southern and south-western British range since 2000 due to systematic recording for county Floras. It may occasionally be over-recorded for dwarf forms of *B. hordeaceus* subsp. *hordeaceus*.

Biogeography Oceanic Temperate element; restricted to the Atlantic coast of north-western Europe.

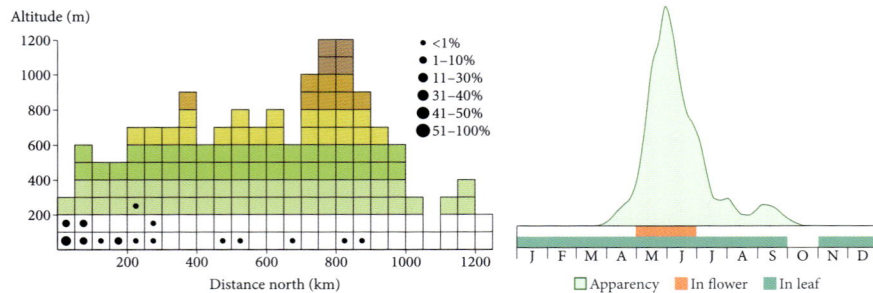

	GB	IR
Long term	No trend	No trend
Short term	No trend	No trend

Native	GB	IR
2000–19	60	0
1987–99	78	2
1970–86	39	1
pre-1970	75	0

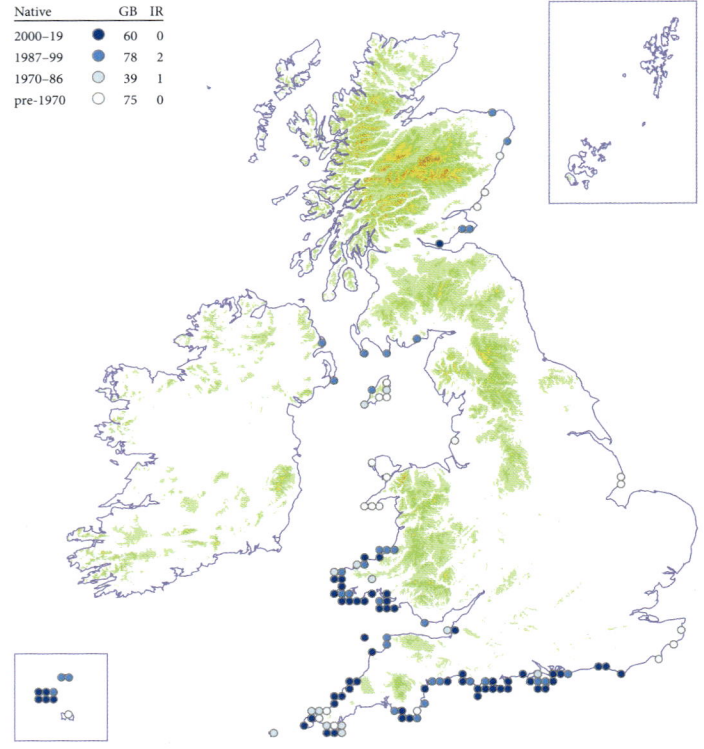

Key refs Cope & Gray (2009), Smith (1968).

D.A. PEARMAN

(N) *Bromus hordeaceus* subsp. *thominei* Sand Soft-brome
(Hardouin) Braun-Blanq.

A winter-annual of coastal fixed dunes, grassy cliff-tops and slopes, and other sandy places by the sea. Inland, it is recorded from sandy soils and ruderal habitats. Lowland.

Trends This taxon was redefined by Smith (1968); the map in Perring & Sell (1968) represents the earlier, broader circumscription. Its distribution remains very uncertain and only confirmed inland records have been accepted; the remainder have been treated as probable errors for *B. ×pseudothominei*.

Biogeography Suboceanic Temperate element.

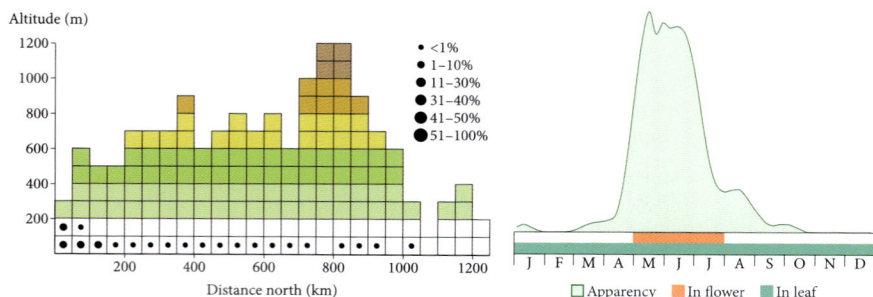

	GB	IR
Long term	No trend	No trend
Short term	No trend	No trend

Native	GB	IR
2000–19	50	1
1987–99	52	0
1970–86	39	0
pre-1970	48	0

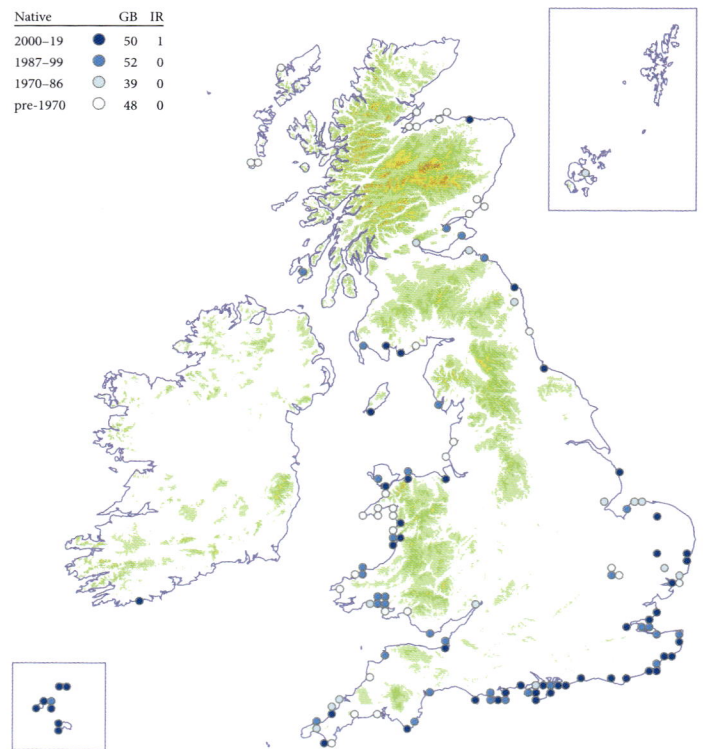

Key refs Cope & Gray (2009), Smith (1968).

D.A. PEARMAN

N *Bromus hordeaceus* subsp. *longipedicellatus*

Spalton

An annual grass of road verges and banks, on waysides, on the edges of arable fields (especially wheat), on waste ground and less frequently in pasture. Lowland.

Trends The precise range of subsp. *longipedicellatus* is still unknown, as the subspecies was described as recently as 2001 (Spalton, 2001). It is not known whether it is a native taxon, or one introduced as a contaminant of introduced grass and cereal seeds; all records are therefore mapped without status. Some authorities regard it as simply a variant of subsp. *hordeaceus* (Cope & Gray, 2009).

Biogeography Possibly endemic although further research is needed to establish its true taxonomic status.

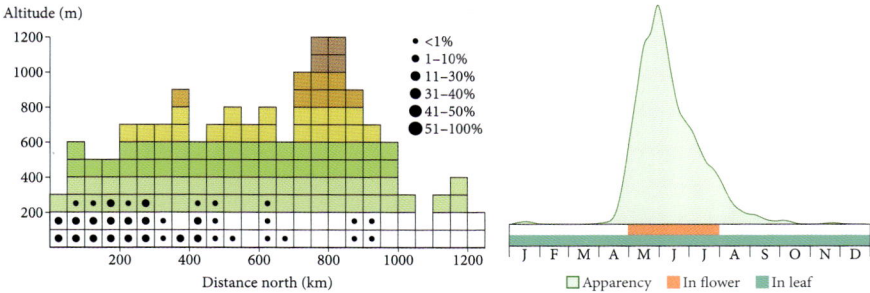

	GB	IR
Long term	No trend	No trend
Short term	No trend	No trend

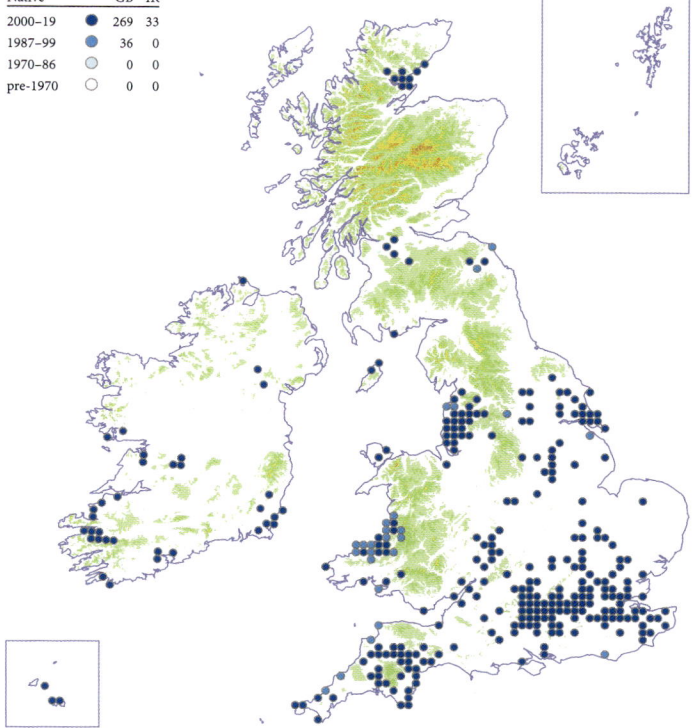

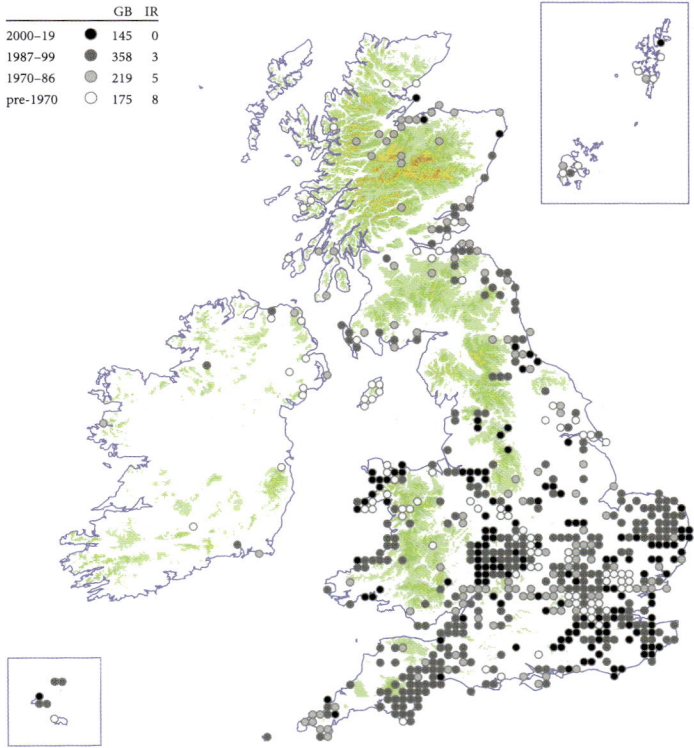

Native	GB	IR
2000–19	269	33
1987–99	36	0
1970–86	0	0
pre-1970	0	0

Key refs Cope & Gray (2009), Spalton (2001).

Altitude (m)

<1%
1–10%
11–30%
31–40%
41–50%
51–100%

Distance north (km)

J F M A M J J A S O N D

☐ Apparency ■ In flower ■ In leaf

D.A. PEARMAN

Hy *Bromus hordeaceus* × *lepidus* = *B.* ×*pseudothominei* Lesser Soft-brome

P.M.Sm.

An annual grass which is most frequent as an impurity on newly sown roadside verges and embankments, sown pastures and cultivated fields, and disturbed sites such as old sand- and stone-quarries, disused railway tracks and sidings, riverside towpaths, waste ground and refuse tips. It is also occasionally found in coastal habitats such as cliff tops, shingle spits and the margins of sand dunes. It is fully fertile, and often occurs in the absence of both its putative parents. Lowland.

A spontaneous hybrid (native × alien).

Trends *B.* ×*pseudothominei* was described by Smith (1968) as a hybrid of *B. hordeaceus* subsp. *hordeaceus* and *B. lepidus*. It was previously confused with the maritime *B. hordeaceus* subsp. *thominei* and was mapped with that taxon by Perring & Sell (1968). It is almost certainly under-recorded, though in recent years Spalton (2001) doubted the distinction of the putative hybrid from *B. hordeaceus* subsp. *hordeaceus*, and Cope & Gray (2009) treat them as synonymous.

Biogeography Widespread in Europe, but with a poorly documented distribution.

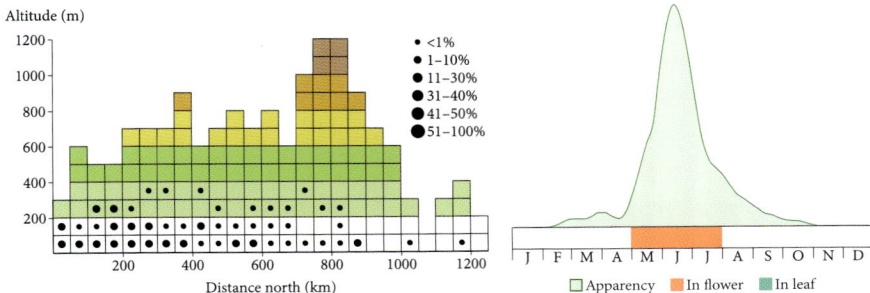

	GB	IR
Long term	No trend	No trend
Short term	No trend	No trend

	GB	IR
2000–19	145	0
1987–99	358	3
1970–86	219	5
pre-1970	175	8

Key refs Cope & Gray (2009), Smith (1968), Spalton (2001), Stace *et al.* (2015).

Altitude (m)

<1%
1–10%
11–30%
31–40%
41–50%
51–100%

Distance north (km)

J F M A M J J A S O N D

☐ Apparency ■ In flower ■ In leaf

C.A. STACE, C.D. PRESTON & D.A. PEARMAN

Ne *Bromus lepidus* Slender Soft-brome
Holmb.

An annual grass, found on arable margins, on arable land sown to pasture, in other leys sown with *Lolium multiflorum* and *L. perenne*, and on the verges of tracks and roads, on waste ground and in gardens. Probably always arising as a contaminant of grass-seed mixtures. Lowland.

Trends *B. lepidus* was first recorded from the wild in 1836 (Cheltenham, East Gloucestershire), not long after the first major imports of seeds for grass leys, and it seems to be an introduced species. The reason for the paucity of modern records is uncertain; it may be less common, or recent recorders may have failed to distinguish it from *B. hordeaceus*, or it may have been over-recorded in the past. Whatever the reason it is now much less frequently recorded.

Biogeography Native range unknown; the species is recorded as an apparent introduction in north-western and north-central Europe and southern Scandinavia. It may have evolved in its man-made habitat.

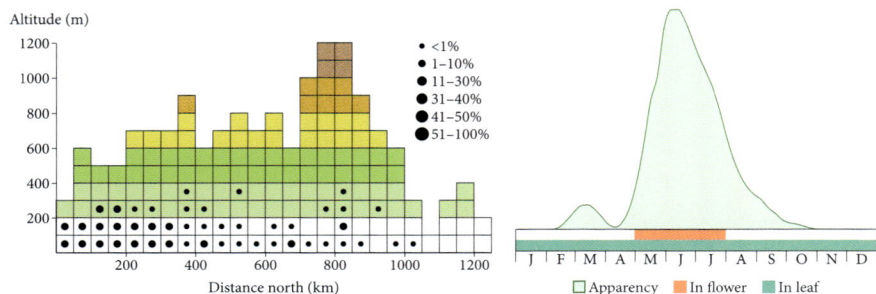

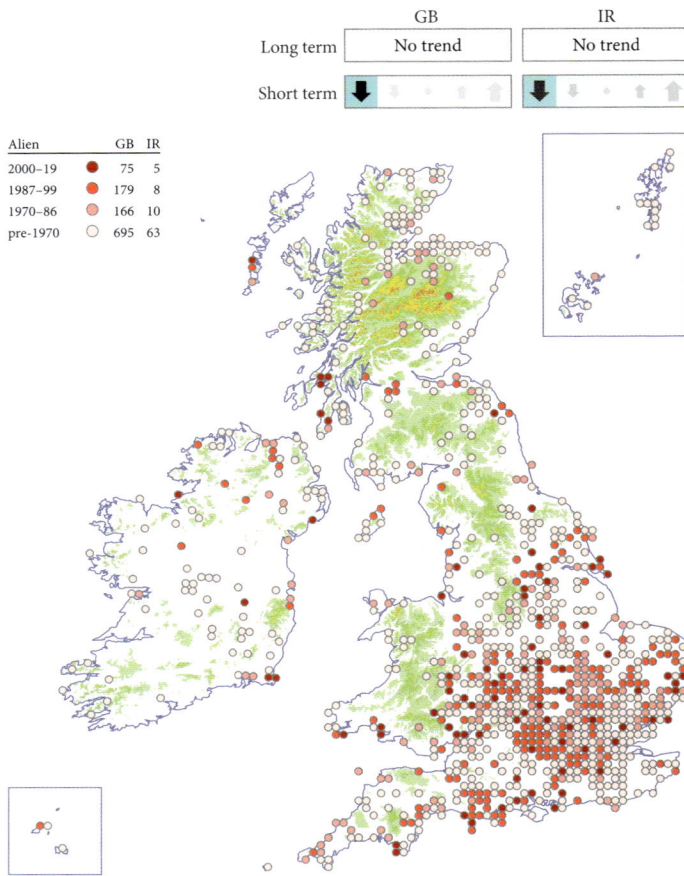

Alien	GB	IR
2000–19	75	5
1987–99	179	8
1970–86	166	10
pre-1970	695	63

	GB	IR
Long term	No trend	No trend
Short term	↓	↓

Key refs Cope & Gray (2009), Smith (1968).

D.A. PEARMAN & K.J. WALKER

N *Bromus interruptus* Interrupted Brome
(Hack.) Druce

An annual grass of light soils in cultivated fields, especially in crops of *Onobrychis viciifolia*, *Lolium* or *Trifolium*, and on waysides. Lowland.

Trends *B. interruptus* occupies a paradoxical position in the British flora as an endemic which has also widely been considered to be a neophyte. It had previously thought to have been unintentionally introduced as a fodder crop seed contaminant from overseas, but excepting two 20th century casual occurrences in the Netherlands at Ermelo (1933) and in Amsterdam docks (1934), the species has never been recorded outside of England. It is now considered to be a native mutation of *B. hordeaceus* which occurred in England and was then dispersed locally. *B. interruptus* was first collected in 1849 at Odsey (Cambridgeshire/Hertfordshire border) and was last seen in 1972, beside a farm track at Pampisford, Cambridgeshire. Though extinct in the wild, it was retained in cultivation in botanic gardens, and since 2003, introductions have been attempted at 11 locations in eight 10km squares within the former range; these are mapped as alien. In 2019 it persisted at four localities.

Biogeography Endemic to England.

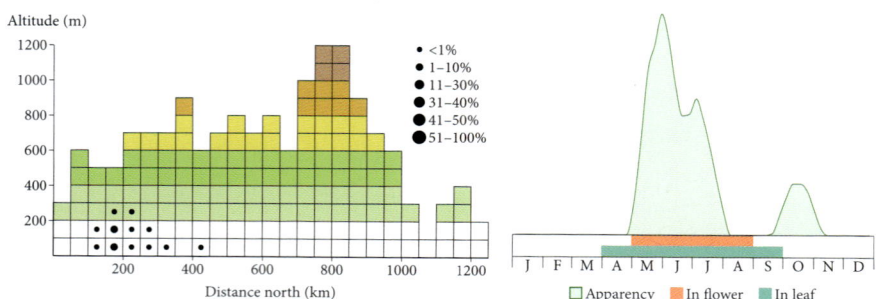

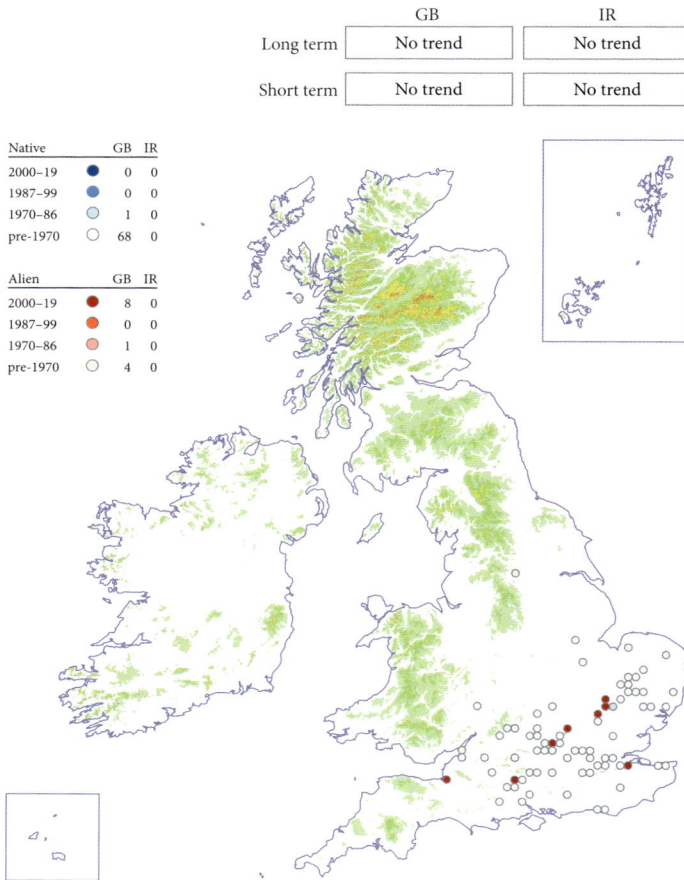

Native	GB	IR
2000–19	0	0
1987–99	0	0
1970–86	1	0
pre-1970	68	0

Alien	GB	IR
2000–19	8	0
1987–99	0	0
1970–86	1	0
pre-1970	4	0

	GB	IR
Long term	No trend	No trend
Short term	No trend	No trend

Key refs Cope & Gray (2009), Donald (1980), Lyte & Cope (1999), Rich & Lockton (2002), Rumsey & Stroh (2020).

F.J. RUMSEY, P.A. STROH & D.A. PEARMAN

Ar *Bromus secalinus* Rye Brome

L.

An annual or biennial grass of cereal fields, also found as a casual on waste ground, and occasionally in improved leys. Lowland.

An archaeophyte in Britain and the Channel Islands and a neophyte in Ireland.

Trends *B. secalinus* has probably been present in Britain since prehistoric times, initially as an arable weed or perhaps as an alternative source of grain when the main cereal crops failed. It was frequent in the 19th and early 20th centuries, but then underwent a sharp decline and by the late 20th century it was absent from large swathes of lowland England. However, since the 1990s its distribution has dramatically increased due to herbicide resistance, and it is flourishing, along with some other species of *Bromus* and *Alopecurus myosuroides*,

under direct-drilling regimes (Davies *et al.*, 2020). The cessation of stubble-burning in arable cultivation may also have assisted its recent resurgence. *B. secalinus* is sometimes confused with *B. pseudosecalinus*.

Biogeography *B. secalinus* may have evolved in cultivation, and must have spread widely in prehistoric times as a weed, perhaps as a 'seed mimic' of rye.

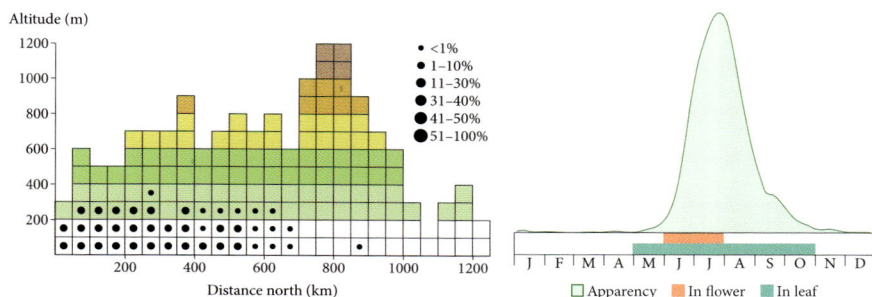

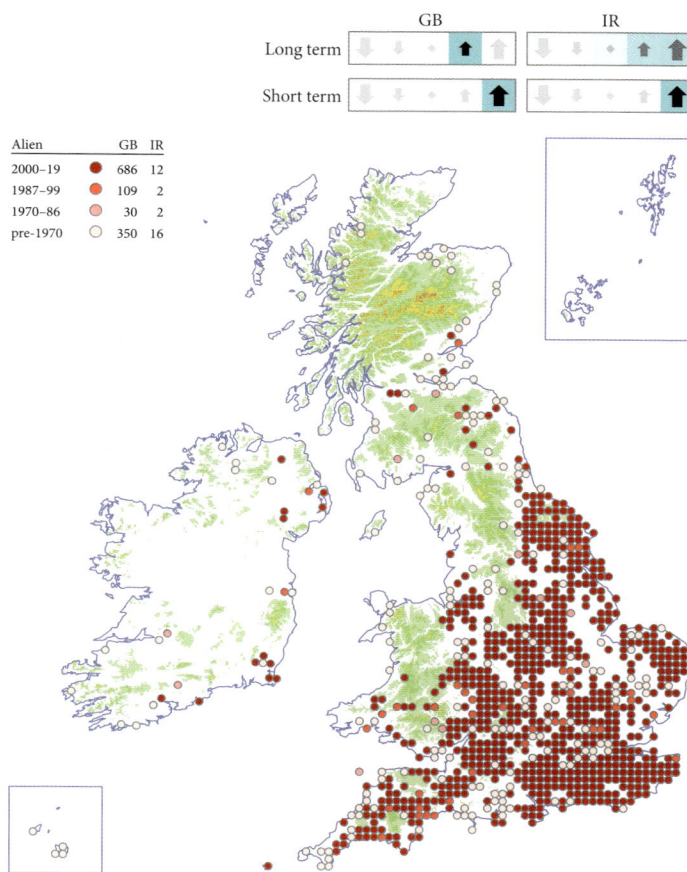

Alien		GB	IR
2000–19	●	686	12
1987–99	●	109	2
1970–86	●	30	2
pre-1970	○	350	16

Key refs Beckett & Bull (1999), Cheffings & Farrell (2005), Cope & Gray (2009), Davies *et al.* (2020).

S.J. Leach & D.A. Pearman

Ne *Anisantha diandra* Great Brome

(Roth) Tutin ex Tzvelev

An annual grass of arable fields, waste ground and roadsides, and in open grassland and heathland on sandy soils. It is sometimes well-established on sand dunes. It is a grain, birdseed and formerly wool alien. Lowland.

Trends *A. diandra* was first recorded from the wild in 1689 (Jersey). In the 1962 *Atlas* it was treated as possibly native in the Channel Islands, though native status there is now considered most unlikely. Its range increased dramatically in the latter part of the 20th century, consolidating its distribution in East Anglia. Since 2000 it has continued to significantly expand its range and distribution to become frequent in many parts of southern, central and north-eastern England, and eastern and north-eastern Scotland. The same is true in south-eastern Ireland. This increase may be a result of milder winters in

combination with herbicide resistance, the increased use of conservation tillage, and a lower diversity of crop rotations. It may be conspecific with *A. rigida*.

Biogeography Native of the Mediterranean region and south-western Asia; naturalized in western Europe, North and South America, southern Africa and elsewhere.

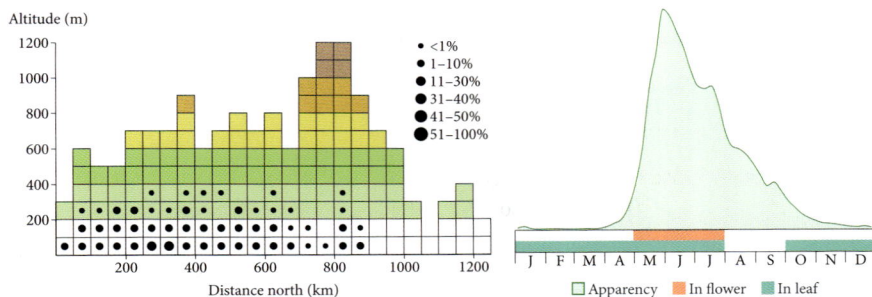

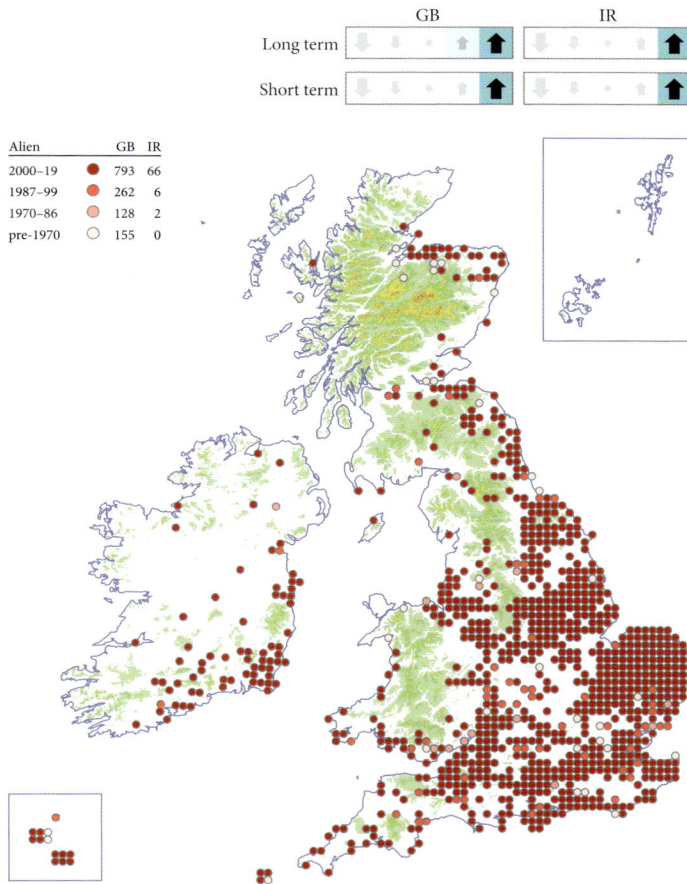

Alien		GB	IR
2000–19	●	793	66
1987–99	●	262	6
1970–86	●	128	2
pre-1970	○	155	0

Key refs Cope & Gray (2009), Ryves *et al.* (1996).

S.J. Leach & D.A. Pearman

Ne *Anisantha rigida* Ripgut Brome
(Roth) Hyl.

An annual grass of waysides, open grassland and disturbed or cultivated ground on light soils, usually not persisting but well-established on sand dunes and other sandy places near the sea in southern England and on the Channel Islands. Lowland.

Trends *A. rigida* is a wool, grain and agricultural seed alien, and was first recorded in the wild in 1834 (St Davids, Fife). It has previously been treated as native in the Channel Islands, although it is more likely to have been introduced there. It seems to have increased since the 1960s, although recent Floras for East Anglian counties have tended to treat this species as a variant of *A. diandra*.

Biogeography Native of the Mediterranean region; closely related to and perhaps only subspecifically distinct from *A. diandra*.

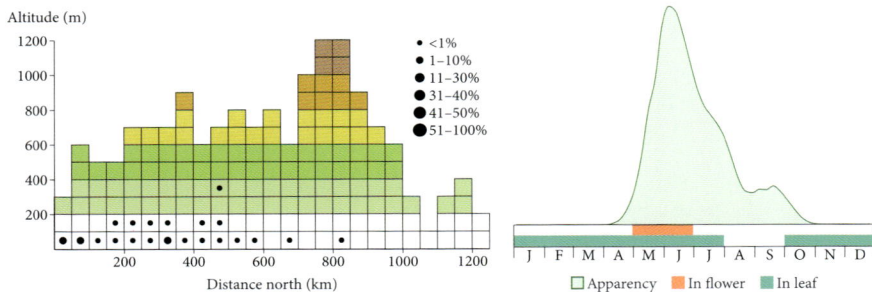

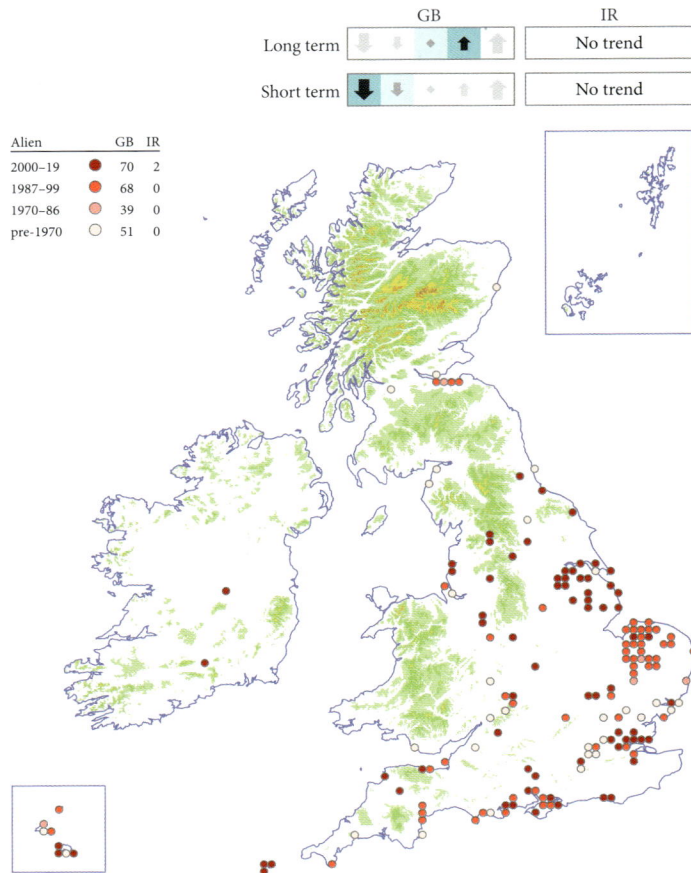

Alien	GB	IR
2000–19	70	2
1987–99	68	0
1970–86	39	0
pre-1970	51	0

Key refs Cope & Gray (2009), Ryves *et al.* (1996).

S.J. Leach & D.A. Pearman

Ar *Anisantha sterilis* Barren Brome
(L.) Nevski

An annual grass of roadsides, railway banks, open grassland, gardens and waste ground. It can be a serious weed in fields where winter cereals are grown repeatedly using minimum cultivation techniques, especially in southern Britain (Grime *et al.*, 2007). In the past it was frequently introduced with wool shoddy. Generally lowland, but reaching 365 m in Derbyshire.

Trends The 10 km distribution of *A. sterilis* remains stable, though locally its distribution is much better known due to increased recording effort this century, and it may be genuinely spreading in some areas of southern England.

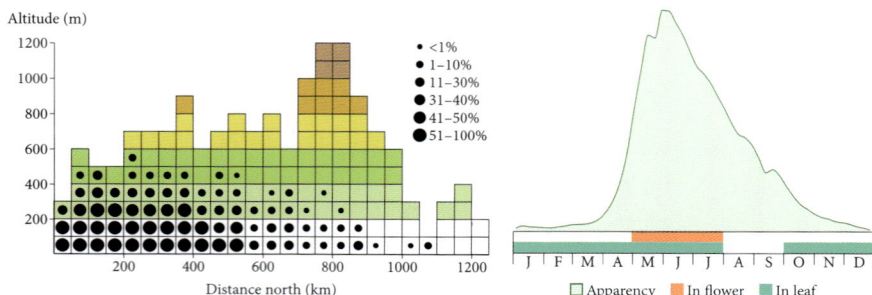

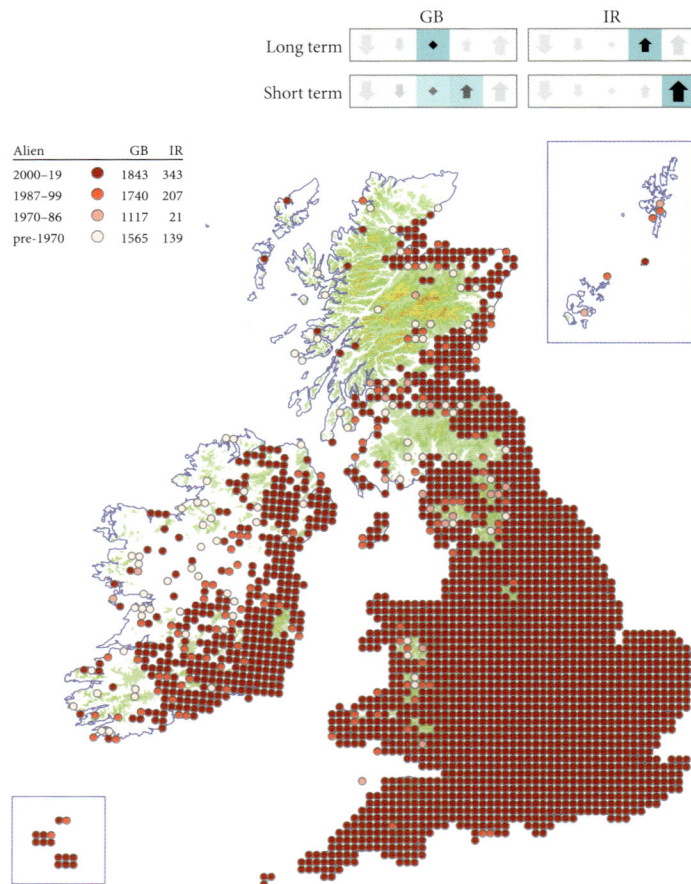

Biogeography As an archaeophyte, *A. sterilis* has a European Southern-temperate distribution; it is widely naturalized outside this range.

Alien	GB	IR
2000–19	1843	343
1987–99	1740	207
1970–86	1117	21
pre-1970	1565	139

Key refs Cope & Gray (2009), Gray (1981), Grime *et al.* (2007).

S.J. Leach & D.A. Pearman

Ne *Anisantha tectorum* Drooping Brome

(L.) Nevski

An annual grass of waste ground, roadsides and grassy places on sandy soils. It is a casual from grain, wool shoddy and grass-seed, but can be naturalized on sandy banks, field margins and grass heaths in Breckland. Many recent records are from newly sown road verges. Lowland.

Trends *A. tectorum* has been known in the wild since 1847 (Hoddesdon, Hertfordshire). It appears to have declined in Breckland, where it was formerly abundant between Brandon and Thetford but has not been seen there since the early 1980s (Beckett *et al.*, 1999); it still occurs in neighbouring West Suffolk and on the adjacent eastern border of Cambridgeshire.

Biogeography A Eurosiberian Southern-temperate species, extending as a native to northern France and southern Scandinavia; it is naturalized in North America, where it can be very invasive, and is known as 'cheatgrass' in Australasia and elsewhere.

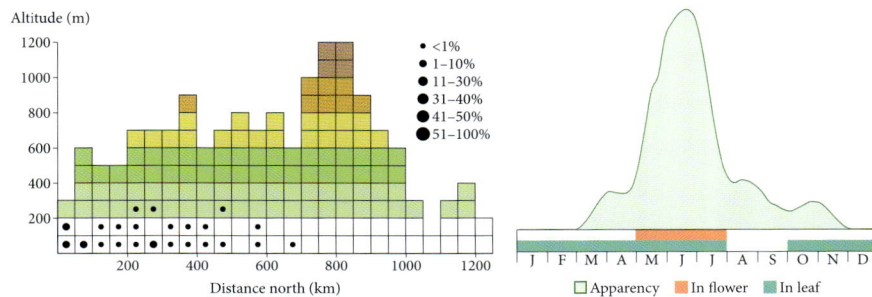

Alien	GB	IR
2000–19	31	3
1987–99	30	1
1970–86	32	0
pre-1970	86	0

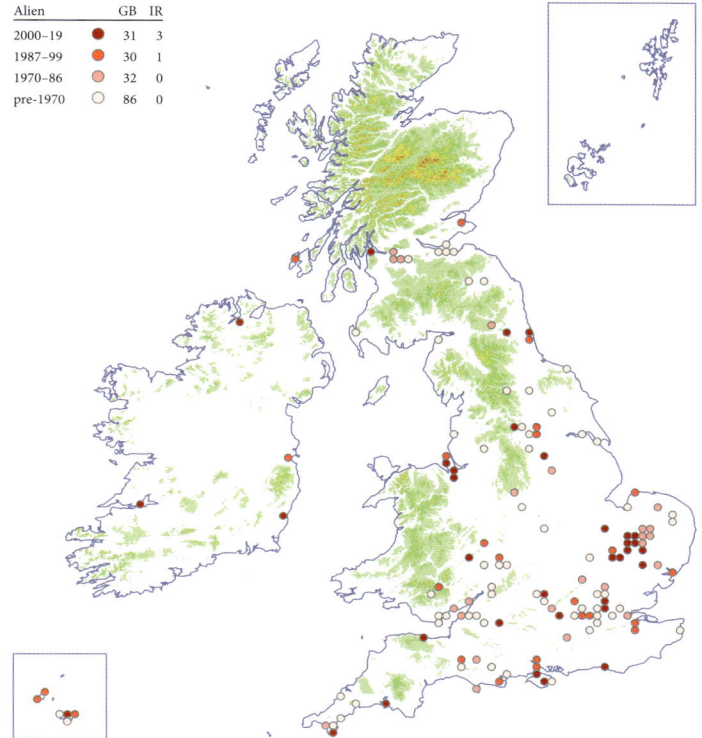

	GB	IR
Long term	No trend	No trend
Short term	↓	No trend

Key refs Beckett & Bull (1999), Cope & Gray (2009), Ryves *et al.* (1996), Upadhyaya *et al.* (1986).

S.J. Leach & D.A. Pearman

Ne *Anisantha madritensis* Compact Brome

(L.) Nevski

An annual grass of waste land, cultivated ground, roadside banks, walls and ruins; also around docks and on refuse tips, on sand dunes and in other sandy or rocky places near the sea. It is long-established (and considered by some to be possibly native) at a few sites in south-western Britain and the Channel Islands, though it is more likely to be an ancient introduction there (Pearman, 2007). Otherwise, it is widespread as a casual. Lowland.

Trends The 10km sqaure distribution of *A. madritensis*, known from the wild in Britain since 1716 (Sandown Castle, East Kent), has increased since the 1960s, and the species has consolidated its range in southern Wales.

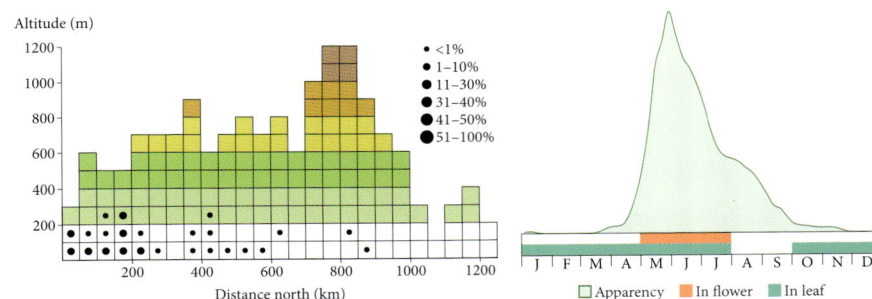

Biogeography Native of the Mediterranean region and south-western Asia; naturalized in North and South America, Australia and elsewhere.

Alien	GB	IR
2000–19	112	8
1987–99	61	4
1970–86	35	3
pre-1970	92	5

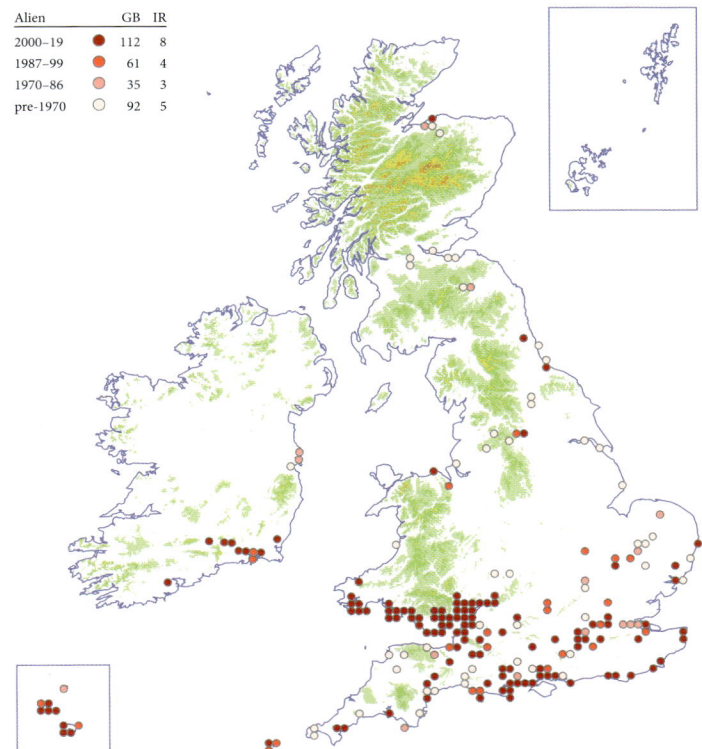

	GB	IR
Long term	No trend	No trend
Short term	↑	↑

Key refs Cope & Gray (2009), Pearman (2007), Wigginton (1999).

S.J. Leach & D.A. Pearman

Bromopsis ramosa Hairy-brome
(Huds.) Holub

A tufted perennial grass of shaded habitats on moist, moderately base-rich soils, including woodlands and hedgerows; it occasionally persists on sites of former woodland. Some bare soil is necessary for successful establishment from seed. Generally lowland lowland, but reaching 490 m at Cwar yr Hendre (Breconshire).

Trends The overall 10 km square distribution of *B. ramosa* appears to have remained relatively stable since the 1960s, although at a more local scale sites have been lost following the clear-felling of woodland.

Biogeography European Temperate element.

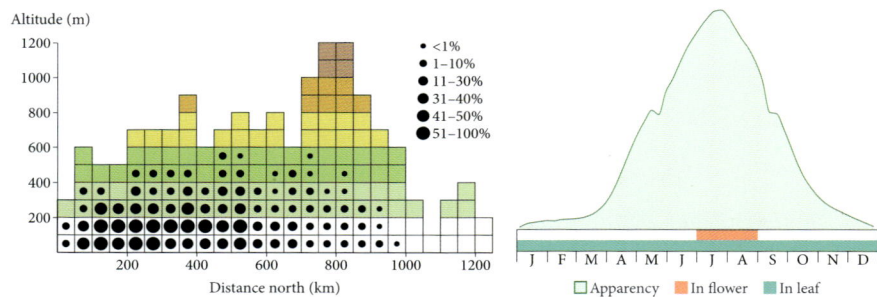

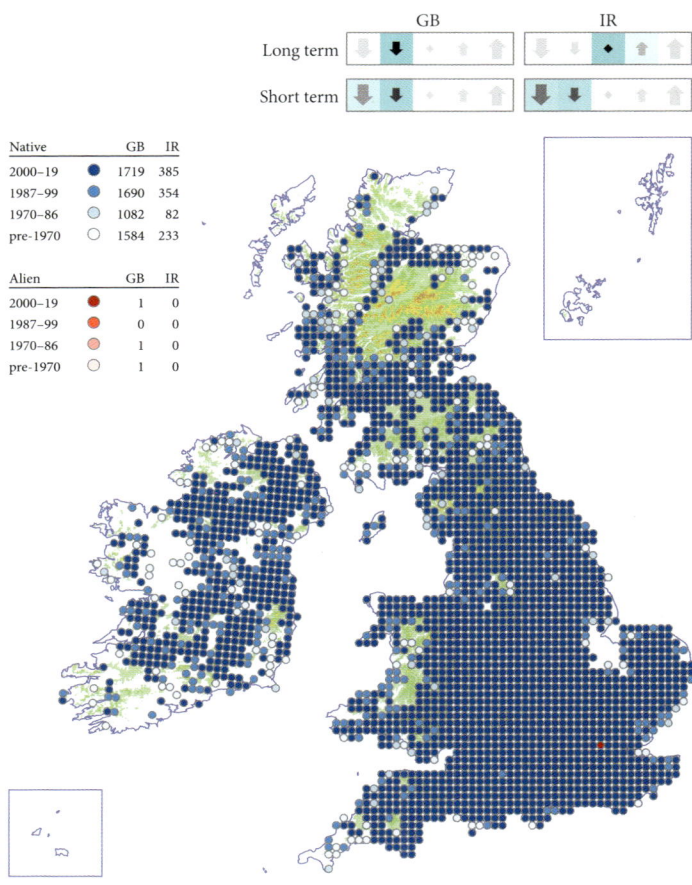

Native		GB	IR
2000–19	●	1719	385
1987–99	●	1690	354
1970–86	●	1082	82
pre-1970	○	1584	233

Alien		GB	IR
2000–19	●	1	0
1987–99	●	0	0
1970–86	●	1	0
pre-1970	○	1	0

Key refs Cope & Gray (2009), Grime *et al.* (2007).

D.A. PEARMAN

Bromopsis benekenii Lesser Hairy-brome
(Lange) Holub

A tufted perennial grass of lightly shaded places in woodland, especially beech woods; also found in scrub and hedgerows. It grows mainly in humus-rich but shallow calcareous soils, often on a slight slope. Lowland.

Trends Although *B. benekenii* is now better recorded than it once was, it is almost certainly still under-recorded in some areas. It is often difficult to separate from the very similar *B. ramosa*, with which it often grows, and possibly only reliably by its chromosome number; consequently it is possibly best treated as a subspecies of that species (Cope & Gray, 2009). It follows that some of the records mapped may be errors for *B. ramosa*.

Biogeography European Temperate element, with a continental distribution in western Europe; also in central Asia.

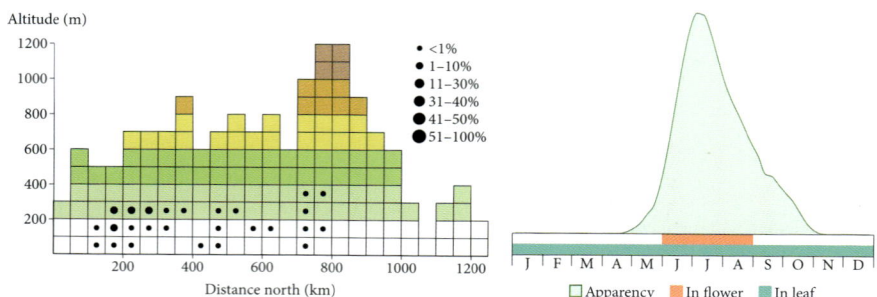

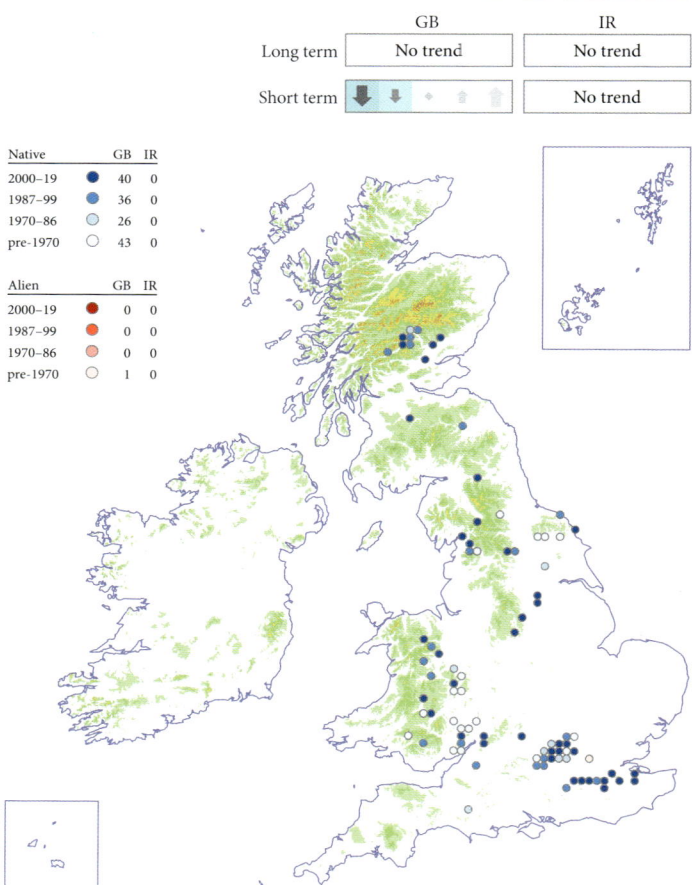

Native		GB	IR
2000–19	●	40	0
1987–99	●	36	0
1970–86	●	26	0
pre-1970	○	43	0

Alien		GB	IR
2000–19	●	0	0
1987–99	●	0	0
1970–86	●	0	0
pre-1970	○	1	0

Key refs Cope & Gray (2009), Stewart *et al.* (1994).

D.A. PEARMAN

(N) *Bromopsis erecta* Upright Brome
(Huds.) Fourr.

A tufted winter-green perennial grass of dry, relatively infertile calcareous soils, growing in chalk and limestone grasslands where it often forms dense stands with *Festuca ovina* or *Brachypodium pinnatum s.l.* in undergrazed swards. It also occurs on calcareous sand dunes, roadside banks and verges, quarry spoil and occasionally waste ground, but avoids wet or arable sites. It spreads by seeds which attach very effectively to the coats of animals. Predominantly lowland, but up to 440 m on limestone pavement at Tennant Gill Farm (Mid-west Yorkshire).

Trends *B. erecta* has increased in grasslands where grazing pressures have relaxed, especially following the reduction of the rabbit population through myxomatosis and the loss of livestock grazing on many lowland sites (including nature reserves) since the

1960s. Its lack of rhizomes and reliance on regeneration by seed means that it is often sub-dominant when growing with its frequent associate, *Brachypodium pinnatum s.l.*, especially in undergrazed swards overlying limestone. The origin of new populations in northern England and Scotland are unknown but at least some appear to be only casual occurrences on roadsides.

Biogeography European Temperate element; widely naturalized outside its native range.

Native	GB	IR
2000–19	627	40
1987–99	660	33
1970–86	456	24
pre-1970	620	18

Alien	GB	IR
2000–19	28	0
1987–99	18	0
1970–86	20	0
pre-1970	39	0

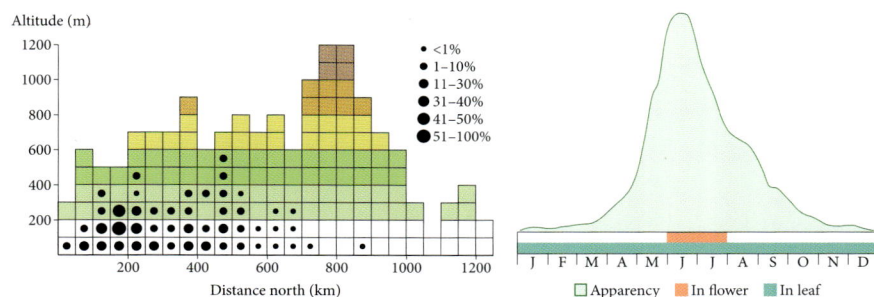

Key refs Cope & Gray (2009), Grime *et al.* (2007).

D.A. PEARMAN & K.J. WALKER

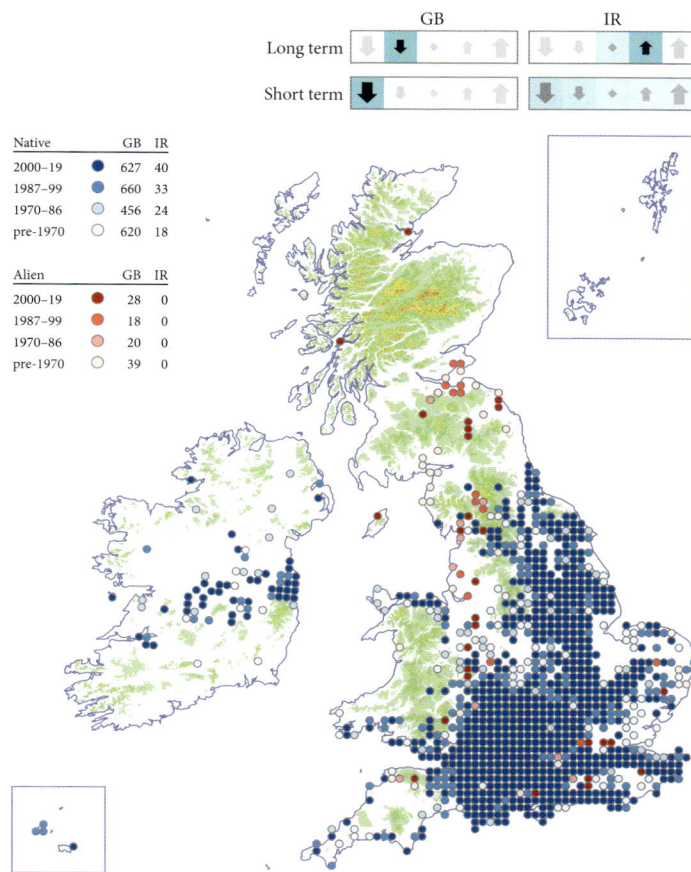

(Ne) *Bromopsis inermis* Hungarian Brome
(Leyss.) Holub

A strongly rhizomatous, winter-green perennial grass that is well naturalized on the banks and verges of roads and on field margins. It tolerates drought and often persists on sandy, well-drained soils. It occurs as a casual elsewhere. Lowland.

Trends *B. inermis*, which was first cultivated in Britain in 1794, was formerly sown as a fodder grass, but it is now introduced only as a seed contaminant. It has been known in the wild since 1890 (Reading, Berkshire), and is continuing to spread in some areas on road verges and on waste ground.

Biogeography *B. inermis* subsp. *inermis* is a Eurosiberian Temperate species; subsp. *pumpelliana* is native to North America.

Alien	GB	IR
2000–19	191	3
1987–99	191	0
1970–86	111	0
pre-1970	95	0

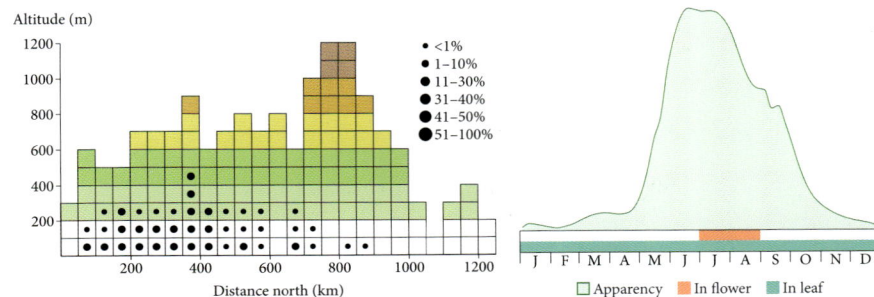

Key refs Cope & Gray (2009), Otfinowski *et al.* (2007), Ryves *et al.* (1996).

D.A. PEARMAN

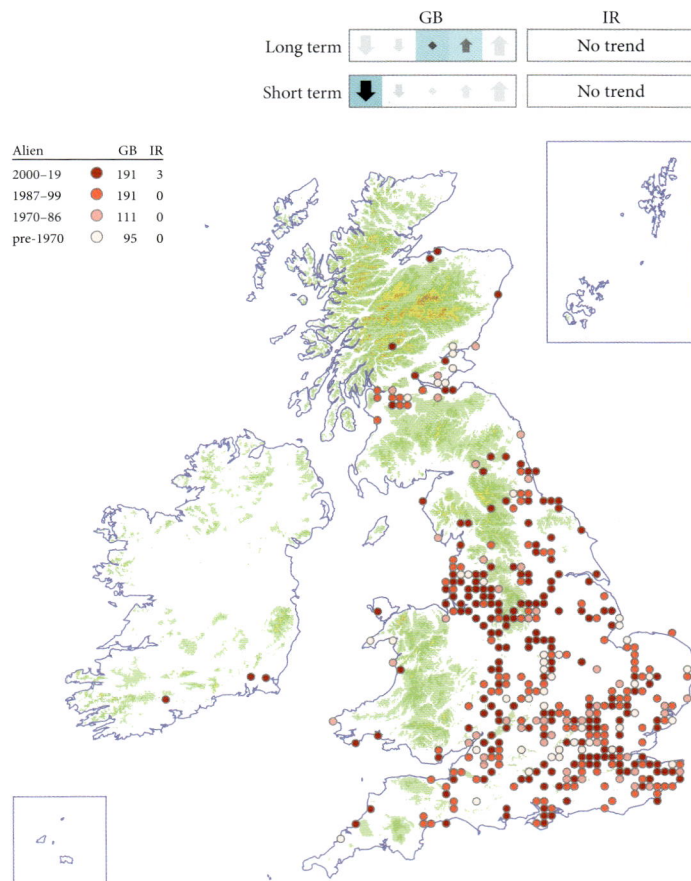

Ⓝⓔ *Ceratochloa carinata* California Brome

(Hook. & Arn.) Tutin

An annual to short-lived winter-green perennial grass, found mostly on the verges of paths, tracks and roads, but also on arable field margins, on waste ground, by rivers and in gardens. It is cleistogamous, and seed can be produced almost all year round. Lowland.

Trends *C. carinata* was apparently originally introduced as a fodder grass but is also a contaminant of agricultural seed and a garden ornamental. It was first recorded as an escape from the Royal Botanic Gardens, Kew (Surrey), in about 1919, but it did not begin to spread until 1945. There were still only a very few records in the 1960s but since then it has spread rapidly, particularly on lighter soils. The new cultivar 'Deborah' was developed in *c.*1975.

Biogeography Native of western North America.

Alien	GB	IR
2000–19	245	2
1987–99	169	1
1970–86	58	0
pre-1970	55	0

Key refs Clement (1981a), Cope & Gray (2009), Ryves *et al.* (1996).

D.A. PEARMAN & K.J. WALKER

Ⓝⓔ *Ceratochloa cathartica* Rescue Brome

(Vahl) Herter

An annual to short-lived winter-green perennial, found mostly on the verges of paths, tracks and roads, but also on refuse tips, pavements, waste ground and the borders of fields, and in arable crops. Whilst it often occurs as a casual, it is increasingly found naturalized in southern and eastern England. Lowland.

Trends *C. cathartica* was introduced as a fodder grass in 1788, and also occurs as a grain- and wool-alien. It was first recorded in the wild in 1854 (Newton in Cleveland, North-east Yorkshire); its distribution has increased markedly since the 1960s possibly due to the widespread sowing of seed mixes on roadsides and in amenity areas. It is persistent and well-naturalized in many localities.

Biogeography Native of South America.

Alien	GB	IR
2000–19	185	1
1987–99	94	0
1970–86	36	0
pre-1970	111	1

Key refs Cope & Gray (2009), Ryves *et al.* (1996).

D.A. PEARMAN

Ⓝ *Elymus caninus* Bearded Couch

(L.) L.

A loosely tufted non-rhizomatous perennial grass of partially shaded sites in woodland, on riverbanks and roadside margins on free-draining, mainly base-rich, soils. It is also found in mountainous areas in gullies, on cliffs and rock-ledges. It regenerates from seed and is intolerant of grazing and mowing. 0–810 m (Creag na Caillich, Mid Perthshire).

Trends The overall distribution of *E. caninus* appears to be stable. A variant with unawned lemmas, var. *donianus*, occurs on limestone rocks in central and northern Scotland.

Biogeography Eurosiberian Boreo-temperate element.

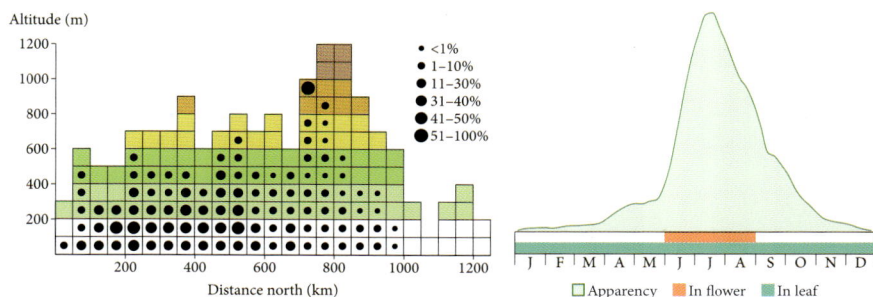

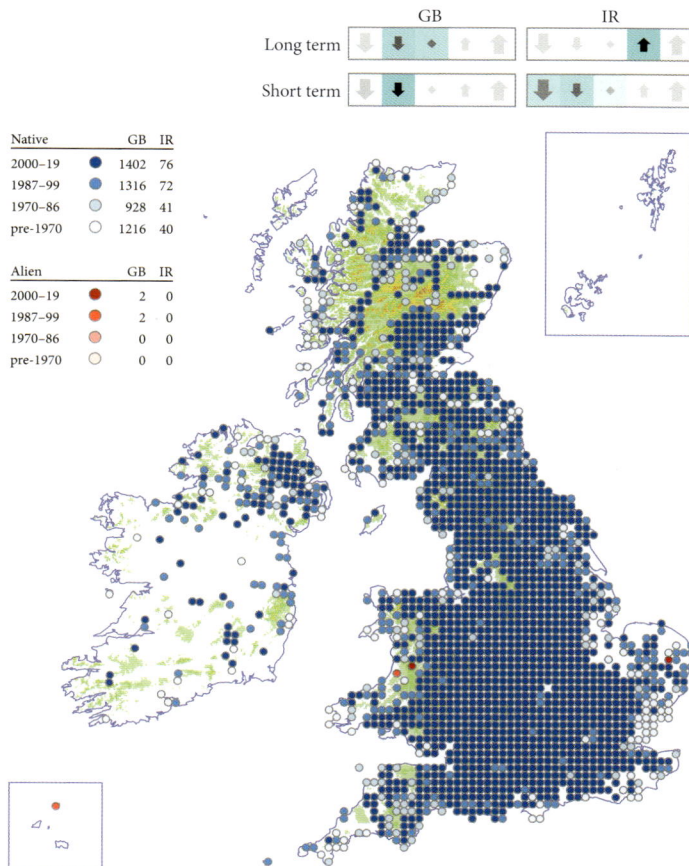

Native	GB	IR
2000–19	1402	76
1987–99	1316	72
1970–86	928	41
pre-1970	1216	40

Alien	GB	IR
2000–19	2	0
1987–99	2	0
1970–86	0	0
pre-1970	0	0

Key refs Cope & Gray (2009), Grime *et al.* (2007).

F.H. Perring & D.A. Pearman

Ⓝ *Elymus repens* Common Couch

(L.) Gould

A rhizomatous perennial grass of a wide range of disturbed, fertile grassland habitats including waste ground, roadsides, railway banks, arable land and derelict grassland; also in coastal areas on sand dunes, shingle, sea-walls and the margins of saltmarshes. It is a notorious weed of gardens and agricultural land. 0–430 m (Nenthead, Cumberland) and exceptionally at 845 m on Great Dun Fell (Westmorland).

Trends *E. repens* is a very widespread species and its 10 km square distribution appears to be stable. There are two subspecies in our area: subsp. *repens*, which occurs throughout the range of the species; and subsp. *arenosus*, which is a coastal species closely resembling *E. athericus* and therefore often confused with it.

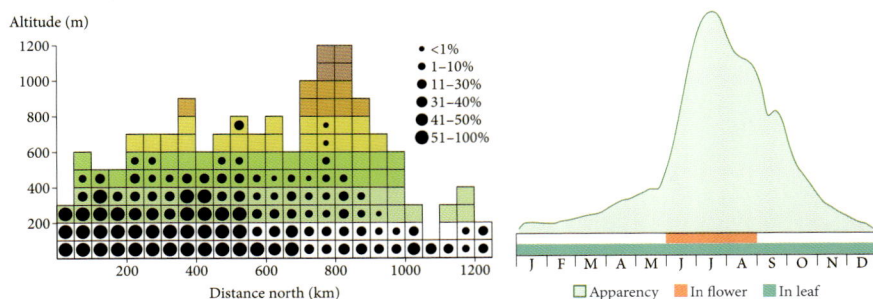

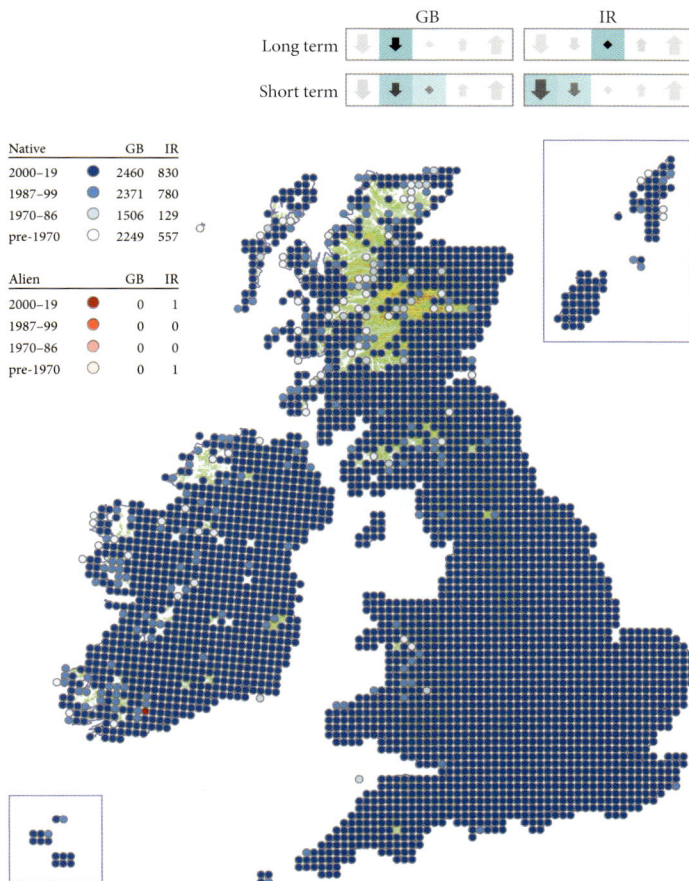

Biogeography Eurosiberian Wide-temperate element, but widely naturalized so that the distribution is now Circumpolar Wide-temperate.

Native	GB	IR
2000–19	2460	830
1987–99	2371	780
1970–86	1506	129
pre-1970	2249	557

Alien	GB	IR
2000–19	0	1
1987–99	0	0
1970–86	0	0
pre-1970	0	1

Key refs Cope & Gray (2009), Grime *et al.* (2007), Palmer & Sagar (1963), Werner & Rioux (1977).

S.J. Leach & D.A. Pearman

Hy *Elymus repens × athericus = E. ×drucei*

(Stace) Stace

The parents of *E. ×drucei* are not always easy to distinguish, making hybrid identification difficult without ascertaining fertility. It is found in similar habitats to the parents, sometimes in abundance, typically growing by tidal creeks, at the upper end of saltmarshes, on sand dunes, shingle, sea-walls and waste ground by the sea. Lowland.

A spontaneous hybrid (native × native).

Trends *E. ×drucei* was first mapped in Stace *et al.* (2015). In north Wales, Lancashire and Cumbria, *E. athericus* has been greatly over-recorded in the past for this hybrid and, to a lesser extent, other hybrids and glaucous variants of *E. repens*; indeed, there is some doubt as to whether *E. athericus* occurs in Cumbria (Halliday, 1997; Greenwood, 2004). It has in recent years also been found at inland salt-laden roadside verges (*e.g.* near the Humber estuary, South-east Yorkshire), and it may be overlooked in this habitat in other areas. It is better recorded on the coast of Ireland this century, but is probably still under-recorded.

Biogeography Widespread on the coast of western Europe.

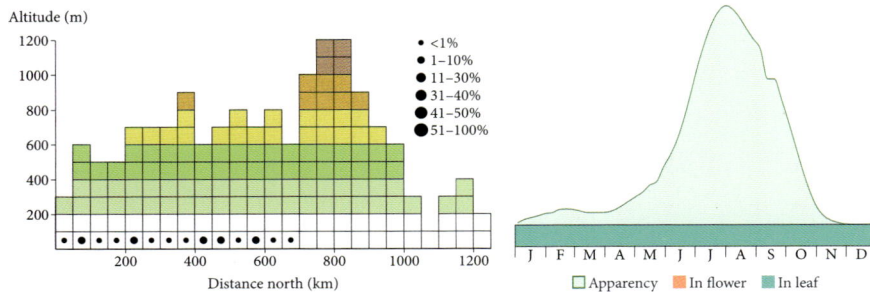

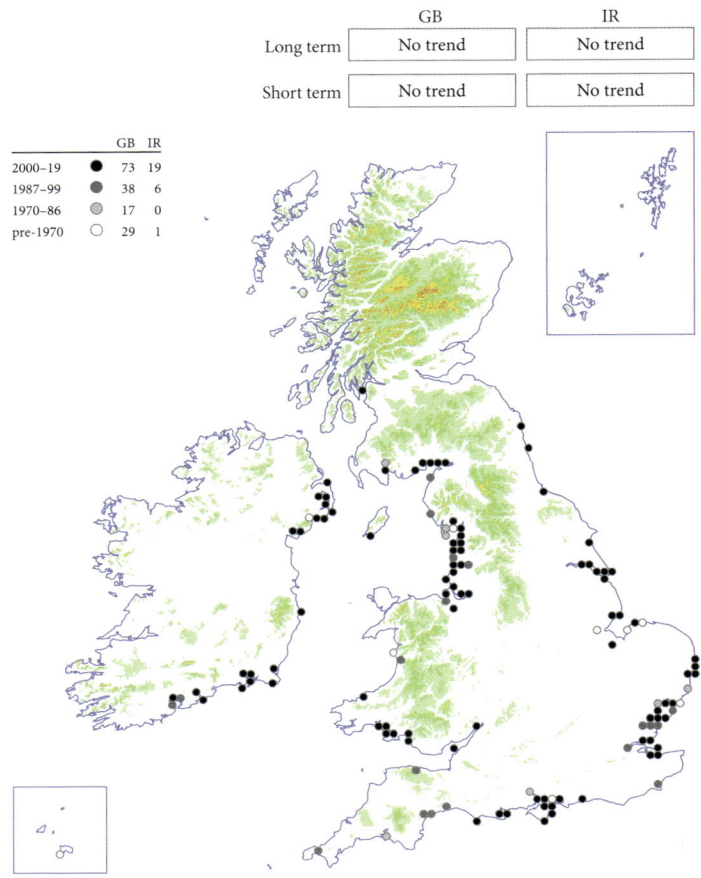

	GB	IR
Long term	No trend	No trend
Short term	No trend	No trend

		GB	IR
2000–19	●	73	19
1987–99	●	38	6
1970–86	●	17	0
pre-1970	○	29	1

Key refs Greenwood (2004), Halliday (1997).

C.A. Stace, C.D. Preston & D.A. Pearman

Hy *Elymus repens × junceiformis = E. ×laxus*

(Fr.) Melderis & D.C.McClint.

This hybrid is a pioneer species of mobile sand, growing on fore-dunes, sandy beaches and occasionally shingle beaches. It is also found, sometimes as large stands, on sandy shores, sand-covered cliffs and sand dunes, and on sandy gravel at the upper edges of beaches, as well as on muddy shores, sandy saltmarshes and shingle. It is usually found with both parents but occasionally persists in the absence of one or both of them. Lowland.

A spontaneous hybrid (native × native).

Trends *E. ×laxus* was not mapped in the 1962 *Atlas* and there is no reliable long-term information on trends in its distribution. Though better recorded this century, many fieldworkers are still likely to overlook it. There may also be some confusion with the hybrid between *E. athericus* and *E. junceiformis* (*E. ×obtusiusculus*).

Biogeography Widespread on the Mediterranean and Atlantic coasts of Europe.

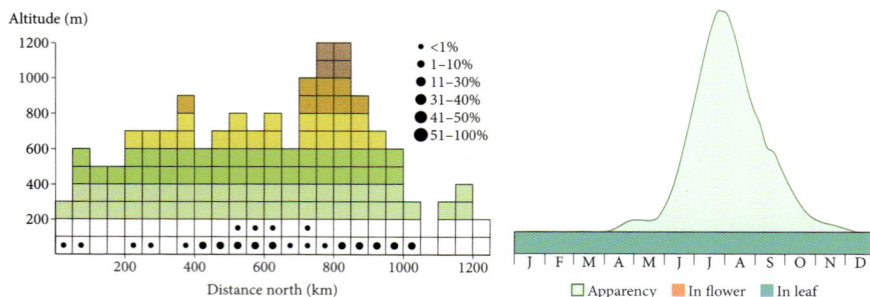

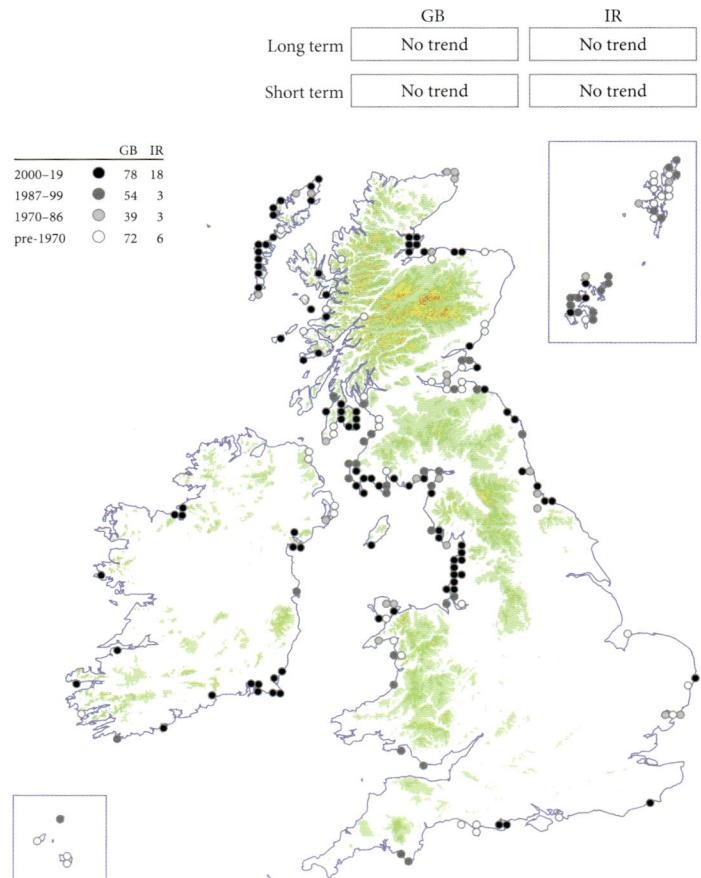

	GB	IR
Long term	No trend	No trend
Short term	No trend	No trend

		GB	IR
2000–19	●	78	18
1987–99	●	54	3
1970–86	●	39	3
pre-1970	○	72	6

Key refs Stace *et al.* (2015).

C.A. Stace, C.D. Preston & D.A. Pearman

Elymus athericus Sea Couch

N

(Link) Kerguélen

A rhizomatous perennial grass of the margins of brackish creeks, saltmarshes, saltmarsh-sand dune transitions, and shingle banks and sea-walls; it is also found on salt-treated road verges. In ungrazed situations it can form dense stands covering large areas to the almost total exclusion of all other plant species. Lowland.

Trends There has been little change in the 10 km square distribution of *E. athericus* since the 1960s. The sterile hybrid with *E. repens* (*E. ×drucei*) has sometimes been misrecorded as *E. athericus*, thus obscuring the northern limit of this species (Halliday, 1997; Greenwood, 2004).

Biogeography European Southern-temperate element.

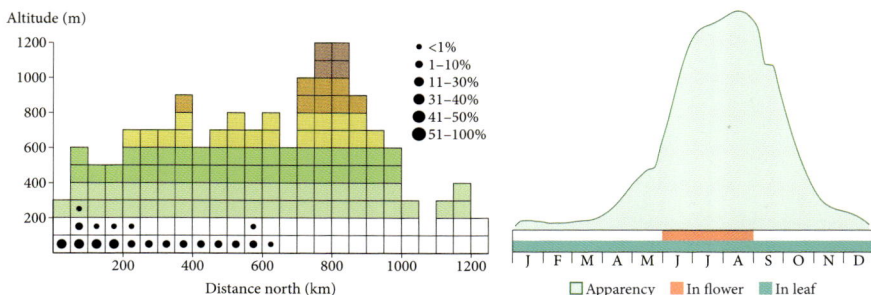

Native	GB	IR
2000–19	388	60
1987–99	321	38
1970–86	240	9
pre-1970	265	12

Alien	GB	IR
2000–19	2	0
1987–99	1	0
1970–86	0	0
pre-1970	0	0

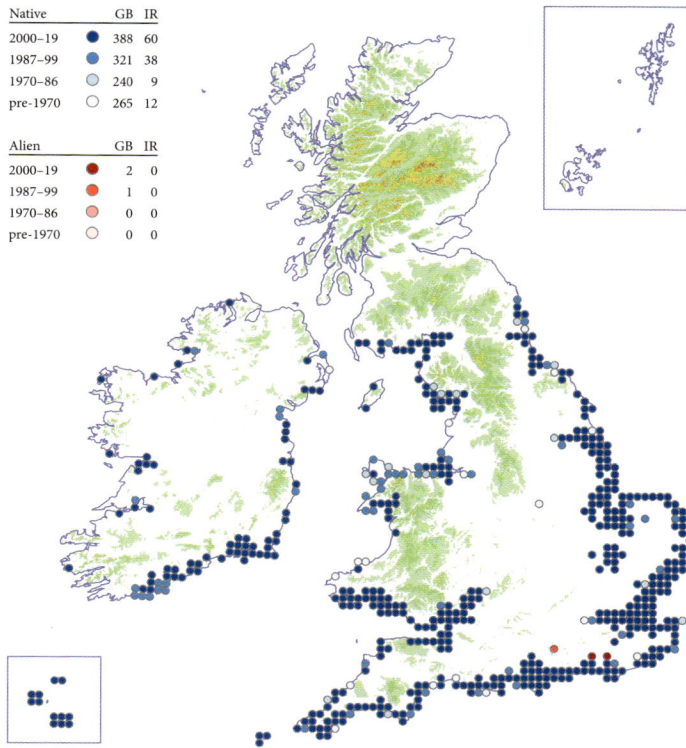

Key refs Cope & Gray (2009), Greenwood (2004), Halliday (1997).

S.J. Leach & D.A. Pearman

Elymus athericus × junceiformis = E. ×obtusiusculus

Hy

(Lange) Melderis & D.C.McClint.

This hybrid grass has a wider habitat range than *E. junceiformis*, growing at the upper edge of saltmarshes, in soft mud at the foot of sea-cliffs and by tidal rivers, as well as on sand dunes, shingle, and sea-walls. It is sometimes present as large stands where it may be more frequent than either parent. Lowland.

A spontaneous hybrid (native × native).

Trends There is no reliable information on trends in the distribution of this taxon. It is under-recorded, as many fieldworkers overlook it for one or the other parent. There may also be some confusion with the hybrid between *E. repens* and *E. junceiformis* (*E. ×laxus*).

Biogeography Widespread on the Mediterranean and Atlantic coasts of Europe, and established as a ballast alien on the Baltic coast, well outside of the range of *E. athericus*.

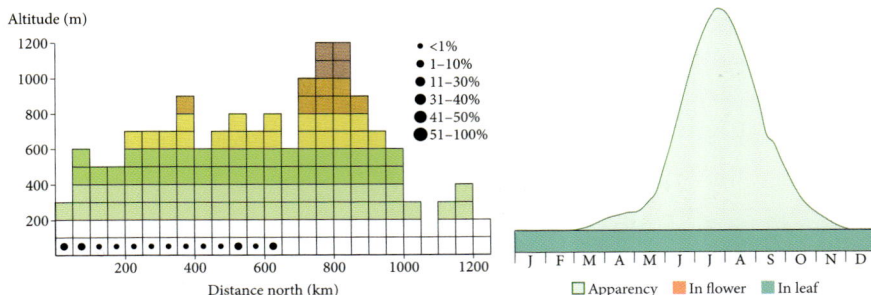

	GB	IR
2000–19	49	11
1987–99	35	8
1970–86	37	1
pre-1970	76	5

	GB	IR
Long term	No trend	No trend
Short term	No trend	No trend

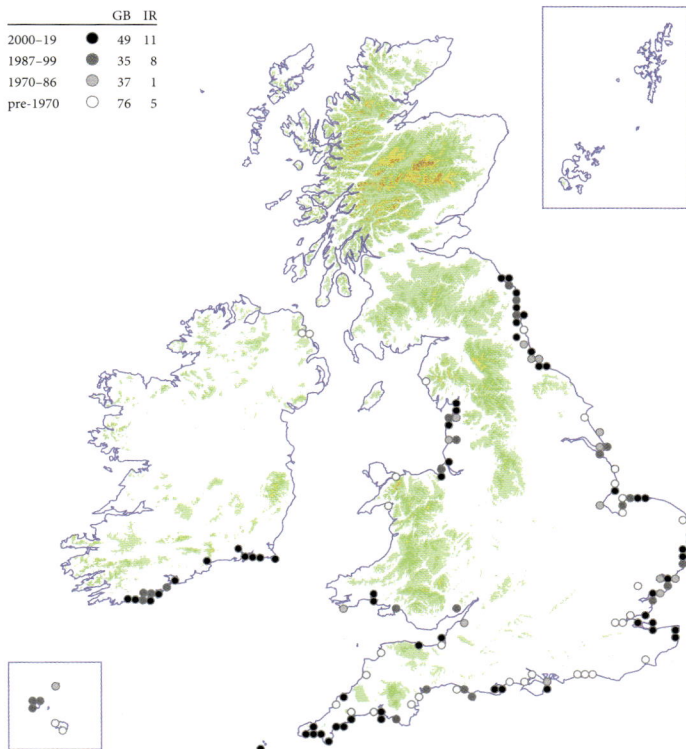

Key refs Stace *et al.* (2015).

C.A. Stace, C.D. Preston & D.A. Pearman

N *Elymus junceiformis* Sand Couch
(Á.Löve & D.Löve) Hand & Buttler

A rhizomatous perennial grass growing on or just above the strandline in loose sand, sometimes also on shingle. It is well known as a sand stabilizer on dune systems, forming low hummocky foredunes on the seaward side of the main *Ammophila arenaria* dunes. Lowland.

Trends There has been little change in the overall 10 km square distribution of *E. junceiformis* since the 1960s, though there have been a few local losses where sand dune systems have been damaged.

Biogeography European Southern-temperate element.

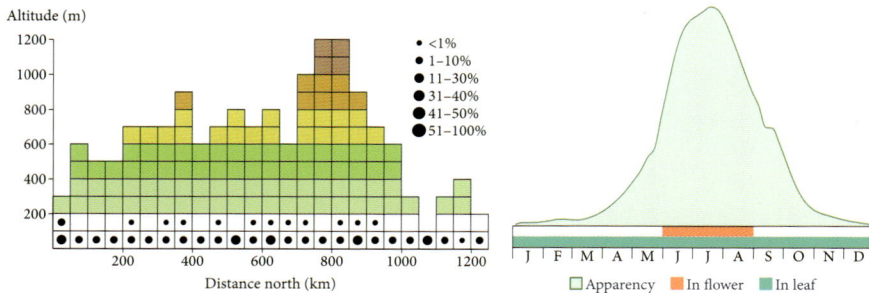

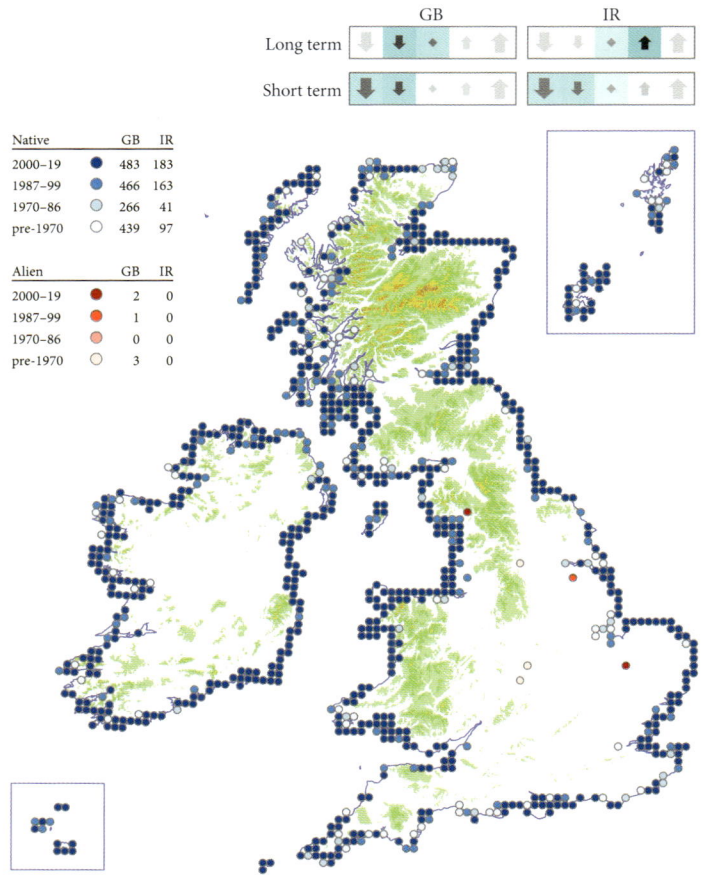

Native	GB	IR
2000–19	483	183
1987–99	466	163
1970–86	266	41
pre-1970	439	97

Alien	GB	IR
2000–19	2	0
1987–99	1	0
1970–86	0	0
pre-1970	3	0

	GB	IR
Long term		
Short term		

Key refs Cope & Gray (2009).

S.J. LEACH & D.A. PEARMAN

N *Leymus arenarius* Lyme-grass
(L.) Hochst.

A rhizomatous perennial grass growing on coastal sand dunes, sometimes also on fine shingle; it is well known as an important species in the stabilization of mobile dunes and widely planted as a sand binder. It is a rare casual or naturalized garden escape inland. Lowland.

Trends There is no evidence of appreciable change in the 10 km square distribution of *L. arenarius* since the 1960s. Though there have some losses in southern England, it is now known in many more squares in both Ireland and Scotland, probably as a result of more systematic recording. The widespread planting of *L. arenarius* on eroding sand dunes may be underestimated on the map. Isolated populations are frequently destroyed by storms.

Biogeography European Boreo-arctic Montane element; also in eastern Asia and North America.

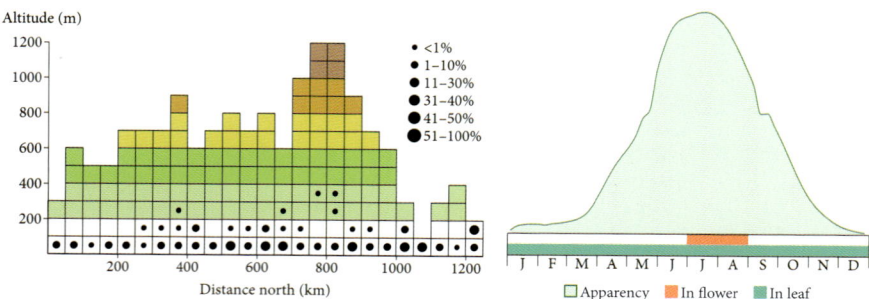

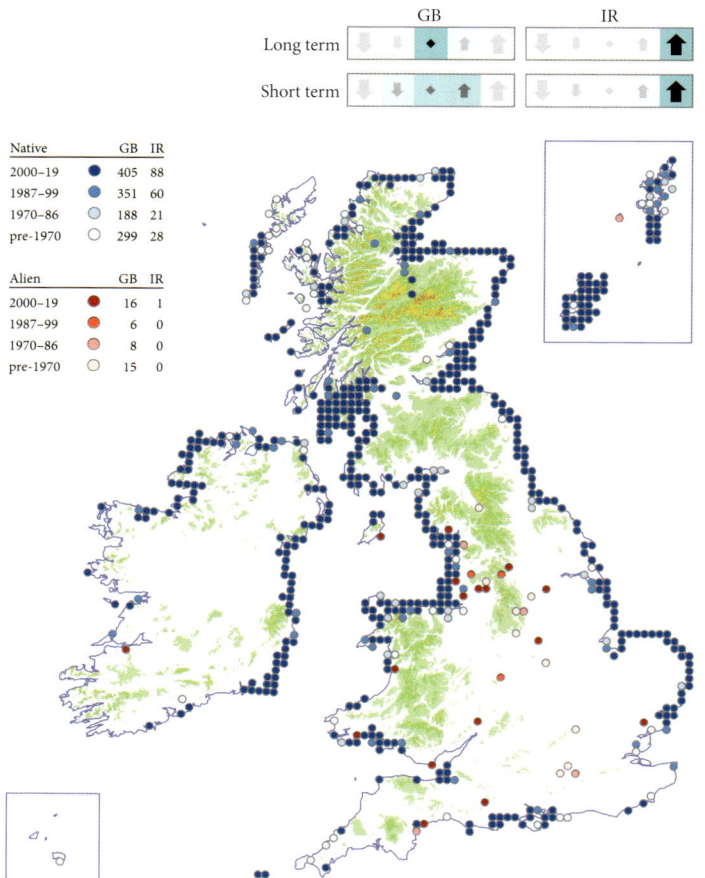

Native	GB	IR
2000–19	405	88
1987–99	351	60
1970–86	188	21
pre-1970	299	28

Alien	GB	IR
2000–19	16	1
1987–99	6	0
1970–86	8	0
pre-1970	15	0

	GB	IR
Long term		
Short term		

Key refs Bond (1952), Cope & Gray (2009).

S.J. LEACH & D.A. PEARMAN

N

Hordelymus europaeus Wood Barley
(L.) Jess. ex Harz

A tall, short-lived perennial grass of chalk and limestone soils and calcareous boulder clay, found in woods and copses and edge habitat such as medieval boundary banks and old hedgerows. Generally lowland, but reaching 440 m at Brough (Westmorland).

Trends *H. europaeus* has been better recorded since the 1960s, but over the same period has seen a slow but steady decline both at the edge of its range and in its historic heartlands due to the removal of hedgebanks, coniferization of deciduous woodland and a lack of disturbance associated with a widespread decline in woodland management. It was refound in Ireland at its historical site in County Antrim in 2011.

Biogeography European Temperate element.

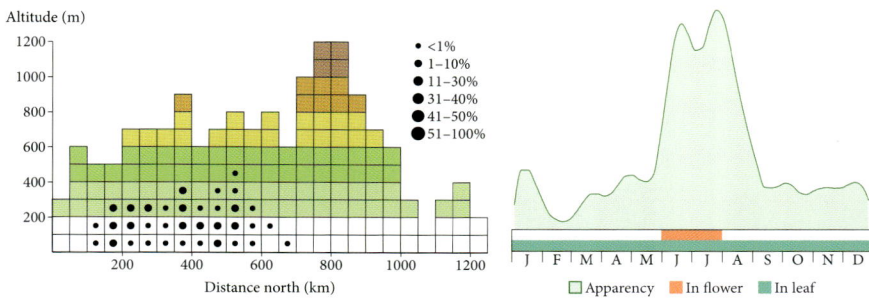

Native	GB	IR
2000–19	94	1
1987–99	116	0
1970–86	108	0
pre-1970	138	1

Alien	GB	IR
2000–19	1	0
1987–99	0	0
1970–86	0	0
pre-1970	0	0

	GB	IR
Long term		No trend
Short term		No trend

Key refs Cope & Gray (2009), Stewart *et al.* (1994).

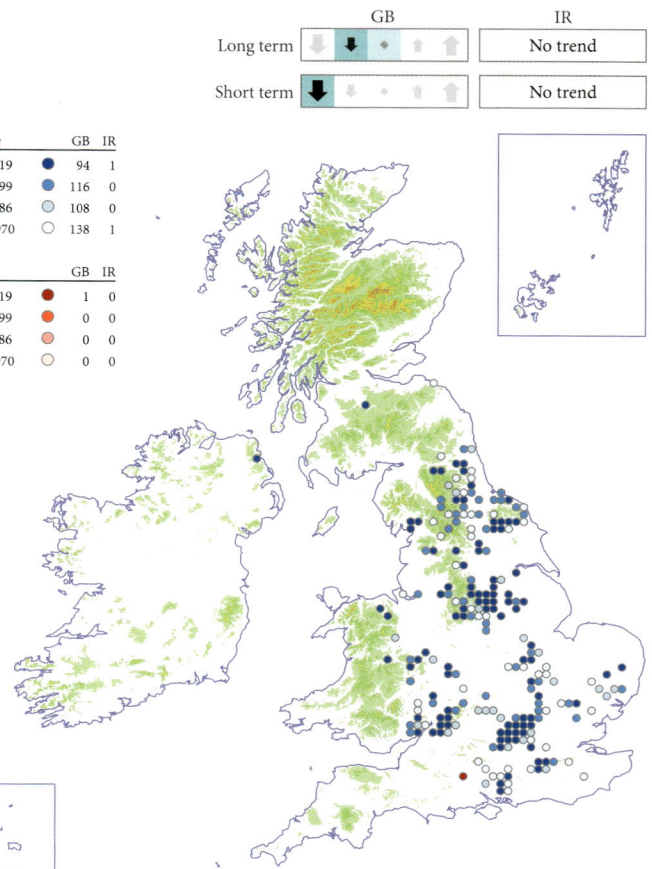

S.J. LEACH & D.A. PEARMAN

Ne

Hordeum vulgare Six-rowed Barley
L.

An annual grass, formerly grown as a cereal crop, sometimes found on arable land as a relic of cultivation, and on roadsides and waste ground as a birdseed and grain casual. Lowland.

Trends *H. vulgare* was known from the wild in Britain by 1846 (Cobham Lodge, Surrey). It is now seldom grown as a crop in our area, and has thus probably decreased as a casual, though its decline in arable habitats may have been offset to some extent by recent introductions as a birdseed casual. It is almost certainly ignored by many recorders; cereal relics were rarely recorded before 1970, but must have been just as frequent then as now.

Biogeography Originated in cultivation; grown in temperate climates worldwide.

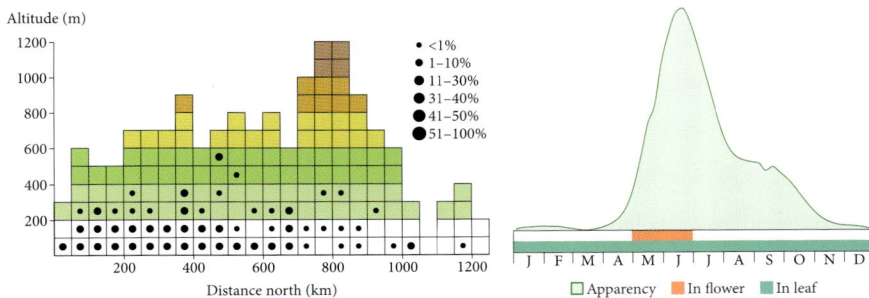

	GB	IR
Long term	No trend	No trend
Short term	No trend	No trend

Alien	GB	IR
2000–19	449	54
1987–99	207	10
1970–86	90	2
pre-1970	60	2

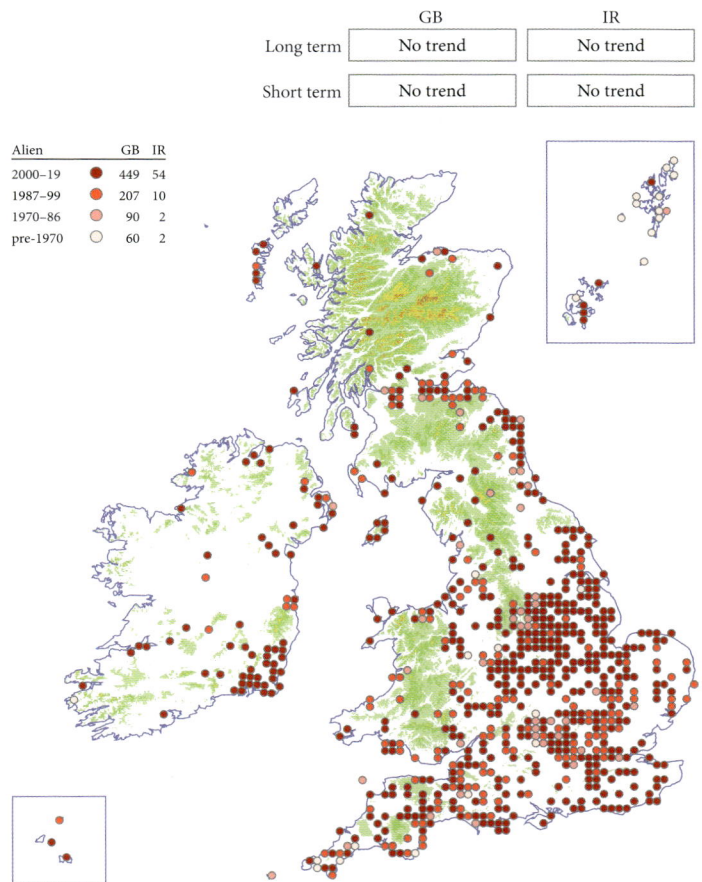

Key refs Cope & Gray (2009), Ryves *et al.* (1996), Zohary & Hopf (2000).

S.J. LEACH & D.A. PEARMAN

Ne *Hordeum distichon s.l.* Two-rowed Barley

Cultivated barley occurs frequently but rarely persists in waste places, fields, waysides and around farm buildings. It is mainly a relic of cultivation, but also occurs on roadsides from spilt grain, birdseed and, formerly, as a casual from wool shoddy. Generally lowland, but to 410 m in Eisteddfa Gurig (Cardiganshire).

Trends Barley has been cultivated in Britain for thousands of years, but was not recorded from the wild until 1852 (Hammersmith, Middlesex). The map includes records of the now commonly cultivated *H. distichon* and also *H. vulgare*, which is now rarely cultivated and is mapped separately. The two species are sometimes confused and often ignored by recorders; as a consequence they are certainly under-recorded in some areas. Both are treated by Stace & Crawley (2015) as cultivated archaeophytes.

Biogeography Unknown as a wild plant; widely cultivated in temperate regions throughout the world.

Alien	GB	IR
2000–19	1258	240
1987–99	703	82
1970–86	230	3
pre-1970	119	2

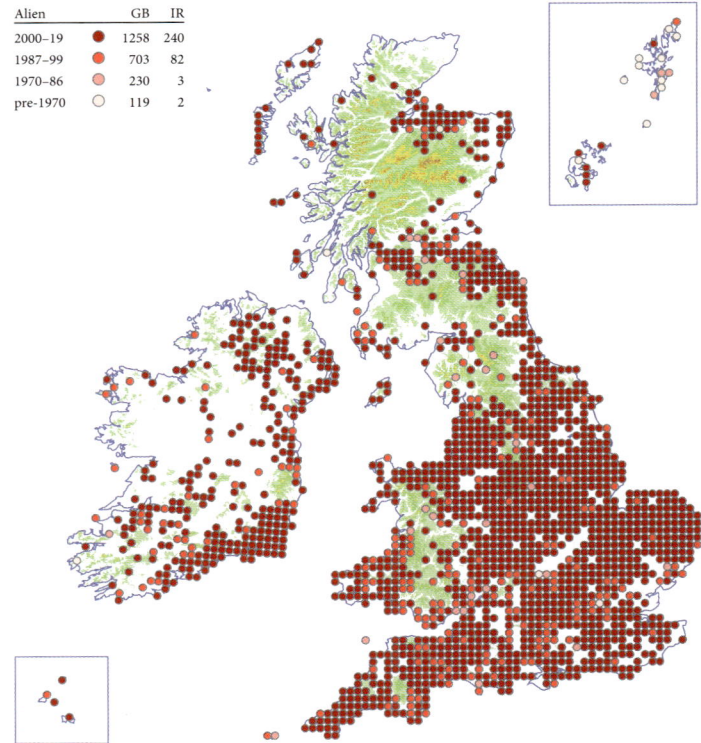

Key refs Cope & Gray (2009), Ryves *et al.* (1996), Stace & Crawley (2015).

S.J. Leach & D.A. Pearman

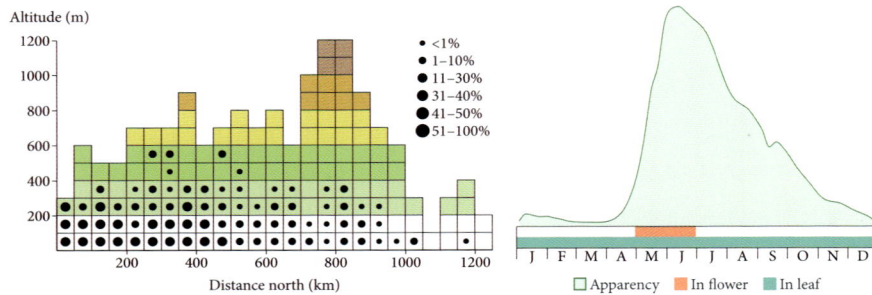

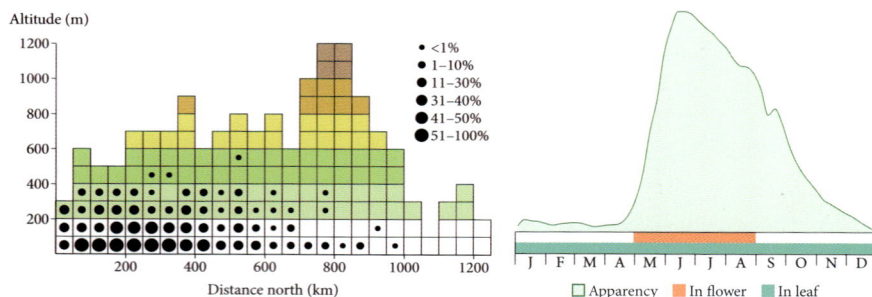

Altitude (m) / Distance north (km)

● <1%
● 1–10%
● 11–30%
● 31–40%
● 41–50%
● 51–100%

Apparency   In flower   In leaf

Ar *Hordeum murinum* Wall Barley
L.

An annual grass, growing in all kinds of fertile, disturbed ground, on roadsides, pavements, walls, railway banks and rough grassland. Generally lowland, but reaching 450 m on the Kirkstone Pass (Westmorland).

Trends The distribution of this ancient introduction is stable in southern, central and eastern England, and throughout much of Wales, but appears to be more patchy this century in the north-west of England, and in Scotland. In Ireland, where it is more likely to be a neophyte, it has been found in several new areas, but also not recorded from past locations. Three subspecies occur in our area: the archaeophyte subsp. *murinum* is common throughout the range, while the neophytes subsp. *glaucum* and subsp. *leporinum* are infrequent casuals from wool shoddy and esparto.

Biogeography As an archaeophyte, *H. murinum* has a Eurosiberian Southern-temperate distribution, but it is widely naturalized so that its distribution is now Circumpolar Southern-temperate.

Alien	GB	IR
2000–19	1357	39
1987–99	1378	44
1970–86	870	4
pre-1970	1246	17

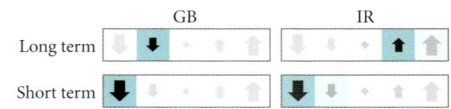

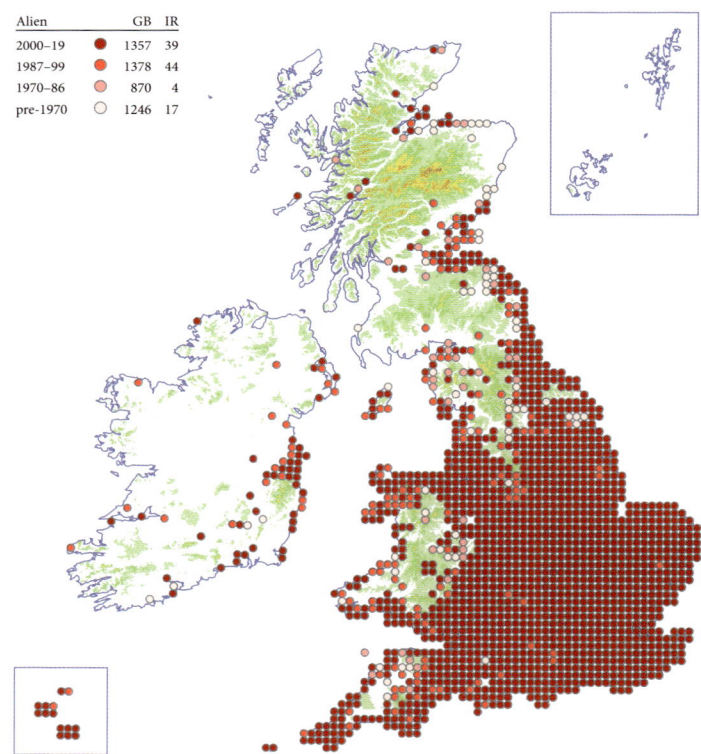

Key refs Cope & Gray (2009), Davison (1970), Davison (1971), Ryves *et al.* (1996).

S.J. Leach & D.A. Pearman

Altitude (m) / Distance north (km)

● <1%
● 1–10%
● 11–30%
● 31–40%
● 41–50%
● 51–100%

Apparency   In flower   In leaf

Ne *Hordeum jubatum* Foxtail Barley
L.

A short-lived perennial grass of road verges, re-sown grassland and waste places, occurring as a casual from birdseed, as a contaminant of commercial grass-seed mixtures and, formerly, as a casual arising from wool shoddy. It is often found with maritime species beside salt-treated roads where it can be very persistent. Generally lowland, but reaching 410 m (Devil's Beef Tub, Dumfriesshire).

Trends *H. jubatum* was introduced as a fodder grass in 1782 and has been recorded from the wild since 1890 (Cross Ness, Thamesmead, West Kent). It was not mapped in the 1962 *Atlas*, but it increased after 1970, particularly along inland roadsides treated with de-icing salt, and possibly as a result of being widely sold as an ornamental grass. It is perhaps now declining but the reasons for this are not clear.

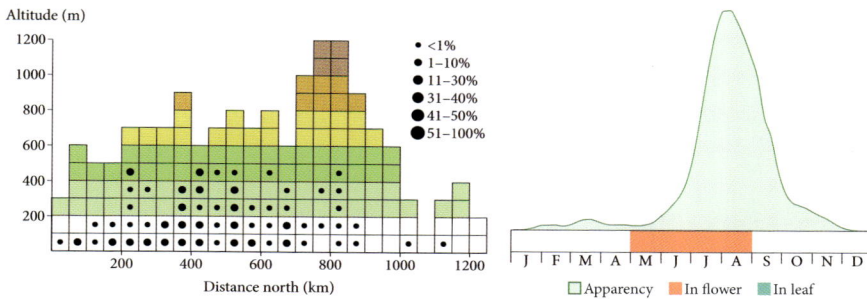

Biogeography Native of North America and eastern Asia; widely naturalized in northern and western Europe.

Alien	GB	IR
2000–19	153	1
1987–99	211	3
1970–86	172	2
pre-1970	112	2

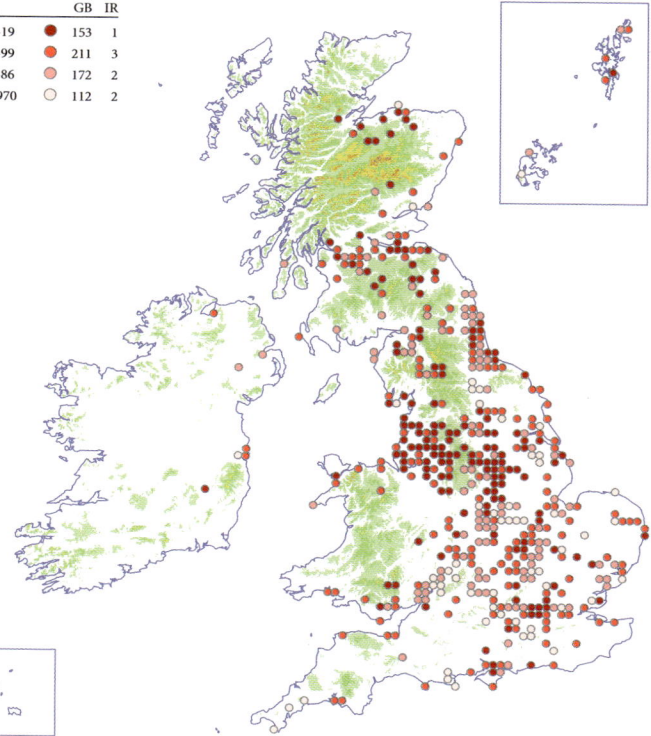

Key refs Best *et al.* (1978), Coombe (1994), Cope & Gray (2009), Ryves *et al.* (1996).

S.J. LEACH & D.A. PEARMAN

N *Hordeum secalinum* Meadow Barley
Schreb.

A perennial grass of meadows, pastures and roadsides, often in river valley floodplains and showing a strong preference for sticky clay soils. In coastal areas it is frequently abundant in grazing marsh grasslands and on earthen sea-walls. Mainly lowland, but reaching 350 m at Llangurig (Montgomeryshire), and up to 540 m near to Pumlumon lead mine (Cardiganshire) as an alien.

Trends The map suggests little apparent change in the 10 km square distribution of *H. secalinum* since the 1960s. However, in some counties it is reported to be decreasing locally due to drainage, re-seeding and the conversion of grassland to arable. It can, however, withstand modest improvement. Its overall distribution is stable in Ireland.

Biogeography European Temperate element.

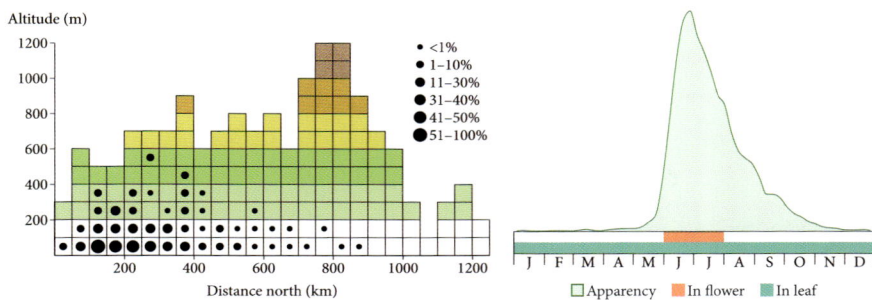

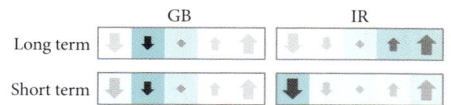

Native	GB	IR
2000–19	870	17
1987–99	794	14
1970–86	483	3
pre-1970	770	23

Alien	GB	IR
2000–19	17	0
1987–99	5	0
1970–86	3	0
pre-1970	14	2

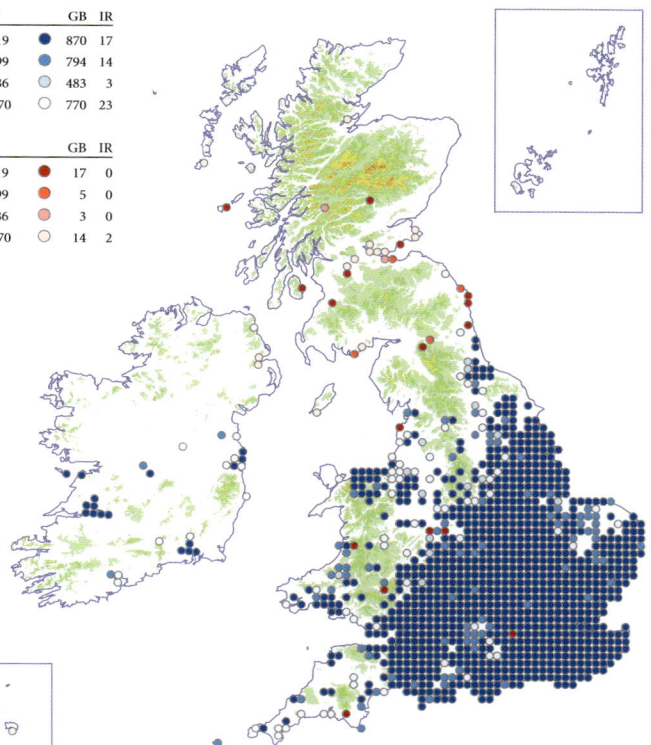

Key refs Cope & Gray (2009).

S.J. LEACH & D.A. PEARMAN

(N) *Hordeum marinum* Sea Barley

Huds.

An annual grass of barish places by the sea, on the trampled margins of dried-up pools and ditches in grazing marshes, on tracks and sea-walls, and in the uppermost parts of saltmarshes; also, very locally, beside salt-treated roads inland. Lowland.

Trends *H. marinum* has decreased in Britain, particularly along the coast from The Wash northwards. This is thought to be due to the rebuilding of sea defences, infilling of pools and ditches, the wholesale conversion of coastal grazing marshes to arable land, and the cessation of grazing. It is spreading very locally inland along salt-treated roadsides, such as in Cambridgeshire, Northamptonshire and Somerset. It is occasionally misrecorded for forms of *H. murinum*.

Biogeography Mediterranean-Atlantic element; also in central Asia and widely naturalized outside its native range.

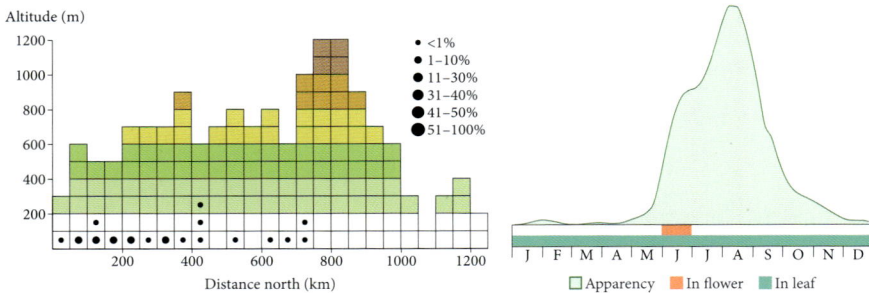

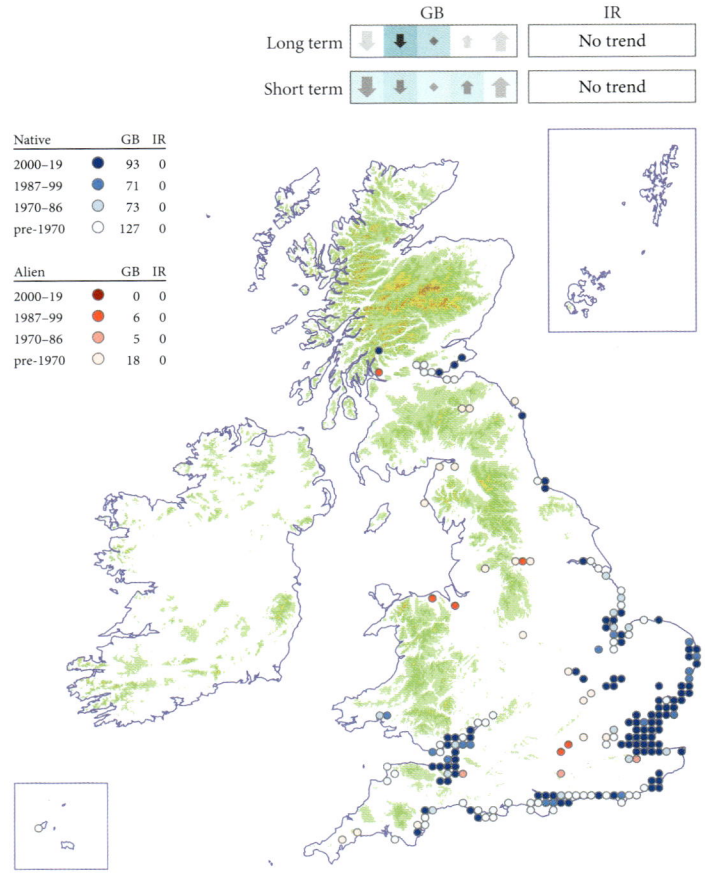

	GB	IR
Long term		No trend
Short term		No trend

Native	GB	IR
2000–19	93	0
1987–99	71	0
1970–86	73	0
pre-1970	127	0

Alien	GB	IR
2000–19	0	0
1987–99	6	0
1970–86	5	0
pre-1970	18	0

Key refs Cope & Gray (2009), Stewart *et al.* (1994).

S.J. LEACH & D.A. PEARMAN

(Ne) *Secale cereale* Rye

L.

An annual grass, sometimes occurring in wheat and barley fields as a grain alien or relic of cultivation. It is also found, usually as a casual from grass-seed or birdseed, on roadsides, manure heaps, refuse tips, waste ground and even the cracks in pavements. Lowland.

Trends *S. cereale* was formerly widely cultivated, but is now relatively rarely grown in our area with only around 12,000 ha sown each year. It can grow on much drier and infertile soils than other cereals and is grown for rye bread, green manure and, increasingly, for bio-gas. It was recorded in the wild by 1858 (Wandsworth, Surrey), but current distributional trends are unclear. It is treated by Stace & Crawley (2015) as a cultivated archaeophyte.

Biogeography Only known in cultivation; widely grown in temperate regions throughout the world.

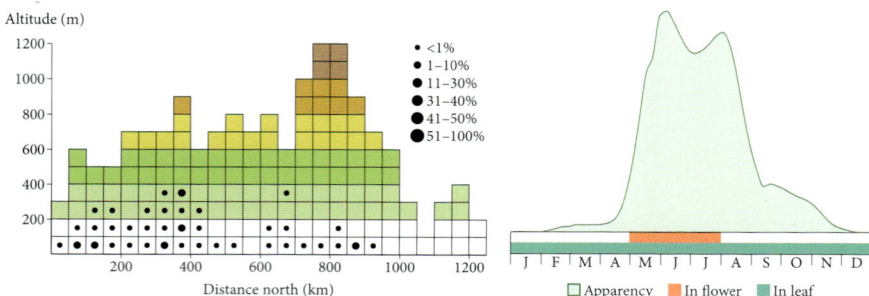

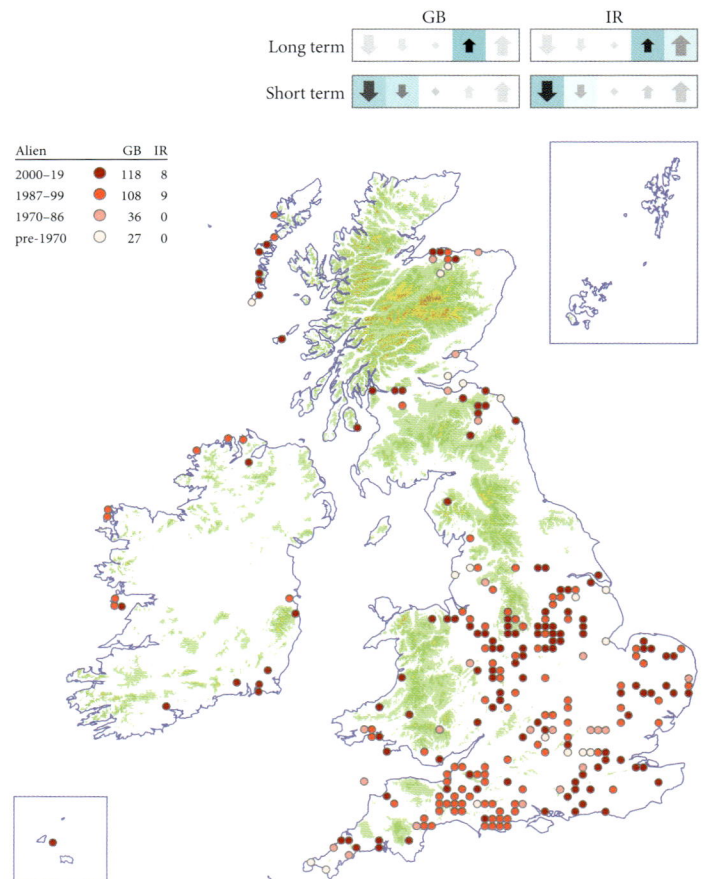

	GB	IR
Long term		
Short term		

Alien	GB	IR
2000–19	118	8
1987–99	108	9
1970–86	36	0
pre-1970	27	0

Key refs Cope & Gray (2009), Ryves *et al.* (1996), Stace & Crawley (2015), Vaughan & Geissler (2009), Zohary & Hopf (2000).

S.J. LEACH & D.A. PEARMAN

Hy × *Triticosecale rimpaui* Triticale

Wittm. ex A.Camus

An annual cereal, widely grown as a grain crop and also on a small scale as game cover and feed, found as a casual relic of cultivation at the edge of cultivated fields and on refuse tips. Lowland.

A cultivated hybrid (native × alien).

Trends Despite a long history as an artificial hybrid, it was only in the 1970s that plant breeders began to develop worthwhile cultivars of × *Triticosecale*. These were the subject of widespread trials in the 1980s and by 1989 it was being grown on a large scale in many countries, especially for animal feed or forage. The area cultivated in England has increased from 7,600 ha in 1990 to 13,500 ha in 2000 and 14,900 ha by 2010; the equivalent figures for Scotland, Wales and Ireland are much lower. The map shows that it is very unevenly recorded and possibly ignored by many recorders.

Biogeography A hybrid of agricultural origin.

	GB	IR
2000–19 ●	54	1
1987–99 ●	3	0
1970–86 ●	0	0
pre-1970 ○	0	0

Key refs Stace *et al.* (2015).

C.A. STACE, C.D. PRESTON & D.A. PEARMAN

Ne *Triticum turgidum* Rivet Wheat

L.

An annual grass which is now rarely grown as a crop, but is found as a relic of cultivation in fields and on roadsides; it also grows on refuse tips and waste ground where it arises as a contaminant of grain and from birdseed. Lowland.

Trends It is uncertain when *T. turgidum* was first cultivated in Britain, but it was certainly before 1800. It was first recorded from the wild in 1887 (Leith Docks, Midlothian). It may be misidentified for *T. aestivum*.

Biogeography Derived in cultivation from wild ancestors which occur in the Middle East and south-western Asia; widely naturalized in these areas and elsewhere.

Alien	GB	IR
2000–19 ●	21	0
1987–99 ●	23	0
1970–86 ●	17	0
pre-1970 ○	5	0

Key refs Cope & Gray (2009), Prance (2005), Ryves *et al.* (1996), Zohary & Hopf (2000).

T.D. DINES & D.A. PEARMAN

1433

Ne *Triticum aestivum* Bread Wheat

L.

A self-pollinating annual grass, widely cultivated and found as a casual in and around arable fields, on track and road verges where it has been spilled during transportation, around farm buildings, on refuse tips and as a weed of streets, gardens and waste places. Occurring as a relic of cultivation or as a birdseed alien. Generally lowland, but reaching 410 m at Eisteddfa Gurig (Cardiganshire).

Trends *T. aestivum* is one of the commonest cereal crops in the lowlands. It usually occurs as single plants and rarely persists, and has often been ignored by recorders. It was not noted in the wild until 1891, but must have been just as frequent then, as cereal relics were rarely recorded before 1970. This taxon, along with primitive wheats, are treated as cultivated archaeophytes by Stace & Crawley (2015).

Biogeography Not known as a wild plant; originated in cultivation and now grown in suitable climates throughout the world.

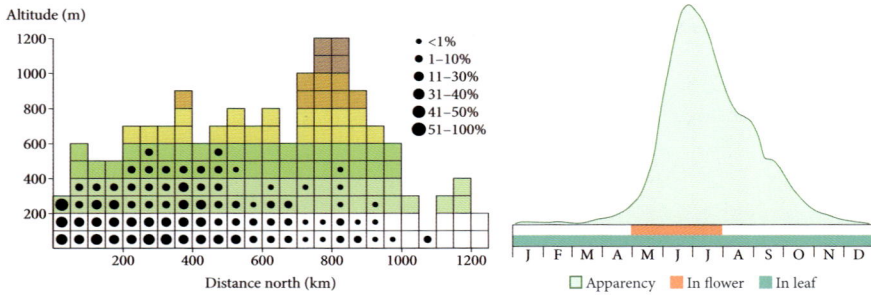

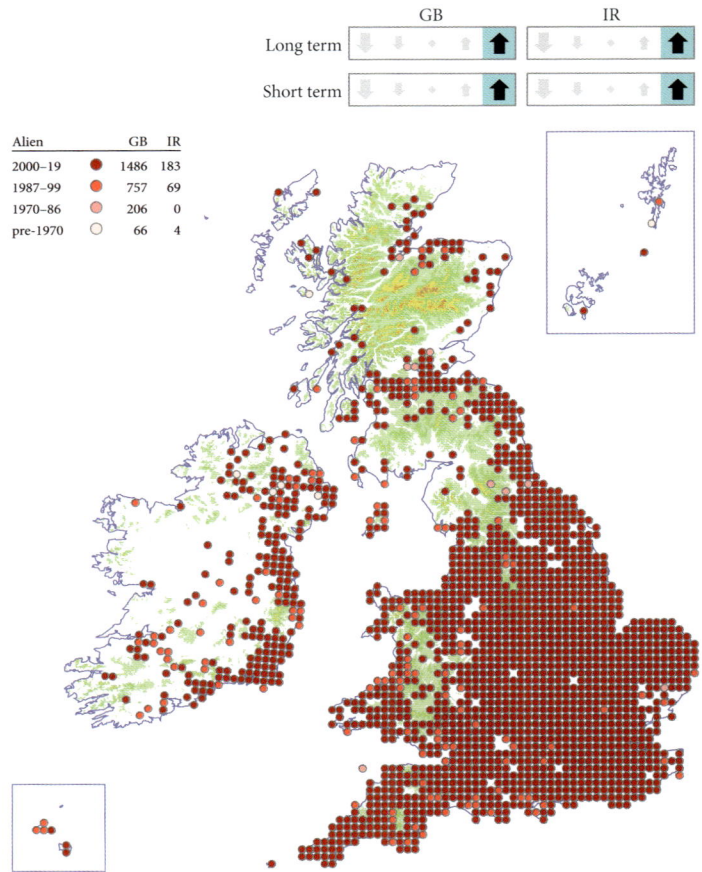

Alien	GB	IR
2000–19	1486	183
1987–99	757	69
1970–86	206	0
pre-1970	66	4

Key refs Cope & Gray (2009), Lupton (1985), Ryves *et al.* (1996), Stace & Crawley (2015), Vaughan & Geissler (2009), Zohary & Hopf (2000).

D.A. PEARMAN

Ne *Digitaria ischaemum* Smooth Finger-grass

(Schreb. ex Schweigg.) Muhl.

An annual grass, found on cultivated ground, pavements, refuse tips, railway sidings and waste ground. It arises from birdseed, soya bean waste and cotton. Some populations in light, sandy, arable fields are well-established and long-lived (especially in south-east England). Lowland.

Trends This species was first recorded in the wild in Britain in 1805 (Brandon, West Norfolk). It remains rare, but has increased in the last two decades.

Biogeography Native of temperate Eurasia; widely naturalized in North America, Australasia and elsewhere.

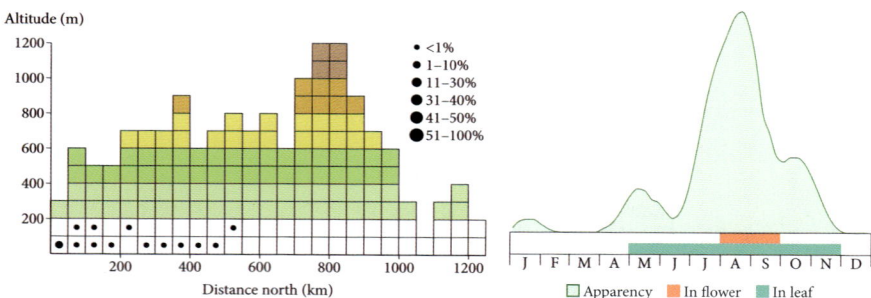

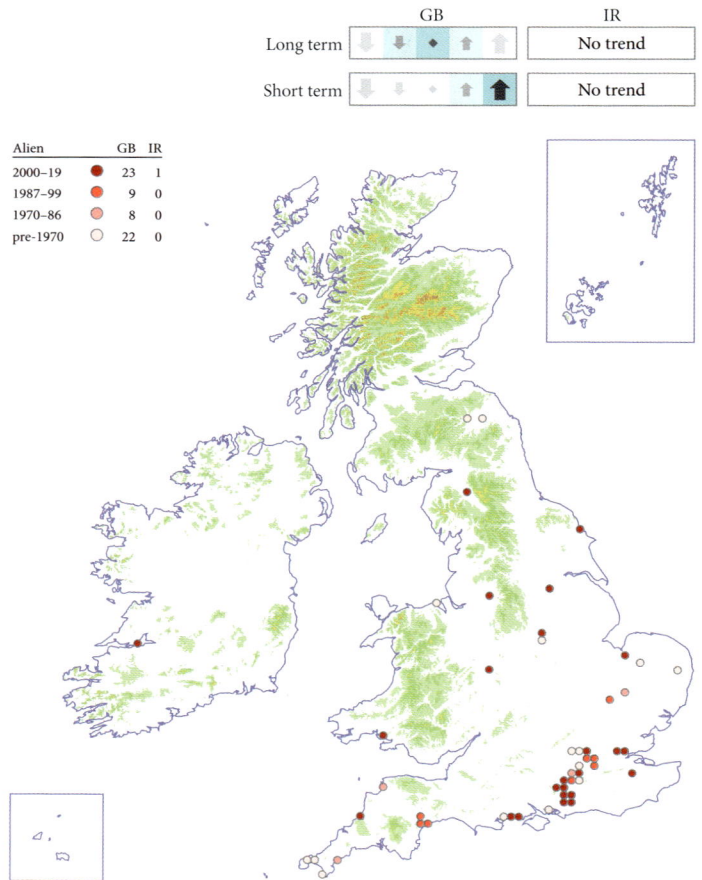

Alien	GB	IR
2000–19	23	1
1987–99	9	0
1970–86	8	0
pre-1970	22	0

Key refs Cope & Gray (2009), Ryves *et al.* (1996).

T.D. DINES & D.A. PEARMAN

Ne *Digitaria sanguinalis* Hairy Finger-grass

(L.) Scop.

An annual grass of bulb-fields and waste places on light soils in the Channel Islands and the Isles of Scilly, where it is relatively persistent. On the mainland it is spreading as a weed of garden centres, flower borders, urban shrubberies, road gutters and pavement cracks; also, as a casual, on refuse tips. Lowland.

Trends *D. sanguinalis* is a bulb-field alien, and increasingly a birdseed and horticultural weed. It was formerly a grain and wool alien, which explains many of the old records on the map. It was first recorded in the wild in 1762 (Battersea, Surrey).

Biogeography Native of southern Europe, the Mediterranean region and south-western Asia; now an almost cosmopolitan weed in warm-temperate and subtropical areas.

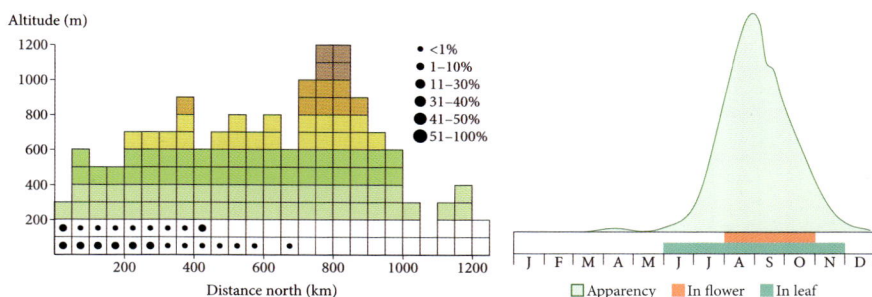

Alien		GB	IR
2000–19	●	240	1
1987–99	●	82	0
1970–86	●	57	1
pre-1970	○	67	0

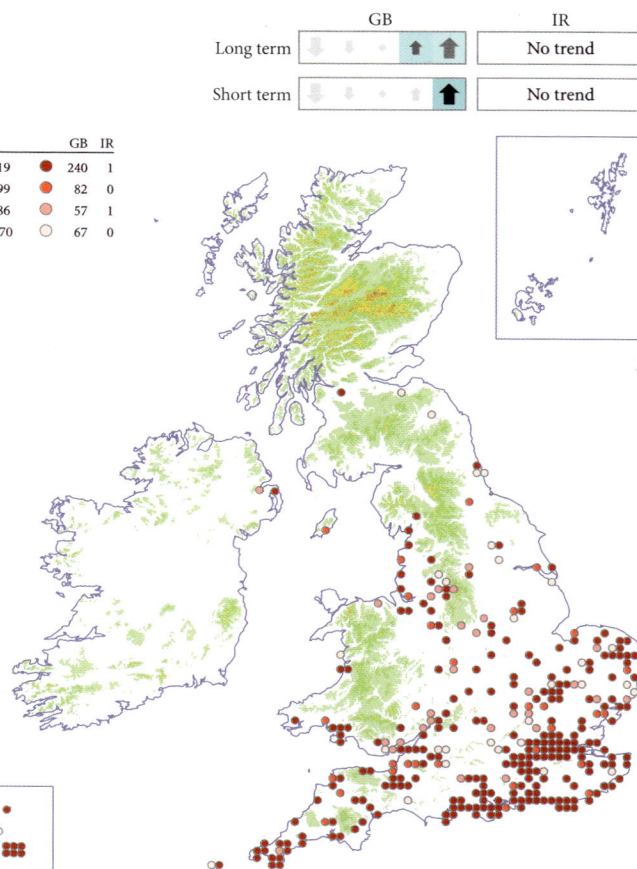

Key refs Cope & Gray (2009), Ryves *et al.* (1996).

S.J. LEACH & D.A. PEARMAN

Ne *Echinochloa crus-galli* Cockspur

(L.) P.Beauv.

A rather stout annual grass, found as a casual of refuse tips, waste places, roadsides and cultivated ground, especially maize crops, mainly originating from birdseed but also from wool shoddy, soya bean and other sources; it is increasingly sown as food for gamebirds (Beckett *et al.*, 1999). Lowland.

Trends *E. crus-galli* has been known in our area since 1620, when it was described from Petersfield (North Hampshire), but increased after the 1940s when it was introduced with North American seed (Rodwell, 2000). Since 2000 there has been an extraordinary increase in records, spreading rapidly along motorways and major road networks (*e.g.* Leach, 2006a). It is persistent at some arable and urban sites in southern England.

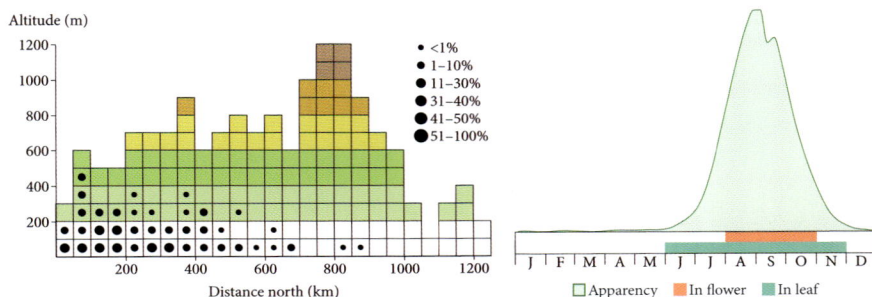

Biogeography Native of warm-temperate and tropical regions of Europe, Asia and North America; widely introduced as a fodder grass elsewhere.

Alien		GB	IR
2000–19	●	920	39
1987–99	●	238	3
1970–86	●	110	0
pre-1970	○	195	3

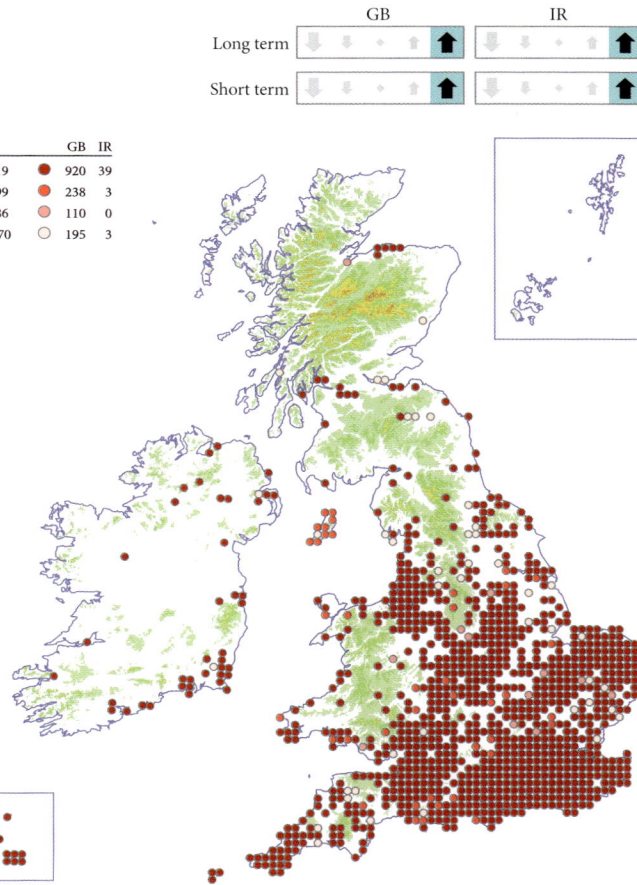

Key refs Beckett & Bull (1999), Cope & Gray (2009), Leach (2006a), Maun & Barrett (1986), Rodwell (2000), Ryves *et al.* (1996).

S.J. LEACH & D.A. PEARMAN

Ne *Echinochloa esculenta* Japanese Millet

(A.Braun) H.Scholz

An annual found as a casual on refuse tips and waste ground, arising as a constituent of birdseed mixtures. It is also sown as a food-source for game. Lowland.

Trends It is difficult to establish the date of the first record of this species in the wild due to taxonomic confusion, but it was certainly known by 1971 (Harford, East Norfolk). It may be increasing, although some older records may represent misidentifications of *E. frumentacea*.

Biogeography Originated in cultivation in Japan as a derivative of *E. crus-galli*.

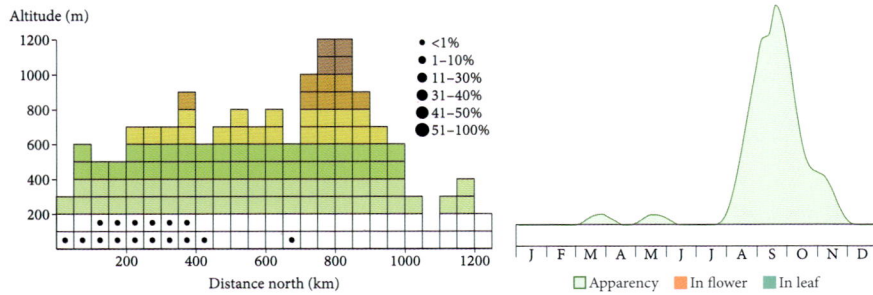

	GB	IR
Long term	No trend	No trend
Short term	⬇⬇◆⬆⬆	No trend

Alien		GB	IR
2000–19	●	51	1
1987–99	●	32	0
1970–86	●	38	0
pre-1970	○	11	0

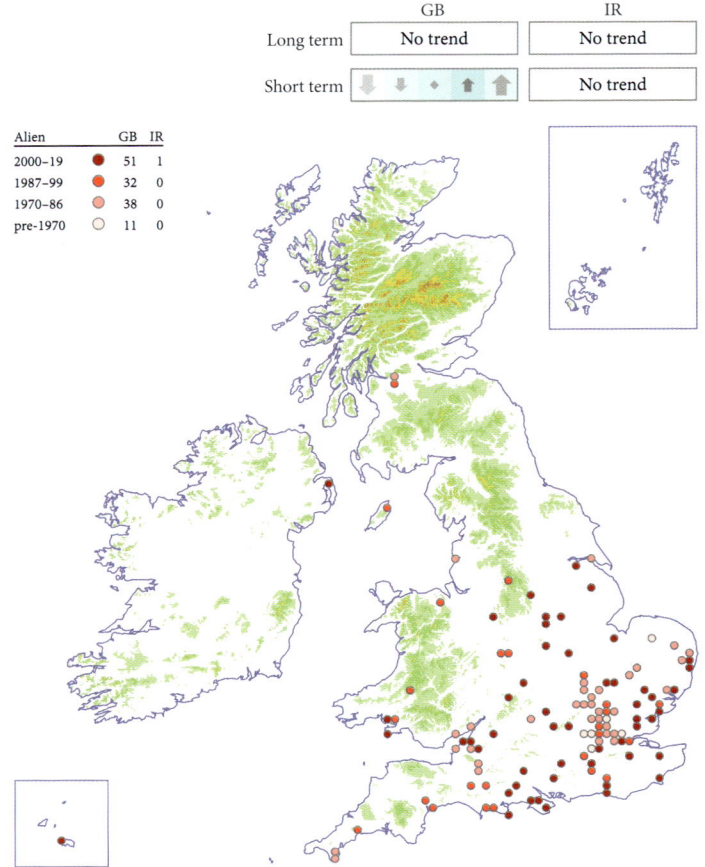

Altitude (m)

- <1%
- 1–10%
- 11–30%
- 31–40%
- 41–50%
- 51–100%

Distance north (km)

Apparency In flower In leaf

Key refs Cope & Gray (2009), Ryves *et al.* (1996).

D.A. Pearman

Ne *Echinochloa colona* Shama Millet

(L.) Link

An annual grass, found on refuse tips, waysides, waste ground and in pavement cracks, where it arises from birdseed, wool shoddy and soya bean waste. Lowland.

Trends *E. colona* was cultivated in Britain by 1699. It was recorded from the wild in 1906 (Reading, Berkshire) and appears to be increasing.

Biogeography Widespread in the tropical and warm temperate regions of the Old and New World; it is thought to be native to Africa and Asia but introduced to North America.

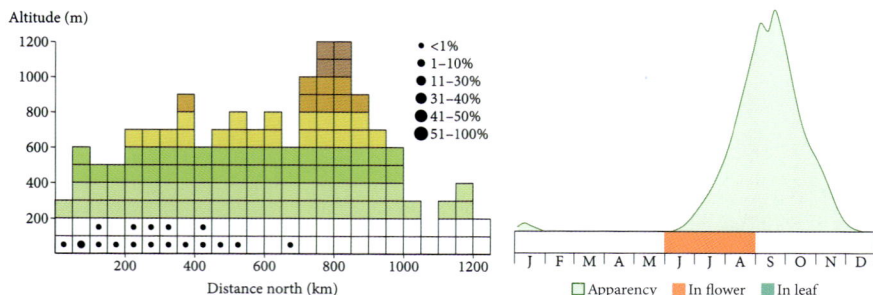

	GB	IR
Long term	No trend	No trend
Short term	⬇⬇◆⬆⬆	No trend

Alien		GB	IR
2000–19	●	47	3
1987–99	●	29	1
1970–86	●	16	0
pre-1970	○	17	0

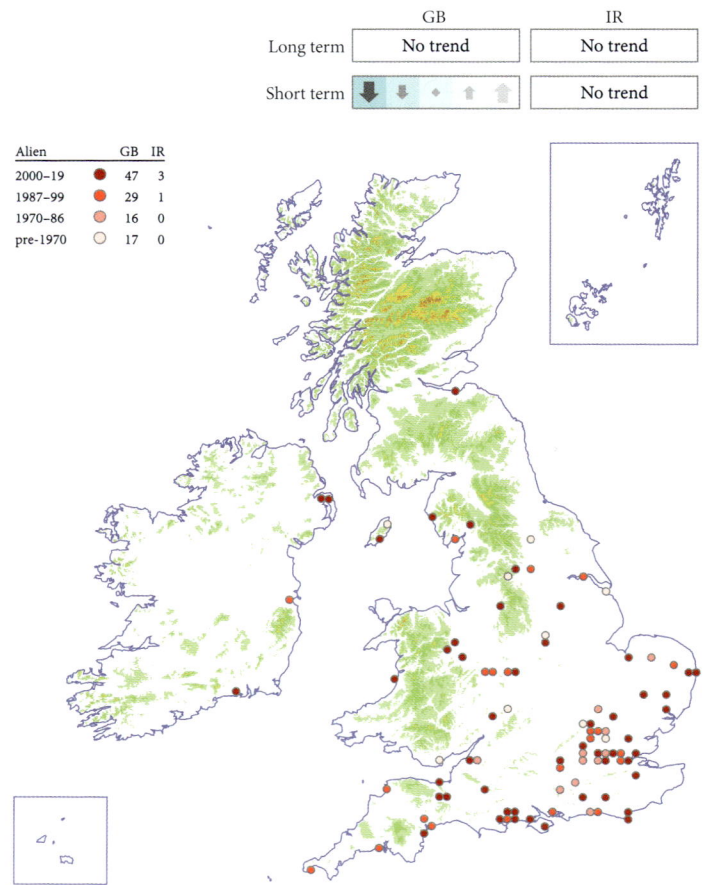

Altitude (m)

- <1%
- 1–10%
- 11–30%
- 31–40%
- 41–50%
- 51–100%

Distance north (km)

Apparency In flower In leaf

Key refs Cope & Gray (2009), Ryves *et al.* (1996).

T.D. Dines & D.A. Pearman

Ne *Echinochloa frumentacea* White Millet

Link

An annual grass, found as a casual on refuse tips, waysides, waste ground and in pavement cracks, where it arises from birdseed, wool shoddy and soya bean waste. Lowland.

Trends This species was recorded from the wild in Britain in 1918 (Bradford, South-west Yorkshire) and has been confused with *E. esculenta*. Its overall distribution appears to be stable.

Biogeography Native of Asia; widely naturalized, especially in the Indian sub-continent, through its use as a cereal, Sawa Millet.

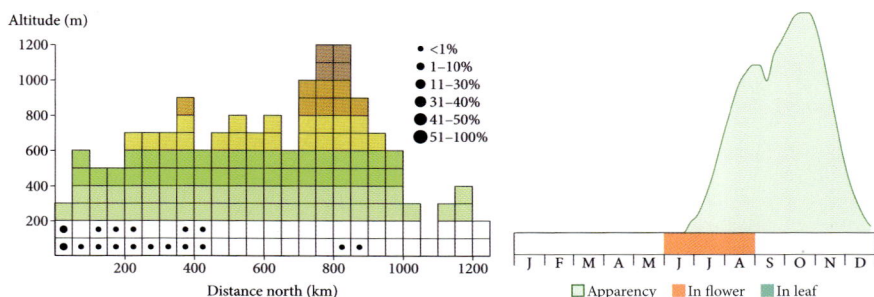

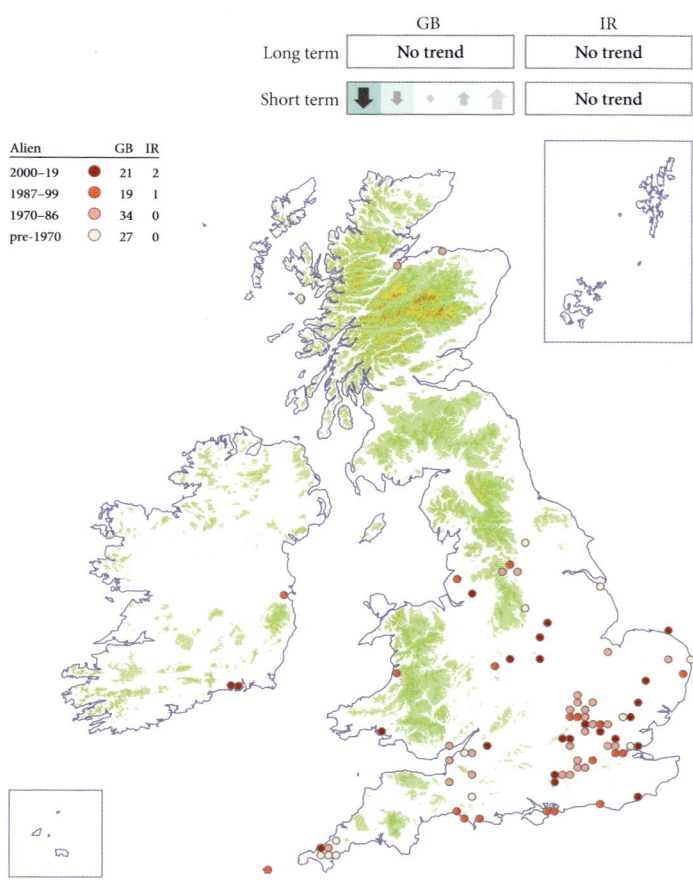

	GB	IR
Long term	No trend	No trend
Short term		No trend

Alien	GB	IR
2000–19	21	2
1987–99	19	1
1970–86	34	0
pre-1970	27	0

Key refs Cope & Gray (2009), Ryves *et al.* (1996).

T.D. Dines & D.A. Pearman

Altitude (m)

<1%
1–10%
11–30%
31–40%
41–50%
51–100%

Distance north (km)

J F M A M J J A S O N D

☐ Apparency ☐ In flower ☐ In leaf

Ne *Panicum capillare* Witch-grass

L.

An annual grass, usually found as a casual of waste places, docks and rubbish tips, arising from birdseed and oil-seed, wool shoddy and as a contaminant of agricultural seed; also occurring as a garden escape. Lowland.

Trends *P. capillare* was cultivated in Britain by 1758 and was first recorded in the wild in 1867 (East Gloucestershire). It is increasingly grown in gardens for its beautiful panicles and, although still a rare casual, is increasing in the wild.

Biogeography Native of North America; widely naturalized in central and southern Europe and elsewhere.

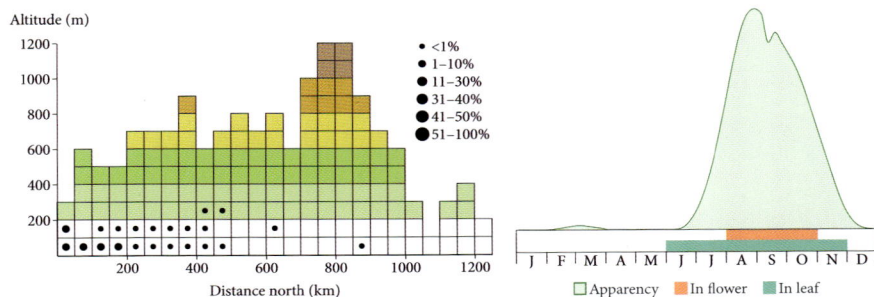

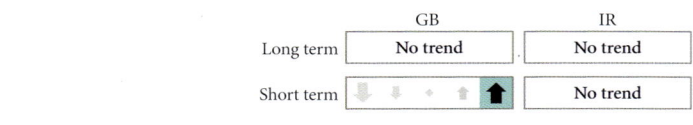

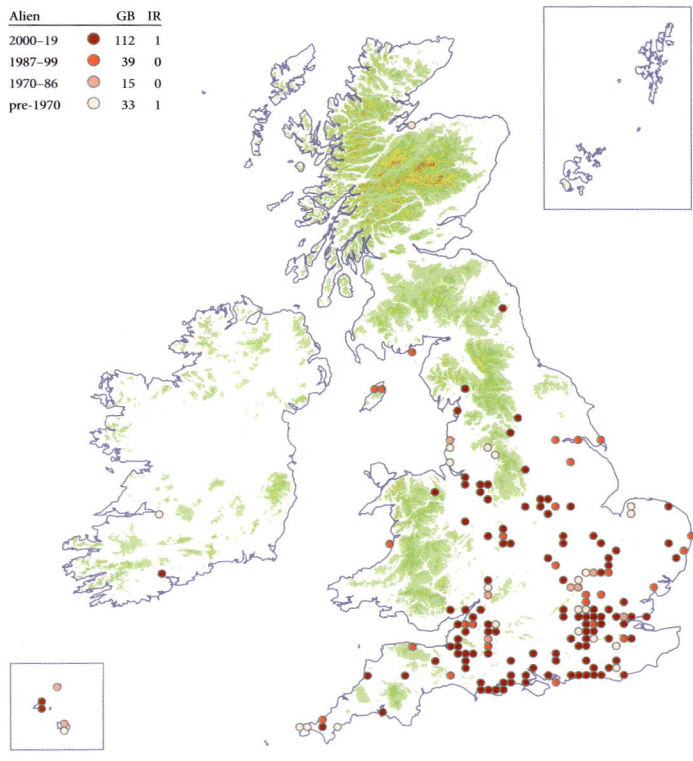

	GB	IR
Long term	No trend	No trend
Short term		No trend

Alien	GB	IR
2000–19	112	1
1987–99	39	0
1970–86	15	0
pre-1970	33	1

Key refs Clements *et al.* (2004), Cope & Gray (2009), Ryves *et al.* (1996).

D.A. Pearman

Altitude (m)

<1%
1–10%
11–30%
31–40%
41–50%
51–100%

Distance north (km)

J F M A M J J A S O N D

☐ Apparency ☐ In flower ☐ In leaf

Ne *Panicum miliaceum* Common Millet
L.

A large, tufted annual grass, found as a frequent birdseed and oil-seed casual on refuse tips, waste ground and in woodland around pheasant feeding areas; also occurring as a grain contaminant in arable crops, especially maize. Lowland.

Trends *P. miliaceum* was grown as a curiosity by 1596 and was first recorded in the wild in Britain in 1865 (Gloucester, East Gloucestershire). It appears to be increasing in many areas, although this may be in part be due to the more systematic recording of aliens in recent decades.

Biogeography Originally domesticated in central and eastern Asia but now grown in warm-temperate and tropical regions throughout the world.

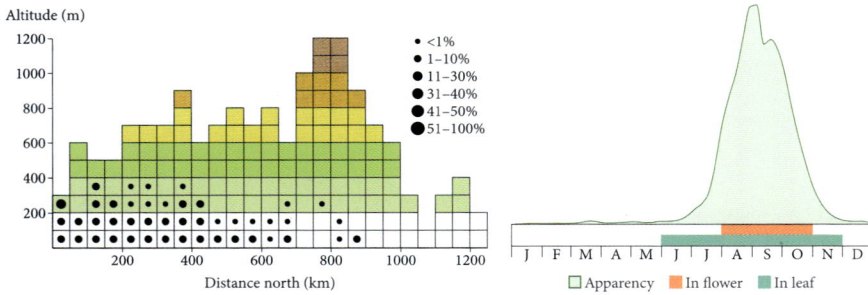

Alien	GB	IR
2000–19	653	17
1987–99	289	3
1970–86	150	2
pre-1970	125	1

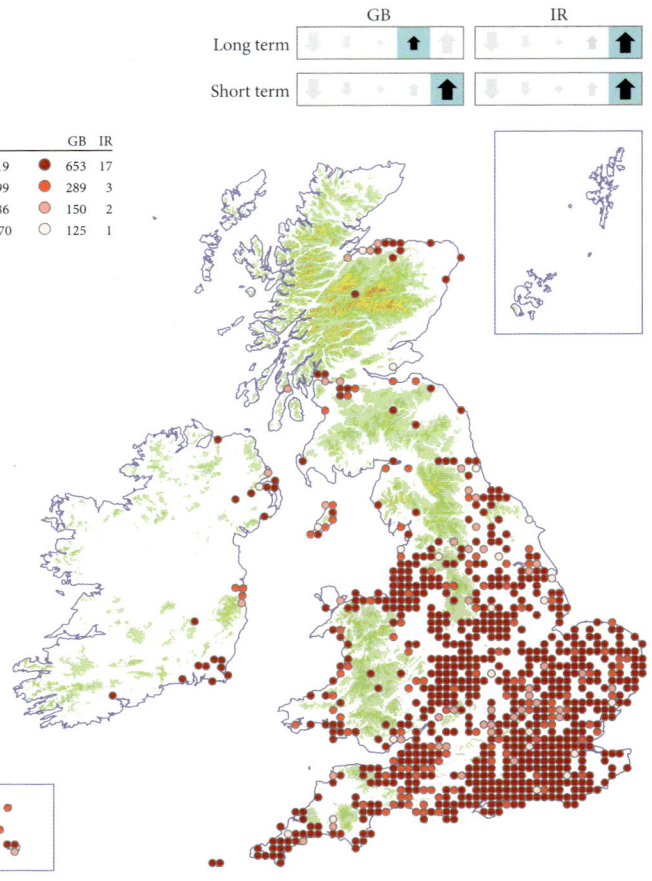

Key refs Cope & Gray (2009), Green *et al.* (1997), Ryves *et al.* (1996), Vaughan & Geissler (2009), Zohary & Hopf (2000).

S.J. LEACH & D.A. PEARMAN

Ne *Setaria pumila* Yellow Bristle-grass
(Poir.) Roem. & Schult.

An annual grass, found as a casual on refuse tips, cultivated and waste ground, mainly from wool and birdseed but also from grain, agricultural seed and oil-seed. It is becoming more frequent as a constituent of seed mixes used for pheasant- or game cover, and can be found self-sown along verges, field margins and pavements near to crops. Lowland.

Trends It is not known when *S. pumila* was first cultivated in Britain, or introduced here, but it was first recorded in the wild from Kew (Surrey) before 1805. The number of records has greatly increased over the last 50 years, and it appears to have a persistent seed bank.

Biogeography Native range uncertain but probably centred on the Mediterranean region and south-western Asia; the species is now naturalized in warm-temperate and subtropical areas throughout the Northern Hemisphere and elsewhere.

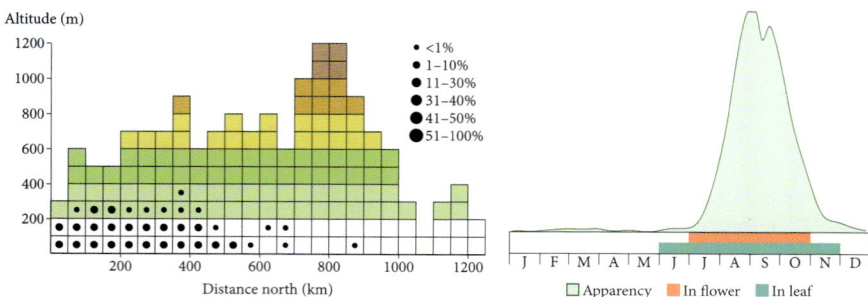

Alien	GB	IR
2000–19	520	10
1987–99	239	2
1970–86	98	0
pre-1970	105	0

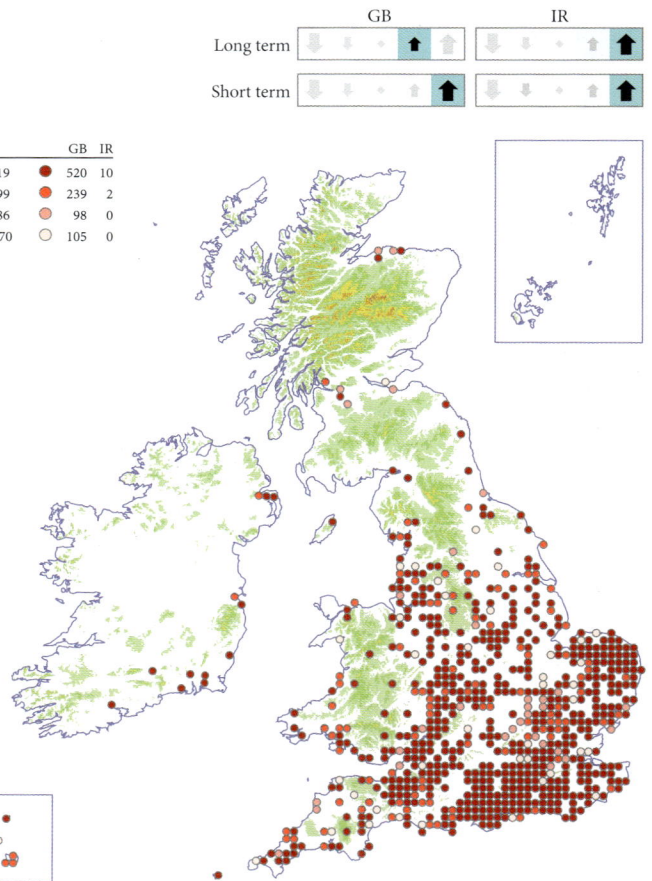

Key refs Cope & Gray (2009), Ryves *et al.* (1996).

S.J. LEACH & D.A. PEARMAN

Ne *Setaria verticillata* Rough Bristle-grass
(L.) P.Beauv.

An annual grass, found on refuse tips, dock quaysides, roadsides and waste ground; also, rarely, as a weed of arable land or garden centres. *S. verticillata* is a birdseed, oil-seed, wool, cotton and esparto alien, usually occurring as a casual but sometimes persisting for a few years in southern England. Lowland.

Trends *S. verticillata* was known from the wild by 1688 (Chelsea, Middlesex). Perhaps its occurrence as a contaminant of birdseed mixtures accounts for a substantial increase in recent records.

Biogeography Native of Eurasia, but precise range obscured by its spread as a weed; it now grows in warm-temperate and subtropical areas of Eurasia, Central and South America, Africa, Australia and elsewhere.

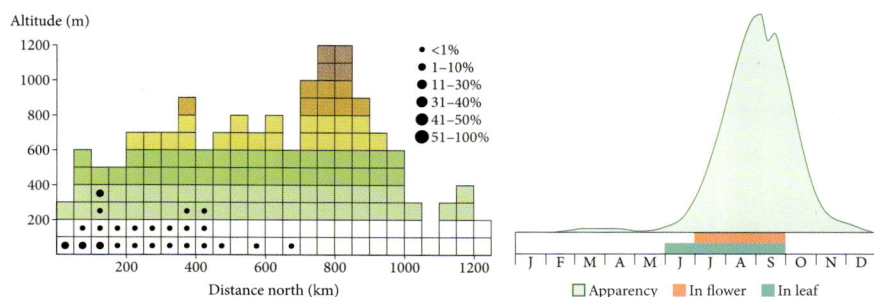

	GB	IR
Long term	↑	No trend
Short term	↑	No trend

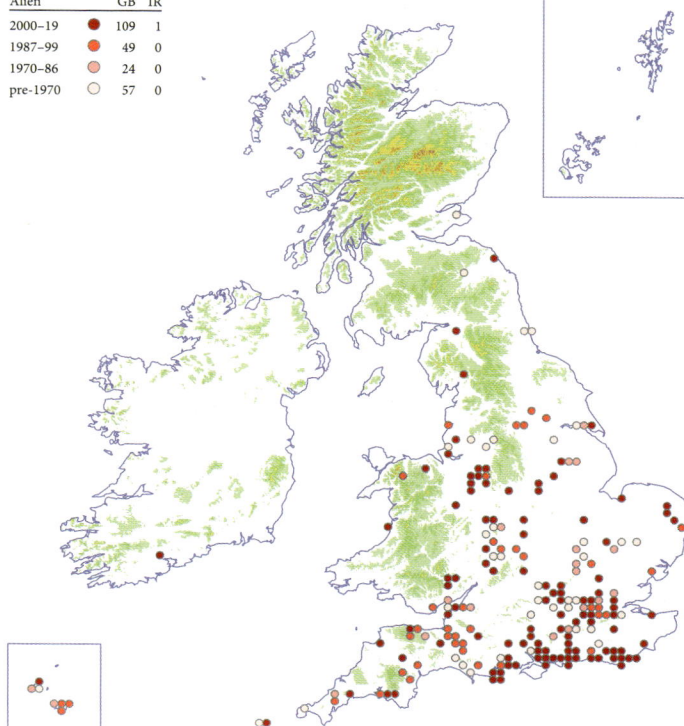

Alien	GB	IR
2000–19	109	1
1987–99	49	0
1970–86	24	0
pre-1970	57	0

Altitude (m) / Distance north (km)

| Apparency | In flower | In leaf |

Key refs Cavers *et al.* (1983), Ryves *et al.* (1996).

S.J. LEACH & D.A. PEARMAN

Ne *Setaria viridis* Green Bristle-grass
(L.) P.Beauv.

An annual grass, usually found as a casual of cultivated and waste ground, the verges of paths, tracks and roads, in car parks, along railway sidings, and in refuse tips. It is mainly introduced in birdseed or for use as pheasant- or game-cover, but also from wool shoddy, oil-seed, esparto and grain. Lowland.

Trends *S. viridis* was first recorded in the wild in Britain in 1666 (Hampton Court, Middlesex). There are many more records than there were 50 years ago, which seem to be the result of better recording as well as a genuine increase in contaminated seed and its intentional sowing in arable margins.

Biogeography A native of Eurasia, which now occurs in temperate and subtropical regions throughout the Northern Hemisphere; this spread has obscured its putative native range.

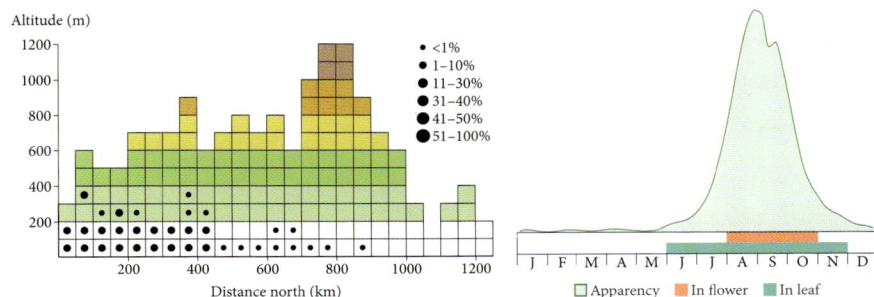

	GB	IR
Long term	↑	↑
Short term	↑	↓

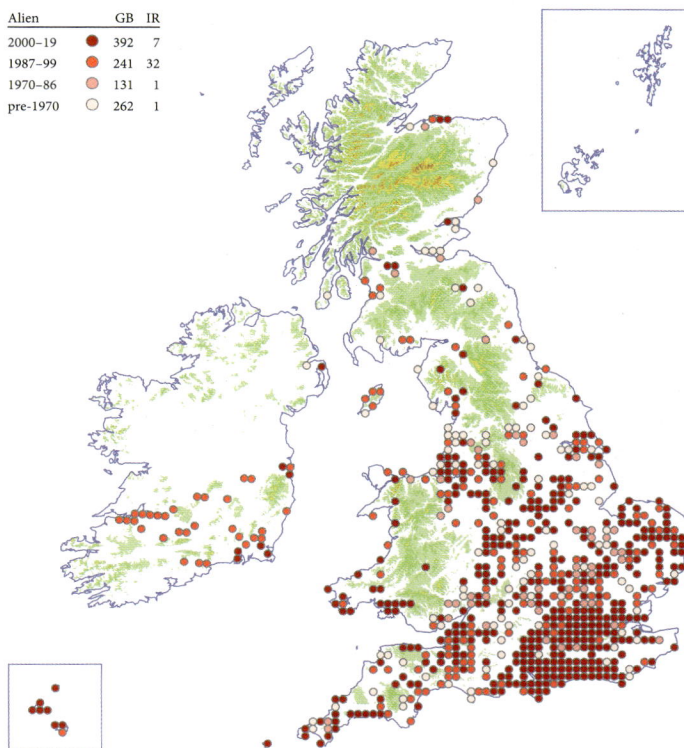

Alien	GB	IR
2000–19	392	7
1987–99	241	32
1970–86	131	1
pre-1970	262	1

Altitude (m) / Distance north (km)

| Apparency | In flower | In leaf |

Key refs Cope & Gray (2009), Douglas *et al.* (1985), Ryves *et al.* (1996).

S.J. LEACH & D.A. PEARMAN

1439

Ne *Setaria italica* Foxtail Bristle-grass

(L.) P.Beauv.

An annual grass found as a casual of refuse tips, docks and waste ground, mainly introduced in birdseed and as a contaminant of grain. Lowland.

Trends *S. italica* is the familiar 'millet' fed to caged birds. It was known from the wild by at least 1899 (Hull, South-east Yorkshire). It is now only a rare casual.

Biogeography Originated in cultivation, perhaps by selection from *S. viridis*; now cultivated and often naturalized in warm-temperate and subtropical regions throughout the world.

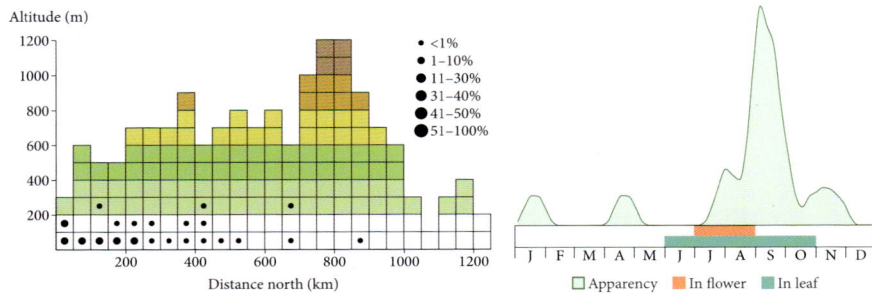

		GB	IR
Long term		No trend	No trend
Short term	⬇		No trend

Alien		GB	IR
2000–19	●	22	0
1987–99	●	49	0
1970–86	●	70	0
pre-1970	○	83	1

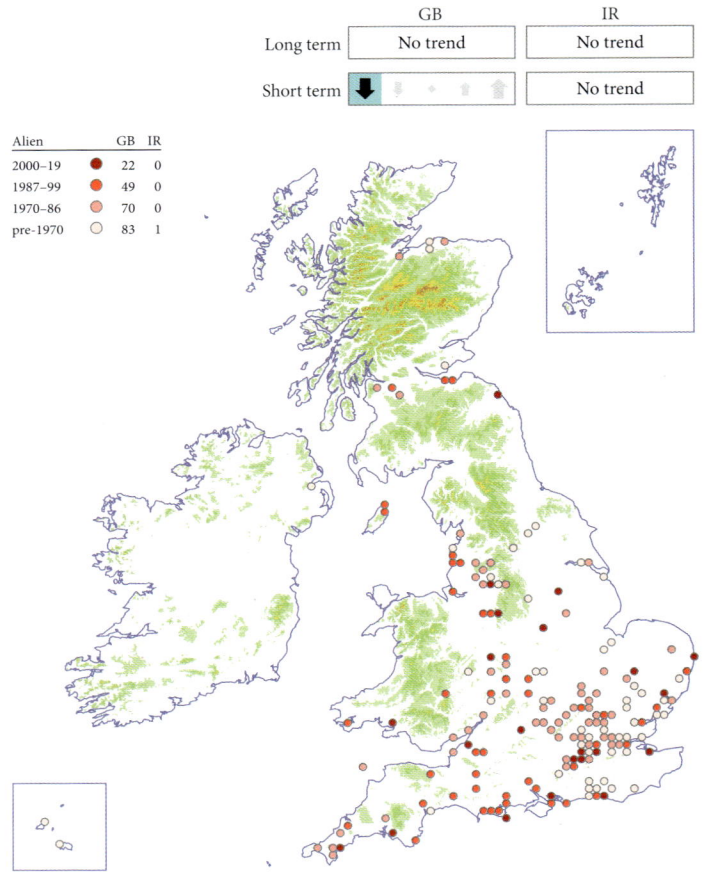

Key refs Cope & Gray (2009), Ryves *et al.* (1996), Zohary & Hopf (2000).

S.J. LEACH & D.A. PEARMAN

Ne *Sorghum halepense* Johnson-grass

(L.) Pers.

A tall rhizomatous perennial grass, found as a casual of refuse tips, railway sidings and waste ground, introduced from birdseed, wool, grain, soya-bean waste and as a component of gamebird food and cover crops. Lowland.

Trends *S. halepense* was first recorded from the wild in 1909 (Weymouth, Dorset). It is probably increasing, though some of the apparent increase could be due to the more systematic recording of alien species in recent decades.

Biogeography Perhaps native to the Mediterranean region, but has spread worldwide in cultivation or as a very persistent weed in warm-temperate and tropical areas and as a casual in temperate zones.

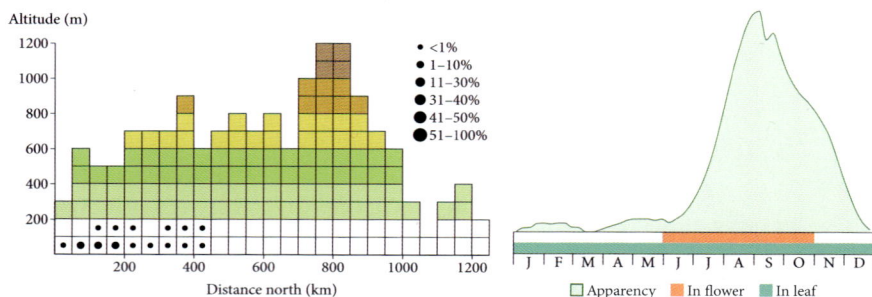

		GB	IR
Long term		No trend	No trend
Short term	⬇		No trend

Alien		GB	IR
2000–19	●	54	1
1987–99	●	47	0
1970–86	●	34	0
pre-1970	○	22	0

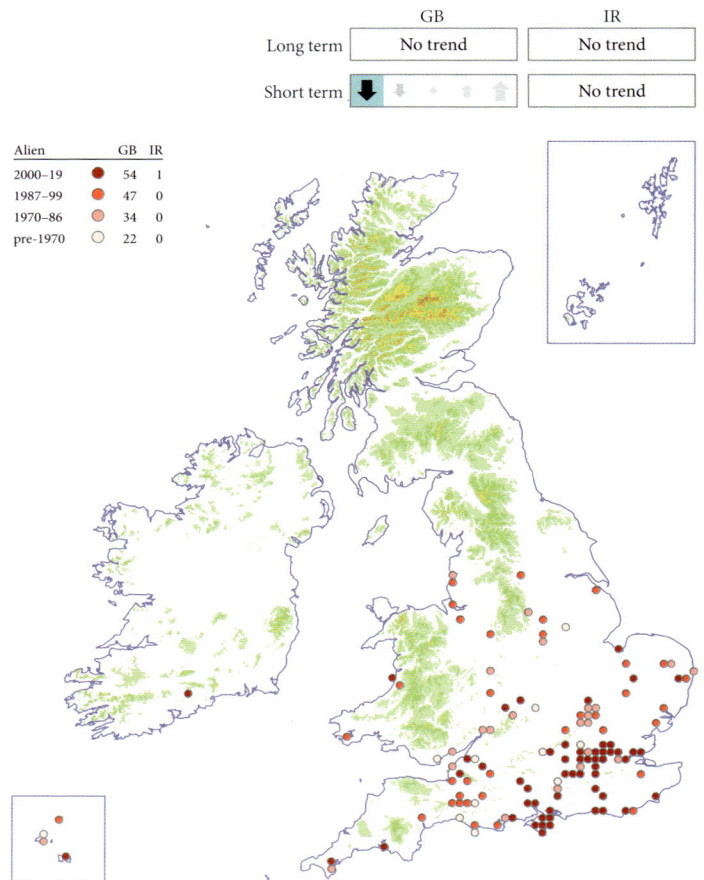

Key refs Ryves *et al.* (1996), Vaughan & Geissler (2009).

S.J. LEACH & D.A. PEARMAN

Ne *Sorghum bicolor* Great Millet
(L.) Moench

An annual grass, found around docks and on cultivated ground, refuse tips and waste ground, where it arises from birdseed and, formerly, wool shoddy. Lowland.

Trends *S. bicolor* was first recorded from the wild in 1890 near Theale (Berkshire) and is increasingly recorded as a casual, presumably due to the increased use of birdseed and greater willingness of recorders to record aliens that emerge from it.

Biogeography The wild variants of *S. bicolor* occur in Africa south of the Sahara, and it was probably domesticated in this area. It is widely grown as a crop in Africa, south-western Asia and India and from the late 18th century in North and South America.

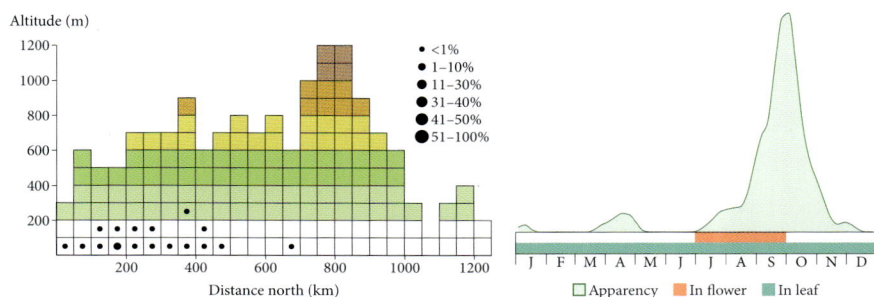

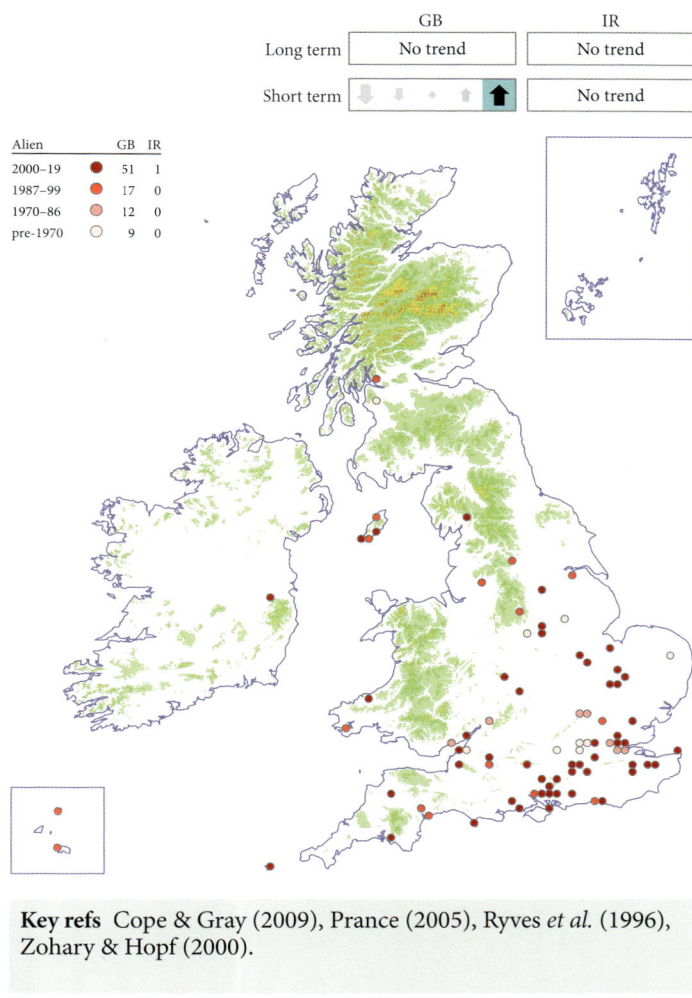

Alien	GB	IR
2000–19	51	1
1987–99	17	0
1970–86	12	0
pre-1970	9	0

Key refs Cope & Gray (2009), Prance (2005), Ryves *et al.* (1996), Zohary & Hopf (2000).

T.D. DINES

Ne *Miscanthus sinensis* Chinese Silver-grass
Andersson

A stoutly rhizomatous, clump-forming perennial grass, much grown in gardens and occasionally escaping into the wild. It readily produces seed and can be self-sown on urban pavements (Leslie, 2009). Lowland.

Trends *M. sinensis* was first recorded in the wild in 1979 (Berkshire) but it is not clear whether that was a planted specimen or a garden escape. It is widely planted, with a very wide range of named cultivars, and many of the mapped records might not be of wild plants. It is apparently rarely grown for biofuel production, unlike the sterile hybrid *M. ×giganteus*.

Biogeography A native of eastern Asia.

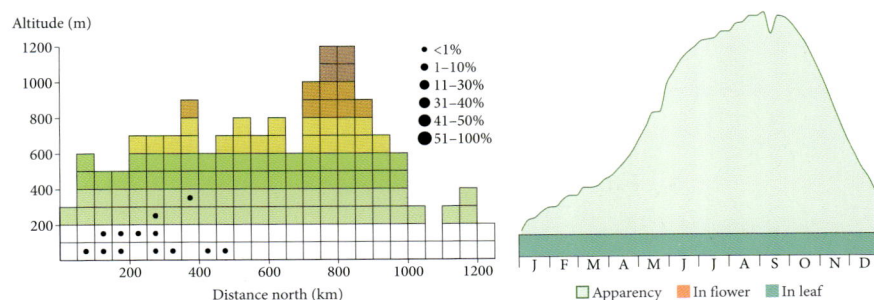

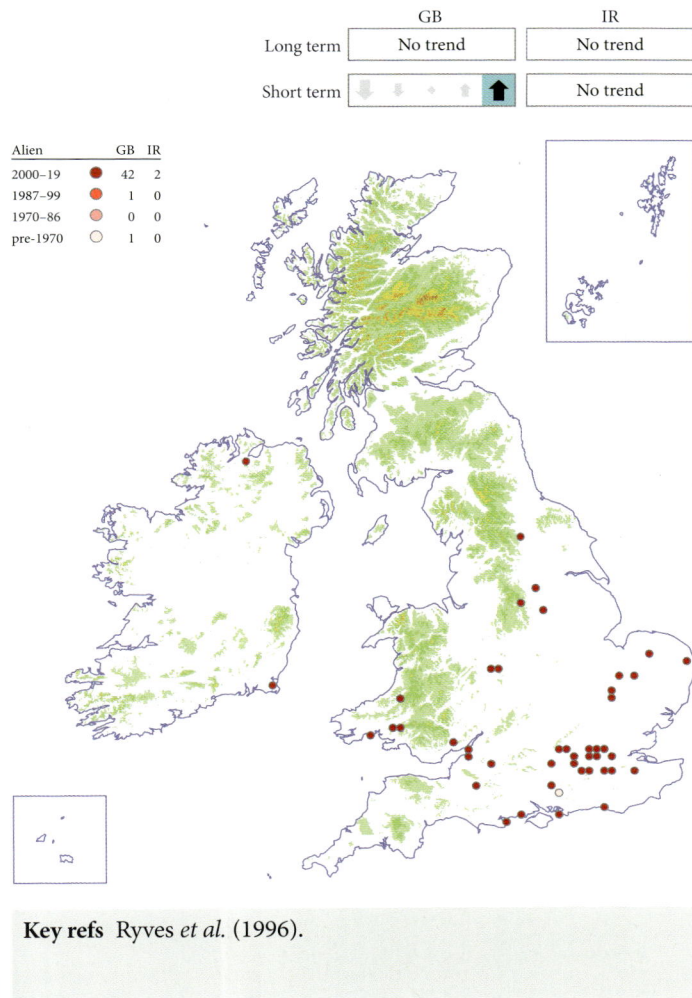

Alien	GB	IR
2000–19	42	2
1987–99	1	0
1970–86	0	0
pre-1970	1	0

Key refs Ryves *et al.* (1996).

D.A. PEARMAN

1441

Ne *Zea mays* Maize
L.

An annual grass, widely grown on a field scale mainly as a fodder crop, but also on a small scale in gardens and found as a relic or escape from cultivation on field margins, refuse tips and waste ground, and also as a casual of birdseed and kitchen waste in these habitats. The male and female flowers are borne on separate inflorescences; pollination is by wind and the seeds are not dispersed but are retained on the cob. Lowland.

Trends *Z. mays* was being grown in Britain by 1562, but only extensively cultivated in southern Britain since the 1970s, mainly for livestock feed and, on a smaller scale, for game cover and human consumption. It was first recorded from the wild by 1876 (Glamorganshire) and is certainly increasing, though never persisting.

Biogeography Not known in the wild, although probably originated in Mexico. Maize has long been cultivated in the Americas and is now grown in some temperate and most tropical and subtropical regions.

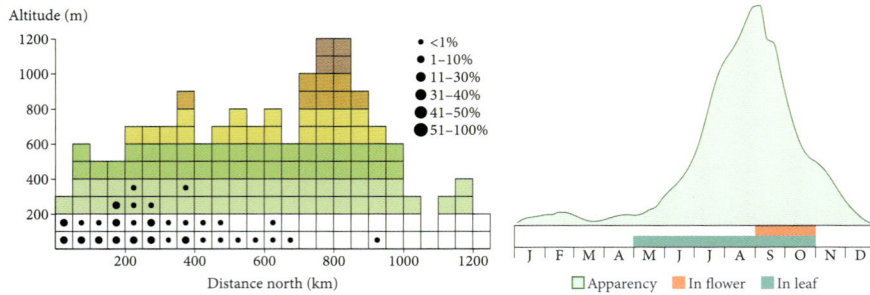

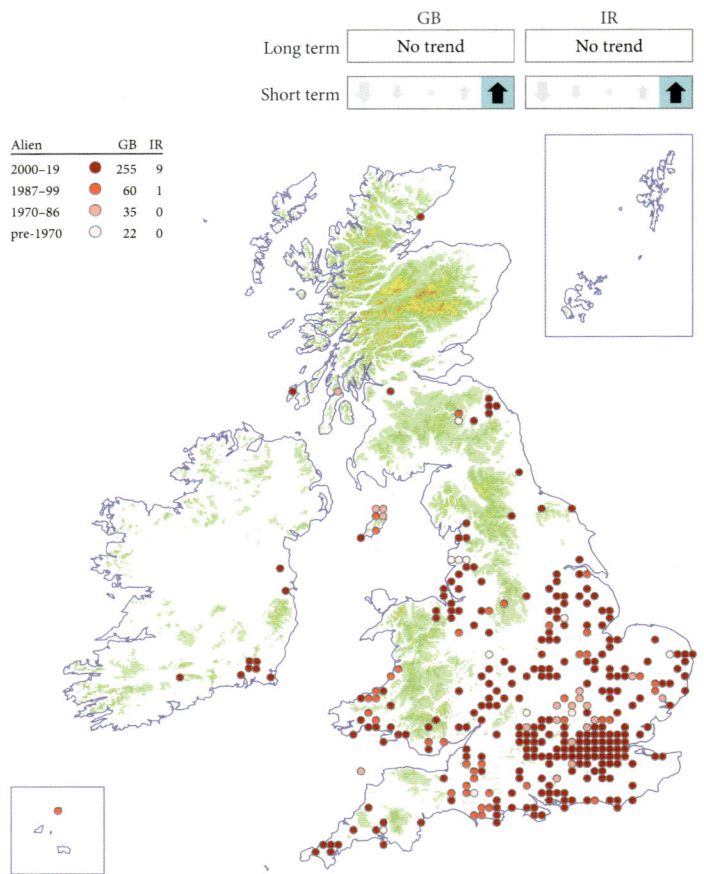

Alien	GB	IR
2000–19	255	9
1987–99	60	1
1970–86	35	0
pre-1970	22	0

	GB	IR
Long term	No trend	No trend
Short term	↑	↑

Key refs Cope & Gray (2009), Robinson & Treharne (1985), Ryves *et al.* (1996), Smart & Simmonds (1995), Vaughan & Geissler (2009).

S.J. LEACH & D.A. PEARMAN

N *Molinia caerulea* Purple Moor-grass
(L.) Moench

A deciduous perennial grass of a wide range of habitats, particularly abundant in wet heaths, moorlands, blanket bogs, mires and fens, more scattered in open birchwoods, montane grassland and cliffs and stony lake margins. It is found on mildly basic to strongly acidic peats and mineral soils which are permanently or seasonally wet. 0–1,000 m (Ben Macdui, South Aberdeenshire).

Trends *M. caerulea*, mapped as 'all records' in the 1962 *Atlas*, has declined in some lowland areas through drainage and habitat destruction. Conversely, it has increased in frequency where grazing has ceased, especially on lowland heaths, where it often forms virtually impenetrable stands, suppressing most other vegetation. Likewise, in the uplands, it has increased in heath and bog habitats that have been degraded by burning, drainage and afforestation.

Subsp. *caerulea* is found throughout the range of the species, subsp. *arundinacea* is widespread but scattered in fens and by rivers and canals.

Biogeography Eurosiberian Boreo-temperate element.

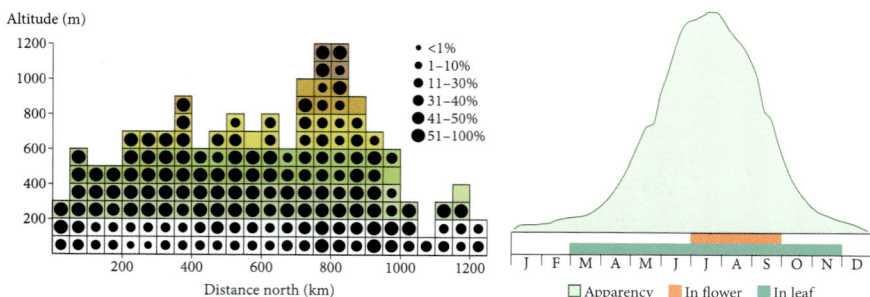

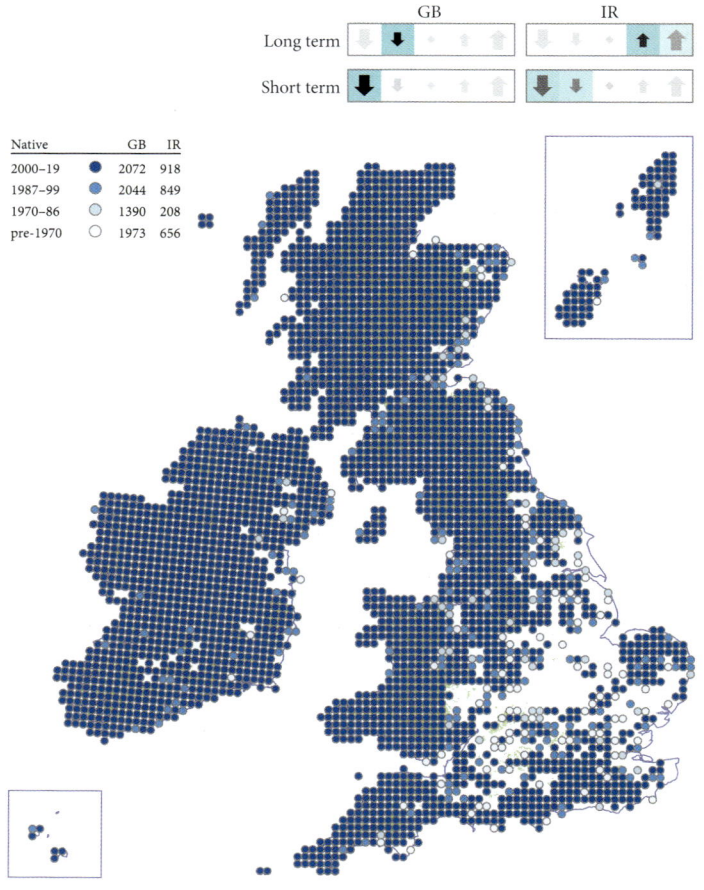

Native	GB	IR
2000–19	2072	918
1987–99	2044	849
1970–86	1390	208
pre-1970	1973	656

	GB	IR
Long term	↓	↑
Short term	↓	↓

Key refs Grime *et al.* (2007), Taylor *et al.* (2001), Trist & Sell (1988).

F.H. PERRING & D.A. PEARMAN

N *Phragmites australis* Common Reed
(Cav.) Trin. ex Steud.

A rhizomatous and stoloniferous grass of swamps and fens, forming large stands in shallow water in ditches, rivers, lakes and ponds; also in brackish swamps and lagoons, and in freshwater seepages on sheltered sea-cliffs. It is frequently planted beside artificial water bodies. Generally lowland, but reaching 470 m on Brown Clee Hill (Shropshire).

Trends The 10 km square distribution is broadly stable, though local losses have been noted, such as the die-back of reedbeds in the Norfolk Broads. However, it has increased in many areas due to eutrophication and lack of grazing. Over recent decades large areas of reedbeds have been created for breeding birds by planting *P. australis*, or for use as a means of filtration to remove contaminants in waste water.

Biogeography Circumpolar Wide-temperate element.

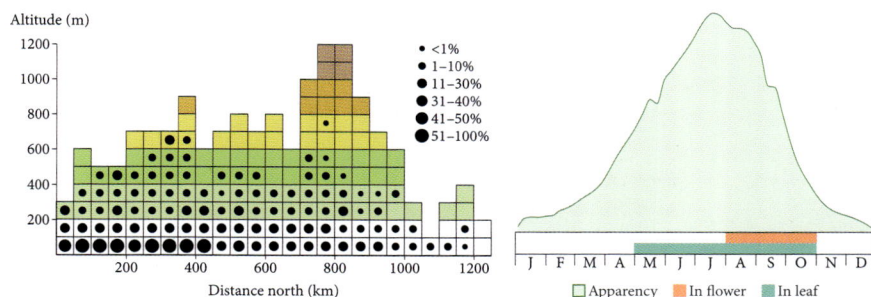

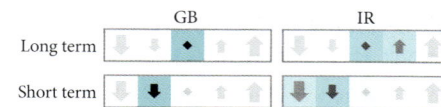

Native	GB	IR
2000–19	2129	792
1987–99	1991	735
1970–86	1379	156
pre-1970	1747	539

Alien	GB	IR
2000–19	7	0
1987–99	3	0
1970–86	0	0
pre-1970	0	0

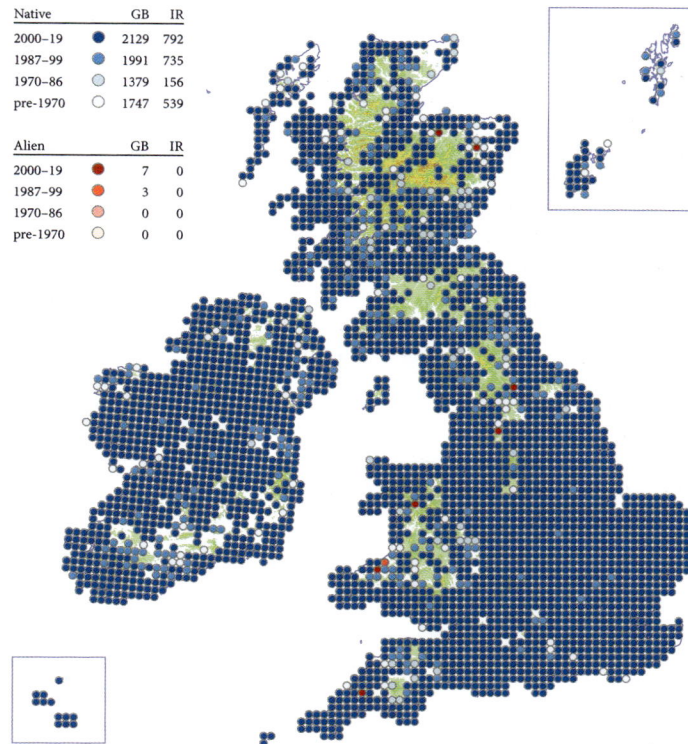

Key refs Cope & Gray (2009), Grime *et al.* (2007), Haslam (1972), Haslam & McDougall (1972), Packer *et al.* (2017), Preston & Croft (1997).

S.J. LEACH & D.A. PEARMAN

N *Danthonia decumbens* Heath-grass
(L.) DC.

A densely tufted perennial grass of infertile pastures, heathy grassland and moorland, favouring mildly acidic soils. It is also found in calcareous swards, including chalk and limestone grassland, but is then rooted into more acidic, superficial or leached horizons. It is frequent too in damp montane grassland. It spreads by seed and seems to have a persistent seed bank. 0–920 m Glas Tulaichean (East Perthshire) and reportedly at 1,040 m on Macgillycuddy's Reeks (South Kerry).

Trends *D. decumbens* has declined markedly throughout lowland regions in Britain and Ireland since the 1960s. The principal causes for this decline are the destruction of infertile habitats by the ploughing-up of permanent pastures, the widespread use of fertilizers and increased atmospheric deposition of nutrients. It distribution is more stable in the uplands. It is easily overlooked and this may account for some recent losses although there have also been many new discoveries, presumably due to more systematic recording. It was mapped as 'all records' in the 1962 *Atlas*.

Biogeography European Temperate element.

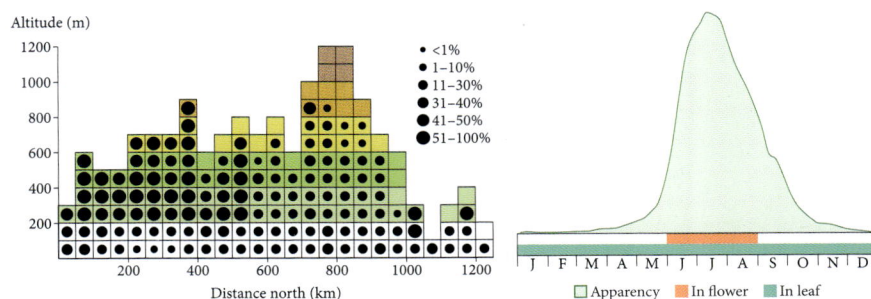

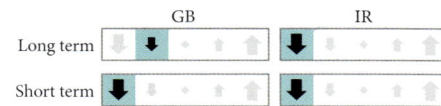

Native	GB	IR
2000–19	2119	656
1987–99	2037	651
1970–86	1270	115
pre-1970	1974	632

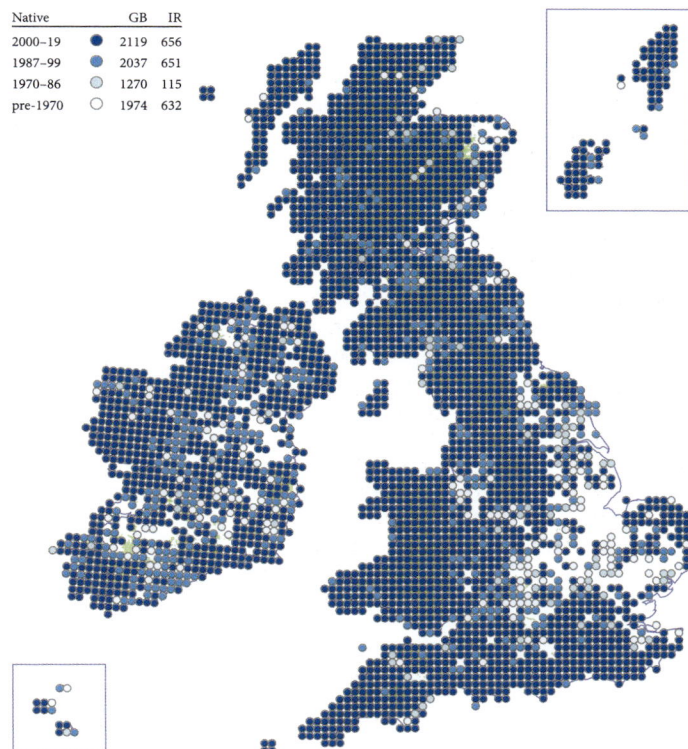

Key refs Cope & Gray (2009), Grime *et al.* (2007).

D.A. PEARMAN & K.J. WALKER

Ne *Cortaderia selloana* Pampas-grass

(Schult. & Schult.f.) Asch. & Graebn.

A large, densely clump-forming, dioecious perennial grass, widely grown in gardens since the 19th century and occasionally planted on roadsides outside gardens and along railway lines. It is naturalized on roadsides, railway banks and rubbish dumps, and in rough grassland on sheltered sea-cliffs and sand dunes. Lowland.

Trends *C. selloana* has been cultivated in Britain since 1839 and is commonly grown in municipal parks and gardens. It was first recorded in the wild in 1906 (St Catherine, Jersey). Most wild populations are reported as originating from garden throw-outs or deliberate planting and are persistent and long-lived. However, both male and female plants are now in cultivation, and in places the species is freely self-seeding (Leslie, 2009;

Gray & Cope, 2009). It is increasing, particularly in south-west England.

Biogeography Native of South America.

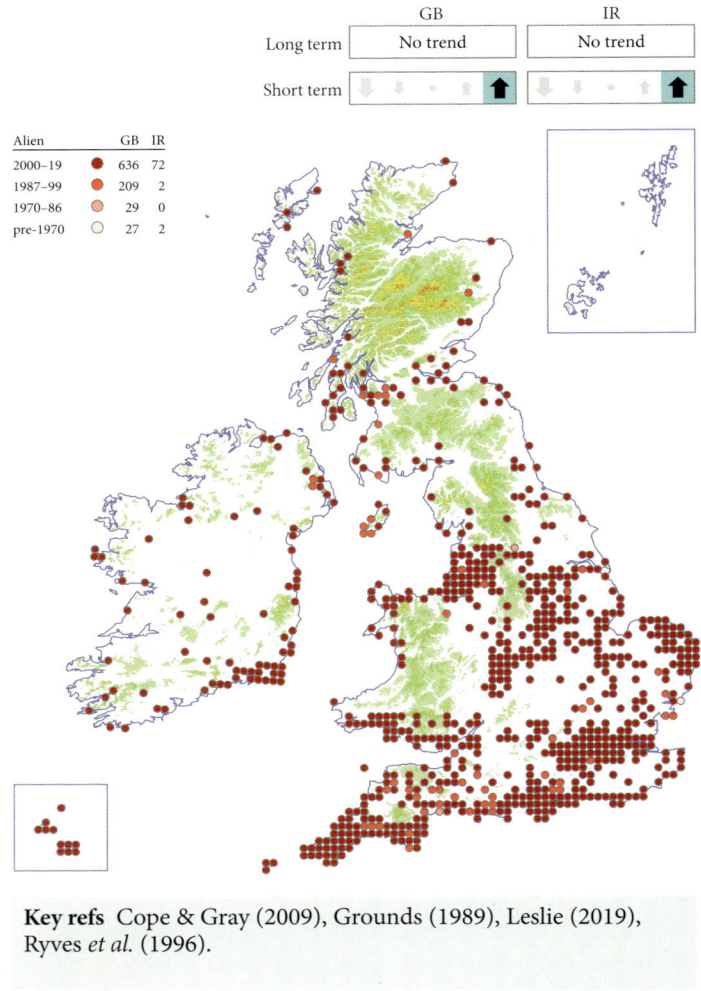

Alien	GB	IR
2000–19	636	72
1987–99	209	2
1970–86	29	0
pre-1970	27	2

	GB	IR
Long term	No trend	No trend
Short term		

Key refs Cope & Gray (2009), Grounds (1989), Leslie (2019), Ryves *et al.* (1996).

S.J. LEACH, D.A. PEARMAN & K.J. WALKER

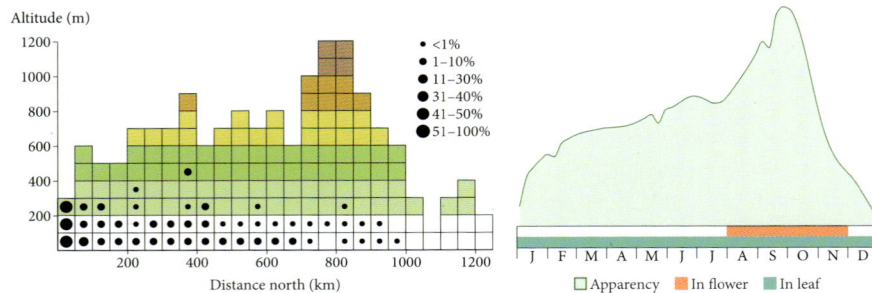

Ne *Cortaderia richardii* Early Pampas-grass

(Endl.) Zotov

A large, densely clump-forming perennial grass, widely grown in gardens and occasionally planted elsewhere. It originates as a garden escape and reproduces freely by seed, and becomes naturalized on cliffs and waste ground. It flowers considerably earlier than *C. selloana*, and prefers the wetter, milder climate of the north and west. Lowland.

Trends *C. richardii* is known as Toetoe Grass in New Zealand. It was introduced to Britain in the 1840s and is occasionally grown in gardens, and seedlings were apparently first recorded from the wild in in 1966 (Helensburgh, Dumbartonshire). The current map shows an extraordinary increase in the number of records. It is not clear whether this is a result of spread, or, possibly more likely, because it is now differentiated from *C. selloana* by many recorders.

Biogeography Native of South Island, New Zealand; naturalized in Australia.

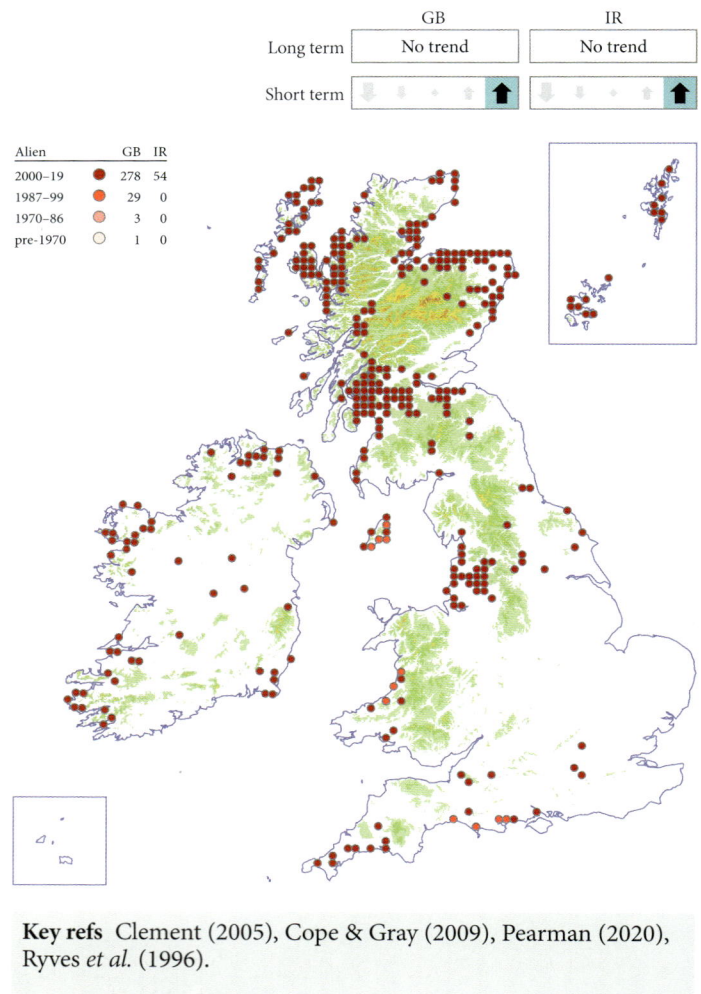

Alien	GB	IR
2000–19	278	54
1987–99	29	0
1970–86	3	0
pre-1970	1	0

	GB	IR
Long term	No trend	No trend
Short term		

Key refs Clement (2005), Cope & Gray (2009), Pearman (2020), Ryves *et al.* (1996).

T.D. DINES, D.A. PEARMAN & K.J. WALKER

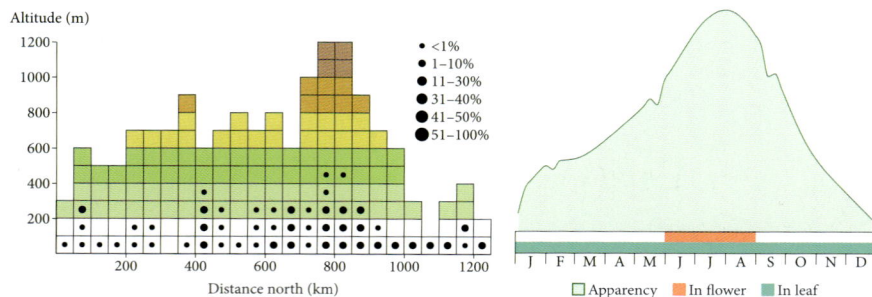

N *Spartina maritima* Small Cord-grass
(Curtis) Fernald

A perennial grass of tidal mud-flats, generally at higher elevations than *S. anglica*, such as in saltmarsh creeks and pans, and on bare ground behind sea-walls. It rarely sets seed in Britain, relying instead on vegetative spread by means of extensively creeping rhizomes. Lowland.

Native in Britain and a neophyte in Ireland.

Trends The 10 km square range of *S. maritima* has contracted during the past century, probably more due to habitat loss – whether through successional changes, coastal erosion or land-claim – and cessation of grazing on many coastal marshes than to the spread of *S. anglica*, which occupies a different niche in the saltmarsh zone. It is thought by some to be an ancient introduction.

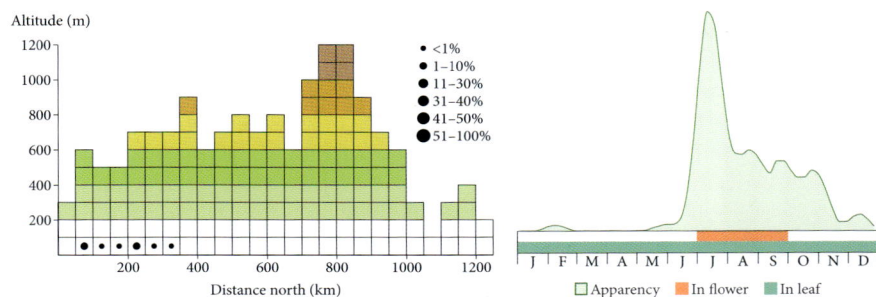

Biogeography Suboceanic Southern-temperate element.

Native	GB	IR
2000–19	23	0
1987–99	29	0
1970–86	24	0
pre-1970	53	0

Alien	GB	IR
2000–19	2	1
1987–99	1	0
1970–86	1	2
pre-1970	2	0

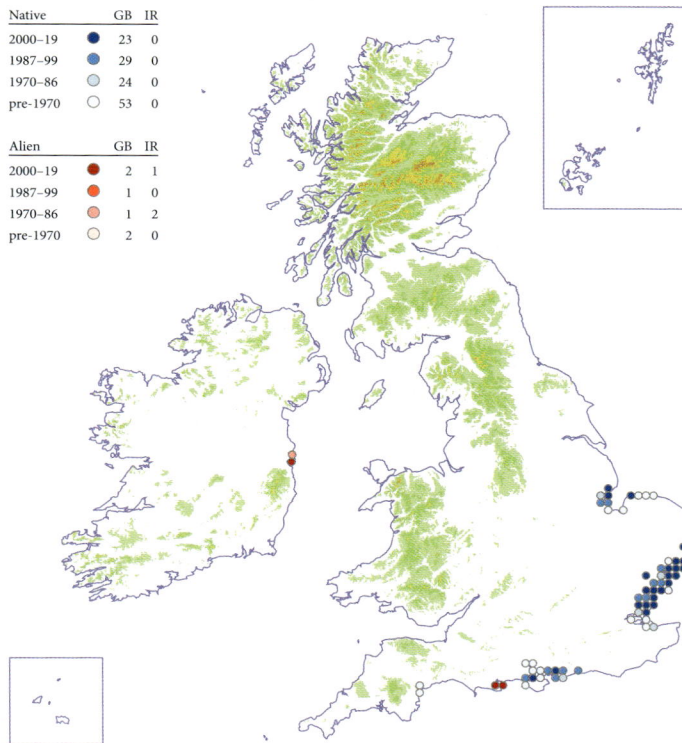

	GB	IR
Long term	↓	No trend
Short term	↓	No trend

Key refs Adam (1990), Cope & Gray (2009), Marchant & Goodman (1969), Stewart *et al.* (1994).

S.J. LEACH & D.A. PEARMAN

Altitude (m) / Distance north (km) — <1%, 1–10%, 11–30%, 31–40%, 41–50%, 51–100%

Apparency / In flower / In leaf

Hy *Spartina alterniflora × maritima = S. ×townsendii*
Townsend's Cord-grass
H.Groves & J.Groves

A rhizomatous, stand-forming perennial grass of tidal mud-flats and saltmarshes that arose naturally but has since been widely planted as a mud-binder. It is sterile and reproduces vegetatively. Lowland.

A spontaneous hybrid (native × alien).

Trends *S. alterniflora*, a frequent species on the coast of eastern North America, was first collected from the banks of the River Itchen (South Hampshire) in 1816, a site to which it had presumably been introduced with shipping. Broomfield (1836) noted that it grew "in vast profusion … scattered over the great beds of mud and ooze" on both sides of the river above Itchen Ferry, Southampton, whereas *S. maritima*, our only native species of *Spartina* until the 19th century, was confined to the lowest part of the river, where it grew adjacent to but not mixed with the alien taxon. The hybrid between these two species, *S. ×townsendii*, arose naturally and was first collected at Itchen Ferry in 1846, and then at Hythe, on the opposite side of Southampton Water, in 1870. It spread rapidly in the 20th century. In recent decades attempts have been made to limit its spread, while in southern England it appears to have declined due to 'die-back' in many sites, possibly due to anaerobic conditions in the mud which develop as a direct result of colonization. *S. anglica*, an amphidiploid derivative of *S. ×townsendii* and now far more widespread than *S. ×townsendii*, was included with the hybrid in the 1962 *Atlas* map, but has since been mapped separately.

Biogeography This hybrid originated in Southampton Water (South Hampshire).

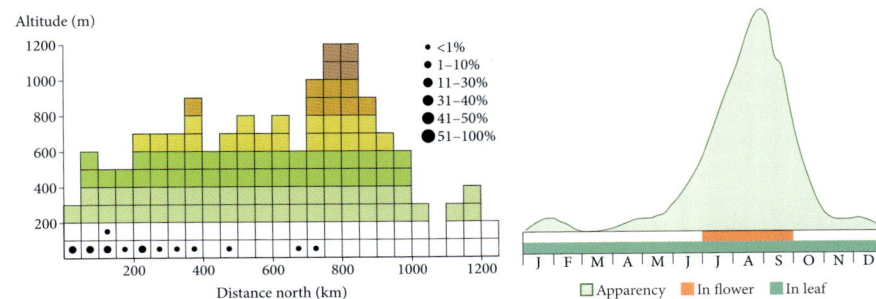

	GB	IR
2000–19	52	1
1987–99	52	0
1970–86	54	1
pre-1970	57	1

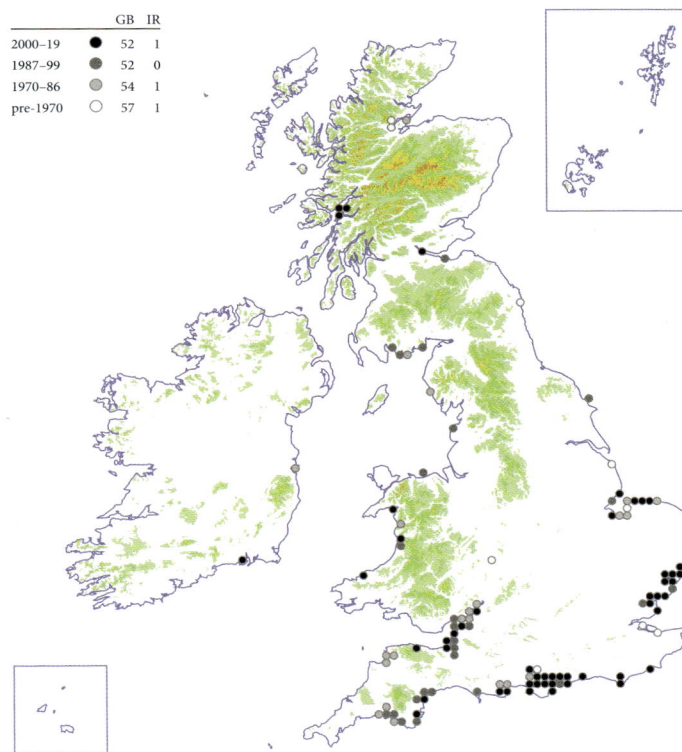

	GB	IR
Long term	↓	No trend
Short term	↓	No trend

Key refs Stace *et al.* (2015).

C.A. STACE, C.D. PRESTON & D.A. PEARMAN

Altitude (m) / Distance north (km) — <1%, 1–10%, 11–30%, 31–40%, 41–50%, 51–100%

Apparency / In flower / In leaf

N *Spartina anglica* Common Cord-grass
C.E.Hubb.

A rhizomatous perennial grass of tidal mud-flats and saltmarshes, much planted as a mud-binder and forming extensive stands in many estuaries. It originated in Southampton Water (South Hampshire) in about 1890 as a fertile amphidiploid derivative of the hybrid between native *S. maritima* and the North American *S. alterniflora* (*S. ×townsendii*). Lowland.

Trends The taxon was included within *S. ×townsendii* in the 1962 *Atlas*, by which time it had become widespread both through deliberate planting and natural colonization. It has not been possible to differentiate between these introduced and native populations and so all records are mapped without status. In recent decades there have been reports of local regression throughout its range due to herbivory and pathogens.

Biogeography Endemic as a native to Britain, but widely planted in western Europe and other parts of the world.

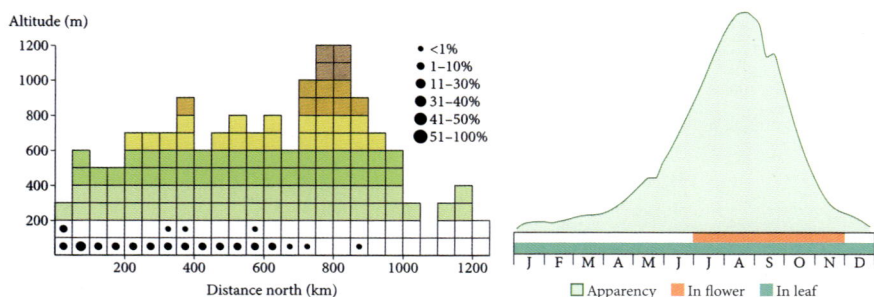

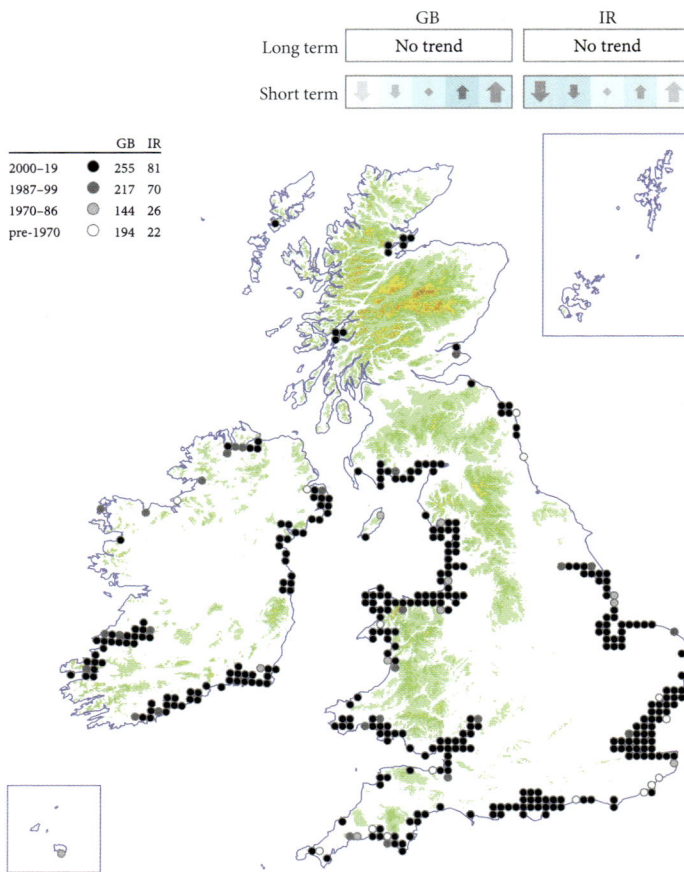

	GB	IR
2000–19	255	81
1987–99	217	70
1970–86	144	26
pre-1970	194	22

	GB	IR
Long term	No trend	No trend
Short term		

Key refs Adam (1990), Cope & Gray (2009), Ferris *et al.* (1997), Goodman *et al.* (1959), Goodman & Williams (1961), Gray & Benham (1990), Lambert *et al.* (1969), Raybould *et al.* (1991).

S.J. LEACH & D.A. PEARMAN

Altitude (m) / Distance north (km) chart; phenology chart (Apparency, In flower, In leaf)

Ne *Cynodon dactylon* Bermuda-grass
(L.) Pers.

A mat-forming perennial herb, found on eroding fore-dunes in dry sandy places and short grassland by the sea, including lawns and sea-front promenades, and inland on lawns and roadside verges. It is also found around docks, on refuse tips and as a casual from wool shoddy and other sources. Lowland.

Trends *C. dactylon* was first recorded in the wild in 1688 (Penzance, West Cornwall), where it persists to this day. In the past it has been considered possibly native there and in the Channel Islands too (Wigginton, 1999), but more likely is a long-standing ballast alien. Elsewhere it is considered a certain introduction, though some of the sites are of long standing. There has been little change in its distribution over the last 30 to 40 years.

Biogeography Eurasian Southern-temperate element.

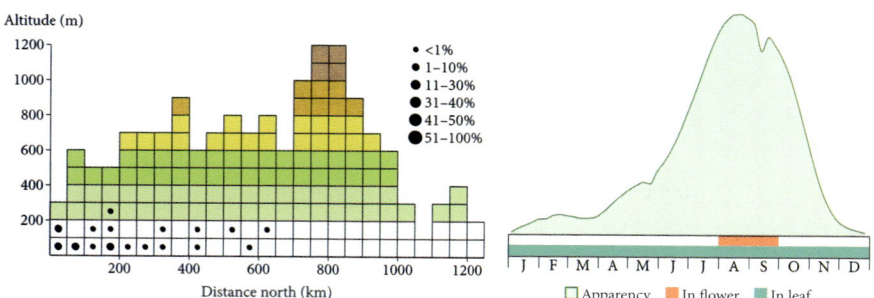

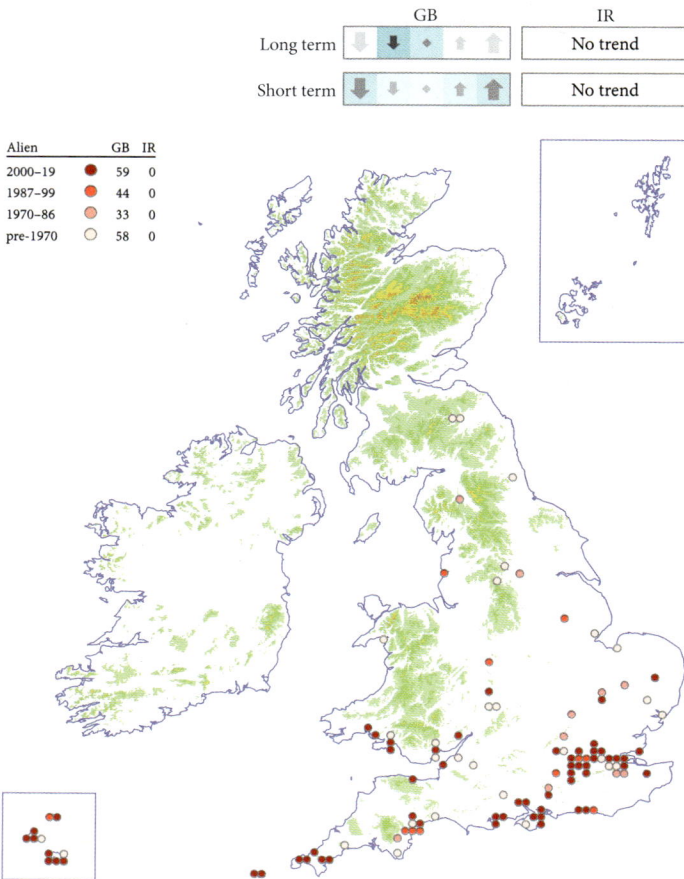

Alien	GB	IR
2000–19	59	0
1987–99	44	0
1970–86	33	0
pre-1970	58	0

	GB	IR
Long term		No trend
Short term		No trend

Key refs Cope & Gray (2009), Wigginton (1999).

Altitude (m) / Distance north (km) chart; phenology chart (Apparency, In flower, In leaf)

S.J. LEACH & D.A. PEARMAN

Chara aculeolata Hedgehog Stonewort

Kütz.

A hard-water species, particularly associated with small water bodies such as pools in calcareous fens and ponds in former clay pits, where it often occurs with other calcicolous species such as *Potamogeton coloratus* and usually with a range of other stoneworts. It can also occur in larger calcareous lakes, typically in fairly shallow water up to 1 m depth. Lowland.

Trends *C. aculeolata* is very sensitive to the secondary effects of nutrient pollution and this has resulted in a significant decline throughout its range. Many sites are also small water bodies which are liable to loss from succession and drainage.

Biogeography Endemic to Europe.

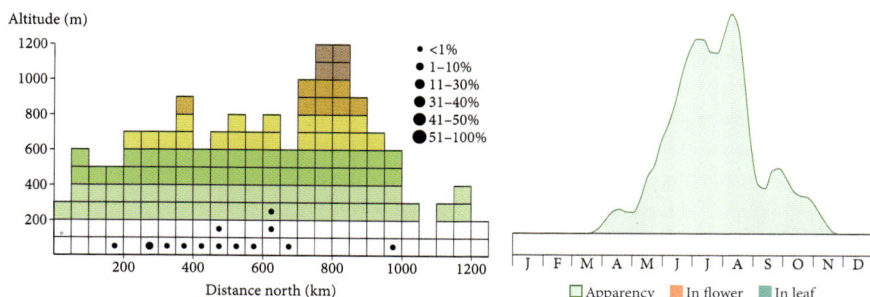

	GB	IR
Long term	No trend	No trend
Short term	No trend	No trend

Native	GB	IR
2000–19	22	50
1987–99	17	36
1970–86	8	18
pre-1970	42	62

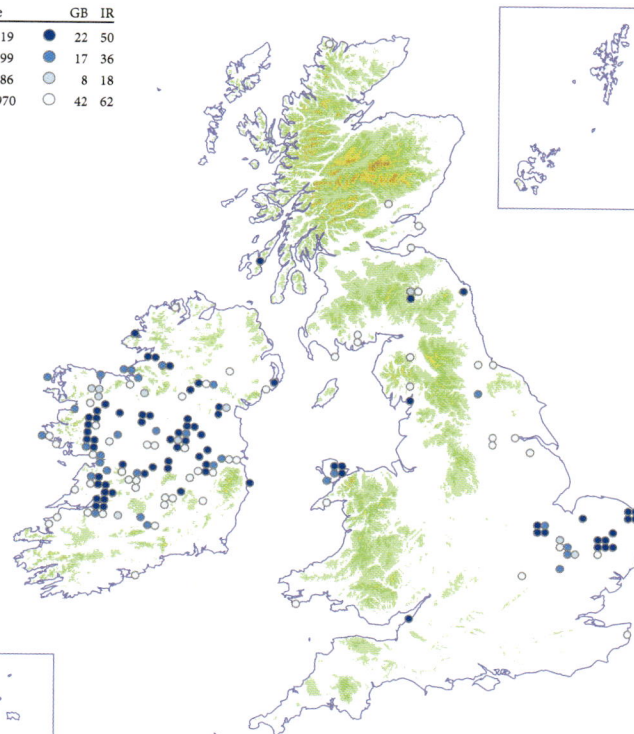

- <1%
- 1–10%
- 11–30%
- 31–40%
- 41–50%
- 51–100%

Altitude (m) / Distance north (km)

Apparency In flower In leaf

Key refs John *et al.* (2021).

N.F. Stewart

Chara aspera Rough Stonewort

Dethard. ex Willd.

C. aspera typically occurs in calcareous lakes, pools and ditches, often on marl or sand. It is tolerant of mildly brackish water, sometimes forming extensive beds in dune pools and machair lakes and even extending into softer waters when there is some salinity. In southern and eastern England, it is associated with gravel and clay pits but elsewhere it is more often found in natural lakes. It particularly occurs in shallow water up to 1 m deep where it is often associated with *Stuckenia filiformis*. It can withstand significant wave-wash and in some stony sites can be restricted to sandy accumulations on the wind-exposed north-eastern sides/ends. However, it can also form significant stands in deeper water in low-nutrient, hard-water sites. Predominately lowland, but up to 516 m at Lochan a'Chleirich, Sutherland.

Trends Although there remain strong populations in western and northern regions, this species has declined significantly throughout the rest of its range. The primary concern is the secondary effects of nutrient enrichment, through increased turbidity and competition from larger vegetation and algae. Its preference for sand and clay substrates can also be affected by the increase in organic deposition in more enriched systems. Its ability to withstand wave-wash means that it can persist in the shallows where turbulence disperses the organic sediment, though competition from *Crassula helmsii* may be an issue in this niche.

Biogeography Occurring in Europe, Turkey, Bangladesh, northern Africa and North America.

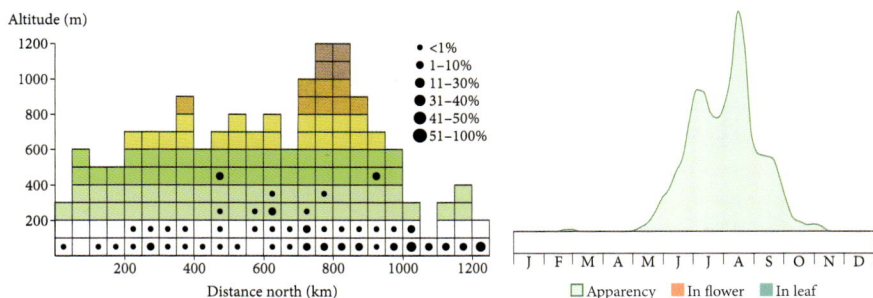

	GB	IR
Long term	No trend	No trend
Short term	No trend	No trend

Native	GB	IR
2000–19	128	63
1987–99	109	53
1970–86	47	30
pre-1970	116	92

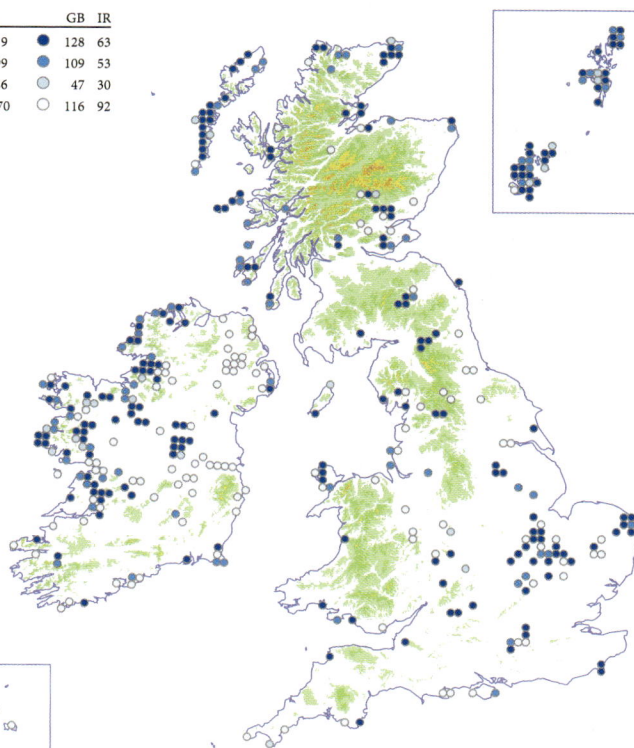

- <1%
- 1–10%
- 11–30%
- 31–40%
- 41–50%
- 51–100%

Altitude (m) / Distance north (km)

Apparency In flower In leaf

Key refs John *et al.* (2021).

N.F. Stewart

Ⓝ *Chara baltica* Baltic Stonewort
Bruzelius

Found in lakes and pools near the sea, where it grows in mildly brackish water on a variety of silts, sand or gravel. It prefers lower salinities than *Lamprothamnium papulosum* and *Tolypella nidifica*, with which it grows in two of its Scottish sites. Here it is often restricted to the lower salinities above the halocline and is therefore restricted to shallower water less than 50 cm deep in salinities up to 11 psu (Loch an Dùin, Outer Hebrides). In its English, Irish and Welsh sites, the salinities are lower and it grows at depths up to 1·5 metres, often with other large stoneworts, principally *C. papillosa* and *C. hispida*, or mixed with a diverse aquatic vascular plant flora. In its Welsh site it grows in several sand dune pools. Lowland.

Trends Populations in the Norfolk Broads have fluctuated considerably over the last few decades due to nutrient enrichment problems. For a brief period in 1999–2000 there was good water clarity throughout the system resulting in a flourishing of the aquatic vegetation. Since 2000 the water quality has deteriorated again with massive reductions in the extent of stonewort communities. These are still present but fluctuate, with periods of increase and then collapse. Sites in Kent, Dorset and Orkney have been lost due to changes in salinity. It has not been seen in Wales since 2007 despite some positive management; the reason for its apparent disappearance is unclear. Sites in western Scotland and Ireland seem more secure but salinity changes as a result of sea level rise may become an issue.

Biogeography *C. baltica* occurs in Baltic and northern Atlantic Europe. The taxon here is not true *C. baltica* and may belong to a species not otherwise recorded in our area; further investigation is needed.

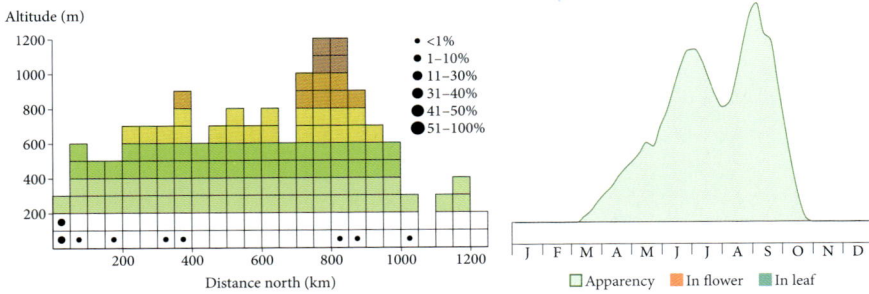

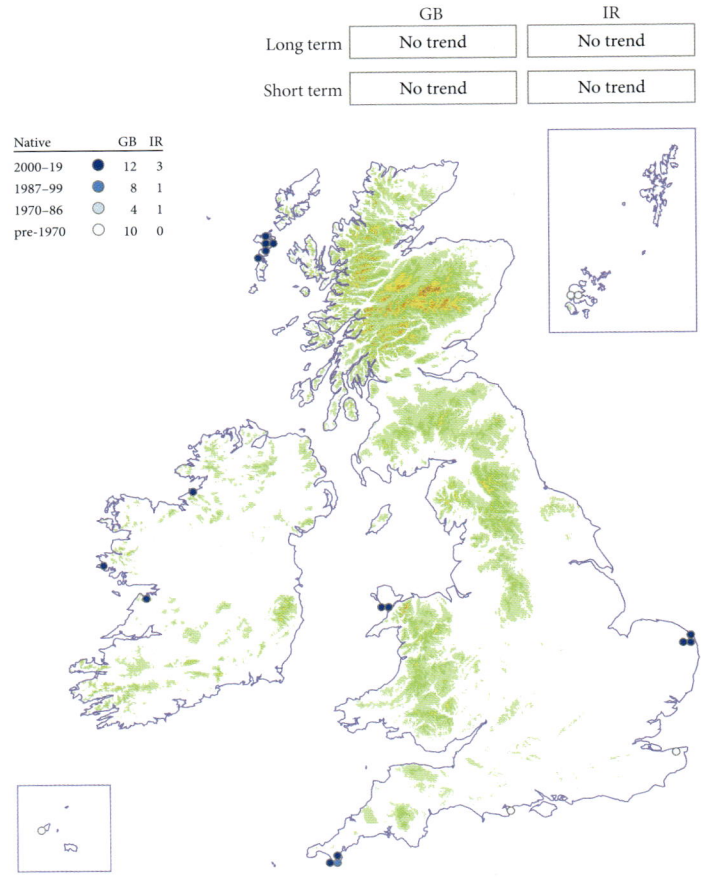

	GB	IR
Long term	No trend	No trend
Short term	No trend	No trend

Native	GB	IR
2000–19	12	3
1987–99	8	1
1970–86	4	1
pre-1970	10	0

Key refs ICIT (2004), Martin (2001), Martin *et al.* (2002), Schubert & Blindow (2003), Scott *et al.* (2011), Stewart (1995b), Stewart (2003c).

N.F. Stewart

Ⓝ *Chara baltica* var. *affinis* Lizard Stonewort
H.Groves & J.Groves

C. baltica var. *affinis* is restricted to the area of serpentinite geology in West Cornwall where it has been recorded in quarry pools and sluggish areas in streams. It mainly grows in shallow water less than 50 cm deep but at one site grows in up to 3 m of water. Associated species include *C. fragifera*, *Myriophyllum alterniflorum*, *Potamogeton polygonifolius*, *Eleogiton fluitans* and *P. natans*. In Guernsey it occurred in pools and ditches in an area of grazing marsh, while in France it grows in brackish water (I. Blindow, pers. comm.). Though described as a variety of *C. baltica*, it clearly does not belong to that species. Pending further research for the forthcoming *European Charophyte Flora*, it has been included here provisionally. Lowland.

Trends In Cornwall there are records from seven sites, including five since 1990, but it may be extant in only two of these and all populations are/were small. Most sites are small water bodies, and the principal threat is from competition from other aquatic vegetation, succession to swamp vegetation and colonization of scrub. One site was also partly infilled and another has issues of nutrient enrichment.

Biogeography **Native of** West Cornwall, Guernsey and western France.

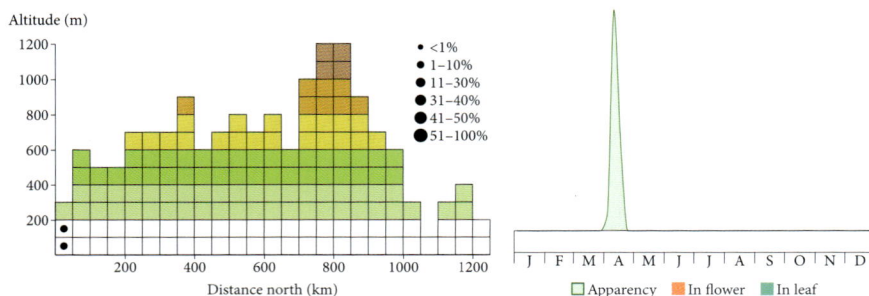

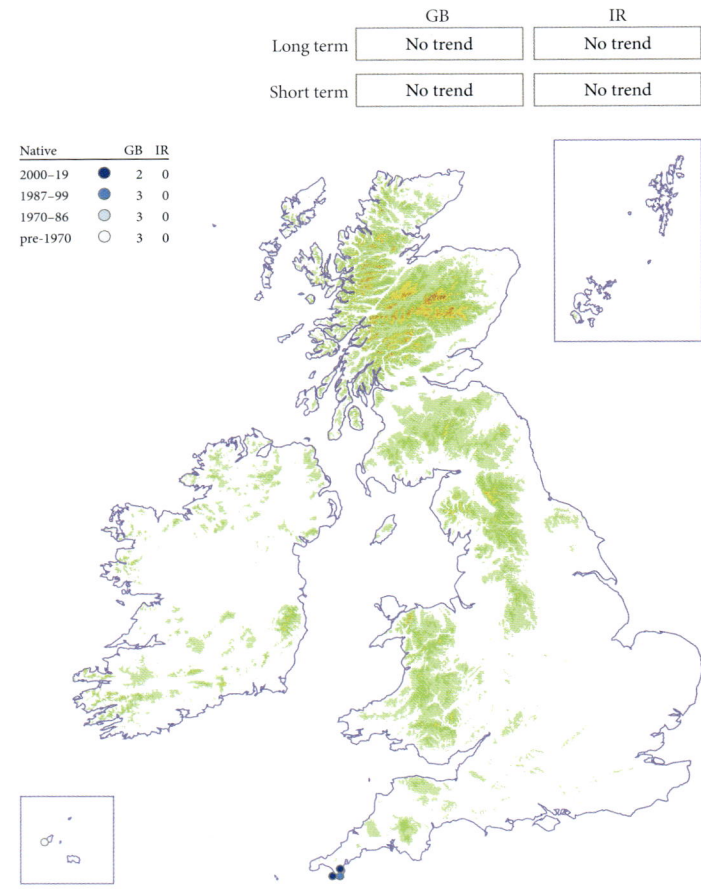

	GB	IR
Long term	No trend	No trend
Short term	No trend	No trend

Native	GB	IR
2000–19	2	0
1987–99	3	0
1970–86	3	0
pre-1970	3	0

Key refs John *et al.* (2021).

N.F. Stewart

Ne *Chara braunii* Braun's Stonewort
C.C.Gmel.

	GB	IR
Long term	No trend	No trend
Short term	No trend	No trend

The only British site for this species in the wild was in the Stockport branch of the Ashton Canal, where it grew in heated water effluent from steam-powered mills. Lowland.

Trends *C. braunii* is thought to have been introduced, along with *Najas graminea*, as a contaminant of Egyptian cotton which was processed in the mill adjacent to where it was first found. It was first discovered in 1883 at Reddish (South Lancashire) at which time it was already well established. By 1948 it had spread to two other locations between here and Lancashire Hill, 2 km to the south. The milling of cotton ceased soon after 1948 and the stonewort was last seen in 1952. The lack of warm water is probably the reason for loss though the canal had fallen into disuse and by the early 1960s the section at Reddish, at least, was mainly dominated by swamp. By the mid-1970s the canal had been completely infilled, although the old condensation tank is still visible beside the former canal line outside one of the mills. In 2009 a few plants were present in a garden centre in Devon, growing in a water-lily pot.

Biogeography A cosmopolitan species recorded throughout the world between 65°N and 35°S.

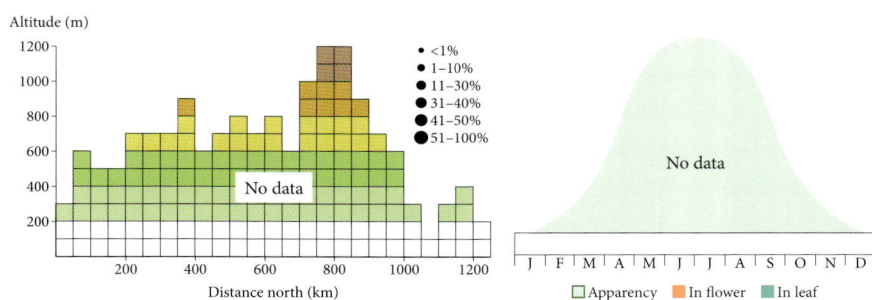

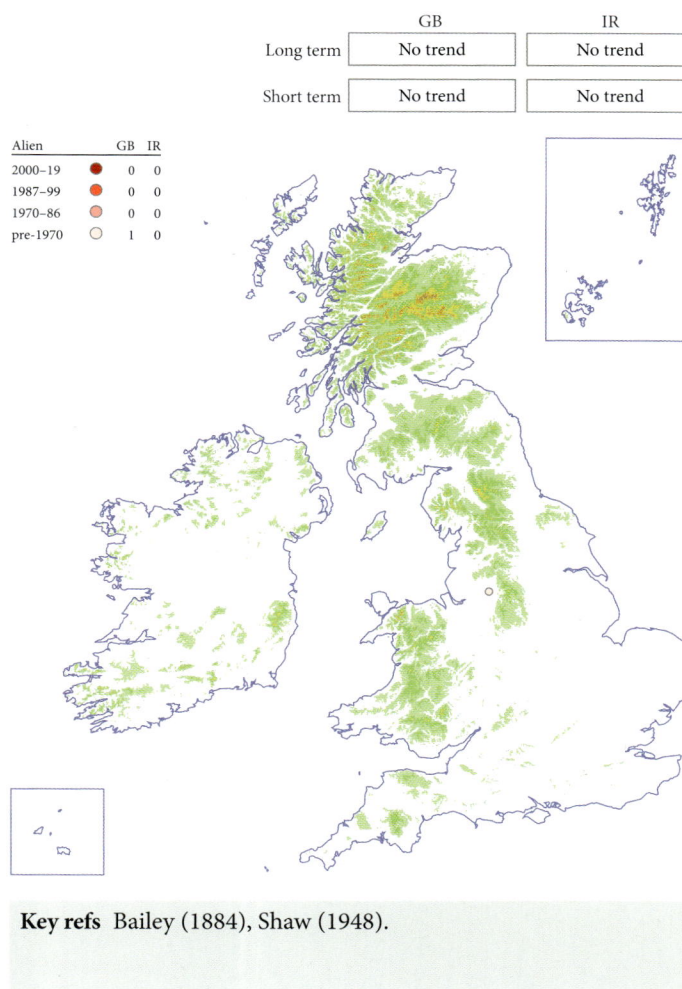

Alien	GB	IR
2000–19	0	0
1987–99	0	0
1970–86	0	0
pre-1970	1	0

Key refs Bailey (1884), Shaw (1948).

N.F. STEWART

N *Chara canescens* Bearded Stonewort
Desv. & Loisel.

	GB	IR
Long term	No trend	No trend
Short term	No trend	No trend

C. canescens is generally confined to calcareous brackish waters with high pH but it can tolerate a wide range of salinities from 1–32 psu and even marked fluctuations in salinity (Schubert & Blindow, 2003). It can grow in large or small water bodies and on sandy or muddy substrates. In shallow water it usually grows as an annual but it is capable of perennating in water up to 5 m deep. It appears to have a limited ability to compete with dense vascular plant growth and to be dependent on factors which suppress the growth of other plants (Stewart & Church, 1992). The preference for calcareous sites is evident in the Outer Hebrides and western Ireland where this species occurs in sites associated with calcareous machair sand but is absent from the rock-bound brackish lakes which support other halophilic stoneworts. Only female plants are known in Britain and it reproduces apomictically. Lowland.

Trends In England there is a cluster of sites in disused brick pits near Peterborough with low salinities (<1 psu). It is thought that high levels of other salts in the brick clays may be the factor allowing it to grow here (Lambert, 2007), and populations may persist for up to 25 years in certain conditions. The considerable reduction of brick clay extraction since 2000, however, has resulted in a sharp decline and it is now mainly restricted to sites with positive management. It has appeared sporadically on the eastern and southern coasts of Britain, possibly carried here by birds from the Baltic Sea where it is more frequent. These populations persist for a few years but tend to be lost due to changes in salinity.

Biogeography Known from Europe, North America, Greenland, northern Africa and Asia.

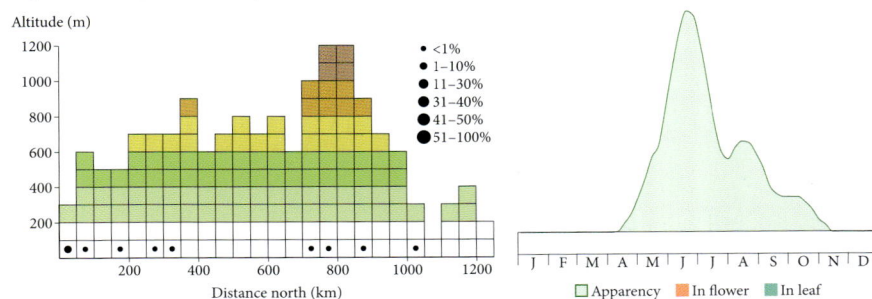

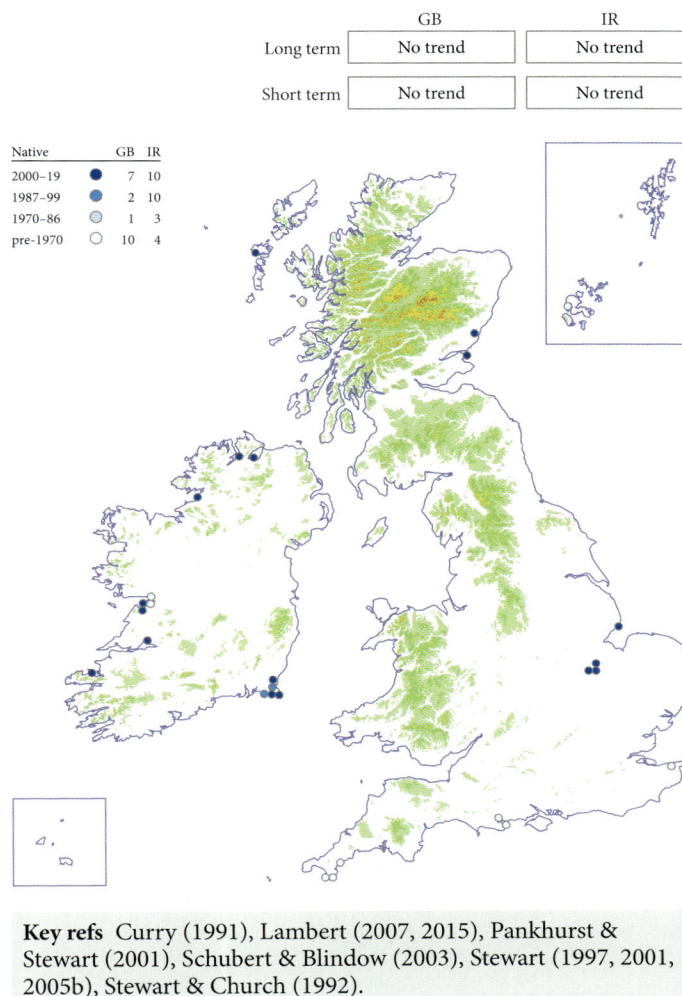

Native	GB	IR
2000–19	7	10
1987–99	2	10
1970–86	1	3
pre-1970	10	4

Key refs Curry (1991), Lambert (2007, 2015), Pankhurst & Stewart (2001), Schubert & Blindow (2003), Stewart (1997, 2001, 2005b), Stewart & Church (1992).

N.F. STEWART

Ⓝ *Chara connivens* Convergent Stonewort
Salzm. ex A.Braun

A plant of alkaline permanent water bodies such as lakes, ponds and ditches where it grows on sandy or marly substrates in depths of up to 3 m. In northern Europe it often occurs near the sea, and normally prefers at least slight salinity, up to 8 psu (Schubert & Blindow, 2003). However, it can sometimes occur inland and two sites in County Wexford and North Devon are quarry ponds some distance from the sea. Lowland.

Trends This species can only be reliably differentiated from the much more common *C. globularis* when it is fertile (usually between May and September). This means that although it is suspected still to be present at some sites it has not been possible to confirm this. It has been lost from sites due to nutrient enrichment, competition from other vegetation or habitat change, while nutrient enrichment is continuing to cause instability in the populations in the Norfolk Broads. Conversely, some new sites have recently been discovered, one of which (Hodbarrow Lagoon, Cumberland) has a strong population.

Biogeography Found in northern Africa, Asia and throughout much of Europe, from the Mediterranean region north to southern Scandinavia.

	GB	IR
Long term	No trend	No trend
Short term	No trend	No trend

Native		GB	IR
2000–19	●	5	1
1987–99	●	3	0
1970–86	○	1	0
pre-1970	○	7	2

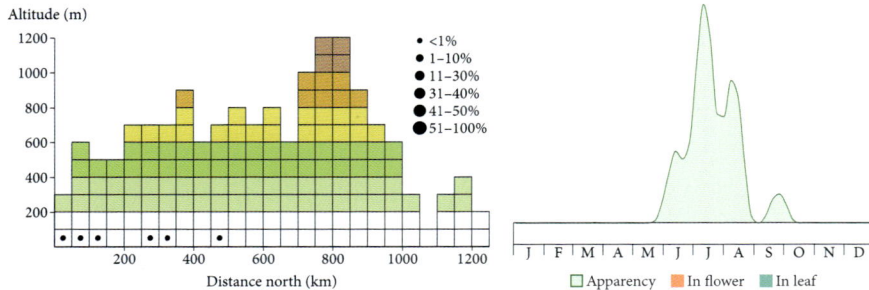

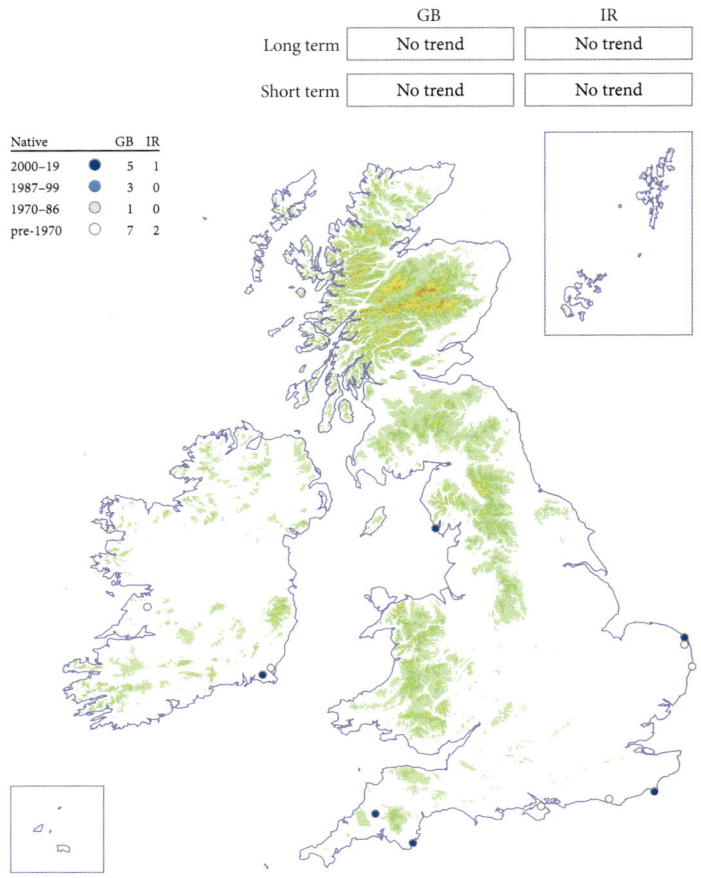

Key refs Schubert & Blindow (2003).

N.F. STEWART

Ⓝ *Chara contraria* Opposite Stonewort
A.Braun ex Kütz.

C. contraria occurs in a wide range of calcareous water bodies, with a greater preference towards lakes compared to its more common relative *C. vulgaris*. In alkaline lakes it can form extensive beds in deep water but often in this situation it can become replaced by *Elodea* species. It also frequently occurs in small water bodies where it often grows in the shallower edges which dry out for part of the year. It can be particularly prominent as an early pioneer in new water bodies such as clay pits. Here it often gradually declines with increasing vegetation and higher organic accumulation in the sediment, as it prefers sandy or marly substrates, though it may persist in the shallow edges where wave-wash keeps the habitat more open. Up to 580 m on the Ben Lawers ridge between Meall Creigh and Lochan Creag (Mid Perthshire).

Trends *C. contraria* is sensitive to nutrient pollution but, compared to other stonewort species, there is an indication of a relatively small decline based on the numbers of recent and historic records. Apparent absence could be due to its ability to move around as habitat suitability varies. Alternatively, it may have been under-recorded due to its similarity to the more common *C. vulgaris*.

Biogeography A cosmopolitan species, widespread throughout mainland Europe.

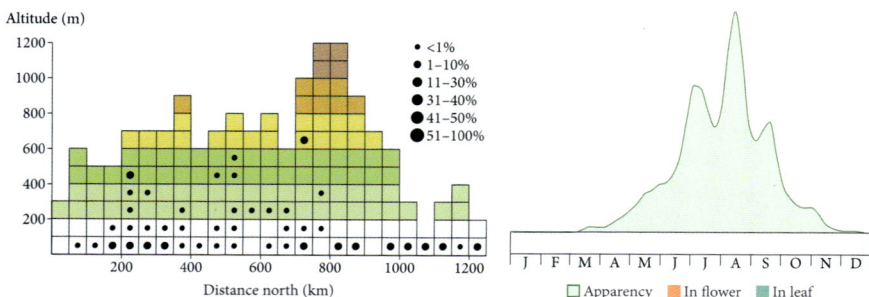

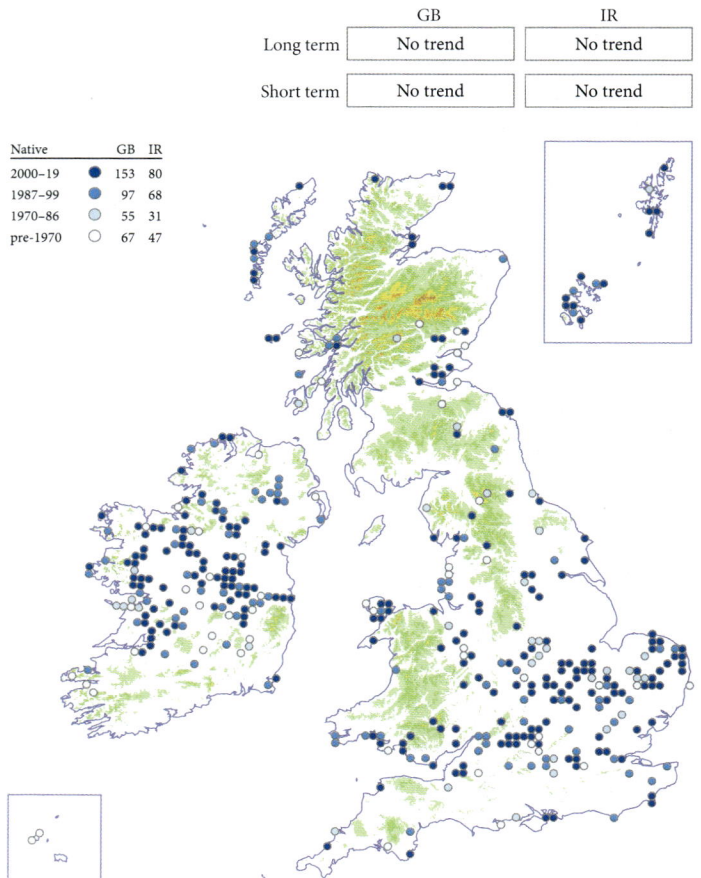

	GB	IR
Long term	No trend	No trend
Short term	No trend	No trend

Native		GB	IR
2000–19	●	153	80
1987–99	●	97	68
1970–86	○	55	31
pre-1970	○	67	47

Key refs John *et al.* (2021).

N.F. STEWART

(N) *Chara curta* Lesser Bearded Stonewort

Nolte ex Kütz.

A plant of calcareous mesotrophic water on peaty, sandy or marly substrates, restricted to areas with a base-rich geology. In Scotland and Ireland, it is found in lakes on limestone or calcareous sandstone but it can also occur in smaller water bodies such as gravel-pits and fen pools and ditches. Its habitat overlaps with that of *C. aspera* with which it sometimes grows. In stony marl lakes in central Ireland, which is its global stronghold, it is characteristic of a zone at around 1–2 m depth between the cyanobacterial crust ("krustenstein") zone in the shallows and beds of larger stoneworts in deeper water (Roden *et al.*, 2020) and it occurs in similar situations on Lismore (Main Argyll). In gravel-pits, however, it is more characteristic of the shallows where wave turbulence keeps a more open community. Lowland.

Trends The main threat to this species is from the secondary effects of nutrient enrichment, resulting in increased turbidity and competition from larger vegetation and algae. It prefers mineral substrates which can also be affected by the increase in organic deposition in more enriched systems. In smaller water bodies such as ditches and pools it may require periodic disturbance to prevent it from becoming overgrown by swamp and scrub. This species is taxonomically close to *C. aspera*, from which it was not fully distinguished until 1924, though it was first recognized as a subspecies (*C. aspera* subsp. *descmacantha*) in 1898. It was again treated as a variety of *C. aspera* for a period following Moore (1986). In some situations, the distinctive clustered spine-cells can be difficult to discern and this has led to some continuing confusion.

Biogeography This species has its global stronghold in Britain and Ireland, and also occurs in Germany, Austria, Spain, Italy and Sweden and possibly elsewhere in Europe.

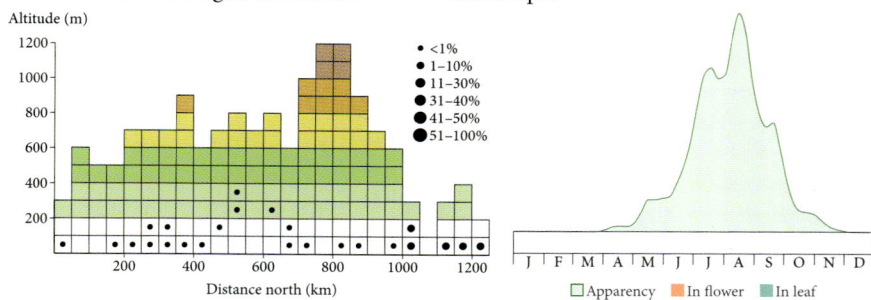

Native	GB	IR
2000–19	49	68
1987–99	36	55
1970–86	11	24
pre-1970	35	48

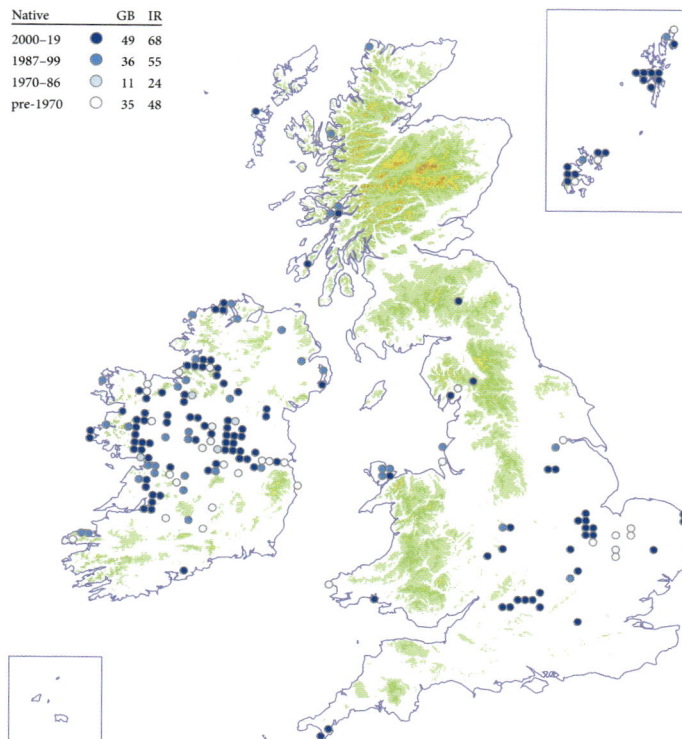

	GB	IR
Long term	No trend	No trend
Short term	No trend	No trend

Key refs Moore (1986), Roden *et al.* (2020), Stewart (2004b).

N.F. Stewart

(N) *Chara dissoluta*

A.Braun ex Leonh.

This a species of clear, hard-water lakes where it grows in depths from 2 m to 10 m, often in lakes which have a strong development of cyanobacterial crust on stones in the shallows. It forms a distinct zone at the bottom of the euphotic zone in these marl lakes, often as monospecific stands but sometimes with *Potamogeton* ×*angustifolius*, *Nitella flexilis* agg. and *Tolypella glomerata* as associates (Roden *et al.*, 2020). Lowland.

Trends *C. dissoluta* has been recorded from a total of 11 sites on the limestones in central and western Ireland. It is vulnerable to the effects of nutrient enrichment, not least because it is a deep-water species that requires good light penetration. At least one site has been lost as a result of enrichment and this is a concern at several others. It may also have been lost from one site where peat-staining of the water has increased, and another site has been lost due to drainage.

Biogeography Thinly scattered throughout Europe, and a rare taxon in South Africa.

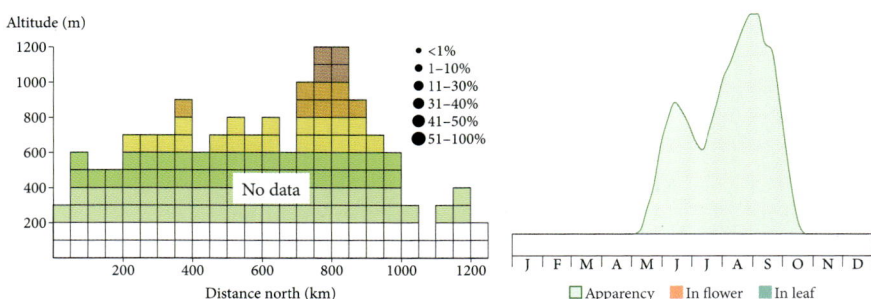

Native	GB	IR
2000–19	0	13
1987–99	0	2
1970–86	0	9
pre-1970	0	1

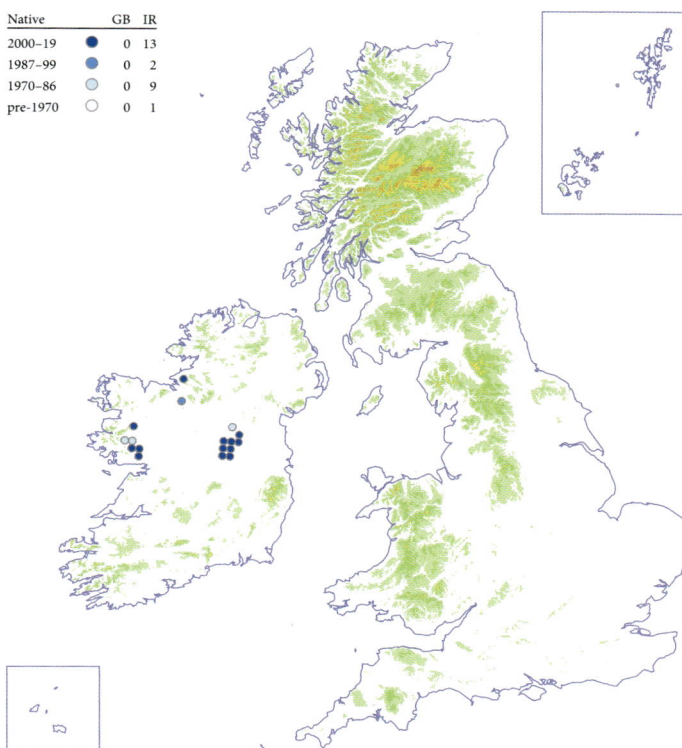

	GB	IR
Long term	No trend	No trend
Short term	No trend	No trend

Key refs Roden *et al.* (2020).

N.F. Stewart

Ⓝ *Chara fragifera* Strawberry Stonewort
Durieu

C. fragifera is a species of shallow, standing or slowly moving water which is low in nutrients (oligotrophic), and it can grow on peaty, clayey or more rarely gravelly substrates. Many sites dry out or at least have substantial water level drop during the summer months. On the Lizard Peninsula (West Cornwall) it occurs in three main situations: in small quarry-pits excavated in the past for serpentinite, in rutted trackways where it is confined to lower areas that remain inundated for longest, and in large but shallow pools. More rarely, it has been recorded from slow-moving areas in streams, and once from a large reservoir. Typical associates include the aquatic form of *Juncus bulbosus*, *Eleogiton fluitans*, *Helosciadium inundatum*, *Potamogeton polygonifolius*, and *Littorella uniflora*. It is unable to persist in taller swamps or under shade. Similarly, it is unable to compete with dense growths of permanent aquatics such as *Myriophyllum alterniflorum* and *P. natans*. Lowland.

Trends In recent times this species has been restricted to the Lizard Peninsula but it previously had a wider distribution in south-west Cornwall (West Penwith and the Isles of Scilly). Losses have occurred due to changes in the management of trackways, natural succession, nutrient enrichment and direct habitat loss through drainage, infilling or agricultural improvement. However, some new populations have appeared as a result of pond restoration and creation.

Biogeography *C. fragifera* has an Atlantic-Mediterranean distribution, reaching its northern limit in Cornwall.

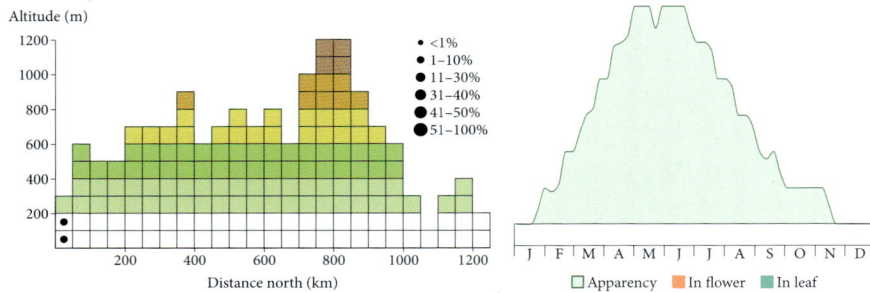

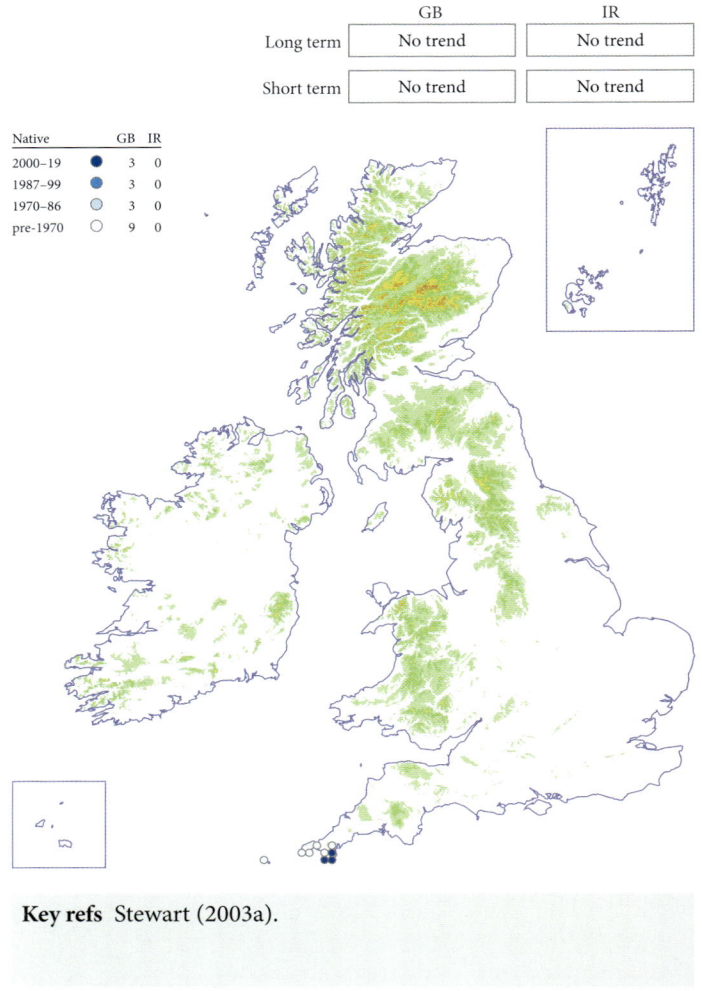

	GB	IR
Long term	No trend	No trend
Short term	No trend	No trend

Native		GB	IR
2000–19	●	3	0
1987–99	●	3	0
1970–86	●	3	0
pre-1970	○	9	0

Altitude (m)

- ● <1%
- ● 1–10%
- ● 11–30%
- ● 31–40%
- ● 41–50%
- ● 51–100%

Distance north (km)

☐ Apparency ■ In flower ■ In leaf

Key refs Stewart (2003a).

N.F. STEWART

Ⓝ *Chara globularis* Fragile Stonewort
Thuill.

C. globularis is recorded from permanent pools and lakes, canals and ditches, often in water greater than 1 m depth. In certain conditions, particularly in alkaline water, it can form dominant stands but it more frequently occurs mixed with other stoneworts or vascular plants. It is apparently restricted to calcareous and moderately nutrient-rich habitats. Up to 375 m at Malham Tarn (Mid-west Yorkshire).

Trends Records for this species (as *C. fragilis*) before 1924 should be treated with considerable caution as *C. virgata* was included as a variety until that time. The distribution map may therefore overestimate the degree of decline, although some loss has almost certainly occurred. It seems to be less sensitive to nutrient enrichment compared to most stoneworts and there are several examples where it has managed to persist in lakes with unstable vegetation due to elevated nutrient levels. Nevertheless, it is sensitive to the secondary effects of higher levels of nutrient enrichment. Its preference for deeper water also means that it is outcompeted by dense growths of *Elodea* species.

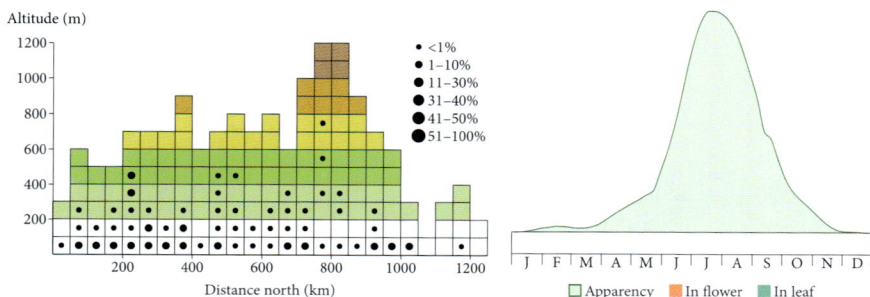

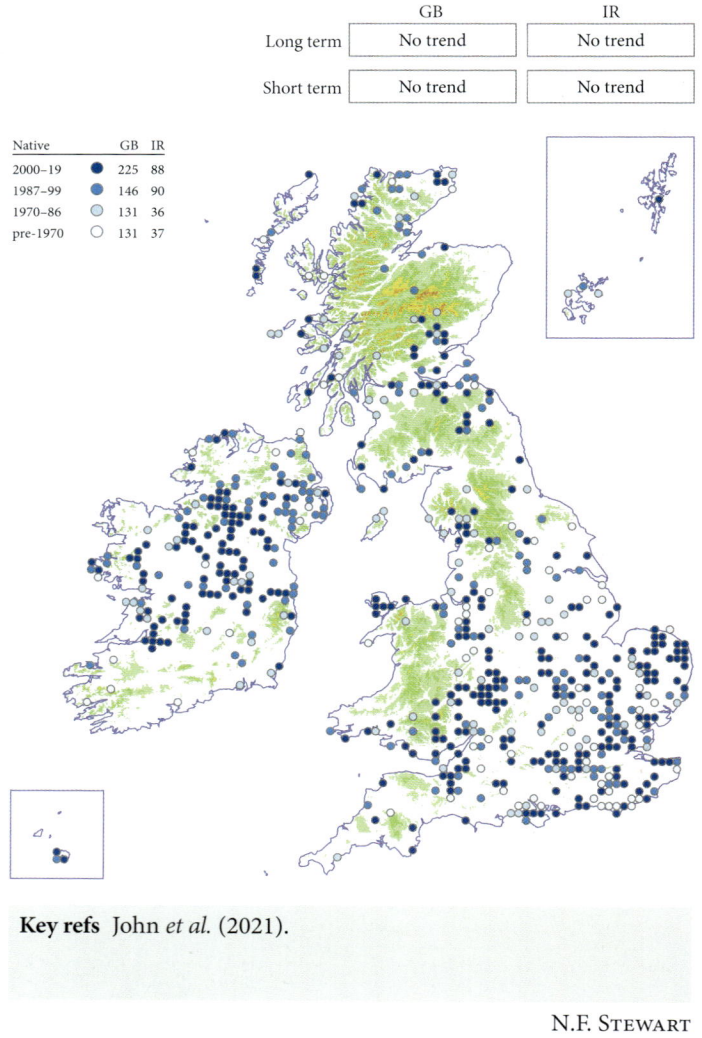

Biogeography A cosmopolitan species, widespread throughout Europe.

	GB	IR
Long term	No trend	No trend
Short term	No trend	No trend

Native		GB	IR
2000–19	●	225	88
1987–99	●	146	90
1970–86	●	131	36
pre-1970	○	131	37

Altitude (m)

- ● <1%
- ● 1–10%
- ● 11–30%
- ● 31–40%
- ● 41–50%
- ● 51–100%

Distance north (km)

☐ Apparency ■ In flower ■ In leaf

Key refs John *et al.* (2021).

N.F. STEWART

Chara hispida Bristly Stonewort
L.

C. hispida occurs in a variety of pools, lakes and ditches, often with a substrate of either clay, marl or silt, and requires calcareous water that is low in nitrates and phosphates. It often forms dense perennial beds which can out-compete other aquatic vegetation and in marl lakes it is often the dominant charophyte when water quality is good. However, in central and western Ireland it is much less frequent in large lakes than its relative *C. subspinosa*, preferring smaller water bodies. In Scotland it becomes restricted to near the coast and all previous inland records have been found to be *C. subspinosa*. It can also occur as scattered plants in mixed vegetation, and in such situations is often associated with a diverse aquatic flora. In mineral extraction sites it is not uncommon in former clay-pits, such as on the Oxford Clay in Bedfordshire and around Peterborough, but is rather less frequent in former gravel-pits. Up to 375 m at Malham Tarn (Mid-west Yorkshire).

Trends *C. hispida* is sensitive to nutrient pollution and this is probably the main cause of the decline throughout its range. In marl lakes, where in good conditions it would form extensive beds to 4 m or 5 m depth, it becomes more restricted to the shallows when nutrient levels increase. It tends to persist longest where there is freshwater seepage from adjacent fens.

Biogeography *C. hispida* occurs in Europe, Siberia and North Africa.

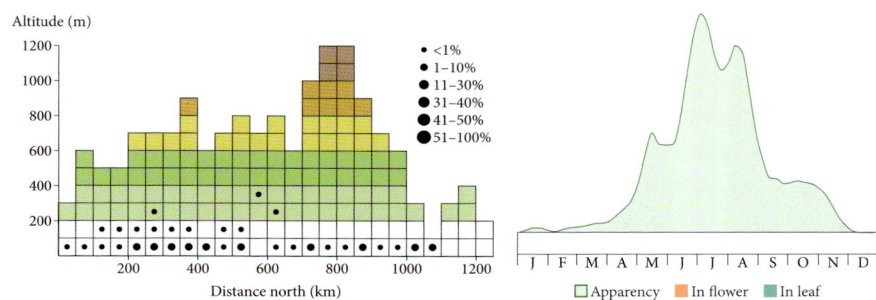

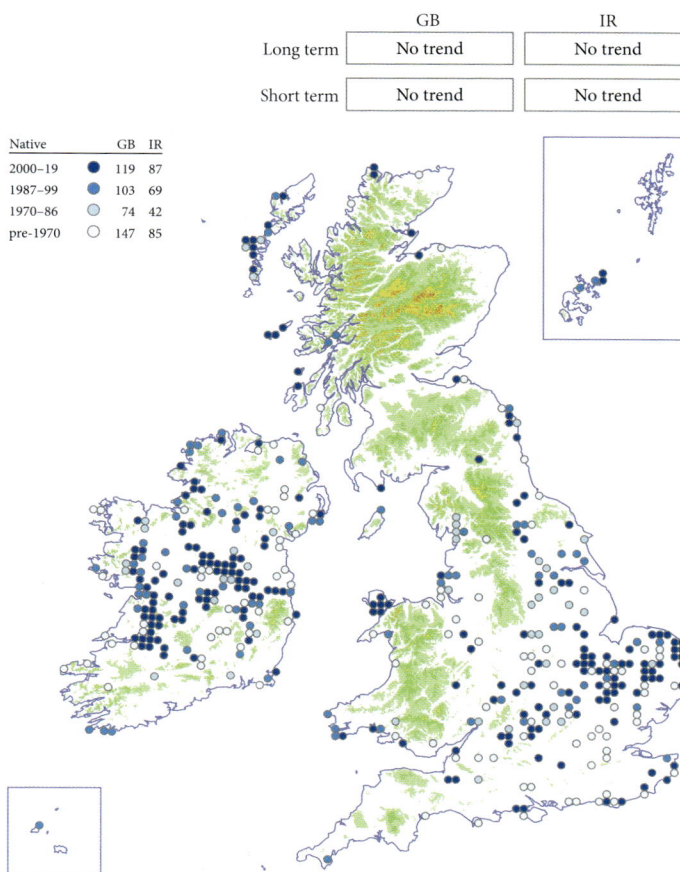

Native	GB	IR
2000–19	119	87
1987–99	103	69
1970–86	74	42
pre-1970	147	85

	GB	IR
Long term	No trend	No trend
Short term	No trend	No trend

Key refs John *et al.* (2021).

N.F. STEWART

Chara muscosa Mossy Stonewort
J.Groves & Bull.-Webst.

C. muscosa and *C. contraria* are closely related and it is possible that *C. muscosa* does not deserve specific rank. It may be that it is a contracted form of *C. contraria* growing in wave-washed conditions akin to similar contracted forms of *C. virgata* (called var. *annulata*) and *C. aspera* (called var. *lacustris*). However, further work is needed to clarify the situation, including genetic study. Lowland.

Trends There have been very few records for this enigmatic plant and the map here includes all records ascribed to this species, except known errors. It was described from Lough Mullaghderg (West Donegal) where it has not been found since the 1930s and is thought to have been lost due to part of the lake being infilled. Specimens from Mill Dam of Rango (Orkney) collected in the 1920s were also ascribed to this species by James Groves but re-examination of the specimens seems to place it within the range of *C. contraria*. More recently, plants from Lough Aughrusbeg (West Galway) and Loch na Cleabaig, (Outer Hebrides) seemed to fit this species but when specimens from the latter were later grown *ex situ* in the Royal Botanic Gardens Edinburgh they developed into *C. contraria*.

Biogeography A European endemic with few records from Ukraine, Serbia, Germany and Spain.

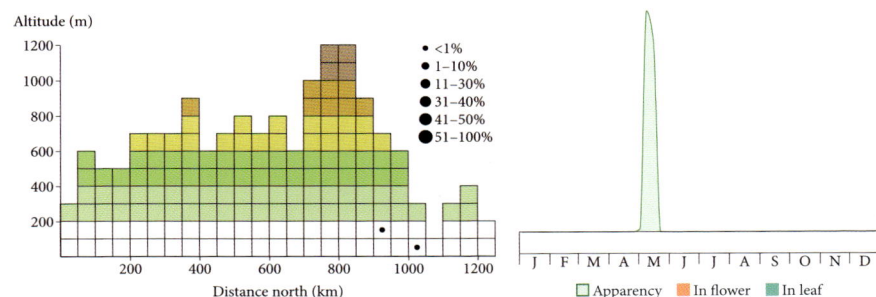

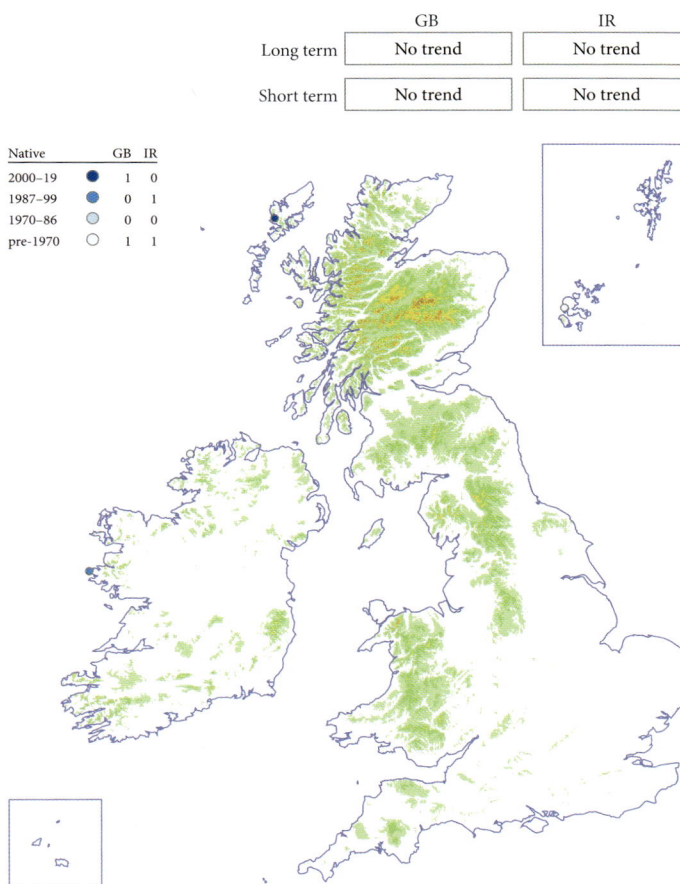

Native	GB	IR
2000–19	1	0
1987–99	0	1
1970–86	0	0
pre-1970	1	1

	GB	IR
Long term	No trend	No trend
Short term	No trend	No trend

Key refs John *et al.* (2021).

N.F. STEWART

N *Chara papillosa*
Kütz.

	GB	IR
Long term	No trend	No trend
Short term	No trend	No trend

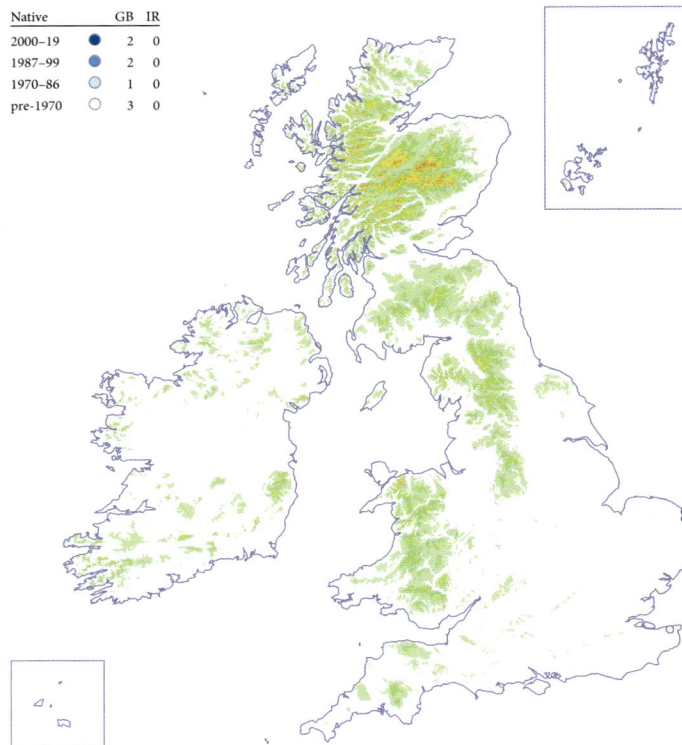

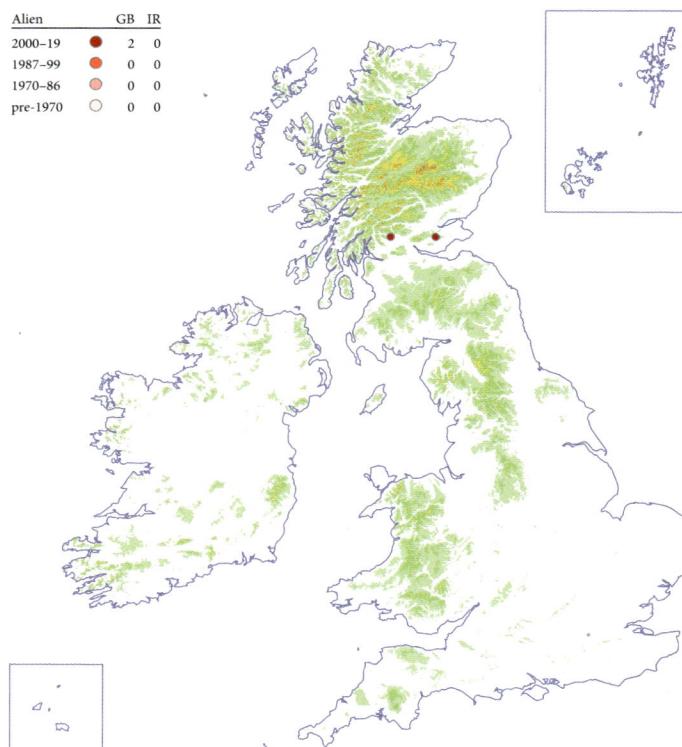

Native	GB	IR
2000–19	2	0
1987–99	2	0
1970–86	1	0
pre-1970	3	0

C. papillosa occurs in calcareous lakes near the sea, where it grows among perennial stonewort communities which may include *C. baltica*, *C. connivens*, *C. globularis*, *C. hispida* and *Nitellopsis obtusa*. It grows at depths of 1–3 m, typically on soft silt substrates. Although it fruits freely, the establishment of seedlings in the soft sediment can be difficult; more frequently it spreads by layering out from dense patches and by regrowth from stem fragments. There was previously much confusion with the taxonomy of this section of the *C. hispida* group, but recent work on the European stonewort flora has clarified that *C. papillosa* is the correct name for this taxon, rather than *C. intermedia*, which for many years has been the name in use in our area. Lowland.

Trends *C. papillosa* is now restricted to the River Thurne system of the Norfolk Broads, although there is a historic record from East Kent. For a brief period at the end of the 20th century there was good water clarity throughout the Thurne system, resulting in a flourishing of the aquatic vegetation, including *C. papillosa* which was recorded from nine water bodies, in some cases (*e.g.* Hickling Broad) in such abundance that it caused an impediment to boat traffic (Harris, 2001; Holman & White, 2008). Since 2000, however, the water quality has deteriorated again with massive reductions in the extent of stonewort communities. These are still present but at a much lower level, and the extent fluctuates from year to year or goes through cycles of increase and collapse over several years.

Biogeography Sparsely scattered across Europe from Britain east to Russia, south to Spain and the Balkans. Its distribution outside Europe is uncertain but it has been recorded from Africa and Asia.

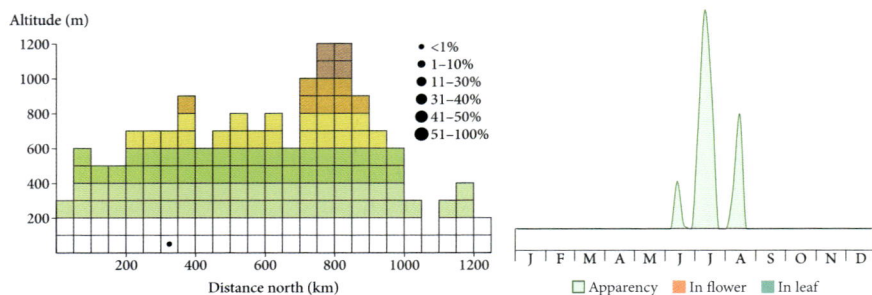

Key refs Broads Authority (1983–2016), Harris (2001), Holman & White (2008).

N.F. STEWART

Ne *Chara socotrensis*
Nordst.

	GB	IR
Long term	No trend	No trend
Short term	No trend	No trend

Alien	GB	IR
2000–19	2	0
1987–99	0	0
1970–86	0	0
pre-1970	0	0

C. socotrensis is unusual in being a *Chara* with a very reduced cortex and could therefore be overlooked as a *Nitella*. Both of its Scottish sites (Loch Leven, Fife; Lake of Menteith, West Perthshire) are large mesotrophic to eutrophic lakes, well known for their rich aquatic flora. It grew in water at 1 m to 3 m depth in an open community mixed among other vegetation. Lowland.

Trends *C. socotrensis* was recorded in 2004 in two lakes about 50 miles apart in central Scotland. Both sites are well-used by anglers and it is possible that the plant was brought in from a trout hatchery when the lakes were stocked with fish. Although not found in either site since is discovery, at least one of the sites needs further exploration. As a subtropical species it is likely that the climate was unsuitable.

Biogeography A poorly understood species with a few widely scattered records from tropical parts of eastern Africa, southern Asia and South America.

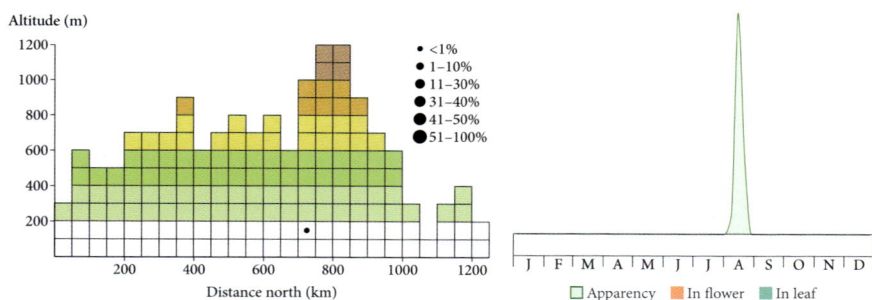

Key refs John *et al.* (2021).

N.F. STEWART

N *Chara subspinosa* Rugged Stonewort

Rupr.

This perennial species, formerly known as *C. rudis*, grows in alkaline fresh waters at depths of up to 7 m, where it can form dense tangled stands with few other species. It will grow in large or small lakes, ponds, abandoned peat cuttings and slowly running water. It also very rarely occurs in shallow pools or ditches but probably never in sites that dry out seasonally. In Irish marl lakes it forms a characteristic zone in around 2–3 m depths between the *C. curta* zone on the shallower side and *C. virgata* in the deeper water (Roden *et al.*, 2020). It probably mainly reproduces vegetatively by lateral branching from old nodes or from loose nodal fragments. In Britain it appears to be restricted to very clean water but in Ireland it seems to have a greater tolerance of enrichment. It avoids brackish conditions and is very rare near the coast. Up to 330 m

at Locker Tarn, Carperby (North-west Yorkshire), and possibly 420 m at Loch Choin (West Perthshire).

Native in Britain and Ireland and a neophyte in the Channel Islands.

Trends *C. subspinosa* has suffered significant declines, principally from the effects of nutrient enrichment. Increasing turbidity and competition results in the break-up of deep-water beds with remaining populations increasingly restricted to niches in the shallows with some clean water influence before disappearing completely. However, water quality improvements at a site in Wales resulted in its reappearance in 2014 after an absence of over 70 years.

Biogeography Occurs in Europe and western Asia.

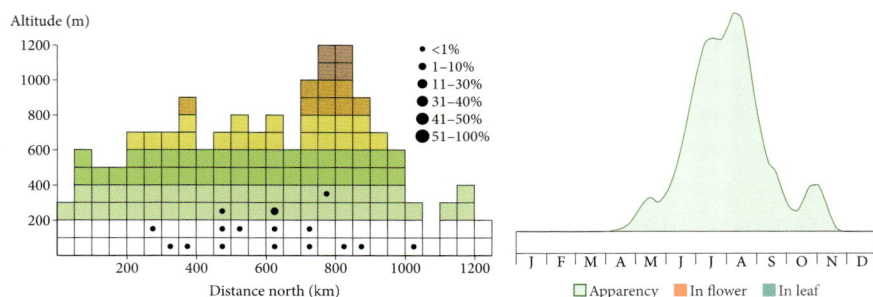

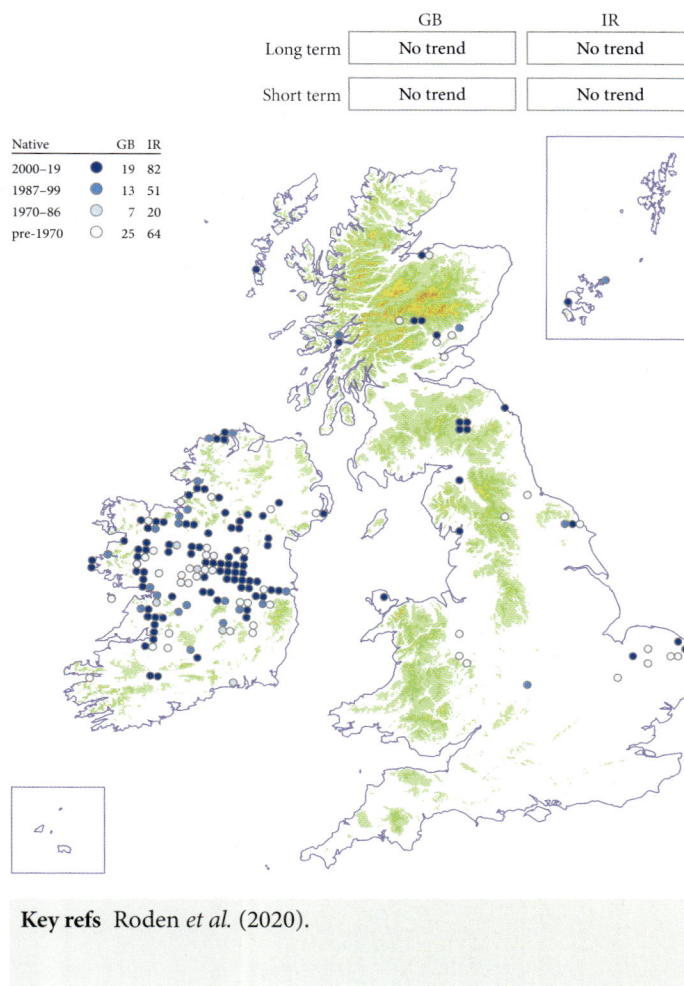

	GB	IR
Long term	No trend	No trend
Short term	No trend	No trend

Native	GB	IR
2000–19	19	82
1987–99	13	51
1970–86	7	20
pre-1970	25	64

Key refs Roden *et al.* (2020).

N.F. Stewart

N *Chara tomentosa* Coral Stonewort

L.

C. tomentosa is a species of strongly calcareous, clear water marl lakes where it grows particularly in depths up to 3 m, but sometimes up to 5 m. It typically occurs in the cyanobacterial crust (termed krustenstein) and *C. curta* zones, growing with a variety of other stonewort species and *Myriophyllum verticillatum* (Roden *et al.*, 2020). Lowland.

Trends This species is restricted to central and western Ireland where it has been recorded from 14 sites. It is vulnerable to the effects of nutrient enrichment and is now rare in the River Shannon and associated lakes. At least one site has been lost as a result of enrichment and this is a concern at several others. It may also have been lost from a site where peat-staining of the water has increased and another site has been lost due to drainage.

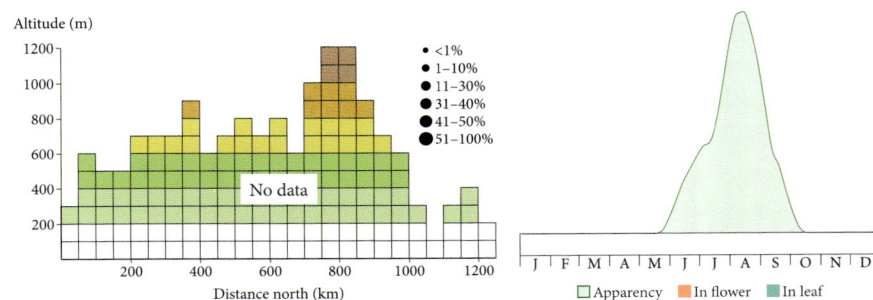

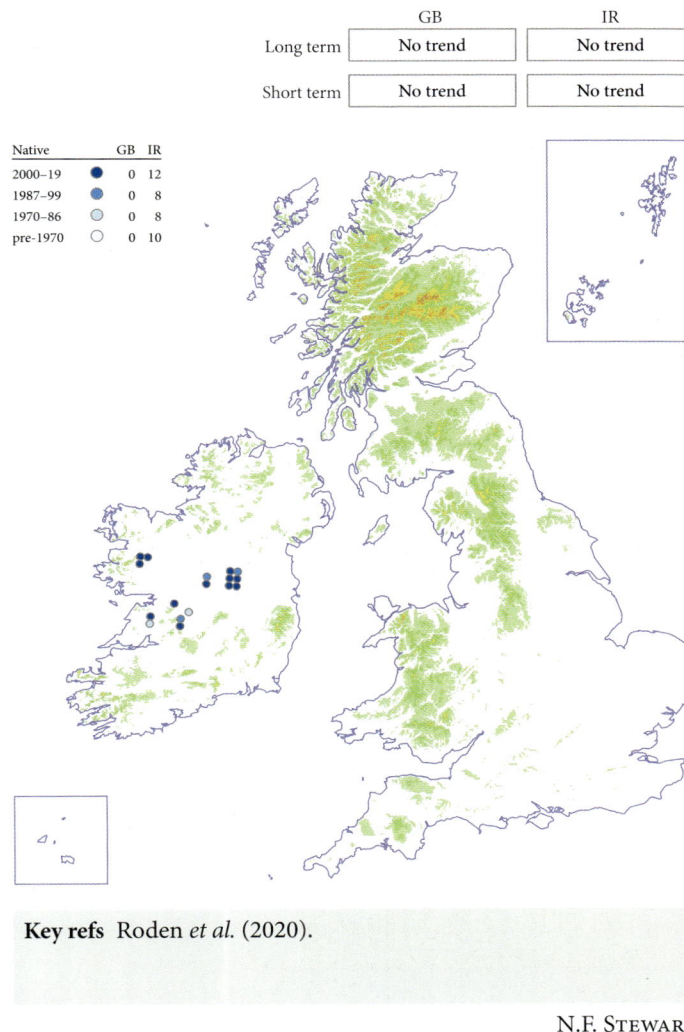

Biogeography Occurs throughout Europe, with its core distribution along the Baltic coast; there are also records from northern Africa and Asia.

	GB	IR
Long term	No trend	No trend
Short term	No trend	No trend

Native	GB	IR
2000–19	0	12
1987–99	0	8
1970–86	0	8
pre-1970	0	10

Key refs Roden *et al.* (2020).

N.F. Stewart

Ⓝ *Chara virgata* Delicate Stonewort
Kütz.

This species has been recorded from a wide range of aquatic habitats, from seasonal pools and flushes to large lakes. In the latter it can occur as tufts in the shallows (sometimes differentiated as var. *annulata*) or as extensive beds in deep water. It is more frequent in acidic water than any other species of *Chara*, for example growing with *Potamogeton polygonifolius* and *Utricularia minor*, and as a result it is most frequent in upland regions. It is also not uncommon in alkaline water providing nutrient levels are low. Up to 748 m at Loch Vrotachan (South Aberdeenshire).

Trends *C. virgata* was not fully differentiated from *C. globularis* until 1924 and a significant number of earlier records for the latter (under the name *C. fragilis*) probably belong here. As a result, the decline may be greater than appears in the distribution map. There seem to have been marked losses in some areas, particularly in lowland England and eastern Ireland. Nevertheless, many records from the 1980s and 1990s originate from systematic lake surveys which have not been repeated since (*e.g.* in Scotland and Northern Ireland) and the plant may still be present in a significant number of these sites.

Biogeography *C. virgata* is found in Europe, India, Japan, and North America.

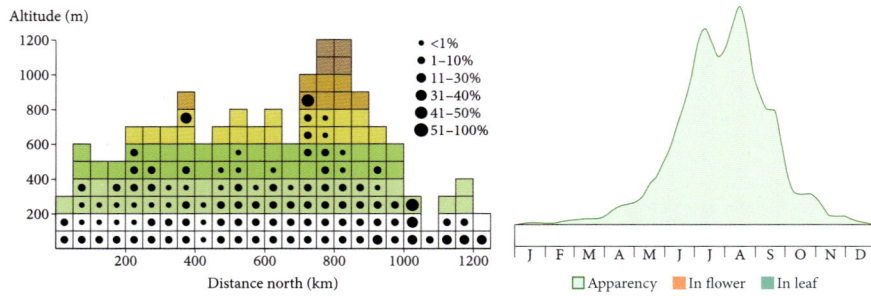

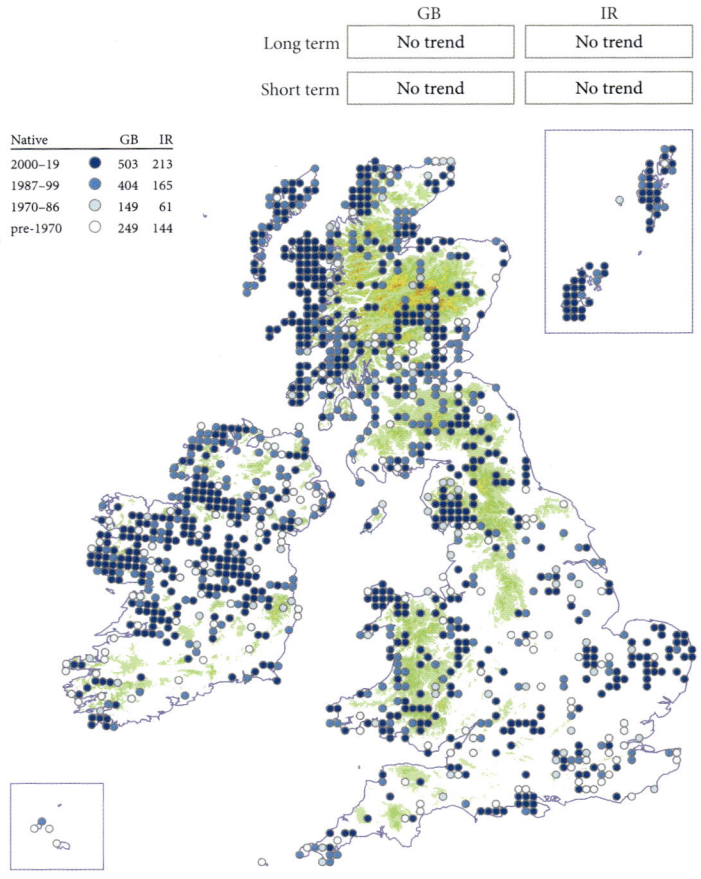

	GB	IR
Long term	No trend	No trend
Short term	No trend	No trend

Native		GB	IR
2000–19	●	503	213
1987–99	●	404	165
1970–86	◐	149	61
pre-1970	○	249	144

Key refs John *et al.* (2021).

N.F. STEWART

Ⓝ *Chara vulgaris* Common Stonewort
L.

C. vulgaris occurs in all kinds of wetland habitats, from puddles, flushes and ditches to lakes, but it is most typically a species of small water bodies. It is able to withstand drying out for periods in the summer. Often it can be the first colonist of new habitats such as gravel workings or clay-pits. Though it may be outcompeted over time by vascular plants, it can persist for longer periods, particularly in more alkaline but nutrient-poor conditions. It requires some form of calcareous influence in the water and consequently becomes quite rare in upland regions. Up to 533 m on Ben Vurich (East Perthshire).

Trends Some of the apparent decline is due to the ability of the species to move between sites as habitat suitability varies, though overall it is thought that there has been a real decline. It appears to be tolerant of some nutrient enrichment (compared to other stoneworts) but it is more usually an indicator of clean water conditions.

Biogeography A cosmopolitan species, widespread throughout mainland Europe.

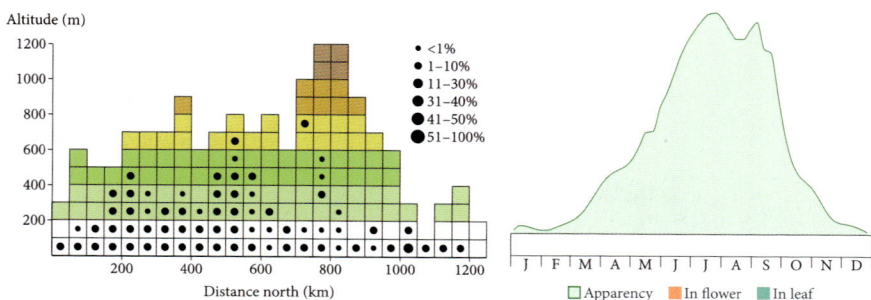

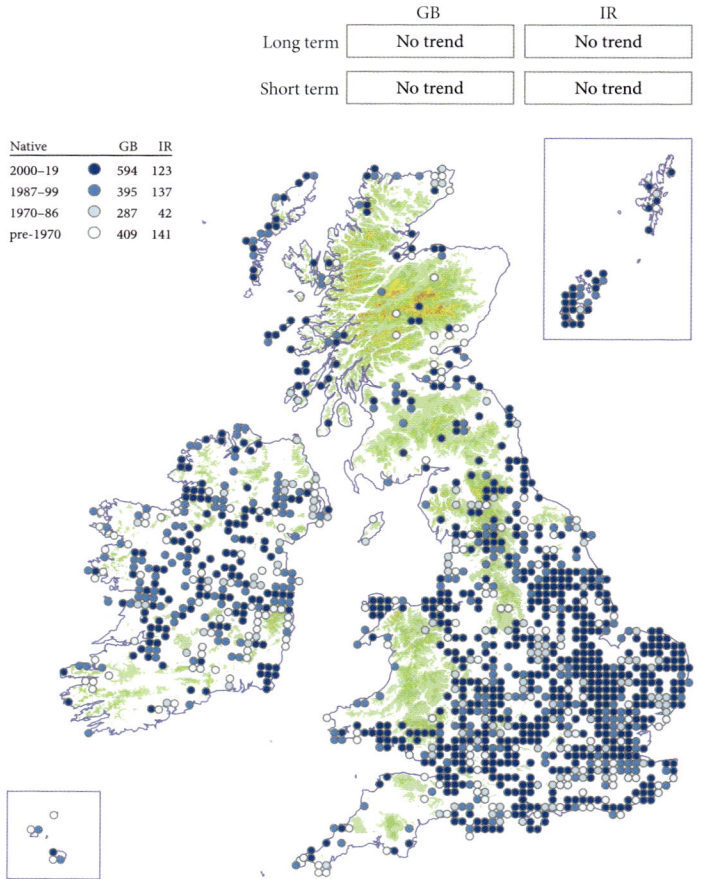

	GB	IR
Long term	No trend	No trend
Short term	No trend	No trend

Native		GB	IR
2000–19	●	594	123
1987–99	●	395	137
1970–86	◐	287	42
pre-1970	○	409	141

Key refs John *et al.* (2021).

N.F. STEWART

Lamprothamnium papulosum Foxtail Stonewort
(Wallr.) J.Groves

L. papulosum grows in natural and artificial brackish lagoons with salinities in the range of 8–25 psu (Schubert & Blindow, 2003). It is most often found growing on sand, gravel or pebbles in less than 2 m of water, but it is intolerant of strong flow or wave action. It usually occurs with *Ruppia* species, but does not compete well with dense vascular plant growth or abundant filamentous algae. It is often to be found in areas where there is some disturbance from birds or other animals or in shallow water where fluctuations in the water level result in more open vegetation. It can grow as a summer annual, germinating in early summer and producing spores from July to October or, particularly in milder climates, it can overwinter as a perennial. It spreads partly by spores and partly by bulbils (Stewart and Church, 1992). Lowland.

Trends Populations in western Scotland and Ireland are reasonably secure and perhaps some of the least threatened in Europe. However, in southern England it has suffered badly from the effects of nutrient enrichment, particularly increased competition from filamentous algae, combined with salinity modifications, and recent surveys have located it in only three of its former sites. There are similar concerns about nutrient enrichment in south-eastern Ireland. Nevertheless, it was recently discovered in Wales for the first time in 2017 in a lagoon that had been reclaimed from the sea.

Biogeography *L. papulosum* occurs sporadically along the coast of Europe from Norway and the Baltic Sea to the Iberian Peninsula. In the Mediterranean it extends east to Tunisia and Sicily, with isolated records from Greece, Cyprus and the Black Sea.

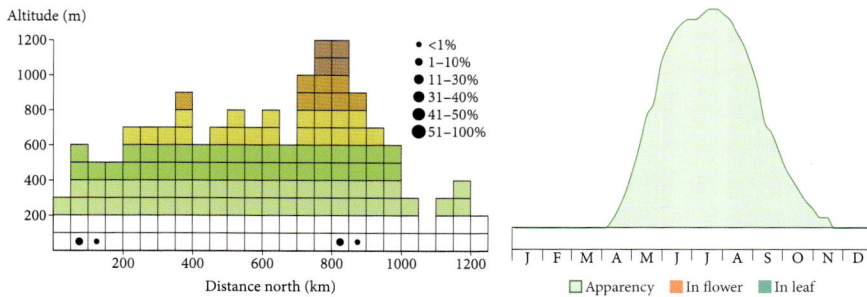

	GB	IR
Long term	No trend	No trend
Short term	No trend	No trend

Native	GB	IR
2000–19	8	7
1987–99	12	10
1970–86	6	3
pre-1970	5	0

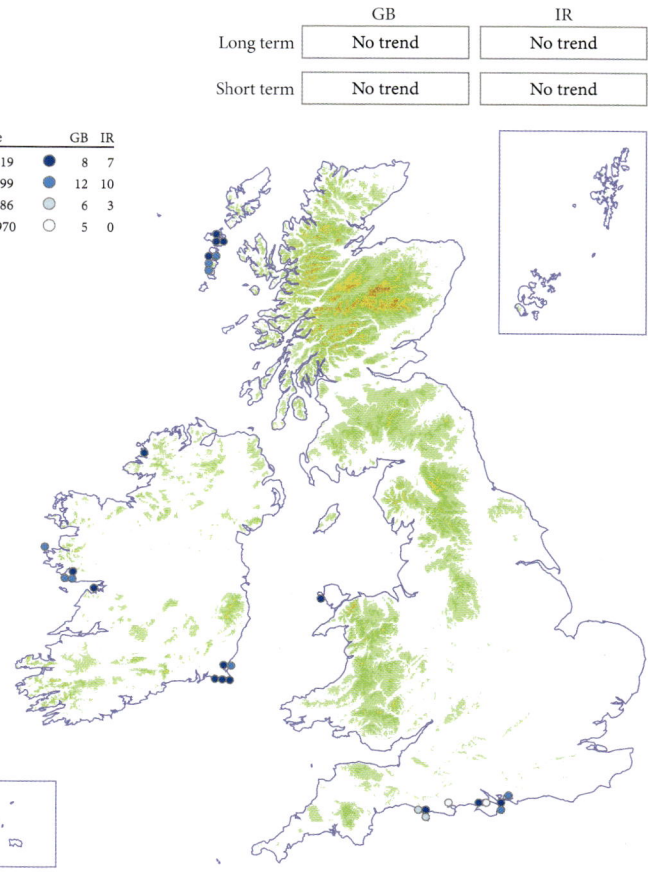

Key refs Abraham (2020), Blindow & Langangen (1995a, 1995b), Lansdown (2021b), Martin (2001), Martin *et al.* (2002), Schubert & Blindow (2003), Stewart & Church (1992).

N.F. STEWART

Nitella capillaris Slimy-fruited Stonewort
(Krock.) J.Groves & Bull.-Webst.

A species of open situations and a poor competitor among dense vegetation. The historic British records were from a grazing marsh ditch and from a river into which the ditch flowed. The new Suffolk records (see below) are from recently restored ponds in arable farmland and are field-edge ponds buffered with grass margins. *N. capillaris* grows as monospecific patches or mixed with other stoneworts (*Chara vulgaris*, *C. virgata*, *Tolypella intricata* and *T. glomerata*) but *Ranunculus aquatilis* agg. and *Potamogeton crispus* are also sometimes present. As an early summer species, it is best looked for between late April and mid-June. Elsewhere in north-west Europe it seems mainly a species of small water bodies such as ditches, ponds and pools in fens, where it grows in oligotrophic to mesotrophic and sometimes eutrophic water that is low in nitrates and phosphates. Lowland.

Trends *N. capillaris* occurred in the Ouse Washes (Cambridgeshire) where it grew in two interconnected locations. It was last seen there in 1959 and was thought to be extinct in our area. However, in 2019 it was found in East Suffolk as a result of the restoration of several overgrown farm ponds. It has now been recorded in six ponds several miles apart and it is probable that these represent overlooked populations rather than new colonization events. Other records from north Wales, Yorkshire and Aberdeenshire are now considered to be erroneous.

Biogeography Widely but sparsely scattered across much of Europe, and with sporadic records from Asia and northern Africa.

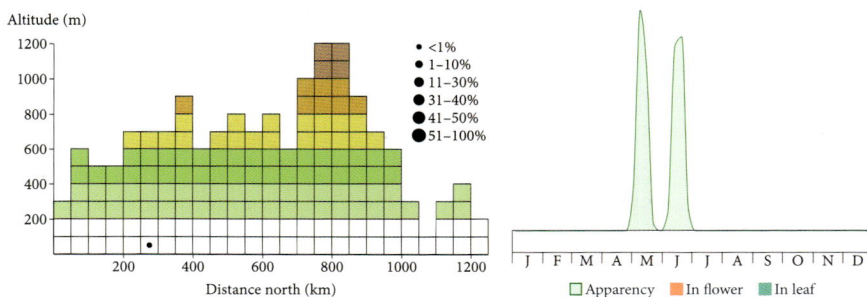

	GB	IR
Long term	No trend	No trend
Short term	No trend	No trend

Native	GB	IR
2000–19	1	0
1987–99	0	0
1970–86	0	0
pre-1970	2	0

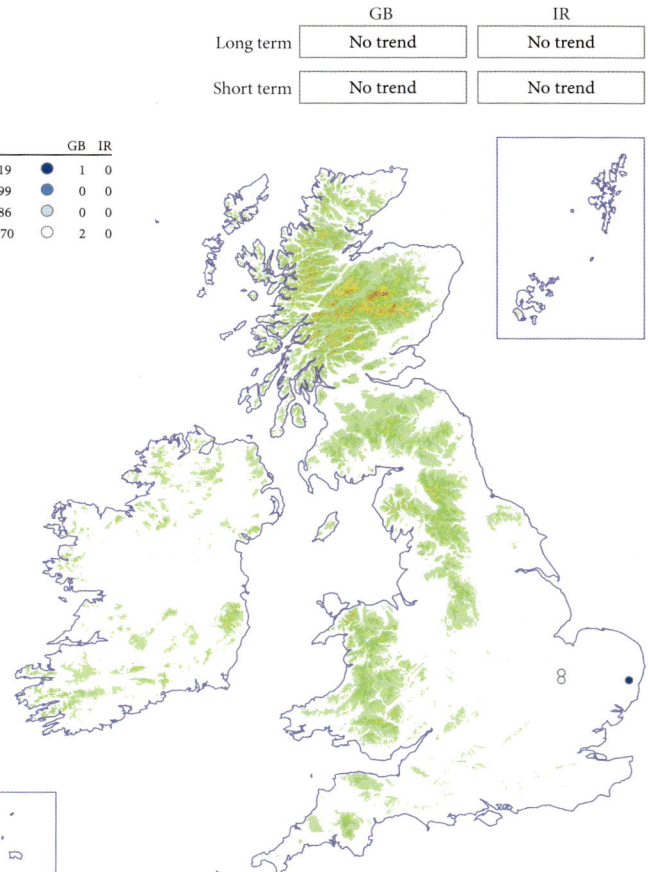

Key refs Hawkins (2020)

N.F. STEWART

Ⓝ *Nitella confervacea* Least Stonewort
(Bréb.) A.Braun ex Leonh.

N. confervacea is an annual recorded from oligotrophic to mesotrophic lakes and pools, growing on peat, peaty silt or firm silt typically in 1–2 m depth. Due to its small size it is easily outcompeted by other vegetation and tends to occur where there are gaps in the vegetation cover. In Scotland and Ireland, it is commonly associated with *Najas flexilis*. It requires clear water and low nutrient levels as it is easily smothered by filamentous algae and loses anchorage when the substrate becomes too soft. Up to 405 m at Dock Tarn (Cumberland).

Trends This species is most frequent in western parts, particularly in Ireland where there are over 30 sites, but also occurs sparsely in upland areas farther east. It is a small species that is easily overlooked and was discovered in England as recently as 2007. However, it has not been found in Wales, despite apparently suitable habitats. Although many western sites are fairly secure it has disappeared from several sites due to changes caused by nutrient enrichment, particularly increased competition and increases in turbidity.

Biogeography *N. confervacea* has a cosmopolitan distribution, occurring throughout central and northern areas of Europe, and rarely into the Mediterranean basin. It is also found in northern Africa, North America, Asia and Australasia.

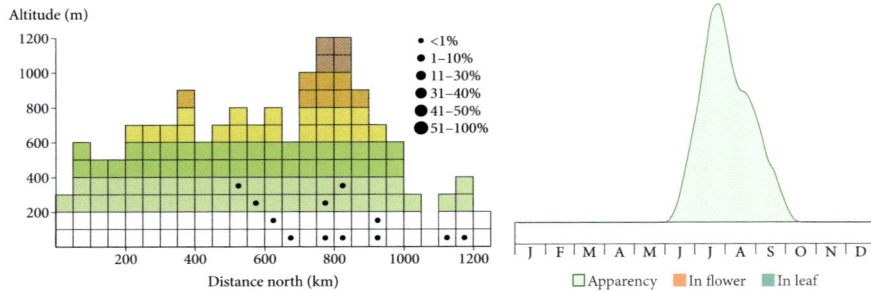

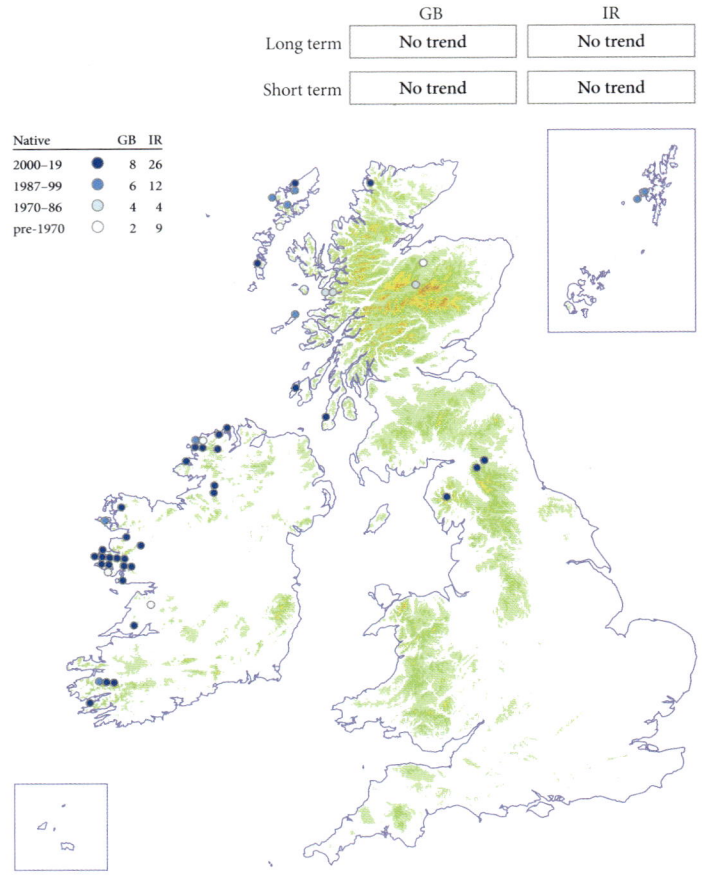

		GB	IR
Long term	No trend		No trend
Short term	No trend		No trend

Native		GB	IR
2000–19	●	8	26
1987–99	●	6	12
1970–86	○	4	4
pre-1970	○	2	9

Key refs Stewart & Preston (2000).

N.F. STEWART

Ⓝ *Nitella flexilis* agg.

N. flexilis agg. comprises the segregates *N. flexilis* s.s. and *N. opaca*, which can only be separated when fertile. They occur in a wide range of habitats including mesotrophic to mildly eutrophic lakes, clay- and gravel-pits, ponds, ditches, canals and seasonal pools.

Trends Though the two taxa were well recognized as separate species over 130 years ago, for a period in the 1980s and 1990s they were united under one taxon (*N. flexilis* var. *flexilis sensu* Moore, 1986), and to complicate matters subsequent nomenclatural confusion in the main field recording databases resulted in records for the aggregate being erroneously translated as *N. flexilis* in the strict sense. *N. opaca* is very much the more common of the two segregates, except perhaps in south-eastern England, and the map shown here is probably a better representation of the distribution of this species.

Biogeography Widely distributed in Europe, Asia, Africa and North and South America.

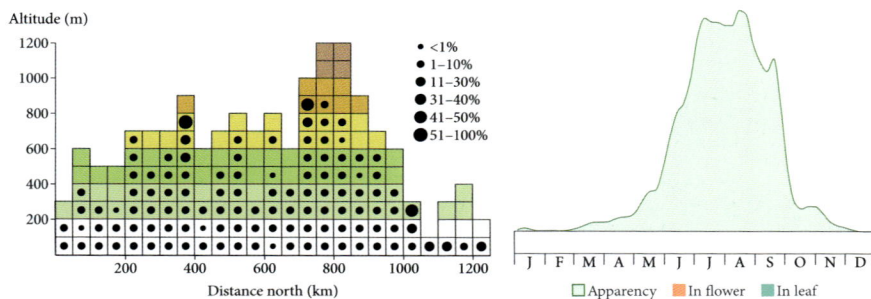

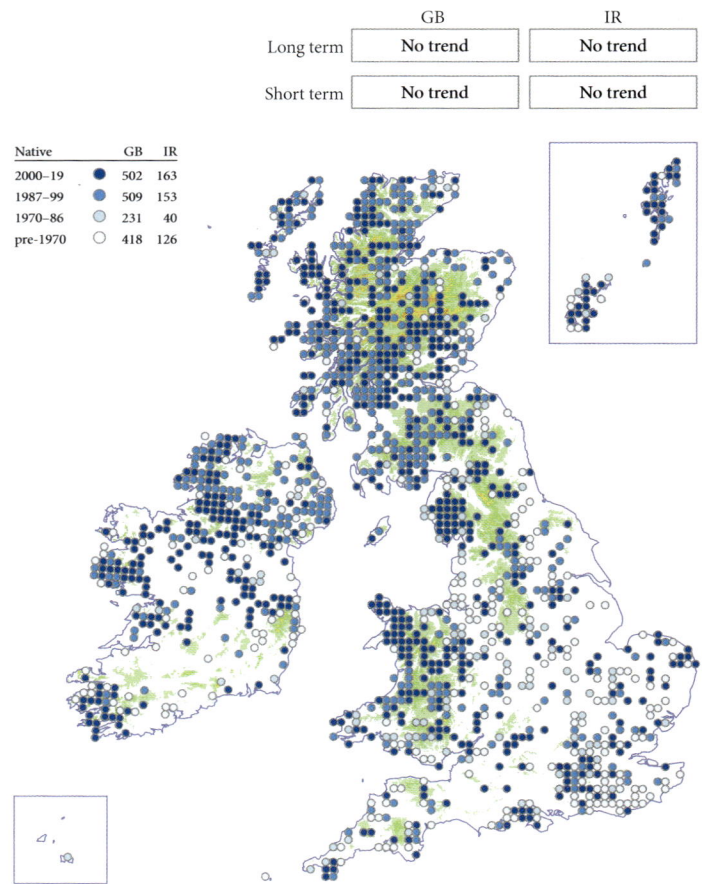

		GB	IR
Long term	No trend		No trend
Short term	No trend		No trend

Native		GB	IR
2000–19	●	502	163
1987–99	●	509	153
1970–86	○	231	40
pre-1970	○	418	126

Key refs John *et al.* (2021).

N.F. STEWART

Ⓝ *Nitella flexilis* Smooth Stonewort
(L.) C.Agardh

N. flexilis s.s. is primarily a species of mesotrophic to mildly eutrophic lakes, pools, ditches and canals where it grows in permanent water, generally in 1–3 m depth. There are some records from soft waters although it is much less common than *N. opaca* in these habitats, with which it is often confused, as the two taxa can only be separated when fertile. Reaching 428 m at Wildmoor Pool (Shropshire), and possibly higher at Widdybank, Teesdale (County Durham).

Trends Although *N. flexilis s.s.* and *N. opaca* were well recognized as separate species over 130 years ago, for a period in the 1980s and 1990s they were united under one taxon (*N. flexilis* var. *flexilis sensu* Moore, 1986). Since then, a further complication has arisen due to nomenclatural confusion in the dictionaries of the main field recording databases which has resulted in records

for the aggregate being translated as *N. flexilis* in the strict sense. The map here attempts to include only records where it is clear that the segregate was intended but this is not always clear. As a result, there is a need for a complete review of all records, including historical records where vouchers exist. The prevalence of old records reflects the reduced recording of the segregates in recent decades.

Biogeography Widely distributed in Europe, Asia, Africa and North and South America.

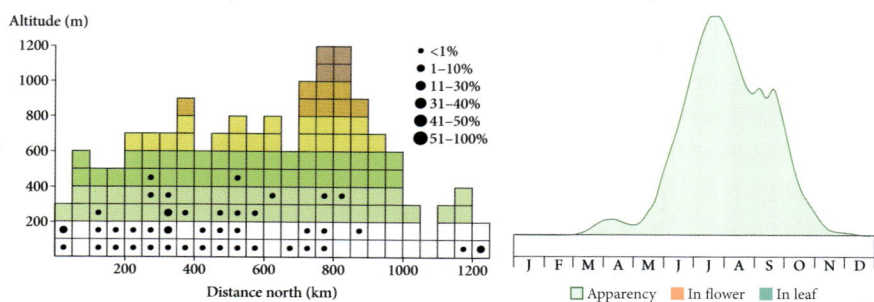

	GB	IR
Long term	No trend	No trend
Short term	No trend	No trend

Native	GB	IR
2000–19	35	21
1987–99	17	3
1970–86	19	4
pre-1970	68	20

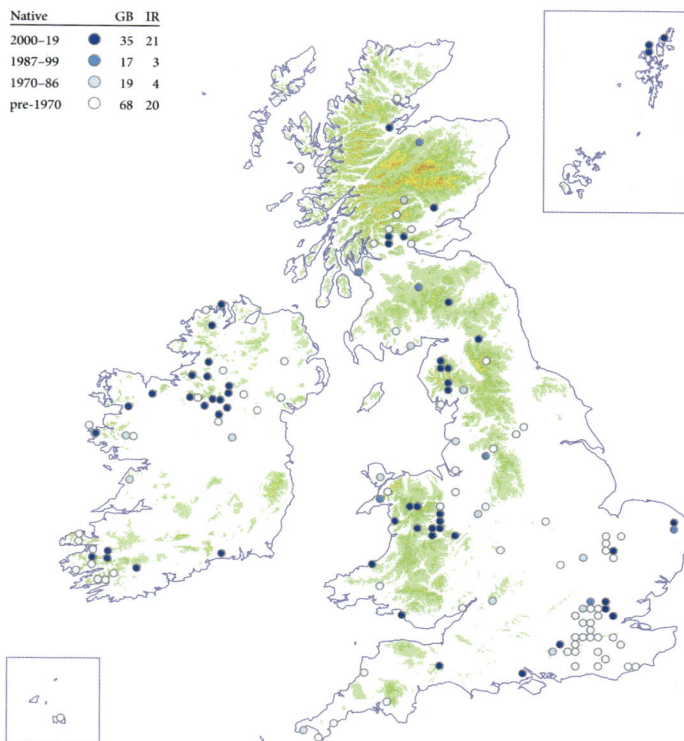

Key refs John *et al.* (2021).

N.F. STEWART

Ⓝ *Nitella opaca* Dark Stonewort
(C.Agardh ex Bruzelius) C.Agardh

N. opaca occurs in a wide range of habitats including lakes, clay- and gravel-pits, ponds, ditches, canals and seasonal pools. It is also one of the few stoneworts that is capable of growing in moderately fast-flowing water. It is most frequent in low pH habitats, where it may be dominant in deeper water over 1 m depth but also as scattered tufts in the shallows. However, it can also grow in alkaline waters, providing nutrient levels are low. *N. opaca* can only be separated from the very similar *N. flexilis s.s.* when fertile; otherwise they are included within *N. flexilis* agg. Reaching 950 m on Beinn Heasgarnich (Mid Perthshire).

Trends *N. opaca* has declined significantly in much of lowland England and in eastern Ireland. It is sensitive to the secondary effects of nutrient pollution, particularly through increased turbidity and competition

from other plants and algae. In deeper water it is often out-competed by dense growths of *Elodea* species, and these can severely reduce the available habitat. In smaller water bodies there have been losses due to succession, drainage and infill. The map includes only records that have been confirmed to the segregate.

Biogeography *N. opaca* occurs in Europe, Asia, northern Africa and the Americas.

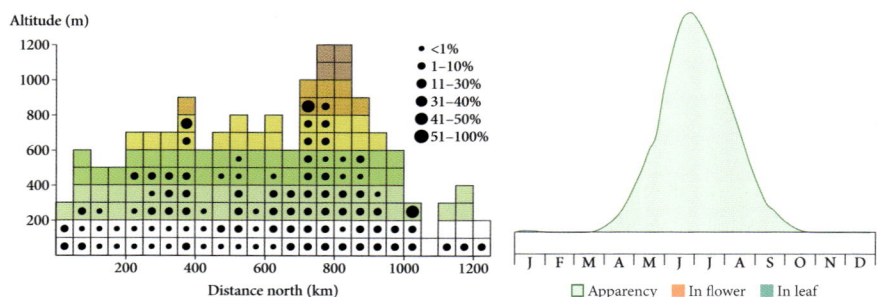

	GB	IR
Long term	No trend	No trend
Short term	No trend	No trend

Native	GB	IR
2000–19	205	67
1987–99	203	19
1970–86	45	12
pre-1970	287	93

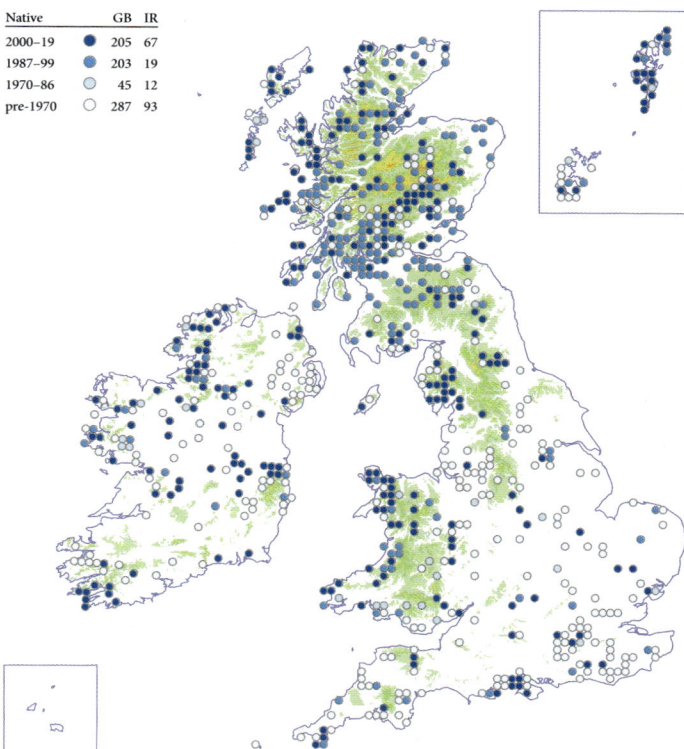

Key refs John *et al.* (2021).

N.F. STEWART

N *Nitella gracilis* Slender Stonewort
(Sm.) C.Agardh

A plant of acidic, nutrient-poor lakes. In larger lakes it typically occurs at the lower edge of vegetation in depths of 2–4 m, growing as scattered tufts where the vascular plant vegetation has become sparse (Jones & Stewart, 2001). It also grows in smaller lochs and lochans on more peaty substrates in depths of up to 1 m. As a poor competitor it relies on the presence of openings in the vascular plant vegetation. In some sites it seems to be associated with patches of floating *Nymphaea alba*, *Nuphar lutea* or *Potamogeton natans* which may reduce the amount of competing underwater vegetation. Up to 439 m at Llyn Berwyn (Cardiganshire).

Trends A number of new sites have been discovered in recent years, particularly in Wales and south-west Ireland, but it is still evidently a rare species in our area for reasons that are unclear. Given its small size and the frequent availability of suitable habitat in upland regions, it is doubtless under-recorded in some areas. However, it has certainly been lost from some localities, most notably in England where it now appears to be extinct. *N. gracilis* is very sensitive to nutrient enrichment, being easily overwhelmed by other vegetation and filamentous algae. In deeper water locations, increases in turbidity are a particular issue and peat-staining of the water can also reduce light penetration. Most extant sites are upland lakes where nutrient pressures are low and unlikely to increase significantly. The possibility that some of the new records this century represent recovery from the previous impacts of acid rain cannot be ruled out.

Biogeography A cosmopolitan species, probably widely but sparsely distributed across much of Europe.

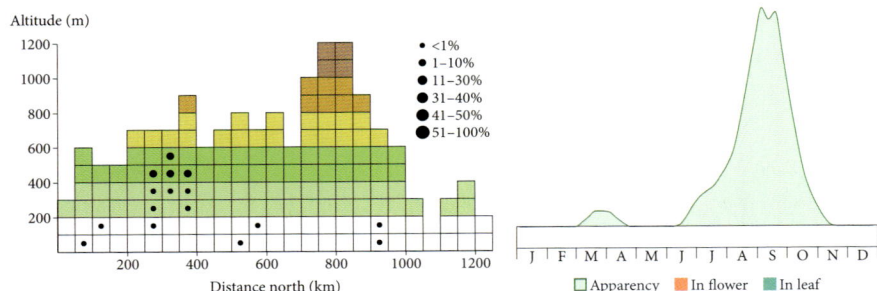

	GB	IR
Long term	No trend	No trend
Short term	No trend	No trend

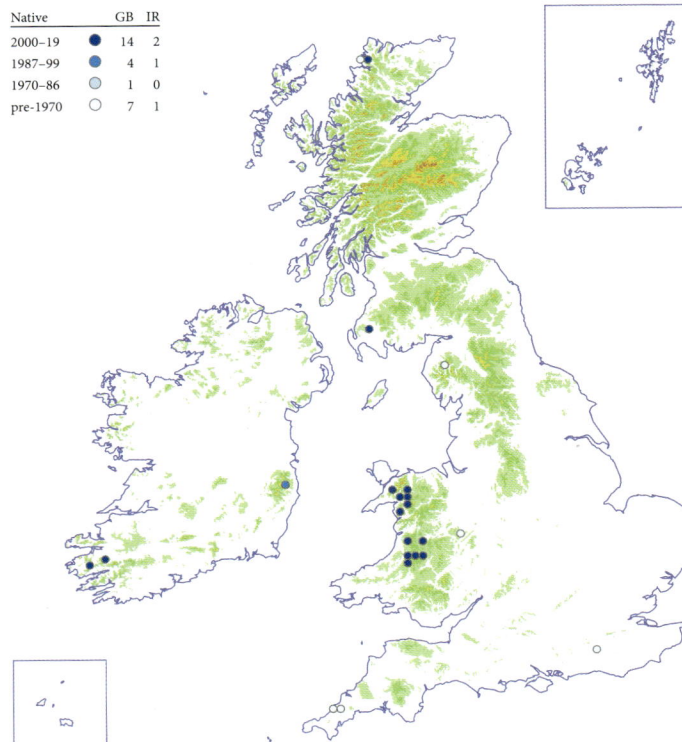

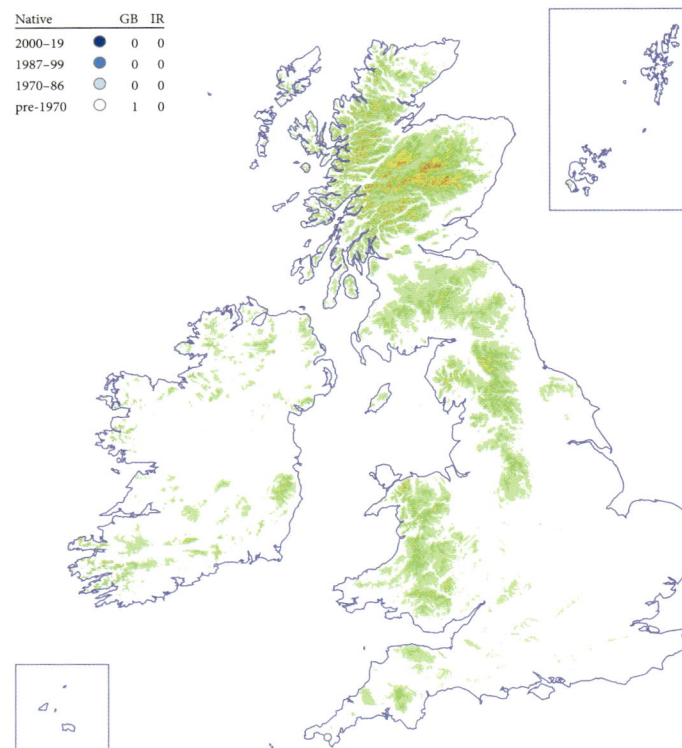

Native	GB	IR
2000–19	14	2
1987–99	4	1
1970–86	1	0
pre-1970	7	1

Key refs Holden (1959), Jones & Stewart (2001), Stewart (2001), Stewart (2005a), Stewart & Scott (2003).

N.F. STEWART

N *Nitella hyalina* Many-branched Stonewort
(DC.) C.Agardh

At the sole site in our area *N. hyalina* grew on mud in depths of about 1–2 m in a mesotrophic lake with a mixed flora of pondweeds such as *Potamogeton perfoliatus* and *P. pusillus*. This seems to be broadly similar to its habitat elsewhere in Europe where it grows in mesotrophic to slightly eutrophic lakes and it is able to tolerate a small amount of salt. However, it requires good water quality with low levels of nitrates and phosphates (Arbeitsgruppe Characeeen Deutschlands, 2016). Lowland.

Trends This species has only ever been recorded from Loe Pool (West Cornwall). Other records from north Wales and Cambridgeshire are now considered errors. It was last seen in Loe Pool in 1914 and it is probable that the species was lost due to a combination of being outcompeted by the newly arrived *Elodea canadensis* and by significant sedimentation of mine waste washed in via the River Cober. More recently Loe Pool has had significant problems with nutrient enrichment which caused the complete loss of aquatic vegetation for a period. There is a possibility that *N. hyalina* was itself an introduction brought in with water-lily roots in the 1890s (Stewart, 1999b).

Biogeography *N. hyalina* is a cosmopolitan species occurring widely around the world between 70° N and 40° S.

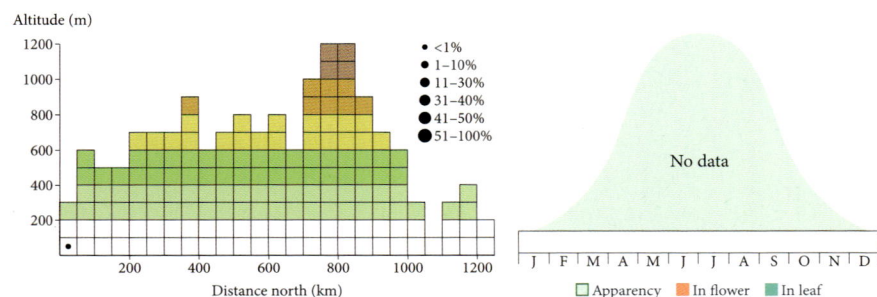

	GB	IR
Long term	No trend	No trend
Short term	No trend	No trend

Native	GB	IR
2000–19	0	0
1987–99	0	0
1970–86	0	0
pre-1970	1	0

Key refs Arbeitsgruppe Characeen Deutschlands (2016), Stewart (1999b).

N.F. STEWART

Nitella mucronata Pointed Stonewort

(A.Braun) Miq.

A species of lakes, canals and ponds, typically growing in 1–3 m depth, occurring in the gaps among denser vegetation or where the vegetation becomes sparser at the lower edge of the photic zone. It can occur in mesotrophic to eutrophic water and appears to tolerate higher levels of nutrients than most stoneworts. Two varieties are recognized in our area: var. *mucronata* and var. *gracillima*. However, the distinction between them is not well-marked, though the former may be more vulnerable to nutrient enrichment than the latter. Lowland.

Native in Britain and the Channel Islands and a neophyte in Ireland.

Trends *N. mucronata* var. *mucronata* was first recorded in the 1720s and is considered to be native, while var. *gracillima* was first recorded in Gloucestershire in 1917 and may have been introduced. The latter has since spread gradually through much of England and to a lesser extent Wales, reaching Scotland in 2015. It has been noted in a few English garden centres dating back to the 1970s and it seems likely that spread has been horticulturally assisted. In Ireland, aside from a pond in Glasnevin Botanic Garden (County Dublin), the variety was first recorded in the Upper Lough Erne system in 1988 and has since become frequent there. More recently it has also started appearing in the Shannon system (Minchin *et al.*, 2019; 2021). Meanwhile, var. *mucronata* is now very rare; it is possible that it has been seen recently in West Sussex, including near Henfield where it was recorded in the 1820s (Abraham, 2020) and North-east Yorkshire (Leven Canal), but further work is needed to confirm these and other recent records.

Biogeography Widely distributed in Europe, Asia, Africa and the Americas.

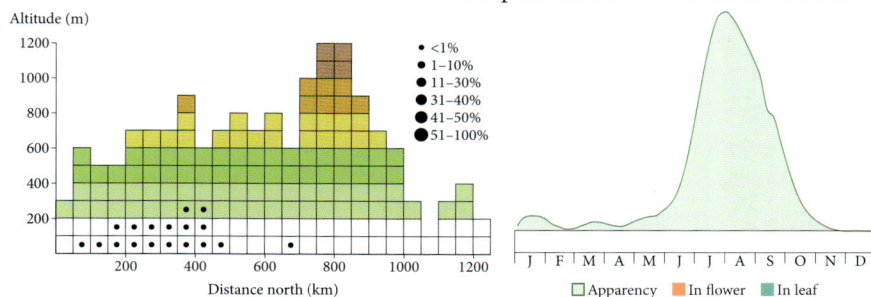

	GB	IR
Long term	No trend	No trend
Short term	No trend	No trend

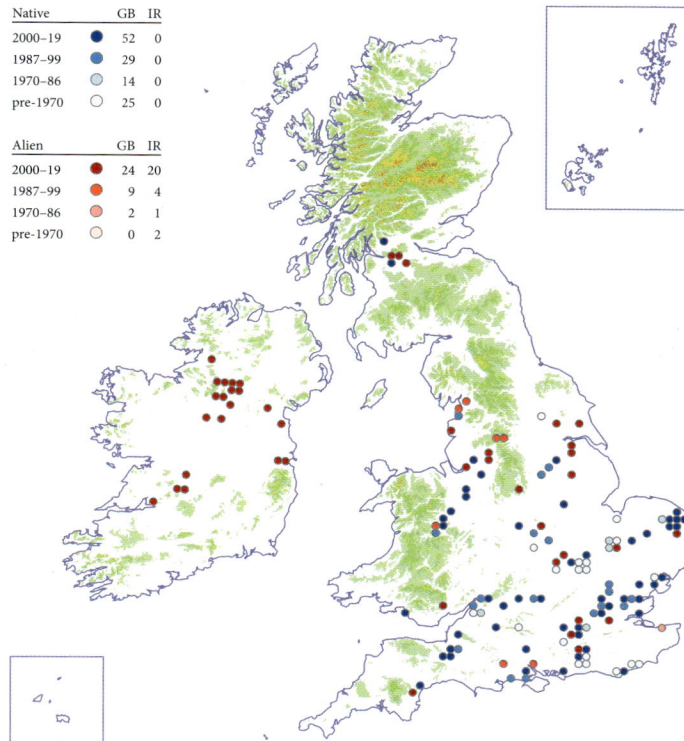

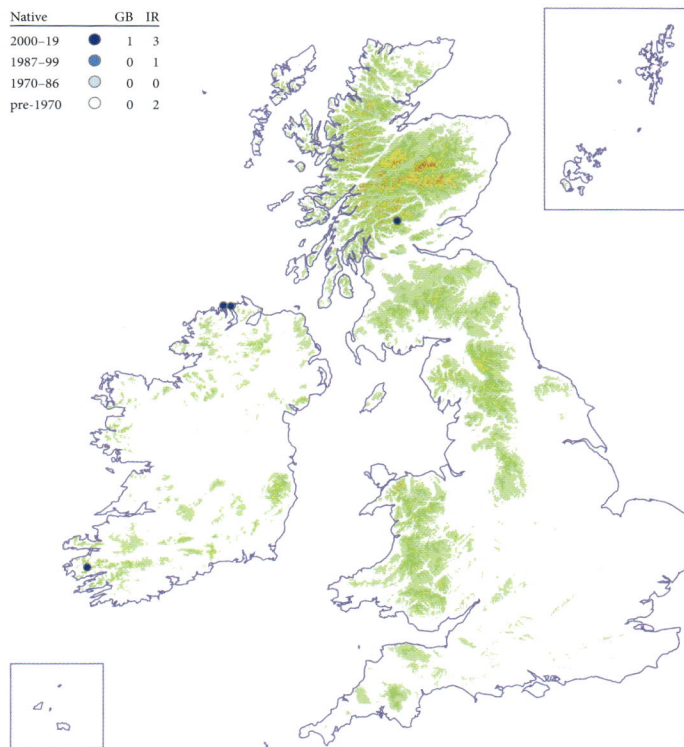

Native	GB	IR
2000–19	52	0
1987–99	29	0
1970–86	14	0
pre-1970	25	0

Alien	GB	IR
2000–19	24	20
1987–99	9	4
1970–86	2	1
pre-1970	0	2

Key refs Abraham (2020), Minchin *et al.*(2019), Minchin *et al.* (2021b).

N.F. Stewart

Altitude (m) histogram legend:
- <1%
- 1–10%
- 11–30%
- 31–40%
- 41–50%
- 51–100%

Distance north (km)

Apparency — In flower — In leaf

Nitella spanioclema Few-branched Stonewort

J.Groves & Bull.-Webst. ex Bull.-Webst.

The ecology of this species is poorly known. The records mapped are from sites which are mesotrophic or are oligotrophic with a calcareous influence. It grows in 1–3 m of water, often in monospecific stands. Lowland.

Trends *N. spanioclema* was described from a site in West Donegal, and has been treated as a separate taxon in British and Irish texts since then. However, Krause (1992) considered it to be only a modification of *N. flexilis*. Nevertheless, there are forms that fit this taxon which appear to be distinct, both in Ireland (C. Roden, pers. comm.) and possibly in Scotland, and this map includes all of these. Further work is needed to clarify whether these deserve specific rank.

Biogeography Possibly endemic to our area.

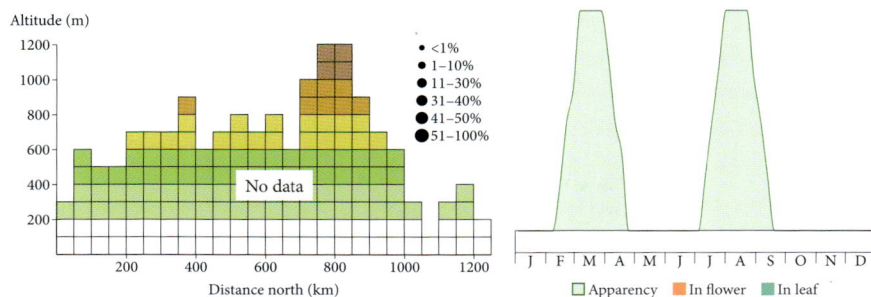

	GB	IR
Long term	No trend	No trend
Short term	No trend	No trend

Native	GB	IR
2000–19	1	3
1987–99	0	1
1970–86	0	0
pre-1970	0	2

Key refs John *et al.* (2021).

N.F. Stewart

Altitude (m) histogram legend:
- <1%
- 1–10%
- 11–30%
- 31–40%
- 41–50%
- 51–100%

No data

Distance north (km)

Apparency — In flower — In leaf

Ne *Nitella syncarpa* Many-fruited Stonewort
(Thuill.) Chevall.

	GB	IR
Long term	No trend	No trend
Short term	No trend	No trend

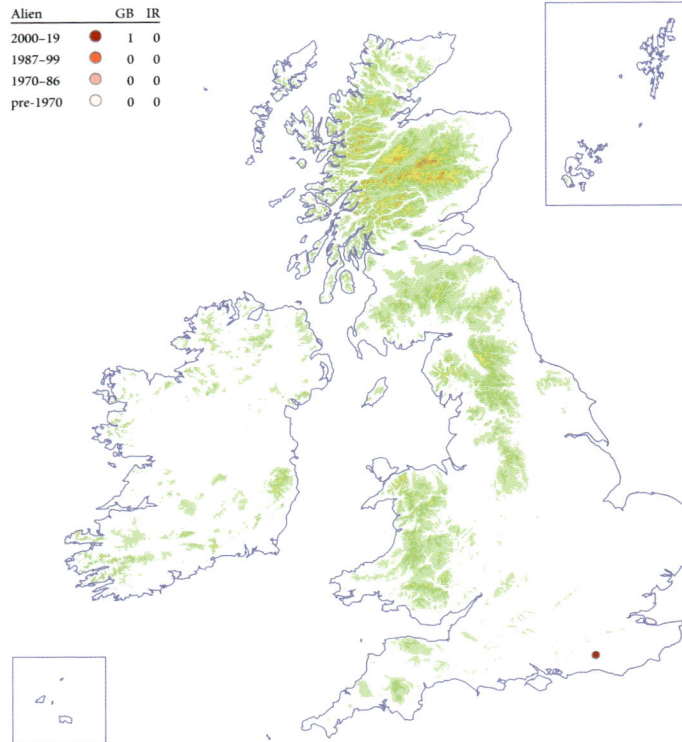

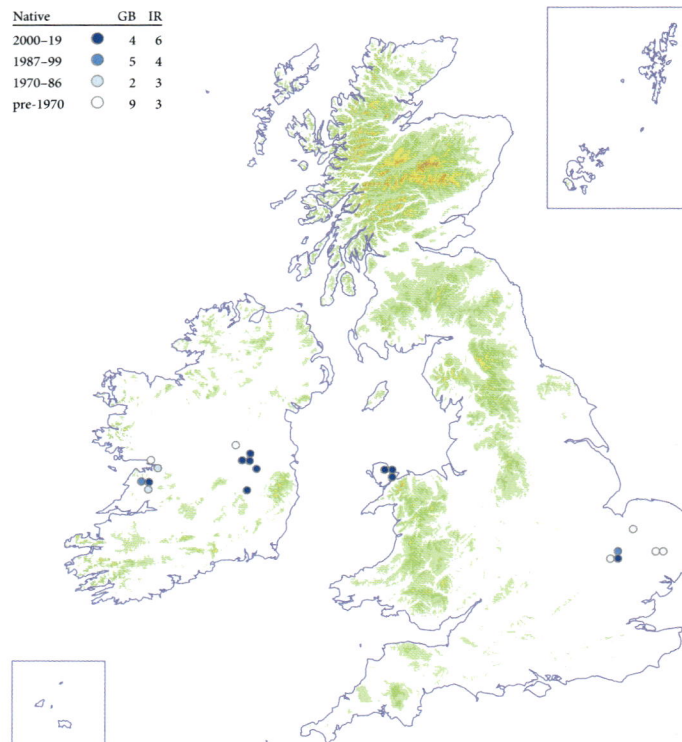

Only recorded once in our area, from a cleaned pond in West Sussex in 2001. Elsewhere in Europe it grows in mesotrophic to slightly eutrophic lakes and ponds in a variety of depths and situations. It can also tolerate slightly brackish conditions. It is a summer annual, germinating in the spring and fruiting freely between July and September (Schubert & Blindow, 2003; Arbeitsgruppe Characeeen Deutschlands, 2016). The names *Chara syncarpa* and *N. syncarpa* were frequently used in the mid-19th century for what is now called *N. opaca*. All old records under this name should be disregarded. Lowland.

Trends *N. syncarpa* was not refound at its sole locality when the site was visited in 2005 nor on subsequent surveys (Abraham, 2020). It is presumed that it was introduced there, mainly because of its lack of persistence and the presence of other introduced aquatics (*e.g. Myriophyllum aquaticum*). However, it occurs in northern France and the Netherlands and its occurrence in Sussex could be natural, reappearing from dormant spores.

Biogeography A European species widely distributed across the continent from southern Scandinavia to the northern parts of the Mediterranean countries. It is locally frequent in central Europe but becomes rare towards the edges of its range.

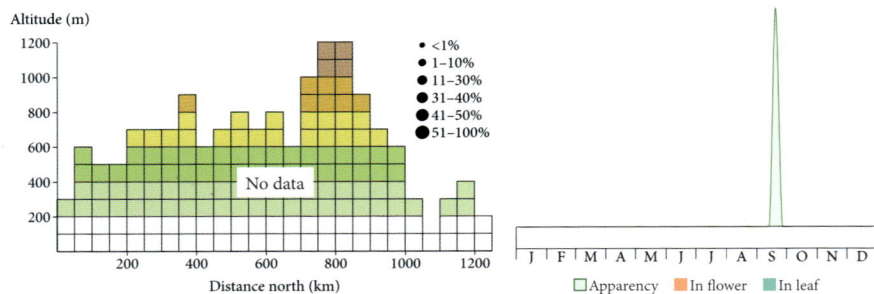

Alien	GB	IR
2000–19	1	0
1987–99	0	0
1970–86	0	0
pre-1970	0	0

Key refs Abraham (2020), Arbeitsgruppe Characeen Deutschlands (2016), Schubert & Blindow (2003).

N.F. STEWART

N *Nitella tenuissima* Dwarf Stonewort
(Desv.) Kütz.

	GB	IR
Long term	No trend	No trend
Short term	No trend	No trend

A plant of calcareous fenland where it occurs in open areas in *Schoenus nigricans* flushes and *Cladium* fen, and in shallow peaty pools and ditches in depths of up to 1 m. It requires bare peat surfaces and does not compete well with other algae or vascular plants (Stewart, 2004a). It is therefore an early colonist in new pools but usually disappears within a few years as other vegetation takes over. Nevertheless, there are some pools where it has survived for over ten years. In flush systems it can probably persist for longer periods provided grazing is sufficient to keep the habitat open. In Ireland it also occurs in calcareous water in canals where it grows in bare areas at the margins, particularly where there is a shallow water shelf. Lowland.

Trends This species has been lost from several sites because of enrichment pollution which favours the growth of filamentous algae and encourages competition from larger plants. Several sites have also been lost through drainage. It requires periodic disturbance to maintain open habitats and, in the past, may have benefitted from peat cutting. In recent years there has been a programme of grazing and pond clearance/creation at several sites which has maintained some of the sub-populations but others have become overgrown. Fortunately, the spores of this species are known to remain viable in the substrate for decades. For example, in its last English site (Wicken Fen, Cambridgeshire) it has been recorded roughly every 10–20 years when there has been some sort of disturbance event (Cadbury, 2001).

Biogeography *N. tenuissima* occurs in Europe, southern Africa, India, North and Central America, and Madagascar.

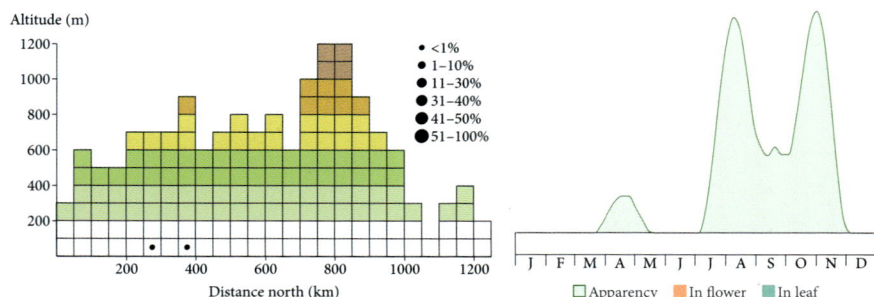

Native	GB	IR
2000–19	4	6
1987–99	5	4
1970–86	2	3
pre-1970	9	3

Key refs Allen (1950), Allen (1951), Bullock-Webster (1901), Cadbury (2001), Friday (1997), Preston (1993b), Stewart (2001), Stewart (2004a), Walters (1958).

N.F. STEWART

N *Nitella translucens* Translucent Stonewort
(Pers.) C.Agardh

N. translucens grows in low pH, nutrient-poor pools and lakes on peat or peaty silt and in open swamp communities. It can occur in shallow water in small pools but in larger lakes it is more frequent in slightly deeper water, growing with *N. opaca* and *Isoetes lacustris*. It cannot tolerate brackish water but some sites are close to the sea and may receive wind-blown salt. Up to 550 m at Coomcalee (South Kerry).

Trends The main strongholds for this species are in western parts of our area where it is locally frequent. There are also scattered populations in upland areas farther east but it is surprisingly absent from some areas (*e.g.* Orkney and the Wicklow Mountains). Elsewhere in lowland Britain and Ireland it is rare and declining, due to a combination of habitat loss and enrichment pollution. Competition from invasive species

such as *Crassula helmsii* is also a serious issue in south-eastern England.

Biogeography *N. translucens* occurs in Europe and northern Africa.

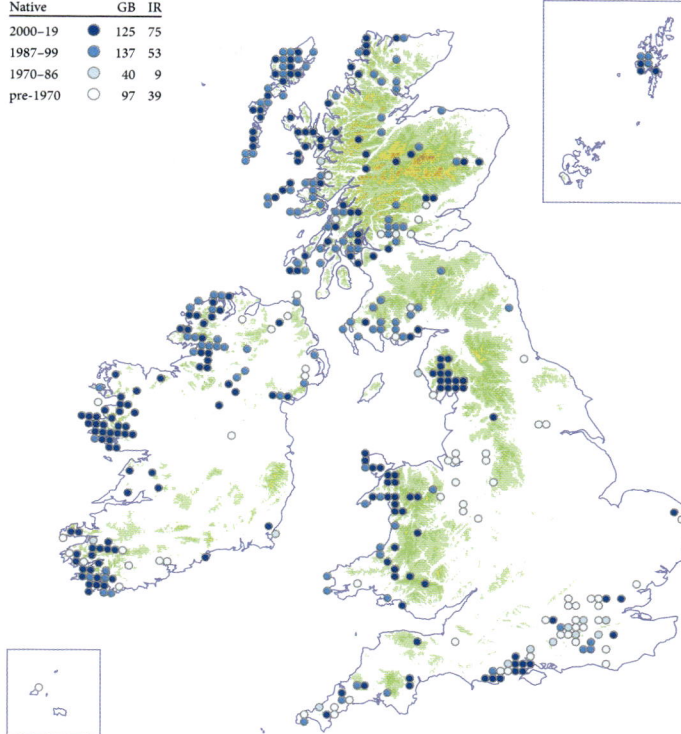

		GB	IR
Long term		No trend	No trend
Short term		No trend	No trend

Native		GB	IR
2000–19	●	125	75
1987–99	●	137	53
1970–86	○	40	9
pre-1970	○	97	39

Key refs John *et al.* (2021).

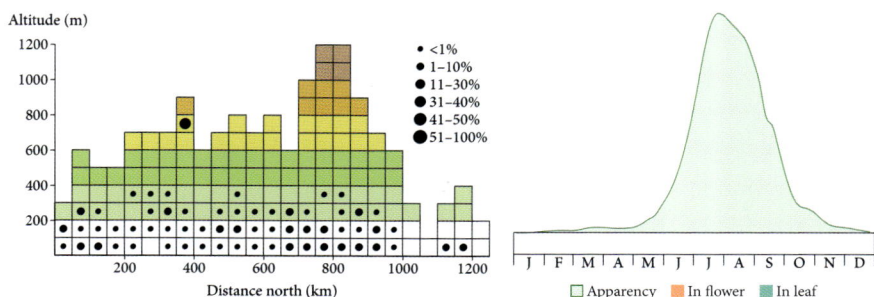

Altitude (m)

● <1%
● 1–10%
● 11–30%
● 31–40%
● 41–50%
● 51–100%

Distance north (km)

☐ Apparency ☐ In flower ☐ In leaf

N.F. STEWART

N *Nitellopsis obtusa* Starry Stonewort
(Desv.) J.Groves

Typically a lake species of deep base-rich water, generally between 1 m and 6 m depth, although it has been recorded from depths of up to 30 m elsewhere in Europe. Although primarily a freshwater species it can tolerate low levels of salinity (Schubert & Blindow, 2003). Starry stonewort is usually a summer annual, but in favourable conditions and mild winters it may not die back completely. Spore production is from July to September and may be controlled by light intensity (Stewart & Church, 1992). Lowland.

Trends There are a few 19th century records from Devon, Hampshire, Greater London and Northamptonshire, but for much of the 20th century this species was confined to the Norfolk Broads. It is still present there, although populations fluctuate unstably because of raised nutrient levels. In recent decades it has been gradually spreading elsewhere; it was first recorded in

Gloucestershire in 1995 and has since been recorded in 19 lakes across southern England, particularly in gravel-pits around the west side of London. It was first recorded in Wales in 2007 and is now known from three sites there; in Ireland it was first collected in 2009 and appears to be increasing in the lower Shannon system (Minchin *et al.*, 2017; 2021). *N. obtusa* was thought to produce spores rarely, reproducing mainly by the star-shaped bulbils, which can remain viable for several years. However, there are suggestions that the current spread may be linked with increased fertility and some of the west London gravel pits have supported abundantly fertile populations.

Biogeography Widely distributed across Europe and Asia, east to Japan. It has recently appeared as a non-native in the central United States where it is regarded as a pest.

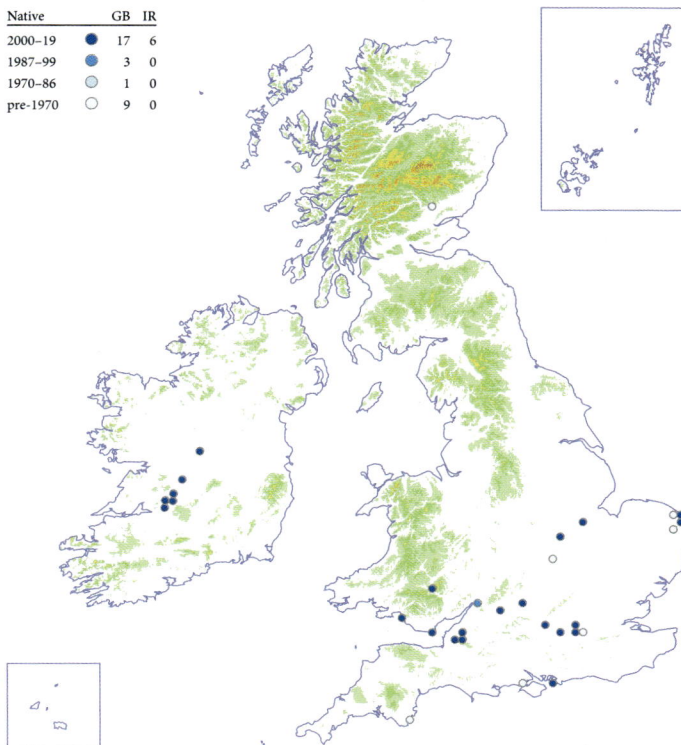

		GB	IR
Long term		No trend	No trend
Short term		No trend	No trend

Native		GB	IR
2000–19	●	17	6
1987–99	●	3	0
1970–86	○	1	0
pre-1970	○	9	0

Key refs Minchin *et al.* (2017), Minchin *et al.* (2021b), Schubert & Blindow (2003), Stewart (2003b), Stewart & Church (1992), Stewart & Hatton-Ellis (2020).

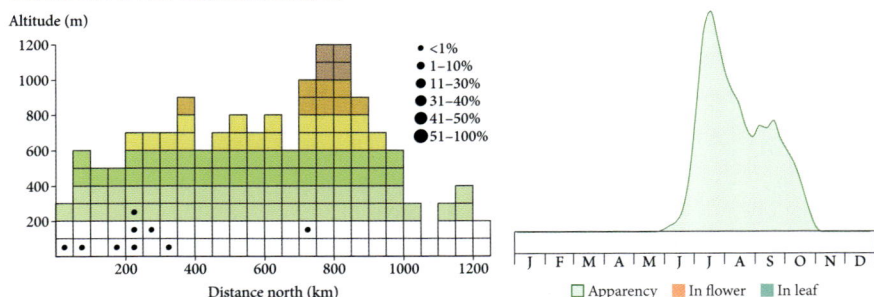

Altitude (m)

● <1%
● 1–10%
● 11–30%
● 31–40%
● 41–50%
● 51–100%

Distance north (km)

☐ Apparency ☐ In flower ☐ In leaf

N.F. STEWART

(N) *Tolypella glomerata* Clustered Stonewort
(Desv.) Leonh.

T. glomerata typically occurs in alkaline pools and the shallow edges and sides of ditches, lakes and canals, often in those parts that dry out in summer. It is tolerant of mildly brackish water and is sometimes locally frequent in dune pools. It is usually a winter annual, visible from October to May, but it can occasionally grow throughout the year in the deeper water of low nutrient, large alkaline lakes. Populations vary considerably depending on habitat; substantial populations can occur for a period in newly created gravel-pits and on occasionally disturbed quarry floors but are normally transient. However, many populations are small. Persistent populations can occur where there is regular drying out or disturbance, such as in dune-slack pools, ponds where there is periodic livestock disturbance, and in the inundation zone at the edges of lakes. Up to 375 m at Malham Tarn (Mid-west Yorkshire).

Trends Though the map shows decline, there may be a degree of under-recording as *T. glomerata* has normally disappeared by the beginning of June, whilst aquatic surveys are often undertaken later in the year. It is also frequently associated with sites with recent disturbance such as cleaned out ditches or re-excavated ponds where spores may have been dormant for decades, and it probably has some ability to migrate to new sites where the habitat is suitable. These factors may contribute to an overestimation of the degree of decline though it is probable that some of the decline is real; it is sensitive to the secondary effects of water pollution and usually occurs in locations where there is some isolation from nutrient enrichment.

Biogeography A cosmopolitan species, found throughout Europe, northern Africa, North America, Asia, and Australasia.

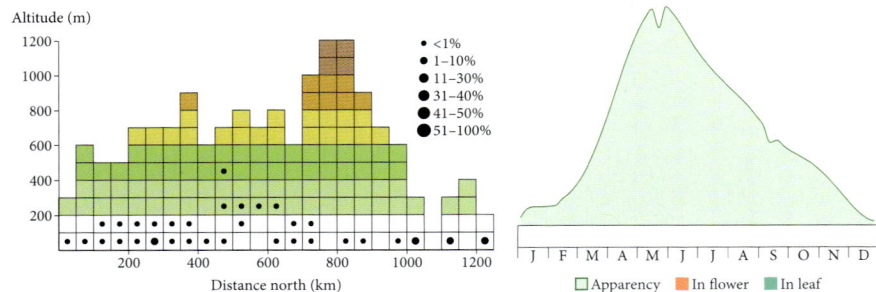

	GB	IR
Long term	No trend	No trend
Short term	No trend	No trend

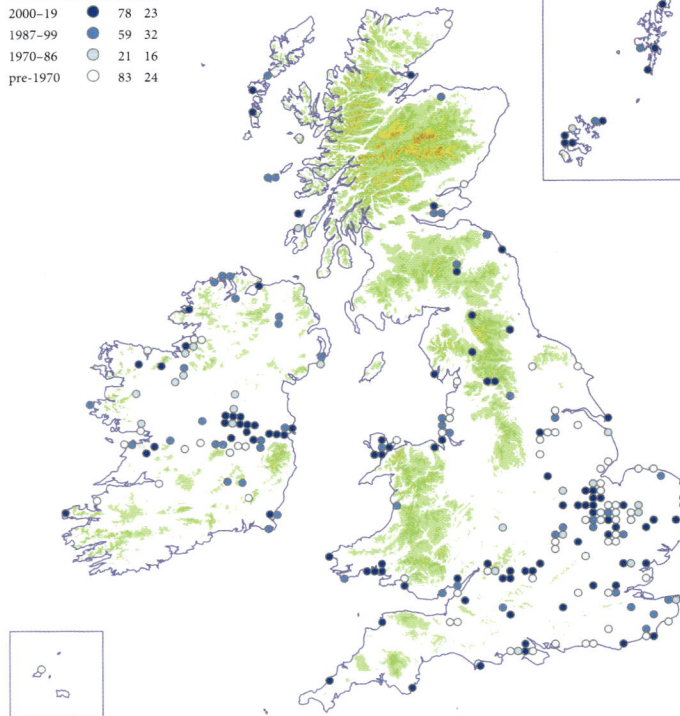

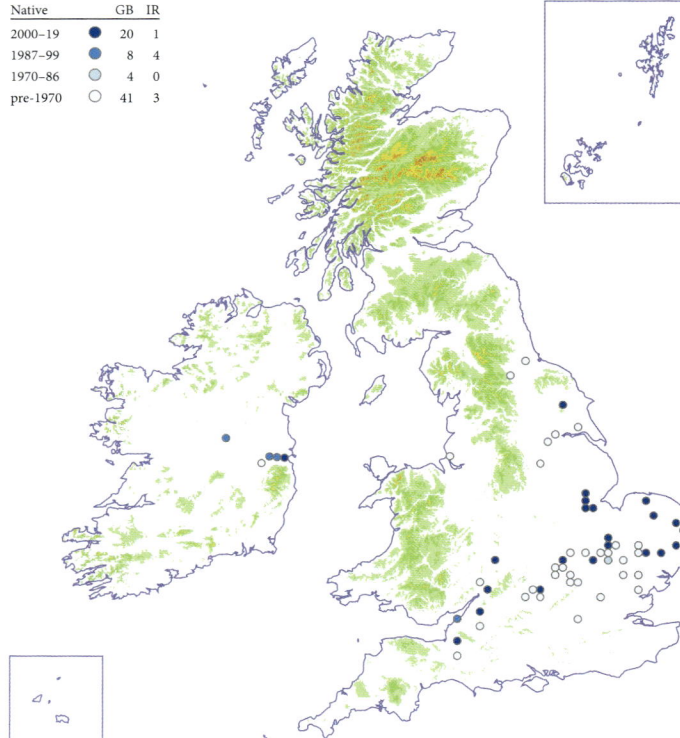

Native	GB	IR
2000–19	78	23
1987–99	59	32
1970–86	21	16
pre-1970	83	24

Key refs John *et al.* (2021).

N.F. STEWART

(N) *Tolypella intricata* Tassel Stonewort
(Trentep. ex Roth) Leonh.

T. intricata grows in alkaline water in pools, canals, ditches and shallow water bodies that dry up in summer. It is a winter annual which usually germinates in the autumn, overwintering in a vegetative state, and is able to withstand being frozen. The spores ripen between April and June and the plant has usually disappeared by early July, although in the deeper water systems in the Lincolnshire drains it appears capable of persisting throughout the year. It is a poor competitor and benefits from disturbance which keeps down other vegetation, sometimes appearing in considerable quantities for a year or two after major disturbance. It appears to be able to tolerate some shade and this may help to limit the competition from vascular plants such as *Glyceria fluitans* and *Juncus effusus*. However, it is easily suppressed by leaf-litter fall unless this is broken up by livestock or other

disturbance. Spores can remain viable in the substrate for decades, waiting for suitable conditions to return. Lowland.

Trends The fragmentation of grazing systems has probably contributed to the decline of this species, although small metapopulations do persist at Otmoor (Oxfordshire) and the Inglestone Common area (Gloucestershire). There is also a stronghold in ground-water-fed ditches in South Lincolnshire. A number of new sites have been discovered in recent years, probably due to more intensive surveys. In Ireland it benefitted considerably from a period of restoration of the canals in and west of Dublin in the early 1990s, but it has since become extremely rare again.

Biogeography Widely but sparsely distributed across Europe south to northern Africa; it is also known from North America.

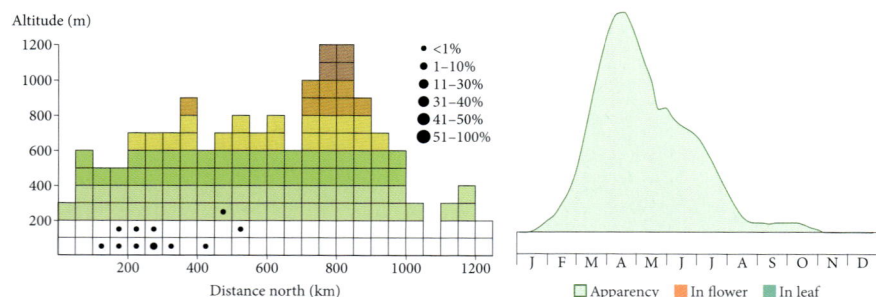

	GB	IR
Long term	No trend	No trend
Short term	No trend	No trend

Native	GB	IR
2000–19	20	1
1987–99	8	4
1970–86	4	0
pre-1970	41	3

Key refs Hawkins (2020), Lambert (2008), Lansdown (2013), Lansdown & Stewart (1999), Williams *et al.* (2003).

N.F. STEWART

Tolypella nidifica Bird's-nest Stonewort

(O.F.Müll.) Leonh.

This is an annual species of brackish water usually growing in salinities of 4–18 psu but sometimes in salinities ranging from 3–30 psu. In our area it grows in lakes and lagoons, and in the Baltic Sea it grows widely along the open coast. It is found at a broad range of depths and substrates but a key feature is the requirement for open conditions with little competing vegetation. In shallow water this can be provided by wave turbulence and water level fluctuation and in deep water it can form a band along the lower margin of aquatic vegetation (Schubert & Blindow, 2003). It can exploit openings created in various ways, such as in the Outer Hebrides where it has been observed where there is bioturbation by lugworms and on sand swept clean by the fronds of *Fucus* species attached to adjacent rocks (Scott *et al.*, 2011). It is a summer annual, germinating in May to June and fruiting from July to October. Lowland.

Trends This is a very rare species restricted to two sites in the Outer Hebrides and one in County Wexford. Records from elsewhere are either extremely doubtful or have been shown to be errors (usually for *T. glomerata*). It has been lost from three sites in Orkney, probably due to changes in salinity levels, although one of the sites is also now affected by enrichment pollution. The latter is also a significant issue in its Irish site where excessive growths of algae are a concern. In its Hebridean sites, the pressures are low but both extant locations have direct connections to the sea which are likely to be affected by rises in sea level.

Biogeography Occurring throughout the northern hemisphere and possibly also in Australia. In Europe, its main stronghold is in the Baltic Sea but away from our area there are also scattered records from Norway, the Iberian Peninsula and southern France.

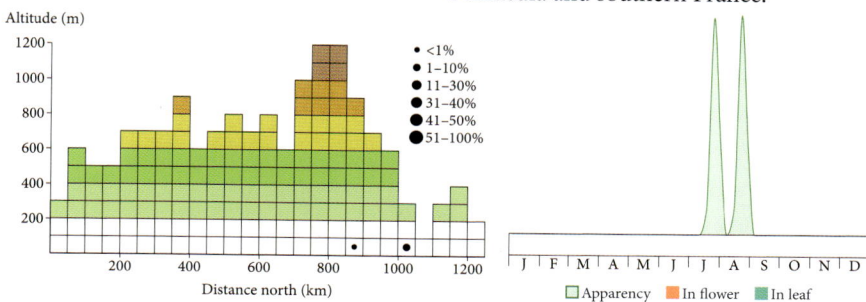

	GB	IR
Long term	No trend	No trend
Short term	No trend	No trend

Native		GB	IR
2000–19	●	4	1
1987–99	●	4	1
1970–86	○	0	0
pre-1970	○	3	1

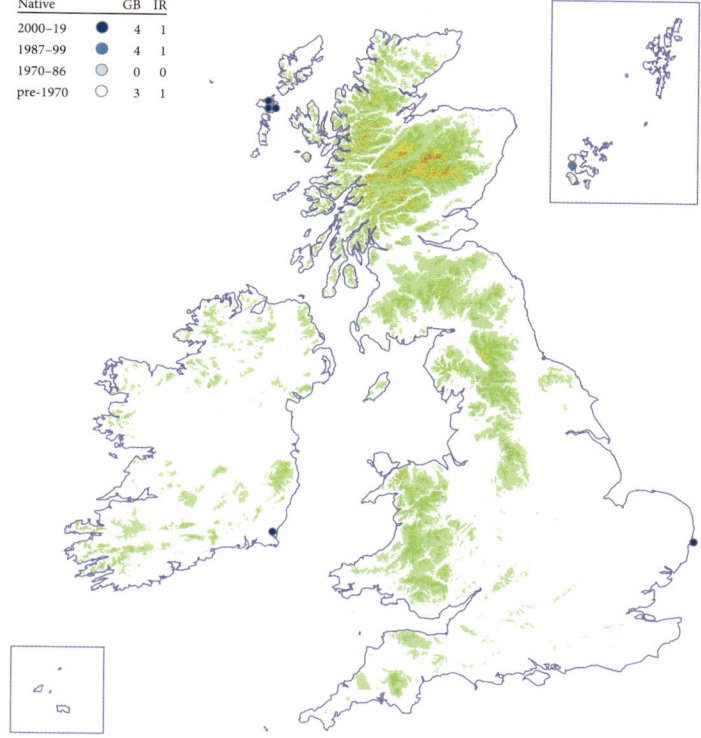

Altitude (m)

● <1%
● 1–10%
● 11–30%
● 31–40%
● 41–50%
● 51–100%

☐ Apparency ■ In flower ■ In leaf

Key refs Angus *et al.* (2015), ICIT (2004), Martin (2001), Martin *et al.* (2002), Murphy & Wallace (2004), Schubert & Blindow (2003), Scott *et al.* (2011).

N.F. STEWART

Tolypella prolifera Great Tassel Stonewort

(Ziz ex A.Braun) Leonh.

T. prolifera is a species of mesotrophic water typically occurring in ditches that are farthest away from poor quality arterial drains or where there is upwelling of cleaner groundwater from underlying gravels. It does not generally compete well with other vegetation and usually requires some form of disturbance that creates bare underwater areas. In ditches it is usually only seen in the first or second summer after a ditch has been dredged and subsequently the abundance of other ditch vegetation often becomes too dense for the plant to survive. In such cases it can persist as spores in the bottom sediments until the ditch is disturbed again and indeed it seems to have a 'sit and wait' strategy rather than moving to new places. Its occurrence in lakes in the lower Thames valley and in central Ireland is a rather different ecology and one that needs further study. In both areas it appears

to be a recent arrival (2016 and 2009 respectively) in sites where *Nitellopsis obtusa* is also a recent arrival and where nutrient levels are slightly higher than the optimum for most stoneworts. Lowland.

Trends This species has declined significantly in England although there is still a stronghold in northern Cambridgeshire and South Lincolnshire. In Ireland, prior to its recent rediscovery it was known only from a single record in the 1870s in the Royal Canal in Dublin.

Biogeography *T. prolifera* is known from Europe, North and South America, and Asia.

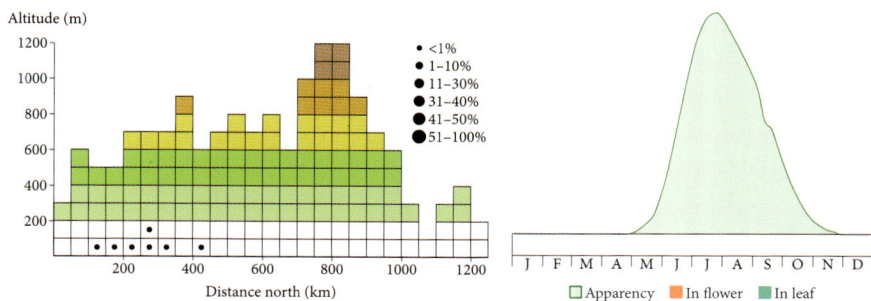

	GB	IR
Long term	No trend	No trend
Short term	No trend	No trend

Native		GB	IR
2000–19	●	18	2
1987–99	●	6	1
1970–86	○	2	0
pre-1970	○	33	1

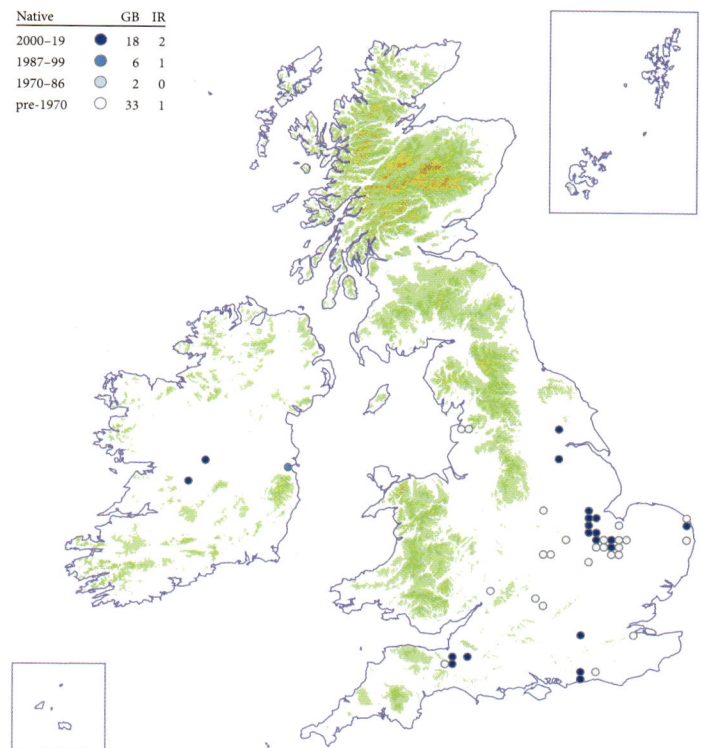

Altitude (m)

● <1%
● 1–10%
● 11–30%
● 31–40%
● 41–50%
● 51–100%

☐ Apparency ■ In flower ■ In leaf

Key refs Lansdown (2013), Plantlife (2001), Stewart & Lansdown (1999), Stewart & Pankhurst (2000), Williams & Stewart (2002).

N.F. STEWART

Bibliography

Aarssen, L.W. 1981. The biology of Canadian weeds. 50. *Hypochoeris radicata* L. *Canadian Journal of Plant Science* **61**: 365–381.

Aarssen, L.W., Hall, I.V. & Jensen, J.I.N. 1986. The biology of Canadian weeds. 76. *Vicia angustifolia* L., *V. cracca* L., *V. sativa* L., *V. tetrasperma* (L.) Schreb. and *V. villosa* Roth. *Canadian Journal of Plant Science* **66**: 711–737.

Abbott, P.P. 2005. *Plant Atlas of Mid-West Yorkshire*. Yorkshire Naturalists' Union.

Abbott, R.J., James, J.K., Irwin, J.A. & Comes, H.P. 2000. Hybrid origin of the Oxford Ragwort, *Senecio squalidus* L. *Watsonia* **23**: 123–138.

Abbott, R.J. & Lowe, A.J. 2004. Origins, establishment and evolution of new polyploid species: *Senecio cambrensis* and *S. eboracensis* in the British Isles. *Biological Journal of the Linnean Society* **82**: 467–474.

Abbott, R.J., Brennan, A.C., James, J.K., Forbes, D.G., Hegarty, M.J. & Hiscock, S.J. 2009. Recent hybrid origin and invasion of the British Isles by a self-incompatible species, Oxford ragwort (*Senecio squalidus* L., Asteraceae). *Biological Invasions* **11**: 1145–1158.

Abraham, F. 2020. *The stoneworts of Sussex*. Sussex Botanical Recording Society/ Brambletye Publishing.

Abraham, F. & Rose, F. 2000. Large-leaved limes on the South Downs. *British Wildlife* **12**: 86–90.

Adam, P. 1990. *Saltmarsh ecology*. Cambridge University Press, Cambridge.

Adams, A.W. 1955. Biological Flora of the British Isles. No. 52. *Succisa pratensis* Moench. *Journal of Ecology* **43**: 709–718.

Adams, K.J. 2003. Changes in the Status and Distribution of *Oenanthe pimpinelloides* Corky-fruited Water Dropwort, in Essex. *Essex Naturalist* **21**: 150–153.

Adams, K.J. 2017. Thin-leaved Horned-pondweed new to the U.K. *Essex Botany, Bryology & Mycology* **6**: 8–9.

Adams, K.J. 2020. Essex Knapweeds. *Essex Botany, Bryology & Mycology* **12**: 4–7.

Agnew, A.D.Q. 1968. The interspecific relationships of *Juncus effusus* and *J. conglomeratus* in Britain. *Watsonia* **6**: 377–388.

Aiken, S.G., Newroth, P.R. & Wile, I. 1979. The biology of Canadian weeds. 34. *Myriophyllum spicatum* L. *Canadian Journal of Plant Science* **59**: 201–215.

Akeroyd, J.R. 1984. *Parapholis incurva* (L.) C. E. Hubbard – a grass overlooked in Ireland. *Irish Naturalists' Journal* **21**: 228–230.

Akeroyd, J.R. 1991. *Anthyllis vulneraria* L. subsp. *polyphylla* (DC.) Nyman, an alien kidney-vetch in Britain. *Watsonia* **18**: 401–403.

Akeroyd, J.R. 1993. The distribution and status of *Rumex pulcher* L. in Ireland. *Irish Naturalists' Journal* **24**: 284–285.

Akeroyd, J.R. 1996. Coastal ecotypic variants of two vetches, *Vicia sepium* L. and *V. sylvatica* L. (Fabaceae), in Britain and Ireland. *Watsonia* **21**: 71–78.

Akeroyd, J.R. 2014. *Docks and knotweeds of Britain and Ireland*. BSBI Handbook No. 3. Edn. 2. Botanical Society of Britain and Ireland, London.

Akeroyd, J.R., Warwick, S.L. & Briggs, D. 1978. Variations in four populations of *Senecio viscosus* L. as revealed by a cultivation experiment. *New Phytologist* **81**: 391–400.

Akeroyd, J.R. & Briggs, D. 1983a. Genecological studies of *Rumex crispus* L. I. Garden experiments using transplanted material. *New Phytologist* **94**: 309–323.

Akeroyd, J.R. & Briggs, D. 1983b. Genecological studies of *Rumex crispus* L. II. Variation in plants grown from wild-collected seed. *New Phytologist* **94**: 325–343.

Akeroyd, J.R. & Preston, C.D. 1984. *Halimione portulacoides* (L.) Aellen on coastal rocks and cliffs. *Watsonia* **15**: 95–103.

Akeroyd, J.R. & Preston, C.D. 1987. Additional records of *Halimione portulacoides* (L.) Aellen on coastal rocks and cliffs. *Watsonia* **16**: 427–428.

Akeroyd, J.R. & Clarke, K. 1993. *Dianthus armeria* L. new to Ireland and other rare plants in West Cork. *Watsonia* **19**: 185–187.

Akeroyd, J.R. & Beckett, G. 1995. *Petrorhagia prolifera* (L.) P.W. Ball & Heywood (Caryophyllaceae), an overlooked native species of eastern England. *Watsonia* **20**: 405–407.

Al-Bermani, A.K.K.A. 1991. *Taxonomic, cytogenetic and breeding relationships of* Festuca rubra *sensu lato*. University of Leicester.

Albernternst, B. & Nawrath, S. 2002. *Lysichiton americanus* newly established in Continental Europe. Is there a chance for control in the early phase of naturalization? *Neobiota* **1**: 91–99.

Allan, B., Woods, P. & Clarke, S. 1993. *Wild orchids of Scotland*. HMSO, Edinburgh.

Allan, E. & Pannell, J.R. 2009. Rapid divergence in physiological and life-history traits between northern and southern populations of the British introduced neo-species, *Senecio squalidus*. *Oikos* **118**: 1053–1061.

Allan, H.H. 1961. *Flora of New Zealand. Vol. 1, Indigenous Tracheophyta*. P. D. Hasselberg, Wellington.

Allen, D.E. 1957. *Leontodon autumnalis* var. *salinus* (Aspegren) Lange. *Proceedings of the Botanical Society of the British Isles* **2**: 240–241.

Allen, D.E. 1968. *Neotinea intacta* (Link) Reichb. in the Isle of Man. *Proceedings of the Botanical Society of the British Isles* **7**: 165–168.

Allen, D.E. 1984. *Flora of the Isle of Man*. The Manx Museum and National Trust, Douglas.

Allen, G.O. 1950. Four days stonewort collecting in the Ely District. *Watsonia* **1**: 10–11.

Allen, G.O. 1951. *Nitella tenuissima* Kütz. *Watsonia* **2**: 110.

Alliende, M.C. & Harper, J.L. 1989. Demographic studies of a dioecious tree, 1. Colonization, sex and age structure of a population of *Salix cinerea*. *Journal of Ecology* **77**: 1029–1047.

Alston, A.H.G. 1949. *Equisetum ramosissimum* as a British plant. *Watsonia* **1**: 149–153.

Amor, R.L. & Richardson, R.G. 1980. The biology of Australian weeds. 2. *Rubus fruticosus* agg. *Journal of the Australian Institute of Agricultural Science* **46**: 87–97.

Amphlett, A. 2019a. Inland populations of *Juncus balticus* (Juncaceae) in Scotland. *British & Irish Botany* **1**: 202–218.

Amphlett, A. 2019b. *Salix euxina* (Eastern Crack-willow) naturalised along the River Spey, Scotland. *BSBI News* **142**: 20–22.

Amphlett, A. 2020. *Lysimachia minima* (Chaffweed) – another roadside halophyte? *BSBI News* **145**: 14–15.

Amphlett, A. 2021. Identification and taxonomy of *Betula* (Betulaceae) in Great Britain and Ireland. *British & Irish Botany* **3**: 99–135.

Anderson, D.E. 1961. Taxonomy and distribution of the genus *Phalaris*. *Iowa State Journal of Science* **36**: 1–96.

Anderson, R.C. & Beare, M.H. 1983. Breeding system and pollination ecology of *Trientalis borealis* (Primulaceae). *American Journal of Botany* **70**: 408–415.

Anderson, R.C., Dhillon, S.S. & Kelley, T.M. 1996. Aspects of the ecology of an invasive plant, garlic mustard (*Alliaria petiolata*), in Central Illinois. *Restoration Ecology* **4**: 181–191.

Anderson, V.L. 1927. Studies on the vegetation of the English chalk. V. The water economy of the chalk flora. *Journal of Ecology* **15**: 72–129.

Angus, S., Scott, S., Darwell, A. & Stewart, N.F. 2015. Bird's nest stonewort. Version 1.0. In Gaywood, M.J., Boon, P.J., Thompson, D.B.A. & Strachan, I.M. (Eds.) *The Species Action Framework Handbook* Scottish Natural Heritage, Battleby, Perth.

Antrobus, S. & Lack, A.J. 1993. Genetics of colonising and established populations of *Primula veris*. *Heredity* **71**: 252–258.

Arbeitsgruppe Characeen Deutschlands 2016. *Armleuchteralgen: Die Characeen Deutschlands*. Springer, Berlin.

Arrigo, N., Buerki, S., Sarr, A., Guadagnuolo, R. & Kozlowski, G. 2011. Phylogenetics and phylogeography of the monocot genus *Baldellia* (Alismataceae): Mediterranean refugia, suture zones and implications for conservation. *Molecular Phylogenetics and Evolution* **58**: 33–42.

Ash, G.J., Cother, E.J. & Tarleton, J. 2004. Variation in lanceleaved waterplantain (*Alisma lanceolatum*) in southeastern Australia. *Weed Science* **52**: 413–417.

Ashburner, K. & McAllister, H.A. 2013. *The Genus* Betula. *A Taxonomic Revision of Birches*. Kew Publishing, Kew.

Atkinson, M.D. 1992. Biological Flora of the British Isles. No. 175. *Betula pendula* Roth (*B. verrucosa* Ehrh.) and *B. pubescens* Ehrh. *Journal of Ecology* **80**: 837–870.

Atkinson, M.D. 1996. The distribution and naturalisation of *Lathraea clandestina* L. (Orobanchaceae) in the British Isles. *Watsonia* **21**: 119–128.

Atkinson, M.D. & Atkinson, E. 2002. Biological Flora of the British Isles. No. 225. *Sambucus nigra* L. *Journal of Ecology* **90**: 895–923.

Atkinson, M.D. & Atkinson, E. 2020. Biological Flora of the British Isles. No. 293. *Lathraea clandestina*. *Journal of Ecology* **108**: 2145–2168.

Auquier, P. 1971a. *Festuca rubra* L. subsp. *pruinosa* (Hack.) Piper: morphologie, écologie, taxonomie. *Lejeunia* **56**: 1–16.

Auquier, P. 1971b. Le problème de *Festuca rubra* L. subsp *arenaria* (Osb.) Richt. et de ses relations avec *F. juncifolia* St-Amans. *Lejeunia* **57**: 1–24.

Auquier, P. 1973. Une fétuque nouvelle de Bretagne: *Festuca huonii*. *Candollea* **28**: 15–19.

Babington, C.C. 1863. On the discovery of *Gladiolus illyricus* as a British plant. *Journal of Botany* **1**: 97–98.

Badmin, J.S. 1979. Recent records of *Puccinellia* Parl. in East Kent. *Watsonia* **12**: 390.

Bailey, C. 1884. Notes on the structure, the occurrence in Lancashire, and the source of origin of *Naias graminea* Delile var. *delilei* Magnus. *Journal of Botany, British and Foreign* **22**: 305–333.

Bailey, J.P. & Conolly, A.P. 1985. Chromosome number, morphology, pairing and DNA values of species and hybrids in the genus *Fallopia* (Polygonaceae). *Plant Systematics and Evolution* **180**: 29–52.

Bailey, J.P., Child, L.E. & Conolly, A.P. 1996. A survey of the distribution of *Fallopia ×bohemica* (Chrtek & Chrtkova) J.P. Bailey (Polygonaceae) in the British Isles. *Watsonia* **15**: 162–163.

Bailey, J.P. & Connolly, A.P. 2000. Prize-winners to pariahs - A history of Japanese Knotweed s.l. (Polygonaceae) in the British Isles. *Watsonia* **23**: 93–110.

Bailey, J.P. & Preston, C.D. 2011. Spatial separation of diploid and triploid *Butomus umbellatus* in Britain and Ireland. *New Journal of Botany* **1**: 28–32.

Bailey, T. & McPherson, S. 2016. *Carnivorous Plants of Britain and Ireland*. Redfern Natural History Productions, Poole.

Bain, J.F. 1991. The biology of Canadian weeds. 96. *Senecio jacobaea* L. *Canadian Journal of Plant Science* **71**: 127–140.

Bain, J.F., Desrochers, A.M. & Warwick, S.I. 1988. The biology of Canadian weeds. 89. *Carduus nutans* L. and *Carduus acanthoides* L. *Canadian Journal of Plant Science* **68**: 1053–1068.

Baker, A. & Pescott, O. 2014. How did *Polypogon viridis* (Water Bent) find itself on the streets of the British Isles? *BSBI News* **125**: 51–52.

Baker, H.G. 1947. Biological Flora of the British Isles. No. 19. *Melandrium* genus (Roehling emend.) Fries (pp. 271–274); *Melandrium album* (Mill.) Garcke (pp. 274–282); *Melandrium dioicum* (L. emend.) Coss. & Germ. (pp. 283–292). *Journal of Ecology* **35**: 271–292.

Baker, H.G. 1955. *Geranium purpureum* Vill. and *G. robertianum* L. in the British Flora: I. *Geranium purpureum*. *Watsonia* **3**: 160–167.

Baker, J.G. 1870. *Kniphofia praecox*. *Refugium Botanicum* **3**: 169.

Baker, K., Richards, A.J. & Tremayne, M. 1994. Fitness constraints on flower number, seed number and seed size in the dimorphic species *Primula farinosa* L. and *Armeria maritima* (Miller) Willd. *New Phytologist* **128**: 563–570.

Balao, F., Tannhauser, M., Lorenzo, M.T., Hedrén, M. & Paun, O. 2016. Genetic differentiation and admixture between sibling allopolyploids in the *Dactylorhiza majalis* complex. *Heredity* **116**: 351–361.

Balkow, K. 2020. A large colony of *Lysimachia europaea* (Chickweed Wintergreen) on Houndkirk Moor, Sheffield (vc. 57). *BSBI News* **145**: 26–227.

Ball, P.W. & Tutin, T.G. 1959. Notes on annual species of *Salicornia* in Britain. *Watsonia* **4**: 193–205.

Ballantyne, G.H. 1992. *Orobanche alba* Steph. ex Willd. in Fife (v.c. 85). *Watsonia* **19**: 39–41.

Ballantyne, G. 2013. *Pentaglottis sempervirens* (Green Alkanet) again. *BSBI News* **123**: 64.

Balme, O.E. 1954. Biological Flora of the British Isles. No. 40. *Viola lutea* Huds. *Journal of Ecology* **42**: 234–240.

Bangerter, E.B. 1964. *Veronica peregrina* L. in the British Isles. *Proceedings of the Botanical Society of the British Isles* **5**: 303–313.

Bangerter, E.B. 1966. Further notes on *Veronica peregrina* L. *Proceedings of the Botanical Society of the British Isles* **6**: 215–220.

Bangerter, E.B. & Kent, D.H. 1957. *Veronica filiformis* Sm. in the British Isles. *Proceedings of the Botanical Society of the British Isles* **2**: 197–217.

Bangerter, E.B. & Kent, D.H. 1962. Further notes on *Veronica filiformis*. *Proceedings of the Botanical Society of the British Isles* **4**: 384–397.

Bangerter, E.B. & Kent, D.H. 1965. Additional notes on *Veronica filiformis*. *Proceedings of the Botanical Society of the British Isles* **6**: 113–118.

Bangerter, E.B., Cannon, J.F.M. & Jermy, A.C. 1978. Ferns and their allies. In Jermy, A.C. & Crabble, J.A. (Eds.) *The Island of Mull: a survey of its flora and environment* pp. 12.1–12.7 British Museum (Natural History), London.

Bannister, P. 1965. Biological Flora of the British Isles. No. 100. *Erica cinerea* L. *Journal of Ecology* **53**: 527–542.

Bannister, P. 1966. Biological Flora of the British Isles. No. 102. *Erica tetralix* L. *Journal of Ecology* **54**: 795–813.

Barling, D.M. 1955. *Tragopogon pratensis* in the central Cotswolds. *Watsonia* **3**: 210–212.

Barling, D.M. 1959. Biological studies in *Poa angustifolia*. *Watsonia* **4**: 147–168.

Barling, D.M. 1962. Studies in the biology of *Poa subcaerulea* Sm. *Watsonia* **5**: 163–173.

Barling, D.M. 1967. *Poa pratensis* L., *P. angustifolia* L. and *P. subcaerulea* Sm. *Proceedings of the Botanical Society of the British Isles* **6**: 363–364.

Barlow, D. 2020. *Rare Plant Register for V.C. 62 (North-east Yorkshire)*.

Barnard, K. 2014. Monitoring Populations of *Saxifraga cespitosa* in Scotland. *Sibbaldia: The Journal of Botanic Garden Horticulture* **12**: 99–110.

Barrat-Segretain, M.H., Elger, A., Sagnes, P. & Puijalon, S. 2002. Comparison of three life-history traits of invasive *Elodea canadensis* Michx. and *Elodea nuttallii* (Planch.) H. St. John. *Aquatic Botany* **74**: 299–313.

Barty-King, H. 1977. *A tradition of English wine*. Oxford Illustrated Press, Oxford.

Baskin, J.M. & Baskin, C.C. 1990. Role of temperature and light in the germination ecology of buried seeds of *Potentilla recta*. *Annals of Applied Biology* **117**: 611–616.

Bassett, I.J. & Crompton, C.W. 1975. The biology of Canadian weeds. 11. *Ambrosia artemisiifolia* L. and *A. psilostachya* DC. *Canadian Journal of Plant Science* **55**: 463–476.

Bassett, I.J., Crompton, C.W. & Woodland, D.W. 1977. The biology of Canadian weeds. 21. *Urtica dioica* L. *Canadian Journal of Plant Science* **57**: 491–498.

Bassett, I.J. & Crompton, C.W. 1978. The biology of Canadian weeds. 32. *Chenopodium album* L. *Canadian Journal of Plant Science* **58**: 1061–1072.

Bassett, I.J. & Munro, D.B. 1985. The biology of Canadian weeds. 67. *Solanum ptycanthum* Dun., *S. nigrum* L. and *S. sarrachoides* Sendt. *Canadian Journal of Plant Science* **65**: 401–414.

Bassett, I.J. & Munro, D.B. 1987. The biology of Canadian weeds. 81. *Atriplex patula* L., *A. prostrata* Boucher ex DC, and *A. rosea* L. *Canadian Journal of Plant Science* **67**: 1069–1082.

Bateman, R.M. 1981. The Hertfordshire Orchidaceae. *Transactions of the Hertfordshire Natural History Society* **28(4)**: 56–79.

Bateman, R.M. 2004. Hybridisation evidence supports the new improved *Anacamptis*. *Journal of the Hardy Orchid Society* **1**: 34–42.

Bateman, R.M. 2006. How many orchid species are currently native to the British Isles? In Bailey, J.P. & Ellis, R.G. (Eds.) *Current taxonomic research on the British and European flora* pp. 89–110 + Plate 1 BSBI Conference Report No. 25 Botanical Society of the British Isles, London.

Bateman, R.M. 2007. Whatever happened to the genus *Orchis*? *Orchid Review* **115**: 322–329.

Bateman, R.M. 2009. Evolutionary classification of European orchids: the crucial importance of maximising explicit evidence and minimising authoritarian speculation. *Journal Europäischer Orchideen* **41**: 243–318.

Bateman, R.M. 2010. The Ghost Orchid vividly illustrates why the term 'extirpation' is an essential element of plant conservation. *BSBI News* **113**: 8–10.

Bateman, R.M. 2011a. Two steps forward, one step back: deciphering British and Irish marsh-orchids. *Journal of the Hardy Orchid Society* **8**: 48–59.

Bateman, R.M. 2011b. Glacial progress: do we finally understand the narrow-leaved marsh-orchids? *New Journal of Botany* **1**: 2–15.

Bateman, R.M. 2012a. Circumscribing genera in the European orchid flora: a subjective critique of recent contributions. *Berichte aus den Arbeitskreisen Heimische Orchideen* **29**: 92–124.

Bateman, R.M. 2012b. Circumscribing species in the European orchid flora: multiple datasets interpreted in the context of speciation mechanisms. *Berichte aus den Arbeitskreisen Heimische Orchideen* **29**: 160–212.

Bateman, R.M. 2018a. Two bees or not two bees? An overview of *Ophrys* systematics. *Berichte aus den Arbeitskreisen Heimische Orchideen* **35**: 5–46.

Bateman, R.M. 2018b. Systematics research into hardy orchids: recent successes and future prospects. *Journal of the Hardy Orchid Society* **15**: 114–132.

Bateman, R.M. 2019. Next-generation Dactylorchids. *Journal of the Hardy Orchid Society* **16**: 114–128.

Bateman, R.M. 2020a. Residual myths in molecular systematics. *BSBI News* **145**: 5–13.

Bateman, R.M. 2020b. False Pugsley's Marsh-orchid. *Journal of the Hardy Orchid Society* **17**: 87–97.

Bateman, R.M. 2020c. Implications of next-generation sequencing for the systematics and evolution of the terrestrial orchid genus *Epipactis*, with particular reference to the British Isles. *Kew Bulletin* **75**: 1–22.

Bateman, R.M. 2021a. *Epipactis* 'neglecta var. collina' fails the tests of biological cohesion and basic logic. *Berichte aus den Arbeitskreisen Heimische Orchideen* **38**: 1–8.

Bateman, R.M. 2021b. Challenges of applying monophyly in the phylogenetic shallows: taxonomic reappraisal of the *Dactylorhiza maculata* group. *Kew Bulletin* **76**: 675–704.

Bateman, R.M. 2021c. Phenotypic versus genotypic disparity in the Eurasian orchid genus *Gymnadenia*: exploring the limits of phylogeny reconstruction. *Systematics and Biodiversity* **19**: 400–422.

Bateman, R.M. 2022. Systematics and conservation of British and Irish orchids: a "state of the union" assessment to accompany Atlas 2020. *Kew Bulletin* **77**: 355–402.

Bateman, R.M. & Denholm, I. 1983a. A reappraisal of the British and Irish dactylorchids, 1. The tetraploid marsh-orchids. *Watsonia* **14**: 347–376.

Bateman, R.M. & Denholm, I. 1983b. *Dactylorhiza incarnata* (L.) Soó. subsp. *ochroleuca* (Boll) P. F. Hunt & Summerhayes. *Watsonia* **14**: 410–411.

Bateman, R.M. & Denholm, I. 1985. A reappraisal of the British and Irish dactylorchids, 2. The diploid marsh-orchids. *Watsonia* **15**: 321–355.

Bateman, R.M. & Farrington, O.S. 1989. Morphometric comparison of populations of *Orchis simia* Lam. (Orchidaceae) from Oxfordshire and Kent. *Botanical Journal of the Linnean Society* **100**: 205–218.

Bateman, R.M. & Denholm, I. 1989. A reappraisal of the British and Irish dactylorchids, 3. The spotted-orchids. *Watsonia* **17**: 319–349.

Bateman, R.M., Pridgeon, A.M. & Chase, M.W. 1997. Phylogenetics of subtribe Orchidinae (Orchidoideae, Orchidaceae) based on nuclear ITS sequences. 2. Infrageneric relationships and taxonomic revision to achieve monophyly of *Orchis* sensu stricto. *Lindleyana* **12**: 113–141.

Bateman, R.M. & Denholm, I. 2003. The Heath Spotted-orchid (*Dactylorhiza maculata* (L.) Soó) in the British Isles: a cautionary case-study in delimitating infraspecific taxa and inferring their evolutionary relationships. *Journal Europäischer Orchideen* **35**: 3–36.

Bateman, R.M., Hollingsworth, P.M., Preston, J., Luo, Y.-B., Pridgeon, A.M. & Chase, M.W. 2003. Molecular phylogenetics and evolution of Orchidinae and selected Habenariinae (Orchidaceae). *Botanical Journal of the Linnean Society* **142**: 1–40.

Bateman, R.M., Hollingsworth, P.M., Squirrell, J. & Hollingsworth, M.L. 2005. Phylogenetics: Neottieae. In Pridgeon, A.M., Cribb, P.L., Chase, M.W. & Rasmussen, F.N. (Eds.) *Genera Orchidacearum, 4. Epidendroideae 1* pp. 487–495 Oxford University Press, Oxford.

Bateman, R.M., Smith, R.J. & Fay, M.F. 2008. Morphometric and population-genetic analyses elucidate the origin, evolutionary significance and conservation implications of *Orchis ×angusticruris* (*O. purpurea* × *O. simia*), a hybrid orchid new to Britain. *Botanical Journal of the Linnean Society* **157**: 687–711.

Bateman, R.M. & Rudall, P.J. 2011. The life and death of a mythical British endemic, *Orchis militaris* L. var. *tenuifrons* P.D. Sell: why infraspecific taxonomy requires a field-based morphometric approach. *New Journal of Botany* **1**: 98–110.

Bateman, R.M., Bradshaw, E., Devey, D.S., Glover, B.J., Malmgren, S., Sramko, G., Thomas, M.M. & Rudall, P.J. 2011. Species arguments: clarifying concepts of species delimitation in the pseudo-copulatory orchid genus *Ophrys*. *Botanical Journal of the Linnean Society* **165**: 336–347.

Bateman, R.M. & Denholm, I. 2012. Taxonomic reassessment of the British and Irish tetraploid marsh-orchids. *New Journal of Botany* **2**: 37–55.

Bateman, R.M., James, K.E. & Rudall, P.J. 2012. Contrast in morphological versus molecular divergence between two closely related Eurasian species of *Platanthera* (Orchidaceae) suggests recent evolution with a strong allometric component. *New Journal of Botany* **2**: 110–148.

Bateman, R.M., Rudall, P.J., Hawkins, J.A. & Sramkó, G. 2013. *Himantoglossum hircinum* (Lizard Orchid) reviewed in the light of new morphological and molecular observations. *New Journal of Botany* 3: 122–140.

Bateman, R.M. & Rudall, P.J. 2014. Bumblebee-mediated pollination of English populations of the Military Orchid (*Orchis militaris* L.): its possible relevance to functional morphology, life history and climate change. *New Journal of Botany* 4: 122–133.

Bateman, R.M., Rudall, P.J., Bidartondo, M.I., Cozzolino, S., Tranchida-Lombardo, V., Carine, M.A. & Moura, M. 2014. Speciation via floral heterochrony and presumed mycorrhizal host-switching of endemic butterfly orchids on the Azorean archipelago. *American Journal of Botany* 101: 979–1001.

Bateman, R.M. & Rudall, P.J. 2017. Clarified relationship between *Dactylorhiza viridis* and *Dactylorhiza iberica* renders obsolete the former genus *Coeloglossum* (Orchidaceae: Orchidinae). *Kew Bulletin* 73: 4.

Bateman, R.M., Rudall, P.J. & Denholm, I. 2017a. Morphometric comparison of British *Pseudorchis albida* with Icelandic *Pseudorchis straminea* (Orchidaceae: Orchidinae). *New Journal of Botany* 7: 78–93.

Bateman, R.M., Molnár, A.V. & Sramkó, G. 2017b. *In situ* morphometric survey elucidates the evolutionary systematics of the Eurasian *Himantoglossum* clade (Orchidaceae: Orchidinae). *PeerJ* 5: e2893.

Bateman, R.M. & Rudall, P.J. 2018. Clarified relationship between *Dactylorhiza viridis* and *Dactylorhiza iberica* renders obsolete the former genus *Coeloglossum* (Orchidaceae: Orchidinae). *Kew Bulletin* 73: 1–17.

Bateman, R.M., Sramkó, G. & Paun, O. 2018a. Integrating restriction site-associated DNA sequencing (RAD-seq) with morphological cladistic analysis clarifies evolutionary relationships among major species groups of bee orchids. *Annals of Botany* 121: 85–105.

Bateman, R.M., Murphy, A.R.M., Hollingsworth, P.M., Hart, M.L., Denholm, I. & Rudall, P.J. 2018b. Molecular and morphological phylogenetics of the digitate-tubered clade within subtribe Orchidinae s.s. (Orchidaceae: Orchidinae). *Kew Bulletin* 73: 54.

Bateman, R.M. & Denholm, I. 2019. Mapping the near-cryptic Fragrant Orchids of Britain and Ireland. *BSBI News* 140: 6–12.

Bateman, R.M., Rudall, P.J., Murphy, A.R.M., Cowan, R.S., Devey, D.S. & Pérez-Escobar, O.A. 2021a. Even whole plastomes are not enough: phylogenomic and morphometric exploration at multiple demographic levels of the bee orchid clade *Ophrys* sect. Sphegodes. *Journal of Experimental Botany* 72: 654–681.

Bateman, R.M., Denholm, I. & Rudall, P.J. 2021b. *In situ* morphometric survey elucidates the evolutionary systematics of the orchid genus *Gymnadenia* in the British Isles. *Systematics and Biodiversity* 19: 571–600.

Baude, M., Kunin, W., Boatman, N., Conyers, S., Davies, N., Gillespie, M.A.K., Morton, R.D., Smart, S.M. & Memmott, J. 2016. Historical nectar assessment reveals the fall and rise of floral resources in Britain. *Nature* 530: 85–88.

Baum, A. & Baum, H. 2017. *Platanthera muelleri* – eine dritte Art in der *Platanthera bifolia/chlorantha* Gruppe in Mitteleuropa. *Journal Europäischer Orchideen* 49: 133–152.

Baumel, A., Youssef, S., Ongamo, G. & Médail, F. 2013. Habitat suitability assessment of the rare perennial plant *Armeria arenaria* (Pers.) Schult. (Plumbaginaceae) along the French Mediterranean coastline. *Candollea* 68: 221–228.

Beales, P.W. 1980. The Late Devensian and Flandrian vegetational history of Crose Mere, Shropshire. *New Phytologist* 85: 133–161.

Bean, W.J. 1970. *Trees and shrubs hardy in the British Isles* I (A-C) Edn. 8. John Murray, London.

Bean, W.J. 1973. *Trees and shrubs hardy in the British Isles* II (D-M) Edn. 8. John Murray, London.

Bean, W.J. 1976. *Trees and shrubs hardy in the British Isles* III (N-Rh) Edn. 8. John Murray, London.

Bean, W.J. (Ed.) 1980. *Trees and shrubs hardy in the British Isles* IV (Ri-Z) Edn. 8. John Murray, London.

Beattie, A.J. 1972. The pollination ecology of *Viola*. 2, Pollen loads of insect-visitors. *Watsonia* 9: 13–25.

Beatty, G.E., McEvoy, P.M., Sweeney, O. & Provan, J. 2008. Range-edge effects promote clonal growth in peripheral populations of the one-sided wintergreen *Orthilia secunda*. *Diversity and Distributions* 14: 546–555.

Beatty, G.E. & Provan, J. 2013. Post-glacial dispersal, rather than *in situ* glacial survival, best explains the disjunct distribution of the Lusitanian plant species *Daboecia cantabrica* (Ericaceae). *Journal of Biogeography* 40: 335–344.

Beatty, G.E., Reid, N. & Provan, J. 2014. Restrospective genetic monitoring of the threatened Yellow marsh saxifrage (*Saxifraga hirculus*) reveals genetic erosion but provides valuable information for conservation strategies. *Diversity and Distributions* 20: 529–537.

Beatty, G.E., Lennon, J.J., O'Sullivan, C.J. & Provan, J. 2015. The not-so-Irish spurge: *Euphorbia hyberna* (Euphorbiaceae) and the Littletonian plant 'steeplechase'. *Biological Journal of the Linnean Society* 114: 249–259.

Beck, H.M. 2022. Viola rupestris *on Ingleborough: A New Perspective*. Unpublished report for Natural England.

Beckett, G. & Bull, A. 1999. *A Flora of Norfolk*. Self-published, Norwich.

Beddows, A.R. 1959. Biological Flora of the British Isles. No. 68. *Dactylis glomerata* L. *Journal of Ecology* 47: 223–239.

Beddows, A.R. 1961. Biological Flora of the British Isles. No. 77. *Holcus lanatus* L. *Journal of Ecology* 49: 421–430.

Beddows, A.R. 1967. Biological Flora of the British Isles. No. 107. *Lolium perenne* L. *Journal of Ecology* 55: 567–587.

Beddows, A.R. 1973. Biological Flora of the British Isles. No. 131. *Lolium multiflorum* Lam. *Journal of Ecology* 61: 587–600.

Beecroft, R., Cadbury, C.J. & Mountford, J.O. 2007. Water Germander *Teucrium scordium* in Cambridgeshire: back from the brink of extinction. *Watsonia* 26: 303–316.

Beerling, D.J. 1998. Biological Flora of the British Isles. No. 202. *Salix herbacea* L. *Journal of Ecology* 86: 872–895.

Beerling, D.J. & Perrins, J.M. 1993. Biological Flora of the British Isles. No. 177. *Impatiens glandulifera* Royle. *Journal of Ecology* 81: 367–382.

Beerling, D.J., Bailey, J.P. & Conolly, A.P. 1994. Biological Flora of the British Isles. No. 183. *Fallopia japonica* (Houtt.) Ronse Decraene. *Journal of Ecology* 82: 959–979.

Beitel, J. & Buck, W.R. 1988. The use of subspecies in the *Dryopteris affinis* complex. *Fiddlehead Forum* 15: 15–16.

Bell, M. 2000. *The Gardener's guide to growing Temperate Bamboos*. David & Charles, Newton Abbot.

Bell, J.N.B. & Tallis, J.H. 1973. Biological Flora of the British Isles. No. 130. *Empetrum nigrum* L. *Journal of Ecology* 61: 289–305.

Belyaeva, I.M. 2009. Nomenclature of *Salix fragilis* L. and a new species, *Salix euxina* (Salicaceae). *Taxon* 58: 1344–1348.

Bennallick, I. 2010. *Centaurium scilloides, Juncus subnodulosus* and *Phegopteris connectilis* rediscovered in Cornwall after many years. *BSBI News* 115: 30–34.

Bennion, H., Sayer, C.D., Clarke, S.J., Davidson, T.A., Rose, N.L., Goldsmith, B., Rawcliffe, R., Burgess, A., Clarke, G., Turner, S. & Wiik, E. 2018. Sedimentary macrofossil records reveal ecological change in English lakes: implications for conservation. *Journal of Paleolimnology* 60: 329–348.

Bergfeld, D. 2017. Beobachtungen an skandinavischen Orchideen. *Journal Europäischer Orchideen* 49: 3–47.

Berry, P.M., Dawson, T.P., Harrison, P.A., Pearson, R. & Butt, N. 2003. The sensitivity and vulnerability of terrestrial habitats and species in Britain and Ireland to climate change. *Journal for Nature Conservation* 11: 15–23.

Bertelli, C.M., Robinson, M.T., Mendzil, A.F., Pratt, L.R. & Unsworth, R.K. 2018. Finding some seagrass optimism in Wales, the case of *Zostera noltii*. *Marine Pollution Bulletin* 134: 216–222.

Best, K.F. 1977. The biology of Canadian weeds. 22. *Descurainia sophia* (L.) Webb. *Canadian Journal of Plant Science* 57: 499–507.

Best, K.F. & McIntyre, G.I. 1975. The biology of Canadian weeds. 9. *Thlaspi arvense* L. *Canadian Journal of Plant Science* 55: 279–292.

Best, K.F., Banting, J.D. & Bowess, G.G. 1978. The biology of Canadian weeds. 31. *Hordeum jubatum* L. *Canadian Journal of Plant Science* 58: 699–708.

Best, K.F., Bowes, G.G., Thomas, A.G. & Maw, M.G. 1980. The biology of Canadian weeds. 39. *Euphorbia esula* L. *Canadian Journal of Plant Science* 60: 651–663.

Bezzant, L. 1992. *Lychnis flos-cuculi* - dwarf form. *Rock garden* 22: 423.

Biesmeijer, J.C., Roberts, S.P.M., Reemer, M., Ohlemüller, R., Edwards, M., Peeters, T., Schaffers, A.P., Potts, S.G., Kleukers, R., Thomas, C.D., Settele, J. & Kunin, W.E. 2006. Parallel declines in pollinators and insect-pollinated plants in Britain and the Netherlands. *Science* 213: 351–354.

Bijlsma, R.-J. 2013. *The estimation of species richness of Dutch bryophytes between 1900 and 2011. Documentation of VBA-procedures based on the Frescalo program*. BLWG-report 15. Dutch Bryological and Lichenological Society, Gouda, the Netherlands.

Birkinshaw, C.R. 1994. Aspects of the ecology and conservation of *Damasonium alisma* Miller in Western Europe. *Watsonia* 20: 33–39.

Birkinshaw, C.R. & Sanford, M.N. 1996. *Pulmonaria obscura* Dumort. (Boraginaceae) in Suffolk. *Watsonia* 21: 169–178.

Birkinshaw, N., Kemp, E. & Clarke, S. 2013. *The ecology of grass-wrack pondweed* Potamogeton compressus. Natural England Commissioned Reports, Number 130. Natural England, Peterborough.

Birse, E.M. 1997. Creeping spearwort, *Ranunculus reptans* L., at the Loch of Strathbeg. *BSBI News* 74: 17–19.

Bishop, G.F. & Davy, A.J. 1994. Biological Flora of the British Isles. No. 180. *Hieracium pilosella* L. *Journal of Ecology* 82: 195–210.

Bishop, G.F., Davy, A.J. & Costa, C.S.B. 2001. *Salicornia* L. (*Salicornia pusilla* J. Woods, *S. ramosissima* J. Woods, *S. europaea* L., *S. obscura* P.W. Ball & Tutin, *S. nitens* P.W. Ball & Tutin, *S. fragilis* P.W. Ball & Tutin and *S. dolichostachya* Moss). *Journal of Ecology* 89: 681–707.

Bishop, I.J., Bennion, H., Sayer, C.D., Patmore, I.R. & Yang, H. 2019. Filling the "data gap": Using paleoecology to investigate the decline of *Najas flexilis* (a rare aquatic plant). *Geo: Geography and Environment* 6.

Bishop, M., Davis, A. & Grimshaw, J. 2006. *Snowdrops: A Monograph of Cultivated Galanthus*. Griffin Press, Cheltenham.

Bittrich, V. & Kadereit, J. 1988. Cytogenetical and geographical aspects of sterility in *Lysimachia nummularia*. *Nordic Journal of Botany* 8: 325–328.

Bizot, A. 2015. Biométrie stomatique et identification des taxons du complexe *Dryopteris affinis*. *Bulletin de la Société d'Histoire Naturelle des Ardennes* 104: 69–85.

Black, L. & Warwick, S.I. 1982. The biology of Canadian weeds. 52. *Achillea millefolium* L. *s.l. Canadian Journal of Plant Science* 62: 163–182.

Blackhall-Miles, R. 2021. Discovery of a second extant plant of Arran's false rowan (*Sorbus pseudomeinichii* Ashley Robertson). *BSBI News* 146: 15–16.

Blackman, G.E. & Rutter, A.J. 1954. Biological Flora of the British Isles. No. 45. *Endymion non-scriptus* (L.) Garcke. *Journal of Ecology* **42**: 629–638.

Blackstock, T.H. 1981. The distribution of *Juncus filiformis* L. in Britain. *Watsonia* **13**: 209–214.

Blackstock, T.H., Howe, E.A. & Rimes, C.A. 1991. Whorled Caraway, *Carum verticillatum* (L.) Koch in Lleyn. *BSBI Welsh Bulletin* **51**: 8–10.

Blackstock, T.H. & Roberts, R.H. 1998. *Trifolium occidentale* D. E. Coombe (Fabaceae) in Anglesey (v.c. 52). *Watsonia* **22**: 182–184.

Blackstock, N. & Jermy, A.C. 2001. Identification – Yellow-sedges *Carex flava* aggregate. *British Wildlife* **12**: 345–351.

Blackstock, N. & Ashton, P.A. 2001. A reassessment of the putative *Carex flava* agg. (Cyperaceae) hybrids at Malham Tarn (v.c. 64): A morphometric analysis. *Watsonia* **23**: 505–516.

Blanchard, J.W. 1990. *Narcissus - A guide to wild daffodils*. Alpine Garden Society, Woking.

Bleasdale, A. 1994. *The Arable Weed Flora of the Rye Crop on the Aran Islands, Co. Galway*. Unpublished report for the National Parks and Wildlife Service of the Office of Public Works.

Blindow, I. & Langangen, A. 1995a. *Lamprothamnium papulosum* (Wallr) J. Groves, a threatened stonewort in Scandinavia. *Cryptogamie Algologie* **16**: 47–55.

Blindow, I. & Langangen, A. 1995b. Kransalgen *Lamprothamnium papulosum* i Sverige [The stonewort *Lamprothamnium papulosum* in Sweden]. *Svensk Botanisk Tidskrift* **89**: 171–174.

Blockeel, T.L., Bosanquet, S.D.S., Hill, M.O. & Preston, C.D. (Eds.) 2014. *Atlas of British & Irish Bryophytes*, 2 vols. Pisces Publications, Newbury.

Blomgren, E. 1992. Portlakmålla *Halimione portulacoides*, funnen i Bohuslån. *Halimione portulacoides* found on the western coast of Sweden. *Svensk Botanisk Tidskrift* **86**: 61–62.

Böcher, T.W. 1940. Studies on the plant-geography of the North-Atlantic heath-formation I. The heaths of the Faroes. In *Det Kongelige Danske Videnskabernes Selskabs* pp. 1–64 Biologiske Meddelelser. XV, 3. E. Munksgaard, Copenhagen.

Bolton, J. 1790. *Filices Britannicae - an History of the British proper ferns*. John Binns, Leeds.

Bond, T.E.T. 1952. Biological Flora of the British Isles. No. 35. *Elymus arenarius* L. *Journal of Ecology* **40**: 217–227.

Boon, C.R. & Outen, A.R. 2011. *Flora of Bedfordshire*. Bedfordshire Natural History Society, Bedford.

Boorman, L.A. 1967. Biological Flora of the British Isles. No. 106. *Limonium vulgare* Mill. and *Limonium humile* Mill. *Journal of Ecology* **55**: 221–229.

Boorman, L.A. & Fuller, R.M. 1984. The comparative ecology of two sand dune biennials: *Lactuca virosa* L. & *Cynoglossum officinale* L. *New Phytologist* **96**: 609–629.

Booy, O., Wade, M. & Roy, H. 2015. *Field guide to invasive plants and animals in Britain*. Bloomsbury Publishing, London.

Borrell, J.S., Wang, N., Nichols, R.A. & Buggs, R.J. 2018. Genetic diversity maintained among fragmented populations of a tree undergoing range contraction. *Heredity* **121**: 304–318.

Borrer, W. 1832. *Rumex pratensis*. In Hooker, W.J. (Ed.) *Supplement to the English Botany of the Late Sir J.E. Smith and Mr Sowerby* **2**: t2757.

Borum, J., Duarte, C.M., Krause-Jensen, D. & Greve, T.M. (Eds.) 2004. *European seagrasses: an introduction to monitoring and management*. Monitoring and Managing of European Seagrasses Project.

Boucher, A. & Partridge, J. 2006. *Urtica membranacea*, an annual nettle, in Warwick: a first British record? *BSBI News* **103**: 29–30.

Bournérias, M. & Prat, D. (Eds.) 2005. *Les orchidées de France, Belgique et Luxembourg*. Edn. 2. Biotope: Mezé.

Bowen, H.J.M. 1968. *The Flora of Berkshire*. Holywell Press, Oxford.

Bowen, H. 2000. *The Flora of Dorset*. Pisces publications, Berkshire.

Bowra, J.C. 1992. Prickly Lettuce (*Lactuca serriola*) - a population explosion in Warwickshire. *BSBI News* **60**: 12–16.

Bowra, J.C. 1999. *Oenothera* (evening-primroses) - the way forward. *BSBI News* **81**: 24–26.

Boyce, P. 1993. *The genus Arum*. HMSO, London.

Boyd, R.J., Powney, G.D., Burns, F., Danet, A., Duchenne, F., Grainger, M.J., Jarvis, S.G., Martin, G., Nilsen, E.B., Porcher, E., Stewart, G.B., Wilson, O.J. & Pescott, O.L. 2022. ROBITT: A tool for assessing the risk-of-bias in studies of temporal trends in ecology. *Methods in Ecology and Evolution* **13**: 1497–1507,.

Bożek, M. 2019. Characteristics of blooming, pollen production, and insect visitors of *Polemonium caeruleum* L. – a species with a potential to enrich pollinator-friendly urban habitats. *Acta Agrobotanica* **72**: 1795.

Bradshaw, M.E. 1962. The distribution and status of five species of the *Alchemilla vulgaris* L. aggregate in Upper Teesdale. *Journal of Ecology* **50**: 681–706.

Bradshaw, M.E. 2009. The decline of Lady's-mantles (*Alchemilla vulgaris* L. agg.) and other hay-meadow species in Northern England since the 1950s. *Watsonia* **27**: 315–321.

Braithwaite, M.E. 1991. The Scottish cabbage patch. New Zealand Bittercress, *Cardamine uniflora*. *BSBI News* **58**: 38–39.

Braithwaite, M.E. 2004. *Tofieldia pusilla* (Michx.) Pers. at the Scottish Border. *Watsonia* **25**: 207–208.

Braithwaite, M.E. 2010a. A wake-up call for the future of Britain's montane flora? *Sedum villosum* in decline in Berwickshire. *BSBI News* **115**: 15–17.

Braithwaite, M.E. 2010b. Berwickshire's disappearing scarce plants. *Watsonia* **28**: 129–140 .

Braithwaite, M.E. 2014. *A short Flora of Berwickshire*. Privately published, Roxburghshire.

Braithwaite, M.E. 2021. Scotland's heritage of naturalised medicinal plants. *British & Irish Botany* **3**: 74–89.

Braithwaite, M.E., Ellis, R.W. & Preston, C.D. 2006. *Change in the British Flora 1987– 2004*. Botanical Society of the British Isles, London.

Brandrud, M.K., Paun, O., Lorenz, R., Baar, J. & Hedrén, M. 2019. Restriction-site associated DNA sequencing supports a sister group relationship of *Nigritella* and *Gymnadenia*. *Molecular Phylogenetics and Evolution* **136**: 21–28.

Brandrud, M.K., Baar, J., Lorenzo, M.T., Athanasiadis, A., Bateman, R.M., Chase, M.W., Hedrén, M. & Paun, O. 2020. Phylogenomic relationships of diploids and the origins of allotetraploids in *Dactylorhiza* (Orchidaceae): RADseq data track reticulate evolution. *Systematic Biology* **61**: 91–109.

Breitkopf, H., Schlüter, P.M., Xu, S., Schiestl, F.P., Cozzolino, S. & Scopece, G. 2013. Pollinator shifts between *Ophrys sphegodes* populations: might adaptation to different pollinators drive population divergence? *Journal of Evolutionary Biology* **26**: 2197–2208.

Brenan, J.P.M. 1950. *Artemisia verlotorum* Lamotte and its occurrence in Britain. *Watsonia* **1**: 209–223.

Brenan, J.P.M. 1961. *Amaranthus* in Britain. *Watsonia* **6**: 261–280.

Brennan, R.M. 2006. Currants and Gooseberries. *Ribes* species. Saxifragaceae. In Janick, J. & Paull, R.E. (Eds.) *Encyclopedia of Fruit and Nut Crops* CABI.

Brewis, A., Bowman, R.P. & Rose, F. 1996. *The Flora of Hampshire*. Harley Books, Colchester.

Brickell, C. (Ed.) 2016. *RHS A-Z encyclopedia of garden plants*. Edn. 4. Dorling Kindersley, London.

Briggs, D., Block, M. & Jennings, S. 1989. The possibility of determining the age of colonies of clonally propagating herbaceous species from historic records: the case of *Aster novi-belgii* L. (first recorded as *A. salignus* Willd.) at Wicken Fen Nature Reserve, Cambridgeshire, England. *New Phytologist* **112**: 577–584.

Briggs, D. & Walters, S.M. 1984. *Plant Variation and Evolution*. Edn. 2. Cambridge University Press, Cambridge.

Briggs, J. 1999. *Kissing Goodbye to Mistletoe*. Plantlife and the Botanical Society of the British Isles, London.

Briggs, M. 1997. *Phacelia tanacetifolia*. *BSBI News* **74**: 48.

Brightmore, D. 1968. Biological Flora of the British Isles. No. 112. *Lobelia urens* L. *Journal of Ecology* **56**: 613–620.

Brightmore, D. 1979. Biological Flora of the British Isles. No. 146. *Frankenia laevis* L. *Journal of Ecology* **67**: 1097–1107.

Brightmore, D. & White, P.H.F. 1963. Biological Flora of the British Isles. No. 94. *Lathyrus japonicus* Willd. *Journal of Ecology* **51**: 795–801.

Britton, A.J., Marrs, R., Pakeman, R. & Carey, P. 2003. The influence of soil-type, drought and nitrogen addition on interactions between *Calluna vulgaris* and *Deschampsia flexuosa*: implications for heathland regeneration. *Plant Ecology* **166**: 93–105.

Britton, A.J., Beale, C., Towers, W. & Hewison, R.L. 2009. Biodiversity gains and losses: Evidence for homogenisation of Scottish alpine vegetation. *Biological Conservation* **142**: 1728–1739.

Broads Authority 1983 – 2016. *Broads annual plant monitoring reports*. Broads Authority, Norwich.

Brock, T.C.M., Mielo, H. & Oostermeijer, G. 1989. On the lifecycle and germination of *Hottonia palustris* L. in a wetland forest. *Aquatic Botany* **35**: 153–166.

Broderick, D.H. 1990. The biology of Canadian weeds. 93. *Epilobium angustifolium* L. (Onagraceae). *Canadian Journal of Plant Science* **70**: 247–259.

Brown, J.M.B. 1953. *Studies on British beechwoods. Forestry Commission Bulletin No. 20*. HMSO, London.

Bruinsma, J.H.P. 1996. Het voorkomen van Haarfonteinkruid (*Potamogeton trichoides* Cham. ex Schld.) op het Plistoceen van Zuid-Nederland. [*Potamogeton trichoides* Cham. ex Schld. on Pleistocene soils in the southern part of the Netherlands.]. *Gorteria* **22**: 6–13.

Brummitt, R.K. 1996. Two subspecies of *Calystegia silvatica* (Kit.) Griseb. Convolvulaceae in the mediterranean region. *Lagascalia* **18**: 338–340.

Brummitt, R.K. & Heywood, V.H. 1960. Pink-flowered Calystegiae of the *Calystegia sepium* complex in the British Isles. *Proceedings of the Botanical Society of the British Isles* **3**: 384–388.

Brummitt, R.K. & Chater, A.O. 2000. *Calystegia* (Convolvulaceae) hybrids in West Wales. *Watsonia* **23**: 161–165.

Bruun, H.H. 2005. Biological Flora of the British Isles. No. 239. *Rosa rugosa* Thunb. ex Murray. *Journal of Ecology* **93**: 441–470.

Brys, R. & Jacquemyn, H. 2009. Biological Flora of the British Isles. No. 253. *Primula veris* L. *Journal of Ecology* **97**: 581–600.

Brys, R. & Jacquemyn, H. 2016. Severe outbreeding and inbreeding depression maintain mating system differentiation in *Epipactis* (Orchidaceae). *Journal of Evolutionary Biology* **29**: 352–359.

Brysting, A.K. 2008. The arctic mouse-ear in Scotland – and why it is not arctic. *Plant Ecology & Diversity* **1**: 321–327.

Brysting, A.K., Gabrielsen, T.M., Sørlibråten, O., Ytrehorn, O. & Brochmann, C. 1996. The Purple Saxifrage, *Saxifraga oppositifolia*, in Svalbard: two taxa or one? *Polar Research* **15**: 93–105.

Brzosko, E., Wróblewska, A., Jermakowicz, E. & Hermaniuk, A. 2013. High level of genetic variation within clonal orchid *Goodyera repens*. *Plant Systematics and Evolution* **299**: 1537–1548.

Buckland, M. 2022. *The Rare Plant Register of Wiltshire*. Wiltshire Botanical Society.

Bujnoch, W. 2015. A contribution to the phylogeny of *Dryopteris remota* by genotyping of a fragment of the nuclear PgiC gene. *Fern Gazette* **20**: 79–89.

Bullard, E.R., Shearer, H.D.H., Day, J.D. & Crawford, R.M.M. 1987. Survival and flowering of *Primula scotica* Hook. *Journal of Ecology* **75**: 589–602.

Bullock, J.M. & Kirchner, F. 1999. Taxonomic separation of *Ulex minor* Roth. and *U. gallii* Planch.: morphometrics and chromosome counts. *Watsonia* **22**: 365–376.

Bullock, J.M., Chapman, D., Schafer, S., Roy, D., Girardello, M., Haynes, T., Beal, S., Wheeler, S., Dickie, I., Phang, Z., Tinch, R., Čivić, K., Delbaere, B., Jones-Walters, L., Hilbert, A., Schrauwen, A., Prank, M., Sofiev, M., Niemelä, S., Räisänen, P., Lees, B., Skinner, M., Finch, S. & Brough, C. 2012. *Assessing and controlling the spread and the effects of common ragweed in Europe*. Final Report to the European Commission, DG Environment. NERC Centre for Ecology and Hydrology, Wallingford.

Bullock-Webster, G.R. 1901. New Characeae Records. *Journal of Botany, British and Foreign* **39**: 101–102.

Bungard, S.J. & Leach, S. 1991. *Atriplex littoralis* by the way. *BSBI News* **59**: 11–12.

Bunting, E.S. 1988. Exploited plants. Oilseed Rape. *Biologist* **35**: 95–100.

Burdon, J.J. 1983. Biological Flora of the British Isles. No. 154. *Trifolium repens* L. *Journal of Ecology* **71**: 307–330.

Burkill, I.H. 1944. Biological Flora of the British Isles. No. 12. *Tamus communis* L. *Journal of Ecology* **32**: 121–129.

Burnett, J. 1997. Notes on *Veronica anagallis-aquatica* **agg.** *BSBI News* **75**: 15–17.

Burns, F., Eaton, M.A., Barlow, K.E., Beckmann, B., Brereton, T., Brooks, D.R., Brown, P.M.J., Fulaij, N.A., Henderson, I., Noble, D.G., Parsons, M., Powney, G.D., Roy, H.E., Stroh, P., Walker, K.J., Wilkinson, J.W., Wotton, S.R. & Gregory, R.D. 2016. Agricultural management and climatic change are the major drivers of biodiversity change in the UK. *PLoS ONE* **11**: e0151595.

Burton, R.M. 1979. Two species of *Senecio* L. from E. Kent. *Watsonia* **12**: 392.

Burton, R.M. 1983. *Flora of the London area*. London Natural History Society, London.

Butcher, R.W. 1947. Biological Flora of the British Isles. No. 18. *Atropa belladonna* L. *Journal of Ecology* **34**: 345–353.

Butcher, R.W. 1954. Biological Flora of the British Isles. No. 42. *Colchicum autumnale* L. *Journal of Ecology* **42**: 249–257.

Butterfield, L. 1999. Boscregan – last refuge of the Purple Viper's-bugloss? *British Wildlife* **10**: 166–171.

Byfield, A. 1993. *The status and ecology of* Cephalanthera longifolia *in Britain, with conservation recommendations*. Plantlife and Hampshire Wildlife Trust.

Byfield, A., Pearman, D., Royal Society for the Protection of Birds & Plantlife 1996. *Dorset's disappearing heathland flora: Changes in the Distribution of Dorset's Rarer Heathland Species, 1931 to 1993*. Plantlife, London.

Cadbury, C.J. 2001. *Nitella tenuissima* Dwarf Stonewort reappears at Wicken Fen, Cambs. *Nature in Cambridgeshire* **43**: 34–35.

Cadbury, C.J. 2008. Greater Water-parsnip (*Sium latifolium*) at the Ouse Washes, Cambridgeshire and West Norfolk: a large population and its ecology. *Nature in Cambridgeshire* **50**: 59–66.

Cadbury, C.J., Halshaw, L. & Tidswell, R. 1994. The ditch flora of the Ouse Washes (Cambridgeshire and West Norfolk): a comparison between 1978 and 1992. *Nature in Cambridgeshire* **36**: 17–33.

Cadbury, C.J., Prosser, M. & Wallace, H. 2003. Ditch flora of the Ouse Washes (Cambridgeshire/Norfolk) revisited in 2001. *Nature in Cambridgeshire* **45**: 37–49.

Cadbury, D.A., Hawkes, J.G. & Readett, R.C. 1971. *A computer-mapped flora: a study of the county of Warwickshire*. Academic Press, London.

Caffrey, J.M. & Monahan, C. 2006. Control of *Myriophyllum verticillatum* L. in Irish canals by turion removal. *Hydrobiologia* **570**: 211–215.

Caffrey, J., Millane, M., Evers, S.L. & Moran, H. 2011. Management of *Lagarosiphon major* (Ridley) Moss in Lough Corrib - a review. *Biology and Environment: proceedings of the Royal Irish Academy* **111B**: 205–212.

Callaghan, D.A. 1998. Biological Flora of the British Isles. No. 203. *Lythrum hyssopifolia* L. *Journal of Ecology* **86**: 1065–1072.

Callaghan, T.V., Svensson, B.M. & Headley, A.D. 1986. The modular growth of *Lycopodium annotinum*. *Fern Gazette* **13**: 65–76.

Callaghan, T.V., Brooker, R.W. & Carlsson, B.A. 2001. *Carex bigelowii* Torrey Ex Schweinitz (*C. rigida* Good., Non Schrank; *C. hyperborea* Drejer). *Journal of Ecology* **89**: 1072–1095.

Cameron, K.C. 2005. Leave it to the leaves: a molecular phylogenetic study of Malaxideae (Epidendroideae, Orchidaceae). *American Journal of Botany* **92**: 1025–1032.

Campbell, C.S., Burgess, M.B., Cushman, K.R., Doucette, E.T., Dibble, A.C. & Frye, C.T. 2014. *Amelanchier*. In Flora of North America Editorial Committee (Eds.) *Flora of North America: North of Mexico. Volume 9: Magnoliophyta: Picramniaceae to Rosaceae* Oxford University Press, New York and Oxford.

Campbell, V.V., Rowe, G., Beebee, T.J.C. & Hutchings, M.J. 2007. Genetic differentiation amongst fragrant orchids (*Gymnadenia conopsea* s.l.) in the British Isles. *Botanical Journal of the Linnean Society* **155**: 349–360.

Campoy, J.G., Acosta, A.T.R., Affre, L., Barreiro, R., Brundu, G., Buisson, E., González, L., Lema, M., Novoa, A., Retuerto, R., Roiloa, S.R. & Fagúndez, J. 2018. Monographs of invasive plants in Europe: *Carpobrotus*. *Botany Letters* **165**: 440–475.

Cannell, M.G.R. 1984. Exploited plants. Sitka spruce. *Biologist* **31**: 255–261.

Cannon, J.F.M. 1964. Infraspecific variation in *Lathyrus nissolia* L. *Watsonia* **6**: 28–35.

Carey, P.D. 1998. Modelling the spread of *Himantoglossum hircinum* (L.) Spreng. at a site in the south of England. *Journal of the Linnean Society* **126**: 159–172.

Carey, P.D. 1999. Changes in the distribution and abundance of *Himantoglossum hircinum* (L.) Sprengel (Orchidaceae) over the last 100 years. *Watsonia* **22**: 353–364.

Carey, P.D., Watkinson, A.R. & Gerard, F.F.O. 1995. The determinants of the distribution and abundance of the winter annual grass *Vulpia ciliata* subsp. *ambigua*. *Journal of Ecology* **83**: 177–187.

Carey, P.D. & Farrell, L. 2002. Biological Flora of the British Isles. No. 221. *Himantoglossum hircinum* (L.) Sprengel. *Journal of Ecology* **90**: 206–218.

Carlisle, A. & Brown, A.H.F. 1968. Biological Flora of the British Isles. No. 109. *Pinus sylvestris* L. *Journal of Ecology* **56**: 269–307.

Carlsson, R. 1980. Quantity and Quality of Leaf Protein Concentrates from *Atriplex hortensis* L., *Chenopodium quinoa* Willd. and *Amaranthus caudatus* L, grown in Southern Sweden. *Acta Agriculturae Scandinavica* **30**: 418–426.

Carter, R.N. & Prince, S.D. 1985. The geographical distribution of Prickly Lettuce (*Lactuca serriola*). I. A general survey of its habitats and performance in Britain. *Journal of Ecology* **73**: 27–38.

Catling, P.M. & Dobson, I. 1985. The biology of Canadian weeds. 69. *Potamogeton crispus* L. *Canadian Journal of Plant Science* **65**: 655–668.

Catling, P.M., Mitrow, G., Haber, E., Posluszny, U. & Charlton, W.A. 2003. The biology of Canadian weeds. 124. *Hydrocharis morsus-ranae* L. *Canadian Journal of Plant Science* **83**: 1001–1016.

Cavers, P.B. & Harper, J.L. 1967. The comparative biology of closely related species living in the same area. IX. *Rumex*: the nature of adaptation to a sea-shore habitat. *Journal of Ecology* **55**: 73–82.

Cavers, P.B., Turkington, R.A. & Rempel, E. 1978. The biology of Canadian weeds. 29. *Melilotus alba* Desv. and *M. officinalis* (L.) Lam. *Canadian Journal of Plant Science* **58**: 523–537.

Cavers, P.B., Heagy, M.I. & Kokron, R.F. 1979. The biology of Canadian weeds. 35. *Alliaria petiolata* (M. Bieb) Cavara and Grande. *Canadian Journal of Plant Science* **59**: 217–229.

Cavers, P.B., Bassett, I.J. & Crompton, C.W. 1980. The biology of Canadian weeds. 47. *Plantago lanceolata* L. *Canadian Journal of Plant Science* **60**: 1269–1282.

Cavers, P.B., Steel, M.G. & Lee, S.M. 1983. The biology of Canadian weeds. 59. *Setaria glauca* (L.) Beauv. and *S. verticillata* (L.) Beauv. *Canadian Journal of Plant Science* **63**: 711–725.

Chadwick, M.J. 1960. Biological Flora of the British Isles. No. 73. *Nardus stricta* L. *Journal of Ecology* **48**: 255–267.

Chalk, D. 1986. Hedge *Veronica* (*Hebe ×franciscana* (Eastwood) Souster). *BSBI News* **43**: 17–18.

Challice, J. & Kovanda, M. 1978. Chemotaxonomic survey of the genus *Sorbus* in Europe. *Naturwissenschaften* **65**: 111–112.

Chapman, V.J. 1947a. Biological Flora of the British Isles. No. 20. *Suaeda maritima* (L.) Dum. *Journal of Ecology* **35**: 293–302.

Chapman, V.J. 1947b. Biological Flora of the British Isles. No. 21. *Suaeda fruticosa* Forsk. *Journal of Ecology* **35**: 303–310.

Chapman, V.J. 1950. Biological Flora of the British Isles. No. 29. *Halimione portulacoides* (L.) Aell. *Journal of Ecology* **38**: 214–222.

Chapurlat, E., Le Ronce, I., Agren, J. & Sletvold, N. 2020. Divergent selection on flowering phenology but not only floral morphology between two closely related orchids. *Ecology and Evolution* **10**: 537–547.

Chater, A.O. 1990. *Ceredigion Rare Plant Register, VC46, February 1990*. Unpublished report.

Chater, A.O. 1992. *Laburnum anagyroides* and *L. alpinum* as hedge plants in Cardiganshire, v.c. 46. *BSBI Welsh Bulletin* **52**: 4–5.

Chater, A.O. 2010a. *Betula celtiberica* in Wales. *BSBI Welsh Bulletin* **85**: 17–19.

Chater, A.O. 2010b. *Flora of Cardiganshire*. privately published.

Chater, A.O. & Rich, T.C.G. 1995. *Rorippa islandica* (Oeder ex Murray) Borbás (Brassicaceae) in Wales. *Watsonia* **20**: 229–238.

Chater, A.O., Oswald, P.H. & Preston, C.D. 2000. Street floras in Cambridge and Aberystwyth. *Nature in Cambridgeshire* **42**: 3–26.

Chatters, C. 1991. The status of *Pulicaria vulgaris* Gaertner in Britain in 1990. *Watsonia* **18**: 405–406.

Chatters, C. 2017. *Saltmarsh*. Bloomsbury, London.

Chatters, C. 2020a. 'By a fayre down', the breck heaths of the West Midlands. *British Wildlife* **32**: 26–33.

Chatters, C. 2020b. *Control of Pitcher Plant* Sarracenia purpurea *in the New Forest 2009 to 2019*. Report for The New Forest Non-native Plants Project. Hampshire and Isle of Wight Wildlife Trust.

Chatters, C. 2021. Small Fleabane: A Miscellany. *Flora News* **60**: 14–15.

Cheffings, C.M. 2004. New plant status lists for Great Britain. *BSBI News* **95**: 36–43.

Cheffings, C.M. & Farrell, L. (Eds.) 2005. *The Vascular Plant Red Data List for Great Britain*. Species Status, 7: 1–116. Joint Nature Conservation Committee, Peterborough.

Chiapella, J. 2000. The *Deschampsia cespitosa* complex in central and northern Europe: a morphological analysis. *Botanical Journal of the Linnean Society* **134**: 495–512.

Christie, M. 1910. *Lathyrus tuberosus* in Britain. *Journal of Botany* **48**: 170–177.

Cierjacks, A., Kowarik, I., Joshi, J., Hempel, S., Ristow, M., von der Lippe, M. & Weber, E. 2013. Biological Flora of the British Isles. No. 273. *Robinia pseudoacacia*. *Journal of Ecology* **101**: 1623–1640.

Clabby, G. & Osborne, B.A. 1999. Biological Flora of the British Isles. No. 204. *Mycelis muralis* (L.) Dumort. (*Lactuca muralis* L.). *Journal of Ecology* **87**: 156–172.

Claessens, J. & Kleynen, J. 2011. *The flower of the European orchid: form and function*. Voerendaal, Netherlands.

Clapham, A.R. 1969. *Flora of Derbyshire*. County Borough of Derby Museums and Art Gallery, Derby.

Clapham, A.R., Pearsall, W.H. & Richards, P.W. 1942. Biological Flora of the British Isles. No. 8. *Aster tripolium* L. *Journal of Ecology* **30**: 385–395.

Clapham, A.R., Tutin, T.G. & Warburg, E.F. 1952. *Flora of the British Isles*. Cambridge University Press, Cambridge.

Clapham, A.R., Tutin, T.G. & Warburg, E.F. 1962. *Flora of the British Isles*. Edn. 2. Cambridge University Press, Cambridge.

Clapham, A.R., Tutin, T.G. & Moore, D.M. 1987. *Flora of the British Isles*. Edn. 3. Cambridge University Press, Cambridge.

Clark, M.J. 2011. Studies on *Epipactis helleborine* s.l. at Kenfig NNR. *Journal of the Hardy Orchid Society* **8**: 24–28.

Clark, S.C. 1974. Biological Flora of the British Isles. No. 136. *Catapodium rigidum* (L.) C. E. Hubbard. *Journal of Ecology* **62**: 937–958.

Clarke, W.G. 1925. *In Breckland Wilds*. Robert Scott, London.

Clay, D.V. & Drinkall, M.J. 2001. The occurrence, ecology and control of *Buddleja davidii* in the UK. *Avon Vegetation Research Limited* **13**: 155–160.

Clement, E.J. 1978a. Adventive News 11. *BSBI News* **19**: 12–17.

Clement, E.J. 1978b. Adventive News 12. *BSBI News* **20**: 9–14.

Clement, E.J. 1981a. Sweet Bromegrass in Britain. *BSBI News* **28**: 12–14.

Clement, E.J. 1981b. Cockleburs in Britain. *BSBI News* **29**: 13.

Clement, E.J. 1983. Some rare alien Polygonaceae. *BSBI News* **34**: 29–31.

Clement, E.J. 1985a. Hedge *Veronica* (*Hebe* × *franciscana*) and allies in Britain. *BSBI News* **41**: 18.

Clement, E.J. 1985b. Selfheals (*Prunella* spp.) in Britain. *BSBI News* **41**: 20.

Clement, E.J. 1993. Buttonweed (*Cotula coronopifolia* L.), new to S. Hants (v.c. 11). *BSBI News* **64**: 43–46.

Clement, E.J. 1997. Can *Euphorbia robbiae* be revived? *BSBI News* **76**: 58–60.

Clement, E.J. 1999. Misconceptions about *Amsinckia lycopsoides* Lehm. *BSBI News* **80**: 44–45.

Clement, E.J. 2000. *Ludwigia* × *kentiana* E.J.Clement: a new hybrid aquatic. *Watsonia* **23**: 167–172.

Clement, E.J. 2001. *Ludwigia grandiflora* established at Barton-on-Sea (v.c.11, S. Hants). *BSBI News* **87**: 52–54.

Clement, E.J. 2002. Dangerous Laurels - not Laurels in danger. *BSBI News* **90**: 45.

Clement, E.J. 2003. How is *Chenopodium quinoa* faring? *BSBI News* **93**: 56–57.

Clement, E.J. 2004. *Gnaphalium luteoalbum* needs no special protection. *BSBI News* **95**: 43–44.

Clement, E.J. 2005. *Cortaderia richardii* (Endl.) Zotov and allies. *BSBI News* **99**: 48–50.

Clement, E.J. 2006. Could *Artemisia campestris* subsp. *maritima* be native? *BSBI News* **103**: 4.

Clement, E.J. 2012. Problems over identification of *Pyracantha* bushes. *BSBI News* **119**: 53–55.

Clement, E.J. & Foster, M.C. 1994. *Alien plants of the British Isles*. Botanical Society of the British Isles, London.

Clements, D.R., DiTommaso, A., Darbyshire, S.J., Cavers, P.B. & Sartonov, A.D. 2004. The biology of Canadian weeds. 127. *Panicum capillare* L. *Canadian Journal of Plant Science* **84**: 327–341.

Coats, A.M. 1963. *Garden shrubs and their histories*. Vista Books, London.

Cody, W.J. & Crompton, C.W. 1975. The biology of Canadian weeds. 15. *Pteridium aquilinum* (L.) Kuhn. *Canadian Journal of Plant Science* **55**: 1059–1072.

Cody, W.J. & Wagner, V. 1980. The biology of Canadian weeds. 49. *Equisetum arvense* L. *Canadian Journal of Plant Science* **61**: 123–133.

Coker, P.D. 1962. Biological Flora of the British Isles. No. 86. *Corrigiola litoralis* L. *Journal of Ecology* **50**: 833–840.

Coker, P.D. 1966. Biological Flora of the British Isles. No. 104. *Sibbaldia procumbens* L. *Journal of Ecology* **54**: 823–831.

Coker, P.D. & Coker, A.M. 1973. Biological Flora of the British Isles. No. 133. *Phyllodoce caerulea* (L.) Bab. *Journal of Ecology* **61**: 901–913.

Coldea, G. (Ed.) 2012. *Les associations végétales de Roumaine. Tome 2. Les associations anthropogènes*. Presa Universitară Clujeană, Cluj-Napoca.

Cole, H. 2012. *The Status of* Erigeron borealis *(Vierh) Simmons on Ben Lawers NNR*. National Trust for Scotland Report.

Cole, S. 2014. History and status of the Ghost Orchid (*Epipogium aphyllum*, Orchidaceae) in England. *New Journal of Botany* **4**: 13–24.

Cole, S. & Waller, M. 2020. *Britain's orchids*. Princeton University Press, Princeton, New Jersey.

Coleman, M., A'Hara, S.W., Tomlinson, P.R. & Davey, P.J. 2016. Elm clone identification and the conundrum of the slow spread of Dutch Elm Disease on the Isle of Man. *New Journal of Botany* **6**: 79–89.

Compton, S.G. & Key, R.S. 2000. Biological Flora of the British Isles. No. 211. *Coincya wrightii* (O.E. Schulz) Stace. *Journal of Ecology* **88**: 535–548.

Conaghan, J.P. & Sheehy Skeffington, M. 2009. The distribution and conservation of *Eriophorum gracile* Koch ex Roth (Cyperaceae), Slender Cotton-grass, in Ireland. *Watsonia* **27**: 229–238.

Conolly, A.P. 1977. The distribution and history in the British Isles of some alien species of *Polygonum* and *Reynoutria*. *Watsonia* **11**: 291–311.

Conolly, A.P. 1991. *Polygonum lichiangense* W. Smith: rejected as a naturalized British species. *Watsonia* **18**: 351–358.

Conran, J., MacLunas, E. & MacLunas, K. 2011. *Serapias lingua* L. (tongue orchid) naturalised in the Adelaide Hills, South Australia: caveat cultivator. *The Orchadian* **16**: 556–561.

Conway, V.M. 1942. Biological Flora of the British Isles. No. 6. *Cladium mariscus* (L.) R. Br. *Journal of Ecology* **30**: 211–216.

Cook, C.D.K. 1962. Biological Flora of the British Isles. No. 82. *Sparganium erectum* L. *Journal of Ecology* **50**: 247–255.

Cook, C.D.K. 1966. A monographic study of *Ranunculus* subg. *Batrachium* (DC.) A. Gray. *Mitteilungen der Botanischen Staatssammlung München* **6**: 47–237.

Cook, C.D.K. & Urmi-König, K. 1983. A revision of the genus *Stratiotes* (Hydrocharitaceae). *Aquatic Botany* **16**: 213–249.

Cook, P.J. 1997. 'Summer Cypress' (*Bassia scoparia*) on Yorkshire roadsides. *BSBI News* **74**: 48–49.

Cook, P.J. 1998. *Bassia scoparia* in v.cc. 28, 53 and 54. A possible connection with east coast ports. *BSBI News* **78**: 63.

Coombe, D.E. 1956a. Biological Flora of the British Isles. No. 60. *Impatiens parviflora* DC. *Journal of Ecology* **44**: 701–713.

Coombe, D.E. 1956b. Notes on some British plants seen in Austria. *Veröffentlichungen des Geobotanisches Institutes Rübel in Zürich* **35**: 128–137.

Coombe, D.E. 1961. *Trifolium occidentale*, a new species related to *T. repens* L. *Watsonia* **5**: 68–87.

Coombe, D.E. 1973. The prostrate junipers at Gew Graze. *The Lizard* **5(1)**: 7–12.

Coombe, D.E. 1994. 'Maritime' plants of roads in Cambridgeshire (v.c. 29). *Nature in Cambridgeshire* **36**: 37–60.

Cooper, M.R. & Johnson, A.W. 1988. *Poisonous plants in Britain and their effects on animals and man*. Her Majesty's Stationery Office, London.

Cope, T. 2009. *The wild flora of Kew Gardens. A cumulative checklist from 1759*. Royal Botanic Gardens, Kew, Richmond, Surrey.

Cope, T.A. & Stace, C.A. 1978. The *Juncus bufonius* L. aggregate in western Europe. *Watsonia* **12**: 113–128.

Cope, T.A. & Stace, C.A. 1983. Variation in the *Juncus bufonius* L. aggregate in western Europe. *Watsonia* **14**: 263–272.

Cope, T.A. & Stace, C.A. 1985. Cytology and hybridization in the *Juncus bufonius* L. aggregate in western Europe. *Watsonia* **15**: 309–320.

Cope, T. & Gray, A. 2009. *Grasses of the British Isles*. BSBI Handbook No. 13. Botanical Society of the British Isles, London.

Coppins, S. & Coppins, B.J. 2012. *Atlantic hazel: Scotland's special woodlands*. Atlantic Hazel Action Group.

Corner, R.W.M. 1957. Notes on the Scottish Flora. *Koenigia islandica* L. *Transactions and Proceedings of the Botanical Society of Edinburgh* **XXXVII**: 129.

Corner, R.W.M. 1969. Plant Notes: *Carex appropinquata* Schumach. – in Scotland. *Proceedings of the Botanical Society of the British Isles* **7**: 562.

Corner, R.W.M. 1989. Observations on inland populations of *Viola canina* L. in south-eastern Scotland and north-western England. *Watsonia* **17**: 351–352.

Corner, R.W.M. 1997. A Pennine 'saltmarsh' flora. *BSBI News* **77**: 40–41.

Corner, R.W.M. 1999. Observations on a low altitude site for *Draba norvegica* and *Poa glauca* in West Sutherland v.c. 108. *Botanical Journal of Scotland* **51**: 127–129.

Corner, R.W.M. 2002. The enigma of montane *Sagina maritima* Don. *Watsonia* **24**: 215–7.

Corner, R.W.M. & Roberts, F.J. 1989. *Carex ornithopoda* Willd. in Cumberland. *Watsonia* **17**: 437–438.

Cotton, D.C.F. 1999. Least duckweed *Lemna minuta* Kunth, in Ireland. *Irish Naturalists' Journal* **26**: 199–200.

Cotton, D.C.F., Cawley, M. & Roden, C. 1994. On the occurrence of *Pseudorchis albida* in Sligo, Leitrim and Galway. *Irish Naturalist's Journal* **24**: 468–471.

Cowan, R.S., Smith, R.J., Fay, M.F. & Rich, T.C.G. 2008. Genetic variation in Irish Whitebeam, *Sorbus hibernica* E. F. Warb. (Rosaceae) and its relationship to a *Sorbus* from the Menai Strait, North Wales. *Watsonia* **27**: 99–108.

Cox, J. 1997. Hampshire purslane found in Dorset. *Recording Dorset* **7**: 20–21.

Crackles, F.E. 1995. A graphical analysis of the characters of *Calamagrostis stricta* (Timm) Koeler, *C. canescens* (Wigg.) Roth and their hybrid populations in S. E. Yorks, v.c. 61, northern England. *Watsonia* **20**: 397–404.

Crackles, F.E. 1997. Variation in some populations of *Calamagrostis stricta* (Timm) Koeler in the British Isles and the putative past hybridization with *C. canescens* (Wigg.) Roth. *Watsonia* **21**: 341–354.

Crawford, R.M.M. 2008. Cold climate plants in a warmer world. *Plant Ecology & Diversity* **1**: 285–297.

Crawley, M.J. 2005. *The Flora of Berkshire*. Brambleby Books, Harpenden.

BIBLIOGRAPHY

Croft, J. 2000. Fen Violet *Viola persicifolia* at Wicken Fen: a reinforcement population. *Nature in Cambridgeshire* **42**: 27–33.

Crompton, C.W., Hall, I.V., Jensen, K.I.N. & Hildebrand, P.D. 1988. The biology of Canadian weeds. 83. *Hypericum perforatum* L. *Canadian Journal of Plant Science* **68**: 149–162.

Crompton, G. 2001. *Cambridgeshire flora records since 1538.*

Cronquist, A. & Gleason, H.A. 1991. *Manual of Vascular Plants on Northeastern United States and adjacent Canada.* Edn. 2. New York Botanical Garden, New York.

Cross, J.R. 1975. Biological Flora of the British Isles. No. 137. *Rhododendron ponticum* L. *Journal of Ecology* **63**: 345–364.

Crouch, H.J. & Rumsey, F.J. 2015. *Dryopteris remota*: a new species in the English flora. *Pteridologist* **6**: 150–151.

Cuizhi, G. & Spongberg, S.A. 2003. *Pyracantha*. In *Flora of China* **Vol. 9.**

Cullen, J. 1986. *Anthyllis* in the British Isles. *Notes from the Royal Botanic Garden Edinburgh* **43**: 277–281.

Cullen, J. 2011. Naturalised rhododendrons widespread in Great Britain and Ireland. *Hanburyana* **5**: 11–32.

Curry, P. 1991. *Distribution, translocation and monitoring of* Chara canescens *at the Peterborough Brickpits.* Bedfordshire and Cambridgeshire Wildlife Trust report.

Curtis, T.G.F. 1981. A further station for *Mercurialis perennis* L. in the Burren with comments on its status there. *Irish Naturalists' Journal* **20**: 184–185.

Curtis, T.G.F. & McGough, H.N. 1988. *The Irish Red Data Book. 1. Vascular Plants.* Stationery Office, Dublin.

Curtis, T.G.F. & FitzGerald, R.A. 1994. The re-discovery of *Carex divisa* Hudson, Divided Sedge, in Ireland. *Irish Naturalists' Journal* **24**: 496–498.

Curtis, T. & Thompson, R. 2009. *The Orchids of Ireland.* National Museums Northern Ireland, Belfast.

Dalby, D.H. & Rich, T.C.G. 1995. *The history, taxonomy, distribution and ecology of Mountain scurvy-grass (*Cochlearia micacea *Marshall). Back from the Brink Project Report, No. 42. (Contractor: Plantlife).* Scottish Natural Heritage, Edinburgh.

Dalby, K. 1989. An experts approach to the *Salicornia* problem. *BSBI News* **53**: 9–10.

Dale, H.M. 1974. The biology of Canadian weeds: 5. *Daucus carota. Canadian Journal of Plant Science* **54**: 673–685.

Dalrymple, S.E. 2007. Biological Flora of the British Isles. No. 246. *Melampyrum sylvaticum* L. *Journal of Ecology* **95**: 583–597.

Dandelot, S., Verlaque, R., Dutartre, A. & Cazaubon, A. 2005. Ecological, dynamic and taxonomic problems due to *Ludwigia* (Onagraceae) in France. *Hydrobiologia* **551**: 131–136.

Daniels, R.E., McDonnell, E.J. & Raybould, A.F. 1998. The current status of *Rumex rupestris* Le Gall (Polygonaceae) in England and Wales. and threats to its survival and genetic diversity. *Watsonia* **22**: 33–39.

Davey, A.J. 1961. Biological Flora of the British Isles. No. 80. *Epilobium nerterioides* A.Cunn. *Journal of Ecology* **49**: 753–759.

David, R.W. 1978a. The distribution of *Carex digitata* L. in Britain. *Watsonia* **12**: 47–49.

David, R.W. 1978b. The distribution of *Carex elongata* L. in the British Isles. *Watsonia* **12**: 158–160.

David, R.W. 1980. The distribution of *Carex ornithopoda* Willd. in Britain. *Watsonia* **13**: 53–54.

David, R.W. 1981. The distribution of *Carex ericetorum* Poll. in Britain. *Watsonia* **13**: 225–226.

David, R.W. 1983. The distribution of *Carex tomentosa* (*C. filiformis* auct.) in Britain. *Watsonia* **14**: 412–414.

David, R.W. & Kelcey, J.G. 1985. Biological Flora of the British Isles. No. 159. *Carex muricata* L. aggregate. *Journal of Ecology* **73**: 1021–1039.

Davidson, T.A., Sayer, C.D., Bennion, H., David, C., Rose, N. & Wade, M.P. 2005. A 250 year comparison of historical, macrofossil and pollen records of aquatic plants in a shallow lake. *Freshwater Biology* **50**: 1671–1686.

Davies, J.H. 1898. *Epilobium roseum* in Ireland; is it native? *The Irish Naturalist* **7**: 41–43.

Davies, L.R., Onkokesung, N., Brazier-Hicks, M., Edwards, R. & Moss, S. 2020. Detection and characterization of resistance to acetolactate synthase inhibiting herbicides in *Anisantha* and *Bromus* species in the United Kingdom. *Pest Management Science* **76**: 2473–2482.

Davis, A. 1992. Exploited plants. White clover. *Biologist* **39**: 129–133.

Davis, A.P. 1999. *The genus Galanthus.* Timber Press, Portland, Oregon.

Davison, A.W. 1970. The ecology of *Hordeum murinum* L. I. Analysis of the distribution in Britain. *Journal of Ecology* **58**: 453–466.

Davison, A.W. 1971. The ecology of *Hordeum murinum* L. II. The ruderal habitat. *Journal of Ecology* **59**: 493–506.

Davy, A.J. 1980. Biological Flora of the British Isles. No. 149. *Deschampsia caespitosa* (L.) Beauv. *Journal of Ecology* **68**: 1075–1096.

Davy, A.J. & Bishop, G.F. 1991. Biological Flora of the British Isles. No. 172. *Triglochin maritima* L. *Journal of Ecology* **79**: 531–555.

Davy, A.J., Scott, R. & Cordazzo, C.V. 2006a. Biological Flora of the British Isles. No. 243: *Cakile maritima* Scop. *Journal of Ecology* **94**: 695–711.

Davy, A.J., Bishop, G.F., Mossman, H., Redondo-Gomez, S., Castillo, J.M., Castellanos, E.M., Luque, T. & Figueroa, M.E. 2006b. Biological Flora of the British Isles. No. 244: *Sarcocornia perennis* (Miller) A.J. Scott. *Journal of Ecology* **94**: 1035–1048.

De Bolòs, O. & Vigo, J. 1984. *Flora dels Països Catalans, I. Introducció. Licopodiàcies-Capparàcies.* Editorial Barcino, Barcelona.

De Bolòs, O. & Vigo, J. 1990. *Flora dels Països Catalans, II. Crucíferes-Amarantàcies.* Editorial Barcino, Barcelona.

De Bolòs, O. & Vigo, J. 1995. *Flora dels Països Catalans, III. Piròlacies-Compostes.* Editorial Barcino, Barcelona.

De Frenne, P., Brunet, J., Cougnon, M., Decocq, G., Graae, B.J., Hagenblad, J., Hermy, M., Kolb, A., Lemke, I.H., Ma, S., Orczewska, A., Plue, J., Vranckx, G., Wulf, M. & Verheyen, K. 2017. Biological Flora of the British Isles. No. 282. *Millium effusum* L. *Journal of Ecology* **105**: 839–858.

de Gasper, A.L., Dittrich, V.A.O., Smith, A.R. & Salino, A. 2016. A classification for Blechnaceae (Polypodiales: Polypodiopsida): New genera, resurrected names, and combinations. *Phytotaxa* **275**: 191–227.

de Groot, W.J., Thomas, P.A. & Wein, R.W. 1997. Biological Flora of the British Isles. No. 194. *Betula nana* L. and *B. glandulosa* Michx. *Journal of Ecology* **85**: 241–264.

de Jong, T.G., Klinkhamer, P.G.L. & Boorman, L.A. 1990. Biological Flora of the British Isles. No. 170. *Cynoglossum officinale* L. *Journal of Ecology* **78**: 1123–1144.

De Rougemont, G.M. 1989. *A field guide to the crops of Britain and Europe.* Collins, London.

de Vere, N. 2007. Biological Flora of the British Isles. No. 247. *Cirsium dissectum* (L.) Hill (*Cirsium tuberosum* (L.) All. subsp. *anglicum* (Lam.) Bonnier; *Cnicus pratensis* (Huds.) Willd., Non Lam.; *Cirsium anglicum* (Lam.) DC.). *Journal of Ecology* **95**: 876–94.

de Vere, N., Jones, L., Cleary, K. & Allainguillaume, J. 2012. *The current status of* Campanula patula *within the UK: distribution, genetics and conservation recommendations.* Unpublished report for the National Botanical Garden of Wales.

Dean, M., Hutcheon, K., Jermy, A.C., Cayouette, J. & Ashton, P.A. 2005. *Carex salina* - a new species of sedge for Britain. *BSBI News* **99**: 17–19.

Dearnley, T.C. & Duckett, J.G. 1999. Juniper in the Lake District National Park. A review of condition and regeneration. *Watsonia* **22**: 261–267.

Dehnen-Schmutz, K., Pescott, O.L., Booy, O. & Walker, K.J. 2022. Integrating expert knowledge at regional and national scales improves impact assessments of non-native species. *NeoBiota* **77**: 79–100.

Delforge, P. 1995. *Epipactis dunensis* (T. & T.A. Stephenson) Godfery et *E. muelleri* Godfery dans les îles Britanniques. *Naturalistes Belges* **76**: 103–123.

Delforge, P. & Gévaudan, A. 2002. Contribution taxonomique et nomenclaturale au groupe d'*Epipactis leptochila*. *Naturalistes Belges* **84**: 19–36.

den Hartog, C. 1970. *The sea-grasses of the world.* North-Holland Publishing Company, Amsterdam.

den Hartog, C. & Triest, L. 2020. A profound view and discourse on the typification and status of three confused taxa: *Ruppia maritima, R. spiralis* and *R. cirrhosa. Botanica Marina* **63**: 229–239.

den Nijs, J.C.M. 1984. Biosystematic studies of the *Rumex acetosella* complex (Polygonaceae). VIII. A taxonomic revision. *Feddes Repertorium* **95**: 43–66.

Denness, A., Armitage, J.D. & Culham, A. 2013. A contribution towards the identification of the giant hogweed species (*Heracleum*, Apiaceae) naturalised in the British Isles with comments concerning their furanocoumarin content. *New Journal of Botany* **3**: 183–196.

Desjardins, S., Hoare, A.G. & Stace, C.A. 2016. A new natural hybrid in the genus *Petasites: P. japonicus × P. pyrenaicus* (Asteraceae). *New Journal of Botany* **6**: 2–3.

Devey, D.S., Bateman, R.M., Fay, M.F. & Hawkins, J.A. 2008. Friends or relatives? Phylogenetics and species delimitation in the controversial European orchid genus *Ophrys. Annals of Botany* **101**: 385–402.

Devey, D.S., Bateman, R.M., Fay, M.F. & Hawkins, J.A. 2009. Genetic structure and systematic relationships within the *Ophrys fuciflora* aggregate (Orchidinae: Orchidaceae): high diversity in Kent and a wind-induced discontinuity bisecting the Adriatic. *Annals of Botany* **104**: 483–495.

Devos, N., Raspé, O., Jacquemart, A.-L. & Tyteca, D. 2006. On the monophyly of *Dactylorhiza* Necker ex Nevski (Orchidaceae): is *Coeloglossum* (L.) Hartman a *Dactylorhiza? Botanical Journal of the Linnean Society* **162**: 261–269.

Dickson, J.H., Hunter, R. & Walters, S.M. 1993. *Alchemilla acutiloba* Opiz new to Scotland. *Botanical Journal of Scotland* **46**: 499–502.

Dickson, J.H., MacPherson, P. & Watson, K. 2000. *The Changing Flora of Glasgow. Urban and Rural Plants through the Centuries.* Edinburgh University Press Ltd, Edinburgh.

Dietrich, W. 1991. The status of *Oenothera cambrica* Rostanski and *O. novae-scotiae* Gates (Onagraceae). *Watsonia* **18**: 407–408.

Dines, T.D. 2008. *A Vascular Plant Red Data List for Wales.* Plantlife International, Salisbury.

Dines, T.D. & Preston, C.D. 2000. *Eleocharis parvula* discovered in Scotland. *Watsonia* **23**: 341–342.

Dines, T.D. & Daniels, A. 2006. *Welsh Juniper Inventory.* Unpublished report.

Dinsdale, J., Dale, M. & Kent, M. 2000. Microhabitat availability and seedling recruitment of *Lobelia urens*: A rare plant species at its geographical limit. *Seed Science Research* **10**: 471–487.

Dixon, J.M. 1982. Biological Flora of the British Isles. No. 151. *Sesleria albicans* Kit. ex Schultes. *Journal of Ecology* **70**: 667–684.

Dixon, J.M. 1991. Biological Flora of the British Isles. No. 173. *Avenula pratensis* (L.) Dumort. (pp. 829–846), *A. pubescens* (Hudson) Dumort. (pp. 846–865). *Journal of Ecology* **79**: 829–865.

Dixon, J.M. 1995. Biological Flora of the British Isles. No. 187. *Trisetum flavescens* (L.) Beauv. *Journal of Ecology* **83**: 895–909.

Dixon, J.M. 2000. Biological Flora of the British Isles. No. 212. *Koeleria macrantha* (Ledeb.) Schultes. *Journal of Ecology* **88**: 709–726.

Dixon, J.M. 2002. Biological Flora of the British Isles. No. 224. *Briza media* L. *Journal of Ecology* **90**: 737–752.

Dixon, J.M., Aksoy, A. & Hale, W.H.G. 1998. Biological Flora of the British Isles. No. 199. *Capsella bursa-pastoris* (L.) Medikus (*Thlaspi bursa-pastoris* L., *Bursa bursa-pastoris* (L.) Shull, *Bursa pastoris* (L.) Weber). *Journal of Ecology* **86**: 171–186.

Dodds, J.G. 1953. Biological Flora of the British Isles. No. 38. *Plantago coronopus* L. *Journal of Ecology* **41**: 467–478.

Donald, D. 1980. *Bromus interruptus* (Hack.) Druce: dodo or phoenix? *Nature in Cambridgeshire* **23**: 48–50, 51.

Dony, C. 1994. *Chenopodium capitatum* in Southern England. *BSBI News* **67**: 55–56.

Dony, J.G. 1953. *Flora of Bedfordshire*. The Corporation of Luton Museum and Art Gallery, Luton.

Dony, J.G. 1967. *The Flora of Hertfordshire*. Hitchin Museum, Hitchin.

Doogue, D. & Akeroyd, J.R. 1988. *Plantago major* L. subsp. *intermedia* (DC.) Arcangeli (Plantaginaceae) in Ireland. *Irish Naturalists' Journal* **22**: 441–443.

Doogue, D., Nash, D., Parnell, J., Reynolds, S. & Wyse Jakson, P. 1998. *Flora of County Dublin*. Dublin Naturalists' Field Club, Dublin.

Doohan, D.J. & Monaco, T.J. 1992. The biology of Canadian weeds. 99. *Viola arvensis* Murr. *Canadian Journal of Plant Science* **72**: 187–201.

Dostálek, J. & Jehlík, V. 2004. *Chenopodium probstii* and *C. missouriense*: Two North American plant species in the Czech Republic, Slovak Republic and neighbouring countries. *Feddes Repertorium* **115**: 483–503.

Douglas, B.J., Thomas, A.G., Morrison, I.N. & Maw, M.G. 1985. The biology of Canadian weeds. 70. *Setaria viridis* (L.) Beauv. *Canadian Journal of Plant Science* **65**: 669–690.

Downey, E.L., Pearman, D.A. & Rich, T.C.G. 2021. Conservation status of the rare endemic *Centaurium tenuiflorum* subsp. *anglicum*, English centaury (Gentianaceae). *British & Irish Botany* **3**: 161–167.

Doyle, G. 1999. Laurophyllisation in Ireland - the case of *Rhododendron ponticum*. In Klötzli, F. & Walther, G.R. (Eds.) *Conference on Recent Shifts in Vegetation Boundaries of Deciduous Forests, Especially Due to General Global Warming* Monte Verità (Proceedings of the Centro Stefano Franscini Ascona) Birkhäuser, Basel.

Doyle, G.J., Foss, P.J. & Nelson, E.C. 1987. The distribution of *Erica erigena* R.Ross in Ireland. *Watsonia* **16**: 311–327.

Druce, G.C. 1897. *The Flora of Berkshire*. Clarendon Press, Oxford.

Druce, G.C. 1903. *Campanula persicifolia* L. in Britain. *Journal of Botany* **41**: 289–290.

Druce, G.C. 1913. *Linaria purpurea × repens = L. × dominii*. *Report of the Botanical Society and Exchange Club of the British Isles* **3**: 168–169.

Druce, G.C. 1922. *Tillaea aquatica* L. *Report of the Botanical Society and Exchange Club of the British Isles* **6**: 281–282.

Druce, G.C. 1926. *Flora of Buckinghamshire*. T. Buncle & Co, Arbroath.

Druce, G.C. 1927. *Flora of Oxfordshire*. Edn. 2. Clarendon Press, Oxford.

Druce, G.C. 1928. *British plant list*. Edn. 2. T. Buncle & Co, Arbroath.

Dudman, A.A. & Richards, A.J. 1997. *Dandelions of Great Britain and Ireland*. *Botanical Society of the British Isles Handbook no. 9*. Botanical Society of the British Isles, London.

Dueck, L.A., Aygoren, D. & Cameron, K.M. 2014. A molecular framework for understanding the phylogeny of *Spiranthes* (Orchidaceae), a cosmopolitan genus with a North American center of diversity. *American Journal of Botany* **101**: 1551–1571.

Duffy, K.J., Kingston, N.E., Sayers, B., Roberts, D.L. & Stout, J.C. 2008. Inferring national and regional declines of rare orchid species with probabilistic models. *Conservation Biology* **23**: 184–195.

Duffy, K.J., Scopece, G., Cozzolino, S., Fay, M.F., Smith, R.J. & Stout, J.C. 2009. Ecology and genetic diversity of the dense-flowered orchid, *Neotinea maculata*, at the centre and edge of its range. *Annals of Botany* **104**: 507–516.

Duffy, K.J., Fay, M.F., Smith, R.J. & Stout, J.C. 2011. Population genetics and conservation of the small white orchid *Pseudorchis albida* in Ireland. *Biology and Environment: Proceedings of the Royal Irish Academy* **111B**: 73–81.

Dufrene, M., Gathoye, J.-L. & Tyteca, D. 1991. Biostatistical studies on western European *Dactylorhiza* (Orchidaceae) – the *D. maculata* group. *Plant Systematics and Evolution* **175**: 55–72.

Duncan, U.K. 1980. *Flora of East Ross-shire*. Botanical Society of Edinburgh, Edinburgh.

Dunn, A.J. 1997. Biological Flora of the British Isles. No. 196. *Stachys germanica* L. *Journal of Ecology* **85**: 531–539.

Dunn, S.T. 1905. *Alien Flora of Britain*. West, Newman & Co, London.

Dupont, P. 1962. *La flore atlantique européenne. Documents pour les cartes des productions végétales serie Europe-Atlantique, vol. 1*. Faculté des Sciences, Toulouse.

Durka, W., Baum, A., Baum, H. & Michalski, S.G. 2017. Darwin's legacy in *Platanthera*: are there more than two species in the *Platanthera bifolia/chlorantha* group? *Plant Systematics and Evolution* **303**: 419–431.

Dyderski, M.K., Chmura, D., Dylewski, L., Horodecki, P., Jagodziński, A.M., Pietras, M., Robakowski, P. & Woziwoda, B. 2020. Biological Flora of the British Isles. No. 291. *Quercus rubra*. *Journal of Ecology* **108**: 1199–1225.

Dyer, A.F., Lindsay, S. & Parks, J.C. 2000. Allozyme, spore and frond variation in some Scottish populations of the ferns *Cystopteris dickieana* and *C. fragilis*. *Edinburgh Journal of Botany* **57**: 83–105.

Dyer, A.G., Whitney, H.M., Arnold, S.E.J., Glover, B.J. & Chittka, L. 2007. Mutations perturbing petal cell shape and anthocyanin synthesis influence bumblebee perception of *Antirrhinum majus* flower colour. *Arthropod-Plant Interactions* **1**: 45–55.

Earle, C.J. 2021. The Gymnosperm Database (https://conifers.org/).

Easy, G. 1979. *Malva alcea* L. and *M. moschata* L. in Cambridgeshire. *Watsonia* **23**: 24–25.

Easy, G.M. 2006. Cambridgeshire Verbascums. *Nature in Cambridgeshire* **48**: 16–19.

Eccarius, W. 2016. *Die Orchideengattung* Dactylorhiza. Self-published, Eisenach, Germany.

Eckenwalder, J.E. 2009. *Conifers of the World*. Timber Press, London.

Edees, E.S. 1972. *Flora of Staffordshire*. David & Charles, Newton Abbott.

Edees, E.S. & Newton, A. 1988. *Brambles of the British Isles*. The Ray Society, London.

Edgington, J.A. 2004. *Sagina maritima* Don (Caryophyllaceae) and other halophytes in London. *Watsonia* **25**: 121–126.

Edgington, J.A. 2011. *Asplenium fontanum*. *Pteridologist* **5**: 286–7.

Edgington, M.J. 1999. *Erica ciliaris* L. (Ericaceae) discovered in the Blackdown Hills, on the Somerset-Devon border (v.c. 3). *Watsonia* **22**: 426–428.

Egea, G., Pérez-Urrestarazu, L., González-Pérez, J., Franco-Salas, A. & Fernández-Cañero, R. 2014. Lighting systems evaluation for indoor living walls. *Urban Forestry & Urban Greening* **13**: 475–483.

Egolf, D.R. & Andrick, A.O. 1995. *A Checklist of* Pyracantha *Cultivars*. United States National Arboretum Contribution Number 8. USDA Agricultural Research Service, Washington DC.

Elkington, T.T. 1963. Biological Flora of the British Isles. No. 91. *Gentiana verna* L. *Journal of Ecology* **51**: 755–767.

Elkington, T.T. 1964. Biological Flora of the British Isles. No. 96. *Myosotis alpestris* F.W. Schmidt. *Journal of Ecology* **52**: 709–722.

Elkington, T.T. 1969. Cytotaxonomic variation in *Potentilla fruticosa* L. *New Phytologist* **68**: 151–160.

Elkington, T.T. 1971. Biological Flora of the British Isles. No. 124. *Dryas octopetala* L. *Journal of Ecology* **59**: 887–905.

Elkington, T.T. 1972. Variation in *Gentiana verna* L. *New Phytologist* **71**: 1203–1211.

Elkington, T.T. & Woodell, S.R.J. 1963. Biological Flora of the British Isles. No. 92. *Potentilla fruticosa* L. *Journal of Ecology* **51**: 769–781.

Ellis, K.B. 1994. *The distribution of* Acaena novae-zelandiae *T. Kirk. (the Piri-Piri Burr) on Lindisfarne National Nature Reserve*. Masters thesis, Durham University.

Ellison, W.G. 2010. *Second Atlas of the Breeding Birds of Maryland and the District of Columbia*. The John Hopkins University Press.

Ennis, T. 2007. The occurrence of *Dactylorhiza lapponica* in Co. Antrim: a new Irish record. *BSBI News* **105**: 13–15.

Environment Agency, 2019. *The State of the Environment: soil*.

Ernst, A., Sauer, J., Wittig, R. & Nowak, C. 2013. Local genetic structure of a montane herb among isolated grassland patches: implications for the preservation of genetic diversity under climate change. *Population Ecology* **55**: 417–431.

Ernst, W.H.O. & Malloch, A.J.C. 1994. Biological Flora of the British Isles. No. 181. *Phleum arenarium* L. *Journal of Ecology* **82**: 403–413.

Erskine, S.E., Killick, H.J., Lambrick, C.R. & Lee, E.M. 2018. *Oxfordshire's Threatened Plants*. Pisces Publications, Berkshire.

Essl, F., Biró, K., Brandes, D., Broennimann, O., Bullock, J.M., Chapman, D.S., Chauvel, B., Dullinger, S., Fumanal, B., Guisan, A., Karrer, G., Kazinczi, G., Kueffer, C., Laitung, B., Lavoie, C., Leitner, M., Mang, T., Moser, D., Müller-Schärer, H., Petitpierre, B., Richter, R., Schaffner, U., Smith, M., Starfinger, U., Vautard, R., Vogl, G., von der Lippe, M. & Follak, S. 2015. Biological Flora of the British Isles. No. 278. *Ambrosia artemisiifolia*. *Journal of Ecology* **103**: 1069–1098.

Evans, L.D.I. & Rich, T.C.G. 2021. Current status of the rare British endemic *Gentianella amarella* subsp. *occidentalis*, Dune Gentian (Gentianaceae). *British & Irish Botany* **3**: 136–151.

Evans, P.A., Evans, I.M. & Rothero, G.P. 2002. *Flora of Assynt*. Privately published.

Evans, T.G. 2007. *Flora of Monmouthshire*. Chepstow Society, Chepstow.

Everett, D. 2013. *The Genus* Tulipa: *Tulips of the World*. Kew Garden Press, Richmond.

Everett, S. 1999. Alder death cause revealed. *British Wildlife* **10**: 365.

Everitt, J.H., Lonard, R.L. & Little, C.R. 2007. *Weeds in South Texas and Northern Mexico*. Texas Tech University Press, Lubbock.

Farjon, A. 1990. *Pinaceae*. Koeltz Scientific Books, Germany.

Farjon, A. 2005a. *A monograph of the Cupressaceae and* Sciadopitys. Royal Botanic Gardens, Kew, Richmond.

Farjon, A. 2005b. *Pines*. Edn. 2. Brill Scientific Publishers, Leiden.

Farmer, A.M. 1989. Biological Flora of the British Isles. No. 165. *Lobelia dortmanna* L. *Journal of Ecology* **77**: 1161–1173.

Farrell, L. 1979. The distribution of *Leucojum aestivum* L. in the British Isles. *Watsonia* **12**: 325–332.

Farrell, L. 1985. Biological Flora of the British Isles. No. 160. *Orchis militaris* L. (*O. galatea* Poir, *O. rivini* Gouan, *O. tephrosanthes* Willd. & Sw.). *Journal of Ecology* **73**: 1041–1053.

Faulkner, J.S. 1972. Chromosome studies on *Carex* section Acutae in north-west Europe. *Botanical Journal of the Linnean Society* **65**: 271–301.

Fay, M.F., Bone, R., Cook, P., Kahandawala, I., Greensmith, J., Harris, S., Pedersen, H.A., Ingrouille, M.J. & Lexer, C. 2009. Genetic diversity in *Cypripedium calceolus* (Orchidaceae) with a focus on north-western Europe, as revealed by plastid DNA length polymorphisms. *Annals of Botany* **104**: 517–525.

Fearn, G.M. 1973. Biological Flora of the British Isles. No. 134. *Hippocrepis comosa* L. *Journal of Ecology* **61**: 915–926.

Fearn, G.M. 1987. Exploited plants. Sainfoin. *Biologist* **34**: 93–97.

Feng, H.-Z., Wei, S.-J., Wang, L.-Y., Chen, S.-F., Fan, Q. & Liao, W.-B. 2021. A taxonomic revision of the *Pyracantha crenulata* complex (Rosaceae, Maleae). *Phytotaxa* **478**: 239–252.

Ferguson, D. & Sang, T. 2001. Speciation through homoploid hybridization between allotetraploids in peonies (*Paeonia*). *Proceedings of the National Academy of Sciences USA* **98**: 3915–3919.

Ferguson, I.K. & Ferguson, L.F. 1974. *Polygonum maritimum* L. new to Ireland. *Irish Naturalists' Journal* **18**: 95.

Ferrarini, A., Alsafran, M.H., Dai, J. & Alatalo, J.M. 2019. Improving niche projections of plant species under climate change: *Silene acaulis* on the British Isles as a case study. *Climate Dynamics* **52**: 1413–1423.

Ferris, C., King, R.A. & Gray, A.J. 1997. Molecular evidence for the maternal parentage in the hybrid origin of *Spartina anglica* C. E. Hubbard. *Molecular Ecology* **6**: 185–187.

Ferry, B., Banks, B., Sears, J. & Sculley, C. 2010. Stinking Hawk's-beard - a reluctant candidate for Species Recovery. *British Wildlife* **21**: 255–260.

Fiala, J.L. 1988. *Lilacs*. Christopher Helm, London.

Fichtner, A. & Wissemann, V. 2021. Biological Flora of the British Isles. No. 295. *Crataegus monogyna*. *Journal of Ecology* **109**: 541–571.

Field, M.H. 1994. The status of *Bupleurum falcatum* L. (Apiaceae) in the British flora. *Watsonia* **20**: 115–117.

Filippov, E.G., Andronova, E.V. & Kazlova, V.M. 2017. Genetic structure of populations of *Dactylorhiza ochroleuca* and *D. incarnata* (Orchidaceae) in the area of their joint growth in Russia and Belarus. *Russian Journal of Genetics* **53**: 661–671.

Firbank, L.G. 1988. Biological Flora of the British Isles. No. 165. *Agrostemma githago* L. *Journal of Ecology* **76**: 1232–1246.

Firbank, L.G., Heard, M.S., Woiwood, I.P., Hawes, C., Haughton, A.J., Champion, G.T., Scott, R.J., Hill, M.O., Dewar, A.M., Squire, G.R., May, M.J., Brooks, D.R., Bohan, D.A., Daniels, R.E., Osborne, J.L., Roy, D.B., Black, H.I.J., Rothery, P. & Perry, J.N. 2003. An introduction to the Farm-Scale Evaluations of genetically modified herbicide-tolerant crops. *Journal of Applied Ecology* **40**: 2–16.

Fischer, M. 1975. The *Veronica hederifolia* group: taxonomy, ecology and phylogeny. In Walters, S.M. (Ed.) *European floristic and taxonomic studies* pp. 48–60 E. W. Classey, Faringdon.

Fischer, M.A. 1987. On the origin of *Veronica persica* (Scrophulariaceae) - a contribution to the history of a neophytic weed. *Plant Systematics and Evolution* **155**: 105–132.

Fitter, A., Hammond, M., Huby, M., Walker, K.J. & Whelpdale, P. 2021. The status of *Carex elongata* (Cyperaceae) in Yorkshire. *British & Irish Botany* **3**: 482–489.

FitzGerald, R. 1990. *Rare Plant Survey of South-West England. Vol. 3. Cornwall. CSD Report, no. 1060*. Nature Conservancy Council, Peterborough.

FitzGerald, R. 1998. Althaea hirsuta - *Hairy Mallow - status of British records between 1792 and 1997. Back from the Brink Project Report No. 98*. Plantlife, London.

FitzGerald, R. & Jermy, C. 1987. *Equisetum ramosissimum* in Somerset. *Pteridologist* **1**: 178–181.

Flora of North America Editorial Committee 1997. *Flora of North America north of Mexico. Vol. 3. Magnoliophyta: Magnoliidae and Hamamelidae*. Oxford University Press, New York.

Flora of North America Editorial Committee 2000. *Flora of North America north of Mexico. Vol. 22. Magnoliophyta: Alismatidae, Arecidae, Commelinidae (in part), and Zingiberidae*. Oxford University Press, New York.

Flora of North America Editorial Committee, Welsh, S.L., Crompton, C.W. & Clemants, S.E. (Eds.) 1993. *Flora of North America North of Mexico [Online]* **4**: 277–278 eFloras.

Fogg, G.E. 1950. Biological Flora of the British Isles. No. 31. *Sinapis arvensis* L. *Journal of Ecology* **38**: 415–429.

Foley, M.J.Y. 1992. The current distribution and abundance of *Orchis ustulata* L. (Orchidaceae) in the British Isles: an updated summary. *Watsonia* **19**: 121–126.

Foley, M.J.Y. 1993. *Orobanche reticulata* Wallr. populations in Yorkshire (north-east England). *Watsonia* **19**: 247–257.

Foley, M.J.Y. 2000a. A morphological comparison between some British *Orobanche* species (Orobanchaceae) and their closely-related non-British counterparts from continental Europe: *Orobanche reticulata* Wallr. s.l. *Watsonia* **23**: 257–267.

Foley, M.J.Y. 2000b. *Dactylorhiza incarnata* subsp. *ochroleuca* (Wüstnei ex Böll) P.F. Hunt & Summerhayes (Orchidaceae): a comparison of British and European plants. *Watsonia* **23**: 299–303.

Foley, M.J.Y. 2004. A summary of the past and present status of *Spiranthes aestivalis* (Poir.) Rich. (Orchidaceae) in north-west Europe. *Watsonia* **25**: 193–201.

Foley, M.J.Y. & Porter, M.S. 2000. *Carex muricata* subsp. *muricata* (Cyperaceae) – a review of its present status in Britain. *Watsonia* **23**: 279–286.

Foley, M.J.Y. & Clarke, S. 2005. *Orchids of the British Isles*. Griffin Press, Cheltenham, Gloucestershire.

Foley, M.J.Y. & Porter, M.S. 2006. *Calamagrostis scotica* (Druce) Druce (Poaceae), a Red Data Book Plant: its history, taxonomy, ecology and genetics. *Watsonia* **26**: 51–55.

Fone, A.L. 1989. Competition in mixtures of the annual *Hypochoeris glabra* and perennial *H. radicata*. *Journal of Ecology* **77**: 484–494.

Forbes, R.S. & Northridge, R.H. 2012. *The Flora of County Fermanagh*. National Museums Northern Ireland, Holywood, County Down.

Forestry Commission Scotland 2009. *Scottish forestry strategy: 'Action for juniper', PDF. (with later revisions)*. Forestry Commission Scotland, Edinburgh.

Forrest, A.D., Hollingsworth, M.L., Hollingsworth, P.M., Sydes, C. & Bateman, R.M. 2004. Population genetic structure in European populations of *Spiranthes romanzoffiana* set in the context of other genetic studies on orchids. *Heredity* **92**: 218–227.

Forrest, G.I., Cottrell, J.E. & White, I.M.S. 1997. The use of RAPD analysis to study diversity in British black poplar (*Populus nigra* L. subsp. *betulifolia* (Pursh) W. Wettst. (Salicaceae)). *Watsonia* **21**: 305–312.

Forster, T.F. & Forster, T. 1842. *Flora Tonbrigensis by the late T.F. Forster with additions by T. Forster*. J. Clifford, Tonbridge Wells.

Foss, P.J. & O'Connell, C.A. 1985. Notes on the ecology of *Sarracenia purpurea* L. on Irish peatlands. *Irish Naturalists' Journal* **21**: 440–443.

Foss, P.J. & Doyle, G.J. 1990. The history of *Erica erigena* R. Ross, an Irish plant with a disjunct European distribution. *Journal of Quaternary Science* **5**: 1–16.

Foust, C.M. 1992. *Rhubarb: the wondrous drug*. Princeton University Press, Princeton, New Jersey.

Fowler, N., Zasada, J. & Harper, J.L. 1983. Genetic components of morphological variation in *Salix repens*. *New Phytologist* **95**: 121–131.

Francis, A. & Warwick, S.I. 2003. The biology of Canadian weeds. 120. *Neslia paniculata* (L.) Desv. *Canadian Journal of Plant Science* **83**: 441–451.

Francis, A., Cavers, P.B. & Warwick, S.I. 2009. The biology of Canadian weeds. 140. *Hesperis matronalis* L. *Canadian Journal of Plant Science* **89**: 191–206.

Fraser, L., Turkington, R. & Chanway, C.P. 1993. The biology of Canadian weeds. 102. *Gaultheria shallon* Pursh. *Canadian Journal of Plant Science* **73**: 1233–1247.

Fraser-Jenkins, C.R. 2007. The species and subspecies in the *Dryopteris affinis* group. *Fern Gazette* **18**: 1–26.

Freijsen, A.H.J. & Heeres, E. 1972. Welke soort rood zwenkgras (*Festuca rubra* s.l.) komt voor in de jonge kustduinen van Voorne en die van overig Nederland? *Gorteria* **6**: 57–60.

French, C.N. 2020. *A Flora of Cornwall*. Wheal Seton Press, Camborne.

French, C.N., Murphy, R.J. & Atkinson, M.G.C. 1999. *Flora of Cornwall*. Wheal Seton Press, Camborne.

French, G.C., Hollingsworth, P.M., Corner, R.W.M., Roberts, F.J. & Taylor, I. 2005. Clonal diversity in two recently discovered English populations of *Carex vaginata* Tausch (Cyperaceae). *Watsonia* **25**: 389–395.

French, G.C., Hollingsworth, P.M., Silverside, A.J. & Ennos, R.A. 2008. Genetics, taxonomy and the conservation of British *Euphrasia*. *Conservation Genetics* **9**: 1547–1562.

Friday, L. (Ed.) 1997. *Wicken Fen: the making of a nature reserve*. Harley Books, Colchester.

Fryer, J. & Hylmö, B. 1994. The native British *Cotoneaster* – Great Orme Berry – renamed. *Watsonia* **20**: 61–63.

Fryer, J. & Hylmö, B. 2009. *Cotoneasters*. Timber Press, Portland, Oregon & London.

Fukatsu, M., Horie, S., Maki, M. & Dohzono, I. 2018. Hybridization, coexistence, and possible reproductive interference between native *Oxalis corniculata* and alien *O. dillenii* in Japan. *Plant Systematics and Evolution* **305**: 127–137.

Galán, A. & Castroviejo, S. 2007. *Zantedeschia*. In Castroviejo, S. (Ed.) *Flora Iberica, vol. 18* pp. 308–310 Real Jardín Botánico, Madrid.

Gantt, E. & Arnott, H.J. 1965. Spore germination and development of the young gametophyte of the Ostrich Fern (*Matteuccia struthiopteris*). *American Journal of Botany* **52**: 82–94.

García-Gonzalez, A. & Clark, S.C. 1989. The distribution of *Minuartia verna* and *Thlaspi alpestre* in the British Isles in relation to 13 soil metals. *Vegetatio* **84**: 87–98.

Gardiner, A.S. 1974. A history of the taxonomy and distribution of the native oak species. In Perring, F.H. & Morris, M.G. (Eds.) *The British Oak* pp. 13–26 Classey, Faringdon.

Gardiner, A.S. 1984. Taxonomy of infraspecific variation in *Betula pubescens* Ehrh., with particular reference to the Scottish Highlands. *Proceedings of the Royal Society of Edinburgh* **85B**: 13–26.

Gargiulo, R., Worswick, G., Arnold, C., Pike, L.J., Cowan, R.S., Hardwick, K.A., Chapman, T. & Fay, M. 2019. Conservation of the threatened species, *Pulsatilla vulgaris* Mill. (Pasqueflower), is aided by reproductive system and polyploidy. *Journal of Heredity* **110**: 618–628.

Geddes, C. & Payne, S. 2006. Loss of Highland Cudweed *Gnaphalium norvegicum* from the Caenlochan area, Angus Scotland. *BSBI News* **102**: 26–27.

Gelin, Z., Wu, Z.Y., Raven, P.H., Hong, D.Y., Mosyakin, S.L. & Clemants, S.E. (Eds.) 2003. *Flora of China* 5: 383 eFloras Missouri Botanical Garden Press, St. Louis.

Geltman, D.V. 1992. *Urtica galeopsifolia* Wierzb. ex Opiz (Urticaceae) in Wicken Fen (E. England). *Watsonia* 19: 127–129.

Gent, G. & Wilson, R. 1995. *The Flora of Northamptonshire and the Soke of Peterborough*. Kettering and District Natural History Society and the Northamptonshire Flora Group.

George, J.P., Woodman, J., Hampton, M., Konrad, H. & Geburek, T. 2016. True Service-tree (*Sorbus domestica*, Rosaceae) in the British Isles: Rare but diverse. *New Journal of Botany* 6: 21–30.

George, M. 1992. *The land use, ecology and conservation of Broadland*. Packard Publishing, Chichester.

Gibbons, E.J. & Lousley, J.E. 1958. An inland *Armeria* overlooked in Britain. Part 1. *Watsonia* 4: 125–135.

Gibson, C. 2000. Notes on Essex specialities. 3: Annual Sea-purslane *Atriplex pedunculata* L. *Essex Naturalist (new series)* 17: 129–132.

Gibson, D.J. & Newman, J.A. 2001. Biological Flora of the British Isles. No. 217. *Festuca arundinacea* Schreber (*F. elatior* subsp. *arundinacea* (Schreber) Hackel). *Journal of Ecology* 89: 304–324.

Gibson, D.J. & Taylor, I. 2005. *Festuca longifolia* Thuill. (*F. glauca* auct. non Vill., *F. glauca* var. *caesia* (Sm.) Howarth, *F. caesia* Sm.). *Journal of Ecology* 93: 214–226.

Gilbert, D. 2011. *Interactions between climate and land use which drive dynamics in treeline ecotone scrub in Scotland*. Ph.D. thesis, University of Edinburgh.

Gilbert, J.L. 1956. Flora Report. *Huntingdonshire Fauna and Flora Society* 9: 10–16.

Gilbert, O.L. 1970. Biological Flora of the British Isles. No. 118. *Dryopteris villarii* (Bellardi) Woynar. *Journal of Ecology* 58: 301–313.

Gilbert, O.L. 1990. Wild figs by the River Don, Sheffield. *Watsonia* 18: 84–85.

Gilbert, O.L. 1995. Biological Flora of the British Isles. No. 184. *Symphoricarpos albus* (L.) S.F. Blake. *Journal of Ecology* 83: 159–166.

Gilián, L.D., Endrédi, A., Zsinka, B., Neményi, A. & Nagy, J.G. 2019. Morphological and reproductive trait-variability of a food deceptive orchid, *Cephalanthera rubra* along different altitudes. *Applied Ecology and Environmental Research* 17: 5619–5639.

Gill, J.A. & Davy, A.J. 1983. Variation and polyploidy within lowland populations of the *Betula pendula / B. pubescens* complex. *New Phytologist* 94: 433–451.

Gillam, B. 1993. *The Wiltshire Flora*. Pisces Publications, Newbury.

Gimingham, C.H. 1960. Biological Flora of the British Isles. No. 74. *Calluna vulgaris* (L.) Hull. *Journal of Ecology* 48: 455–483.

Gioria, M. & Osborne, B.A. 2013. Biological Flora of the British Isles. No. 270. *Gunnera tinctoria*. *Journal of Ecology* 101: 243–264.

Godwin, H. 1943. Biological Flora of the British Isles. No. 11. Rhamnaceae (pp. 66–68). *Rhamnus cathartica* L. (pp. 69–76), *Frangula alnus* Miller (*Rhamnus frangula* L.) (the genus *Rhamnus* sensu lato, L.) (pp. 77–92). *Journal of Ecology* 31: 66–92.

Godwin, H. 1975. *The history of the British Flora: A Factual Basis for Phytogeography*. Edn. 2. Cambridge University Press, Cambridge.

Goldblatt, P., Manning, J. & Dunlop, G. 2004. Crocosmia & Chasmanthe. Royal Horticultural Society Plant Collector Guide. Timber Press, Portland.

Good, R. 1936. On the distribution of lizard orchid (*Himantoglossum hircinum* Koch). *New Phytologist* 35: 142–170.

Goodman, P.J., Braybrooks, E.M. & Lambert, J.M. 1959. Investigations into 'die-back' in *Spartina townsendii* agg. I. The present status of *Spartina townsendii* in Britain. *Journal of Ecology* 47: 651–677.

Goodman, P.J. & Williams, W.T. 1961. Investigations into 'die-back' in *Spartina townsendii* agg. III. Physiological correlates of 'die-back'. *Journal of Ecology* 49: 391–398.

Goodway, K.M. 1957. The species problem in *Galium pumilum*. In Lousley, J.E. (Ed.) *Progress in the study of the British Flora* pp. 116–118 BSBI Conference Report No. 5 British Museum, London.

Goodwillie, R. 1999a. *Campanula trachelium* L. in Clare (H9), new to the Burren. *Irish Naturalists' Journal* 26: 286.

Goodwillie, R. 1999b. *Alopecurus aequalis* Sobol. new to Clare (H9) and S. E. Galway (H15). *Irish Naturalists' Journal* 26: 286–287.

Gorer, R. 1970. *The development of garden flowers*. Eyre & Spottiswoode, London.

Gornall, R.J. 1988. The coastal ecodeme of *Parnassia palustris* L. *Watsonia* 17: 139–143.

Gosler, A.G. 1990. Introgressive hybridization between *Crataegus monogyna* Jacq. and *C. laevigata* (Poiret) DC. in the Upper Thames valley, England. *Watsonia* 18: 49–62.

Grace, J. & Nelson, M. 1981. Insects and their pollen loads in a hybrid *Heracleum* site. *New Phytologist* 87: 413–423.

Grace, J.B. & Harrison, J.S. 1986. The biology of Canadian weeds. 73. *Typha latifolia* L., *Typha angustifolia* & *Typha* ×*glauca* Godr. *Canadian Journal of Plant Science* 66: 361–379.

Graham, G.G. 1988. *The Flora and Vegetation of County Durham*. Durham Flora Committee and Durham County Conservation Trust, Durham.

Graham, G.G. & Primavesi, A.L. 1993. *Roses of Great Britain and Ireland*. BSBI Handbook no. 7. Botanical Society of the British Isles, London.

Graham, J.J. & Preston, C.D. 2012. *Potamogeton compressus* recolonises Cambridgeshire, 2004–2010. *Nature in Cambridgeshire* 54: 3–11.

Graham, R.A. 1950. Mint notes, II. *Mentha gracilis* Sole, and its relationship to *Mentha cardiaca* Baker. *Watsonia* 1: 276–278.

Graham, R.A. 1958. Mint notes, VIII. A new mint from Scotland. *Watsonia* 4: 119–121.

Grassly, N.C., Harris, S.A. & Cronk, Q.C.B. 1996. British *Apium repens* (Jacq.) Lag. (Apiaceae) status assessed using random amplified polymorphic DNA (RAPD). *Watsonia* 21: 103–111.

Gray, A.J. & Scott, R. 1977. Biological Flora of the British Isles. No. 140. *Puccinellia maritima* (Huds.) Parl. *Journal of Ecology* 65: 699–716.

Gray, A.J. & Benham, P.E.M. 1990. Spartina anglica - a research review. ITE Research Publication no. 2. HMSO, London.

Gray, G.R. 1981. *Aspects of the ecology of Barren Brome (Bromus sterilis L.)*. University of Oxford.

Green, A.E., Unsworth, R.K.F., Chadwick, M.A. & Jones, P.J.S. 2021. Historical analysis exposes catastrophic seagrass loss for the United Kingdom. *Frontiers in Plant Science* 12.

Green, D. 2015. *Sorbus* of the Doward. *BSBI News* 130: 12–16.

Green, I. 1998. *Hordeum marinum* along the A5 in Somerset, V.C. 6. *BSBI News* 79: 52.

Green, P.S. 1954. *Stellaria nemorum* L. subspecies *glochidisperma* Murbeck in Britain. *Watsonia* 3: 122–126.

Green, P.S. 1973. *Hebe* × *franciscana* (Eastwood) Souter, not *H.* × *lewisii* - naturalised in Britain. *Watsonia* 9: 371–372.

Green, P.R. 2000. *Pontederia cordata* and *Sagittaria rigida* new to Ireland. *BSBI News* 83: 44.

Green, P.R. 2007. *Minuartia recurva* found in Co. Waterford. *BSBI News* 104: 4.

Green, P.R. 2008. *Flora of County Waterford*. National Botanic Gardens of Ireland, Dublin.

Green, P.R. 2018. *Atriplex praecox* (Early Orache) a new native species to Ireland in 2017. *BSBI News* 137: 27–28.

Green, P.R., Green, I.P. & Crouch, G.A. 1997. *The Atlas Flora of Somerset*. Privately published, Wayford and Yeovil.

Green, S., Elliot, M., Armstrong, A. & Hendry, S.J. 2015. *Phytophthora austrocedrae* emerges as a serious threat to juniper (*Juniperus communis*) in Britain. *Plant Pathology* 64: 456–466.

Greenwood, E.F. 2004. Coastal *Elytrigia* species and hybrids in North-western England and northern Wales. *BSBI News* 95: 15–19.

Greenwood, E.F. 2012. *Flora of North Lancashire*. Palatine Books, Lancaster.

Greig-Smith, J. & Sagar, G.R. 1981. Biological causes of local rarity in *Carlina vulgaris*. In Synge, H. (Ed.) *The Biological Aspects of Rare Plant Conservation* pp. 389–400 BSBI Conference Report no.17 John Wiley & Sons, Chichester.

Greig-Smith, P. 1948. Biological Flora of the British Isles. No. 23. *Urtica* genus L. (pp. 339–343), *U. dioica* L. (pp. 343–351), *U. urens* L. (pp. 351–355). *Journal of Ecology* 36: 339–355.

Grenfell, A.L. 1982. Adventive News 24. *BSBI News* 33: 10–13.

Grenfell, A.L. 1983. Adventive ferns - 1. *BSBI News* 35: 12.

Grenfell, A.L. 1984. Cucurbitaceae in Britain. *BSBI News* 38: 13–18.

Grey-Wilson, C. 1993. *Poppies. A Guide to the Poppy Family in the Wild and in Cultivation*. Timber Press, Portland, Oregon.

Grey-Wilson, C. 1997. *Cyclamen: a guide for gardeners, horticulturalists and botanists*. B.T. Batsford, London.

Grey-Wilson, C. & Mathew, B. 1981. *Bulbs*. Collins, London.

Grey-Wilson, C. & Matthews, V. 1983. *Gardening on walls*. William Collins Sons and Co. Ltd, London.

Grey-Wilson, C., Leeds, R. & Rolfe, R. 2020. Colchicum - the complete guide. Royal Horticultural Society, Peterborough.

Grieve, M. 1974. *A Modern Herbal, new edition by C. F. Leyel*. Jonathan Cape, London.

Griffiths, M.E. & Proctor, M.C.F. 1956. *Helianthemum canum* (L.) Baumg. In: M. C. F. Proctor, Biological Flora of the British Isles. No. 58. *Helianthemum* Mill. *Journal of Ecology* 44: 677–682.

Grigson, G. 1955. *The Englishman's Flora*. Phoenix House, London.

Grime, J.P., Hodgson, J.G. & Hunt, R. 2007. *Comparative Plant Ecology*. Edn. 2. Castlepoint Press and Botanical Society of the British Isles.

Groom, Q.J. 2013. Some poleward movement of British native vascular plants is occurring, but the fingerprint of climate change is not evident. *PeerJ* 1: e77.

Groom, Q., Walker, K.J. & McIntosh, J. 2011. *BSBI Recording the British and Irish flora 2010–2020. Annex 1: Guidance on sampling approaches*. Botanical Society of the British Isles, London.

Groom, Q.J., Durkin, J., O'Reilly, J., Mclay, A., Richards, A., Angel, J., Horsley, A., Rogers, M. & Young, G. 2015. A benchmark survey of the common plants of South Northumberland and Durham, United Kingdom. *Biodiversity Data Journal* 3: e7318.

Groom, Q., Strubbe, D., Adriaens, T., Davis, A.J.S., Desmet, P., Oldoni, D., Reyserhove, L., Roy, H.E. & Vanderhoeven, S. 2019a. Empowering citizens to inform decision-making as a way forward to support invasive alien species policy. *Citizen Science: Theory and Practice* 4: 33.

Groom, Q.J., Van der Straeten, J. & Hoste, I. 2019b. The origin of *Oxalis corniculata* L. *PeerJ* 7: e6384.

Grose, D. 1957. *The Flora of Wiltshire*. Natural History Section, Wiltshire Archaeological and Natural History Society, Devizes.

Gross, K.L. & Werner, P.A. 1978. The biology of Canadian weeds. 28. *Verbascum thapsus* L. and *V. blattaria* L. *Canadian Journal of Plant Science* **58**: 401–413.

Gross, R.S., Werner, P.A. & Hawthorn, W.R. 1980. The biology of Canadian weeds. 38. *Arctium minus* (Hill) Bernh. and A. *Lappa* L. *Canadian Journal of Plant Science* **60**: 621–634.

Grounds, R. 1989. *Ornamental grasses*. C. Helm, London.

Grubb, P.J., Crowder, A.A., Pearson, M.C. & Langlois, P.H. 1990. Biological Flora of the British Isles. No. 167. *Drosera* genus L. (p. 233); *D. rotundifolia* L. (pp. 233–252); *D. anglica* Huds. (pp. 252–257); *D. intermedia* Drev. & Hayne (pp. 257–267). *Journal of Ecology* **78**: 233–267.

Gruntman, M., Groß, D., Májeková, M. & Tielbörger, K. 2017. Decision-making in plants under competition. *Nature Communications* **8**: 1–8.

Gulden, R.H., Warwick, S.I. & Thomas, A.G. 2008. The Biology of Canadian Weeds. 137. *Brassica napus* L. and *B. rapa*. *Canadian Journal of Plant Science* **88**: 951–996.

Gulliver, R.L. 1996. The status of *Spiranthes romanzoffiana* Cham. (Orchidaceae), Irish Lady's Tresses, on Colonsay (v.c. 102) in 1995; with special reference to associated plant communities. *Watsonia* **21**: 202–204.

Gulliver, R.L. 1997. Pyramidal Bugle (*Ajuga pyramidalis*) on Colonsay (VC 102). *Glasgow Naturalist* **23(2)**: 55.

Gunn, I.D.M. & Carvallo, L. 2020. *Slender Naiad (*Najas flexilis*) Habitat Quality Assessment. CRW2018_27*. Scotland's Centre of Expertise for Waters (CREW).

Gurney, M. 2000. *Population genetics and conservation biology of* Primula elatior. Ph.D. thesis, University of Cambridge.

Gurney, M., Preston, C.D., Barrett, J. & Briggs, D. 2007. Hybridisation between Oxlip *Primula elatior* (L.) Hill and Primrose *P. vulgaris* Hudson, and the identification of their variable hybrid *P.* ×*digenea* A. Kerner. *Watsonia* **26**: 239–251.

Gynn, E.G. & Richards, A.J. 1985. Biological Flora of the British Isles. No. 161. *Acaena novae-zelandiae* T. Kirk. *Journal of Ecology* **73**: 1055–1063.

Hackney, P. 1992. *Stewart & Corry's Flora of the North-east of Ireland*. Edn. 3. Queen's University, Belfast.

Haggar, J. 2004a. The early marsh orchid (*Dactylorhiza incarnata*) in Northern Europe. III. The British and Irish fen, marsh and bog forms. *Journal of the Hardy Orchid Society* **31**: 18–23.

Haggar, J. 2004b. The early marsh orchid (*Dactylorhiza incarnata*) in Northern Europe. IV. Northern forms, blotched leaves and polymorphism. *Journal of the Hardy Orchid Society* **32**: 45–51.

Haggar, J. 2005a. The early marsh orchid (*Dactylorhiza incarnata*) in Northern Europe. V. Red flowers and dune forms. *Journal of the Hardy Orchid Society* **36**: 51–59.

Haggar, J. 2005b. The early marsh orchid (*Dactylorhiza incarnata*) in Northern Europe. VI. The significance of yellow flowers. *Journal of the Hardy Orchid Society* **38**: 116–124.

Haines, A. 2003. *The families Huperziaceae and Lycopodiaceae of New England*. V.F. Thomas Co, Bar Harbor, Maine.

Hall, I.V., Steiner, E., Threadgill, P. & Jones, R.W. 1988. The biology of Canadian weeds. 84. *Oenothera biennis* L. *Canadian Journal of Plant Science* **68**: 163–173.

Halliday, G. 1960. *Taxonomic and ecological studies in the* Arenaria ciliata *and* Minuartia verna *complexes*. Ph.D. thesis, University of Cambridge.

Halliday, G. 1995. Two subspecies of *Festuca rubra* L. new to England. *Watsonia* **20**: 412.

Halliday, G. 1997. *A Flora of Cumbria*. Centre for North-West Regional Studies, University of Lancaster, Lancaster.

Hambler, D.J. & Dixon, J.M. 2003. Biological Flora of the British Isles. No. 230. *Primula farinosa* L. *Journal of Ecology* **91**: 694–705.

Hamet-Ahti, L. 1987. Mountain birch and mountain woodland in NW Europe. *Phytocoenologia* **15**: 449–453.

Hampton, M. 2015. *Sorbus domestica* in the Wye Valley. *BSBI News* **130**: 30–33.

Hamston, T.J., Wilson, R.J., de Vere, N., Rich, T.C.G., Stevens, J.R. & Cresswell, J.E. 2017. Breeding system and spatial isolation from congeners strongly constrain seed set in an insect-pollinated apomictic tree: *Sorbus subcuneata* (Rosaceae). *Scientific Reports* **7**: 45122.

Hamston, T.J., de Vere, N., King, R.A., Pellicer, J., Fay, M.F., Cresswell, J.E. & Stevens, J.R. 2018. Apomixis and Hybridization Drives Reticulate Evolution and Phyletic Differentiation in *Sorbus* L.: Implications for Conservation. *Frontiers in Plant Science* **9**: 1796.

Handley, R.J. & Davy, A.J. 2000. Discovery of male plants of *Najas marina* L. (Hydrocharitaceae) in Britain. *Watsonia* **23**: 331–334.

Hanrahan, S.A. 2018. *The ecology and conservation of* Arctostaphylos uva-ursi *Bearberry heath habitats in the Burren, Western Ireland*. Ph.D. Thesis, NUI Galway.

Hanson, C.G. & Mason, J.L. 1985. Bird seed aliens in Britain. *Watsonia* **15**: 237–252.

Hanson, G. 2002. Yet more *Persicaria capitata*. *BSBI News* **89**: 52.

Harley, R.M. 1956. *Rubus arcticus* L. in Britain. *Watsonia* **3**: 237–238.

Harmes, P.A. & Spiers, A. 1993. *Polygonum maritimum* L. in East Sussex (v.c. 14). *Watsonia* **19**: 271–273.

Harpenslager, S.F., Lamers, L.P.M., van der Heide, T., Roelofs, J.G.M. & Smolders, A.J.P. 2015. Harnessing facilitation: Why successful re-introduction of *Stratiotes aloides* requires high densities under high nitrogen loading. *Biological Conservation* **195**: 17–23.

Harper, J.L. 1957. Biological Flora of the British Isles. No. 61. *Ranunculus acris* L. (pp. 289–314), *R. repens* L. (pp. 314–325), *R. bulbosus* L. (pp. 325–342). *Journal of Ecology* **45**: 289–342.

Harper, J.L. & Wood, W.A. 1957. Biological Flora of the British Isles. No. 62. *Senecio jacobaea* L. *Journal of Ecology* **45**: 617–637.

Harper, J.L. & Cavers, P.B. 1964. Biological Flora of the British Isles. No. 98. *Rumex obtusifolius* L., *R. crispus* L. *Journal of Ecology* **52**: 737–754, 754.

Harper, M. 2000. *At war with aliens*. Plantlife, London.

Harrap, A. & Harrap, S. 2009. *Orchids of Britain & Ireland*. Edn. 2. A. & C. Black, London.

Harrap, S. 2009. What is the British distribution of *Epipactis leptochila* (Narrow-lipped Helleborine)? *BSBI News* **111**: 12–14.

Harrap, S. 2017. Saltmarsh Goosefoot *Chenopodium chenopodioides*: new for West Norfolk (v.c.28)? *BSBI News* **134**: 19–20.

Harris, G.R. & Lovell, P.H. 1980. Localised spread of *Veronica filiformis*, *V. agrestis* and *V. persica*. *Journal of Applied Ecology* **17**: 815–826.

Harris, J. 2001. *Survey of the aquatic plants of the Upper Thurne Broads and Rivers*. Report to English Nature.

Harris, S.A. 2002. Introduction of Oxford Ragwort, *Senecio squalidus* L. (Asteraceae), to the United Kingdom. *Watsonia* **24**: 31–43.

Harrison, S.G. 1968. A New Zealand Willow-herb in Wales. *Nature in Wales* **11**: 74–78.

Harrold, P. 1978. A glabrous variety of *Sagina subulata* (Sw.) C. Presl. in Britain. *Transactions of the Botanical Society of Edinburgh* **43**: 1–5.

Harron, J. 1986. *Flora of Lough Neagh*. University of Ulster, Belfast: Irish Naturalists' Journal Committee & Coleraine.

Harron, J. 1992. The present distribution of the dark-leaved willow *Salix myrsinifolia* Salisb., in north-east Ireland. *Irish Naturalists' Journal* **24**: 8–11.

Harvey, H.J. & Meredith, T.C. 1981. The biology and conservation of Milk-Parsley, *Peucedanum palustre* at Wicken Fen. *Nature in Cambridgeshire* **24**: 38–42.

Harvey, J. 1981. *Mediaeval gardens*. B.T. Batsford, London.

Harvey, J.H. 1996. Fritillary and martagon - wild or garden? *Garden History* **24**: 30–38.

Harvey, M.J. 1966. An experiment with *Epilobium angustifolium*. *Proceedings of the Botanical Society of the British Isles* **6**: 229–231.

Haskell, G. 1960. The Raspberry wild in Britain. *Watsonia* **4**: 238–255.

Haslam, S.M. 1972. Biological Flora of the British Isles. No. 128. *Phragmites communis* Trin. *Journal of Ecology* **60**: 585–610.

Haslam, S.M. & McDougall, D.S.A. 1972. *The Reed ('Norfolk Reed')*. Edn. 2. Norfolk Reed Growers' Association.

Hatcher, P.E. 2003. Biological Flora of the British Isles. No. 177. *Impatiens noli-tangere* L. *Journal of Ecology* **91**: 147–167.

Hatcher, P.E., Wilkinson, M.J., Albani, M.C. & Hebbern, C.A. 2004. Conserving marginal populations of the food plant (*Impatiens noli-tangere*) of an endangered moth (*Eustroma reticulatum*) in a changing climate. *Biological Conservation* **116**: 305–317.

Hauke, R.L. 1965. An Analysis of a Variable Population of *Equisetum arvense* and *E.* × *litorale*. *American Fern Journal* **55**: 123–135.

Hawkes, J.G. 1990. *The potato: evolution, biodiversity and genetic resources*. Edn. 3. Belhaven Press, London.

Hawkins, J. 2020. The discovery and conservation of rare stoneworts in Suffolk farmland ponds. *Suffolk Natural History* **59**: 109–125.

Hawksford, J.E. & Hopkins, I.J. 2011. *The Flora of Staffordshire*. Staffordshire Wildlife Trust, Stafford.

Hawthorn, W.R. 1974. The biology of Canadian weeds. 4. *Plantago major* and *P. rugelli*. *Canadian Journal of Plant Science* **54**: 383–396.

Hayward, C.M. 1995. *The spread of* Epilobium brunnescens, *a non-indigenous species, in Cwm Idwal NNR, its effects on the local indigenous flora and the possible effect of climate change on its spread*. University of Wales, Bangor.

Hayward, I.M. & Druce, G.C. 1919. *The adventive flora of Tweedside*. T. Buncle & Co., Arbroath.

Headley, A.D. & Callaghan, T.V. 1990. Modular growth of *Huperzia selago* (Lycopodiaceae: Pteridophyta). *Fern Gazette* **13**: 361–372.

Hedberg, K.O. 1992. Taxonomic differentiation in *Saxifraga hirculus* L. (Saxifragaceae), a circumpolar Arctic-Boreal species of Central Asiatic origin. *Botanical Journal of the Linnean Society* **109**: 377–393.

Hedley, R. 1998. *The flowering and fruiting performance of* Cephalanthera longifolia, *with implications for conservation*. Hampshire Wildlife Trust.

Hedley, S. 2015. Potentilla fruticosa L. Shrubby Cinquefoil. *Species Account*. Botanical Society of Britain and Ireland.

Hedley, S. & Walker, K.J. 2015. Saxifraga hirculus L. Marsh Saxifrage. *Species Account*. Botanical Society of Britain and Ireland.

Hedrén, M. & Nordström, S. 2009a. Polymorphic populations of *Dactylorhiza incarnata* s.l. (Orchidaceae) on the Baltic island of Gotland: morphology, habitat preference and genetic differentiation. *Annals of Botany* **104**: 527–542.

Hedrén, M. & Nordström, S. 2009b. Genetic diversity and differentiation of allopolyploid *Dactylorhiza* (Orchidaceae), with particular focus on the *Dactylorhiza majalis* ssp. *traunsteineri/lapponica* complex. *Botanical Journal of the Linnean Society* **97**: 52–67.

Hedrén, M., Nordström, S. & Bateman, R.M. 2011a. Plastid and nuclear DNA marker data support the recognition of four tetraploid marsh orchids (*Dactylorhiza majalis* s.l., Orchidaceae) in Britain and Ireland. *Biological Journal of the Linnean Society* **104**: 107–128.

Hedrén, M., Paun, O. & Sayers, B. 2011b. The polymorphic early marsh orchids, *Dactylorhiza incarnata* s.l. (Orchidaceae), at Loch Gealain, Ireland. *New Journal of Botany* **1**: 16–23.

Hegarty, M.J., Abbott, R.J. & Hiscock, S.J. 2012. Allopolyploid Speciation in Action: The Origins and Evolution of *Senecio cambrensis*. In Soltis, P.S. & Soltis, D.E. (Eds.) *Polyploidy and Genome Evolution* Springer-Verlag, Berlin, Heidelberg.

Heide, O.M. 2005. Ecotypic variation among European arctic and alpine populations of *Oxyria digyna*. *Arctic, Antarctic, and Alpine Research* **37**: 233–238.

Heinze, B. 1997. A PCR marker for a *Populus deltoides* allele and its use in studying introgression with native European *Populus nigra*. *Belgian Journal of Botany* **129**: 123–130.

Henrys, P.A., Stevens, C.J., Smart, S.M., Maskell, L.C., Walker, K.J., Preston, C.D., Crowe, A., Rowe, E.C., Gowing, D.J. & Emmett, B.A. 2011. Impacts of nitrogen deposition on vascular plants in Britain: an analysis of two national observation networks. *Biogeosciences* **8**: 3501–3518.

Hepburn, I. 1952. *Flowers of the coast*. Collins, London.

Hepper, F.N. 1956. Biological Flora of the British Isles. No. 59. *Silene nutans* L. *Journal of Ecology* **44**: 693–700.

Heslop Harrison, J. 1953. The North American and Lusitanian elements in the flora of the British Isles. In Lousley, J.E. (Ed.) *The Changing Flora of Britain* pp. 105–123 BSBI Conference Report no.3 Botanical Society of the British Isles, London.

Heslop-Harrison, Y. 1953. *Nuphar intermedia* Ledeb., a presumed relict hybrid, in Britain. *Watsonia* **3**: 7–25.

Heslop-Harrison, Y. 1955a. Biological Flora of the British Isles. No. 49. *Nuphar* genus Sm. (pp. 342–343), *N. lutea* (L.) Sm. (pp. 344–355), *N. pumila* (Timm) DC. (pp. 355–360), *N. × intermedia* Ledeb. (pp. 360–364). *Journal of Ecology* **43**: 342–364.

Heslop-Harrison, Y. 1955b. Biological Flora of the British Isles. No. 53. *Nymphaea* L. em. Sm. genus (pp. 719–721), *Nymphaea alba* L. (pp. 722–734). *Journal of Ecology* **43**: 719–734.

Heslop-Harrison, Y. 2004. Biological Flora of the British Isles. No. 441. *Pinguicula* L. *Journal of Ecology* **92**: 1071–1118.

Hewett, D.G. 1964. Biological Flora of the British Isles. No. 97. *Menyanthes trifoliata* L. *Journal of Ecology* **52**: 723–735.

Hibberd, D. 1994. *Hardy Geraniums*. Cassell & Royal Horticultural Society, London.

Hicks, H., Lambert, J., Pywell, R., Hulmes, L., Hulmes, S., Walker, K.J., Childs, D.Z. & Freckleton, R.P. 2020. Characterising the environmental drivers of the abundance and distribution of *Alopecurus myosuroides* on a national scale. *Pest Management Science* **77**: 2726–2736.

Hill, D.J. & Price, B. 2000. Biological Flora of the British Isles. No. 210. *Ornithogalum pyrenaicum* L. *Journal of Ecology* **88**: 354–365.

Hill, M.O. 2012. Local frequency as a key to interpreting species occurrence data when recording effort is not known. *Methods in Ecology and Evolution* **3**: 195–205.

Hill, M.O. & Preston, C.D. 2015. Disappearance of boreal plants in southern Britain: habitat loss or climate change? *Biological Journal of the Linnean Society* **115**: 598–610.

Hill, M.O., Preston, C.D. & Roy, D.B. 2004. *PLANTATT. Attributes of British and Irish Plants: Status, Size, Life History, Geography and Habitats*. NERC Centre for Ecology and Hydrology, Cambridgeshire.

Hills, L.D. 1976. *Comfrey past, present and future*. Faber & Faber, London.

Hipkin, C.R. & Facey, P.D. 2009. Biological Flora of the British Isles: *Coincya monensis* (L.) Greuter & Burdet ssp. *monensis* (*Rhyncosinapis monensis* (L.) Dandy Ex A.R. Clapham) and ssp. *cheiranthos* (Vill.) Aedo, Leadley & Muñoz Garm. (*Rhyncosinapis cheiranthos* (Vill.) Dandy). *Journal of Ecology* **97**: 1101–1116.

Hitchcock, C.L. & Cronquist, A. 1973. *Flora of the Pacific Northwest*. University of Washington Press.

Hobson, D.D. 1991. The status of *Populus nigra* L. in the Republic of Ireland. *Watsonia* **18**: 303–305.

Hobson, D.D. 1993. *Populus nigra* L. in Ireland – an indigenous species? *Irish Naturalists' Journal* **24**: 244–247.

Hocking, P.J. 1982. Salt and mineral nutrient levels in fruits of two strand species, *Cakile maritima* and *Arctotheca populifera*, with special reference to the effect of salt on the germination of *Cakile*. *Annals of Botany n.s* **50**: 335–343.

Hodd, R.L. & Rumsey, F.J. 2020. *Stenogrammitis myosuroides* (Polypodiaceae): a new addition to the European flora from southwest Ireland. *British & Irish Botany* **2**: 158–168.

Hodgson, J. 2005. *Geranium purpureum* in North Nottinghamshire. *BSBI News* **99**: 22.

Holden, A.V. 1959. *Fertilization experiments in Scottish freshwater lochs, II. Sutherland 1954*. Freshwater and Salmon Fisheries Research, Report no.24. HMSO.

Holland, S.C., Caddick, H.M. & Dudley-Smith, D.S. 1986. *Supplement to the Flora of Gloucestershire*. Grenfell Publications, Bristol.

Hollings, E. & Stace, C.A. 1978. Morphological variation in the *Vicia sativa* L. aggregate. *Watsonia* **12**: 1–14.

Hollingsworth, P.M., Tebbitt, M., Watson, K.J. & Gornall, R.J. 1998. Conservation genetics of an arctic species, *Saxifraga rivularis* L., in Britain. *Botanical Journal of the Linnean Society* **128**: 1–14.

Hollingsworth, P.M. & Swan, G.A. 1999. Genetic differentiation and hybridisation among subspecies of Deergrass (*Trichophorum cespitosum* (L.) Hartman) in Northumberland. *Watsonia* **22**: 235–242.

Hollingsworth, M.L. & Bailey, J.P. 2000. Hybridisation and clonal diversity in some introduced *Fallopia* species (Polygonaceae). *Watsonia* **23**: 111–121.

Hollingsworth, P.M., Squirrell, J., Hollingsworth, M.L., Richards, A.J. & Bateman, R.M. 2006. Taxonomic complexity, conservation and recurrent origins of self-pollination in *Epipactis* (Orchidaceae). In Bailey, J.P. & Ellis, R.G. (Eds.) *Current taxonomic research on the British and European flora* pp. 27–44 BSBI Conference Report No. 25 Botanical Society of the British Isles, London.

Holm, L.G., Doll, J., Holm, E., Pancho, J.V. & Herberger, J.P. 1997. *World Weeds: Natural Histories and Distribution*. John Wiley & Sons Inc, New York.

Holman, I.P. & White, S.M. 2008. *Synthesis of the Upper Thurne research and recommendations for management*. Report by Cranfield University for the Broads Authority.

Holub, P., Tůma, I., Záhora, J. & Fiala, K. 2012. Different nutrient use strategies of expansive grasses *Calamagrostis epigejos* and *Arrhenatherum elatius*. *Biologia* **67**: 673–680.

Holyoak, D.T. 1999. *Gentianella uliginosa* (Willd.) Börner (Gentianaceae) rediscovered in north Devon. *Watsonia* **22**: 428–429.

Hopkins, J.J. 1996. Scrub ecology and conservation. *British Wildlife* **8**: 28–36.

Horn, P.C. 1993. *Report on the decline and conservation of* Cerastium brachypetalum *Pers. in Bedfordshire*. The Wildlife Trust of Bedfordshire and Cambridgeshire.

Horn, P.C. 2006. *Cerastium brachypetalum* in a Bedfordshire railway cutting. *BSBI News* **101**: 25.

Hornemann, G., Michalski, S.G. & Durka, W. 2012. Short- term fitness and long-term population trends in the orchid *Anacamptis morio*. *Plant Ecology* **213**: 1583–1595.

Horrill, A.D. 1972. Biological Flora of the British Isles. No. 125. *Melampyrum cristatum* L. *Journal of Ecology* **60**: 235–244.

Horsman, F. 2005. Some observations on *Spiranthes romanzoffiana* in the British Isles. *BSBI News* **99**: 37–40.

Horton, P. & Jefferson, R.G. 2006. The Wiltshire Snake's head fritillary meadows: a case study in habitat degradation. *British Wildlife* **17**: 176–184.

Houston, L., Lovatt, C.M., Frost, L.C. & Beckett, A. 1991. *Allium sphaerocephalon* L. and introduced *A. carinatum* L., *A. roseum* L. and *Nectaroscordum siculum* (Ucria) Lindley on St Vincent's Rocks, Bristol. *Watsonia* **18**: 381–385.

Houston, L., Humphries, R.N., Whittington, W.J. & Wilson, G.B. 2000. Biological Flora of the British Isles. No. 213. *Veronica spicata* L. ssp. *spicata* and ssp. *hybrida* (L.) Gaudin. *Journal of Ecology* **88**: 890–909.

Houston, L., Robertson, A. & Rich, T.C.G. 2008. The distribution, population size and growth of the rare English endemic *Sorbus bristoliensis* A. J. Wilmott, Bristol Whitebeam (Rosaceae). *Watsonia* **27**: 37–49.

Houston, L., Robertson, A., Jones, K., Smith, S.C.C., Hiscock, S.J. & Rich, T.C.G. 2009. An account of the Whitebeams (*Sorbus* L., Rosaceae) of Cheddar Gorge, England, with description of three new species. *Watsonia* **27**: 283–300.

Houston Durrant, T., de Rigo, D. & Caudullo, G. 2016. *Salix alba* in Europe: distribution, habitat, usage and threats. In San-Miguel-Ayanz, J., de Rigo, D., Caudullo, G., Houston Durrant, T. & Mauri, A. (Eds.) *European Atlas of Forest Tree Species*. Publications Office of the European Union, Luxembourg.

Howard, H.W. & Lyon, A.G. 1952. Biological Flora of the British Isles. No. 36. *Nasturtium officinale* R. Br. (pp. 228–238), *N. microphyllum* Boenningh. ex Rchb. (pp. 239–245). *Journal of Ecology* **40**: 228–245.

Howard-Williams, E. 2013. *A phylogeographic study of* Arenaria ciliata *and* Arenaria norvegica *in Ireland and Europe*. Ph.D. thesis, National University of Ireland, Maynooth.

Howarth, S.E. & Williams, J.T. 1968. Biological Flora of the British Isles. No. 110. *Chrysanthemum leucanthemum* L. *Journal of Ecology* **56**: 585–595.

Howarth, S.E. & Williams, J.T. 1972. Biological Flora of the British Isles. No. 127. *Chrysanthemum segetum* L. *Journal of Ecology* **60**: 573–584.

Howitt, R.C.L. & Howitt, B.M. 1990. Willows. In *A Guide to Some Difficult Plants* pp. 28–40 Wild Flower Society, London.

Howland, D.E., Oliver, R.P. & Davy, A.J. 1995. Morphological and molecular variation in natural populations of *Betula*. *New Phytologist* **130**: 117–124.

Hubbard, C.E. 1954. *Grasses*. Penguin Books, Harmondsworth.

Huiskes, A.H.L. 1979. Biological Flora of the British Isles. No. 144. *Ammophila arenaria* (L.) Link. *Journal of Ecology* **67**: 363–382.

Hultén, E. 1968. *Flora of Alaska and neighboring territories*. Stanford University Press, Stanford.

Hultén, E. 1971. The circumpolar plants. II. Dicotyledons. *Kungliga Svenska Vetenskapsakademiens Handlingar, Fjärde Serien* **13**: 1–463.

Hultén, E. & Fries, M. 1986. *Atlas of north European vascular plants north of the Tropic of Cancer. 3 vols*. Koeltz Scientific Books, Königstein.

Hultgård, U.M. 1987. *Parnassia palustris* L. in Scandinavia. *Symbolae Botanicae Upsaliensis* **28**: 1–128.

BIBLIOGRAPHY

Hume, L., Martinez, J. & Best, K. 1983. The biology of Canadian weeds. 60. *Polygonum convolvulus* L. *Canadian Journal of Plant Science* **63**: 959–971.

Hurry, J.B. 1930. *The woad plant and its dye.* Oxford University Press, Oxford.

Hurst, C.P. 1901. The range of *Diotis candidissima* Desf., in England and Wales, and in Ireland. *Memoirs and Proceedings of the Manchester Literary and Philosophical Society* **46**: 1–8.

Hutchings, M.J. 2010. The population biology of the early spider orchid *Ophrys sphegodes* Mill. III. Demography over three decades. *Journal of Ecology* **98**: 867–878.

Hutchings, M.J., Mendoza, A. & Havers, W. 1998. Demographic properties of an outlier population of *Orchis militaris* L. (Orchidaceae). *Journal of the Linnean Society* **126**: 95–107.

Hutchings, M.J. & Price, E.A.C. 1999. Biological Flora of the British Isles. No. 205. *Glechoma hederacea* L. (*Nepeta glechoma* Benth., *N. hederacea* (L.) Trev.). *Journal of Ecology* **87**: 347–364.

Hutchinson, C.S. & Seymour, G.B. 1982. Biological Flora of the British Isles. No. 153. *Poa annua* L. *Journal of Ecology* **70**: 887–901.

Hutchinson, J., Lewin, R.A. & Colosi, J. 1984. The biology of Canadian weeds. 63. *Sonchus asper* (L.) Hill and *S. oleraceus* L. *Canadian Journal of Plant Science* **64**: 731–744.

Hutchinson, T.C. 1966. The occurrence of living and sub-fossil remains of *Betula nana* L. in Upper Teesdale. *New Phytologist* **65**: 351–357.

Hutchinson, T.C. 1968. Biological Flora of the British Isles. No. 115. *Teucrium scorodonia* L. *Journal of Ecology* **56**: 901–911.

ICIT 2004. *Review of biological communities in the Lochs of Stenness and Harray, Orkney.* Scottish Natural Heritage Commissioned Report 066 (Part 2 of 12), Battleby, Perth.

Ingram, M. 1958. The ecology of the Cairngorms, IV. The *Juncus* zone: *Juncus trifidus* communities. *Journal of Ecology* **46**: 707–737.

Ingram, R. & Noltie, H.J. 1981. *The flora of Angus (Forfar, V.C. 90).* Dundee Museum and Art Galleries, Dundee.

Ingram, R. & Noltie, H.J. 1995. Biological Flora of the British Isles. No. 186. *Senecio cambrensis* Rosser. *Journal of Ecology* **83**: 537–546.

Ingrouille, M.J. 1985. The *Limonium auriculae-ursifolium* (Pourret) Druce group (Plumbaginaceae) in the Channel Isles. *Watsonia* **15**: 221–229.

Ingrouille, M. 1989. A non-expert's approach to the *Salicornia* problem. *BSBI News* **53**: 11–12.

Ingrouille, M.J. 2006. What use is sex? In Ellis, R.G. & Bailey, J.P. (Eds.) *Current taxonomic research on the British and European flora* BSBI Conference Report No. 25 Botanical Society of Britain and Ireland, London.

Ingrouille, M.J. & Stace, C.A. 1986. The *Limonium binervosum* aggregate (Plumbaginaceae) in the British Isles. *Journal of the Linnean Society* **92**: 177–217.

Ingrouille, M.J. & Smirnoff, N. 1986. *Thlaspi caerulescens* J. & C. Presl (*T. alpestre* L.) in Britain. *New Phytologist* **102**: 219–233.

Ingrouille, M.J. & Dawson, H.J. 1995. A biometric survey of *Limonium vulgare* Miller and *L. humile* Miller in the British Isles. *Watsonia* **20**: 239–254.

Intermap Technologies. 2009. *NEXTMap British Digital Terrain 50m resolution (DTM10) Model Data by Intermap.* NERC Earth Observation Data Centre.

Irish, M. & Irish, G. 2000. *Agaves, Yucca and related plants.* Timber Press, Portland, Oregon.

Isermann, M. & Rooney, P. 2014. Biological Flora of the British Isles. No. 274. *Eryngium maritimum.* *Journal of Ecology* **102**: 789–821.

Ivimey-Cook, R.B. 1959. Biological Flora of the British Isles. No. 71. *Agrostis setacea* Curt. *Journal of Ecology* **47**: 697–706.

Ivimey-Cook, R.B. 1963. Biological Flora of the British Isles. No. 88. *Hypericum linariifolium* Vahl. *Journal of Ecology* **51**: 727–732.

Ivimey-Cook, R.B. 1969. Investigations into the phenetic relationships between species of *Ononis* L. *Watsonia* **7**: 1–23.

Jackson, A. 1995. The Plymouth Pear - the recovery programme for one of Britain's rarest trees. *British Wildlife* **6**: 272–278.

Jackson, A., Erry, B. & Culham, A. 1997. Genetic aspects of the Species Recovery Programme for the Plymouth Pear (*Pyrus cordata* Desv.). In Tew, T.E., Crawford, T.J., Spencer, J.W., Stevens, D.P., Usher, M.B. & Warren, J. (Eds.) *The role of genetics in conserving small populations* pp. 112–121 JNCC, Peterborough.

Jackson, A.B. 1916. Two new pyracanthas from China. *The Gardeners' Chronicle* **60**: 309.

Jackson, M.T. 1986. Exploited plants. The potato. *Biologist* **33**: 161–167.

Jacquemart, A.L. 1996. Biological Flora of the British Isles. No. 193. *Vaccinium uliginosum* L. *Journal of Ecology* **84**: 771–785.

Jacquemart, A.L. 1997. *Vaccinium oxycoccos* L. (*Oxycoccus palustris* Pers.) and *Vaccinium microcarpum* (Turcz. ex Rupr.) Schmalh. (*Oxycoccus microcarpus* Turcz. ex Rupr.). *Journal of Ecology* **85**: 381–396.

Jacquemart, A.L. 1998. Biological Flora of the British Isles. No. 200. *Andromeda polifolia* L. *Journal of Ecology* **86**: 527–541.

Jacquemyn, H., Brys, R. & Hutchings, M.J. 2008. Biological Flora of the British Isles. No. 250. *Paris quadrifolia* L. *Journal of Ecology* **96**: 833–844.

Jacquemyn, H., Brys, R., Adriaens, D., Honnay, O. & Roldan-Ruiz, I. 2009a. Effects of population size and forest management on genetic diversity and structure of the tuberous orchid *Orchis mascula. Conservation Genetics* **10**: 161–168.

Jacquemyn, H., Wiegand, T., Vandepitte, K., Brys, R., Roldan-Ruiz, I. & Honnay, O. 2009b. Multigenerational analysis of spatial structure in the terrestrial, food-deceptive orchid *Orchis mascula. Journal of Ecology* **97**: 206–216.

Jacquemyn, H., Brys, R., Honnay, O. & Hutchings, M.J. 2009c. Biological Flora of the British Isles. No. 252. *Orchis mascula* (L.) L. *Journal of Ecology* **97**: 360–377.

Jacquemyn, H., Endels, P., Brys, R., Hermy, M. & Woodell, S.R.J. 2009d. Biological Flora of the British Isles. No. 254. *Primula vulgaris* Huds (*P. acaulis* (L.) Hill). *Journal of Ecology* **97**: 812–833.

Jacquemyn, H. & Hutchings, M.J. 2010. Biological Flora of the British Isles. No. 258. *Spiranthes spiralis* (L.) Chevall. *Journal of Ecology* **98**: 1253–1267.

Jacquemyn, H., Brys, R. & Hutchings, M.J. 2011. Biological Flora of the British Isles. No. 264. *Orchis anthropophora* (L.) All. (*Aceras anthropophorum* (L.) W.T. Aiton). *Journal of Ecology* **99**: 1551–1565.

Jacquemyn, H., Brys, R. & Hutchings, M.J. 2014. Biological Flora of the British Isles. No. 276. *Epipactis palustris. Journal of Ecology* **102**: 1341–1355.

Jacquemyn, H. & Hutchings, M.J. 2015. Biological Flora of the British Isles. No. 280. *Ophrys sphegodes. Journal of Ecology* **103**: 1680–1696.

Jacquemyn, H., De Kort, H., Broeck, A.V. & Brys, R. 2018. Immigrant and extrinsic hybrid seed inviability contribute to reproductive isolation between forest and dune ecotypes of *Epipactis helleborine* (Orchidaceae). *Oikos* **127**: 73–84.

Jakubska-Busse, A., Zolubak, E., Jarzembowski, P. & Prockow, J. 2017. Morphological variability in *Epipactis purpurata* s. stricto (Orchidaceae) – an analysis based on herbarium material and field observations. *Annales Botanici Fennici* **54**: 55–56.

Jalas, J. & Sell, P. 1967. Taxonomic and Nomenclatural Notes on the British Flora: *Cerastium fontanum* Baumg. *Watsonia* **6**: 298–301.

Jalas, J. & Suominen, J. (Eds.) 1972. *Atlas Florae Europaeae* **1** Committee for Mapping the Flora of Europe and Societas Biologica Fennica Vanamo, Helsinki.

Jalas, J. & Suominen, J. (Eds.) 1973. *Atlas Florae Europaeae* **2** Committee for Mapping the Flora of Europe and Societas Biologica Fennica Vanamo, Helsinki.

Jalas, J. & Suominen, J. (Eds.) 1976. *Atlas Florae Europaeae* **3** Committee for Mapping the Flora of Europe and Societas Biologica Fennica Vanamo, Helsinki.

Jalas, J. & Suominen, J. (Eds.) 1979. *Atlas Florae Europaeae* **4** Committee for Mapping the Flora of Europe and Societas Biologica Fennica Vanamo, Helsinki.

Jalas, J. & Suominen, J. (Eds.) 1980. *Atlas Florae Europaeae* **5** Committee for Mapping the Flora of Europe and Societas Biologica Fennica Vanamo, Helsinki.

Jalas, J. & Suominen, J. (Eds.) 1983. *Atlas Florae Europaeae* **6** Committee for Mapping the Flora of Europe and Societas Biologica Fennica Vanamo, Helsinki.

Jalas, J. & Suominen, J. (Eds.) 1986. *Atlas Florae Europaeae* **7** Committee for Mapping the Flora of Europe and Societas Biologica Fennica Vanamo, Helsinki.

Jalas, J. & Suominen, J. (Eds.) 1989. *Atlas Florae Europaeae* **8** Committee for Mapping the Flora of Europe and Societas Biologica Fennica Vanamo, Helsinki.

Jalas, J. & Suominen, J. (Eds.) 1991. *Atlas Florae Europaeae* **9** Committee for Mapping the Flora of Europe and Societas Biologica Fennica Vanamo, Helsinki.

Jalas, J. & Suominen, J. (Eds.) 1994. *Atlas Florae Europaeae* **10** Committee for Mapping the Flora of Europe and Societas Biologica Fennica Vanamo, Helsinki.

Jalas, J. & Suominen, J. (Eds.) 1996. *Atlas Florae Europaeae* **11** Committee for Mapping the Flora of Europe and Societas Biologica Fennica Vanamo, Helsinki.

Jalas, J. & Suominen, J. (Eds.) 1999. *Atlas Florae Europaeae* **12** Committee for Mapping the Flora of Europe and Societas Biologica Fennica Vanamo, Helsinki.

James, C.M., Wurzell, B.S. & Stace, C.A. 2000. A new hybrid between a European and a Chinese species of *Artemisia* (Asteraceae). *Watsonia* **23**: 139–147.

James, N.D.G. 1982. *The Forester's Companion.* Blackwell, Oxford.

James, R., Mitchell, S.C., Kett, J. & Leaton, R. 1981. The natural history of *Quercus ilex* L. in Norfolk. *Watsonia* **13**: 271–286.

James, T.J. 2009. *Flora of Hertfordshire.* Hertfordshire Natural History Society, Hertfordshire.

James, T.J. 2013. *Pentaglottis sempervirens* (Green Alkanet) in Hertfordshire. *BSBI News* **123**: 65.

James, T.J., Porter, M.S. & Jiménez-Mejías, P. 2012. The occurrence in Britain of *Carex cespitosa*, a Eurasian sedge rare in western Europe. *New Journal of Botany* **2**: 20–25.

Janes, R. 1998a. Growth and survival of *Azolla filiculoides* in Britain I. Vegetative reproduction. *New Phytologist* **138**: 367–375.

Janes, R. 1998b. Growth and survival of *Azolla filiculoides* in Britain II. Sexual reproduction. *New Phytologist* **138**: 377–384.

Janes, R.A., Eaton, J.W. & Hardwick, K. 1996. The effects of floating mats of *Azolla filiculoides* Lam. and *Lemna minuta* Kunth on the growth of submerged macrophytes. *Hydrobiologia* **340**: 23–26.

Jannink, M. & Rich, T. 2010. Ghost Orchid rediscovered in Britain after 23 years. *Journal of the Hardy Orchid Society* **7**: 14–15.

Jefferson, R.G. 2008. Biological Flora of the British Isles. No. 249. *Mercurialis perennis* L. *Journal of Ecology* **96**: 386–412.

Jefferson, R.G. & Walker, K.J. 2017. Biological Flora of the British Isles. No. 284. *Serratula tinctoria. Journal of Ecology* **105**: 1438–1458.

Jenkinson, M.N. 1991. *Wild orchids of Dorset.* Orchid Sundries, Gillingham.

Jepson, P., Welch, D. & Bailey, J.P. 2012. A new *Myosotis* hybrid, *Myosotis ×bollandica* (Boraginaceae). *New Journal of Botany* **2**: 2–8.

Jerling, L. 1988. Population dynamics of *Glaux maritima* (L.) along a distributional cline. *Vegetatio* **74**: 161–170.

Jerling, L. & Elmgren, G. 1996. Phenotypic variation in clonal growth of *Glaux maritima* along an environmental cline. *Acta Botanica Neerlandica* **45**: 367–380.

Jermy, A.C. 1989. The history of *Diphasiastrum issleri* (Lycopodiaceae) in Britain and a review of its taxonomic status. *Fern Gazette* **13**: 257–265.

Jermy, A.C. & Crabbe, J.A. (Eds.) 1978. *The Island of Mull - a survey of its flora and environment.* British Museum (Natural History), London.

Jermy, A.C., Arnold, H.R., Farrell, L. & Perring, F.H. 1978. *Atlas of ferns of the British Isles.* Botanical Society of the British Isles & British Pteridological Society, London.

Jermy, A.C., Chater, A.O. & David, R.W. 1982. *Sedges of the British Isles.* BSBI Handbook No. 1. Edn. 2. Botanical Society of the British Isles, London.

Jermy, A.C. & Camus, J.C. 1991. *The illustrated field guide to ferns and allied plants of the British Isles.* Natural History Museum, London.

Jermy, A.C., Simpson, D.A., Foley, M.J.Y. & Porter, M.S. 2007. *Sedges of the British Isles.* BSBI Handbook No. 1. Edn. 3. Botanical Society of the British Isles, London.

Jermyn, S.T. 1974. *Flora of Essex.* Essex Naturalists' Trust, Colchester.

Jersákova, J., Malinova, T., Jerabková, K. & Dötterl, S. 2011. Biological Flora of the British Isles. No. 263. *Pseudorchis albida* (L.) A. & D. Löve. *Journal of Ecology* **99**: 1282–1298.

Jobling, J. 1990. *Poplars for wood production and amenity. Forestry Commission Bulletin no. 92.* HMSO, London.

John, D.M., Whitton, B.A. & Brook, A.J. (Eds.) 2021. *The Freshwater Algal Flora of the British Isles.* Edn. 2. Cambridge University Press, Cambridge.

John, R.F. 1992. *Genetic variation, reproductive biology and conservation in isolated populations of rare plant species.* University of Wales, Swansea.

Johnson, O. 2011. *Champion Trees of Britain & Ireland.* The Tree Register Handbook. Royal Botanic Gardens, Kew, Surrey.

Johnson, O. 2015. *Arboretum. A history of the trees grown in Britain and Ireland.* Whittet Books, Stansted.

Jones, A. 1991. Welsh Mudwort? *BSBI Welsh Bulletin* **52**: 6–8.

Jones, A. 2018. Changing, Early and 'Doubtful' Forget-me-nots. *BSBI Welsh Bulletin* **101**: 37–41.

Jones, A. 2020a. Native or Neophyte? *Euphorbia stricta*, the Tintern Spurge. *BSBI Welsh Bulletin* **105**: 21–24.

Jones, A. 2020b. Two Interesting Species: Welsh Mudwort, *Limosella australis* and Limestone Woundwort, *Stachys alpina* on the GB Vascular Plants "Waiting List". *BSBI Welsh Bulletin* **106**: 24–27.

Jones, A. & Rumsey, F. 2019. *Myosotis stricta*: a likely native and overlooked forget-me-not in Britain. *BSBI News* **141**: 8–9.

Jones, A. & Rumsey, F. in press. The status of *Artemisia campestris* L. subsp. *maritima* (DC.) Arcang. (syn. *Artemisia crithmifolia* L.) in the British Isles. *British & Irish Botany*.

Jones, B. & Gliddon, C. 1999. Reproductive biology and genetic structure in *Lloydia serotina*. *Plant Ecology* **141**: 151–161.

Jones, B.L. & Unsworth, R.K.F. 2016. The perilous state of seagrass in the British Isles. *Royal Society Open Science* **3**: 1–14.

Jones, B.M.G. 1959b. Distribution of *Bunias orientalis* in Britain. *Proceedings of the Botanical Society of the British Isles* **3**: 330.

Jones, B.M.G. & Wilcock, C.C. 1974. The identification and origin of *Stachys ×ambigua* Sm. *Watsonia* **10**: 139–147.

Jones, D.A. & Bonnemaison, F. 1986. Variation in alien *Lotus corniculatus* L.1. Morphological differences between alien and native British plants. *Heredity* **56**: 129–138.

Jones, D.A. & Turkington, R. 1986. Biological Flora of the British Isles. No. 163. *Lotus corniculatus* L. *Journal of Ecology* **74**: 1185–1212.

Jones, E.M. 1975. Taxonomic studies of the genus *Atriplex* (Chenopodiaceae). *Watsonia* **10**: 233–251.

Jones, E.W. 1945. Biological Flora of the British Isles. No. 13. *Acer* L. genus (pp. 215–219), *A. pseudo-platanus* L. (pp. 220–237), *A. platanoides* L. (p. 238), *A. campestre* L. (pp. 239–252). *Journal of Ecology* **32**: 215–252.

Jones, E.W. 1959a. Biological Flora of the British Isles. No. 67. *Quercus* L. genus, *Q. robur* L. and *Q. petraea* (Matt.) Liebl. (pp. 169–216), *Q. borealis* Mich. var. *maxima* Sarg. (p. 216), *Q. cerris* L. (pp. 216–217), *Q. ilex* L. (pp. 218–222). *Journal of Ecology* **47**: 169–222.

Jones, M. 1984. The plant remains. In Cunliffe, B. (Ed.) *Danebury: an Iron Age hillfort in Hampshire. Vol. 2. The excavations, 1969-1978: the finds.* Council for British Archaeology Research Report no. 52 pp. 483–495.

Jones, M. 1987. *Orobanche hederae* Duby in the British Isles. In Weber, H.C. & Forstreuter, W. (Eds.) *Parasitic Flowering Plants. Proceedings of the 4th International Symposium on Parasitic Flowering Plants. Marburg* pp. 457–471.

Jones, P.S. 1998. Aspects of the population biology of *Liparis loeselii* (L.) Rich. var. *ovata* Ridd. ex Godfery (Orchidaceae) in the dune slacks of South Wales, UK. *Botanical Journal of the Linnean Society* **126**: 123–139.

Jones, R.A. 2011. Conservation genetics and the need for historic and field data: three case studies from research into scarce and declining lowland plants. In Blackstock, T.H., Howe, E.A., Rothwell, J.P., Duigan, C.A. & Jones, P.S. (Eds.) *Proceedings of the memorial conference for David Stevens, 1958-2007. Grassland ecologist and conservationist* pp. 29–34 CCW Staff Science Report No: 10/03/05 Countryside Council for Wales, Bangor.

Jones, R.A. 2015. *Baldellia ranunculoides* (Lesser Water-plantain) ssp. *ranunculoides* & ssp. *repens. BSBI News* **129**: 4–5.

Jones, R.A. & Stewart, N.F. 2001. *Nitella gracilis* (Smith) Agardh, an elusive stonewort new to Cardiganshire (V.C. 46). *Watsonia* **23**: 443–453.

Jones, V. & Richards, P.W. 1954. Biological Flora of the British Isles. No. 46. *Juncus acutus* L. *Journal of Ecology* **42**: 639–650.

Jones, V. & Richards, P.W. 1956. Biological Flora of the British Isles. No. 57. *Saxifraga oppositifolia* L. *Journal of Ecology* **44**: 300–316.

Jones, V. & Richards, P.W. 1962. Biological Flora of the British Isles. No. 83. *Silene acaulis* (L.) Jacq. *Journal of Ecology* **50**: 475–487.

Jonsell, B. 1968. Studies in the north-west European species of *Rorippa s.str. Symbolae Botanicae Upsaliensis* **19**: 1–222.

Jonsell, B. (Ed.) 2000. *Flora Nordica* **1**. *Lycopodiaceae to Polygonaceae.* The Bergius Foundation. The Royal Swedish Academy of Sciences, Stockholm.

Jonsell, B. (Ed.) 2001. *Flora Nordica* **2**. *Chenopodiaceae to Fumariaceae.* The Bergius Foundation. The Royal Swedish Academy of Sciences, Stockholm.

Jonsell, B., Nordal, I. & Roberts, F.J. 2000. *Viola rupestris* and its hybrids in Britain. *Watsonia* **23**: 269–278.

Jowsey, W.H. (Comp.) 1978. *Botanical Atlas of the Harrogate District.* Harrogate District Naturalists' Society, Harrogate.

Joyce, D. 2019. *The Bardfield Oxlip.* Great Bardfield Historical Society.

Joys, A., Fuller, R.J. & Dolman, P.M. 2004. Influences of deer browsing, coppice history, and standard trees on the growth and development of vegetation structure in coppiced woods in lowland England. *Forest Ecology and Management* **202**: 23–37.

Jung, T., Orlikowski, L., Henricot, B., Abad-Campos, P., Aday, A.G., Aguín Casal, O., J., B., Cacciola, S.O., Cech, T., Chavarriaga, D., Corcobado, T., Cravador, A., Decourcelle, T., Denton, G. *et al.* 2016. Widespread *Phytophthora* infestations in European nurseries put forest, semi-natural and horticultural ecosystems at high risk of *Phytophthora* diseases. *Forest Pathology* **46**: 134–163.

Jutila, H.M. 1996. Seed bank and emergent vascular flora of ballast areas in Reposaari, Finland. *Annales Botanici Fennici* **33**: 165–182.

Kadereit, G., Ball, P., Beer, S., Mucina, L., Sokoloff, D., Teege, P., Yaprak, A.E. & Freitag, H. 2007. A taxonomic nightmare comes true: Phylogeny and biogeography of glassworts (*Salicornia* L., Chenopodiaceae). *Taxon* **56**: 1143–1170.

Kadereit, G., Piirainen, M., Lambinon, J. & Vanderpoorten, A. 2012. Cryptic taxa should have names: Reflections in the glasswort genus *Salicornia* (Amaranthaceae). *Taxon* **61**: 1227–1239.

Kadereit, J.W. 1986a. *Papaver somniferum* L. (Papaveraceae): a triploid hybrid? *Botanische Jahrbucher fur Systematik, Pflanzengeschichte und Pflanzengeographie* **106**: 221–244.

Kadereit, J.W. 1986b. A revision of *Papaver* section *Argemonidium*. *Notes from the Royal Botanic Garden Edinburgh* **44**: 25–43.

Kadereit, J.W. 1987. Experimental evidence on the affinities of *Papaver somniferum* (Papaveraceae). *Plant Systematics and Evolution* **156**: 189–195.

Kadereit, J.W. 1989. A revision of *Papaver* L. section *Rhoeadium* Spach. *Notes from the Royal Botanic Garden Edinburgh* **45**: 225–286.

Kadereit, J.W. & Sell, P.D. 1986. Variation in *Senecio jacobaea* L. (Asteraceae) in the British Isles. *Watsonia* **16**: 21–23.

Kadereit, J.W., Preston, C.D. & Valtueña, F.J. 2011. Is Welsh Poppy, *Meconopsis cambrica* (L.) Vig. (Papaveraceae), truly a *Meconopsis*? *New Journal of Botany* **1**: 80–88.

Kadereit, J.W., Laux, P. & Dillenberger, M.S. 2021. A conspectus of *Tephroseris* (Asteraceae: Senecioneae) in Europe outside Russia and notes on the decline of the genus. *Willdenowia* **51**: 271–317.

Kaligaric, M., Bohanec, B., Simonovik, B. & Sajna, N. 2008. Genetic and morphologic variability of annual glassworts (*Salicornia* L.) from the Gulf of Trieste (Northern Adriatic). *Aquatic Botany* **89**: 275–282.

Kaplan, Z. & Štěpánek, J. 2003. Genetic variation within and between populations of *Potamogeton pusillus* agg. *Plant Systematics and Evolution* **239**: 95–112.

Kaplan, Z., Šumberová, K., Formanová, I. & Ducháček, M. 2014. Re-establishment of an extinct population of the endangered aquatic plant *Potamogeton coloratus*. *Aquatic Botany* **119**: 91–99.

Kay, G.M. 1998a. A tale of two *Bidens*. *BSBI News* **78**: 64–65.

Kay, Q.O.N. 1969. The origin and distribution of diploid and tetraploid *Tripleurospermum inodorum* (L.) Schultz Bip. *Watsonia* **7**: 130–141.

Kay, Q.O.N. 1971a. Biological Flora of the British Isles. No. 122. *Anthemis cotula* L. *Journal of Ecology* **59**: 623–636.

Kay, Q.O.N. 1971b. Biological Flora of the British Isles. No. 123. *Anthemis arvensis* L. *Journal of Ecology* **59**: 637–648.

Kay, Q.O.N. 1972. Variation in sea mayweed (*Tripleurospermum inodorum* (L.) Koch) in the British Isles. *Watsonia* **9**: 81–107.

Kay, Q.O.N. 1985. Hermaphrodites and subhermaphrodites in a reputedly dioecious plant, *Cirsium arvense* (L.) Scop. *New Phytologist* **100**: 457–472.

Kay, Q.O.N. 1994. Biological Flora of the British Isles. No. 182. *Tripleurospermum inodorum* (L.) Schultz Bip. *Journal of Ecology* **82**: 681–697.

Kay, Q.O.N. 1998b. Genetic variation, origins, history and conservation of *Sorbus domestica*, *S. leyana* and *S. minima*. In Jackson, A. & Flanagan, M. (Eds.) *The conservation status of* Sorbus *in the UK* pp. 5–14 Royal Botanic Gardens, Kew, London.

Kay, Q.O.N. & Harrison, J. 1970. Biological Flora of the British Isles. No. 119. *Draba aizoides* L. *Journal of Ecology* **58**: 877–888.

Kay, Q.O.N. & John, R. 1994. *Population genetics and demographic ecology of some scarce and declining vascular plants of Welsh lowland grassland and related habitats. Science Report No. 93.* Countryside Council for Wales, Bangor.

Kay, Q.O.N. & John, R. 1995. *The conservation of scarce and declining plant species in lowland Wales: population genetics, demographic ecology and recommendations for future conservation in 32 species of lowland grassland and related habitats. Science Report No. 110.* Countryside Council for Wales, Bangor.

Kay, Q.O.N., John, R.F. & Jones, R.A. 1999. Biology, genetic variation and conservation of *Luronium natans* (L.) Raf. in Britain and Ireland. *Watsonia* **22**: 301–315.

Kay, S. & Proctor, J. 2003. Population dynamics of two Scottish ultramafic (serpentine) rarities with contrasting life histories. *Botanical Journal of Scotland* **55**: 269–285.

Kelleher, C.T., Kelly, D.L. & Hodkinson, T.R. 2004. Species status, hybridisation and geographic distribution of Irish populations of *Quercus petraea* (Matt.) Liebl. and *Q. robur* L. *Watsonia* **25**: 83–97.

Kelly, D.L. 1990. *Cornus sericea* L. in Ireland: an incipient weed of wetlands. *Watsonia* **18**: 33–36.

Kenneth, A.G. & Tennant, D.J. 1987. Further notes on *Dactylorhiza incarnata* subsp. *cruenta* in Scotland. *Watsonia* **16**: 332–334.

Kent, D.H. 1963. *Pteris cretica* L. *Proceedings of the Botanical Society of the British Isles* **5**: 121.

Kent, D.H. 1965. The taxonomy of *Asplenium trichomanes* in Europe. *British Fern Gazette* **9**: 147–160.

Kent, D.H. 1968. *Echinops. Proceedings of the Botanical Society of the British Isles* **7**: 243–244.

Kent, D.H. 1975. *The historical flora of Middlesex.* Ray Society, London.

Kenward, H.K. & Hall, A.R. 1995. Biological evidence from Anglo-Scandinavian deposits at 16–22 Coppergate. *The Archaeology of York* **14**: 435–797 i.

Killick, H.J. 1975. The decline of *Vicia sativa* L. *sensu stricto* in Britain. *Watsonia* **10**: 288–289.

Killick, H.J., Perry, R. & Woodell, S. 1998. *The Flora of Oxfordshire.* Pisces Publications, Newbury.

Kirby, K.J. 2001. The impact of deer on the ground flora of British broadleaved woodland. *Forestry: An International Journal of Forest Research* **74**: 219–229.

Kirby, K.J. 2020. *Woodland Flowers.* Bloomsbury, London.

Kirschner, J. & Rich, T.C.G. 1996. *Luzula multiflora* subsp. *hibernica*, a new tetraploid taxon of *Luzula* sect. *Luzula* (Juncaceae) from Ireland. *Watsonia* **21**: 89–97.

Kitchen, M.A.R. 1994. *Cerastium pumilum.* In Stewart, A., Pearman, D.A. & Preston, C.D. (Eds.) *Scarce plants in Britain* Joint Nature Conservation Committee (JNCC), Peterborough.

Kitchener, G.D. 1983. Maritime plants on inland roadsides of West Kent. *Transactions of the Kent Field Club* **9(2)**: 87–94.

Kitchener, G.D. 2021. Kent Botany 2020 (https://bsbi.org/wp-content/uploads/dlm_uploads/Kent-Botany-2020-final.pdf).

Kitchener, G.D. 2022. *Kent Rare Plant Register; Draft species accounts.*

Kitchener, G.D. & McKean, D.R. 1998. Hybrids of *Epilobium brunnescens* (Cockayne) Raven & Englehorn (Onagraceae) and their occurrence in the British Isles. *Watsonia* **22**: 49–60.

Kiviniemi, K. 2002. Population dynamics of *Agrimonia eupatoria* and *Geum rivale*, two perennial grassland species. *Plant Ecology* **159**: 153–169.

Klinkhamer, P.G.L. & de Jong, T.G. 1993. Biological Flora of the British Isles. No. 176. *Cirsium vulgare* (Savi) Ten. *Journal of Ecology* **81**: 177–191.

Kohn, D.D., Hulme, P.E., Hollingsworth, P.M. & Butler, A. 2009. Are native bluebells (*Hyacinthoides non-scripta*) at risk from alien congenerics? Evidence from distributions and co-occurrence in Scotland. *Biological Conservation* **142**: 61–74.

Kohn, D.D., Ruhsam, M., Hulme, P.E., Barrett, S.C.H. & Hollingsworth, P.M. 2019. Paternity analysis reveals constraints on hybridization potential between native and introduced bluebells (*Hyacinthoides*). *Conservation Genetics* **20**: 571–584.

Kollmann, J. & Grubb, P.J. 2002. Biological Flora of the British Isles. No. 226. *Viburnum lantana* L. and *Viburnum opulus* L. (*V. lobatum* Lam., *Opulus vulgaris* Borkh.). *Journal of Ecology* **90**: 1044–1070.

Kotlinek, M., Tesitelová, T. & Jersáková, J. 2015. Biological Flora of the British Isles. No. 279. *Neottia ovata. Journal of Ecology* **103**: 1345–1366.

Kotlinek, M., Tatarenko, I. & Jersáková, J. 2018. Biological Flora of the British Isles: *Neottia cordata. Journal of Ecology* **106**: 444–460.

Kozlowski, G., Jones, R.A. & Nicholls-Vuille, F.-L. 2008. Biological Flora of Central Europe: *Baldellia ranunculoides* (Alismataceae). *Perspectives in Plant Ecology, Evolution and Systematics* **10**: 109–142.

Kozlowski, G. & Vallelian, S. 2009. Eutrophication and endangered aquatic plants: an experimental study on *Baldellia ranunculoides* (L.) Parl. (Alismataceae). *Hydrobiologia* **635**: 181–187.

Kozlowski, G., Rion, S., Python, A. & Riedo, S. 2009. Global conservation status assessment of the threatened aquatic plant genus *Baldellia* (Alismataceae): challenges and limitations. *Biodiversity and Conservation* **18**: 2307–2325.

Kretzschmar, H., Eccarius, W. & Dietrich, H. 2007. *The orchid genera* Anacamptis, Orchis *and* Neotinea. EchinoMedia, Bürgel, Germany.

Kreutz, C.A.J. 2008. Update on British orchids. *Journal of the Hardy Orchid Society* **5**: 11–16.

Kreutz, C.A.J. & Dekker, H. 2016. *Dactylorhiza purpurella*, eine neue Art die Niederlande? *Journal Europäischer Orchideen* **48**: 71–89.

Kuitert, W. & Peterse, A. 1999. *Japanese Flowering Cherries.* Timber Press, Oregon.

Kull, T. 1999. Biological Flora of the British Isles. No. 208. *Cypripedium calceolus* L. *Journal of Ecology* **87**: 913–924.

Kurtto, A., Lampinen, R. & Junikka, L. (Eds.) 2004. *Atlas Florae Europaeae. Distribution of Vascular Plants in Europe. 13. Rosaceae* (Spiraea *to* Fragaria, *excl.* Rubus*).* The Committee for Mapping the Flora of Europe & Societas Biologica Fennica Vanamo, Helsinki.

Kytövuori, I. 1969. *Epilobium davuricum* Fisch. (Onagraceae) in Eastern Fennoscandinavia compared with *E. palustre* L. A morphological, ecological and distributional study. *Annales Botanici Fennici* **6**: 35–58.

Kytövuori, I. 1972. The Alpinae group of the genus *Epilobium* in northernmost Fennoscandinavia. A morphological, taxonomical and ecological study. *Annales Botanici Fennici* **9**: 163–203.

Lallemand, F., Logacheva, M., Le Clainche, I., Bérard, A., Zheleznaia, E., May, M., Jakalski, M., Delannoy, É., Le Paslier, M.-C. & Selosse, M.-A. 2019. Thirteen new plastid genomes from mixotrophic and autotrophic species provide insights into heterotrophy evolution in Neottieae orchids. *Genome Biology and Evolution* **11**: 2457–2467.

Lambert, J.M. 1947. Biological Flora of the British Isles. No. 17. *Glyceria maxima* (Hartm.) Holmb. *Journal of Ecology* **34**: 310–344.

Lambert, J.M., Marchant, C.J., Goodman, P.J. & Braybrooks, E.M. 1969. Biological Flora of the British Isles. No. 116. *Spartina* ×*townsendii* H. & J. Groves *sensu lato, Spartina alterniflora* × *S. maritima. Journal of Ecology* **57**: 298–313.

Lambert, S.J. 2007. *The environmental range and tolerance limits of British stoneworts (Charophytes).* Ph.D. thesis, University of East Anglia.

Lambert, S.J. 2008. *A preliminary survey of Cantley Marsh, Gillingham Marsh and Sculthorpe Moor (Norfolk) to determine the feasibility of translocation and re-introduction of* Tolypella intricata. First Report to the Norfolk Biodiversity Partnership.

Lambert, S.J. 2011. *Stonewort survey of Dogsthorpe Star Pit August / September 2011.* Report for The Wildlife Trust for Bedfordshire, Cambridgeshire and Northamptonshire.

Lambert, S.J. 2015. *Orton Pit SSSI/SAC, Cambridgeshire: Aquatic Plant Monitoring for CES.* Report for Froglife.

Lang, D.C. 2001. *Wild Orchids of Sussex.* Pomegranate Press, Lewes.

Langeland, K.A. 1996. *Hydrilla verticillata* (L.F.) Royle (Hydrocharitaceae), "The Perfect Aquatic Weed". *Castanea* **61**: 293–304.

Lansdown, R.V. 2008. *Water starworts of Europe.* BSBI Handbook No. 11. Botanical Society of the British Isles, London.

Lansdown, R.V. 2011. *Conservation of ribbon-leaved water-plantain: Current status, the species recovery programme and future outlook.* Natural England Commissioned Reports, Number 74. Natural England, Peterborough.

Lansdown, R.V. 2013. *Surveys of vegetation of ditches in the catchment of the South Forty-foot Drain, Lincolnshire.* Unpublished report to CH2M Hill, Norwich.

Lansdown, R.V. 2015. *An ecological profile of Starfruit (*Damasonium alisma*).* Unpublished report to Natural England.

Lansdown, R.V. 2017. *Development of a conservation plan for Least Water-lily (*Nuphar pumila*) in England.* Natural England Commissioned Reports, Number 243. Natural England, York.

Lansdown, R.V. 2021a. *An ecological profile of Sharp-leaved Pondweed (*Potamogeton acutifolius*).* Unpublished report to Natural England.

Lansdown, R.V. 2021b. *Survey of sites formerly supporting Foxtail Stonewort (*Lamprothamnium papulosum*) in England.* Report for Natural England.

Lansdown, R.V. & Stewart, N.F. 1999. *The conservation status of Tassel Stonewort (*Tolypella intricata*) in Britain. Interim Report No. 1.* Plantlife Report No. 122. Plantlife, London.

Lansdown, R.V. & Wade, P.M. 2003. *Ecology of the Floating Water-plantain,* Luronium natans. Conserving Natura 2000 Rivers Ecology Series No. 9. English Nature, Peterborough.

Lansdown, R.V., Sayer, C.D., Shaw, M.M. & Stevens, P. 2016. Two new occurrences of *Najas marina* outside its traditional British range. *BSBI News* **131**: 18–19.

Lansdown, R.V., Cousins, M., Gargiulo, R. & Fay, M. 2018. Hybridisation and the conservation of *Nuphar pumila* (Least Water-lily). *BSBI News* **137**: 14–19.

Lansdown, R.V. & McVeigh, A. 2019. *Notes on surveys of sites known to have supported* Damasonium alisma *in recent years.* Freshwater Habitats Trust.

Lansdown, R.V., Kitchener, G. & Jones, E. 2022. *Wolffia columbiana* and *W. globosa* new to Britain. *British & Irish Botany* **4**: 14–26.

Lavin, J.C. & Wilmore, G.T.D. 1994. *The West Yorkshire Plant Atlas.* City of Bradford Metropolitan Council, Bradford.

Lawrence, P.A. and Ashenden, T.W. 1993. Effects of acidic gases and mists on the reproductive capability of three fern species. *Environmental Pollution* **79**: 267–270.

Leach, S.J. 1984. Notes on the distribution of *Artemisia maritima* L. in eastern Scotland. *Watsonia* **15**: 36–38.

Leach, S.J. 1986. The rediscovery of *Carex maritima* Gunn. on the fairways at St. Andrews Links, Fife. *Watsonia* **16**: 80–81.

Leach, S.J. 1988. Rediscovery of *Halimione pedunculata* (L.) Aellen in Britain. *Watsonia* **17**: 170–171.

Leach, S.J. 1989. *Halimione portulacoides* (L.) Aellen in Co Down. *Irish Naturalists' Journal* **23**: 74–75.

Leach, S.J. 1990. *Cochlearia danica* on inland roadsides. *BSBI News* **55**: 20–21.

Leach, S.J. 1997. *Phacelia tanacetifolia* as a 'green manure'. *BSBI News* **75**: 40–41.

Leach, S.J. 1999a. *Atriplex littoralis* on inland roadsides. *BSBI News* **81**: 36–37.

Leach, S.J. 1999b. *Lotus angustissimus* L. (Fabaceae) Slender Bird's-foot trefoil. In Wigginton, M.J. (Ed.) *British Red Data Books. 1. Vascular plants* pp. 232–233 Edn. 3. Joint Nature Conservation Committee, Peterborough.

Leach, S.J. 2006a. *Echinochloa crus-galli* (Cockspur) on roadsides in S. England. *BSBI News* **101**: 37–38.

Leach, S.J. 2006b. Recent surveys of endemic *Limonium* (Rock Sea-lavender) taxa in S. Devon (v.c. 3). In Leach, S.L., Page, C.N., Peytoureau, Y. & Sanford, M.N. (Eds.) *Botanical Links in the Atlantic Arc* BSBI Conference Report No. 24 Botanical Society of the British Isles, London.

Leach, S.J. 2017. The Vascular Plant Red Data List for Great Britain: a summary of amendments in years 10 and 11 (2015– 16) of the annual amendments process. *BSBI News* **135**: 59–62.

Leach, S.J. & Pearman, D.A. 2003. An assessment of the status of *Gaudinia fragilis* (L.) P. Beauv. (Poaceae) in the British Isles. *Watsonia* **23**: 469–487.

Leach, S.J. & Pearman, D.A. 2006. A review of recent work on the *Limonium binervosum* aggregate (Rock Sea-lavenders) in the British Isles. In Leach, S.L., Page, C.N., Peytoureau, Y. & Sanford, M.N. (Eds.) *Botanical Links in the Atlantic Arc* BSBI Conference Report No. 24 Botanical Society of the British Isles, London.

Leach, S.J. & Martin, J.P. 2014. Would anyone believe us if we said we had seen *Suaeda vera* (Shrubby Sea-blite) on the M6 in Warwickshire? *BSBI News* **125**: 34.

Leaney, R.M. 2014. A further update on the Norfolk comfrey (*Symphytum* × *norvicense*) and another overlooked comfrey hybrid in Norfolk. *BSBI News* **125**: 21–25.

Leaney, R.M. 2015. Probable yellow flowered *Symphytum* ×*uplandicum* and some thoughts on the derivation and status of some of the *Symphytum officinale* complex. *BSBI News* **129**: 22–26.

Leaney, R.M. 2016. Pink-yellow-cream flowered forms of *Symphytum* ×*uplandicum* in Yorkshire and Cambridgeshire. *BSBI News* **131**: 26–30.

Leather, S.R. 1996. Biological Flora of the British Isles. No. 189. *Prunus padus* L. *Journal of Ecology* **84**: 125–132.

Le Sueur, F. 1984. *Flora of Jersey*. Societe Jersiaise, Jersey.

Lee, J.A. 1977. The vegetation of British inland salt marshes. *Journal of Ecology* **65**: 673–698.

Lemna, W.K. & Messersmith, C.G. 1990. The biology of Canadian weeds. 94. *Sonchus arvensis* L. *Canadian Journal of Plant Science* **70**: 509–532.

Leslie, A.C. 1978. *The taxonomy of* Ranunculus auricomus *L. in the British Isles.* Ph.D. thesis, University of Cambridge.

Leslie, A.C. 1981. A note on naturalized *Doronicum* in Britain. *BSBI News* **27**: 22–23.

Leslie, A.C. 1984. Some new *Typha* records. *Watsonia* **15**: 168.

Leslie, A.C. 2019. *Flora of Cambridgeshire*. Royal Horticultural Society, Peterborough.

Lewin, R.A. 1948. Biological Flora of the British Isles. No. 22. *Sonchus* L. genus (pp. 203), *S. oleraceus* L. emend Gouan (pp. 204–216), *S. asper* (L.) Hill (pp. 216–223). *Journal of Ecology* **36**: 203–223.

Lewis, L. 2003. Dune forms of *Epipactis helleborine* at Kenfig. *Hardy Orchid Society Newsletter* **28**: 15–17.

Lewis, L. 2017. Green-flowered Helleborine, *Epipactis phyllanthes* in England and Wales. *Journal Europäischer Orchideen* **49**: 153–165.

Lewis, L. & Spencer, E.J. 2005. *Epipactis phyllanthes* var. *cambrensis* (C.A. Thomas) P.D. Sell and other unusual *Epipactis* at Kenfig National Nature Reserve. *Watsonia* **25**: 290–295.

Liljefors, A. 1955. Cytological studies in *Sorbus. Acta Horti Bergiani* **17**: 47–113.

Lockton, A. & Whild, S. 2015. *The Flora and Vegetation of Shropshire*. Shropshire Botanical Society, Shrewsbury.

Lodge, R.W. 1959. Biological Flora of the British Isles. No. 70. *Cynosurus cristatus* L. *Journal of Ecology* **47**: 511–518.

Lõhmus, A. & Runnel, K. 2014. Ash dieback can rapidly eradicate isolated epiphyte populations in production forests: A case study. *Biological Conservation* **169**: 185–188.

Long, D. & Williams, J. 2007. *Juniper in the British uplands: the Plantlife Juniper Survey results*. Plantlife Scotland, Stirling.

Long, M.P., Breen, C., Conaghan, J., Denyer, J., Faulkner, J., MacGowan, F., McCorry, M., Northbridge, R. & O'Meara, P. 2017. Telling the story of eight uncommon/declining Irish plant species – first results of the Irish Species Project (ISP). *Irish Botanical News* **27**: 55–77.

Lönn, M., Alexandersson, R. & Gustafsson, S. 2006. Hybrids and fruit set in a mixed flowering-time population of *Gymnadenia conopsea* (Orchidaceae). *Hereditas* **143**: 222–228.

Looman, J. 1978. Biological Flora of the Canadian Prairie Provinces. V. *Koeleria gracilis* Pers. *Canadian Journal of Plant Science* **58**: 459–466.

Lousley, J.E. 1944. Notes on British rumices: II. *Report of the Botanical Society and Exchange Club of the British Isles* **12**: 547–585.

Lousley, J.E. 1947. *Typha angustifolia* L. × *latifolia* L. *Report of the Botanical Society and Exchange Club of the British Isles* **13**: 174.

Lousley, J.E. 1948a. *Calystegia sylvestris* (Willd.) R.&S. *Report of the Botanical Society and Exchange Club of the British Isles* **13**: 265–268.

Lousley, J.E. 1948b. *Ficus carica* L. in Britain. *Report of the Botanical Society and Exchange Club of the British Isles* **13**: 330–333.

Lousley, J.E. 1958. *Plantago intermedia* in Britain? *Proceedings of the Botanical Society of the British Isles* **3**: 33–36.

Lousley, J.E. 1961. A census list of wool aliens found in Britain, 1946–1960. *Proceedings of the Botanical Society of the British Isles* **4**: 221–247.

Lousley, J.E. 1968. A glabrous perennial *Sonchus* in Britain. *Proceedings of the Botanical Society of the British Isles* **7**: 151–157.

Lousley, J.E. 1971. *Flora of the Isles of Scilly*. David & Charles, Newton Abbot.

Lousley, J.E. 1976. *Flora of Surrey*. David & Charles, London and Newton Abbot.

Lovatt, C.M. 1982. *The history, ecology and status of the rare plants and the vegetation of the Avon Gorge, Bristol*. University of Bristol.

Lovett-Doust, J., Lovett-Doust, L. & Groth, A.T. 1990. The biology of Canadian weeds. 95. *Ranunculus repens* L. *Canadian Journal of Plant Science* **70**: 1123–1141.

Lovis, J.D. 1955. The problem of *Asplenium trichomanes*. In Lousley, J.E. (Ed.) *Species studies in the British Flora* pp. 99–103 BSBI Conference Report no. 4 Botanical Society of the British Isles, London.

Low, E.G. 2007. *Shingle biodiversity and habitat disturbance*. University of Sussex, Brighton.

Lowe, A.J. & Abbott, R.J. 2003. A new British species, *Senecio eboracensis* (Asteraceae), another hybrid derivative of *S. vulgaris* L. and *S. squalidus* L. *Watsonia* **24**: 375–388.

Lucey, J. 2019. Irish Spurge (*Euphorbia hyberna*) in England: native or naturalised? *British & Irish Botany* **1**: 243–249.

Ludwig, S., Robertson, A., Rich, T.C.G., Djordjević, M., Cerović, R., Houston, L., Harris, S.A. & Hiscock, S.J. 2013. Breeding systems, hybridisation and continuing evolution in Avon Gorge *Sorbus. Annals of Botany* **111**: 563–575.

Luer, C.A. 1975. *The native orchids of the United States and Canada, excluding Florida*. New York Botanical Garden, New York.

Lupton, D. & Sheehy Skeffington, M. 2020. A review of the ecology and status of the Kerry Lily *Simethis mattiazzii* (*S. planifolia*) Asphodelaceae in Ireland. *British & Irish Botany* **2**: 309–334.

Lupton, F.G.H. 1985. Exploited plants. Wheat. *Biologist* **32**: 97–105.

Lusby, P. 1998. On the extinct plants of Scotland. In Lambert, R.A. (Ed.) *Species history in Scotland* pp. 45–62 Scottish Cultural Press, Edinburgh.

Lusby, P. & Wright, J. 2001. *Scottish Wild Plants, Their History, Ecology & Conservation*. Edn. 2. Royal Botanic Garden Edinburgh.

Lynes, M. 2019. *Alchemilla sciura* (Rosaceae), a new species of Lady's-mantle. *British & Irish Botany* **1**: 335–341.

Lynes, M. 2021. Three new species of *Alchemilla* (Rosaceae) from northern Britain. *British & Irish Botany* **3**: 334–348.

Lynes, M. 2022. Alchemilla: *Lady's-mantles of Britain and Ireland*. BSBI Handbook no. 24. Botanical Society of Britain and Ireland, Durham.

Lyte, B. & Cope, T. 1999. Plants in Peril, 25. *Bromus interruptus. Curtis's Botanical Magazine* **16**: 296–300.

Mabey, R. 1996. *Flora Britannica*. Sinclair-Stevenson, London.

MacDonald, M.A. & Cavers, P.B. 1991. The biology of Canadian weeds. 97. *Barbarea vulgaris* R.Br. *Canadian Journal of Plant Science* **71**: 149–166.

Mackenzie, N.A. 2000. *Low Alpine, Subalpine & Coastal Scrub Communities in Scotland*. A Report to Highland Birchwoods. Highland Birchwoods, Munlochy.

Mackinnon, A., Lovett-Doust, J. & Lovett-Doust, L. 1985. Biology of Canadian weeds. 71. *Oxalis stricta* L., *O. corniculata* L., *O. dillenii* Jacq. ssp. *dillenii* and *O. dillenii* Jacq. ssp. *filipes* (Small) Eiten. *Canadian Journal of Plant Science* **65**: 691–709.

Macpherson, P., Dickson, J.H., Ellis, R.G., Kent, D.H. & Stace, C.A. 1996. Plant status nomenclature. *BSBI News* **72**: 13–16.

Madge, S. 1994. The status of *Serapias parviflora* Parl. in Britain. *Botanical Cornwall* **6**: 51–52.

Mal, T.K., Lovett-Doust, J., Lovett-Doust, L. & Mulligan, G.A. 1992. The biology of Canadian weeds. 100. *Lythrum salicaria. Canadian Journal of Plant Science* **72**: 1305–1330.

Malik, N. & Vanden Born, W.H. 1988. The biology of Canadian weeds. 86. *Galium aparine* L. and *Galium spurium* L. *Canadian Journal of Plant Science* **68**: 481–499.

Malloch, A.J.C. & Okusanya, O.T. 1979. An experimental investigation into the ecology of some maritime cliff species I. Field observations. *Journal of Ecology* **67**: 283–292.

Manton, I. 1950. *Problems of Cytology and Evolution in the Pteridophyta*. Cambridge University Press, Cambridge.

Marchant, C.J. & Goodman, P.J. 1969. Biological Flora of the British Isles. No. 116. *Spartina maritima* (Curtis) Fernald (pp. 287–291), 2. *S. alterniflora* Loisel. (pp. 291–295), 3. *S. glabra* Muhl. (pp. 295–297). *Journal of Ecology* **57**: 287–297.

Marciniuk, J., Marciniuk, P. & Rymuza, K. 2010. Effects of site conditions on sexual dimorphism and sex ratio in lowland populations of *Aruncus sylvestris* Kostel. (Rosaceae). *Polish Journal of Ecology* **58**: 249–257.

Mardon, D.K. 1990. Conservation of montane willow scrub in Scotland. *Transactions of the Botanical Society of Edinburgh* **45**: 427–436.

Mardon, D.K. & Watts, S.H. 2019. Population dynamics and life history of the rare arctic-alpine plant *Sagina nivalis* (Caryophyllaceae) on the Ben Lawers range, Scotland, UK. *British & Irish Botany* **1**: 50–69.

Margetts, L.J. & David, R.W. 1981. *A review of the Cornish flora 1980*. Institute of Cornish Studies, Redruth.

Margetts, L.J., Murphy, R.J., Rich, T.C.G. & Holyoak, D.T. 1997. Hybridisation between *Gentianella amarella* (L.) Boerner and *G. anglica* (Pugsley) E. F. Warb. (Gentianaceae). *Watsonia* 21: 313–325.

Marren, P.R. 1971. The Lundy Cabbage. *Annual Report of the Lundy Field Society* 22: 27–31.

Marren, P.R. 1972. Addenda to The Lundy Cabbage. *Annual Report of the Lundy Field Society* 23: 51–52.

Marren, P.R. 1981. A possible origin of *Carum verticillatum* (L.) Koch in north-eastern Scotland. *Watsonia* 13: 323.

Marren, P.R. 1983. The history of Dickie's fern in Kincardineshire. *Transactions of the Botanical Society of Edinburgh* 44: 157–164.

Marren, P.R. 1988. The past and present distribution of *Stachys germanica* L. in Britain. *Watsonia* 17: 59–68.

Marren, P.R. 1999. *Britain's rare flowers*. T. & A.D. Poyser, London.

Marren, P.R. 2000. *Where have all the flowers gone? A study of local extinctions as recorded in the county Floras*. Plantlife, London.

Marren, P.R., Payne, A.G. & Randall, R.E. 1986. The past and present status of *Cicerbita alpina* (L.) Wallr. in Britain. *Watsonia* 16: 131–142.

Marrinan, L. & Rich, T.C.G. 2019. *101 rare plants of Wales*. Graffeg, Llanelli.

Marriott, R.W., Mchaffie, H. & Mardon, D.K. 2015. Woolly willow. In Gaywood, M.J., Boon, P.J., Thompson, D.B.A. & Strachan, I.M. (Eds.) *The Species Action Framework Handbook* Scottish Natural Heritage, Battleby, Perth.

Marrs, R.H. 1993. An assessment of change in *Calluna* heathlands in Breckland, eastern England, between 1983 and 1991. *Biological Conservation* 65: 133–139.

Marrs, R.H. & Watt, A.S. 2006. Biological Flora of the British Isles. No. 245. *Pteridium aquilinum* (L.) Kuhn. *Journal of Ecology* 94: 1272–1321.

Marrs, R.H., Le Duc, M.G., Smart, S.M., Kirby, K.J., Bunce, R.G.H. & Corney, P.M. 2010. Aliens or natives: Who are the 'thugs' in British woods? *Kew Bulletin* 65: 583–594.

Marrs, R.H., Lee, H., Blackbird, S., Connor, L., Girdwood, S.E., O'Connor, M., Smart, S.M., Rose, R.J., O'Reilly, J. & Chiverrell, R.C. 2020. Release from sheep-grazing appears to put some heart back into upland vegetation: A comparison of nutritional properties of plant species in long-term grazing experiments. *Annals of Applied Biology* 177: 152–162.

Marsden-Jones, E.M. & Turrill, W.B. 1957. *The Bladder Campions*. Ray Society, London.

Marshall, E.S. 1914. *Betula*. In Moss, C.E. (Ed.) *The Cambridge British Flora* Volume 2. Cambridge University Press, Cambridge.

Marshall, E.S. 1916. Notes on *Sorbus*. *Journal of Botany* 54: 10–14.

Marshall, J.K. 1967. Biological Flora of the British Isles. No. 105. *Corynephorus canescens* (L.) Beauv. *Journal of Ecology* 55: 207–220.

Marston, A. 2007. The distribution and abundance of Wood Calamint on the Isle of Wight 1999– 2005. *Proceedings of the Isle of Wight Natural History and Archaeological Society* 22: 42–60.

Martin, A. 2001. *The ecology and palaeoecology of the charophyte* Lamprothamnium papulosum *in U.K. coastal lagoons*. Ph.D. thesis, University College, London.

Martin, A., Carvalho, L. & Downie, A.J. 2002. Rare charophytes in Scotland's coastal saline lagoons. *Botanical Journal of Scotland* 54: 23–35.

Martin, J. 1993. *Cotula coronopifolia* established in Yorkshire. *BSBI News* 64: 42–43.

Martin, M.H. & Frost, L.C. 1980. Autecological studies of *Trifolium molinerii* at the Lizard Peninsula, Cornwall. *New Phytologist* 86: 329–344.

Martinsson, K. 1991a. *Callitriche* in Sweden: case studies of reproductive biology and intraspecific variation in a semi-aquatic plant genus. *Acta Universitatis Upsaliensis* 327.

Martinsson, K. 1991b. Geographical variation in fruit morphology in Swedish *Callitriche hermaphroditica* (Callitrichaceae). *Nordic Journal of Botany* 11: 497–512.

Maskell, L.C., Smart, S.M., Bullock, J.M., Thompson, K. & Stevens, C.J. 2010. Nitrogen deposition causes widespread loss of species richness in British habitats. *Global Change Biology* 16: 671–679.

Maskell, L.C., Henrys, P., Pescott, O.L. & Smart, S.M. 2020. Long-term trends in the distribution, abundance and impact of native "injurious" weeds. *Applied Vegetation Science* 23: 635–647.

Maskew, R. 2014. *The Flora of Worcestershire*. Self-published, Tenbury Wells.

Mathew, B. 1981. *The Iris*. Batsford, London.

Mathew, B. 1982. *The Crocus*. Batsford, London.

Mathew, B. 1996. *A review of* Allium *section* Allium. Royal Botanic Gardens, Kew.

Matthews, J., Beringen, R., Boer, E., Duistermaat, H. & Odé, B. 2015. *Risks and management of non-native* Impatiens *species in the Netherlands*. Reports Environmental Science 491. Radboud University.

Matthews, P. & Davison, A.W. 1976. Maritime species on roadside verges. *Watsonia* 11: 146–147.

Maun, M.A. & Barrett, S.C.H. 1986. The biology of Canadian weeds. 77. *Echinochloa crus-galli* (L.) Beauv. *Canadian Journal of Plant Science* 66: 739–759.

Maycock, R. & Woods, A. 2005. *A Checklist of the Plants of Buckinghamshire (including Milton Keynes and Slough)*. Milton Keynes Natural History Society, Milton Keynes.

Mayland-Quellhorst, E., Föller, J. & Wissemann, V. 2012. Biological Flora of the British Isles. No. 265. *Rosa spinosissima* L. *Journal of Ecology* 100: 561–576.

McAllister, H.A. 1999. *Lysimachia punctata* L. and *L. verticillaris* Sprengel (Primulaceae) naturalised in the British Isles. *Watsonia* 22: 279–281.

McAllister, H.A. & Rutherford, A. 1990. *Hedera helix* L. and *H. hibernica* (Kirchner) Bean (Araliaceae) in the British Isles. *Watsonia* 18: 7–15.

McAllister, H.A. & Marshall, A. 2017. Hedera: *the complete guide*. Royal Horticultural Society, Peterborough.

McCallum Webster, M. 1978. *Flora of Moray, Nairn & East Inverness*. Aberdeen University Press, Aberdeen.

McCarthy, W.N. & Bratton, J.H. 2010. *The status of rare grassland plants and their habitats on eastern Great Orme in 2010*. Unpublished report for Plantlife.

McClean, C.J., Van Den Berg, L.J., Ashmore, M.R. & Preston, C.D. 2011. Atmospheric nitrogen deposition explains patterns of plant species loss. *Global Change Biology* 17: 2882–2892.

McClintock, D. 1972. Short Notes. *Gaudinia fragilis* (L.) Beauv. *Watsonia* 9: 143–146.

McClintock, D. 1975. *The wildflowers of Guernsey*. Collins, London.

McClintock, D. 1982. *Guernsey's Earliest Flora*. Ray Society, London.

McClintock, D. 1986. The Guernsey Millet: a new subspecies. *Report and Transactions La Société Guernesiaise* 21: 698–700.

McClintock, D. 1987. *Supplement to The Wild Flowers of Guernsey (Collins, 1975)*. La Société Guernesiaise, St Peter Port.

McCollin, D. & Geraghty, E. 2015. Change and causes of change in the vascular plant flora of Ireland: 1970–1999. *Biology and Environment: Proceedings of the Royal Irish Academy*, 115B: 67–81.

McCosh, D.J. & Rich, T.C.G. 2018. *Atlas of British and Irish Hawkweeds (*Pilosella Hill *and* Hieracium *L.)*. Edn. 2. Botanical Society of Britain and Ireland, Harpenden.

McDonnell, E.J. 1995. *The status of Toadflax-leaved St. John's-wort (*Hypericum linariifolium *Vahl) in Britain in 1994*. Back from the Brink Project Report no. 40. Plantlife, London.

McHaffie, H.S. 2005. Biological Flora of the British Isles. No. 241. *Athyrium distentifolium* Tausch ex Opiz (*A. alpestre* (Hoppe) Rylands ex T. Moore-non-Clairv.) including *A. distentifolium* var. *flexile* (Newman) Jermy. *Journal of Ecology* 93: 839–851.

McKee, J. & Richards, A.J. 1998. The effect of temperature on reproduction in five *Primula* species. *Annals of Botany* 82: 359–374.

McMullen, R. 2016. Beggarticks (*Bidens frondosa*) in Grand Canal Docks, Dublin, (H21). *Irish Botanical News* 26.

McNaughton, I.H. & Harper, J.L. 1964. Biological Flora of the British Isles. No. 99. *Papaver rhoeas* L. (pp. 767–779), *P. dubium* L. (pp. 780–783), *P. lecoqii* Lamotte (pp. 783–786), *P. argemone* L. (pp. 786–789), *P. hybridum* L. (pp. 789–793). *Journal of Ecology* 52: 767–793.

McNeill, J. 1977. The biology of Canadian weeds. 25. *Silene alba* (Miller) E.H.L. Krause. *Canadian Journal of Plant Science* 57: 1103–1114.

McNeill, J. 1980. The biology of Canadian weeds. 46. *Silene noctiflora* L. *Canadian Journal of Plant Science* 60: 1243–1253.

McVean, D.N. 1953. Biological Flora of the British Isles. No. 37. *Alnus glutinosa* (L.) Gaertn. *Journal of Ecology* 41: 447–466.

McVean, D.N. 1955a. Ecology of *Alnus glutinosa* (L.) Gaertn. I. Fruit formation. *Journal of Ecology* 43: 46–60.

McVean, D.N. 1955b. Ecology of *Alnus glutinosa* (L.) Gaertn. II. Seed distribution and germination. *Journal of Ecology* 43: 61–71.

McVean, D.N. 1961. Post-glacial history of juniper in Scotland. *Proceedings of the Linnean Society of London* 172: 53–55.

McVean, D.N. & Ratcliffe, D.A. 1962. *Plant communities of the Scottish Highlands*. Monographs of the Nature Conservancy No. 1. Her Majesty's Stationery Office, London.

McVeigh, A., Carey, J.E. & Rich, T.C.G. 2005. Chiltern Gentian, *Gentianella germanica* (Willd.) Börner (Gentianaceae) in Britain: distribution and current status. *Watsonia* 25: 339–367.

Meade, M. 1989. Year-by-year observations of *Selinum carvifolia, Parnassia palustris* and other species on Sawston Hall Moor. *Nature in Cambridgeshire* 31: 43–45.

Measures, G. & Thomas, S. 2011. *Horizon-scanning for invasive non-native plants in Great Britain*. Natural England Commissioned Reports, Number 53.

Meatyard, B. 1999. *Koenigia islandica* (Iceland Purslane) A Case Study of a Potential Indicator of Climate Change in the UK. In Visconti, G., Beniston, M., Iannorelli, E.D. & Barba, D. (Eds.) *Global Change and Protected Areas* pp. 209–217 Advances in Global Change Research, vol 9 Springer, Dordrecht.

Meekers, T., Hutchings, M.J., Honnay, O. & Jacquemyn, H. 2012. Biological Flora of the British Isles. No. 268: *Gymnadenia conopsea* s.l. *Journal of Ecology* 100: 1269–1288.

Meerts, P. 1988. Une famille nouvelle pour la flore adventice de la Belgique: les Pontederiaceae. *Dumortiera* 41: 1–3.

Meeus, S., Brys, R., Honnay, O. & Jacquemyn, H. 2013. Biological Flora of the British Isles. No. 272. *Pulmonaria officinalis*. *Journal of Ecology* 101: 1353–1368.

Meikle, R.D. 1984. *Willows and Poplars of Great Britain and Ireland*. BSBI Handbook no. 4. Botanical Society of the British Isles, London.

Meikle, R.D. 1992. British willows; some hybrids and some problems. *Proceedings of the Royal Society of Edinburgh* 98B: 13–20.

Meng, X.L. 2018. Statistical paradises and paradoxes in big data (I): Law of large populations, big data paradox, and the 2016 US presidential election. *The Annals of Applied Statistics* 12: 685–726.

Mercer, R.J. 1981. *Grimes Graves, Norfolk excavations 1971–72: volume 1.* Department of the Environment Archaeological Reports no. 11. Her Majesty's Stationery Office, London.

Merceron, N.R., Lamarque, L.J., Delzon, S. & Porté, A.J. 2016. Killing it Softly: Girdling as an Efficient Eco-friendly Method to Locally Remove Invasive *Acer negundo. Ecological Restoration* 34: 297–305.

Meredith, T.C. & Grubb, P.J. 1993. Biological Flora of the British Isles. No. 179. *Peucedanum palustre* (L.) Moench. *Journal of Ecology* 81: 813–826.

Merryweather, J. 2020. *Britain's Ferns.* Princeton University Press, Oxfordshire.

Mesters, C.M.L. 1995. Shifts in macrophyte species composition as a result of eutrophication and pollution in Dutch transboundary streams over the past decades. *Journal of Aquatic Ecosystem Health* 4: 295–305.

Metherell, C. & Rumsey, F.J. 2018. *Eyebrights (*Euphrasia*) of the UK and Ireland.* BSBI Handbook No. 18. Botanical Society of Britain and Ireland, Bristol.

Meusel, H., Jäger, E. & Weinert, E. 1965. *Vergleichende Chorologie der zentraleuropäischen Flora. Volume 1. 2 vols.* Gustav Fischer, Jena.

Meusel, H., Jäger, E., Rauschert, S. & Weinert, E. 1978. *Vergleichende Chorologie der zentraleuropäischen Flora. Volume 2. 2 vols.* Gustav Fischer, Jena.

Meusel, H. & Jäger, E.J. 1992. *Vergleichende Chorologie der zentraleuropäischen Flora. Volume 3. 2 vols.* Gustav Fischer, Jena.

Mhic Daeid, C. & Reynolds, S. 1999. *Phalaris minor* Retz. in Meath (H22) and Wexford (H12), and Other Alien Grasses in Arable Habitats. *Irish Naturalists' Journal* 26: 198–199.

Micheneau, C., Duffy, K.J., Smith, R.J., Stevens, L.J., Stout, J.C., Civeyrel, L., Cowan, R.S. & Fay, M.F. 2010. Plastid microsatellites for the study of genetic variability in the widespread *Cephalanthera longifolia, C. damasonium* and *C. rubra* (Neottieae, Orchidaceae), and cross-amplification in other *Cephalanthera* species. *Botanical Journal of the Linnean Society* 163: 181–193.

Michl, T., Huck, S., Schmitt, T., Liebrich, A., Haase, P. & Buedel, B. 2010. The molecular population structure of the tall forb *Cicerbita alpina* (Asteraceae) supports the idea of cryptic glacial refugia in central Europe. *Botanical Journal of the Linnean Society* 164: 142–154.

Millar, N. 2012. Invasive alien - *Pentaglottis sempervirens* (Green Alkanet). *BSBI News* 121: 58.

Miller, G.R. 2004. Size and longevity of seedbanks of Alpine Gentian (*Gentiana nivalis* L.). *Botanical Journal of Scotland* 56: 93–102.

Miller, D. & Grant, M. 1998. *Lavatera olbia* × *L. thuringiaca* in gardens. *BSBI News* 79: 67.

Miller, G.R., Geddes, C. & Mardon, D.K. 1999. Response of alpine gentian (*Gentiana nivalis* L.) to protection from grazing by sheep. *Biological Conservation* 87: 311–318.

Miller, G.R. & Geddes, C. 2004. Seed-setting by Alpine Gentian (*Gentiana nivalis* L.). *Botanical Journal of Scotland* 56: 85–91.

Millett, J. & Edmondson, S. 2015. The impact of 36 years of grazing management on soil nitrogen (N) supply rate and *Salix repens* N status and internal cycling in dune slacks. *Plant Soil* 396: 411–420.

Milne-Redhead, E. 1947. *Cerastium brachypetalum* Pers. in Britain. *The Naturalist* 822: 95–96.

Milne-Redhead, E. 1990. The B.S.B.I. Black Poplar survey, 1973–88. *Watsonia* 18: 1–5.

Minchin, D., Boelens, R. & Roden, C. 2017. The first record of *Nitellopsis obtusa* (N.A. Devaux) J. Groves (Charophyceae, Characeae) in Ireland (H9, H10). *The Irish Naturalists' Journal* 35: 105–109.

Minchin, D., Boelens, R. & Roden, C. 2019. The non-indigenous stonewort *Nitella mucronata gracillima* (A. Braun) Miquel (Charophyta; Characeae) established in Lough Derg, Co. Tipperary (H9). *The Irish Naturalists' Journal* 36: 137–138.

Minchin, D., Boelens, R. & Higgins, D. 2021a. Expansion of a localised population of the introduced *Stratiotes aloides* (Hydrocharitaceae) in Lough Derg, Ireland. *British & Irish Botany* 3: 455–468.

Minchin, D., Boelens, R. & Roden, C. 2021b. Non-indigenous and cryptogenic charophytes (Characeae) forming meadows in the Shannon River, Ireland. *Irish Naturalists' Journal* 38: 5–13.

Mitchell, A. 1996a. *A Field Guide to the Trees of Britain and Northern Europe.* Edn. 3. Collins, London.

Mitchell, A.F. 1972. *Conifers in the British Isles. A descriptive handbook.* Her Majesty's Stationery Office, London.

Mitchell, A.F. 1996b. *Alan Mitchell's Trees of Britain.* Harper Collins, London.

Mitchell, J. 1981. *Elatine hydropiper* at Kilmannan Reservoir. *Glasgow Naturalist* 20: 185–186.

Mitchell, R.J., Beaton, J.K., Bellamy, P.E., Broome, A., Chetcuti, J., Eaton, S., Ellis, C.J., Gimona, A., Harmer, R., Hester, A.J., Hewison, R.L., Hodgetts, N.G., Iason, G.R., Kerr, G., Littlewood, N.A., Newey, S., Potts, J.M., Pozsgai, G., Ray, D., Sim, D.A., Stockan, J.A., Taylor, A.F.S. & Woodward, S. 2014. Ash dieback in the UK: A review of the ecological and conservation implications and potential management options. *Biological Conservation* 175: 95–109.

Miyanishi, K., Eriksson, O. & Wein, R.W. 1991. The biology of Canadian weeds. 98. *Potentilla anserina* L. *Canadian Journal of Plant Science* 71: 791–801.

Mjelde, M. & Faafeng, B.A. 1997. *Ceratophyllum demersum* hampers phytoplankton development in some small Norwegian lakes over a wide range of phosphorus concentrations and geographical latitude. *Freshwater Biology* 37: 355–365.

Moody, M.L. & Les, D.H. 2002. Evidence of hybridity in invasive watermilfoil (*Myriophyllum*) populations. *Proceedings of the National Academy of Sciences USA* 99: 14867–14871.

Mooney, H.A. & Billings, W.D. 1961. Comparative physiological ecology of arctic and alpine populations of *Oxyria digyna. Ecological Monographs* 31: 1–29.

Moore, D.M. 1958. Biological Flora of the British Isles. No. 66. *Viola lactea* Sm. *Journal of Ecology* 46: 527–535.

Moore, J.A. 1986. *Charophytes of Great Britain and Ireland.* BSBI Handbook no.5. Botanical Society of the British Isles, London.

Moore, J.J. 1966. *Minuartia recurva* (All.) Schinz and Thell. new to the British Isles. *Irish Naturalists' Journal* 15: 130–132.

Moore, J.R. 2011. *Wood properties and uses of Sitka Spruce in Britain.* Forestry Commission, Edinburgh.

Moore, R.J. 1975. The biology of Canadian weeds. 13. *Cirsium arvense* (L.) Scop. *Canadian Journal of Plant Science* 55: 1033–1048.

Morecroft, M.D., Stokes, V.J., Taylor, M.E. & Morison, J.I.L. 2008. Effects of climate and management history on the distribution and growth of sycamore (*Acer pseudoplatanus* L.) in a southern British woodland in comparison to native competitors. *Forestry: An International Journal of Forest Research* 81: 59–74.

Morris, W.F. & Doak, D.F. 1998. Life history of the long-lived gynodioecious cushion plant *Silene acaulis* (Caryophyllaceae), inferred from size-based population projection matrices. *American Journal of Botany* 85: 784–793.

Morrow, S.B. & Forbes, R.S. 2012. Agriculture in County Fermanagh, *In:* Forbes, R.S. & Northridge, R.H. (Eds.), *The Flora of County Fermanagh*, pp. 45–56. National Museums of Northern Ireland, Holywood, County Down.

Morton, J.K. 1973. A cytological study of the British Labiatae (excluding *Mentha*). *Watsonia* 9: 239–246.

Moss, S., Perryman, S. & Tatnell, L. 2007. Managing Herbicide-resistant Blackgrass (*Alopecurus myosuroides*): Theory and Practice. *Weed Technology* 21: 300–309.

Moughan, M., McGinn, K.J., Jones, L., Rich, T.C.G., Waters, E. & de Vere, N. 2021. Biological Flora of the British Isles. No. 297. *Salvia pratensis. Journal of Ecology* 12: 4171–4190.

Mountford, J.O. 1994. Floristic change in English grazing marshes: the impact of 150 years of drainage and land-use change. *Watsonia* 20: 3–24.

Mountford, J.O. & Graham, J.J. 2021. *Diplotaxis erucoides* – the 'Cabbage-patch Rocket': the spread and status of a speciality of the Lincolnshire Fenland. *The Lincolnshire Naturalist (Transactions of the Lincolnshire Naturalists' Union)* 30: 76–78.

Muldoon, C.S. 2011. *Conservation biology of* Saxifraga hirculus *L. in Ireland.* Unpublished Ph.D. thesis, University of Dublin, Trinity College.

Mulligan, G.A. & Findlay, J.N. 1974. The biology of Canadian weeds. 3. *Cardaria draba, C. chalepensis* and *C. pubescens. Canadian Journal of Plant Science* 54: 149–160.

Mulligan, G.A. & Bailey, L.G. 1975. The biology of Canadian weeds. 8. *Sinapis arvensis* L. *Canadian Journal of Plant Science* 55: 171–183.

Mulligan, G.A. & Munro, D.B. 1981. The biology of Canadian weeds. 48. *Cicuta maculata* L., *C. douglasii* (DC.) Coult. & Rose and *C. virosa* L. *Canadian Journal of Plant Science* 61: 93–105.

Mundell, A.R.G. & Carter, C.I. 2001. A Couple of Chenopodiums. *BSBI News* 87: 58–59.

Munz, P.A. & Keck, D.D. 1959. *A California Flora (and 1968 Supplement).* University of California Press.

Murphy, K.J. & Wallace, G. 2004. *Macrophyte survey of the Loch of Boardhouse, Orkney.* Scottish Natural Heritage Commissioned Report 021 (ROAME No. F03LA10), Battleby, Perth.

Murphy, R.J. 1994. Progress report. *Botanical Cornwall* 6: 1–7.

Murphy, R.J. 2009. *Fumitories of Britain and Ireland.* BSBI Handbook No. 12. Botanical Society of the British Isles, London.

Murphy, R.J. 2016. *Evening-primroses (*Oenothera*) of Britain and Ireland.* BSBI Handbook No. 16. Botanical Society of Britain and Ireland, Bristol.

Murphy, R.J. & Page, C.N. 1996. *Polypodium* ×*mantoniae* Rothm. & U.Schneider (*P. vulgare* × *P. interjectum*) in Cornwall. *Botanical Cornwall* 7: 33–36.

Murphy, R.J. & Rumsey, F.J. 2005. *Cystopteris diaphana* (Bory) Blasdell (Woodsiaceae) an overlooked native new to the British Isles. *Watsonia* 25: 255–263.

Myerscough, P.J. 1980. Biological Flora of the British Isles. No. 148. *Epilobium angustifolium* L. *Journal of Ecology* 68: 1047–1074.

Myerscough, P.J. & Whitehead, F.H. 1966. Comparative biology of *Tussilago farfara* L., *Chamaenerion angustifolium* (L.) Scop., *Epilobium montanum* L., and *Epilobium adenocaulon* Hausskn. I. General biology and germination. *New Phytologist* 65: 192–210.

Myerscough, P.J. & Whitehead, F.H. 1967. Comparative biology of *Tussilago farfara* L., *Chamaenerion angustifolium* (L.) Scop., *Epilobium montanum* L., and *Epilobium adenocaulon* Hausskn. II. Growth and ecology. *New Phytologist* 66: 785–823.

Nagengast, B. & Gąbka, M. 2017. Niche partitioning of two congeneric submerged macrophytes in small water bodies: The case of *Ceratophyllum demersum* L. and *C. submersum* L. *Aquatic Botany* 137: 1–8.

Nagy, L. 2013. Biological Flora of the British Isles. No. 271. *Silene suecica. Journal of Ecology* 101: 532–544.

BIBLIOGRAPHY

Naylor, R.E.L. 1972. Biological Flora of the British Isles. No. 129. *Alopecurus myosuroides* Huds. *Journal of Ecology* **60**: 611–622.

Neff, J. 2000. *Atlas 2000 Irish Scarce Plants Project Report November 2000*. Unpublished report prepared for Dúchas, The Heritage Service, Department of Arts, Heritage, Gaeltacht and the Islands, Dublin.

Nelson, E.C. 1977. The discovery in 1810 and subsequent history of *Phyllodoce caerulea* (L.) Bab. in Scotland. *The Western Naturalist* **6**: 45–72.

Nelson, E.C. 1993. Who was the author of *Montbretia crocosmiflora*? *Watsonia* **19**: 265–267.

Nelson, E.C. 2000. A history, mainly nomenclatural, of St Dabeoc's Heath. *Watsonia* **23**: 47–58.

Nelson, E.C. 2004. The enigma of the alien heathers of Britain, especially *Erica* × *darlyensis*. *Heath Society Bulletin* **6**: 4–6.

Nethercott, P.J.M. 1998. Conservation status of *Sorbus* in the Avon Gorge. In Jackson, A. & Flanagan, M. (Eds.) *The conservation status of* Sorbus *in the UK* pp. 40–43 Royal Botanic Gardens, Kew, London.

Neumann, D., Nieden, U., Schwieger, W., Leopold, I. & Lichtenberger, O. 1997. Heavy metal tolerance of *Minuartia verna*. *Journal of Plant Physiology* **151**: 101–108.

New, J.K. 1961. Biological Flora of the British Isles. No. 76. *Spergula arvensis* L. *Journal of Ecology* **49**: 205–215.

Newbold, C. 2003a. Water quality and the aquatic flora of the Ouse Washes: an historical perspective. *Nature in Cambridgeshire* **45**: 64–69.

Newbold, C. 2003b. *The ecology and status of* Potamogeton acutifolius*, Link, (Sharp-leaved pondweed) in 2003*. Contract report to English Nature EIT34-01-07. English Nature, Peterborough.

Newcombe, M. 1991. Sea Heath and other plants on a degraded cliff face. *Transactions of the Kent Field Club* **11**(2): 93.

Newlands, C. & Smith, H. 1998. Management and conservation status of sites with *Orobanche reticulata* Wallr. Populations. *The Naturalist* **123**: 70–75.

Newman, J.R. & Dawson, F.H. 1999. Ecology, distribution and chemical control of *Hydrocotyle ranunculoides* in the U.K. *Hydrobiologia* **415**: 295–298.

Newman, J.R. & Duenas, M. 2006. *CEH Information Sheet 24:* Hydrocotyle ranunculoides. NERC Centre for Ecology and Hydrology.

Newman, R.D., Showler, A.J., Harvey, M.C. & Showler, D.A. 2007. Hand pollination to increase seed-set of red helleborine *Cephalanthera rubra* in the Chiltern Hills, Buckinghamshire, England. *Conservation Evidence* **4**: 88–93.

Newsholme, C. 1992. *Willows, the genus* Salix, Batsford Ltd.

Nicolle, D. 1991. *Scilla bithynica*. *BSBI News* **58**: 40–41.

Nielsen, U.N., Riis, T. & Brix, H. 2006. The importance of vegetative and sexual dispersal of *Luronium natans*. *Aquatic Botany* **84**: 165–170.

Nixon, C.J. & Worrell, R. 1999. *The potential for natural regeneration of conifers in Britain. Forestry Commission Bulletin no. 120*. Forestry Commission, Edinburgh.

Nobis, A., Nowak, A. & Rola, K. 2018. Do invasive alien plants really threaten river bank vegetation? A case study based on plant communities typical for *Chenopodium ficifolium* - an indicator of large river valleys. *PloS one* **13**: e0194473.

Noble, J.C. 1982. Biological Flora of the British Isles. No. 152. *Carex arenaria* L. *Journal of Ecology* **70**: 867–886.

Norton, M. & Roberts, J. 2020. *Calamagrostis purpurea* (Scandinavian Small-reed), in Co Meath (H22), first report from Ireland. *BSBI News* **144**: 16–21.

Nunez, D.R., De Castro, C.O., Ruiz, S.R. & Ariza, F.A. 2003. O'Donovan, J.T. & Sharma, M.P. 1987. The biology of Canadian weeds. 78. *Galeopsis tetrahit* L. *Canadian Journal of Plant Science* **67**: 787–796.

O'Leary, M. 1989. The habitat of *Selinum carvifolia* in Cambridgeshire. *Nature in Cambridgeshire* **31**: 36–43.

O'Mahony, T. 1976. *Carex depauperata* Curt. in NE Cork (H5) a sedge new to Ireland. *Irish Naturalists' Journal* **18**: 296–298.

O'Mahony, T. 1985. The history of *Geranium purpureum* Vill. in the Irish flora. *Irish Naturalists' Journal* **21**: 517–521.

O'Mahony, T. 2006. *Mibora minima* (L.) Desv., Early Sand-grass (Poaceae) in West Cork (H3): an addition to the Irish flora. *Irish Botanical News* **16**: 5–13.

O'Mahony, T. 2008. The diagnostic characters of *Rosa stylosa* Desv. (Short-styled Field-rose) (Rosaceae): a brief account of its history, distribution and habitat preferences in the Irish Flora, and its current-known distribution in Co. Cork (v.cc. H3-H5). *Irish Botanical News* **18**: 5–18.

O'Mahony, T. 2009. *Wildflowers of Cork City and County*. The Collins Press, Cork.

O'Neill, F.H., Hodd, R.L. & Long, M.P. 2019. *Results of a monitoring survey of the Annex II species* Saxifraga hirculus *(Marsh Saxifrage) in Ireland 2015–2018*. Irish Wildlife Manuals, No. 112. National Parks and Wildlife Service, Dublin.

O'Reilly, C. 2006. What is *Symphytum officinale* subsp. *bohemicum* (Schmidt) Čelak? *BSBI News* **102**: 46–48.

Ockendon, D.J. 1968. Biological Flora of the British Isles. No. 113. *Linum perenne* L. ssp. *anglicum* (Miller) Ockendon. *Journal of Ecology* **56**: 871–882.

Ockendon, D.J. & Walters, S.M. 1970. Studies in *Potentilla anserina* L. *Watsonia* **8**: 135–144.

Ohwi, J. 1965. *Flora of Japan (in English)*. Smithsonian Institution, Washington, D.C.

Okusanya, O.T. 1979a. An experimental investigation into the ecology of some maritime cliff species II. Germination studies. *Journal of Ecology* **67**: 293–304.

Okusanya, O.T. 1979b. An experimental investigation into the ecology of some maritime cliff species III. Effects of water on growth. *Journal of Ecology* **67**: 579–590.

Okusanya, O.T. 1979c. An experimental investigation into the ecology of some maritime cliff species IV. Cold sensitivity and competition studies. *Journal of Ecology* **67**: 591–600.

Olesen, I. & Warncke, E. 1992. Breeding system and seasonal variation in seed set in a population of *Potentilla palustris*. *Nordic Journal of Botany* **12**: 373–380.

Oleskevich, C., Shamoun, S.F. & Punja, Z.K. 1996. The biology of Canadian weeds. 105. *Rubus strigosus* Michx., *Rubus parviflorus* Nutt., and *Rubus spectabilis* Pursh. *Canadian Journal of Plant Science* **76**: 187–201.

Oliver, J. 1998. North American asters in Wiltshire. *Wiltshire Archaeological and Natural History Magazine* **91**: 128–138.

Oostermeijer, J.G.B., Luisten, S.H., Ellis-Adam, A.C. & den Nijs, J.C.M. 2002. Future prospects for the rare, late-flowering *Gentianella germanica* and *Gentianopsis ciliata* in Dutch, nutrient-poor calcareous grasslands. *Biological Conservation* **104**: 339–350.

Oswald, P.H. 1992. The Fritillary in Britain - a historical perspective. *British Wildlife* **3**: 200–210.

Oswald, P.H. 1993. Native and naturalised garlics in the Cambridge University Botanic Garden. *Nature in Cambridgeshire* **35**: 67–75.

Oswald, P.H. 2000. Historical records of *Lactuca serriola* L. and *L. virosa* L. in Britain, with special reference to Cambridgeshire (v.c. 29). *Watsonia* **23**: 149–159.

Otfinowski, R., Kenkel, N.C. & Catling, P.M. 2007. The biology of Canadian weeds. 134. *Bromus inermis* Leyss. *Canadian Journal of Plant Science* **87**: 183–198.

Ovington, J.D. & Scurfield, G. 1956. Biological Flora of the British Isles. No. 54. *Holcus mollis* L. *Journal of Ecology* **44**: 272–280.

Pacha, M.J. & Petit, S. 2008. The effect of landscape structure and habitat quality on the occurrence of *Geranium sylvaticum* in fragmented hay meadows. *Agriculture, Ecosystems and Environment* **123**: 81–87.

Packer, J.G., Meyerson, L.A., Skálová, H., Pyšek, P. & Kueffer, C. 2017. Biological Flora of the British Isles. No. 283. *Phragmites australis*. *Journal of Ecology* **105**: 1123–1162.

Packham, J.R. 1978. Biological Flora of the British Isles. No. 141. *Oxalis acetosella* L. *Journal of Ecology* **66**: 669–693.

Packham, J.R. 1983. Biological Flora of the British Isles. No. 155. *Lamiastrum galeobdolon* (L.) Ehrend. & Polatschek. *Journal of Ecology* **71**: 975–997.

Packham, J.R., Thomas, P.A., Atkinson, M.D. & Degen, T. 2012. Biological Flora of the British Isles. No. 269. *Fagus sylvatica*. *Journal of Ecology* **100**: 1557–1608.

Page, C.N. 1982. The history and spread of bracken in Britain. *Proceedings of the Royal Society of Edinburgh* **81B**: 3–10.

Page, C.N. 1997. *The ferns of Britain and Ireland*. Edn. 2. Cambridge University Press, Cambridge.

Page, K.W. 1987. Hybrid bluebells. *BSBI News* **46**: 9.

Palin, M.A. 1988. Biological Flora of the British Isles. No. 164. *Ligusticum scoticum* L. *Journal of Ecology* **76**: 889–902.

Palmer, J.H. & Sagar, G.R. 1963. Biological Flora of the British Isles. No. 93. *Agropyron repens* (L.) Beauv. *Journal of Ecology* **51**: 783–794.

Palmer, J.R. 1991. Mexican orange, *Choisya ternata*, naturalised in a west Kent woodland. *BSBI News* **58**: 41.

Pan, J.T. 1988. A conspectus of the genus *Bergenia* Moench. *Acta Phytotaxonomica Sinica* **26**: 120–129 [in Chinese with an English summary].

Pankhurst, R.J. & Mullin, J.M. 1991. *Flora of the Outer Hebrides*. Natural History Museum Publications, London.

Pankhurst, T.J. 2014. Turf removal to stimulate natural regeneration of Spanish Catchfly *Silene otites* (L.) Wibel at Cranwich Camp, Norfolk, UK. *Conservation Evidence* **11**: 66–69.

Pankhurst, T.J. & Stewart, N.F. 2001. *Survey of Aquatic Plants, Hampton, Peterborough, Cambridgeshire*. Unpublished report for Green Environmental Consultants.

Pankhurst, T.J., Shellswell, C.H., Cooke, E., Moyse, R. & Waller, M. 2021. *Looking after Fingered Speedwell* Veronica triphyllos. Ecology and Conservation Portfolio. Plantlife, Salisbury.

Park, K.J.F., Rawes, M. & Allen, S.E. 1962. Grassland studies on the Moor House National Nature Reserve. *Journal of Ecology* **50**: 53–62.

Parker, D.M. 1979. *Saxifraga rosacea* and *S. hypnoides* in the British Isles. *BSBI News* **21**: 22–23.

Parker, D.M. 1981. The re-introduction of *Saxifraga cespitosa* to North Wales. In Synge, H. (Ed.) *The Biological Aspects of Rare Plant Conservation* pp. 506–508 BSBI Conference Report no.17 John Wiley & Sons, Chichester.

Parker, D.M. 1996. Tufted Saxifrage. *British Wildlife* **7**: 201.

Parnell, J.A.N. 1985. Biological Flora of the British Isles. No. 157. *Jasione montana* L. *Journal of Ecology* **73**: 341–358.

Parnell, J. & Needham, M. 1998. Morphometric variation in Irish *Sorbus* L. (Rosaceae). *Watsonia* **22**: 153–161.

Parslow, R. & Bennallick, I. 2017. *The New Flora of the Isles of Scilly*. Parslow Press, Cornwall.

Partridge, J.W. 2001. Biological Flora of the British Isles. No. 218. *Persicaria amphibia* (L.) Gray (*Polygonum amphibium* L.). *Journal of Ecology* **89**: 487–501.

Paternoster, R., Brame, R., Mazerolle, P. & Piquero, A. 1998. Using the correct statistical test for the equality of regression coefficients. *Criminology* **36**: 859–866.

Paton, A. 1967. True service trees of Worcestershire. *Proceedings of the Botanical Society of the British Isles* 7: 9–13.

Paul, A.M. 1987. The status of *Ophioglossum azoricum* (Ophioglossaceae: Pteridophyta) in the British Isles. *Fern Gazette* 13: 173–187.

Paul, V.N. 1965. *Chiltern Research Committee Survey, I. Orchids of the Chilterns*. Chiltern Research Committee, Reading.

Paule, J. 2010. *Evolutionary patterns and processes in the genus* Potentilla *L. (Rosaceae)*. Ph.D. thesis, University of Heidelberg, Germany.

Paun, O., Bateman, R.M., Fay, M.F., Hedrén, M., Civeyrel, L. & Chase, M.W. 2010. Stable epigenetic effects impact evolution and adaptation in allopolyploid orchids. *Molecular Biology and Evolution* 27: 2465–2473.

Paun, O., Bateman, R.M., Luna, J.A., Moat, J., Fay, M.F. & Chase, M.W. 2011. Altered gene expression and ecological divergence in sibling allopolyploids of *Dactylorhiza* (Orchidaceae). *BMC Evolutionary Biology* 11: 113.

Pearman, D.A. 1988. *Chenopodium vulvaria* in Dorset. *BSBI News* 50: 13–14.

Pearman, D.A. 1994. *Sedges and their Allies in Dorset*. Dorset Environmental Records Centre, Dorchester.

Pearman, D.A. 1997. *Carex humilis* Leysser in Dorset (v.c. 9). *Watsonia* 21: 368–374.

Pearman, D.A. 2007. 'Far from any house' – assessing the status of doubtfully native species in the flora of the British Isles. *Watsonia* 26: 271–290.

Pearman, D.A. 2008. The status of Coral-necklace *Illecebrum verticillatum* L. (Caryophyllaceae) in Great Britain. *Watsonia* 27: 143–148.

Pearman, D.A. 2013. Late-discovered petaloid monocotyledons: separating the native and alien flora. *New Journal of Botany* 3: 24–32.

Pearman, D.A. 2017a. The population dynamics of rare annual plants on the Lizard Peninsula, Cornwall, UK, 2009–2016. *New Journal of Botany* 7: 11–24.

Pearman, D.A. 2017b. *The Discovery of the Native Flora of Britain & Ireland*. Botanical Society of Britain and Ireland, Bristol.

Pearman, D.A. 2020. *Cortaderia richardii* (Early Pampas-grass) – a different view of its distribution in Britain and Ireland. *BSBI News* 142: 62–63.

Pearman, D.A. 2022. The status of *Pancratium maritimum* L. (Sea Daffodil) in Britain and Ireland. *BSBI News* 150: 66–68.

Pearman, D.A. & Preston, C.D. 2000. *A Flora of Tiree, Gunna and Coll*. Privately published, Dorchester.

Pearman, D.A. & Edwards, B. 2002. *Valerianella eriocarpa* Desv. in Dorset, and a reassessment of its status as a presumed introduction in Britain. *Watsonia* 24: 81–89.

Pearman, D.A. & Rumsey, F.J. 2004. *Drosera* ×*belezeana* Camus confirmed for the British Isles. *Watsonia* 25: 115–119.

Pearman, D.A. & Walker, K.J. 2004a. Rare plant introductions in the UK: creative conservation or wildlife gardening? *British Wildlife* 15: 174–182.

Pearman, D.A. & Walker, K.J. 2004b. An examination of J. W. Heslop Harrison's unconfirmed plant records from Rum. *Watsonia* 25: 45–63.

Pearman, D.A. & Preston, C.D. 2005. *Hybridisation and the Flora of the British Isles*: a new edition of Clive Stace's 1975 work. *BSBI News* 99: 10–16.

Pearman, D.A., Braithwaite, M., Ellis, R.G. & Lockton, A. 2005. Atlas Updating Project. *BSBI Recorder, Newsletter for the BSBI County Recorders 2005*. 5–6.

Pearman, D.A., Preston, C.D., Rothero, G.P. & Walker, K.J. 2008. *The Flora of Rum: An Atlantic Island Reserve*. Privately published, Truro.

Pearman, D.A., Rumsey, F.J. & Bennallick, I.J. 2014. Monitoring change in *Isoetes histrix* Bory (Isoetaceae) at its northern distributional limit. *Fern Gazette* 19: 297–306.

Pedersen, H.A. 2001. Late-flowering dune populations of *Dactylorhiza incarnata* (Orchidaceae): variation patterns and taxonomic inferences. *Nordic Journal of Botany* 21: 177–186.

Pedersen, H.A. 2007. Taxonomic revision of the *Dactylorhiza majalis* subsp. *purpurella* complex (Orchidaceae): a morphometric approach. *Journal Europäischer Orchideen* 39: 341–366.

Pedersen, H.A. 2010. Genetic and morphological variation of the Southern Marsh-orchid in western Europe: implications for taxonomy and nomenclature. *Journal Europäischer Orchideen* 42: 83–110.

Pegoraro, L., De Vos, J.M., Cozzolino, S. & Scopece, G. 2019. Shift in flowering time allows diploid and autotetraploid *Anacamptis pyramidalis* (Orchidaceae) to coexist by reducing competition for pollinators. *Botanical Journal of the Linnean Society* 191: 274–284.

Pemberton, R.W. 2000. Waterblommejie (*Aponogeton distachyos*, Aponogetonaceae), a recently domesticated aquatic food crop in Cape South Africa with unusual origins. *Economic Botany* 54: 144–149.

Pennell, F.W. 1921. *Veronica* in North and South America. *Rhodora* 23: 29–41.

Perring, F.H. 1960. Report on the survey of *Arctium* L. agg. in Britain, 1959. *Proceedings of the Botanical Society of the British Isles* 4: 33–37.

Perring, F.H. 1973. Mistletoe. In Green, P.S. (Ed.) *Plants-wild and Cultivated: A Conference on Horticulture and Field Botany* pp. 139–145 BSBI Conference Report No. 13 Botanical Society of the British Isles, Hampton.

Perring, F.H. 1994. *Symphytum* - Comfrey. In Perry, A.R. & Ellis, R.G. (Eds.) *The common ground of wild and cultivated plants*. pp. 65–70 BSBI Conference Report no. 22 National Museum of Wales, Cardiff.

Perring, F.H. & Walters, S.M. (Eds.) 1962. *Atlas of the British Flora*. Thomas Nelson & Sons, London.

Perring, F.H., Sell, P.D., Walters, S.M. & Whitehouse, H.L.K. 1964. *A Flora of Cambridgeshire*. Cambridge University Press, Cambridge.

Perring, F.H. & Sell, P.D. (Eds.) 1968. *Critical supplement to the Atlas of the British Flora*. Thomas Nelson & Sons, London.

Perring, F.H. & Farrell, L. 1977. *British Red Data Books: 1. Vascular Plants*. Society for Nature Conservation, Lincoln.

Perring, F.H. & Farrell, L. 1983. *British Red Data Books: 1. Vascular Plants*. Edn. 2. Society for Nature Conservation, Lincoln.

Perring, F.H. & Walters, S.M. (Eds.) 1976. *Atlas of the British Flora*. Edn. 2. EP Publishing, Wakefield.

Perring, F.H. & Scott, D.[W.] 1977. Common species in the British Isles. *Watsonia* 11: 430.

Perring, F.H. & Walters, S.M. (Eds.) 1982. *Atlas of the British Flora*. Edn. 3. EP Publishing, Wakefield.

Perrins, J., Fitter, A. & Williamson, M. 1993. Population biology and rates of invasion of three introduced *Impatiens* species in the British Isles. *Journal of Biogeography* 20: 33–44.

Persson, N.L., Eriksson, T. & Smedmark, J.E.E. 2020. Complex patterns of reticulate evolution in opportunistic weeds (*Potentilla* L., Rosaceae), as revealed by low-copy nuclear markers. *BMC Evolutionary Biology* 20: 1–17.

Pescott, O.L., Walker, K.J., Pocock, M.J.O., Jitlal, M., Outhwaite, C.L., Cheffings, C.M., Harris, F. & Roy, D.B. 2015. Ecological monitoring with citizen science: the design and implementation of schemes for recording plants in Britain and Ireland. *Biological Journal of the Linnean Society* 115: 505–521.

Pescott, O.L., Humphrey, T.A. & Walker, K.J. 2018. *A short guide to using British and Irish plant occurrence data for research*. Wallingford, NERC/Centre for Ecology & Hydrology.

Pescott, O.L., Walker, K.J., Harris, F., New, H., Cheffings, C.M., Newton, N., Jitlal, M., Redhead, J., Smart, S.M. & Roy, D.B. 2019a. The design, launch and assessment of a new volunteer-based plant monitoring scheme for the United Kingdom. *PLoS ONE* 14: e0215891.

Pescott, O.L., Humphrey, T.A., Stroh, P.A. & Walker, K.J. 2019b. Temporal changes in distributions and the species atlas: How can British and Irish plant data shoulder the inferential burden? *British & Irish Botany* 1: 250–282.

Pescott, O.L., Stroh, P.A., Humphrey, T.A. & Walker, K.J. 2022. Simple methods for improving the communication of uncertainty in species' temporal trends. *Ecological Indicators* 141: 109117.

Petch, C.P. & Swann, E.L. 1968. *Flora of Norfolk*. Jarrold & Sons, Norwich.

Peterken, G.F. 1974. A method for assessing woodland flora for conservation using indicator species. *Biological Conservation* 6: 239–245.

Peterken, G.F. 1975. Holly survey. *Watsonia* 10: 297–299.

Peterken, G.F. 1981. *Woodland conservation and management*. Chapman & Hall, London.

Peterken, G.F. 2013. *Meadows*. British Wildlife Publishing, Dorset.

Peterken, G.F. & Lloyd, P.S. 1967. Biological Flora of the British Isles. No. 108. *Ilex aquifolium* L. *Journal of Ecology* 55: 841–858.

Peterson, S.R. 1969. Biology of the mouse-ear chickweed, *Cerastium vulgatum*. *The Michigan Botanist* 8: 151–157.

Petraglia, A., Tomaselli, M., Mondoni, A., Brancaleoni, L. & Carbognani, M. 2014. Effects of nitrogen and phosphorus supply on growth and flowering phenology of the snowbed forb *Gnaphalium supinum* L. *Flora - Morphology, Distribution, Functional Ecology of Plants* 209: 271–278.

Pfeifer, M., Wiegand, K., Heinrich, W. & Jetschke, G. 2006. Long-term demographic fluctuations in an orchid species driven by weather: implications for conservation planning. *Journal of Applied Ecology* 3: 313–324.

Pfitzenmeyer, C.D.C. 1962. Biological Flora of the British Isles. No. 81. *Arrhenatherum elatius* (L.) J. & C. Presl. *Journal of Ecology* 50: 235–245.

Phillips, M.E. 1954. Biological Flora of the British Isles. No. 43. *Eriophorum angustifolium* Roth. *Journal of Ecology* 42: 612–622.

Phillips, R. & Rix, M. 1993. *Vegetables*. Pan Books, London.

Pickering, C.M., Mount, A., Wichmann, M.C. & Bullock, J.M. 2011. Estimating human-mediated dispersal of seeds within an Australian protected area. *Biological Invasions* 13: 1869–1880.

Pigott, A.C. 1997. *Morphotypes of the* Dryopteris affinis *complex in Britain and Ireland*. Affinis Watch Newsletter Special Issue.

Pigott, C.D. 1955. Biological Flora of the British Isles. No. 50. *Thymus* L. genus (pp. 365–368), *T. drucei* (pp. 369–379), *T. serpyllum* subsp. *serpyllum* (pp. 379–382), *T. pulegioides* (pp. 383–387). *Journal of Ecology* 43: 365–387.

Pigott, C.D. 1958. Biological Flora of the British Isles. No. 65. *Polemonium caeruleum* L. *Journal of Ecology* 46: 507–525.

Pigott, C.D. 1968. Biological Flora of the British Isles. No. 111. *Cirsium acaulon* (L.) Scop. *Journal of Ecology* 56: 597–612.

Pigott, C.D. 1981. The status, ecology and conservation of *Tilia platyphyllos* in Britain. In Synge, H. (Ed.) *The Biological Aspects of Rare Plant Conservation* pp. 305–317 BSBI Conference Report no.17 John Wiley & Sons, Chichester.

Pigott, C.D. 1988. The reintroduction of *Cirsium tuberosum* (L.) All. in Cambridgeshire. *Watsonia* 17: 149–152.

Pigott, C.D. 1991. Biological Flora of the British Isles. No. 174. *Tilia cordata* Miller. *Journal of Ecology* 79: 1147–1207.

Pigott, C.D. 2020. Biological Flora of the British Isles. No. 294: *Tilia platyphyllos*. *Journal of Ecology* 108: 2638–2676.

Pigott, C.D. & Woodward, F.I. 1975. The climatic control of the altitudinal distribution of *Sedum rosea* (L.) Scop. and *S. telephium* L. I. Field observations. *New Phytologist* 74: 323–334.

BIBLIOGRAPHY

Pilkington, M. 2020. *The effect of climate change on the abundance and distribution of the nationally rare plant* Koenigia islandica *on Mull, Scotland, UK*. B.Sc. dissertation, Manchester Metropolitan University.

Pilkington, S. 2007. *Wiltshire Rare Plant Register: The rare and threatened vascular plants of north and south Wiltshire*. Wiltshire Botanical Society and the Wiltshire Natural History Publications Trust.

Pillon, Y., Qamaruz-Zaman, F., Fay, M.F., Hendoux, F. & Piquot, Y. 2006. Genetic diversity and ecological differentiation of the endangered Fen Orchid (*Liparis loeselii*). *Conservation Genetics* **8**: 177–184.

Pillon, Y., Fay, M.F., Hedrén, M., Bateman, R.M., Devey, D.S., van der Bank, M., Shipunov, A.B. & Chase, M.W. 2007. Evolution and temporal diversification of European species complexes in *Dactylorhiza* (Orchidaceae). *Taxon* **56**: 1185–1208 + E1–E17.

Piqueras, J. & Klimes, L. 1998. Demography and modelling of clonal fragments in the pseudoannual plant *Trientalis europaea*. *Plant Ecology* **136**: 213–227.

Piñeiro Fernández, L., Byers, K.J.R.P., Cai, J., Sedeek, K.E.M., Kellenberger, R.T., Russo, A., Qi, W., Aquino-Fournier, C. & Schlüter, P.M. 2019. A phylogenomic analysis of the floral transcriptomes of sexually deceptive and rewarding European orchids, *Ophrys* and *Gymnadenia*. *Frontiers in Plant Science* **10**: 1553.

Plantlife 2001. *Species Action Plan for Great Tassel Stonewort*. Plantlife, London.

Plassmann, K., Brown, N., Jones, M.L.M. & Edwards-Jones, G. 2008. Can atmospheric input of nitrogen affect seed bank dynamics in habitats of conservation interest? The case of dune slacks. *Applied Vegetation Science* **11**: 413–420.

Plassmann, K., Brown, N., Jones, M.L.M. & Edwards-Jones, G. 2009. Can soil seed banks contribute to the restoration of dune slacks under conservation management? *Applied Vegetation Science* **12**: 199–210.

Plue, J., Cousins, S.A.O., De Pauw, K., Diekmann, M., Hagenblad, J., Helsen, K., Hermy, M., Liira, J., Orczewska, A., Vanneste, T., Wulf, M. & De Frenne, P. 2020. Biological Flora of the British Isles. No. 292. *Poa nemoralis* L. *Journal of Ecology* **108**: 1750–1774.

Poland, J. & Clement, E.J. 2020. *The Vegetative Key to the British Flora*, Edn. 2. John Poland, Southampton.

Pollard, K.M., Varia, S., Seier, M.K. & Ellison, C.A. 2021. Battling the biotypes of balsam: the biological control of *Impatiens glandulifera* using the rust fungus *Puccinia komarovii* var. *glanduliferae* in GB. *Fungal Biology* **125**: 637–645.

Pope, C. 2002. Bay (*Laurus nobilis*) as an invasive species. *BSBI News* **90**: 43.

Pope, C., Snow, L. & Allen, D.E. 2003. *The Isle of Wight Flora*. The Dovecote Press, Dorset.

Pope, C. & Stanley, P. 2018. Caravan touring sites – an overlooked habitat for introduced species. *BSBI News* **139**: 53–55.

Popiela, A.A., Łysko, A., Wieczorek, A. & Nalepka, D. 2011. The distribution of *Elatine hexandra* (Lapierre) DC. (Elatinaceae). *Acta Societatis Botanicorum Poloniae* **80**: 27–32.

Popiela, A.A., Łysko, A.R., Wieczorek, A. & Molnár, A. 2012. The distribution of *Elatine hexandra* (Lapierre) DC. (Elatinaceae). *Acta Societatis Botanicorum Poloniae* **81**: 137–143.

Porley, R.D. 1999. Separation of *Carex vulpina* L. and *C. otrubae* Podp. (Cyperaceae) using transverse leaf sections. *Watsonia* **22**: 431–432.

Porter, M.S. & Roberts, F.J. 1997. Bird's-foot Sedge (*Carex ornithopoda* Willd.) in Cumbria. *The Carlisle Naturalist* **5**: 18–23.

Porter, M.S. & Halliday, G. 2014. *The Rare Plant Register of Cumbria*. Trollius Publications, Cumbria.

Porter, M.S. & Foley, M.J.Y. 2017. *Violas of Britain and Ireland*. BSBI Handbook No. 17. Botanical Society of Britain and Ireland, Bristol.

Praeger, R.L. 1934. *The Botanist in Ireland*. Hodges, Figgis, & Co, Dublin.

Praeger, R.L. 1951. Hybrids in the Irish flora: a tentative list. *Proceedings of the Royal Irish Academy, B* **54**: 1–14.

Prance, G. (Ed.) 2005. *The Cultural History of Plants*. Routledge, Oxford.

Prelli, R. 2001. *Les Fougeres et plantes alliees de France et d'Europe occidentale*. Editions Belin, Paris.

Preston, C.D. 1988. The spread of *Epilobium ciliatum* Raf. in the British Isles. *Watsonia* **17**: 279–288.

Preston, C.D. 1993a. The distribution of the Oxlip *Primula elatior* (L.) Hill in Cambridgeshire. *Nature in Cambridgeshire* **35**: 29–60.

Preston, C.D. 1993b. Charophyte records. *Nature in Cambridgeshire* **35**: 86.

Preston, C.D. 1995a. *Potamogeton ×schreberi* G. Fisch. (*P. natans* L. × *P. nodosus* Poir.) in Dorset, new to the British Isles. *Watsonia* **20**: 255–262.

Preston, C.D. 1995b. *Pondweeds of Great Britain and Ireland*. BSBI Handbook no. 8. Botanical Society of the British Isles, London.

Preston, C.D. 1997. The genus *Rosa* in Cambridgeshire (v.c. 29): an interim account. *Nature in Cambridgeshire* **39**: 40–53.

Preston, C.D. 2002. 'Babingtonia pestifera' - the explosive spread of *Elodea canadensis* and its intellectual reverberations. *Nature in Cambridgeshire* **44**: 40–49.

Preston, C.D. 2007. Which vascular plants are found at the northern or southern edges of their European range in the British Isles? *Watsonia* **26**: 253–269.

Preston, C.D. 2013. Following the BSBI's lead: the influence of the *Atlas of the British flora*, 1962–2012. *New Journal of Botany* **3**: 2–14.

Preston, C.D. & Whitehouse, H.L.K. 1986. The habitat of *Lythrum hyssopifolia* L. in Cambridgeshire, its only surviving English locality. *Biological Conservation* **35**: 41–62.

Preston, C.D. & Sell, P.D. 1989. The Aizoaceae naturalized in the British Isles. *Watsonia* **17**: 217–245.

Preston, C.D. & Croft, J.M. 1997. *Aquatic plants in Britain and Ireland*. Harley Books, Colchester.

Preston, C.D. & Hill, M.O. 1997. The geographical relationships of British and Irish vascular plants. *Botanical Journal of the Linnean Society* **124**: 1–120.

Preston, C.D. & Pearman, D.A. 1998. J. E. Dandy's & G. Taylor's unpublished study of *Potamogeton × sudermanicus* Hagstr. in Britain, with an account of the current distribution of the hybrid. *Watsonia* **22**: 163–172.

Preston, C.D. & Pearman, D.A. 2000. *Centaurium littorale* as a saltmarsh species in Scotland. *BSBI Scottish Newsletter* **22**: 14–16.

Preston, C.D., Pearman, D.A. & Dines, T.D. (Comps. & Eds.) 2002a. *New Atlas of the British and Irish Flora*. Oxford University Press, Oxford.

Preston, C.D., Telfer, M.G., Arnold, H.R., Carey, P.D., Copper, J.M., Dines, T.D., Hill, M.O., Pearman, D.A., Roy, D.B. & Smart, S.M. 2002b. *The Changing Flora of the UK*. Department for the Environment, Food and Rural Affairs, London.

Preston, C.D., Telfer, M.G., Roy, D.B., Carey, P.D., Hill, M.O., Meek, W.R., Rothery, P., Smart, S.M., Smith, G.M., Walker, K.J. & Pearman, D.A. 2003. *The Changing Distribution of the Flora of the United Kingdom: Technical Report*. NERC Centre for Ecology & Hydrology, Huntingdon, Cambridgeshire.

Preston, C.D., Pearman, D.A. & Hall, A.R. 2004. Archaeophytes in Britain. *Botanical Journal of the Linnean Society* **145**: 257–294.

Prieto, J.A.F., Cires, E., Perez, R. & Bueno, A. 2012. A new endemism for the Azores: the case of *Centaurium scilloides* (L. f.) Samp. *Plant Systematics and Evolution* **298**: 1867–1879.

Prime, C.T. 1954. Biological Flora of the British Isles. No. 41. *Arum neglectum* (Towns.) Ridley. *Journal of Ecology* **42**: 241–248.

Prime, C.T. 1960. *Lords & Ladies*. Collins, London.

Prince, S.D. & Hare, A.D.R. 1981. *Lactuca saligna* and *Pulicaria vulgaris* in Britain. In Synge, H. (Ed.) *The Biological Aspects of Rare Plant Conservation* pp. 379–388 BSBI Conference Report no.17 John Wiley & Sons, Chichester.

Pring, M.E. 1961. Biological Flora of the British Isles. No. 78. *Arabis stricta* Huds. *Journal of Ecology* **49**: 431–437.

Pritchard, N.M. 1959. *Gentianella* in Britain. I. *G. amarella, G. anglica* and *G. uliginosa*. *Watsonia* **4**: 169–193.

Pritchard, N.M. 1960. *Gentianella* in Britain. II. *Gentianella septentrionalis* (Druce) E. F. Warb. *Watsonia* **4**: 218–237.

Proctor, M.C.F. 1956. Biological Flora of the British Isles. No. 58. *Helianthemum* Mill. genus (pp. 675–677), *H. chamaecistus* Mill. (pp. 683–688), *H. apenninum* (L.) Mill. (pp. 688–692). *Journal of Ecology* **44**: 675–692.

Proctor, M.C.F. 1960. Biological Flora of the British Isles. No. 72. *Tuberaria guttata* (L.) Fourreau. *Journal of Ecology* **48**: 243–253.

Proctor, M.C.F. 1965. The distinguishing characters and geographical distributions of *Ulex minor* and *Ulex gallii*. *Watsonia* **6**: 177–187.

Proctor, M.C.F. & Groenhof, A.C. 1992. Peroxidase isoenzyme and morphological variation in *Sorbus* L. in South Wales and adjacent areas, with particular reference to *S. porrigentiformis* E. F. Warb. *Watsonia* **19**: 21–37.

Proctor, M.C.F., Yeo, P.F. & Lack, A.J. 1996. *The natural history of pollination*. HarperCollins, London.

Pryce, R.D. 1999. *Carmarthenshire rare plant register*. privately published, Llanelli.

Pryce, R.D. 2004. The Rhos pastures of south-west Wales and their conservation. Presidential address, 10th May 2003. *Watsonia* **25**: 1–16.

Pryce, R.D. & Chater, A.O. 2000. Overlooking *Sibthorpia*. *BSBI News* **84**: 50–51.

Pryor, K.V., Young, J.E., Rumsey, F.J., Edwards, K.J., Bruford, M.W. & Rogers, H.J. 2001. Diversity, genetic structure and evidence of outcrossing in British populations of the rock fern *Adiantum capillus-veneris* using microsatellites. *Molecular Ecology* **10**: 1881–1894.

Pugsley, H.W. 1924. A new *Statice* in Britain. *Journal of Botany* **62**: 129–134.

Puzey, J. & Vallejo-Marín, M. 2014. Genomics of invasion: Diversity and selection in introduced populations of monkeyflowers (*Mimulus guttatus*). *Molecular Ecology* **23**: 4472–4485.

Pyne, K. 1997. *Mespilus germanica* in southern Britain. *BSBI News* **75**: 49–50.

Pyšek, P., Cock, M.J.W., Nentwig, W. & Ravn, H.P. (Eds.) 2007. *Ecology and Management of Giant Hogweed (*Heracleum mantegazzianum*)*. CAB International, Wallingford.

Pywell, R.F., Pakeman, R.J., Allchen, E.A., Bourn, N.A.D., Warman, E.A. & Walker, K.J. 2002. The potential for lowland heath regeneration following plantation removal. *Biological Conservation* **108**: 247–258.

Pywell, R.F., Bullock, J.M., Walker, K.J., Coulson, S.J., Gregory, S.J. & Stevenson, M.J. 2004. Facilitating grassland diversification using the hemiparasitic plant *Rhinanthus minor*. *Journal of Applied Ecology* **41**: 880–887.

Rackham, O. 1961. Ecological significance of hybridisation between *Rumex sanguineus* and *R. conglomeratus*. *Proceedings of the Botanical Society of the British Isles* **4**: 332.

Rackham, O. 1975. *Hayley Wood*. Cambridgeshire and Isle of Ely Naturalists' Trust, Cambridge.

Rackham, O. 1980. *Ancient woodland: its history, vegetation and uses in England*. Edward Arnold, London.

Rackham, O. 1986. *The History of the Countryside*. J.M. Dent & Sons, London.

Rackham, O. 1990. *Trees and woodland in the British Landscape*. Edn. 2. J. M. Dent & Sons, London.

Rackham, O. 1999. The woods 30 years on: where have the Primroses gone? *Nature in Cambridgeshire* **41**: 73–87.

Rackham, O. 2014. *The Ash Tree*. Little Toller Books, Dorset.

Radcliffe-Smith, A. 1985. Taxonomy of North American leafy spurge. In Watson, A.K. (Ed.) *Leafy Spurge. Monograph Series of the Weed Science Society of America* **3**: 14–25 Weed Science Society of America.

Rahn, K. 1989. A survey of the genus *Sorbaria* (Rosaceae). *Nordic Journal of Botany* **8**: 557–563.

Ralph, P.J. & Short, F.T. 2002. Impact of the wasting disease pathogen, *Labyrinthula zosterae*, on the photobiology of eelgrass *Zostera marina*. *Marine Ecology Progress Series* **226**: 265–271.

Ramsey, M.M. & Stewart, J. 1998. Re-establishment of the lady's slipper orchid (*Cypripedium calceolus* L.) in Britain. *Botanical Journal of the Linnean Society* **126**: 173–181.

Rand, M. 2003. *Ludwigia grandiflora* - a view from across the Channel. *BSBI News* **93**: 57–59.

Rand, M. 2005. *Gladiolus illyricus* in Hampshire. *BSBI News* **98**: 21–23.

Rand, M. & Leach, S.J. 2007. *Dittrichia graveolens* - a new roadside colonist in S. Hants (v.c.11). *BSBI News* **104**: 45–47.

Rand, M. & Chatters, C. 2010. Vascular Plants. In Newton, A.C. (Ed.) *Biodiversity in the New Forest* Pisces Publications, Newbury.

Rand, M. & Mundell, T. 2011. *Hampshire Rare Plant Register*. Trollius Publications.

Randall, R.E. 1977. The past and present status and distribution of Sea Pea, *Lathyrus japonicus* Willd., in the British Isles. *Watsonia* **11**: 247–251.

Randall, R.E. 1988. *A field survey of* Mertensia maritima *(L.) Gray, Oyster plant, in Britain during 1986 and 1987*. Contract Surveys no. 20. Nature Conservancy Council, Peterborough.

Randall, R.E. 2003. *Smyrnium olusatrum* L. *Journal of Ecology* **91**: 325–340.

Randall, R.E. 2004. Biological Flora of the British Isles. No. 233. *Viola kitaibeliana* Schult(es). *Journal of Ecology* **92**: 361–369.

Randall, R.E. & Thornton, G. 1996. Biological Flora of the British Isles. No. 191. *Peucedanum officinale* L. *Journal of Ecology* **84**: 475–485.

Raspé, O. 1996. *Genetic variation of* Sorbus aucuparia *at the western European scale*. Unité d'Ecologie et de Biogéographie, Université Catholique, Louvain.

Raspé, O. & Jacquemart, A.L. 1998. Allozyme diversity and genetic structure of European populations of *Sorbus aucuparia* L. (Rosaceae: Maloideae). *Heredity* **81**: 537–545.

Raspé, O., Findlay, C. & Jacquemart, A.L. 2000. Biological Flora of the British Isles. No. 214. *Sorbus aucuparia* L. *Journal of Ecology* **88**: 910–930.

Ratcliffe, D. 1959a. Biological Flora of the British Isles. No. 69. *Hornungia petraea* (L.) Rchb. *Journal of Ecology* **47**: 241–247.

Ratcliffe, D.A. 1959b. The habitat of *Koenigia islandica* L. in Scotland. *Transactions and Proceedings of the Botanical Society of Edinburgh* **37**: 272–275.

Ratcliffe, D. 1960. Biological Flora of the British Isles. No. 75. *Draba muralis* L. *Journal of Ecology* **48**: 737–744.

Rautiainen, P., Koivula, K. & Hyvärinen, M. 2004. The effect of within-genet and between-genet competition on sexual reproduction and vegetative spread in *Potentilla anserina* subsp. *egedii*. *Journal of Ecology* **92**: 505–511.

Raven, J.E. 1952. *Koenigia islandica* in Scotland. *Watsonia* **2**: 188–190.

Raven, P.H. 1963. *Circaea* in the British Isles. *Watsonia* **5**: 262–272.

Raven, P.H. & Raven, T.E. 1976. The genus *Epilobium* (Onagraceae) in Australasia: a systematic and evolutionary study. *New Zealand Department of Scientific and Industrial Research Bulletin* **216**.

Raven, P.H., Dietrich, W. & Wagner, W.L. 1997. Systematics of *Oenothera* section *Oenothera* subsection *Oenothera* (Onagraceae). *Systematic Botany Monographs* **50**: 1–234.

Rawes, M. & Welch, D. 1972. Trials to recreate floristically-rich vegetation by plant introduction in the Northern Pennines, England. *Biological Conservation* **4**: 135–140.

Ray, J. 1677. *Catalogus Plantarum Angliae, et Insularum Adjacentium*. Edn. 2. London.

Raybould, A.F., Gray, A.J., Lawrence, M.J. & Marshall, D.F. 1991. The evolution of *Spartina anglica* C. E. Hubbard (Gramineae) - origin and genetic variability. *Biological Journal of the Linnean Society* **43**: 111–126.

Rebele, F. & Lehmann, C. 2001. Biological Flora of Central Europe: *Calamagrostis epigejos* (L.) Roth. *Flora* **196**: 325–344.

Rechinger, K.H. 1961. Notes on *Rumex acetosa* L. in the British Isles. (Beitrag zur Kenntnis von *Rumex*, no. XV). *Watsonia* **5**: 64–66.

Rees, E.I.S. 2018. *Atriplex praecox* (Early Orache) on a shore in the Menai Strait. *BSBI News* **137**: 24–26.

Reid, J.A. 1975. The distinction between *Oxalis corniculata* L. and *O. exilis* A. Cunn. *Watsonia* **10**: 290–291.

Reinhammar, L.-G. 1998. Systematics of *Pseudorchis albida* s.l. (Orchidaceae) in Europe and North America. *Botanical Journal of the Linnean Society* **126**: 363–382.

Reinhammar, L.-G., Olsson, E.G. & Sormerland, E. 2002. Conservation biology of an endangered grassland plant species, *Pseudorchis albida*, with some references to the closely related alpine *P. straminea* (Orchidaceae). *Botanical Journal of the Linnean Society* **139**: 47–66.

Renals, T.J. 2017. *The GB Water Primrose* Ludwigia grandiflora *Eradication Programme: 2017 Progress Report*. Environment Agency.

Revels, R., Boon, C. & Bellamy, G. 2015. *Wild Orchids of Bedfordshire*. Bedfordshire Natural History Society, Bedford.

Reynolds, S. 1994. *Chenopodium capitatum* in Ireland. *BSBI News* **66**: 36.

Reynolds, S. 1997. *Conyza bilbaoana* also in Ireland. *BSBI News* **74**: 44–46.

Reynolds, S. 1999. *Lactuca serriola* L. in Dublin (H21). *Irish Naturalists' Journal* **26**: 285–286.

Reynolds, S.C.P. 2002. *A Catalogue of Alien Plants in Ireland*. National Botanic Gardens, Glasnevin, Dublin.

Rich, T.C.G. 1987. The genus *Barbarea* R. Br. (Cruciferae) in Britain and Ireland. *Watsonia* **16**: 389–396.

Rich, T. 1988. A little cabbage patch V. Food for thought, or the rape of mustard and cress. *BSBI News* **49**: 12–13.

Rich, T.C.G. 1991. *Crucifers of Great Britain and Ireland*. BSBI Handbook No. 6. Botanical Society of the British Isles, London.

Rich, T.C.G. 1994a. Ragweeds (*Ambrosia* L.) in Britain. *Grana* **33**: 38–43.

Rich, T.C.G. 1994b. *Luzula pallidula* Kirschner in Ireland. *Irish Botanical News* **4**: 26–28.

Rich, T.C.G. 1994c. *Pedicularis sylvatica* L. subsp. *hibernica* D. A. Webb (Scrophulariaceae) new to Wales. *Watsonia* **20**: 70–71.

Rich, T.C.G. 1996. Is *Gentianella uliginosa* (Willd.) Boerner (Gentianaceae) present in England? *Watsonia* **21**: 208–209.

Rich, T.C.G. 1997a. Early gentian (*Gentianella anglica* (Pugsley) E.F.Warb.) present in Wales. *Watsonia* **21**: 289–290.

Rich, T.C.G. 1997b. *The management of semi-natural lowland grassland for selected rare and scarce vascular plants: a review. English Nature Research Report no. 216*. English Nature and the Wildlife Trusts, Peterborough.

Rich, T.C.G. 1999a. Conservation of Britain's biodiversity IV: *Filago pyramidata* (Asteraceae), Broad-leaved cudweed. *Edinburgh Journal of Botany* **56**: 61–73.

Rich, T.C.G. 1999b. Conservation of Britain's biodiversity: *Filago lutescens* Jordan (Asteraceae), Red-tipped cudweed. *Watsonia* **22**: 251–260.

Rich, T.C.G. 1999c. Conservation of Britain's biodiversity: *Cyperus fuscus* L. (Cyperaceae), Brown Galingale. *Watsonia* **22**: 397–403.

Rich, T.C.G. 1999d. The potential for seed dispersal by sea water in *Coincya wrightii* (O. E. Schulz) Stace and *C. monensis* (L.) W. Greuter & Burdet subsp. *monensis*. *Watsonia* **22**: 422–423.

Rich, T.C.G. 2003. Flowering plants. In Hawksworth, D.L. (Ed.) *The changing wildlife of Great Britain and Ireland* Taylor & Francis, London.

Rich, T.C.G. 2005. Could *Centaurium scilloides* (L. f.) Samp. (Gentianaceae), Perennial Centaury, have colonised Britain by sea? *Watsonia* **25**: 397–401.

Rich, T.C.G. 2022. *A review of limestone woundwort* Stachys alpina *L. with special reference to Wales*. Natural Resources Wales Report No. 463.

Rich, T.C.G. & Baecker, M. 1986. The distribution of *Sorbus lancastriensis* E.F.Warburg. *Watsonia* **16**: 83–85.

Rich, T.C.G. & Rich, M.D.B. 1988. *Plant Crib*. Botanical Society of the British Isles, London.

Rich, T.C.G. & Woodruff, E.R. 1990. *The BSBI Monitoring Scheme, 1987–1988. 2 vols. Nature Conservancy Council Report no. 1265*. Botanical Society of the British Isles, London.

Rich, T.C.G. & Baecker, M. 1992. Additional records of *Sorbus lancastriensis* E. F. Warburg (Rosaceae). *Watsonia* **19**: 138–140.

Rich, T.C.G. & Woodruff, E.R. 1992. Recording bias in botanical surveys. *Watsonia* **19**: 73–95.

Rich, T.C.G. & Baecker, M. 1992. Additional records of *Sorbus lancastriensis* E. F. Warburg (Rosaceae). *Watsonia* **19**: 138–140.

Rich, T.C.G. & Palmer, J. 1994. *Grey Mouse-ear (Cerastium brachypetalum Pers.) under threat from the Channel Tunnel Rail Link*. Plantlife 'Back from the Brink' Project. Plantlife, Salisbury.

Rich, T.C.G., Richardson, S.J. & Rose, F. 1995. Tunbridge Filmy-fern, *Hymenophyllum tunbrigense* (Hymenophyllaceae: Pteridophyta), in South-East England in 1994/1995. *Fern Gazette* **15**: 51–63.

Rich, T.C.G. & Smith, P.A. 1996. Botanical recording, distribution maps and species frequency. *Watsonia* **21**: 161–173.

Rich, T.C.G. & Woodruff, E.R. 1996. Changes in the vascular plant floras of England and Scotland between 1930–1960 and 1987–1988: the BSBI monitoring scheme. *Biological Conservation* **75**: 217–229.

Rich, T.[C.G.], Donovan, P., Harmes, P., Knapp, A., McFarlane, M., Marrable, C., Muggeridge, N., Nicholson, R., Reader, M., Reader, P., Rich, E. & White, P. 1996. *Flora of Ashdown Forest*. Sussex Botanical Recording Society.

Rich, T.C.G. & Baeker, M. 1998. The distribution of *Sorbus lancastriensis* E.F.Warburg. In Jackson, A. & Flanagan, M. (Eds.) *The conservation status of* Sorbus *in the UK* pp. 44–47 Royal Botanic Gardens, Kew, London.

Rich, T.C.G. & Jermy, A.C. 1998. *Plant Crib 1998*. Botanical Society of the British Isles, London.

Rich, T.C.G., Lambrick, C.R., Kitchen, C. & Kitchen, M.A.R. 1998a. Conserving Britain's biodiversity. 1. *Thlaspi perfoliatum* L. (Brassicaceae), Cotswold Pennycress. *Biology in Conservation* **7**: 915–926.

Rich, T.C.G., FitzGerald, R. & Sydes, C. 1998b. Distribution and ecology of Small Cow-wheat (*Melampyrum sylvaticum* L.; Scrophulariaceae) in the British Isles. *Botanical Journal of Scotland* **50**: 29–46.

Rich, T.C.G. & Lewis, J. 1999. Use of herbarium material for mapping the distribution of *Erophila* (Brassicaceae) taxa *sensu* Filfilan & Elkington in Britain and Ireland. *Watsonia* **22**: 377–385.

Rich, T.C.G., Gibson, C. & Marsden, M. 1999a. Re-establishment of the extinct native plant *Filago gallica* L. (Asteraceae), narrow-leaved cudweed, in Britain. *Biological Conservation* **91**: 1–8.

Rich, T.C.G., Kay, G.M. & Sydes, C. 1999b. Distribution and ecology of Pyramidal Bugle (*Ajuga pyramidalis* L., Lamiaceae) in the British Isles. *Botanical Journal of Scotland* **51**: 181–193.

Rich, T.C.G., Lambrick, C.R. & McNab, C. 1999c. Conservation of Britain's biodiversity: *Salvia pratensis* L. (Lamiaceae), Meadow Clary. *Watsonia* **22**: 405–411.

Rich, T.C.G. & Brown, N. 2000. *Suaeda vera* Forssk. ex J. F. Gmel. (Chenopodiaceae), shrubby sea-blite, present in Anglesey (v.c. 52), Wales. *Watsonia* **23**: 343–344.

Rich T.C.G., Beesley, S. & Goodwillie, R. 2001. Changes in the vascular plant flora of Ireland between pre-1960 and 1987–1988: the BSBI monitoring scheme. *The Irish Naturalists' Journal* **26**: 333–350.

Rich, T.C.G. & Fitzgerald, R. 2002. Life cycle, ecology and distribution of *Schoenoplectus triqueter* (L.) Palla (Cyperaceae), Triangular Club-rush, in Britain and Ireland. *Watsonia* **24**: 57–67.

Rich, T.C.G. & Lockton, A.J. 2002. *Bromus interruptus* (Hack.) Druce (Poaceae) - An extinct English endemic. *Watsonia* **24**: 69–80.

Rich, T.C.G., Bennallick, I.J., Cordrey, L., Kay, Q.O.N., Lockton, A. & Rich, L.K. 2002. Distribution and population sizes of *Asparagus prostratus* Dumort., Wild Asparagus, in Britain. *Watsonia* **24**: 183–192.

Rich, T.C.G. & Pryor, K.V. 2003. *Galeopsis segetum* Neck. (Lamiaceae), Downy Hemp-nettle: native or introduced in Britain? *Watsonia* **24**: 401–411.

Rich, T.C.G. & Houston, L. 2004. The distribution and population sizes of the rare English endemic *Sorbus wilmottiana* E. F. Warburg, Wilmott's Whitebeam (Rosaceae). *Watsonia* **25**: 185–191.

Rich, T.C.G., Lockton, A.J. & Parnell, J. 2005a. Distribution of the Irish Whitebeam *Sorbus hibernica* E. F. Warb.(Rosaceae). *Watsonia* **25**: 369–380.

Rich, T.C.G., Motley, G.S. & Kay, Q.O.N. 2005b. Population sizes of three rare Welsh endemic *Sorbus* species (Rosaceae). *Watsonia* **25**: 381–388.

Rich, T.C.G. & Houston, L. 2006. *Sorbus whiteana* (Rosaceae), a new endemic tree from Britain. *Watsonia* **26**: 1–7.

Rich, T.C.G. & Cann, D.C.G. 2009. A survey of *Sorbus* species at Watersmeet, North Devon, September 2007. *Transactions of the Devonshire Association for the Advancement of Science* **140**: 185–198.

Rich, T.C.G. & Proctor, M.C.F. 2009. Some new British and Irish *Sorbus* L. taxa (Rosaceae). *Watsonia* **27**: 207–216.

Rich, T.C.G., Charles, C.A., Houston, L. & Tillotson, A. 2009. The diversity of *Sorbus* L. (Rosaceae) in the Lower Wye Valley. *Watsonia* **27**: 301–313.

Rich, T.C.G., Houston, L., Robertson, A. & Proctor, M.C.F. 2010. *Whitebeams, Rowans and Service Trees of Britain and Ireland. A monograph of British and Irish* Sorbus *L.* BSBI Handbook No. 14. Botanical Society of the British Isles, London.

Rich, T.C.G. & Whild, S.J. 2012. The Whitebeams (*Sorbus*) of Blodwel Rocks. *Shropshire Botanical Society Newsletter* **24**: 10.

Rich, T.C.G., McVeigh, A., Hodd, R. & Wyse Jackson, M.B. 2013. The genus *Sorbus* in the Killarney area, Co. Kerry, Ireland. *Irish Botanical News* **23**: 11–20.

Rich, T.C.G., Green, D., Houston, L., Lepší, M., Ludwig, S. & Pellicer, J. 2014. British *Sorbus* (Rosaceae): Six new species, two hybrids and a new subgenus. *New Journal of Botany* **4**: 2–12.

Rich, T.C.G. & Lavery, L. 2018. *Gentianella uliginosa* (Willd.) Börner does not occur in Scotland. *BSBI News* **139**: 26–27.

Rich, T.C.G., McVeigh, A. & Stace, C.A. 2018. New taxa and new combinations in the British flora. *Edinburgh Journal of Botany* **76**: 173–180.

Rich, T.C.G. & McVeigh, A. 2019. *Gentians of Britain and Ireland*. BSBI Handbook No. 19. Botanical Society of Britain and Ireland, Harpenden.

Rich, T.C.G., Houston, L., Goodwin, A., Morgan, V., Bird, S., Jones, R., May, R., Shiel, D. & Stockdale, R. 2019. Conservation status of *Sorbus cuneifolia* (Rosaceae), Llangollen whitebeam. *British & Irish Botany* **1**: 231–242.

Richards, A.J. 1973. An upland race of *Potentilla erecta* (L.) Rausch. in the British Isles. *Watsonia* **9**: 301–317.

Richards, A.J. 1989. *Primulas of the British Isles*. Shire Publications, Princes Risborough.

Richards, A.J. 1993. *Primula*. B.T. Batsford, London.

Richards, A.J. 1994. *Epipactis leptochila s.l.* In Stewart, A., Pearman, D.A. & Preston, C.D. (Eds.) *Scarce plants in Britain* Joint Nature Conservation Committee, Peterborough.

Richards, A.J. 2009. *Alchemilla micans* at Keepershield Quarry, S. Northumb. (v.c.67). *BSBI News* **112**: 10–11.

Richards, A.J. 2015a. Ribes spicatum *Robson. Downy Currant Species Account*. Botanical Society of Britain and Ireland.

Richards, A.J. 2015b. Festuca altissima *All. Wood Fescue Species Account*. Botanical Society of Britain and Ireland.

Richards, A.J. 2021. *Field Handbook to British and Irish Dandelions*. BSBI Handbook No. 23. Botanical Society of Britain and Ireland, Durham.

Richards, A.J. & Swan, G.A. 1976. *Epipactis leptochila* (Godf.) Godf. and *E. phyllanthes* G.E.Sm. occurring in South Northumberland on lead and zinc soils. *Watsonia* **11**: 1–5.

Richards, A.J. & Mitchell, N.D. 1979. Biological Flora of the British Isles. No. 145. *Brassica oleracea* L. ssp. *oleracea*. *Journal of Ecology* **67**: 1087–1096.

Richards, A.J. & Squirrell, J. 2009. *Epipactis leptochila* complex in Britain. *BSBI News* **112**: 8–9.

Richards, P.W. 1943a. Biological Flora of the British Isles. No. 9. *Juncus macer* S. F. Gray. *Journal of Ecology* **31**: 51–59.

Richards, P.W. 1943b. Biological Flora of the British Isles. No. 10. *Juncus filiformis* L. *Journal of Ecology* **31**: 60–65.

Richards, P.W. & Clapham, A.R. 1941a. Biological Flora of the British Isles. No. 2. *Juncus inflexus* L. *Journal of Ecology* **29**: 369–374.

Richards, P.W. & Clapham, A.R. 1941b. Biological Flora of the British Isles. No. 4. *Juncus conglomeratus* L. *Journal of Ecology* **29**: 381–384.

Richards, P.W. & Clapham, A.R. 1941c. Biological Flora of the British Isles. No. 5. *Juncus subnodulosus* Schrank. *Journal of Ecology* **29**: 385–391.

Richards, P.W. & Evans, G.B. 1972. Biological Flora of the British Isles. No. 126. *Hymenophyllum tunbrigense* (L.) Sm. (pp. 245–258), *H. wilsonii* Hooker (258–268). *Journal of Ecology* **60**: 245–268.

Richens, R.H. 1947. Biological Flora of the British Isles. No. 16. *Allium vineale* L. *Journal of Ecology* **34**: 209–226.

Richens, R.H. 1983. *Elm*. Cambridge University Press, Cambridge.

Richens, R.H. 1987. The history of the elms in Wales. *Nature in Wales* **5**: 3–11.

Rickard, M.H. 1989. Two spleenworts new to Britain - *Asplenium trichomanes* subsp. *pachyrachis* and *Asplenium trichomanes* nothosubsp. *staufferi*. *Pteridologist* **1**: 244–248.

Riddelsdell, H.J. 1905. Lightfoot's visit to Wales in 1773. *Journal of Botany* **43**: 290–307.

Ritchie, J.C. 1954. Biological Flora of the British Isles. No. 44. *Primula scotica* Hook. *Journal of Ecology* **42**: 623–628.

Ritchie, J.C. 1955. Biological Flora of the British Isles. No. 51. *Vaccinium vitis-idaea* L. *Journal of Ecology* **43**: 701–708.

Ritchie, J.C. 1956. Biological Flora of the British Isles. No. 56. *Vaccinium myrtillus* L. *Journal of Ecology* **44**: 291–299.

Rixen, C., Wipf, S., Frei, E. & Stöckli, V. 2014. Faster, higher, more? Past, present and future dynamics of alpine and arctic flora under climate change. *Alpine Botany* **124**: 77–79.

Roach, F.A. 1985. *Cultivated fruits of Britain: their origin and history*. Basil Blackwell, Oxford.

Robbirt, K.M., Roberts, D.L., Hutchings, M.J. & Davy, A.J. 2014. Potential disruption of pollination in a sexually deceptive orchid by climatic change. *Current Biology* **24**: 2845–2849.

Robe, W.E. & Griffiths, H. 1992. Seasonal variation in the ecophysiology of *Littorella uniflora* (L.) Ascherson in acidic and eutrophic habitats. *New Phytologist* **120**: 289–304.

Robe, W.E. & Griffiths, H. 1994. The impact of NO_3 loading on the freshwater macrophyte *Littorella uniflora*: N utilization strategy in a slow-growing species from oligotrophic habitats. *Oecologia* **100**: 368–378.

Roberts, R.H. 1964. *Mimulus* hybrids in Britain. *Watsonia* **6**: 70–75.

Roberts, R.H. 1968. The hybrids of *Mimulus cupreus*. *Watsonia* **6**: 371–376.

Roberts, R.H. 1975. *Frankenia laevis* L. in Anglesey. *Watsonia* **10**: 291–292.

Roberts, F.J. 1977. *Viola rupestris* Schmidt and *Juncus alpinus* Vill. in Mid-W. Yorkshire. *Watsonia* **11**: 385–386.

Roberts, F.J. 2009a. Northern Deergrass (*Trichophorum cespitosum*) in upper Teesdale. *BSBI News* **111**: 22–26.

Roberts, F.J. 2009b. Crepis praemorsa *(L.) F. Walther at Orton in 2009*. Unpublished report to Natural England.

Roberts, H.A. & Feast, P.M. 1973. Emergence and longevity of seeds of annual weeds in cultivated and undisturbed soil. *Journal of Applied Ecology* **10**: 133–143.

Roberts, H.A. & Boddrell, J.E. 1983a. Seed survival and periodicity of seedling emergence in ten species of annual weeds. *Annals of Applied Biology* **102**: 523–532.

Roberts, H.A. & Boddrell, J.E. 1983b. Seed survival and periodicity of seedling emergence in eight species of Cruciferae. *Annals of Applied Biology* **103**: 301–309.

Roberts, H.A. & Boddrell, J.E. 1984. Seed survival and periodicity of seedling emergence in four weedy species of *Papaver*. *Weed Research* **24**: 195–200.

Robertson, A., Newton, A.C. & Ennos, R.A. 2004a. Breeding systems and continuing evolution in the endemic *Sorbus* taxa on Arran. *Heredity* **93**: 487–495.

Robertson, A., Newton, A.C. & Ennos, R.A. 2004b. Multiple hybrid origins, genetic diversity and population genetic structure of two endemic *Sorbus* taxa on the Isle of Arran, Scotland. *Molecular Ecology* **13**: 123–143.

Robertson, A. & Sydes, C. 2006. *Sorbus pseudomeinichii*, a new endemic *Sorbus* (Rosaceae) microspecies from Arran, Scotland. *Watsonia* **26**: 9–14.

Robertson, A., Rich, T.C.G., Allen, A.M., Houston, L., Roberts, C., Bridle, J.R., Harris, S.A. & Hiscock, S.J. 2010. Hybridization and polyploidy as drivers of continuing evolution and speciation in *Sorbus* L. (Rosaceae). *Molecular Ecology* **19**: 1675–1690.

Robinson, L. 2003. Observations on *Alopecurus borealis* at Green Fell in the northern Pennines, Cumbria, after foot and mouth. *BSBI News* **93**: 11–12.

Robinson, L. 2007. The discovery of *Alopecurus borealis* and *Carex vaginata* in the Yorkshire Dales (v.c. 65) with observations on *Saxifraga hirculus*. *BSBI News* **107**: 6–7.

Robinson, L. 2009. *Cotula alpina* (Hook. f.) Hook. f. (Alpine Cotula) in North-west Yorkshire (v.c.65), Mid-west Yorkshire (v.c.64) and North-East Yorkshire (v.c.62), new to Britain and Europe. *BSBI News* **113**: 52–54.

Robinson, J.B.D. & Treharne, K.J. 1985. Exploited plants. Maize. *Biologist* **32**: 199–207.

Robson, N.K.B. 1958. *Hypericum maculatum* in Britain and Europe. *Proceedings of the Botanical Society of the British Isles* **3**: 99–100.

Robson, N.K.B. 1985. Studies in the genus *Hypericum* L. (Guttiferae) 3. Sections 1. Campylosporus to 6a. Umbraculoides. *Bulletin of the British Museum (Natural History) Botany* **12**: 163–325.

Robson, N.K.B. 1990. British and Irish St. John's-worts. In *A Guide to Some Difficult Plants* pp. 90–108 Wild Flower Society, London.

Robson, N.K.B. 1996. Studies in the genus *Hypericum* L. (Guttiferae) 6. Sections 20. Myriandra to 28. Elodes. *Bulletin of the British Museum (Natural History) Botany* **26**: 75–217.

Roden, C., Murphy, P. & Ryan, J. 2020. *Benthic vegetation in Irish marl lakes: monitoring habitat 3140 condition 2011 to 2018.* Irish Wildlife Manuals, No. 124. National Parks and Wildlife Service, Dublin.

Rodwell, J.S. (Ed.) 1991. *British plant communities, 1. Woodlands and scrub.* Cambridge University Press, Cambridge.

Rodwell, J.S. (Ed.) 1992*a*. *British plant communities, 2. Mires and heaths.* Cambridge University Press, Cambridge.

Rodwell, J.S. (Ed.) 1992*b*. *British plant communities, 3. Grasslands and montane communities.* Cambridge University Press, Cambridge.

Rodwell, J.S. (Ed.) 1995. *British plant communities, 4. Aquatic communities, swamps and tall-herb fens.* Cambridge University Press, Cambridge.

Rodwell, J.S. (Ed.) 2000. *British plant communities, 5. Maritime communities and vegetation of open communities.* Cambridge University Press, Cambridge.

Roe, R.G.B. 1978. *Veronica crista-galli* Stev. in the British Isles. *Watsonia* **12**: 129–132.

Roger, G. 1952. *Diapensia lapponica* in Scotland. *Transactions and Proceedings of the Botanical Society of Edinburgh* **36**: 34–36.

Rogers, J.A. & Pearson, M.C. 1962. Biological Flora of the British Isles. No. 85. *Hippophaë rhamnoides* L. *Journal of Ecology* **50**: 501–513.

Roper, P. 1993. The distribution of the Wild Service Tree, *Sorbus torminalis* (L.) Crantz, in the British Isles. *Watsonia* **19**: 209–229.

Rose, F. 1948. Biological Flora of the British Isles. No. 25. *Orchis purpurea* Huds. *Journal of Ecology* **36**: 366–377.

Rose, F. 1988a. Plants to look for in the British Isles some of which might be expected to occur as natives. *BSBI News* **49**: 11–12.

Rose, F. 1988b. *Gymnadenia*. In Rich, T.C.G. & Jermy, A.C. (Eds.) *The Plant Crib* pp. 118–119 Edn. 1. Botanical Society of the British Isles, London.

Rose, R.J., Bannister, P. & Chapman, S.B. 1996. Biological Flora of the British Isles. No. 192. *Erica ciliaris* L. *Journal of Ecology* **84**: 617–628.

Ross, L.C., Woodin, S.J., Hester, A.J., Thompson, D.B.A. & Birks, H.J.B. 2012. Biotic homogenisation of upland vegetation: patterns and drivers at multiple spatial scales over five decades. *Journal of Vegetation Science* **23**: 755–770.

Rostański, K. 1982. The species of *Oenothera* L. in Britain. *Watsonia* **14**: 1–34.

Rowell, T.A. 1984. Further discoveries of the Fen Violet (*Viola persicifolia* Schreber) at Wicken Fen, Cambridgeshire. *Watsonia* **15**: 122–123.

Rowell, T.A., Walters, S.M. & Harvey, H.J. 1982. The rediscovery of the Fen Violet, *Viola persicifolia* Schreber, at Wicken Fen, Cambridgeshire. *Watsonia* **14**: 183–184.

Roy, H.E., Peyton, J., Aldridge, D.C., Bantock, T., Blackburn, T.M., Britton, R., Clark, P., Cook, E., Dehnen-Schmutz, K., Dines, T., Dobson, M., Edwards, F., Harrower, C., Harvey, M.C., Minchin, D., Noble, D.G., Parrott, D., Pocock, M.J.O., Preston, C.D., Roy, S., Salisbury, A., Schönrogge, K., Sewell, J., Shaw, R.H., Stebbing, P., Stewart, A.J.A. & Walker, K.J. 2014. Horizon scanning for invasive alien species with the potential to threaten biodiversity in Great Britain. *Global Change Biology* **20**: 3859–3871.

Roy, H.E., Rorke, S.L., Beckmann, B., Booy, O., Botham, M.S., Brown, P.M.J., Harrower, C., Noble, D., Sewell, J. & Walker, K.J. 2015. The contribution of volunteer recorders to our understanding of biological invasions. *Biological Journal of the Linnaean Society* **115**: 678–689.

Rudall, P.J., Perl, C.D. & Bateman, R.M. 2013. Organ homologies in orchid flowers re-interpreted using the Musk Orchid as a model. *PeerJ* **1**: e26.

Ruhsam, M., Jacobs, T., Watson, K. & Hollingsworth, P.M. 2015. Is hybridisation a threat to *Rumex aquaticus* in Britain? *Plant Ecology & Diversity* **8**: 465–474.

Ruksans, J. 2017. *The World of Crocuses.* Latvian Academy of Sciences, Riga.

Rumsey, F.J. 1997. *Asplenium viride* Hudson (Aspleniaceae) in Greater London. *Watsonia* **21**: 376–378.

Rumsey, F.J. 2007a. An overlooked boreal clubmoss *Lycopodium lagopus* (Laest. Ex Hartm.) Zinserl. Ex Kusen. (Lycopodiaceae) in Britain. *Watsonia* **26**: 477–480.

Rumsey, F.J. 2007b. An early specimen of *Cystopteris diaphana* (Bory) Blasdell supports its native status. *Watsonia* **26**: 489–490.

Rumsey, F.J. 2012. *Diphasiastrum tristachyum* (Pursh) Holub (Lycopodiaceae: Lycopodiophyta) – an overlooked extinct British Native. *Fern Gazette* **19**: 55–62.

Rumsey, F.J. 2016. Taxonomic changes to British cinquefoils. *BSBI News* **132**: 18–21.

Rumsey, F.J. 2017. What should we do about *Dryopteris affinis* – thoughts on a critical complex. *Pteridologist* **6**: 330–331.

Rumsey, F.J. 2018. The status of *Teucrium chamaedrys* (Wall Germander) in the British Isles. *BSBI News* **137**: 20–23.

Rumsey, F.J. 2019. *Lathyrus hirsutus* L. Native or not… and should it really matter. *BSBI News* **140**: 16–20.

Rumsey, F.J. 2021. *The subspecies of Annual Knawel* (Scleranthus annuus *L.) A taxonomic review and conservation assessment.* Unpublished report to Natural England.

Rumsey, F.J., Sheffield, E. & Farrar, D.R. 1990. British filmy-fern gametophytes. *Pteridologist* **2**: 40–42.

Rumsey, F.J. & Jury, S.L. 1991. An account of *Orobanche* L. in Britain and Ireland. *Watsonia* **18**: 257–295.

Rumsey, F.J. & Headley, A.D. 1998. Are British *Orobanche* species in decline? *The Naturalist* **123**: 76–85.

Rumsey, F.J., Jermy, A.C. & Sheffield, E. 1998. The independent gametophytic stage of *Trichomanes speciosum* Willd. (Hymenophyllaceae), the Killarney Fern and its distribution in the British Isles. *Watsonia* **22**: 1–19.

Rumsey, F.J. & Lansdown, R.V. 2012. Duckweeds and other simple floating plants. *British Wildlife* **23**: 326–334.

Rumsey, F.J., Crouch, H.J., Lansdown, R.V. & Spencer, M.A. 2019. Pedunculate Club-rush *Bolboschoenus laticarpus* - an overlooked native or a spreading neophyte? *British & Irish Botany* **1**: 91–106.

Rumsey, F.J. & Stroh, P.A. 2020. Will de-extinction be forever? Lessons from the re-introductions of *Bromus interruptus* (Hack.) Druce. *Journal for Nature Conservation* **56**: 125835.

Rumsey, F.J., Metherell, C. & Metherell, H. 2021. *Diphasiastrum* ×*issleri* (Lycopodiaceae) in England and Wales. *British & Irish Botany* **3**: 33–51.

Rünk, K., Zobel, M. & Zobel, K. 2012. Biological Flora of the British Isles. No. 267. *Dryopteris carthusiana, D. dilatata* and *D. expansa. Journal of Ecology* **100**: 1039–1063.

Rutherford, A. & Stirling, A.McG. 1987. Variegated archangels. *BSBI News* **46**: 9–11.

Ryves, T.B. 1984. *Artemisia* L. species in the British Isles. *Watsonia* **15**: 109–112.

Ryves, T.B., Clement, E.J. & Foster, M.C. 1996. *Alien grasses of the British Isles.* Botanical Society of the British Isles, London.

Saber, M.A., Clements, D.R., Hall, M.R., Doohan, D.J. & Crompton, C.W. 1995. The biology of Canadian weeds. 105. *Linaria vulgaris* Mill. *Canadian Journal of Plant Science* **75**: 525–537.

Sagar, G.R. & Harper, J.L. 1964. Biological Flora of the British Isles. No. 95. *Plantago major* L. (pp. 189–205), *P. media* L. (pp. 205–210), *P. lanceolata* L. (pp. 211–218). *Journal of Ecology* **52**: 189–221.

Salisbury, E.J. 1952. *Downs and dunes.* G. Bell & Sons, London.

Salisbury, E.J. 1953. A changing flora as shown in the study of weeds of arable land and waste places. In Lousley, J.E. (Ed.) *The Changing Flora of Britain* pp. 130–139 BSBI Conference Report no.3 Botanical Society of the British Isles, London.

Salisbury, E.J. 1961. *Weeds & Aliens.* Collins, London.

Salisbury, E.J. 1963. Fertile seed production and self-incompatability of *Hypericum calycinum* in England. *Watsonia* **5**: 368–376.

Salisbury, E.J. 1964. *Weeds & Aliens.* Edn. 2. Collins, London.

Salisbury, E.J. 1969a. A note on fertile seed production by *Hypericum calycinum. Watsonia* **7**: 24.

Salisbury, E.J. 1969b. The reproductive biology and occasional seasonal dimorphism of *Anagallis minima* and *Lythrum hyssopifolia. Watsonia* **7**: 25–39.

Salisbury, E.J. 1974. The reproduction of *Juncus tenuis* and its dispersal. *Transactions of the Botanical Society of Edinburgh* **42**: 187–190.

Salmon, C.E. 1926. A new *Myosotis* from Britain. *Journal of Botany* **64**: 289–295.

Salmon, C.E., Pearsall, W.H. (Ed.) 1931. *Flora of Surrey.* G. Bell & Sons, London.

Sand-Jensen, K., Pedersen, N.L., Thorsgaard, I., Moeslund, B., Borum, J. & Brodersen, K.P. 2008. 100 years of vegetation decline and recovery in Lake Fure, Denmark. *Journal of Ecology* **96**: 260–271.

Sanderson, N.A. 2012. *Ecological importance of Holmsley Bog in relation to the exotic pitcher plant* Sarracenia purpurea. Report for the New Forest Non-native Plants Project. Hampshire and Isle of Wight Wildlife Trust.

Sanford, M.N. 1991. *The orchids of Suffolk.* Suffolk Naturalists' Society, Ipswich.

Sanford, M.N. & Fisk, R. 2010. *A Flora of Suffolk.* D.K. & M.N. Sandford, Suffolk.

Santos, G. & Sayers, B. 2020. *Epipactis dunensis* (Orchidaceae): a confirmed new addition for the Irish flora. *Irish Botanical News* **30**: 8–11.

Sanyal, A. & Decocq, G. 2015. Biological Flora of the British Isles. No. 277. *Crambe maritima. Journal of Ecology* **103**: 769–88.

Sarbu, I., Stefan, N. & Oprea, A. 2013. *Plante Vasculare din Romania.* Editura Victor, Bucharest.

Sargent, C. 1985. *Britain's railway vegetation.* Institute of Terrestrial Vegetation, Cambridge.

Sargent, C., Mountford, O. & Greene, D. 1986. The distribution of *Poa angustifolia* L. in Britain. *Watsonia* **16**: 31–36.

Sark, C., Michalski, S.G., Babik, W., Winterfeld, G. & Durka, W. 2011. Strong genetic differentiation between *Gymnadenia conopsea* and *G. densiflora* despite morphological similarity. *Plant Systematics and Evolution* **293**: 213–226.

Savidge, J.P., Heywood, V.H. & Gordon, V. 1963. *Travis's Flora of South Lancashire.* Liverpool Botanical Society, Liverpool.

Scally, L. & Waldren, S. 1993. Ecological factors controlling the distribution of *Saxifraga spathularis* and *S. hirsuta* in Ireland. In Costello, M.J. & Kelly, K.S. (Eds.) *Biogeography of Ireland: past, present, and future* pp. 45–55 Irish Biogeographical Society, Dublin.

Scannell, M.J.P. 1973. *Juncus planifolius* R. Br. in Ireland. *Irish Naturalists' Journal* **17**: 308–309.

Scannell, M.J.P. 1975. The known distribution of *Juncus planifolius* R. Br. in Ireland. *Watsonia* **10**: 418–419.

Scannell, M.J.P. & Webb, D.A. 1976. The identity of the Renvyle *Hydrilla*. *Irish Naturalists' Journal* **18**: 327–331.

Scannell, M.J.P. & Synnott, D.M. 1987. *Census catalogue of the flora of Ireland*. Edn. 2. Stationery Office, Dublin.

Schmidt, T., Arens, P., Smulders, M.J., Billeter, R., Liira, J., Augenstein, I. & Durka, W. 2009. Effects of landscape structure on genetic diversity of *Geum urbanum* L. populations in agricultural landscapes. *Flora – Morphology, Distribution, Functional Ecology of Plants* **204**: 549–559.

Schmitz, U., Köhler, S. & Hussner, A. 2014. First records of American *Wolffia columbiana* in Europe – Clandestine replacement of native *Wolffia arrhiza*? *Bioinvasions Records* **3**: 213–216.

Schnittler, M., Horn, K., Kaufmann, R., Rimgailė-Voicik, R., Klahra, A., Bog, M., Fuchs, J. & Bennert, H.W. 2019. Genetic diversity and hybrid formation in Central European club-mosses (*Diphasiastrum*, Lycopodiaceae) – New insights from cp microsatellites, two nuclear markers and AFLP. *Molecular Phylogenetics and Evolution* **131**: 181–192.

Schotsman, H.D. 1967. *Les Callitriches: espèces de France et taxa nouveaux d'Europe*. Éditions Paul Lechevalier, Paris.

Schroeder, F.G. 1970. Exotic *Amelanchier* species naturalised in Europe and their occurrence in Great Britain. *Watsonia* **8**: 155–162.

Schubert, H. & Blindow, I. 2003. *Charophytes of the Baltic Sea*. The Baltic Marine Biologists Publication No. 19. A.R.G.Gantner Verlag Kommanditgesellschaft, Ruggell.

Schütz, W. 1995. Vegetation of running waters in Southwestern Germany - pristine conditions and human impact. *Acta botanica gallica* **142**: 571–584.

Scobie, A.R. 2007. Evidence of pollination and seed-set in Scottish populations of *Spiranthes romanzoffiana*. *BSBI News* **106**: 9–12.

Scopece, G., Cozzolino, S. & Bateman, R.M. 2010. Just what is a genus? Comparing levels of postzygotic isolation to test alternative taxonomic hypotheses in Orchidaceae subtribe Orchidinae. *Taxon* **59**: 1754–1764.

Scott, D.W. (Ed.) 1975. *B.S.B.I. Mapping Scheme. Distribution maps of 50 common plants*. Biological Records Centre, Abbots Ripton.

Scott, G.A.M. 1963a. Biological Flora of the British Isles. No. 89. *Mertensia maritima* (L.) S. F. Gray. *Journal of Ecology* **51**: 733–742.

Scott, G.A.M. 1963b. Biological Flora of the British Isles. No. 90. *Glaucium flavum* Crantz. *Journal of Ecology* **51**: 743–754.

Scott, G.A.M. & Randall, R.E. 1976. Biological Flora of the British Isles. No. 139. *Crambe maritima* L. *Journal of Ecology* **64**: 1077–1091.

Scott, M. 2016a. Diapensia: mystery on the mountain. *British Wildlife* **27**: 404–408.

Scott, M. 2016b. *Mountain Flowers*. British Wildlife Collection, No. 4. Bloomsbury Press, London.

Scott, M., Scott, S. & Sydes, C. 1999. A Scottish perspective on the conservation of pillwort. *British Wildlife* **10**: 297–302.

Scott, N.E. 1985. The updated distribution of maritime species on British roadsides. *Watsonia* **15**: 381–386.

Scott, N.E. & Davison, A.W. 1980. The distribution and ecology of coastal halophytes on roadsides. *Vegetatio* **62**: 433–440.

Scott, N.E. & Davison, A.W. 1982. De-icing salt and the invasion of road verges by maritime plants. *Watsonia* **14**: 41–52.

Scott, S., Darwell, A. & Stewart, N.F. 2011. *Bird's Nest Stonewort* Tolypella nidifica in Loch an t-Sruith Mhòir and Loch an Dùin, North Uist. Report for Scottish Natural Heritage. Scott, W. & Palmer, R. 1987. *The flowering plants and ferns of the Shetland Islands*. The Shetland Times Ltd., Lerwick.

Scott, W. 1968. *Pilosella flagellaris* (Willd.) Sell & C. West subsp. *bicapitata* Sell & C. West – in Zetland. *Proceedings of the Botanical Society of the British Isles* **7**: 192–193.

Scott, W., Harvey, P., Riddington, R. & Fisher, M. 2002. *Rare plants of Shetland*. Shetland Amenity Trust, Lerwick.

Scully, R.W. 1916. *Flora of County Kerry*. Hodges, Figgis & Co, Dublin.

Scurfield, G. 1954. Biological Flora of the British Isles. No. 39. *Deschampsia flexuosa* (L.) Trin. *Journal of Ecology* **42**: 225–233.

Scurfield, G. 1962. Biological Flora of the British Isles. No. 84. *Cardaria draba* (L.) Desv. (*Lepidium draba* L.). *Journal of Ecology* **50**: 489–499.

Sealy, J.R. & Webb, D.A. 1950. Biological Flora of the British Isles. No. 30. *Arbutus* L., *Arbutus unedo* L. *Journal of Ecology* **38**: 223–236.

Seebens, H., Blackburn, T.M., Dyer, E.E., Genovesi, P., Hulme, P.E., Jeschke, J.M., Pagad, S., Pysek, P., Winter, M., Arianoutsou, M., Bacher, S., Blasius, B., Brundu, G., Capinha, C., Celesti-Grapow, L., Dawson, W., Dullinger, S., Fuentes, N., Jager, H., Kartesz, J., Kenis, M., Kreft, H., Kuhn, I., Lenzner, B., Liebhold, A., Mosena, A., Moser, D., Nishino, M., Pearman, D., Pergl, J., Rabitsch, W., Rojas-Sandoval, J., Roques, A., Rorke, S., Rossinelli, S., Roy, H.E., Scalera, R., Schindler, S., Stajerova, K., Tobarska-Guzik, B., Kleunen, M. van, Walker, K.J., Weigelt, P., Yamanaka, T. & Essle, F. 2016. No saturation in the accumulation of alien species worldwide. *Nature Communications* **8**: 14435.

Sell, P.D. 1967. Taxonomic and nomenclatural notes on the British flora. *Watsonia* **6**: 292–318.

Sell, P.D. 1981. *Lapsana intermedia* Bieb. or *Lapsana communis* L. subsp. *intermedia* (Bieb.) Hayek? *Watsonia* **13**: 299–302.

Sell, P.D. 1986. The genus *Cicerbita* Wallr. in the British Isles. *Watsonia* **16**: 121–129.

Sell, P.D. 1989. The *Sorbus latifolia* (Lam.) Pers. aggregate in the British Isles. *Watsonia* **17**: 385–399.

Sell, P.D. 1991. The cherries and plums of Cambridgeshire. *Nature in Cambridgeshire* **33**: 29–39.

Sell, P.D. 1992. More plums. *Nature in Cambridgeshire* **34**: 59–60.

Sell, P.D. 1994. *Ranunculus ficaria* L. sensu lato. *Watsonia* **20**: 41–50.

Sell, P.D. & Murrell, G. 1996. *Flora of Great Britain and Ireland, volume 5: Butomaceae-Orchidaceae*. Cambridge University Press, Cambridge.

Sell, P.D. & Murrell, G. 2006. *Flora of Great Britain and Ireland, volume 4: Campanulaceae-Asteraceae*. Cambridge University Press, Cambridge.

Sell, P.D. & Murrell, G. 2009. *Flora of Great Britain and Ireland, volume 3: Mimosaceae-Lentibulariaceae*. Cambridge University Press, Cambridge.

Sell, P.D. & Murrell, G. 2014. *Flora of Great Britain and Ireland, volume 2: Capparaceae-Rosaceae*. Cambridge University Press, Cambridge.

Sell, P.D. & Murrell, G. 2018. *Flora of Great Britain and Ireland, volume 1: Lycopodiaceae-Salicaceae*. Cambridge University Press, Cambridge.

Selosse, M.-A., Weiss, M., Jany, J.L. & Tillier, A. 2002. Communities and populations of sebacinoid basidiomycetes associated with the achlorophyllous orchid *Neottia nidus-avis* (L.) L.C.M. Rich. and neighbouring tree ectomycorrhizae. *Molecular Ecology* **11**: 1831–1844.

Sennikov, A.N. 2011. Chamerion or Chamaenerion (Onagraceae)? The old story in new words. *Taxon* **60**: 1485–1488.

Shamsi, S.R.A. & Whitehead, F.H. 1974. Comparative eco-physiology of *Epilobium hirsutum* L. and *Lythrum salicaria* L. I. General biology, distribution and germination. *Journal of Ecology* **62**: 279–290.

Sharma, M.P. & Vanden Born, W.H. 1978. The biology of Canadian weeds. 27. *Avena fatua* L. *Canadian Journal of Plant Science* **58**: 141–157.

Shaw, S. 1948. *Chara braunii* Gmelin. *The North Western Naturalist* **23**: 166–167.

Shaw, N.L. 2004. *Holodiscus discolor*. In Francis, J.K. (Ed.) *Wildland shrubs of the United States and its territories: Thamnic descriptions, Vol. 1* pp. 379–381 General Technical Report - International Institute of Tropical Forestry, USDA Forest Service. No.IITF-GTR-26 U.S. Department of Agriculture, Forest Service, Fort Collins, C.O.

Shaw, M. 2020. *Hawkweeds of south-east England*. BSBI Handbook no. 20. Botanical Society of Britain and Ireland, Durham.

Shaw, R.F., Iason, G.R., Pakeman, R.J. & Young, M.R. 2010. Regeneration of *Salix arbuscula* and *Salix lapponum* within a large mammal exclosure: the impacts of microsite and herbivory. *Restoration Ecology* **18**: 1–9.

Sheehy Skeffington, M. 2015. An alien immigrant? The story of Mackay's Heath (*Erica mackayana*) in Ireland. *Moorea* **17**: 61–70.

Sheehy Skeffington, M. & Hall, K. 2011. The ecology, distribution and invasiveness of *Gunnera* L. species in Connemara, Western Ireland. *Biology and Environment: Proceedings of the Royal Irish Academy* **111B**: 157–175.

Sheehy Skeffington, M. & van Doorslaer, L. 2015. Distribution and habitats of *Erica mackayana* and *Erica × stuartii* (Ericaceae): new insights and ideas regarding their origins in Ireland. *New Journal of Botany* **5**: 164–177.

Sheehy Skeffington, M. & Scott, N. 2021. Is the Strawberry Tree, *Arbutus unedo* (Ericaceae), native to Ireland, or was it brought by the first copper miners? *British & Irish Botany* **3**: 385–341.

Shefferson, R.P., Roy, M., Püttsepp, U. & Selosse, M.-A. 2016. Demographic shifts related to mycoheterotrophy and their fitness impacts in two *Cephalanthera* species. *Ecology* **97**: 1452–1462.

Shellswell, C.H., Gibbons, H., Mitchell, A., Moyse, R. & Waller, M. (Eds.) 2021. *Looking after Broad-fruited Cornsalad* Valerianella rimosa. Ecology and Conservation Portfolio. Plantlife, Salisbury.

Shenstone, J.C. 1910. *Lathyrus tuberosus* in Britain. *Journal of Botany* **48**: 327–331.

Sheppard, A.W. 1991. Biological Flora of the British Isles. No. 171. *Heracleum sphondylium* L. *Journal of Ecology* **79**: 235–258.

Shimwell, D.W. 2006. A shoddy tale: perspectives on the wool alien flora in West Yorkshire in the twenty-first century. *Watsonia* **26**: 127–137.

Shirreffs, D.A. 1985. Biological Flora of the British Isles. No. 158. *Anemone nemorosa* L. *Journal of Ecology* **73**: 1005–1020.

Shivas, M.G. 1961. Contribution to the cytology and taxonomy of species of *Polypodium* in Europe and America, II. Taxonomy. *Botanical Journal of the Linnean Society* **58**: 27–38.

Showler, A.J. & Rich, T.C.G. 1993. *Cardamine bulbifera* (L.) Crantz (Cruciferae) in the British Isles. *Watsonia* **19**: 231–245.

Silverside, A.J. 1983. *Euphrasia heslop-harrisonii* Pugsl. - An overlooked saltmarsh taxon? *Watsonia* **14**: 456.

Silverside, A.J. 1990a. Dandelions and their allies. In *A Guide to Some Difficult Plants* pp. 41–67 Wild Flower Society, London.

Silverside, A.J. 1990b. The nomenclature of some hybrids of the *Spiraea salicifolia* group naturalized in Britain. *Watsonia* **18**: 147–151.

Silverside, A.J. 1991. The identity of *Euphrasia officinalis* L. and its nomenclatural implications. *Watsonia* **18**: 343–350.

Silverside, A.J. 1994. *Mimulus*: 180 years of confusion. In Perry, A.R. & Ellis, R.G. (Eds.) *The common ground of wild and cultivated plants.* pp. 59–64 BSBI Conference Report no. 22 National Museum of Wales, Cardiff.

Silverside, A.J. 1998. *Euphrasia.* In Rich, T.C.G. & Jermy, A.C. (Eds.) *Plant Crib 1998* pp. 269–272 Botanical Society of the British Isles, London.

Silvertown, J., Wells, D.A., Gillman, M., Dodd, M.E., Robertson, H. & Lakhani, K. 1993. Short-term effects and long-term after-effects of fertilizer application on the flowering population of green-winged orchid *Orchis morio. Biological Conservation* **69**: 191–197.

Simmonds, N.W. 1945. Biological Flora of the British Isles. No. 14. *Polygonum* L. em. Gaertn. (pp. 117–120), *P. persicaria* L. (pp. 121–131), *P. lapathifolium* L. (*P. tomentosum* Schr. of many continental authors) (pp. 121–131), *P. petecticale* (Stokes) Druce (*P. maculatum* Trimen & Dyer, *P. nodosum* Persoon, etc) (pp. 140–143). *Journal of Ecology* **33**: 117–143.

Simmonds, N.W. 1946. Biological Flora of the British Isles. No. 15. *Gentiana pneumonanthe* L. *Journal of Ecology* **33**: 295–307.

Simpson, F.W. 1982. *Simpson's Flora of Suffolk.* Suffolk Naturalists' Society, East Bergholt.

Simpson, B.B., Neff, J.L. & Seigler, D.S. 1983. Floral biology and floral rewards of *Lysimachia* (Primulaceae). *American Midland Naturalist* **110**: 249–256.

Sing, Y., van Wyk, A.E. & Baijnath, H. 1996. Floral biology of *Zantedeschia aethiopica* (L.) Spreng. (Araceae). *South African Journal of Botany* **62**: 146–150.

Sinker, C.A., Packham, J.R., Trueman, I.C., Oswald, P.H., Perring, F.H. & Prestwood, W.V. 1985. *The Ecological Flora of the Shropshire Region.* Shropshire Trust for Nature Conservation, Shrewsbury.

Skene, K.R., Sprent, J.I., Raven, J.A. & Herdman, L. 2000. Biological Flora of the British Isles. No. 215. *Myrica gale* L. *Journal of Ecology* **88**: 1079–1094.

Skyring, I. (Ed.) 2019. *The North Face Survey: Discovering the hidden side of Ben Nevis.* The Nevis Landscape Partnership, Fort William.

Slater, F.M. 1990. Biological Flora of the British Isles. No. 168. *Gagea bohemica* (Zauschner) J. A. & J. H. Schultes (*G. saxatilis* Koch). *Journal of Ecology* **78**: 535–546.

Sledge, W.A. 1975. Further comments on the supposed occurrence of *Euphrasia salisburgensis* in Yorkshire. *The Naturalist* **934**: 87–89.

Small, E. & Cronquist, A. 1976. A practical and natural taxonomy for *Cannabis. Taxon* **25**: 405–435.

Small, E., Pocock, T. & Cavers, P.B. 2003. The biology of Canadian weeds. 119. *Cannabis sativa* L. *Canadian Journal of Plant Science* **83**: 217–237.

Smart, J. & Simmonds, N.W. 1995. *Evolution of crop plants.* Edn. 2. Longman, London.

Smart, S.M., Henrys, P.A., Norton, L.R., Wallace, H., Wood, C.M., Williams, B. & Bunce, R.G.H. 2017. Changes in the frequency of common plant species across linear features in Wales from 1990 to 2016: implications for potential delivery of ecosystem services. *New Journal of Botany* **7**: 112–124.

Smillie, C. 2015. *Salicornia* spp. as a biomonitor of Cu and Zn in salt marsh sediments. *Ecological Indicators* **56**: 70–78.

Smit, P.G. 1973. A revision of *Caltha* (Ranunculaceae). *Blumea* **21**: 119–150.

Smith, A.J.E. 1963b. Variation in *Melampyrum pratense* L. *Watsonia* **5**: 336–367.

Smith, B.M., Diaz, A., Winder, L. & Daniels, R. 2005. The effect of provenance on the establishment and performance of *Lotus corniculatus* L. in a re-creation environment. *Biological Conservation* **125**: 37–46.

Smith, G.L. 1963a. Studies in *Potentilla*, 1. Embryological investigations into the mechanism of agamospermy in British *P. tabernaemontani* Aschers. *New Phytologist* **62**: 264–282.

Smith, M. 2013a. *Polycarpon tetraphyllum* (Four-leaved Allseed) established in South Essex, and some interesting plants nearby. *BSBI News* **124**: 19–20.

Smith, M. 2013b. *Pentaglottis sempervirens. BSBI News* **124**: 54.

Smith, P. 2017. Some interesting salt-tolerant plants of roadsides in the Outer Hebrides. *Hebridean Naturalist*, **16**: 15-23.

Smith, P.A., Strachan, I.M. & Coupar, A.M. 2021a. An overview of *Scheuchzeria palustris* in Scotland and a new locality in Westerness (vc97). *British & Irish Botany* **3**: 58–64.

Smith, P.A., Lutz, M., Chater, A.O. & Woods, R.G. 2021b. Anther smuts on Butterworts (*Pinguicula* spp.). *Field Mycology* **22**: 5–11.

Smith, P.H. 1984. The distribution, status and conservation of *Juncus balticus* Willd. in England. *Watsonia* **15**: 15–26.

Smith, P.H. 2005. *Schoenoplectus pungens* on the Sefton Coast. *BSBI News* **98**: 30–33.

Smith, P.H. & Wilcox, M.P. 2006. *Artemisia campestris* subsp. *maritima*, new to Britain, on the Sefton coast, Merseyside. *BSBI News* **103**: 3.

Smith, P.H. & Lockwood, P.A. 2011. Grazing is the key to the conservation of *Gentianella campestris* (L.) Börner (Gentianaceae): evidence from the north Merseyside sand-dunes. *New Journal of Botany* **1**: 127–136.

Smith, P.M. 1968. The *Bromus mollis* aggregate in Britain. *Watsonia* **6**: 327–344.

Smith, P.M., Dixon, R.O.D. & Cochrane, M.P. (Eds.) 2002. *Plant Life of Edinburgh and the Lothians.* Edinburgh University Press, Edinburgh.

Smith, R., Hodgson, B. & Ison, J. 2016. *A New Flora of Devon.* Devonshire Association for the Advancement of the Arts, Science and Literature, Exeter.

Smith, R.S., Buckingham, H., Bullard, M.J., Shiel, R.S. & Younger, A. 1996. The conservation management of mesotrophic (meadow) grassland in northern England. 1. Effects of grazing, cutting date and fertilizer on the vegetation of a traditionally managed sward. *Grass and Forage Science* **51**: 278–291.

Smith, R.T. & Taylor, J.A. 1995. *Bracken: an environmental issue. International Bracken Group Special Publication no. 2.* University of Leeds Printing Service.

Smith, T. & Buckley, P. 2020. Biological Flora of the British Isles. No. 290. *Crassula helmsii. Journal of Ecology* **108**: 797–813.

Smith, U.K. 1979. Biological Flora of the British Isles. No. 147. *Senecio integrifolius* (L.) Clairv. (*Senecio campestris* (Retz.) DC.). *Journal of Ecology* **67**: 1109–1124.

Snogerup, B. 1982. *Odontites litoralis* Fries subsp. *litoralis* in the British Isles. *Watsonia* **14**: 35–39.

Snogerup, S. 1993. A revision of *Juncus* subgen. *Juncus* (Juncaceae). *Willdenowia* **23**: 23–73.

Snyder, E., Francis, A. & Darbyshire, S.J. 2016. Biology of invasive alien plants in Canada. 13. *Stratiotes aloides* L. *Canadian Journal of Plant Science* **96**: 225–242.

Sobey, D.G. 1981. Biological Flora of the British Isles. No. 150. *Stellaria media* (L.) Vill. *Journal of Ecology* **69**: 311–335.

Soldaat, L.L., Pannekoek, J., Verweij, R.J., van Turnhout, C.A. & van Strien, A.J. 2017. A Monte Carlo method to account for sampling error in multi-species indicators. *Ecological Indicators* **81**: 340–347.

Soltis, D.E. 1984. Autopolyploidy in *Tolmiea menziesii* (Saxifragaceae). *Journal of Botany* **71**: 1171–1174.

Somme, L., Mayer, C., Raspé, O. & Jacquemart, A.L. 2014. Influence of spatial distribution and size of clones on the realized outcrossing rate of the marsh cinquefoil (*Comarum palustre*). *Annals of Botany* **113**: 477–487.

Sowter, F.A. 1949. Biological Flora of the British Isles. No. 27. *Arum* L., *Arum maculatum* L. *Journal of Ecology* **37**: 207–219.

Spalton, L.M. 2001. A new subspecies of *Bromus hordeaceus* L. (Poaceae). *Watsonia* **23**: 525–531.

Sparling, J.H. 1968. Biological Flora of the British Isles. No. 114. *Schoenus nigricans* L. (*Chaetospora nigricans* Kunth). *Journal of Ecology* **56**: 883–899.

Speaka, A.F., Rothwella, J.J., Lindleya, S.J. & Smith, C.L. 2012. Urban particulate pollution reduction by four species of green roof vegetation in a UK city. *Atmospheric Environment* **61**: 283–293.

Species Recovery Trust 2016. *Field Cow-wheat at Portsdown.* Site status report. Species Recovery Trust, Salisbury.

Species Recovery Trust 2017. *Archaeophytes project.* Progress Report. Species Recovery Trust, Salisbury.

Spencer, J. 2000. A bleak future for *Gaultheria shallon* in the New Forest. *BSBI News* **84**: 47–48.

Spicer, K.W. & Catling, P.M. 1988. The biology of Canadian weeds. 88. *Elodea canadensis* Michx. *Canadian Journal of Plant Science* **68**: 1035–1051.

Spinage, C. 2000. The Wild Pear tree – one of Britain's rarest trees or a garden escape? *British Wildlife* **11**: 313–318.

Spooner, B.M. 1982. *Salvia reflexa* Hornem. in Britain. *BSBI News* **31**: 17–18.

Squirrell, J., Hollingsworth, P.M., Bateman, R.M., Dickson, J.H., Light, M.H.S., Mcconaill, M. & Tebbitt, M.C. 2001. Partitioning and diversity of nuclear and organelle markers in native and introduced populations of *Epipactis helleborine* (Orchidaceae). *American Journal of Botany* **88**: 1409–1418.

Squirrell, J., Hollingsworth, P.M., Bateman, R.M., Tebbitt, M.C. & Hollingsworth, M.L. 2002. Taxonomic complexity and breeding system transitions: conservation genetics of the *Epipactis leptochila* complex. *Molecular Ecology* **11**: 1957–1964.

Squirrell, J., Hollingsworth, P.M., Sears, J., Banks, B., Ferry, B. & de Graaf, D.T. 2006. Assessment of the genetic diversity in populations of *Crepis foetida* L. (Asteraceae). *Watsonia* **26**: 121–126.

Sramkó, G., Molnár, A.V., Hawkins, J.A. & Bateman, R.M. 2014. Molecular phylogenetics and evolution of the Eurasiatic orchid genus *Himantoglossum* s.l. *Annals of Botany* **114**: 1609–1626.

Sramkó, G., Paun, O., Brandrud, M.K., Laczko, L., Molnár, A.V. & Bateman, R.M. 2019. Iterative allogamy–autogamy transitions drive actual and incipient speciation during the ongoing evolutionary radiation within the orchid genus *Epipactis* (Orchidaceae). *Annals of Botany* **124**: 481–497.

Srutek, M. & Teckelmann, M. 1998. Review of biology and ecology of *Urtica dioica. Preslia (Praha)* **70**: 1–19.

Stace, C.A. 1961. *Nardurus maritimus* (L.) Murb. in Britain. *Proceedings of the Botanical Society of the British Isles* **4**: 248–261.

Stace, C.A. 1972. The history and occurrence in Britain of hybrids in *Juncus* subgenus *Genuini. Watsonia* **9**: 1–11.

Stace, C.A. (Ed.) 1975. *Hybridisation and the flora of the British Isles.* Academic Press, London.

Stace, C.A. 1991. *New Flora of the British Isles.* Edn. 1. Cambridge University Press, Cambridge.

Stace, C.A. 1997. *New Flora of the British Isles.* Edn. 2. Cambridge University Press, Cambridge.

Stace, C.A. 2010. *New Flora of the British Isles.* Edn. 3. Cambridge University Press, Cambridge.

Stace, C.A. 2019. *New Flora of the British Isles.* Edn. 4. C&M Floristics, Suffolk.

Stace, C.A. & Wilkinson, M.J. 1989. The taxonomic relationships and typification of *Festuca brevipila* Tracey and *F. lemanii* Bastard (Poaceae). *Watsonia* **17**: 289–299.

Stace, C.A., Al Bermani, A.K.K.A. & Wilkinson, M.J. 1992. The distinction between the *Festuca ovina* L. and *Festuca rubra* L. aggregates in the British Isles. *Watsonia* **19**: 107–112.

BIBLIOGRAPHY

Stace, C.A. & Crawley, M.J. 2015. *Alien plants*. New Naturalist 129. Harper Collins, London.

Stace, C.A., Preston, C.D. & Pearman, D.A. (Comps. & Eds.) 2015. *Hybrid Flora of the British Isles*. Botanical Society of Britain and Ireland, Bristol.

Stadtlander, T., Förster, S., Rosskothern, D. & Leiber, F. 2019. Slurry-grown duckweed (*Spirodela polyrhiza*) as a means to recycle nitrogen into feed for rainbow trout fry. *Journal of Cleaner Production* 228: 86–93.

Stahlberg, D. & Hedrén, M. 2008. Systematics and phylogeography of the *Dactylorhiza maculata* complex (Orchidaceae) in Scandinavia: insights from cytological, morphological and molecular data. *Plant Systematics and Evolution* 273: 107–132.

Stahlberg, D. & Hedrén, M. 2010. Evolutionary history of the *Dactylorhiza maculata* polyploid complex (Orchidaceae). *Biological Journal of the Linnean Society* 101: 503–525.

Stanek, M., Piechnik, L. & Stefanowicz, A.M. 2020. Invasive red oak (*Quercus rubra* L.) modifies soil physicochemical properties and forest understory vegetation. *Forest Ecology and Management* 472: 118253.

Stanley, P.A. 1996. *Conyza bilbaoana* J. Remy - new to South Hampshire (VC11) and to Britain. *BSBI News* 73: 47–49.

Stead, J. 1980. Plant portraits, 1. *Salix reticulata*, the net-veined willow. *Quarterly Bulletin of the Alpine Garden Society* 48: 59–60.

Stensvold, M.C. & Farrar, D.R. 2017. Genetic diversity in the worldwide *Botrychium lunaria* (Ophioglossaceae) complex, with new species and new combinations. *Brittonia* 69: 148–175.

Stephenson, R. 1994. Sedum: *cultivated stonecrops*. Timber Press, Portland, Oregon.

Stevens, D.P. 1990. The distribution of gender in *Petasites hybridus* (Butterbur). *BSBI News* 55: 10–11.

Stevens, C.J., Smart, S.M., Henrys, P., Maskell, L.C., Walker, K.J., Preston, C.D., Crowe, A., Rowe, E., Gowing, D.J. & Emmett, B.A. 2011. *Collation of evidence of nitrogen impacts on vegetation in relation to UK biodiversity objectives*. JNCC Report, No. 447. Joint Nature Conservation Committee, Peterborough.

Stevens, C.J., Wilson, J. & McAllister, H.A. 2012. Biological Flora of the British Isles. No. 266. *Campanula rotundifolia*. *Journal of Ecology* 100: 821–39.

Stewart, A., Pearman, D.A. & Preston, C.D. 1994. *Scarce plants in Britain*. Joint Nature Conservation Committee, Peterborough.

Stewart, G.B., Tyler, C. & Pullin, A.S. 2005. *Effectiveness of current methods for the control of Bracken (*Pteridium aquilinum*)*. Centre for Evidence-based Conservation, University of Birmingham.

Stewart, N.F. 1995a. *A stonewort survey of Orton Pit, Peterborough Southern Township*. Unpublished report to English Nature.

Stewart, N.F. 1995b. *A survey of Orkney stoneworts*. Report for Scottish Natural Heritage.

Stewart, N.F. 1997. *Bearded Stonewort (*Chara canescens*): Species Action Plan*. Edn. 2. Unpublished report to English Nature.

Stewart, N.F. 1999a. *A stonewort survey of clay and gravel pits in the Peterborough area*. Unpublished report to English Nature.

Stewart, N.F. 1999b. *Survey of the botany and vegetation of Loe Pool, Helston*. Unpublished report for National Trust.

Stewart, N.F. 2001. *Review of the status of Biodiversity Action Plan stonewort species*. Plantlife report no. 170.

Stewart, N.F. 2003a. A review of the records for *Chara fragifera* in Britain. *Botanical Cornwall* 12: 51–72.

Stewart, N.F. 2003b. *Species dossier: Starry Stonewort Nitellopsis obtusa in Scotland*. Report for Scottish Natural Heritage.

Stewart, N.F. 2003c. *Aquatic plants and vegetation of the Lochs of Harray and Stenness, August 2002*. Report by the International Centre for Island Technology for Scottish Natural Heritage.

Stewart, N.F. 2004a. *Dwarf Stonewort Nitella tenuissima in Britain*. Report for North Wales Wildlife Trust.

Stewart, N.F. 2004b. *Species dossier: Lesser Bearded Stonewort Chara curta in Scotland*. Report for Scottish Natural Heritage.

Stewart, N.F. 2005a. *Slender Stonewort Nitella gracilis in Cornwall*. Report to Environmental Records Centre for Cornwall and the Isles of Scilly.

Stewart, N.F. 2005b. *Stoneworts at Orton Pit, Peterborough, 7th report*. Unpublished report for Froglife.

Stewart, N.F. & Church, J.M. 1992. *Red Data Books of Britain and Ireland: Stoneworts*. Joint Nature Conservation Committee.

Stewart, N.F. & Lansdown, R.V. 1999. *The conservation status of Great Tassel Stonewort (*Tolypella prolifera*) in Britain. Interim report No. 1*. Plantlife Report No. 121. Plantlife, London.

Stewart, N.F. & FitzGerald, R. 2000. *Three-lobed Water Crowfoot, Ranunculus tripartitus - report for 1999*. Plantlife Report No. 157. Plantlife, London.

Stewart, N.F. & Pankhurst, T.J. 2000. *The conservation status of Great Tassel Stonewort (*Tolypella prolifera*) in Britain. Interim report No. 2*. Plantlife Report No. 153. Plantlife, London.

Stewart, N.F. & Preston, C.D. 2000. Stoneworts of Coll and Tiree. *Botanical Journal of Scotland* 52: 91–100.

Stewart, N.F. & Scott, S. 2003. *Species dossier: Slender Stonewort Nitella gracilis in Scotland*. Report for Scottish Natural Heritage.

Stewart, N.F. & Hatton-Ellis, T. 2020. *A Red List of Stoneworts in Wales*. Natural Resources Wales Evidence Report No. 406. Natural Resources Wales, Bangor.

Stewart, O. 1987. *Juncus subulatus* at Grangemouth, V.C. 86. *BSBI Scottish Newsletter* 9: 12.

Stokes, K.E., Bullock, J.M. & Watkinson, A.R. 2003. Biological Flora of the British Isles. No. 232. *Ulex gallii* Planch and *Ulex minor* Roth. *Journal of Ecology* 91: 1106–1124.

Stone, D.A. & Russell, R.V. 2000. *Population biology of late spider orchid* Ophrys fuciflora – a study at Wye National Nature Reserve, 1987–1998. English Nature Research Report 389. English Nature, Peterborough.

Strachan, I. 2015. Plants - Scotland. *British Wildlife* 26: 442–444.

Strachan, I. 2019. *A survey of the distribution and abundance of Scottish Small-reed Calamagrostis scotica at Loch of Durran SSSI, Caithness*. Unpublished report to NatureScot.

Strayer, D.L., D'Antonio, C.M., Essl, F., Fowler, M.S., Geist, J., Hilt, S., Jarić, I., Jöhnk, K., Jones, C.G., Lambin, X., Latzka, A.W., Pergl, J., Pyšek, P., Robertson, P., von Schmalensee, M., Stefansson, R.A., Wright, J. & Jeschke, J.M. 2017. Boom-bust dynamics in biological invasions: towards an improved application of the concept. *Ecology Letters* 20: 1337–1350.

Streeter, D.T. 2021. *Bunium bulbocastanum* on the South Downs. *BSBI News* 147: 5–11.

Strid, A. 1986. *Mountain Flora of Greece. Vol. 1*. Cambridge University Press, Cambridge.

Stroh, P.A. 2007. The current distribution of Green-winged Orchid *Orchis morio* L. in Huntingdonshire (vc31), the Soke of Peterborough (vc32) and old Cambridgeshire (vc29). *Nature in Cambridgeshire* 49: 3–10.

Stroh, P.A. 2014a. Allium oleraceum *L. Field Garlic. Species Account*. Botanical Society of Britain and Ireland, Durham.

Stroh, P.A. 2014b. Spiranthes spiralis *(L.) Chevall. Autumn Ladies-tresses. Species Account*. Botanical Society of Britain and Ireland, Durham.

Stroh, P.A. 2015a. Anacamptis morio *(L.) Bateman, Pridgeon & Chase. Green-winged Orchid. Species Account*. Botanical Society of Britain and Ireland, Durham.

Stroh, P.A. 2015b. Ophrys insectifera *L. Fly Orchid. Species Account*. Botanical Society of Britain and Ireland, Durham.

Stroh, P.A. 2015c. Sibthorpia europaea *L. Cornish Moneywort. Species Account*. Botanical Society of Britain and Ireland.

Stroh, P.A. 2015d. Hammarbya paludosa *L. Bog Orchid Species Account*. Botanical Society of Britain and Ireland.

Stroh, P.A. 2015e. *Hordeum marinum* in Northamptonshire. *BSBI News* 130: 29.

Stroh, P.A. 2016. Orchis militaris *L. Military Orchid. Species Account*. Botanical Society of Britain and Ireland, Durham.

Stroh, P.A. 2019. Wild Liquorice (*Astragalus glycyphyllos*) in Cambridgeshire. *Nature in Cambridgeshire* 61: 42–50.

Stroh, P.A. 2020. An update on the history, ecology and fate of Fen Ragwort (*Jacobaea paludosa*) in Britain. *Nature in Cambridgeshire* 62: 39–45.

Stroh, P.A., Mountford, J.O. & Hughes, F.M.R. 2011. The potential for the endozoochorous dispersal of temperate fen species by free-roaming horses. *Applied Vegetation Science* 15: 359–368.

Stroh, P.A., Leach, S.J., August, T.A., Walker, K.J., Pearman, D.A., Rumsey, F.J., Harrower, C.A., Fay, M.F., Martin, J.P., Pankhurst, T., Preston, C.D. & Taylor, I. 2014. *A Vascular Plant Red List for England*. Botanical Society of Britain and Ireland, Bristol.

Stroh, P.A. & Croft, J.M. 2015. Emerging from slumber – Fen Violet (*Viola persicifolia*) at Wicken Fen National Nature Reserve, Cambridgeshire. *Nature in Cambridgeshire* 57: 91–96.

Stroh, P.A. & Scott, W. 2017. *Angelica archangelica* subsp. *littoralis* (Apiaceae) – a new native taxon for Britain. *New Journal of Botany* 7: 57–58.

Stroh, P.A., Pescott, O.L. & Mountford, J.O. 2017. Long-term changes in lowland calcareous grassland plots using *Tephroseris integrifolia* subsp. *integrifolia* as an indicator species. *Plant Ecology* 218: 1269–1281.

Stroh, P.A., Walker, K.J., Smith, S.L.N., Jefferson, R.G., Pinches, C.E. & Blackstock, T.H. 2019. *Grassland plants of the British and Irish lowlands: ecology, threats and management*. Botanical Society of Britain and Ireland, Durham.

Styles, B.T. 1962. The taxonomy of *Polygonum aviculare* and its allies in Britain. *Watsonia* 5: 177–214.

Styles, B.T. 1976. *Stachys annua*. *BSBI News* 12: 12.

Suggitt, A.J., Wilson, R.J., Isaac, N.J.B., Beale, C.M., Auffret, A.G., August, T.A., Bennie, J.J., Crick, H.Q.P., Duffield, S., Fox, R., Hopkins, J.J., Macgregor, N.A., Morecroft, M.D., Walker, K.J. & Maclean, I.M.D. 2018. Extinction risk from climate change is reduced by microclimatic buffering. *Nature Climate Change* 8: 713–717.

Sullivan, G. 2003. *Extent and condition of Juniper scrub in Scotland*. Report to Scottish Natural Heritage. Contract no. BAT/AC205/01/02/96.

Summerfield, R.J. 1974. Biological Flora of the British Isles. No. 135. *Narthecium ossifragum* (L.) Huds. *Journal of Ecology* 62: 325–339.

Summerhayes, V.S. 1968. *Wild orchids of Britain*. Edn. 2. Collins, London.

Sumpter, J.P., D'Ayala, R., Parfitt, A.J., Pratt, P. & Raper, C. 2004. The current status of Military (*Orchis militaris*) and Monkey (*Orchis simia*) Orchids in the Chilterns. *Watsonia* 25: 175–183.

Sussex Botanical Recording Society. 2018. *The Flora of Sussex* (Abraham, F., Briggs, M., Harmes, P., Hoare, A., Knapp, A., Lording, T., Scott, B., Shaw, M., Streeter, D. & Sturt, N. Eds.). Pisces Publications, Newbury.

Sutherland, W.J. 1990. Biological Flora of the British Isles. No. 169. *Iris pseudacorus* L. *Journal of Ecology* **78**: 833–848.

Sutton, J. 2001. *The Plantfinder's guide to Daisies.* David & Charles, Newton Abbot.

Svensson, R. & Wigren, M. 1986. Sminkrotens historia och biologi i Sverige. (History and biology of *Lithospermum arvense* in Sweden). *Svensk Botanisk Tidskrift* **80**: 107–131.

Swan, G.A. 1993. *Flora of Northumberland.* Natural History Society of Northumbria, Newcastle upon Tyne.

Swan, G.A. 1999. Identification, distribution and a new nothosubspecies of *Trichophorum cespitosum* (L.) Hartman (Cyperaceae) in the British Isles and N.W. Europe. *Watsonia* **22**: 209–233.

Swanton, C.J., Cavers, P.B., Clements, D.R. & Moore, M.J. 1992. The biology of Canadian weeds. 101. *Helianthus tuberosus* L. *Canadian Journal of Plant Science* **72**: 1367–1382.

Sydes, C. 2008. Can we protect threatened Scottish arctic-alpine higher plants? *Plant Ecology and Diversity* **1**: 339–349.

Synnott, D.M. 1983. Notes on *Salix phylicifolia* L. and related Irish willows. *Glasra* **7**: 1–10.

Tabbush, P. & Beaton, A. 1998. Hybrid poplars: present status and potential in Britain. *Forestry* **71**: 355–364.

Takagi-Arigho, R. 1995. Plant records. *Festuca huonii. Watsonia* **20**: 299.

Tali, K., Foley, M.J.Y. & Kull, T. 2004. Biological Flora of the British Isles. No. 232. *Orchis ustulata* L. *Journal of Ecology* **92**: 174–184.

Tali, K., Fay, M.F. & Bateman, R.M. 2006. Little genetic differentiation across Europe between early-flowering and late-flowering populations of the rapidly declining orchid *Neotinea ustulata. Biological Journal of the Linnean Society* **87**: 13–25.

Tansley, A.G. 1939. *The British Islands and their vegetation.* Cambridge University Press, Cambridge.

Tarpey, T. & Heath, J. 1990. *Wild flowers of North East Essex.* Colchester Natural History Society, Colchester.

Taschereau, P.M. 1977. *Atriplex praecox* Hülphers: a species new to the British Isles. *Watsonia* **11**: 195–198.

Taschereau, P.M. 1985a. Taxonomy of *Atriplex* species indigenous to the British Isles. *Watsonia* **15**: 183–209.

Taschereau, P.M. 1985b. Field studies, cultivation experiments and the taxonomy of *Atriplex longipes* Dejer in the British Isles. *Watsonia* **15**: 211–219.

Taylor, F.J. 1956. Biological Flora of the British Isles. No. 55. *Carex flacca* Schreb. *Journal of Ecology* **44**: 281–290.

Taylor, K. 1971. Biological Flora of the British Isles. No. 121. *Rubus chamaemorus* L. *Journal of Ecology* **59**: 293–306.

Taylor, K. 1997a. Biological Flora of the British Isles. No. 197. *Geum urbanum* L. *Journal of Ecology* **85**: 705–720.

Taylor, K. 1997b. Biological Flora of the British Isles. No. 198. *Geum rivale* L. *Journal of Ecology* **85**: 721–731.

Taylor, K. 1999a. Biological Flora of the British Isles. No. 207. *Galium aparine* L. *Journal of Ecology* **87**: 713–730.

Taylor, K. 1999b. Biological Flora of the British Isles. No. 209. *Cornus suecica* L. (*Chamaepericlymenum suecicum* (L.) Ascherson & Graebner). *Journal of Ecology* **87**: 1068–1077.

Taylor, K. 2009. Biological Flora of the British Isles. No. 256. *Urtica dioica* L. *Journal of Ecology* **97**: 1436–1458.

Taylor, K. & Markham, B. 1978. Biological Flora of the British Isles. No. 142. *Ranunculus ficaria* L. *Journal of Ecology* **66**: 1011–1031.

Taylor, K., Rowland, A.P. & Jones, H.E. 2001. Biological Flora of the British Isles. No. 216. *Molinia caerulea* (L.) Moench. *Journal of Ecology* **89**: 126–144.

Taylor, K., Havill, D.C., Pearson, J. & Woodall, J. 2002. Biological Flora of the British Isles. No. 222. *Trientalis europaea* L. *Journal of Ecology* **90**: 404–418.

Taylor, K. & Rumsey, F.J. 2003. Biological Flora of the British Isles. No. 231. *Bartsia alpina* L. *Journal of Ecology* **91**: 908–921.

Taylor, K. & Woodell, S.R.J. 2008. Biological Flora of the British Isles. No. 251. *Primula elatior* (L.) Hill. *Journal of Ecology* **96**: 1098–1116.

Taylor, K. & Rowland, P. 2010. Biological Flora of the British Isles. No. 259. *Stachys sylvatica* L. *Journal of Ecology* **98**: 1476–1489.

Taylor, K. & Rowland, P. 2011. Biological Flora of the British Isles. No. 262. *Stachys palustris* L. *Journal of Ecology* **99**: 1081–1090.

Taylor, L. & Roberts, D.L. 2011. Biological Flora of the British Isles. No. 261. *Epipogium aphyllum* Sw. *Journal of Ecology* **99**: 878–890.

Taylor, P. 1989. *The genus Utricularia: a taxonomic monograph. Kew Bulletin Additional Series XIV.* Her Majesty's Stationery Office, London.

Taylor, P. 1991. *The genus Utricularia - A taxonomic monograph. Kew Bulletin Additional series XIV.* HMSO, London.

Teege, P., Kadereit, J.W. & Kadereit, G. 2011. Tetraploid European *Salicornia* species are best interpreted as ecotypes of multiple origins. *Flora* **206**: 910–920.

Telfer, M.G., Preston, C.D. & Rothery, P. 2002. A general method for the calculation of relative change in range size from biological atlas data. *Biological Conservation* **107**: 99–109.

Tennant, D.J. 1995. *Cystopteris fragilis* var. *alpina* Hook. in Britain. *The Naturalist* **120**: 45–50.

Tennant, D.J. 1996. *Cystopteris dickieana* R. Sim in the central and eastern Scottish Highlands. *Watsonia* **21**: 135–139.

Tennant, D.J. 2010. The British records of *Cystopteris alpina* (Lam.) Desv. *Watsonia* **28**: 57–63.

Thirsk, J. 1997. *Alternative agriculture.* Oxford University Press, Oxford.

Thomas, A.G., Maw, M.G. & Stahevitch, A. 1985. The biology of Canadian weeds. 66. *Artemisia absinthum* L. *Canadian Journal of Plant Science* **65**: 389–400.

Thomas, P.A. 2016. Biological Flora of the British Isles. No. 281. *Fraxinus excelsior. Journal of Ecology* **104**: 1158–1209.

Thomas, P.A. 2017. Biological Flora of the British Isles. No. 286. *Sorbus torminalis. Journal of Ecology* **105**: 1806–1831.

Thomas, P.A. & Polwart, A. 2003. Biological Flora of the British Isles. No. 229. *Taxus baccata* L. *Journal of Ecology* **91**: 489–524.

Thomas, P.A., El-Barghathi, M. & Polwart, A. 2007. Biological Flora of the British Isles. No. 248. *Juniperus communis* L. *Journal of Ecology* **95**: 1404–1440.

Thomas, P.A., El-Barghathi, M. & Polwart, A. 2011. Biological Flora of the British Isles. No. 260. *Euonymus europaeus* L. *Journal of Ecology* **99**: 345–365.

Thomas, P.A. & Mukassabi, T.A. 2014. Biological Flora of the British Isles. No. 275. *Ruscus aculeatus. Journal of Ecology* **102**: 1083–1100.

Thomas, P.A., Stone, D. & La Porta, N. 2018. Biological Flora of the British Isles. No. 288. *Ulmus glabra. Journal of Ecology* **106**: 1724–1766.

Thomas, P.A., Alhamd, O., Iszkuło, G., Dering, M. & Mukassabi, T.A. 2019. Biological Flora of the British Isles. No. 289. *Aesculus hippocastanum. Journal of Ecology* **107**: 992–1030.

Thomas, P.A., Leski, T., La Porta, N. & Dering, M. 2021. Biological Flora of the British Isles. No. 296. *Crataegus laevigata. Journal of Ecology* **109**: 572–596.

Thompson, J.D. & Turkington, R. 1988. The biology of Canadian weeds. 82. *Holcus lanatus* L. *Canadian Journal of Plant Science* **68**: 131–147.

Thompson, N.A. 2013. Will *Frankenia* be the next *Cochlearia danica*? *BSBI News* **123**: 48.

Thompson, P.A. 1973. Effects of Cultivation on the Germination Character of the Corn Cockle (*Agrostemma githago* L.). *Annals of Botany* **149**: 133–154.

Thor, G. 1979. *Utricularia* i Sverige, speciellt de förbisedda arterna *U. australis* och *U. ochroleuca*. [*Utricularia* in Sweden, especially the overlooked species *U. australis* and *U. ochroleuca*]. *Svensk Botanisk Tidskrift* **73**: 381–395.

Thor, G. 1987. Sumpbläddra, *Utricularia stygia*, en ny svensk art. [*Utricularia stygia* Thor, a new *Utricularia* species in Sweden]. *Svensk Botanisk Tidskrift* **81**: 273–280.

Thor, G. 1988. The genus *Utricularia* in the Nordic countries, with special emphasis on *U. stygia* and *U. ochroleuca. Nordic Journal of Botany* **8**: 213–225.

Thorogood, C.J., Rumsey, F.J. & Hiscock, S.J. 2009. Host-specific races in the holoparasitic angiosperm *Orobanche minor*: implications for speciation in parasitic plants. *Annals of Botany* **103**: 1005–1014.

Thorogood, C.J. & Rumsey, F.J. 2020. An account of Common Broomrape *Orobanche minor* (Orobanchaceae) in the British Isles. *British & Irish Botany* **2**: 223–239.

Thorogood, C.J. & Rumsey, F.J. 2021. *Broomrapes of Britain and Ireland.* BSBI Handbook No. 22. Botanical Society of Britain and Ireland, Durham.

Thurston, J.M. 1954. Survey of Wild Oats (*Avena fatua* and *A. ludoviciana*) in England and Wales in 1951. *Annals of Applied Biology* **41**: 619–636.

Tiley, G.E.D. 2010. Biological Flora of the British Isles. No. 257: *Cirsium arvense* (L.) Scop. *Journal of Ecology* **98**: 938–83.

Tiley, G.E.D., Dodd, F.S. & Wade, P.M. 1996. Biological Flora of the British Isles. No. 190. *Heracleum mantegazzianum* Sommier & Levier. *Journal of Ecology* **84**: 297–319.

Timson, J. 1963. The taxonomy of *Polygonum lapathifolium* L., *P. nodosum* Pers. and *Polygonum tomentosum* Schrank. *Watsonia* **5**: 386–395.

Timson, J. 1966. Biological Flora of the British Isles. No. 103. *Polygonum hydropiper* L. *Journal of Ecology* **54**: 815–821.

Tison, J.-M. & Girod, C.J. 2014. Synopsis du genre *Gladiolus* L. (Iridaceae) en France. *Journal de Botanique. Société Botanique de France* **68**: 69–75.

Tofts, R.J. 1999. Biological Flora of the British Isles. No. 206. *Cirsium eriophorum* (L.) Scop. *Journal of Ecology* **87**: 529–542.

Tofts, R.J. 2004a. *Geranium robertianum* L. *Journal of Ecology* **92**: 537–555.

Tofts, R.J. 2004b. *Geranium purpureum* Vill. *Journal of Ecology* **92**: 720–731.

Townsend, C.C. 1962. Some notes on *Galeopsis ladanum* L. and *G. angustifolia* Ehrh. ex Hoffm. *Watsonia* **5**: 143–149.

Townsend, F. 1904. *The Flora of Hampshire.* Lowell Reeve, London.

Trávníček, P., Jersáková, J., Kubátová, B., Krejčíková, J., Bateman, R.M., Lučanová, M., Krajníková, E., Těšitelová, T., Štípková, Z., Amardeilh, J.-P., Brzosko, E., Jermakowicz, E., Cabanne, O., Durka, W., Efimov, P., Hedrén, M., Hermosilla, C.E., Kreutz, K., Kull, T., Tali, K., Marchand, O., Rey, M., Schiestl, F.P., Čurn, V. & Suda, J. 2012. Minority cytotypes in European populations of the *Gymnadenia conopsea* complex (Orchidaceae) greatly increase intraspecific and intrapopulation diversity. *Annals of Botany* **110**: 977–986.

Tremayne, M. & Richards, A.J. 1997. The effects of breeding system and seed weight on plant fitness in *Primula scotica* Hooker. In Tew, T.E., Crawford, T.J., Spencer, J.W., Stevens, D.P., Usher, M.B. & Warren, J. (Eds.) *The role of genetics in conserving small populations* pp. 133–142 JNCC, Peterborough.

Trewick, S. & Wade, P.M. 1986. The distribution and dispersal of two alien species of *Impatiens*, waterway weeds in the British Isles. In *Proceedings EWRS/AAB 7th Symposium on Aquatic Weeds* pp. 351–356.

Trewren, K. 2014. *Some taxa within the* Dryopteris affinis *complex.* British Pteridological Society, London.

Trist, P.J.O. 1971. *A survey of the agriculture of Suffolk*. Royal Agricultural Society of England, London.

Trist, P.J.O. 1973. *Festuca glauca* Lam. and its var. *caesia* (Sm.) K. Richt. *Watsonia* **9**: 257–262.

Trist, P.J.O. 1979. *An ecological Flora of Breckland*. EP Publishing, East Ardsley.

Trist, P.J.O. 1986. The distribution, ecology, history and status of *Gastridium ventricosum* (Gouan) Schinz & Thell. in the British Isles. *Watsonia* **16**: 43–54.

Trist, P.J.O. 1989. Spreading meadow-grass *Poa subcaerulea* Sm. *Nature in Cambridgeshire* **31**: 57–60.

Trist, P.J.O. 1998. The distribution and status of *Corynephorus canescens* (L.) P.Beauv. (Poaceae) in Britain and the Channel Islands with particular reference to conservation. *Watsonia* **22**: 41–47.

Trist, P.J.O. & Sell, P.D. 1988. Two subspecies of *Molinia caerulea* (L.) Moench in the British Isles. *Watsonia* **17**: 153–157.

Trist, P.J.O. & Butler, J.K. 1995. *Puccinellia distans* (Jacq.) Parl. subsp. *borealis* (O. Holmb.) W. E. Hughes (Poaceae) in mainland Scotland and the Outer Isles. *Watsonia* **20**: 391–396.

Trueman, I., Morton, A. & Wainwright, M. 1995. *The flora of Montgomeryshire*. Montgomeryshire Field Society and the Montgomeryshire Wildlife Trust, Welshpool.

Trueman, I., Poulton, M. & Reade, P. 2013. *Flora of Birmingham and the Black Country*. Pisces Press, Newbury.

Turkington, R. & Cavers, P.B. 1979. The biology of Canadian weeds. 33. *Medicago lupulina* L. *Canadian Journal of Plant Science* **59**: 99–110.

Turkington, R. & Franko, G.D. 1980. The biology of Canadian weeds. 41. *Lotus corniculatus* L. *Canadian Journal of Plant Science* **60**: 965–979.

Turkington, R., Kenkel, N.C. & Franko, G.D. 1980. The biology of Canadian weeds. 42. *Stellaria media* (L.) Vill. *Canadian Journal of Plant Science* **60**: 981–992.

Turkington, R. & Burdon, J.J. 1983. The biology of Canadian weeds. 57. *Trifolium repens* L. *Canadian Journal of Plant Science* **63**: 243–266.

Turkington, R. & Aarssen, L.W. 1983. Biological Flora of the British Isles. No. 156. *Hypochoeris radicata* L. *Journal of Ecology* **71**: 999–1022.

Turner, W. 1548. *The names of herbes*. London. Reprinted in 1965 by The Ray Society.

Tutin, T.G. 1942. Biological Flora of the British Isles. No. 7. *Zostera* genus L. (pp. 217), *Z. marina* L. (pp. 217–224), *Z. hornemanniana* Tutin (pp. 224–226). *Journal of Ecology* **30**: 217–226.

Tutin, T.G. 1947. *Typha angustifolia* L. × *latifolia* L. *Report of the Botanical Society and Exchange Club of the British Isles* **13**: 173–174.

Tutin, T.G. 1950. *Milium scabrum* Merlet. *Watsonia* **1**: 345–348.

Tutin, T.G. 1957. Biological Flora of the British Isles. No. 63. *Allium ursinum* L. *Journal of Ecology* **45**: 1003–1010.

Tutin, T.G. 1980. *Umbellifers of the British Isles*. BSBI Handbook No. 2. Botanical Society of the British Isles, London.

Tutin, T.G., Heywood, V.H., Burges, N.A., Valentine, D.H., Walters, S.M. & Webb, D.A. 1964. *Flora Europaea. Volume 1, Lycopodiaceae to Platanaceae*. Cambridge University Press, Cambridge.

Tutin, T.G. & Chater, A.O. 1974. *Asperula occidentalis* Rouy in the British Isles. *Watsonia* **10**: 170–171.

Tyteca, D. & Esposito, F. 2018. Recent proposals in *Platanthera* (Orchidaceae) systematics in Western Europe, with a focus on intermediate looking plants. *Journal Europäischer Orchideen* **50**: 393–408.

Tyteca, D., Pessoa, J., Pereira, A., Pereira, C., Borges, L., Caperta, A.D., Areias, F. & Monteiro, J. 2018a. The orchid flora of Portugal – Addendum N. 7 – *Gymnadenia borealis* new for Portugal and Galicia. *Journal Europäischer Orchideen* **50**: 235–246.

Tyteca, D., Esposito, F., Vereecken, N., Gammella, M., Rinaldi, R. & Laurent, P. 2018b. Characterization of sympatric *Platanthera bifolia* and *Platanthera chlorantha* (Orchidaceae) populations with intermediate plants. *PeerJ* **6**: e4256.

Ubsdell, R.A.E. 1976a. Studies on variation and evolution in *Centaurium erythraea* Rafn. and *C. littorale* (D. Turner) Gilmour in the British Isles. 1: Taxonomy and biometrical studies. *Watsonia* **11**: 7–31.

Ubsdell, R.A.E. 1976b. Studies on variation and evolution in *Centaurium erythraea* Rafn. and *C. littorale* (D. Turner) Gilmour in the British Isles. 2: Cytology. *Watsonia* **11**: 33–43.

Ubsdell, R.A.E. 1979. Studies on variation and evolution in *Centaurium erythraea* Rafn. and *C. littorale* (D. Turner) Gilmour in the British Isles. 3: Breeding systems, floral biology and general discussion. *Watsonia* **12**: 225–232.

Uotila, P. 1978. Variation, distribution and taxonomy of *Chenopodium suecicum* and *C. album*, in N. Europe. *Acta Botanica Fennica* **108**: 1–35.

Upadhyaya, M.K., Turkington, R. & McIlvride, D. 1986. The biology of Canadian weeds. 75. *Bromus tectorum* L. *Canadian Journal of Plant Science* **66**: 689–709.

Upadhyaya, M.K., Tilsner, H.R. & Pitt, M.D. 1988. The biology of Canadian weeds. 87. *Cynoglossum officinale* L. *Canadian Journal of Plant Science* **68**: 763–774.

Upson, T. & Andrews, S. 2004. *The Genus* Lavandula. Kew Publishing, Surrey.

Valentine, D.H. 1947. The distribution of sexes in Butterbur. *North Western Naturalist* **22**: 111–114.

Valentine, D.H. 1980. Ecotypic and polymorphic variation in *Centaurea scabiosa* L. *Watsonia* **13**: 103–109.

Vallejo-Marín, M. 2012. *Mimulus peregrinus* (Phrymaceae): A new British allopolyploid species. *Phytokeys* **14**: 1–14.

Vallejo-Marín, M. & Lye, G.C. 2013. Hybridisation and genetic diversity in introduced *Mimulus* (Phrymaceae). *Heredity* **110**: 111–122.

Vallejo-Marín, M., Buggs, R.J.A., Cooley, A.M. & Puzey, J.R. 2015. Speciation by genome duplication: Repeated origins and genomic composition of the recently formed allopolyploid species *Mimulus peregrinus*. *Evolution* **69**: 1487–1500.

Vallejo-Marín, M., Cooley, A.M., Lee, M.Y.Q., Folmer, M.R., McKain, M.R. & Puzey, J.R. 2016. Strongly asymmetric hybridization barriers shape the origin of a new polyploid species and its hybrid ancestor. *American Journal of Botany* **103**: 1–17.

Valtueña, F.J., Preston, C.D. & Kadereit, J.W. 2011. Evolutionary significance of the invasion of introduced populations into the native range of *Meconopsis cambrica*. *Molecular Ecology* **20**: 4318–4331.

Valtueña, F.J., Dillenberger, M.S., Kadereit, J.W., Moore, A.J. & Preston, C.D. 2015. What is the origin of the Scottish populations of the European endemic *Cherleria sedoides* (Caryophyllaceae)? *New Journal of Botany* **5**: 13–25.

Valverde, T. & Silvertown, J. 1997. A metapopulation model for *Primula vulgaris*, a temperate forest understorey herb. *Journal of Ecology* **85**: 193–210.

van den Berg, L.J.L., Vergeer, P., Rich, T.C.G., Smart, S.M., Guest, D. & Ashmore, M.R. 2010. Direct and indirect effects of nitrogen deposition on species composition change in calcareous grasslands. *Global Change Biology* **17**: 1871–1883.

van Rossum, F., Leprince, N., Mayer, C., Raabová, J., Hans, G. & Jacquemart, A.L. 2015. What influences pollen dispersal in the clonal distylous *Menyanthes trifoliata* (Menyanthaceae)? *Plant Ecology and Evolution* **148**: 199–212.

Vanderpoorten, A., Hardy, O.J., Lambinon, J. & Raspé, O. 2011. Two reproductively isolated cytotypes and a swarm of highly inbred, disconnected populations: a glimpse into *Salicornia*'s evolutionary history and challenging taxonomy. *Journal of Evolutionary Biology* **24**: 630–644.

Väre, H. 2001. Mountain birch taxonomy and floristics of mountain birch woodlands. In Wielgolaski, F.E. (Ed.) *Nordic mountain birch ecosystems* pp. 35–46 Man and the biosphere series 27 UNESCO, Paris and Parthenon, New York.

Varia, S., Wood, S.V., Allen, R.M.S. & Murphy, S.T. 2022. Assessment of the host-range and impact of the mite, *Aculus crassulae*, a potential biological control agent for Australian swamp stonecrop, *Crassula helmsii*. *Biological Control* **167**: 104854.

Vaughan, J.G. & Geissler, C.A. 1997. *The new Oxford Book of Food Plants*. Oxford University Press, Oxford.

Vaughan, J.G. & Geissler, C.A. 2009. *The New Oxford book of Food Plants*. Edn. 2. Oxford University Press, Oxford.

Verdcourt, B. 1948. Biological Flora of the British Isles. No. 24. *Cuscuta* L. genus (p. 356–358), *C. europaea* L. (pp. 358–365). *Journal of Ecology* **36**: 356–365.

Verloove, F. 2014. Potentilla norvegica (http://alienplantsbelgium.be/) at *Manual of the Alien Plants of Belgium*. Botanic Garden, Meise.

Verloove, F. 2015. Pontederia cordata (http://alienplantsbelgium.be/) at *Manual of the Alien Plants of Belgium*. Botanic Garden, Meise.

Verloove, F. & Lambinon, J. 2006. The non-native vascular flora of Belgium: a new nothospecies and three new combinations. *Systematics and Geography of Plants* **76**: 217–220.

Vogel, J.C., Rumsey, F.J., Russell, S.J., Cox, C.J., Holmes, J.S., Bujnoch, W., Stark, C., Barrett, J.A. & Gibby, M. 1999. Genetic structure, reproductive biology and ecology of isolated populations of *Asplenium csikii* (Aspleniaceae, Pteridophyta). *Heredity* **83**: 604–612.

Wade, A.E. 1958. The history of *Symphytum asperum* Lepech. and *S.* ×*uplandicum* Nyman in Britain. *Watsonia* **4**: 117–118.

Wade, A.E., Kay, Q.O.N., Ellis, R.G. & National Museum of Wales 1994. *Flora of Glamorgan*. HMSO, London.

Waite, S. & Farrell, L. 1998. Population biology of the rare military orchid (*Orchis militaris* L.) at an established site in Suffolk, England. *Botanical Journal of the Linnean Society* **126**: 109–121.

Waldren, S. 1982. *Frankenia laevis* L. in Mid Glamorgan. *Watsonia* **14**: 185–186.

Walker, K.J. 2000. The distribution, ecology and conservation of *Arenaria norvegica* subsp. *anglica* Halliday (Caryophyllaceae). *Watsonia* **23**: 197–208.

Walker, K.J. 2003. *Eriophorum gracile* formerly present in Northamptonshire (v.c.32). *BSBI News* **92**: 16–17.

Walker, K.J. 2009. Water-borne dispersal of *Cardamine bulbifera* (L.) Crantz (Brasssicaceae) in Mid-West Yorkshire (V.C. 64). *Watsonia* **27**: 250–253.

Walker, K.J. 2014a. *Sarracenia purpurea* subsp. *purpurea* (Sarraceniaceae) naturalised in Britain and Ireland: distribution, ecology, impacts and control. *New Journal of Botany* **4**: 33–41.

Walker, K.J. 2014b. Alopecurus magellanicus *Lam.* Alpine Foxtail. *Species Account*. Botanical Society of Britain and Ireland.

Walker, K.J. 2014c. Pseudorchis albida *(L.) Á. and D. Löve. Small White Orchid. Species Account*. Botanical Society of Britain and Ireland, Durham.

Walker, K.J. 2015a. Epipactis atrorubens *(Hoffm.) Besser. Dark-red Helleborine Species Account*. Botanical Society of Britain and Ireland, Bristol.

Walker, K.J. 2015b. Minuartia stricta *(Sw.) Hiern. Teesdale Sandwort. Species Account*. Botanical Society of Britain and Ireland.

Walker, K.J. 2015c. Myosotis alpestris *F.W. Schmidt. Alpine Forget-me-not. Species Account*. Botanical Society of Britain and Ireland.

Walker, K.J. 2015d. Potentilla crantzii *(Crantz) G. Beck ex Fritsch. Alpine Cinquefoil. Species Account.* Botanical Society of Britain and Ireland.

Walker, K.J. 2021. Snake's-head Fritillary *Fritillaria meleagris* (Liliaceae) in Britain: its distribution, habitats and status. *British & Irish Botany* 3: 262–278.

Walker, K.J., Critchley, C.N.R. & Sherwood, A.J. 2007. The effectiveness of new agri-environment scheme options in conserving rare arable plants. *Aspects of Applied Biology* 81: 301–308.

Walker, K.J., Preston, C.D. & Boon, C.R. 2009a. Fifty years of change in an area of intensive agriculture: plant trait responses to habitat modification and conservation, Bedfordshire, England. *Biodiversity and Conservation* 18: 3597–3613.

Walker, K.J., Ward, S. & Parr, S. 2009b. The re-discovery of *Arenaria norvegica* subsp. *norvegica* in Ireland. *Watsonia* 27: 248–250.

Walker, K.J. & Pinches, C.E. 2011. Reduced grazing and the decline of *Pulsatilla vulgaris* Mill. (Ranunculaceae) in England, UK. *Biological Conservation* 144: 3098–3105.

Walker, K.J. & Pearman, D.A. 2012. *The distribution and status of Critically Endangered archaeophytes in England.* Unpublished report to Natural England, Botanical Society of Britain and Ireland.

Walker, K.J., Howard-Williams, E. & Meade, C. 2013. The distribution and ecology of *Arenaria norvegica* Gunn. in Ireland. *Irish Naturalists' Journal* 32: 1–12.

Walker, K.J. & Hedley, S. 2014. *The Rare and Threatened Plants of Moor House and Upper Teesdale National Nature Reserve.* Unpublished report to Natural England.

Walker, K.J., Auld, C., Austin, E. & Rook, J. 2016a. Effectiveness of methods to control the invasive non-native pitcherplant *Sarracenia purpurea* L. on a European mire. *Journal for Nature Conservation* 31: 1–8.

Walker, K.J., Pearman, D.A. & Stroh, P.A. 2016b. Where and what do we record? BSBI News 133: 35.

Walker, K.J., Stroh, P.A. & Ellis, R.W. 2017. *Threatened plants in Britain and Ireland.* Botanical Society of Britain and Ireland, Bristol.

Walker, K.J., Leach, S.J., Preston, C.D., Humphrey, T.A., James, T.J., Pearman, D.A. & Smith, P.A. 2019. Recording plant status and regeneration during single visits. *British & Irish Botany* 1: 283–291.

Walker, K.J. & Stroh, P.A. 2020. Changes in the distribution and abundance of *Carex ericetorum* in Britain since the 1970s. *British & Irish Botany* 2: 77–92.

Walker, K.J., Robinson, L. & Donald, D. 2020. *Cotula alpina* (Asteraceae) naturalised in the British Isles. *British & Irish Botany* 2: 43–55.

Wallace, G. 2005. *The functional ecology of* Potamogeton rutilus *Wolfg.* Ph.D. thesis, University of Glasgow.

Walters, S.M. 1946. Observations on varieties of *Viola odorata* L. *Report of the Botanical Society and Exchange Club of the British Isles* 12: 834–839.

Walters, S.M. 1949a. Biological Flora of the British Isles. No. 26. *Eleocharis* genus R.Br. (pp. 192–194), *E. palustris* (L.) R.Br. em. R.&S. (pp. 194–202), *E. uniglumis* (Link) Schult. (pp. 203–206). *Journal of Ecology* 37: 192–206.

Walters, S.M. 1949b. *Aphanes microcarpa* (Boiss. et Reut.) Rothm. in Britain. *Watsonia* 1: 163–169.

Walters, S.M. 1953. *Montia fontana* L. *Watsonia* 3: 1–6.

Walters, S.M. 1954. The distribution maps scheme. *Proceedings of the Botanical Society of the British Isles* 1: 212–130.

Walters, S.M. 1958. Exhibition meeting, 1957; *Nitella tenuissima*, a rare British stonewort. *Proceedings of the Botanical Society of the British Isles* 3: 104.

Walters, S.M. 1963. *Eleocharis austriaca* Hayek, a species new to the British Isles. *Watsonia* 5: 329–335.

Walters, S.M. 1979. *Epilobium lanceolatum* Seb. & Mauri - a plant to look for in your garden. *Watsonia* 12: 399.

Walters, S.M. 1993. *Wild & garden plants.* HarperCollins, London.

Walton, J. & Walton, M. 2013. *Frankenia laevis* (Sea-heath) in Warwickshire. *BSBI News* 122: 12.

Wang, N., Borrell, J.S., Bodles, W.J., Kuttapitiya, A., Nichols, R.A. & Buggs, R.J. 2014. Molecular footprints of the Holocene retreat of dwarf birch in Britain. *Molecular Ecology* 23: 2771–2782.

Wanntorp, L., Wanntorp, H.-E. & Källersjö, M. 2002. The identity of *Gunnera manicata* Linden ex André resolving a Brazilian-Colombian enigma. *Taxon* 51: 493–497.

Ward, L.K. 1973. The conservation of juniper I. Present status of juniper in southern England. *Journal of Applied Ecology* 10: 165–188.

Ward, L.K. 1981. The demography, fauna and conservation of *Juniperus communis* in Britain. In Synge, H. (Ed.) *The Biological Aspects of Rare Plant Conservation* pp. 319–329 BSBI Conference Report no.17 John Wiley & Sons, Chichester.

Ward, L.K. & Shellswell, C.W. 2017. *Looking after Juniper: ecology, conservation and folklore.* Ecology and Conservation Portfolio. Plantlife, Salisbury.

Wardlaw, A.C. 2005. What happened to *Asplenium fontanum* in Britain? *Pteridologist* 4: 100–101.

Wardle, D.A. 1987. The ecology of ragwort (*Senecio jacobaea* L.) - a review. *New Zealand Journal of Ecology* 10: 67–76.

Wardle, P. 1961. Biological Flora of the British Isles. No. 79. *Fraxinus excelsior* L. *Journal of Ecology* 49: 739–751.

Warwick, S.I. 1979. The biology of Canadian weeds. 37. *Poa annua* L. *Canadian Journal of Plant Science* 59: 1053–1066.

Warwick, S.I. & Sweet, R.D. 1983. The biology of Canadian weeds. 58. *Galinsoga parviflora* and *G. quadriradiata* (= *G. ciliata*). *Canadian Journal of Plant Science* 63: 695–709.

Warwick, S.I., Black, L.D. & Zilkey, B.F. 1985. Biology of Canadian weeds. 72. *Apera spica-venti. Canadian Journal of Plant Science* 65: 711–721.

Warwick, S.I. & Black, L.D. 1988. The biology of Canadian weeds. 90. *Abutilon theophrasti. Canadian Journal of Plant Science* 68: 1069–1085.

Warwick, S.I. & Wall, D.A. 1998. The biology of Canadian Weeds. 108. *Erucastrum gallicum* (Willd.) O.E. Schulz. *Canadian Journal of Plant Science* 78: 155–165.

Warwick, S.I. & Francis, A. 2005. The biology of Canadian weeds. 132. *Raphanus raphanistrum* L. *Canadian Journal of Plant Science* 85: 709–733.

Warwick, S.I. & Francis, A. 2009. The biology of Canadian Weeds. 142. *Camelina alyssum* (Mill.) Thell.; *C. microcarpa* Andrz. ex DC.; *C. sativa* (L.) Crantz. *Canadian Journal of Plant Science* 89: 791–810.

Watkins, F. 2011. Veronica praecox, *Breckland Speedwell: 2010: Twelve years on.* Unpublished report for the Ashmolean Natural History Society of Oxfordshire Rare Plants Group.

Watkinson, A.R. 1978. Biological Flora of the British Isles. No. 143. *Vulpia fasciculata* (Forskål) Samp. *Journal of Ecology* 66: 1033–1049.

Watkinson, A.R., Newsham, K.K. & Forrester, L. 1998. Biological Flora of the British Isles. No. 201. *Vulpia ciliata* Dumort. ssp. *ambigua* (Le Gall) Stace & Auquier. *Journal of Ecology* 86: 690–705.

Watson, D. 2019. *Glencoe vascular plant Site Condition Monitoring report, 4th cycle.* National Trust for Scotland Report, Lynedoch, Killin.

Watson, K. 1988. Notable canal plants. *Glasgow naturalist* 21: 486–487.

Watson, M.F. 1997. *Oxalis.* In Cullen, J. *et al.* (Eds.) *European Garden Flora, Vol. 5, Dicotyledons (Part III)* pp. 18–26 Cambridge University Press, Cambridge.

Watson, W. 1904. *Nicotiana sanderae. Flora & Slyva* 2: 216–217.

Watt, A.S. 1931. Preliminary observations on Scottish beechwoods. Introduction and Part I. *Journal of Ecology* 19: 137–157.

Watt, A.S. 1934. The vegetation of the Chiltern Hills, with special reference to the beechwoods and their seral relationships. *Journal of Ecology* 22: 445–507.

Watts, S.H. 2014. *A census of snow pearlwort* Sagina nivalis *on Ben Lawers SSSI.* National Trust for Scotland Report, Lynedoch, Killin.

Watts, S.H. 2016. *Monitoring* Veronica fruticans *at Ben Lawers SSSI.* National Trust for Scotland Report, Lynedoch, Killin.

Watts, S.H. 2018. *Monitoring* Saxifraga cernua *on Ben Lawers SSSI.* National Trust for Scotland Report, Lynedoch, Killin.

Watts, S.H. 2019a. *Monitoring* Salix lapponum *on Ben Lawers SSSI.* National Trust for Scotland Report, Lynedoch, Killin.

Watts, S.H. 2019b. *A census of snow pearlwort* Sagina nivalis *on Ben Lawers SSSI.* National Trust for Scotland Report, Lynedoch, Killin.

Watts, S.H., Griffith, A. & Mackinlay, L. 2019. Grazing exclusion and vegetation change in an upland grassland with patches of tall herbs. *Applied Vegetation Science* 22: 383–393.

Watts, S.H., Mardon, D.K., Mercer, C., Watson, D., Cole, H., Shaw, R.F. & Jump, A.S. 2022. Riding the elevator to extinction: Disjunct arctic-alpine plants of open habitats decline as their more competitive neighbours expand. *Biological Conservation* 272: 109620.

Weaver, S.E. & McWilliams, E.L. 1980. The biology of Canadian weeds. 44. *Amaranthus retroflexus* L., *A. powellii* S. Wats. and *A. hybridus* L. *Canadian Journal of Plant Science* 60: 1215–1234.

Weaver, S.E. & Riley, W.R. 1982. The biology of Canadian weeds. 53. *Convolvulus arvensis* L. *Canadian Journal of Plant Science* 62: 461–472.

Weaver, S.E. & Lechowicz, M.J. 1983. The biology of Canadian weeds. 56. *Xanthium strumarium* L. *Canadian Journal of Plant Science* 63: 211–225.

Weaver, S.E. & Warwick, S.I. 1984. The biology of Canadian weeds. 64. *Datura stramonium* L. *Canadian Journal of Plant Science* 64: 979–991.

Webb, C.J., Sykes, W.R. & Garnock-Jones, P.J. 1988. *Flora of New Zealand. Vol. IV. Naturalised Pteridophytes, Gymnosperms, Dicotyledons.* Botany Division, D.S.I.R, Christchurch, New Zealand.

Webb, D.A. 1950. Biological Flora of the British Isles. No. 28. *Saxifraga* genus L. (Section Dactyloides Tausch) (pp. 185–194), *S. cespitosa* L. (incl. *S. groenlandica* L.) (pp. 194–197), *S. hartii* Webb (pp. 197–199), *S. rosacea* Moench. (pp. 199–206), *S. hypnoides* L. (emend Webb) (pp. 206–213). *Journal of Ecology* 38: 185–213.

Webb, D.A. 1955a. Biological Flora of the British Isles. No. 47. *Erica mackaiana* Bab. *Journal of Ecology* 43: 319–330.

Webb, D.A. 1955b. The Distribution Maps Scheme: A provisional extension to Ireland of the British National Grid. *Proceedings of the Botanical Society of the British Isles* 1: 316–319.

Webb, D.A. 1956. A new subspecies of *Pedicularis sylvatica* L. *Watsonia* 3: 239–241.

Webb, D.A. 1957. *Hypericum canadense* L., a new American plant in Western Ireland. *Irish Naturalists' Journal* 12: 113–116.

Webb, D.A. 1958. *Hypericum canadense* L. in Western Ireland. *Watsonia* 4: 140–144.

Webb, D.A. 1984. *Polygonum mite* Schrank in Ireland. *Irish Naturalists' Journal* 21: 283–286.

Webb, D.A. 1985. What are the criteria for presuming native status? *Watsonia* 15: 231–236.

Webb, D.A. & Halliday, G. 1973. The distribution, habitat and status of *Hypericum canadense* L. in Ireland. *Watsonia* **9**: 333–344.

Webb, D.A. & Scannell, M.J.P. 1983. *Flora of Connemara and the Burren*. Royal Dublin Society & Cambridge University Press, Cambridge.

Webb, D.A. & Gornall, R.J. 1989. *Saxifrages of Europe*. Christopher Helm, London.

Webb, D.A. & Akeroyd, J.R. 1991. Inconstancy of seashore plants. *Irish Naturalists' Journal* **23**: 384–385.

Webber, J., Gibbs, J. & Hendry, S. 2004. Phytophthora disease of Alder. Forestry Commission Information Note (FCIN6). In *Phytophthora disease of Alder Forestry Commission Information Note (FCIN6)* Forestry Commission, Edinburgh.

Weber, C. 1963. Cultivars in the genus *Chaenomeles*. *Arnoldia* **23**: 17–75.

Weber, C. 1964. The genus *Chaenomeles* (Rosaceae). *Journal of the Arnold Arboretum* **45**: 161–205.

Webster, M.M. 1978. *Flora of Moray, Nairn & East Inverness*. Aberdeen University Press, Aberdeen.

Webster, S.D. 1988. *Ranunculus penicillatus* (Dumort.) Bab. in Great Britain and Ireland. *Watsonia* **17**: 1–22.

Wegmüller, S. 1971. A cytotaxonomic study of *Lamiastrum galeobdolon* (L.) Ehrend. & Polatschek in Britain. *Watsonia* **8**: 277–288.

Wein, R.W. 1973. Biological Flora of the British Isles. No. 132. *Eriophorum vaginatum* L. *Journal of Ecology* **61**: 601–615.

Welch, D. 1966. Biological Flora of the British Isles. No. 101. *Juncus squarrosus* L. *Journal of Ecology* **54**: 535–548.

Welch, D. 1967. Notes on *Myosotis scorpioides* agg. *Watsonia* **6**: 276–279.

Welch, D. 1993. *Flora of North Aberdeenshire*. Privately published, Banchory.

Welch, D. 1995. An early Scottish record of *Rubus arcticus* L. (Rosaceae). *Watsonia* **20**: 418.

Welch, D. 2001. Colonisation by *Cochlearia danica* L. along trunk roads in central Scotland from 1996 to 2000. *Watsonia* **23**: 446–449.

Welch, D. 2003. A reconsideration of the native status of *Linnaea borealis* L. (Caprifoliaceae) in lowland Scotland. *Watsonia* **24**: 427–432.

Welch, D. 2005. Further colonisation by *Cochlearia* species in N.E. Scotland. *BSBI News* **100**: 18–19.

Welch, D. & Welch, M.J. 1998. Colonisation by *Cochlearia officinalis* L. (Brassicaceae) and other halophytes on the Aberdeen-Montrose main road in north-east Scotland. *Watsonia* **22**: 190–193.

Welch, D. & Innes, M. 1999. Southward recolonisation by *Mertensia maritima* (L.) Gray on the coast of north-eastern Scotland. *Watsonia* **22**: 424–426.

Welch, D., Scott, D. & Doyle, S. 2000. Studies on the paradox of seedling rarity in *Vaccinium myrtillus* L. in N.E. Scotland. *Botanical Journal of Scotland* **52**: 17–30.

Wells, T.C.E. 1967. Changes in a population of *Spiranthes spiralis* (L.) Chevall. at Knocking Hoe National Nature Reserve, Bedfordshire, 1962–65. *Journal of Ecology* **55**: 83–99.

Wells, T.C.E. 1976. Biological Flora of the British Isles. No. 138. *Hypochoeris maculata* L. *Journal of Ecology* **64**: 757–774.

Wells, T.C.E. 2003. *The Flora of Huntingdonshire and the Soke of Peterborough*. Huntingdonshire Fauna and Flora Society and the author, Huntingdon.

Wells, T.C.E. & Barling, D.M. 1971. Biological Flora of the British Isles. No. 120. *Pulsatilla vulgaris* Mill. *Journal of Ecology* **59**: 275–292.

Wells, T.C.E. & Cox, R. 1989. Predicting the probability of the bee orchid (*Ophrys apifera*) flowering or remaining vegetative from the size and number of leaves. In Pritchard, H.W. (Ed.) *Modern methods in orchid conservation* pp. 127–139 Cambridge University Press, Cambridge.

Wells, T.C.E. & Cox, R. 1991. Demographic and biological studies on *Ophrys apifera*: some results from a 10 year study. In Wells, T.C.E. & Willems, J.H. (Eds.) *Population ecology of terrestrial orchids* pp. 47–51 SPB Academic Publishing, The Hague.

Wells, T.C.E., Rothery, P., Cox, R. & Bamford, S. 1998. Flowering dynamics of *Orchis morio* L. and *Herminium monorchis* (L.) R.Br. at two sites in eastern England. *Botanical Journal of the Linnean Society* **126**: 39–48.

Wentworth, J.E. & Gornall, R.J. 1996. Cytogenetic evidence for autopolyploidy in *Parnassia palustris*. *New Phytologist* **134**: 641–648.

Werner, P.A. & Soule, J.D. 1976. The biology of Canadian weeds. 18. *Potentilla recta* L., *P. norvegica* L. and *P. argentea* L. *Canadian Journal of Plant Science* **56**: 591–603.

Werner, P.A. & Rioux, R. 1977. The biology of Canadian weeds. 24. *Agropyron repens* (L.) Beauv. *Canadian Journal of Plant Science* **57**: 905–919.

Werner, P.A. & Hawthorn, W.R. 1980. The biology of Canadian weeds. 38. *Arctium minus* (Hill) Bernh. and *A. lappa* L. *Canadian Journal of Plant Science* **60**: 621–634.

Werner, P.A., Bradbury, I.K. & Gross, R.S. 1980. The biology of Canadian weeds. 45. *Solidago canadensis* L. *Canadian Journal of Plant Science* **60**: 1393–1409.

West, R.G. 2000. *Plant Life of the Quaternary Cold Stages. Evidence from the British Isles*. Cambridge University Press, Cambridge.

Westbury, D.B. 2004. Biological Flora of the British Isles. No. 433. *Rhinanthus minor* L. *Journal of Ecology* **92**: 906–927.

Westerhoff, D. & Clark, M.J. 1992. *The New Forest heathlands, grasslands and mires. A management review and strategy*. English Nature, Lyndhurst.

Wheeler, B.D. 1998. Cephalanthera longifolia *in England, 1997*. Plantlife Report 89. Plantlife, Salisbury.

Wheeler, B.D., Lambley, P.W. & Geeson, J. 1998. *Liparis loeselii* (L.) Rich. in eastern England: constraints on distribution and population development. *Botanical Journal of the Linnean Society* **126**: 141–158.

Wheeler, B.R. & Hutchings, M.J. 1999. The history and distribution of *Phyteuma spicatum* L. (Campanulaceae) in Britain. *Watsonia* **22**: 387–395.

Wheeler, B.R. & Hutchings, M.J. 2002. *Phyteuma spicatum* L. Biological Flora of the British Isles No. 223. *Journal of Ecology* **90**: 581–591.

Wheldon, J.A. 1897. Variations in *Erythraea*. *Science Gossip, new series* **4**: 110–111.

White, J.E.J. 1992. Ornamental uses of willow in Britain. *Proceedings of the Royal Society of Edinburgh* **98B**: 183–192.

White, J.W. 1912. *The Flora of Bristol*. John Wright & Sons, Bristol.

Whitehouse, C. 2016. *Kniphofia - the complete guide*. Royal Horticultural Society, Peterborough.

Whittington, G. & Edwards, K.T. 2000. *Illecebrum verticillatum* L. in the Outer Hebrides. *Botanical Journal of Scotland* **52**: 101–104.

Wiberg, R.A.W., Scobie, A.R., A'Hara, S.W., Ennos, R.A. & Cottrell, J.E. 2016. The genetic consequences of long term habitat fragmentation on a self-incompatible clonal plant, *Linnaea borealis* L. *Biological Conservation* **201**: 405–413.

Wiegleb, G., Brux, H. & Herr, W. 1991. Human impact on the ecological performance of *Potamogeton* species in northwestern Germany. *Vegetatio* **97**: 161–172.

Wigginton, M.J. 1999. *British Red Data Books. 1. Vascular plants*. Edn. 3. Joint Nature Conservation Committee, Peterborough.

Wigston, D.L. 1979. *Nothofagus* Blume in Britain. *Watsonia* **12**: 344–345.

Wilcox, M.P. 2015. *Geum ×convallis* (*G. macrophyllum × G. urbanum*, Rosaceae): a new *Geum* hybrid from England. *New Journal of Botany* **5**: 26–31.

Wilcox, M.P. 2016. *Myosotis stolonifera* (Pale Forget-me-not) on Exmoor, Somerset. *BSBI News* **133**: 26.

Wilcox, M.P. 2019. The putative hybrid *Limonium ×neumanii* (*L. vulgare × L. humile*). *BSBI News* **140**: 31–33.

Wilcox, M.P. & Ruhsam, M. 2020. The Genus *Cymbalaria* Hill (Toadflaxes) in Britain and the discovery of *C. muralis × C. pallida*. *BSBI News* **143**: 13–21.

Wilford, R. 2006. *Tulips: Species and Hybrids for the Gardener*. Timber Press, Portland, Oregon.

Wilkinson, M.J. & Stace, C.A. 1991. A new taxonomic treatment of the *Festuca ovina* L. aggregate (Poaceae) in the British Isles. *Botanical Journal of the Linnean Society* **106**: 347–397.

Willems, J.H. & Melser, C. 1998. Population dynamics and life-history of *Coeloglossum viride* (L.) Hartm.: an endangered orchid species in The Netherlands. *Botanical Journal of the Linnean Society* **126**: 83–93.

Williams, J.T. 1963. Biological Flora of the British Isles. No. 87. *Chenopodium album* L. *Journal of Ecology* **51**: 711–725.

Williams, J.T. 1969. Biological Flora of the British Isles. No. 117. *Chenopodiunn rubrum* L. *Journal of Ecology* **57**: 831–841.

Williams, L.R. 2000. Annual variations in the size of a population of *Cardamine impatiens* L. *Watsonia* **23**: 209–212.

Williams, P. & Stewart, N.F. 2002. *The conservation status of Great Tassel Stonewort* (Tolypella prolifera) *in Britain 2000–2001*. Plantlife Report No. 215. Plantlife, London.

Williams, P.J., Lansdown, R.V., Pankhurst, T.J. & Stewart, N.F. 2003. *The status of tassel stonewort (*Tolypella intricata) *in 2002*. Plantlife Report No. 224. Plantlife, London.

Williamson, M., Stout, J.C., Dehnen-Schmutz, K., Milbau, A. & Hall, A.R. 2008. A provisional list of Irish archaeophytes. *The Irish Naturalists' Journal* **29**: 30–35.

Williamson, R. 1978. *The Great Yew Forest: the natural history of Kingley Vale*. Macmillan, London.

Willis, A.J. & Davies, E.W. 1960. *Juncus subulatus* Forsk. in the British Isles. *Watsonia* **4**: 211–217.

Willmot, A. & Moyes, N. 2015. *The Flora of Derbyshire*. Pisces Press, Newbury.

Wilmore, G.T.D. 2000. *Alien Plants of Yorkshire*. Yorkshire Naturalists' Union, York.

Wilson, G.B., Whittington, W.J. & Humphries, R.N. 1995a. Biological Flora of the British Isles. No. 185. *Potentilla rupestris* L. *Journal of Ecology* **83**: 335–343.

Wilson, G.B., Wright, J., Lusby, P., Whittington, W.J. & Humphries, R.N. 1995b. Biological Flora of the British Isles. No. 188. *Lychnis viscaria* L. *Journal of Ecology* **83**: 1039–1051.

Wilson, J.B., Daker, M.G. & Savidge, J.P. 1990. A phenetic comparison of some *Fumaria* spp (Fumariaceae). *Plant Systematics and Evolution* **172**: 51–63.

Wilson, P.J. 1990. *The ecology and conservation of rare arable weed species and communities*. University of Southampton.

Wilson, P.J. 1991. Britain's arable weeds. *British Wildlife* **3**: 149–161.

Wilson, P.J. 1999. *The status and distribution of* Dianthus armeria *L. in Britain. Report for 1998. Back from the Brink Report No. 117*. Plantlife, London.

Wilson, P.J. & Aebischer, N.J. 1995. The distribution of dicotyledonous arable weeds in relation to distance from the field edge. *Journal of Applied Ecology* **32**: 295–310.

Wilson, Z.A., Dawson, J., Russell, J. & Mulligan, B.J. 1991. Exploited plants. *Arabidopsis thaliana*. *Biologist* **38**: 163–169.

Wimmer, F. 1866. *Salices Europaeae*. Fernandi Hirt, Breslau.

Winfield, M.O., Wilson, P.J., Labra, M. & Parker, J.S. 2003. A brief evolutionary excursion comes to an end: the genetic relationship of British species of *Gentianella* sect. *Gentianella* (Gentianaceae). *Plant Systematics and Evolution* **237**: 137–151.

Wingfield, R.A., Murphy, K.J., Hollingsworth, P. & Gaywood, M.J. 2004. *The ecology of* Najas flexilis. Scottish Natural Heritage Commissioned Report no. 017. Scottish Natural Heritage, Edinburgh.

Wolf, D. & Lundholm, J.T. 2008. Water uptake in green roof microcosms: Effects of plant species and water availability. *Ecological Engineering* **33**: 179–186.

Wolff, K. & Morgan-Richards, M. 1999. The use of RAPD data in the analysis of population genetic structure: case studies in *Alkanna* (Boraginaceae) and *Plantago* (Plantaginaceae). In Hollingsworth, P.M., Bateman, R.M. & Gornall, R.J. (Eds.) *Molecular systematics and plant evolution* pp. 51–73 Taylor & Francis, London.

Wollaston, T.V. 1845. Note on the Entomology of Lundy Island. *Zoologist* **3**: 897–900.

Wood, J. & Ramsay, M. 2004. Plate 482. *Anacamptis laxiflora* (Orchidaceae). *Curtis's Botanical Magazine* **21**: 26–33.

Wood, S.N. 2017. *Generalized Additive Models. An Introduction with R.* 2nd ed. Chapman and Hall/CRC, New York.

Wood, S.N. 2022. *mgcv: Mixed GAM Computation Vehicle with Automatic Smoothness Estimation. Reference manual. March 29, 2022.* https://cran.r-project.org/web/packages/mgcv/mgcv.pdf [Accessed 21st September 2022].

Woodell, S.R.J. 1958. Biological Flora of the British Isles. No. 64. *Daboecia cantabrica* K. Koch. *Journal of Ecology* **46**: 205–216.

Woodell, S.R.J. & Dale, A. 1993. Biological Flora of the British Isles. No. 178. *Armeria maritima* (Mill.) Willd. *Journal of Ecology* **81**: 573–588.

Woodhead, N. 1951a. Biological Flora of the British Isles. No. 32. *Lloydia serotina* (L.) Rchb. *Journal of Ecology* **39**: 198–203.

Woodhead, N. 1951b. Biological Flora of the British Isles. No. 33. *Lobelia* genus L. (pp. 456–457), and *L. dortmanna* L. (pp. 458–464). *Journal of Ecology* **39**: 456–464.

Woodhead, N. 1951c. Biological Flora of the British Isles. No. 34. *Subularia aquatica* L. *Journal of Ecology* **39**: 465–469.

Woods, R.G. 1993. *Flora of Radnorshire*. National Museum of Wales & Bentham-Moxon Trust, Cardiff.

Woods, R.G. 1998. The conservation of some *Sorbus* species in Wales. In Jackson, A. & Flanagan, M. (Eds.) *The conservation status of* Sorbus *in the UK* pp. 32–39 Royal Botanic Gardens, Kew, London.

Woods, R.G. & Rix, E.M. 1981. *Gagea bohemica* (Zauschner) J. A. & J. H. Schultes in the British Isles, and a general review of the *G. bohemica* species complex. *Watsonia* **13**: 265–270.

Woodward, F.I. 1975. The climatic control of the altitudinal distribution of *Sedum rosea* (L.) Scop. and *S. telephium* L. II. The analysis of plant growth in controlled environments. *New Phytologist* **74**: 335–348.

Woodward, F.I. 1997. Life at the edge: a 14 year study of a *Verbena officinalis* population's interactions with climate. *Journal of Ecology* **85**: 899–906.

Woodward, I. & Webster, M. 2021. A 'natural regeneration' approach to wild flower meadow creation results in the appearance of *Helosciadium repens* (Creeping Marshwort) in West Suffolk. *BSBI News* **146**: 3–6.

Worrell, R. & Malcolm, D.C. 1998. Anomalies in the distribution of silver birch (*Betula pendula* Roth) populations in Scotland. *Botanical Journal of Scotland* **50**: 1–10.

Worrell, R., Ruhsam, M. & Renny, J. 2021. Discovering Britain's truly Wild Apples. *British Wildlife* **32**: 237–244.

Wright, I.R. & Bartel, T.W. 2017. Effect of varying coppice height on tree survival and ground flora in Brasenose Wood, Oxfordshire, UK. *Conservation Evidence* **14**: 1–4.

Wright, J.A. & Lusby, P.S. 1999. The past and present status of *Moneses uniflora* (L.) Gray (Pyrolaceae) in Scotland. *Watsonia* **22**: 343–352.

Wu, L. & Jain, S. 1980. Self-fertility and seed set in natural populations of *Anthoxanthum odoratum* L. *Botanical Gazette* **141**: 300–304.

Wurzell, B. 1988. *Conyza sumatrensis* (Retz.) E.Walker established in England. *Watsonia* **17**: 145–148.

Wurzell, B. 1990. Truth is stranger than fitches. *BSBI News* **54**: 24–25.

Wurzell, B. 1992a. Spring flowering crocuses. *BSBI News* **60**: 36–38.

Wurzell, B. 1992b. Foreign *Crataegus* in Britain: a thorny problem. *BSBI News* **61**: 42–45.

Wurzell, B. 1994. A history of *Conyza* in London. *BSBI News* **65**: 34–39.

Wynne, G. 1993. *Flora of Flintshire*. Gee & Son, Denbigh.

Wyse Jackson, M., FitzPatrick, Ú., Cole, E., Jebb, M., McFerran, D., Sheehy Skeffington, M. & Wright, M. 2016. *Ireland Red List No. 10: Vascular Plants*. National Parks and Wildlife Service, Department of Arts, Heritage, Regional, Rural and Gaeltacht Affairs, Dublin.

Wyse Jackson, P.S. 1991. A note on *Cochlearia scotica* Druce (Cruciferae). *Botanical Journal of the Linnean Society* **106**: 118–119.

Yeloff, D.E., Labadz, J.C. & Hunt, C.O. 2006. Causes of degradation and erosion of a blanket mire in the southern Pennines, UK. *Mires and Peat* **1**: 1–18.

Yeo, P.F. 1966. A revision of the genus *Bergenia* Moench (Saxifragaceae). *Kew Bulletin* **20**: 113–148.

Yeo, P.F. 1973. *Acaena*. In Green, P.S. (Ed.) *Plants-wild and Cultivated: A Conference on Horticulture and Field Botany* pp. 51–55 & Appendix III (193–221) BSBI Conference Report No. 13 Botanical Society of the British Isles, Hampton.

Yeo, P.F. 1975. The Yorkshire records of *Euphrasia salisburgensis*. *The Naturalist* **934**: 83–87.

Yeo, P.F. 1978. A taxonomic revision of *Euphrasia* in Europe. *Botanical Journal of the Linnean Society* **77**: 223–334.

Yeo, P.F. 1985. *Hardy Geraniums*. Croom Helm, London.

Yeo, P.F. 2003. The taxonomic and conservation status of *Geranium purpureum* (Little-Robin) subsp. *forsteri*. *BSBI News* **93**: 30–33.

Yerka, M., Wiersma, A., Lindenmayer, R., Westra, P., Johnson, W., De Leon, N. & Stoltenberg, D. 2013. Reduced Translocation Is Associated with Tolerance of Common Lambsquarters (*Chenopodium album*) to Glyphosate. *Weed Science* **61**: 353–360.

Young, D.P. 1948. Studies in the British *Epipactis*, 1. *Epipactis dunensis* and *E. pendula*. *Watsonia* **1**: 102–112.

Young, D.P. 1958. *Oxalis* in the British Isles. *Watsonia* **4**: 51–69.

Young, D.P. 1962. Studies in the British *Epipactis*, 5. *Epipactis leptochila*; with some notes on *E. dunensis* and *E. muelleri*. *Watsonia* **5**: 127–135.

Zhou, T. & Jin, X.H. 2018. Molecular systematics and the evolution of mycoheterotrophy of tribe Neottieae (Orchidaceae, Epidendroideae). *Phytokeys* **94**: 39–49.

Zohary, D. & Hopf, M. 2000. *Domestication of plants in the Old World*. Edn. 3. Oxford University Press, Oxford.

Zohren, J., Wang, N., Kardailsky, I., Borrell, J.S., Joecker, A., Nichols, R.A. & Buggs, R.J.A. 2016. Unidirectional diploid–tetraploid introgression among British birch trees with shifting ranges shown by restriction site-associated markers. *Molecular Ecology* **25**: 2413–2426.

Index

This index covers taxa included in both Volume 1 and Volume 2 of this publication, as well as taxa that are included in the *Online Plant Atlas* (plantatlas2020.org) only: these are indicated as "online". Volume 1 includes taxon accounts up to *page 758* (the end of Rubiaceae) and Volume 2 covers taxon accounts from *page 759* (Gentianaceae onwards). The page numbers for taxa included in Volume 1 are in **bold type**; those included in Volume 2 are in regular type. Scientific names for taxa that are the subject of an account in these volumes are in ***bold italics***; vernacular names are in **regular bold** type. Taxa that are "online" only are included using non-bold type:

scientific names in *italics*; vernacular names in regular type. Stace (2019) included a number of nomenclatural changes from his earlier edition (Stace, 2010); we have included recent synonyms for all taxa that are mapped in these volumes and in the *Online Plant Atlas*. These Stace (2010) synonyms are included within the index and shown in *italicized* text, with their updated Stace (2019) name placed in brackets alongside. The page number given for each family (presented in CAPITALS) indicates the first page where a taxon account appears. Incidental mentions in a species account of other taxa are not indexed.